Offer your students tutoring assistance—FREE upon adoption!

Prentice Hall offers a wealth of tutorial resources for students **free** of charge:

→ **Tutorial Videos** are available on **www.prenhall.com/horngren**.

→ **Live Tutoring** provides gentle coaching on core topics.

→ **Tutorial Software** is available at **www.prenhall.com/horngren** on core management accounting topics.

→ **Horngren's Online Study Guides** on the **free** text Companion Web site let students take 3–5 quizzes per text chapter and receive immediate scoring and feedback (results may be sent to faculty). Quizzes include true/false, multiple-choice, essay, fill-in-the-blank, and matching questions.

Get your students up and running in Excel—Free/Minimal charge.

Each instructor has specific requirements for how students use Excel. Horngren and Prentice Hall offer options for all your requirements:

→ **Learn Excel** using the Excel Tutorial at **www.prenhall.com/horngren**.

→ **Students work with existing templates** at **www.prenhall.com/horngren** for in-text assignments.

→ For even more review, *MS Excel for Accounting: The First Course* may be packaged with new texts at a valuable discount or are available as stand-alone items.

Offer your students Practice Sets—50% off with new texts!

Horngren and Prentice Hall offer an extensive series of manual and computerized Practice Sets—many include Peachtree and QuickBooks exercises. Go to **www.prenhall.com/accounting** for a complete list.

Text Web site **www.prenhall.com/horngren**.

Horngren's Companion Web site offers a robust assortment of resources for students and faculty including PowerPoints, online study guides, current events articles, software downloads, and much more!

D002630l

Introduction to Management Accounting

Thirteenth Edition

Charles T. Horngren
Stanford University

Gary L. Sundem
University of Washington—Seattle

William O. Stratton
Pepperdine University

PEARSON
Prentice Hall

Upper Saddle River, New Jersey 07458

Library of Congress Cataloging-in-Publication Data

Horngren, Charles T.
    Introduction to management accounting/Charles T. Horngren, Gary L. Sundem, William
O. Stratton — 13th ed.
      p. cm. — (Charles T. Horngren series in accounting)
    ISBN 0-13-144131-0
      1. Managerial accounting. I. Sundem, Gary L. II. Stratton, William O. III. Title.
IV. Series.

HF5635.H814 2005
658.15′11 — dc22   2003069027

Editor-in-Chief: Jeff Shelstad
Senior Editorial Assistant: Jane Avery
Director of Development: Steve Deitmer
Development Editor: Elisa Adams
Assistant Editor: Sam Goffinet
Senior Project Manager, Media: Nancy Welcher
Executive Marketing Manager: Beth Toland
Marketing Assistant: Melissa Owens
Managing Editor (Production): Cynthia Regan
Production Editor: Michael Reynolds
Production Assistant: Joe DeProspero
Production Manager, Manufacturing: Arnold Vila
Design Manager: Maria Lange
Art Director: Janet Slowik
Interior Design: Craig Ramsdell
Cover Design: Maria Lange
Cover Illustration/Photo: Brian Hagiwara/Foodpix, Inc.
Art Studio: Matrix Art Services
Associate Director, Multimedia Production: Karen Goldsmith
Manager, Print Production: Christy Mahon
Print Production Liaison: Ashley Scattergood
Composition/Full-Service Project Management: Progressive Information Technologies
Printer/Binder: Von Hoffman

Credits and acknowledgments borrowed from other sources and reproduced, with permission, in this textbook appear on appropriate page within text (or on page P1).

Pearson Education LTD.
Pearson Education Singapore, Pte. Ltd
Pearson Education, Canada, Ltd
Pearson Education–Japan

Pearson Education Australia PTY, Limited
Pearson Education North Asia, Ltd
Pearson Educación de Mexico, S.A. de C.V.
Pearson Education Malaysia, Pte. Ltd

10 9 8 7 6 5 4 3 2 1
ISBN 0-13-144131-0

To Joan, Chelsea, Erik, Marissa,

Liz, Garth, Jens, Reed, Grant,

Norma, Gina, Adam, Nisha, and Tiana

Charles T. Horngren   (*center*) is the Edmund W. Littlefield Professor of Accounting, emeritus, at Stanford University. A graduate of Marquette University, he received his MBA from Harvard University and his Ph.D. from the University of Chicago. He is also the recipient of honorary doctorates from Marquette University and DePaul University.

A certified public accountant, Horngren served on the Accounting Principles Board for six years, the Financial Accounting Standards Board Advisory Council for five years, and the Council of the American Institute of Certified Public Accountants for three years. For six years, he served as a trustee of the Financial Accounting Foundation, which oversees the Financial Accounting Standards Board and the Government Accounting Standards Board.

Horngren is a member of the Accounting Hall of Fame.

A member of the American Accounting Association, Horngren has been its president and its director of research. He received its first annual Outstanding Accounting Educator Award.

The California Certified Public Accountants Foundation gave Horngren its Faculty Excellence Award and its Distinguished Professor Award. He is the first person to have received both awards.

The American Institute of Certified Public Accountants presented its first Outstanding Educator Award to Horngren.

Horngren was named Accountant of the Year, Education, by the national professional accounting fraternity, Beta Alpha Psi.

Professor Horngren is also a member of the Institute of Management Accountants, where he has received its Distinguished Service Award. He was a member of the Institute's Board of Regents, which administers the Certified Management Accountant examinations.

Horngren is the author of other accounting books published by Prentice Hall: *Cost Accounting: A Managerial Emphasis*, Eleventh Edition, 2003 (with Srikant Datar and George Foster); *Introduction to Financial Accounting*, Eighth Edition, 2002 (with Gary L. Sundem and John A. Elliott); *Accounting*, Sixth Edition, 2005 (with Walter T. Harrison Jr. and Linda Bamber); and *Financial Accounting*, Fifth Edition, 2004 (with Walter T. Harrison Jr.).

Horngren is the Consulting Editor for the Charles T. Horngren Series in Accounting.

Gary L. Sundem   (*left*) is the Julius A. Roller Professor of Accounting at the University of Washington, Seattle. He received his B.A. degree from Carleton College and his MBA and Ph.D. degrees from Stanford University.

Professor Sundem was the 1992–1993 President of the American Accounting Association. He was Executive Director of the Accounting Education Change Commission, 1989–1991, and served as Editor of *The Accounting Review*, 1982–1986.

A member of the Institute of Management Accountants, Sundem is past president of the Seattle chapter. He has served on IMA's national board of directors and chaired its Academic Relations and Professional Development committees.

Professor Sundem has numerous publications in accounting and finance journals including *Issues in Accounting Education, The Accounting Review, Journal of Accounting*

Research, and *The Journal of Finance*. He was selected as the Outstanding Accounting Educator by the American Accounting Association in 1998 and by the Washington Society of CPAs in 1987. He has made more than 200 presentations at universities in the United States and abroad.

William O. Stratton   (*right*) is Professor of Accounting at Pepperdine University. He received B.S. degrees from Florida State University and Pennsylvania State University, his MBA from Boston University, and his Ph.D. from the Claremont Graduate University.

A certified management accountant, Stratton has lectured extensively at management accounting conferences in North America, South America, and Europe. He has developed and delivered professional workshops on activity-based management and performance achievement to manufacturing and service organizations throughout the United States and South America. In 1993, Professor Stratton was awarded the Boeing Competition prize for classroom innovation.

Stratton has numerous publications in accounting and international business journals including *Management Accounting, CMA Management, Decision Sciences, IIE Transactions, The Journal of Cost Management,* and *Synergie*.

BRIEF CONTENTS

CONTENTS

Part 2 | **Accounting for Planning and Control**

Part 3 | Capital Budgeting

Part 4 | Product Costing

Part 5 │ Basic Financial Accounting

PREFACE

 Now more than ever, managers have to understand how their decisions effect costs.

Management accounting is an essential tool that enhances a manager's ability to make effective economic decisions. Because understanding concepts is more important than memorizing techniques, *Introduction to Management Accounting*, 13/e describes both theory and common practices so students understand how to produce information that's useful in day-to-day decision making. From the first chapter, we encourage students to think about why companies use various techniques, not to blindly apply the techniques.

Introduction to Management Accounting, 13/e deals with all business sectors—non-profit, retail, wholesale, service, selling, and administrative situations—as well as manufacturing. The focus is on planning and control decisions, not on product costing for inventory valuation and income determination.

Our Philosophy

 Introduce concepts and principles early, then revisit them at more complex levels as students gain understanding, and provide appropriate real-company examples at every stage.

As management accounting builds on financial accounting, the concepts within management accounting build on one another. Students begin their understanding of managerial decisions by asking, "How will my decisions affect the costs and revenues of the organization?" Students then progress to more complex questions: "What is the most appropriate cost-management system for the company?" "What products or services should we emphasize?" "What do our budget variances mean?"

Our goals are to choose relevant subject matter and to present it clearly and accessibly using many examples drawn from actual companies. Companies such as Starbucks, Boeing, AT&T, McDonald's, Microsoft, and more set the stage for chapter material and are revisited throughout so that students understand management accounting concepts in a real-company context.

 Take your pick—two different text versions fit any course structure.

Introduction to Management Accounting, 13/e (Chapters 1–14) provides a concise treatment of management accounting topics suitable for a one-term course.

Introduction to Management Accounting, 13/e (Chapters 1–17) includes three financial accounting chapters in addition to the fourteen management accounting chapters. This version is especially suited to continuing education or MBA courses where students need to learn financial and management accounting in a one-term course. The financial accounting chapters also provide material for any student who may need a financial accounting review.

Introduction to Financial Accounting, 8/e and *Introduction to Management Accounting*, 13/e provide a seamless presentation for any first year accounting course. Please contact your Prentice Hall representative about cost-savings discounts when both books are adopted.

New Edition Enhancements

- **NEW and revised Business First boxes** provide insights into operations at well-known domestic and international companies, including technology and e-Commerce companies such as Reichhold Inc., DaimlerChrysler, IBM, Battelle, and EncripTix.
- **NEW and revised chapter opening vignettes** help students understand accounting's role in current business practice. We revisit the chapter opening company later in chapter discussions so students can see how accounting decisions effect real company practices. Starbucks, General Motors, L. A. Darling, AT&T, Boeing, Nantucket Nectars, and McDonald's are just some of the companies students will recognize.
- **NEW Making Managerial Decisions boxes** in all chapters allow students to take what they've learned, apply this material to a real business situation, and then plot a course of action.
- **NEW assignment material in all chapters**, including an Excel Application Exercise, new end-of-chapter summaries, and Fundamental Assignment Problems in selected chapters, and a general updating of most exercises and problems to reflect significant text changes.
- **NEW Ethics problems or cases** in each chapter.

Updated Material

- Chapter 1—includes significantly more ethics coverage including new Business First boxes; coverage of ERP and XBRL added.
- Chapter 2—clarified distinction between total and unit contribution margin, including new exhibit comparing gross margin and contribution margin; two new Business First boxes; new Boeing examples throughout the chapter discussion.
- Chapter 3—Discussion of capacity decisions expanded; new problem material on data presentation and analysis.
- Chapter 4—major chapter revision focusing on simplifying the presentation as well as adding more examples and illustrations; ABC coverage simplified with more examples and illustrations and complex multistage ABC moved to an appendix; includes new section on process mapping.
- Chapter 5—new, expanded ethics discussions as well as expanded coverage of target costing; new assignments on ABC and target costing.
- Chapter 6—new Nantucket Nectars examples throughout chapter; new Business First box on outsourcing; shortened and simplified discussion of more advanced material by placing it in Summary Problem for Your Review with solution; several new questions, exercises, and problems using the chapter-opening company.
- Chapter 7—new Business First box on budgeting as a value driver; new section on activity-based master budgets; new Making Managerial Decisions boxes.
- Chapter 8—simplified coverage of variance analysis; McDonald's, chapter-opening company, is revisited throughout the chapter discussion.
- Chapter 9—balanced scorecard moved to a section on nonfinancial measures and heavily revised with a new example; "Goal Congruence, Managerial Effort, and Motivation" heavily revised for clearer presentation; added coverage of Six Sigma and two new Business First boxes.
- Chapter 10—heavily revised and reorganized section on transfer pricing is now covered later in the chapter; EVA material revised; new section, "Budgeting, Performance Targets, and Ethics."
- Chapter 11—inflation now covered in an appendix; added coverage on internal rate of return (IRR), real options, and ethical issues concerning tax avoidance and evasion.

- Chapter 12—extensive chapter revision includes revised exhibits as well as new discussions involving chapter-opening company, L. A. Darling; Exhibit 12-1 revised to set overall framework for chapter discussions; problems 12-34 through 12-36 added to illustrate and apply chapter discussion for service-department cost allocation, process maps, ABC product costing, and ABC customer profitability.
- Chapter 13—combines the coverage of overhead in two chapters of the Twelfth edition into one logical discussion; the major illustration used in both Chapters 13 and 14 is based on same company, allowing students to study Chapter 14 before 13 or study only Chapter 14; discussion simplified by eliminating many journal entries; chapter illustrations use Dell Computer Corporation, the chapter-opening company; simplified discussion by deleting sections on *selection of expected activity level for computing the fixed-overhead rate* and *actual, normal, and standard costing*.
- Chapter 14—consolidates coverage of these two product-costing systems into one new chapter; the process-costing section of the chapter opens with a vignette that combines two companies: one with a job-costing system and the other with a process-costing system; Summary Problem for Your Review applies concepts to chapter-opening company; simplified coverage of process costing by deleting first-in, first-out method for process-costing systems.
- Chapter 15—Microsoft used extensively throughout chapter discussions; added material on ethics, including Business First box; improved explanation of cash versus accrual accounting.
- Chapter 16—extensively rewritten coverage of statement of cash flows, including discussion of free cash flow; new appendix on accounting for inventory (in Chapter 19 of Twelfth edition).
- Chapter 17—consolidated goodwill discussion; revised and updated financial ratios; now includes General Motors consolidated statements; new appendix on changing prices and income measurement (in Chapter 19 of Twelfth edition).
- Financial Accounting review streamlined and covered in three rather than four chapters.

Supplements for Instructors and Students

INSTRUCTOR'S RESOURCE CD-ROM A complete, one-step resource for instructors, including all faculty and student supplements as well as testing software. Available upon request from your local Pearson Prentice Hall representative.

INSTRUCTOR'S RESOURCE MANUAL BY SCOTT YETMAR (CLEVELAND STATE UNIVERSITY) Substantially revised, this resource manual provides insightful and useful tips on how to best manage course content when using *Introduction to Management Accounting*, 13/e in class. Chapter-by-chapter explanations and pedagogical philosophies are clearly delineated and oriented to greatly aid the teaching process.

SOLUTIONS MANUAL AND SOLUTIONS TRANSPARENCIES BY CHARLES T. HORNGREN (EMERITUS STANFORD UNIVERSITY), GARY L. SUNDEM (UNIVERSITY OF WASHINGTON, SEATTLE), AND WILLIAM O. STRATTON (PEPPERDINE UNIVERSITY) Comprehensive solutions for all end-of-chapter material. Also available in acetate form for in-class presentation.

TEST ITEM FILE BY SCOTT YETMAR (CLEVELAND STATE UNIVERSITY) A ready-to-use bank of testing material. Each chapter includes a variety of types of questions, including true/false, multiple choice, and critical thinking problems. Intended for ease of use, each question is linked to chapter objectives, and also provides suggested difficulty level and reference to text pages where answers can be found.

TestGenEQ by Tamarack Software, Inc.   Testing software designed to aid in creating custom tests in minutes. Features include question randomization, a point-and-drag interface, and extensive customizable settings.

PowerPoint Presentation by Olga Quintana (University of Miami) Complete PowerPoint presentations for each chapter. Instructors may download and use each presentation as is or customize the slides to create a tailor-made slide show. Each presentation allows instructors to offer a more interactive presentation using colorful graphics, outlines of chapter material, and graphical explanations of difficult topics. Available online at http://www.prenhall.com/horngren and on the Instructor's Resource CD-ROM.

Course Web site at http://www.prenhall.com/horngren   A complete online resource that offers a variety of Internet-based teaching and learning support. Our Web site provides a wealth of resources for students and faculty.
Resources include

- an online study guide;
- downloadable supplements, including PowerPoint and General Ledger Software for student use;
- learning assessment sections;
- practice tests with immediate feedback for self-study use.

Student Study Guide by Frank R. Selto (University of Colorado)   The Student Study Guide contains a wealth of resources designed to aid students in text comprehension. Each chapter includes chapter overviews, study tips, self-test questions, demonstration problems and worked-out solutions, and more.

Spreadsheet Templates by Albert Fisher (Community College of Southern Nevada)   Ready-made templates to accompany selected end-of-chapter problems can be found at http://www.prenhall.com/horngren.

Excel Application Exercises   The Excel Application Exercises were prepared by Glenda C. Levendowski, CPA, Mesa Community College and Terry Levendowski, CMA, CPA, Consultant.

ACKNOWLEDGMENTS

We have received ideas, assistance, miscellaneous critiques, and assorted assignment material in conversations with and by mail from many students, professors, and business leaders. Each has our gratitude, but the list is too long to enumerate here. We wish to thank the following reviewers whose feedback was critical to this new revision:

Mark E. Bettini, University of California, Berkeley

Phillip A. Blanchard, University of Arizona

Wayne G. Bremser, Villanova University

C. Douglas Cloud, Pepperdine University

Kenneth P. Couvillion, San Joaquin Delta College

Jan M. Duffy, Iowa State University

Suzanne Lowensohn, Colorado State University

Roderick B. Posey, University of Southern Mississippi

George L. Schatz, Maine Maritime Academy

James K. Smith, University of San Diego

Wendy Tietz, Kent State University

We also thank Kathy Hertz for help in proofing the manuscript and checking the solutions manual. Finally, students in our classes have provided invaluable feedback on previous editions, for which we are grateful.

Many people at Prentice Hall also earn our deepest thanks for their thoughtful contributions. We note especially Michael Reynolds, Elisa Adams, and Jane Avery for their efforts. We also thank P. J. Boardman, Sam Goffinet, Nancy Welcher, Beth Toland, Melissa Owens, Cynthia Regan, Joe DeProspero, Suzanne Grappi, Arnold Vila, Maria Lange, Janet Slowik, Karen Goldsmith, Christy Mahon, Carolyn Streuly, and Ashley Scattergood.

Charles T. Horngren
Gary L. Sundem
William O. Stratton

Managerial Accounting and the Business Organization

CHAPTER 1

LEARNING OBJECTIVES

When you have finished studying this chapter, you should be able to:

1. Describe the major users and uses of accounting information.

2. Explain why ethics is important to management accountants.

3. Describe the cost-benefit and behavioral issues involved in designing an accounting system.

4. Explain the role of budgets and performance reports in planning and control.

5. Discuss the role accountants play in the company's value chain functions.

6. Contrast the functions of controllers and treasurers.

7. Explain why accounting is important in a variety of career paths.

8. Identify current trends in management accounting.

9. Appreciate the importance of a code of ethical conduct to professional accountants.

When Mei-Hwa Zhang walks into a Starbucks in Beijing, she has much the same experience as Mohammad Kumar does in a Starbucks in Kuwait or Franz Mueller does in one in Zurich. How does Starbucks manage to keep its 7,000 coffee stores the same throughout the world?

All Starbucks' managers, from baristas to store managers to its chairman, Howard Schultz, have common objectives. They assess how well their department meets these objectives partly by looking at accounting reports. Accounting provides a common language to help managers around the world communicate financial information. Without this information, managers would find their task much more difficult. By the time you finish reading this book, you will be comfortable with much of the accounting information managers use to make their decisions. You will be able to use this information, along with other information, to develop plans, make short-term and long-term decisions, assess performance, and, in general, be a better manager.

Starbucks is a young, fast-growing company that has established a worldwide reputation in a short time. Recently it was named one of the Top 5 Global Brands of the Year by Brandchannel.com's Readers Choice survey. It has consistently been among *Fortune* magazine's 100 Best Companies to Work For. *Business Ethics* magazine selected it among its 100 Best Corporate Citizens. The chairman of Starbucks, Howard Schultz, was selected by *Business Week* as one of the Top 25 Best Managers in the country. Finally, *Fortune* named Starbucks the Most Admired Brand in the food services category two years in a row. How did Starbucks accomplish all of this?

If you had asked most people a decade or two ago whether consumers around the world would pay a premium price for a "better" cup of coffee, few would have

Starbucks stores, such as this one at Yu Garden in Shanghai, look very much alike, and the products and services are consistent throughout the world. This is a result of good management, and good management is a result of good information. Management accounting information is essential to managers of Starbucks, as it is to managers in any organization, large or small, for-profit or nonprofit, regardless of its location in the world.

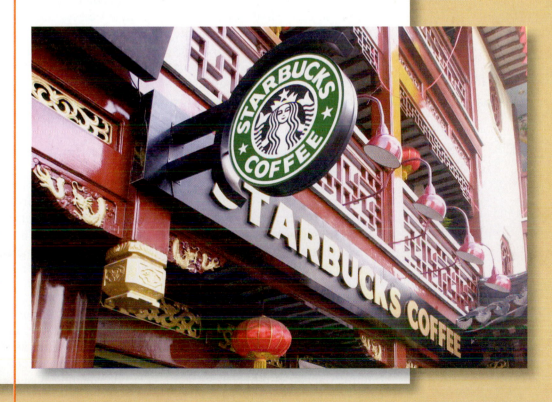

answered yes. Nevertheless, the expansion of Starbucks has been nothing short of phenomenal. In 2002, Starbucks' total revenues—the amount the company received for all the items sold—were $3.3 billion, compared with only $700 million in 1996. The net income—the profit that Starbucks made—was $215 million, up from only $42 million in 1996. Total assets—the recorded value of the items owned by Starbucks—grew from less than $900 million in 1996 to nearly $2.3 billion in 2002. All these numbers are accounting measures of Starbucks' success. It is the detailed numbers behind these figures that managers use to make day-to-day decisions and measure performance. The cumulative success of numerous managers of Starbucks' stores in many countries adds up to these company-wide numbers.

As we embark on our journey into the world of management accounting, we will explore what it takes for a company such as Starbucks to manage its activities with ease and how managers throughout the company use accounting information to better carry out their jobs. Keep this in mind: The same basic accounting needs and procedures that supported managers in the small coffee company that Starbucks was in 1990 support the managers in the larger company it is today, and indeed they support businesses big and small, old and new, worldwide. The accounting systems may be larger and more elaborate, but the principles that govern them remain the same.

Just as at Starbucks, managerial accounting can help managers in all types of organizations answer vital questions. Consider the decisions you might face as a manager in the following situations:

- Suppose you are a **Boeing** engineer preparing manufacturing specifications for a new airplane, the 777-X. There are three possible ways to organize the assembly of the plane. Which is the most cost-effective approach?
- Suppose you are a product manager at **General Mills** and you are designing a new marketing plan for Cheerios. Market research predicts that distributing free samples in the mail will increase annual sales by 4%. Will the cost of the free samples (including the cost of distributing them) be more or less than the profits from the added sales?
- **Bank of America** offers free checking to customers who keep a minimum balance of $500 in their FirstChoice™ Minimum Balance account. How much does it cost the bank to provide this free service?
- Kitsap County Special Olympics holds a series of athletic events for disabled youth. As executive director, you must decide how much money the group's annual fund drive must raise to support its planned activities.
- Chez Bonaparte is a dinner-only restaurant located in a middle-class neighborhood. Suppose you are the proprietor and are considering opening for lunch. To be competitive, you must price the average lunch at about $7, and you can serve about 40 patrons. Can the restaurant produce a lunch that meets its quality standards at an average cost of less than $7?
- The Seattle School District is negotiating with the teachers' union. Among the issues are teachers' salaries, class size, and number of extracurricular activities offered. The union and the district have both made several proposals. If you were superintendent of schools, you would want to know how much each of the various proposals will cost. You would also like to know the added cost of increasing class size by one student per class, and whether this cost would differ for elementary, junior high, and high school levels.

In making decisions such as these, managers turn to management accountants for information. In this chapter, we consider the purposes and roles of accounting and accountants in different types of organizations, as well as some of the trends and challenges faced by accountants today. We place a special emphasis on ethics. Information is useful only if it is believable. Accountants must have the highest integrity or their information will have little value. ■

Accounting and Decision Making

The basic purpose of accounting information is to help you make decisions, whether you are a company president, a production manager, a hospital or school administrator, an investor—the list could go on and on. Regardless of who is making the decision, understanding accounting information allows for a more informed, and better, decision.

OBJECTIVE 1

Describe the major users and uses of accounting information.

Users of Accounting Information

Users of accounting information fall into two general categories:

1. Internal managers who use the information for day-to-day operating decisions and for long-range strategic decisions.
2. External parties, such as investors and government authorities, who use the information for making decisions about the company.

Both internal parties (managers) and external parties use accounting information, but they often demand different types of information and use it in different ways. **Management accounting** produces information for managers within an organization. It is the process of identifying, measuring, accumulating, analyzing, preparing, interpreting, and communicating information that helps managers fulfill organizational objectives. In contrast, **financial accounting** produces information for external parties such as stockholders, suppliers, banks, and government regulatory agencies.[1] We list the major differences between management accounting and financial accounting in Exhibit 1-1. Despite these differences, most organizations use a general-purpose accounting system that meets most of the needs of both types of users. However, as we consider the needs of managers, we should realize that sometimes companies compromise managers' needs to gain the efficiency—and cost savings—of a single accounting system that serves all users.

What kinds of accounting information do managers need? Good accounting information helps an organization achieve its goals and objectives by helping to answer three types of questions:

1. Scorecard questions: Am I doing well or poorly? **Scorekeeping** is the accumulation and classification of data. This aspect of accounting enables both internal and external parties to evaluate organizational performance. Starbucks' annual income statement, balance sheet, and cash flow statement and its income tax filings with the government are part of the scorekeeping function performed by the company's accountants.
2. Attention-directing questions: Which problems should I look into? **Attention directing** means reporting and interpreting information that helps managers to focus on operating problems, imperfections, inefficiencies, and opportunities. Attention directing usually involves routine reports that compare actual results to before-the-fact expectations. For example, a Starbucks store may report profits of $120,000 when budgeted profit was $150,000. The accounting report will include information explaining why the store did not achieve its budget.
3. Problem-solving questions: Of the several alternatives being considered, which is the best? The **problem-solving** aspect of accounting often involves a special study to assess possible courses of action and recommend the best course to follow. For example, Starbucks recently experimented with adding food service to its coffee stores. After a special analysis of the revenues and costs of such an operation, management decided not to expand its food operations.

---

management accounting
The branch of accounting that produces information for managers within an organization. It is the process of identifying, measuring, accumulating, analyzing, preparing, interpreting, and communicating information that helps managers fulfill organizational objectives.

financial accounting
The branch of accounting that develops information for external decision makers such as stockholders, suppliers, banks, and government regulatory agencies.

scorekeeping
The accumulation and classification of data.

attention directing
Reporting and interpreting information that helps managers to focus on operating problems, imperfections, inefficiencies, and opportunities.

problem-solving
The aspect of accounting that often involves a special study to assess possible courses of action and recommends the best course to follow.

---

[1]For a book-length presentation of the subject, see Charles T. Horngren, Gary L. Sundem, and John A. Elliott, *Introduction to Financial Accounting* (Upper Saddle River, NJ: Prentice Hall, 2006), the companion to this textbook.

Exhibit 1-1
Distinctions Between
Management
Accounting and
Financial Accounting

	Management Accounting	Financial Accounting
Primary users	Organization managers at various levels.	Outside parties such as investors and government agencies but also organization managers.
Freedom of choice of accounting measures	No constraints other than costs in relation to benefits of improved management decisions.	Constrained by generally accepted accounting principles (GAAP).
Behavioral measure implications in selecting accounting measures	Choice should consider how measurements and reports will influence managers' daily behavior.	Choice based on how to and communicate economic phenomena. Behavioral considerations are secondary, although executive compensation based on reported results may have behavioral impacts.
Time focus of reports	Future orientation: formal use of budgets as well as historical records. Example: 20X2 budget versus 20X2 actual performance.	Past orientation: historical evaluation. Example: 20X2 actual performance versus 20X1 actual performance.
Time span of reports	Flexible, varying from hourly to 10 to 15 years.	Less flexible; usually one year or one quarter.
Types of reports	Detailed reports: includes details about parts of the entity, products, departments, territories, etc.	Summary reports: primarily report on the entity as a whole.
Delineation of	Field is less sharply defined.	Field is more sharply defined.

The scorecard and attention-directing uses of information are closely related. The same information may serve a scorecard function for a manager and an attention-directing function for the manager's superior. For example, many accounting systems provide performance reports that compare actual results of decisions and activities with previously determined plans. By pinpointing where actual results differ from plans, such performance reports can show managers how they are doing and show the managers' superiors where to take action. Companies produce most scorecard and attention-directing information on a routine basis evey day, month, quarter, or year.

In contrast, managers use problem-solving information when they make long-range plans or special, nonrecurring decisions, such as whether to make or to buy parts, replace equipment, or add or drop a product. They produce this information only when there is a specific decision to make or plan to prepare. For example, Starbucks uses problem-solving information when deciding whether to run ads during the Super Bowl broadcast.

MAKING MANAGERIAL DECISIONS

Managers use accounting information for many different types of decisions. Accountants must make sure that they produce information that is useful for these various decisions. What type of information—scorekeeping, attention directing, or problem solving—would managers use for each of the following decisions? Why?

1. Deciding whether to replace a traditional assembly line with a fully automated robotic process.
2. Evaluating the performance of a particular division for the preceding year.
3. Identifying which products exceeded their budgeted profitability and which ones fell short of budget.

Answers

1. Problem solving. This is a one-time decision for which managers need information targeted at the specific alternatives under consideration.
2. Scorekeeping. This is a routine evaluation of an organizational unit for which managers want systematic data on a regular basis.
3. Attention directing. Managers want information that highlights deviations from budget to make them aware of products that need attention.

Influences on Accounting Systems

Accounting information for managers usually comes from the company's general-purpose accounting system. An **accounting system** is a formal mechanism for gathering, organizing, and communicating information about an organization's activities. Managers may prefer that their needs be given first priority in designing an accounting system. However, often that is not the case. External forces (for example, income tax authorities and regulatory bodies such as the U.S. Securities and Exchange Commission and the California Health Facility Commission) often limit management's choices of accounting methods for external reports. Many organizations develop systems primarily to satisfy legal requirements imposed by external parties. After all, most external reports are mandatory, while information for managers is optional. Thus, managers must justify their information needs on a cost-benefit basis—the benefit of better managerial decisions must exceed the cost of the information.

One major influence on accounting systems is the need for public companies to issue annual financial reports. These reports must adhere to a set of standards known as **generally accepted accounting principles (GAAP).** However, internal accounting reports are not restricted by GAAP. Managers can create whatever kind of internal accounting system they want—provided they are willing to pay the cost of developing and operating the system.

Another external influence on accounting systems is governmental regulations. A specific example of this is government contracting. Universities, defense contractors, and others contracting with the U.S. government must allocate costs to government contracts in specified ways or risk the government's refusal to pay. A more far-reaching example is the **Foreign Corrupt Practices Act,** a U.S. law forbidding bribery and other corrupt practices. The title is misleading because the act's provisions apply to all publicly held companies, even if they conduct no business outside the United States. This law requires that companies maintain their accounting records in reasonable detail and accuracy and that they have an appropriate system of **internal control**—policies to protect and make the most efficient use of an organization's assets. Internal auditors help review and evaluate systems, including their internal controls, to help

accounting system
A formal mechanism for gathering, organizing, and communicating information about an organization's activities.

generally accepted accounting principles (GAAP)
A set of standards to which public companies' published financial statements must adhere.

Foreign Corrupt Practices Act
A U.S. law forbidding bribery and other corrupt practices. The law also requires all public companies to maintain their accounting records in reasonable detail and accuracy and have an appropriate system of internal controls.

Internal controls
Policies to protect and make the most efficient use of an organization's assets.

management audit
A review to determine whether managers are implementing the policies and procedures specified by top management.

Sarbanes-Oxley Act
A 2002 law that requires more top-management oversight of a company's accounting policies and procedures.

minimize errors, fraud, and waste. They also conduct **management audits**—reviews to determine whether managers are implementing the policies and procedures specified by top management. In general, the act focused attention on the quality of information in accounting systems. In 2002, the **Sarbanes-Oxley Act** added an extra level of government regulation. Driven by corporate bankruptcies blamed in part on accounting lapses (as well as deficiencies in corporate governance, lax securities regulation, and executive greed), the bill requires more top-management oversight of a company's accounting policies and procedures. By requiring chief executive officers to sign a statement certifying the accuracy of the company's financial statements, the act makes accounting numbers the concern of all managers, not just the accountants. The overall impact of Sarbanes-Oxley, as well as other government regulations, is controversial. Many managers insist that the extra costs of compliance exceed any possible benefits. One benefit, however, is that operating managers, now more than ever, must become more intimately familiar with their accounting systems. The resulting changes in the systems sometimes provide stronger controls and more informative reports.

Importance of Ethics

OBJECTIVE 2
Explain why ethics is important to management accountants.

Most regulation of accounting systems seeks to ensure the reliability of the information that accountants provide. However, no regulation can be as effective in ensuring reliability as holding accountants to high ethical standards. As recently as five years ago, surveys showed high public confidence in the integrity of accountants, but because of accounting's role in the corporate collapses early in this decade, public regard for accountants has since plummeted. A reputation for high integrity develops slowly and requires much effort, but reputation can be quickly lost. The accounting profession is now trying to rebuild its reputation.

Why is integrity so important to accountants? Think of it this way: If you buy a car, you can see many of the quality details. Further, if something goes wrong with the car, you will certainly know it. You don't have to rely on the word of the salesperson. But accounting information is different. You can't see its quality. You might not notice for years that something is wrong—probably not until it's too late to do anything about it. Thus, you rely on the integrity of accountants who tell you that the information about a company is correct. If you cannot trust the accountant, then the information is nearly worthless.

In companies such as **Enron, WorldCom, Tyco, Global Crossing, Adelphia, Xerox**, and many others, the accounting information provided was faulty. The courts will decide whether there were illegalities, but there surely was misleading information offered to a trusting public. What did accountants have to do with this? In a very few cases, accountants apparently participated in fradulent activities. But most of the time, they simply did not step up and challenge what they surely knew (or at least should have known) were misleading practices. Exceptions were accountants who became whistle-blowers, as illustrated in the Business First box on page 9. Integrity takes more than not lying. Most of these accountants did not blatantly lie. But neither did they tell the truth—that is, they did not correct the false or confusing information. They did not make sure that the information provided was reliable, a prime duty of accountants.

Why is this important to you? Because ethical habits you develop as a student will carry over into your life as a manager or an accountant. A recent survey of university students in the United States showed that 80% of them were appalled at the ethical behavior of corporate executives. Yet 59% of the students admitted to cheating while at the university. Cheating is not unique to U.S. universities. In a survey in Australia, 79% of undergraduates and 54% of graduate students admitted to cheating. There may be a difference in magnitude between the actions of the executives or accountants and the

Companies often rely on accountants to safeguard company ethics. Accountants have a special responsibility to make sure that managers act with integrity and that information disclosed to customers, suppliers, regulators, and the public is accurate. If accountants do not take this responsibility seriously, or if the company ignores the accountants' reports, dire consequences can follow. Just ask WorldCom or Enron. In both companies, an accountant decided to be a *whistle-blower*, one who reports wrongdoings to his or her supervisor. The WorldCom and Enron whistle-blowers became two of the three 2002 Persons of the Year in *Time* magazine.

In June 2002, Cynthia Cooper, vice president of internal audit for WorldCom, told the company's board of directors that fraudulent accounting entries had turned a $662 million loss into a $2.4 billion profit in 2001. This disclosure led to additional discoveries totaling $9 billion in erroneous accounting entries—the largest accounting fraud in history. Cooper was proud of WorldCom and highly committed to its success. Nevertheless, when she and her internal audit team discovered the unethical actions of superiors she admired, she did not hesitate to do the right thing. She saw no joy when CEO Bernie Ebbers and CFO Scott Sullivan were handcuffed and led away. She simply applied what she had learned when she sat in the middle of the front row of seats in her accounting classes at Mississippi State University. Accountants ask hard questions, find the answers, and act with integrity. Being a whistle-blower has not been easy for Cooper. She is a hero to some, a villian to others. But regardless of the reaction of others, Cooper knows that she did what any good accountant should do—no matter how painful it is to tell the truth.

At Enron, Sherron Watkins had a different experience. An accounting major at the University of Texas at Austin who started her career at Arthur Andersen, Watkins moved out of accounting when she took a position at Enron in 1993. But in the spring of 2001 she moved back into the financial arena, working directly for CFO Andrew Fastow. As she became more familiar with the accounting at Enron, she discovered the off-the-books liabilities that have now become famous. In August, she wrote a memo to CEO Kenneth Lay and met with him personally, explaining to him "an elaborate accounting hoax." Later she discovered that, rather than the hoax being investigated, her report had generated a memo from Enron's legal counsel titled "Confidential Employee Matter" that included the following: ". . . how to manage the case with the employee who made the sensitive report. . . . Texas law does not currently protect corporate whistle-blowers. . . ." In addition, her boss confiscated her hard drive, and she was demoted. She now regrets that she did not take the matter to higher levels, but she thought that Lay would take her allegations seriously. In the end, Watkins proved to be right. While many at Enron knew what was happening, they ignored it. Watkins's accounting background made her both able to spot the irregularities and impelled to report them. Another Enron employee, Lynn Brewer, said that "hundreds, perhaps thousands, of people inside the company knew what was going on, and chose to look the other way." Watkins made the ethical decision and did not look the other way.

Sources: "The Party Crasher," *Time*, December 30, 2002–January 6, 2003, pp. 52–56; "The Night Detective," *Time*, December 30, 2002–January 6, 2003, pp. 45–50; M. Flynn, "Enron Insider Shares Her Insights," *Puget Sound Business Journal*, March 7–13, 2003, p. 50.

type of cheating by university students, but the reasoning is often the same: "Everyone is doing it." "It won't hurt just this one time." "This assignment (or earnings report) is so important that the benefit of cheating is greater than the cost." "There is very little chance that I will get caught." None of these is a legitimate justification for unethical behavior.

Later in this chapter, we will address some specific ethical standards for professional accountants. But for now, just remember that information from an unreliable source has little value. For accountants to provide reliable information, not only must they *be* ethical, users of the information must *believe* that the accountants are ethical. Integrity is hard to establish, but easy to lose.

Management Accounting in Service and Nonprofit Organizations

Accountants in manufacturing organizations developed the basic ideas of management accounting. These ideas, however, have evolved so that they apply to all types of organizations, including service organizations. Service organizations, for our purposes, are organizations that do not make or sell tangible goods. Public accounting firms, law firms, management consultants, real estate firms, transportation companies, banks, insurance companies, and hotels are profit-seeking service organizations.

Most nonprofit organizations, such as hospitals, schools, libraries, museums, and government agencies, are also service organizations. Managers and accountants in nonprofit organizations have much in common with their counterparts in profit-seeking organizations. They raise and spend money. They prepare budgets and design and implement control systems. All managers have an obligation to use resources wisely. If used intelligently, accounting contributes to efficient operations and helps both profit-seeking and nonprofit organizations achieve their objectives.

The characteristics of service organizations, whether profit-seeking or nonprofit, include the following:

1. Labor is intensive: The highest proportions of expenses in schools and law firms are wages, salaries, and payroll-related costs, not the costs relating to the use of machinery, equipment, and physical facilities.
2. Output is usually difficult to define: The output of a university might be defined as the number of degrees granted, but many critics would maintain that the real output is what is contained in the students' brains. Therefore, measuring output is often considered impossible.
3. Service organizations cannot store their major inputs and outputs: An airline cannot save an empty airline seat for a later flight, and a hotel's available labor force and rooms are either used or unused as each day occurs.

Simplicity is the watchword for installation of systems in service industries and nonprofit organizations. Why? Because many professionals, such as physicians, professors, or government officials, are too busy to try to grapple with a complex system. For them to use the information, it must be in a form that is easy to understand. In fact, simplicity is a fine watchword for the design of any accounting system. Complexity tends to generate costs of gathering and interpreting data that often exceed prospective benefits. Concern for simplicity is sometimes expressed as KISS ("keep it simple, stupid," or, better yet, "keep it simple for success").

Cost-Benefit and Behavioral Considerations

cost-benefit balance
Weighing estimated costs against probable benefits, the primary consideration in choosing among accounting systems and methods.

In addition to simplicity, managers should keep two other ideas in mind when designing accounting systems: (1) cost-benefit balances and (2) behavioral implications.

The **cost-benefit balance**—weighing estimated costs against probable benefits—is the primary consideration in choosing among accounting systems and methods. Therefore, we will refer again and again to cost-benefit considerations throughout this book. For now, consider accounting systems to be economic goods—like office supplies or labor—available at various costs. Which system does a manager want to buy? A simple file drawer for amassing receipts and canceled checks? An elaborate budgeting system based on computerized models of the organization and its subunits? Or something in between?

The answer depends on the buyer's perceptions of the expected benefits in relation to the costs. For example, consider a manager at University Hospital who is considering installing a ConTrol®-computerized system made by Advanced Medical Systems for controlling hospital operations. Users need to enter a piece of information only once and the system automatically

OBJECTIVE 3

Describe the cost-benefit and behavioral issues involved in designing an accounting system.

incorporates it into budgeting, purchasing, and payables records. Such a system is highly efficient and is subject to few errors, but is it a good buy? That depends on its expected benefit. If its value to the hospital is greater than its cost of $300,000, then it is a good buy. If not, the manager should consider another accounting system.

The value of a loaf of bread may exceed a cost of $0.50 a loaf, but it is not likely to exceed a cost of $5 per loaf. Similarly, a particular accounting system may be a wise investment if its cost is sufficiently small. Like a consumer who switches from bread to potatoes if the cost of bread is too high, managers seek other sources of information if accounting systems are too expensive. In many organizations, it may be more economical to gather some kinds of data by one-shot special efforts than by a ponderous system that repetitively gathers data that are rarely used.

In estimating the benefits of an accounting system, managers should also consider **behavioral implications,** that is, the system's effect on the behavior, specifically the decisions, of managers. The system must provide accurate, timely budgets and performance reports in a form useful to managers. If managers do not use accounting reports, the reports create no benefits.

Management accounting reports also affect employees' feelings and behavior. Consider a performance report that a manager's superiors use to evaluate the operations for which he is responsibile. If the report unfairly attributes excessive costs to the operation, the manager may lose confidence in the system and not let it influence future decisions. In contrast, a system that managers believe in and trust can greatly influence their decisions and actions.

In a nutshell, think of management accounting as a balance between costs and benefits of accounting information coupled with an awareness of the importance of behavioral effects. Therefore, management accountants must understand related disciplines, such as economics, the decision sciences, and the behavioral sciences, to make intelligent decisions about the best information to supply to managers.

> **behavioral implications**
> *The accounting system's effect on the behavior, specifically the decisions, of managers.*

The Management Process and Accounting

Regardless of the type of organization, managers benefit when accounting provides information that helps them plan and control the organization's operations.

The Nature of Planning and Controlling

The management process is a series of activities in a cycle of planning and control. **Decision making**—the purposeful choice from among a set of alternative courses of action designed to achieve some objective—is the core of the management process. Decisions range from the routine (making daily production schedules) to the nonroutine (launching a new product line).

There are two basic types of decisions within an organization: (1) planning decisions and (2) control decisions. In practice, planning and control are so intertwined that it seems artificial to separate them. In studying management, however, we find it useful to concentrate on either the planning phase or the control phase to simplify our analysis.

The left side of Exhibit 1-2 demonstrates the planning and control cycle of current operations that could be used by a particular Starbucks store. **Planning** (the top box) refers to setting objectives for an organization and outlining how it will attain them. Thus, planning provides the answers to two questions: What is desired? When and how is it to be accomplished? For the Starbucks store, management wants to improve profitability. The store will accomplish this by adding new drinks and improving advertising. In contrast, **controlling** (actions) refers to implementing plans and using feedback to attain objectives (evaluation). The Starbucks store will expand its menu offerings and expand advertising. Management will evaluate the effectiveness of these actions based on selected

> **decision making**
> *The purposeful choice from among a set of alternative courses of action designed to achieve some objective.*

> **planning**
> *Setting objectives for an organization and outlining how it will attain them.*

> **controlling**
> *Implementing plans and using feedback to attain objectives.*

Exhibit 1-2
Starbucks Store.
Accounting
Framework for
Planning and Control

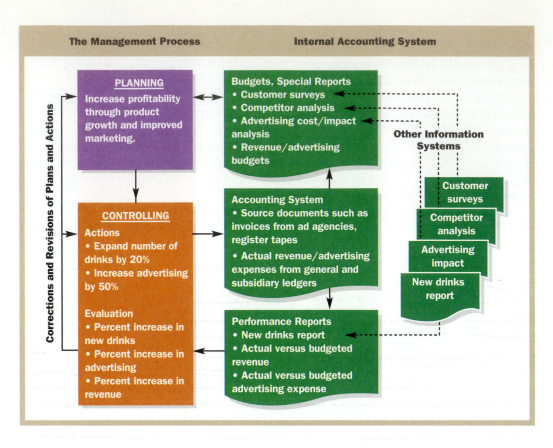

performance measures such as the percent increase in new drinks. Feedback is crucial to the cycle of planning and control. Planning determines action, action generates feedback, and the control phase uses this feedback to influence further planning and actions. Timely, systematic reports provided by the internal accounting system are the chief source of useful feedback. None of this cycle would be possible without accounting.

O B J E C T I V E 4

Explain the role of budgets and performance reports in planning and control.

budget
A quantitative expression of a plan of action and an aid to coordinating and implementing the plan.

performance reports
Feedback provided by comparing results with plans and by highlighting variances.

variances
Deviations from plans.

Management by Exception

The right side of Exhibit 1-2 shows that accounting formalizes plans by expressing them as budgets. A **budget** is a quantitative expression of a plan of action. The Starbucks store would express its plan for product growth and improved marketing through revenue and advertising budgets. Budgets also help to coordinate and implement plans. They are the chief devices for disciplining management planning. Without budgets, planning may not get the front-and-center focus that it usually deserves.

The accounting system supports both planning and controlling. The system records, measures, and classifies actions to produce performance reports (the last box). **Performance reports** provide feedback by comparing results with plans and by highlighting **variances,** which are deviations from plans. For example, managers of the Starbucks store would evaluate the effectiveness of its advertising plan by comparing the increase in revenue and profits to the increase in advertising. Based on their evaluation, managers at Starbucks would make corrections and revisions to their plans.

Exhibit 1-3 shows a simple performance report for a hypothetical Starbucks store, the Mayfair Starbucks. Organizations use performance reports to judge managers' decisions and the productivity of organizational units. By comparing actual results to budgets, performance reports motivate managers to achieve the objectives.

The first column of Exhibit 1-3 is the budget for March 20X1. It is based on a predicted level of sales and the estimated costs needed to support that level of sales. After managers and their superiors agree on a budget, it becomes the managers' target for the month.

	Budget	Actual	Variance
Sales	$50,000	$50,000	0
Less:			
Ingredients	22,000	$ 24,500	$2,500 U
Store labor (barristas, etc.)	12,000	11,600	400 F
Other labor (managers, supervisors)	6,000	6,050	50 U
Utilities, maintenance, etc.	4,500	4,500	0
Total expenses	44,500	46,650	2,150 U
Total operating income	$5,500	$3,350	$2,150 U

U = Unfavorable—actual exceeds budget

Exhibit 1-3
Mayfair Starbucks Store. Performance Report for the Month Ended March 31, 20X1

As the store sells its products and incurs costs, Starbucks' accounting system collects the revenue and cost information. At the end of the month (or weekly, or possibly even daily, if managers need quick feedback), the accounting department prepares a store-level performance report such as the one in Exhibit 1-3. Actual reports will usually contain more details, but the format will be similar to that shown here.

Store managers and their superiors use the performance report to help appraise how effectively and efficiently the store is operating. Their focus is on the variances—the deviations from the budget. The Mayfair store report shows that the store met its targeted sales, but ingredient costs were $2,500 over budget, store labor costs were $400 under budget, and other labor was $50 over budget. By investigating such variances, managers may find better ways of doing things. Since ingredients had by far the largest variance, management would undoubtedly investigate it first.

Performance reports spur investigation of exceptions—items for which actual amounts differ significantly from budgeted amounts. Managers then revise operations to conform with the plans or revise the plans. This process is **management by exception,** which means concentrating on areas that deviate from the plan and ignoring areas that are presumed to be running smoothly. Thus, the management-by-exception approach frees managers from needless concern with those phases of operations that are adhering to plans. However, well-conceived plans should incorporate enough discretion or flexibility so that the manager may feel free to pursue any unforeseen opportunities. In other words, control should not be a straightjacket. When unfolding events call for actions not specifically authorized in the plan, managers should have the freedom to take these actions.

management by exception
Concentrating on areas that deviate from the plan and ignoring areas that are presumed to be running smoothly.

Notice that although budgets aid planning and performance reports aid control, it is not accountants but other managers and their subordinates who evaluate accounting reports and actually plan and control operations. Accounting assists the managerial planning and control functions by providing prompt measurements of actions and by systematically pinpointing trouble spots.

Planning and Control for Product Life Cycles and the Value Chain

Many management decisions relate to a single good or service, or to a group of related products. To effectively plan for and control production of such goods or services, accountants and other managers must consider the product's life cycle. **Product life cycle** refers to the various stages through which a product passes, from conception and development to introduction into the market to maturation and, finally, withdrawal from the market. At each stage, managers face differing costs and potential returns. Exhibit 1-4 shows a typical product life cycle.

Product life cycles range from a few months (for fashion clothing or faddish toys) to many years (for automobiles or refrigerators). Some products, such as many computer

product life cycle
The various stages through which a product passes, from conception and development to introduction into the market to maturation and, finally, withdrawal from the market.

Exhibit 1-4
Typical Product Life Cycle

software packages, have long development stages and relatively short market lives. Others, such as Boeing 777 airplanes, have a market life many times longer than their development stage.

In the planning process, managers must recognize revenues and costs over the entire life cycle—however long or short. Accounting needs to track actual costs and revenues throughout the life cycle, too. Periodic comparisons between planned costs and revenues and actual costs and revenues allow managers to assess the current profitability of a product, determine its current product life-cycle stage, and make any needed changes in strategy.

For example, suppose **Pfizer, Inc.,** is developing a new drug to reduce high blood pressure. The budget for the product should plan for costs without revenues in the product development stage. Most of the revenues are realized in the introduction and mature-market stages, and a pricing strategy should recognize the need for revenues to cover both development and phaseout costs as well as the direct costs of producing the drug. During phaseout, Pfizer must balance the costs of producing the drug with both the revenue generated and the need to keep the drug on the market for those who have come to rely on it.

The Value Chain

In addition to considering a product's life cycle, managers making planning and controlling decisions must recognize those activities necessary for a company to create the goods or services that it sells. Whether making doughnuts in a shopping mall or making $50 million airplanes, all organizations try to create goods or services that their customers value. The **value chain** is the set of business functions or activities that add value to the products or services of an organization. These functions are as follows:

- Research and development—the generation of, and experimentation with, ideas related to new products, services, or processes.
- Design of products, services, or processes—the detailed design and engineering of products.
- Production—the coordination and assembly of resources to produce a product or deliver a service.
- Marketing—the manner by which individuals or groups learn about the value and features of products or services (for example, advertising or selling activities).
- Distribution—the mechanism by which a company delivers products or services to the customer.
- Customer service—the support activities provided to the customer.
- Support functions—the support activities provided to other internal business functions (for example, management information systems, accounting).

Exhibit 1-5 shows these business functions. Not all are of equal importance to the success of a company. Senior management must decide which of these functions enables the company to gain and maintain a competitive edge. For example, **Dell Computers** considers the design function a critical success factor. The features designed into Dell's computers create higher quality. In addition, the design of efficient processes used to

value chain
The set of business functions or activities that add value to the products or services of an organization.

Exhibit 1-5
The Value Chain of
Business Functions

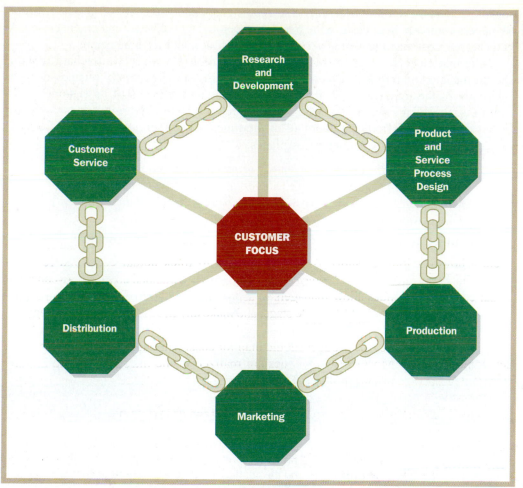

Support activities such as management information systems and accounting are not shown. These activities support all other value chain functions.

make and deliver computers lowers costs and speeds up delivery to its customers. Of course, Dell also performs the other value-chain functions, but it concentrates on being the best process designer in the computer market.

Accountants play a key role in all value-chain functions. Most obvious is the production stage, where accountants measure the costs of production and help track the effects of continuous improvement programs. They facilitate cost planning and control through the use of budgets and performance reporting, as described in the previous section. However, accounting can also have a great influence on the two preproduction value-chain functions. For example, accountants provide estimated revenue and cost data during the research and development stage and especially the design stage of the value chain. These data enable managers and engineers to reduce the life-cycle costs of products or services by changing product and process designs. Using computer-based planning software, accountants can give managers rapid feedback on ideas for cost reductions long before the company must make a commitment to purchase expensive equipment.

Accountants also play a central role in postproduction value-chain functions. For example, marketing decisions have a significant impact on sales, but the cost of promotional programs is also significant. Accountants analyze the trade-off between increased costs and revenues. In addition, accounting information can influence decisions about distributing products or services to customers. Should a company sell its products directly to a chain of retail stores, or should it sell to a wholesaler? What transportation system should be used—trucks or trains? Accountants provide important information about the costs of each alternative. Finally, accountants provide cost data for customer

OBJECTIVE 5

Discuss the role accountants play in the company's value chain functions.

service activities, such as warranty and repair costs and the costs of goods returned. Managers compare these costs to the benefits generated by the better customer service. As you can see, cost management is very important throughout the value chain.

Note that customer focus is at the center of Exhibit 1-5. Each value-chain function should focus on activities that create value to the customer. Successful businesses never lose sight of the importance of maintaining a focus on the needs of its customers. For example, one of the main principles in Starbucks' mission statement is to "develop enthusiastically satisfied customers all of the time." Customers are also the focus of a very different business, commercial airplanes:

> *Customers, by the choices they make, grant companies a future or condemn them to extinction. We will continuously strive to achieve total customer satisfaction. . . . We will seek to truly understand the complexity of our customers' needs, not push our own ideas or technology.*
>
> Philip Condit, chairman and chief executive officer, Boeing Company

The value chain and the concepts of adding value and focusing on the customer are extremely important to companies. Accountants must focus on the values created compared to the costs incurred in each link of the value chain. Therefore, we will return to the value chain and use it as a focus for discussion throughout this book.

MAKING MANAGERIAL DECISIONS

Measuring costs at various stages of the value chain is important to Starbucks. Suppose that you are a Starbucks manager or accountant. For each of the following activities, indicate the value-chain function that is being performed and what accounting information might be helpful to managers in the function.

1. Process engineers investigate methods to reduce the time to roast coffee beans and to better preserve their flavor.
2. A direct-to-your-home mail-order system is established to sell custom-blended coffees.
3. Arabica coffee beans are purchased and transported to company processing plants.
4. Focus groups investigate the feasibility of a new line of Frappuccino drinks.
5. A telephone hot line is established for mail-order customers to call with comments on the quality and speed of delivery.
6. Each company-owned retail store undertakes a campaign to provide information to customers about the processes used to make its coffee products.

Answers

1. Design. Both the design of products and, as here, design of production processes are part of the entire design function. Managers need the costs of various possible production processes to decide among the alternatives.
2. Distribution. This provides an additional way to deliver products to customers. Managers need information on the costs of a mail-order system to compare to the added profit from mail-order sales.
3. Production. The purchase price of beans and transportation (or freight-in) costs are part of product costs incurred during the production function. Starbucks purchases only premium beans, but the company is still concerned about the price paid and the added costs of transportation.
4. Research and development. These costs (mostly wages) are incurred prior to management's final decision to design and produce a new product. Predicted revenues and costs from the Frappuccino market can help managers design a drink that is both marketable and profitable.
5. Customer service. These costs include all expenditures made after Starbucks has delivered the product to the customer; in this case, Starbucks obtains feedback on the quality and speed of delivery. Managers will trade off the cost of the hot line and the value of the information generated from the calls.
6. Marketing. These costs are for activities that enhance the existing or potential customers' awareness and opinion of the product. Like many advertising expenses, it is easy to estimate the costs of such a program but hard to quantify the benefits.

Accounting's Position in the Organization

The role of management accountants in organizations has been changing rapidly during the last decade or so. Consider the following four work activities of management accountants:

- Collecting and compiling information.
- Preparing standardized reports.
- Interpreting and analyzing information.
- Being involved in decision making.

Recent surveys show that a majority of management accountants are spending less time on the first two activities and more time on the last two. In addition, more than 80% of the respondents to these surveys think this trend will be even more pronounced in the future. In essence, the management accountant is becoming an internal consultant on information-related issues—that is, an advisor for managers about what information would be useful, what information is available, and how to get the needed information.

Line and Staff Authority

As an organization grows, it must divide responsibilities among a number of managers and executives. In traditionally organized companies, this meant increasing specialization. **Line managers** were directly involved with making and selling the organization's products or services. Their decisions led directly to meeting (or not meeting) the organization's objectives. In contrast, **staff managers** were advisory—they supported the line managers. They had no authority over line managers, but they helped the line managers by providing information and advice. The organization chart in Exhibit 1-6 shows how a traditional manufacturing company divides responsibilities between line and staff managers. Notice that Sales, Engineering, Personnel, and Financial provide staff support at the corporate level, and Receiving and Storeroom, Inspection, Tool Room, Purchasing, Production Control, and Maintenance provide staff support at the factory. They all support the line managers located in Manufacturing.

Many modern organizations are abandoning the type of hierarchical structure shown in Exhibit 1-6 and replacing it with a "flatter" organization. Specialization by individuals is giving way to decision making by cross-functional teams. In such an organization, management accountants are still the information specialists, but they are not isolated in one branch of the organization chart. They do not sit in their offices and issue reports that managers use to make decisions. Instead, the management accountants are physically located with the line managers, and they work together to determine the optimal information support for the managers. We highlight some other recent changes in the role of accountants in the Business First box on p. 19.

Controller and Treasurer Functions

We have referred to the role of management accountants in an organization. However, seldom does anyone have the title "management accountant." Those carrying out management accounting functions have a variety of titles. The **chief financial officer (CFO),** a top executive who deals with all finance and accounting issues, oversees the accounting function in most organizations. Both the treasurer and controller generally report to the CFO, as shown in Exhibit 1-6. The **treasurer** is concerned mainly with the company's financial matters such as raising and managing cash, the **controller** (also called **comptroller** in many government organizations) with operating matters such as aiding management decision making. Finance classes address most treasury activities; accounting is concerned mainly with the controllership activities. The

---

line managers
Managers who are directly involved with making and selling the organization's products or services.

staff managers
Managers who are advisory to the line managers. They have no authority over line managers, but they help the line managers by providing information and advice.

chief financial officer (CFO)
The top executive who deals with all finance and accounting issues in an organization. The CFO generally oversees the accounting function.

treasurer
A manager who is concerned mainly with the company's financial matters such as raising and managing cash.

controller (comptroller)
The top accounting officer of an organization who deals mainly with operating matters such as aiding management decision making.

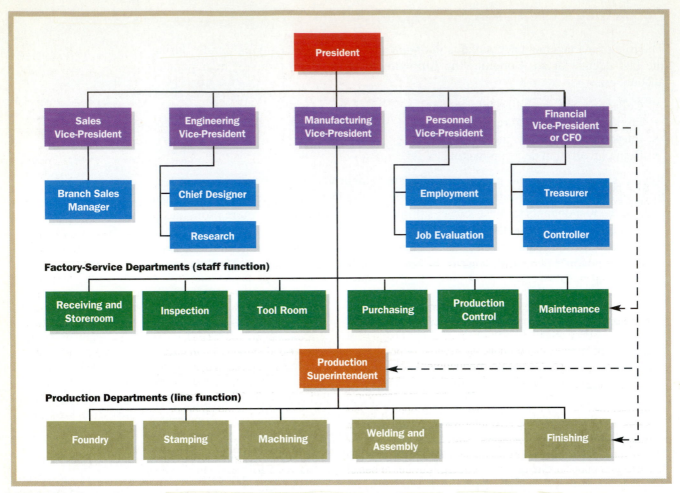

Exhibit 1-6
Partial Organization Chart of a Manufacturing Company

Contrast the functions of controllers and treasurers.

controller is the organization's top accounting officer. The controller's department provides managers with specialized services, including advice and help in budgeting, analyzing variances, pricing, and making special decisions. The controller often also prepares the financial statements for external users.

The Financial Executives Institute, an association of corporate treasurers and controllers, distinguishes the two as follows:

Controllership	**Treasurership**
1. Planning for control	1. Provision of capital
2. Reporting and interpreting	2. Investor relations
3. Evaluating and consulting	3. Short-term financing
4. Tax administration	4. Banking and custody
5. Government reporting	5. Credits and collections
6. Protection of assets	6. Investments
7. Economic appraisal	7. Risk management (insurance)

Management accounting is the primary means of implementing the first three functions of controllership. In a small company, one person may perform both treasury and controllership functions. Nevertheless, it is useful to differentiate the two different roles.

THE ACCOUNTANT'S ROLE AT THE MARMON GROUP

The Marmon Group, Inc., embodies nearly all of the reasons why management accounting is a vital and growing function in today's leading companies. Marmon, headquartered in Chicago, is an international association of more than 100 manufacturing, distribution, and service companies with annual revenues in excess of $6.4 billion and assets of $7.4 billion. It is one of the 20 largest privately held companies in the United States. Because operations are spread out in more than 40 different countries with thousands of diverse products and services (such as workers' gloves, water coolers, railroad tank cars, medical products, and credit services for banks), managers at Marmon make extensive use of management accounting information when undertaking important decisions.

What exactly is the role of management accountants at Marmon? According to Jim Smith, Marmon's former director of cost management, "The role of the management accountant is changing dramatically in most of our companies." In the past, Marmon's management accountants were basically clerical workers who spent most of their time analyzing monthly cost variances. Now, however, Marmon's management accountants work closely with operating and sales managers, providing cost information in a format that makes sense to those managers. Says Smith, "In the past few years the management accountant has become much more of a financial and business strategy adviser to senior management. Operating and sales managers are demanding meaningful cost information, and management accountants are helping them see how their actions affect costs and the bottom line."

Management accountants have become more important to Marmon, according to Smith, because recessions and foreign competition over the past ten years have awakened the understanding in most managers that managing costs is an important function. Knowing what a product truly costs or the cost of servicing a particular customer has become essential to Marmon's profitability.

"To help manage costs," says Smith, "accountants and managers are shying away from using one cost, often the cost used for financial reporting purposes, as the only important cost." Instead, they are now using costs calculated for the decision at hand. As Smith indicated, "Depending on the decision, any of the cost methods described in *Introduction to Management Accounting* are relevant." He believes this is a very positive change, "since it allows and, in fact, requires the management accountant to understand all of the functions in a business and how each one adds value to the product or service."

Source: The Marmon Group Web site (http://www.marmon.com); discussions with James Smith, former director of cost management, the Marmon Group, Inc.

Summary Problem For Your Review

PROBLEM

Following are quotes by or about controllers or treasurers. Indicate whether each refers to a treasury or controllership function and why.

1. "At **Lucent**, Ms. Hund-Mejean was responsible for executing over $12 billion in corporate financings, the management of customer financings activities, oversight of investor relations, and the management of over $30 billion in employee benefit assets."
2. "At [a California distribution company] we're implementing a company-wide budget for capital spending and expect to reduce capital spending by 10%."
3. "At **DRS Technologies**, Mr. Hardman will be responsible for . . . arranging short- and long-term financing, maintaining relationships with commercial and investment banks and credit rating agencies, overseeing domestic and international cash management, forecasting, developing and executing foreign exchange strategies, and providing interest-rate risk management and capital-structure analysis."

SOLUTION

1. These are all financial activities, thus Ms. Hund-Mejean must be a treasurer.
2. Budgeting and advising on capital spending are functions of the controller.
3. All of the items mentioned are financing activities, so Mr. Hardman is the treasurer at DRS Technologies.

Career Opportunities in Management Accounting

OBJECTIVE 7

Explain why accounting is important in a variety of career paths.

The many types and levels of accounting personnel found in the typical organization mean that there are broad opportunities awaiting those who master the accounting discipline. Average starting salaries for accounting graduates are higher than those for other business graduates. In 2002, starting accounting salaries were nearly $2,000 a year more than ecomomics/finance and management information systems salaries and nearly $6,000 higher than marketing and general business administration salaries, according to a survey by the National Association of Colleges and Employers. In addition, managers throughout an organization, from entry level to CEO, find that management accounting skills help them be better managers or executives.

Certified Management Accountant

certified public accountant (CPA)
In the United States, independent accountants who reassure the public about the reliability of companies' published financial statements.

chartered accountant (CA)
The equivalent to the CPA in many countries.

certified management accountant (CMA)
The management accountant's counterpart to the CPA.

Institute of Management Accountants (IMA)
The largest U.S. professional organization of accountants focused on internal accounting. It oversees the CMA program.

When accounting is mentioned, most people think first of independent auditors—**certified public accountants (CPAs)** in the United States and **chartered accountants (CAs)** in many other nations—who reassure the public about the reliability of companies' published financial statements. However, the majority of accountants work in private industry and government. While they produce the organizations' financial statements, they also produce management accounting information for managers.

The **certified management accountant (CMA)** designation is the internal accountant's counterpart to the CPA. The **Institute of Management Accountants (IMA),** the largest U.S. professional organization focused on internal accounting, oversees the CMA program. CMAs must pass a four-part examination: (1) economics, finance, and management; (2) financial accounting and reporting; (3) management reporting, analysis, and behavioral issues; and (4) decision analysis and information systems.[2] Like the CPA designation, the CMA confers higher status on its holders, and it also leads to more responsible positions and higher pay.

Training for Top Management Positions

Why should you study management accounting if you do not plan to become an accountant—either a CPA or CMA? In addition to preparing you to be an accountant, studying accounting helps you to understand the decision making process and how information can improve decisions in purchasing, manufacturing, wholesaling, retailing, marketing, and many other functional areas. You will develop skills that will help you to be a better manager, regardless of the type of managerial position you hold.

In addition to studying accounting, working as an accountant, at least early in your career, can give you exposure to many parts of an organization. By learning about all aspects of an organization, you will be better prepared for positions as, for example,

---

[2]Information can be obtained from the IMA, 10 Paragon Drive, Montvale, NJ 07645, or at http://www.imanet.org.

a production or marketing executive. Why? Because you will interact with managers in those areas, learn from them, and have an opportunity to impress them. According to an article in *Business Week*, "the main reason the controller is getting the ear of top management these days is that he or she is virtually the only person familiar with all the working parts of the company." A recent survey by *Financial Executive* magazine showed that 33% of chief executive officers (CEOs) in companies with revenues greater than $500 million had risen through the finance/accounting ranks, compared with 26% from operations and 21% from sales and marketing. CEOs of companies such as **Pfizer** and **Burger King** have finance backgrounds. Thus, you can see that management accounting can be a ladder to the highest-level executive positions in an organization.

Adaptation to Change

The job of the CFO and the function of management accounting in general have changed in the last decade or two. Business has become more competitive, and the role of information has become more important. Many companies today derive their competitive advantage from their information, not their physical facilities. Such companies have focused much attention on improving accounting information. The information that supported traditional companies in the 1980s and 1990s does not support the modern business environment of the twenty-first century.

Changes in the business environment have caused most of the changes in accounting. Because those changes have led to a more prominent role for information, including accounting information, they have also elevated the influence and prestige of accountants within organizations. The managing director of a prominent executive search firm, quoted in *Financial Executive,* summarized it well: "Today, executive searches focus on finding a CFO who not only has financial acumen but who can be a true business partner with the CEO — and who has the breadth and depth to serve as the organization's number two executive."

Current Trends

Four major business trends are causing changes in management accounting today:

1. Shift from a manufacturing-based to a service-based economy in the United States
2. Increased global competition
3. Advances in technology
4. Changes in business processes

OBJECTIVE 8

Identify current trends in management accounting.

We will discuss the first three in this section and the fourth in the following section.

The service sector now accounts for almost 80% of the employment in the United States. Service industries are becoming increasingly competitive, and their use of accounting information is growing. Many examples in this book are from service companies.

Global competition has increased in recent years as many countries have lowered international barriers to trade, such as tariffs and duties. In addition, there has been a worldwide trend toward deregulation. The result has been a shift in the balance of economic power in the world. Nowhere has this been more evident than in the United States. To regain their competitive edge, many U.S. companies redesigned their accounting systems to provide more accurate and timely information about the cost of activities, products, or services. To be competitive, managers must understand the effects of their decisions on costs, and accountants must help managers predict such effects.

By far the most dominant influence on management accounting over the past decade has been technological change. This change has affected both the production and the use of accounting information. The increasing capabilities and decreasing cost of computers, especially personal computers (PCs), has changed how accountants gather, store, manipulate, and report data. In many cases, the use of spreadsheet software and graphics packages enables managers to access data directly and to generate their own reports and analyses. Thus, today managers and accountants must work together to assure the availability of the needed data and to be sure managers know how to assemble and use the data.

One of the most rapidly growing uses of technology is **electronic commerce** or **e-commerce**—conducting business online. The media focuses on business-to-consumer (**B2C**) transactions, but nearly 90% of e-commerce is business-to-business (**B2B**) transactions. A survey by the Boston Consulting Group predicted U.S. e-commerce sales of $4.8 trillion by 2004, up from only $1.2 trillion in 2000. The business slowdown of 2001 and 2002 slowed the growth in e-commerce, but the future is still bright—especially for B2B transactions. B2C may create convenience, but B2B creates real savings to the companies involved. For example, some companies have reduced procurement processing costs by as much as 70% by automating the process. Accounting for e-commerce transactions differs from traditional accounting because there is no paper trail of evidence for accountants to rely on to assure the accuracy of their data and reports.

The most direct effect of technology changes on accounting systems has been the growing use of **enterprise resource planning (ERP) systems**—integrated information systems that support all functional areas of a company. Accounting is just one part of such a system. For example, J. D. Edwards, now part of People Soft, describes its ERP system as one that helps companies "with managing finance, assets (including inventory, fixed assets, and real estate), people, projects, suppliers, and the fulfillment and manufacturing processes." Other well-known ERP system providers are Oracle, SAP, and Baan. Accountants must work with managers throughout the organization to ensure that the ERP system effectively and efficiently provides the financial information those managers need.

Finally, the development of **XBRL** (eXtensible Business Reporting Language), an XML-based accounting language, helps communicate financial information electronically. This language is likely to greatly influence both internal and external reporting by making comparisons across companies much simpler.

Changes in Business Processes

Management accounting exists to support business decisions. When businesses change the way they operate, their information needs change, and therefore they should consider altering their accounting systems. In recent years, advances in technology have been a prime driver of changes in management practices.

Some companies implement sweeping changes in operations through **business process reengineering,** the fundamental rethinking and radical redesign of business processes to improve performance in areas such as cost, quality, service, and speed. This technique has been especially popular in the United States, and government as well as business organizations have applied it. Examples are the U.S. Joint Forces Command in Norfolk, Virginia, and Bank One in Chicago.

A more targeted change leading to increased efficiency in U.S. factories has been the adoption of a **just-in-time (JIT) philosophy.** Originally, JIT referred only to an inventory system that minimized inventories by arranging for materials and subcomponents to arrive just as they were needed and for goods to be made just in time to be shipped to customers—no sooner and no later. But JIT has become the cornerstone of a broad management philosophy. It originated in Japanese companies such as Toyota and Kawasaki, and now has been adopted by many large U.S. companies including Hewlett-Packard, Goodyear, General Motors, Intel, and Xerox. Many small firms have also embraced JIT. The essence of the JIT philosophy is to eliminate waste. Managers try to (1) reduce the

---

electronic commerce (e-commerce)
Conducting business online.

B2C
Electronic commerce from business to consumer.

B2B
Electronic commerce from one business to another business.

enterprise resource planning (ERP) systems
Integrated information systems that support all functional areas of a company.

XBRL
An XML-based accounting language that helps communicate financial information electronically.

business process reengineering
The fundamental rethinking and radical redesign of business processes to improve performance in areas such as cost, quality, service, and speed.

just-in-time (JIT) philosophy
A philosophy to eliminate waste by reducing the time products spend in the production process and eliminating the time products spend on activities that do not add value.

time that products spend in the production process and (2) eliminate the time that products spend in activities that do not add value (such as inspection and waiting time).

Companies can reduce process time by redesigning, simplifying, and automating the production process. They can use computer-aided design (CAD) to design products that can be manufactured efficiently and computer-aided manufacturing (CAM) to direct and control production equipment. **Computer-integrated manufacturing (CIM) systems** use CAD, CAM, robots, and computer-controlled machines. The costs of such a system are quite different from those of a less-automated system. Companies that install a full CIM system use very little labor. Instead, they must acquire the robots and computer-controlled machines needed to perform the routine jobs that were previously accomplished by assembly-line workers. Besides automating production, companies have found that a focus on quality is important in today's competitive environment. In the 1980s and 1990s, many companies undertook **total quality management (TQM)** initiatives. TQM minimizes costs by maximizing quality. It focuses on continuous improvement in quality and has come to represent a focus on satisfying one's customers. Recently the focus on quality has shifted to **Six Sigma**, a continuous process improvement effort designed to reduce costs by improving quality. For many companies, it has become a management philosophy used to transform their business. Six Sigma essentially ensures that internal processes are running as efficiently as possible.

Why do these business process changes affect management accounting? They all have a direct effect on costs, and accountants often measure the actual cost savings, predict anticipated cost savings, and develop costs for products or services that differ for different production environments. For example, one midwestern factory saved production time by redesigning its plant layout so that the distance products traveled from one operation to the next during production was reduced from 1,384 feet to 350 feet. Accountants measured the cost the company saved by the reduced production time. A British company reduced the time to manufacture a vacuum pump from three weeks to six minutes by switching from long assembly lines to manufacturing cells that accomplish the entire process in quick succession. Again, accountants measured the benefits created by the reduced production time. In general, when companies change their production processes to accomplish economic objectives, accountants predict and measure the economic impact.

computer-integrated manufacturing (CIM) systems
Systems that use computer-aided design, computer-aided manufacturing, robots, and computer-controlled machines.

total quality management (TQM)
Initiatives that minimize costs by maximizing quality.

Six Sigma
A continuous process improvement effort designed to reduce costs by improving quality.

MAKING MANAGERIAL DECISIONS

Suppose you are a manager of a **DuPont** chemical plant. The plant has just undertaken a business process reengineering project and, as a result, has substantially changed its production process. It is much more automated, with newly acquired equipment replacing labor-intensive operations. The plant is also making more use of electronic commerce and moving toward a just-in-time inventory policy. You have a meeting with your accountant to discuss possible changes in your accounting system. What types of accounting-system changes might be warranted?

Answer
Major changes in production processes generally lead to different information needs. The old accounting system may have focused on accounting for labor; the new system should carefully monitor and report on the use of the automated equipment. This will direct attention to the most important costs in the process and make sure that they are not out of control. Problem-solving needs will also be different. Initially, the plant's managers will probably want comparative data on the costs of the new process versus the cost of the old. In the future, they will need information about how best to use a capacity that the plant owns (the equipment) rather than how much labor to use for the planned level of production.

Implications of Process Changes for the Study of Management Accounting

As you read the remainder of this book, remember that accounting systems change as the world changes. You will find the techniques presented in this book applied in real organizations today. Tomorrow, however, everything may be different. To adapt to changes, you must understand *why* companies are using the techniques, not just *how* they are using them. We urge you to resist the temptation simply to memorize rules and techniques. Instead, develop your understanding of the underlying concepts and principles. These will continue to be useful in developing and understanding new techniques for changing environments.

Ethical Conduct for Professional Accountants

Business processes and accounting systems change. However, the need for accountants to adhere to high ethical standards of professional conduct will never change. Integrity has always been important, but after the ethical lapses revealed in 2001 and 2002, it has taken on added urgency. Accountants must reestablish a stellar reputation for ethics and integrity that the events of recent years have diminished. First we should define *ethics*. The Institute of Management Accountants says that "ethics, in its broader sense, deals with human conduct in relation to what is morally good and bad, right and wrong. It is the application of values to decision making. These values include honesty, fairness, responsibility, respect and compassion." We like to think of **ethics** as simply doing what is right.

ethics
Doing what is right.

Standards of Ethical Conduct

Until recently, public opinion surveys consistently ranked accountants high in terms of their professional ethics. Ethical standards require CPAs and CMAs to adhere to codes of conduct regarding competence, confidentiality, integrity, and objectivity. Exhibit 1-7 contains the **Standards of Ethical Conduct for Practitioners of Management Accounting and Financial Management** developed by the IMA. Professional accounting organizations have procedures for reviewing alleged behavior not consistent with the standards.

Standards of Ethical Conduct for Practitioners of Management Accounting and Financial Management
Codes of conduct developed by the Institute of Management Accountants; these codes include competence, confidentiality, integrity, and objectivity.

Within organizations, the CFO is often the ethical gatekeeper and company conscience. Not only should CFOs have high personal integrity, often they are also responsible for assuring high ethical conduct throughout the organization. There should be no difference between personal and business ethics. Managers who check their ethical standards at the door when they report to work, rationalizing that "business is business," will eventually lead an organization into trouble. Realizing this, many companies have hiring practices that include ethical profiling—trying to hire only managers with high ethical standards.

OBJECTIVE 9

Appreciate the importance of a code of ethical conduct to professional accountants.

The ethical organization also has policies in place to motivate ethical actions. Top management sets the tone. Complete integrity and outspoken support for ethical standards by senior managers, in both word and deed, are the greatest motivators of ethical behavior throughout an organization. To use an old cliché, top management must "walk the walk" as well as "talk the talk." A **code of conduct**—a document specifying the ethical standards of an organization—is the centerpiece of most ethics programs. (See the Business First box, "Ethics and Corporate Codes of Conduct," on p. 27.) But having a code is not sufficient. Actual policies and practices influence behavior. This means that managers' evaluations must include an assessment of ethical conduct. Unethical behavior that leads to apparently high performance cannot be tolerated. An accountant who can hide losses by manipulating the accounting reports should be penalized, not rewarded. For example, WorldCom, Global Crossing, Qwest, and other companies created accounting entries to

code of conduct
A document specifying the ethical standards of an organization.

Exhibit 1-7
Standards of
Ethical Conduct
for Practitioners
of Management
Accounting and
Financial
Management

Practitioners of management accounting and financial management have an obligation to the public, their profession, the organization they serve, and themselves to maintain the highest standards of ethical conduct. In recognition of this obligation, the Institute of Management Accountants has promulgated the following standards of ethical conduct for practitioners of management accounting and financial management. Adherence to these standards, both professionally and internationally, is integral to achieving the Objectives of Management Accounting. Practitioners of management accounting and financial management shall not commit acts contrary to these standards nor shall they condone the commission of such acts by others within their organizations.

Competence

Practitioners of management accounting and financial management have a responsibility to

- Maintain an appropriate level of professional competence by ongoing development of their knowledge and skills.
- Perform their professional duties in accordance with relevant laws, regulations, and technical standards.
- Prepare complete and clear reports and recommendations after appropriate analyses of relevant and reliable information.

Confidentiality

Practitioners of management accounting and financial management have a responsibility to

- Refrain from disclosing confidential information acquired in the course of their work except when authorized, unless legally obligated to do so.
- Inform subordinates as appropriate regarding the confidentiality of information acquired in the course of their work and monitor their activities to assure the maintenance of that confidentiality.
- Refrain from using or appearing to use confidential information acquired in the course of their work for unethical or illegal advantage either personally or through third parties.

Integrity

Practitioners of management accounting and financial management have a responsibility to

- Avoid actual or apparent conflicts of interest and advise all appropriate parties of any potential conflict.
- Refrain from engaging in any activity that would prejudice their ability to carry out their duties ethically.
- Refuse any gift, favor, or hospitality that would influence or would appear to influence their actions.
- Refrain from either actively or passively subverting the attainment of the organization's legitimate and ethical objectives.
- Recognize and communicate professional limitations or other constraints that would preclude responsible judgment or successful performance of an activity.
- Communicate unfavorable as well as favorable information and professional judgments or opinions.
- Refrain from engaging in or supporting any activity that would discredit the profession.

Objectivity

Practitioners of management accounting and financial management have a responsibility to

- Communicate information fairly and objectively.
- Disclose fully all relevant information that could reasonably be expected to influence an intended user's understanding of the reports, comments, and recommendations presented.

Exhibit 1-7
Continued

Resolution of Ethical Conflict

In applying the standards of ethical conduct, practitioners of management accounting and financial management may encounter problems in identifying unethical behavior or in resolving an ethical conflict. When faced with significant ethical issues, practitioners of management accounting and financial management should follow the established policies of the organization bearing on the resolution of such conflict. If these policies do not resolve the ethical conflict, such practitioners should consider the following courses of action.

- Discuss such problems with the immediate superior except when it appears that the superior is involved, in which case the problem should be presented initially to the next higher managerial level. If a satisfactory resolution cannot be achieved when the problem is initially presented, submit the issues to the next higher managerial level. If the immediate superior is the chief executive officer, or equivalent, the acceptable reviewing authority may be a group such as the audit committee, executive committee, board of directors, board of trustees, or owners. Contact with levels above the immediate superior should be initiated only with the superior's knowledge, assuming the superior is not involved. Except where legally prescribed, communication of such problems to authorities or individuals not employed or engaged by the organization is not considered appropriate.
- Clarify relevant ethical issues by confidential discussion with an objective advisor (for example, IMA Ethics Counseling service) to obtain a better understanding of possible courses of action. Consult your own attorney as to legal obligations and rights concerning the ethical conflict.
- If the ethical conflict still exists after exhausting all levels of internal review, there may be no other recourse on significant matters than to resign from the organization and to submit an informative memorandum to an appropriate representative of the organization. After resignation, depending on the nature of the ethical conflict, it may also be appropriate to notify other parties.

Source: Institute of Management Accountants, Ethical Standards, http://www.imanet.org.

---

make their financial reports look better than their actual performances. Such entries were misleading—and some downright illegal. At first, managers were rewarded for coming up with such innovative schemes. But in the end, they and their schemes were the downfall of their companies. Once exposed, they revealed the companies' lack of integrity and caused investors and others to question many aspects of the companies' operations.

Many companies make ethics a top priority. For example, Starbucks includes ethical principles in the first line of its mission statement: "To establish Starbucks as the premier purveyor of the finest coffee in the world while maintaining our uncompromising principles as we grow." **Ben & Jerry's,** the ice cream company, has a high reputation for ethics that focuses more on its external social obligations, as recognized in its mission statement: "To operate the Company in a way that actively recognizes the central role that business plays in the structure of society by initiating innovative ways to improve the quality of life of a broad community—local, national, and international." There are many more companies with high ethical standards than with large ethical violations. It is unfortunate that the latter receive most of the publicity.

To maintain high ethical standards, accountants and others need to recognize situations that create pressures for unethical behavior. Four such temptations, summarized in *Financial Executive,* are

1. Emphasis on short-term results. This may have been the largest issue in the recent spate of ethical breakdowns. If "making the numbers" is goal number one, accountants may do whatever is necessary to produce the expected profit numbers.

ETHICS AND CORPORATE CODES OF CONDUCT

The Sarbanes-Oxley Act of 2002 requires companies "to disclose whether or not, and if not, the reason therefore, such issuer has adopted a code of ethics for senior financial officers, applicable to its principal financial officer and comptroller or principal accounting officer, or persons performing similar functions." This has created increased interest in corporate codes of conduct. However, a code of conduct means different things to different companies. Some of the items included in companies' codes of conduct include maintaining a dress code, avoiding illegal drugs, following instructions of superiors, being reliable and prompt, maintaining confidentiality, not accepting personal gifts from stakeholders as a result of company role, avoiding racial or sexual discrimination, avoiding conflict of interest, complying with laws and regulations, not using organization's property for personal use, not discriminating against race or age or sexual orientation, and reporting illegal or questionable activity. Even before the Enron and other corporate scandals, over 80% of U.S. companies had a code of conduct, according to a survey by the Financial Executives Institute. But the codes differed in type and in level of enforcement.

One company had only one rule: "Don't do anything you would be embarrassed to read about in tomorrow's newspaper." Others have detailed lists of dos and don'ts. Some companies use consulting firms to advise them on their codes. Although the codes and their development differ, the goal is generally the same—to motivate employees to act with integrity.

To encourage development of codes of conduct, the Financial Executives Institute includes examples of codes on its Web site. Two extremes among those presented are those of **Wiremold** and **CSX Corporation**. Wiremold has a simple, seven-point code: (1) respect others, (2) tell the truth, (3) be fair, (4) try new ideas, (5) ask why, (6) keep your promises, and (7) do your share. In contrast, CSX has 26 paragraphs detailing expectations of employees under the following headings: Employee Relationships and Conflicts of Interest, Political Contributions and Public Service Involvement, Misrepresentations and False Statements, Employee Discrimination and Harassment, Competition, and Safety and the Environment.

The existence of a code of conduct is not sufficient. After all, Enron's code of conduct specified that "business is to be conducted in compliance . . . with the highest professional and ethical standards." Top management must set the tone and get out the message. They must recognize and reward honesty and integrity. As Clarence Otis, CFO of **Darden Restaurants**, says, "Our senior managers care about honesty and integrity and doing things right, and that influences how they do their job." The corporate culture, more than codes of conduct, is the real influence on the ethical climate of an organization. Codes of conduct can be a part, but only a part, of developing a culture of integrity.

Sources: *Sarbanes-Oxley Act of 2002*, HR 3763; RedHawk Productions Web site (http://redhawkproductions.com); Financial Executives Institute Web site (http://www.fei.org); D. Blank, "A Matter of Ethics," *Internal Auditor*, February 2003, pp. 27–31; Enron Corporation 2000 Corporate Responsibility Report, p. 3.

2. **Ignoring the small stuff.** Most ethical compromises start out small. The first step may seem insignificant, but large misdeeds are often the result of many small steps. Toleration of even small lapses can lead to large problems.
3. **Economic cycles.** A down market can reveal what an up market conceals. When Enron was flying high, no one seemed to question its financial reports. When the economy took a downward turn, managers made ethical compromises to keep pace with expectations of an up market. The result was a huge crisis when scrutiny revealed the many questionable practices. To prevent disclosure of ethical problems in bad times, companies need to be especially vigilant in good times.
4. **Accounting rules.** Accounting rules have become more complex and less intuitive, making abuse of the rules harder to identify. Further, ethical accountants do not just meet the "letter of the law," they hold a higher standard for full and fair disclosure. They do not try to find loopholes in the regulations. Instead, they seek transparency—conveying to users the real economic performance and position of the company.

Few organizations are intentionally unethical. Even **Arthur Andersen,** the accounting firm destroyed by failed audits at Enron, Sunbeam, Global Crossing, and others, had a formal ethical structure, including a partner in charge of ethics. Nevertheless, other pressures, especially the pressure for growing revenues, overrode the ethical controls and caused many bad decisions.

Ethical Dilemmas

What makes an action by an accountant unethical? An unethical act is one that violates the ethical standards of the profession. The standards, however, leave much room for individual interpretation and judgment. A first step is to ask two questions: Is this action unethical? Would it be unethical not to take this action? If the answers to these questions are clear, then the ethical action is clear. For example, if WorldCom's accountants had asked whether their recording of expenses as assets was unethical, they would have no choice but to have answered "yes." However, ethical dilemmas faced by managers are often made more complex because there are no legal guidelines or even clear-cut ethical standards. Ethical dilemmas exist when managers must choose an alternative and there are (1) significant value conflicts among differing interests, (2) real alternatives that are both justifiable, and (3) significant consequences on stakeholders in the situation.

Suppose you are an accountant who has been asked to supply the company's banker with a profit forecast for the coming year. A badly needed bank loan rides on the prediction. The company president is absolutely convinced that profits will be at least $500,000—anything less than that and the loan is not likely to be approved.

Your analysis shows that if the planned introduction of a new product goes extraordinarily well, profits will exceed $500,000. The most likely outcome, however, is for a modestly successful introduction and a $100,000 profit. If the product fails, the company stands to lose $600,000. Without the loan, the new product cannot be taken to the market, and there is no way the company can avoid a loss for the year. Bankruptcy is a real possibility.

What forecast would you make? A forecast of less than $500,000 seems to guarantee financial problems, perhaps even bankruptcy. This would hurt stockholders, management, employees, suppliers, and customers. But a forecast of $500,000 may not be fair and objective. It may mislead the bank. Still, the president apparently thinks a $500,000 forecast is reasonable, and you know that there is some chance it will be achieved. Perhaps the potential benefit to the company of an overly optimistic forecast is greater than the possible cost to the bank.

There is no right answer to this dilemma. It is one of those gray areas where neither action is without its risks. But remember that a series of gray areas can create a black area. That is, a series of actions that push the boundary of ethical behavior can add up to a clearly unethical situation. Accountants must draw the line someplace, and it is usually better to be conservative than to push the boundary too far. Enron was the champion of pushing the boundaries. If its managers had done this once or twice, providing that they did not step over into a completely unethical area, it might have been acceptable. But the accumulation of questionable actions revealed an environment where ethical cosiderations were secondary at best.

Resolution of Ethical Conflicts

Ethical dilemmas often do not end with deciding what is ethical and what is not. If you discover unethical behavior in an organization, you are obligated to try to halt that behavior. However, you still have confidentiality issues to confront. The section on Resolution of Ethical Conflict in Exhibit 1-7 provides guidance. Most often you can bring the issue to the attention of your supervisor or a special ethics officer (often called an ombudsperson) in the organization. However, if there is not an ethics officer and you suspect your supervisor is involved in unethical activity, your decision becomes more complex. As was the case for the two whistle-blowers described in the Business First box on p. 9, you may need to go directly to the top levels in the company. Ultimately, the board of directors may become involved. If the case involves legal issues and the board is not responsive, approaching the Securities and Exchange Commission (the body that regulates corporate reporting) or other legal authorities may be necessary. However, rarely is it appropriate to go directly to the media.

Summary Problem For Your Review

PROBLEM

Yang Electronics Company (YEC) developed a high-speed, low-cost copying machine. The company marketed the machine primarily for home use. However, as YEC customers learned how easy and inexpensive it was to make copies with it, its use by small businesses grew. Sales soared as some businesses ordered large numbers of the copiers. However, the heavier use by these companies caused breakdowns in a certain component of the equipment. The copiers were warranted for two years, regardless of the amount of usage. Consequently, YEC experienced high costs for replacing the damaged components.

As the quarterly meeting of YEC's board of directors approached, Mark Chua, assistant controller, was asked to prepare a report on the situation. Unfortunately, it was hard to predict the exact effects. However, it seemed that many business customers were starting to switch to more expensive copiers sold by competitors. And it was clear that the increased maintenance costs would significantly affect YEC's profitability. Mark summarized the situation as best he could for the board.

Alice Martinez, YEC's controller, was concerned about the impact of the report on the board. She did not disagree with the analysis, but thought it would make management look bad and might even lead the board to discontinue the product. She was convinced from conversations with the head of engineering that the copier could be slightly redesigned to meet the needs of high-volume users, so discontinuing it may pass up a potentially profitable opportunity.

Martinez called Chua into her office and asked him to delete that part of his report dealing with the component failures. She said it was all right to mention this orally to the board, noting that engineering is nearing a solution to the problem. However, Chua felt strongly that such a revision in his report would mislead the board about a potentially significant, negative impact on the company's earnings.

Explain why Martinez's request to Chua is unethical. How should Chua resolve this situation?

SOLUTION

According to the Standards of Ethical Conduct for Practitioners of Management Accounting and Financial Management in Exhibit 1-7, Martinez's request violates requirements for competence, integrity, and objectivity. It violates competence because she is asking Chua to prepare a report that is not complete and clear, one that omits potentially relevant information. Therefore, the board will not have all the information it should to make a decision about the component failure problem.

The request violates the integrity requirement because the revised report may subvert the attainment of the organization's objectives to achieve Martinez's objectives. Management accountants are specifically responsible for communicating unfavorable as well as favorable information.

Finally, the revised report would not be objective. It would not disclose all relevant information that could be expected to influence the board's understanding of operations and therefore its decisions.

Chua's responsibility is to discuss this issue with increasingly higher levels of authority within YEC. First, he should let Martinez know about his misgivings. Possibly the issue can be resolved by her withdrawing the request. If not, he should inform her that he intends to take up the matter with her superior and then continue up to higher levels of authority, even to the board, if necessary, until the issue is resolved. So that Chua does not violate the standard of confidentiality, he should not discuss the matter with persons outside of YEC.

Highlights to Remember

1 Describe the major users and uses of accounting information. Internal managers use accounting information for making short-term planning and control decisions, for making nonroutine decisions, and for formulating overall policies and long-range plans. External users such as investors and regulators use published financial statements to make investment decisions, regulatory rulings, and many other decisions. Managers use accounting information to answer scorekeeping, attention-directing, and problem-solving questions.

2 Explain why ethics is important to management accountants. Integrity is essential to accountants because they provide information that users must trust to be right. Users cannot directly assess the quality of accounting data, and if they cannot rely on accountants to produce unbiased information, the information will have little value to the users.

3 Describe the cost-benefit and behavioral issues involved in designing an accounting system. Companies design management accounting information systems for the benefit of managers. These systems should be judged by a cost-benefit criterion—the benefits of better decisions should exceed the cost of the system. Behavioral factors—how the system affects managers and their decisions—greatly affect the benefit of a system.

4 Explain the role of budgets and performance reports in planning and control. Budgets and performance reports are essential tools for planning and control. Budgets result from the planning process. Managers use them to translate the organization's goals into action. A performance report compares actual results to the budget. Managers use these reports to monitor, evaluate, and reward performance and thus exercise control.

5 Discuss the role accountants play in the company's value-chain functions. Accountants play a key role in planning and control. Throughout the company's value chain, accountants gather and report cost and revenue information for decision makers.

6 Contrast the functions of controllers and treasurers. Accountants are staff employees who provide information and advice for line managers. The head of accounting is often called the controller. Unlike the treasurer, who is concerned mainly with financial matters such as raising capital and investing excess funds, the controller measures and reports on operating performance.

7 Explain why accounting is important in a variety of career paths. Accounting skills are useful in many functional areas of an organization. Management accountants often work with managers throughout the company and learn much from them. This exposure makes management accountants prime candidates for promotions to operating and executive positions.

8 Identify current trends in management accounting. Many factors have caused changes in accounting systems in recent years. Most significant are globalization, technology, and changed business processes. Without continuous adaptation and improvement, accounting systems would soon become obsolete.

9 Appreciate the importance of a code of ethical conduct to professional accountants. Users of accounting information expect both external and internal accountants to adhere to high standards of ethical conduct. Many ethical dilemmas, however, require value judgments, not the simple application of standards.

Accounting Vocabulary

Vocabulary is an essential and often troublesome phase of the learning process. A fuzzy understanding of terms hampers the learning of concepts and the ability to solve accounting problems.

Before proceeding to the assignment material or to the next chapter, be sure you understand the words and terms listed below. Their meaning is explained in the chapter and in the glossary at the end of this book.

accounting system, p. 7
attention directing, p. 5
B2B, p. 22
B2C, p. 22
behavioral implications, p. 11
budget, p. 12
business process reengineering, p. 22
certified management accountant (CMA), p. 20
certified public accountant (CPA), p. 20
chartered accountant (CA), p. 20
chief financial officer (CFO), p. 17
code of conduct, p. 24
controller (comptroller), p. 17
computer-integrated manufacturing (CIM) systems, p. 23

controlling, p. 11
cost-benefit balance, p. 10
decision making, p. 11
electronic commerce, p. 22
enterprise resource planning system (ERP), p. 22
e-commerce, p. 22
ethics, p. 24
financial accounting, p. 5
Foreign Corrupt Practices Act, p. 7
generally accepted accounting principles (GAAP), p. 7
Institute of Management Accountants (IMA), p. 20
internal controls, p. 7
just-in-time (JIT) philosophy, p. 22
line managers, p. 17
management accounting, p. 5

management audit, p. 8
management by exception, p. 13
performance reports, p. 12
planning, p. 11
problem solving, p. 5
product life cycle, p. 13
Sarbanes-Oxley Act, p. 8
scorekeeping, p. 5
Six Sigma, p. 23
staff managers, p. 17
Standards of Ethical Conduct for Practitioners of Management Accounting and Financial Management, p. 24
total quality management (TQM), p. 23
treasurer, p. 17
variances, p. 12
value chain, p. 14
XBRL, p. 22

Fundamental Assignment Material

The assignment material for each chapter is divided into two groups: fundamental and additional. The fundamental assignment material consists of two sets of parallel problems that convey the essential concepts and techniques of the chapter. The additional assignment material consists of questions, critical thinking exercises, exercises, problems, cases, excel application exercises, a collaborative learning exercise, and an Internet exercise that cover the chapter in more detail.

1-A1 Scorekeeping, Attention Directing, and Problem Solving

For each of the following activities, identify the function that the accountant is performing—scorekeeping, attention directing, or problem solving—and explain why it fits that category.

1. Preparing the budget for the maintenance department of Providence Hospital.
2. Analyzing, for a **Sony** production superintendent, the impact on costs of purchasing some new assembly equipment.
3. Preparing a scrap report for the finishing department of a **Toyota** parts factory.
4. Interpreting why a Springfield foundry did not adhere to its production schedule.
5. Explaining the stamping department's performance report.
6. Preparing a monthly statement of European sales for the **Ford Motor Company's** vice president of marketing.
7. Preparing, for the manager of production control of an **Inland Steel** plant, a cost comparison of two computerized manufacturing control systems.
8. Interpreting variances on the Harvard University purchasing department's performance report.
9. Analyzing, for a **Boeing** international manufacturing manager, the desirability of having some airplane parts made in Korea.
10. Preparing a schedule of depreciation for forklift trucks in the receiving department of a **General Electric** factory in Scotland.

1-A2 Management by Exception

Beta Gamma Sigma (BGS), the business honorary fraternity, held a homecoming party. The fraternity expected attendance of 80 persons and prepared the following budget:

Room rental	$ 140
Food	800
Entertainment	600
Decorations	220
Total	$1,760

After BGS paid all the bills for the party, the total cost came to $1,938, or $178 over budget. Details are $140 for room rental; $1,008 for food; $600 for entertainment; and $190 for decorations. Ninety-five persons attended the party.

1. Prepare a performance report for the party that shows how actual costs differed from the budget. That is, include in your report the budgeted amounts, actual amounts, and variances.
2. Suppose the fraternity uses a management-by-exception rule. Which costs deserve further examination? Why?

1-A3 Professional Ethics

Exhibit 1-7 lists four main categories of ethical standards for management accountants: competence, confidentiality, integrity, and objectivity. For each of the following situations, indicate which of these four should influence the manager and what the appropriate action should be:

1. At a dinner party, a guest asked a **General Mills** manager how a major new cereal was doing. The manager had just read a report that said sales lagged much below expectation. What should he say?
2. Roberto just graduated from business school with an accounting major and joined the controller's department of Belltown Enterprises. His boss asked him to evaluate a market analysis for a potential new product prepared by the marketing department. Roberto knows very little about the industry, and he never had a class to teach him how to make a market analysis. Should he just wade in, without asking for help?
3. Helen prepared a budget for a division of Yankton Electronics. Her supervisor, the division manager, was not happy that she included results for an exciting new product that was to be introduced in a month. He asked her to leave the results for the product out of the budget. That way, the financial results for the product would boost actual profits well above the amount budgeted, resulting in favorable reviews for the division and its managers. What should Helen do?

1-B1 Scorekeeping, Attention Directing, and Problem Solving

For each of the following activities, identify the function the accountant is performing—scorekeeping, attention directing, or problem solving. Explain each of your answers.

1. Posting daily cash collections to customers' accounts. *Scorekeeping*
2. Recording daily material purchase vouchers. *Scorekeeping*
3. Analyzing the costs of acquiring and using each of two alternate types of welding equipment. *Problem Solving*
4. Preparing a report of overtime labor costs by production department. *Attention direct*
5. Estimating the costs of moving corporate headquarters to another city. *Problem solving*
6. Interpreting increases in nursing costs per patient-day in a hospital. *Attention directing*
7. Analyzing deviations from the budget of the factory maintenance department. *Attention directing*
8. Assisting in a study by the manufacturing vice president to determine whether to buy certain parts needed in large quantities for manufacturing products or to acquire facilities for manufacturing these parts. *Problem Solving*
9. Allocating factory service department costs to production departments. *Scorekeeping*
10. Recording overtime hours of the product finishing department. *Scorekeeping*
11. Compiling data for a report showing the ratio of advertising expenses to sales for each branch store. *Attention directing*
12. Investigating reasons for increased returns and allowances for drugs purchased by a hospital. *A Directing*
13. Preparing a schedule of fuel costs by months and government departments. *Att. Dire.*
14. Estimating the operating costs and outputs that could be expected for each of two large metal-stamping machines offered for sale by different manufacturers. Only one of these machines is to be acquired by your company. *Problem Solving* *A-Dr*
15. Computing and recording end-of-year adjustments for expired fire insurance on the factory warehouse for materials. *Scorekeeping*

1-B2 Management by Exception

The Tulalip Indian tribe sells fireworks for the five weeks preceding July 4. The tribe's stand at the corner of Highway 104 and Eagle Drive had budgeted sales for 20X5 of $75,000. Expected expenses were as follows:

Cost of fireworks	$35,000
Labor cost	15,000
Other costs	8,000
Total costs	$58,000

Actual sales were $74,860, almost equal to the budget. The tribe spent $39,500 for fireworks, $13,000 for labor, and $8,020 for other costs.

1. Compute budgeted profit and actual profit.
2. Prepare a performance report to help identify those costs that were significantly different from the budget.
3. Suppose the tribe uses a management-by-exception rule. What costs deserve further explanation? Why?

1-B3 Accounting's Position in the Organization: Controller and Treasurer

For each of the following activities, indicate whether it is most likely to be performed by the controller or by the treasurer. Explain each answer.

1. Meet with financial analysts from Wall Street.
2. Help managers prepare budgets.
3. Advise which alternative action is least costly.
4. Prepare divisional financial statements.
5. Arrange short-term financing.
6. Prepare tax returns.
7. Arrange insurance coverage.
8. Prepare credit checks on customers.

Additional Assignment Material

Questions

1-1 Who uses information from an accounting system?

1-2 "The emphases of financial accounting and management accounting differ." Explain.

1-3 "The field is less sharply defined. There is heavier use of economics, decision sciences, and behavioral sciences." Identify the branch of accounting described in the quotation.

1-4 Distinguish among scorekeeping, attention directing, and problem solving.

1-5 "Generally accepted accounting principles (GAAP) assists the development of management accounting systems." Do you agree? Explain.

1-6 "The Foreign Corrupt Practices Act applies to bribes paid outside the United States." Do you agree? Explain.

1-7 Why is integrity so important to accountants?

1-8 Give three examples of service organizations. What distinguishes them from other types of organizations?

1-9 What two major considerations affect all accounting systems? Explain each.

1-10 "The accounting system is intertwined with operating management. Business operations would be in a hopeless tangle without the paperwork that is so often regarded with disdain." Do you agree? Explain, giving examples.

1-11 Distinguish among a budget, a performance report, and a variance.

1-12 "Management by exception means abdicating management responsibility for planning and control." Do you agree? Explain.

1-13 "Good accounting provides automatic control of operations." Do you agree? Explain.

1-14 Why are accountants concerned about product life cycles?

1-15 Name the six primary business functions (excluding support functions) that make up the value chain, and briefly describe each.

1-16 "Accountants in every company should measure and report on every function in the company's value chain." Do you agree? Explain.

1-17 Distinguish between the duties of line managers and staff managers.

1-18 The role of management accountants is changing, especially in companies with a "flatter" organizational structure. What are some of the changes?

1-19 Does every company have both a controller and a treasurer? Explain.

1-20 Describe the four parts of the qualifying examination for becoming a CMA.

1-21 "The problem with accounting is that accountants never get to become top managers such as CEOs." Do you agree? Explain.

1-22 How are changes in technology affecting management accounting?

1-23 What is the essence of the JIT philosophy?

1-24 Briefly describe how a change in a plant's layout can make its operation more efficient.

1-25 Standards of ethical conduct for management accountants have been divided into four major responsibilities. Describe each of the four in 20 words or less.

1-26 "Why are there ethical dilemmas? I thought accountants had standards that specified what is ethical behavior." Discuss this quote.

Critical Thinking Exercises

1-27 Finance and Management Accounting

Often there is confusion between the roles played by the controller and treasurer in an organization. In fact, in many small companies, a single person performs activities related to both functions.

Distinguish between the controller and the treasurer functions by listing typical activities that are associated with each.

1-28 Marketing and Management Accounting

A cross-functional team of managers, including the management accountant, performs each of the following activities. However, depending on the nature of the decision to be made, one functional area will take the leadership role. Which of these activities is primarily a marketing decision? What would the management accountant contribute to each of the marketing decisions?

1. **Porsche Motor Company** must decide whether to buy a part for one of its cars or to make the part at one of its plants.
2. **Boeing Company** must decide the price for spare parts it sells over the Internet using its Spare Parts Web site.
3. St. Steven's Hospital must decide how to finance the purchase of expensive new medical analysis equipment.
4. **Amazon.com** must forecast the impact on video sales of a new advertising program.
5. TexMex Foods, Inc., a regional market leader in the production and distribution of tortillas to retail and food service industries, must decide whether to accept a special order for tortilla chips by a large, national retail chain.
6. **Target Stores, Inc.**, must decide whether to close one of its retail stores that is operating at a loss.

1-29 Production and Management Accounting

A cross-functional team of managers, including the management accountant, performed each of the following activities. However, depending on the nature of the decision to be made, one functional area will take the leadership role. Which of these activities is primarily a production decision? What would the management accountant contribute to each of the production decisions?

1. **Porsche Motor Company** must decide whether to buy a part for one of its cars or to make the part at one of its plants.
2. **Boeing Company** must decide the price for spare parts it sells over the Internet using its Spare Parts Web site.
3. St. Steven's Hospital must decide how to finance the purchase of expensive new medical analysis equipment.
4. **Amazon.com** must forecast the impact on video sales of a new advertising program.
5. TexMex Foods, Inc., a regional market leader in the production and distribution of tortillas to retail and food service industries, must decide whether to accept a special order for tortilla chips by a large national retail chain.

6. **Kmart** must evaluate its overall vision and strategic goals in the light of competitive pressures from Target, **Sears,** and **Wal-Mart**.
7. **Dell Computers** must decide whether to spend money on training workers to perform setups and changeovers faster. This will free up capacity to be used to make more computers without purchasing more equipment.
8. **General Motors** must decide whether to keep or replace four-year-old equipment used in one of its Saturn plants.

Exercises

1-30 Management Accounting and Financial Accounting
Consider the following short descriptions. Indicate whether each description more closely relates to a major feature of financial accounting or management accounting.

1. Has a future orientation
2. Provides internal consulting advice to managers
3. Has less flexibility
4. Is characterized by detailed reports
5. Field is less sharply defined
6. Is constrained by generally accepted accounting principles
7. Behavioral impact is secondary

1-31 Planning and Control, Management by Exception
Study Exhibit 1-2 on p. 12 and the illustration of a **Starbucks** store. Suppose that for 20X1 a particular store budgeted revenue of $220,000, a 10% increase over the current revenue of $200,000. The actions listed in Exhibit 1-2 resulted in six new budgeted products and a total advertising budget of $15,000. Actual results were

New drinks added	7
Advertising	$16,500
Revenues	$228,000

1. Prepare a performance report using the format of Exhibit 1-3.
2. Net income results were not available until several months after the store implemented the plan. The net income results were disappointing to management because profits actually declined even though revenues increased. Why? Because costs increased by more than revenues. List some factors that might have caused costs to increase so much and that management may not have considered when they formulated the store's plan.

1-32 Line Versus Staff and Value-Chain Responsibility
For each of the following, indicate whether the employee has line or staff responsibility and which value-chain business function is most closely related to activities performed by the employee.

1. President
2. Cost accountant
3. Market research analyst
4. District sales manager
5. Head of the legal department
6. Production superintendent

1-33 Microsoft's Value Chain
Microsoft is the world's largest software company. For each of the following value-chain functions, discuss briefly what Microsoft managers would do to achieve that function and how important it is to the overall success of Microsoft.

R&D	Product & Service Process Design
Production	Marketing
Distribution	Customer Service
Support functions	

1-34 Objectives of Management Accounting
The Institute of Management Accountants (IMA) is composed of more than 60,000 members. The IMA "Objectives of Management Accounting" states, "The management accountant participates, as

part of management, in assuring that the organization operates as a unified whole in its long-run, intermediate, and short-run best interests."

Based on your reading in this chapter, prepare a 100-word description of the principal ways that accountants participate in managing an entity.

1-35 Cost-Benefit of the Ethical Environment

A poor ethical environment results in costs to the company. Examples include the cost of internal theft and the cost of absenteeism. On the other hand, a good ethical environment creates benefits. Examples include reduced risk of legal fines and sanctions and improved employee morale and productivity.

List several additional costs of a poor ethical environment and benefits of a good ethical environment.

1-36 Early Warning Signs of Ethical Conflict

The following statements are early warning signs of ethical conflict:

- "I don't care how you do it, just get it done!"
- "No one will ever know."

List several other statements that are early warning signs of ethical conflict.

Problems

1-37 Management and Financial Accounting

Grace Choi, an able mechanical engineer, was informed that she would be promoted to assistant factory manager. Grace was pleased but uncomfortable. In particular, she knew little about accounting. She had taken one course in financial accounting.

Grace planned to enroll in a management accounting course as soon as possible. Meanwhile, she asked Burt Greenspan, a cost accountant, to state three or four of the principal distinctions between financial and management accounting.

Prepare Burt's written response to Grace.

1-38 Use of Accounting Information in Hospitals

Most U.S. hospitals do not derive their revenues directly from patients. Instead, revenues come through third parties such as insurance companies and government agencies. Until the 1980s, these payments generally reimbursed the hospital's costs of serving patients. Such payments, however, are now generally flat fees for specified services. For example, the hospital might receive $5,000 for an appendectomy or $25,000 for heart surgery — no more, no less.

How might the method of payment change the demand for accounting information in hospitals? Relate your answer to the decisions of top management.

1-39 Costs and Benefits

Marks & Spencer, a huge retailer in the United Kingdom with sales of more than £8 billion, was troubled by its paper bureaucracy. Looked at in isolation, each document seemed reasonable, but overall a researcher reported that there was substantial effort in each department to verify the information. Basically, the effort seemed out of proportion to any value received, and, eventually, the company simplified or eliminated many of the documents.

Describe the rationale that should govern systems design. How should a company such as Marks & Spencer decide what documents it needs and which can be eliminated?

1-40 Importance of Accounting

Some companies are run by engineers and other technical specialists. For example, a manager in a division that is now part of **ArvinMeritor,** a $7 billion automotive parts supplier, once said that "there'd be sixty or seventy guys talking technical problems, with never a word on profits." Other companies, especially consumer products companies such as General Mills, fill top management positions primarily with marketing executives. And still others, like **Berksire Hathaway** with Warren Buffett as CEO, have top managers with strong finance skills.

How might the role of management accountants differ in these types of companies?

1-41 Changes in Accounting Systems

In the 1990s, the **Boeing Company** undertook a large-scale study of its accounting system. The study led to several significant changes. None of these changes were for reporting to external parties.

Management believed, however, that the new system gave more accurate costs of the airplanes and other products produced.

1. Boeing had been a very successful company using its old accounting system. What might have motivated it to change the system?
2. When Boeing changed its system, what criteria might its managers have used to decide whether to invest in the new system?
3. Is changing to a system that provides more accurate product costs always a good strategy? Why or why not?

1-42 Value Chain

Nike is an Oregon-based company that focuses on the design, development, and worldwide marketing of high-quality sports footwear, apparel, equipment, and accessory products. Nike is the largest seller of athletic footwear and athletic apparel in the world. The company sells its products to approximately 18,000 retail accounts in the United States and through a mix of independent distributors, licensees, and subsidiaries in approximately 140 countries around the world. Independent contractors manufacture virtually all of the company's products. Nike produces most footwear products outside the United States, while it produces apparel products both in the United States and abroad.

1. Identify one decision that Nike managers make in each of the six value-chain functions.
2. For each decision in requirement 1, identify one piece of accounting information that would aid the manager's decision.

1-43 Role of Controller

Juanita Palencia, newly hired controller of Braxton Industries, had been lured away from a competitor to revitalize the controller's department. Her first day on the job proved to be an eye-opener. One of her first interviews was with Bill Belton, production supervisor in the Cleveland factory. Belton commented, "I really don't want to talk to anyone from the controller's office. The only time we see those accountants is when our costs go over their budget. They wave what they call a 'performance report,' but it's actually just a bunch of numbers they make up. It has nothing to do with what happens on the shop floor. Besides, my men can't afford the time to fill out all the paperwork those accountants want, so I just plug in some numbers and send it back. Now, if you'll let me get back to important matters. . . ." Palencia left quickly, but she was already planning for her next visit with Belton.

1. Identify some of the problems in the relationship between the controller's department and the production departments (assuming that the Cleveland factory is representative of the production departments).
2. What should Juanita Palencia do next?

1-44 The Accountant's Role in an Organization

Marmon Group is a collection of more than 100 different operating companies with more than 500 facilities in 45 countries. It has annual revenues of more than $6.4 billion. Its member companies manufacture such diverse products as copper tubing, water purification products, railroad tank cars, and store fixtures, and they provide services such as credit information for banks.

The Business First box on page 19 described the role of accountants in Marmon. Others have described accountants as "internal consultants." Using the information in the box, discuss how accountants at Marmon can act as internal consultants. What kind of background and knowledge would an accountant require to be an effective internal consultant?

1-45 Ethics and Accounting Personnel

McMillan Shipping Company has an equal opportunity employment policy. This policy has the full support of the company's president, Beverly Paluska, and is included in all advertisements for employee positions.

Hiring in the accounting department is done by the controller, D. W. "Butch" Brigham. The assistant controller, Jack Myers, also interviews candidates, but Brigham makes all decisions. In the last year, the department hired five new people from a pool of 175 applicants. Thirteen had been interviewed, including four minority candidates. The five hired included three sons of Brigham's close friends and no minorities. Myers had felt that at least two of the minority candidates were very well qualified and that the three sons of Brigham's friends were definitely not among the most qualified.

When Myers questioned Brigham concerning his reservations about the hiring practices, he was told that these decisions were Brigham's and not his, so he should not question them.

1. Explain why Brigham's hiring practices were probably unethical.
2. What should Myers do about this situation?

1-46 Ethical Issues

Suppose you are controller of a medium-size oil exploration company in west Texas. You adhere to the standards of ethical conduct for management accountants. How would those standards affect your behavior in each of the following situations?

1. Late one Friday afternoon you receive a geologist's report on a newly purchased property. It indicates a much higher probability of oil than had previously been expected. You are the only one to read the report that day. At a party on Saturday night, a friend asks about the prospects for the property.
2. An oil industry stock analyst invites you and your spouse to spend a week in Hawaii free of charge. All she wants in return is to be the first to know about any financial information your company is about to announce to the public.
3. It is time to make a forecast of the company's annual earnings. You know that some additional losses will be recognized before the final statements are prepared. The company's president has asked you to ignore these losses in making your prediction because a lower-than-expected earnings forecast could adversely affect the chances of obtaining a loan that is being negotiated and that will be completed before actual earnings are announced.
4. You do not know whether a particular expense is deductible for income tax purposes. You are debating whether to research the tax laws or simply to assume that the item is deductible. After all, if you are not audited, no one will ever know the difference. If you are audited, you can plead ignorance of the law.

1-47 Hundred Best Corporate Citizens

Each year *Business Ethics* magazine publishes its list of the 100 best corporate citizens. The magazine rates companies on seven dimensions reflecting quality of service to seven stakeholder groups: (1) stockholders, (2) community, (3) minorities and women, (4) employees, (5) environment, (6) non–U.S. stakeholders, and (7) customers. In 2002, the top ten corporate citizens were **IBM**, **Hewlett-Packard**, **Fannie Mae**, **St. Paul Companies**, **Procter & Gamble**, **Motorola**, **Cummins Engine**, **Herman Miller**, **General Mills**, and **Avon Products**.

For each of the seven dimensions on which the magazine rated companies, give a one-sentence description of what you think would make for good corporate citizenship. Based on your knowledge of these ten companies, however limited that is, predict the top two companies in each of the seven rated categories.

Cases

1-48 Line and Staff Authority

Fairmont Leasing Company (FLC) leases office equipment to a variety of customers. The company's organization chart is at the top of page 39.

The four positions in blue in the chart are described below.

- J. P. Chen, assistant controller—special projects. Chen works on projects assigned to him by the controller. The most recent project was to design a new accounts payable system.
- Betty Hodge, leasing contracts manager. Hodge coordinates and implements leasing transactions. Her department handles all transactions after the sales department gets a signed contract. This includes requisitioning equipment from the purchasing department, maintaining appropriate insurance, delivering equipment, issuing billing statements, and seeking renewal of leases.
- Larry Paperman, chief accountant. Paperman supervises all the accounting functions. He produces reports for the four supervisors in the functional areas.
- Dawn Burgstahler, director of human resources. Burgstahler works with all departments of FLC in hiring personnel. Her department advertises all positions and screens candidates, but the individual departments conduct interviews and make hiring decisions. Burgstahler also coordinates employee evaluations and administers the company's salary schedule and fringe benefit program.

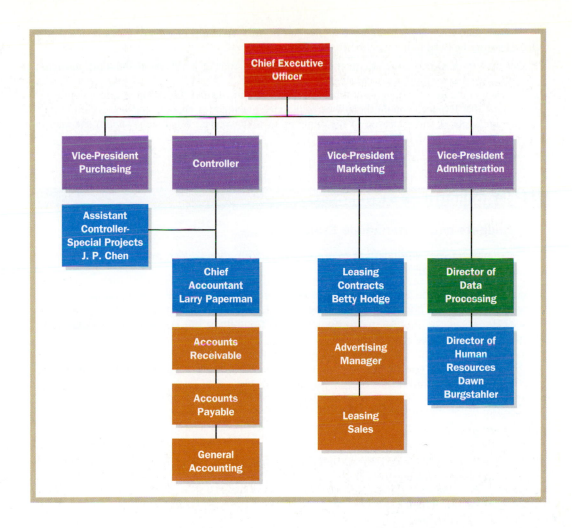

1. Distinguish between line and staff positions in an organization and discuss why conflicts might arise between line and staff managers.
2. For each of the four managers described, identify whether their position is a line or staff position and explain why you classified it that way. Also, indicate any potential conflicts that might arise with other managers in the organization.

1-49 Professional Ethics and Toxic Waste

Yukon Mining Company extracts and processes a variety of ores and minerals. One of its operations is a coal-cleaning plant that produces toxic wastes. For many years, the wastes have been properly disposed of through National Disposal, an experienced company. However, disposal of the toxic wastes is becoming an economic hardship because increasing government regulations caused the cost of such disposal to quadruple in the last six years.

Rebecca Long, director of financial reporting for Yukon Mining, was preparing the company's financial statements for the year ended June 30, 2004. In researching the material needed for preparing a footnote on environmental contingencies, Rebecca found the following note scribbled in pencil at the bottom of a memo to the General Manager of the coal cleaning plant. The body of the memo gave details on the increases in the cost of toxic waste disposals:

> *Ralph — We've got to keep these costs down or we won't meet budget. Can we mix more of these wastes with the shipments of refuse to the Oak Hill landfill? Nobody seems to notice the coal-cleaning fluids when we mix it in well.*

Rebecca was bothered by the note. She considered ignoring it, pretending that she had not seen it. But after a couple of hours, her conscience would not let her do it. Therefore, she pondered the following three alternative courses of action:

- Seek the advice of her boss, the vice president of finance for Yukon.
- Anonymously release the information to the local newspaper.

- Give the information to an outside member of Yukon's board of directors, whom she knew because he lived in her neighborhood.

1. Discuss why Rebecca Long has an ethical responsibility to take some action about her suspicion of the illegal dumping of toxic wastes.
2. For each of the three alternative courses of action, explain whether the action is appropriate.
3. Assume that Rebecca sought the advice of the vice president of finance and discovered that he both knew about and approved of the dumping of toxic wastes. What steps should she take to resolve the conflict in this situation?

EXCEL Application Exercise

1-50 Budgets and Performance Evaluation

Goal: Create an Excel spreadsheet to prepare a performance report, and use the results to answer questions about your findings.

Scenario: Beta Gamma Sigma, the business honorary fraternity, has asked you to prepare a performance report about a homecoming party that they recently held. The background data for Beta Gamma Sigma's performance report appears in the Fundamental Assignment Material 1-A2.

When you have completed your spreadsheet, answer the following questions:
1. Based on the formatting option used in the exercise, do the negative (red) variances represent amounts that are over or under budget?
2. Which cost/costs changed because the number of attendees increased?
3. Did the fraternity stay within the budgeted amount for food on a per person basis?

Step-by-Step:
1. Open a new Excel spreadsheet.
2. In column A, create a bold-faced heading that contains the following:
   Row 1: Chapter 1 Decision Guideline
   Row 2: Beta Gamma Sigma Homecoming Party
   Row 3: Performance Report
   Row 4: Today's Date
3. Merge and center the date across columns A through D.
4. In Row 7, create the following bold-faced, right-justified column headings:
   Column B: Budget
   Column C: Actual
   Column D: Variance
5. In Column A, create the following row headings:
   Row 8: Room rental
   Row 9: Food
   Row 10: Entertainment
   Row 11: Decorations
   Row 12: Total costs
   Skip a row
   Row 14: Attendees
   Skip a row
   Row 16: Food per person
6. Use the data from Fundamental Assignment Material 1-A2 and enter the Budget and Actual amounts for room, food, entertainment, decorations, and attendees.
7. Use Budget minus Actual formulas to generate variances for each of the cost categories.
8. Use the SUM function to generate total costs for the budget, actual, and variance columns.
9. Use a formula to generate the "per person" food amount for the budget and actual columns.
10. Format all amounts as:

Number tab:	Category:	Currency
	Decimal places:	0
	Symbol:	None
	Negative numbers:	Red with parentheses

11. Change the format of the food per person amounts to display two decimal places and a dollar symbol.

12. Change the format of the room rental and total cost amounts to display a dollar symbol.

13. Change the format of the total costs data (Row 12) to display as bold-faced.

14. Change the format of the total costs heading to display as indented:

Alignment tab:	Horizontal:	Left (Indent)
	Indent:	1

15. Save your work to disk, and print a copy for your files.

Collaborative Learning Exercise

1-51 The Future Management Accountant

Students should gather in groups of four to six each. Half of each group should read the first of the following articles and half should read the second article. (Alternatively, you can do this exercise as a whole class, with half of the class reading one article and half reading the other).

- Kulesza, C., and G. Siegel, "It's Not Your Father's Management Accounting," *Management Accounting,* May 1997, pp. 56–59.
- Russell, K., G. Siegel, and C. Kulesza, "Counting More, Counting Less: Transformations in the Management Accounting Profession," *Strategic Finance*, September 1999, pp. 39–44.

1. Individually, write down the three most important lessons you learned from the article you read.
2. As a group, list all the lessons identified in requirement 1. Combine those that are essentially the same.
3. Prioritize the list you developed in requirement 2 in terms of their importance to someone considering a career in management accounting.
4. Discuss whether this exercise has changed your impression of management accounting and, if so, how your impression has changed.

Internet Exercise ● www.prenhall.com/horngren

1-52 Institute of Management Accountants

The Institute of Management Accountants (IMA) is a major professional organization that is geared toward managerial accounting and finance. The IMA has chapters throughout the United States as well as international chapters. The IMA is very concerned about ethics. Log on to http://www.imanet.org, the Web site for the IMA.

1. Click on About IMA. What is the IMA devoted to?
2. Follow the link that shows the Mission Statement for the IMA. What is the mission of the IMA?
3. One of the stated missions of the IMA is to help its members' professional development through education. Click on the Professional Development link. What options does the IMA provide to help educate the members?
4. Click on the Ethics Center link. Follow the link to code of ethics. Read the code and comment on its importance to management accountants.
5. The IMA is made up of individual chapters where members can interact with other management accountants. Click on the Chapters and Councils link to see if there is a chapter in your state. List the chapters in your state. Does the chapter closest to your school have a Web site? You may wish to contact the chapter to find out about student involvement and scholarships.

Introduction to Cost Behavior and Cost-Volume Relationships

C H A P T E R 2

LEARNING OBJECTIVES

When you have finished studying this chapter, you should be able to:

1. Explain how cost drivers affect cost behavior.

2. Show how changes in cost-driver activity levels affect variable and fixed costs.

3. Calculate break-even sales volume in total dollars and total units.

4. Create a cost-volume-profit graph and understand the assumptions behind it.

5. Calculate sales volume in total dollars and total units to reach a target profit.

6. Differentiate between contribution margin and gross margin.

7. Explain the effects of sales mix on profits (Appendix 2A).

8. Compute cost-volume-profit relationships on an after-tax basis (Appendix 2B).

In 1915, William Boeing, a Seattle timberman, assem-

bled his first airplane in a boathouse. Today, the **Boeing Company** produces 20 to 25 commercial jetliners each month and has annual revenues of nearly $60 billion. The company has about half of the world's market share in airplane sales, but that could change as the competition steps up to meet growing demand. How will Boeing maintain its competitive edge and profitability margin? With increased competition, Boeing knows that it can improve profits more by controlling (reducing) costs than by increasing prices to customers. So, should it build bigger airplanes or more of the existing size but with improvements in features and efficiencies that will lower customers' costs? Which alternative has lower costs for Boeing and its customers? To answer these questions, Boeing had to understand its own costs as well as the costs of its customers. The real question to ask is, What do customers value in return for a price tag in excess of $50 million per airplane? This chapter begins your study of costs so that you, too, can assess the costs that are important to Boeing and other companies, big and small, as they make crucial decisions about their products and production processes.

Consider a recent decision Boeing faced regarding production of a proposed Sonic Cruiser. In 1999, the company began its R & D program for this unique airplane with a delta wing, rear-mounted engines, and two horizontal fins at the back of the airplane instead of the standard horizontal and vertical tail section found on today's jetliners. The Sonic Cruiser was designed to reduce travel time by about 20%. An important part of its research was the assessment of its customers' costs—both of operating their existing fleet of planes and of the costs of the new Sonic Cruisers. In early 2001, discussions with airlines in North America, Asia, and Europe confirmed

The Boeing facility pictured here illustrates both fixed and variable costs. The entire cost of the facility, including heating and lighting, is a fixed cost. It does not depend on the number of airplanes being produced. In contrast, the cost of the bodies and other parts of the airplanes, as well as the cost of much of the labor used to produce the airplanes, are variable costs. To produce another airplane requires more of these costs.

the design offered exactly what airlines and passengers are looking for: the ability to fly quickly and directly to their destinations while avoiding time-consuming and costly stops at major hubs—a concept known as point-to-point service. In late 2002, after more than three years of research, the company had completed the design of the new airplane and was faced with the final decision to launch. A decision to launch would involve a huge immediate investment in costly plant and equipment resources. To pay for these assets and make a profit, it had to be confident that its customers would be willing to pay more for the airplane than it cost Boeing to produce it.

But production ultimately hinged on whether customers wanted a faster airplane that used the most up-to-date technology both in operating the airplane and producing it. Despite the years of development activities, Boeing decided not to proceed with the Sonic Cruiser. The economic recession and the terrorist attacks of Septermber 11, 2001, had changed the airline industry's needs. Instead, Boeing management decided to dedicate its resources to developing an as-yet-unnamed "super-efficient" version of its existing 777 jetliner. According to Alan Mulally, chief executive officer of Boeing Commercial Airplanes, the airlines made it clear that they wanted a cheaper plane rather than a faster plane. Just a year and a half earlier, Boeing had scrapped plans for a stretched version of its 747, the 747X. Boeing's managers made both decisions after a careful analysis of its own production costs and the airlines' operating costs, comparing them to the predicted demands for airline travel in the next decade.

Managers need to understand costs. For example, how much would it cost Boeing to produce each Sonic Cruiser? How much cost does **Northwest Airlines** incur when it adds one more passenger at the last moment to an existing flight, or when it adds one more flight to the schedule? What does it cost **Toyota** to develop a new line of luxury autos, as it did with the Lexus? How much does it cost to produce one more Lexus? How will an increase in Arizona's population affect the costs needed to run the State's Department of Motor Vehicles? What does it cost **Nestle Purina** to meet **Wal-Mart's** specifications for shipments of pet-care products? What activities contribute most to Nestle Purina's cost to serve Wal-Mart stores? These questions are really different forms of one general question: What will happen to financial results if a company or organization changes its level of activity?

Although financial results are based on revenues and costs, we will focus primarily on costs in this chapter. After all, as we saw in the case of Boeing, companies usually have more control over their costs than they do over their revenues. In fact, one of the main goals of management accounting is controlling (and reducing) costs. But managers cannot control costs unless they understand **cost behavior**—how the activities of an organization affect its costs.

cost behavior
How the activities of an organization affect its costs.

Identifying Activities, Costs, and Cost Drivers

OBJECTIVE 1

Explain how cost drivers affect cost behavior.

Different types of costs behave in different ways. Consider Boeing Company's costs of an existing plant that makes 737 business jets. As Boeing produces more airplanes, the cost of materials such as electrical wire, seats, and aluminum increases. But the cost of the plant and salaries of key managers stay the same, regardless of the number of airplanes made. Associating cost behavior with units of product produced gives us an overall view of how costs behave, but it does little to help managers control costs on a day-to-day basis.

On a day-to-day basis, managers focus their efforts on managing the activities to make, sell, and deliver products or services—not necessarily on the products and services themselves. A production manager needs to know how routine activities such as machine maintenance and repairs affect costs. So, because understanding costs is so important for cost control, associating costs with activities is a key factor in controlling costs.

For example, one of the activities performed at Boeing's plant is receiving parts to be installed on the airplane. Receiving managers need to know how their activities affect costs. Costs such as depreciation of the equipment used to move parts from one location in the plant to another do not change when receiving activity increases or decreases. However, costs such as fuel for the same moving equipment do vary with the rate of activity. Actually, we should say that activities such as receiving require resources such as moving equipment and fuel and that these resources cost money.

But how exactly do accountants relate activities to resource costs in a way that makes cost control possible? Accountants first identify the activities in their organization and determine measures of output for each activity. They then relate each output measure to the resources that are necessary to produce it. Any output measure that causes costs (that is, causes the use of costly resources) is a **cost driver.** In our receiving example, the cost driver or output measure of receiving activity could be "number of parts received" or "weight of parts received." The receiving manager can easily understand how an increase in the number of parts received or the weight of parts received can increase or *drive* the use (and therefore the cost) of fuel and moving equipment.

An organization has many cost drivers across its value chain. Exhibit 2-1 lists examples of costs and potential cost drivers for each of the value-chain functions. How well the accountant can identify the most appropriate cost drivers determines how well managers understand cost behavior and how well managers can control costs.

cost driver
Any output measure that causes costs (that is, causes the use of costly resources).

Exhibit 2-1
Examples of Value-Chain Functions, Costs, and Cost Drivers

Value-Chain Function and Example Costs	Example Cost Drivers
Research and development	
• Salaries of marketing research personnel, costs of market surveys	Number of new product proposals
• Salaries of product and process engineers	Complexity of proposed products
Design of products, services, and processes	
• Salaries of product and process engineers	Number of engineering hours
• Cost of computer-aided design equipment, cost to develop prototype of product for testing	Number of parts per product
Production	
• Labor wages	Labor hours
• Supervisory salaries	Number of people supervised
• Maintenance wages	Number of mechanic hours
• Depreciation of plant and machinery, supplies	Number of machine hours
• Energy cost	Kilowatt hours
Marketing	
• Cost of advertisements	Number of advertisements
• Salaries of marketing personnel, travel costs, entertainment costs	Sales dollars
Distribution	
• Wages of shipping personnel	Labor hours
• Transportation costs including depreciation of vehicles and fuel	Weight of items delivered
Customer service	
• Salaries of service personnel	Hours spent servicing products
• Costs of supplies, travel	Number of service calls

Comparing Variable and Fixed Costs

To understand cost behavior, a first step is to distinguish variable costs from fixed costs. Accountants classify costs as variable or fixed depending on how much they change as the level of a particular cost driver changes. A **variable cost** changes in direct proportion to changes in the cost-driver level. In contrast, changes in the cost-driver level do not immediately affect a **fixed cost.** Suppose units of production is the cost driver of interest. A 10% increase in the units of production would produce a 10% increase in variable costs. However, the fixed costs would remain unchanged.

Consider some variable costs. Suppose Watkins Products, the 135-year-old health food company, pays its sales personnel a 40% straight commission on sales. The total cost of sales commissions to Watkins is 40% of sales dollars—a variable cost with respect to sales revenues. Or suppose Long Lake Bait Shop buys bags of fish bait for $2 each. The total cost of fish bait is $2 times the number of bags purchased—a variable cost with respect to units (number of bags) purchased. Notice that variable costs do not change per unit, but that the total costs change in direct proportion to the cost-driver activity. Exhibit 2-2 shows these relationships between total cost and cost-driver activity graphically.

Now consider a fixed cost. Suppose **Sony** rents a factory to produce DVD players for $500,000 per year. The total cost of $500,000 is not affected by the number of DVD players produced. The unit cost of rent applicable to each DVD player, however, does depend on the total number of DVD players produced. If Sony produces 100,000 DVD players, the unit cost will be $500,000 ÷ 100,000 = $5. If it produces 50,000 DVD players, the unit cost will be $500,000 ÷ 50,000 = $10. Therefore, a fixed cost does not change *in total,* but the *per-unit* fixed cost becomes progressively smaller as the volume increases.

Note carefully from these examples that the "variable" or "fixed" characteristic of a cost relates to its total dollar amount and not to its per-unit amount. The following table summarizes these relationships.

If Cost-Driver Activity Level Increases (or Decreases)		
Type of Cost	**Total Cost**	**Cost per Unit***
Fixed costs	No change	Decrease (or increase)
Variable costs	Increase (or decrease)	No change

*Per unit of activity volume, for example, product units, passenger-miles, orders processed, or sales dollars.

When analyzing costs, you may find these two rules of thumb useful:

1. Think of fixed costs as a total. Total fixed costs remain unchanged regardless of changes in cost-driver activity.

Exhibit 2-2
Variable-Cost
Behavior

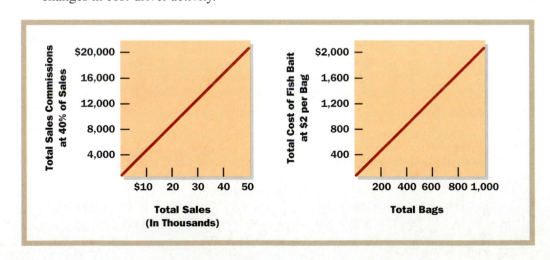

2. Think of variable costs on a per-unit basis. The per-unit variable cost remains unchanged regardless of changes in cost-driver activity. As a result, the total variable cost varies proportionately with the level of cost-driver activity.

MAKING MANAGERIAL DECISIONS

A key factor in helping managers understand cost behavior is distinguishing between variable and fixed costs. Test your understanding by answering the following questions.

1. A producer of premium ice cream uses "gallons of ice cream produced" as a cost driver for dairy ingredients. Is the cost of dairy ingredients a variable or a fixed cost?
2. The same company uses "square feet occupied" as a cost driver for occupancy costs such as building depreciation and insurance. Is occupancy cost variable or fixed?

Answer

The best way to determine whether the cost of a resource is fixed or variable is to ask the question, "If the level of the cost driver changes, what will happen to the cost?" If the company increases (decreases) its production of ice cream, then the cost of dairy ingredients will also increase (decrease). Thus, the cost of dairy ingredients is variable. If the square feet occupied by a particular unit in an organization increases (decreases), the building depreciation and insurance on the building will not change. Thus, building occupancy costs such as depreciation and insurance are fixed costs.

Relevant Range

Although we have just described fixed costs as unchanging regardless of changes in the given cost driver, this rule of thumb holds true only within reasonable limits. For example, rent costs, which are generally fixed, will rise if increased production requires a larger or additional building—or if the landlord just decides to raise the rent. Conversely, rent costs may go down if decreased production causes the company to move to a smaller plant. The **relevant range** is the limit of cost-driver activity level within which a specific relationship between costs and the cost driver is valid. Even within the relevant range, though, a fixed cost remains fixed only over a given period of time—usually the budget period. Fixed costs may change from budget year to budget year solely because of changes in insurance and property tax rates, executive salary levels, or rent levels. But these items are unlikely to change within a given year.

relevant range
The limit of cost-driver activity level within which a specific relationship between costs and the cost driver is valid.

For example, suppose that the relevant range for a **General Electric** lightbulb plant is between 40,000 and 85,000 cases of lightbulbs per month and that total monthly fixed costs within the relevant range are $100,000. Within the relevant range, fixed costs will remain the same. If production falls below 40,000 cases, changes in personnel and salaries would slash fixed costs to $60,000. If operations rise above 85,000 cases, increases in personnel and salaries would boost fixed costs to $115,000.

These assumptions—a given period and a given activity range—are shown graphically at the top of Exhibit 2-3. It is highly unusual, however, for monthly operations to be outside the relevant range. Therefore, the three-level refinement at the top of Exhibit 2-3 is usually not graphed. Instead, a single horizontal line is typically extended through the plotted activity levels, as at the bottom of the exhibit. Often a dashed line is used outside the relevant range.

The basic idea of a relevant range also applies to variable costs. That is, outside a relevant range, some variable costs, such as fuel consumed, may behave differently per unit of cost-driver activity. For example, the variable cost of a canning machine at **Del Monte** might be $5 for every hour it is used, assuming that it will be used between 30 and 50 hours each week. However, if it is used for more than 50 hours a week, the added wear and tear might increase variable costs to $6 for those hours beyond 50.

Exhibit 2-3
Fixed Costs and
Relevant Range

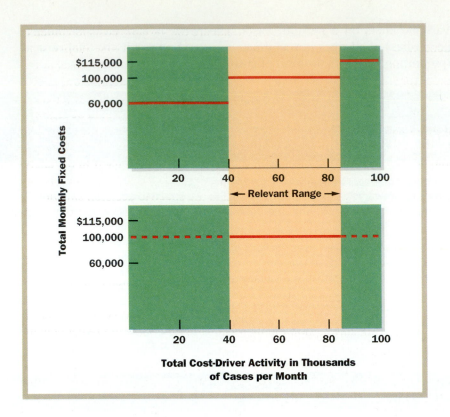

Differences in Classifying Costs

Is it difficult to classify a cost as exactly variable or exactly fixed? As you may suspect, it often is. Many complications arise, including the possibility of costs behaving in some nonlinear way (not producing a straight-line graph). For example, as tax preparers learn to process the new year's tax forms, their productivity rises. This means that total costs may actually behave as in panel A that follows, and not as in panel B.

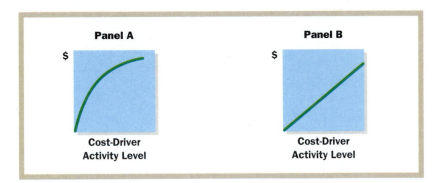

Moreover, more than one cost driver may simultaneously affect costs. For example, both the weight and the number of units handled may affect the costs of shipping labor at an **Amazon.com** warehouse. We shall investigate various facets of this problem in succeeding chapters; for now, we shall assume that we can classify every cost as either totally variable or totally fixed. We assume also that only one volume-related cost driver affects a given variable cost and that the relationship between the cost and the cost driver is linear.

Whether we classify costs as fixed or variable depends on the situation. More costs are fixed and fewer are variable when decisions for which we use the cost information involve very short time spans and very small changes in activity level. Suppose a **United Airlines** plane with several empty seats will depart from its gate in two minutes. A potential passenger is running down a corridor bearing a transferable ticket from a competing airline. Unless the airplane is held for an extra 30 seconds, the passenger will miss the departure and will not switch to United for the planned trip. What are the variable costs to United of delaying the departure and placing one more passenger in an otherwise empty seat? Variable costs (for example, one more meal) are negligible. Virtually all the costs in this situation are fixed (for example, flight crew and maintenance crew salaries). Now, in contrast, suppose United's decision is whether to add another flight, acquire another gate, add another city to its routes, or acquire another airplane. Many more costs would be regarded as variable and fewer as fixed. For example, in the case of adding a flight, the salaries of the flight and maintenance crews would now be variable.

This example underscores the importance of the decision situation itself in the analysis of cost behavior. Whether costs are really "fixed" depends heavily on the relevant range, the length of the planning period in question, and the specific decision situation.

Cost-Volume-Profit Analysis

Managers often classify costs as fixed or variable when making decisions that affect the volume of output. Consider the decision about how many units of a product to produce in the coming year. Managers realize that many factors in addition to the volume of output will affect costs. Yet, a useful starting point in their decision process is to predict how the choice of production level will affect costs.

The managers of profit-seeking organizations usually study the effects of output volume on revenue (sales), expenses (costs), and net income (net profit). We call this study **cost-volume-profit (CVP) analysis.** The managers of nonprofit organizations also benefit from the study of CVP relationships. Why? No organization has unlimited resources, and knowledge of how costs fluctuate with changes in volume helps managers to understand how to control costs. For example, administrators of nonprofit hospitals are concerned about the behavior of costs as the volume of patients fluctuates.

To apply CVP analysis, managers usually resort to some simplifying assumptions. The major one is that we can classify costs as either variable or fixed with respect to a single measure of the volume of output activity. This chapter focuses on such a simplified relationship.

cost-volume-profit
(CVP) analysis
The study of the effects of output volume on revenue (sales), expenses (costs), and net income (net profit).

CVP Scenario

Amy Winston, the manager of food services for one of Boeing's plants, is trying to decide whether to rent a line of snack vending machines. Although individual snack items have various acquisition costs and selling prices, Winston has decided that an average selling price of 50¢ per unit and an average acquisition cost of 40¢ per unit will suffice for purposes of this analysis. She predicts the following revenue and expense relationships:

	Per Unit	Percentage of Sales
Selling price	$ .50	100%
Variable cost of each item	.40	80
Selling price less variable cost	$ .10	20%
Monthly fixed expenses		
Rent	$1,000	
Wages for replenishing and servicing	4,500	
Other fixed expenses	500	
Total fixed expenses per month	$6,000	

We will now use these data in examining several applications of CVP analysis.

OBJECTIVE 3
Calculate break-even sales volume in total dollars and total units.

Break-Even Point—Contribution-Margin and Equation Methods

The most basic CVP analysis computes the monthly break-even point in number of units and in dollar sales. The **break-even point** is the level of sales at which revenue equals

break-even point
The level of sales at which revenue equals expenses and net income is zero.

TECH FIRMS LOWER BREAK-EVEN POINTS

In late 2002 and early 2003, many high technology companies reported on their attempts to achieve profitability in spite of declining sales. They often focused on how their efforts to control costs reduced their break-even points. If a company faces rapidly falling sales, it must restructure its costs to be able to break even at a lower volume.

The early twenty-first century was hard on technology companies. After the bursting of the stock-price bubble of the 1990s, demand for most technology products plummeted. Nearly all technology companies experienced declines in sales. Most lost money in 2001 and 2002, but because of restructured operations, most predicted a return to profitability in 2003.

Consider Alcatel, the French telecommunications company. CEO Serge Tchuruk indicated that the company cut its break-even point, which was Euro 6 billion in the fourth quarter of 2001, to Euro 4.1 billion by the last quarter of 2002. It planned to further cut its quarterly break-even point to Euro 3 billion by the end of 2003. One way that Alcatel accomplished this is by outsourcing much of its manufacturing, thus greatly reducing its fixed costs.

Lucent Technologies, a U.S. telecom company, faced a similar situation. Sales in 2002 were only 43% of those in 2000, and Lucent lost nearly $12 billion in 2002. CEO Patricia Russo indicated that the company "intends to lower its break-even point on a quarterly revenue basis to between $2.5 billion and $3 billion," and cited a need to possibly reduce Lucent's break-even point even further because its anticipated quarterly sales were only $2.5 to $3 billion, leaving little margin for error.

Like Lucent, Nortel, the Canadian telecom company, had sales in 2002 that were less than half of those at its peak. By mid-2002 it had reduced its quarterly break-even point to about $2.6 billion, but since third-quarter 2002 sales were only $2.36 billion, the company sought a further reduction of its break-even by $200 million.

Stockholders responded to these efforts to lower the break-even point. In early 2003, stock prices for Alcatel, Lucent, and Nortel doubled, tripled, and quadrupled, respectively. The media attributed this to two factors: "First, each company announced staff reductions that promise to lower their quarterly break-even rates. Second, demand for telecom equipment no longer appears to be plunging at a neck-snapping rate."

The need to cut break-even points was not confined to telecom companies. Sun Microsystems, the developer of products and services for network computing, said it would "bring the group's quarterly break-even point to $3.2 billion–$3.3 billion." With quarterly sales running under $3 billion, even that goal would not bring automatic profitability. And Hector de Jesus Ruiz, president and chief executive officer of chip-maker Advanced Micro Devices (AMD), "reaffirmed his goal of reducing expenses to a break-even point of $775 million by the end of the second quarter of 2003." With 2002 sales down 30% and averaging $675 million a quarter, the expense reduction will have to be combined with a sales increase of about $100 million a quarter before AMD breaks even.

A look at many other cases would reveal the same picture. Technology companies of all types had net losses in 2001 and 2002, and profitability in 2003 would depend on reducing their break-even point to a level consistent with realistic sales expectations.

Sources: "Alcatel Plans to Lower Break-Even Point to Euro 3 Billion," *Europe Information Service*, January 30, 2003; "Russo Sees Lower Lucent Break-Even," *Financial Post*, September 19, 2002; "Nortel to Slash Costs by $1.25B," *Edmonton Journal*, October 12, 2002; "AMD Firing 2,000," *San Francisco Chronicle*, November 15, 2002; 2002 annual reports for Alcatel, Lucent, Nortel, Sun Microsystems, and Advanced Micro Devices.

expenses and net income is zero. The business press frequently refers to break-even points. For example, a news story on hotel occupancy rates in San Francisco stated that "seventy percent [occupancy] is considered a break-even for hoteliers." Another news story stated that "the Big Three auto makers have slashed their sales break-even point in North America from 12.2 million cars and trucks to only 9.1 million this year." Finally, an article on **Outboard Marine Corporation** reported that, as a result of restructuring, the company's "break-even point will be $250 million lower" than it was before the restructuring. When a company's sales begin to fall, it may try to lower its break-even point to avoid losing money. The Business First box above describes this situation for some high-tech firms.

Some people call the study of cost-volume-profit relationships break-even analysis. However, this term is misleading. Why? Because CVP analysis does much more than compute the break-even point. It is often an important part of a company's planning process. It helps managers to predict how their decisions will affect sales, costs, and net income. Nevertheless, computing a break-even point is a first step in applying CVP analysis.

We next illustrate the two basic methods for computing a break-even point: the contribution-margin method and the equation method.

Contribution-Margin Method Consider the following commonsense arithmetic approach. Every unit sold generates a **unit contribution margin** or **marginal income,** which is the unit sales price minus the variable cost per unit. For the vending machine snack items, the unit contribution margin is $.10:

Unit sales price	$.50
– Unit variable cost	–.40
= Unit contribution margin	$.10

unit contribution margin (marginal income)
The sales price minus the variable cost per unit.

When do we reach the break-even point? When we sell enough units to generate a **total contribution margin** (total number of units sold × unit contribution margin) equal to the total fixed costs. Divide the $6,000 in fixed costs by the $.10 unit contribution margin. The number of units that we must sell to break even is $6,000 ÷ $.10 = 60,000 units. The sales revenue at the break-even point is 60,000 units × $.50 per unit, or $30,000. (Note that some managers and accountants use the term **contribution margin** to mean either unit contribution margin or total contribution margin, assuming that the context makes clear which they mean.)

total contribution margin
Total number of units sold times the unit contribution margin.

contribution margin
A term used for either unit contribution margin or total contribution margin.

Think about the contribution margin of the snack items. Each unit sold generates extra revenue of $.50 and extra cost of $.40. Fixed costs are unaffected. If we sell zero units, we incur a loss equal to the fixed cost of $6,000. Each unit reduces the loss by $.10 until sales reach the break-even point of 60,000 units. After that point, each unit adds (or contributes) $.10 to profit.

The condensed income statement at the break-even point is

	Total	Per Unit	Percentage
Units	60,000		
Sales	$30,000	$.50	100%
Variable costs	24,000	.40	80
Contribution margin*	$ 6,000	$.10	20%
Fixed costs	6,000		
Net income	$ 0		

*Sales less variable costs.

Many companies sell multiple products and therefore have no single unit price and unit variable cost. For example, a grocery store sells hundreds of products at many different prices. In such a company, it would not be meaningful to compute a break-even point in overall units sold. Instead, we can use total sales and total variable costs to calculate the variable costs percentage and the contribution margin percentage:

Variable-cost percentage = total variable costs ÷ total sales
Contribution-margin percentage = total contribution margin ÷ total sales = 100% – variable cost percentage

variable-cost percentage
Total variable costs divided by total sales.

contribution-margin percentage
Total contribution margin divided by sales or 100% minus the variable cost percentage.

Consider our vending machine example:

Sales price	100%
– Variable expenses as a percentage of dollar sales	– 80
= Contribution-margin percentage	20%

variable-cost ratio
Variable cost percentage expressed as a ratio.

contribution-margin ratio
Contribution margin percentage expressed as a ratio.

The variable cost percentage is 80%, and the contribution margin percentage is 20%. We can also express these percentages as ratios, the **variable-cost ratio** and **contribution-margin ratio,** which are .80 and .20, respectively. Therefore, 20% of each sales dollar is available for the recovery of fixed expenses and the making of net income. Thus, we need $6,000 ÷ .20 = $30,000 of sales to break even. We base the contribution-margin percentage on dollar sales, and we can also express it as a ratio (.20 instead of 20%). Using the contribution-margin percentage, we can compute the break-even volume in dollar sales without determining the break-even point in units.

Equation Method The equation method is the most general form of analysis, one you can adapt to any conceivable cost-volume-profit situation. You are familiar with a typical income statement. We can express any income statement in equation form, or as a mathematical model, as follows:

$$\text{sales} - \text{variable expenses} - \text{fixed expenses} = \text{net income} \qquad (1)$$

That is,

$$\left(\begin{matrix}\text{Unit sales} \\ \text{price}\end{matrix} \times \begin{matrix}\text{number} \\ \text{of units}\end{matrix}\right) - \left(\begin{matrix}\text{unit} \\ \text{variable cost}\end{matrix} \times \begin{matrix}\text{number} \\ \text{of units}\end{matrix}\right) - \begin{matrix}\text{fixed} \\ \text{expenses}\end{matrix} = \begin{matrix}\text{net} \\ \text{income}\end{matrix}$$

At the break-even point net income is zero:

$$\text{sales} - \text{variable expenses} - \text{fixed expenses} = 0$$

Let N = number of units to be sold to break even. Then, for the vending machine example,

$$\$.50N - \$.40N - \$6,000 = 0$$
$$\$.10N = \$6,000$$
$$N = \$6,000 \div \$.10$$
$$N = 60,000 \text{ units}$$

Total sales in the equation is a price-times-quantity relationship, which we expressed in our example as $.50N. To find the dollar sales, multiply 60,000 units by $.50, which yields the break-even dollar sales of $30,000.

You can also solve the equation for sales dollars without computing the unit break-even point by using the relationship of variable costs and profits as a percentage of sales:

$$\begin{matrix}\text{variable-cost} \\ \text{ratio or percentage}\end{matrix} = \frac{\text{variable cost per unit}}{\text{sales price per unit}} = \frac{\$.40}{\$.50} = .80 \text{ or } 80\%$$

Let S = sales in dollars needed to break even. Then

$$S - .80S - \$6,000 = 0$$
$$.20S = \$6,000$$
$$S = \$6,000 \div .20$$
$$S = \$30,000$$

Relationship Between the Two Methods You may have noticed that the contribution-margin method is merely a shortcut version of the equation method. Look at the last three lines in the two solutions given for equation 1. They read

Break-Even Volume	
Units	**Dollars**
$\$.10N = \$6,000$	$.20S = \$6,000$
$N = \dfrac{\$6,000}{\$.10}$	$S = \dfrac{\$6,000}{.20}$
$N = 60,000\text{ units}$	$S = \$30,000$

From these equations, we can derive the following general shortcut formulas:

$$\text{break-even volume in units} = \frac{\text{fixed expenses}}{\text{unit contribution margin}} \qquad (2)$$

$$\text{break-even volume in dollars} = \frac{\text{fixed expenses}}{\text{contribution-margin ratio}} \qquad (3)$$

Which should you use, the equation or the contribution-margin method? Use either. Both yield the same results, so the choice is a matter of personal preference or convenience in a particular case.

MAKING MANAGERIAL DECISIONS

Managers use CVP analysis to predict effects of changes in sales or costs. Using shortcut formulas (2) and (3), answer the following questions. Remember that the contribution margin per unit equals the sales price per unit minus the variable costs per unit.

1. What would be the effect on the unit and dollar break-even level if fixed costs increase (and there are no other changes)?
2. What would be the effect on the unit and dollar break-even level if variable cost per unit decreases (and there are no other changes)?
3. What would be the effect on the unit and dollar break-even level if sales volume increases (and there are no other changes)?

Answers

1. The break-even level in both units and sales dollars would increase if fixed costs increase.
2. The break-even level in both units and sales dollars would decrease if variable cost per unit decreases.
3. Think before answering this question. The actual (or even planned) volume of sales in units has nothing to do with determining the break-even point. This is why unit volume does not appear in either equation (2) or (3).

Graphing the Break-Even Point Exhibit 2-4 is a graph of the cost-volume-profit relationship in our vending machine example. If you fully understand the contribution margin or equation method, you do not need to also learn the graphical method. However, most students find that a careful study of the graphical method leads to a better understanding of CVP analysis. Study the graph as you read the procedure for constructing it.

O B J E C T I V E 4

Create a cost-volume-profit graph and understand the assumptions behind it.

1. Draw the axes. The horizontal axis is the sales volume, and the vertical axis is dollars of cost and revenue.

Exhibit 2-4
Cost-Volume-Profit
Graph

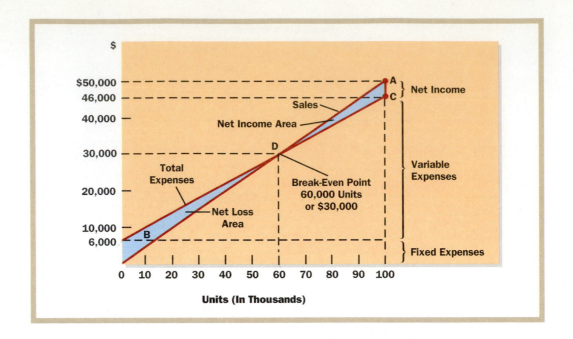

2. Plot sales volume. Select a convenient sales volume, say, 100,000 units, and plot point A for total sales dollars at that volume: $100,000 \times \$.50 = \$50,000$. Draw the revenue (that is, sales) line from point A to the origin, point 0.
3. Plot fixed expenses. Draw the line showing the $6,000 fixed portion of expenses. It should be a horizontal line intersecting the vertical axis at $6,000, point B.
4. Plot variable expenses. Determine the variable portion of expenses at a convenient level of activity: $100,000$ units $\times \$.40 = \$40,000$. Add this to the fixed expenses: $\$40,000 + \$6,000 = \$46,000$. Plot point C for 100,000 units and $46,000. Then draw a line between this point and point B. This is the total expenses line.
5. Locate the break-even point—where the total expenses line crosses the sales line, 60,000 units or $30,000, namely, where total sales revenues exactly equal total costs, point D.

The break-even point is only one part of this cost-volume-profit graph. The graph also shows the profit or loss at any rate of activity. At any given volume, the vertical distance between the sales line and the total expenses line measures the net income or net loss.

Managers often use break-even graphs because these graphs show potential profits over a wide range of volume more easily than numerical exhibits. Whether you use graphs or other presentations depends largely on your preferences. However, if you need to explain a CVP model to an audience, a graphical approach can be most helpful.

Note that the concept of relevant range applies to the entire break-even graph. Almost all break-even graphs show revenue and cost lines extending back to the vertical axis as shown in Exhibit 2-5(A). This approach is misleading because the relationships depicted in such graphs are valid only within a particular relevant range of volume. Exhibit 2-5(B), a modification of the conventional break-even graph, demonstrates the applicability of the graph only over the relevant range.

Regardless of the method used for CVP analysis, it is based on a set of important assumptions. Some of these assumptions follow.

1. We can classify expenses into variable and fixed categories. Total variable expenses vary directly with activity level. Total fixed expenses do not change with activity level.
2. The behavior of revenues and expenses is linear over the relevant range. The principal differences between the accountant's break-even chart and the economist's are that (a) the accountant's sales line is drawn on the assumption that selling prices do not

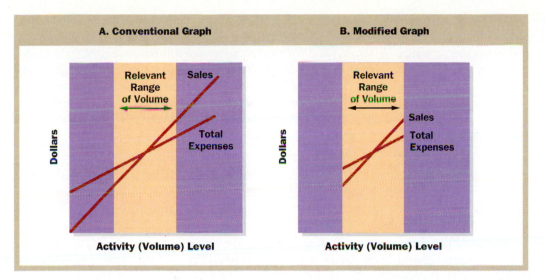

Exhibit 2-5
Conventional and Modified Break-Even Graphs

change with production or sales, while the economist assumes that reduced selling prices are normally associated with increased sales volume; and (b) the accountant usually assumes a constant variable expense per unit, while the economist assumes that variable expense per unit changes with production levels. Within the relevant range, the accountant's and the economist's sales and expense lines are usually close to one another, although the lines may diverge greatly outside the range.

3. We expect no change in efficiency or productivity.

4. Sales mix remains constant. The **sales mix** is the relative proportions or combinations of quantities of products that constitute total sales. (See Appendix 2A for more on sales mixes.)

5. The difference in inventory level at the beginning and at the end of a period is insignificant. That is, number of units sold equals number of units produced.

sales mix
The relative proportions or combinations of quantities of products that constitute total sales.

Changes in Fixed Expenses Changes in fixed expenses cause changes in the break-even point. For example, if we double the $1,000 monthly rent of the vending machines, what would be the monthly break-even point in number of units and dollar sales?

The fixed expenses would increase from $6,000 to $7,000, so

$$\text{break-even volume in units} = \frac{\text{fixed expenses}}{\text{unit contribution margin}}$$

$$= \frac{\$7,000}{\$.10}$$

$$= 70,000 \text{ units}$$

$$\text{break-even volume in dollars} = \frac{\text{fixed expenses}}{\text{contribution margin ratio}}$$

$$= \frac{\$7,000}{.20}$$

$$= \$35,000$$

Note that a one-sixth increase in fixed expenses altered the break-even point by one-sixth: from 60,000 to 70,000 units and from $30,000 to $35,000. This type of relationship always exists between fixed expenses and the break-even point if everything else remains constant.

Companies frequently lower their break-even points by reducing their total fixed costs. For example, closing or selling factories decreases property taxes, insurance, depreciation, and managers' salaries. When demand for Boeing airplanes fell because of the slumping economy and the September 11, 2001, terrorist attacks, the company made structural changes to reduce fixed costs. If Boeing had merely produced fewer airplanes with the same fixed/variable cost structure, its volume would have fallen below its break-even point. By reducing fixed costs, the company lowered its break-even point and remained profitable.

Changes in Unit Contribution Margin   Changes in variable costs also cause the break-even point to shift. Companies can reduce their break-even points by increasing their unit contribution margins through either increases in sales prices or decreases in unit variable costs, or both.

For example, assume that the fixed rent for the vending machines is still $1,000. (1) If the rental charge includes 1¢ per unit sold in addition to the fixed rent, find the monthly break-even point in number of units and in dollar sales. (2) If Winston reduces the selling price from 50¢ to 45¢ per unit and the original variable expenses per unit are unchanged, find the monthly break-even point in number of units and in dollar sales.

Here's what happens to the break-even point:

1. The variable expenses would increase from 40¢ to 41¢, the unit contribution margin would decline from 10¢ to 9¢, and the contribution-margin ratio would become $.09 ÷ $.50 = .18.

   The original fixed expenses of $6,000 would stay the same, but the denominators would change from those previously used. Thus,

$$\text{break-even point in units} = \frac{\$6,000}{\$.09} = 66,667 \text{ units}$$

$$\text{break-even point in dollars} = \frac{\$6,000}{.18} = \$33,333$$

2. If Winston reduces the selling price from 50¢ to 45¢ and the original variable expenses are unchanged, the unit contribution would fall from 50¢ − 40¢ = 10¢ to 45¢ − 40¢ = 5¢, and the break-even point would soar to $6,000 ÷ $.05 = 120,000 units. The break-even point in dollars would also change because the selling price and contribution-margin ratio change. The contribution-margin ratio would be $.05 ÷ $.45 = .11111. The break-even point, in dollars, would be 120,000 units × $.45 = $54,000 or, using the formula:

$$\text{break-even volume in dollars} = \frac{\$6,000}{.11111} = \$54,000$$

You can see that small changes in price or variable costs can lead to large changes in the unit contribution margin and, hence, to large changes in the break-even point.

Target Net Profit and an Incremental Approach

OBJECTIVE 5

Calculate sales volume in total dollars and total units to reach a target profit.

Managers can also use CVP analysis to determine the total sales, in units and dollars, needed to reach a target profit. For example, in our snack vending example, suppose Winston considers $480 per month the minimum acceptable net income. How many units will she have to sell to justify the adoption of the vending machine plan? How does this figure "translate" into dollar sales?

To compute the target sales volume in units needed to meet the desired or target net income, we adapt the basic break-even formula (equation 1 on p. 52):

$$\text{target sales} - \text{variable expenses} - \text{fixed expenses} = \text{target net income} \qquad (4)$$

or

$$\text{target sales volume in units} = \frac{\text{fixed expenses} + \text{target net income}}{\text{unit contribution margin}}$$

$$= \frac{\$6,000 + \$480}{\$.10} = 64,800 \text{ units} \qquad (5)$$

The only real difference from the normal break-even analysis is that here we use a positive target net income instead of a break-even net income of $0.

Another way of getting the same answer is to use your knowledge of the break-even point and adopt an incremental approach. The phrase **incremental effect** refers to the change in total results (such as revenue, expenses, or income) under a new condition in comparison with some given or known condition.

In this case, the given condition is the 60,000-unit break-even point. We would recover all expenses at that volume. Therefore the change or increment in net income for every unit of sales beyond 60,000 would be equal to the unit contribution margin of $.50 − $.40 = $.10. If $480 were the target net profit, $480 ÷ $.10 would show that the target volume must exceed the break-even volume by 4,800 units; it would therefore be 60,000 + 4,800 = 64,800 units.

To find the answer in terms of dollar sales, multiply 64,800 units by $.50 or use the formula

$$\text{target sales volume in dollars} = \frac{\text{fixed expenses} + \text{target net income}}{\text{contribution-margin ratio}}$$

$$= \frac{\$6,000 + \$480}{.20} = \$32,400 \qquad (6)$$

To solve directly for sales dollars with the incremental approach, we would start at the break-even point in dollar sales of $30,000. Every sales dollar beyond that point contributes $.20 to net profit. Divide $480 by $.20. Dollar sales must exceed the break-even volume by $2,400 to produce a net profit of $480. Thus the total dollar sales would be $30,000 + $2,400 = $32,400.

The following table summarizes these computations:

	Break-Even Point	Increment	New Condition
Volume in units	60,000	4,800	64,800
Sales	$30,000	$2,400	$32,400
Variable expenses	24,000	1,920	25,920
Contribution margin	$ 6,000	$ 480	$ 6,480
Fixed expenses	6,000	—	6,000
Net income	$ 0	$ 480	$ 480

Multiple Changes in Key Factors

So far, we have seen changes in only one CVP factor at a time. In the real world, managers often make decisions about the probable effects of multiple factor changes. For example, **Boeing** may cut the price of its airplanes to stimulate a larger volume of sales. **Mars** might decrease the size of its Snickers candy bar, saving variable costs and increasing the unit contribution margin, but also decreasing sales volume. Or **Medtronics, Inc.** might

incremental effect
The change in total results (such as revenue, expenses, or income) under a new condition in comparison with some given or known condition.

automate the production of its insulin infusion pump, replacing variable costs of labor with fixed costs of equipment.

Consider our vending-machine example. Suppose Winston is considering locking the vending machines from 6:00 P.M. to 6:00 A.M., which she estimates will save $820 in wages monthly. However, the cutback from 24-hour service would hurt volume substantially because many nighttime employees use the machines. (Assume that the cutback will not affect morale; it is strictly a financial decision.) Should the machines remain available 24 hours per day? Assume that monthly sales would decline by 10,000 units from the current sales level. We will perform the analysis assuming two different levels of current sales volume: (1) 62,000 units and (2) 90,000 units.

We will consider two approaches. One is to construct and solve equations for conditions that prevail under each alternative and select the volume level that yields the highest net income.

Regardless of the current volume level, be it 62,000 or 90,000 units, if we accept the prediction that sales will decline by 10,000 units, closing from 6:00 P.M. to 6:00 A.M. will decrease net income by $180:

	Decline from 62,000 to 52,000 Units		Decline from 90,000 to 80,000 Units	
Units	62,000	52,000	90,000	80,000
Sales	$31,000	$26,000	$45,000	$40,000
Variable expenses	24,800	20,800	36,000	32,000
Total contribution margin	$ 6,200	$ 5,200	$ 9,000	$ 8,000
Fixed expenses	6,000	5,180	6,000	5,180
Net income	$ 200	$ 20	$ 3,000	$ 2,820
Change in net income		($180)		($180)

A second approach—an incremental approach—is quicker and simpler. Simplicity is important to managers because it keeps the analysis from being cluttered by irrelevant and potentially confusing data.

What does the insightful manager see in this situation? First, whether the vending machines sell 62,000 or 90,000 units is irrelevant to the decision at hand. The issue is the decline in volume, which is 10,000 units in either case. The essence of this decision is whether the prospective savings in fixed costs exceed the prospective loss in total contribution-margin dollars.

Lost total contribution margin, 10,000 units @ .10	$1,000
Less savings in fixed expenses	− 820
Prospective decline in net income	$ 180

The incremental analysis also shows that locking the vending machines from 6:00 P.M. to 6:00 A.M. would cause a $180 decrease in monthly net income. Whichever way you analyze it, locking the machines is not a sound financial decision.

CVP Analysis and Computer-Based Spreadsheets

The use of spreadsheets simplifies the examination of multiple changes in key factors in a CVP model. Managers in a variety of organizations use a personal computer and a spreadsheet-based CVP modeling program to study combinations of changes in selling prices, unit variable costs, fixed costs, and desired profits. Many nonprofit organizations also use computerized CVP modeling. For example, some private universities have models that help measure how decisions such as raising tuition, adding programs, and closing dormitories during winter holidays will affect financial results. The computer quickly calculates the results of changes and can display them both numerically and graphically.

	A	B	C	D	E
1				Sales Required to Earn	
2	Fixed	Variable		Annual Net Income of	
3	Expenses	Expense %	$2,000	$ 4,000	$ 6,000
4					
5	$4,000	0.40	$10,000*	$13,333	$16,667
6	$4,000	0.44	$10,714*	$14,286	$17,857
7	$4,000	0.48	$11,538*	$15,385	$19,231
8	$6,000	0.40	$13,333	$16,667	$20,000
9	$6,000	0.44	$14,286	$17,857	$21,429
10	$6,000	0.48	$15,385	$19,231	$23,077
11	$8,000	0.40	$16,667	$20,000	$23,333
12	$8,000	0.44	$17,857	$21,429	$25,000
13	$8,000	0.48	$19,231	$23,077	$26,923
15					
16	*(A5 + C3)/(1 − B5) = ($4,000 + $2,000)/(1 − $.40) = $10,000				
17	(A6 + C3)/(1 − B6) = ($4,000 + $2,000)/(1 − $.44) = $10,714				
18	(A7 + C3)/(1 − B7) = ($4,000 + $2,000)/(1 − $.48) = $11,538				
19					

Exhibit 2-6
Spreadsheet Analysis of CVP Relationships

Consider our vending machine example. Exhibit 2-6 is a sample spreadsheet that shows what the sales level would have to be at three different fixed expense levels and three different variable expense levels to reach three different income levels. The computer calculates the 27 different sales levels rapidly and without error. Managers can insert any numbers they want for fixed expenses (column A), variable expense percentage (column B), target net income (row 3 of columns C, D, and E), and the computer will compute the sales level.

In addition to speed and convenience, computers allow a more sophisticated approach to CVP analysis than the one illustrated in this chapter. The assumptions we listed on pages 54–55 are necessary to simplify the analysis enough for most managers to construct a CVP model by hand. Computer analysts, however, can construct a model that does not require all the simplifications. Computer models can include multiple cost drivers, nonlinear relationships between costs and cost drivers, varying sales mixes, and analyses that need not be restricted to a relevant range.

Use of computer models is a cost-benefit issue. The reliability of these models depends on the accuracy of their underlying assumptions about how revenues and costs will actually be affected. More complex models often require fewer assumptions and thus are more reliable. However, sometimes the costs of modeling exceed the value of the improved quality of management decisions. In small organizations, simplified CVP models often are accurate enough; more sophisticated (and more expensive) modeling may be unwarranted.

Additional Uses of Cost-Volume Analysis

Best Cost Structure

Analyzing cost-volume-profit relationships is an important management responsibility. Managers usually try to find the most profitable cost structure—the combination of variable- and fixed-cost factors. For example, purchasing automated machinery may raise fixed costs but reduce labor cost per unit. Conversely, it may be wise to reduce fixed costs to obtain a more favorable combination. Thus, a company may decide to compensate its sales force via sales commissions (variable costs) rather than pay them salaries (a fixed cost).

DID BLOCKBUSTER VIOLATE DISNEY CONTRACT?
ACCOUNTING DISAGREEMENT OR ETHICAL ISSUE?

In early 2003, the Walt Disney Company sued Blockbuster, claiming that Blockbuster had violated a 1997 agreement between the two companies. Prior to the agreement, Blockbuster purchased videos from Disney for about $65 each and kept all the rental revenue. Under the pact, Blockbuster agreed to purchase movies from Disney for $7 a copy and then pay the studio a portion of the revenue from each rental.

The contract allowed Blockbuster to buy more copies of each video, which led to the guarantee that customers could rely on Blockbuster to have a copy of any movie they wanted or else the rental was free. With this policy, Blockbuster increased its market share of the video rental market from 28% to 40%. Essentially, Blockbuster turned a fixed cost, $65 per tape, into primarily a variable cost, with a small $7 fixed-cost portion and a larger variable-cost portion that depended on how much revenue Blockbuster generated from its rentals.

The arrangement was similar to that between the owners of shopping malls and many of their retail store tenants. Each store pays a monthly rental fee plus a percentage of its sales. Just as shopping mall owners rely on their tenants to truthfully report their sales, Disney relied on Blockbuster to correctly account for its video rentals.

In addition, Blockbuster and Disney also agreed on when Blockbuster could sell old rental tapes. Since these were so inexpensive for Blockbuster, selling them could be a lucrative business. But Disney did not want these low-cost tapes competing with its own videotape sales. Thus, it placed restrictions on when Blockbuster could sell them.

In the suit, Disney claimed that Blockbuster improperly deducted "promotional" credits from its gross rental fees, failed to account for "hundreds of thousands" of missing videos, and sold videos prematurely. Disney had to rely on Blockbuster to correctly account for its rental revenues and inventory of tapes. Blockbuster claimed that its accounting was in accordance with the original agreement.

This is an example where good ethics and good accounting are both important. The original agreement promised benefits to both companies—more rental income for Disney on hit movies and more cost-structure flexibility for Blockbuster. But such a contract will not work if each party cannot trust the other. It's not clear who is right in this case, but both companies were hurt by the allegations. At a minimum, both will need to include better monitoring provisions in future contracts because other companies will suspect Disney of trying to get more than it deserves and Blockbuster of playing accounting tricks to minimize its payment to Disney.

Source: "Disney Sues Blockbuster Over Contract," *New York Times*, January 4, 2003; "Disney Sues Top Video Chain," *Los Angeles Times*, January 3, 2003.

Another example of exchanging a fixed cost for a variable cost is a contract **Blockbuster** signed with **Disney** and other major studios. Instead of buying video tapes for $65 each, a fixed cost for each tape, Blockbuster paid only a $7 fixed cost and an additional variable cost equal to a percentage of the rental revenues. You can see one result of this contract in the Business First box above.

Generally, companies that spend heavily for advertising are willing to do so because they have high contribution-margin percentages (e.g., airlines and cigarette and cosmetic companies). Conversely, companies with low contribution-margin percentages usually spend less for advertising and promotion (e.g., manufacturers of industrial equipment). As a result, two companies with the same unit sales volumes at the same unit prices could have different attitudes toward risking an advertising outlay. Assume the following:

	Perfume Company	Janitorial Service Company
Unit sales volume	200,000 bottles	200,000 square feet
Dollar sales at $10 per unit	$2,000,000	$2,000,000
Variable costs	200,000	1,700,000
Total contribution margin	$1,800,000	$ 300,000
Contribution-margin percentage	90%	15%

Suppose each company can increase sales volume by 10% with the same expenditure for advertising:

	Perfume Company	Janitorial Service Company
Increase in sales volume, 20,000 × $10	$200,000	$200,000
Increase in total contribution margin, 90%, 15%	180,000	30,000

The perfume company would be inclined to increase advertising considerably to boost the total contribution margin by $180,000. In contrast, the janitorial service company would be foolhardy to spend large amounts to increase the total contribution margin by $30,000.

Note that when the contribution margin as a percentage of sales is low, great increases in volume are necessary before significant increases in net profits can occur. On the other hand, decreases in profit are also small as volume decreases. High contribution-margin ratios have the opposite effect—large increases in profits as sales grow but also large decreases in profits if sales fall.

Operating Leverage

In addition to weighing the varied effects of changes in fixed and variable costs, managers need to consider their firm's ratio of fixed to variable costs, called **operating leverage**. In highly leveraged companies—those with high fixed costs and low variable costs—small changes in sales volume result in large changes in net income. Changes in sales volume have a smaller effect on companies with less leverage (that is, lower fixed costs and higher variable costs).

operating leverage
A firm's ratio of fixed to variable costs.

Exhibit 2-7 shows cost behavior relationships at two firms, one highly leveraged and one with low leverage. The firm with higher leverage has fixed costs of $14,000 and variable cost per unit of $.10. The firm with lower leverage has fixed costs of only $2,000 but variable costs of $.25 per unit. Expected sales at both companies are 80,000 units at $.30 per unit. At this sales level, both firms would have net incomes of $2,000. If sales fall short of 80,000 units, profits drop most sharply for the highly leveraged business. If sales exceed 80,000 units, however, profits also increase most sharply for the highly leveraged concern.

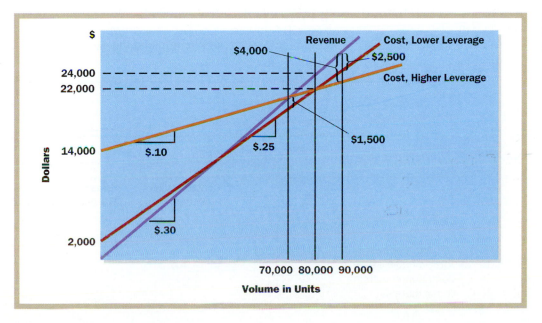

Exhibit 2-7
High Versus Low Leverage

The highly leveraged alternative is more risky. Why? Because it provides the highest possible net income and the highest possible losses. In other words, net income is highly variable, depending on the actual level of sales. The low-leverage alternative is less risky because variations in sales lead to only small variability in net income. At sales of 90,000 units, net income is $4,000 for the higher-leveraged firm but only $2,500 for the lower-leveraged firm. At sales of 70,000 units, however, the higher-leveraged firm has zero profits, compared to $1,500 for the lower-leveraged firm.

Margin of Safety

margin of safety
The planned unit sales less the break-even unit sales; it shows how far sales can fall below the planned level before losses occur.

CVP analysis can also help managers assess risk by providing a measure of the margin of safety. The **margin of safety** shows how far sales can fall below the planned level of sales before losses occur. It compares the level of planned sales with the break-even point:

$$\text{margin of safety} = \text{planned unit sales} - \text{break-even unit sales}$$

The larger the margin of safety, the less likely it is that the company will have an operating loss, that is, operate below the break-even point. A small margin of safety may indicate a more risky situation. If Amy Winston in our vending-machine example had predicted a sales volume of 8,000 units, the margin of safety would be 2,000 units:

$$\text{margin of safety} = 8{,}000 \text{ units} - 6{,}000 \text{ units} = 2{,}000 \text{ units}$$

Contribution Margin and Gross Margin

gross margin (gross profit)
The excess of sales over the total cost of goods sold.

cost of goods sold
The cost of the merchandise that a company acquires or produces and then sells.

This chapter has focused on the contribution margin. However, accountants also use a similar term, *gross margin,* to mean something quite different. Too often people confuse the terms *contribution margin* and *gross margin.* **Gross margin,** also called **gross profit,** is the excess of sales over the cost of goods sold. **Cost of goods sold** is the cost of the merchandise that a company acquires or produces and then sells. Compare the gross margin with the contribution margin:

$$\text{gross margin} = \text{sales price} - \text{cost of goods sold}$$
$$\text{contribution margin} = \text{sales price} - \text{all variable expenses}$$

OBJECTIVE 6

Differentiate between contribution margin and gross margin.

Exhibit 2-8 shows costs divided on two different dimensions. As shown at the bottom of the exhibit, the gross margin uses the division on the production or acquisition cost versus selling and administrative cost dimension, and the contribution margin uses the division based on the variable-cost versus fixed-cost dimension.

In our vending-machine illustration, the contribution margin and the gross margin are identical because the cost of goods sold is the only variable cost:

Sales	$.50
Variable costs: acquisition cost of unit sold	.40
Contribution margin and gross margin are equal	$.10

Now, suppose the firm had to pay a commission of 4¢ per unit sold:

		Contribution Margin	Gross Margin
Sales		$.50	$.50
Acquisition cost of unit sold	$.40		.40
Variable commission	.04		
Total variable expense		.44	
Contribution margin		$.06	
Gross margin			$.10

Exhibit 2-8
Costs for Gross Margin and Contribution Margin

contribution margin = sales − total variable costs = sales − (A + C)
gross margin = sales − total production or acquisition cost = sales − (A + B)

As the preceding tabulation indicates, contribution margin and gross margin are not the same concepts. Contribution margin focuses on sales in relation to all variable costs, whereas gross margin focuses on sales in relation to cost of goods sold. For example, consider **MascoTech,** a Detroit-based auto parts supplier. A newspaper article reported that MascoTech's "gross profit margin on sales is about 21% today, but for each additional sales dollar the contribution margin is more like 30%."

Nonprofit Application

Consider how cost-volume-profit relationships apply to nonprofit organizations. Suppose a city has a $100,000 lump-sum budget appropriation to conduct a counseling program for drug addicts. The variable costs for counseling are $400 per patient per year. Fixed costs are $60,000 in the relevant range of 50 to 150 patients. If the city spends the entire budget appropriation, how many patients can it serve in a year?

We can use the break-even equation to solve the problem. Let N be the number of patients, substitute the $100,000 lump-sum budget for sales, and note that sales equals variable expenses plus fixed expenses if the city completely spends its budget.

$$\text{sales} = \text{variable expenses} + \text{fixed expenses}$$
$$\$100,000 \text{ lump sum} = \$400N + \$60,000$$
$$\$400N = \$100,000 - \$60,000$$
$$N = \$40,000 \div \$400$$
$$N = 100 \text{ patients}$$

The city can serve 100 patients. Now, suppose the city cuts the total budget appropriation for the following year by 10%. Fixed costs will be unaffected, but service will decline.

$$\text{sales} = \text{variable expenses} - \text{fixed expenses}$$
$$\$90,000 = \$400N + \$60,000$$
$$\$400N = \$90,000 - \$60,000$$
$$N = \$30,000 \div \$400$$
$$N = 75 \text{ patients}$$

The percentage reduction in service is $(100 - 75) \div 100 = 25\%$, which is more than the 10% reduction in the budget. Unless the city restructures its operations, the service volume must fall by 25% to stay within budget.

A graphical presentation of this analysis is in Exhibit 2-9. Note that lump-sum revenue is a horizontal line on the graph.

Exhibit 2-9
Graphical
Presentation of
Nonprofit Application

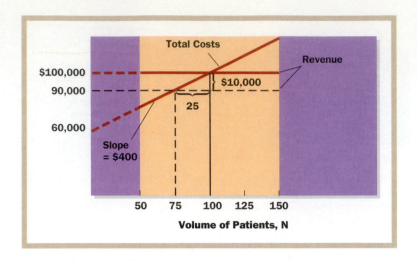

Summary Problem For Your Review

PROBLEM

A summary of the budgeted income statement of Port Williams Gift follows:

Net revenue	$800,000
Less expenses, including $400,000 of fixed expenses	880,000
Net loss	$ (80,000)

The manager believes that an additional outlay of $200,000 for advertising will increase sales substantially.

1. At what sales volume will the store break even after spending $200,000 on advertising?
2. What sales volume will result in a net profit of $40,000 after spending the $200,000 on advertising?

SOLUTION

1. Note that all data are in dollars, not units. Most companies have many products, so the overall break-even analysis deals with dollar sales, not units. The variable expenses are $880,000 − $400,000 = $480,000. The variable-expense ratio is $480,000 ÷ $800,000 = .60. (Remember to divide variable costs by sales, not by total costs.) Therefore, the contribution-margin ratio is .40. Let S = break-even sales in dollars. Then

$$S - \text{variable expenses} - \text{fixed expenses} = \text{net profit}$$

$$S - .60S - (\$400{,}000 + \$200{,}000) = 0$$

$$.40S = \$600{,}000$$

$$S = \frac{\$600{,}000}{.40} = \frac{\text{fixed expenses}}{\text{contribution - margin ratio}}$$

$$S = \$1{,}500{,}000$$

2.

$$\text{required sales} = \frac{(\text{fixed expenses} + \text{target net profit})}{\text{contribution - margin ratio}}$$

$$\text{required sales} = \frac{(\$600{,}000 + \$40{,}000)}{.40} = \frac{\$640{,}000}{.40}$$

$$\text{required sales} = \$1{,}600{,}000$$

Alternatively, we can use an incremental approach and reason that all dollar sales beyond the $1.5 million break-even point will result in a 40% contribution to net profit. Divide $40,000 by .40. Sales must therefore be $100,000 beyond the $1.5 million break-even point to produce a net profit of $40,000.

Highlights to Remember

1 **Explain how cost drivers affect cost behavior.** A cost driver is an output measure that causes the use of costly resources. When the level of an activity changes, the level of the cost driver or output measure will also change, causing changes in costs.

2 **Show how changes in cost-driver activity levels affect variable and fixed costs.** Different types of costs behave in different ways. If the cost of the resource used changes in proportion to changes in the cost driver level, the resource is a variable-cost resource (its costs are variable). If the cost of the resource used does not change because of cost-driver level changes, the resource is a fixed-cost resource (its costs are fixed).

3 **Calculate break-even sales volume in total dollars and total units.** We can approach CVP analysis (sometimes called break-even analysis) graphically or with equations. To calculate the break-even point in total units, divide the fixed costs by the unit contribution margin. To calculate the break-even point in total dollars (sales dollars), divide the fixed costs by the contribution-margin ratio.

4 **Create a cost-volume-profit graph and understand the assumptions behind it.** We can create a cost-volume-profit graph by drawing revenue and total cost lines as functions of the cost-driver level. Be sure to recognize the limitations of CVP analysis and that it assumes constant efficiency, sales mix, and inventory levels.

5 **Calculate sales volume in total dollars and total units to reach a target profit.** Managers use CVP analysis to compute the sales needed to achieve a target profit or to examine the effects on profit of changes in factors such as fixed costs, variable costs, or cost driver volume.

6 **Differentiate between contribution margin and gross margin.** The contribution margin—the difference between sales price and variable costs—is an important concept. Do not confuse it with gross margin, the difference between sales price and cost of goods sold.

Appendix 2A: Sales-Mix Analysis

To emphasize fundamental ideas, the cost-volume-profit analysis in this chapter focused on a single product. Nearly all companies, however, sell more than one product. Thus, they must be concerned with sales mix, which you will recall from p. 55 is the relative proportions or combinations of quantities of products that comprise total sales. If the proportions of the mix change, the cost-volume-profit relationships also change.

Suppose Ramos Company has two products, wallets (W) and key cases (K). The income budget follows:

OBJECTIVE 7

Explain the effects of sales mix on profits.

	Wallets (W)	Key Cases (K)	Total
Sales in units	300,000	75,000	375,000
Sales @ $8 and $5	$2,400,000	$375,000	$2,775,000
Variable expenses @ $7 and $3	2,100,000	225,000	2,325,000
Contribution margins @ $1 and $2	$ 300,000	$150,000	$ 450,000
Fixed expenses			180,000
Net income			$ 270,000

What is the break-even point? The typical answer assumes a constant mix of 4 units of W for every unit of K. Therefore, let K = number of units of product K to break even, and 4K = number of units of product W to break even:

$$\text{sales} - \text{variable expenses} - \text{fixed expenses} = \text{zero net income}$$
$$[\$8(4K) + \$5(K)] - [\$7(4K) + \$3(K)] - \$180{,}000 = 0$$
$$\$32K + \$5K - \$28K - \$3K - \$180{,}000 = 0$$
$$\$6K = \$180{,}000$$
$$K = 30{,}000$$
$$4K = 120{,}000 = W$$

The break-even point is 30,000K + 120,000W = 150,000 units.

This is the only break-even point for a sales mix of four wallets for every key case. Clearly, however, there are other break-even points for other sales mixes. For instance, suppose Ramos Company sells only key cases and fixed expenses stay at $180,000.

$$\text{break-even point} = \frac{\text{fixed expenses}}{\text{contribution margin per unit}}$$
$$= \frac{\$180{,}000}{\$2}$$
$$= 90{,}000 \text{ key cases}$$

If Ramos sells only wallets:

$$\text{break-even point} = \frac{\$180{,}000}{\$1} = 180{,}000 \text{ wallets}$$

We can see that the break-even point could be 180,000 units (of wallets), 90,000 units (of key cases), or 150,000 units (30,000 key cases and 120,000 wallets).

Managers are not interested in the break-even point for its own sake. Instead, they want to know how changes in a planned sales mix will affect net income. When the sales mix changes, the break-even point and the expected net income at various sales levels change also. For example, suppose overall actual total sales were equal to the budget of 375,000 units. However, Ramos sold only 50,000 key cases.

	Wallets (W)	Key Cases (K)	Total
Sales in units	325,000	50,000	375,000
Sales @ $8 and $5	$2,600,000	$250,000	$2,850,000
Variable expenses @ $7 and $3	2,275,000	150,000	2,425,000
Contribution margins @ $1 and $2	$ 325,000	$100,000	$ 425,000
Fixed expenses			180,000
Net income			$ 245,000

The change in sales mix has resulted in a $245,000 actual net income rather than the $270,000 budgeted net income, an unfavorable difference of $25,000. The budgeted and actual sales in number of units were identical, but the proportion of sales of the product bearing the higher unit contribution margin declined.

Managers usually want to maximize the sales of all their products. Faced with limited resources and time, however, executives prefer to generate the most profitable sales mix achievable. For example, **Clorox Company** included the following in the report of its first-quarter 2003 results: "The revised projection reflects benefits from . . . a more favorable mix of products sold during the quarter." **U.S. Home Systems, Inc.,** had the opposite experience in 2002: "The loss in the third quarter resulted . . . [partly from the] mix of products sold."

Profitability of a given product helps guide executives who must decide to emphasize or deemphasize particular products. For example, given limited production facilities or limited time of sales personnel, should we emphasize wallets or key cases? Of course, other factors beyond the contribution margin can affect these decisions. Chapter 5 explores some of these factors, including the importance of the amount of profit per unit of time rather than per unit of product.

Appendix 2B: Impact of Income Taxes

Thus far we have (as so many people would like to) ignored income taxes. In most nations, however, private enterprises must pay income taxes. Reconsider the vending machine example in this chapter. As part of our CVP analysis, we discussed the sales necessary to achieve a target income before income taxes of $480. If Boeing pays income tax at a rate of 40%, the new result would be

O B J E C T I V E   8

Compute cost-volume-profit relationships on an after-tax basis.

Income before income tax	$480	100%
Income tax	192	40
Net income	$288	60%

Note that

$$\text{net income} = \text{income before income taxes} - .40\,(\text{income before income taxes})$$
$$\text{net income} = .60\,(\text{income before income taxes})$$
$$\text{income before income taxes} = \frac{\text{net income}}{.60}$$

or

$$\text{target income before income taxes} = \frac{\text{target after-tax net income}}{1 - \text{tax rate}}$$

$$\text{target income before income taxes} = \frac{\$288}{1 - .40} = \frac{\$288}{.60} = \$480$$

Suppose the target net income after taxes was $288. The only change in the general equation approach would be on the right-hand side of the following equation:

$$\text{target sales} - \text{variable expenses} - \text{fixed expenses} = \frac{\text{target after-tax net income}}{1 - \text{tax rate}}$$

Thus, letting N be the number of units to be sold at $.50 each with a variable cost of $.40 each and total fixed costs of $6,000,

$$\$.50N - \$.40N - \$6,000 = \frac{\$288}{1 - .4}$$

$$\$.10N = \$6,000 + \frac{\$288}{.6}$$

$$\$.06N = \$3,600 + \$288 = 3,888$$

$$N = \$3,888 \div \$.06 = 64,800 \text{ units}$$

Sales of 64,800 units produce an after-tax profit of $288 as shown here and a before-tax profit of $480 as shown in the chapter.

Suppose the target net income after taxes was $480. The volume needed would rise to 68,000 units, as follows:

$$\$.50N - \$.40N - \$6,000 = \frac{\$480}{1 - .4}$$

$$\$.10N = \$6,000 + \frac{\$480}{.6}$$

$$\$.06N = \$3,600 + \$480 = 4,080$$

$$N = \$4,080 \div \$.06 = 68,000 \text{ units}$$

As a shortcut to computing the effects of volume on the change in after-tax income, use the formula

$$\text{change in net income} = \left(\begin{array}{c}\text{change in volume}\\ \text{in units}\end{array}\right) \times \left(\begin{array}{c}\text{contribution margin}\\ \text{per unit}\end{array}\right) \times \left(1 - \text{tax rate}\right)$$

In our example, suppose operations were at a level of 64,800 units and $288 after-tax net income. The manager is wondering how much after-tax net income would increase if sales become 68,000 units.

$$\text{change in net income} = (68{,}000 - 64{,}800) \times \$.10 \times (1 - .4)$$
$$= 3{,}200 \times \$.10 \times .60 = 3{,}200 \times \$.06$$
$$= \$192$$

In brief, each unit beyond the break-even point adds to after-tax net profit at the unit contribution margin multiplied by $(1 - \text{income tax rate})$.

Throughout our illustration, the break-even point itself does not change. Why? Because there is no income tax at a level of zero profits.

Accounting Vocabulary

break-even point, p. 49
contribution margin, p. 51
contribution-margin percentage, p. 51
contribution-margin ratio, p. 52
cost behavior, p. 44
cost driver, p. 45
cost of goods sold, p. 62

cost-volume-profit (CVP) analysis, p. 49
fixed cost, p. 46
gross margin, p. 62
gross profit, p. 62
incremental effect, p. 57
marginal income, p. 51
margin of safety, p. 62

operating leverage, p. 61
relevant range, p. 47
sales mix, p. 55
total contribution margin, p. 51
unit contribution margin, p. 51
variable cost, p. 46
variable-cost percentage, p. 51
variable-cost ratio, p. 52

Fundamental Assignment Material

2-A1 Cost-Volume-Profits and Vending Machines

Riccardo Food Services Company operates and services soft drink vending machines located in restaurants, gas stations, and factories in four southeastern states. The machines are rented from the manufacturer. In addition, Riccardo must rent the space occupied by its machines. The following expense and revenue relationships pertain to a contemplated expansion program of 40 machines.

Fixed monthly expenses follow:

Machine rental: 40 machines @ $53.50	$2,140
Space rental: 40 locations @ $38.80	1,552
Part-time wages to service the additional 40 machines	2,008
Other fixed costs	300
Total monthly fixed costs	$6,000

Other data follow:

	Per Unit	Per $100 of Sales
Selling price	$1.00	100%
Cost of snack	.80	80
Contribution margin	$ .20	20%

These questions relate to the above data unless otherwise noted. Consider each question independently.

1. What is the monthly break-even point in number of units? In dollar sales?
2. If 40,000 units were sold, what would be the company's net income?
3. If the space rental cost were doubled, what would be the monthly break-even point in number of units? In dollar sales?
4. If, in addition to the fixed rent, Riccardo Food Services Company paid the vending-machine manufacturer 2¢ per unit sold, what would be the monthly break-even point in number of units? In dollar sales? Refer to the original data.
5. If, in addition to the fixed rent, Riccardo paid the machine manufacturer 4¢ for each unit sold in excess of the break-even point, what would the new net income be if 40,000 units were sold? Refer to the original data.

2-A2 Exercises in Cost-Volume-Profit Relationships

Barkins Moving Company specializes in hauling heavy goods over long distances. The company's revenues and expenses depend on revenue miles, a measure that combines both weights and mileage. Summarized budget data for next year are based on predicted total revenue miles of 800,000. At that level of volume, and at any level of volume between 700,000 and 900,000 revenue miles, the company's fixed costs are $120,000. The selling price and variable costs are

Per Revenue Mile	
Average selling price (revenue)	$1.50
Average variable expenses	1.30

1. Compute the budgeted net income. Ignore income taxes.
2. Management is trying to decide how various possible conditions or decisions might affect net income. Compute the new net income for each of the following changes. Consider each case independently.
   a. A 10% increase in sales price
   b. A 10% increase in revenue miles
   c. A 10% increase in variable expenses
   d. A 10% increase in fixed expenses
   e. An average decrease in selling price of 3¢ per revenue mile and a 5% increase in revenue miles. Refer to the original data.
   f. An average increase in selling price of 5¢ and a 10% decrease in revenue miles
   g. A 10% increase in fixed expenses in the form of more advertising and a 5% increase in revenue miles

2-B1 Basic CVP Exercises

Each problem is unrelated to the others.

1. Given: Selling price per unit, $20; total fixed expenses, $5,000; variable expenses per unit, $16. Find break-even sales in units.
2. Given: Sales, $40,000; variable expenses, $30,000; fixed expenses, $8,000; net income, $2,000. Find break-even sales.
3. Given: Selling price per unit, $30; total fixed expenses, $33,000; variable expenses per unit, $14. Find total sales in units to achieve a profit of $7,000, assuming no change in selling price.
4. Given: Sales, $50,000; variable expenses, $20,000; fixed expenses, $20,000; net income, $10,000. Assume no change in selling price; find net income if activity volume increases 10%.
5. Given: Selling price per unit, $40; total fixed expenses, $80,000; variable expenses per unit, $30. Assume that variable expenses are reduced by 20% per unit, and the total fixed expenses are increased by 10%. Find the sales in units to achieve a profit of $20,000, assuming no change in selling price.

2-B2 Basic CVP Analysis

Rudy LaConte opened Rudy's Corner, a small day care facility, just over two years ago. After a rocky start, Rudy's Corner has been thriving. LaConte is now preparing a budget for November 20X5.

Monthly fixed costs for Rudy's Corner are

Rent	$ 800
Salaries	1,400
Other fixed costs	100
Total fixed costs	$2,300

The salary is for Ann Penilla, the only employee, who works with Rudy by caring for the children. LaConte does not pay himself a salary, but he receives the excess of revenues over costs each month.

The cost driver for variable costs is "child-days." One child-day is one day in day care for one child, and the variable cost is $10 per child-day. The facility is open from 6:00 A.M. to 6:00 P.M. weekdays (that is, Monday through Friday), and there are 22 weekdays in November 20X5. An average day has 8 children attending Rudy's Corner. State law prohibits Rudy's Corner from having more than 14 children, a limit it has never reached. LaConte charges $30 per day per child, regardless of how long the child is at the facility.

1. Suppose attendance for November 20X5 is equal to the average, resulting in $22 \times 8 = 176$ child-days. What amount will LaConte have left after paying all his expenses?
2. Suppose both costs and attendance are difficult to predict. Compute the amount LaConte will have left after paying all his expenses for each of the following situations. Consider each case independently.
    a. Average attendance is 9 children per day instead of 8, generating 198 child-days.
    b. Variable costs increase to $12 per child-day.
    c. Rent increases by $220 per month.
    d. LaConte spends $300 on advertising (a fixed cost) in November, which increases average daily attendance to 9.5 children.
    e. LaConte begins charging $33 per day on November 1, and average daily attendance slips to 7 children.

Additional Assignment Material

Questions

2-1 "Cost behavior is simply identification of cost drivers and their relationships to costs." Comment.

2-2 Give two rules of thumb to use when analyzing cost behavior.

2-3 Give three examples of variable costs and of fixed costs.

2-4 "Fixed costs decline as volume increases." Do you agree? Explain.

2-5 "It is confusing to think of fixed costs on a per-unit basis." Do you agree? Why or why not?

2-6 "All costs are either fixed or variable. The only difficulty in cost analysis is determining which of the two categories each cost belongs to." Do you agree? Explain.

2-7 "The relevant range pertains to fixed costs, not variable costs." Do you agree? Explain.

2-8 Identify the major simplifying assumption that underlies CVP analysis.

2-9 "Classification of costs into variable and fixed categories depends on the decision situation." Explain.

2-10 "Contribution margin is the excess of sales over fixed costs." Do you agree? Explain.

2-11 Why is "break-even analysis" a misnomer?

2-12 "Companies in the same industry generally have about the same break-even point." Do you agree? Explain.

2-13 "It is essential to choose the right CVP method—equation, contribution margin, or graphical. If you pick the wrong one, your analysis will be faulty." Do you agree? Explain.

2-14 Describe three ways of lowering a break-even point.

2-15 "Incremental analysis is quicker, but it has no other advantage over an analysis of all costs and revenues associated with each alternative." Do you agree? Why or why not?

2-16 "CVP analysis is a common management use of personal computers." Do you agree? Explain.

2-17 Explain operating leverage and why a highly leveraged company is risky.

2-18 "The contribution margin and gross margin are always equal." Do you agree? Explain.

2-19 "CVP relationships are unimportant in nonprofit organizations." Do you agree? Explain.

2-20 Study Appendix 2A. A company sold two products. Total budgeted sales and total actual sales in number of units were identical. Actual unit variable costs and sales prices were the same as budgeted. Actual contribution margin was lower than budgeted. What could be the reason for the lower contribution margin?

2-21 Study Appendix 2B. Given a target after-tax net income, present the CVP formula for computing the income before income taxes.

2-22 Study Appendix 2B. Present the CVP formula for computing the effects of a change in volume on after-tax income.

2-23 "As I understand it, costs such as the salary of the vice president of transportation operations are variable because the more traffic you handle, the less your unit cost. In contrast, costs such as fuel are fixed because each ton-mile should entail consumption of the same amount of fuel and hence bear the same unit cost." Do you agree? Explain.

Critical Thinking Exercises

2-24 Marketing Function of Value-Chain and Cost Behavior
Refer to Exhibit 2-1. For the two examples of marketing costs given in Exhibit 2-1, describe their cost behavior in relation to the cost driver listed.

2-25 Production Function of Value-Chain and Cost Behavior
Refer to Exhibit 2-1. For the labor wages and depreciation of plant and machinery examples of production costs given in Exhibit 2-1, describe their cost behavior in relation to the cost driver listed.

2-26 Tenneco Automotive's Value Chain
Tenneco Automotive is one of the world's largest makers of ride-control and exhaust systems, with annual revenues in excess of $3 billion. After reporting weak earnings, the company undertook a strategy to reduce its break-even point by 25% by selling excess capacity, reducing head count, and introducing new high-contribution-margin products. The company's senior vice president listed the key elements of the company's strategy, stating, "We are gaining momentum and transforming our North American aftermarket business with new products, new technology, new positioning strategies, and new pricing." For each of these "new" elements of Tenneco's aftermarket business strategy, list the value-chain function that is most applicable.

Exercises

2-27 Identifying Cost Drivers
The following list identifies several potential cost drivers for a manufacturing company that makes eight products. The company uses a just-in-time (JIT) production system so it stores finished product for a very limited time. The eight products vary substantially in size from small (plastic casings for pens) to large (plastic casings for truck instrument panels).

- Number of setups
- Setup time
- Square feet
- Cubic feet
- Cubic feet weeks

For each situation described below (activity and related resource), identify the best cost driver from the list and briefly justify your choice.

1. To produce a product, production mechanics must set up machinery. It takes about the same time to set up for a production run regardless of the product being produced. What is the best cost driver for mechanic wages?
2. Instead of the situation described in number 1, what driver should the company use for mechanic wages if it takes longer to set up for complex products such as the instrument panel casings than for simple products such as pen casings?
3. What driver should the company use for warehouse occupancy costs (depreciation and insurance)? The company uses the warehouse to store finished product.
4. What driver should the company use for the warehouse occupancy costs if it did not use a JIT system (that is, the company maintains inventories), and upon inspection, one of the products had a thick layer of dust on it.

2-28 Basic Review Exercises
Fill in the blanks for each of the following independent cases (ignore income taxes):

	Sales	Variable Expenses	Contribution Margin	Fixed Expenses	Net Income
1.	$900,000	$500,000	$ —	$330,000	$ —
2.	800,000	450,000	350,000	620 —	80,000
3.	240 —	600,000	360,000	250,000	— 230

2-29 Basic Review Exercises

Fill in the blanks for each of the following independent cases:

Case	(a) Selling Price per Unit	(b) Variable Cost per Unit	(c) Total Units Sold	(d) Total Contribution Margin	(e) Total Fixed Costs	(f) Net Income
1	$25	$— 19	120,000	$720,000	$650,000	$ — 790,000
2	10	6	100,000	—	320,000	
3	20	15	—	100,000	—	15,000
4	30	20	60,000	600—	—	12,000
5	2 —	9	80,000	160,000	110,000	—

2-30 Basic Cost-Volume-Profit Graph

Refer to Exercise 2-29. Construct a cost-volume-profit graph for Case 2 that depicts the total revenue, total variable cost, total fixed cost, and total cost lines. Estimate the break-even point in total units sold and the net income for 100,000 units sold.

2-31 Basic Cost-Volume-Profit Graph

Refer to Exercise 2-29. Construct a cost-volume-profit graph for Case 4 that depicts the total revenue, total variable cost, total fixed cost, and total cost lines. Estimate the break-even point in total units sold and the net income (loss) for 50,000 units sold.

2-32 Hospital Costs and Pricing

St. Vincent Hospital has overall variable costs of 30% of total revenue and fixed costs of $42 million per year.

1. Compute the break-even point expressed in total revenue.
2. A patient-day is often used to measure the volume of a hospital. Suppose there are to be 50,000 patient-days next year. Compute the average daily revenue per patient necessary to break even.

2-33 Motel Rentals

Suppose a particular **Motel 6** ("We'll leave the light on for you") has annual fixed costs of $3.4 million for its 400-room motel, average daily room rents of $50, and average variable costs of $10 for each room rented. It operates 365 days per year.

1. How much net income on rooms will Motel 6 generate (a) if the motel is completely full throughout the entire year and (b) if the motel is half full?
2. Compute the break-even point in number of rooms rented. What percentage occupancy for the year is needed to break even?

2-34 Variable Cost to Break Even

General Mills makes Wheaties, Cheerios, Betty Crocker cake mixes, and many other food products. Suppose the product manager of a new General Mills cereal has determined that the appropriate wholesale price for a carton of the cereal is $48. Fixed costs of the production and marketing of the cereal is $19 million.

1. The product manager estimates that she can sell 800,000 cartons at the $48 price. What is the largest variable cost per carton that General Mills can pay and still achieve a profit of $1 million?
2. Suppose the variable cost is $25 per carton. What profit (or loss) would General Mills expect?

2-35 Basic Relationships, Hotel

The Seaview Hotel in Portland has 400 rooms, with a fixed cost of $400,000 per month during the busy season. Room rates average $62 per day, with variable costs of $12 per rented room per day. Assume a 30-day month.

1. How many rooms must be occupied per day to break even?
2. How many rooms must be occupied per month to make a monthly profit of $100,000?
3. Assume that the Seaview Hotel does more than rent rooms. It has the following average contribution margins per month from activities in other spaces in its hotel:

Leased shops in hotel	$60,000
Meals served, conventions	30,000
Dining room and coffee shop	30,000
Bar and cocktail lounge	20,000

$140,000 cont. Mu

Assume that the hotel averages 80% occupancy per day. What average rate per day must the hotel charge to make a profit of $100,000 per month?

2-36 Sales-Mix Analysis

Study Appendix 2A. Matsunaga Farms produces strawberries and raspberries. Annual fixed costs are $15,600. The cost driver for variable costs is pints of fruit produced. The variable cost is $.75 per pint of strawberries and $.95 per pint of raspberries. Strawberries sell for $1.10 per pint, raspberries for $1.45 per pint. Two pints of strawberries are produced for every pint of raspberries.

1. Compute the number of pints of strawberries and the number of pints of raspberries produced and sold at the break-even point.
2. Suppose only strawberries are produced and sold. Compute the break-even point in pints.
3. Suppose only raspberries are produced and sold. Compute the break-even point in pints.

2-37 Income Taxes

Review the illustration in Appendix 2B. Suppose the income tax rate were 20% instead of 40%. How many units would the company have to sell to achieve a target after-tax net income of (1) $288 and (2) $480? Show your computations.

2-38 Income Taxes and Cost-Volume-Profit Analysis

Study Appendix 2B. Suppose Hernandez Construction Company has a 40% income tax rate, a contribution-margin ratio of 30%, and fixed costs of $470,000. What sales volume is necessary to achieve an after-tax income of $42,000?

Problems

2-39 Fixed Costs and Relevant Range

Bridger Canyon Systems Group (BCSG) has a substantial year-to-year fluctuation in billings to clients. Top management has the following policy regarding the employment of key professional personnel:

If Gross Annual Billings Are	Number of Persons to Be Employed	Key Professional Annual Salaries
$2,000,000 or less	10	$1,000,000
$2,000,001–2,400,000	11	$1,100,000
$2,400,001–2,800,000	12	$1,200,000

Top management believes that the group should maintain a minimum of ten individuals for a year or more even if billings drop drastically below $2 million.

For the past five years, gross annual billings for BCSG have fluctuated between $2,020,000 and $2,380,000. Expectations for next year are that gross billings will be between $2,100,000 and $2,300,000. What amount should the group budget for key professional personnel salaries? Graph the relationships on an annual basis, using the two approaches illustrated in Exhibit 2-3 on page 48. Indicate the relevant range on each graph. You need not use graph paper; simply approximate the graphical relationships.

2-40 Comparing Contribution Margin Percentages

Below are actual statements of operating income for **Microsoft** and **Procter & Gamble** (in millions):

Microsoft		Procter & Gamble	
Revenues	$28,365	Net sales	$40,238
Cost of revenue	5,191	Cost of products sold	20,989
Research and development	4,307	Marketing, research,	
Sales and Marketing	5,407	and administrative expenses	12,571
General and administrative	1,550	Operating income	$ 6,678
Operating income	$11,910		

Assume that the only variable cost for Microsoft is "cost of revenue" and for Procter & Gamble it is "cost of products sold."

1. Compute the contribution-margin percentage of Microsoft and that of Procter & Gamble. Why do you suppose the percentages are so different?
2. Suppose each company increases its revenue by $10 million. Compute the increase in operating income for each company.
3. Explain how the contribution margin percentage helps you predict the effects on operating income of changes in sales volume. What assumptions do you make in forming such a prediction?

2-41 Movie Manager

Malia Mahler is the manager of Stanford's traditional Sunday Flicks. Each Sunday, a film has two showings. The admission price is deliberately set at a very low $3. She sells a maximum of 500 tickets for each showing. The rental of the auditorium is $330 and labor is $435, including $90 for Mahler. Mahler must pay the film distributor a guarantee, ranging from $300 to $900, or 50% of gross admission receipts, whichever is higher.

Before and during the show, she sells refreshments; these sales average 12% of gross admission receipts and yield a contribution margin of 40%.

1. On June 3, Mahler screened *The Lord of the Rings: The Two Towers*. The film grossed $2,250. The guarantee to the distributor was $750, or 50% of gross admission receipts, whichever is higher. What operating income was produced for the Students' Association, which sponsored the showings?
2. Recompute the results if the film grossed $1,400.
3. The "four-wall" concept is increasingly being adopted by movie producers. In this plan, the movie's producer pays a fixed rental to the theater owner for, say, a week's showing of a movie. As a theater owner, how would you evaluate a "four-wall" offer?

2-42 Promotion of a Rock Concert

BBT Productions, Ltd., is promoting a rock concert in London. The bands will receive a flat fee of £7 million in cash. The concert will be shown worldwide on closed-circuit television. BBT will collect 100% of the receipts and will return 30% to the individual local closed-circuit theater managers. BBT expects to sell 1.1 million seats at a net average price of £13 each. BBT will also receive £300,000 from the London arena (which has sold out its 19,500 seats, ranging from £150 for box seats to £20 for general admission, for a gross revenue of £1.25 million); BBT will not share the £300,000 with the local promoters.

1. The general manager of BBT Productions is trying to decide what amount to spend for advertising. What is the most BBT could spend and still break even on overall operations, assuming sales of 1.1 million tickets?
2. If BBT desires an operating income of £500,000, how many seats would it have to sell? Assume that the average price is £13 and the total fixed costs (including £2,000,000 in advertising) are £9 million.

2-43 Basic Relationships, Restaurant

Jacqui Giraud owns and operates a restaurant. Her fixed costs are $21,000 per month. She serves luncheons and dinners. The average total bill (excluding tax and tip) is $19 per customer. Giraud's present variable costs average $10.60 per meal.

1. How many meals must she serve to attain a profit before taxes of $8,400 per month?
2. What is the break-even point in number of meals served per month?
3. Giraud's rent and other fixed costs rise to a total of $29,925 per month and variable costs also rise to $12.50 per meal. If Giraud increases her average price to $23, how many meals must she serve to make $8,400 profit per month?
4. Assume the same situation described in number 3. Giraud's accountant tells her she may lose 10% of her customers if she increases her prices. If this should happen, what would be Giraud's profit per month? Assume that the restaurant had been serving 3,500 customers per month.
5. Assume the same situation described in number 4. To help offset the anticipated 10% loss of customers, Giraud hires a pianist to perform for four hours each night for $2,000 per month. Assume that this would increase the total monthly meals from 3,150 to 3,450. Would Giraud's total profit change? By how much?

2-44 Changing Fixed Costs to Variable Costs at Blockbuster Video

According to an article in *Business Week*, when John F. Antioco took charge of **Blockbuster Video**, he changed the company's strategy. Traditionally, Blockbuster had bought videotapes from the movie studios for an average cost of about $65 each, planning to rent them out often enough to make a profit.

Mr. Antioco replaced this strategy with one that allows Blockbuster to purchase videos for an average of $7 per tape and pay the studio 40% of any rental fee received for the tape. With this arrangement, Blockbuster could afford to stock more copies of each tape and guarantee customers that the tape they want will be in stock—or the rental is free. Suppose that Blockbuster rents videotapes for $2.00 a day. Assume that operating costs are all fixed.

1. Under the traditional strategy, how many days must each tape be rented before Blockbuster will break even on the tape?
2. Under the new strategy, how many days must each tape be rented before Blockbuster will break even on the tape?
3. Suppose customers rented a particular copy of *Chicago* for 50 days. What profit would Blockbuster make on rentals of the tape (considering only the direct costs of the tape, not the costs of operating the rental store) under the traditional strategy? Under the new strategy?
4. Suppose customers rented a particular copy of *About Schmidt* for only six days. What profit would Blockbuster make on rentals of the tape (considering only the direct costs of the tape, not the costs of operating the rental store) under the traditional strategy? Under the new strategy?
5. Comment on how the new arrangement affects the risks Blockbuster accepts when purchasing an additional copy of a particular videotape.

2-45 Cost-Volume-Profit Analysis, Barbering

Hun-Tong's Hair Styling in Singapore has five barbers. (Hun-Tong is not one of them.) Hun-Tong pays each barber $9.90 per hour. The barbers work a 40-hour week and a 50-week year, regardless of the number of haircuts. Rent and other fixed expenses are $1,750 per month. The variable cost of supplies is $1 per haircut. Assume that the only service performed is the giving of haircuts, the unit price of which is $13.

1. Find the contribution margin per haircut. Assume that the barbers' compensation is a fixed cost.
2. Determine the annual break-even point, in number of haircuts.
3. What will be the operating income if 20,000 haircuts are performed?
4. Suppose Hun-Tong revises the compensation method. He now pays the barbers $4 per hour plus $6 for each haircut. What is the new contribution margin per haircut? What is the annual break-even point (in number of haircuts)?
5. Ignore requirements 3 and 4 and assume that the barbers cease to be paid by the hour but receive $7 for each haircut. What is the new contribution margin per haircut? The annual break-even point (in number of haircuts)?
6. Refer to requirement 5. What would be the operating income if 20,000 haircuts are performed? Compare your answer with the answer in requirement 3.
7. Refer to requirement 5. If 20,000 haircuts are performed, at what rate of commission (that is, percentage of selling price) would Hun-Tong earn the same operating income as he earned in requirement 3?

2-46 CVP and Financial Statements

ConAgra, Inc., is an Omaha-based company that produces food products under brand names such as Healthy Choice, Armour, and Banquet. The company's 2002 income statement showed the following (in millions):

Net sales	$27,630
Costs of goods sold	23,537
Selling, administrative, and general expense	2,423
Interest expense	402
Income before income tax	$ 1,268

Suppose that the cost of goods sold is the only variable cost; selling, administrative, general, and interest expenses are fixed with respect to sales.

Assume that ConAgra had a 10% increase in sales in 2003 and that there was no change in costs except for increases associated with the higher volume of sales. Compute the predicted 2003 income before income tax for ConAgra and its percentage increase. Explain why the percentage increase in income differs from the percentage increase in sales.

2-47 Bingo and Leverage

Many churches sponsor bingo games, a tradition stemming from the time when only specific non-profit institutions were allowed to sponsor games of chance. Reverend Justin Olds, the pastor of a new parish in Orange County, is investigating the desirability of conducting weekly bingo nights.

The parish has no hall, but a local hotel would be willing to commit its hall for a lump-sum rental of $600 per night. The rent would include cleaning, setting up and taking down the tables and chairs, and so on.

1. A local printer would provide bingo cards in return for free advertising. Local merchants would donate door prizes. The services of clerks, callers, security force, and others would be donated by volunteers. Admission would be $4 per person, entitling the player to one card; extra cards would be $1.50 each. Many persons buy extra cards, so there would be an average of four cards played per person. What is the maximum in total cash prizes that the church may award and still break even if 200 persons attend each weekly session?
2. Suppose the total cash prizes are $1,100. What will be the church's operating income if 100 persons attend? If 200 persons attend? If 300 persons attend? Briefly explain the effects of the cost behavior on income.
3. After operating for ten months, Reverend Olds is thinking of negotiating a different rental arrangement but keeping the prize money unchanged at $1,100. Suppose the rent is $200 weekly plus $2 per person. Compute the operating income for attendance of 100, 200, and 300 persons, respectively. Explain why the results differ from those in requirement 2.

2-48 Leverage at eBay

eBay, Inc., is one of the survivors of the technology collapse in 2001 and 2002. eBay's mission is to "provide a global trading platform where practically anyone can trade practically anything." In the first quarter of 2001, eBay reported revenue of $154 million and operating expenses of $123 million, for an operating profit of $31 million. In the first quarter of 2002, eBay reported that revenue had increased 59%, to $245 million. eBay's fixed costs were $37 million and variable costs vary with the amount of revenue.

1. Compute eBay's operating income for the first quarter of 2002 and its percentage increase in operating income between 2001 and 2002.
2. Explain how eBay managed to increase its income so much with only a 59% increase in revenue.

2-49 Adding a Product

Mac's Brew Pub, located near State University, serves as a gathering place for the university's more social scholars. Mac sells beer on draft and all brands of bottled beer at a contribution margin of 60¢ a beer.

Mac is considering also selling hamburgers during selected hours. His reasons are twofold. First, sandwiches would attract daytime customers. A hamburger and a beer are a quick lunch. Second, he has to meet competition from other local bars, some of which provide more extensive menus.

Mac analyzed the costs as follows:

	Per Month			Per Hamburger
Monthly fixed expenses		Variable expenses		
Wages of part-time cook	$1,200	Rolls		$.12
Other	360	Meat @ $2.80 per pound		
Total	$1,560	(7 hamburgers per pound)		.40
		Other		.18
		Total		$.70

Mac planned a selling price of $1.20 per hamburger to lure many customers. For all questions, assume a 30-day month.

1. What are the monthly and daily break-even points, in number of hamburgers?
2. What are the monthly and daily break-even points, in dollar sales?
3. At the end of two months, Mac finds he has sold 3,600 hamburgers. What is the operating profit per month on hamburgers?
4. Mac thinks that at least 60 extra beers are sold per day because he has these hamburgers available. This means that 60 extra people come to the bar or that 60 buy an extra beer because they are attracted by the hamburgers. How does this affect Mac's monthly operating income?
5. Refer to number 3. How many extra beers would have to be sold per day so that the overall effects of the hamburger sales on monthly operating income would be zero?

2-50 Cost-Volume-Profit Relationships and a Dog Track

The Key West Kennel Club is a dog-racing track. Its revenue is derived mainly from attendance and a fixed percentage of the pari-mutuel betting. Its expenses for a 90-day season are as follows:

Wages of cashiers and ticket takers	$150,000
Commissioner's salary	20,000
Maintenance (repairs, etc.)	20,000
Utilities	40,000
Other expenses (depreciation, insurance, advertising, etc.)	100,000
Purses: total prizes paid to winning racers	810,000

The track made a contract with PK, Inc., to park patrons' cars. PK charged the track $4.80 per car. A survey revealed that on the average three persons arrived in each car and that half the attendees arrived by private automobiles. The others arrived by taxi or public bus.

The track's sources of revenue are

Rights for concession and vending	$60,000
Admission charge (deliberately low)	$1 per person
Percentage of bets placed	10%

Assume that each person bets $25 a night.

1. a. How many persons have to be admitted for the track to break even for the season?
   b. If the desired operating profit for the year is $270,000, how many people would have to attend?
2. If a policy of free admission brought a 20% increase in attendance, what would be the new level of operating profit? Assume that the previous level of attendance was 600,000 people.
3. If the purses were doubled in an attempt to attract better dogs and thus increase attendance, what would be the new break-even point? Refer to the original data and assume that each person bets $25 a night.

2-51 Traveling Expenses

Yukio Asaka is a traveling inspector for the state treasurer's office. He uses his own car, and the agency reimburses him at 23¢ per mile. Asaka claims he needs 27¢ per mile just to break even.

Marilyn McDyess, the district manager, looks into the matter and compiles the following information about Asaka's expenses:

Oil change every 3,000 miles	$ 30
Maintenance (other than oil) every 6,000 miles	240
Yearly insurance	700
Auto cost $13,500 with an average cash trade-in value of $6,000; has a useful life of three years.	
Gasoline is approximately $1.70 per gallon and Asaka averages 17 miles per gallon.	

When Asaka is on the road, he averages 120 miles a day. McDyess knows that Asaka does not work Saturdays or Sundays, has 10 working days vacation and 6 holidays, and spends approximately 15 working days in the office.

1. How many miles per year would Asaka have to travel to break even at the current rate of reimbursement?
2. What would be an equitable mileage rate?

2-52 Government Organization

A social welfare agency has a government budget appropriation for 20X2 of $900,000. The agency's major mission is to help disabled persons who are unable to hold jobs. On the average, the agency supplements each person's income by $5,000 annually. The agency's fixed costs are $280,000. There are no other costs.

1. How many disabled persons were helped during 20X2?
2. For 20X3, the agency's budget appropriation has been reduced by 15%. If the agency continues the same level of monetary support per person, how many disabled persons will be helped in 20X3? Compute the percentage decline in the number of persons helped.
3. Assume a budget reduction of 15%, as in number 2. The manager of the agency has discretion as to how much to supplement each disabled person's income. She does not want to reduce the number of persons served. On the average, what is the amount of the supplement that can be given to each person? Compute the percentage decline in the annual supplement.

2-53 Airline CVP

Airline companies regularly provide operating statistics with their financial statements. In 2002, **Continental Airlines** reported that it had approximately 80,122 million seat-miles available, of which 74.1% were filled. (A seat-mile is one seat traveling one mile. For example, if an airplane with 100 seats traveled 400 miles, capacity would have been $100 \times 400 = 40,000$ seat miles.) The average revenue was $.132 per revenue-passenger-mile, where a revenue-passenger-mile is one seat occupied by a passenger traveling one mile. In 2001, 84,485 million seat-miles were available, but only 72.4% of them were filled at an average revenue of $.138 per filled seat-mile. Continental calls the percentage of seat-miles available that are filled with passengers their load factor.

1. Compute Continental's passenger revenue for 2002 and 2001.
2. Assume that Continental's variable costs were $.08 per revenue-passenger-mile in both 2001 and 2002 and that annual fixed costs are $3,000 million each year.
   a. Compute Continental's break-even point at the 2001 level of revenue per passenger mile. Express it in both revenue-passenger-miles and as a load factor (that is, as a percentage of available capacity used).
   b. Compute Continental's break-even point at the 2002 level of revenue per passenger mile. Express it in both revenue-passenger-miles and as a load factor (that is, as a percentage of available capacity used).
3. Suppose Continental maintained the same level of seat-miles available in 2003 as it had in 2002, had revenue of $.135 per revenue-passenger-mile, and maintained the same total fixed cost and unit variable costs as in the previous two years. Compute the load factor necessary to achieve an operating income of $400 million.

2-54 Gross Margin and Contribution Margin

Eastman Kodak Company produces and sells cameras, film, and other imaging products. A condensed 2001 income statement follows (in millions):

Sales	$13,234
Costs of goods sold	8,670
Gross margin	4,564
Other operating expenses	4,219
Operating income	$ 345

Assume that $1,800 million of the cost of goods sold is a fixed cost representing depreciation and other production costs that do not change with the volume of production. In addition, $3,000 million of the other operating expenses is fixed.

1. Compute the total contribution margin for 2001 and the contribution margin percentage. Explain why the contribution margin differs from the gross margin.
2. Suppose that sales for Eastman Kodak were predicted to increase by 10% in 2002 and that the cost behavior was expected to continue in 2002 as it did in 2001. Compute the predicted operating income for 2002. By what percentage did this predicted 2002 operating income exceed the 2001 operating income?
3. What assumptions were necessary to compute the predicted 2002 operating income in number 2?

2-55 Choosing Equipment for Different Volumes

MetroCinema owns and operates a nationwide chain of movie theaters. The 500 properties in the chain vary from low-volume, small-town, single-screen theaters to high-volume, big-city, multiscreen theaters.

The management is considering installing machines that will make popcorn on the premises. These machines would allow the theaters to sell freshly popped popcorn rather than the prepopped, prebagged corn that it currently sells. This proposed feature would be properly advertised and is intended to increase patronage at the company's theaters.

The machines can be purchased in several different sizes. The annual rental costs and operating costs vary with the size of the machines. The machine capacities and costs are as follows:

	Popper Model		
	Standard	**Deluxe**	**Jumbo**
Annual capacity	50,000 boxes	120,000 boxes	300,000 boxes
Costs			
Annual machine rental	$7,840	$11,200	$20,200
Popcorn cost per box	.14	.14	.14
Cost of each box	.09	.09	.09
Other variable costs per box	.22	.14	.05

1. Calculate the volume level in boxes at which the standard and deluxe poppers would earn the same operating profit (loss).
2. The management can estimate the number of boxes to be sold at each of its theaters. Present a decision rule that would enable MetroCinema management to select the most profitable machine without having to make a separate cost calculation for each theater. That is, at what anticipated range of unit sales should the theater use the standard model? The deluxe model? The jumbo model?
3. Could the management use the average number of boxes sold per seat for the entire chain and the capacity of each theater to develop this decision rule? Explain your answer.

2-56 Boeing Break Even

Boeing is the largest commercial airplane manufacturer in the world. One of its airplanes is the 757-300, a 240-passenger plane with a range up to 4,010 miles. The 757 series has the lowest operating cost per seat-mile of any mid-sized or single-aisle jetliner. First deliveries of 757-300s took place in 1999.

Assume that Boeing's annual fixed costs for the 757-300 are $800 million, its variable cost per airplane is $45 million, and the selling price is $65 million per plane.

1. Compute Boeing's break-even point in number of 757-300 airplanes and in dollars of sales.
2. Suppose Boeing plans to sell forty-two 757-300 airplanes in 2005. Compute Boeing's projected operating profit.
3. Suppose Boeing increased its fixed costs by $84 million and reduced variable costs per airplane by $2 million. Compute its operating profit if it sells forty-two 757-300 airplanes. Compute the break-even point. Comment on your results.
4. Ignore number 3. Suppose fixed costs do not change but variable costs increase by 10% before deliveries of 757-300 airplanes begin in 2005. Compute the new break-even point. What strategies might Boeing use to help assure profitable operations in light of increases in variable cost?

2-57 Sales Compensation, Variable/Fixed Costs, and Ethics

Most companies compensate their sales forces with a combination of a fixed salary and a commission that is a percentage of sales. Consider two companies competing for the same customers—for example, **Kelloggs** and **Post** cereals. Suppose that Kelloggs pays its sales force a large fixed salary and a small commission, while Post pays its sales force a small fixed salary and a large commission. The total pay on average was the same for both companies.

1. Compare the sales cost structure of Kelloggs with that of Post. Which has the larger fixed cost? Which has the larger variable cost? How will this affect each company's risk? (Focus on how the company's profits change with changes in volume.)
2. What incentives does each pay system provide for the sales force?
3. Might either incentive system create potential ethical dilemmas for the sales personnel? Explain.

2-58 Sales-Mix Analysis

Study Appendix 2A. The Rocky Mountain Catering Company specializes in preparing Mexican dinners that it freezes and ships to restaurants in the Denver area. When a diner orders an item, the restaurant heats and serves it. The budget data for 20X5 are

	Product	
	Chicken Tacos	**Beef Enchiladas**
Selling price to restaurants	$5	$7
Variable expenses	3	4
Contribution margin	$2	$3
Number of units	250,000	125,000

The company prepares the items in the same kitchens, delivers them in the same trucks, and so forth. Therefore, decisions about the individual products do not affect the fixed costs of $735,000.

1. Compute the planned net income for 20X5.
2. Compute the break-even point in units, assuming that the company maintains its planned sales mix.
3. Compute the break-even point in units if the company sells only tacos and if it sells only enchiladas.
4. Suppose the company sells 78,750 units of enchiladas and 236,250 units of tacos, for a total of 315,000 units. Compute the net income. Compute the new break-even point with this new sales mix. What is the major lesson of this problem?

2-59 Hospital Patient Mix

Study Appendix 2A. Hospitals measure their volume in terms of patient-days. We calculate patient-days by multiplying the number of patients by the number of days that the patients are hospitalized. Suppose a large hospital has fixed costs of $54 million per year and variable costs of $600 per patient-day. Daily revenues vary among classes of patients. For simplicity, assume that there are two classes: (1) self-pay patients (S) who pay an average of $1,000 per day and (2) non–self-pay patients (G) who are the responsibility of insurance companies and government agencies and who pay an average of $800 per day. Twenty percent of the patients are self-pay.

1. Compute the break-even point in patient-days, assuming that the hospital maintains its planned mix of patients.
2. Suppose that the hospital achieves 225,000 patient-days but that 25% of the patient-days were self-pay (instead of 20%). Compute the net income. Compute the break-even point.

2-60 Income Taxes on Hotels

Study Appendix 2B. The Four Winds Hotel in downtown Phoenix has annual fixed costs applicable to rooms of $9.2 million for its 600-room hotel, average daily room rates of $105, and average variable costs of $25 for each room rented. It operates 365 days per year. The hotel is subject to an income tax rate of 40%.

1. How many rooms must the hotel rent to earn a net income after taxes of $720,000? Of $360,000?
2. Compute the break-even point in number of rooms rented. What percentage occupancy for the year is needed to break even?
3. Assume that the volume level of rooms sold is 150,000. The manager is wondering how much income could be generated by adding sales of 15,000 rooms. Compute the additional net income after taxes.

2-61 Tax Effects, Multiple Choice

Study Appendix 2B. Victor Company is a wholesaler of compact disks. The projected after-tax net income for the current year is $120,000, based on a sales volume of 200,000 CDs. Victor has been selling the CDs at $16 each. The variable costs consist of the $10 unit purchase price and a handling cost of $2 per unit. Victor's annual fixed costs are $600,000, and the company is subject to a 40% income tax rate.

Management is planning for the coming year when it expects that the unit purchase price will increase 30%.

1. Victor Company's break-even point for the current year is (a) 150,000 units, (b) 100,000 units, (c) 50,000 units, (d) 60,000 units, or (e) some amount other than those given.
2. An increase of 10% in projected unit sales volume for the current year would result in an increased after-tax income for the current year of (a) $80,000, (b) $32,000, (c) $12,000, (d) $48,000, or (e) some amount other than those given.
3. The volume of sales in dollars that Victor Company must achieve in the coming year to maintain the same after-tax net income as projected for the current year if unit selling price remains at $16 is (a) $12,800,000, (b) $14,400,000, (c) $11,520,000, (d) $32,000,000, or (e) some amount other than those given.
4. To cover a 30% increase in the unit purchase price for the coming year and still maintain the current contribution-margin ratio, Victor Company must establish a selling price per unit for the coming year of (a) $19.60, (b) $20.00, (c) $20.80, (d) $19.00, or (e) some amount other than those given.

Cases

2-62 Hospital Costs

Gotham City Hospital is unionized. In 20X1, nurses received an average annual salary of $45,000. The hospital administrator is considering changes in the contract with nurses for 20X2. In turn, the hospital may also change the way it charges nursing costs to each department.

The hospital holds each department accountable for its financial performance, and it allocates revenues and expenses to departments. Consider the expenses of the obstetrics department in 20X1.

Variable expenses (based on 20X1 patient-days) are

Meals	$ 610,000
Laundry	260,000
Laboratory	900,000
Pharmacy	850,000
Maintenance	150,000
Other	530,000
Total	$3,300,000

Fixed expenses (based on number of beds) are

Rent	$3,000,000
General administrative services	2,200,000
Janitorial	200,000
Maintenance	150,000
Other	350,000
Total	$5,900,000

Management assigns nurses to departments on the basis of annual patient-days as follows:

Volume Level in Patient-Days	Number of Nurses
10,000–12,000	30
12,000–16,000	35

Total patient-days are the number of patients multiplied by the number of days they are hospitalized. The hospital charges each department for the salaries of the nurses assigned to it.

During 20X1 the obstetrics department had a capacity of 60 beds, billed each patient an average of $810 per day, and had revenues of $12.15 million.

1. Compute the 20X1 volume of activity in patient-days.
2. Compute the 20X1 patient-days that would have been necessary for the obstetrics department to recoup all fixed expenses except nursing expenses.
3. Compute the 20X1 patient-days that would have been necessary for the obstetrics department to break even including nurses' salaries as a fixed cost.
4. Suppose obstetrics must pay $200 per patient-day for nursing services. This plan would replace the two-level, fixed-cost system employed in 20X1. Compute what the break-even point in patient-days would have been in 20X1 under this plan.

2-63 CVP and Prediction of Income

According to an article in *Business Week*, T. J. Izzo had a great idea after a bad back almost forced him to give up golf. His problem was carrying a golf bag, not swinging a club. So he designed a harness-like golf bag strap that distributes the weight equally on both shoulders. Two years after forming **Izzo Systems, Inc.**, Izzo made operating income of $12,000 on revenue of $1 million from selling 75,000 straps. The next year Izzo expected to sell 92,000 straps for $1.7 million.

1. Suppose that variable costs per strap are $10. Compute total fixed and total variable costs for the sales level of 75,000 straps.
2. What price did Izzo charge for the straps to generate its $1 million of revenue? What price does the company expect to charge for the 92,000 straps it predicts it will sell the next year?
3. Suppose the cost behavior does not change. Estimate Izzo's operating income next year (a) with sales at the predicted 92,000 straps, (b) with unit sales 10% above the predicted level, and (c) with unit sales 10% below the predicted level.
4. Explain why the predicted operating income at 92,000 straps was so much greater than the previous year's operating income for 75,000 straps.

2-64 CVP in a Modern Manufacturing Environment

A division of **Hewlett-Packard Company** changed its production operations from one where a large labor force assembled electronic components to an automated production facility dominated by computer-controlled robots. The change was necessary because of fierce competitive pressures. Improvements in quality, reliability, and flexibility of production schedules were necessary just to match the competition. As a result of the change, variable costs fell and fixed costs increased, as shown in the following assumed budgets:

	Old Production Operation	New Production Operation
Unit variable cost		
Material	$ .88	$ .88
Labor	1.22	.22
Total per unit	$ 2.10	$ 1.10
Monthly fixed costs		
Rent and depreciation	$450,000	$ 875,000
Supervisory labor	80,000	175,000
Other	50,000	90,000
Total per month	$580,000	$1,140,000

Expected volume is 600,000 units per month, with each unit selling for $3.10. Capacity is 800,000 units.

1. Compute the budgeted profit at the expected volume of 600,000 units under both the old and the new production environments.
2. Compute the budgeted break-even point under both the old and the new production environments.
3. Discuss the effect on profits if volume falls to 500,000 units under both the old and the new production environments.
4. Discuss the effect on profits if volume increases to 700,000 units under both the old and the new production environments.
5. Comment on the riskiness of the new operation versus the old operation.

2-65 Multiproduct Break-Even in a Restaurant

Study Appendix 2A. An article in *Washington Business* included an income statement for **La Brasserie,** a French restaurant in Washington, D.C. A simplified version of the statement follows:

Revenues	$2,098,400
Cost of sales, all variable	1,246,500
Gross profit	851,900
Operating expenses	
Variable	222,380
Fixed	170,940
Administrative expenses, all fixed	451,500
Net income	$ 7,080

The average dinner tab at La Brasserie is $40, and the average lunch tab is $20. Assume that the variable cost of preparing and serving dinner is also twice that of a lunch. The restaurant serves twice as many lunches as dinners. Assume that the restaurant is open 305 days a year.

1. Compute the daily break-even volume in lunches and dinners for La Brasserie. Compare this to the actual volume reflected in the income statement.
2. Suppose that an extra annual advertising expenditure of $15,000 would increase the average daily volume by three dinners and six lunches, and that there is plenty of capacity to accommodate the extra business. Prepare an analysis for the management of La Brasserie, explaining whether this would be desirable.
3. La Brasserie uses only premium food, and the cost of food makes up 25% of the restaurant's total variable costs. Use of average rather than premium ingredients could cut the food cost by 20%. Assume that La Brasserie uses average-quality ingredients and does not change its prices. How much of a drop-off in volume could it endure and still maintain the same net income? What factors in addition to revenue and costs would influence the decision about the quality of food to use?

2-66 Effects of Changes in Costs, Including Tax Effects

Study Appendix 2B. Pacific Fish Company is a wholesale distributor of salmon. The company services grocery stores in the Chicago area.

Small but steady growth in sales has been achieved by Pacific Fish over the past few years, while salmon prices have been increasing. The company is formulating its plans for the coming fiscal year. Presented next are the data used to project the current year's after-tax net income of $128,250.

Average selling price per pound	$	5.00
Average variable costs per pound		
Cost of salmon	$	2.50
Shipping expenses		.50
Total	$	3.00
Annual fixed costs		
Selling	$	210,000
Administrative		356,250
Total	$	566,250
Expected annual sales volume (390,000 pounds)		$1,950,000
Tax rate		40%

Fishing companies have announced that they will increase prices of their products by an average of 15% in the coming year, owing mainly to increases in labor costs. Pacific Fish Company expects that all other costs will remain at the same rates or levels as in the current year.

1. What is Pacific Fish Company's break-even point in pounds of salmon for the current year?
2. What selling price per pound must Pacific Fish Company charge to cover the 15% increase in the cost of salmon and still maintain the current contribution-margin ratio?
3. What volume of sales in dollars must the Pacific Fish Company achieve in the coming year to maintain the same net income after taxes as projected for the current year if the selling price of salmon remains at $5 per pound and the cost of salmon increases 15%?
4. What strategies might Pacific Fish Company use to maintain the same net income after taxes as projected for the current year?

EXCEL Application Exercise

2-67 CVP and Break-Even

Goal: Create an Excel spreadsheet to perform CVP analysis and show the relationship between price, costs, and break-even points in terms of units and dollars. Use the results to answer questions about your findings.

Scenario: Phonetronix, Inc., is a small manufacturer of telephone and communications devices. Recently, company management decided to investigate the profitability of cellular phone production. They have three different proposals to evaluate. Under all of the proposals, the fixed costs for the new phone would be $110,000. Under proposal A, the selling price of the new phone would be $99 and the variable cost per unit would be $55. Under proposal B, the selling price of the phone would be $129 and the variable cost would remain the same. Under proposal C, the selling price would be $99 and the variable cost would be $49.

When you have completed your spreadsheet, answer the following questions:
1. What are the break-even points in units and dollars under proposal A?
2. How did the increased selling price under proposal B impact the break-even points in units and dollars compared to the break-even points calculated under proposal A?
3. Why did the change in variable cost under proposal C not impact the break-even points in units and dollars as significantly as proposal B did?

Step-by-Step:
1. Open a new Excel spreadsheet.
2. In column A, create a bold-faced heading that contains the following:
   Row 1: Chapter 2 Decision Guideline
   Row 2: Phonetronix, Inc.
   Row 3: Cost-Volume-Profit (CVP) Analysis
   Row 4: Today's Date
3. Merge and center the four heading rows across columns A through D.
4. In Row 7, create the following bold-faced, right-justified column headings:
   Column B: Proposal A
   Column C: Proposal B
   Column D: Proposal C
   Note: Adjust cell widths when necessary as you work.

5. In Column A, create the following row headings:
   Row 8: Selling price
   Row 9: Variable cost
   Row 10: Contribution margin
   Row 11: Contribution margin ratio
   Skip a row
   Row 13: Fixed cost
   Skip a row
   Row 15: Break-even in units
   Skip a row
   Row 17: Break-even in dollars
6. Use the scenario data to fill in the selling price, variable cost, and fixed cost amounts for the three proposals.
7. Use the appropriate formulas from Chapter 2 to calculate contribution margin, contribution margin ratio, break-even in units, and break-even in dollars.
8. Format all amounts as:

Number tab:	Category:	Currency
	Decimal places:	0
	Symbol:	None
	Negative numbers:	Red with parenthesis

9. Change the format of the selling price, contribution margin, fixed cost, and break-even in dollars amounts to display a dollar symbol.
10. Change the format of both contribution margin headings to display as indented:

| **Alignment tab:** | Horizontal: | Left (Indent) |
| | Indent: | 1 |

11. Change the format of the contribution margin amount cells to display a top border, using the default line style.

| **Border tab:** | Icon: | Top Border |

12. Change the format of the contribution margin ratio amounts to display as a percentage with two decimal places.

| **Number tab:** | Category: | Percentage |
| | Decimal places: | 2 |

13. Change the format of all break-even headings and amounts to display as bold-faced.
14. Activate the ability to use heading names in formulas under Tools > Options:

Calculation tab: Check the box: Accept labels in formulas

15. Replace the cell-based formulas with "word-based" equivalents for each formula used in Proposal A.
    Example: Contribution margin for proposal B would be:
    = ('Selling price' 'Proposal B') − ('Variable cost' 'Proposal B')
    Note: The tic marks used in the example help avoid naming errors caused by data having similar titles, i.e., "contribution margin" and "contribution margin ratio." The parentheses help clarify groupings.

    Help: Ask the Answer Wizard about "Name cells in a workbook."
    Select "Learn about labels and names in formulas" from the right-hand panel.
16. Save your work to a disk, and print a copy for your files.

Collaborative Learning Exercise

2-68 CVP for a Small Business

Form into groups of two to six students. Each group should select a very simple business, one with a single product or one with approximately the same contribution margin percentage for all products. Some possibilities are

   A child's lemonade stand
   A retail video rental store

An espresso cart
A retail store selling compact disks
An athletic shoe store
A cookie stand in a mall

However, you are encouraged to use your imagination rather than just select one of these examples. The following tasks might be split up among the group members:

1. Make a list of all fixed costs associated with running the business you selected. Estimate the amount of each fixed cost per month (or per day or per year, if one of them is more appropriate for your business).
2. Make a list of all variable costs associated with making or obtaining the product or service your company is selling. Estimate the cost per unit for each variable cost.
3. Given the fixed and variable costs you have identified, compute the break-even point for your business in either units or dollar sales.
4. Assess the prospects of your business making a profit.

Internet Exercise ● www.prenhall.com/horngren

2-69 Cost Behavior at Southwest Airlines

It is critical that managers understand how costs and revenues behave. One company that is affected by changes in costs and may not have the capability to rapidly change revenues because of competition is Southwest Airlines. Let's take a closer look at SWA and its costs and revenues. Log on to SWA's Web site at http://www.southwest.com. This Web site serves many purposes for the airline, such as providing flight schedules, making reservations and selling tickets, and displaying vacation and airfare specials.

1. Click on the reservations icon. How many cities does SWA serve? What is the closest city served by SWA to your current location? Click on that city as the departure city and then select any city you like for the arrival city. Now select a date about a month from now for leaving and one for returning. Click to continue to the next screen. What types of fares are available? Why do you think that there are different types of fares offered? Click on one of the fare-type captions to see if Southwest places any restrictions on this fare. If there are any restrictions, what purpose do they serve?
2. Return to the reservations screen and select a departure date that is less than a week away. What types of fare choices are available now? Are the rates the same as those that you found for a trip more than a month away? Why do you think that the choices remaining are for the most part the higher-priced ones? Is there any advantage to the fare(s) still available? Who is the most likely user of a ticket purchased at the last minute?
3. Now that you have looked at the revenue side, let's focus on the expense side. Individuals on the same flight may pay different prices for the ticket. Do you think that the cost of flying a passenger differs due to the price that they pay for the ticket? Why or why not?
4. Return to SWA's home page. Take a look at the costs that SWA actually incurs. Click on the "About SWA" icon and then click on "Investor Relations." Click on the "Annual Reports" icon and then select the most recent annual report. Open the annual report using Adobe Acrobat Reader. When you have located the annual report, notice the summary information that the company has provided in the "Consolidated Highlights" section. Give the most recent year's operating revenues and operating expenses. How much has each changed over the prior year? What does this imply for Southwest's profitability?
5. Now find "Management's Discussion and Analysis of Financial Condition and Results of Operations." Examine the table that shows "Operating Expenses per ASM." (ASM stands for available seat miles, a measure of capacity.) Which of these costs is primarily fixed with respect to ASM? Which is primarily variable? What other cost drivers might be important causes of costs for Southwest?

Measurement of Cost Behavior

CHAPTER 3

LEARNING OBJECTIVES
When you have finished studying this chapter, you should be able to:

1. Explain step- and mixed-cost behavior.

2. Explain management influences on cost behavior.

3. Measure and mathematically express cost functions and use them to predict costs.

4. Describe the importance of activity analysis for measuring cost functions.

5. Measure cost behavior using the engineering analysis, account analysis, high-low, visual-fit, and least-squares regression methods.

With annual revenues of more than $2 billion, America West is the ninth-largest U.S. commercial airline. The company focuses on the low-fare, full-service markets in the United States, Mexico, and Canada with more than 800 daily departures. Its primary operations (hubs) are in Phoenix and Las Vegas. America West rode the wave of a booming economy to increased revenues in the late 1990s. As a result, management decided to expand by introducing service to new destinations including Acapulco, Miami, and Detroit, and by adding more daily flights to existing markets, including Las Vegas, Mexico City, and Boston. To accomplish this, the company had to expand its labor force, add new aircraft, and spend more than $40 million on new technology.

Management at America West did not take lightly the decision to invest large amounts of money in aircraft and equipment. They knew that their decision would have a significant influence on costs, and thus profits, for many years. They also knew that most of the costs would be fixed but the revenues would fluctuate with the economy. When the economy is bad, revenues may not cover these costs.

How does an airline protect itself against losses when the economy turns down? According to Richard Goodmanson, former president and chief executive officer of America West, "management has a goal to have from 5% to 10% of the fleet of aircraft leased and thus subject to annual renewal. This enhances the company's ability to decrease capacity (and related costs) in the event of an industry downturn." This example illustrates that understanding how costs behave, as well as how managers' decisions can influence costs, helped the airline improve its cost control.

An America West flight departing from Phoenix's Sky Harbor International airport. America West serves the low-cost, full-service market at more than 144 destinations in the United States, Canada, and Mexico. Understanding its costs is an important factor in developing the company's competitive strategy, so managers carefully measure cost behavior.

measurement of cost behavior
Understanding and quantifying how activities of an organization affect its levels of costs.

Chapter 2 demonstrated the importance of understanding the cost structure of an organization and the relationships between an organization's activities and its costs, revenues, and profits. This chapter focuses on **measurement of cost behavior,** which means understanding and quantifying how activities of an organization affect its levels of costs. Recall that activities use resources, and these resources have costs. We measure the relationship between activity and cost using cost drivers. Understanding relationships between costs and their cost drivers allows managers in all types of organizations—profit-seeking, nonprofit, and government—to

- Evaluate strategic plans and operational improvement programs (Chapter 4)
- Make proper short-run marketing decisions (Chapter 5)
- Make short-run production decisions (Chapter 6)
- Plan or budget the effects of future activities (Chapters 7 and 8)
- Design effective management control systems (Chapters 9 and 10)
- Make proper long-run decisions (Chapter 11)
- Design accurate and useful product costing systems (Chapters 12 to 14)

As you can see, understanding cost behavior is fundamental to management accounting. There are numerous real-world cases in which managers have made very poor decisions to drop product lines, close manufacturing plants, or bid too high or too low on jobs because they had erroneous cost-behavior information. This chapter, therefore, deserves careful study.

Cost Drivers and Cost Behavior

linear-cost behavior
Activity that can be graphed with a straight line because costs are assumed to be either fixed or variable.

Accountants and managers often assume that cost behavior is linear over some relevant range of activity levels or cost-driver levels. We can graph **linear-cost behavior** with a straight line because we assume each cost to be either fixed or variable. Recall that the relevant range specifies the limits of cost-driver activity within which a specific relationship between a cost and its cost driver will be valid. Managers usually define the relevant range based on their previous experience with different levels of activity and cost.

Many activities can influence costs. However, in this chapter we focus on those costs for which the volume of a product produced or service provided is the primary driver. These costs are easy to identify with, or trace to, products or services. Examples of volume-driven costs include the costs of printing labor, paper, ink, and binding to produce all the copies of this textbook. The number of copies printed obviously affects the total printing labor, paper, ink, and binding costs. Equally important, we could relatively easily trace the use of these resources to the number of copies of the text printed. Schedules, payroll records, and other documents show how much of each resource was used to produce the copies of this text.

Activities not directly related to volume also affect costs. Such costs often have multiple cost drivers. For example, the wages and salaries of the editorial staff of the publisher of this textbook are not easy to identify with or trace to outputs. These editorial personnel produce many different textbooks, and it would be very difficult to determine exactly what portion of their wages and salaries went into a specific book, such as *Introduction to Management Accounting*.

Understanding and measuring costs that are difficult to trace to outputs can be especially challenging. In practice, many organizations use a linear relationship with a single cost driver to describe each cost, even though many costs have multiple causes. This approach is easier and less expensive than using nonlinear relationships or multiple cost drivers. If we use it carefully, this method often provides cost estimates that are accurate enough for most decisions. It may seem at odds with reality and economic theory, but the added benefit of understanding "true" cost behavior may be less than the cost of determining it.

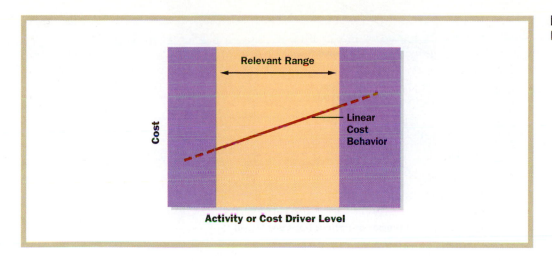

Exhibit 3-1
Linear-Cost Behavior

Accountants usually describe cost behavior in visual or graphical terms. Exhibit 3-1 shows linear-cost behavior, the relevant range, and an activity or cost driver. Note the similarity to the CVP charts of Chapter 2.

Step- and Mixed-Cost Behavior Patterns

Chapter 2 described two patterns of cost behavior: variable costs and fixed costs. Recall that a purely variable cost changes in proportion to changes in its cost driver's activity, while the cost-driver level does not affect a fixed cost. In addition to these pure versions of cost, two additional types of costs combine characteristics of both fixed- and variable-cost behavior. These are step costs and mixed costs.

OBJECTIVE **1**

Explain step- and mixed-cost behavior.

Step Costs Step costs change abruptly at intervals of activity because the resources and their costs are only available in indivisible chunks. If the individual chunks of cost are relatively large and apply to a specific, broad range of activity, we consider the cost a fixed cost over that range of activity. An example is in panel A of Exhibit 3-2, which shows the cost of leasing oil and gas drilling equipment. When oil and gas exploration activity reaches a certain level in a given region, the company must lease an entire additional rig.

step costs
Costs that change abruptly at intervals of activity because the resources and their costs come in indivisible chunks.

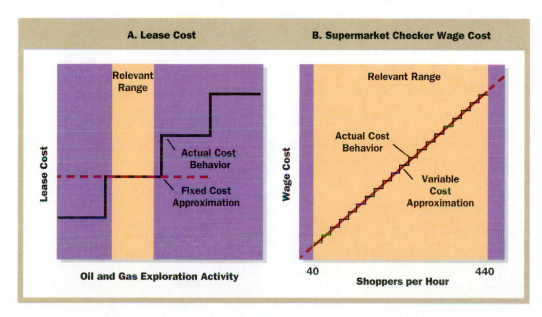

Exhibit 3-2
Step-Cost Behavior

Exhibit 3-3
Mixed-Cost Behavior

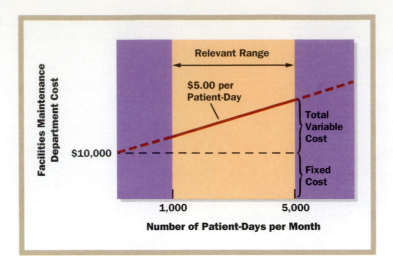

One level of oil and gas rig leasing, however, will support all volumes of exploration activity within a relevant range of drilling. Within each relevant range, this step cost behaves as a fixed cost. The total step cost at a level of activity is the amount of fixed cost appropriate for the range containing that activity level.

In contrast, accountants often describe step costs as variable when the individual chunks of costs are relatively small and apply to a narrow range of activity. Panel B of Exhibit 3-2 shows the wage cost of cashiers at a supermarket. Suppose one cashier can serve an average of 20 shoppers per hour and that within the relevant range of shopping activity, the number of shoppers can range from 40 per hour to 440 per hour. The corresponding number of cashiers would range between 2 and 22. Because the steps are relatively small, this step cost behaves much like a variable cost, and we could use it as such for planning with little loss of accuracy.

mixed costs

Costs that contain elements of both fixed- and variable-cost behavior.

Mixed Costs Mixed costs contain elements of both fixed- and variable-cost behavior. The fixed-cost element is unchanged over a range of cost-driver activity levels. The variable-cost element of the mixed cost is a purely variable cost that varies proportionately with cost-driver activity within the relevant range. You might think of the fixed cost as the cost of having available the capacity necessary to operate at any volume within the relevant range and the variable cost as the additional cost of using that capacity to produce outputs.

Many costs are mixed costs. For example, consider the monthly facilities maintenance department cost of the Parkview Medical Center, shown in Exhibit 3-3. Salaries of the maintenance personnel and costs of equipment are fixed at $10,000 per month. In addition, cleaning supplies and repair materials vary at a rate of $5 per patient-day[1] delivered by the hospital.

The chief administrator at Parkview Medical Center used knowledge of the facilities maintenance department cost behavior to

1. Plan costs: In May, the hospital expected to service 4,000 patient-days. May's predicted facilities maintenance department costs are $10,000 fixed plus the variable cost of $20,000 (4,000 patient-days times $5 per patient-day) for a total of $30,000.
2. Provide feedback to managers: In May, the actual facilities maintenance costs were $34,000 in a month when 4,000 patient-days were serviced as planned. The administrator wanted to know why the hospital overspent by $4,000 ($34,000 less the planned $30,000) so that managers could take corrective action.
3. Make decisions about the most efficient use of resources: For example, managers might weigh the long-run trade-offs of increased fixed costs of highly automated floor cleaning equipment against the variable costs of extra hours needed to clean floors manually.

---

[1] A patient-day is one patient spending one day in the hospital. One patient spending five days in the hospital is five patient-days of service.

We can see that managers not only passively measure how costs behave, they also take actions that influence the cost structure of an organization. Let's explore in more detail how managers influence cost behavior.

Management Influence on Cost Behavior

In addition to measuring and evaluating current cost behavior, managers can influence cost behavior through decisions about such factors as product or service attributes, capacity, technology, and policies to create incentives to control costs.

OBJECTIVE 2
Explain management influences on cost behavior.

Product and Service Decisions and the Value Chain

Throughout the value chain, managers influence cost behavior. This influence occurs through their choices of process and product design, quality levels, product features, distribution channels, and so on. Each of these decisions contributes to the organization's performance, and managers should consider the costs and benefits of each decision. For example, Hertz, the car rental company, would add a feature to its services only if the cost of the feature—for example, free mileage—could be more than recovered in profit from increased business.

Capacity Decisions

Strategic decisions about the scale and scope of an organization's activities generally result in fixed levels of capacity costs. **Capacity costs** are the fixed costs of being able to achieve a desired level of production or to provide a desired level of service while maintaining product or service attributes, such as quality. Most companies make a capacity decision infrequently. They consider strategic decisions as strategic because large amounts of resources are involved. An incorrect capacity decision can have serious consequences for the competitivness of a company. However, some companies make capacity decisions so frequently that they almost become routine operating decisions, such as opening a new Starbucks or McDonald's. In this case, the decision to open a new Starbucks is still strategic, but it becomes highly structured.

capacity costs
The fixed costs of being able to achieve a desired level of production or to provide a desired level of service while maintaining product or service attributes, such as quality.

Companies in industries with long-term variations in demand must be careful when making capacity decisions. Companies cannot recover fixed capacity costs when demand falls during an economic downturn. Consider the dilemma facing automakers such as Ford and General Motors. Demand for new cars in the auto industry varies substantially over time. It is not unusual for an assembly or production plant to operate at ranges of capacity from 60% to 100%. During boom times—such as in the mid-1990s—Ford was operating at full capacity. To meet demand, workers were on overtime, and Ford even outsourced some of its auto prodution. Ford had to choose either to build new plants and assembly lines or to continue to pay premiums for overtime and outsourced production. Building new plants would enable Ford to produce cars at lower cost, but it would not be able to reduce the fixed capacity costs if production volumes were to fall. Overtime and outsourcing production were expensive, but Ford could eliminate these variable costs during any business downturn when it did not need the extra cars. What did Ford do? Ford chose not to build expensive new plants. According to executives at Ford, it was worth it to keep costs under control: "Sooner or later there's going to be a downturn and we'll be running down days and short weeks even with the capacity we have." Ford's decision to limit its fixed costs even in the face of higher variable costs helped the company to endure the business downturn in the early 2000s. Ford was better able to reduce its costs as demand for autos fell.

Capacity decisions also entail an ethical commitment to a company's employees. Most companies try to keep a stable employment policy so that they do not need to fire or lay off employees unless there are huge shifts in demand. In the economic downturn of the early

2000s, news stories about companies "downsizing" (or, using a term that became more politically correct, "rightsizing") abounded. But other companies managed the decrease in demand without imposing large emotional costs on their employees. Companies that plan their capacity to allow flexibility in meeting demand generally survive economic hard times better, without the emotional upheaval caused by widespread firings and layoffs.

Committed Fixed Costs

committed fixed costs
Costs arising from the possession of facilities, equipment, and a basic organization.

Even if, like Ford, a company has chosen to minimize fixed capacity costs, every organization has some costs to which it is committed, perhaps for quite a few years. **Committed fixed costs** usually arise from the possession of facilities, equipment, and a basic organization. They include mortgage or lease payments, interest payments on long-term debt, property taxes, insurance, and salaries of key personnel. Only major changes in the philosophy, scale, or scope of operations could change these committed fixed costs in future periods. Recall the example of the facilities maintenance department for the Parkview Medical Center. The capacity of the facilities maintenance department was a management decision, and in this case the decision determined the magnitude of the equipment cost. Suppose Parkview Medical Center were permanently to increase its patient-days per month beyond the relevant range of 5,000 patient-days. Because Parkview would need more capacity, the committed equipment cost would rise to a new level per month.

Discretionary Fixed Costs

discretionary fixed costs
Costs determined by management as part of the periodic planning process in order to meet the organization's goals. They have no obvious relationship with levels of capacity or output activity.

Some costs are fixed at certain levels only because management decided to incur these levels of cost to meet the organization's goals. These **discretionary fixed costs** have no obvious relationship to levels of capacity or output activity. Companies determine them as part of the periodic planning process. Each planning period, management will determine how much to spend on discretionary items such as advertising and promotion costs, public relations, research and development costs, charitable donations, employee training programs, and purchased management consulting services. These costs then become fixed until the next planning period.

Managers can alter discretionary fixed costs easily—up or down—even within a budget period, if they decide that different levels of spending are desirable. Conceivably, managers could eliminate such discretionary costs almost entirely for a given year in dire times, whereas they could not reduce committed costs. Discretionary fixed costs may be essential to the long-run achievement of the organization's goals, but managers can vary spending levels broadly in the short run.

Consider Marietta Corporation, which is experiencing financial difficulties. Sales for its major products are down, and Marietta's management is considering cutting back on costs temporarily. Marietta's management must determine which of the following fixed costs it can reduce or eliminate and how much money each would save:

Fixed Costs	Planned Amounts
Advertising and promotion	$ 30,000
Depreciation	400,000
Employee training	100,000
Management salaries	800,000
Mortgage payment	250,000
Property taxes	600,000
Research and development	1,500,000
Total	$3,680,000

Can Marietta reduce or eliminate any of these fixed costs? The answer depends on Marietta's long-run outlook. Marietta could reduce costs but also greatly reduce its ability to compete in the future if it cuts carelessly. Rearranging these costs by categories of committed and discretionary costs yields the following analysis:

Fixed Costs	Planned Amounts
Committed	
Depreciation	$ 400,000
Mortgage payment	250,000
Property taxes	600,000
Total committed	$1,250,000
Discretionary (potential savings)	
Advertising and promotion	$ 30,000
Employee training	100,000
Management salaries	800,000
Research and development	1,500,000
Total discretionary	$2,430,000
Total committed and discretionary	$3,680,000

Eliminating all discretionary fixed costs would save Marietta $2,430,000 per year. However, Marietta would be unwise to cut all discretionary costs completely. This would severely impair the company's long-run prospects. Nevertheless, distinguishing committed and discretionary fixed costs would be the company's first step in identifying where costs could be reduced.

Technology Decisions

One of the most critical decisions that managers make is choosing the type of technology the organization will use to produce its products or deliver its services. Choice of technology (for example, labor-intensive versus robotic manufacturing, traditional banking services versus automated tellers, or e-commerce versus in-store or mail-order sales) positions the organization to meet its current goals and to respond to changes in the environment (for example, changes in customer needs or actions by competitors). The use of high technology methods rather than labor usually means a much greater fixed-cost component to the total cost. This type of cost behavior creates greater risks for companies with wide variations in demand.

Cost-Control Incentives

Finally, the incentives that management creates for employees can affect future costs. Managers use their knowledge of cost behavior to set cost expectations, and employees may receive compensation or other rewards that are tied to meeting these expectations. For example, the administrator of Parkview Medical Center could give the supervisor of the facilities maintenance department a favorable evaluation if the supervisor maintained quality of service and kept department costs below the expected amount for the actual level of patient-days. This feedback motivated the supervisor to watch department costs carefully and to find ways to reduce costs without reducing quality of service.

Cost Functions

As a manager, you will use cost functions often as a planning and control tool. A few of the reasons why cost functions are important are listed here.

1. Planning and controlling the activities of an organization require accurate and useful estimates of future fixed and variable costs.

2. Understanding relationships between costs and their cost drivers allows managers in all types of organizations—profit-seeking, nonprofit, and government—to make better operating, marketing, and production decisions, to plan and evaluate actions, and determine appropriate costs for short-run and long-run decisions.

cost measurement
Estimating or predicting
costs as a function of
appropriate cost drivers.

The first step in estimating or predicting costs is **cost measurement**—measuring cost behavior as a function of appropriate cost drivers. The second step is to use these cost measures to estimate future costs at expected levels of cost-driver activity. We begin by looking at the form of cost functions and the criteria for choosing the most appropriate cost drivers.

Form of Cost Functions

O B J E C T I V E 3

Measure and mathematically express cost functions and use them to predict costs.

cost function
An algebraic equation used
by managers to describe
the relationship between a
cost and its cost driver(s).

To describe the relationship between a cost and its cost driver(s), managers often use an algebraic equation called a **cost function.** When there is only one cost driver, the cost function is similar to the algebraic CVP relationships discussed in Chapter 2. Consider the mixed cost graphed in Exhibit 3-3 on page 90, the facilities maintenance department cost:

$$\begin{array}{l} \text{monthly facilities} \\ \text{maintenance} \\ \text{department costs} \end{array} = \begin{array}{l} \text{monthly fixed} \\ \text{maintenance cost} \end{array} + \begin{array}{l} \text{monthly variable} \\ \text{maintenance cost} \end{array}$$

$$= \begin{array}{l} \text{monthly fixed} \\ \text{maintenance cost} \end{array} + \left(\begin{array}{l} \text{variable cost per} \\ \text{patient-day} \end{array} \times \begin{array}{l} \text{number of patient-days} \\ \text{in the month} \end{array} \right)$$

Let

Y = monthly facilities maintenance department cost

F = monthly fixed maintenance cost

V = variable cost per patient-day

X = cost-driver activity in number of patient-days per month

We can rewrite the mixed-cost function as

$$Y = F + VX$$

or

$$Y = \$10,000 + \$5.00X \tag{1}$$

This mixed-cost function has the familiar form of a straight line—it is called a linear-cost function. When we graph a cost function, F is the intercept, the point on the vertical axis where the cost function begins. In Exhibit 3-3, the intercept is the $10,000 fixed cost per month. V, the variable cost per unit of activity, is the slope of the cost function. In Exhibit 3-3, the cost function slopes upward at the rate of $5 for each additional patient-day.

In our example, we use the cost driver patient-days. How did we choose this cost driver? Why not use number of patients or number of operations? In general, how do we develop cost functions?

Developing Cost Functions

Managers should apply two criteria to obtain accurate and useful cost functions: plausibility and reliability.

1. The cost function must be plausible, that is, believable. Personal observation of costs and activities, when it is possible, provides the best evidence of a plausible relationship between a resource cost and its cost driver. Some cost relationships, by nature, are not directly observable, so the cost analyst must be confident that the proposed relationship is sound. Many costs may move together with a number of cost drivers, but no cause-and-effect relationships may exist. A cause-and-effect relationship (that is, the cost driver causes the resource cost) is desirable for cost functions to be accurate and useful. For example, consider three possible cost drivers for the total cost of an America West round-trip flight from Phoenix to San Diego: miles flown, number of passengers, and passenger-miles (number of passengers times miles flown). Which of these possible cost drivers makes most sense? The answer is passenger-miles—the cost driver used by almost all airlines.

2. In addition to being plausible, a cost function's estimates of costs at actual levels of activity must reliably conform with actually observed costs. We assess reliability in terms of "goodness of fit"—how well the cost function explains past cost behavior. If the fit is good and conditions do not change, the cost function should be a reliable predictor of future costs.

Managers use these criteria *together* in choosing a cost function. Each is a check on the other. Knowledge of operations and the way accountants record costs is helpful in choosing a plausible and reliable cost function that links cause and effect. For example, companies often perform maintenance when output is low, because that is when they can take machines out of service. Lower output does not cause increased maintenance costs, however, nor does increased output cause lower maintenance costs. A more plausible explanation is that over a longer period increased output causes higher maintenance costs, but daily or weekly recording of maintenance costs and outputs may make it appear otherwise. Understanding the nature of maintenance costs should lead managers to a reliable, long-run cost function.

MAKING MANAGERIAL DECISIONS

A cost function is a mathematical expression of the components of a particular cost. However, an intuitive understanding of cost functions is just as important as being able to write the mathematical formula. Suppose you have been using a cost function to predict total order-processing activity costs. The cost function is total costs = $25,000 + $89 × (number of orders processed). This formula is based on data that are in the range of 500 to 700 orders processed. Now, you need to predict the total cost for 680 orders. You have a few questions to answer before you are comfortable using the cost function in this situation. Why is it important to know the relevant range? What does it mean when a cost function is linear? Why do managers want to know whether a cost is linear?

the relevant range—500 to 700, in this case—gives you confidence in the predicted total cost. A linear cost function means that there are two parts to the cost. One part is fixed—that is, it's independent of the cost driver. The other part varies in proportion to the cost driver—that is, if the cost driver increases by X%, this part of the cost also increases by X%. Knowing that a cost is linear allows a manager to separate the cost into fixed and variable components—a simplification that helps understand how decisions will affect costs. Incidentally, the predicted total cost for 680 orders is $25,000 + $89 × 680 = $85,520.

Answer

As long as the operating conditions that existed when the data were collected have not changed significantly, then knowing that the number of orders processed is within

Choice of Cost Drivers: Activity Analysis

OBJECTIVE 4

Describe the importance of activity analysis for measuring cost functions.

activity analysis

The process of identifying appropriate cost drivers and their effects on the costs of making a product or providing a service.

How do managers choose reliable and plausible cost functions? Well, you cannot have a good cost function without knowing the right cost drivers, so choosing a cost function starts with choosing cost drivers—the X in equation (1) on page 94. Managers use **activity analysis** to identify appropriate cost drivers and their effects on the costs of making a product or providing a service. The final product or service may have several cost drivers because production may involve many separate activities. The greatest benefit of activity analysis is that it directs management accountants to the appropriate cost drivers for each cost.

Consider Northwestern Computers, which makes two products for personal computers: a plug-in music board (Mozart-Plus) and a hard-disk drive (Powerdrive). In the past, most of the work on Northwestern's products was done by hand. Thus, most costs other than the cost of materials were related to (driven by) labor cost. On average, support costs were twice as much as labor costs.

Northwestern has just finished upgrading the production function. Now the company uses computer-controlled assembly equipment, which has increased the costs of support activities such as engineering and maintenance and has reduced labor cost. Labor cost is now only 5% of the total costs at Northwestern. Furthermore, activity analysis has shown that most of today's support costs are driven by the number of components added to products (a measure of product complexity), not by labor cost. Mozart-Plus has five component parts, and Powerdrive has nine.

Suppose Northwestern wants to predict how much support cost it will incur in producing one Mozart-Plus and how much for one Powerdrive. Using the old cost driver, labor cost, the prediction of support costs would be

	Mozart-Plus	Powerdrive
Labor cost	$ 8.50	$130.00
Support cost		
2 × direct labor cost	$17.00	$260.00

Using the more appropriate cost driver, the number of components added to products, the predicted support costs are

	Mozart-Plus	Powerdrive
Support cost at $20 per component		
$20 × 5 components	$100.00	
$20 × 9 components		$180.00
Difference in predicted support cost	$ 83.00	$ 80.00
	higher	lower

By using an appropriate cost driver, Northwestern can predict its support costs much more accurately. Managers will make better decisions with this more accurate information. For example, they can relate prices charged for products more closely to the costs of production. To see how an actual organization uses activity analysis, see the Business First box on page 97.

One major question remains in our discussion of the measurement of cost behavior— how are the estimates of fixed costs and variable cost per cost-driver unit determined? Equation (1) on page 94 denotes these amounts by F = monthly fixed maintenance cost and V = variable cost per patient-day. In practice, organizations use several methods of measuring cost functions. Let's look at each of these methods.

ACTIVITY ANALYSIS FOR A HOSPICE

Manufacturing companies were the first organizations to use activity analysis. However, its use has spread to many service industries and nonprofit organizations. A recent article described how a health-care organization, **Hospice and Palliative Care of Central Kentucky (HPCCK)**, undertook an activity analysis to better understand its costs.

HPCCK is a Medicare/Medicaid–certified program providing medical care to the terminally ill in ten counties in central Kentucky. In addition to seeing to the medical needs of its patients, HPCCK has social workers, home health aides, volunteers, and chaplains. It also provides an 18-month bereavement program for families of patients.

Many of HPCCK's costs were related directly to patients, and understanding these costs posed no problems. However, support costs were large, and HPCCK had little information about what caused these costs. Before undertaking an activity analysis, HPCCK simply assumed that the patient-day was the only cost driver for all support costs. All that HPCCK knew about support costs was that they were $35.53 per patient-day.

Because HPCCK felt the squeeze of increasing costs and constant reimbursements from HMOs and insurance companies, management at HPCCK wanted better cost information to make various decisions. To do this, the organization undertook an activity analysis to determine the appropriate cost drivers for support costs. This consisted of two basic tasks: (1) identify the activities being performed and (2) select a cost driver for each activity.

To identify the activities and the costs related to each activity, HPCCK formed a cross-functional team. Identifying the activities takes a thorough understanding of all the operations of the hospice, so a team of only finance or accounting professionals would not be knowledgeable enough for this task. The team included the director of operations, the bereavement coordinator, the billing coordinator, a nurse, and a representative of the community service program. Among them they knew all aspects of the hospice's operations.

The team identified 14 activities. The next step was to select a cost driver for each activity. Some of the activities and their related cost drivers are

Activity	Cost Driver
Referral	Number of (indexed) referrals
Admission	Number of admissions
Bereavement	Number of deaths
Accounting/finance	Number of (indexed) patient-days
Billing	Number of billings
Volunteer services	Number of volunteers

Using the cost information from the activity analysis, management was able to learn how much each different activity cost and could recognize that patients requiring use of expensive activities were more expensive to treat. Management could then try to reduce the costs of activities that were not worth the amount being spent for them, and they could better negotiate contracts so that HMOs and insurance companies would provide more support for patients that required the most expensive activities.

Source: Adapted from Sidney J. Baxendale and Victoria Dornbusch, "Activity-Based Costing for a Hospice," *Strategic Finance*, March 2000, pp. 65–70; Hospice and Palliative Care of Central Kentucky's Web site (http://www.hospices.org/Central_Kentucky.htm).

Methods of Measuring Cost Functions

After determining the most plausible drivers behind different costs, managers can choose from a broad selection of methods of approximating cost functions. These methods include (1) engineering analysis, (2) account analysis, (3) high-low analysis, (4) visual-fit analysis, and (5) least-squares regression analysis. These methods are not mutually exclusive; managers frequently use two or more together to avoid major errors in measuring cost behavior. The first two methods rely primarily on logical analysis, whereas the last three involve analysis of past costs.

OBJECTIVE 5

Measure cost behavior using the engineering analysis, account analysis, high-low, visual-fit, and least-squares regression methods.

Engineering Analysis

engineering analysis
The systematic review of materials, supplies, labor, support services, and facilities needed for products and services; measuring cost behavior according to what costs should be, not by what costs have been.

The first method, **engineering analysis,** measures cost behavior according to what costs should be, not by what costs have been. It entails a systematic review of materials, supplies, labor, support services, and facilities needed for products and services. Analysts can even use engineering analysis successfully for new products and services, as long as the organization has had experience with similar costs. Why? Because they can base measures on information from personnel who are directly involved with the product or service. In addition to actual experience, analysts learn about new costs from experiments with prototypes, accounting and industrial engineering literature, the experience of competitors, and the advice of management consultants. From this information, cost analysts determine what future costs should be. If the cost analysts are experienced and understand the activities of the organization, then their engineering cost predictions may be quite reliable and useful for decision making. The disadvantages of engineering cost analysis are that the efforts are costly and often not timely.

Weyerhauser Company, producer of wood products, used engineering analysis to determine the cost functions for its 14 corporate service departments. These cost functions measure the cost of corporate services used by three main business groups. For example, accounts payable costs for each division are a function of three cost drivers: the number of hours spent on each division, number of documents, and number of invoices. Nearly any service organization could use this approach to measuring cost behavior.

At Parkview Medical Center, introduced earlier, an assistant to the hospital administrator interviewed facilities maintenance personnel and observed their activities on several random days for a month. From these data, she confirmed that the most plausible cost driver for facilities maintenance cost is the number of patient-days. She also estimated from current department salaries and equipment charges that monthly fixed costs approximated $10,000 per month. Using interviews and observing supplies usage during the month, she estimated that variable costs are $5 per patient-day. She gave this information to the hospital administrator but cautioned that the cost measures may be wrong because

1. The month observed may be abnormal.
2. The facilities maintenance personnel may have altered their normal work habits because the assistant was observing them.
3. The facilities maintenance personnel may not have told the complete truth about their activities because of their concerns about the use of the information they revealed.

However, if we assume the observed and estimated information is correct, we could predict facilities maintenance cost in any month by first forecasting that month's expected patient-days and then entering that figure into the following algebraic, mixed-cost function:

$$Y = \$10{,}000 \text{ per month} + (\$5 \times \text{patient-days})$$

For example, if the administrator expects 4,000 patient-days next month, the prediction of facilities maintenance costs would be

$$Y = \$10{,}000 + (\$5 \times 4{,}000 \text{ patient-days}) = \underline{\underline{\$30{,}000}}$$

Account Analysis

account analysis
Selecting a plausible cost driver and classifying each account as a variable cost or as a fixed cost.

In contrast to engineering analysis, users of **account analysis** look to the accounting system for information about cost behavior. The simplest method of account analysis selects a plausible cost driver and classifies each account as a variable or fixed cost with respect to the cost driver. The cost analyst then looks at each cost account balance and estimates either the variable cost per unit of cost-driver activity or the periodic fixed cost.

To illustrate this approach to account analysis, let's return to the facilities maintenance department at Parkview Medical Center and analyze costs for the month of January.

Recall that the most plausible driver for these costs is the number of patient-days serviced per month. The table below shows costs recorded in a month with 3,700 patient-days:

Monthly Cost	January Amount
Supervisor's salary and benefits	$ 3,800 F ⟍ 9,673
Hourly workers' wages and benefits	14,674 V
Equipment depreciation and rentals	5,873 F ⟍ 27,750
Equipment repairs	5,604 V
Cleaning supplies	7,472 V
Total facilities maintenance cost	$37,423

Next, the analyst determines which costs may be fixed and which may be variable. Assume that the analyst has made the following judgments:

Monthly Cost	Amount	Fixed	Variable
Supervisor's salary and benefits	$ 3,800	$3,800	
Hourly workers' wages and benefits	14,674		$14,674
Equipment depreciation and rentals	5,873	5,873	
Equipment repairs	5,604		5,604
Cleaning supplies	7,472		7,472
Total facilities maintenance costs	$37,423	$9,673	$27,750

Measuring total facilities maintenance cost behavior, then, requires only simple arithmetic. Add all the fixed costs to get the total fixed cost per month. Divide the total variable costs by the units of cost-driver activity to get the variable cost per unit of cost driver.

$$\text{Fixed cost per month} = \$9,673$$
$$\text{Variable cost per patient-day} = \$27,750 \div 3,700 \text{ patient-days}$$
$$= \$7.50 \text{ per patient-day}$$

The algebraic, mixed-cost function, measured by account analysis, is

$$Y = \$9,673 \text{ per month} + (\$7.50 \times \text{patient-days})$$

Account-analysis methods are less expensive to conduct than engineering analyses, but they require recording of relevant cost accounts and cost drivers. In addition, like engineering analysis, account analysis is subjective because the analysts decide whether each cost is variable or fixed based on their own judgment.

Summary Problem For Your Review

PROBLEM

The Reliable Insurance Company processes a variety of insurance claims for losses, accidents, thefts, and so on. Account analysis using one cost driver has estimated the variable cost of processing the claims for each automobile accident at 0.5% (.005) of the dollar value of all claims related to a particular accident. This estimate seemed reasonable because high-cost claims often involve more analysis before settlement. To control processing costs better, however, Reliable conducted an activity analysis of claims processing. The analysis suggested that there are three main cost drivers for the costs of processing claims for automobile accidents. The drivers and cost behavior are

0.2% of Reliable Insurance policyholders' property claims
+ 0.6% of other parties' property claims
+ 0.8% of total personal injury claims

Data from two recent automobile accident claims follow:

	Automobile Claim No. 607788	Automobile Claim No. 607991
Policyholder claim	$ 4,500	$23,600
Other party claim	0	3,400
Personal injury claim	12,400	0
Total claim amount	$16,900	$27,000

1. Estimate the cost of processing each claim using data from (a) the single-cost-driver analysis and (b) the three-cost-driver analysis.
2. How would you recommend that Reliable Insurance estimate the cost of processing claims?

SOLUTION

1. Costs are summarized in the table here.

	Automobile Claim No. 607788		Automobile Claim No. 607991	
	Claim Amount	Processing Cost	Claim Amount	Processing Cost
Using single-cost-driver analysis				
Total claim amount	$16,900		$27,000	
Estimated processing cost at 0.5%		$ 84.50		$135.00
Using three-cost-driver analysis				
Policyholder claim	$ 4,500		$23,600	
Estimated processing cost at 0.2%		$ 9.00		$ 47.20
Other party claim	0		3,400	
Estimated processing cost at 0.6%		0		20.40
Personal injury claim	12,400		0	
Estimated processing cost at 0.8%		99.20		0
Total estimated processing cost		$108.20		$ 67.60

2. The three-cost-driver analysis estimates of processing costs are considerably different from those using a single cost driver. If the activity analyses are reliable, then automobile claims that include personal injury losses are more costly to process than property damage claims. If these estimates are relatively inexpensive to keep current and to use, then it seems reasonable to adopt the three-cost-driver approach. Reliable will have more accurate cost estimates and will be better able to plan its claims processing activities. Reliable processes many different types of claims, however. Extending activity analysis to identify multiple cost drivers for all types of claims would result in a complicated system for predicting costs—much more complex (and costly) than simply using the total dollar value of claims. Whether to undertake an activity analysis for all types of policies depends on cost-benefit considerations. Managers can address such considerations by first adopting activity analysis for one type of claim and assessing the usefulness and cost of the more accurate information.

High-Low, Visual-Fit, and Least-Squares Methods

When enough cost data are available, we can use historical data to measure the cost function mathematically. Three popular methods that use such data are the high-low, visual-fit, and least-squares methods. All three of these methods are more objective than the engineering-analysis and activity-analysis methods because each is based on hard evidence as well as on judgment and they use more than one period's cost and activity information. Account analysis and engineering analysis will probably remain primary methods of measuring cost behavior because the three mathematical methods require more past cost data. Products, services, technologies, and organizations are changing rapidly in response to increased global competition and technological advances. In some cases, by the time enough historical data are collected to support these analyses, the data are obsolete—the organization has changed, the production process has changed, or the product has changed. The cost analyst must be careful that the historical data are from a past environment that still closely resembles the future environment for which a manager wants to predict costs. Another concern is that historical data may hide past inefficiencies that the company could reduce if it could identify them.

Data for Illustration In discussing the high-low, visual-fit, and least-squares regression methods, we will continue to use the Parkview Medical Center's facilities maintenance department costs. The following table shows monthly data collected on facilities maintenance department costs and on the number of patient-days serviced over the past year:

Facilities Maintenance Department Data

Month	Facilities Maintenance Department Cost (Y)	Number of Patient-Days (X)
January	$37,000	3,700
February	23,000	1,600
March	37,000	4,100
April	47,000	4,900
May	33,000	3,300
June	39,000	4,400
July	32,000	3,500
August	33,000	4,000
September	17,000	1,200
October	18,000	1,300
November	22,000	1,800
December	20,000	1,600

High-Low Method When sufficient cost data are available, the cost analyst may use historical data to measure the cost function mathematically. The simplest of the three methods to measure a linear-cost function from past cost data is the **high-low method** shown in Exhibit 3-4.

The first step in the high-low method is to plot the historical data points on a graph. This visual display helps the analyst see whether there are obvious errors in the data. Even though many points are plotted, the focus of the high-low method is normally on the highest- and lowest-activity points. However, if one of these points is an outlier that seems in error or non-representative of normal operations, we will need to use the next-highest or next-lowest activity point. For example, you should not use a point from a period with abnormally low activity caused by a labor strike or fire. Why? Because that point is not representative of a normal relationship between the cost and the cost driver.

After selecting the representative high and low points, we can draw a line between them, extending the line to the vertical (Y) axis of the graph. Note that this extension in Exhibit 3-4

high-low method
A simple method for measuring a linear-cost function from past cost data, focusing on the highest-activity and lowest-activity points and fitting a line through these two points.

Exhibit 3-4

High-Low Method

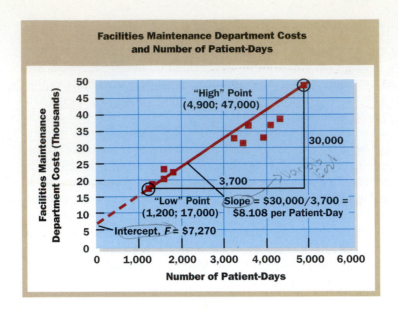

is a dashed line, as a reminder that costs may not be linear outside the range of activity for which we have data (the relevant range). Also, managers usually are concerned with how costs behave within the relevant range, not with how they behave either at zero activity or at impossibly high activity levels. Measurements of costs within the relevant range probably are not reliable measures or predictors of costs outside the relevant range.

The point at which the line intersects the Y-axis is the intercept, F, or estimate of fixed cost. The slope of the line measures the variable cost, V, per patient-day. The clearest way to measure the intercept and slope with the high-low method is to use algebra:

Month	Facilities Maintenance Department Cost (Y)	Number of Patient-Days (X)
High: April	$47,000	4,900
Low: September	17,000	1,200
Difference	$30,000	3,700

Variable cost per patient-day,

$$V = \frac{\text{change in costs}}{\text{change in activity}} = \frac{\$47,000 - \$17,000}{4,900 - 1,200 \text{ patient-days}}$$

$$V = \frac{\$30,000}{3,700} \qquad = \underline{\$8.1081} \text{ per patient-day}$$

Fixed cost per month, F = total mixed cost less total variable cost

$$\text{At X (high): } F = \$47,000 - (\$8.1081 \times 4,900 \text{ patient-days})$$
$$= \$47,000 - \$39,730$$
$$= \underline{\underline{\$7,270}} \text{ per month}$$

$$\text{At X (low): } F = \$17,000 - (\$8.1081 \times 1,200 \text{ patient-days})$$
$$= \$17,000 - \$9,730$$
$$= \underline{\underline{\$7,270}} \text{ per month}$$

Therefore, the facilities maintenance department cost function, measured by the high-low method, is

$$Y = \$7,270 \text{ per month} + (\$8.1081 \times \text{patient-days}$$

The high-low method is easy to apply and illustrates mathematically how a change in a cost driver can change total cost. The cost function that resulted in this case is plausible. Before the widespread availability of computers, managers often used the high-low method to measure a cost function quickly. Today, however, the high-low method is not used as often because it makes inefficient use of information, basing the cost function on only two periods' cost experience, regardless of how many relevant data points have been collected.

Summary Problem For Your Review

PROBLEM

The Reetz Company has its own photocopying department. Reetz's photocopying costs include costs of copy machines, operators, paper, toner, utilities, and so on. We have the following cost and activity data:

Month	Total Photocopying Cost	Number of Copies
1	$25,000	320,000
2	29,000	390,000
3	24,000	300,000
4	23,000	310,000
5	28,000	400,000

1. Use the high-low method to measure the cost behavior of the photocopy department in formula form.
2. What are the benefits and disadvantages of using the high-low method for measuring cost behavior?

SOLUTION

1. The lowest and highest activity levels are in months 3 (300,000 copies) and 5 (400,000 copies).

$$\text{Variable cost per copy} = \frac{\text{change in cost}}{\text{change in activity}} = \frac{\$28,000 - \$24,000}{400,000 - 300,000}$$

$$= \frac{\$4,000}{100,000} = \$0.04 \text{ per copy}$$

fixed cost per month = total cost less variable cost

at 400,000 copies: $28,000 − ($0.04 × 400,000) = $12,000 per month

at 300,000 copies: $24,000 − ($0.04 × 300,000) = $12,000 per month

Therefore, the photocopy cost function is

Y (total cost) = $12,000 per month + $0.04 × number of copies

2. The benefits of using the high-low method are
   - The method is easy to use.
   - Not many data points are needed.

The disadvantages of using the high-low method are

- The choice of the high and low points is subjective.
- The method does not use all available data.
- The method may not be reliable.

visual-fit method

A method in which the cost analyst visually fits a straight line through a plot of all the available data.

Visual-Fit Method Because it uses all the available data instead of just two points, the **visual-fit method** is more reliable than is the high-low method. In the visual-fit method, we draw a straight line through a plot of all the available data, using judgment to fit the line as close as possible to all the plotted points. If the cost function for the data is linear, it is possible to draw a straight line through the scattered points that comes reasonably close to most of them and thus captures the general tendency of the data. We can extend that line back until it intersects the vertical axis of the graph.

Exhibit 3-5 shows this method applied to the facilities maintenance department cost data for the past 12 months. By measuring where the line intersects the cost axis, we can estimate the monthly fixed cost—in this case, about $10,000 per month. To find the variable cost per patient-day, select any activity level (say, 1,000 patient-days) and find the total cost at that activity level ($17,000). Then divide the variable cost (which is total cost less fixed cost) by the units of activity.

$$\text{Variable cost per patient-day} = (\$17,000 - \$10,000) \div 1,000 \text{ patient-days}$$
$$= \$7 \text{ per patient-day}$$

The linear-cost function measured by the visual-fit method is

$$Y = \$10,000 \text{ per month} + (\$7 \times \text{patient-days})$$

Although the visual-fit method uses all the data, the placement of the line and the measurement of the fixed and variable costs are subjective. This subjectivity is the main reason that many companies with sufficient data prefer to use least-squares regression analysis rather than the visual-fit method.

Exhibit 3-5
Visual-Fit Method

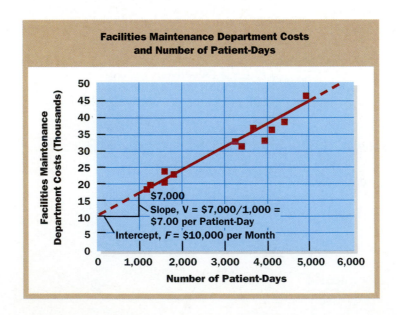

Least-Squares Regression Method Least-squares regression (or simply **regression analysis**) measures a cost function more objectively (with statistics rather than human eyesight) than does the visual-fit method. Least-squares regression analysis uses statistics to fit a cost function to all the historical data. A simple regression uses one cost driver to measure a cost function while a multiple regression uses two or more cost drivers. We will discuss only simple regression analysis in this section of the chapter. Appendix 3 presents some statistical properties of regression and shows how to use computer regression software.

> *least-squares regression (regression analysis)*
> *Measuring a cost function objectively by using statistics to fit a cost function to all the data.*

Regression analysis measures cost behavior more reliably than other cost measurement methods. In addition, regression analysis yields important statistical information about the reliability of cost estimates, so analysts can assess confidence in the cost measures and select the best cost driver. One such measure of reliability, or goodness of fit, is the **coefficient of determination, R^2** (or R-squared), which measures how much of the fluctuation of a cost is explained by changes in the cost driver. Appendix 3 explains R^2 and discusses how to use it to select the best cost driver.

> *coefficient of determination (R^2)*
> *A measurement of how much of the fluctuation of a cost is explained by changes in the cost driver.*

Exhibit 3-6 shows the linear, mixed-cost function for facilities maintenance costs as measured by simple regression analysis. The fixed-cost measure is $9,329 per month. The variable-cost measure is $6.951 per patient-day. The linear-cost function is

facilities maintenance department cost = $9,329 per month + $6.951 per patient-day

or

$$Y = \$9{,}329 + \$6.951 \times \text{patient-days}$$

Compare the cost measures produced by each of the five approaches:

Method	Fixed Cost per Month	Variable Cost per Patient-Day
Engineering analysis	$10,000	$5.000
Account analysis	9,673	7.500
High-low	7,270	8.108
Visual-fit	10,000	7.000
Regression	9,329	6.951

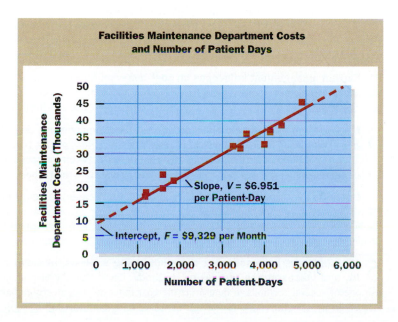

Facilities Maintenance Department Costs and Number of Patient Days

Slope, V = $6.951 per Patient-Day

Intercept, F = $9,329 per Month

Exhibit 3-6
Least-Squares
Regression Method

To see the differences in results between methods, we will use account-analysis and regression-analysis measures to predict total facilities maintenance department costs at 1,000 and 5,000 patient-days, the approximate limits of the relevant range:

	Account Analysis	Regression Analysis	Difference
1,000 patient-days:			
Fixed cost	$ 9,673	$ 9,329	$ 344
Variable costs			
$7.500 × 1,000	7,500		
$6.951 × 1,000		6,951	549
Predicted total cost	$17,173	$16,280	$ 893
5,000 patient-days:			
Fixed cost	$ 9,673	$ 9,329	$ 344
Variable costs			
$7.500 × 5,000	37,500		
$6.951 × 5,000		34,755	2,745
Predicted total cost	$47,173	$44,084	$3,089

At lower levels of patient-day activity the difference between cost predictions is small. At higher levels of patient-day activity, however, the account-analysis cost function predicts much higher costs. The difference between the predicted total costs is due primarily to the higher variable cost per patient-day (approximately $0.55 more) measured by account analysis. Because of their grounding in statistical analysis, the regression-cost measures are probably more reliable than are the other methods. Managers would thus have more confidence in cost predictions from the regression-cost function.

Highlights to Remember

1 **Explain step- and mixed-cost behavior.** Cost behavior refers to how costs change as levels of an organization's activities change. Costs can behave as fixed, variable, step, or mixed costs. Step and mixed costs both combine aspects of variable- and fixed-cost behavior. Step costs form graphs that look like steps. Costs will remain fixed within a given range of activity or cost-driver level, but then will rise or fall abruptly when the cost-driver level is outside this range. Mixed costs involve a fixed element and a variable element of cost behavior. Unlike step costs, mixed costs have a single fixed cost at all levels of activity, and in addition have a variable cost element that increases proportionately with activity.

2 **Explain management influences on cost behavior.** Managers can affect the costs and cost behavior patterns of their companies through the decisions they make. Decisions on product and service features, capacity, technology, and cost-control incentives, for example, can all affect cost behavior.

3 **Measure and mathematically express cost functions and use them to predict costs.** The first step in estimating or predicting costs is measuring cost behavior. This is done by finding a cost function. This is an algebraic equation that describes the relationship between a cost and its cost driver(s). To be useful for decision-making purposes, cost functions should be plausible and reliable.

4 **Describe the importance of activity analysis for measuring cost functions.** Activity analysis is the process of identifying the best cost drivers to use for cost estimation and prediction and determining how they affect the costs of making a product or service. This is an essential step in understanding and predicting costs.

5 **Measure cost behavior using the engineering analysis, account analysis, high-low, visual-fit, and least-squares regression methods.** Once analysts have identified cost drivers, they can use one of several methods to determine the cost function. Engineering analysis focuses on what costs should be by systematically reviewing the materials, supplies, labor, support services, and facilities needed for a given level of production. Account analysis involves examining all accounts in terms of an appropriate cost driver and classifying each account as either fixed or variable with respect to the driver. The cost function consists of the variable cost per cost-driver unit multiplied by the amount of the cost driver plus the total fixed cost. The high-low, visual-fit, and least-squares methods all use historical costs to determine cost functions. Of these three methods, high-low is the easiest, although least-squares is the most reliable.

Appendix 3: Use and Interpretation of Least-Squares Regression

We can apply regression analysis of historical cost data with no more than a simple calculator. It would be unusual, however, to find cost analysts doing regression analysis by hand—computers are much faster and less prone to error. Therefore, we focus on using a computer to perform regression analysis and on interpretation of the results.

This appendix is not a substitute for a good statistics class. More properly, think of it as a motivator for studying statistics so that you can provide and interpret top-quality cost estimates.

Assume that there are two potential cost drivers for the costs of the facilities maintenance department in Parkview Medical Center: (1) number of patient-days and (2) total value of hospital room charges. Regression analysis helps to determine which activity is the better cost driver. Exhibit 3-7 shows the past 12 months' cost and cost-driver data for the facilities maintenance department.

Regression Analysis Procedures

Most spreadsheet software available for PCs offers basic regression analysis in the Data Analysis or Tools commands. We will use these spreadsheet commands to illustrate regression analysis because many readers will be familiar already with spreadsheet software.

Entering Data
First create a spreadsheet with the historical cost data in rows and columns. Each row should be data from one period. Each column should be a cost category or a cost driver. For ease of analysis, all the potential cost drivers should be in adjacent columns. Each row and column should be complete (no missing data) and without errors.

Plotting Data
There are two main reasons why the first step in regression analysis should be to plot the cost against each of the potential cost drivers: (1) Plots may show obvious nonlinear trends in the data; if so, linear regression analysis may not be appropriate for the entire range of the data. (2) Plots help

Month	Facilities Maintenance Cost (Y)	Number of Patient-Days (X_1)	Value of Room Charges (X_2)
January	$37,000	3,700	$2,183,000
February	23,000	1,600	2,735,000
March	37,000	4,100	2,966,000
April	47,000	4,900	2,846,000
May	33,000	3,300	2,967,000
June	39,000	4,400	2,980,000
July	32,000	3,500	3,023,000
August	33,000	4,000	2,352,000
September	17,000	1,200	1,825,000
October	18,000	1,300	1,515,000
November	22,000	1,800	1,547,000
December	20,000	1,600	2,117,000

Exhibit 3-7
Facilities Maintenance Department Data

identify outliers—costs that are in error or are otherwise obviously inappropriate. There is little agreement about what to do with any outliers that are not the result of data-entry errors or nonrepresentative cost and activity levels (e.g., periods of labor strikes or natural catastrophes). After all, if the data are not in error and are representative, the process that is being studied generated them. Even so, some analysts recommend removing outliers from the data set. Leaving these outliers in the data makes regression analysis statistically less appealing, because data far removed from the rest of the data set will not fit the line well. The most conservative action is to leave all data in the data set unless you discover uncorrectable errors or unless you know the data to be not representative of the process.

Plotting with spreadsheets uses Graph commands on the columns of cost and cost-driver data. These Graph commands typically offer many optional graph types (such as bar charts and pie charts), but the most useful plot for regression analysis usually is called the *XY* graph. This graph is the type shown earlier in this chapter—the *X*-axis is the cost driver, and the *Y*-axis is the cost. The *XY* graph should be displayed without lines drawn between the data points (called data symbols)—an optional command. (Consult your spreadsheet manual for details, because each spreadsheet program is different.)

Regression Output

The format of the regression output is different for each software package. However, every package will identify the cost to be explained ("dependent variable") and the cost driver(s) ("independent variable[s]").

Producing regression output with spreadsheets is simple: Just select the Regression command, specify (or highlight) the *X*-dimension[s] (the cost driver[s]), and specify the *Y*-dimension or "series" (the cost). Next specify a blank area on the spreadsheet where the output will be displayed, and select Go. Below is a regression analysis of facilities maintenance department costs using one of the two possible cost drivers, number of patient-days, X_1.

Facilities Maintenance Department Cost Explained by Number of Patient-Days	
Regression Output	
Constant	9,329
R^2	0.955
X coefficient(s)	6.951

Interpretation of Regression Output

The fixed-cost measure, labeled "constant" or "intercept" by most programs, is $9,329 per month. The variable cost measure, labeled "*X* coefficient(s)" (or something similar in other spreadsheets), is $6.951 per patient-day. The linear cost function is

$$Y = \$9{,}329 \text{ per month} + (\$6.951 \times \text{patient-days})$$

Typically, the computer output gives a number of statistical measures that indicate how well each cost driver explains the cost and how reliable the cost predictions are likely to be. A full explanation of the output is beyond the scope of this text. One of the most important statistics, the coefficient of determination, or R^2, is very important to assessing the goodness of fit of the cost function to the actual cost data.

What the visual-fit method tries to do with eyesight, regression analysis accomplishes more reliably. In general, the better a cost driver is at explaining a cost, the closer the data points will lie to the line, and the higher will be the R^2, which varies between 0 and 1. An R^2 of 0 would mean that the cost driver does not explain variability in the cost data, whereas an R^2 of 1 would mean that the cost driver explains the variability perfectly. The R^2 of the relationship measured with number of patient-days as the cost driver is 0.955, which is quite high. This value indicates that number of patient-days explains facilities maintenance department cost extremely well. In fact, the number of patient-days explains 95.5% of the past fluctuation in facilities maintenance department cost.

In contrast, performing a regression analysis on the relationship between facilities maintenance department cost and value of hospital room charges produces the following results:

Facilities Maintenance Department Cost Explained by Value of Hospital Room Charges	
Regression Output	
Constant	$ 924
R^2	0.511
X coefficient(s)	0.012

The R^2 value, 0.511, indicates that the cost function using value of hospital room charges does not fit facilities maintenance department cost as well as the cost function using number of patient-days.

To use the information generated by regression analysis fully, an analyst must understand the meaning of the statistics and must be able to determine whether the statistical assumptions of regression are satisfied by the cost data. Indeed, one of the major reasons why cost analysts study statistics is to understand the assumptions of regression analysis better. With this understanding, analysts can provide their organizations with top-quality estimates of cost behavior.

Summary Problem For Your Review

PROBLEM

Comtell, Inc., makes computer peripherals (disk drives, tape drives, and printers). Until recently, managers predicted production scheduling and control (PSC) costs to vary in proportion to labor costs according to the following cost function:

$$\text{PSC costs} = 200\% \text{ of labor}$$

or

$$Y = 2 \times \text{labor cost}$$

Because PSC costs have been growing at the same time that labor cost has been shrinking, Comtell is concerned that its cost estimates are neither plausible nor reliable. Comtell's controller has just completed activity analysis to determine the most appropriate drivers of PSC costs. She obtained two cost functions using different cost drivers:

$$Y = 2 \times \text{labor cost}$$
$$R^2 = 0.233$$

and

$$Y = \$10,000/\text{month} + (11 \times \text{number of components used})$$
$$R^2 = 0.782$$

1. What would be good tests of which cost function better predicts PSC costs?
2. During a subsequent month, Comtell's labor costs were $12,000, and it used 2,000 product components. Actual PSC costs were $31,460. Using each of the preceding cost functions, prepare reports that show predicted and actual PSC costs and the difference or variance between the two.
3. What is the meaning and importance of each cost variance?

SOLUTION

1. A statistical test of which function better explains past PSC costs compares the R^2 of each function. The second function, based on the number of components used, has a considerably higher R^2, so it better explains the past PSC costs. If the environment is essentially unchanged in the future, the second function probably will predict future PSC costs better than the first.

   A useful predictive test would be to compare the cost predictions of each cost function with actual costs for several months that were not used to measure the cost functions. The function that more closely predicted actual costs is probably the more reliable function.

2. Note that more actual cost data would be desirable for a better test, but the procedure would be the same. PSC cost predicted on a labor-cost basis follows:

Predicted Cost	Actual Cost	Variance
$2 \times \$12,000 = \$24,000$	$31,460	$7,460 underestimate

PSC cost predicted on a component basis follows:

Predicted Cost	Actual Cost	Variance
$\$10,000 + (\$11 \times 2,000) = \$32,000$	$31,460	$540 overestimate

3. The cost function that relies on labor cost underestimated PSC cost by $7,460. The cost function that uses the number of components closely predicted actual PSC costs (off by $540). Planning and control decisions would have been based on more accurate information using this prediction than using the labor cost-based prediction. An issue is whether the benefits of collecting data on the number of components used exceeded the added cost of so doing.

Accounting Vocabulary

account analysis, p. 98
activity analysis, p. 96
capacity costs, p. 91
coefficient of determination (R^2), p. 105
committed fixed costs, p. 92
cost function, p. 94

cost measurement, p. 94
discretionary fixed costs, p. 92
engineering analysis, p. 98
high-low method, p. 101
least-squares regression, p. 105
linear-cost behavior, p. 88

measurement of cost behavior, p. 88
mixed costs, p. 90
regression analysis, p. 105
step costs, p. 89
visual-fit method, p. 104

Fundamental Assignment Material

3-A1 Types of Cost Behavior

Identify the following planned costs as (a) purely variable costs, (b) discretionary fixed costs, (c) committed fixed costs, (d) mixed costs, or (e) step costs. For purely variable costs and mixed costs, indicate the most likely cost driver.

1. Total repairs and maintenance of a university classroom building. *Committed*
2. Sales commissions based on revenue dollars. Payments to be made to advertising salespersons employed by radio station WCCO, Minneapolis. *Mixed*
3. Jet fuel costs of **Southwest Airlines**.
4. Total costs of renting trucks by the city of Nashville. Charge is a lump sum of $300 per month plus $.20 per mile.
5. Straight-line depreciation on desks in the office of an attorney. *Fixed*
6. Advertising costs, a lump sum, planned by ABC, Inc. *D*
7. Rental payment by the Internal Revenue Service on a five-year lease for office space in a private office building. *C*

8. Advertising allowance granted to wholesalers by **7-Up Bottling** on a per-case basis. *D*
9. Compensation of lawyers employed internally by **Microsoft.** *C*
10. Crew supervisor in a **Lands' End, Inc.,** mail-order house. A new supervisor is added for every 12 workers employed. *C*
11. Public relations employee compensation to be paid by **Intel.** *C*

3-A2 Activity Analysis

Evergreen Signs makes customized wooden signs for businesses and residences. These signs are made of wood, which the owner glues and carves by hand or with power tools. After carving the signs, she paints them or applies a natural finish. She has a good sense of her labor and materials cost behavior, but she is concerned that she does not have good measures of other support costs. Currently, she predicts support costs to be 60% of the cost of materials. Close investigation of the business reveals that $40 times the number of power tool operations is a more plausible and reliable support cost relationship.

Consider estimated support costs of the following two signs that Evergreen Signs is making:

	Sign A	Sign B
Materials cost	$300	$150
Number of power tool operations	3	6
Support cost	?	?

1. Prepare a report showing the support costs of both signs using each cost driver and showing the differences between the two.
2. What advice would you give Evergreen Signs about predicting support costs?

3-A3 Division of Mixed Costs into Variable and Fixed Components

Martina Fernandez, president of Evert Tool Co., has asked for information about the cost behavior of manufacturing support costs. Specifically, she wants to know how much support cost is fixed and how much is variable. The following data are the only records available:

Month	Machine Hours	Support Costs
May	850	$ 9,000
June	1,400	12,500
July	1,000	7,900
August	1,250	11,000
September	1,750	13,500

1. Find monthly fixed support cost and the variable support cost per machine hour by the high-low method.
2. A least-squares regression analysis gave the following output:

$$\text{Regression equation: } Y = \$2,728 + \$6.77X$$

What recommendations would you give the president based on these analyses?

3-B1 Identifying Cost Behavior Patterns

At a seminar, a cost accountant spoke on identification of different kinds of cost behavior. Tammy Li, a hospital administrator who heard the lecture, identified several hospital costs of concern to her. After her classification, Li presented you with the following list of costs and asked you to (1) classify their behavior as one of the following: variable, step, mixed, discretionary fixed, committed fixed, and (2) to identify a likely cost driver for each variable or mixed cost.

1. Training costs of an administrative resident
2. Straight-line depreciation of operating room equipment
3. Costs of services of King Hospital Consulting
4. Nursing supervisors' salaries (a supervisor is needed for each 45 nursing personnel)
5. Operating costs of X-ray equipment ($95,000 a year plus $3 per film)
6. Health insurance for all full-time employees
7. Costs incurred by Dr. Rath in cancer research
8. Repairs made on hospital furniture

3-B2 Activity Analysis

Boise Technology, an Idaho manufacturer of printed circuit boards, has always estimated the production cost of its circuit boards with a 100% "markup" over its material costs. An activity analysis suggests that support costs are driven primarily by the number of manual operations performed on each board, estimated at $4 per manual operation. Compute the estimated support costs of two typical circuit boards below using the traditional markup and the activity analysis results:

	Board Z15	Board Q52
Material cost	$30.00	$55.00
Manual operations	16	7

Why are the cost estimates different?

3-B3 Division of Mixed Costs into Variable and Fixed Components

The president and the controller of Monterrey Transformer Company (Mexico) have agreed that refinement of the company's cost measurements will aid planning and control decisions. They have asked you to measure the function for mixed-cost behavior of repairs and maintenance from the following sparse data. Currency is the Mexican peso (P).

Monthly Activity in Machine Hours	Monthly Repair and Maintenance Cost
8,000	P190,000,000
12,000	P260,000,000

Additional Assignment Material

Questions

3-1 What is a cost driver? Give three examples of costs and their possible cost drivers.

3-2 Explain linear-cost behavior.

3-3 "Step costs can be fixed or variable, depending on your perspective." Explain.

3-4 Explain how mixed costs are related to both fixed and variable costs.

3-5 How do management's product and service choices affect cost behavior?

3-6 Why are fixed costs also called capacity costs?

3-7 How do committed fixed costs differ from discretionary fixed costs?

3-8 Why are committed fixed costs the most difficult of the fixed costs to change?

3-9 What are the primary determinants of the level of committed costs? Discretionary costs?

3-10 "Planning is far more important than day-to-day control of discretionary costs." Do you agree? Explain.

3-11 How can a company's choice of technology affect its costs?

3-12 Explain the use of incentives to control cost.

3-13 Why is it important for managers and accountants to measure cost functions?

3-14 Explain *plausibility* and *reliability* of cost functions. Which is preferred? Explain.

3-15 What is activity analysis?

3-16 What is engineering analysis? Account analysis?

3-17 Describe the methods for measuring cost functions using past cost data.

3-18 How could account analysis be combined with engineering analysis?

3-19 Explain the strengths and weaknesses of the high-low and visual-fit methods.

3-20 In the high-low method, does the *high* and *low* refer to cost-driver levels or to total cost levels? Explain.

3-21 Why is regression analysis usually preferred to the high-low method?

3-22 "You never know how good your fixed- and variable-cost measures are if you use account analysis or if you visually fit a line on a data plot. That's why I like least-squares regression analysis." Explain.

3-23 (Appendix 3) Why should an analyst always plot cost data in addition to applying least-squares regression analysis?

3-24 (Appendix 3) What can we learn from R^2, the coefficient of determination?

3-25 At a conference, a consultant stated, "Before you can control, you must measure." An executive complained, "Why bother to measure when work rules and guaranteed employment provisions in labor contracts prevent discharging workers, using part-time employees, and using overtime?" Evaluate these comments. Summarize your personal attitudes toward the usefulness of engineering analysis.

Critical Thinking Exercises

3-26 Mixed Costs and the Sales Force

Wysocki Company pays its sales force a fixed salary plus a 5% commission on all sales. Explain why sales force costs would be considered a mixed cost.

3-27 Committed and Discretionary Fixed Costs in Manufacturing

Among the fixed costs of Howarth Company are depreciation and research and development (R&D). Using these two costs as examples, explain the difference between committed and discretionary fixed costs.

3-28 Cost Functions and Decision Making

Why is it important that decision makers in a corporation know the cost function for producing the companies' products?

3-29 Statistical Analysis and Cost Functions

What advantages does using regression analysis have over the visual-fit method for determining cost functions?

Exercises

3-30 Step Costs

Which of the following are step costs? Why?

    a. Rent on a warehouse that is large enough for all anticipated orders.
    b. Teachers for a private elementary school. One teacher is needed for each 15 students.
    c. Sheet steel for a producer of machine parts. Steel is purchased in carload shipments, where each carload contains enough steel for 1,000 parts.

3-31 Mixed Costs

The following cost function is a mixed cost. Explain why it is a mixed cost and not a fixed, variable, or step cost.

$$\text{total cost} = \$5,000 + \$45 \times \text{units produced}$$

3-32 Various Cost-Behavior Patterns

In practice, there is often a tendency to simplify approximations of cost-behavior patterns, even though the "true" underlying behavior is not simple. Choose from graphs A through H on the top of page 114, the one that matches the numbered items. Indicate by letter which graph best fits each of the situations described. Next to each number-letter pair, identify a likely cost driver for that cost.

    The vertical axes of the graphs represent total dollars of costs incurred, and the horizontal axes represent levels of cost driver activity during a particular time period. The graphs may be used more than once.

1. Cost of machining labor that tends to decrease as workers gain experience   G
2. Price of an increasingly scarce raw material as the quantity used increases   B
3. Guaranteed annual wage plan, whereby workers get paid for 40 hours of work per week even at   C zero or low levels of production that require working only a few hours weekly
4. Water bill, which entails a flat fee for the first 10,000 gallons used and then an increasing unit cost for every additional 10,000 gallons used   H
5. Availability of quantity discounts, where the cost per unit falls as each price break is reached   A
6. Depreciation of office equipment   E
7. Cost of sheet steel for a manufacturer of farm implements   D
8. Salaries of supervisors, where one supervisor is added for every 12 phone solicitors   F
9. Natural gas bill consisting of a fixed component, plus a constant variable cost per thousand cubic feet after a specified number of cubic feet are used   C

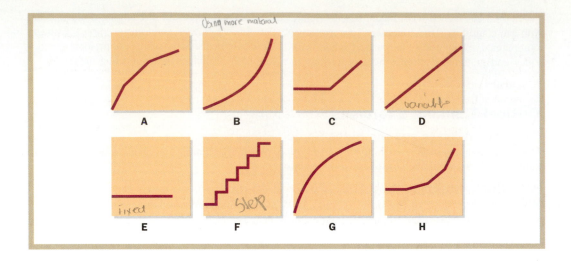

3-33 Plotting Data

The following graph was constructed and data plotted to apply the visual-fit method. Then, the predicted total order-department costs if 90 orders were processed was computed. Comment on the accuracy of the analysis. Do your own analysis and explain any differences. Assume the data in parentheses are accurate in thousands of dollars and number of orders.

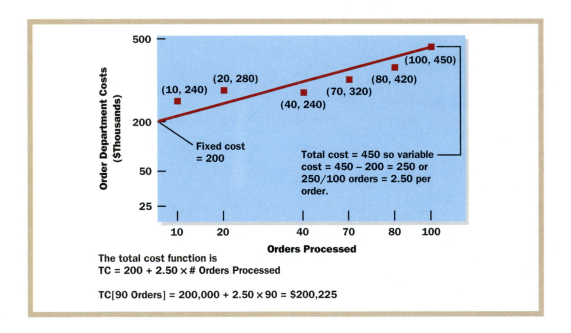

3-34 Cost Function for Expedia

Expedia, Inc., provides travel services on the Internet. In the first quarter of 2001, Expedia reported an operating loss of $19 million on sales revenue of $57 million. In the first quarter of 2002, sales revenue had more than doubled to $116 million, and Expedia had operating income of $18 million. Assume that fixed costs were the same in 2002 as in 2001.

1. Compute the operating expenses for Expedia in the first quarter of 2001. In the first quarter of 2002.
2. Determine the cost function for Expedia, that is, the total fixed cost and the variable cost as a percentage of sales revenue. Use the same form as equation (1) on page 94.
3. Explain how Expedia's operating income could increase by $37 million with an increase in sales of $59 million, while it had an operating loss of $19 million on its $57 million of sales in the first quarter of 2001.

3-35 Predicting Costs

Given the following four cost behaviors and expected levels of cost-driver activity, predict total costs:

1. Fuel costs of driving vehicles, $0.20 per mile, driven 15,000 miles per month
2. Equipment rental cost, $6,000 per piece of equipment per month for seven pieces for three months
3. Ambulance and EMT personnel cost for a soccer tournament, $1,100 for each 250 tournament participants; the tournament is expecting 2,400 participants
4. Purchasing department cost, $7,500 per month plus $4 per material order processed at 4,000 orders in one month

3-36 Identifying Discretionary and Committed Fixed Costs

Identify and compute total discretionary fixed and total committed fixed costs from the following list prepared by the accounting supervisor for Huang Building Supply, Inc.:

Advertising	$20,000 D
Depreciation	47,000 C
Company health insurance	15,000 C
Management salaries	85,000 C
Payment on long-term debt	50,000 C
Property tax	32,000 C
Grounds maintenance	9,000 C
Office remodeling	21,000 C
Research and development	36,000 D

3-37 Cost Effects of Technology

Recreational Sports, Inc., an outdoor sports retailer, is planning to add a Web site for online sales. The estimated costs of two alternative approaches are as follows:

	Alternative 1	Alternative 2
Annual fixed cost	$200,000	$400,000
Variable cost per order	$8	$4
Expected number of orders	70,000	70,000

At the expected level of orders, which online approach has the lower cost? What is the indifference level of orders, or the "break-even" level of orders? What is the meaning of this level of orders?

3-38 Mixed Cost, Choosing Cost Drivers, and High-Low and Visual-Fit Methods

Cedar Rapids Implements Company produces farm implements. Cedar Rapids is in the process of measuring its manufacturing costs and is particularly interested in the costs of the manufacturing maintenance activity, since maintenance is a significant mixed cost. Activity analysis indicates that maintenance activity consists primarily of maintenance labor setting up machines using certain supplies. A setup consists of preparing the necessary machines for a particular production run of a product. During setup, machines must still be running, which consumes energy. Thus, the costs associated with maintenance include labor, supplies, and energy. Unfortunately, Cedar Rapid's cost accounting system does not trace these costs to maintenance activity separately. Cedar Rapids employs two full-time maintenance mechanics to perform maintenance. The annual salary of a maintenance mechanic is $25,000 and is considered a fixed cost. Two plausible cost drivers have been suggested: "units produced" and "number of setups."

Data had been collected for the past 12 months and a plot made for the cost driver—units of production. The maintenance cost figures collected include estimates for labor, supplies, and energy. Cory Fielder, controller at Cedar Rapids, noted that some types of activities are performed each time a batch of goods is processed rather than each time a unit is produced. Based on this concept, he has gathered data on the number of setups performed over the past 12 months. The plots of monthly maintenance costs versus the two potential cost drivers follow on page 116.

1. Find monthly fixed maintenance cost and the variable maintenance cost per driver unit using the visual-fit method based on each potential cost driver. Explain how you treated the April data.

2. Find monthly fixed maintenance cost and the variable maintenance cost per driver unit using the high-low method based on each potential cost driver.
3. Which cost driver best meets the criteria for choosing cost functions? Explain.

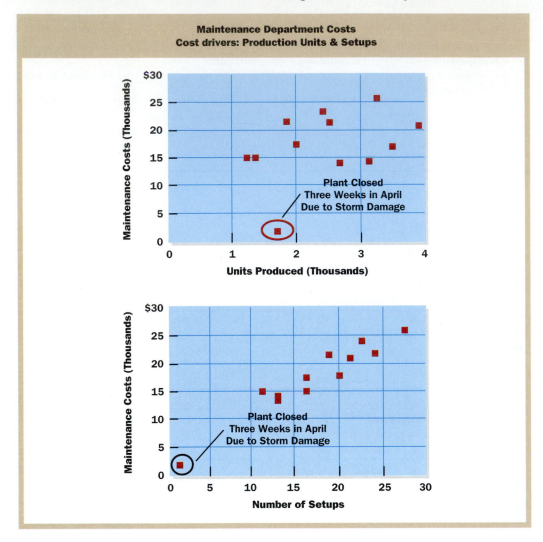

3-39 Account Analysis

Custom Computers, Inc., is a company started by two engineering students to assemble and market personal computers to faculty and students. The company operates out of the garage of one of the students' homes. From the following costs of a recent month, compute the total cost function and total cost for the month:

- Telephone $ 50, fixed
- Utilities   260: fixed, 25% attributable to the garage, 75% to the house
- Advertising   75, fixed
- Insurance   80, fixed
- Materials   7,500, variable, for five computers
- Labor   1,800: $1,300 fixed plus $500 for hourly help for assembling five computers

3-40 Linear Cost Functions

Let Y = total costs, X_1 = production volume, and X_2 = number of setups. Which of the following are linear cost functions? Which are mixed cost functions?

a. $Y = \$1,000$
b. $Y = \$8X_1$
c. $Y = \$5,000 + \$4X_1$
d. $Y = \$3,000 + \$6X_1 + \$30X_2$

e. $Y = \$9{,}000 + \$3(X_1 \times X_2)$

f. $Y = \$8{,}500 + \$1.50X_1^2$

3-41 High-Low Method

Manchester Foundry produced 45,000 tons of steel in March at a cost of £1,150,000. In April, the foundry produced 35,000 tons at a cost of £950,000. Using only these two data points, determine the cost function for Manchester.

3-42 Economic Plausibility of Regression Analysis Results

The head of the Warehousing Division of Lachton Co. was concerned about some cost behavior information given to him by the new assistant controller, who was hired because of his recent training in cost analysis. His first assignment was to apply regression analysis to various costs in the department. One of the results was presented as follows:

> *A regression on monthly data was run to explain building maintenance cost as a function of direct labor hours as the cost driver. The results are*

$$Y = \$6{,}810 - \$.47X$$

> *I suggest that we use the building as intensively as possible to keep the maintenance costs down.*

The department head was puzzled. How could increased use cause decreased maintenance cost? Explain this counterintuitive result to the department head. What step(s) did the assistant controller probably omit in applying and interpreting the regression analysis?

Problems

3-43 Controlling Risk, Capacity Decisions, Technology Decisions

Consider the earlier discussion of **Ford Motor** on page 91. Ford had been outsourcing production to Mazda and using overtime for as much as 20% of production—Ford's plants and assembly lines were running at 100% of capacity and demand was sufficient for an additional 20%. Ford had considered building new, highly automated assembly lines and plants to earn more profits since overtime premiums and outsourcing were costly. However, the investment in high technology and capacity expansion was rejected.

Assume that all material and labor costs are variable with respect to the level of production and that all other costs are fixed. Consider one of Ford's plants that makes the Probe model. The cost to convert the plant to use fully automated assembly lines is $20 million. The resulting labor costs would be significantly reduced. The costs, in millions of dollars, of the build option and the outsource/overtime option are given in the table below:

	Build Option		
Percent of capacity	60	100	120
Material costs	$18	$30	$36
Labor costs	6	10	12
Other costs	40	40	40
Total costs	$64	$80	$88

	Outsource/Overtime Option		
Percent of capacity	60	100	120
Material costs	$18	$30	$ 36
Labor costs	18	30	44
Other costs	20	20	20
Total costs	$56	$80	$100

1. Prepare a line graph showing total costs for the two options: (a) build new assembly lines, and (b) continue to use overtime and outsource production of Probes. Give an explanation of the cost behavior of the two options.

2. Which option enables Ford management to control risk better? Explain. Assess the cost-benefit trade-offs associated with each option.
3. A solid understanding of cost behavior is an important prerequisite to effective managerial control of costs. Suppose you are an executive at Ford and currently the production (and sales) level is approaching the 100% level of capacity and the economy is expected to remain strong for at least one year. While sales and profits are good now, you are aware of the cyclical nature of the automobile business. Would you recommend committing Ford to building automated assembly lines in order to service potential near-term increases in demand or would you recommend against building, looking to the likely future downturn in business? Discuss your reasoning.

3-44 Step Costs

Algona Beach Jail requires a staff of at least one guard for every four prisoners. The jail will hold 48 prisoners. Algona Beach attracts numerous tourists and transients in the spring and summer. However, the town is rather sedate in the fall and winter. The jail's fall-winter population is generally between 12 and 16 prisoners. The numbers in the spring and summer can fluctuate from 12 to 48, depending on the weather, among other factors (including phases of the moon, according to some longtime residents).

Algona Beach has four permanent guards, hired on a year-round basis at an annual salary of $36,000 each. When additional guards are needed, they are hired on a weekly basis at a rate of $600 per week. (For simplicity, assume that each month has exactly four weeks.)

1. Prepare a graph with the weekly planned cost of jail guards on the vertical axis and the number of prisoners on the horizontal axis.
2. What would be the budgeted amount for jail guards for the month of January? Would this be a fixed or a variable cost?
3. Suppose the jail population of each of the four weeks in July was 25, 38, 26, and 43, respectively. The actual amount paid for jail guards in July was $19,800. Prepare a report comparing the actual amount paid for jail guards with the amount that would be expected with efficient scheduling and hiring.
4. Suppose Algona Beach treated jail-guard salaries for nonpermanent guards as a variable expense of $150 per week per prisoner. This variable cost was applied to the number of prisoners in excess of 16. Therefore, the weekly cost function was

$$\text{Weekly jail-guard cost} = \$3,000 + \$150 \times (\text{total prisoners} - 16)$$

Explain how this cost function was determined.
5. Prepare a report similar to that in number 3 except that the cost function in number 4 should be used to calculate the expected amount of jail-guard salaries. Which report, this one or the one in number 3, is more accurate? Is accuracy the only concern?

3-45 Government Service Cost Analysis

Auditors for the Internal Revenue Service scrutinize income tax returns after they have been prescreened with the help of computer tests for normal ranges of deductions claimed by taxpayers. The IRS uses an expected cost of $7 per tax return, based on measurement studies that allow 20 minutes per return. Each agent has a workweek of five days of eight hours per day. Twenty auditors are employed at a salary of $830 each per week.

The audit supervisor has the following data regarding performance for the most recent 4-week period, when 8,000 returns were processed:

Actual Cost of Auditors	Expected Cost for Processing Returns	Difference or Variance
$66,400	?	?

1. Compute the planned cost and the variance.
2. The supervisor believes that audit work should be conducted more productively and that superfluous personnel should be transferred to field audits. If the foregoing data are representative, how many auditors should be transferred?
3. List some possible reasons for the variance.
4. Describe some alternative cost drivers for processing income tax returns.

3-46 Cost Analysis at America West

America West is one of the nation's leading commercial air carriers, with hubs in Phoenix and Las Vegas. Listed below are some of the costs incurred by America West. For each cost, select an appropriate cost driver and indicate whether the cost is likely to be fixed, variable, or mixed in relation to your cost driver.

a. Airplane fuel
b. Flight attendants' salaries
c. Baggage handlers' salaries
d. In-flight meals
e. Pilots' salaries
f. Airplane depreciation
g. Advertising

3-47 Separation of Drug Testing Laboratory Mixed Costs into Variable and Fixed Components

A staff meeting has been called at SportsLab, Inc., a drug-testing facility retained by several professional and college sports leagues and associations. The chief of testing, Dr. Hyde, has demanded an across-the-board increase in prices for a particular test because of the increased testing and precision that are now required.

The administrator of the laboratory has asked you to measure the mixed-cost behavior of this particular testing department and to prepare a short report she can present to Dr. Hyde. Consider the following limited data:

	Average Test Procedures per Month	Average Monthly Cost of Test Procedures
Monthly averages, 20X4	500	$ 60,000
Monthly averages, 20X5	600	70,000
Monthly averages, 20X6	700	144,000

3-48 University Cost Behavior

Lakeview School, a private high school, is preparing a planned income statement for the coming academic year ending August 31, 20X4. Tuition revenues for the past two years ending August 31 were 20X3: $720,000, and 20X2: $770,000. Total expenses for 20X3 were $710,000 and in 20X2 were $730,000. No tuition rate changes occurred in 20X2 or 20X3, nor are any expected to occur in 20X4. Tuition revenue is expected to be $710,000 for 20X4. What net income should be planned for 20X4, assuming that the implied cost behavior remains unchanged?

3-49 Activity Analysis

Des Moines Software develops and markets computer software for the agriculture industry. Because support costs are a large portion of the cost of software development, the director of cost operations of Des Moines, Leslie Paton, is especially concerned with understanding the effects of support cost behavior. Paton has completed a preliminary activity analysis of one of Des Moines's primary software products: FertiMix (software to manage fertilizer mixing). This product is a software template that is customized for specific customers, who are charged for the basic product plus customizing costs. The activity analysis is based on the number of customized lines of FertiMix code. Currently, support cost estimates are based on a fixed rate of 50% of the basic cost. Data are shown for two recent customers:

	Customer	
	West Acres Plants	Beautiful Blooms
Basic cost of FertiMix	$12,000	$12,000
Lines of customized code	490	180
Estimated cost per line of customized code	$23	$23

1. Compute the support cost of customizing FertiMix for each customer using each cost-estimating approach.
2. If the activity analysis is reliable, what are the pros and cons of adopting it for all of Des Moines's software products?

3-50 High-Low, Regression Analysis

On November 15, 2004, Sandra Cook, a newly hired cost analyst at Demgren Company, was asked to predict overhead costs for the company's operations in 2005, when 510 units are expected to be produced. She collected the following quarterly data:

Quarter	Production in Units	Overhead Costs
1/01	76	$ 721
2/01	79	715
3/01	72	655
4/01	136	1,131
1/02	125	1,001
2/02	128	1,111
3/02	125	1,119
4/02	133	1,042
1/03	124	997
2/03	129	1,066
3/03	115	996
4/03	84	957
1/04	84	835
2/04	122	1,050
3/04	90	991

1. Using the high-low method to estimate costs, prepare a prediction of overhead costs for 2005.
2. Sandy ran a regression analysis using the data she collected. The result was

$$Y = \$337 + \$5.75X$$

Using this cost function, predict costs for 2005.
3. Which prediction do you prefer? Why?

3-51 Interpretation of Regression Analysis

Study Appendix 3. The Tent Division of Arizona Outdoor Equipment Company has had difficulty controlling its use of supplies. The company has traditionally regarded supplies as a purely variable cost. Nearly every time production was above average, however, the division spent less than predicted for supplies; when production was below average, the division spent more than predicted. This pattern suggested to Yuki Li, the new controller, that part of the supplies cost was probably not related to production volume, or was fixed.

She decided to use regression analysis to explore this issue. After consulting with production personnel, she considered two cost drivers for supplies cost: (1) number of tents produced, and (2) square feet of material used. She obtained the following results based on monthly data.

	Cost Driver	
	Number of Tents	Square Feet of Material Used
Constant	2,300	1,900
Variable coefficient	.033	.072
R^2	.220	.686

1. Which is the preferred cost function? Explain.
2. What percentage of the fluctuation of supplies cost depends on square feet of materials? Do fluctuations in supplies cost depend on anything other than square feet of materials? What proportion of the fluctuations is not explained by square feet of materials?

3-52 Regression Analysis

Study Appendix 3. Liao, Inc., a manufacturer of fine china and stoneware, is troubled by fluctuations in productivity and wants to compute how manufacturing support costs are related to the various sizes of batches of output. The following data show the results of a random sample of ten batches of one pattern of stoneware:

Sample	Batch Size, X	Support Costs, Y
1	15	$180
2	12	140
3	20	230
4	17	190
5	12	160
6	25	300
7	22	270
8	9	110
9	18	240
10	30	320

1. Plot support costs, Y, versus batch size, X.
2. Using regression analysis, measure the cost function of support costs and batch size.
3. Predict the support costs for a batch size of 25.
4. Using the high-low method, repeat numbers 2 and 3. Should the manager use the high-low or regression method? Explain.

3-53 Choice of Cost Driver

Study Appendix 3. Richard Ellis, the director of cost operations of American Micro Devices, wishes to develop an accurate cost function to explain and predict support costs in the company's printed circuit board assembly operation. Mr. Ellis is concerned that the cost function that he currently uses—based on direct labor costs—is not accurate enough for proper planning and control of support costs. Mr. Ellis directed one of his financial analysts to obtain a random sample of 25 weeks of support costs and three possible cost drivers in the circuit-board assembly department: direct labor hours, number of boards assembled, and average cycle time of boards assembled. (Average cycle time is the average time between start and certified completion—after quality testing—of boards assembled during a week.) Much of the effort in this assembly operation is devoted to testing for quality and reworking defective boards, all of which increase the average cycle time in any period. Therefore, Mr. Ellis believes that average cycle time will be the best support cost driver. Mr. Ellis wants his analyst to use regression analysis to demonstrate which cost driver best explains support costs.

Week	Circuit Board Assembly Support Costs, Y	Direct Labor Hours, X_1	Number of Boards Completed, X_2	Average Cycle Time (Hours), X_3
1	$66,402	7,619	2,983	186.44
2	56,943	7,678	2,830	139.14
3	60,337	7,816	2,413	151.13
4	50,096	7,659	2,221	138.30
5	64,241	7,646	2,701	158.63
6	60,846	7,765	2,656	148.71
7	43,119	7,685	2,495	105.85
8	63,412	7,962	2,128	174.02
9	59,283	7,793	2,127	155.30
10	60,070	7,732	2,127	162.20
11	53,345	7,771	2,338	142.97
12	65,027	7,842	2,685	176.08
13	58,220	7,940	2,602	150.19
14	65,406	7,750	2,029	194.06
15	35,268	7,954	2,136	100.51
16	46,394	7,768	2,046	137.47
17	71,877	7,764	2,786	197.44
18	61,903	7,635	2,822	164.69
19	50,009	7,849	2,178	141.95
20	49,327	7,869	2,244	123.37

21	44,703	7,576	2,195	128.25
22	45,582	7,557	2,370	106.16
23	43,818	7,569	2,016	131.41
24	62,122	7,672	2,515	154.88
25	52,403	7,653	2,942	140.07

1. Plot support costs, Y, versus each of the possible cost drivers, X_1, X_2, and X_3.
2. Use regression analysis to measure cost functions using each of the cost drivers.
3. According to the criteria of plausibility and reliability, which is the best cost driver for support costs in the circuit board assembly department?
4. Interpret the economic meaning of the best cost function.

3-54 Use of Cost Functions for Pricing

Study Appendix 3. Read the previous problem. If you worked this problem, use your measured cost functions. If you did not work the previous problem, assume the following measured cost functions:

$$Y = \$9{,}000/\text{week} + (\$6 \times \text{direct labor hours}); \ R^2 = .10$$

$$Y = \$20{,}000/\text{week} + (\$14 \times \text{number of boards completed}); \ R^2 = .40$$

$$Y = \$5{,}000/\text{week} + (\$350 \times \text{average cycle time}); \ R^2 = .80$$

1. Which of the support cost functions would you expect to be the most reliable for explaining and predicting support costs? Why?
2. Assume that American Micro Devices prices its products by adding a percentage markup to its product costs. Product costs include assembly labor, components, and support costs. Using each of the cost functions, compute the circuit board portion of the support cost of an order that used the following resources:

   a. Effectively used the capacity of the assembly department for three weeks
   b. Assembly labor hours: 20,000
   c. Number of boards: 6,000
   d. Average cycle time: 180 hours

3. Which cost would you recommend that American Micro Devices use? Why?
4. Assume that the market for this product is extremely cost competitive. What do you think of American Micro Devices's pricing method?

3-55 Review of Chapters 2 and 3

Madison Musical Education Company (MME) provides instrumental music education to children of all ages. Payment for services comes from two sources: (1) a contract with Country Day School to provide private music lessons for up to 150 band students a year (where a year is nine months of education) for a fixed fee of $150,000, and (2) payment from individuals at a rate of $100 per month for nine months of education each year. In the 2003–2004 school year, MME made a profit of $5,000 on revenues of $295,000:

Revenues:		
Country Day School contract	$150,000	
Private students	145,000	
Total revenues		$295,000
Expenses:		
Administrative staff	$ 75,000	
Teaching staff	81,000	
Facilities	93,500	
Supplies	40,500	
Total expenses		290,000
Profit		$ 5,000

MME conducted an activity analysis and found that teaching staff wages and supplies costs are variable with respect to student-months. (A student-month is one student educated for one month.) Administrative staff and facilities costs are fixed within the range of 2,000 to 3,000 student-months. At volumes between 3,000 and 3,500 student-months, an additional facilities charge of $8,000 would be incurred. During the last year, a total of 2,700 student-months of education were provided, 1,450 of which were for private students and 1,250 of which were offered under the contract with Country Day School.

1. Compute the following using cost information from year 2003–2004 operations:
   Fixed cost per year
   Variable cost per student-month
2. Suppose that in 2004–2005 Country Day School decreased its use of MME to 120 students (that is, 1,080 student-months). The fixed contract price of $150,000 was still paid. If everything else stayed as it was in 2003–2004, what profit or loss would be made in 2004–2005?
3. Suppose that at the beginning of 2004–2005 Country Day School decided not to renew its contract with MME and the management of MME decided to try to maintain business as usual with only private students. How many students (each signing up for nine months) would MME require to continue to make a profit of $5,000 per year?

Cases

3-56 Government Health Cost Behavior

Dr. Stephanie White, the chief administrator of Uptown Clinic, a community mental health agency, is concerned about the dilemma of coping with reduced budgets in the next year and into the foreseeable future, despite increasing demand for services. In order to plan for reduced budgets, she first must identify where costs can be cut or reduced and still keep the agency functioning. Below are some data from the past year:

Program Area	Costs
Administration	
Salaries	
Administrator	$60,000
Assistant	35,000
Two secretaries	42,000
Supplies	35,000
Advertising and promotion	9,000
Professional meetings, dues, and literature	14,000
Purchased services	
Accounting and billing	15,000
Custodial and maintenance	13,000
Security	12,000
Consulting	10,000
Community mental health services	
Salaries (two social workers)	46,000
Transportation	10,000
Outpatient mental health treatment	
Salaries	
Psychiatrist	86,000
Two social workers	70,000

1. Identify which costs you think are likely to be discretionary or committed costs.
2. One possibility is to eliminate all discretionary costs. How much would be saved? What do you think of this recommendation?
3. How would you advise Dr. White to prepare for reduced budgets?

3-57 Activity Analysis

The costs of the Systems Support (SS) department (and other service departments) of Southeast Pulp and Paper, Inc., have always been charged to the three business divisions (Forest Management, Lumber Products, and Paper Products) based on the number of employees in each division. This measure is easy to obtain and update, and until recently none of the divisions had complained about the charges. The Paper Products division has recently automated many of its operations and has reduced the number of its employees. At the same time, however, to monitor its new process, Paper Products has increased its requests for various reports provided by the SS department. The other divisions have begun to complain that they are being charged more than their fair share of SS department costs. Based on activity analysis of possible cost drivers, cost analysts have suggested using the number of reports prepared as a means of charging for SS costs and have gathered the following information:

	Forest Management	Lumber Products	Paper Products
2003 number of employees	762	457	502
2003 number of reports	410	445	377
2003 SS costs: $300,000			
2004 number of employees	751	413	131
2004 number of reports	412	432	712
2004 SS costs: $385,000			

1. Discuss the plausibility and probable reliability of each of the cost drivers—number of employees or number of reports.
2. What are the 2003 and 2004 SS costs per unit of cost driver for each division using each cost driver? Do the Forest Management and Lumber Products divisions have legitimate complaints? Explain.
3. What are the incentives that are implied by each cost driver?
4. Which cost driver should Southeast Pulp and Paper use to charge its divisions for SS services? For other services? Why?

3-58 Identifying Relevant Data

eComp.com manufactures personal digital assistants (PDAs). Because these very small computers compete with laptops that have more functions and flexibility, understanding and using cost behavior is very critical to eComp.com's profitability. eComp.com's controller, Kelly Hudson, has kept meticulous files on various cost categories and possible cost drivers for most of the important functions and activities of eComp.com. Because most of the manufacturing at eComp.com is automated, labor cost is relatively fixed. Other support costs comprise most of eComp.com's costs. Partial data that Hudson has collected over the past 25 weeks on one of these support costs, logistics operations (materials purchasing, receiving, warehousing, and shipping), follow:

Week	Logistics Costs, Y	Number of Orders, X
1	$23,907	1,357
2	18,265	1,077
3	24,208	1,383
4	23,578	1,486
5	22,211	1,292
6	22,862	1,425
7	23,303	1,306
8	24,507	1,373
9	17,878	1,031
10	18,306	1,020
11	20,807	1,097
12	19,707	1,069
13	23,020	1,444
14	20,407	733
15	20,370	413
16	20,678	633
17	21,145	711
18	20,775	228
19	20,532	488
20	20,659	655
21	20,430	722
22	20,713	373
23	20,256	391
24	21,196	734
25	20,406	256

1. Plot logistics cost, Y, versus number of orders, X. What cost behavior is evident? What do you think happened in week 14?
2. What is your recommendation to Kelly Hudson regarding the relevance of the past 25 weeks of logistics cost and number of orders for measuring logistics cost behavior?
3. Hudson remarks that one of the improvements that eComp.com has made in the past several months was to negotiate just-in-time deliveries from its suppliers. This was made possible by substituting an automated ordering system for the previous manual (labor-intensive) system. Although fixed costs increased, the variable cost of placing an order was expected to drop greatly. Do the data support this expectation? Do you believe that the change to the automated ordering system was justified? Why or why not?

EXCEL Application Exercise

3-59 Fixed and Variable Cost Data

Goal: Create an Excel spreadsheet to calculate fixed and variable cost data for evaluating alternative approaches. Use the results to answer questions about your findings.

Scenario: Recreational Sports, Inc., has asked you to evaluate two alternative cost approaches for their new Web site. They would like you to calculate fixed and variable costs at different numbers of orders. The background data for your analysis appear in exercise 3–37.

When you have completed your spreadsheet, answer the following questions:
1. At what number of orders are the Total Costs for the two approaches the same? What does this mean?
2. Which alternative should be selected if the expected number of orders is less than the breakeven level of orders? If the expected number of orders is greater than the break-even level of orders?
3. What conclusion regarding cost predictions can be drawn from your analysis?

Step-by-Step:
1. Open a new Excel spreadsheet.
2. In column A, create a bold-faced heading that contains the following:
   Row 1: Chapter 3 Decision Guideline
   Row 2: Recreational Sports, Inc.
   Row 3: Analysis of Alternative Cost Approaches
   Row 4: Today's Date
3. Merge and center the four heading rows across columns A through K.
4. In row 7, create the following bold-faced, right-justified column headings:
   Column A: Number of Orders
   Column B: Alternative 1
   Column C: Alternative 2
   Note: Adjust column widths as necessary.

5. In column A, Rows 8 through 12, enter order levels from 40,000 to 80,000 in 10,000-unit increments.
6. Use the Scenario data to create formulas in columns B and C for calculating the total costs (fixed plus variable costs) for each alternative at the order level in column A.
7. Format all amounts as

Number tab:	Category:	Number
	Decimal places:	0
	Use 1000 Separator (,):	Checked

8. Modify the Page Setup by selecting File, Page Setup.

Page tab:	Orientation:	Landscape
Margins tab:	Top:	.5
	Bottom:	.5

9. Select the data in columns A through C, Rows 7 through 12, and start the Chart Wizard either by inserting a chart (Insert, Chart) or by clicking the Chart Wizard icon on the toolbar.

Step 1 of 4—Chart Type
    a. **Custom Types tab:**
    b. Chart Type: Smooth Lines
    c. Click "Next >" button
    Note: List is alphabetical.

Step 2 of 4—Chart Source Data
    d. **Data Range tab:**
    e. Modify Data range to: *=SheetName!*$B$7:$C$12
    f. Series in: Columns
    g. **Series tab:**
    h. Category (X) axis labels: *=SheetName!*$A$8:$A$12
    i. Click "Next >" button

Step 3 of 4—Chart Options
    j. **Titles tab:**
    k. Chart Title: Analysis of Alternative Cost Approaches
    l. Category (X) axis: Number of Orders
    m. Value (Y) axis: Total Costs
    n. **Gridlines tab:**
    o. Category (X) axis: Major Gridlines (checked)
    p. Value (Y) axis: Major Gridlines (checked)
    q. Click "Next >" button

Step 4 of 4—Chart Location
    r. As object in *SheetName*   Checked
    s. Click "Finish" button

10. Move the chart so the upper-left corner is on the left margin, row 14.
Left-mouse click the upper-left handle and drag it to the designated location.
11. Resize the chart so the lower-right corner fills cell K37.
Left-mouse click the lower-right handle and drag it to the designated location.
12. Format the Y-axis amounts (Total Costs) to display a dollar symbol by doing the following:
Double-click any cost amount on the Y-axis to open the 'Format Axis' dialog box.

Scale tab:		Minimum:	300,000
Number tab:		Category:	Currency
		Decimal Places:	0
		Symbol:	$

13. Save your work to disk, and print a copy for your files.
Note: Select cell A8 before printing if you want both the data and the chart to print. If you want only the chart to print, ignore the "Select cell A8" instruction.
Print your spreadsheet using landscape in order to ensure that all columns appear on one page.

Collaborative Learning Exercise

3-60 Cost-Behavior Examples

Select about ten students to participate in a "cost-behavior bee." The game proceeds like a spelling bee—when a participant is unable to come up with a correct answer, he or she is eliminated from the game. The last one in the game is the winner.

The object of the game is to identify a type of cost that fits a particular cost-behavior pattern. The first player rolls a die.[2] If a 1 or a 6 comes up, the die passes to the next player (and the roller makes it to the next round). If a 2, 3, 4, or 5 comes up, the player has to identify one of the following types of costs:

If a 2 is rolled, identify a variable cost.
If a 3 is rolled, identify a fixed cost.

---

[2]Instead of rolling a die, players could draw one of the four cost categories out of a hat (or similar container) or from a deck of four 3×5 cards. This eliminates the chance element that can let some players proceed to a later round without having to give an example of a particular cost behavior. However, the chance element can add to the enjoyment of the game.

If a 4 is rolled, identify a mixed cost.

If a 5 is rolled, identify a step cost.

A scribe should label four columns on the board, one for each type of cost, and list the costs that are mentioned for each category. Once a particular cost has been used, it cannot be used again.

Each player has a time limit of 10 seconds to produce an example. (For a tougher game, make the time limit 5 seconds.) The instructor is the referee, judging if a particular example is acceptable. It is legitimate for the referee to ask a player to explain why he or she thinks the cost mentioned fits the category before making a judgment.

After each player has had a turn, a second round begins with the remaining players taking a turn in the same order as in the first round. The game continues through additional rounds until all but one player has failed to give an acceptable answer within the time limit. The remaining player is the winner.

Internet Exercise ● **www.prenhall.com/horngren**

3-61 Cost Behavior at Southwest Airlines

In this exercise, we will look at some costs and see if we can determine the type of behavior associated with those costs. While firms are concerned about trying to label costs as either variable or fixed to help in planning, very few costs are completely variable or fixed. The information provided by firms to external users also often precludes a user from determining specifics about the cost behaviors—they don't want to give the competitors too much information!

Log on to the **Southwest Airlines** Web site at http://www.iflyswa.com. Click on the information icon "About SWA," and then click on "Investor Relations." This will take you to the site where you can then access the financial information.

1. Click on the "Annual Reports" icon and then select the most recent annual report. Looking at the table of contents, find the page where the ten-year summary starts. Go to this section of the report. What type of information do you find there?

2. When you look at the operating revenue information, what do you see? Look at the information provided concerning operating expenses. Is it categorized in the same manner as the revenues? If the information is not in the same categories, why do you think Southwest did not match it up in the same manner?

3. Now look at the section on consolidated operating statistics. Southwest measures activity in Revenue Passenger Miles (RPMs) and capacity in Available Seat Miles (ASMs). Which of these is larger? How are the RPM and ASM determined? Is it possible for the two numbers to be the same? What information is provided for each of these items in the consolidated operating statistics section?

4. Compute the total operating expense per RPM.

5. Using data from the most recent year and three years earlier, use the high-low method to compute the variable operating expense per RPM. Compare the total operating expense per RPM and the variable expense per RPM. Is this relationship what you expected? Why or why not?

6. Airlines are often considered to be high-fixed-cost companies. Is this consistent with your findings in requirement 5? Explain why the high-low method over this time might overestimate the amount of variable costs.

Cost Management Systems and Activity-Based Costing

CHAPTER 4

LEARNING OBJECTIVES

When you have finished studying this chapter, you should be able to:

1. Describe the purposes of cost management systems.

2. Explain the relationship among cost, cost objective, cost accumulation, and cost assignment.

3. Distinguish among direct, indirect, and unallocated costs.

4. Explain how the financial statements of merchandisers and manufacturers differ because of the types of goods they sell.

5. Understand the main differences between traditional and activity-based costing (ABC) systems and why ABC systems provide value to managers.

6. Design a cost accounting system that includes activity-based costing.

7. Use activity-based cost information to make strategic and operational control decisions.

8. Understand why multistage ABC systems give more value than two-stage ABC systems for strategic planning and operational control (Appendix 4).

Companies face good times and bad. They grow quickly at times, and at other times may not grow at all. Their reputations rise and fall. But good companies adapt to the changes in their environments, and they survive the bad times and flourish in the good. A survey several years ago asked 1,000 adults for their choice of a "really good company." The company named most often was **AT&T**. Chances are, AT&T has reached out and touched you, too. With 54 million customers, it has annual revenues of more than $52 billion and net income exceeding $7.7 billion. However, AT&T today is not the same as it was when the survey was taken.

A communications revolution is taking place on a global scale. Today, we communicate using wireless cell phones and computer online services, in addition to the traditional telephone. How does AT&T, a company that has been synonymous with communications for more than 100 years, ensure that it remains competitive? Certainly AT&T has the people, technology, brand, market presence, and financial resources to get the job done—but it takes more. Like any other company, AT&T's managers, from top executives to local service managers, must understand their customers, their competitors, and their costs. This understanding is a common theme among all successful businesses.

Consider AT&T's Business Communication Services unit (BCS). With annual revenue of more than $28 billion, BCS is responsible for domestic and international voice and data communications services. To keep the unit's competitive edge, management began using a new cost accounting system in the mid-1990s. Accountants and managers designed the new costing system "to help operating managers gain a better understanding of the costs of each kind of service (product)." The old cost system gathered financial data used primarily by top management and accountants.

AT&T Wireless Services customers can use their cell phones in more than 5,500 locations across the United States and Canada, as well as in Europe, Asia, and Australia. People are able to call cell phone users nearly anywhere on earth by dialing the recipient's local wireless number. It is important to AT&T Wireless managers to know the cost of serving its customers.

The new cost system measures the costs of the key business processes in the BCS and the costs of the activities that the unit performs to support its various services. ■

Cost Management Systems

To support managers' decisions, accountants go beyond simply determining the cost of products and services; they develop cost management systems. A **cost management system (CMS)** is a collection of tools and techniques that identifies how management's decisions affect costs. The primary purposes of a cost management system are to provide

1. cost information for strategic management decisions,
2. cost information for operational control, and
3. aggregate measures of inventory value and cost of goods manufactured for external reporting to investors, creditors, and other external stakeholders.

External users of cost information, such as investors and creditors, need aggregate measures of inventory value and the cost of goods sold. They do not need accurate cost information on individual products or services. It is only the first and second purposes of a CMS that generate the need for more elaborate tools and techniques. Internal managers need accurate and timely cost information for strategic reasons, such as deciding on the optimal product and customer mix, choosing the value-chain functions to receive special focus or to outsource, and making investment decisions. For these decisions, managers want to know the costs of individual products, services, customers, and processes associated with value-chain functions. For example, until 1998, AT&T focused primarily on one product—long-distance voice service. Management realized that increased competition and new calling alternatives such as wireless, online chat, and e-mail would result in declining revenue. So, from 1998 to 2001, AT&T invested over $35 billion to expand its core products and to transform AT&T from a domestic long-distance company to a global communications and information services company. To make this strategic decision, AT&T management needed detailed information concerning the costs of the various new services.

The assessment of process improvement efforts and other operational cost control programs also requires accurate and timely feedback on costs. Consider the billing center at AT&T Business Communication Services. The cost system reported the costs of various activities performed in the center, including the costs of investigating incorrect bills. The cost was so high that BCS managers started a process improvement program to reduce the costs of incorrect bills. The result was annual cost savings of about $500,000.

Often, companies make strategic and operational control decisions simultaneously. AT&T made the strategic decision to change the way it billed corporate customers from the traditional paper-based system to e-billing. It made this decision primarily to serve its customers better (faster)—a strategic decision. Yet, this change in the way AT&T did business had a dramatic effect on its costs. With a paper-based billing system, a large corporate customer recieves about 17,000 pages in invoices over the course of a year. Just the postage for these bills is $800. Paper and postage account for nearly 75% of the cost of billing. AT&T's strategic decision to change how it billed customers also helped the company meet its environmental impact goals. In total, AT&T saves 3,000,000 sheets of paper each year—equivalent to 260 trees and 6,000 gallons of oil!

Throughout this text, we describe many CMS tools and techniques. Examples are the contribution margin technique and cost-volume-profit analysis from Chapter 2. The usefulness of a report that lists the contribution margins for the products of AT&T depends on the accuracy of the cost data that it uses. Clearly, inaccurate cost data can lead AT&T managers to make incorrect decisions. The cost data that managers use for decision making come from the cost accounting system—the most fundamental component of a cost management system. The cost accounting system supports all other cost management system tools and techniques. The major focus of this chapter is **cost accounting systems**—the techniques used to determine the cost of a product, service, customer, or other cost objective. In other chapters, we will focus on cost management—using the output of cost accounting systems to manage the organization.

Cost Accounting Systems

All kinds of organizations—manufacturing firms, service companies, and nonprofit organizations—need some form of **cost accounting,** that part of the cost management system that measures costs for the purposes of management decision making and financial reporting.

Managers rely on accountants to design a cost accounting system that measures costs to meet each of the three purposes of a CMS. Consider the following commentaries on the modern role of management accountants and cost accounting systems.

> *We (management accountants) have to understand what the numbers mean, relate the numbers to business activity, and recommend alternative courses of action. Finally, we have to evaluate alternatives and make decisions to maximize business efficiency.*
>
> —South Central Bell

> *Because the ABC (activity-based costing) system now mirrors the manufacturing process, the engineers and production staff believe the cost data produced by the cost accounting system. Engineering and production regularly ask accounting to help find the product design combination that will optimize costs. . . . The accountants now participate in product design decisions. They help engineering and production understand how costs behave. . . . The ABC system makes the professional lives of the accountants more rewarding.*
>
> —Hewlett-Packard Company

The cost accounting system typically includes two processes:

1. **Cost accumulation:** Collecting costs by some "natural" classification such as materials or labor, or by activities performed such as order processing or machine processing.
2. **Cost assignment:** Tracing or allocating costs to one or more cost objectives such as activities, processes, departments, customers, or products.

Exhibit 4-1 is a very simple illustration of these two basic processes. First, the system collects the costs of all materials. Then it assigns these costs to the departments that use the materials and further to the specific activities performed in these departments. Last, the system assigns the accumulated costs of materials used in the various activities to the products made—cabinets, tables, and chairs. The total materials cost of a particular product is the sum of the materials costs assigned to it in the various departments. For example, the cost of a finished desk would include the following materials costs:

- Metal top, sides, and legs assembled during the various activities in the machining department
- Bolts, brackets, screws, drawers, handles, and knobs pieced together by finishing department activities

The importance of a company's cost accounting system cannot be stressed enough. Any manager who makes a decision based on financial data relies on the accuracy of the cost

---

cost accounting systems
The techniques used to determine the cost of a product, service, customer, or other cost objective.

cost accounting
That part of the cost management system that measures costs for the purposes of management decision making and financial reporting.

cost accumulation
Collecting costs by some natural classification such as activities performed, labor, or materials.

cost assignment
Tracing or allocating costs to one or more cost objectives such as activities, departments, customers, or products.

O B J E C T I V E
Explain the relationship between cost, cost objective, cost accumulation, and cost assignment.

Exhibit 4-1
Cost Accumulation
and Assignment

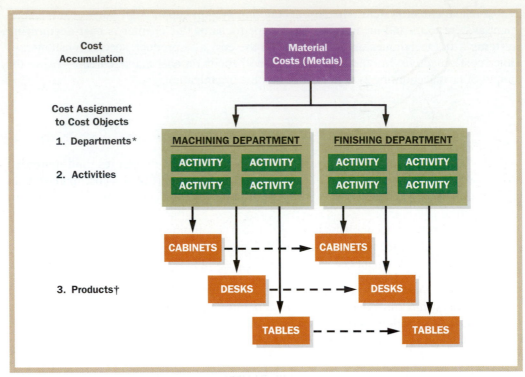

*Purpose: to evaluate performance of manufacturing departments.
†Purpose: to obtain costs of various products for valuing inventory, determining income, and judging product profitability.

accounting system. In today's business environment, characterized by highly-competitive global markets and complex operating systems, designing costing systems that provide accurate and useful information is a key success factor for all types of organizations.

This chapter describes the major types of cost accounting systems and how managers use the costs that these systems provide. However, before describing the types of cost accounting systems, we need to develop an understanding of the various cost terms that managers and accountants commonly use. We will start with a discussion of cost terms that are important for strategic decision making and operational control purposes.

Cost Terms Used for Strategic Decision Making and Operational Control Purposes

Cost accounting systems need to provide accurate and useful cost information to help managers make decisions. In fact, without accurate and useful cost information, many decisions can be downright harmful. For example, an extremely large U.S. grocery chain, A&P, ran into profit difficulties and began retrenching by closing many stores. Management's lack of adequate cost information about individual store operations made the closing program a hit-or-miss affair. A news story reported the following:

> *Because of the absence of detailed profit-and-loss statements, and a cost-allocation system that did not reflect true costs, A&P's strategists could not be sure whether an individual store was really unprofitable. For example, distribution costs were shared equally among all the stores in a marketing area without regard to such factors as a store's distance from the warehouse. Says one close observer of the company: "When they wanted to close a store, they had to wing it. They could not make rational decisions, because they did not have a fact basis."*

We can classify and report costs in many ways—far too many for us to cover in a single chapter. We have already seen costs classified by their behavior—fixed, variable, step, and mixed. This section concentrates on the big picture of how accounting systems accumulate, classify, and report costs. We will look at important attributes of costs, each playing an important role in subseqent cost-management tools and techniques. We begin by defining costs and cost objectives.

Cost Objectives

A **cost** is a sacrifice or giving up of resources for a particular purpose. For many organizations, the largest single cost is the cost of labor. The resource the organization gives up is cash and the purpose is to pay laborers for the activities they perform in producing products or services. We generally measure costs by the monetary units (for example, dollars, yen, or euros) that an organization must pay for goods and services. Accountants initially record costs by category, such as repairs or advertising. Then they group costs in different ways to help managers make decisions, such as evaluating subordinates and subunits of the organization, expanding or deleting products or territories, and replacing equipment.

As a manager, you will often want to know the cost of something to help make a decision. We call this 'something' a **cost objective** or **cost object,** defined as anything for which decision makers desire a separate measurement of costs. Although you will most often want to know the cost of a product or service, there are many other cost objectives that you might use. Examples of cost objectives include customers, departments, territories, and activities such as processing orders or moving materials. For example, one large manufacturer of pet food products recently changed its cost management system to report both the cost of products it makes and the cost to serve the company's major retail customers. It discovered that all its products were profitable, but the cost to sell to and service some customers was greater than the profit margin on the products sold to these customers. Thus, by using a combination of two cost objectives, it learned that some customers were a serious drain on the company's profit. The company was able to develop a strategy to improve the profitability of these customers and change the way it conducted business to reduce its operating costs.

In the next section, we will describe the three major types of costs and how they relate to cost objectives. You will often use these cost types during your business career, so give this section special attention.

Direct, Indirect, and Unallocated Costs

A major characteristic of a cost is its relationship to a particular cost objective. We can classify all costs in one of three ways: direct, indirect, or unallocated with respect to a particular cost objective. Accountants can identify **direct costs** specifically and exclusively with a given cost objective in an economically feasible way. Parts and materials included in a product are the most common type of direct cost. For example, to determine the cost of parts assembled into a Dell laptop computer, Dell's accountants simply look at the purchase orders for the specific parts used.

Accountants cannot specifically and exclusively identify **indirect costs** with a given cost objective in an economically feasible way. However, through **cost allocation,** we can assign these costs to cost objects by identifying plausible and reliable output measures (cost drivers) with which to allocate these indirect costs among cost objects. How would Dell's accountants determine how much assembly-equipment depreciation the company should assign to a particular model of laptop? This is a more difficult challenge because Dell uses this equipment to produce many different products. The depreciation on Dell's assembly equipment is an example of an indirect cost. Dell's accountants might allocate

cost
A sacrifice or giving up of resources for a particular purpose, frequently measured by the monetary units that an organization must pay for goods and services.

cost objective (cost object)
Anything for which decision makers desire a separate measurement of costs. Examples include departments, products, activities, and territories.

OBJECTIVE 3
Distinguish between direct, indirect, and unallocated costs.

direct costs
Costs that can be identified specifically and exclusively with a given cost objective in an economically feasible way.

indirect costs
Costs that cannot be identified specifically and exclusively with a given cost objective in an economically feasible way.

cost allocation
Assigning indirect costs to cost objects using plausible and reliable cost drivers.

this indirect cost to Dell's various products based on the output measure "machine hours." If making a Latitude laptop uses twice as many machine hours as making an Inspiron laptop, then Dell would allocate twice as much machine depreciation cost to the Latitude. Whenever an accountant uses the term *allocated,* we know the related cost is an indirect cost.

Finally, there are some costs for which we can identify no relationship to a cost objective. These are **unallocated costs.** Unallocated costs might include research and development, process design, legal expenses, accounting, information services, and executive salaries. Keep in mind, though, that an unallocated cost for one company may be an indirect or even a direct cost for another. Why? Because businesses vary considerably in their value chains and operating systems. For example, in some businesses the design function is a critical success factor and therefore managers are willing to spend the time and effort to deploy sophisticated operating systems and to implement equally sophisticated accounting systems to allocate or even directly trace the costs incurred.

Consider the statement of operating income in panel A of Exhibit 4-2. It represents a manufacturing company that makes cabinets, tables, and chairs. Each item in panel A represents accumulated totals for all products sold for an entire reporting period. To help make a strategic decision regarding which of the three products to emphasize, it would be useful to "unbundle" these totals to find the profitability amounts for individual products. How can we do this?

First, note that we can directly trace or allocate to individual products all cost items except administrative salaries and other administrative expenses. Consider cost of goods sold. Most companies find that it is easy to trace material costs to individual products. However, some other manufacturing costs, often even labor, are more difficult to trace directly, so these costs are indirect, and we allocate them to products. It is

unallocated costs
Costs for which we can identify no relationship to a cost objective.

Panel A Statement of Operating Income [External Reporting Purpose]		Panel B Contribution to Corporate Costs and Profit [Internal Strategic Decision-Making Purpose]			
		Cabinets	**Tables**	**Chairs**	**Cost Type, Assignment Method**
Sales	$470,000	$280,000	$100,000	$90,000	
Cost of goods sold:					
Direct material	120,000	50,000	30,000	40,000	Direct, direct trace
Indirect manufacturing	110,000	45,000	30,000	35,000	Indirect, allocation based on machine hours
	230,000	95,000	60,000	75,000	
Gross profit	240,000	185,000	40,000	15,000	
Operating expenses:					
Sales salaries	47,000	28,000	10,000	9,000	Direct, direct trace
Distribution	30,000	12,000	8,000	10,000	Indirect, allocation based on
Total operating expenses	77,000	40,000	18,000	19,000	weight
Contribution to corporate expenses and profit	**163,000**	**$145,000**	**$ 22,000**	**$(4,000)**	
Corporate expenses (unallocated):					
Administrative salaries	40,000				
Other administrative	60,000				
Total unallocated expenses	100,000				
Operating income	$ 63,000				

Exhibit 4-2
Direct, Indirect, and Unallocated Costs

not unusual for the amount of indirect costs to be a large component of total company costs. As a result, many companies develop sophisticated cost allocation systems for these indirect costs. The complexity of cost allocation depends on the complexity of the associated production system.

Let's assume that the use of machine hours to allocate the indirect manufacturing costs gives a reasonable degree of costing accuracy. Then, managers responsible for each of the products would be satisfied that the cost of goods sold and gross profit amounts are a good estimate of the "true" cost and profit for these products. Last year 9,000, 6,000, and 7,000 machine hours were used to make cabinets, tables, and chairs, respectively. So we would calculate the allocation of the $110,000 indirect manufacturing costs to cabinets as $110,000 \times (9,000/22,000) = $45,000. Exhibit 4-2 shows all three allocations of the indirect manufacturing costs.

In our example, we can directly trace sales salaries to individual products because the company pays its sales force on a strictly commission basis. In addition, we can allocate the expenses for the distribution of products to warehouses in a fair manner based on weight. Last year, shipments of cabinets, tables, and chairs weighed 6,000, 4,000, and 5,000 pounds; respectively. We would calculate the allocation of the $30,000 total distribution costs to cabinets as $30,000 \times (6,000/15,000) = $12,000. Exhibit 4-2 shows all three allocations of the distribution costs.

So, while the managers in charge of chairs may not be happy with the reported loss of $4,000, they would feel that it is a reasonable measure of profitability. Top management would also have useful financial information to aid in their strategic decision regarding the most profitable product mix.

In our example, we assume that managers could find no reasonable means to allocate administrative salaries or other administrative expenses. So these corporate-level expenses remain unallocated. Why not allocate the administrative salaries and other administrative expenses to the products by using some simple measure such as "percent of total revenue generated" or "number of units sold?" The answer is, because managers want allocations to be a fair measure of the costs incurred on their behalf. In our case, the work performed by the administrative personnel was not a simple function of the volume of units sold or revenue generated. If a company cannot find such a measure, it often chooses not to allocate.

Whenever it is economically feasible, managers prefer costs to be direct rather than indirect. This gives them greater confidence in the reported costs of products, services, or other cost objectives. To be economically feasible, a system for tracing costs to cost objectives cannot be too expensive in relation to expected benefits. For example, it may be economically feasible to trace the exact cost of steel and fabric (direct cost) to a specific lot of desk chairs. However, it may be economically infeasible to trace the exact cost of rivets or thread (indirect costs) to the chairs, even though such a tracing is technically possible.

Another factor that influences whether we consider a cost direct, indirect, or unallocated is the particular cost objective. For example, suppose the manager of a local telephone company is faced with two decisions: what price to charge for installing new phone service, and what amount of costs to use for the installation department's budget. Among the various costs relevant to both decisions is the salary of a supervisor in the installation department. The supervisor oversees both phone installations and routine service calls. For the pricing decision, the supervisor's salary is an indirect cost. Why? Because accountants cannot physically trace this cost to the phone installations or service calls and therefore must allocate the cost. However, for the department budget, the supervisor's salary is a direct cost. Why? Because accountants can physically identify 100% of the cost as belonging to the department. In general, many more costs are direct when a department is the cost objective than when a product or service such as a telephone installation or service call is the cost objective.

Frequently, managers want to know both the costs of running departments and the costs of products, services, activities, or resources. Companies inevitably allocate costs to more than one cost objective. Thus, a particular cost may simultaneously be direct and indirect. As you have just seen, a supervisor's salary can be both direct with respect to his or her department and indirect with respect to the department's individual products or services.

We conclude our discussion of costs to serve different purposes by describing cost terms that accountants use for external financial reporting.

Cost Terms Used for External Reporting Purposes

One of the three purposes of cost management systems is to provide aggregate measures of inventory value and cost of goods manufactured for external reporting to investors, creditors, and other external stakeholders. We will discuss four attributes of these costs: manufacturing costs, product versus period costs, costs on the balance sheet, and costs on the income statement.

Categories of Manufacturing Costs

Manufacturing companies differ from merchandising companies in the way they accumulate and report the cost of inventories. In manufacturing operations, which transform materials into other goods through the use of labor and factory facilities, products are frequently the cost objective. Thus, these firms have their own way of classifying costs. Manufacturing companies classify costs that they assign to products as either (1) direct material, (2) direct labor, or (3) indirect manufacturing costs.

direct-material costs
The acquisition costs of all materials that a company identifies as a part of the manufactured goods and traces to the manufactured goods in an economically feasible way.

direct-labor costs
The wages of all labor that a company can trace specifically and exclusively to the manufactured goods in an economically feasible way.

indirect production costs (indirect manufacturing costs, factory burden, factory overhead, manufacturing overhead)
All costs other than direct material or direct labor that are associated with the manufacturing process.

1. **Direct-material costs** include the acquisition costs of all materials that a company identifies as a part of the manufactured goods and that it can trace to the manufactured goods in an economically feasible way. Examples are iron castings, lumber, aluminum sheets, and subassemblies. Direct materials often do not include minor items such as tacks or glue because the costs of tracing these items are greater than the possible benefits of having more precise product costs. Such items, often called supplies or indirect materials, are a part of indirect production costs.

2. **Direct-labor costs** include the wages (and, in some companies, related benefits) paid to employees that a company can trace specifically and exclusively to the manufactured goods in an economically feasible way. Examples are the wages of machine operators and assemblers. In highly automated factories with a flexible workforce, there may be no direct labor costs. Why? Because workers spend time on numerous products, which makes it economically infeasible to physically trace any labor cost directly to specific products.

3. **Indirect production costs** (or **indirect manufacturing costs**, **factory overhead**, **factory burden**, or **manufacturing overhead**) include all costs associated with the production process that a company cannot trace to the goods or services produced in an economically feasible way. Because managers and accountants use all of these terms, we will use them interchangeably throughout this textbook. Accountants consider many labor costs, such as that of janitors, forklift truck operators, plant guards, and storeroom clerks, to be indirect labor because it is impossible or economically infeasible to trace such activity to specific products. Other examples of factory overhead costs are power, supplies, supervisory salaries, property taxes, rent, insurance, and depreciation.

The application of computer technology has allowed modern cost systems to physically trace more costs to products in an economically feasible manner. Thus, costs that were previously indirect costs become direct costs. For example, meters wired to computers can monitor the electricity used to produce each product, and managers can trace the costs of setting up a batch production run to the items produced in the run. In general, the more manufacturing costs we can trace directly to products, the more accurate the product cost.

In addition to direct-material, direct-labor, and indirect production costs, all manufacturing companies also incur costs associated with the other value-chain functions (research and development, design, marketing, distribution, and customer service). Accounting information systems accumulate these costs by departments such as R&D, advertising, and sales. Most firms' financial statements report these costs as selling and administrative expenses. In short, these costs do not become a part of the reported inventory cost of the manufactured products.

Product Costs and Period Costs

Regardless of the type of cost accounting system we use for internal decision-making purposes, the resulting costs appear in a company's financial statements for external financial reporting purposes. Costs appear both on the income statement, as cost of goods sold, and on the balance sheet, as inventory amounts. When preparing both income statements and balance sheets, accountants frequently distinguish between product costs and period costs. **Product costs** are costs identified with goods produced or purchased for resale. Product costs first become part of the inventory on hand. These inventoriable costs become expenses in the form of cost of goods sold only when the company sells the inventory. In contrast, **period costs** become expenses during the current period without going through an inventory stage.

For example, look at the top half of Exhibit 4-3. A merchandising company such as a retailer or wholesaler acquires goods for resale without changing their basic form. The only product cost is the purchase cost of the merchandise. The company holds unsold goods as merchandise inventory and shows their costs as an asset on a balance sheet. As the company sells the goods, their costs become expenses (often referred to as expiration) in the form of "cost of goods sold."

A merchandising company also has a variety of selling and administrative expenses. These costs are period costs because the company deducts them from revenue as expenses without ever being regarded as a part of inventory.

The bottom half of Exhibit 4-3 illustrates product and period costs in a manufacturing company. Note that the company transforms direct materials into salable items with the help of direct-labor and indirect manufacturing costs. All these costs are product costs that the company shows as inventory until it sells the goods. As in merchandising accounting, the selling and administrative expenses are period costs, not product costs.

Be sure you are clear on the differences between merchandising accounting and manufacturing accounting for such costs as insurance, depreciation, and wages. In merchandising accounting, all such items are period costs and are expenses of the current period. In manufacturing accounting, many of these items are related to production activities and thus, as indirect manufacturing, are product costs that appear initially on the balance sheet as inventory. These costs become expenses on the income statement in the form of cost of goods sold when the company sells the inventory.

In both merchandising and manufacturing accounting, selling and general administrative costs are period costs. Thus, the inventory cost of a manufactured product excludes sales salaries, sales commissions, advertising, legal, public relations, and the president's salary. Manufacturing overhead is part of finished-goods inventory cost, but selling expenses and general administrative expenses are not.

How do balance sheets and income statements of merchandising and manufacturing companies differ in presenting costs? Would the basic structure of these financial statements be different for a merchandising company like **Sears** compared to a manufacturing

product costs
Costs identified with goods produced or purchased for resale.

period costs
Costs that become expenses during the current period without going through an inventory stage.

Exhibit 4-3
Relationships of
Product Costs and
Period Costs

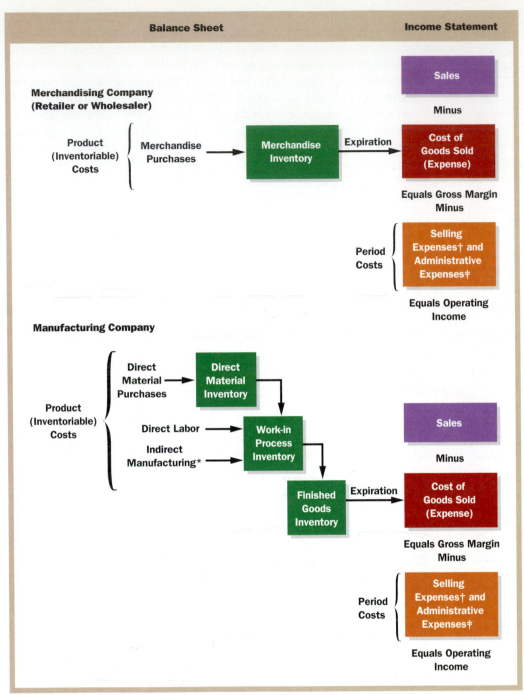

*Examples: indirect labor, factory supplies, insurance, and depreciation on plant.
†Examples: insurance on salespersons' cars, depreciation on salespersons' cars, salespersons' salaries.
‡Examples: insurance on corporate headquarters building, depreciation on office equipment, clerical salaries.
Note particularly that when insurance and depreciation relate to the manufacturing function, they are inventoriable, but when they relate to selling and administration, they are not inventoriable.

OBJECTIVE 4

Explain how the financial statements of merchandisers and manufacturers differ because of the types of goods they sell.

company like **Goodyear**? Let's take a closer look at how these two primary financial statements differ between manufacturing and merchandising organizations.

Balance Sheet Presentation of Costs

Examining Exhibit 4-3, you can see that the balance sheets of manufacturers and merchandisers differ with respect to inventories. Instead of one inventory account, a manufacturing concern has three inventory accounts that help managers trace all product costs through the production process to the time of sales. These accounts are

- Direct-material inventory: Material on hand and awaiting use in the production process.
- Work-in-process inventory: Goods undergoing the production process but not yet fully completed. Costs include appropriate amounts of the three major manufacturing costs: direct material, direct labor, and indirect production costs.
- Finished-goods inventory: Goods fully completed but not yet sold.

Current Asset Sections of Balance Sheets

Manufacturer			Retailer or Wholesaler	
Cash		$ 4,000	Cash	$ 4,000
Receivables		25,000	Receivables	25,000
Finished goods	$ 32,000			
Work in process	22,000			
Direct material	23,000			
Total inventories		77,000	Merchandise inventories	77,000
Other current assets		1,000	Other current assets	1,000
Total current assets		$107,000	Total current assets	$107,000

The difference between the balance sheet of a manufacturer and that of a retailer or wholesaler is apparent from the inventory accounts from the 2002 annual reports of Goodyear and Sears (in millions):

Goodyear Tire & Rubber Company		**Sears, Roebuck and Co.**	
Raw materials	$ 451.0	Merchandise inventories	$5,115
Work in process	100.0		
Finished goods	1,820.6		
Total	$2,371.6		

Income Statement Presentation of Costs

In income statements, the detailed reporting of selling and administrative expenses is typically the same for manufacturing and merchandising organizations, but the cost of goods sold is different.

Manufacturer	**Retailer or Wholesaler**
Manufacturing cost of goods produced and then sold, usually composed of the three major categories of cost: direct material, direct labor, and indirect manufacturing costs.	Merchandise cost of goods sold, usually composed of the purchase cost of items, including freight in, that are acquired and then resold.

Consider the additional details that we present in the model income statement of a manufacturing company in Exhibit 4-4. The $40 million cost of goods manufactured includes subdivisions for direct materials, direct labor, and indirect manufacturing. In contrast, a wholesale or retail company would replace the entire cost-of-goods-manufactured section with a single line, cost of goods purchased.

Accountants and managers often use the terms *costs* and *expenses* loosely. Expenses denote all costs deducted from revenue in a given period. On the other hand, cost is a much broader term that we use to describe both an asset such as the cost of inventory and an expense such as the cost of goods sold. Thus, manufacturing costs become an expense on an income statement via the multistep inventory procedure shown earlier in Exhibit 4-3.

Exhibit 4-4
Model Income
Statement,
Manufacturing
Company

Sales (8,000,000 units @ $10)		$80,000,000
Cost of goods manufactured and sold		
Beginning finished-goods inventory		$ –0–
Cost of goods manufactured		
Direct material used	$20,000,000	
Direct labor	12,000,000	
Indirect manufacturing	8,000,000	40,000,000
Cost of goods available for sale		$40,000,000
Ending finished-goods inventory,		
2,000,000 units @ $4		8,000,000
Cost of goods sold (an expense)		32,000,000
Gross margin or gross profit		$48,000,000
Less: other expenses		
Selling costs (an expense)	$30,000,000	
General and administrative costs		
(an expense)	8,000,000	38,000,000
Operating income*		$10,000,000

*Also net income in this example because other expenses, such as interest and income taxes, are ignored here for simplicity.

In contrast, selling and general administrative costs become expenses immediately as they are incurred in all types of companies.

Now that we understand cost classifications, let's turn our attention to the types of cost accounting systems that accumulate and report costs. There are many different types of cost accounting systems, but we can describe most of the important features of these systems by looking at two general types—traditional and activity-based cost accounting systems.

Traditional and Activity-Based Cost Accounting Systems

OBJECTIVE 5

Understand the main differences between traditional and activity-based costing systems and why ABC systems provide value to managers.

Companies adopt cost accounting systems that are consistent with their management philosophies and production technologies. Changes in philosophies or technologies often prompt corresponding changes in cost accounting systems.

For example, when **Borg-Warner's** Automotive Chain Systems Operation transformed its manufacturing operation to a just-in-time manufacturing system with work cells, it also changed its cost accounting system. This change in the way Borg-Warner operated made the existing cost accounting system obsolete. A new cost accounting system, coupled with the new production systems, "improved the overall reporting, controls, and efficiency dramatically."[1] In recent years, many other companies also recognized the need to improve the accuracy and usefulness of their cost information. The accounting profession responded by developing new types of cost accounting systems that improve the accuracy of costs and thereby enhance the value to managers who use this information for decision-making purposes.

traditional costing systems

One that does not accumulate or report costs of activities or processes.

Until the 1990s, almost all companies used **traditional costing systems**—those that do not accumulate or report costs of activities or processes. Traditional costing systems work well with simple production and operating systems. Consider a company that makes only a few products for which direct-material and direct-labor costs are a very high percentage of total costs. Indirect manufacturing costs are a small percentage of total costs, so the system combines them and allocates them to products using only one cost

[1]Phillips and Don Collins, "How Borg-Warner Made the Transition from Pile Accounting to JIT," *Management Accounting*, October 1990, pp. 32–35.

driver—such as direct-labor hours. Such a company can achieve a high level of accuracy of product costs with a traditional costing system.

As companies grow and their operations become more complex, they often need to refine their traditional costing systems to maintain the accuracy of product or service costs. They often do this by accumulating indirect costs into several **cost pools**—a group of individual costs that a company allocates to activities or cost objectives using a single cost driver. Consider a company that has two operating departments, assembly and finishing. The resources in the assembly department are dominated by large, expensive machines. The finishing department has only a few machines but many laborers. A traditional costing system for this situation might use machine hours as a cost driver for the manufacturing overhead in the assembly department and labor hours as a cost driver for manufacturing overhead in the finishing department.

But what about a more complex situation where a company makes hundreds or thousands of different products and indirect production costs are a large percentage of total costs? What if the many different products consume resources at widely varing rates? Achieving a high level of cost accuracy in such an operating environment requires a more elaborate cost accounting system. A popular elaborate cost accounting system is an **activity-based costing (ABC) system**—a system that first accumulates indirect resource costs for each of the activities of a particular plant, department, value-chain function or organization and then assigns the costs of activities to the products, services, or other cost objects that require that activity. ABC systems provide highly accurate product or customer costs that a company can use for strategic decisions. Further, accumulating and reporting costs by activities helps managers to understand the cause-effect relationships between day-to-day activities and product or customer costs and thereby aids the operational control purpose of cost management systems. Let's take a closer look at how ABC differs from traditional costing.

> **cost pool**
> *A group of individual costs that a company allocates to cost objectives using a single cost driver.*

> **activity-based costing (ABC) systems**
> *A system that first accumulates overhead costs for each of the activities of the area being costed, and then assigns the costs of activities to the products, services, or other cost objects that require that activity.*

Activity-Based Costing and Traditional Costing

One of the most important differences between traditional and ABC systems is the extent of allocation across the value chain. Traditional systems generally allocate only indirect production costs to the products. These are the only costs that can be added to the inventory value of a product for financial reporting purposes, and traditional systems often focus on simply measuring such inventory values. They normally do not allocate the costs of other value-chain functions because these are not appropriate costs to include in inventory. Activity-based costing systems, in contrast, focus on the costs that are important to decision makers. They often expand allocation of costs beyond production to processes such as design, marketing, order processing, and customer service. As a result, ABC systems are more complex but promise more accurate and useful costs to aid decision making. The Business First box on page 142 reports on a recent survey listing reasons why companies use ABC. Let's look at a simple example that demonstrates the main differences between traditional and ABC and the value of ABC to managers.

A Simple Illustration of Traditional and ABC Systems and Activity-Based Management Simple Plastics Company makes just two product lines, plastic casings for pens and plastic casings for cell phones. The company had an operating loss last quarter of $64,500. Management needs to take immediate actions to improve profitability.

You are the vice president of operations. You have to decide which of the two product lines to emphasize in order to improve profitability. You also wish to reduce costs—especially in the production function of the value chain. Simple Plastics currently uses a traditional cost accounting system but you are considering deploying an ABC system to

Why do managers use ABC? The most frequent applications are for product and service costing, process and activity analysis, and performance measurement. These are the primary purposes of strategic decision making and operational control that we discussed at the beginning of this chapter. A recent survey asked companies that use ABC to indicate how many managers routinely used the ABC system. The vast majority, 62%, indicated that from 10 to 24 managers used ABC; 23% of the companies reported that between 25 and 99 managers used ABC information.

BlueCross BlueShield of Florida (BCBSF) is an example of one company that uses ABC. BCBSF's major customers include local groups (persons in companies with headquarters in Florida), direct pay (individuals), national and corporate accounts (persons in companies with headquarters outside Florida), and government programs (persons 65 years or older with Medicare benefits). During the early 1990s, BCBSF faced increased competition for its health care products and services. But its cost management system did not adequately meet the needs of managers.

The primary goal of BCBSF's management was to develop a new cost management system that would help identify opportunities for increased operating control and cost reduction in administrative expenses. Administrative expenses are all the costs of doing business other than claims payments. In 1996, they were $588 million, or 20% of total revenue. The company goal was to reduce administrative costs from 20% of revenue to less than 10%. The cost-management-system technique BCBSF used was an ABC system. This new cost accounting system provided more accurate and timely measurements of

1. customer and product profitability—a strategic purpose,
2. activities that provided the most value to managers and customers—an operational control purpose, and
3. costs of non-value-added activities—an operational control purpose.

Sources: Mohan Nair, "Activity-Based Costing: Who's Using It and Why?" *Management Accounting Quarterly,* Spring 2000, pp. 29–33; K. Thurston, D. Keleman, and J. MacArthur, "Cost for Pricing at BlueCross BlueShield of Florida," *Management Accounting Quarterly,* Spring 2000, pp. 4–13.

support strategic decision making and operational control. Exhibit 4-5 shows the company's traditional cost accounting system in panel A, and the related two financial reports for the most recent quarter in panel B. Notice the three types of costs: direct, indirect, and unallocated, in Simple Plastics' traditional cost accounting system. In the traditional costing system, the portion of total indirect costs ($220,000) allocated to a product depends on the proportion of total direct-labor hours consumed in making the product. Last period, the company used 4,500 and 500 direct-labor hours to make pen casings and cell phone casings, respectively. So it allocated 4,500/5,000 = 90% of the indirect costs to pen casings. The gross profit margin for both product lines, shown at the bottom of panel B, indicates that cell phone casings is the most profitable product line.

As is the case for Simple Plastics, many traditional systems use only one cost driver as a basis for allocating indirect manufacturing costs. When does a traditional costing system provide accurate product costs? When there is a plausible and reliable relationship between the single cost driver and all the indirect resource costs being allocated. In today's complex business environments, this is rare. Let's take a careful look at Simple Plastics' production requirements to see if the traditional cost accounting system is providing the costing accuracy required for strategic decision making and operational control.

Pen casings have a simple design and thus require a simple production process. The company produces them in high volumes, using 90% of its direct-labor time and machine-processing time. Pen casings rarely require special customer support or engineering work. This means that indirect production support costs such as design engineering of the pen casings will be small.

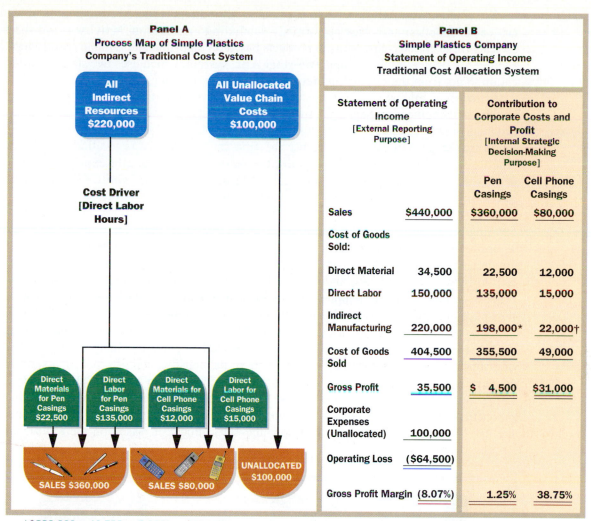

Panel A
Process Map of Simple Plastics Company's Traditional Cost System

All Indirect Resources $220,000

All Unallocated Value Chain Costs $100,000

Cost Driver [Direct Labor Hours]

Direct Materials for Pen Casings $22,500

Direct Labor for Pen Casings $135,000

Direct Materials for Cell Phone Casings $12,000

Direct Labor for Cell Phone Casings $15,000

SALES $360,000

SALES $80,000

UNALLOCATED $100,000

Panel B
Simple Plastics Company Statement of Operating Income Traditional Cost Allocation System

	Statement of Operating Income [External Reporting Purpose]	Contribution to Corporate Costs and Profit [Internal Strategic Decision-Making Purpose]	
		Pen Casings	Cell Phone Casings
Sales	$440,000	$360,000	$80,000
Cost of Goods Sold:			
Direct Material	34,500	22,500	12,000
Direct Labor	150,000	135,000	15,000
Indirect Manufacturing	220,000	198,000*	22,000†
Cost of Goods Sold	404,500	355,500	49,000
Gross Profit	35,500	$ 4,500	$31,000
Corporate Expenses (Unallocated)	100,000		
Operating Loss	($64,500)		
Gross Profit Margin	(8.07%)	1.25%	38.75%

*$220,000 × (4,500 ÷ 5,000) = $198,000
†$220,000 × (500 ÷ 5,000) = $22,000

Exhibit 4-5
Simple Plastics Company's Traditional Costing System and Statement of Operating Income

On the other hand, cell phone casings have a more complex design, and the company produces them in small volumes, accounting for only 10% of its direct labor and machine processing time. Customers who buy cell phone casings have specific design requirements that cause much engineering work. We have learned that most of the engineering work performed at Simple Plastics supports the production of cell phones. So, common sense tells us that we should allocate most of the costs of engineering to the cell phone casings. How significant is the cost of engineering-related work? Of the $220,000 total indirect cost, engineering-related costs are $40,000.

But Simple Plastics uses a traditional cost system. It does not separately identify or report the indirect costs of engineering activity. Instead, the $40,000 of resources used for engineering activity—such as engineer labor and depreciation of computer-aided design (CAD) equipment—is part of the single indirect resource cost pool. It allocates all $40,000 of these indirect costs using the volume-based cost driver of direct-labor time. Thus, it allocates only 10% of the engineering costs to the cell phone casings. This simply does not make sense. We conclude that the traditional system probably does not provide the level of costing accuracy needed. So, how can we improve Simple Plastics' costing accuracy? How can we change the design of the company's cost accounting system to better support strategic decision making and operational control?

two-stage ABC system

A costing system with two stages of allocation to get from the original cost to the final product or service cost. The first stage allocates resource costs to activity-cost pools. The second stage allocates activity costs to products or services.

We could use an ABC system to accumulate all indirect resource costs into the most critical production activities performed—including engineering activity—and then allocate these activity-cost pools to products based on plausible and reliable cost drivers. Exhibit 4-6 depicts a fairly simple **two-stage ABC system,** which uses two stages of allocation to get from the original indirect resource cost to the final product or service cost. The first stage allocates indirect resource costs to two activity-cost pools, processing activity and engineering-support activity. The second stage allocates activity costs to the products or services.

In two-stage ABC systems, we use the first-stage cost drivers to allocate indirect resource costs to activities that require the resources. We usually express the cost drivers as percentages. Consider the indirect resource *engineers and CAD equipment* in Exhibit 4-6. Most of the $40,000 cost of these resources is the salaries of the engineers. Engineers generally spend, on average, about 48 minutes each hour performing production-support activities such as designing casings. They spend the other 12 minutes supervising the processing activity. Thus, we allocate 80% and 20% of engineering salaries to the production support and processing activities, respectively. Similarly, we allocated 75% and 25% of the plant and machinery resource costs to the processing and production-support activities, respectively, based on a measure such as the space occupied by processing and engineering personnel.

Now consider the second-stage allocation. The cost driver for the production-support activity costs might be "number of customer-generated engineering changes" or "number of distinct parts," whichever is a better measure of the consumption of production-support activity. Suppose pen casings have only 5 distinct parts compared to 20 for cell phone casings. Using "number of distinct parts" as the cost driver, we allocate $20 \div (20 + 5) = 80\%$ of the production-support activity costs to cell phone casings. This 80% allocation better measures the use of engineering services than does the 10% allocation based on the traditional

Exhibit 4-6
Simple Plastics Company's ABC System

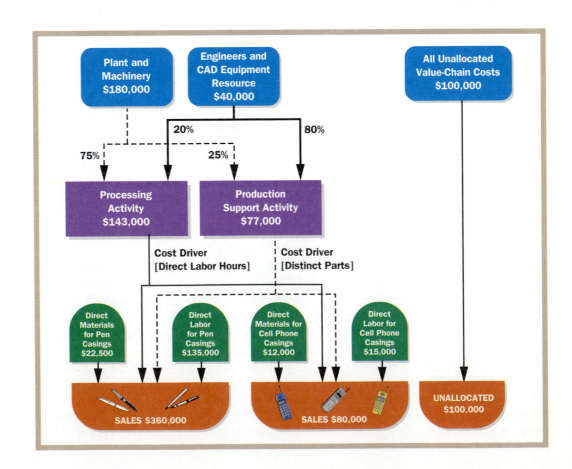

system. Note the two essential improvements of the ABC system that result from measuring costs by activity and using plausible and reliable cost drivers—better costing accuracy and better operational information in the form of activity costs.

MAKING MANAGERIAL DECISIONS

Suppose you have been asked to attend a meeting of top management; when the meeting begins, you are asked to explain in general terms the main differences and similarities in traditional and ABC systems. You have only Exhibits 4-5 and 4-6 as a guide, so you quickly draw these exhibits on a white board and, after taking a deep breath, begin to talk. List as many differences as you can between the two systems, based on Exhibits 4-5 and 4-6.

Answer

1. Traditional costing systems are much simpler than ABC systems and are usually less costly to maintain.
2. Traditional systems and ABC systems both have all three types of costs: direct, indirect, and unallocated.
3. ABC systems unbundle indirect resources into many subgroups, each being assigned to consuming activities.
4. ABC systems assign indirect resource costs to cost objectives in two stages of allocation, whereas traditional systems normally assign indirect resource costs in just one stage.
5. Both traditional and ABC systems use average prices and consumption rates for products lines. Prices and costs within each product line do not vary significantly, so the accuracy of product and customer costs is maintained.
6. ABC systems accumulate and report activity costs in several activity-cost pools.
7. ABC systems require many more cost drivers than do traditional systems. When these cost drivers are both plausible and reliable, the overall accuracy of product, service, or customer cost is improved. Further, more operational information is provided, which can be used to improve operational control.

We now are in a position to complete our ABC analysis and answer our strategic issue regarding our product mix strategy. We do this in the following Summary Problem for Your Review. It is important for you to carefully work this problem to gain a clear understanding of the basic concepts and value of an ABC system.

Summary Problem For Your Review

PROBLEM

Refer to the Simple Plastics illustration, especially the financial reports based on the traditional cost accounting system in panel B of Exhibit 4-5. Based on these reports, the marketing department manager has proposed a plan that emphasizes cell phone casings due to their large gross profit margin (38.75%) compared to that of pen casings (1.25%).

Now management implements the ABC system shown in Exhibit 4-6. The first stage of the two-stage ABC system has been completed and the results are the activity-cost-pool figures given in Exhibit 4-6—processing activity costs of $143,000 and production-support activity costs of $77,000. You need to perform the second-stage allocations to determine the profitability of each product line. The cost driver for processing activity is direct-labor hours and the cost driver for production support activity is distinct parts. Data on the use of these cost drivers for the last quarter is:

	Pen Casings	Cell Phone Casings
Direct labor hours	4,500	500
Distinct parts	5	20

Calculate the gross profit margin for both products based on ABC. Do your results differ significantly from those based on the traditional cost accounting system? Explain. Evaluate marketing's plan. Propose a product-mix strategy for the company.

SOLUTION

The table below shows the gross profit for each product using ABC costs.

Financial Reports for Simple Plastics Company
Activity-Based Cost Allocation System

	Panel A Statement of Operating Income [External Reporting Purpose]	Panel B Contribution to Corporate Costs and Profit [Internal Strategic Decision-Making and Operational-Control Purposes]	
		Pen Casings	Cell Phone Casings
Sales	$440,000	$360,000	$ 80,000
Cost of goods sold:			
Direct material	34,500	22,500	12,000
Direct labor	150,000	135,000	15,000
Processing activity	143,000	128,700*	14,300
Production support activity	77,000	15,400†	61,600
Cost of goods sold	404,500	301,600	102,900
Gross profit	35,500	$ 58,400	$ (22,900)
Corporate expenses			
(Unallocated):	100,000		
Operating loss	$ (64,500)		
Gross profit margin	8.07%	16.22%	(28.63%)

* The cost driver is direct-labor hours. The company used 4,500/(4,500 + 500) = 90% of direct-labor hours to produce pen casings. Thus, the allocation is $143,000 × .90 = $128,700.
† The cost driver is distinct parts. The company used 5/(20 + 5) = 20% of distinct parts to make pen casings. Thus, the allocation is $77,000 × .20 = $15,400.

The ABC system yields results that are dramatically different from those of the traditional cost allocation system. Pen casings are generating substantial profits for the company, while cell phone casings are losing money. Why is there such a dramatic difference between the two cost accounting systems? Because of differences in the production process for each of the two products. Only the cell phone casings require large amounts of the production-support activity. The ABC system correctly allocates most of this cost to the cell phone casings, while the traditional system allocates most of it to the pen casings. The ABC system first separates the processing-related costs from the production-support costs. Then it allocates each activity cost to the products based on the proportion of the activity used by each product.

Marketing's plan most likely will result in significantly lower profitability, assuming that the ABC results are accurate. The company's top management should probably make the strategic decision to emphasize the pen casings product line due to its large gross profit margin. The cell phone casing line is losing money and needs to be carefully evaluated. Possible actions include raising prices, changing the design by reducing the number of distinct parts, working with suppliers to reduce the cost of direct materials, and improving the efficiency of direct labor.

Let's take a closer look at how ABC can add value to a manager's decision-making responsibility.

Activity-Based Management: A Cost Management System Tool

ABC systems not only develop more accurate costs, they also aid control of costs. Recall that managers' day-to-day focus is on managing activities, not costs. So, because ABC systems also focus on activities, they are a very useful tool in cost management systems. **Activity-based management (ABM)** is using the output of an activity-based cost accounting system to aid strategic decision making and to improve operational control of an organization. The strategic decision to emphasize the pen casing products at Simple Plastics is an example of ABM. In the broadest terms, activity-based management aims to improve the value received by customers and to improve profits by identifying opportunities for improvements in strategy and operations.

One of the most useful applications of ABM is distinguishing between value-added costs and non-value-added costs. A **value-added cost** is the cost of an activity that a company cannot eliminate without affecting a product's value to the customer. Value-added costs are necessary (as long as the activity that drives such costs is performed efficiently). In contrast, companies try to minimize **non-value-added costs,** costs that a company can eliminate without affecting a product's value to the customer. Activities such as handling and storing inventories, transporting partly finished products from one part of the plant to another, and changing the setup of production-line operations to produce a different model of the product are all non-value-adding activities. A company can reduce, if not eliminate, them by careful redesign of the plant layout and the production process.

Another ABC-related technique that has gained popularity is **benchmarking,** the continuous process of comparing products, services, and activities to the best industry standards. Benchmarking is a tool to help an organization measure its competitive posture. Benchmarks can come from within the organization, from competing organizations, or from other organizations having similar processes.

Consider the billing center at AT&T's Business Communication Services unit (BCS) discussed in the chapter opening vignette. Unit costs for key activities provided the basis for benchmarking the work groups within the billing center as well as between different billing centers in the AT&T system. AT&T used the cost drivers for key activities—for example, the time to process a work order—as operational benchmarks. The most efficient work groups and centers shared their ideas for process improvements with other groups and centers.

Companies must exercise caution when benchmarking, especially when using financial benchmarks. Consider a California bank with branches located in Chico and several in San Francisco. The bank's benchmarking system uses the financial measure cost per deposit as a benchmark for the deposit-processing efficiency. The benchmark has been consistently set by a small branch located in Chico, a small city in the north central part of the state.

Tellers at the Chico branch use the same processing equipment as other branches. However, unlike the San Francisco branches, Chico's ABC system does not allocate the costs of the equipment to the deposit-processing activity; these costs are unallocated. The most costly resource used (and captured in Chico's ABC system) is teller labor.

The San Francisco branches cannot come close to matching this benchmark. Why? There can be numerous reasons but we point out two that are fairly common. The most obvious reason is the difference in the salaries of tellers. Tellers in metropolitan areas are paid much higher wages because of the higher cost of living. The higher costs are reflected in the numerator of the benchmark measure.

activity-based management (ABM)
Using an activity-based costing system to improve the operations of an organization.

value-added cost
The necessary cost of an activity that cannot be eliminated without affecting a product's value to the customer.

non-value-added costs
Costs that a company can eliminate without affecting a product's value to the customer.

benchmarking
The continuous process of comparing products, services, and activities against the best industry standards.

A second reason is the difference in the scope of the ABC system. The costs of processing equipment at the San Francisco branches is captured by their ABC systems and allocated to the processing activity. This will cause the numerator of the benchmark measure to be higher at the San Francisco branches.

As a result, even if the tellers process deposits faster and more accurately at the San Francisco branches, their performance will not appear to be as good as the tellers at the Chico branch. Perhaps a better measure of the deposit process would be the time to process a deposit, a strictly non-financial benchmark.

Benefits of Activity-Based Costing and Activity-Based Management

Activity-based costing systems are more complex and costly than traditional systems. So companies that have relatively simple operating systems may not realize sufficient benefits and thus may not want to use ABC systems. But more and more organizations in both manufacturing and nonmanufacturing industries are adopting activity-based costing systems for a variety of reasons:

- Fierce competitive pressure has resulted in shrinking profit margins. Companies may know their overall margin, but they often do not have confidence in the accuracy of the margins for individual products or services. Some are winners and some are losers—but which ones? Accurate costs are essential for answering this question. Consider **Taylor Corporation**, one of the largest specialty printers in the United States with annual sales of more than $1.3 billion. Its products include wedding invitations, company stationery, Post-it Notes, greeting cards, and calendars. One of its operating divisions implemented an ABC system to provide better information on the profitability of more than 3,500 products. Managers used the ABC information to set an optimal product mix and to estimate the profit margins of new products.
- Greater diversity in the types of products and services as well as customer classes results in greater business operating complexity. Therefore, the consumption of a company's shared resources also varies substantially across products and customers.
- New production techniques have increased the proportion of indirect costs. That is, indirect costs are far more important in today's world-class manufacturing environment than they have been in the past. In many industries automated equipment is replacing direct labor. Indirect costs are sometimes more than 50% of total cost.
- The rapid pace of technological change has shortened product life cycles. Hence, companies do not have time to make price or cost adjustments once they discover costing errors.
- The costs associated with bad decisions that result from inaccurate cost determinations are substantial. Examples include bids lost due to overcosted products, hidden losses from undercosted products, and failure to detect activities that are not cost effective. Companies with accurate costs have a huge advantage over those with inaccurate costs.
- Computer technology has reduced the costs of developing and operating ABC systems.

Detailed Illustration of Traditional and Activity-Based Cost Accounting Systems[2]

As we have mentioned, ABC systems are much more complex than traditional systems. In this section, we go a bit further in depth than the Simple Plastics Company example. You will notice however, that the main concepts are exactly the same—only the details will change.

Suppose the billing department of one of AT&T's smaller customer care centers requires accurate and useful information about the cost of providing account inquiry

---

[2]If your goal is simply a general understanding of ABC systems and ABM without the details about how a company might design and implement and use such a system, you can skip the rest of this chapter.

and bill printing services for its 120,000 residential and 20,000 commercial customer accounts. A local service bureau has offered to provide all the functions currently performed by the billing department at $4.30 per residential account and $8.00 per commercial account. To make informed decisions, AT&T's managers need accurate estimates of the department's own cost per residential account and cost per commercial account. They also need to know the costs of the key activities performed in the department to determine whether they can achieve cost savings through better control of their activities.

Exhibit 4-7 depicts the residential and commercial customer classes (cost objects) and the resources used to support the billing department. All the costs incurred in the billing department are indirect. There are no direct costs or unallocated costs. The billing department uses a traditional costing system that allocates all indirect production costs based on the number of account inquiries.

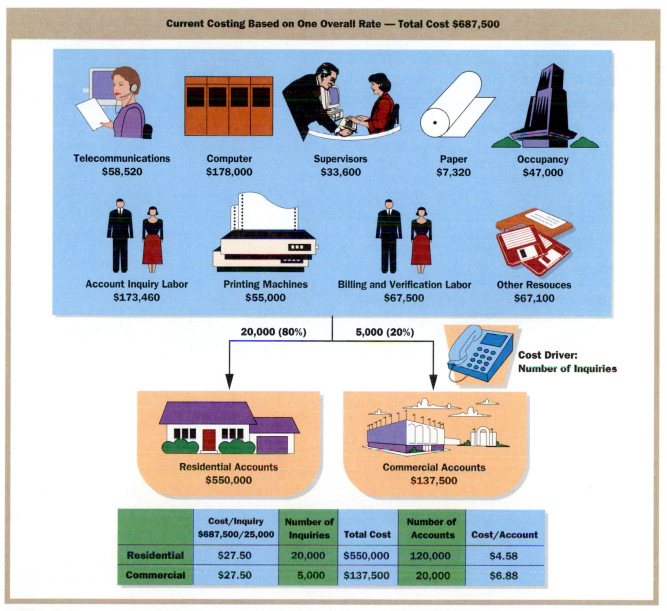

	Cost/Inquiry $687,500/25,000	Number of Inquiries	Total Cost	Number of Accounts	Cost/Account
Residential	$27.50	20,000	$550,000	120,000	$4.58
Commercial	$27.50	5,000	$137,500	20,000	$6.88

Exhibit 4-7
Traditional Costing System at the Billing Department

Exhibit 4-7 shows that the resources used in the billing department last month cost $687,500. The cost accounting system is very simple. It adds together all indirect costs and then allocates them based on the number of inquiries the department receives from each customer class. The billing department received 25,000 account inquiries during the month, so the cost per inquiry was $687,500 ÷ 25,000 = $27.50. There were 20,000 residential account inquiries, 80% of the total. Thus, we assign 80% of the indirect production cost to residential accounts and 20% to commercial accounts. The resulting cost per account is ($687,500 × .8) ÷ 120,000 = $4.58 and ($687,500 × .2) ÷ 20,000 = $6.88 for residential and commercial accounts, respectively. Does this traditional cost accounting system provide managers with accurate estimates of the cost to serve residential and commercial customers? If the answer is yes, the billing department management would accept the service bureau's proposal to service residential accounts because of the apparent savings of $4.58 − $4.30 = $.28 per account. The billing department would continue to service its commercial accounts because its costs are $8.00 − $6.88 = $1.12 less than the service bureau's bid.

MAKING MANAGERIAL DECISIONS

Suppose AT&T's management believes that a more plausible and reliable cost driver is "number of printed lines." Each residential bill averages 12 lines and each commercial bill averages 50 lines. What would be the new cost per account for residential and commercial customers based on number of lines per bill? How would this new cost accounting information affect the outsourcing decision?

Answer

The total costs would be the same, but the allocation of the total cost to each customer class would change. Instead of allocating 80% of total costs to residential customers, we would allocate only (12 × 120,000) ÷ (12 × 120,000 + 50 × 20,000) = 59% of total costs to residential customers and the other 41% to commercial accounts. The cost per account for residential customers would then be (59% × $687,500) ÷ 120,000 = $3.38, and the cost per commercial account would be (41% × $687,500) ÷ 20,000 = $14.09. The outsourcing decision would likely change. We would outsource commercial accounts but not residential accounts. A key issue is how much confidence management has in the costs it uses for decision making. Poor cost data can lead to poor decisions.

Now suppose you are the billing department manager and you know that billing laborers spend much of their time verifying the accuracy of commercial bills and no time verifying residential bills. Yet the traditional cost accounting system allocates 80% of the costs of this work to residential customers. Does this make any sense to you? Do you have some doubt about the accuracy of the cost-per-account data? You also know that commercial accounts average 50 lines or two pages per bill, compared with only 12 lines or one page for residential accounts. This means that the billing department uses much more paper, computer time, and printing machine time for each commercial account. Again, this does not agree with the percentage of allocations based on number of inquiries. In addition, you believe that the actual consumption of support resources for commercial accounts is much greater than 20% because of their complexity.

As the billing department manager, you are also concerned about activities such as verification of commercial bills, inquiries from customers, and correspondence resulting from customer inquiries. These activities consume costly resources but do not add value to AT&T's services from the customer's perspective. To reduce these costs, management needs a more thorough understanding of key activities and their relationships to resource costs.

In summary, you would probably conclude that the billing department's traditional cost accounting system needs to be improved because it is not providing managers with useful information for strategic decisions or operational control. This is exactly what AT&T concluded. So, let's see how management might design an activity-based costing system for the billing department.

Design of an Activity-Based Cost Accounting System

How do managers actually design ABC systems? The Business First box on page 152 describes the ABC system of **Reichhold, Inc.,** a leading global manufacturer of polyester and performance resins. At the billing department of AT&T's customer-care center, a team of managers from the billing department and AT&T's regional controller used the following four-step procedure to design their new cost accounting system.

OBJECTIVE 6

Design a cost accounting system that includes activity-based costing.

Step 1: Determine the Key Components of the Activity-Based Cost Accounting System

The key components of an activity-based cost accounting system are cost objectives, key activities, resources, and related cost drivers. These components, together with the purpose of the new system, determine the scope of the ABC system. Management at AT&T wanted the system to (1) determine the billing department cost per account for each customer class in order to support the strategic decision regarding outsourcing accounts to the local service bureau, and (2) enhance the managers' understanding of key billing department activities to support operational cost control. Because the bid from the local service bureau includes performing all the activities of the department, the ABC system must include all department costs. Further, because management wants to understand the key activities and related costs, the team designed an activity-based system.

They identified the following activities and related cost drivers for the billing department through interviews with the department supervisors.

Activity	Cost Driver
Account billing	Number of printed pages
Bill verification	Number of accounts verified
Account inquiry	Number of inquiries
Correspondence	Number of letters
Other activities	Number of printed pages

The four key billing department activities are account billing, bill verification, account inquiry, and correspondence. These activities require the vast majority of the work done in the billing department. There are other activities performed in the billing department, such as routine printer and computer maintenance, training, and preparing monthly reports. These were not identified as individual activities. Instead, the team lumped them together and labeled them "other activities." Why? Because the cost of the resources used for each of these individual activities was relatively small, the team could not find plausible and reliable cost drivers for them, or the cost of collecting data was too high. The cost driver selected for the "other activities" cost pool is number of printed pages, because most of the other activities, such as maintenance and training, are associated with the printing function. Exhibit 4-7 shows the resources used by the billing department.

REICHHOLD DESIGNS COST ACCOUNTING SYSTEM TO MEET ITS COST MANAGEMENT OBJECTIVES

Reichhold, Inc., is a leading global supplier of polyester and performance resins used in products such as boats, bowling balls, paints, and car coatings. The company has manufacturing facilities in 11 countries in the Americas and Europe and employs 2,500 workers. Reichhold recently made a major change in its organizational structure moving from a product-line focused, divisional structure to a team-based structure. At the same time, it changed its marketing strategy to emphasize specialty products with high gross margins. With a new organizational structure and new product family, management needed more accurate cost information to determine the most profitable product mix and to control production costs. Reichhold's management chose an activity-based cost accounting system. The figure below compares the traditional and activity-based cost accounting systems.

For example, two products consumed the same number of reactor hours and so received the same allocation of indirect costs. But managers knew that one of these products consumed much more time in the thin-tank and filtration processes and had much higher waste disposal costs. The new allocation system, as shown below, captures such differences in the rate of consumption of resources. The company's activity-based costing system has just five major activities or processes, but the information provided for cost control was much more useful. With the new ABC system, the cost of the product that consumed more time in the thin-tank and filtrations processes increased from $13 per unit to $18 per unit, reflecting its consumption of costly resources. This new ABC information supported improvements in cost control. Reichhold now produces items with high waste disposal costs in larger batches by combining orders. Overall, the new ABC system improved

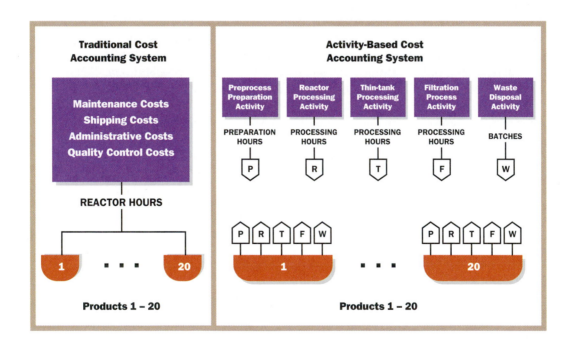

The company had used a traditional cost accounting system where it allocated all indirect production costs to its products based on one cost driver, "number of reactor hours." Company managers believed the traditional system was not providing accurate product costs for strategic or operational control purposes.

capacity management, analysis of product profitability, and strategic pricing decisions.

Source: Adapted from E. Blocher, B. Wong, and C. McKittrick, "Making Bottom-Up ABC Work at Reichhold, Inc.," *Strategic Finance*, April 2002, pp. 51–55.

MAKING MANAGERIAL DECISIONS

Billing department managers debated whether they should allocate the "other activities" cost pool to the two customer classes or leave it unallocated. Although the plausibility and reliability of the cost driver—number of printed pages—was not as high as normally desired, management accepted it because they wanted to allocate all costs to the two customer classes in order to compare full unit costs to the costs bid by the local service bureau. What would be the impact on the costs per account if the billing department did not allocate the "other activities" cost pool?

Answer

The costs per account would be less if the billing department did not allocate the other activities cost pool. This may lead to a bad decision by management to reject the service bureau's offer. The unallocated costs will not go away simply because management does not allocate them to customer classes. This is a common managerial issue—the trade-off between the need for comparability of cost data and the need for plausible and reliable cost drivers used to generate the cost data.

Step 2: Determine the Relationships Among Cost Objectives, Activities, and Resources An important phase of any activity-based analysis is identifying the relationships among key activities and the resources consumed. The management team does this by interviewing personnel and analyzing various internal data. AT&T interviewed all employees as part of its ABC study. For example, they asked supervisors how they spent their time. Based on time records, the supervisors estimated that they spend most of their time (40%) supervising account inquiry activity. They also estimated that they spend about 30% of their time supervising billing activity and about 10% of their time reviewing and signing correspondence. They spend the remaining 20% of their time on all other department activities. Exhibit 4-8 shows the results of the interviews.

Implementing an ABC system requires a careful study of operations. As a result, managers often discover that they can trace directly to cost objectives some previously indirect or even unallocated costs, thus improving the accuracy of product or service

Exhibit 4-8
Analysis of Interviews with Supervisors from the Billing Department

Resource Used to Perform Activity	Account Inquiry Activity	Correspondence Activity	Billing Activity	Verification Activity	All Other Activities	Total
Supervisor	40%	10%	30%		20%	100%
Account inquiry labor	90	10				100%
Billing labor			30	70		100%
Verification labor				100		100%
Paper			100			100%
Computer	45	5	35	10	5	100%
Telecommunications	90				10	100%
Occupancy	65		15		20	100%
Printing machines		5	90		5	100%
All other department resources					100	100%

costs. During interviews with the billing department supervisors, the ABC team learned that several of the billing laborers work exclusively on verification of commercial bills. Thus, the team could trace their salaries—$11,250—directly to the verification activity. Further, because the billing department performs verification activity only for commercial accounts, they could also trace this cost pool directly to the commercial customer cost objective.

Look at the computer resource row in Exhibit 4-8. The supervisor indicated that 45% of this resource supports account inquiry, 5% supports correspondence, and so on. How did the supervisor determine these percentages? Initially, he might simply estimate them. Later, he might gather data to support his estimates. Now consider the occupancy resource row. The percentages used to allocate this resource might be based on the square feet used by the various laborers for each activity compared to the total square feet in the department.

Next, the team determined which activities were needed by each cost object. The supervisors indicated that residential customers needed account inquiry, correspondence, and billing activities. Commercial customers needed account inquiry, correspondence, billing, and verification activities.

process map

A schematic diagram capturing interrelationships between cost objects, activities, and resources.

Many ABC teams find it useful to develop a **process map**—a schematic diagram with symbols that captures the interrelationships between cost objects, activities, and resources. These maps can be an efficient method to enhance managers' understanding of operations. Let's see how process maps are drawn.

Exhibit 4-9 contains three examples to show the basic concepts for drawing process maps. When the cost objective is the product, service, or customer of the company, we will use the ⬤ symbol, and when it is an activity we use a ⬛.

We assume that there is no way to physically trace the costs of resource A to activities 1 and 2, so we must use a cost driver to allocate the costs, making them indirect costs.

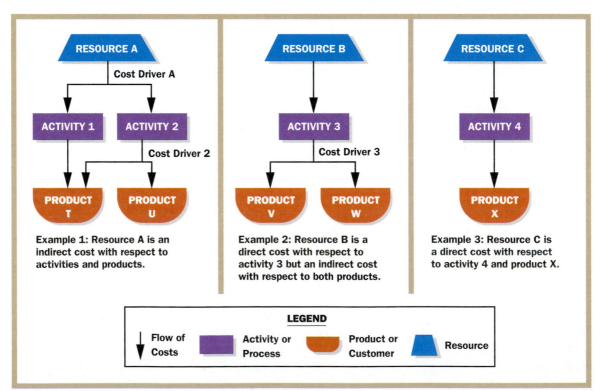

Exhibit 4-9
Basic Concepts for Process Maps

Similarly, we must use cost drivers for the allocation of the costs of activities 2 and 3 to the products. In contrast, any resource cost that is used by only one activity (as for resources B and C) is direct with respect the activity, as is any activity cost that is required by only one product (as for activities 1 and 4). There is no ambiguity about which cost objective is responsible for these direct costs.

In Exhibit 4-9, the costs of resource A are indirect costs to activities 1 and 2, and to products T and U. We will use cost driver A to allocate the cost of resource A to activity cost pools 1 and 2 and cost driver 2 to allocate activity cost pool 2 to products T and U. The cost of resource B is direct with respect to activity 3 but indirect with respect to products V and W. Thus, we use cost driver 3 to allocate the costs of activity 3 to products V and W. The costs of resource C are direct with respect to both activity 4 and product X; no allocation is necessary.

MAKING MANAGERIAL DECISIONS

From Exhibit 4-8, suggest output measures that the billing department might use to determine the percentage of the telecommunications, printing machines, and paper resource costs to allocate to the indicated activities. Which of these costs is a direct cost with respect to the related activity but an indirect cost with respect to the customer cost objectives?

Answer

There are several reasonable output measures for each resource. Accountants often use minutes or hours to allocate telecommunication costs. They can use machine time, lines printed, or pages printed to allocate printing machine costs. Paper is a direct cost to the printing activity, so an output measure is not necessary. Note that the paper resource is an indirect cost with respect to the final cost objecive—customers. It will be part of the printing activity cost pool to be allocated based on pages printed.

A process map depicts in a concise manner the same information that was gathered from interviews. Exhibit 4-10 shows the process map for the billing department. We allocate the costs of the ten resources to the five activities. For example, account inquiry activity consumes 65% of occupancy costs, 90% of telecommunication resources, 45% of computer resources, 40% of supervisor resources, and 90% of account inquiry resources. Then we allocate the costs of the five activities to the two customer cost objectives—residential and commercial. For example, commercial accounts require inquiry, correspondence, billing, verification, and other activities. We allocate the activity costs based on a measure of the amount of activitiy that each customer uses. For example, we allocate the account inquiry activity cost pool based on the number of inquiries received from residential and commerical accounts.

Process maps can be a key tool for managers to gain an understanding of operations. For example, AT&T's managers "considered this document (process map) critical because it revealed how AT&T conducted business. Managers also were able to see how cost flows are a function of operations and how they consume costly resources."[3] Normally, we do

---

[3] T. Hobdy, J. Thomson, and P. Sharman, "Activity-Based Management at AT&T," *Management Accounting*, April 1994, pp. 35–39.

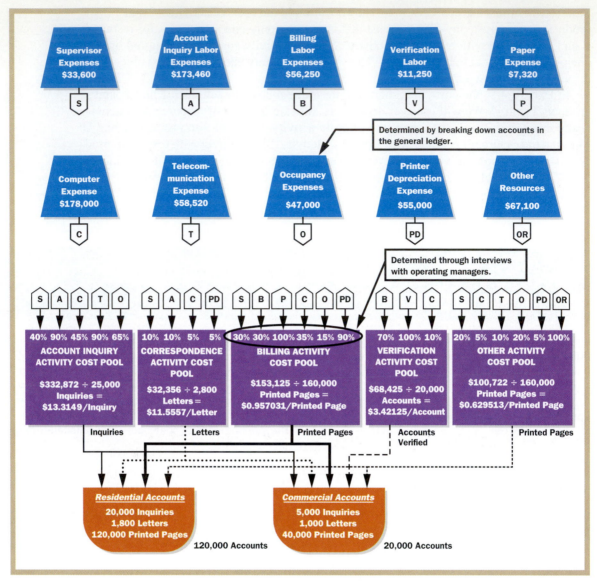

Exhibit 4-10
Two-Stage Cost Allocation for Billing Department Operations

not collect the cost data and the cost driver data shown in Exhibit 4-10 until we have drawn the process map and identified the resources and cost drivers. The ABC team usually uses the process map as a guide for the next step in designing the ABC system—data collection.

Step 3: Collect Relevant Data Concerning Costs and the Physical Flow of the Cost-Driver Units Among Resources and Activities

Using the process map as a guide, billing department managers collected the required cost and operational data by further interviews with relevant personnel. Sources of data include the accounting records, special studies, and sometimes "best estimates of managers." They collected resource cost information from the general ledger (Exhibit 4-7) and data on the flow of cost drivers from various operational reports (Exhibits 4-8 and 4-11). Exhibit 4-10 shows the data collected.

Exhibit 4-11
Number of Cost
Driver Units for the
Billing Department

Activity	Cost Driver Units	Number of Cost Driver Units		
		Residential	**Commercial**	**Total**
Account inquiry	Inquiries	20,000	5,000	25,000
Correspondence	Letters	1,800	1,000	2,800
Bill printing	Printed pages	120,000	40,000	160,000
Verification	Accounts verified		20,000	20,000
Other activities	Printed pages	120,000	40,000	160,000

Management can now use the completed process map to determine costs for the strategic and operational decisions that they must make.

Step 4: Calculate and Interpret the New Activity-Based Cost Information

After collecting all required financial and operational data, we can calculate the new activity-based information. Exhibit 4-12 summarizes stage 1 allocations. It shows the total traceable costs for the five activity cost pools. Notice that the total traceable costs of $332,872 + $32,356 + $153,125 + $68,425 + $100,722 = $687,500 in Exhibit 4-12 equals the total indirect costs in Exhibit 4-7.

Now we can determine the activity-based cost per account for each customer class, (stage 2 allocations), from the data in step 3. Exhibit 4-13 shows the computations.

Examine the last two rows in Exhibit 4-13. Notice that traditional costing overcosted the high-volume residential accounts and substantially undercosted the low-volume, complex commercial accounts. The cost per account for residential accounts using ABC is $3.98, which is $0.60 (or 13%) less than the $4.58 cost generated by the traditional costing system. The cost per account for commercial accounts is $10.50, which is $3.62 (or 53%) more than the $6.88 cost from the traditional costing system. The analysis confirms management's belief that the traditional system undercosted commercial accounts. AT&T's management now has more accurate cost information for strategic

Resource	Cost (from Exhibit 4-7)	Activity Cost Pool				
		Account Inquiry	**Correspondence**	**Billing**	**Verification**	**Other**
Supervisors	$ 33,600	$ 13,440*	$ 3,360**	$ 10,080***		$ 6,720****
Account inquiry labor	173,460	156,114	17,346			
Billing labor	56,250			16,875	$39,375	
Verification labor	11,250				11,250	
Paper	7,320			7,320		
Computer	178,000	80,100	8,900	62,300	17,800	8,900
Telecommunication	58,520	52,668				5,852
Occupancy	47,000	30,550		7,050		9,400
Printers	55,000		2,750	49,500		2,750
Other resources	67,100					67,100
Total traceable cost	$687,500	$332,872	$32,356	$153,125	$68,425	$100,722

* From Exhibits 4-8 and 4-10, account inquiry activity uses 40% of the supervisor resource. So the allocation is 40% × $33,600 = $13,440.
** 10% × $33,600
*** 30% × $33,600
**** 20% × $33,600

Exhibit 4-12
Total Traceable Cost of Activities in the Billing Department

	Driver Costs		
Activity (Driver Units)	Traceable Costs (from Exhibit 4-12) (1)	Total Number of Driver Units (from Exhibit 4-11) (2)	Cost per Driver Unit (1) ÷ (2)
Account inquiry (inquiries)	$332,872	25,000 Inquiries	$13.314880
Correspondence (letters)	$ 32,356	2,800 Letters	$11.555714
Account billing (printed pages)	$153,125	160,000 Printed pages	$ 0.957031
Bill verification (accounts verified)	$ 68,425	20,000 Accounts verified	$ 3.421250
Other activities (printed pages)	$100,722	160,000 Printed pages	$ 0.629513

	Cost per Customer Class				
		Residential		Commercial	
	Cost per Driver Unit	Number of Driver Units	Cost	Number of Driver Units	Cost
Account inquiry	$13.314880	20,000 Inquiries	$266,298	5,000 Inquiries	$ 66,574
Correspondence	$11.555714	1,800 Letters	20,800	1,000 Letters	11,556
Account billing	$ 0.957031	120,000 Pages	114,844	40,000 Pages	38,281
Bill verification	$ 3.421250			20,000 Accts.	68,425
Other activities	$ 0.629513	120,000 Pages	75,541	40,000 Pages	25,181
Total cost			$477,483		$210,017
Number of accounts			120,000		20,000
Cost per account			$ 3.98		$ 10.50
Cost per account, traditional system from Exhibit 4-7			$ 4.58		$ 6.88

Exhibit 4-13
Key Results of Activity-Based Costing Study

decision-making and cost control purposes. Results like these are common when companies perform activity-based costing studies. Traditional systems generally overcost high-volume cost objects with simple processes. Which system makes more sense—the traditional allocation system that "spreads" all support costs to customer classes based solely on the number of inquiries, or the activity-based costing system that identifies key activities and assigns costs based on the consumption of units of cost drivers for each key activity? For AT&T, the probable benefits of the new ABC system appear to outweigh the costs of implementing and maintaining the new cost system.

Strategic Decisions, Operational Cost Control, and ABM

OBJECTIVE 7

Use activity-based cost information to make strategic and operational control decisions.

Now let's see how billing department managers can use the ABC system to improve their strategic decisions and operational cost control. Suppose that the billing department needed to find a way to increase its capacity to handle more accounts due to an expected large increase in demand from a new housing development and a business center. Managers proposed a strategic action—outsource certain customer accounts to a local service bureau. Billing department managers were also interested in reducing the operating costs of the department while not impairing the quality of the service it provided to its customers. To address both of these issues, they used the ABC information from Exhibit 4-13 to identify non-value-added activities that had significant costs. Account inquiry and bill verification activities are non-value-added and costly, so management asked for ideas for cost reductions. The new information provided by the ABC system generated the following ideas.

- Use the service bureau for commercial accounts because of the significant cost savings. From Exhibit 4-13, the service bureau's bid is $8.00 per account, compared to the billing department's activity-based cost of $10.50, a potential savings of $2.50 per account! In addition, department managers would try to eliminate or reduce bill verification, commercial account inquiry, and commercial account correspondence activities, all non-value-adding activities.

Suppose AT&T outsourced commercial customers to the service bureau. Would actual costs immediately decrease by $50,000 ($2.50 for each of 20,000 commercial accounts)? No. Only the variable portion of resource costs such as paper, variable telecommunication charges, variable computer charges, and overtime or part time labor would decrease immediately. The fixed cost portion of all these resources would not change without some specific management actions. For example, suppose billing labor used for verification is a fixed-cost resource. Then the time formerly required for verification is idle time but the company must still pay wages. Management would have to decide whether to lay off billing labor or to keep them in anticipation of the increase in printing activity due to the expected increase in residential customers.

- Exhibit 4-13 indicates that account inquiry activity is very costly, accounting for a significant portion of total billing department costs. A benchmarking analysis showed the cost per inquiry of $13.31 was unusually high compared to similar measures at other customer care centers. The billing department managers developed ideas for process improvements at meetings with the managers from centers that had significantly lower activity cost rates. One idea that resulted from these meetings was to implement a Web-based inquiry system to handle routine questions about bills.

The billing department, like so many companies that have adopted ABM and ABC, improved both strategic and operational decisions.

Summary Problem For Your Review

PROBLEM

Refer to the billing department illustration. Suppose that management at AT&T's Youngstown area customer care center is implementing an ABC system. The center has 98,000 residential customers and 25,000 commercial customers. An ABC team has collected the data shown in Exhibit 4-14. Management has decided not to allocate the other resource costs.

1. Using the same format as Exhibits 4-12 and 4-13, prepare schedules to determine the cost per driver unit for each activity and the activity-based cost per account for each customer type.
2. Consider the verification activity. Suppose the cost per account verified is $0.45. The center verifies 50% of residential and commercial bills. Given that there are, on average, 50 lines on each commercial bill and only 12 lines on each residential bill, criticize the use of accounts verified as a cost driver and suggest a more plausible and reliable cost driver.

SOLUTION

1. Following the format of Exhibit 4-12 we prepare a schedule to determine the traceable cost of the activities of the billing department. This is shown in Exhibit 4-15.

    Now, we can determine the cost per driver unit and the activity-based cost per account for each customer class from the data in Exhibit 4-15, as shown in Exhibit 4-16.
2. The ABC system allocates $49,000 \div (49,000 + 12,500) = 79.7\%$ of verification costs to residential accounts based on the number of accounts verfied. However, the

Resource	Monthly Cost	Percent of Resource Used in Activity				
		Billing	Account Inquiry	Correspondence	Verification	Other
Supervisors	$ 30,500	40%	35%	8%		17%
Account inquiry labor	102,000		85	15		
Billing labor	45,000	70			30	
Paper	5,800	100				
Computers	143,000	30	48	7	10	5
Telecommunications	49,620		85			15
Occupancy	56,000	15	70			15
Printers	75,000	80		5		15
Other	59,000					100
Total	$565,920					

Activity	Cost Driver	Monthly Number of Cost Driver Units		
		Residential	Commercial	Total
Printing	Lines	1,176,000	1,250,000	2,426,000
Account inquiry	Inquiries	9,800	7,500	17,300
Correspondence	Letters	1,960	2,500	4,460
Verification	Accounts	49,000	12,500	61,500

Exhibit 4-14
First Stage Percentage Allocations and Monthly Number of Cost Driver Units

work performed to verify a bill is probably closely related to the number of lines on the bill. Using accounts verified assumes that employees expend the same amount of effort verifying residential accounts and commercial accounts, even though there are many fewer lines on residential bills. Thus, the cost driver "lines verified" is more plausible and reliable. The number of lines verified for commercial accounts

Resource	Cost (from Exhibit 4-14)	Activity				
		Billing	Account Inquiry	Correspondence	Verification	Other
Supervisors	$ 30,500	$ 12,200*	$ 10,675**	$ 2,440***		$ 5,185****
Account inquiry labor	102,000		$ 86,700	15,300		
Billing labor	45,000	31,500			$13,500	
Paper	5,800	5,800				
Computer	143,000	42,900	68,640	10,010	14,300	7,150
Telecommunication	49,620		42,177			7,443
Occupancy	56,000	8,400	39,200			8,400
Printers	75,000	60,000		3,750		11,250
Other resources	59,000					59,000
Total traceable cost	$565,920	$160,800	$247,392	$31,500	$27,800	$98,428

  * 40% × $30,500
 ** 35% × $30,500
*** 8% × $30,500
**** 17% × $30,500

Exhibit 4-15
Total Traceable Cost of Activities in the Billing Department

Driver Costs

Activity (Driver Units)	Traceable Costs (From Exhibit 4-15) (1)	Total Number of Driver Units (From Exhibit 4-14) (2)	Cost per Driver Unit (1) ÷ (2)
Account inquiry (inquiries)	$247,392	17,300 Inquiries	$14.300116
Correspondence (letters)	$ 31,500	4,460 Letters	$ 7.062780
Account billing (lines)	$160,800	2,426,000 Lines	$ 0.066282
Bill verification (accounts verified)	$ 27,800	61,500 Accounts Verified	$ 0.452033

Cost per Customer Class

| | Cost per Driver Unit | Residential | | Commercial | |
		Number of Driver Units	Cost	Number of Driver Units	Cost
Account inquiry	$14.300116	9,800 Inquiries	$140,141	7,500 Inquiries	$107,251
Correspondence	$ 7.062780	1,960 Letters	13,843	2,500 Letters	17,657
Account billing	$ 0.066282	1,176,000 Lines	77,947	1,250,000 Lines	82,853
Bill verification	$ 0.452033	49,000 Accounts	22,149	12,500 Accounts	5,650
Total cost			$254,081		$213,411
Number of accounts			98,000		25,000
Cost per account			$ 2.59		$ 8.54

Exhibit 4-16
Cost Per Driver Unit and Activity-Based Cost Per Account

are 50 lines per account × 12,500 accounts = 625,000 lines and for residential accounts are 12 lines per account × 49,000 accounts = 588,000 lines. Thus, we would allocate 588,000 ÷ (588,000 + 625,000) = 48.5% of verification costs to residential accounts based on lines verified. ABC teams should always exercise care when choosing cost drivers. The Youngstown team might also want to investigate the plausibility and reliability of the "number of inquiries" cost driver because this assumes that residential and commercial customer inquiries require the same amount of work.

Highlights to Remember

1 **Describe the purposes of cost management systems.** Cost management systems provide cost information for external financial reporting, for strategic decision making, and for operational cost control.

2 **Explain the relationship between cost, cost objective, cost accumulation, and cost assignment.** Cost accounting systems provide cost information about various types of objectives—products, customers, activities, and so on. To do this, a system first accumulates resource costs by natural classifications such as materials, labor, and energy. Then it assigns these costs to cost objectives, either tracing them directly or assigning them indirectly through allocation.

3 **Distinguish between direct, indirect, and unallocated costs.** Accountants can specifically and exclusively identify direct costs with a cost object in an economically feasible way. When this is not possible, accountants may allocate costs to cost objectives using a cost driver. Such costs are called indirect costs. The greater the proportion of direct costs, the greater the accuracy of the cost system. When the proportion of indirect costs is significant, accountants must take care to find the most appropriate cost drivers. Some costs are unallocated because the accountants can determine no plausible and reliable relationship between resource costs and cost objectives.

4 **Explain how the financial statements of merchandisers and manufacturers differ because of the types of goods they sell.** The primary difference between the financial statements of a merchandiser and a manufacturer is the reporting of inventories. A merchandiser has only one type of inventory whereas a manufacturer has three types of inventory—raw materials, work-in-process, and finished goods.

5 **Understand the main differences between traditional and activity-based costing systems and why ABC systems provide value to managers.** Traditional systems usually allocate only the indirect costs of the production function. ABC systems allocate many (and sometimes all) of the costs of the value-chain functions. Traditional costing accumulates costs using categories such as direct material, direct labor, and production overhead. ABC systems accumulate costs by activities required to produce a product or service. The key value of ABC systems is in their increased costing accuracy and better information provided that can lead to process improvements.

6 **Design a cost accounting system that includes activity-based costing.** Designing and implementing an activity-based costing system involves four steps. First, managers determine the cost objectives, key activities, and resources used, and they identify cost drivers (output measures) for each resource and activity. Second, they determine the relationship among cost objectives, activities, and resources. The third step is collecting cost and operating data. The last step is to calculate and interpret the new activity-based information. Often, this last step requires the use of a computer due to the complexity of many ABC systems.

7 **Use activity-based cost information to make strategic and operational control decisions.** Activity-based management is using ABC information to improve operations. A key advantage of an activity-based costing system is its ability to aid managers in decision making. ABC improves the accuracy of cost estimates, including product and customer costs and the costs of value-added versus non-value-added activities. ABC also improves managers' understanding of operations. Managers can focus their attention on making strategic decisions, such as product mix, pricing, and process improvements.

8 **Understand why multistage ABC (MSABC) systems give more value than two-stage ABC systems for strategic planning and operational control (Appendix 4).** For some organizations that have operations that are highly complex, two-stage ABC systems do not offer enough costing accuracy or decision-making information. The three key attributes of MSABC systems that lead to more value for these organizations include more than two stages of allocation, cost behavior of resources, and much more operational information.

Appendix 4: Multistage ABC (MSABC) Systems

OBJECTIVE 8

Understand why multistage ABC systems give more value than two-stage ABC systems for strategic planning and operational control.

multistage ABC (MSABC) systems
Costing systems with more than two stages of allocations and cost drivers other than percentages.

Two-stage ABC systems are the simplest ABC systems. The first stage allocates costs to activities, and the second stage allocates the activity costs to products, customers, or other cost objectives. They have a financial accounting flavor because the general ledger is at the heart of all the cost data used. While two-stage ABC systems meet the decision-making needs of many organizations, some organizations (such as **FedEx**, **Boeing**, **Allstate Insurance**, and the United States Department of Labor) prefer to design **multistage ABC (MSABC)** with more than two stages of allocations and resource cost drivers other than percentages.

There is a distinctive operational flavor to MSABC systems because much of the required data comes from operational data sources, not just the general ledger. Many companies, such as **Pillsbury** and **AT&T**, began their use of ABC by using the two-stage approach. However, they later converted to the multistage approach because of its focus on operations and its tendency to enhance operating managers' understanding of the business. According to one manager at Pillsbury,

> *Having already completed an ABC model within our organization using the two-stage ABC approach, my eyes were opened to the importance of the multistage ABC approach and how its scenario-playing capability and flexibility allows an organization to move past just ABC toward ABM.*

> —Pillsbury Company

Managers at companies that use MSABC systems believe that their additional complexity yields more accurate costs and a deeper understanding of operations. A deeper understanding of the business leads to better ideas for process improvement. Process improvements, in turn, lead to more satisfied customers and a competitive edge. Three key attributes distinguish MSABC systems from two-stage ABC systems.

1. There are more than two stages of allocation.
2. Cost behavior of resources is considered.
3. There is a greater use of operational information such as cost drivers and consumption rates.

Let's explore each of these attributes to see why MSABC systems offer so much value to managers.

Key Attributes of Multistage ABC Systems

Understanding the relationships between activities, resources, resource costs, and cost drivers is the key to understanding MSABC systems and how they facilitate managers' understanding of operations. To gain more insight into how an ABC system actually works, we will look at one of the products produced by Woodland Park Company, a manufacturer of plastic components used in commercial trucks and buses.

One of the components Woodland Park makes, 102Z, is a plastic dashboard casing for the control panel of large trucks. Making 102Z requires resin material and several activities, such as receiving, production scheduling, material handling, setup, molding machine processing, assembly, inspection, packaging, and shipping. We will focus on the set-up and molding machine processing activities. The resources required by these activities include an injection-molding machine, operating labor, electrical energy, and the plant itself. Exhibit 4-17 shows the relationships between the setup and machine processing activities and the resources used.

The first key attribute of MSABC systems is the use of more than two stages of allocation. In Exhibit 4-17, notice that the plant resource costs are allocated to the final cost objective—truck dashboard casings—in three stages. In a two-stage ABC system, plant costs would be allocated to the truck casings in only two stages. In the MSABC system we assume machine and labor resources consume plant costs as measured by the square feet that each occupies. In a two-stage ABC system, we would ignore the interrelationship between the plant and the machine and labor resources, and instead use a percentage to allocate plant costs directly to the setup and machine-processing activities. But this is difficult to interpret and does little to enhance our understanding of operations. MSABC systems overcome this problem, allowing for any number of allocations necessary to accurately describe operations.

The second key attribute of MSABC systems is their extensive use of operational information. Look at the cost objective Truck Dashboard Casing in Exhibit 4-17. It takes 15 minutes of machine time to process each casing. This is shown by the activity-consumption rate $r_2 = 0.25$ machine hours per casing. Similarly, r_1 gives the consumption rate for setup activity. Each production run produces 100 casings and requires one setup ($r_1 = 0.01$). Each casing requires 0.6 pounds of resin material. Therefore, the annual demand for 800 casings requires a total of 8 setups ($800 \times .01$), 200 processing hours ($800 \times .25$) and 480 pounds of resin (800×0.6).

A similar interpretation can be made for the activities. For example, each hour of machine-processing activity requires (consumes) one molding machine hour, three operator labor hours, and 0.3 kilowatt hours of energy. We can see that the cost drivers are a measure of the activity level (setups and processing hours) and the amount of resources used (machine hours, labor hours, and kilowatt hours) to produce casings. The resource-consumption rates (the r's on each activity in Exhibit 4-17) give the rates at which the activity uses resources for each cost-driver unit of the activity.

Two-stage ABC systems differ in the treatment of the consumption of resources by activities. In two-stage ABC, percentages would be used to describe the relationships between resources and activities. Managers who use MSABC believe that resource-consumption rates provide more valuable operational information than percentages. In our example, the managers at Woodland Park Company now have cost and operational information that they can use to manage operations more effectively. For example, consider the portion of the process map shown at the top of page 165. There is much more useful operational information in the MSABC map. Operational managers use information such as the labor hours per machine hours or kilowatt hours per machine hour to track operational improvements. Using the cost behavior feature of MSABC, managers can predict the effects on activity costs of such improvements. This is much more difficult—or impossible—using the two-stage approach.

Let's look at an example. Suppose that Woodland Park can increase its sales of truck casings to an annual total of 900 but does not have the machine time available for the extra 100 casings. It would require an additional 25 hours of processing time to meet this new demand. Management believes that by using special quick-change dies, they can reduce the setup time by 75%. Will this process improvement save enough time to produce the extra 100 casings? The new consumption rate for machine time, r_4, is 2 hours per setup. So, the total machine time consumed during setups

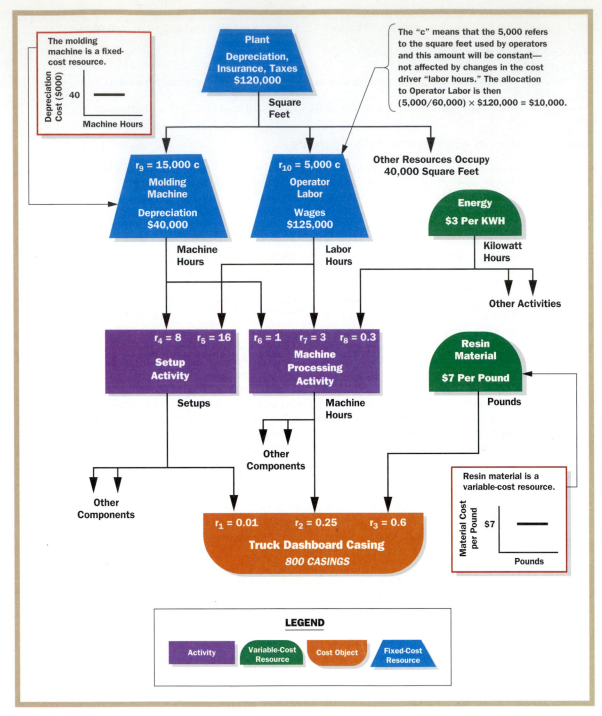

The molding machine is a fixed-cost resource.

Depreciation Cost ($000) 40 — Machine Hours

Plant
Depreciation, Insurance, Taxes $120,000

Square Feet

The "c" means that the 5,000 refers to the square feet used by operators and this amount will be constant— not affected by changes in the cost driver "labor hours." The allocation to Operator Labor is then $(5,000/60,000) \times \$120,000 = \$10,000$.

$r_9 = 15,000$ c
Molding Machine
Depreciation $40,000

$r_{10} = 5,000$ c
Operator Labor
Wages $125,000

Other Resources Occupy 40,000 Square Feet

Energy
$3 Per KWH

Machine Hours   Labor Hours   Kilowatt Hours

Other Activities

$r_4 = 8$ $r_5 = 16$
Setup Activity

$r_6 = 1$ $r_7 = 3$ $r_8 = 0.3$
Machine Processing Activity

Resin Material
$7 Per Pound

Setups   Machine Hours   Pounds

Other Components

Other Components

$r_1 = 0.01$ $r_2 = 0.25$ $r_3 = 0.6$
Truck Dashboard Casing
800 CASINGS

Resin material is a variable-cost resource.

Material Cost per Pound $7 — Pounds

LEGEND

| Activity | Variable-Cost Resource | Cost Object | Fixed-Cost Resource |

Exhibit 4-17
Relationship Between Cost Object, Activities, and Resources in an ABC System

will be 18 hours (900 casings × 0.01 setups per casing × 2 machine hours per setup) compared to the current 64 hours (800 × 0.01 × 8). Thus, the time savings of 46 hours is more than enough to produce the extra 100 casings. If a two-stage ABC system were being used, it would be much more difficult to analyze this improvement idea because we would not have the consumption rate for machine time. Instead, we would have a percentage based on historical relationships and general ledger data.

The third key attribute of MSABC systems is their recognition of cost behavior. In Exhibit 4-17, the variable-cost resources—energy and resin material—are modeled by using this symbol ◼.

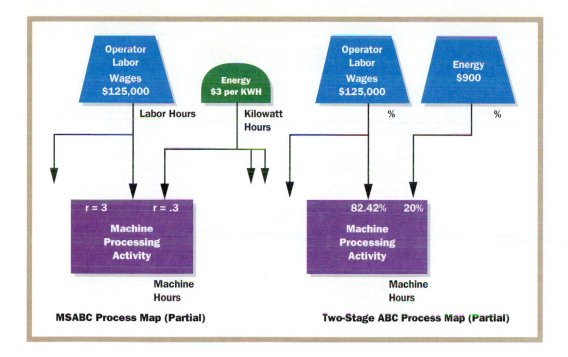

MSABC Process Map (Partial)   **Two-Stage ABC Process Map (Partial)**

Financial data for these resources are expressed as costs per cost-driver unit. For energy, this is $3 per kilowatt hour. Energy cost varies directly with changes in the processing activity because the power company charges Woodland Park based on the kilowatt hours used. One additional processing hour will require .3 additional kilowatt hours that will increase energy cost by $0.90 ($3.00 × .3). Thus, energy is a variable-cost resource, and it is easy to see that processing hours and kilowatt hours are factors that affect energy costs.

The fixed-cost resources—plant, machines, and labor—are modeled by using this symbol 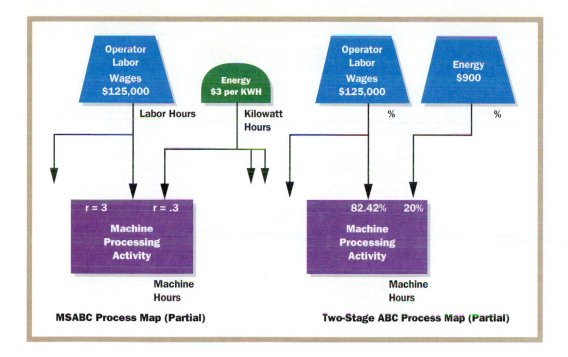. For financial data, we use total costs. The costs of the machine and labor resources are fixed with respect to changes (within the relevant range) in the cost drivers. One additional processing hour requires one additional machine hour and three labor hours, but the costs of the machine (depreciation) and labor (wages) resources do not change as long as machine time and labor time are available. Have we violated our definition of cost driver? Not really. If the number of processing hours increases enough, the required machine hours or labor hours will exceed the capacities of the machine and labor. Management will then decide whether to purchase more machines or to hire additional operating laborers. Costs of fixed-cost resources do not change automatically when cost drivers change—this involves a management decision. However, if cost drivers truly affect costs, good managers will eventually adjust the resource usage as the level of activity changes.

In simple, two-stage ABC systems, the cost behavior of resources is usually ignored. This means that planning for future operations is almost impossible with two-stage ABC because the impact of changes in demand and related cost-driver levels cannot be predicted. For example, if we expect that the demand for casings will increase, a two-stage ABC system will not enable us to predict the increase in variable production costs such as materials and energy, but the MSABC system will correctly predict the variable resin and energy cost increases.

Summary Problem For Your Review

PROBLEM

Refer to the chapter discussion of the billing department at one of AT&T's customer care centers. Suppose the billing department has designed an MSABC system. Exhibit 4-18 shows the process map for the MSABC system. Consider the portion of the billing department's process map shown in Exhibit 4-19. Management wants to reduce activities that do not add value for the customer. One idea

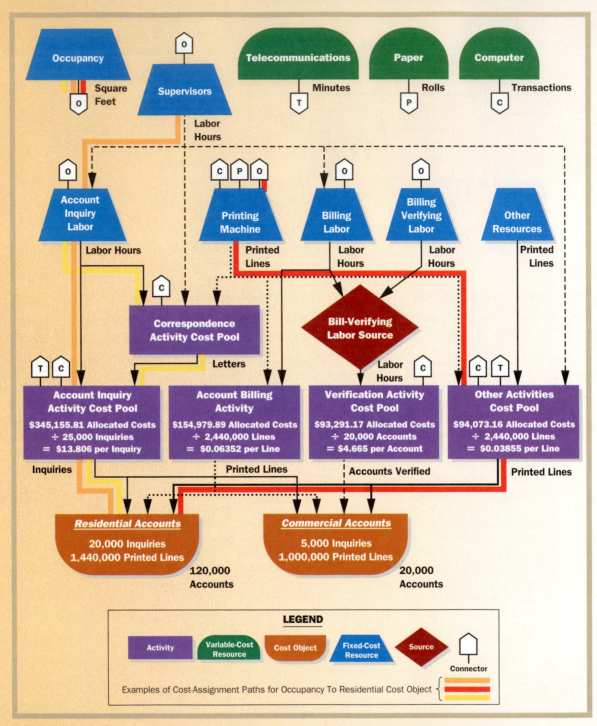

Exhibit 4-18
Multistage ABC System for Billing Department Operations

is to reduce the verification of commercial bills by verifying only 70% of commercial bills (at random) and, further, by verifying only certain parts of each bill. Verifying only part of each bill will reduce the verifying time from 6 minutes to only 3 minutes per bill (account). Management believes that this procedure would not result in any increase in the number of inquiries and that bill accuracy would be unchanged. Since only part of each bill will be verified, the number of computer

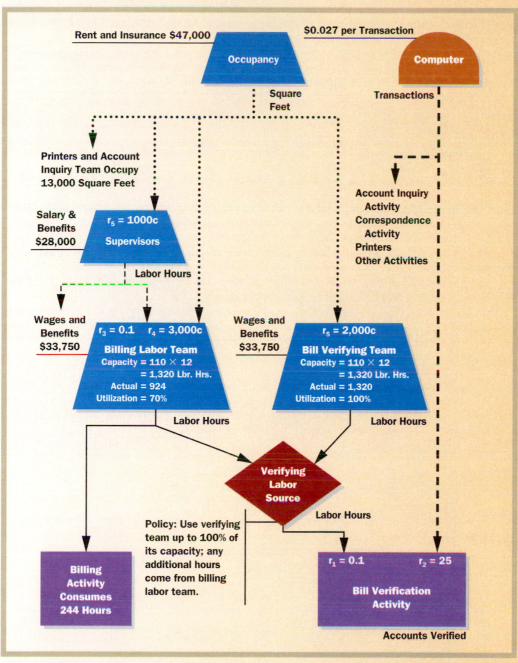

Exhibit 4-19
Billing Department Bill Verification Activity

transactions will also be reduced from 25 to 15 per account. AT&T's labor agreement specifies that whenever labor utilization for the combined billing and verification labor pool falls below 70% due to any process improvement, the company may lay off workers until the utilization level reaches 70%. Currently, billing labor (billing labor plus bill-verifying labor) utilization is at 85% (actual hours consisting of 244 hours for actual billing plus 20,000 accounts × .1 lbr. hrs = 2,000 labor hours for verification activity divided by capacity of 24 × 110 hours per laborer = 2,640). Wages and benefits are $2,812.50 per month per laborer. Each laborer is available for 110 hours a month. Currently, there are 24 billing laborers, 12 of whom are dedicated to verifying bills—the verification team. Because of the negative impact that layoffs have on employee morale, management is hesitant to implement any layoffs unless the cost savings are significant.

1. A comparison of Exhibits 4-10 and 4-18 shows the primary differences between two-stage and MSABC systems: multiple stages of allocations, cost behavior, and more operational information. Look at the occupancy resource in both Exhibits.

   Cost allocation in MSABC systems is complex and requires some form of computer software. To get a feel for this complexity, consider the various cost-allocations required to allocate occupancy cost to the residential accounts. Three of these paths are listed below and are also displayed in Exhibit 4-18.

   Allocation Path 1: Occupancy → Account Inquiry Labor → Correspondence Activity → Account Inquiry Activity → Residential Accounts
   Allocation Path 2: Occupancy → Supervision → Account Inquiry Labor → Account Inquiry Activity → Residential Accounts
   Allocation Path 3: Occupancy → Printers→ Other Activities → Residential Accounts

   A computer program, either a spreadsheet or commercial software, would compute the allocations for each step in these paths based on the percentage of cost drivers used. For example, the first set of allocations of the $47,000 occupancy costs are based on the square feet occupied by account inquiry labor, supervisors, printing machines, billing labor, and bill-verifying labor.

   There are a total of eleven allocation paths to allocate occupancy costs to residential accounts. Give the other eight paths, using the same format shown above.

2. In Exhibit 4-19, the relationship (indicated by arrows and consumption rates) between the computer resource and activities and resources such as account inquiry, correspondence, printing machines, and other activities is *not* shown. Explain why it is not necessary to know these relationships in order to determine the incremental billing labor cost savings from the process improvement.

3. Why is "transactions" a true cost driver for computer costs, whereas supervisor "labor hours" is not a true cost driver of billing labor costs?

4. Determine the billing labor and computer cost savings from this process improvement. What other potential cost savings may result? What action would you recommend?

SOLUTION

1. The remaining eight cost-allocation paths are:

   Allocation Path 4: Occupancy → Account Inquiry Activity → Account Inquiry Labor → Residential Accounts
   Allocation Path 5: Occupancy → Supervision → Account Inquiry Labor → Correspondence → Account Inquiry Activity → Residential Accounts
   Allocation Path 6: Occupancy → Supervision → Correspondence → Account Inquiry Activity → Residential Accounts
   Allocation Path 7: Occupancy → Supervision → Billing Labor → Billing Activity → Residential Accounts
   Allocation Path 8: Occupancy → Billing Labor → Billing Activity → Residential Accounts
   Allocation Path 9: Occupancy → Supervision → Other Activities → Residential Accounts
   Allocation Path 10: Occupancy → Printing Machines → Correspondence → Account Inquiry Activity → Residential Accounts
   Allocation Path 11: Occupancy → Printing Machines → Billing Activity → Residential Accounts

   We note that the number of stages of allocation for the occupancy resource varies from three (paths 4, 8 and 9) to five (path 5). Two-stage ABC has only two stages of allocations for all paths and there are only 3 allocation paths. As managers, you need to decide whether the benefits of increased costing accuracy and operational information exceed the incremental cost to maintain the MSABC system.

2. We can determine how a resource will be affected by an operational change by starting at the point where the change is made and following all possible paths upward through the process map that end at the computer resource. In our case, the starting point is the verification activity. As the

number of verified accounts is reduced, the number of computer transactions will also decline, as will computer costs. In this case, there is only one path linking verification to computers and it is shown in Exhibit 4-18. As can be seen from Exhibit 4-18, the cost-driver levels for account inquiry, correspondence, printers, and other activities will not be affected by a decrease in the number of accounts verified. No other cost driver links to the computer resource changes, so we do not need to show these relationships.

3. Any increase in demand for the computers will result in an immediate and automatic increase in the number of transactions. Since the computer leasing company bills the company on a per transaction basis, the computer costs will "automatically" decrease in response to the decrease in accounts verified. Billing labor hours does not automatically drive the cost of this resource. We use this cost driver as the allocation basis but it would require a decision by management to change the resource cost. As the number of accounts verified decreases, the number of billing labor hours will also decrease but the total wages paid will stay the same—only the utilization rate will decrease. If this rate falls below 70%, management can decide whether to reduce the labor pool and hence the labor cost.

4. Exhibt 4-20 shows the calculation of the predicted cost savings from this process improvement— $41,580. Additional cost savings may result from the reduced utilization of the supervisory resource and the occupancy resource. The space occupied by the eight billing laborers who are let go may either be used for other productive purposes or rented.

	Total Cost Analysis			
Resource	**Current Cost**		**Cost with Process Improvement**	
Computer	20,000 acct × 25 trans/acct × $.027/trans =	$13,500	14,000 accts × 15 trans/acct × $.027/trans =	$ 5,670
Billing labor	$2,812.50/lbr × 24 lbrs =	$67,500	[(14,000 accts × .05 hr/acct) + 244 hr] ÷ .7 = desired capacity of 1,349 hr or 1,349 ÷ 110 ≈ 12 lbr.*	
			Cost is 12 lbr × $2,812.50 =	$33,750
	Total cost	$81,000	Total cost	$39,420
			Cost savings ($81,000 − $39,420)	$41,580

* Check for utilization: capacity = 12 × 110 = 1,320; actual = (14,000 acct × .05 hr/acct) + 244 hr = 944 hr. Utilization = 944 ÷ 1,320 = 71.5%. With 13 people, utilization would be 944 ÷ 1,430 = 66%, so one additional laborer can be laid off.

Exhibit 4-20
Total Cost Analysis of Process Improvement in Verification Activity

Accounting Vocabulary

activity-based costing (ABC) systems, p. 141
activity-based management (ABM), p. 147
benchmarking, p. 147
cost, p. 133
cost accounting, p. 131
cost accounting systems, p. 131
cost accumulation, p. 131
cost allocation, p. 133
cost assignment, p. 131
cost management system (CMS), p. 130

cost object, p. 133
cost objective, p. 133
cost pool, p. 141
direct costs, p. 133
direct-labor costs, p. 136
direct-material costs, p. 136
factory burden, p. 136
factory overhead, p. 136
indirect costs, p. 133
indirect manufacturing costs, p. 136
indirect production costs, p. 136

manufacturing overhead, p. 136
multistage ABC (MSABC) system, p. 162
non-value-added costs, p. 147
period costs, p. 137
process map, p. 154
product costs, p. 137
traditional costing systems, p. 140
two-stage ABC system, p. 144
unallocated costs, p. 134
value-added cost, p. 147

Fundamental Assignment Material

4-A1 Direct, Indirect, and Unallocated Costs, Process Map

Henry Picture Frame Company makes and sells three product lines—custom detailed frames, large standard frames, and small standard frames. The statement of operating income for the most recent period is shown below.

Henry Manufacturing Company
Statement of Operating Income

		Total
Sales		$152,000
Cost of goods sold		
Direct material	$40,000	
Indirect manufacturing	41,000	81,000
Gross profit		71,000
Selling and administrative expenses:		
Commissions	15,000	
Distribution to warehouses	10,400	25,400
Operating income		45,600
Unallocated expenses		
Administrative salaries	8,000	
Other administrative expenses	4,000	12,000
Operating income before taxes		$ 33,600

Henry uses a traditional cost accounting system. A process map has been developed to describe this system as shown in Exhibit 4-21. To aid in the company's analysis of its product mix strategy, you have been asked to determine operating income (loss) for each product line. Use a format similar to Exhibit 4-2 in the text.

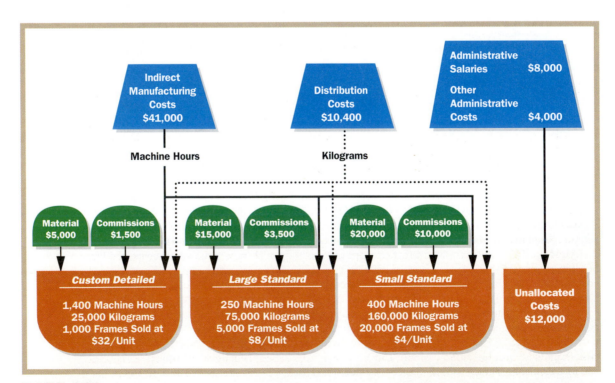

Exhibit 4-21
Process Map for Henry Picture Frame Company's Traditional Cost Allocation System

4-A2 Traditional and ABC Cost Accounting, Activity-Based Management

Refer to the text discussion of Simple Plastics Company on pages 141–145. Assume that the company has the traditional cost accounting system described in Exhibit 4-5. The top management team wants to reverse the pattern of quarterly losses. The company president, Marta Steward, has emphasized the importance of profit improvement by linking future pay raises of the two product-line managers to their respective gross profit margins. She is concerned about the profitability of the pen casing product line while pleased with the profitability of the cell phone casing line. She also believes that the unallocated costs of the company are too high compared to those of competitors.

The office of controller, whose costs are included in the unallocated costs, is responsible for vendor relations and purchasing of direct materials. The controller presents the following idea:

> We should use more standard parts in cell phone casings, which will dramatically
> reduce the purchasing department's work required for purchasing. I believe this should
> cut our office's costs by as much as $25,000 per quarter. In addition, using standard
> parts eliminates the need to purchase several expensive resins. The larger volume of
> purchases of less costly resin from fewer vendors will cut the cell phone casing direct
> material cost by 10%. Product engineering agrees that this idea is not only feasible
> but, if implemented, would improve the overall quality of cell phone casings.

The controller and marketing manager provided the following summary of actions and related effects:

Action	Expected effects
Reduce prices of cell phone casings 25%.	The vice president of sales estimates that the improved quality of cell phone casings combined with the price reduction will yield a 100% increase in demand for cell phone casings per quarter.
Use standard parts wherever possible in cell phone casings.	Total number of parts for each cell phone casing will not change, but the direct material cost per casing will be reduced by 10% due to volume discounts from preferred vendors.
	The use of fewer suppliers will reduce vendor-relations work by the purchasing department. This will result in unallocated costs decreasing by $25,000.
	Processing time, measured in direct-labor hours, will increase by 500 hours due to expected 100% increase in sales and production of cell phone casings, but there is adequate capacity of labor and machine time. Direct-labor costs are fixed as are all of the indirect manufacturing costs.
	Quality of cell phone casings will improve due to reduced complexity of processing.

1. Evaluate this idea using the traditional cost allocation system shown in Exhibit 4-5 on page 143. What would be the predicted profitability for each product line and the company as a whole? What would be the most likely level of support for the controller's idea by the product managers of the pen casing product line and the cell phone casing product line? What would be the level of support by the president?
2. Assume that you have the ABC system described in Exhibit 4-6 on page 144. Often, managers with ABC systems can anticipate more effects of improvement ideas because of their increased understanding of the operating system. In this case, although the total number of parts would not change, the idea would reduce the number of distinct parts for cell phone casings from 20 to 9. Evaluate the controller's idea using the ABC system described in Exhibit 4-6. What would be the predicted profitability for each product line and the company as a whole? What would be the most likely level of support for the controller's idea by the product managers of the pen casing product line and the cell phone casing product line? What would be the level of support by the president?
3. As vice president, you have expressed concern about the traditional cost-allocation system's product-cost accuracy and its ability to provide relevant information for operational control. Does the new ABC system satisfy your concerns? Explain.

4-A3 Activities, Resources, Cost Drivers, and the Banking Industry

Best Bank is a retail branch of an established banking corporation; it is located in a residential area and it services mostly individuals and local businesses. Best Bank's four main services are transaction processing (withdrawals, checks, currency exchange), loans, simple investments (individual clients), and complex investments (portfolios of large businesses).

To support these activities, Best Bank employs ten front-office staff, 12 back-office staff dealing with loan applications and investments, and two people to consult with customers and manage complex portfolio investments. A team of three supervisors manages the overall operations of the bank.

As part of Best Bank's implementation of activity-based costing, it needed to identify activities, resources, and cost drivers. The following table summarizes the cost drivers Best Bank has chosen for its activities and resources:

Cost Driver
number of investments
number of applications
number of loans
number of person hours
number of minutes
number of computer transactions
number of square feet
number of loan inquiries
number of transactions
number of schedules
number of securities

For each brief description below, indicate whether it is an activity or a resource (A or R). For each activity or resource, choose the most appropriate cost driver from the list above and indicate for each resource whether it is a fixed-cost (F) or variable-cost (V) resource. The first two items are completed as a guide.

a. External service bureau providing customer credit checks for loan applications (R; number of loan inquiries; V)
b. Contract maintenance of building and insurance (R; number of square feet; F)
c. Staff for front-line customer service
d. Preparing investment documents for customers
e. Research to evaluate a loan application
f. Overtime by back-office staff
g. Telephones/facsimile
h. Staff for service and background research
i. Establish customer collateral for approved loans
j. External computing services
k. Development of repayment schedules
l. Staff for consulting with customers and arranging the portfolios

4-A4 Cost Allocation, Activity-Based Costing, and Activity-Based Management

Reliable Machining Products (RMP) is an automotive component supplier. RMP has been approached by Toyota with a proposal to significantly increase production of Part T151A to a total annual quantity of 100,000. Toyota believes that by increasing the volume of production of Part T151A, RMP should realize the benefits of economies of scale and hence should accept a lower price than the current $7.50 per unit. Currently, RMP's gross margin on Part T151A is 20%, computed as follows.

	Total	Per Unit ($\div$ 100,000)
Direct materials	$150,000	$1.50
Indirect manufacturing (300% $\times$ direct materials)	450,000	4.50
Total cost	$600,000	$6.00
Sales price		7.50
Gross margin		$1.50
Gross margin percentage		20%

Part T151A seems to be a marginal profit product because the 20% gross margin must cover the costs of other value-chain functions such as design, distribution, customer service, and corporate support. If additional production volume of Part T151A is to be added, RMP management believes that the sales price must be increased, not reduced as requested by Toyota. The management of RMP sees this quoting situation as an excellent opportunity to examine the effectiveness of their traditional costing system versus an activity-based costing system. RMP decided to implement a two-stage ABC system. A team consisting of accounting and engineering analysts has developed a process-based map. Exhibit 4-22 shows the second stage allocations from this map. Data have been collected and entered on the map. For example, the total annual cost for the quality assurance activity is estimated to be $800,000 and the total quantity of the cost driver "number of pieces scrapped" is estimated to be 10,000. Thus, the cost per piece scrapped is $80. Activity-consumption rates have also been entered on the map. The consumption rate for the production activity is 0.005 machine hours per unit of T151A produced. Thus, the expected total number of machine hours required to produce 100,000 units of T151A is 500.

1. Prepare a schedule calculating the unit cost and gross margin percentage of Part T151A using the activity-based costing approach.
2. Based on the ABC results, what course of action would you recommend regarding the proposal by Toyota? List the benefits and costs associated with implementing an activity-based-costing system at RMP.

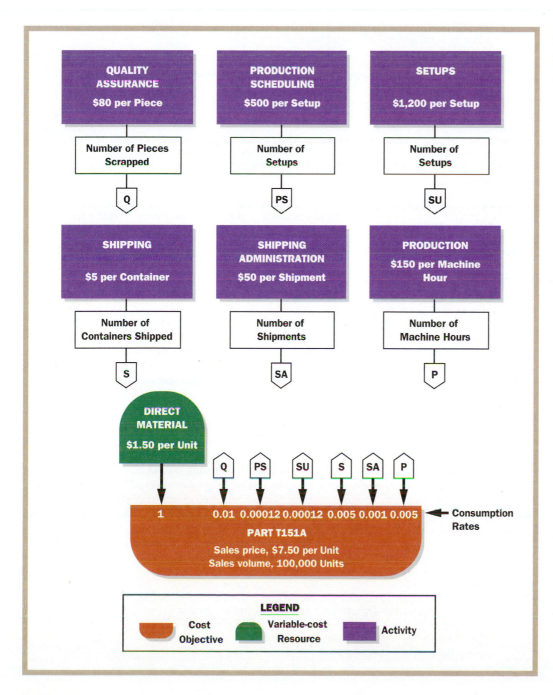

Exhibit 4-22
Reliable Machining Product's ABC System

4-B1 Direct, Indirect, and Unallocated Costs

Rantoul Metals Corporation is a supplier that assembles purchased parts into components for three distinct markets—farm tractor implements, lawn mower parts, and hand tool parts. The statement of operating income for the most recent period is shown below.

Rantoul Metals Corporation:
Statement of Operating Income

		Total
Sales		$1,010,000
Cost of goods sold		
Direct material	400,000	
Indirect manufacturing (allocated based on machine hours)	94,000	494,000
Gross profit		516,000
Selling and administrative expenses:		
Commissions	55,000	
Distribution to warehouses (allocated based on weight in kilograms)	150,000	205,000
Operating income		311,000
Unallocated expenses		
Corporate salaries	7,000	
Other general expenses	5,000	12,000
Operating income before taxes		$ 299,000

Rantoul uses a traditional cost accounting system. Operating data used in the cost accounting system are as follows:

	Tractor Implements	Lawn Mower Parts	Hand Tool Parts
Purchase cost of parts assembled	$175,000	$125,000	$100,000
Machine hours	8,500	1,750	1,500
Weight of parts shipped to distributors (kilograms)	100,000	400,000	250,000
Sales commissions per unit	$ 5.00	$ 0.80	$ 0.20
Units assembled and sold	5,000	25,000	50,000
Sales price per unit	$ 70.00	$ 16.00	$ 5.20

You have been asked to determine operating income (loss) for each product line. Use a format similar to Exhibit 4-2 in the text.

4-B2 Traditional Costing and ABC, Activity-Based Management

Refer to the text discussion of Simple Plastics Company on pages 141–145. Assume that the company has the traditional cost accounting system described in Exhibit 4-5. The top management team wants to reverse the pattern of quarterly losses. The company president, Marta Steward, has emphasized the importance of profit improvement by linking future pay raises of the two product-line managers to their respective gross profit margins. She is concerned about the profitability of the pen casing product line while pleased with the profitability of the cell-phone casing line. She also believes that the unallocated costs of the company are too high compared to competitors.

The office of controller, whose costs are included in the unallocated costs, is responsible for vendor relations and purchasing of direct materials. The controller and head of the engineering department present the following idea:

> *We should use more standard parts in cell phone casings, which will dramatically reduce the purchasing department's work required for purchasing. I believe this should cut our office's costs by as much as $20,000 per quarter. Product engineering agrees that this idea is not only feasible but, if implemented, would substantially reduce the design work required for cell phone casings. Quality would also improve.*

The controller, marketing manager, and head of the engineering department provided the following summary of actions and related effects.

Action	Expected effects
Reduce prices of cell phone casings 25%.	The vice president of sales estimates that the improved quality of cell phone casings, combined with the price reduction will yield a 100% increase in demand for cell phone casings per quarter.
Use standard parts wherever possible in cell phone casings.	The use of fewer suppliers will reduce vendor-relations work by the purchasing department. This will result in unallocated costs decreasing by $20,000.
	One of the two engineers can be let go at an annual cost savings of $80,000.
	Less of the plant and equipment will be used by engineering so the allocation percentages will change from 75% and 25% to 80% and 20%. Much less engineer and CAD equipment costs will be needed for engineering support, so these percentages will change from 80% and 20% to 50% and 50%.
	Processing time, measured in direct-labor hours, will increase by 500 hours due to expected 100% increase in sales and production of cell phone casings, but there is adequate capacity of labor and machine time. Direct-labor costs are fixed as are all of the indirect manufacturing costs.
	Quality of cell phone casings will improve due to reduced complexity of processing.

1. Evaluate this idea using the traditional cost allocation system shown in Exhibit 4-5 on page 143. What would be the predicted profitability for each product line and the company as a whole? What would be the most likely level of support for the controller's idea by the product managers of the pen casing product line and the cell phone casing product line? What would be the level of support by the president?

2. Assume that you have the ABC system described in Exhibit 4-6 on page 144. Often, managers with ABC systems can anticipate more effects of improvement ideas because of their increased understanding of the operating system. In this case, although the total number of parts used would not change, the idea would reduce the number of distinct parts for cell phone casings from 20 to 11. Evaluate the controller's idea using the ABC system described in Exhibit 4-6. What would be the predicted profitability for each product line and the company as a whole? What would be the most likely level of support for the controller's idea by the product managers of the pen casing product line and the cell phone casing product line? What would be the level of support by the president?

3. As vice president, you have expressed concern about the traditional cost-allocation system's product-cost accuracy and its ability to provide relevant information for operational control. Does the new ABC system satisfy your concerns? Explain.

4-B3 Financial Statements for Manufacturing and Merchandising Companies

Outdoor Equipment Company (OEC) and Mountain Supplies, Inc., (MSI) both sell tents. OEC purchases its tents from a manufacturer for $97 each and then sells them for $180. It purchased 10,000 tents in 20X4.

MSI produces its own tents. In 20X4 MSI produced 10,000 tents. Costs were as follows:

Direct materials purchased		$580,000
Direct materials used		$530,000
Direct labor		290,000
Indirect manufacturing:		
Depreciation	$50,000	
Indirect labor	60,000	
Other	40,000	150,000
Total cost of production		$970,000

Assume that MSI had no beginning inventory of direct materials. There was no beginning inventory of finished tents, but ending inventory consisted of 1,000 finished tents. Ending work-in-process inventory was negligible.

Each company sold 9,000 tents for $1,620,000 in 20X4 and incurred the following selling and administrative costs:

Sales salaries and commissions	$100,000
Depreciation on retail store	40,000
Advertising	25,000
Other	15,000
Total selling and administrative cost	$180,000

1. Prepare the inventories section of the balance sheet for December 31, 20X4, for OEC.
2. Prepare the inventories section of the balance sheet for December 31, 20X4, for MSI.
3. Using Exhibit 4-4 on page 140 as a model, prepare an income statement for the year 20X4 for OEC.
4. Using Exhibit 4-4 on page 140 as a model, prepare an income statement for the year 20X4 for MSI.
5. Summarize the differences between the financial statements of OEC, a merchandiser, and MSI, a manufacturer.
6. What purpose of a cost management system is being served by reporting the items in requirements 1–4?

4-B4 Activity-Based Costing in an Electronics Company

The cordless phone manufacturing division of a Denver-based consumer electronics company uses activity-based costing. For simplicity, assume that its accountants have identified only the following three activities and related cost drivers for indirect production costs:

Activity	Cost Driver
Materials handling	Direct-materials cost
Engineering	Engineering change notices
Power	Kilowatt hours

Three types of cordless phones are produced: SA2, SA5, and SA9. Direct costs and cost-driver activity for each product for a recent month are as follows:

	SA2	SA5	SA9
Direct-materials cost	$25,000	$ 50,000	$125,000
Direct-labor cost	$ 4,000	$ 1,000	$ 3,000
Kilowatt hours	50,000	200,000	150,000
Engineering change notices	13	5	2

Indirect production cost for the month was

Materials handling	$ 8,000
Engineering	20,000
Power	16,000
Total indirect production cost	$44,000

1. Compute the indirect production cost allocated to each product with the activity-based costing system.
2. Suppose all indirect production costs had been allocated to products in proportion to their direct-labor costs. Compute the indirect production costs allocated to each product.
3. In which product costs, those in number 1 or those in number 2, do you have the most confidence? Why?

Additional Assignment Material

Questions

4-1 Define a cost management system and give its three purposes.

4-2 Cost management systems have three primary purposes. For each of the decisions listed below, indicate the purpose of the CMS being applied.

a. A production manager wants to know the cost of performing a setup for a production run in order to compare it to a target cost established as part of a process improvement program.

b. Top management wants to identify the profitability of several product lines to establish the optimum product mix.

c. Financial managers want to know the manufactured cost of inventory to appear on the balance sheet of the annual report.

4-3 What is the major purpose of detailed cost accounting systems?

4-4 What are the major processes peformed by a cost accounting system?

4-5 Why are cost accounting systems critically important to managers?

4-6 Name four cost objectives or cost objects.

4-7 "Departments are not cost objects or objects of costing." Do you agree? Explain.

4-8 Distinguish between direct, indirect, and unallocated costs.

4-9 "The same cost can be direct and indirect." Do you agree? Explain.

4-10 "Economic feasibility is an important guideline in designing cost accounting systems." Do you agree? Explain.

4-11 How does the idea of economic feasibility relate to the distinction between direct and indirect costs?

4-12 "The typical traditional accounting system does not allocate costs associated with value-chain functions other than production to units produced." Do you agree? Explain.

4-13 "It is better not to allocate some costs than to use a cost driver that does not make any sense." Do you agree? Explain.

4-14 Production maintenance, sales commissions, and process design costs are part of a company's costs. Identify which of these costs are most likely direct, indirect, and unallocated.

4-15 "For a furniture manufacturer, glue or tacks become an integral part of the finished product, so they would be direct material." Do you agree? Explain.

4-16 "Depreciation is a period expense for financial statement purposes." Do you agree? Explain.

4-17 Distinguish between *costs* and *expenses*.

4-18 "Unexpired costs are always inventory costs." Do you agree? Explain.

4-19 Why is there no direct-labor inventory account on a manufacturing company's balance sheet?

4-20 Distinguish between manufacturing and merchandising companies.

4-21 We refer to resources as variable-cost or fixed-cost resources. Why do we not specify the cost behavior of activities?

4-22 Name four steps in the design and implementation of an activity-based costing system.

4-23 In two-stage ABC systems, percentages are commonly used to allocate resource costs to activity cost pools. Are these percentages cost drivers?

4-24 "ABC systems are always more accurate than traditional costing systems." Do you agree? Explain.

4-25 Why are more and more organizations adopting activity-based costing systems?

4-26 Explain how the layout of a plant's production equipment can reduce non-value-added costs.

4-27 Contrast activity-based costing (ABC) with activity-based management (ABM).

4-28 Why do managers want to distinguish between value-added activities and non-value-added activities?

4-29 What is benchmarking?

4-30 Why should caution be exercised when comparing company performance to benchmarks?

4-31 Cost drivers for resources such as computers, printers, and account inquiry labor are sometimes called resource cost drivers, whereas cost drivers for activities such as inquiry and billing are called activity cost drivers. Explain.

4-32 Refer to the text discussion of Woodland Park Company on pages 163–165. Suppose Winter Park Company has two plants—the Salem plant and the Youngstown plant. The Youngstown plant produces only three components that are very similar in material and production requirements. The Salem plant makes a wide variety of parts. Which type of costing system would you recommend for each plant (traditional or ABC)? Explain.

4-33 Distinguish between two-stage and multi-stage ABC systems.

4-34 (Study Appendix 4) In Exhibits 4-7 and 4-9, the r's represent resource- and activity-consumption rates. Why are these rates important to managers looking for ideas for process improvements?

4-35 (Study Appendix 4) Explain the difference between resource-consumption rates and cost per driver unit.

Critical Thinking Exercises

4-36 Marketing and Capacity Planning

A company has just completed its marketing plan for the coming year and the management accountant has input the increases in sales volume into the process model. The result is that several key resource capacities have been exceeded. What are the three alternative courses of action to solve this dilemma?

4-37 ABC and ABM Compared

During seminars on activity-based management, participants often ask what the difference is between ABC and ABM. Explain briefly.

4-38 ABC and Cost Management Systems

Cost management systems have three primary purposes. Two of these are providing information for strategic and operational purposes. Activity-based costing systems are often adopted to increase the accuracy of cost information used by managers for strategic and operational decisions. Suppose a company produces only one product. This means that 100% of its costs are direct with respect to the product cost objective. The accurate product unit cost is simply all costs incurred divided by the total units produced. Why would this company be interested in an ABC system?

4-39 ABC and Benchmarking

Refer to the illustration of the billing department at one of AT&T's customer care centers in the chapter on pages 149–158. Suppose that, as part of its benchmarking efforts, AT&T compared the activity cost per driver unit for similar activities and cost per customer accounts for the Youngstown area customer care center's billing department with the cost per customer accounts for the billing department illustrated in the text. Are these meaningful comparisons? Why or why not?

4-40 Determining the Number of Cost Objectives

Look at the two cost objectives in Exhibits 4-5 and 4-6. Note that we show four different types of pens and three different types of cell phones within each product line. Why don't we have separate cost objectives for four pen casings and three cell phone casings—a total of seven individual products?

Exercises

4-41 Classification of Manufacturing Costs

Classify each of the following as direct or indirect (D or I) with respect to traceability to product and as variable or fixed (V or F) with respect to whether the cost fluctuates in total as activity or volume changes over wide ranges of activity. You will have two answers, D or I and V or F, for each of the ten items.

1. Supervisor training program
2. Abrasives (e.g., sandpaper)
3. Cutting bits in a machinery department
4. Food for a factory cafeteria
5. Factory rent
6. Salary of a factory storeroom clerk
7. Workers' compensation insurance in a factory
8. Cement for a road builder
9. Steel scrap for a blast furnace
10. Paper towels for a factory washroom

4-42 Confirm your Understanding of the Classification of Manufacturing Costs

Classify each of the following as direct or indirect with respect to traceability to product and as variable or fixed with respect to whether the costs fluctuate in total as volume of production changes over wide ranges.

1. The cost of components that are assembled into a final product.
2. The cost of supplies consumed when maintenance is performed on machines.
3. The cost of training mechanics who service processing machinery.
4. The wages of machine operators who work on only one product.

4-43 Variable Costs and Fixed Costs; Manufacturing and Other Costs

For each of the numbered items, choose the appropriate classifications from the lettered items for a manufacturing company. If in doubt about whether the cost behavior is basically variable or fixed, decide on the basis of whether the total cost will fluctuate substantially over a wide range of volume. Most items have two answers among the following possibilities.

a. Selling cost
b. Manufacturing costs, direct
c. Manufacturing costs, indirect

d. General and administrative cost
e. Fixed cost
f. Variable cost
g. Other (specify)

Examples:

Direct material	b, f
President's salary	d, e
Bond interest expense	e, g (financial expense)

Items for your consideration:

1. Factory power for machines
2. Salespersons' commissions
3. Salespersons' salaries
4. Welding supplies
5. Fire loss
6. Sandpaper
7. Supervisory salaries, production control
8. Supervisory salaries, assembly department
9. Supervisory salaries, factory storeroom
10. Company picnic costs
11. Overtime premium, punch press
12. Idle time, assembly
13. Freight out
14. Property taxes
15. Paint for finished products
16. Heat and air conditioning, factory
17. Materials-handling labor, punch press
18. Straight-line depreciation, salespersons' automobiles

4-44 Direct, Indirect, and Unallocated Costs

Refer to the Simple Plastics Company example on pages 141–145 and to Exhibit 4-6. The following list gives various resources used by Simple Plastics Company. Use the letters D, I, and U to indicate how the cost of each resource cost would be classified; D = direct, I = indirect, and U = unallocated.

1. Salaries of operating labor processing pen casings
2. Salaries of cost accountant
3. Depreciation on computers used by engineers to design cell phone casings
4. Depreciation of the plant
5. Resin used to make pen casings
6. Salaries of engineers
7. Salary of plant manager
8. Travel costs of purchasing agent while investigating potential new suppliers of resin

4-45 Cost Allocation in ABC

Refer to the Simple Plastics Company illustration on pages 141–145 and to Exhibit 4-6. Based on new information, management has adjusted the percentages that apply to the first stage of the ABC system as shown below. Prepare a schedule that shows the gross margins for both products.

	Indirect Resource	
Percent of Resource Used In	Plant and Equipment	Engineers and CAD Equipment
Processing activity	90%	30%
Production support activity	10%	70%

4-46 Two-Stage Activity-Based Costing, Banking

Better Bank is an established banking corporation. Its Colorado City location is a retail branch in a rapidly growing residential area. It services individuals and local businesses. To support its services, the branch employs 14 tellers, three retail sales managers (RSMs), and the branch managing officer. The branch services about 2,900 customers. Each of the 70 branches of Better Bank is implementing ABC in order to improve profitability. About half of the branches are implementing two-stage ABC systems and the other half are implementing multistage ABC systems. Better Bank's branch managing officers have been given the responsibility to implement activity-based costing. The two-stage ABC system is less expensive and can be implemented faster than the multistage ABC systems. However, multistage ABC systems provide more operational information and higher levels of cost accuracy. The managing officer at the Colorado City branch decided to implement the two-stage ABC system. Exhibit 4-23, panel A, depicts the two-stage ABC system. (Panel B will be used in Exercise 4-51.)

The Colorado City branch has the following cost data for the last year:

Teller wages	$ 350,000
RSM salaries and benefits	210,000
Managing officer salary and benefits	100,000
Other bank costs	430,000
Total	$1,090,000

The "other bank costs" include depreciation on the facility including furniture, building, equipment, insurance, rentals of computers, contracted computer services, telecommunications, and utilities. These costs cannot be directly or indirectly related to routine bank activities such as processing new accounts or processing deposits or withdrawals and thus are unallocated. There are no costs that can be traced directly to customers so the Colorado City branch has just two types of costs—indirect and unallocated. All employees have been interviewed as part of the ABC study. For example, tellers were asked how they spent their time. They said that they spent most of their time (60%) processing deposits and withdrawals. They also estimated that they spent about 10% of their time processing new accounts and about 20% of their time processing other transactions. The remaining 10% of their time was spent on all other banking activities. Three major activities were identified. The results of the interviews appear below.

Internal Activity Analysis					
	Open New Accounts	**Process Deposits and Withdrawals**	**Process Other Transactions**	**All Other Banking Activities**	**Total**
Teller wages	10%	60%	20%	10%	100%
Retail sales manager salary	10%	20%	30%	40%	100%
Managing officer salary	0%	10%	30%	60%	100%

Determine the total traceable cost of the three major activities conducted at the Colorado City branch of Better Bank. Use Exhibit 4-23, panel A, as a guide. (Note that this represents the first stage in the two-stage ABC method.)

4-47 Two-Stage Activity-Based Costing, Banking, Benchmarking. (This exercise is a continuation of Exercise 4-46 and should be assigned only if Exercise 4-46 is also assigned.)

A part of the activity analysis conducted at the Colorado City branch of Better Bank was identifying potential cost drivers for each major activity. The following cost drivers were chosen because they were both plausible and reliable and data were available:

Activity	Cost Driver	Annual Flow of Cost Driver
Process new accounts	Number of new accounts	540
Process deposits and withdrawals	Number of deposits and withdrawals	163,000
Process other transactions	Number of other transactions	49,000

Of the 2,900 customers of the branch, only 400 are local businesses. The business customer class generated 40 new accounts, 88,000 deposits and withdrawals, and 24,000 other transactions.

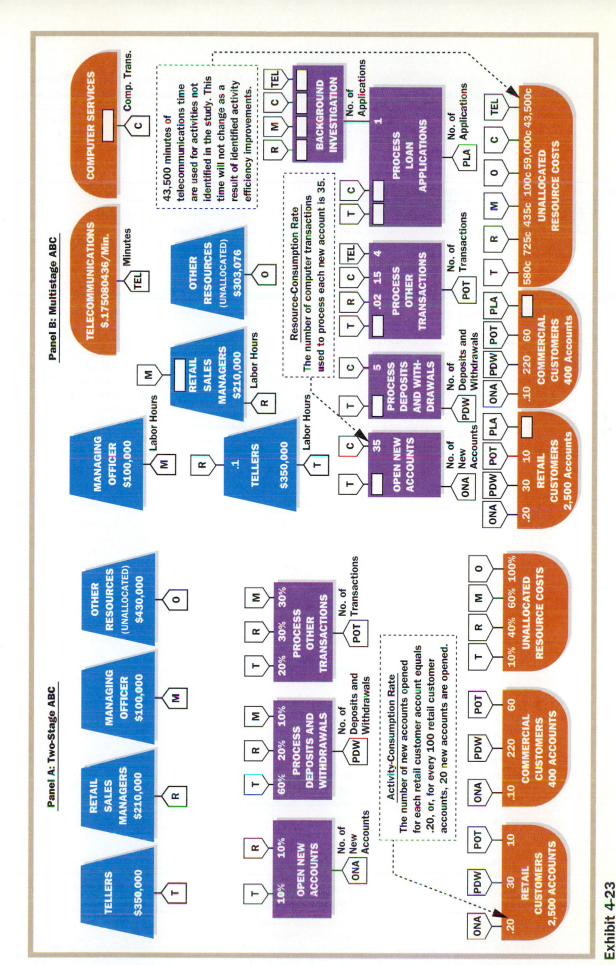

Exhibit 4-23
Comparison of Two-Stage ABC and Process-Based Costing at the Colorado City Branch of Better Bank

The implementation of ABC at all branches of Better Bank provided sufficient data for internal benchmarking. The following are the lowest activity costs among all branches implementing two-stage ABC systems:

Activity	Lowest Activity Cost per Driver Unit
Open new accounts	$81.67 per new account
Process deposits and withdrawals	$.75 per deposit or withdrawal
Process other transactions	$3.05 per transaction

Customer Class	Lowest Customer Cost per Account
Retail	$88
Commercial	$508

1. Determine the allocated (indirect) cost per account for retail and commercial accounts. Use Exhibit 4-23, panel A, as a guide.
2. Under what conditions would benchmarking between the Colorado City branch of Better Bank and the other branches be inappropriate?
3. What do the results of the ABC study suggest?

4-48 Direct, Indirect, and Unallocated Costs

Study Appendix 4. Listed below are several activities and related costs that have been observed at Wardy Company, a manufacturing company. The company makes a variety of products and currently uses a traditional costing system that allocates only production overhead based on direct-labor hours. It is implementing a multistage ABC system for the design, production, and distribution functions of its value chain. You have been asked to complete the table below by indicating for each activity whether the related cost is direct, indirect, or unallocated. For each indirect cost, indicate one appropriate cost driver (more than one cost driver may be appropriate). The first two items have been completed for you.

Activity	Related Cost	Traditional	Multistage ABC
Supervising production	Supervisor salaries	Indirect (direct-labor hours)	Indirect (people supervised)
Designing a prototype for new product	Depreciation of computers	Unallocated	Indirect (number of parts)
Setting up for a production run	Mechanic wages		
Purchasing materials and parts to be used in products	Materials and parts cost		
Shipping sold products to customers (distributors)	Fuel used on company's fleet of trucks		
Market research study conducted by marketing staff to assess demand for potential new product	Salaries of market research staff		
Production scheduling	Salaries of production scheduling managers		
Purchasing materials and parts to be used in products	Salaries of purchasing agents		
Order processing of customer orders	Salaries of order processing staff		
Preparing cost analyses	Cost accountant salary		
Designing a new product	Salaries of design engineers that are fully dedicated to this new product		
Managing overall operations of company	Salary of executive		

4-49 Direct, Indirect, and Unallocated Costs

Study Appendix 4. Listed below are several activities and related costs that have been observed at Henderson Company, a manufacturing company. The company makes a variety of products and currently uses a traditional costing system that allocates only production overhead based on direct labor hours. It is implementing a multistage ABC system for the design, production, and customer service functions of its value chain. You have been asked to complete the table below by indicating for each activity whether the related cost is direct, indirect, or unallocated. For each indirect cost, indicate one appropriate cost driver (more than one cost driver may be appropriate).

Activity	Related Cost	Traditional	Multistage ABC
Supervising production	Supervisor salaries	Indirect (direct-labor hours)	Indirect (people supervised)
Designing a prototype for a new product	Depreciation of computers	Unallocated	Indirect (number of parts)
Setting up for a production run	Depreciation of production processing machinery that must remain idle during setup activity		
Purchasing materials and parts to be used in products	Materials and parts cost		
Shipping sold products to customers (distributors)	Fuel used on company's fleet of trucks		
Market research study conducted by marketing staff to assess demand for potential new product	Salaries of market research staff		
Moving partially completed products from processing to assembly area	Salaries of forklift operators		
Purchasing materials and parts to be used in products	Travel costs to interview potential vendors		
Customer inquiry	Telecommunication costs		
Preparing cost analyses	Cost accountant salary		
Designing a new product	Salaries of design engineers that are fully dedicated to this new product		
President delivering a speech to a trade conference	Travel and entertainment costs at conference		

4-50 Cost Assignment Paths

Study Appendix 4, especially the Summary Problem for your Review on pages 165–169. Exhibit 4-18 shows the MSABC system of the billing department. What costs would be included in the billing labor and bill-verifying labor resources? Compile a list of the cost-allocation paths from these two labor resources to the commercial accounts cost object.

4-51 Cost Assignment Paths

(This exercise is an extension of exercises 4-46 and 4-47. It should only be assigned if both the exercises are also assigned.) Study Appendix 4, especially the Summary Problem for your Review on pages 165–169. Panel B of Exhibit 4-23 shows the MSABC system for the Colorado City branch of

Better Bank. Compile a list of the cost-allocation paths from the managing officer resource to the commercial customers cost object.

Problems

4-52 Cost Accumulation and Allocation

Hwang Manufacturing Company has two departments, machining and finishing. For a given period, the following costs were incurred by the company as a whole: direct material, $130,000; direct labor, $75,000; and indirect manufacturing, $80,000. The grand total was $285,000.

The machining department incurred 70% of the direct-material costs, but only 33-$\frac{1}{3}$% of the direct-labor costs. As is commonplace, indirect manufacturing incurred by each department was allocated to products in proportion to the direct-labor costs of products within the departments. Three products were produced.

Product	Direct Material	Direct Labor
X-1	40%	30%
Y-1	30%	30%
Z-1	30%	40%
Total for the machining department	100%	100%
X-1	33 $\frac{1}{3}$%	40%
Y-1	33 $\frac{1}{3}$%	40%
Z-1	33 $\frac{1}{3}$%	20%
Total added by finishing department	100%	100%

The indirect manufacturing costs incurred by the machining and finishing departments and allocated to all products therein amounted to machining, $38,000 and finishing, $42,000.

1. Compute the total costs incurred by the machining department and added by the finishing department.
2. Compute the total costs of each product that would be shown as finished-goods inventory if all the products were transferred to finished stock on completion. (There were no beginning inventories.)

4-53 Activity-Based Costing and Activity-Based Management, Automotive Supplier

Reliable Machining Products (RMP) is an automotive component supplier. RMP has been approached by General Motors to consider expanding its production of part H707 to a total annual quantity of 2,000 units. This part is a low-volume, complex product with a high gross margin that is based on a proposed (quoted) unit sales price of $7.50. RMP uses a traditional costing system that allocates indirect manufacturing costs based on direct-labor costs. The rate currently used to allocate indirect manufacturing costs is 400% of direct-labor cost. This rate is based on the $3,300,000 annual factory overhead divided by $825,000 annual direct-labor cost. To produce 2,000 units of H707 requires $5,000 of direct materials and $1,000 of direct labor. The unit cost and gross margin percentage for part H707 based on the traditional cost system are computed as follows:

	Total	Per Unit ($\div$2,000)
Direct material	$ 5,000	$2.50
Direct labor	1,000	.50
Indirect manufacturing: (400% $\times$ direct labor)	4,000	2.00
Total cost	$10,000	$5.00
Sales price quoted		7.50
Gross margin		$2.50
Gross margin percentage		33.3%

The management of RMP decided to examine the effectiveness of their traditional costing system versus an activity-based costing system. The following data have been collected by a team consisting of accounting and engineering analysts:

Activity Center	Traceable Factory Overhead Costs (Annual)
Quality	$ 800,000
Production scheduling	50,000
Setup	600,000
Shipping	300,000
Shipping administration	50,000
Production	1,500,000
Total indirect manufacturing cost	$3,300,000

Activity Center: Cost Drivers	Annual Cost-Driver Quantity
Quality: Number of pieces scrapped	10,000
Production scheduling and set up: Number of setups	500
Shipping: Number of containers shipped	60,000
Shipping administration: Number of shipments	1,000
Production: Number of machine hours	10,000

The accounting and engineering team has performed activity analysis and provides the following estimates for the total quantity of cost drivers to be used to produce 2,000 units of part H707:

Cost Driver	Cost-Driver Consumption
Pieces scrapped	120
Setups	4
Containers shipped	10
Shipments	5
Machine hours	15

1. Prepare a schedule calculating the unit cost and gross margin of part H707 using the activity-based costing approach.
2. Based on the ABC results, which course of action would you recommend regarding the proposal by General Motors? List the benefits and costs associated with implementing an activity-based costing system at RMP.

4-54 Library Research in Activity-Based Costing or Activity-Based Management
Select an article from *Strategic Finance*, *Management Accounting Quarterly*, or *Journal of Cost Management* (available in most libraries) that describes a particular company's application of either (a) an activity-based costing system, or (b) activity-based management. Prepare a summary of 300 words or less that includes the following:

- Name of the company (if given)
- Industry of the company
- Description of the particular application
- Assessment of the benefits the company received from the application
- Any difficulties encountered in implementation

4-55 Review of Chapters 2, 3, and 4
The Gomez Hosiery Company provides you with the following miscellaneous data regarding operations in 20X1:

Gross profit	$ 20,000
Net loss	(5,000)
Sales	100,000
Direct material used	35,000
Direct labor	25,000
Fixed manufacturing overhead	15,000
Fixed selling and administrative expenses	10,000

There are no beginning or ending inventories.

Compute (a) variable selling and administrative expenses, (b) contribution margin in dollars, (c) variable manufacturing overhead, (d) break-even point in sales dollars, and (e) manufacturing cost of goods sold.

4-56 Review of Chapters 2, 3, and 4

Stephenson Corporation provides you with the following miscellaneous data regarding operations for 20X1:

Break-even point (in sales dollars)	$ 66,667
Direct material used	24,000
Gross profit	25,000
Contribution margin	30,000
Direct labor	28,000
Sales	100,000
Variable manufacturing overhead	5,000

There are no beginning or ending inventories.

Compute (a) the fixed manufacturing overhead, (b) variable selling and administrative expenses, and (c) fixed selling and administrative expenses.

4-57 Review of Chapters 2, 3, and 4

U. Grant Company manufactured and sold 1,000 sabres during November. Selected data for this month follow:

Sales	$100,000
Direct materials used	21,000
Direct labor	16,000
Variable manufacturing overhead	13,000
Fixed manufacturing overhead	14,000
Variable selling and administrative expenses	?
Fixed selling and administrative expenses	?
Contribution margin	40,000
Operating income	22,000

There were no beginning or ending inventories.

1. What were the variable selling and administrative expenses for November?
2. What were the fixed selling and administrative expenses for November?
3. What was the cost of goods sold during November?
4. Without prejudice to your earlier answers, assume that the fixed selling and administrative expenses for November amounted to $4,000.
   a. What was the break-even point in units for November?
   b. How many units must be sold to earn a target operating income of $12,000?
   c. What would the selling price per unit have to be if the company wanted to earn an operating income of $18,000 on the sale of 900 units?

4-58 Distribution Company, Activity-Based Management, Capacity Planning

Study Appendix 4. Southeast Distributors is in the business of distributing a variety of products to different classifications of customers from small corner grocery stores to large megastores. There are 16 activities in the company's ABC system. Some of these activities are processing orders, receiving, warehousing, unpacking and stacking, picking, unstacking and packing, repackaging in boxes, repackaging in cartons, shipping, and returns processing. The company's activity-based model computes the profitability of its major customer types. The process map has 91 symbols and 200 financial categories. The figure at the top of page 187 shows a small portion of this map, the order-processing (OP) department (8 symbols) for the month of April. The department performs three primary activities—regular order processing, returns processing, and order changes. Costs shown are the resource costs to be allocated to the department. Department total costs are to be allocated to departmental activities based on the number of OP documents processed. Note that each type of document (order changes, returns, and orders) takes about the same amount of work to process (hence the consumption rates are all 1).

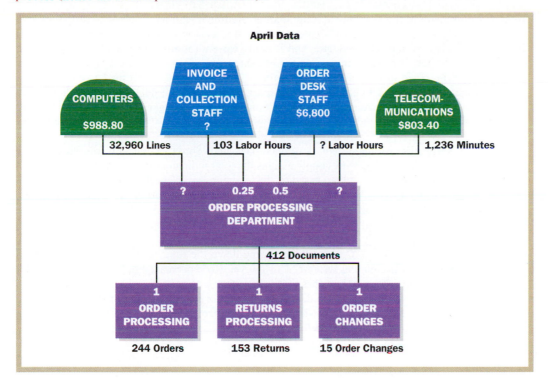

Southeast Distributors receives telephone orders for cases of different products from the various customer types. In some situations, prior to shipment the customer can change orders. Orders are handled by the order desk staff and subsequently processed by invoicing and collections staff. Resources used by the department include computers, invoicing and collections staff, order desk staff, and telecommunications. The average total cost incurred for each OP document processed is $28.1364, based on April data.

a. What is the resource-consumption rate for the computer and variable telecommunication resources?
b. What is the total cost of the invoicing and collections staff that supports the department?
c. How many labor hours of order desk staff support the department activities?
d. What is the activity-based cost of the three primary activities in the order processing department?
e. There is one person in the invoice and collections staff and two people in the order desk staff. Up until now, all staff worked an average of 135 hours each month. However, a new collective bargaining agreement lowers the number of available labor hours to 120 hours per month. April is a slow month for Southeast. The heaviest sales come in November when there are 19 order changes, 190 returns, and 300 orders. With the new union agreement, will the company be able to meet the processing needs in November? Explain.
f. Assume that one or more of the staff labor pools will not be able to meet the demand for processing in November. What alternative courses of action can management take?

4-59 Multistage Activity-Based Costing at AT&T

Study Appendix 4. Refer to the chapter discussion of the billing department at one of AT&T's customer care centers. Suppose the billing department has designed an MSABC system. Exhibit 4-18 on page 166 shows the process map for the MSABC system.

1. Using a format similar to the lower half of Exhibit 4-13 on page 158, calculate the cost per account for residential and commercial customers.
2. Based on this new MSABC information, what recommendation would you make to the billing department management concerning outsourcing to the local service bureau?
3. Prepare a table or chart that contrasts the residential cost per account to the commercial cost per account using the traditional, two-stage ABC, and MSABC systems. Comment on the results, indicating which system gives a greater level of accuracy and more information for management's strategic planning and operational control purposes.

Cases

4-60 ABC and Customer Profitability In Financial Services

To increase its share of the checking account market, Belltown National Bank in Seattle took two actions: It established a customer call center to respond to customer inquiries about account balances, checks cleared, fees charged, etc., and it paid year-end bonuses to branch managers who met their branch's target increase in the number of customers. While 80% of the branch managers met the target increase in the number of customers, Belltown National's profits continued to decline. Roger Welton, the CEO, didn't understand why profits were declining, even though the bank was serving more customers. The Pierce County branch manager, Rose Martinez, noticed that while small retail customers flocked to the bank, the number of business customers was declining.

Belltown National's costing system, developed back in 1988, is straightforward. No costs are traced directly to customers. The bank simply assigns the total indirect costs to customer lines (retail customer line or business customer line) based on the total number of checks processed.

Martinez suspected that Belltown National's cost system might be part of the problem. Martinez learned about activity-based costing (ABC) in school, but the applications involved manufacturing firms. She wonders whether Belltown National could develop an ABC system, with the customer-line as the primary cost object.

Rose's boss was skeptical. ("Our profits are going down the tubes and you want me to spend money developing a new accounting system???") However, Rose persuaded her boss to allow a pilot ABC study, using the three Tacoma branches for the pilot test.

The ABC implementation team included Martinez, the managers of each of the three Tacoma branches, a bank teller, and a customer service representative from the customer call center. The team began by identifying the following three activities:

- Check payments
- Teller withdrawals and deposits
- Customer service call center

The ABC team then scrutinized the Tacoma branches' total indirect cost of $2,850,000. They classified the components of this total indirect cost into the appropriate activity pool, coming up with the following estimates (in thousands of dollars):

Cost	Activity Cost Pool to Which Cost Is Assigned	Estimated Total Costs for Tacoma Branches
Salaries of check-processing personnel	Check payments	$ 440
Depreciation on check-processing equipment	Check payments	700
Teller salaries	Teller withdrawals and deposits	1,200
Salaries of customer representatives at call center	Customer service call center	450
Toll-free phone lines at customer call center	Customer service call center	60
Total indirect costs		$2,850

The team then identified the following cost drivers for each activity cost pool:

Activity Cost Pool	Activity Cost Driver
Check payments	number of checks processed
Teller withdrawals and deposits	number of teller transactions
Customer service call center	number of calls

The ABC team estimated that for the Tacoma branches, the retail customer line and the business customer line would require the following total resources (in thousands):

Activity Cost Driver	Number of Units of Activity Cost Driver Used by Retail Customers	Number of Units of Activity Cost Driver Used by Business Customers	Total
Checks processed	1,140	4,560	5,700
Teller transactions	320	80	400
Customer calls to call center	95	5	100
Checking accounts	150	50	200

That is, the retail customers have 320,000 teller transactions, make 95,000 calls to the customer service center, and so on.

On average, Belltown National Bank earns revenue from each type of account (from interest earned on checking account balances) as follows:

Average revenue per retail customer account $10
Average revenue per business customer account $40

1. Using the original (old) cost system:
   a. Compute the indirect cost allocation rate.
   b. Determine the total indirect cost assigned to the retail customer line and the business customer line.
   c. Compute the proportion of the total indirect cost assigned to the retail customer line and the business customer line.
   d. Determine the indirect cost per retail account and the indirect cost per business account.
   e. Assuming that there are no direct costs, compute the average profit per account for retail customers and for business customers.
   f. Assess the likely business strategy that might be adopted by managers using data from this original cost system.
2. What are the signs that Belltown National's original cost system was broken or in need of refinement?
3. Using the new activity-based costing system:
   a. Compute the indirect cost allocation rates for each of the three activities:
      • Check payments
      • Teller withdrawals and deposits
      • Customer call center
   b. Use the schedule below to compute the total indirect cost allocated to each customer line:

Activity	Total Indirect Cost Assigned to Retail Customer Line	Total Indirect Cost Assigned to Business Customer Line
Check payments		
Teller withdrawals and deposits		
Customer call center		
Total indirect costs		

   c. What proportion of each activity's resources are used by the retail customer line and the business customer line?
   d. Using the ABC data from number 4, compute the indirect cost per retail customer account and the indirect cost per business customer account.
   e. Explain why the results in number 1d and number 6 differ in the direction they do. Be precise and specific.
   f. Using the new ABC data, compute the average profit per account for both retail and business customers. Assess the likely business strategy that might be adopted by managers using data from this ABC cost system.
4. Be prepared to discuss the following questions:
   a. Was Belltown National Bank's bonus-based incentive plan to increase the number of checking account customers a wise strategy? Would you suggest any change in the strategy based on the ABC analysis?
   b. What benefits can Belltown National reap from the ABC analysis?
   c. Why might Rose Martinez have suspected that the benefits of ABC would likely outweigh the costs of implementing ABC at Belltown National Bank?
   d. Why is it important for non-accounting managers to understand ABC?

4-61 Identifying Activities, Resources, and Cost Drivers in Manufacturing

Extrusion Plastics is a multinational, diversified organization. One of its manufacturing divisions, Northeast Plastics Division, has become less profitable due to increased competition. The division produces three major lines of plastic products within its single plant. Product Line A is high-volume, simple pieces produced in large batches. Product Line B is medium-volume, more complex pieces. Product Line C is low-volume, small-order, highly complex pieces.

Currently, the division allocates indirect manufacturing costs based on direct labor. The vice president of manufacturing is uncomfortable using the traditional cost figures. He thinks the company is underpricing the more complex products. He decides to conduct an activity-based costing analysis of the business.

Interviews were conducted with the key managers in order to identify activities, resources, cost drivers, and their interrelationships.

Interviewee: Production Manager

Q1: What activities are carried out in your area?
A1: All products are manufactured using three similar, complex, and expensive molding machines. Each molding machine can be used in the production of the three product lines. Each setup takes about the same time irrespective of the product.

Q2: Who works in your area?
A2: Last year, we employed 30 machine operators, two maintenance mechanics, and two supervisors.

Q3: How are the operators used in the molding process?
A3: It requires nine operators to support a machine during the actual production process.

Q4: What do the maintenance mechanics do?
A4: Their primary function is to perform machine setups. However, they were also required to provide machine maintenance during the molding process.

Q5: Where do the supervisors spend their time?
A5: They provide supervision for the machine operators and the maintenance mechanics. For the most part, the supervisors appear to spend the same amount of time with each of the employees that they supervise.

Q6: What other resources are used to support manufacturing?
A6: The molding machines use energy during the molding process and during the setups. We put meters on the molding machines to get a better understanding of their energy consumption. We discovered that for each hour that a machine ran, it used 6.3 kilowatts of energy. The machines also require consumable shop supplies (e.g., lubricants, hoses, and so on). We have found a direct correlation between the amount of supplies used and the actual processing time.

Q7: How is the building used, and what costs are associated with it?
A7: We have a 100,000-square-foot building. The total rent and insurance costs for the year were $675,000. These costs are allocated to production, sales, and administration based on square footage.

1. Identify the activities and resources for the division. For each activity, suggest an appropriate cost driver.
2. For each resource identified in number 1, indicate its cost behavior with respect to the activities it supports (assume a planning period of 1 month).

4-62 Multistage Activity-Based Costing, Customer Costing, Benchmarking, Banking

Study Appendix 4. Refer to Exercises 4-46 and 4-47. Independent of your answer to Exercise 4-47, assume that the results of the two-stage ABC study are as shown below.

Activity	Lowest Activity Cost per Driver Unit*	Colorado City Branch Cost per Driver Unit
Process new accounts	$81.67 per new account	$103.70
Process deposits and withdrawals	$ 0.75 per deposit or withdrawal	$ 1.61
Process other transactions	$ 3.05 per transaction	$ 3.33

Customer Class	Lowest Customer Cost per Account*	Colorado City Branch Cost per Account
Retail	$ 88	$102
Business	$508	$564

*These benchmarks are based on only those branches that implemented two-stage ABC systems.

The branch managing officer at the Colorado City branch of Better Bank is concerned that branch costs are high compared to the benchmarks within the Better Bank system. In particular, she is not sure how to proceed with a process improvement program because there are insufficient operational data resulting from the study.

For example, although she knows that the cost of the activity "processing deposits and withdrawals" is clearly too high (reflecting operational inefficiencies) compared to the benchmark, she has no operational information from which to begin. When she asked the RSMs to suggest ideas for improvement, their typical response was, "These percentages do not help us any. We need more information, like the time it takes tellers to process deposits and withdrawals and how much supervision is needed for this process." Managers also noted that the unallocated costs amounted to over half of the total branch costs. So the branch managing officer decided to refine the two-stage ABC by implementing multistage ABC.

In order to convert the two-stage ABC to a multistage ABC model the following had to be done:

- For each activity in the two-stage model, determine if other activities are required. This is done through more extensive interviews and data analysis. Typically, the more in-depth analysis yields additional activities, and more resources can be allocated.
- For each resource, determine a cost driver and cost behavior.
- For activities and related resources, determine the resource consumption rates. Replace the percentages in the two-stage model with these rates.

The result was a complete process map for the operations of the Colorado City branch. This map was the document used to enter the model into a computer program. The process map is shown in Exhibit 4-23, panel B, on page 181. Key results of the interviews, data analysis, and computer analysis are given on the next page.

Collaboration with other branches that were implementing multistage ABC as well as further interviews with branch managers resulted in two additional activities being identified that could be allocated: processing loans and the background investigation (credit and employment history). The cost driver for both of these activities is the number of loan applications. In addition, two variable-cost resources were identified: telecommunications and computer services. The cost driver for telecommunications is minutes and the cost driver for computer services is online computer transactions. The cost data for each of these variable-cost resources were specified on a per cost-driver unit basis, and it is assumed that these rates would apply across the relevant range of activity. The resulting unallocated resource costs were reduced from $430,000 to $303,076.

A transcript of some interviews with assistant operations managers follows:

Q1: Can you identify other activities beyond those in the first ABC study that use up significant amounts of resources?

A1: Yes, although we do not process many loan applications compared to deposits and withdrawals, when we do process them, it takes lots of time. Last year, we had 250 retail loan applications and 100 commercial applications. Tellers process applications, and RSMs do a lot of loan research. We use the computers and are on the phone a lot of the time. Even the branch manager reviews each application.

Q2: Can you estimate, in terms of labor hours, how tellers spend their time on the four activities?

A2: It takes about one and one-half labor hours for tellers to process a new account. Our records show that on average it takes about three minutes to process a deposit or withdrawal and about nine minutes to process the other transactions. That is why I mentioned the loans. Each loan application takes about 20 to 30 minutes. I would estimate that 24 minutes would be a good average.

Q3: How many computer transactions and how much phone time did you say it takes to process loans?

A3: Based on our records, tellers use the computer about 15 minutes and make about 38 computer transactions for each loan application. RSMs use the computer ten minutes and make about 45 computer transactions for background investigation. Tellers do not use the phone, but between the assistant manager and branch manager, I would say that about 35 minutes of phone time is used for background investigation on each application.

Q4: Do you lease computer time or own your computers?

A4: We lease computers as well as an online computer service. We are charged by the number of online computer transactions we make, and the current rate is $.05 per computer transaction. For example, it may take 15 to 20 transactions to process a deposit for an account but most of these will be off-line. There would be only four to six transactions made online for a deposit. The financial services firm we use has a new software program for processing deposits and withdrawals and an excellent training program. However, we have not purchased this program nor have we used their training. Last year, the total cost of computer time was $82,847.50 and our records show that we were billed for 1,656,950 computer transactions.

Q5: You mentioned that both RSMs and the managing officer were involved with loan applications. Can you specify how much time they spend?

A5: Yes, most of the work in doing loan research is done by the RSMs. They spend close to two hours investigating each loan. In fact, the average last year was 1.75 hours per application. The final approval of a loan is made by the managing officer after her review. This takes about a half hour per application.

Q6: You mentioned her review. Did you mean her review of the assistant managers' work or her separate analysis?

A6: What I mean is her separate analysis takes 30 minutes. She also supervises all of their work. I would estimate that she spends about nine minutes each hour with the RSMs.

For those branches that implemented multistage ABC, much more benchmarking data were generated than for the two-stage method due to the operational focus. The following is benchmark data for those activities and resources where significant differences existed between the Colorado City branch and the best practices in the Better Bank system.

Selected Operational Benchmarks for Better Bank System

Activity and Related Resource	Benchmark
Processing new accounts—labor time	1 hour per new account
Processing deposits and withdrawals—labor time	2 minutes per deposit or withdrawal
Processing loan applications—labor time	15 minutes per application
Processing loan applications—computer	22 computer transactions per application
Background investigations—analysis time (RSMs)	1 hour per application
Background investigations—telecommunications time	20 minutes per application
Processing other transactions—labor time	6 minutes per transaction
Processing other transactions—computer	9 computer transactions per transaction

Selected Financial Benchmarks for Better Bank System

Processing cost per new account	$35
Processing cost per deposit or withdrawal	$.85
Processing cost of other transactions (per transaction)	$6.25
Processing cost of a loan application	$102
Cost per retail customer	$75
Cost per commercial customer	$640

Once the operational and financial data were collected and input into a computer program, the traceable costs for each of the four primary activities were calculated (rounded to the nearest dollar).

Activity	Traceable Cost
Open new accounts	$ 22,824
Process deposits and withdrawals	$260,896
Process other transactions	$332,908
Process loan applications	$ 61,371

Required

1. Refer to Exhibit 4-23 on page 181, panel B. Complete the business process map for the Colorado City branch by determining the missing data (13 data items depicted by □). Use the interview information.
2. Determine the activity cost per driver unit for each of the four primary activities.
3. Determine the cost per account for both retail and commercial customers.
4. What does your analysis suggest about the operations at the Colorado City branch?
5. The branch manager has decided to implement a process improvement program. The program has two components: (a) teller efficiency improvement including their use of computers (the use of computers for processing other transactions is entirely by tellers) and (b) RSM efficiency improvement including their use of telecommunications for researching loans. The goal of the program is to attain benchmark efficiency levels. The teller efficiency component would involve RSMs spending more time to train tellers. This additional time would add three minutes each hour to the existing time RSMs spend supervising tellers. The RSM component would involve self-improvement and the adoption of credit scoring. In credit scoring, a point system is used to evaluate the risk of applicants. If the applicant's initial score is higher than a specified cutoff, then the RSM automatically approves the loan without any background investigation.

The managing officer needs an analysis of the expected cost savings associated with each program. It was assumed that efficiency improvements in activities (processing deposits and withdrawals, and so on) did not have an impact on unallocated resources. For example, the teller labor hours that are associated with unallocated resources (580) remained unchanged.

Cost savings from lower levels of teller labor or assistant managers will be realized through attrition rather than layoffs. Currently, there are 14 tellers who are available for a total of 1,500 hours each year. Management has set a policy that efficiency gains in labor will not result in any layoffs but that, through attrition, the number of tellers will be reduced by the full-time equivalent positions saved [that is, (savings in hours) ÷ 1,500 rounded down].

A partially completed analysis is presented in Exhibit 4-24. Complete this analysis by doing the teller labor analysis section and determining the total expected cost savings.

4-63 Library Research and AT&T Corporation

AT&T Corporation was highlighted on page 129. AT&T used multistage ABC as described in Appendix 4 of our chapter. In fact, AT&T first tried the two-stage ABC approach but was not happy with it. A detailed description of AT&T's experience with ABM is given in the article "Activity-Based Management at AT&T," by T. Hobdy, J. Thomson, and P. Sharman, *Management Accounting* (April 1994).

Compare the approach to designing and implementing an ABC and ABM system described in the text to that described in the article by answering the following questions.

1. In the article, how were "some billing costs" allocated to different customer classes (invoice types) prior to implementing the process modeling approach to ABC?
2. In the article, what business unit was selected for the pilot ABC project and what were the overall goals of the pilot study from the managers' perspective?
3. From the article, give examples of cost objects, activities, resources, and cost drivers.
4. For AT&T, "the cost of service support to these individual customers was determined by identifying activity and driver consumption characteristics." For the bill verification activity described in Exhibit 4-19, what is meant by the cost consumption characteristics for the labor resource.
5. Exhibit 4-18 on page 166 shows the operations of the Billing Department at AT&T. A similar flowchart is described in the article. What function did it perform?
6. In the article, "each cost object was costed by multiplying the quantity of driver units of each activity consumed by the cost per driver unit." Using the data from Exhibit 4-18, explain how this method applies for the residential customer class.
7. In the article, the ABC study revealed that "25% of total center costs were assignable to message investigation (account inquiry and correspondence)." For the text illustration, what is the percent of total billing department costs assigned to account inquiry investigation?
8. What process improvements were implemented at AT&T for the message investigation activity?

EXCEL Application Exercise

4-64 Traditional Costing versus Activity-Based Costing

Goal: Create an Excel spreadsheet to compare traditional costing versus activity-based costing. Use the results to answer questions about your findings.

Scenario: Circuitech Corporation is one of Dell's circuit board suppliers. Circuitech currently uses traditional costing for making business decisions. At the urging of Dell, however, the company has decided to move to activity-based costing for circuit board production related to products LP-7310 and PC-33. As one of the company's accountants, you have been asked to prepare a spreadsheet comparing the two costing methods for the next company board meeting. Your supervisor has given you the following quarterly data:

Total Indirect Costs for the Quarter:

Assembly	$630,000	
Soldering	$270,000	
Inspection	$160,000	

	LP-7310	PC-33
Direct costs (materials, labor)	$162,400	$178,240
Machine hours (assembly)	480	1,080
Number of units produced (soldering)	6,000	4,000
Testing hours (inspection)	6,000	8,000

Teller Labor Analysis

	Open New Accounts	Process Deposits and Withdrawals	Process other Transactions	Process Loan Applications	Background Investigations	Supervision of Tellers	Total
Current resource consumption (hours):							
Current rate × Current driver units							
Benchmark resource consumption (hours):							
Benchmark rate × Current driver units							
Teller labor time savings (hours)							
Teller labor cost savings							

Retail Sales Manager Labor Analysis

	Open New Accounts	Process Deposits and Withdrawals	Process other Transactions	Process Loan Applications	Background Investigations	Supervision of Tellers	Total
Current resource consumption (hours):					1.75 × 350 = 612.5	0.10 × 17,030 = 1,703	
Current rate × Current driver units							
Benchmark resource consumption (hours):					1.0 × 350 = 350.0	0.15 × 11,540.29 = 1,731	
Benchmark rate × predicted driver units							
RSM time savings (hours)					262.5	(28.6)	234.5
RSM cost savings							$ -0- *

Computer Resource Analysis

	Open New Accounts	Process Deposits and Withdrawals	Process other Transactions	Process Loan Applications	Background Investigations	Supervision of Tellers	Total
Current resource consumption (computer transactions):			15 × 49,000 = 735,000	38 × 350 = 13,300			
Benchmark resource consumption:			9 × 49,000 = 441,000	22 × 350 = 7,700			
Computer time savings (minutes)			294,000	5,600			299,600
Computer cost savings (299,600 × $0.05)							$14,980

Telecommunications Resource Analysis

	Open New Accounts	Process Deposits and Withdrawals	Process other Transactions	Process Loan Applications	Background Investigations	Supervision of Tellers	Total
Current resource consumption (minutes):					35 × 350 = 12,250		
Benchmark resource consumption (minutes):					20 × 350 = 7,000		
Telecommunications time savings (minutes)					5,250		5,250
Telecommunications time savings 5,250 × .175080436							$919
TOTAL COST SAVINGS							?

*Assuming that no retail sales managers would be laid off.

Exhibit 4-24
Benchmark Program Cost Analysis for the Colorado City Branch of Better Bank

When you have completed your spreadsheet, answer the following questions:

a. What is the total manufacturing cost per unit using traditional costing for LP-7310? For PC-33?

b. What is the total manufacturing cost per unit using activity-based costing for LP-7310? For PC-33?

c. What conclusions can be drawn from your spreadsheet results?

Step-by-Step:

1. Open a new Excel spreadsheet.
2. In column A, create a bold-faced heading that contains the following:
   Row 1: Chapter 4 Decision Guideline
   Row 2: Circuitech Corporation
   Row 3: Traditional vs. Activity-based Costing
   Row 4: Today's Date

   Note: Adjust column widths as follows: Column A (41.57), Columns B, C, and D (21.0). Column D is for check figures only. The column widths have been designed to ensure that Column D will not print on the final version of the spreadsheet if only page 1 is printed.

3. Merge and center the four heading rows across columns A through C.
4. In Column A, create the following row headings:
   Row 7: Raw Data
   Row 8: Indirect costs for the quarter:
   Row 9: Assembly
   Row 10: Soldering
   Row 11: Inspection
   Row 12: Total indirect costs
   Skip 2 rows
   Row 15: Direct costs (Materials, labor)
   Row 16: Machine hours (Assembly)
   Row 17: Number of units produced (Soldering)
   Row 18: Testing hours (Inspection)
   Skip 2 rows
   Row 21: Traditional costing system
   Row 22: Indirect cost driver (machine hours)
   Row 23: Allocated indirect costs
   Skip a row
   Row 25: Cost per product
   Row 26: Direct costs
   Row 27: Manufacturing overhead
   Row 28: Total manufacturing costs per product
   Skip a row
   Row 30: Number of units
   Row 31: Total manufacturing costs per unit
   Skip 2 rows
   Row 34: Activity-based costing system
   Row 35: Assembly cost driver (machine hours)
   Row 36: Allocated assembly cost
   Row 37: Soldering cost driver (units)
   Row 38: Allocated soldering cost
   Row 39: Inspection cost driver (testing hours)
   Row 40: Allocated inspection cost
   Skip a row
   Row 42: Cost per product
   Row 43: Direct costs
   Row 44: Manufacturing overhead:
   Row 45: Assembly
   Row 46: Soldering
   Row 47: Inspection
   Row 48: Total manufacturing costs per product
   Skip a row

Row 50: Number of units
Row 51: Total manufacturing costs per unit

4. Change the format of Raw Data (Row 7), Traditional costing system (Row 21), and Activity-based costing system (Row 34) to bold-faced headings.

    Hint: Use the control key for highlighting multiple cells or rows when making changes.

5. Change the format of Cost per product (Rows 25 and 42) to underlined headings.
6. In Rows 14, 21, 25, 34, and 42 create the following bold-faced, right-justified column headings:
    Column B: LP-7310
    Column C: PC-33
7. In Rows 21 and 34 create the following bold-faced, right-justified column headings:
    Column D: Total
8. Use the scenario data to fill in the Raw Data section.
    Use the SUM function to calculate Total indirect costs (Row 12).
9. Traditional costing system:
    Fill in rows 26 and 30 with information from the Raw Data section.
    Use appropriate formulas from Chapter 4 to calculate the cost driver and allocated costs.
    Use the SUM function to calculate the Total column for manufacturing overhead costs.
    Complete the remainder of the Cost per product data using formulas and calculations.
    Calculate the Total manufacturing costs per product.
10. Activity-based costing system:
    Fill in Rows 43 and 50 with information from the Raw Data section.
    Use appropriate formulas from Chapter 4 to calculate the cost drivers and allocated costs.
    Use the SUM function to calculate the Total columns for all allocated costs.
    Complete the remainder of the Cost per product data using formulas and calculations.
    Calculate the Total manufacturing costs per product.

    Hint: If using the SUM function to calculate Total manufacturing costs, verify range.

11. Format all amounts as:

Number tab:	
	Category: Currency
	Decimal places: 2
	Symbol: None
	Negative numbers: Red with parentheses

12. Change the format of hours and units in rows 16–18, 30, and 50 to display no decimal places.
13. Change the format of the amounts in rows 9, 12, 15, 23, 26, 28, 31, 36, 38, 40, 43, 48, and 51 to display a dollar symbol.
14. Change the format of the row headings in rows 9–11, 15–18, 23, 36, 38, 40, and 45–47 to display as indented.

Alignment tab:	
	Horizontal: Left (Indent)
	Indent: 1

15. Change the format of the amounts in rows 12, 28, and 48 to display a top border, using the default Line Style.

Border tab:	
	Icon: Top Border

16. Change the format of the cost driver calculations in rows 22, 35, 37, and 39 to display as left-justified percentages with two decimal places.

Number tab:	
	Category: Percentage
	Decimal places: 2

Alignment tab:	
	Horizontal: Left (Indent)
	Indent: 0

17. Accentuate the Cost per product information for each costing method by applying cell-shading to columns A, B, and C of rows 25–31 and 42–51.

Patterns tab:	
	Color: Lightest grey

18. Save your work to disk, and print a copy for your files.

    Note: The final version of the spreadsheet will be on page 1. You do not need to print page 2 as it should contain only the check figures.

Collaborative Learning Exercise

4-65 Internet Research, ABC, and ABM

Form groups of three to five people each. Each member of the group should pick one of the following industries:

- Manufacturing
- Insurance
- Health care
- Government
- Service

Each person should explore the Internet for an example of a company that implemented activity-based costing and activity-based management. One way to do this is to go to the Web site http://www.Hyperion.com and choose one company from the industry chosen. Prepare and give a briefing for your group. Do this by completing the following:

1. Describe the company and its business.
2. What was the scope of the ABC/ABM project?
3. What were the goals for the ABC/ABM project?
4. Summarize the results of the project.

After each person has briefed the group on his or her company, discuss within your group the commonalities between the ABC/ABM applications.

Internet Exercise   ●   www.prenhall.com/horngren

4-66 Vermont Teddy Bear Factory

Costs are very important to any manager. Managers focus on trying to keep costs as low as possible. There are many ways to report costs such as the total amount that is often seen on the income statement to an individual cost for a particular component part.

1. Go to the home page of Vermont Teddy Bear Factory at http://www.vermontteddybear.com. When you click onto the Web site, what does it suggest that you should do? What is the current headline offering on the site?
2. Click to learn more about what a Bear-Gram gift is and what it contains.
3. What is unique about a Vermont Teddy Bear? What color can a teddy bear be? Can you choose what type of outfit you would like your bear to sport? What do you notice about the accessories?
4. Take a tour of the factory. Click on "Online Factory Tour" in the QUICK LINKS section. What bear can we see being born online? Take the online tour. List several activities shown in the tour. What are some resources that are consumed by these activities? For one of the activities you listed, give at least one fixed-cost and one variable-cost resource. Suggest a cost driver for one of the activities you listed.
5. Do you think that the Vermont Teddy Bear factory would be a good candidate for using activity-based costing? Explain.
6. Find the company's most recent annual report by clicking "investor relations" at ir.vtbearcompany.com. What information can you find about the types of inventory accounts that the company has? Where did you find this information? What was the value of the inventory accounts for the past year? Is this amount increasing or decreasing?
7. Would you say the firm is a manufacturer or merchandiser, based on the financial statements? Does the income statement provided give you a clue as to the type of firm this is? Explain. In the chapter, we discussed the differences in the financial statements for a manufacturer and a merchandiser — do these differences really show up in the annual report?

Relevant Information and Decision Making: Marketing Decisions

CHAPTER 5

LEARNING OBJECTIVES

When you have finished studying this chapter, you should be able to:

1. Discriminate between relevant and irrelevant information for making decisions.

2. Apply the decision process to make business decisions.

3. Decide to accept or reject a special order using the contribution margin technique.

4. Choose whether to add or delete a product line using relevant information.

5. Compute a measure of product profitability when production is constrained by a scarce resource.

6. Identify the factors that influence pricing decisions in practice.

7. Compute a target sales price by various approaches, and compare the advantages and disadvantages of these approaches.

8. Use target costing to decide whether to add a new product.

While you are on vacation, the last thing you want to

worry about is transportation. For visitors to Grand Canyon National Park, the **Grand Canyon Railway** provides a relaxing alternative to driving to the canyon. Why drive when you can sit back and enjoy the scenery across 65 miles of beautiful Arizona countryside from the comfort of a fully reconditioned steam-powered train? Strolling musicians serenade you, and western characters stage attacks and holdups that offer a glimpse into what train travel might have been like for old-west loggers, miners, and ranchers at the turn of the century. The Grand Canyon Railway thus offers a ride not only to the canyon itself but into the past as well.

Of course, rides into the past aren't exactly cheap. Tracks for the narrow-gauge train as well as the authentic steam engines and passenger cars cost an awful lot to buy new or to recondition. The company spent upward of $20 million before opening. Recovering that initial investment while earning a profit is not easy. According to the company controller, Kevin Call, "Pricing is really the key in running a successful operation."

The railway offers five different classes of service, and setting the pricing on each one determines the profit and return on investment the company's going to make. To set prices, management uses the contribution margin technique introduced in Chapter 2. Among the influences on pricing discussed in this chapter, costs and customer demands are the most important to the railway. The prices charged must not only ensure a reasonable profit, but also must be attractive to the customer.

Costs are important in the marketing decisions of many types of companies. What price should a **Safeway** store charge for a pound of hamburger? What should **Boeing** charge for a 777 airplane? Should a clothing manufacturer accept a special discount

The Grand Canyon Railway offers classic train rides to the southern rim of the Grand Canyon. The train departs from the railway's Williams, Arizona, depot for the 65-mile trip. Managers use relevant cost and revenue information to set prices for the various classes of passenger service.

order from **Wal-Mart**? Should an appliance manufacturer add a new product, say, an automatic bread machine, to its product line? Or should the company drop an existing product? Marketing managers rely on accounting information to answer these questions and make important decisions on a daily basis. Without accounting information, it would be impossible for a firm to determine a marketing strategy. However, not all accounting information applies to each type of decision. In this chapter, we'll focus on identifying relevant information for marketing decisions. The ability to separate relevant from irrelevant information is often the difference between success and failure in modern business.[1] ■

The Concept of Relevance

What information is relevant? That depends on the decision being made. Decision making is essentially choosing among several courses of action. The available actions are identified by an often time-consuming formal or informal search and screening process, perhaps carried out by a company team that includes engineers, accountants, and operating executives.

Accountants play an important role in the decision-making process, not as decision makers but as collectors, reporters, and analyzers of relevant information. Although many managers want the accountant to recommend the proper decision, the final choice always rests with the operating executive. The accountant's role in decision making is primarily that of a technical expert on financial analysis who helps managers focus on the relevant information that will lead to the best decision.

What Is Relevance?

OBJECTIVE 1

Discriminate between relevant and irrelevant information for making decisions.

relevant information
The predicted future costs and revenues that will differ among alternative courses of action.

Making business decisions requires managers to compare two or more alternative courses of action. Accountants should use two criteria to determine whether information is relevant: (1) Information must be an expected future revenue or cost, and (2) it must have an element of difference among the alternatives. **Relevant information** is the predicted future costs and revenues that will differ among the alternatives.

Note that relevant information is a prediction of the future, not a summary of the past. Historical (past) data have no direct bearing on a decision. Such data can have an indirect bearing on a decision because they may help in predicting the future. But past figures, in themselves, are irrelevant to the decision itself. Why? Because the decision cannot affect past data. Decisions affect the future. Nothing can alter what has already happened.

Of the expected future data, only those that will differ from alternative to alternative are relevant to the decision. Any item that will remain the same regardless of the alternative selected is irrelevant. For instance, if a department manager's salary will be the same regardless of the products produced, the salary is irrelevant to the selection of products.

Here are some examples to help you clarify the sharp distinctions between relevant and irrelevant information.

Suppose you always buy gasoline from either of two nearby gasoline stations. Yesterday you noticed that one station was selling gasoline at $1.50 per gallon. The other was selling it at $1.40. Your automobile needs gasoline, and in making your choice of stations, you assume that these prices have not changed. The relevant costs are $1.50 and $1.40, the expected future costs that will differ between the alternatives. You use your past experience (that is, what you observed yesterday) for predicting today's price. Note that the relevant cost is not what you paid in the past, or what you observed yesterday, but what you expect to pay when you drive in to get gasoline. This cost meets our two criteria: (1) It is the expected future cost, and (2) it differs between the alternatives.

---

[1] Throughout this and the next chapter, to concentrate on the fundamental ideas, we shall ignore the time value of money and income taxes (discussed in Chapter 11).

You may also plan to have your car lubricated. The recent price at each station was $12, and this is what you anticipate paying. This expected future cost is irrelevant because it will be the same under either alternative. It does not meet our second criterion.

On a business level, consider the following decision. A food container manufacturer is thinking of using aluminum instead of tin in making a line of large cans. The cost of direct material will decrease from 30¢ to 20¢ per can if aluminum is used.

The cost of tin used for this comparison probably came from historical cost records on the amount paid most recently for tin, but the relevant cost in the foregoing analysis is the expected future cost of tin compared with the expected future cost of aluminum.

The direct-labor cost will continue to be 70¢ per unit regardless of the material used. It is irrelevant because our second criterion—an element of difference between the alternatives—is not met.

	Aluminum	Tin	Difference
Direct material	$.20	$.30	$.10
Direct labor	.70	.70	—

Therefore, we can safely exclude direct labor from the comparison of alternatives.

A Decision Model

Exhibit 5-1 illustrates this simple decision, and it serves to show the appropriate framework for more complex decisions. Box 1(A) represents historical data from the accounting system. Box 1(B) represents other data, such as price indices or industry statistics, gathered from outside the accounting system. Regardless of their source, the data in step 1 help the formulation of predictions in step 2. (Remember that, although historical data may act as a guide to predicting, they are irrelevant to the decision itself.)

In step 3, these predictions become inputs to the decision model. A **decision model** is any method used for making a choice. Such models sometimes require elaborate quantitative procedures, such as a petroleum refinery's mathematical method for choosing what products to manufacture for any given day or week. A decision model, however, may also be simple. It may be confined to a single comparison of costs for choosing between two materials. In this example, our decision model is to compare the predicted unit costs and select the alternative with the lesser cost.

We will be referring to Exhibit 5-1 frequently because it illustrates the main concept in this chapter. In fact, this decision process applies to all business decisions, no matter how simple or complicated they may be. By using this process, you will be able to focus squarely on the relevant information—the predicted future differences between alternatives—in any decision. In the rest of this chapter, we will use this decision process to apply the concept of relevance to several specific marketing decisions.

Accuracy and Relevance

In the best of all possible worlds, the information managers use for decision making would be perfectly relevant and accurate. However, in reality, such information is often too difficult or too costly to obtain. Accountants are thus sometimes forced to trade relevance for accuracy.

Precise but irrelevant information is worthless for decision making. For example, a university president's salary may be $140,000 per year, to the penny, but may have no bearing on the question of whether to buy or rent data-processing equipment. However, imprecise but relevant information can be useful. For example, sales predictions for a new product may be subject to error, but they still are helpful to the decision of whether to manufacture the product. Of course, relevant information must be reasonably accurate but not precisely so.

OBJECTIVE 2

Apply the decision process to make business decisions.

decision model
Any method for making a choice, sometimes requiring elaborate quantitative procedures.

Exhibit 5-1
Decision Process and
Role of Information

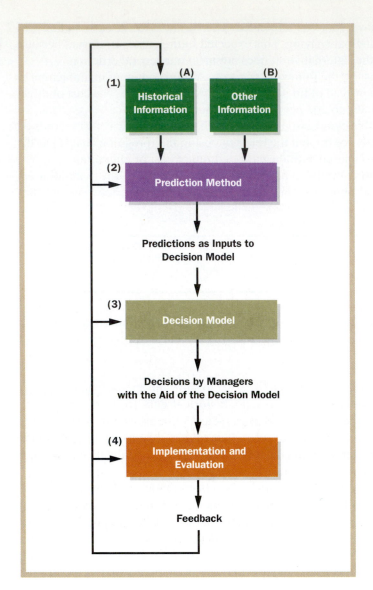

The degree to which information is relevant or precise often depends on the degree to which it is qualitative or quantitative. Qualitative aspects are those for which measurement in dollars and cents is difficult and imprecise; quantitative aspects are those for which measurement is easy and precise. Accountants, statisticians, and mathematicians try to express as many decision factors as feasible in quantitative terms, because this approach reduces the number of qualitative factors to be judged. Just as we noted that relevance is more crucial than precision in decision making, so qualitative aspects may easily carry more weight than measurable (quantitative) financial impacts in many decisions. For example, the extreme opposition of a militant union to new labor-saving machinery may cause a manager to forgo installation of such machinery even if it would save money. Alternatively, to avoid a long-range dependence on a particular supplier, a company may pass up the opportunity to purchase a component from the supplier at a price below the cost of producing it themselves.

Similarly, managers sometimes introduce new technology (for example, advanced computer systems or automated equipment) even though the expected quantitative results seem unattractive. Managers defend such decisions on the grounds that failure to keep abreast of new technology will surely bring unfavorable financial results sooner or later.

The Special Sales Order

The first decision for which we examine relevant information is the special sales order.

Illustrative Example

In our illustration, we'll focus on the Cordell Company. Suppose Cordell makes and sells 1 million units of seat covers for seats on airplanes, buses, and railroad passenger cars. Cordell sells these to companies such as America West and the Grand Canyon Railway Company. The total manufacturing cost of making 1,000,000 seat covers is $30,000,000. The unit manufacturing cost of the product is $30,000,000 ÷ 1,000,000, or $30 per unit. Suppose Branson Gray Line Tours offered Cordell $26 per unit for a 100,000-unit special order that (1) would not affect Cordell's regular business in any way, (2) would not raise any antitrust issues concerning price discrimination, (3) would not affect total fixed costs, (4) would not require any additional variable selling and administrative expenses, and (5) would use some otherwise idle manufacturing capacity. Should Cordell accept the order?

Perhaps we should state the question more succinctly: What is the difference in the short-run financial results between not accepting and accepting? As usual, the key question is, What are the differences between alternatives? Exhibit 5-2 presents the projected income statement of the Cordell Company without the special order, using the contribution margin technique.

OBJECTIVE 3

Decide to accept or reject a special order using the contribution margin technique.

Correct Analysis—Focus on Relevant Information and Cost Behavior

The correct analysis focuses on determining relevant information and cost behavior. It employs the contribution margin technique. As Exhibit 5-3 shows, this particular order affects only variable manufacturing costs, at a rate of $24 per unit. All other variable costs and all fixed costs are unaffected and thus irrelevant, so a manager may safely ignore them in making this special-order decision. Note how the contribution margin technique's distinction between variable- and fixed-cost behavior patterns aids the necessary cost analysis. Total short-run income will increase by $200,000 if Cordell accepts the order—despite the fact that the unit selling price of $26 is less than the total unit manufacturing cost of $30.

Why did we include fixed costs in Exhibit 5-3? After all, they are irrelevant. We included them because management wants to know the difference in short-run financial results between not accepting and accepting the special order. The analysis could have ended with the contribution margin line, but we wanted to show how the difference would affect the bottom line—operating income. There will be occasions when irrelevant data will be included in the accountant's presentation of analysis. Why? To suit the preferences of managers who will use the information for decision making.

Contribution Form		
Sales		$40,000
Less: variable expenses		
Manufacturing	$24,000	
Selling and administrative	2,200	26,200
Contribution margin		$13,800
Less: fixed expenses		
Manufacturing	$ 6,000	
Selling and administrative	5,800	11,800
Operating income		$ 2,000

Exhibit 5-2
Cordell Company
Contribution Form of the Income Statement For the Year Ended December 31, 20X1 (thousands of dollars)

	Without Special Order, 1,000,000 Units	Effect of Special Order 100,000 Units		With Special Order, 1,100,000 Units
		Total	Per Unit	
Sales	$40,000,000	$2,600,000	$26	$42,600,000
Less: variable expenses				
Manufacturing	$24,000,000	$2,400,000	$24	$26,400,000
Selling and administrative	2,200,000	—	—	2,200,000
Total variable expenses	$26,200,000	$2,400,000	$24	$28,600,000
Contribution margin	$13,800,000	$ 200,000	$ 2	$14,000,000
Less: fixed expenses				
Manufacturing	$ 6,000,000	—	—	$ 6,000,000
Selling and administrative	5,800,000	—	—	5,800,000
Total fixed expenses	$11,800,000	—	—	$11,800,000
Operating income	$ 2,000,000	$ 200,000	$ 2	$ 2,200,000

Exhibit 5-3
Cordell Company
*Comparative Predicted Income Statements, Contribution Margin Technique
for Year Ended December 31, 20X1*

MAKING MANAGERIAL DECISIONS

Suppose you are at a meeting of Cordell Company managers and someone asked the following questions. Some of the answers given by your colleagues follow.

Q: *What will be the change in the contribution margin if we accept this order?*
A: The contribution margin will increase to $14,000,000.

Q: *In your analysis [Exhibit 5-3], you show that fixed costs do not change if we accept the order. Are these costs relevant?*
A: No. Fixed costs are not relevant.

Q: *OK. But do fixed costs that we incur have an effect on the bottom line of our company?*
A: Certainly. That is why we deduct fixed costs from the contribution margin to get operating income.

Q. *Well, if fixed costs affect the bottom line, how can you say they are not relevant?*

Comment on your colleague's answers, and answer the last question.

Answer

Your colleague's answer to the first question is technically incorrect. The question asks for change, not the new total contribution margin. The correct answer to this question is that contribution margin will increase *by* $200,000 (and therefore *to* $14,000,000). We need to be very careful when answering questions to be sure to differentiate between terms that imply totals and terms that imply changes. In this case, $14,000,000 is the answer to "What is the new total contribution margin if we accept the order?"

Your colleague's responses to the second and third questions are correct. The fixed costs of Cordell are not relevant for this particular special order situation. Nevertheless, the bottom line includes all costs or *total* costs and revenues. Do not confuse this with the *relevant costs*—a term we associated with this specific decision. In a decision situation, relevant costs include only those future costs that will differ if we accept the order. If a manager wants to know the "bottom line" after accepting the order, we would need to include the fixed cost. However, the fixed costs do not affect the *difference* between the preorder bottom line and the bottom line after accepting the order. The difference is the same $200,000 amount by which the contribution margin increases.

Incorrect Analysis—Misuse of Unit Cost

Faulty cost analysis sometimes occurs because of misinterpreting unit fixed costs. For instance, Cordell's managers might erroneously use the $30 per-unit total manufacturing cost to make the following prediction for the year:

Incorrect Analysis	Without Special Order 1,000,000 Units	Incorrect Effect of Special Order 100,000 Units	With Special Order 1,100,000 Units
Sales	$40,000,000	$2,600,000	$42,600,000
Less: manufacturing cost of goods sold @ $30	30,000,000	3,000,000	33,000,000
Gross margin	10,000,000	(400,000)	9,600,000
Selling and administrative expenses	8,000,000	—	8,000,000
Operating income	$ 2,000,000	$ (400,000)	$ 1,600,000

The incorrect prediction of a $3 million increase in costs results from multiplying 100,000 units by $30. Of course, the fallacy in this approach is that it treats a fixed cost (fixed manufacturing cost) as if it were variable. Avoid the assumption that unit costs may be used indiscriminately as a basis for predicting how total costs will behave. Unit costs are useful for predicting variable costs but often misleading when used to predict fixed costs.

Confusion of Variable and Fixed Costs

Consider the relationship between total fixed manufacturing costs and a fixed manufacturing cost per unit of product:

$$\text{fixed manufacturing cost per unit of product} = \frac{\text{total fixed manufacturing costs}}{\text{some selected volume level as the denominator}}$$

$$= \frac{\$6,000,000}{1,000,000 \text{ units}} = \$6 \text{ per unit}$$

As we noted in Chapter 2, the typical cost accounting system serves two purposes simultaneously: planning and control and product costing. We can graph the total fixed cost for budgetary planning and control purposes as a lump sum:

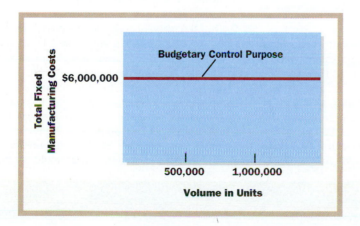

For product-costing purposes, however, using the total unit manufacturing cost implies that these fixed costs have a variable-cost behavior pattern:

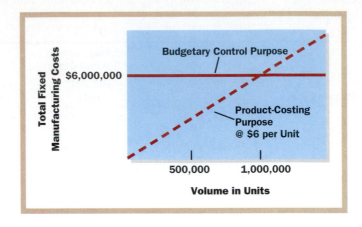

The addition of 100,000 units will not add any total fixed costs as long as total output is within the relevant range. The incorrect analysis, however, includes 100,000 × $6 = $600,000 of fixed cost in the predictions of increases in total costs.

In short, we should compute the increase in manufacturing costs by multiplying 1,000,000 units by $24, not by $30. The $30 includes a $6 component that will not affect the total manufacturing costs as volume changes.

MAKING MANAGERIAL DECISIONS

We have presented two key lessons so far in this chapter: relevant information and misuse of unit costs. We cannot stress enough how important it is to clearly understand the definition and concept of relevant information. It is also important to understand why the use of unit fixed costs can lead to an incorrect analysis.

Suppose you are a manager in a company that makes small appliances. You are deciding whether to accept or reject a special order for 1,000 units. (Assume there is sufficient capacity available for the order.)

1. Which of the following costs are relevant: (a) parts for the order, (b) supervisor's salary, (c) assembly equipment depreciation, (d) power to operate the assembly equipment?
2. Suppose the total unit manufacturing cost for the 1,000 units is $100 per unit. We determined this amount by dividing the total cost by 1,000 units. If the customer decided to double the order to 2,000 units, which costs listed in number 1 would change? Which

costs *per unit* would change? Would the total cost of the order double?

Answers

1. Relevant costs and revenues are predicted future costs and revenues that differ among alternative courses of action. In this case, the cost of parts and power would increase if management accepts the order, and thus they are relevant.
2. Only the relevant costs, in this case, the variable costs, would change: parts and power. Fixed cost would be unaffected. In contrast, the fixed costs *per unit* will change, whereas the variable cost per unit will stay the same. For example, fixed supervisory salaries will be divided by 2,000 units instead of by only 1,000 units, and hence per-unit supervisory cost will decrease. The parts cost per unit would stay the same, as would the power cost per unit. So, the total unit cost would fall, and the total cost of the order would not double.

Activity-Based Costing, Special Orders, and Relevant Costs

To identify relevant costs affected by a special order (or by other special decisions), more and more firms are going a step beyond simply identifying fixed and variable costs. As we pointed out in Chapters 3 and 4, a company's operations include many different activities. Businesses that have identified all their significant activities and related cost drivers can produce more detailed relevant information to predict the effects of special orders more accurately.

Suppose the Cordell Company examined its $24 million of variable manufacturing costs very closely and identified two significant activities and related cost drivers: $18 million of processing activity that varies directly with units produced at a rate of $18 per unit and $6 million of setup activity that varies with the number of production setups. Normally, for processing 1,000,000 units, Cordell has 500 setups at a cost of $12,000 per setup, with an average of 2,000 units processed for each setup. Additional sales generally require a proportional increase in the number of setups.

Now suppose the special order is for 100,000 units that vary only slightly in production specifications. Instead of the normal 50 setups, Cordell will need only 5 setups. So processing 100,000 units will take only $1,860,000 of additional variable manufacturing cost:

Additional unit-based variable manufacturing cost, 100,000 × $18	$ 1,800,000
Additional setup-based variable manufacturing cost, 5 × $12,000	60,000
Total additional variable manufacturing cost	$ 1,860,000

Instead of the original estimate of 100,000 × $24 = $2,400,000 additional variable manufacturing cost, the special order will cost only $1,860,000, or $540,000 less than the original estimate. Therefore, activity-based costing (ABC) allows managers to realize that the special order is $540,000 more profitable than predicted from the simple unit-based assessment of variable manufacturing cost.

A special order may also be more costly than predicted by a simple fixed- and variable-cost analysis. Suppose the 100,000-unit special order called for a variety of models and colors delivered at various times, so that it requires 100 setups. The variable cost of the special order would be $3.0 million.

Additional unit-based variable cost, 100,000 × $18	$ 1,800,000
Additional setup-based variable cost, 100 × $12,000	1,200,000
Total additional variable cost	$ 3,000,000

Activity-based costing systems provide much useful operating information for special-order decisions, but the fundamental concepts remain the same—focus your attention on future costs and revenues that differ because of the special order. Also, be careful to recognize and use terms such as *impact, change,* and *total* properly. The summary problem for your review that follows gives you more practice at analyzing a special order.

Summary Problem For Your Review

PROBLEM

1. Return to the basic illustration in Exhibit 5-3. Suppose the Cordell Company received a special order for 100,000 units that had the following terms: Selling price would be $27.00 instead of $26.00, but if Cordell accepts the order it would have to pay a flat fee

of $80,000 to a manufacturer's agent who had obtained the potential order. Should Cordell accept the special order?

2. What if the order was for 250,000 units at a selling price of $23.00 and there was no $80,000 agent's fee? Some managers have been known to argue for acceptance of such an order as follows: "Of course, we will lose $1.00 each on the variable manufacturing costs, but we will gain $1.20 per unit by spreading our fixed manufacturing costs over 1.25 million units instead of 1 million units. Consequently, we should take the offer because it represents an advantage of $.20 per unit."

Old fixed manufacturing cost per unit, $6,000,000 ÷ 1,000,000	$6.00
New fixed manufacturing cost per unit, $6,000,000 ÷ 1,250,000	4.80
"Saving" in fixed manufacturing cost per unit	$1.20
Loss on variable manufacturing cost per unit, $23.00 − $24.00	1.00
Net saving per unit in manufacturing cost	$ .20

Explain why this is faulty thinking.

SOLUTION

1. Focus on relevant information—the differences in revenues and costs. In this problem, in addition to the difference in variable costs, there is a difference in fixed costs between the two alternatives.

Additional revenue, 100,000 units @ $27.00 per unit	$2,700,000
Less additional costs	
Variable costs, 100,000 units @ $24 per unit	2,400,000
Fixed costs, agent's fee	80,000
Increase in operating income from special order	$ 220,000

So, from a strictly financial perspective, Cordell should accept the special order.

2. The faulty thinking comes from attributing a "savings" to the decrease in unit fixed costs. Regardless of how we "unitize" the fixed manufacturing costs or "spread" them over the units produced, the special order will not change the total of $6 million. Remember that we have a negative contribution margin of $1.00 per unit on this special order. Thus, there is no way we can cover any amount of fixed costs! Fixed costs are not relevant to this decision.

Deletion or Addition of Products, Services, or Departments

OBJECTIVE 4

Choose whether to add or delete a product line using relevant information.

Relevant information also plays an important role in decisions about adding or deleting products, services, or departments.

Avoidable and Unavoidable Costs

Often, existing businesses will want to expand or contract their operations to improve profitability. How can a manufacturer decide whether to add or to drop products? The same way a retailer decides whether to add or to drop departments: by examining all the relevant costs and revenues. For example, consider a discount department store that has three major departments: groceries, general merchandise, and drugs. Management is considering dropping the grocery department, which has consistently shown an operating loss. The following table reports the store's present annual operating income (in thousands of dollars):

| | Total | | Departments | |
		Groceries	General Merchandise	Drugs
Sales	$1,900	$1,000	$ 800	$100
Variable cost of goods sold and expenses*	1,420	800	560	60
Contribution margin	$ 480 (25%)	$ 200 (20%)	$ 240 (30%)	$ 40 (40%)
Fixed expenses (salaries, depreciation, insurance, property taxes, and so on):				
Avoidable	$ 265	$ 150	$ 100	$ 15
Unavoidable	180	60	100	20
Total fixed expenses	$ 445	$ 210	$ 200	$ 35
Operating income	$ 35	$ (10)	$ 40	$ 5

* Examples of variable expenses include product, paper shopping bags, and sales commissions.

Notice that we have divided the fixed expenses into two categories, avoidable and unavoidable. **Avoidable costs**—costs that will not continue if an ongoing operation is changed or deleted—are relevant. In our example, avoidable costs include department salaries and other costs that the store could eliminate by not operating the specific department. **Unavoidable costs**—costs that continue even if a company discontinues an operation—are not relevant in our example because a decision to delete the department does not affect them. Unavoidable costs include many **common costs**, which are those costs of facilities and services that are shared by users.[2] For example, store depreciation, heating, air conditioning, and general management expenses are costs of shared resources used by all departments. For our example, assume first that we will consider only two alternatives, dropping or continuing the grocery department, which shows a loss of $10,000. Assume further that the decision will not affect the total assets invested in the store. The vacated space would be idle, and the unavoidable costs would continue. Which alternative would you recommend? An analysis (in thousands of dollars) follows.

avoidable costs
Costs that will not continue if an ongoing operation is changed or deleted.

unavoidable costs
Costs that continue even if a company discontinues an operation.

common costs
Those costs of facilities and services that are shared by users.

| | Store as a Whole | | |
Income Statements	Total Before Change (a)	Effect of Dropping Groceries (b)	Total After Change (a) − (b)
Sales	$1,900	$1,000	$ 900
Variable expenses	1,420	800	620
Contribution margin	$ 480	$ 200	$ 280
Avoidable fixed expenses	265	150	115
Profit contribution to common space and other unavoidable costs	$ 215	$ 50	$ 165
Common space and other unavoidable costs	180	—	180
Operating income	$ 35	$ 50	$ (15)

[2] The concept of avoidable cost is used by government regulators as well as business executives. For example, Amtrak divides its costs into avoidable—costs that "would cease if the route were eliminated"—and fixed—costs that would "remain relatively constant if a single route were discontinued." The U.S. Interstate Commerce Commission then considers the avoidable costs when considering approval of a railroad's request to abandon a route. Similarly, the Canadian government looks at the avoidable cost when determining the amount of subsidy to give to the country's passenger rail system. The *Montreal Gazette* reported that revenues covered only 35% of the "$7 million in avoidable costs (costs that wouldn't exist if the train disappeared tomorrow—things like staff salaries, food, fuel, and upkeep of train stations)."

The preceding analysis shows that matters would be worse, rather than better, if the store drops the groceries department and leaves the vacated facilities idle. In short, as the income statement shows, groceries bring in a contribution margin of $200,000, which is $50,000 more than the $150,000 fixed expenses that the store would save by closing the grocery department. The grocery department showed a loss in the first income statement because of the unavoidable fixed costs charged to it.

Of course, most companies do not like having space left idle, so perhaps the preceding example was a bit too basic. Assume now that the store could use the space made available by the dropping of groceries to expand the general merchandise department. The space would be occupied by merchandise that would increase sales by $500,000, generate a 30% contribution-margin percentage, and have avoidable fixed costs of $70,000. The $80,000 increase in operating income of general merchandise more than offsets the $50,000 decline from eliminating groceries, providing an overall increase in operating income of $65,000 − $35,000 = $30,000.

			Effects of Changes	
	Total Before Change (a)	Drop Groceries (b)	Expand General Merchandise (c)	Total After Changes (a) − (b) + (c)
(in thousands of dollars)				
Sales	$1,900	$1,000	$500	$1,400
Variable expenses	1,420	800	350	970
Contribution margin	$ 480	$ 200	$150	$ 430
Avoidable fixed expenses	265	150	70	185
Contribution to common space and other unavoidable costs	$ 215	$ 50	$ 80	$ 245
Common space and other unavoidable costs*	180	—	—	180
Operating income	$ 35	$ 50	$ 80	$ 65

* Includes the $60,000 of former grocery fixed costs, which were allocations of unavoidable common costs that will continue regardless of how the space is occupied.

The purpose of deciding whether to add or drop new products, services, or departments is to obtain the greatest contribution possible. The company will use the contribution to pay the unavoidable costs. The unavoidable costs will remain the same regardless of any decision, so the key is picking the alternative that will contribute the most toward paying off these costs. The following analysis illustrates this concept for our example:

	Profit Contribution of Given Space (in thousands of dollars)		
	Groceries	Expansion of General Merchandise	Difference
Sales	$1,000	$500	$500 U
Variable expenses	800	350	450 F
Contribution margin	$ 200	$150	$ 50 U
Avoidable fixed expenses	150	70	80 F
Contribution to common space and other unavoidable costs	$ 50	$ 80	$ 30 F

F = Favorable difference resulting from replacing groceries with general merchandise.
U = Unfavorable difference.

In our example, the general merchandise will not achieve the dollar sales volume that groceries will, but the higher contribution margin percentage and the lower wage costs (mostly because of the diminished need for stocking and checkout clerks) combine to produce a more favorable bottom line.

This example illustrates that relevant costs are not always variable. In the special order decision, the relevant costs were the variable costs, which might have led you to believe that you should always ignore fixed costs and focus only on variable costs. However, the key to decision making is not relying on a hard and fast rule about what to include and what to ignore. Rather, you need to analyze all pertinent costs and revenues to determine what is and what is not relevant. In this case, the relevant costs included the fixed avoidable costs.

It is also important to remember that nonfinancial information can influence decisions to add or delete products or departments. For example, when deciding to delete a product or to close a plant, there are ethical considerations. What happens to the employees in the area being discontinued? What about customers who might be relying on customer support in the future? What about the community in which a discontinued operation is located? While the financial impacts of such considerations are hard to determine, they are still factors a company should consider. In addition, a stable, committed work force and a supportive community can be important assets to a company. This may be a situation where good ethics is good business. Any negative impacts on employees, customers, or communities could create future financial problems for the company that are much larger than short-term cost savings from discontinuing a product or plant.

MAKING MANAGERIAL DECISIONS

When managers face a decision about whether to add or delete a product, service, or department, it is useful to classify the associated fixed costs as avoidable or unavoidable. Indicate whether the following fixed costs are typically avoidable or unavoidable if a company deletes a product. Assume that the company produces many products in a single plant.

1. Depreciation on equipment used to produce the product. The company will sell the equipment if it discontinues the product.
2. Salary of the plant manager.

3. Depreciation on the plant building.
4. Advertising costs for the product. The company places specific ads just for this product.

Answer

Numbers 1 and 4 are avoidable fixed costs. The company is unlikely to change the salary of the plant manager if it discontinues only one product. Thus, it is unavoidable. The same is true for the plant depreciation. Hence, it is also an unavoidable cost.

Optimal Use of Limited Resources

Suppose a plant makes more than one product and is operating at capacity. If demand for its products exceeds the amount the company can produce, managers must decide which orders to accept. The contribution margin technique also applies here, because the product to be emphasized or the order to be accepted is the one that makes the biggest total profit contribution per unit of the limiting factor. A **limiting factor** or **scarce resource** restricts or constrains the production or sale of a product or service. Limiting factors include labor hours and machine hours that limit production (and hence sales) in manufacturing firms, and square feet of floor space or cubic meters of display space that limit sales in department stores.

limiting factor (scarce resource)
The item that restricts or constrains the production or sale of a product or service.

OBJECTIVE 5

Compute a measure of product profitability when production is constrained by a scarce resource.

Managers must use the contribution margin technique wisely. They sometimes mistakenly favor those products with the biggest contribution margin or gross margin per sales dollar, without regard to scarce resources. This could lead to incorrect decisions.

Consider the Grand Canyon Railway. Assume that the railway is considering converting its club-class passenger car to a first-class car. The car has 100 club-class seats. However, it will hold only 50 first-class seats, because each first-class seat takes twice as much space as a club-class seat. Unit data follow.

	Club Class	First Class
Selling price per seat	$ 80	$120
Variable costs per seat	60	84
Contribution margin per seat	$ 20	$ 36
Contribution margin ratio	25%	30%

Which is more profitable, a first-class seat or a club-class seat? On which should the railway spend its resources? The correct answer is, "It depends." Suppose every train runs with some empty seats in both club class and first class. Now a customer approaches and wants to buy a ticket. What ticket would be most profitable, a club-class ticket or a first-class ticket? It would be better to sell a first-class ticket contributing $36 than a club-class ticket contributing $20. In this case, first-class seats generate more profit per ticket. Thus, if the limiting factor is demand, that is, units of sales, the more profitable product is the one with the higher contribution per unit.

Now suppose there is enough demand to fill the car with passengers regardless of whether it has first-class or club-class seats. Capacity is now the limiting factor because there is only one car that can hold either 100 club-class seats or 50 first-class seats. In this case, the club class is more profitable. Why? Because it contributes more profit per car.

	Club Class	First Class
1. Seats per car	100	50
2. Contribution margin per seat	$ 20	$ 36
Contribution margin per car (1) × (2)	$2,000	$1,800

A railway car need not have all first-class or all club-class seats. What our analysis tells us is that club-class seats are a better use of the railway-car space than are first-class seats when there is demand for both. Grand Canyon Railway would want to make sure there are as many club-class seats available as customers demand, and only after satisfying this demand is it worth making first-class seats available.

Of course, this analysis depends on the relative use of capacity by the two products. Suppose the first-class seats took only 1.5 times as much space as the club-class seats. Then, the first-class seats would be the most profitable use of the space. In this case, we could express the contribution per unit of capacity in several different ways including:

	Club Class	First Class
Contribution per car	100 × $20 = $2,000	(100 ÷ 1.5) × $36 = $2,400
Contribution per space for one first-class seat	1.5 × $20 = $30	1 × $36 = $36
Contribution per space for one club-class seat	1 × $20 = $20	2/3 × $36 = $24

Any way we express it, first-class seats will have more contribution per unit of capacity. Note that each of these financial measures shows that first-class seats are 20% more

	Regular Department Store	Discount Department Store
Retail price	$4.00	$3.50
Cost of merchandise and other variable costs	3.00	3.00
Contribution to profit per unit	$1.00 (25%)	$ .50 (14%)
Units sold per year	10,000	22,000
Total contribution to profit, assuming the same space allotment in both stores	$10,000	$11,000

Exhibit 5-4
Effect of Turnover on Profit

profitable than club-class seats. For example, the contribution per car measure for first class is $400 more than for club class, that is, 20% = $400/$2,000 more.

As we said earlier, the criterion for maximizing profits when one factor limits sales is to obtain the greatest possible contribution to profit for each unit of the limiting factor. However, the product that is most profitable when one particular factor limits sales may be the least profitable if a different factor restricts sales.

In retail sales, the limiting resource is often floor space. Thus, retail stores must focus either on products taking up less space or on using the space for shorter periods of time — greater **inventory turnover** (number of times the average inventory is sold per year). Consider an example of two department stores. The conventional gross profit percentage (gross profit ÷ selling price) is an insufficient clue to profitability because, as we said, profits depend on the space occupied and the inventory turnover. Discount department stores such as **Wal-Mart, Target,** and **Kmart** have succeeded in using lower markups than traditional department stores because they have been able to increase turnover and thus increase the contribution to profit per unit of space. Exhibit 5-4 illustrates the same product, taking up the same amount of space, in each of two stores. The contribution margins per unit and per sales dollar are less in the discount store, but faster turnover makes the same product a more profitable use of space in the discount store. In general, retail companies seek faster inventory turnover. A survey of retail shoe stores showed that those with above-average financial performance had an inventory turnover of 2.6 times per year compared to an industry average of 2.0.

inventory turnover
The number of times the average inventory is sold per year.

Pricing Decisions

One of the major decisions managers face is pricing. Actually, pricing can take many forms. Among the many pricing decisions managers make are

1. Setting the price of a new or refined product.
2. Setting the price of products sold under private labels.
3. Responding to a new price of a competitor.
4. Pricing bids in both sealed and open bidding situations.

Pricing decisions are so important, in fact, that we will spend the rest of the chapter discussing the many aspects of pricing. Let us now take a look at some of the basic concepts behind pricing.

The Concept of Pricing

Pricing decisions depend on the characteristics of the market a firm faces. In **perfect competition,** all competing firms sell the same type of product at the same price. Thus, a firm can sell as much of a product as it can produce, all at a single market price. If it

perfect competition
A market in which a firm can sell as much of a product as it can produce, all at a single market price.

Exhibit 5-5
Marginal Revenue
and Cost in Perfect
Competition

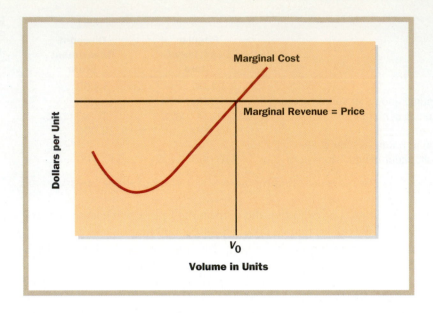

charges more, no customer will buy. If it charges less, it sacrifices profits. Therefore, every firm in such a market will charge the market price, and the only decision for managers to make is how much to produce.

Although costs do not directly influence prices in perfect competition, they do affect the production decision. Consider the marginal cost curve in Exhibit 5-5. The **marginal cost** is the additional cost resulting from producing and selling one additional unit—for the Grand Canyon Railway, one additional passenger; for General Motors, one additional car. The marginal cost often decreases as production increases up to a point because of efficiencies created by larger amounts. At some point, however, marginal costs begin to rise with increases in production because facilities become overcrowded or overused, resulting in inefficiencies.

Exhibit 5-5 also includes a marginal revenue curve. The **marginal revenue** is the additional revenue resulting from the sale of an additional unit. In perfect competition, the marginal revenue curve is a horizontal line equal to the price per unit at all volumes of sales.

As long as the marginal cost is less than the marginal revenue (price), additional production and sales are profitable. When marginal cost exceeds price, however, the firm loses money on each additional unit. Therefore, the profit-maximizing volume is the quantity at which marginal cost equals price. In Exhibit 5-5, the firm should produce V_0 units. Producing fewer units passes up profitable opportunities, and producing more units reduces profit because each additional unit costs more to produce than it generates in revenue.

In **imperfect competition,** the price a firm charges for a unit will influence the quantity of units it sells. At some point, the firm must reduce prices to generate additional sales. Exhibit 5-6 contains a demand curve (also called the average revenue curve) for imperfect competition that shows the volume of sales at each possible price. To sell additional units, the firm must reduce the price of all units sold. Therefore, the marginal revenue curve, also shown in Exhibit 5-6, is below the demand curve. That is, the marginal revenue for selling one additional unit is less than the price at which it is sold because the price of all other units falls as well. For example, suppose a firm can sell 10 units for $50 per unit. However, the firm must drop the price to $49 per unit to sell 11 units, to $48 to sell 12 units, and to $47 to sell 13 units. The fourth column of Exhibit 5-7 shows the marginal revenue for units 11 through 13. Notice that the marginal revenue decreases as volume increases.

marginal cost
The additional cost resulting from producing and selling one additional unit.

marginal revenue
The additional revenue resulting from the sale of an additional unit.

imperfect competition
A market in which the price a firm charges for a unit will influence the quantity of units it sells.

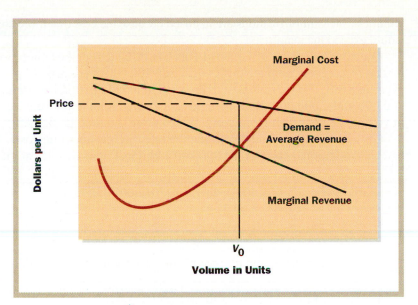

Exhibit 5-6
Marginal Revenue
and Cost in Imperfect
Competition

To estimate marginal revenue, managers must predict the **price elasticity**—the effect of price changes on sales volume. If small price increases cause large volume declines, demand is highly elastic. If prices have little or no effect on volume, demand is highly inelastic.

For the marginal costs shown in the fifth column of Exhibit 5-7, the optimal production and sales level is 12 units. The last column of that exhibit illustrates that the eleventh unit adds $4 to profit, and the twelfth adds $1, but production and sale of the thirteenth unit would decrease profit by $2. In general, firms should produce and sell units until the marginal revenue equals the marginal cost, represented by volume V_0 in Exhibit 5-6. The optimal price charged will be the amount that creates a demand for V_0 units.

Notice that the marginal cost is relevant for pricing decisions. In managerial accounting, marginal cost is essentially the variable cost. What is the major difference between marginal cost and variable cost? Accountants assume that variable cost is constant within a relevant range of volume, whereas marginal cost may change with each unit produced. Within large ranges of production volume, however, changes in marginal cost are often small. Therefore, variable cost can be a reasonable approximation of marginal cost in many situations.

price elasticity
The effect of price changes on sales volume.

Pricing and Accounting

Accountants seldom compute marginal revenue curves and marginal cost curves. Instead, they use estimates based on judgment to predict the effects of additional production and sales on profits. In addition, they examine selected volumes, not the whole range of possible

Units Sold	Price per Unit	Total Revenue	Marginal Revenue	Marginal Cost	Profit from Production and Sale of Additional Unit
10	$50	10 × $50 = $500			
11	49	11 × 49 = 539	$539 − $500 = $39	$35	$39 − $35 = $4
12	48	12 × 48 = 576	576 − 539 = 37	36	37 − 36 = 1
13	47	13 × 47 = 611	611 − 576 = 35	37	35 − 37 = (2)

Exhibit 5-7
Profit Maximization in Imperfect Competition

volumes. Such simplifications are justified because the cost of a more sophisticated analysis would exceed the benefits.

Consider a division of **General Electric (GE)** that makes microwave ovens. Suppose market researchers estimate that GE can sell 700,000 ovens at $200 per unit and 1,000,000 ovens at $180. The variable cost of production is $130 per unit at production levels of both 700,000 and 1,000,000. Both volumes are also within the relevant range, so that changes in volume do not affect fixed costs. Which price should GE charge?

GE's accountant would determine the relevant revenues and costs. The additional revenue and additional costs of the 300,000 additional units of sales at the $180 prices are

Additional revenue: (1,000,000 × $180) − (700,000 × $200) =	$40,000,000
Additional costs: 300,000 × $130 =	39,000,000
Additional profit	$ 1,000,000

Alternatively, the accountant could compare the total contribution for each alternative:

Contribution at $180: ($180 − $130) × 1,000,000 =	$50,000,000
Contribution at $200: ($200 − $130) × 700,000 =	49,000,000
Difference	$ 1,000,000

Notice that comparing the total contributions is essentially the same as computing the additional revenues and costs—both use the same relevant information. Further, both approaches correctly ignore fixed costs, which are unaffected by this pricing decision.

General Influences on Pricing in Practice

OBJECTIVE 6

Identify the factors that influence pricing decisions in practice.

Several factors interact to shape the market in which managers make pricing decisions. Legal requirements, competitors' actions, and customer demands all influence pricing.

Legal Requirements

Managers must consider constraints imposed by U.S. and international laws when making pricing decisions. These laws often protect consumers, but they also help protect other companies from predatory and discriminatory pricing.

Predatory pricing means setting prices so low that they drive competitors out of the market. The predatory pricer then has no significant competition and can raise prices dramatically. For example, lawsuits have accused Wal-Mart of predatory pricing—selling at low cost to drive out local competitors. However, in a 4-to-3 vote, The Arkansas Supreme Court ruled in favor of Wal-Mart. Courts in the United States have generally ruled that pricing is predatory only if companies set prices below their average variable cost and actually lose money in order to drive their competitors out of business.

Discriminatory pricing is charging different prices to different customers for the same product or service. For example, a large group of retail druggists and big drugstore chains sued several large drug companies, alleging that their practice of allowing discounts, some as large as 40%, to mail-order drug companies, health maintenance organizations, and other managed-care entities constitutes discriminatory pricing. However, pricing is not discriminatory if it reflects a cost differential incurred in providing the good or service. A tentative settlement to the $600 million class-action suit was reached, but it did not require the drug companies to alter their pricing practices.

Both predatory and discriminatory pricing practices are not only illegal but unethical business practices. Management accountants have an ethical obligation to perform their

predatory pricing

Establishing prices so low that they drive competitors out of the market. The predatory pricer then has no significant competition and can raise prices dramatically.

discriminatory pricing

Charging different prices to different customers for the same product or service.

duties in accordance with relevant laws and to refrain from engaging in or supporting any activity or practice that would descredit the profession.

Competitors' Actions

Competitors usually react to the price changes of their rivals. Many companies will gather information regarding a rival's capacity, technology, and operating policies. In this way, managers make more informed predictions of competitors' reactions to a company's prices. The study of game theory, for which two economists won a Nobel Prize, focuses on predicting and reacting to competitors' actions.

A manager's expectations of competitors' reactions and of the overall effects of price changes on the total industry demand for the good or service in question heavily influence pricing policies. For example, an airline might cut prices even if it expects price cuts from its rivals, hoping that total customer demand for the tickets of all airlines will increase sufficiently to offset the reduction in the price per ticket. In contrast, they might avoid price reductions if they expect competitors to follow and do not expect an increase in overall industry demand.

Competition is becoming increasingly international. Overcapacity in some countries often causes aggressive pricing policies, particularly for a company's exported goods. As companies' markets expand globally, their pricing policies become even more complex.

Customer Demands

More than ever before, managers are recognizing the needs of customers. Pricing is no exception. If customers believe a price is too high, they may turn to other sources for the product or service, substitute a different product, or decide to produce the item themselves. As the controller for the Grand Canyon Railway states, ". . . prices charged must be attractive to the customer." If not, they can simply drive their own car to the Grand Canyon or choose to ride a bus.

Cost-Plus Pricing

Accounting influences pricing by providing costs. The exact role costs play in pricing decisions depends on both the market conditions and the company's approach to pricing. This section discusses cost-plus pricing, the most common use of costs in pricing decisions.

What Is Cost-Plus Pricing?

Many managers say that they set prices by "cost-plus" pricing. For example, Grand Canyon Railway sets its prices by computing an average cost and then adding a desired **markup**—the amount by which price exceeds cost—that will generate a target return on investment. The key, however, is the "plus" in cost plus. Instead of being a fixed markup, the "plus" will usually depend on both costs and the demands of customers. For example, the railway has a standard (rack rate) price that does not change during the year, but it often offers discounts during the slow winter season.

Prices are most directly related to costs in industries where revenue is based on cost reimbursement. Cost-reimbursement contracts generally specify how to measure costs and what costs are allowable. For example, the government reimburses only coach-class (not first-class) airfares for business travel on defense contracts.

markup
The amount by which price exceeds cost.

Ultimately, though, the market sets prices. Why? Because companies inevitably adjust the price as set by a cost-plus formula "in light of market conditions." The maximum price a company can charge is the one that does not drive the customer away. The minimum price might be considered to be zero (for example, companies may give out free samples to gain entry into a market). A more practical guide is that, in the short run, the minimum price sales personnel should quote on an order is the cost that the company can avoid if it does not land the order—often all variable costs of producing, selling, and distributing the good or service. In the long run, the price must be high enough to cover all costs, including fixed costs.

Cost Bases for Cost-Plus Pricing

OBJECTIVE 7

Compute a target sales price by various approaches, and compare the advantages and disadvantages of these approaches.

To set a desired price or target price for products or services, managers often add a markup to some measure of costs—thus, the term *cost plus*. The size of the "plus" depends on the definition of cost and the target (desired) operating income. Target prices can be based on a host of different markups that are in turn based on a host of different definitions of cost. Thus, there are many ways to arrive at the same target price.

Exhibit 5-8 displays the relationships of costs to target selling prices, assuming a target operating income of $1 million. The percentages there represent four popular markup formulas for pricing: (1) as a percentage of variable manufacturing costs, (2) as a percentage of total variable costs, (3) as a percentage of full costs, and (4) as a percentage of total manufacturing cost.

full cost (fully allocated cost)
The total of all manufacturing costs plus the total of all selling and administrative costs.

Note particularly that **full cost** or **fully allocated cost** means the total of all manufacturing costs plus the total of all selling and administrative costs. As noted in earlier chapters, we use "selling and administrative" to include value-chain functions other than production. Of course, the percentages differ. For instance, the markup on variable manufacturing costs is 66.67%, and on full costs it is only 5.26%. Regardless of the formula used, the pricing decision maker will be led toward the same target price. For a volume of 1 million units, assume that the target selling price is $20 per unit. If the decision maker is unable to obtain such a price consistently, the company will not achieve its $1 million operating income objective.

We have seen that managers can base prices on various types of cost information, from variable manufacturing costs to full costs. Each of these costs can be relevant to the pricing decision. Each approach has advantages and disadvantages.

Exhibit 5-8
Relationships of Costs to Same Target Selling Prices

		Alternative Markup Percentages to Achieve Same Target Sales Prices
Target sales price	$20.00	
Variable cost:		
(1) Manufacturing	$12.00	($20.00 − $12.00) ÷ $12.00 = 66.67%
Selling and administrative*	1.10	
(2) Unit variable costs	$13.10	($20.00 − $13.10) ÷ $13.10 = 52.67%
Fixed costs:		
Manufacturing†	$ 3.00	
Selling and administrative	2.90	
Unit fixed costs	$ 5.90	
(3) Full costs	$19.00	($20.00 − $19.00) ÷ $19.00 = 5.26%
Target operating income	$ 1.00	

* Selling and administrative costs include costs of value chain functions other than production.
† (4) A frequently used formula is based on total manufacturing costs: [$20.00 − ($12.00 + $3.00)] ÷ $15.00 = 33.33%.

Advantages of Contribution Margin Approach in Cost-Plus Pricing

Prices based on variable costs represent a contribution approach to pricing. When used intelligently, the contribution margin approach has some advantages over the total-manufacturing-cost and full-cost approaches, because the latter two often fail to highlight different cost behavior patterns.

Obviously, the contribution margin approach offers more detailed information because it displays variable- and fixed-cost behavior patterns separately. Because the contribution margin approach is sensitive to cost-volume-profit relationships, it is a helpful basis for developing pricing formulas. As a result, this approach allows managers to prepare price schedules at different volume levels.

The correct analysis in Exhibit 5-9 shows how changes in volume affect operating income. The contribution margin approach helps managers with pricing decisions by readily displaying the interrelationships among variable costs, fixed costs, and potential changes in selling prices.

In contrast, target pricing with full costing presumes a given volume level. When volume changes, the unit cost used at the original planned volume may mislead managers. Managers sometimes erroneously assume that they can compute the change in total costs by multiplying any change in volume by the full unit cost.

The incorrect analysis in Exhibit 5-9 shows how using the $19 full cost per unit to predict effects of volume changes on operating income can mislead managers. Suppose a manager uses the $19 figure to predict an operating income of $900,000 if the company sells 900,000 instead of 1,000,000 units. If actual operating income is $310,000 instead, as the correct analysis predicts, that manager may be stunned—and possibly looking for a new job.

The contribution margin approach also offers insight into the short-run versus long-run effects of cutting prices on special orders. For example, assume the same cost behavior patterns as in the Cordell Company example in Exhibit 5-3 (page 204). The 100,000-unit order added $200,000 to operating income at a selling price of $26, which was $14 below the target selling price of $40 and $4 below the total manufacturing

	Correct Analysis			Incorrect Analysis		
Volume in units	900,000	1,000,000	1,100,000	900,000	1,000,000	1,100,000
Sales @ $20.00	$18,000,000	$20,000,000	$22,000,000	$18,000,000	$20,000,000	$22,000,000
Unit variable costs @ $13.10*	11,790,000	13,100,000	14,410,000			
Contribution margin	6,210,000	6,900,000	7,590,000			
Fixed costs†	5,900,000	5,900,000	5,900,000			
Full costs @ $19.00*				17,100,000	19,000,000	20,900,000
Operating income	$ 310,000	$ 1,000,000	$ 1,690,000	$ 900,000	$ 1,000,000	$ 1,100,000

* From Exhibit 5-8

† Fixed manufacturing costs	$3,000,000
Fixed selling and administrative costs	2,900,000
Total fixed costs	$5,900,000

Exhibit 5-9
Analyses of Effects of Changes in Volume on Operating Income

cost of $30. Given all the stated assumptions, accepting the order appeared to be the better choice. As you saw earlier, the contribution margin approach generated the most relevant information. Consider the contribution and total-manufacturing-cost approaches.

	Contribution Margin Technique	Total-Manufacturing-Cost Approach
Sales, 100,000 units @ $26	$2,600,000	$2,600,000
Variable manufacturing costs @ $24	2,400,000	
Total manufacturing costs @ $30		3,000,000
Apparent change in operating income	$ 200,000	($ 400,000)

Under the total-manufacturing-cost approach, the offer is definitely unattractive because the price of $26 is $4 below total manufacturing costs.

Under the contribution margin approach, the decision maker sees a short-run advantage of $200,000 from accepting the offer. Fixed costs will be unaffected by whatever decision is made, and operating income will increase by $200,000. Still, there often are long-run effects to consider. Will acceptance of the offer undermine the long-run price structure? In other words, is the short-run advantage of $200,000 more than offset by highly probable long-run financial disadvantages? The decision maker may think so and may reject the offer. But—and this is important—by doing so the decision maker is, in effect, forgoing $200,000 now to protect certain long-run market advantages. Generally, the decision maker can assess problems of this sort by asking whether the probability of long-run benefits is worth an "investment" equal to the forgone contribution margin ($200,000, in this case). Under full-cost approaches, the decision maker must ordinarily conduct a special study to find the immediate effects. Under the contribution margin approach, the manager has a system that will routinely and more surely provide such information.

Advantages of Total-Manufacturing-Cost and Full-Cost Approaches in Cost-Plus Pricing

Frequently, companies do not employ a contribution margin approach because they fear that managers will indiscriminately substitute variable costs for full costs and will therefore lead to suicidal price cutting. This problem should not arise if managers use the data wisely. However, if top managers perceive a pronounced danger of underpricing when they reveal variable-cost data, they may justifiably prefer a total-manufacturing-cost or full-cost approach for guiding pricing decisions.

Actually, total manufacturing costs or full costs are far more widely used in practice than is the contribution margin approach. Why? In addition to the reasons we have already mentioned, managers have cited the following:

1. In the long run, a firm must recover all costs to stay in business. Sooner or later, fixed costs do indeed fluctuate as volume changes. Therefore, it is prudent to assume that all costs are variable (even if some are fixed in the short run).
2. Computing target prices based on cost plus may indicate what competitors might charge, especially if they have approximately the same level of efficiency as you and also aim at recovering all costs in the long run.
3. Total-manufacturing-cost or full-cost formula pricing meets the cost-benefit test. It is too expensive to conduct individual cost-volume tests for the many products (sometimes thousands) that a company offers.
4. There is much uncertainty about the shape of the demand curves and the correct price-output decisions. Total-manufacturing-cost or full-cost pricing copes with this uncertainty by not encouraging managers to take too much marginal business.

5. Total-manufacturing-cost or full-cost pricing tends to promote price stability. Managers prefer price stability because it eases their professional lives, primarily because it makes planning more dependable.

6. Total-manufacturing-cost or full-cost pricing provides the most defensible basis for justifying prices to all interested parties including government antitrust investigators.

7. Total-manufacturing-cost or full-cost pricing provides convenient reference (target) points to simplify hundreds or thousands of pricing decisions.

Using Multiple Approaches

To say that either a contribution margin approach or a total-manufacturing-cost or full-cost approach provides the "best" guide to pricing decisions is a dangerous oversimplification of one of the most perplexing issues in business. Lack of understanding and judgment can lead to unprofitable pricing regardless of the kind of cost data available or cost accounting system used.

Basically, no single method of pricing is always best. Executives who were interviewed for a study on their pricing methods said that companies often use both full-cost and variable-cost information in pricing decisions.

The history of accounting reveals that most companies have gathered costs via some form of full-manufacturing-cost system because this is what authorities require for financial reporting. Modern accounting systems such as ERP systems often identify variable and fixed costs. However, when companies implement such a system, managers often regard this information as an addition to the existing full-manufacturing-cost information. That is, many managers insist on having information regarding both variable costs per unit and the allocated fixed costs per unit before setting selling prices. Most ERP systems can easily provide both variable-cost and full-cost information. In contrast, most older systems focus on total-manufacturing-cost and do not organize their data collection to distinguish between variable and fixed costs. As a result, special studies or educated guessing must be used to designate costs as variable or fixed.

Managers are especially reluctant to focus on variable costs and ignore allocated fixed costs when their performance evaluations, and possibly their bonuses, are based on income shown in published financial statements. Why? Because most companies base such statements on full costing, and thus allocations of fixed costs affect reported income.

Formats for Pricing

Exhibit 5-8 showed how to compute alternative general markup percentages that would produce the same selling prices if used day after day. In practice, the format and arithmetic of quote sheets, job proposals, or similar records vary considerably.

Exhibit 5-10 is from an actual quote sheet used by the manager of a small job shop that bids on welding machinery orders in a highly competitive industry. The approach in Exhibit 5-10 is a tool for informed pricing decisions. Notice that the maximum price is not a matter of cost at all. It is what you think you can obtain. The minimum price is the total variable cost.

Of course, the manager will rarely bid the minimum price. Businesses do need to make a profit. Still, the manager wants to know the effect of a job on the company's total variable costs. Occasionally, a company will bid near that minimum price to establish a presence in new markets or with a new customer.

Note that Exhibit 5-10 classifies costs specifically for the pricing task. More than one person may make pricing decisions in a particular company. The accountant's responsibility is to prepare an understandable format that requires a minimum of computations.

Exhibit 5-10
Quote Sheet
for Pricing

Direct materials, at cost	$25,000
Direct labor and variable manufacturing overhead,	
600 direct labor hours × $30	18,000
Sales commission (varies with job)	2,000
Total variable costs—minimum price*	45,000
Add fixed costs allocated to job, 600 direct labor hours × $20	12,000
Total costs	57,000
Add desired markup	30,000
Selling price—maximum price that you think you can obtain*	$87,000

* This sheet shows two prices, maximum and minimum. Any amount you can get above the minimum price is a contribution margin.

Exhibit 5-10 combines direct labor and variable manufacturing overhead. It lumps together all fixed costs, whether manufacturing, selling, or administrative, and applies them to the job using a single fixed-overhead rate per direct labor hour. Obviously, if the company wants more accuracy, it could formulate many more detailed cost items and overhead rates. To obtain the desired accuracy, many companies are turning to activity-based costing.

Some managers, particularly in construction and in service industries such as auto repair, compile separate categories of costs of (1) direct materials, parts, and supplies and (2) direct labor. These managers then use different markup rates for each category. They use these rates to provide enough revenue to cover both indirect and unallocated costs and operating profit. For example, an automobile repair shop might have the following format for each job:

	Billed to Customers
Auto parts ($200 cost plus 40% markup)	$280
Direct labor (Cost is $20 per hour. Bill at 300% to recover	
indirect and unallocated costs and provide for operating profit.	
Billing rate is $20 × 300% = $60 per hour. Total billed for 10 hours	
is $60 × 10 = $600)	600
Total billed to customer	$880

Another example is an Italian printing company in Milan that wants to price its jobs so that each one generates a margin of 28% of revenues—14% to cover selling and administrative expenses and 14% for profit. To achieve this margin, the manager uses a pricing formula of 140% times predicted materials cost plus €25 per hour of production time. The latter covers labor and overhead costs of €18 per hour. For a product with €400 of materials cost and 30 hours of production time, the price would be €1,310:

	Cost	Price	Profit
Materials	€400	€ 560	€160
Labor and overhead	540	750	210
Total	€940	€1,310	€370

The profit of €370 is approximately 40% of the cost of €940 and 28% of the price of €1,310.

Thus there are numerous ways to compute selling prices. However, some general words of caution are appropriate here. Managers are better able to understand their options and the effects of their decisions on profits if they know their costs. That is, it is more informative to pinpoint costs first, before adding markups, than to have a variety of markups already embedded in the "costs" used as guides for setting selling prices. For example, if materials cost $1,000, they should be shown on a price quotation guide at $1,000, not at, say, a marked-up $1,400 because that is what the seller hopes to get.

Summary Problem For Your Review

PROBLEM

Custom Graphics is a Chicago printing company that bids on a wide variety of design and printing jobs. The owner of the company, Janet Solomon, prepares the bids for most jobs. Her cost budget for 20X4 follows.

Materials		$ 350,000
Labor		250,000
Overhead		
Variable	$300,000	
Fixed	150,000	450,000
Total production cost of jobs		1,050,000
Selling and administrative expenses*		
Variable	$ 75,000	
Fixed	125,000	200,000
Total costs		$1,250,000

* These expenses include costs of all value chain functions other than production.

Solomon has a target profit of $250,000 for 20X4.
Compute the average target markup percentage for setting prices as a percentage of

1. Materials plus labor
2. Variable production cost of jobs (assume labor is a variable-cost resource)
3. Total production cost of jobs
4. All variable costs
5. All costs

SOLUTION

The purpose of this problem is to emphasize that many different approaches to pricing might be used that, properly employed, would achieve the same target selling prices. To achieve $250,000 of profit, the desired revenue for 20X4 is $1,250,000 + $250,000 = $1,500,000. The target markup percentages are

1. Percent of materials and labor $= \dfrac{(\$1,500,000 - \$600,000)}{(\$600,000)} = 150\%$

2. Percent of variable production cost of jobs $= \dfrac{(\$1,500,000 - \$900,000)}{(\$900,000)} = 66.7\%$

3. Percent of total production cost of jobs $= \dfrac{(\$1,500,000 - \$1,050,000)}{(\$1,050,000)} = 42.9\%$

$$\text{4. Percent of all variable costs} = \frac{(\$1,500,000 - \$975,000)}{(\$975,000)} = 53.8\%$$

$$\text{5. Percent of all costs} = \frac{(\$1,500,000 - \$1,250,000)}{(\$1,250,000)} = 20\%$$

Target Costing

OBJECTIVE 8

Use target costing to decide whether to add a new product.

Consider a company that is deciding whether to develop and market a new product. In evaluating the feasibility of the new product, management must determine both the price it can charge and the expected cost. As we have seen, both market conditions and the actions of management can affect the price and the cost of the new product. The degree to which management actions can affect price and cost determines the most effective approach to use for pricing and cost management purposes. Companies use cost-plus pricing for products where management actions (for example, advertising) can influence the market price. Although cost management is important in this case, there is a strong focus on marketing and the revenue side of the profit equation.

But what if the market conditions are such that management cannot influence prices? If a company is to achieve management's desired profit, it must focus on the product's cost. What management needs is an effective tool to reduce costs without reducing value to the customer. A growing number of companies faced with this situation are adopting target costing. **Target costing** is a cost management tool for making cost reduction a key focus throughout the life of a product. A desired, or target, cost is set before creating or even designing the product. Management bases the target cost on the product's predicted price and the company's desired profit. Managers must then try to reduce and control costs so that the product's cost does not exceed its target cost. Target costing is most effective at reducing costs during the product design phase. Why? Because product design affects a vast majority of costs. For example, the design of the product and the associated production process largely determines the costs of resources such as new machinery, materials, parts, and even future refinements. It is not easy to reduce these costs once production begins. So, the emphasis of target costing is on proactive, up-front planning throughout every activity of the new product development process.

target costing

A cost management tool for making cost reduction a key focus throughout the life of a product.

Target Costing and New Product Development

Exhibit 5-11 shows the target costing process for a new product. Based on the existing technology and related cost structure, the product has three parts, requires direct labor, and has four types of indirect costs. The first step in the target-costing process is to determine the market price. The market sets this price. So why does management have to determine it? Remember that the product is new and has not actually been on the market. So, management has to estimate what the market will pay for the product. There are several tools, such as market focus group studies and surveys, that a firm uses to determine this price. Management also sets a desired gross margin for the new product. The difference between the gross margin and the market price is the target cost for the new product. The company determines the existing cost structure for the product by building up costs on an individual component level. This product has two components. Component 1 consists of parts A and B. Component 2 is part C. Both components and the final assembly use direct labor. Finally, the activities necessary to plan and process the product create indirect costs.

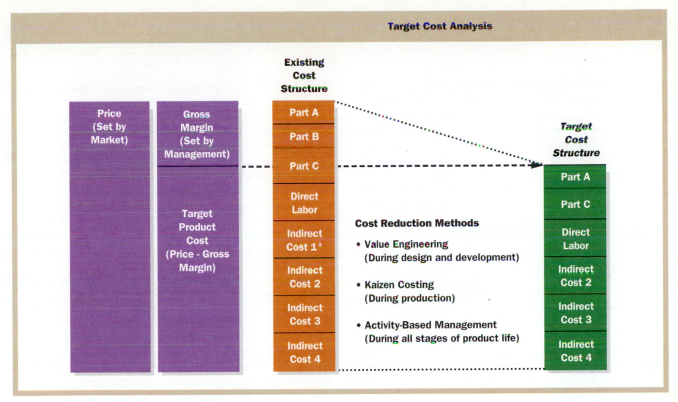

Exhibit 5-11
The Target Costing Process
* Each indirect cost is associated with an indirect activity. Indirect Cost 1 was eliminated in the cost-reduction process.

Marketing plays a large role in target costing. Market research from the marketing department at the beginning of the target costing activity guides the whole product development process by supplying information about customer demands and requirements. In fact, one of the key characteristics of successful target costing is a strong emphasis on understanding customer demands. Many companies actively seek customer input on the design of product features. Then the cost of the feature is compared to its value to determine whether to add it to the product. For example, one of Boeing's customers wanted heated floors in its airplanes. But the cost of the heated floors was too high and the customer reconsidered.

In the example in Exhibit 5-11, the existing cost is too large to generate the desired profit. Does this mean that the new product is not feasible? Not necessarily. A cross-functional team consisting of engineers, sales personnel, key suppliers, and accountants now must determine if the company can implement cost reductions large enough to meet the target cost. In the example in Exhibit 5-11, in the target-cost structure, the company reduced the cost of parts by changing the design of the product so that it could use part C in place of part B.

The company also asked suppliers of parts A and C to reduce their costs. Design and process engineers were also able to eliminate the activity that generated the first type of indirect cost. These cost reductions resulted from **value engineering**—a cost-reduction technique, used primarily during the design stage, that uses information about all value-chain functions to satisfy customer needs while reducing costs. In total, the planned cost reductions were adequate to reduce costs to the target.

However, not all the reductions in cost take place before production begins. **Kaizen costing** is the Japanese term for continuous improvement during manufacturing. How do companies apply kaizen costing? They establish kaizen goals each year as part of

value engineering
A cost-reduction technique, used primarily during design, that uses information about all value chain functions to satisfy customer needs while reducing costs.

kaizen costing
The Japanese term for continuous improvement during manufacturing.

TARGET COSTING, ABC, AND THE ROLE OF MANAGEMENT ACCOUNTING

Many companies use target costing together with an activity-based costing (ABC) system. Target costing requires a company to first determine what a customer will pay for a product and then work backward to design the product and production process that will generate a desired level of profit. ABC provides data on the costs of the various activities needed to produce the product. Knowing the costs of activities allows product and production process designers to predict the effects of their designs on the product's cost. Target costing essentially takes activity-based costs and uses them for strategic product decisions.

For example, Culp, Inc., a North Carolina textile manufacturer, uses target costing and ABC to elevate cost management into one of the most strategically important areas of the firm. Culp found that 80% of its product costs are predetermined at the design stage, but earlier cost control efforts had focused only on the other 20%. By shifting cost management efforts to the design stage and getting accurate costs of the various activities involved in production, cost management at Culp evolved into a process of cutting costs when engineers design a product, not identifying costs that are out of line after the production is complete.

A basic goal of target costing is to reduce costs before they occur. After all, once a company has incurred costs, it cannot change them. Such a strategy is especially important when product life cycles are short. Because most product life cycles are shrinking, use of target costing is expanding. Target costing focuses on reducing costs in the product

design and development stages—when costs can really be affected. For example, target costing heavily influenced DaimlerChrysler's design of the low-priced Neon, and Procter & Gamble's CEO credits target costing for helping eliminate costs that could cause managers to price products too high for the market to bear. "The design process is where you can truly leverage [reduce] your costs," according to Ron Gallaway, CFO of Micrus Semiconductors.

What role does management accounting play in target costing? At Micrus, management accountants are responsible for setting final targets for all components and processes. One survey reports that 86% of companies using target costing take data directly from their cost systems to estimate product costs during product design. At Eastman Kodak, management accountants are a vital part of the cross-functional team that implements target costing. This team includes design and manufacturing engineers, procurement, and marketing, as well as management accounting. Peter Zampino, director of research at the Consortium for Advanced Manufacturing—International, agrees: "It's like anything else; if finance doesn't bless the numbers, they won't have the credibility throughout the organization."

Sources: Adapted from R. Banham, "Off Target," *CFO,* May 2000; J. Bohn, "Chrysler Cuts Costs by Nurturing Links with Suppliers," *Automotive Age,* January 17, 1994, p. 18; G. Boer and J. Ettlie, "Target Costing Can Boost Your Bottom Line," *Strategic Finance,* July 1999, pp. 49–52; J. Brausch, "Target Costing for Profit Enhancement," *Management Accounting,* November 1994, pp. 45–49; G. Hoffman, "Future Vision," *Grocery Marketing,* March 1994, p. 6.

the planning process. Examples include the continual reduction in setup and processing times due to increased employee familiarity with the procedure. In total, target costing during design and kaizen costing during manufacturing may allow the firm to achieve the target cost over the product's life, even if initial cost predictions look too high.

Underlying these cost-reduction methods is the need for accurate cost information. Activity-based costing provides this information. Companies can then use activity-based management (ABM) to identify and eliminate non-value-added activities, waste, and their related costs. ABM is applied throughout both the design and manufacturing stages of the product's life. For examples of how accountants are using ABC in target costing, see the Business First box above.

Illustration of Target Costing

Consider the target-costing system used by ITT Automotive—one of the world's largest automotive suppliers. The company designs, develops, and manufactures a broad range of products, including brake systems, electric motors, and lamps. Also, the company is the

TARGET COSTING AND THE EXTERNAL VALUE CHAIN

The value chain we have defined consists of functions within a company that add value to a product or service. Companies that use target costing often go beyond the internal value chain to involve both customers and suppliers during the design process.

DaimlerChrysler's target-costing team worked actively with customers when analyzing the trade-off between cost and value of lighting for interior controls and under the hood. The value analysis resulted in adding the interior control lighting but not the under-the-hood lighting.

For many companies, a large percentage of the total cost of a product is from materials and parts that are purchased from suppliers—approximately 75% for Daimler Chrysler and Continental Teves—one of largest manufacturers of hydraulic and electronic brake systems, electronic steering systems and air spring systems. Both of these companies have intercompany teams to meet cost-reduction goals. At DaimlerChrysler, each supplier was asked to reduce costs by 5% annually, including improvements that reduce DaimlerChrysler's costs. For example, one supplier suggested changing the front rail system from several pieces to one unit. This improvement reduced Daimler Chrysler's costs so the supplier received credit. Continental Teves uses a cost-modeling tool to determine the target costs for components it outsources. If a supplier fails to meet its target costs, Continental might send a team to analyze the supplier's operations.

Source: Adapted from D. Swenson, S. Ansari, J. Bill, I. Kim, "Best Practices in Target Costing," *Management Accounting Quarterly*, Winter 2003.

worldwide market leader in antilock braking systems (ABS), producing 20,000 such systems per day.

What pricing approach does ITT Automotive use for the ABS? The pricing process starts when one of ITT's customers, say **Mercedes-Benz**, sends an invitation to bid. The market for brake systems is so competitive that very little variance exists in the prices companies can ask (bid). ITT then forms a target-costing group and charges it with determining whether the price and costs allow for enough of a profit margin. This group includes engineers, cost accountants, and sales personnel. Factors the group considers in determining the feasibility of earning the desired target profit margin include competitor pricing, inflation rates, interest rates, and potential cost reductions during both the design (target costing) and production (kaizen costing) stages of the ABS product life. ITT purchases many of the component parts that make up the ABS. Thus, the target-costing group works closely with suppliers. After making product and process design improvements and receiving commitments from suppliers, the company has the cost information needed for deciding the price for the bid.

The target-costing system has worked well at ITT Automotive. The company's bid for the ABS resulted in Mercedes-Benz U.S. International selecting ITT Automotive as the developer and supplier of ABS for the automaker's M-Class All-Activity Vehicle. For another illustration of how target-costing teams at DaimlerChrysler and **Continental Teves** are working closely with both customers and suppliers, see the Business First box, "Target Costing and the External Value Chain" above.

Target Costing and Cost-Plus Pricing Compared

Successful companies understand the market in which they operate and use the most appropriate pricing approach. To see how target costing and cost-plus pricing can lead to different decisions, suppose that ITT Automotive receives an invitation from **Ford** to bid on the ABS to be used in a new model car.

Assume the following data apply:

- The specifications contained in Ford's invitation lead to an estimated current manu-facturing cost (component parts, direct labor, and manufacturing overhead) of $154.
- ITT Automotive had a desired gross margin rate of 30% on sales, which means that actual cost should make up 70% of the price.
- Highly competitive market conditions exist and have established a sales price of $200 per unit.

If ITT had used cost-plus pricing to bid on the ABS, the bid price would be $154 ÷ .7 = $220. Ford would most likely reject this bid because the market price is only $200. ITT Automotive's pricing approach would lead to a lost opportunity.

Suppose that managers at ITT Automotive recognize that market conditions dictate a set price of $200. If ITT used a target-costing system, what would the pricing decision be? The target cost is $140 (that is, $200 × .7), so a required cost reduction of $14 per unit is neces-sary. The target-costing group would work with product and process engineers and suppliers to determine if they could reduce the average unit cost by $14 over the product's life. Note that it is not necessary to get costs down to the $140 target cost before production begins. The ini-tial unit cost will likely be higher, say, $145. Continuous improvement over the product's life will result in the final $5 of cost reductions. If the managers receive commitments for cost reductions, they will decide to bid $200 per unit. Note that if ITT Automotive accepts the bid, it must carry through with its focus on cost management throughout the life of the product.

Target costing originated in Japan and is a common practice there. However, a grow-ing number of companies now use it worldwide, including DaimlerChrysler, Boeing, **Eastman Kodak**, **Honda of America**, Mercedes-Benz, **Procter & Gamble**, **Caterpillar**, and ITT Automotive. Even some hospitals use target costing.

Why the increasing popularity of target costing? With increased global competition in many industries, companies are increasingly limited in influencing market prices. Cost management then becomes the key to profitability. Target costing forces managers to focus on costs to achieve the desired profits.

Highlights to Remember

1 **Discriminate between relevant and irrelevant information for making decisions.** To be relevant to a particular decision, a cost (or revenue) must meet two criteria: (1) It must be an expected future cost (or revenue), and (2) it must have an element of difference among the alternative courses of action.

2 **Apply the decision process to make business decisions.** All managers make business decisions based on some decision process. The best processes help decision making by focusing the manager's attention on relevant information.

3 **Decide to accept or reject a special order using the contribution margin technique.** Decisions to accept or reject a special sales order should use the contribution margin technique and focus on the additional revenues and additional costs of the order.

4 **Choose whether to add or delete a product line using relevant information.** Relevant information also plays an important role in decisions about adding or deleting products, services, or departments. Decisions on whether to delete a department or product line require analysis of the revenues forgone and the costs saved from the deletion.

5 **Compute a measure of product profitability when production is constrained by a scarce resource.** When production is constrained by a limiting resource, the key to obtaining the maximum profit from a given capacity is to obtain the greatest possible contribution to profit per unit of the limiting or scarce resource.

6 **Identify the factors that influence pricing decisions in practice.** Market conditions, the law, customers, competitors, and costs influence pricing decisions. The degree that management actions can affect price and cost determines the most effective approach to use for pricing and cost management purposes.

7 **Compute a target sales price by various approaches, and compare the advantages and disadvantages of these approaches.** Companies use cost-plus pricing for products when management actions can influence the market price. They can add profit markups to a variety of cost bases including variable manufacturing costs, all variable costs, full manufacturing costs, or all costs. The contribution margin approach to pricing has the advantage of providing detailed cost behavior information that is consistent with cost-volume-profit analysis.

8 **Use target costing to decide whether to add a new product.** When market conditions are such that management cannot influence prices, companies must focus on cost control and reduction. They use target costing primarily for new products, especially during the design phase of the value chain. They deduct a desired target margin from the market-established price to determine the target cost. Cost management then focuses on controlling and reducing costs over the product's life cycle to achieve that target cost.

Accounting Vocabulary

avoidable costs, p. 209
common costs, p. 209
decision model, p. 201
discriminatory pricing, p. 216
full cost, p. 218
fully allocated cost, p. 218
imperfect competition, p. 214

inventory turnover, p. 213
kaizen costing, p. 225
limiting factor, p. 211
marginal cost, p. 214
marginal revenue, p. 214
markup, p. 217
perfect competition, p. 213

predatory pricing, p. 216
price elasticity, p. 215
relevant information, p. 200
scarce resource, p. 211
target costing, p. 224
unavoidable costs, p. 209
value engineering, p. 225

Fundamental Assignment Material

5-A1 Special Order

Consider the following details of the income statement of the Manteray Pen Company (MPC) for the year ended December 31, 20X4.

Sales	$10,000,000
Less cost of goods sold	6,500,000
Gross margin or gross profit	$ 3,500,000
Less selling and administrative expenses	2,800,000
Operating income	$ 700,000

MPC's fixed manufacturing costs were $2.9 million and its fixed selling and administrative costs were $2.0 million. Sales commissions of 3% of sales are included in selling and administrative expenses.

The division had sold 2 million pens. Near the end of the year, **Pizza Hut** offered to buy 150,000 pens on a special order. To fill the order, a special Pizza Hut logo would have to be added to each pen. Pizza Hut intended to use the pens in special promotions in an eastern city during early 20X5.

Even though MPC had some idle plant capacity, the president rejected the Pizza Hut offer of $660,000 for the 150,000 pens. He said,

The Pizza Hut offer is too low. We'd avoid paying sales commissions, but we'd have to incur an extra cost of $.20 per pen to add the logo. If MPC sells below its regular selling prices, it will begin a chain reaction of competitors' price cutting and of customers wanting special deals. I believe in pricing at no lower than 8% above our full costs of $9,300,000 ÷ 2,000,000 units = $4.65 per unit plus the extra $.20 per pen less the savings in commissions.

1. Using the contribution margin technique, prepare an analysis similar to that in Exhibit 5-3 on page 204. Use four columns: without the special order, the effect of the special order (one column total and one column per unit), and totals with the special order.
2. By what percentage would operating income increase or decrease if the order had been accepted? Do you agree with the president's decision? Why?

5-A2 Choice of Products

The Ibunez Tool Company has two products: a plain circular saw and a professional circular saw. The plain saw sells for $66 and has a variable cost of $50. The professional circular saw sells for $100 and has a variable cost of $70.

1. Compute contribution margins and contribution-margin ratios for plain and professional saws.
2. The demand is for more units than the company can produce. There are only 20,000 machine hours of manufacturing capacity available. Two plain saws can be produced in the same average time (1 hour) needed to produce one professional saw. Compute the total contribution margin for 20,000 hours for plain saws only and for professional saws only.
3. Use two or three sentences to state the major lesson of this problem.

5-A3 Formulas for Pricing

Randy Azarski, a building contractor, builds houses in tracts, often building as many as 20 homes simultaneously. Azarski has budgeted costs for an expected number of houses in 20X4 as follows:

Direct materials	$3,500,000
Direct labor	1,000,000
Job construction overhead	1,500,000
Cost of jobs	$6,000,000
Selling and administrative costs	1,500,000
Total costs	$7,500,000

The job construction overhead includes approximately $600,000 of fixed costs, such as the salaries of supervisors and depreciation on equipment. The selling and administrative costs include $300,000 of variable costs, such as sales commissions and bonuses that depend fundamentally on overall profitability.

Azarski wants an operating income of $1.5 million for 20X4.

Compute the average target markup percentage for setting prices as a percentage of

1. Direct materials plus direct labor
2. The full "cost of jobs"
3. The variable "cost of jobs"
4. The full "cost of jobs" plus selling and administrative costs
5. The variable "cost of jobs" plus variable selling and administrative costs

5-A4 Target Costing

Lowest Cost Corporation uses target costing to aid in the final decision to release new products to production. A new product is being evaluated. Market research has surveyed the potential market for this product and believes that its unique features will generate a total demand over the product's life of 70,000 units at an average price of $360. The target costing team has members from market research, design, accounting, and production engineering departments. The team has worked closely with key customers and suppliers. A value analysis of the product has determined that the total cost for the various value-chain functions using the existing process technology are as follows:

Value-Chain Function	Total Cost over Product Life
Research and development	$ 2,500,000
Design	950,000
Manufacturing (70% outsourced to suppliers)	8,000,000
Marketing	1,800,000
Distribution	2,400,000
Customer service	950,000
Total cost over product life	$16,600,000

Management has a target contribution to profit percentage of 40% of sales. This contribution provides sufficient funds to cover corporate support costs, taxes, and a reasonable profit.

1. Should the new product be released to production? Explain.
2. Approximately 70% of manufacturing costs for this product consists of materials and parts that are purchased from suppliers. Key suppliers on the target-costing team have suggested process improvements that will reduce supplier cost by 20%. Should the new product be released to production? Explain.
3. New process technology can be purchased at a cost of $220,000 that will reduce nonoutsourced manufacturing costs by 25%. Assuming the supplier's process improvements and new process technology are implemented, should the new product be released to production? Explain.

5-B1 Special Order, Terminology, and Unit Costs

Following is the income statement of Danube Company, a manufacturer of men's blue jeans:

Danube Company
Income Statement for the Year Ended December 31, 20X0

	Total	Per Unit
Sales	$40,000,000	$20.00
Less cost of goods sold	24,000,000	12.00
Gross margin	$16,000,000	$ 8.00
Less selling and administrative expenses	15,000,000	7.50
Operating income	$ 1,000,000	$ .50

Danube had manufactured 2 million pairs of jeans, which had been sold to various clothing wholesalers and department stores. At the start of 20X1, the president, Rosie Valenzuela, died unexpectedly. Her son, Ricardo, became the new president. Ricardo had worked for 15 years in the marketing phases of the business. He knew very little about accounting and manufacturing, which were his mother's strengths. Ricardo has several questions, including inquiries regarding the pricing of special orders.

1. To prepare better answers, you decide to recast the income statement in contribution form. Variable manufacturing cost was $19 million. Variable selling and administrative expenses, which were mostly sales commissions, shipping expenses, and advertising allowances paid to customers based on units sold, were $9 million. Prepare the revised income statement.
2. Ricardo asks, "I can't understand financial statements until I know the meaning of various terms. In scanning my mother's assorted notes, I found the following pertaining to both total and unit costs: full manufacturing cost, variable cost, full cost, fully allocated cost, gross margin, and contribution margin. Using our data for 20X0, please give me a list of these costs, their total amounts, and their per-unit amounts."
3. "Near the end of 20X0, I brought in a special order from Costco for 100,000 jeans at $17 each. I said I'd accept a flat $20,000 sales commission instead of the usual 6% of selling price, but my mother refused the order. She usually upheld a relatively rigid pricing policy, saying that it was bad business to accept orders that did not at least generate full manufacturing cost plus 80% of full manufacturing cost.

   "That policy bothered me. We had idle capacity. The way I figured, our manufacturing costs would go up by $100,000 \times \$12 = \$1,200,000$, but our selling and administrative expenses would go up by only $20,000. That would mean additional operating income of $100,000 \times (\$17 - \$12)$ minus $20,000, or $500,000 minus $20,000, or $480,000. That's too much money to give up just to maintain a general pricing policy. Was my analysis of the impact on operating income correct? If not, please show me the correct additional operating income."
4. After receiving the explanations offered in number 2 and 3, Ricardo said, "Forget that I had the Costco order. I had an even bigger order from Lands' End. It was for 500,000 units and would have filled the plant completely. I told my mother I'd settle for no commission. There would have been no selling and administrative costs whatsoever because Lands' End would pay for the shipping and would not get any advertising allowances.

   "Lands' End offered $9.20 per unit. Our fixed manufacturing costs would have been spread over 2.5 million instead of 2 million units. Wouldn't it have been advantageous to accept the offer? Our old fixed manufacturing costs were $2.50 per unit. The added volume would reduce that cost more than our loss on our variable costs per unit.

   "Am I correct? What would have been the impact on total operating income if we had accepted the order?"

5-B2 Unit Costs and Capacity

Fargo Manufacturing Company produces two industrial solvents for which the following data have been tabulated. Fixed manufacturing cost is applied to products at a rate of $1.00 per machine hour.

Per Unit	XY-7	BD-4
Selling price	$6.00	$4.00
Variable manufacturing costs	3.00	1.50
Fixed manufacturing cost	.80	.20
Variable selling cost	2.00	2.00

The sales manager has had a $160,000 increase in her budget allotment for advertising and wants to apply the money on the most profitable product. The solvents are not substitutes for one another in the eyes of the company's customers.

1. How many machine hours does it take to produce one XY-7? To produce one BD-4? (*Hint:* Focus on applied fixed manufacturing cost.)
2. Suppose Fargo has only 100,000 machine hours that can be made available to produce XY-7 and BD-4. If the potential increase in sales units for either product resulting from advertising is far in excess of these production capabilities, which product should be produced and advertised, and what is the estimated increase in contribution margin earned?

5-B3 Dropping a Product Line

Hambley's Toy Store is on Regent Street in London. It has a magic department near the main door. Suppose that management is considering dropping the magic department, which has consistently shown an operating loss. The predicted income statements, in thousands of pounds (£), follow (for ease of analysis, only three product lines are shown):

	Total	General Merchandise	Electronic Products	Magic Department
Sales	£6,000	£5,000	£400	£ 600
Variable expenses	4,090	3,500	200	390
Contribution margin	£1,910 (32%)	£1,500 (30%)	£200 (50%)	£ 210 (35%)
Fixed expenses (compensation, depreciation, property taxes, insurance, etc.)	1,110	750	50	310
Operating income	£ 800	£ 750	£150	£(100)

The £310,000 of magic department fixed expenses include the compensation of employees of £100,000. These employees will be released if the magic department is abandoned. All of the magic department's equipment is fully depreciated, so none of the £310,000 pertains to such items. Furthermore, disposal values of equipment will be exactly offset by the costs of removal and remodeling.

If the magic department is dropped, the manager will use the vacated space for either more general merchandise or more electronic products. The expansion of general merchandise would not entail hiring any additional salaried help, but more electronic products would require an additional person at an annual cost of £25,000. The manager thinks that sales of general merchandise would increase by £300,000; electronic products, by £200,000. The manager's modest predictions are partially based on the fact that she thinks the magic department has helped lure customers to the store and thus improved overall sales. If the magic department is closed, that lure would be gone.

Should the magic department be closed? Explain, showing computations.

5-B4 Cost-Plus Pricing and Target Costing

A Fortune 100 company, Caterpillar is the world's leading manufacturer of construction and mining equipment, diesel and natural gas engines, and industrial gas turbines. Caterpillar also manufactures custom piston pins for other manufacturers in the same facility used to make pins for its own heavy-duty engines. Piston pins are made with cost effective CNC bar feeders and multispindle barstock machines. This process is a high-output, high-efficiency operation that eliminates the added costs of purchasing special cut-to-length barstock or cutting barstock to specific lengths.

The market research department has indicated that a proposed new piston pin for a manufacturer of truck engines would likely sell for $46. A similar piston pin currently being produced has the following manufacturing costs:

Direct materials	$24.00
Direct labor	10.00
Overhead	16.00
Total	$50.00

Assume that Caterpillar desires a gross margin of 35% of the manufacturing cost.

1. Suppose Caterpillar used cost-plus pricing, setting the price 35% above the manufacturing cost. What price would be charged for the piston pin? Would you produce such a piston pin if you were a manager at Caterpillar? Explain.
2. Caterpillar uses target costing. What price would the company charge for a piston pin? What is the highest acceptable manufacturing cost for which Caterpillar would be willing to produce the piston pin?
3. As a user of target costing, what steps would Caterpillar managers take to try to make production of this product feasible?

Additional Assignment Material

Questions

5-1 "The distinction between precision and relevance should be kept in mind." Explain.

5-2 Distinguish between the quantitative and qualitative aspects of decisions.

5-3 Describe the accountant's role in decision making.

5-4 "Any future cost is relevant." Do you agree? Explain.

5-5 Why are historical or past data irrelevant to special decisions?

5-6 Describe the role of past or historical costs in the decision process. That is, how do these costs relate to the prediction method and the decision model?

5-7 "There is a commonality of approach to various special decisions." Explain.

5-8 "In relevant-cost analysis, beware of unit costs." Explain.

5-9 "The key to decisions to delete a product or department is identifying avoidable costs." Do you agree? Explain.

5-10 "Avoidable costs are variable costs." Do you agree? Explain.

5-11 Give four examples of limiting or scarce factors.

5-12 Why are customers one of the factors influencing pricing decisions?

5-13 What is target cost per unit?

5-14 What is value engineering?

5-15 What is kaizen costing?

5-16 "In target costing, prices determine costs rather than vice versa." Explain.

5-17 Many companies that use target costing involve both customers and suppliers in product and process design. Explain why.

5-18 If a target-costing system is used and the existing cost cannot be reduced to the target cost through cost reductions, management should discontinue producing and selling the product. Do you agree? Explain.

5-19 "Basing pricing on only the variable costs of a job results in suicidal underpricing." Do you agree? Why?

5-20 Provide three examples of pricing decisions other than the special order.

5-21 List three popular markup formulas for pricing.

5-22 Describe two long-run effects that may lead to managers' rejecting opportunities to cut prices and obtain increases in short-run profits.

5-23 Give two reasons why full costs are far more widely used than variable costs for guiding pricing.

5-24 Why do most executives use both full-cost and variable-cost information for pricing decisions?

Critical Thinking Exercises

5-25 Fixed Costs and the Sales Function

Many sales managers have a good intuitive understanding of costs, but they often are imprecise in how they describe the costs. For example, one manager said the following: "Increasing sales will decrease fixed costs because it spreads them over more units." Do you agree? Explain.

5-26 The Economics of the Pricing Decision

Economic theory states that managers should set price equal to marginal cost in perfect competition. Accountants use variable cost to approximate marginal costs. Compare and contrast marginal cost and variable cost, and explain whether using variable costs as an approximation for marginal cost is appropriate for making pricing decisions.

5-27 Pricing Decisions, Ethics, and the Law

Managers should base pricing decisions on both cost and market factors. In addition, they must also consider ethical and legal issues. Describe the influence that ethics and the law have on pricing decisions.

5-28 Target Costing and the Value Chain

According to Keith Hallin, senior manager of finance for decision support initiatives at Boeing Commercial Airplane Group, reaching target costs is a challenge for the company's entire value chain. Explain how managers of the various value-chain functions at Boeing might be involved in the target costing process.

Exercises

5-29 Pinpointing Relevant Costs

Today you are planning to see a motion picture and you can attend either of two theaters. You have only a small budget for entertainment, so prices are important. You have attended both theaters recently. One charged $6 for admission; the other charged $7. You habitually buy popcorn in the theater—each theater charges $2. The motion pictures now being shown are equally attractive to you, but you are virtually certain that you will never see the picture that you reject today.

Identify the relevant costs. Explain your answer.

5-30 Information and Decisions

Suppose the historical costs for the manufacture of a calculator by **Radio Shack** were as follows: direct materials, $5.00 per unit; direct labor, $3.00 per unit. Management is trying to decide whether to replace some materials with different materials. The replacement should cut material costs by 5% per unit. However, direct-labor time will increase by 5% per unit. Moreover, direct-labor rates will be affected by a recent 10% wage increase.

Prepare an exhibit like Exhibit 5-1 (p. 502), showing where and how the data about direct material and direct labor fit in the decision process.

5-31 Identification of Relevant Costs

Paul and Paula Petroceli were trying to decide whether to go to the symphony or to the baseball game. They already have two nonrefundable tickets to "Pops Night at the Symphony" that cost $40 each. This is the only concert of the season they considered attending because it is the only one with the type of music they enjoy. The baseball game is the last one of the season, and it will decide the league championship. They can purchase tickets to the game for $20 each.

The Petroceli will drive 50 miles round-trip to either event. Variable costs for operating their auto are $.14 per mile, and fixed costs average $.13 per mile for the 18,000 miles they drive annually. Parking at the symphony is free, but it costs $6 at the baseball game.

To attend either event, Paul and Paula will hire a baby-sitter at $4 per hour. They expect to be gone 5 hours to attend the baseball game but only 4 hours to attend the symphony.

Compare the cost of attending the baseball game with the cost of attending the symphony. Focus on relevant costs. Compute the difference in cost, and indicate which alternative is more costly to the Petrocelis.

5-32 Special-Order Decision

Belltown Athletic Supply (BAS) makes game jerseys for athletic teams. The F. C. Kitsap soccer club has offered to buy 100 jerseys for the teams in its league for $15 per jersey. The team price for such jerseys normally is $18, an 80% markup over BAS's purchase price of $10 per jersey. BAS adds a name and number to each jersey at a variable cost of $2 per jersey. The annual fixed cost of equipment used in the printing process is $6,000, and other fixed costs allocated to jerseys are $2,000. BAS makes about 2,000 jerseys per year, so the fixed cost is $4 per jersey. The equipment is used only for printing jerseys and stands idle 75% of the usable time.

The manager of BAS turned down the offer, saying, "If we sell at $15 and our cost is $16, we lose money on each jersey we sell. We would like to help your league, but we can't afford to lose money on the sale."

1. Compute the amount by which the operating income of BAS would change if the F. C. Kitsap's offer were accepted.
2. Suppose you were the manager of BAS. Would you accept the offer? In addition to considering the quantitative impact computed in number 1, list two qualitative considerations that would influence your decision—one qualitative factor supporting acceptance of the offer and one supporting rejection.

5-33 Unit Costs and Total Costs

You are a CPA who belongs to a downtown business club. Annual dues are $120. You use the club solely for lunches, which cost $6 each. You have not used the club much in recent years and you are wondering whether to continue your membership.

1. You are confronted with a variable-cost plus a fixed-cost behavior pattern. Plot each on a graph, where the vertical axis is total cost and the horizontal axis is annual volume in number of lunches. Also plot a third graph that combines the previous two graphs.
2. What is the cost per lunch if you pay for your own lunch once a year? Twelve times a year? Two hundred times a year?
3. Suppose the average price of lunches elsewhere is $10. (a) How many lunches must you have at the luncheon club so that the total costs of the lunches would be the same, regardless of where you ate for that number of lunches? (b) Suppose you ate 250 lunches a year at the club. How much would you save in relation to the total costs of eating elsewhere?

5-34 Advertising Expenditures and Nonprofit Organizations

Many colleges and universities have been extensively advertising their services. For example, a university in Philadelphia used a biplane to pull a sign promoting its evening program, and one in Mississippi designed bumper stickers and slogans as well as innovative programs.

Suppose Wilton College charges a comprehensive annual fee of $14,000 for tuition, room, and board, and it has capacity for 2,500 students. The admissions department predicts enrollment of 2,000 students for 20X1. Costs per student for the 20X1 academic year are

	Variable	Fixed	Total
Educational programs	$4,000	$4,200	$8,200
Room	1,300	2,200	3,500
Board	2,600	600	3,200
	$7,900	$7,000*	$14,900

* Based on 2,000 to 2,500 students for the year.

The assistant director of admissions has proposed a two-month advertising campaign, however, using radio and television advertisements, together with an extensive direct mailing of brochures.

1. Suppose the advertising campaign will cost $1.83 million. What is the minimum number of additional students the campaign must attract to make the campaign break even?
2. Suppose the admissions department predicts that the campaign will attract 350 additional students. What is the most Wilton should pay for the campaign and still break even?
3. Suppose a three-month (instead of two-month) campaign will attract 450 instead of 350 additional students. What is the most Wilton should pay for the one-month extension of the campaign and still break even?

5-35 Variety of Cost Terms

Consider the following data:

Variable selling and administrative costs per unit	$ 4.00
Total fixed selling and administrative costs	$2,900,000
Total fixed manufacturing costs	$3,000,000
Variable manufacturing costs per unit	$ 9.00
Units produced and sold	500,000

1. Compute the following per unit of product: (a) total variable costs, (b) full manufacturing, (c) full cost.
2. Give a synonym for full cost.

5-36 Profit per Unit of Space

1. Several successful chains of warehouse stores such as **Costco** and **Sam's Club** have merchandising policies that differ considerably from those of traditional department stores. Name some characteristics of these warehouse stores that have contributed to their success.
2. Food chains such as **Safeway** have typically regarded approximately 20% of selling price as an average target gross profit on canned goods and similar grocery items. What are the limitations of such an approach? Be specific.

5-37 Deletion of Product Line

Zurich American School is an international private elementary school. In addition to regular classes, after-school care is provided between 3:00 P.M. and 6:00 P.M. at SFR 12 per child per hour. Financial results for the after-school care for a representative month are

Revenue, 600 hours @ SFR 12 per hour		SFR 7,200
Less		
Teacher salaries	SFR 5,200	
Supplies	800	
Depreciation	1,300	
Sanitary engineering	100	
Other fixed costs	200	7,600
Operating income (loss)		SFR (400)

The director of Zurich American School is considering discontinuing the after-school care services because it is not fair to the other students to subsidize the after-school care program. He thinks that eliminating the program will free up SFR 400 a month to support regular classes.

1. Compute the financial impact on Zurich American School from discontinuing the after-school care program.
2. List three qualitative factors that would influence your decision.

5-38 Acceptance of Low Bid

The Velasquez Company, a maker of a variety of metal and plastic products, is in the midst of a business downturn and is saddled with many idle facilities. Columbia Health Care has approached Velasquez to produce 300,000 nonslide serving trays. Columbia will pay $1.30 each.

Velasquez predicts that its variable costs will be $1.40 each. Its fixed costs, which had been averaging $1 per unit on a variety of other products, will now be spread over twice as much volume, however. The president commented, "Sure we'll lose $.10 each on the variable costs, but we'll gain $.50 per unit by spreading our fixed costs. Therefore, we should take the offer, because it represents an advantage of $.40 per unit."

Suppose the regular business had a current volume of 300,000 units, sales of $600,000, variable costs of $420,000, and fixed costs of $300,000. Do you agree with the president? Why?

5-39 Pricing by Auto Dealer

Many automobile dealers have an operating pattern similar to that of Austin Motors, a dealer in Texas. Each month, Austin initially aims at a unit volume quota that approximates a break-even point. Until the break-even point is reached, Austin has a policy of relatively lofty pricing, whereby the "minimum deal" must contain a sufficiently high markup to ensure a contribution to profit of no less than $400. After the break-even point is attained, Austin tends to quote lower prices for the remainder of the month.

What is your opinion of this policy? As a prospective customer, how would you react to this policy?

5-40 Pricing to Maximize Contribution

Reynolds Company produces and sells picture frames. One particular frame for 8 × 10 photos was an instant success in the market, but recently competitors have come out with comparable frames. Reynolds has been charging $12 wholesale for the frames, and sales have fallen from 10,000 units last year to 7,000 units this year. The product manager in charge of this frame is considering lowering the price to $10 per frame. He believes sales will rebound to 10,000 units at the lower price, but they will fall to 6,000 units at the $12 price. The unit variable cost of producing and selling the frames is $6, and $40,000 of fixed cost is assigned to the frames.

1. Assuming that the only prices under consideration are $10 and $12 per frame, which price will lead to the largest profit for Reynolds? Explain why.
2. What subjective considerations might affect your pricing decision?

5-41 Target Selling Prices

Consider the following data from Blackmar Company's budgeted income statement (in thousands of dollars).

Target sales	$60,000
Variable costs	
Manufacturing	30,000
Selling and administrative	6,000
Total variable costs	36,000
Fixed costs	
Manufacturing	8,000
Selling and administrative	6,000
Total fixed costs	14,000
Total of all costs	50,000
Operating income	$10,000

Compute the following markup formulas that would be used for obtaining the same target sales as a percentage of (1) total variable costs, (2) full costs, (3) variable manufacturing costs.

5-42 Competitive Bids

Griffy, Rodriguez, and Martinez, a CPA firm, is preparing to bid for a consulting job. Although Alicia Martinez will use her judgment about the market in finalizing the bid, she has asked you to prepare a cost analysis to help in the bidding. You have estimated the costs for the consulting job to be

Materials and supplies, at cost	$ 30,000
Hourly pay for consultants, 2,000 hours @ $35 per hour	70,000
Fringe benefits for consultants, 2,000 hours @ $12 per hour	24,000
Total variable costs	124,000
Fixed costs allocated to the job	
Based on labor, 2,000 hours @ $10 per hour	20,000
Based on materials and supplies, 80% of 30,000	24,000
Total cost	$168,000

Of the $44,000 allocated fixed costs, $35,000 will be incurred even if the job is not undertaken.

Alicia normally bids jobs at the sum of (1) 150% of the estimated materials and supplies cost and (2) $75 per estimated labor hour.

1. Prepare a bid using the normal formula.
2. Prepare a minimum bid equal to the additional costs expected to be incurred to complete the job.
3. Prepare a bid that will cover full costs plus a markup for profit equal to 20% of full cost.

5-43 Target Costing

Quality Corporation believes that there is a market for a portable electronic toothbrush that can be easily carried by business travelers. Quality's market research department has surveyed the features and prices of electronic brushes currently on the market. Based on this research, Quality believes that $65 would be about the right price. At this price, marketing believes that about 80,000 new portable brushes can be sold over the product's life cycle. It will cost about $1,000,000 to design and develop the portable brush. Quality has a target profit of 20% of sales.

Determine the total and unit target cost to manufacture, sell, distribute, and service each portable brush.

5-44 Target Costing

Best Cost Corporation has an aggressive R&D program and uses target costing to aid in the final decision to release new products to production. A new product is being evaluated. Market research has surveyed the potential market for this product and believes that its unique features will generate a total demand of 50,000 units at an average price of $230. Design and production engineering departments have performed a value analysis of the product and have determined that the total cost for the various value-chain functions using the existing process technology are as follows:

Value-Chain Function	Total Cost over Product Life
Research and Development	$ 1,500,000
Design	750,000
Manufacturing	5,000,000
Marketing	800,000
Distribution	1,400,000
Customer Service	750,000
Total Cost over Product Life	$10,200,000

Management has a target profit percentage of 20% of sales. Production engineering indicates that new process technology can reduce the manufacturing cost by 40%, but it will cost $1,000,000.

1. Assuming the existing process technology is used, should the new product be released to production? Explain.
2. Assuming the new process technology is purchased, should the new product be released to production? Explain.

Problems

5-45 Pricing, Ethics, and the Law

Great Lakes Pharmaceuticals, Inc. (GLPI), produces both prescription and over-the-counter medications. In January GLPI introduced a new prescription drug, Capestan, to relieve the pain of arthritis. The company spent more than $50 million over the last five years developing the drug, and advertising alone during the first year of introduction will exceed $10 million. Production cost for a bottle of 100 tablets is approximately $12. Sales in the first three years are predicted to be 500,000, 750,000, and 1,000,000 bottles, respectively. To achieve these sales, GLPI plans to distribute the medicine through three sources: directly to physicians, through hospital pharmacies, and through retail pharmacies. Initially, the bottles will be given free to physicians to give to patients, hospital pharmacies will pay $25 per bottle, and retail pharmacies will pay $40 per bottle. In the second and third year, the company plans to phase out the free distributions to physicians and move all other customers toward a $50-per-bottle sales price.

Comment on the pricing and promotion policies of GLPI. Pay particular attention to the legal and ethical issues involved.

5-46 Pricing and Contribution Margin Technique

The Transnational Trucking Company has the following operating results to date for 20X4:

Operating revenues	$50,000,000
Operating costs	40,000,000
Operating income	$10,000,000

A large Boston manufacturer has inquired about whether Transnational would be interested in trucking a large order of its parts to Chicago. Steve Goldmark, operations manager, investigated the situation and estimated that the "fully allocated" costs of servicing the order would be $45,000. Using his general pricing formula, he quoted a price of $50,000. The manufacturer replied, "We'll give you $39,000, take it or leave it. If you do not want our business, we'll truck it ourselves or go elsewhere."

A cost analyst had recently been conducting studies of how Transnational's operating costs tended to behave. She found that $32 million of the $40 million could be characterized as variable costs. Goldmark discussed the matter with her and decided that this order would probably generate cost behavior little different from Transnational's general operations.

1. Using a contribution margin technique, prepare an analysis for Transnational.
2. Should Transnational accept the order? Explain.

5-47 Cost Analysis and Pricing

The budget for the Oxford University Printing Company for 20X5 follows:

Sales		£1,100,000
Direct material	£280,000	
Direct labor	320,000	
Overhead	400,000	1,000,000
Net income		£ 100,000

The company typically uses a so-called cost-plus pricing system. Direct-material and direct-labor costs are computed, overhead is added at a rate of 125% of direct labor, and 10% of the total cost is added to obtain the selling price.

Edith Smythe, the sales manager, has placed a £22,000 bid on a particularly large order with a cost of £5,600 direct material and £6,400 direct labor. The customer informs her that she can have the business for £19,800, take it or leave it. If Smythe accepts the order, total sales for 20X5 will be £1,119,800.

Smythe refuses the order, saying, "I sell on a cost-plus basis. It is bad policy to accept orders at below cost. I would lose £200 on the job."

The company's annual fixed overhead is £160,000.

1. What would net income have been with the order? Without the order? Show your computations.
2. Give a short description of a contribution margin technique to pricing that Smythe might follow. Include a stipulation of the pricing formula that Smythe should routinely use if she hopes to obtain a target net income of £100,000.

5-48 Pricing of Education

You are the director of continuing education programs for a state university. Courses for executives are especially popular, and you have developed an extensive menu of one-day and two-day courses that are presented in various locations throughout the state. The performance of these courses for the current fiscal year, excluding the final course, which is scheduled for the next Saturday, is

Tuition revenue	$2,000,000
Costs of courses	800,000
Contribution margin	1,200,000
General administrative expenses	400,000
Operating income	$ 800,000

The costs of the courses include fees for instructors, rentals of classrooms, advertising, and any other items, such as travel, that can be easily and exclusively identified as being caused by a particular course.

The general administrative expenses include your salary, your secretary's compensation, and related expenses, such as a lump-sum payment to the university's central offices as a share of university overhead.

The enrollment for your final course of the year is 30 students, who have paid $200 each. Two days before the course is to begin, a city manager telephones your office. "Do you offer discounts to nonprofit institutions?" he asks. "If so, we'll send 10 managers. But our budget will not justify our spending more than $100 per person." The extra cost of including these 10 managers would entail lunches at $20 each and course materials at $40 each.

1. Prepare a tabulation of the performance for the full year including the final course. Assume that the costs of the final course for the 30 enrollees' instruction, travel, advertising, rental of hotel classroom, lunches, and course materials would be $4,000. Show a tabulation in four columns: before final course, final course with 30 registrants, effect of 10 more registrants, and grand totals.
2. What major considerations would probably influence the pricing policies for these courses? For setting regular university tuition in private universities?

5-49 Videotape Sales and Rental Markets

Is it more profitable to sell your product for $50 or $15? This is a difficult question for many movie studio executives. Consider a movie that cost $60 million to produce and required another $40 million to promote. After its theater release, the studio must determine whether to sell videotapes directly to the public at a wholesale price of about $15 per tape or to sell to video rental store distributors for about $50 per tape. The distributors will then sell to about 14,000 video rental stores in the United States.

Assume that the variable cost to produce and ship one video tape is $2.00.

1. Suppose each video rental store would purchase 10 tapes of this movie. How many tapes would need to be sold directly to customers to make direct sales a more profitable option than sales to video store distributors?
2. How does the cost of producing and promoting the movie affect this decision?
3. Walt Disney Co. elected to sell *The Lion King* directly to consumers, and it sold 30 million copies at an average price of $15.50 per tape. How many tapes would each video rental store have to purchase to provide Disney as much profit as the company received from direct sales? Assume that Disney would receive $50 per tape from the distributors.

5-50 Use of Passenger Jets

In a recent year Continental Air Lines, Inc., filled about 50% of the available seats on its flights, a record about 15 percentage points below the national average.

Continental could have eliminated about 4% of its runs and raised its average load considerably. The improved load factor would have reduced profits, however. Give reasons for or against this elimination. What factors should influence an airline's scheduling policies?

When you answer this question, suppose that Continental had a basic package of 3,000 flights per month, with an average of 100 seats available per flight. Also suppose that 52% of the seats were filled at an average ticket price of $200 per flight. Variable costs are about 70% of revenue.

Continental also had a marginal package of 120 flights per month, with an average of 100 seats available per flight. Suppose that only 20% of the seats were filled at an average ticket price of $100 per flight. Variable costs are about 50% of this revenue. Prepare a tabulation of the basic package, marginal package, and total package, showing percentage of seats filled, revenue, variable expenses, and contribution margin.

5-51 Effects of Volume on Operating Income

The Wittred Division of Melbourne Sports Company manufactures boomerangs, which are sold to wholesalers and retailers. The division manager has set a target of 250,000 boomerangs for next month's production and sales. The manager, however, has prepared an analysis of the effects on operating income of deviations from the target:

Volume in units	200,000	250,000	300,000
Sales @ $3.00	$600,000	$750,000	$900,000
Full costs @ $2.50	500,000	625,000	750,000
Operating income	$100,000	$125,000	$150,000

The costs have the following characteristics. Variable manufacturing costs are $.90 per boomerang; variable selling costs are $.20 per boomerang. Fixed manufacturing costs per month are $300,000; fixed selling and administrative costs, $50,000.

1. Prepare a correct analysis of the changes in volume on operating income. Prepare a tabulated set of income statements at levels of 200,000, 250,000, and 300,000 boomerangs. Also show percentages of operating income in relation to sales.
2. Compare your tabulation with the manager's tabulation. Why is the manager's tabulation incorrect?

5-52 Pricing at the Grand Canyon Railway

Suppose a tour guide approached the general manager of the Grand Canyon Railway with a proposal to offer a special guided tour to the agent's clients. The tour would occur 20 times each summer and be part of a larger itinerary that the agent is putting together. The agent presented two options: (a) a special 65-mile tour with the agent's 30 clients as the only passengers on the train, or (b) adding a car to an existing train to accommodate the 30 clients on an already scheduled 65-mile tour.

Under either option, Grand Canyon would hire a tour guide for $150 for the trip. Grand Canyon has extra cars in its switching yard, and it would cost $40 to move a car to the main track and hook it up. The extra fuel cost to pull one extra car is $.20 per mile. To run an engine and a passenger car on the trip would cost $2.20 per mile, and an engineer would be paid $400 for the trip.

Depreciation on passenger cars is $5,000 per year, and depreciation on engines is $20,000 per year. Each passenger car and each engine travels about 50,000 miles a year. They are replaced every 8 years.

The agent offered to pay $30 per passenger for the special tour and $15 per passenger for simply adding an extra car.

1. Which of the two options is more profitable to Grand Canyon? Comment on which costs are irrelevant to this decision.
2. Should Grand Canyon accept the proposal for the option you found best in number 1? Comment on what costs are relevant for this decision but not for the decision in number 1.

5-53 Pricing of Special Order

The Drosselmeier Corporation, located in Munich, makes Christmas nutcrackers and has an annual plant capacity of 2,400 product units. Suppose its predicted operating results (in euros) for the year are

Production and sales of 2,000 units, total sales	€180,000
Manufacturing costs	
Fixed (total)	60,000
Variable (per unit)	26
Selling and administrative expenses	
Fixed (total)	30,000
Variable (per unit)	10

Compute the following, ignoring income taxes:

1. If the company accepts a special order for 300 units at a selling price of €40 each, how would the total predicted net income for the year be affected, assuming no effect on regular sales at regular prices?
2. Without decreasing its total net income, what is the lowest unit price for which the Drosselmeier Corporation could sell an additional 100 units not subject to any variable selling and administrative expenses, assuming no effect on regular sales at regular prices?
3. List the numbers given in the problem that are irrelevant (not relevant) in solving number 2.
4. Compute the expected annual net income (with no special orders) if plant capacity can be doubled by adding additional facilities at a cost of €500,000. Assume that these facilities have an estimated life of five years with no residual scrap value, and that the current unit selling price can be maintained for all sales. Total sales are expected to equal the new plant capacity each year. No changes are expected in variable costs per unit or in total fixed costs except for depreciation.

5-54 Pricing and Confusing Variable and Fixed Costs

Goldwyn Electronics had a fixed factory overhead budget for 20X1 of $10 million. The company planned to make and sell 2 million units of a particular communications device. All variable manufacturing costs per unit were $10. The budgeted income statement contained the following:

Sales	$40,000,000
Manufacturing cost of goods sold	30,000,000
Gross margin	10,000,000
Deduct selling and administrative expenses	4,000,000
Operating income	$ 6,000,000

For simplicity, assume that the actual variable costs per unit and the total fixed costs were exactly as budgeted.

1. Compute Goldwyn's budgeted fixed factory overhead per unit.
2. Near the end of 20X1, a large computer manufacturer offered to buy 100,000 units for $1.2 million on a one-time special order. The president of Goldwyn stated, "The offer is a bad deal. It's foolish to sell below full manufacturing costs per unit. I realize that this order will have only a modest effect on selling and administrative costs. They will increase by a $10,000 fee paid to our sales agent." Compute the effect on operating income if the offer is accepted.
3. What factors should the president of Goldwyn consider before finally deciding whether to accept the offer?
4. Suppose the original budget for fixed manufacturing costs was $10 million, but budgeted units of product were 1 million. How would your answers to numbers 1 and 2 change? Be specific.

5-55 Demand Analysis

Zimmerman Manufacturing Limited produces and sells one product, a three-foot Canadian flag. During 20X4, the company manufactured and sold 50,000 flags at $25 each. Existing production capacity is 60,000 flags per year.

In formulating the 20X5 budget, management is faced with several decisions concerning product pricing and output. The following information is available:

1. A market survey shows that the sales volume depends on the selling price. For each $1 drop in selling price, sales volume would increase by 10,000 flags.
2. The company's expected cost structure for 20X5 is as follows:
   a. Fixed cost (regardless of production or sales activities), $360,000
   b. Variable costs per flag (including production, selling, and administrative expenses), $16
3. To increase annual capacity from the present 60,000 to 90,000 flags, additional investment for plant, building, equipment, and the like of $200,000 would be necessary. The estimated average life of the additional investment would be 10 years, so the fixed costs would increase by an average of $20,000 per year. (Expansion of less than 30,000 additional units of capacity would cost only slightly less than $200,000.)

Indicate, with reasons, what the level of production and the selling price should be for the coming year. Also indicate whether the company should approve the plant expansion. Show your calculations. Ignore income tax considerations and the time value of money.

5-56 Choice of Products

Gulf Coast Fashions sells both designer and moderately priced women's wear in Tampa. Profits have been volatile. Top management is trying to decide which product line to drop. Accountants have reported the following data:

	Per Item	
	Designer	**Moderately Priced**
Average selling price	$240	$150
Average variable expenses	120	85
Average contribution margin	$120	$ 65
Average contribution-margin percentage	50%	43%

The store has 8,000 square feet of floor space. If moderately priced goods are sold exclusively, 400 items can be displayed. If designer goods are sold exclusively, only 300 items can be displayed. Moreover, the rate of sale (turnover) of the designer items will be two-thirds the rate of moderately priced goods.

1. Prepare an analysis to show which product to drop.
2. What other considerations might affect your decision in number 1?

5-57 Analysis of Unit Costs

Home Appliances Company manufactures small appliances such as electric can openers, toasters, food mixers, and irons. The peak manufacturing season is at hand, and the president is trying to decide whether to produce more of the company's standard line of can openers or its premium line that includes a built-in knife sharpener, a better finish, and a higher-quality motor. The unit data follow:

	Product	
	Standard	Premium
Selling price	$28	$38
Direct material	$ 8	$13
Direct labor	2	1
Variable factory overhead	4	6
Fixed factory overhead	6	9
Total cost of goods sold	$20	$29
Gross profit per unit	$ 8	$ 9

The sales outlook is very encouraging. The plant could operate at full capacity by producing either product or both products. Both the standard and the premium products are processed through the same departments. Selling and administrative costs will not be affected by this decision, so they may be ignored.

Many of the parts are produced on automatic machinery. The factory overhead is allocated to products by developing separate rates per machine hour for variable and fixed overhead. For example, the total fixed overhead is divided by the total machine hours to get a rate per hour. Thus the amount of overhead allocated to products is dependent on the number of machine hours used by the product. It takes one hour of machine time to produce one unit of the standard product.

Direct labor may not be proportionate with overhead because many workers operate two or more machines simultaneously.

Which product should be produced? If more than one should be produced, indicate the proportions of each. Show computations. Explain your answers briefly.

5-58 Use of Available Facilities

The Oahu Audio Company manufactures electronic subcomponents that can be sold as is or can be processed further into "plug-in" assemblies for a variety of intricate electronic equipment. The entire output of subcomponents can be sold at a market price of $2.20 per unit. The plug-in assemblies have been generating a sales price of $5.70 for three years, but the price has recently fallen to $5.30 on assorted orders.

Janet Oh, the vice president of marketing, has analyzed the markets and the costs. She thinks that production of plug-in assemblies should be dropped whenever the price falls below $4.70 per unit. However, at the current price of $5.30, the total available capacity should currently be devoted to producing plug-in assemblies. She has cited the data in Exhibit 5-12.

Direct-materials and direct-labor costs are variable. The total overhead is fixed; it is allocated to units produced by predicting the total overhead for the coming year and dividing this total by the total hours of capacity available.

The total hours of capacity available are 600,000. It takes 1 hour to make 60 subcomponents and 2 hours of additional processing and testing to make 60 plug-in assemblies.

1. If the price of plug-in assemblies for the coming year is to be $5.30, should sales of subcomponents be dropped and all facilities devoted to the production of plug-in assemblies? Show computations.

Exhibit 5-12
Oahu Audio Company
Product Profitability
Data

	Subcomponents	
Selling price, after deducting relevant selling costs		$2.20
Direct materials	$1.10	
Direct labor	.30	
Manufacturing overhead	.60	
Cost per unit		2.00
Operating profit		$ .20

	Plug-In Assemblies	
Selling price, after deducting relevant selling costs		$5.30
Transferred-in variable cost for subcomponents	$1.40	
Additional direct materials	1.45	
Direct labor	.45	
Manufacturing overhead	1.20*	
Cost per unit		4.50
Operating profit		$ .80

* For additional processing to make and test plug-in assemblies.

2. Prepare a report for the vice president of marketing to show the lowest possible price for plug-in assemblies that would be acceptable.
3. Suppose 40% of the manufacturing overhead is variable with respect to processing and testing time. Repeat numbers 1 and 2. Do your answers change? If so, how?

5-59 Target Costing

Memphis Electrical, Inc., makes small electric motors for a variety of home appliances. Memphis sells the motors to appliance makers, who assemble and sell the appliances to retail outlets. Although Memphis makes dozens of different motors, it does not currently make one to be used in garage-door openers. The company's market research department has discovered a market for such a motor.

The market research department has indicated that a motor for garage-door openers would likely sell for $25. A similar motor currently being produced has the following manufacturing costs:

Direct materials	$13.00
Direct labor	6.00
Overhead	8.00
Total	$27.00

Memphis desires a gross margin of 15% of the manufacturing cost.

1. Suppose Memphis used cost-plus pricing, setting the price 15% above the manufacturing cost. What price would be charged for the motor? Would you produce such a motor if you were a manager at Memphis? Explain.
2. Suppose Memphis uses target costing. What price would the company charge for a garage-door-opener motor? What is the highest acceptable manufacturing cost for which Memphis would be willing to produce the motor?
3. As a user of target costing, what steps would Memphis managers take to try to make production of this product feasible?

5-60 Target Costing and ABM

Cleveland Plastics makes plastic parts for other manufacturing companies. Cleveland has an ABC system for its production, marketing, and customer service functions. The company uses target costing as a strategic decision-making tool. One of Cleveland's product lines—consumer products—has over 100 individual products with life cycles of less than three years. This means that about 30 to 40 products are discontinued and replaced with new products each year. Cleveland's top management has established the following tool to be used by the target-cost team for evaluating proposed new products:

Required Cost Reduction (RCR) as a Percent of Market Price	Action
RCR ≤ 0%	Release to production
0 < RCR ≤ 5%	Release to production and set kaizen improvement plan
5% < RCR ≤ 25%	Product and process redesign
RCR > 25%	Abandon subject to top management review and approval

The following operational and ABC data are for four proposed new products:

Value-Chain Function	Cost per Driver Unit	Estimated Number of Driver Units over Product Life Cycle			
		C-200472	C-200473	C-200474	C-200475
Production					
Direct Material	$1.60 per pound	2,000	1,000	4,000	800
Setup/Maintenance	$1,015 per setup	10	4	12	5
Processing	$370 per machine hour	20	12	32	12
Marketing	$860 per order	30	10	50	16
Customer Service	$162 per sales call	55	35	20	28
Estimated Life-cycle Demand		2,000 Units	1,400	4,000	600
Estimated Market Price per Unit		$39	28	35	50

Top management has set a desired contribution to cover unallocated value-chain costs, taxes, and profit of 40% of the estimated market price.

Prepare a schedule that shows for each proposed new product, the target cost, estimated cost using existing technology, and any required cost reduction as a percent of the estimated market price. Use the evaluation tool to make a decision regarding the four proposed new products.

5-61 Target Costing Over Product Life Cycle

Southeast Equipment, Inc., makes a variety of motor-driven products for homes and small businesses. The market research department recently identified power lawn mowers as a potentially lucrative market. As a first entry into this market, Southeast is considering a riding lawn mower that is smaller and less expensive than those of most of the competition. Market research indicates that such a lawn mower would sell for about $995 at retail and $800 wholesale. At that price, Southeast expects life cycle sales as follows:

Year	Sales
2004	1,000
2005	5,000
2006	10,000
2007	10,000
2008	8,000
2009	6,000
2010	4,000

The production department has estimated that the variable cost of production will be $475 per lawn mower, and annual fixed costs will be $900,000 per year for each of the seven years. Variable selling costs will be $25 per lawn mower and fixed selling costs will be $50,000 per year. In addition, the product development department estimates that $5 million of development costs will be necessary to design the lawn mower and the production process for it.

1. Compute the expected profit over the entire product life cycle of the proposed riding lawn mower.
2. Suppose Southeast expects pretax profits equal to 10% of sales on new products. Would the company undertake production and selling of the riding lawn mower?
3. Southeast Equipment uses a target costing approach to new products. What steps would management take to try to make a profitable product of the riding lawn mower?

Cases

5-62 Use of Capacity

St. Tropez S.A. manufactures several different styles of jewelry cases in southern France. Management estimates that during the second quarter of 20X5 the company will be operating at 80% of normal capacity. Because the company desires a higher utilization of plant capacity, it will consider a special order.

St. Tropez has received special-order inquiries from two companies. The first is from Lyon, Inc., which would like to market a jewelry case similar to one of St. Tropez's cases. The Lyon jewelry case would be marketed under Lyon's own label. Lyon, Inc., has offered St. Tropez €67.5 per jewelry case for 20,000 cases to be shipped by July 1, 20X5. The cost data for the St. Tropez jewelry case, which would be similar to the specifications of the Lyon special order, are as follows:

Regular selling price per unit	€100
Costs per unit:	
Raw materials	€ 35
Direct labor, .5 hour @ €60	30
Overhead, .25 machine hour @ €40	10
Total costs	€ 75

According to the specifications provided by Lyon, Inc., the special-order case requires less expensive raw materials, which will cost only €32.5 per case. Management has estimated that the remaining costs, labor time, and machine time will be the same as those for the St. Tropez jewelry case.

The second special order was submitted by the Avignon Co. for 7,500 jewelry cases at €85 per case. These cases would be marketed under the Avignon label and would have to be shipped by July 1, 20X5. The Avignon jewelry case is different from any jewelry case in the St. Tropez line. Its estimated per-unit costs are as follows:

Raw materials	€42.5
Direct labor, .5 hour @ €60	30
Overhead, .5 machine hour @ €40	20
Total costs	€92.5

In addition, St. Tropez will incur €15,000 in additional setup costs and will have to purchase a €25,000 special device to manufacture these cases; this device will be discarded once the special order is completed.

The St. Tropez manufacturing capabilities are limited by the total machine hours available. The plant capacity under normal operations is 90,000 machine hours per year, or 7,500 machine hours per month. The budgeted fixed overhead for 20X5 amounts to €2.16 million, or €24 per hour. All manufacturing overhead costs are applied to production on the basis of machine hours at €40 per hour.

St. Tropez will have the entire second quarter to work on the special orders. Management does not expect any repeat sales to be generated from either special order. Company practice precludes St. Tropez from subcontracting any portion of an order when special orders are not expected to generate repeat sales.

Should St. Tropez accept either special order? Justify your answer and show your calculations. (*Hint:* Distinguish between variable and fixed overhead.)

EXCEL Application Exercise

5-63 Optimal Product Mix to Maximize Total Contribution Margin Dollars

Goal: Create an Excel spreadsheet to determine the optimal product mix for a company that wants to maximize total contribution margin dollars. Use the results to answer questions about your findings.

Scenario: The Ibunez Tool Company has two products: a plain circular saw and a professional circular saw. The plain saw sells for $66 and has a variable cost of $50. The professional circular saw sells for $100 and has a variable cost of $70.

The company has only 20,000 machine-hours of manufacturing capacity available. Two plain saws can be produced in the same average time (1 hour) needed to produce one professional saw.

Note: This scenario is based on data in Fundamental Assignment Material 5-A2.

When you have completed your spreadsheet, answer the following questions:

1. What is the contribution margin and contribution margin ratio per unit for the plain circular saw? For the professional circular saw?
2. What is the potential total contribution margin for the plain circular saw if you assume that it is the only saw manufactured by Ibunez? For the professional circular saw?
3. What general conclusion can you draw from the data illustrated by the Excel problem?

Step-by-Step:

1. Open a new Excel spreadsheet.
2. In column A, create a bold-faced heading that contains the following:
   Row 1: Chapter 5 Decision Guideline
   Row 2: Ibunez Tool Company
   Row 3: Product Mix Analysis
   Row 4: Today's Date
3. Merge and center the four heading rows across columns A through E.
4. Adjust column widths as follows:
   Column A: 17
   Column B: 15
   Column C: 10
   Column D: 15
   Column E: 10
5. In row 7, create the following bold-faced column heading:
   Column B: Products
6. Merge and center the Products heading across columns B through E.
7. In row 8, create the following bold-faced column headings:
   Column B: Plain Circular Saw
   Column D: Professional Circular Saw
8. Merge and center the Plain Circular Saw heading across columns B and C.
9. Merge and center the Professional Circular Saw heading across columns D and E.
10. In column A, create the following row headings:
    Row 9: Selling price
    Row 10: Variable cost
    Row 11: Contribution margin
    Skip 2 rows
    Row 14: Available machine hours:
    Row 15: Saws manufactured per machine hour:
    Row 16: Manufacturing capacity:
    Skip 1 row
    Row 18: Potential total contribution margin:
11. Merge the headings in rows 14 through 18 across columns A and B, then right-justify.

      Alignment tab: Horizontal: Right

12. Enter the selling price and variable cost for plain and professional saws in columns B and D respectively.
13. Enter the available machine hours and the number of saws manufactured per machine hour for plain and professionals saws in columns C and E respectively.
14. In row 11, create formulas to calculate the contribution margin for each type of saw in columns B and D respectively.
15. In row 11, create formulas to calculate the contribution margin percent for each type of saw in columns C and E respectively.
16. In row 16, create formulas to calculate the manufacturing capacity for each type of saw in columns C and E, respectively.
17. In row 18, create formulas to calculate potential total contribution margin for each type of saw in columns C and E, respectively.

18. Format all amounts in columns B and D as

    Number tab: Category: Accounting ($ sign is left-justified)

                                Decimal places: 2

                                Symbol: $

19. Modify the format of the variable cost amounts to exclude the dollar ($) sign.

    Number tab: Symbol: None

20. Modify the format of the contribution margin amounts to display a top border, using the default Line Style.

    Border tab: Icon: Top Border

21. Format the contribution margin percent in columns C and E as

    Number tab: Category: Percentage

                                Decimal places: 0

    Alignment tab: Horizontal: Center

22. Format amounts in rows 14 through 16 as

    Number tab: Category: Number

                                Decimal places: 0

                              Use 1000 Separator (,):   Checked

    Alignment tab: Horizontal: Center

23. Format potential total contribution margin amounts as

    Number tab: Category: Accounting

                                Decimal places: 0

                                Symbol: $

24. Save your work to disk, and print a copy for your files.

Collaborative Learning Exercise

5-64 Understanding Pricing Decisions

Form teams of three to six students. Each team should contact and meet with a manager responsible for pricing in a company in your area. This might be a product manager or brand manager for a large company or a vice president of marketing or sales for a smaller company.

Explore with the manager how his or her company sets prices. Among the questions you might ask are:

- How do costs influence your prices? Do you set prices by adding a markup to costs? If so, what measure of costs do you use? How do you determine the appropriate markup?
- How do you adjust prices to meet market competition? How do you measure the effects of price on sales level?
- Do you use target costing? That is, do you find out what a product will sell for and then try to design the product and production process to make a desired profit on the product?
- What is your goal in setting prices? Do you try to maximize revenue, market penetration, contribution margin, gross margin, or some combination of these, or do you have other goals when setting prices?

After each team has conducted its interview, it would be desirable, if time permits, to get together as a class and share your findings. How many different pricing policies did the groups find? Can you explain why policies differ across companies? Are there characteristics of different industries or different management philosophies that explain the different pricing policies?

Internet Exercise   www.prenhall.com/horngren

5-65 Marketing Decisions at Colgate-Palmolive

Managers need information of all types in order to make decisions. Many marketing decisions are strategic, such as setting pricing policies and deciding to add or delete product lines (or even entire business segments). Managers rely on multiple sources to help locate relevant information to support these decisions. Managers must know how to use the information that is available and what weight to assign to the information that is deemed to be useful.

A firm is not going to give us detailed information about its marketing strategy on its Web site. However, we can view a firm's Web site to look at some of the relevant information that managers might use to help make marketing decisions. Let's look at the **Colgate-Palmolive Company** to see what information on their site would be relevant for some marketing decisions.

1. Go to Colgate-Palmolive's home page at http://www.colgate.com. Notice that Colgate has a moving heading line, meaning that by moving across the heading the user can see snapshots of different topics the firm wants to highlight. Move your cursor to the heading "For Investors." Click on "For Investors," then on the most recent annual report, and then on the "Management Letter to Stockholders." In this section, Colgate shares its worldwide strategy. What types of marketing decisions that are discussed in Chapter 5 are part of Colgate's strategy? What does this strategy reveal about the need for relevant information?

2. Many companies place a high priority on ethics. Look through the current annual report to see the importance of ethics at Colgate. Give an example that shows Colgate's commitment to ethical behavior.

3. One area that many companies identify as a key component to strategy is new product development. Visit the Press Room where Colgate highlights its newest products. Based on the information in the press room, when was the last new product news release made? What product was released? Is this a "new" product or is it simply a variation of an existing product?

4. Now look at the products that the firm manufacturers. What format is offered for learning about these products? Look at the laundry products for the North America region. How many detergents does the firm offer? From looking at the information provided, can you tell what differentiates the products? Does the Web site provide any information on how or when to use the products? If you had a particular type of stain, would the information provided on the Web site help determine which detergent was best for this problem? Would you want to make a decision about the "best" detergent for a problem, based on the information found on the Web site? Why or why not?

5. The company indicates three other ways that it plans to meet its worldwide strategy. Let's look at the most recent annual report and see how the firm did in each of those areas. Can you tell from looking at the income statement if each of those target areas was addressed? Can any of the areas be identified from financial statement footnotes? Does this appear to be in keeping with the strategy? Is there any information you are unable to determine for the strategy? Is the company improving profitability?

Relevant Information and Decision Making: Production Decisions

CHAPTER **6**

LEARNING OBJECTIVES

When you have finished studying this chapter, you should be able to:

1. Use opportunity cost to analyze the income effects of a given alternative.

2. Decide whether to make or to buy certain parts or products.

3. Decide whether a joint product should be processed beyond the split-off point.

4. Identify irrelevant information in disposal of obsolete inventory.

5. Decide whether to keep or replace equipment.

6. Explain how unit costs can be misleading.

7. Discuss how performance measures can affect decision making.

8. Construct absorption and contribution format income statements and identify which is better for decision making.

Starting a beverage business can be a complex maze

of decisions. Tom First and Tom Scott should know. After graduating from college, they operated a two-person boat service business off Nantucket Island, provisioning and cleaning yachts during the summer. In 1989, the inspiration for a juice drink made with fresh peaches hit. After a bit of experimentation, the self-proclaimed "juice guys" began bottling and selling their nectar drink from their boat. That first summer, they sold 2,000 bottles at $1.00 each. Today, **Nantucket Nectars** makes 48 different juice blends and sells millions of cases each year. Sales exceed $66 million.

Getting to this point, however, has been anything but smooth sailing. Their early attempts to sell juice to retailers failed. Profits were nonexistent. They sold half the business to an equity partner for $500,000 to venture into distribution, but ended up losing $1 million the first year. Employees stole caseloads of merchandise from the warehouse. And there have been inevitable product disappointments, such as bayberry tea. But the juice guys are quick learners. They got out of distribution, changed their marketing approach, and stopped the flow of red ink.

As the company has grown, it has tackled important production-related decisions. For example, should they build and operate their own bottling facilities? What criteria should be used for developing new products? What's the best approach for tracking and analyzing the growing volume of production, distribution, and sales data?

After examining the cost of building and operating bottling plants, Nantucket Nectars chose to contract with existing beverage co-packers in Rhode Island, Nevada, Florida, Pennsylvania, and Maryland. This approach gives the company broader distribution options without the capital expenditure and overhead of

When you relax with a bottle of Nantucket Nectars juice, you do not consider the various costs that go into producing, selling, and distributing the bottle. But these costs are very important to the managers at Nantucket Nectars.

multiple plants. Its managers scrutinize unit costs associated with new product ideas emerging from the test kitchen to be sure margins are on target. And they meticulously track every detail—from production costs to marketing promotions—through a computerized Enterprise Resource Planning (ERP) information system from **Oracle**.

Throughout it all, the juice guys never wavered in their determination to produce a top-quality product and satisfy customers. They readily admit they both failed their first accounting course in college, but they have come to appreciate its relevance in decision making as they've weathered stormy periods and sailed smooth seas.

As with Nantucket Nectars, managers in other companies must make similar production-related decisions. Should **Toyota** make the tires it mounts on its cars, or should it buy them from suppliers? Should **General Mills** sell the flour it mills, or should it use the flour to make more breakfast cereal? Should **Delta Airlines** add routes to use idle airplanes, or should it sell the planes? These decisions all require a good deal of accounting information. But what information will be relevant to each decision? In Chapter 5, we identified relevant information for decisions in the marketing function of the value chain. We now need to determine relevance in the production function. The basic framework for identifying relevant information remains the same for production as it was for marketing. We are still looking only for future costs that differ among alternatives. However, we now expand our analysis by introducing the concepts of opportunity and differential costs. ■

Opportunity, Outlay, and Differential Costs

differential cost (revenue)
The difference in total cost or revenue between two alternatives.

Management decision making is often a matter of comparing two or more alternative courses of action. (Of course, if there were only one alternative, no decision would be necessary.) Suppose a manager has only two alternatives to compare. The key to determining the financial difference between the alternatives is to identify the differential costs and revenues. **Differential cost/differential revenue** is the difference in total cost or differential revenue between two alternatives. For example, consider the decision about which of two machines to purchase. Both machines perform the same function. The cost is the difference in the price paid for the machines plus the difference in the costs of operating the machines.

incremental cost
Another term for differential cost when one alternative includes all the costs of the other plus some additional costs.

If one alternative includes all the costs of the other plus some additional costs, we often use the term **incremental cost** instead of differential cost. For instance, Nantucket Nectars' incremental costs of increasing production from 1,000 bottles of its NectarFizz juice drink to 1,200 bottles per week are the costs of producing the additional 200 bottles each week. In the reverse situation, the decline in costs caused by reducing production from 1,200 to 1,000 bottles per week are called the *differential* or *incremental savings*.

When there are more than two alternative courses of action, managers often compare one particular action against the entire set of alternatives. For example, Nantucket Nectars might consider introducing a new 100% juice drink, Papaya Mango. There are many alternatives to introducing Papaya Mango, including introducing other new 100% juice dinks, expanding production of existing drinks such as juice cocktails or blended nectars, or producing nonjuice products. Computing the differential costs and revenues for Papaya Mango with every alternative would be cumbersome. Thus, the Nantucket Nectars managers might use a different approach.

outlay cost
A cost that requires a future cash disbursement.

opportunity cost
The maximum available contribution to profit forgone (or passed up) by using limited resources for a particular purpose.

Introducing Papaya Mango would entail two types of costs: **outlay costs,** which require a future cash disbursement, and opportunity costs. An **opportunity cost** is the maximum available contribution to profit forgone (or passed up) by using limited resources for a particular purpose. Opportunity costs apply to resources that are already owned or for which the company already has a commitment to purchase. The decision regarding Papaya Mango will not affect whether the company acquires these resources, only how it uses them. The opportunity cost of such resources depends on the potential uses for the resources, not on the amount paid for them. Why? Because the decision about Papaya Mango will not affect the amount paid. However, the decision to use the resources to produce Papaya Mango precludes using them for other alternatives. The amount that the company would have gained if the resources had been used in their best alternative use (that is, the best use other than using them to produce Papaya Mango) becomes the opportunity cost of the resources.

Suppose Nantucket Nectars has a machine for which it paid $100,000 several years ago and is not being used. It can use the machine to produce Papaya Mango or to increase the production of The Original Peach 100% juice. The contribution margin from the additional sales of The Original Peach would be $60,000. A third alternative is selling the machine for $50,000 cash. What is the opportunity cost of the machine when we analyze the Papaya Mango alternative? It is $60,000, the larger of the $50,000 or $60,000, the two possible gains that the company could achieve using the machine in its alternative uses. The $100,000 paid for the machine is a past cost, and we know from our discussion of relevant costs in Chapter 5 that past costs are irrelevant.

Now suppose that Nantucket Nectars will have total sales over the life cycle of Papaya Mango 100% juice drink of $500,000, and the production and marketing costs (outlay costs), excluding the cost of the machine, are $400,000. The net financial benefit from the Papaya Mango is $40,000.

OBJECTIVE 1

Use opportunity cost to analyze the income effects of a given alternative.

Revenues		$500,000
Costs:		
Outlay costs	$400,000	
Opportunity costs	60,000	
Total cost		460,000
Net financial benefit		$ 40,000

Nantucket Nectars will gain $40,000 more financial benefit using the machine to make Papaya Mango than it would make using it for the next most profitable alternative.

When considering only two alternatives, a manager might use straightforward differential analysis or an opportunity cost analysis. The two approaches are equivalent. To see this, consider Maria Morales, a certified public accountant employed by a large accounting firm for a salary of $60,000 per year. She is considering an alternative use of her time, her most valuable resource. The alternative is to have her own independent accounting practice. A straightforward differential analysis follows:

	Alternatives Under Consideration		
	Remain an Employee	**Open an Independent Practice**	**Difference**
Revenues	$60,000	$200,000	$140,000
Outlay costs (operating expenses)	—	120,000	120,000
Income effects per year	$60,000	$ 80,000	$ 20,000

Maria has revenues of $200,000 — quite a bit more than she would make as an employee of the large firm. However, she would also have to pay $120,000 to rent office space, lease equipment, buy advertising, and cover other out-of-pocket expenses. The $80,000 of operating income is $20,000 more than her salary with the firm.

Now if we look in isolation at the alternative of operating an independent practice, essentially comparing it to all alternative uses of Maria's time (which in this case is simply the alternative of working for the large firm), we must consider another cost. Had Maria remained an employee, she would have made $60,000. By starting her own company, Maria will forego this profit. Thus, the $60,000 is an opportunity cost of starting her own business:

		Alternative Chosen: Independent Practice
Revenue		$200,000
Expenses		
Outlay costs (operating expenses)	$120,000	
Opportunity cost of employee salary	60,000	180,000
Income effects per year		$ 20,000

Ponder the two preceding tabulations. Each produces the correct key difference between alternatives, $20,000. The first tabulation does not mention opportunity cost because we measured the economic impacts (in the form of revenues and outlay costs) individually for each of the alternatives (two in this case). We did not exclude either alternative from consideration. The second tabulation mentions opportunity cost because we included the $60,000 annual economic impact of the best excluded alternative as a cost of the chosen alternative. If we had failed to recognize opportunity cost in the second tabulation, we would have misstated the difference between the alternatives.

The major message here is straightforward: Do not overlook opportunity costs. Consider a homeowner who has made the final payment on a home mortgage. While celebrating, the owner says, "It's a wonderful feeling to know that future occupancy is free of any interest cost!" Many owners have similar thoughts. Why? Because they will have no future outlay costs for interest. Nevertheless, there is an opportunity cost of continuing to live in the home. After all, an alternative would be to sell the home, place the proceeds in some other investment, and rent an apartment. The owner forgoes the interest in the other investment, so this forgone interest income becomes an opportunity cost of home ownership.

MAKING MANAGERIAL DECISIONS

Consider how difficult it is to estimate opportunity costs. There is no sale or purchase to establish an appropriate cost. Further, the opportunity cost depends on the alternatives that are available at a point in time. The same alternatives may not be available at a different time. For example, excess capacity in September does not mean that there will also be excess capacity in October. How might a manager at Mattel, the toy company, estimate the opportunity cost of excess warehouse space in January?

be excess space late in the year as Christmas approaches. Therefore, he or she would look for temporary alternatives, ones that use the space for only a few months. After identifying alternatives, the manager would estimate the value of each. Because most of the alternatives are ones that a company never undertakes, estimating their values is a subjective process. The highest valued alternative would establish the opportunity cost of the space.

Answer
The Mattel manager would know that excess warehouse space is a seasonal phenomenon. There is unlikely to

Make-or-Buy Decisions

Managers often must decide whether to produce a product or service within the firm or purchase it from an outside supplier. They apply relevant cost analysis to a variety of such make-or-buy decisions as the following:

- **Boeing** must decide whether to buy or make many of the tools used in assembling 777 airplanes.
- **IBM** must decide whether to develop its own operating system for a new computer or to buy it from a software vendor.

When managers consider the make-or-buy decision for services, it is often called outsourcing, which is described in the Business First box on page 257.

Basic Make-or-Buy and Idle Facilities

A basic make-or-buy question is whether a company should make its own parts that it will use in its final products or buy the parts from vendors. Sometimes the answer to this question is based on qualitative factors. For example, some manufacturers always make parts because they want to control quality. Alternatively, some companies always purchase parts to protect long-run relationships with their suppliers. These companies may deliberately buy from vendors even during slack times to avoid difficulties in obtaining needed parts during boom times, when there may well be shortages of materials and workers, but no shortage of sales orders.

OBJECTIVE 2

Decide whether to make or buy certain parts or products.

What quantitative factors are relevant to the decision of whether to make or buy? The answer, again, depends on the situation. A key factor is whether there are idle facilities. Many companies make parts only when they cannot use their facilities to better advantage.

Assume that Nantucket Nectars reports the following costs:

Nantucket Nectors Company
Cost of Making 12-Ounce Glass Bottles

	Total Cost for 1,000,000 Bottles	Cost per Bottle
Direct materials	$ 60,000	$ .06
Direct labor	20,000	.02
Variable factory overhead	40,000	.04
Fixed factory overhead	80,000	.08
Total costs	$200,000	$.20

Another manufacturer offers to sell Nantucket Nectars the bottles for $.18. Should Nantucket Nectars make or buy the bottles?

Although the $.20 unit cost seemingly indicates that the company should buy, the answer is rarely so obvious. The essential question is, "What is the difference in expected future costs between the alternatives?" If the $.08 fixed overhead per bottle consists of costs that will continue regardless of the decision, the entire $.08 becomes irrelevant. Examples of such costs include depreciation, property taxes, insurance, and allocated executive salaries.

Again, are only the variable costs relevant? No. Perhaps Nantucket Nectars will eliminate $50,000 of the fixed costs if the company buys the bottles instead of making them. For example, the company may be able to release a supervisor with a $50,000 salary. In other words, fixed costs that the company will be able to avoid in the future are relevant.

For the moment, suppose the capacity now used to make bottles will become idle if the company purchases the bottles. Further, the $50,000 supervisor's salary is the only fixed cost that the company would eliminate. The relevant computations follow.

	Make		Buy	
	Total	**Per Bottle**	**Total**	**Per Bottle**
Purchase cost			$180,000	$.18
Direct materials	$ 60,000	$.06		
Direct labor	20,000	.02		
Variable factory overhead	40,000	.04		
Fixed factory overhead that can be avoided by not making (supervisor's salary)	50,000*	.05*		
Total relevant costs	$170,000	$.17	$180,000	$.18
Difference in favor of making	$ 10,000	$.01		

* Note that unavoidable fixed costs of $80,000 − $50,000 = $30,000 are irrelevant. Thus, the irrelevant costs per unit are $.08 − $.05 = $.03.

The key to wise make-or-buy decisions is identifying and accurately measuring the additional costs for making (or the costs avoided by buying) a part or component. Companies with accurate cost accounting systems, such as activity-based costing systems discussed in Chapter 4, are in a better position to perform make-or-buy analysis.

Make or Buy and the Use of Facilities

Make-or-buy decisions are rarely as simple as the one in our Nantucket Nectars example. As we said earlier, the use of facilities is a key to the make-or-buy decision. For simplicity, we assumed that the Nantucket Nectars facilities would remain idle if the company chose to buy the bottles. This means that the opportunity cost of the facilities is zero. Of course, in most cases companies will not leave their facilities idle. Instead, they will often put idle facilities to some other use, and we must consider the financial outcomes of these uses when choosing to make or buy. The value received from the best of these alternative uses is an opportunity cost for the internal production of the parts or components.

Suppose Nantucket Nectars can use the released facilities in our example in some other manufacturing activity to produce a contribution to profits of $55,000 or can rent them out for $25,000. We now have four alternatives to consider (figures are in thousands):

	Make	Buy and Leave Facilities Idle	Buy and Rent Out Facilities	Buy and Use Facilities for Other Products
Rent revenue	$ —	$ —	$ 25	$ —
Contribution from other products	—	—	—	55
Relevant cost of bottles	(170)	(180)	(180)	(180)
Net relevant costs	$(170)	$(180)	$(155)	$(125)

The final column indicates that buying the bottles and using the vacated facilities for the production of other products would yield the lowest net costs in this case. We can also analyze this choice using opportunity costs. The total cost to make the bottles, including opportunity cost, is $225,000, which is $45,000 higher than the cost of purchasing them.

Cost to Make Bottles (in thousands)	
Outlay cost	$170
Opportunity cost	55
Total cost	$225

AN EXAMPLE OF MAKE OR BUY: OUTSOURCING

Make-or-buy decisions apply to services as well as to products. Companies are increasingly deciding to hire service firms to handle some of their internal operations, an option called *outsourcing*. According to the Outsourcing Institute, outsourcing is "the strategic use of outside resources to perform activities traditionally handled by internal staff and resources."

Companies use outsourcing for many business processes. How do these processes compare to the value-chain functions we have discussed? The companies often outsource the following business functions:

What are the key reasons for outsourcing? Over half of the companies in Outsourcing Institute's 2002 annual survey say they wanted to improve the company's focus and reduce operating costs. According to Todd Kertley, who manages IBM's outsourcing services, "Corporations increasingly want to focus on their core businesses, not technology." As the complexity of data processing and especially networking has grown, companies have found it harder and harder to keep current with the technology. Instead of investing huge sums in personnel and equipment and diverting attention from the value-added activi-

Business Function	Percent of Companies Outsourcing	Value-Chain Function
Information technology	55%	Corporate support
Administration	47%	Corporate support
Distribution and logistics	22%	Distribution
Finance	20%	Corporate support
Human resources	19%	Corporate support
Manufacturing	18%	Production
Contact centers/call centers	15%	Marketing
Sales and marketing	13%	Marketing

The processes listed include almost all the value-chain functions, including corporate support. Research and development and design are the two value-chain functions not frequently outsourced. That makes sense because most companies perceive these functions as core business processes. Although companies can outsource many processes, the Internet has driven much of the recent growth in outsourcing. During the 1990s, many companies installed enterprise resource planning (ERP) systems to handle all their computing needs. However, by the beginning of the twenty-first century, many companies realized that the huge investments necessitated by ERP systems may be unnecessary. They could purchase the required services over the Internet without investing in the systems' purchase and development costs. The formerly expensive process of communication using service providers had become essentially free via the Internet. A new group of computing service providers—called application service providers (ASP)—arose to provide outsourcing opportunities for a variety of computing applications.

ties of their own businesses, many firms have found outsourcing financially attractive. The big stumbling block to outsourcing has been subjective factors, such as control. To make outsourcing attractive, the services must be reliable, be available when needed, and be flexible enough to adapt to changing conditions. Companies that have successful outsourcing arrangements have been careful to include the subjective factors in their decisions.

Outsourcing has become so profitable that more than 75% of Fortune 500 companies outsource some aspect of their business support services. The total value of outsourcing contracts in the United States is more than $10 billion. The Outsourcing Institute was formed to provide "objective, independent information on the strategic use of outside resources."

Sources: Adapted from T. Kearney, "Why Outsourcing Is In," *Strategic Finance*, January 2000, pp. 34–38; R. E. Drtina, "The Outsourcing Decision," *Management Accounting*, March, 1994, pp. 56–62; J. Hechinger, "IBM to Take Over Operations of Auto-Parts Maker Visteon," *Wall Street Journal*, February 12, 2003; and the Outsourcing Institute (http://www.outsourcing.com).

The opportunity cost is the $55,000 that Nantucket Nectars passes up when it cannot use the facilities to make other products.

To summarize, the make-or-buy decision should focus on relevant costs in a particular decision situation. In all cases, companies should relate make-or-buy decisions to the long-run policies for the use of capacity.

MAKING MANAGERIAL DECISIONS

Suppose a company uses its facilities, on average, 80% of the time. However, because of seasonal changes in the demand for its product, the actual demand for the facilities varies from 60% in the off season to over 100% in the peak season when it must outsource production of some parts. Under what circumstances would the company choose to perform special projects during the off season and continue to outsource production of parts during the peak season—that is, why would the company choose not to expand its capacity?

Answer

During the off season, the company may decide to perform special projects for other manufacturers (on a subcontract). There is profit on these projects, but it may not be enough to justify expanding the capacity of the facilities. The company will use facilities for these projects only when their opportunity cost is close to zero, that is, when there are no other more profitable uses for the facilities. In contrast, during the peak season, the company meets the high volume by outsourcing the production of some parts. Again, the cost of purchased parts may be higher than the cost to make them in the company's own facilities if there were idle capacity, but purchasing the parts is less costly than buying the facilities to produce them.

Summary Problem For Your Review

PROBLEM

Exhibit 6-1 contains data for the Block Company for the year just ended. The company makes industrial power drills. Exhibit 6-1 shows the costs of the plastic housing separately from the costs of the electrical and mechanical components. Answer each of the following questions independently.

1. During the year, a prospective customer in an unrelated market offered $82,000 for 1,000 drills. The drills would be manufactured in addition to the 100,000 units sold. Block Company would pay the regular sales commission rate on the 1,000 drills. The president rejected the order because "it was below our costs of $97 per unit." What would operating income have been if Block Company had accepted the order?

2. A supplier offered to manufacture the year's supply of 100,000 plastic housings for $13.50 each. What would be the effect on operating income if the Block Company purchased rather than made the housings? Assume that Block Company would avoid $350,000 of the fixed costs assigned to housings if it purchases the housings.

3. Suppose that Block Company could purchase the housings for $13.50 each and use the vacated space for the manufacture of a deluxe version of its drill. Assume that it could make 20,000 deluxe units (and sell them for $130 each in addition to the sales of the 100,000 regular units) at a unit variable cost of $90, exclusive of housings and exclusive of the 10% sales commission. The company could also purchase the 20,000 extra plastic housings for $13.50 each. All the fixed costs pertaining to the plastic

	A	B	A + B
	Electrical and Mechanical Components*	**Plastic Housing**	**Industrial Drills**
Sales: 100,000 units, @ $100			$10,000,000
Variable costs			
Direct materials	$4,400,000	$ 500,000	$ 4,900,000
Direct labor	400,000	300,000	700,000
Variable factory overhead	100,000	200,000	300,000
Other variable costs	100,000	—	100,000
Sales commissions, @ 10% of sales	1,000,000	—	1,000,000
Total variable costs	$6,000,000	$1,000,000	$ 7,000,000
Contribution margin			$ 3,000,000
Total fixed costs	$2,220,000	$ 480,000	2,700,000
Operating income			$ 300,000

* Not including the costs of plastic housing (column B).

Exhibit 6-1
Block Company Cost of Industrial Drills

housings would continue, because these costs relate primarily to the manufacturing facilities used. What would operating income have been if Block had bought the housings and made and sold the deluxe units?

SOLUTION

1. The costs of filling the special order follow:

Direct materials	$49,000
Direct labor	7,000
Variable factory overhead	3,000
Other variable costs	1,000
Sales commission @ 10% of $82,000	8,200
Total variable costs	$68,200
Selling price	82,000
Contribution margin	$13,800

Operating income would have been $300,000 + $13,800, or $313,800, if Block Company had accepted the order. In a sense, the decision to reject the offer implies that the Block Company is willing to invest $13,800 in immediate gains foregone (an opportunity cost) in order to preserve the long-run selling price structure.

2. Assuming that Block Company could have avoided $350,000 of the fixed costs by not making the housings and that the other fixed costs would have continued, we can summarize the alternatives as follows.

	Make	Buy
Purchase cost		$1,350,000
Variable costs	$1,000,000	
Avoidable fixed costs	350,000	
Total relevant costs	$1,350,000	$1,350,000

If the facilities used for plastic housings became idle, the Block Company would be indifferent whether to make or buy. Operating income would be unaffected.

3. The effect of purchasing the plastic housings and using the vacated facilities for the manufacture of a deluxe version of its drill is

Sales would increase by 20,000 units, @ $130		$2,600,000
Variable costs exclusive of housings would increase by		
20,000 units, @ $90	$1,800,000	
Plus: sales commission, 10% of $2,600,000	260,000	$2,060,000
Contribution margin on 20,000 units		$ 540,000
Housings: 120,000 rather than 100,000 would be needed		
Buy 120,000 @ $13.50	$1,620,000	
Make 100,000 @ $10 (only the variable costs are relevant)	1,000,000	
Excess cost of outside purchase		620,000
Fixed costs, unchanged		—
Disadvantage of making deluxe units		$ 80,000

Operating income would decline to $220,000 ($300,000 − $80,000). The deluxe units bring in a contribution margin of $540,000, but the additional costs of buying rather than making housings is $620,000, leading to a net disadvantage of $80,000.

Joint Product Costs

joint products
Two or more manufactured products that (1) have relatively significant sales values and (2) are not separately identifiable as individual products until their split-off point.

split-off point
The juncture of manufacturing where the joint products become individually identifiable.

separable costs
Any cost beyond the split-off point.

joint costs
The costs of manufacturing joint products prior to the split-off point.

ConAgra, Inc., produces meat products with brand names such as Swift, Armour, and Butterball. ConAgra cannot kill a sirloin steak; it has to purchase and slaughter a steer, which supplies various cuts of dressed meat, hides, and trimmings. So how does ConAgra determine the proper allocation of the purchase cost paid for the steer to the various manufactured meat products? When two or more manufactured products (1) have relatively significant sales values and (2) are not separately identifiable as individual products until their split-off point, we call them **joint products.** The **split-off point** is that juncture of manufacturing where the joint products become individually identifiable. Any costs beyond that stage are **separable costs** because they are not part of the joint process and the accounting system can exclusively identify them with individual products. We call the costs of manufacturing joint products prior to the split-off point **joint costs.** Further examples of joint products include chemicals, lumber, flour, and the products of petroleum refining.

To illustrate joint costs, suppose **Dow Chemical Company** produces two chemical products, X and Y, as a result of a particular joint process. The joint processing cost is $100,000. This includes raw material costs and the cost of processing before the joint products X and Y reach the split-off point. At the split-off point, Dow either sells X and Y or processes them further before selling them to the petroleum industry which uses them as ingredients of gasoline. The relationships follow:

Manufacturers that have joint products frequently face the decision to sell or to process further. Let's see how managers develop relevent information to help them decide whether to sell joint products at the split-off point or to process some or all products further.

Sell or Process Further

Consider again the situation described in the previous section where Dow Chemical has two joint products, X and Y. Suppose Dow can further process the 500,000 liters of Y and sell it to the plastics industry as product YA, an ingredient for plastic sheeting. The additional processing cost would be $.08 per liter for manufacturing and distribution, a total of $40,000 for 500,000 liters. The net sales price of YA would be $.16 per liter, a total of $80,000.

Dow cannot process product X further and will sell it at the split-off point, but management is undecided about product Y. Should the company sell Y at the split-off point, or should it process Y into YA? To answer this question, we need to find the relevant costs involved. Because Dow must incur the joint costs to reach the split-off point, those costs might seem relevant. However, they cannot affect anything beyond the split-off point. Therefore, they do not differ between alternatives and are completely irrelevant to the question of whether to sell or process further. The only approach that will yield valid results is to concentrate on the separable costs and revenue beyond split-off, as shown in Exhibit 6-2.

This analysis shows that it would be $10,000 more profitable to process Y beyond split-off than to sell Y at split-off. Briefly, it is profitable to extend processing or to incur additional distribution costs on a joint product if the additional revenue exceeds the additional expenses.

Exhibit 6-3 illustrates another way to compare the alternatives of (1) selling Y at the split-off point and (2) processing Y beyond split-off. It includes the joint costs, which are the same for each alternative and therefore do not affect the difference.

The allocation of joint costs would not affect the decision, as Exhibit 6-3 demonstrates. In the exhibit we have not allocated the joint costs, but no matter how we might allocate them, the total income effects would not change.

We provide additional coverage of joint costs and inventory valuation in Chapter 12.

OBJECTIVE 3

Decide whether a joint product should be processed beyond the split-off point.

	Sell at Split-Off as Y	Process Further and Sell as YA	Difference
Revenues	$30,000	$80,000	$50,000
Separable costs beyond split off @ $.08	—	40,000	40,000
Income effects	$30,000	$40,000	$10,000

Exhibit 6-2
Illustration of Sell or Process Further

	(1) Alternative One			(2) Alternative Two			(3) Differential Effects
	X	Y	Total	X	YA	Total	
Revenues	$90,000	$30,000	$120,000	$90,000	$80,000	$170,000	$50,000
Joint costs			$100,000			$100,000	—
Separable costs			—		40,000	40,000	40,000
Total costs			$100,000			$140,000	$40,000
Income effects			$ 20,000			$ 30,000	$10,000

Exhibit 6-3
Sell or Process Further Analysis — Firm as a Whole

Irrelevance of Past Costs

OBJECTIVE 4

Identify irrelevant
information in disposal of
obsolete inventory.

The ability to recognize and thereby ignore irrelevant costs is sometimes just as important
to decision makers as identifying relevant costs. How do we know that past costs, although
sometimes good predictors of future costs, are irrelevant in decision making? Let's consider such past costs as obsolete inventory and the book value of old equipment to see why
they are irrelevant to decisions.

Obsolete Inventory

Suppose **General Dynamics** has 100 obsolete aircraft parts in its inventory. The original manufacturing cost of these parts was $100,000. General Dynamics can (1) remachine the parts
for $30,000 and then sell them for $50,000 or (2) scrap them for $5,000. Which should it do?
     This is an unfortunate situation, yet the $100,000 past cost is irrelevant to the decision
to remachine or scrap. The only relevant factors are the expected future revenues and costs:

	Remachine	Scrap	Difference
Expected future revenue	$ 50,000	$ 5,000	$45,000
Expected future costs	30,000	—	30,000
Relevant excess of revenue over costs	$20,000	$ 5,000	$15,000
Accumulated historical inventory cost*	100,000	100,000	—
Net overall loss on project	$(80,000)	$(95,000)	$15,000

* Irrelevant, because it is unaffected by the decision.

     As you can see from the fourth line of the preceding table, we can completely ignore the
$100,000 historical cost and still arrive at the $15,000 difference, the key figure in the analysis.

Book Value of Old Equipment

OBJECTIVE 5

Decide whether to keep or
replace equipment.

depreciation
*The periodic cost of
equipment that a company
spreads over the future
periods in which the
company will use the
equipment.*

*book value
(net book value)*
*The original cost of equip-
ment less accumulated
depreciation*

accumulated depreciation
*The sum of all depreciation
charged to past periods.*

Like obsolete parts, the book value of equipment is not a relevant consideration in deciding
whether to replace the equipment. Why? Because it is a past cost, not a future cost. When a
company purchases equipment, it spreads the cost via a **depreciation** expense over the future
periods in which it will use the equipment. The equipment's **book value,** or **net book value,**
is the original cost less accumulated depreciation. **Accumulated depreciation** is the sum of
all depreciation charged to past periods. For example, suppose a $10,000 machine with a ten-
year life span has depreciation of $1,000 per year. At the end of six years, accumulated depre-
ciation is 6 × $1,000 = $6,000, and the book value is $10,000 − $6,000 = $4,000.
     Consider the following data for a decision whether to replace an old machine:

	Old Machine	Replacement Machine
Original cost	$10,000	$8,000
Useful life in years	10	4
Current age in years	6	0
Useful life remaining in years	4	4
Accumulated depreciation	$ 6,000	0
Book value	$ 4,000	Not acquired yet
Disposal value (in cash) now	$ 2,500	Not acquired yet
Disposal value in four years	0	0
Annual cash operating costs (maintenance, power, repairs, coolants, and so on)	$ 5,000	$3,000

     Let's prepare a comparative analysis of the two alternatives. Before proceeding, consider
some important concepts. The most widely misunderstood facet of replacement decision
making is the role of the book value of the old equipment in the decision. We often call the

book value a **sunk cost,** which is really just another term for historical or past cost, a cost that the company has already incurred and, therefore, is irrelevant to the decision-making process. All past costs are down the drain. Nothing can change what has already happened. The Business First box on page 265 illustrates this concept.

The irrelevance of past costs for decisions does not mean that knowledge of past costs is useless. Often managers use past costs to help predict future costs. In addition, past costs affect future payments for income taxes (as explained in Chapter 11). However, the past cost itself is not relevant. The only relevant cost is the predicted future cost.

In deciding whether to replace or keep existing equipment, we must consider the relevance of four commonly encountered items:[1]

- **Book value** of old equipment: irrelevant, because it is a past (historical) cost. Therefore, depreciation on old equipment is irrelevant.
- **Disposal value** of old equipment: relevant, because it is an expected future inflow that usually differs among alternatives.
- **Gain or loss on disposal:** This is the difference between book value and disposal value. It is therefore a meaningless combination of irrelevant and relevant items. The combination form, loss (or gain) on disposal, blurs the distinction between the irrelevant book value and the relevant disposal value. Consequently, it is best to think of each separately.
- **Cost of new equipment:** relevant, because it is an expected future outflow that will differ among alternatives. Therefore, depreciation on new equipment is relevant.

Exhibit 6-4 shows the relevance of these items in our example. Book value of old equipment is irrelevant regardless of the decision-making technique we use. The "difference" column in Exhibit 6-4 shows that the $4,000 book value of the old equipment does not differ between alternatives. We should completely ignore it for decision-making purposes. The difference is merely one of timing. The amount written off is still $4,000, regardless of any available alternative. The $4,000 appears on the income statement either as a $4,000 deduction from the $2,500 cash proceeds received to obtain a $1,500 loss on disposal in the first year or as $1,000 of depreciation in each of four years. But how it appears is irrelevant to the replacement decision. In contrast, the $2,000 annual depreciation on the new equipment is relevant because the total $8,000 depreciation is a future cost that we can avoid by not replacing. The three relevant items—operating costs, disposal value, and acquisition cost—give replacement a net advantage of $2,500.

sunk cost
A historical or past cost, that is, a cost that the company has already incurred and, therefore, is irrelevant to the decision-making process.

Exhibit 6-4
Cost Comparison— Replacement of Equipment Including Relevant and Irrelevant Items

	Four Years Together		
	Keep	**Replace**	**Difference**
Cash operating costs	$20,000	$12,000	$ 8,000
Old equipment (book value)			
Periodic write-off as depreciation	4,000	—	—
or			
Lump-sum write-off		4,000*	
Disposal value	—	−2,500*	2,500
New machine			
Acquisition cost	—	8,000†	−8,000
Total costs	$24,000	$21,500	$ 2,500

The advantage of replacement is $2,500 for the four years together.

* In a formal income statement, these two items would be combined as "loss on disposal" of $4,000 − $2,500 = $1,500.

† In a formal income statement, written off as straight-line depreciation of $8,000 ÷ 4 = $2,000 for each of four years.

[1]For simplicity, we ignore income tax considerations and the effects of the interest value of money in this chapter. Book value is irrelevant even if income taxes are considered, however, because the relevant item is then the tax cash flow, not the book value. The book value is essential information for predicting the amount and timing of future tax cash flows, but, by itself, the book value is irrelevant. For elaboration, see Chapter 11.

Summary Problem For Your Review

PROBLEM

Exhibit 6-4 is the first example that looks beyond one year. Examining the alternatives over the equipment's entire life ensures that peculiar nonrecurring items, such as loss on disposal, will not obstruct the long-run view vital to many managerial decisions. However, Exhibit 6-4 presents both relevant and irrelevant items. Prepare an analysis that concentrates on relevant items only.

SOLUTION

Exhibit 6-5 presents the analysis with relevant items only—the cash operating costs, the disposal value of the old equipment, and the depreciation on the new equipment. To demonstrate that the amount of the old equipment's book value will not affect the answer, suppose the book value of the old equipment is $500,000 rather than $4,000. Your final answer will not change. The cumulative advantage of replacement is still $2,500. (If you are in doubt, rework this example, using $500,000 as the book value.)

	Four Years Together		
	Keep	**Replace**	**Difference**
Cash operating costs	$20,000	$12,000	$ 8,000
Disposal value of old machine	—	−2,500	2,500
New machine, acquisition cost	—	8,000	−8,000
Total relevant costs	$20,000	$17,500	$ 2,500

Exhibit 6-5
Cost Comparison—Replacement of Equipment, Relevant Items Only

MAKING MANAGERIAL DECISIONS

It is sometimes difficult to accept the proposition that past or sunk costs are irrelevant to decisions. Consider the ticket you have to a major football game in December. After getting the ticket, you learn that the game will be on television, and you really prefer to watch the game in the comfort of your warm home. Does your decision about attending the game or watching it on TV depend on whether you were given the ticket for free or you paid $80 for it? What does this tell you about a manager's decision to replace a piece of equipment?

Answer
The amount paid, whether it be $0, $80, or $1,000, should make no difference to the decision. You have the ticket, and you have paid for it. That cannot be changed. If you really prefer to watch the game on TV, it may have been a bad decision to pay $80 for a ticket. But you cannot erase that bad decision. All you can do is choose the future action that has most value to you. You should not suffer through a less pleasant experience just because you paid $80 for the ticket.

A manager must make the same analysis regarding the replacement of a piece of equipment. What the company spent for the equipment is irrelevant. Keeping equipment that is no longer economical is just like using a ticket for an event that you would rather not attend.

SUNK COSTS AND GOVERNMENT CONTRACTS

It is easy to agree that—in theory—managers should ignore sunk costs when making decisions. But in practice, sunk costs often influence important decisions, especially when a decision maker doesn't want to admit that a previous decision to invest funds was a bad decision.

Consider two examples from the *St. Louis Post Dispatch:* (1) Larry O. Welch, the air force chief of staff, was quoted as saying that "the B-2 already is into production; cancel it and the $17 billion front end investment is lost." (2) Les Aspin, chairman of the House Armed Services Committee, was quoted as stating that "with $17 billion already invested in it, the B-2 is too costly to cancel."

The $17 billion already invested in the B-2 is a sunk cost. It is "lost" regardless of whether the government cancels production of the B-2. And whether B-2 production is too costly to continue depends only on the future costs necessary to complete production compared to the value of the completed B-2s. The $17 billion was relevant when the Defense Department made the original decision to begin development of the B-2, but now that the money has been spent, it is no longer relevant. No decision can affect it.

Why would intelligent leaders consider the $17 billion relevant to the decision on continuing production of the B-2?

Probably because it is difficult to admit that the government would derive no benefit from the $17 billion investment. Those who favor canceling production of the B-2 would consider the outcome of the original investment decision to be unfavorable. With perfect hindsight, they believe the investment should not have been made. It is human nature to find unpleasant the task of admitting that $17 billion was wasted. Yet, it is more important to avoid throwing good money after bad—that is, if the value of the B-2 is not at least equal to the future investment in it, the Defense Department should terminate production, regardless of the amount spent to date.

Failure to ignore sunk costs is not unique to the U.S. government. In reference to Russia's store of bomb-grade plutonium, the country's minister of atomic energy stated, "We have spent too much money making this material to just mix it with radioactive wastes and bury it." Burying the plutonium may or may not be the best decision, but the amount already spent is not relevant to the decision.

Sources: Adapted from J. Berg, J. Dickhaut, and C. Kanodia, "The Role of Private Information in the Sunk Cost Phenomenon," unpublished paper, November 12, 1991; M. Wald and M. Gordon, "Russia Treasures Plutonium, But U.S. Wants to Destroy It," *New York Times,* August 19, 1994, p. A1.

Irrelevance of Future Costs that Will Not Differ

In addition to past costs, some future costs may be irrelevant because they will be the same under all feasible alternatives. These, too, we may safely ignore for a particular decision. The salaries of many members of top management are examples of expected future costs that will be unaffected by the decision at hand.

Other irrelevant future costs include fixed costs that will be unchanged by such considerations as whether machine X or machine Y is selected. However, it is not merely a case of saying that fixed costs are irrelevant and variable costs are relevant. Variable costs can be irrelevant, and fixed costs can be relevant. For instance, sales commissions are a varible cost that is irrelevant to a decision on whether to produce a product in plant G or plant H. The rental cost of a warehouse is a fixed cost that is relevant if one alternative requires the warehouse while the other does not. Variable costs are irrelevant whenever they do not differ among the alternatives at hand, and fixed costs are relevant whenever they differ between the alternatives at hand.

Beware of Unit Costs

The pricing illustration in Chapter 5 showed that managers should analyze unit costs with care in decision making. There are two major ways to go wrong: (1) including irrelevant costs, such as the $.03 allocation of unavoidable fixed costs in the Nantucket

OBJECTIVE 6

Explain how unit costs can be misleading.

Nectars make-or-buy example (p. 255) that would result in a unit cost of $.20 instead of the relevant unit cost of $.17, and (2) comparing unit costs not computed on the same volume basis, as the following example demonstrates. Machinery sales personnel often brag about the low unit costs of using the new machines. Sometimes they neglect to point out that the unit costs are based on outputs far in excess of the volume of activity of their prospective customer. Assume that a new $100,000 machine with a five-year life span can produce 100,000 units a year at a variable cost of $1 per unit, as opposed to a variable cost per unit of $1.50 with an old machine. A sales representative claims that the new machine will reduce cost by $.30 per unit. Is the new machine a worthwhile acquisition?

The new machine is attractive at first glance. If the customer's expected volume is 100,000 units, unit-cost comparisons are valid, provided that new depreciation is also considered. Assume that the disposal value of the old equipment is zero. Because depreciation is an allocation of historical cost, the depreciation on the old machine is irrelevant. In contrast, the depreciation on the new machine is relevant because the new machine entails a future cost that the customer can avoid by not acquiring it.

	Old Machine	New Machine
Units	100,000	100,000
Variable costs	$150,000	$100,000
Straight-line depreciation	—	20,000
Total relevant costs	$150,000	$120,000
Unit relevant costs	$ 1.50	$ 1.20

Apparently, the sales representative is correct. However, if the customer's expected volume is only 30,000 units per year, the unit costs change in favor of the old machine.

	Old Machine	New Machine
Units	30,000	30,000
Variable costs	$45,000	$30,000
Straight-line depreciation	—	20,000
Total relevant costs	$45,000	$50,000
Unit relevant costs	$ 1.50	$1.6667

Generally, be wary of unit fixed costs. Use total costs rather than unit costs to perform cost analyses. Then, if desired, the total costs that result from analyzes may be unitized.

Conflicts Between Decision Making and Performance Evaluation

OBJECTIVE 7

Discuss how performance measures can affect decision making.

You should now know how to make good decisions based on relevant data. However, knowing how to make these decisions and actually making them are two different things. Managers might be tempted to make decisions they know are poor—not in the best interests of the company—if the performance measures in place will reward them for those decisions. To motivate managers to make optimal decisions, methods of evaluating managers' performance should be consistent with their appropriate decision model.

Let's look at an example of a conflict between the analysis for decision making and the method used to evaluate performance. Consider the replacement decision shown in Exhibit 6-5 on page 264, where replacing the machine had a $2,500 advantage over keeping it. To motivate managers to make the right choice, the method used to evaluate performance should be consistent with the decision model—that is, it should show better performance when managers replace the machine than when they keep it. Assume that top management uses accounting income to measure a manager's performance. The accounting income in the first year after replacement compared with that in years 2, 3, and 4 follows:

	Year 1		Years 2, 3, and 4	
	Keep	**Replace**	**Keep**	**Replace**
Cash operating costs	$5,000	$3,000	$5,000	$3,000
Depreciation	1,000	2,000	1,000	2,000
Loss on disposal ($4,000 − $2,500)	—	1,500	—	—
Total charges against revenue	$6,000	$6,500	$6,000	$5,000

First-year costs will be $6,500 − $6,000 = $500 lower and first-year income will be $500 higher if the manager keeps the machine rather than replacing it. Because managers naturally want to make decisions that maximize the measure of their performance, the manager may be inclined to keep the machine.

The conflict is especially severe if a company often transfers managers from one position to another. Why? Because the $500 first-year advantage for keeping the machine will be off-set by a $1,000 annual advantage of replacing in years 2 to 4. (Note that the net difference of $2,500 in favor of replacement over the four years together is the same as in Exhibit 6-5.) A manager who moves to a new position after the first year, however, bears the entire loss on disposal without reaping the benefits of lower operating costs in years 2 to 4.

The decision to replace a machine earlier than planned also reveals a possible error in the original decision to purchase the machine. The company bought the old machine six years ago for $10,000. Its expected life span was ten years. However, if a better machine is now available, then the useful life of the old machine was really six years, not ten. This feedback on the actual life of the old machine has two possible effects, the first good and the second bad. First, managers might learn from the earlier mistake. If the manager over-estimated the useful life of the old machine, how believable is the prediction that the new machine will have a four-year life span? Feedback can help avoid repeating past mistakes. Second, another mistake might be made to cover up the earlier one. A "loss on disposal" could alert superiors to the incorrect economic-life prediction used in the earlier decision. By avoiding replacement, the manager can spread the $4,000 remaining book value over the future as "depreciation," a more appealing term than "loss on disposal." The superiors may never find out about the incorrect prediction of economic life. The accounting income approach to performance evaluation mixes the financial effects of various deci-sions, hiding both the earlier misestimation of useful life and the current failure to replace.

The conflict between decision making and performance evaluation is a widespread problem in practice. Unfortunately, there are no easy solutions. In theory, accountants could evaluate performance in a manner consistent with decision making. In our equip-ment example, this would mean predicting year-by-year income effects over the planning horizon of four years, noting that the first year would be poor, and evaluating actual per-formance against the predictions.

The trouble is that evaluating performance, decision by decision, is a costly procedure. Therefore, we generally use aggregate measures. For example, an income statement shows the results of many decisions, not just the single decision of buying a machine. Consequently, in many cases like our equipment example, the first-year effects on the income statement may be the major influence on managers' decisions. Thus, managers refrain from taking the longer view that would benefit the company.

How Income Statements Influence Decision Making

When executives use income statements to evaluate performance, managers need to know how their decisions will affect income as reported on the statements. Some income state-ments track fixed and variable costs using the contribution approach, whereas others adopt the absorption approach used in reporting to external parties. To highlight the different effects of these approaches, we will assume that in 2004 the Samson Company has direct-materials costs of $7 million and direct-labor costs of $4 million. Assume also that the company incurred the indirect manufacturing costs illustrated in Exhibit 6-6 and the selling and administrative expenses illustrated in Exhibit 6-7. Total sales were $20 million. Finally, assume that Sampson Company produces the same number of units that it sells.

Note that Exhibits 6-6 and 6-7 subdivide costs as variable or fixed. Many companies do not make such subdivisions in their income statements. Furthermore, those that do must sometimes make arbitrary decisions about whether a given cost is variable, fixed, or partially fixed (for example, repairs). Nevertheless, to align income statements with the information that should be used in decision making, many companies are attempting to report the extent to which their costs are approximately variable or fixed.

OBJE8TIVE

Construct absorption and contribution format income statements and identify which is better for decision making.

Exhibit 6-6

Samson Company
Schedules of Indirect Manufacturing Costs for the Year Ended December 31, 2004 (thousands of dollars)

Schedule 1: Variable Costs		
Supplies (lubricants, expendable tools, coolants, sandpaper)	$ 150	
Materials-handling labor (forklift operators)	700	
Repairs	100	
Power	50	$1,000
Schedule 2: Fixed Costs		
Managers' salaries	$ 200	
Employee training	90	
Factory picnic and holiday party	10	
Supervisory salaries	700	
Depreciation, plant and equipment	1,800	
Property taxes	150	
Insurance	50	3,000
Total indirect manufacturing costs		$4,000

Exhibit 6-7

Samson Company
Schedules of Selling and Administrative Expenses for the Year Ended December 31, 2004 (thousands of dollars)

Schedule 3: Selling Expenses		
Variable		
Sales commissions	$ 700	
Shipping expenses for products sold	300	$1,000
Fixed		
Advertising	$ 700	
Sales salaries	1,000	
Other	300	2,000
Total selling expenses		$3,000

Schedule 4: Administrative Expenses		
Variable		
Some clerical wages	$ 80	
Computer time rented	20	$ 100
Fixed		
Office salaries	$ 100	
Other salaries	200	
Depreciation on office facilities	100	
Public-accounting fees	40	
Legal fees	100	
Other	360	900
Total administrative expenses		$1,000

Sales		$20,000
Less: Manufacturing costs of goods sold		
Direct materials	$7,000	
Direct labor	4,000	
Indirect manufacturing (Schedules 1 plus 2)*	4,000	15,000
Gross margin or gross profit		$ 5,000
Selling expenses (Schedule 3)	$3,000	
Administrative expenses (Schedule 4)	1,000	
Total selling and administrative expenses		4,000
Operating income		$ 1,000

* Schedules 1 and 2 are in Exhibit 6-6. Schedules 3 and 4 are in Exhibit 6-7.

Exhibit 6-8
Samson Company
Absorption Income Statement for the Year Ended December 31, 2004 (thousands of dollars)

Absorption Approach

Exhibit 6-8 presents Samson's income statement using the **absorption approach** (absorption costing), the approach used by companies for external financial reporting. Firms that take this approach consider all indirect manufacturing (both variable and fixed) to be product (inventoriable) costs that become an expense in the form of manufacturing cost of goods sold only as sales occur.

    Note in Exhibit 6-8 that gross profit or gross margin is the difference between sales and the manufacturing cost of goods sold. Note too that the primary classifications of costs on the income statement are by three major management functions: manufacturing, selling, and administrative.

absorption approach *A costing approach that considers all indirect manufacturing costs (both variable and fixed) to be product (inventoriable) costs that become an expense in the form of manufacturing cost of goods sold only as sales occur.*

Contribution Approach

In contrast, Exhibit 6-9 presents Samson's income statement using the **contribution approach** (variable costing or direct costing). Authorities do not allow the contribution approach for external financial reporting. However, many companies use this approach for internal or management accounting purposes and an absorption format for external purposes. Why? Because they expect the benefits of making better decisions to exceed the extra costs of using different reporting systems simultaneously.

    For decision purposes, the major difference between the contribution approach and the absorption approach is that the former emphasizes the distinction between variable and

contribution approach *A method of internal (management accounting) reporting that emphasizes the distinction between variable and fixed costs for the purpose of better decision making.*

Sales		$20,000
Less: Variable expenses		
Direct materials	$ 7,000	
Direct labor	4,000	
Variable indirect manufacturing costs (Schedule 1)*	1,000	
Total variable manufacturing cost of goods sold	$12,000	
Variable selling expenses (Schedule 3)	1,000	
Variable administrative expenses (Schedule 4)	100	
Total variable expenses		13,100
Contribution margin		$ 6,900
Less: fixed expenses		
Manufacturing (Schedule 2)	$ 3,000	
Selling (Schedule 3)	2,000	
Administrative (Schedule 4)	900	5,900
Operating income		$ 1,000

* Note: Schedules 1 and 2 are in Exhibit 6-6. Schedules 3 and 4 are in Exhibit 6-7.

Exhibit 6-9
Samson Company
Contribution Income Statement for the Year Ended December 31, 2004 (thousands of dollars)

fixed costs. Its primary classifications of costs are by variable- and fixed-cost behavior patterns, not by business functions.

The contribution income statement provides a contribution margin—revenue less all variable costs including variable selling and administrative costs. This approach makes it easier to understand the impact of changes in sales demand on operating income. It also dovetails neatly with the cost-volume-profit (CVP) analysis illustrated in Chapter 2 and the decision analyses in this chapter and the preceding one.

A major benefit of the contribution approach is that it stresses the role of fixed costs in operating income. Before a company can earn income, it first must recoup the fixed costs it has incurred for manufacturing and other value-chain functions. This highlighting of total fixed costs focuses management attention on fixed-cost behavior and control in making both short-run and long-run plans. Remember that advocates of the contribution approach do not maintain that fixed costs are unimportant or irrelevant. They do stress, however, that the distinctions between behaviors of variable and fixed costs are crucial for certain decisions.

The difference between the gross margin (from the absorption approach) and the contribution margin (from the contribution approach) is striking in manufacturing companies. Why? Because absorption-costing systems regard fixed manufacturing costs as a part of cost of goods sold, and these fixed costs reduce the gross margin accordingly. However, fixed manufacturing costs do not reduce the contribution margin, which is simply the difference between revenues and variable costs.

Comparing Contribution and Absorption Approaches

In essence, the contribution approach deducts variable costs from sales to compute a contribution margin and then deducts fixed costs to measure profit. This approach is generally consistent with analyses used to make decisions. In contrast, the absorption approach deducts manufacturing costs from sales to compute a gross margin and then deducts nonmanufacturing costs to measure profit. This format is less helpful for decision making. Consider the following four-way breakdown of costs:

	Manufacturing Costs	Nonmanufacturing Costs
Variable Costs	A. Variable manufacturing costs	B. Variable nonmanufacturing costs
Fixed Costs	C. Fixed manufacturing costs	D. Fixed nonmanufacturing costs

Contribution and absorption income statements would look as follows:

Contribution Income Statement	Absorption Income Statement
Sales	Sales
Less: A + B	Less: A + C
Contribution margin	Gross margin
Less: C + D	Less: B + D
Profit	Profit

Summary Problem For Your Review

PROBLEM

1. Review the illustrations in Exhibits 6-6 through 6-9. Suppose that all variable costs fluctuate in direct proportion to units produced and sold, and that total fixed costs are the same over a wide range of production and sales. What would operating income

have been if sales (at normal selling prices) had been $20.9 million instead of $20.0 million? Which statement, the absorption income statement or the contribution income statement, did you use as a framework for your answer? Why?

2. Suppose we regarded employee training (Exhibit 6-6) as a variable rather than a fixed cost at a rate of $90,000 ÷ 1,000,000 units, or $.09 per unit. How would your answer in number 1 change?

SOLUTION

1. Operating income would increase from $1,000,000 to $1,310,500, computed as follows:

Increase in revenue	$ 900,000
Increase in total contribution margin:	
Contribution-margin ratio in contribution income statement	
(Exhibit 6-9) is $6,900,000 ÷ $20,000,000 = .345	
Ratio times revenue increase is .345 × $900,000	$ 310,500
Increase in fixed expenses	0
Operating income before increase	$1,000,000
New operating income	$1,310,500

We can easily make these computations by using data from the contribution income statement. In contrast, the traditional absorption-costing income statement must be analyzed and divided into variable and fixed categories before the effect on operating income can be estimated.

2. The original contribution-margin ratio would be lower because the variable costs would be higher by $.09 per unit: ($6,900,000 − $90,000) ÷ $20,000,000 = .3405.

	Given Level	Higher Level	Difference
Revenue	$20,000,000	$20,900,000	$900,000
Variable expense ($13,100,000 + $90,000)	13,190,000	13,783,550*	593,550
Contribution margin at .3405	$ 6,810,000	$ 7,116,450	$306,450
Fixed expenses ($5,900,000 − $90,000)	5,810,000	5,810,000	—
Operating income	$ 1,000,000	$ 1,306,450	$306,450

*$20,900,000 − $7,116,450 or (1 − .3405) × $20,900,000

Chapters 5 and 6 introduced the important topics of relevant information and decision making. Our major focus was on how to determine and use relevant information when faced with various managerial decisions—special sales orders, adding or deleting a product line, service, or department, pricing, make or buy, and equipment replacement. We have emphasized the importance of understanding cost behavior in each of these decision situations. Now, we shift our emphasis from decision-making techniques to planning and control techniques. One of the most important planning techniques you will use as a manager is budgeting—the major topic in Chapters 7 and 8.

Highlights to Remember

1 **Use opportunity cost to analyze the income effects of a given alternative.** One should always consider opportunity costs when deciding on the use of limited resources. The opportunity cost of a course of action is the maximum profit forgone from other alternative actions. Decision makers may fail to consider opportunity costs because accountants do not report them in the financial accounting system.

2 **Decide whether to make or to buy certain parts or products.** One of the most important production decisions is the make-or-buy decision. Should a company make its own parts or products or should it buy them from outside sources? Both qualitative and quantitative factors affect this decision. In applying relevant cost analysis to a make-or-buy situation, a key factor to consider is the use of facilities.

3 **Decide whether a joint product should be processed beyond the split-off point.** Another typical production situation is deciding whether to process further a joint product or sell it at the split-off point. The relevant information for this decision includes the costs that differ beyond the split-off point. Joint costs that occur before split-off are irrelevant.

4 **Identify irrelevant information in disposal of obsolete inventory.** In certain production decisions, it is important to recognize and identify irrelevant costs. In the decision to dispose of obsolete inventory, the original cost of the inventory is irrelevant because there is no way to restore the resources used to buy or produce the inventory.

5 **Decide whether to keep or replace equipment.** In the decision to keep or replace equipment, the book value of old equipment is irrelevant. This sunk cost is a past or historical cost that a company has already incurred. Relevant costs normally include the disposal value of old equipment, the cost of new equipment, and the difference in the annual operating costs.

6 **Explain how unit costs can be misleading.** Unit fixed costs can be misleading because of the differences in the assumed level of volume on which they are based. The more units a company makes, the lower the unit fixed cost will be. If a salesperson assumes a company will produce 100,000 units and it actually produces only 30,000 units, the unit costs will be understated. You can avoid being misled by unit costs by always using total fixed costs.

7 **Discuss how performance measures can affect decision making.** If companies evaluate managers using performance measures that are not in line with relevant decision criteria, there could be a conflict of interest. Managers often make decisions based on how the decision affects their performance measures. Thus, performance measures work best when they are consistent with the long-term good of the company.

8 **Construct absorption and contribution format income statements and identify which is better for decision making.** The major difference between the absorption and contribution formats for the income statement is that the contribution format focuses on cost behavior (fixed and variable), whereas the absorption format reports costs by business functions. The contribution approach makes it easier for managers to evaluate the effects of changes in volume on income and thus it is better for decision making.

Accounting Vocabulary

absorption approach, p. 269
accumulated depreciation, p. 262
book value, p. 262
contribution approach, p. 269
depreciation, p. 262
differential cost, p. 252

differential revenue, p. 252
incremental cost, p. 252
joint costs, p. 260
joint products, p. 260
net book value, p. 262

opportunity cost, p. 252
outlay cost, p. 252
separable costs, p. 260
split-off point, p. 260
sunk cost, p. 263

Fundamental Assignment Material

6-A1 Make or Buy

Sunshine State Fruit Company sells premium-quality oranges and other citrus fruits by mail order. Protecting the fruit during shipping is important, so the company has designed and produces shipping boxes. The annual cost to make 80,000 boxes is

Materials	$120,000
Labor	20,000
Indirect manufacturing costs	
Variable	16,000
Fixed	60,000
Total	$216,000

Therefore, the cost per box averages $2.70.

Suppose **Weyerhaeuser** submits a bid to supply Sunshine State with boxes for $2.40 per box. Sunshine State must give Weyerhaeuser the box design specifications, and the boxes will be made according to those specs.

1. How much, if any, would Sunshine State save by buying the boxes from Weyerhaeuser?
2. What subjective factors should affect Sunshine State's decision whether to make or buy the boxes?
3. Suppose all the fixed costs represent depreciation on equipment that was purchased for $600,000 and is just about at the end of its ten-year life. New replacement equipment will cost $1 million and is also expected to last ten years. In this case, how much, if any, would Sunshine State save by buying the boxes from Weyerhaeuser?

6-A2 Joint Products: Sell or Process Further

The Mussina Chemical Company produced three joint products at a joint cost of $117,000. These products were processed further and sold as follows.

Chemical Product	Sales	Additional Processing Costs
A	$230,000	$190,000
B	330,000	300,000
C	175,000	100,000

The company has had an opportunity to sell at split off directly to other processors. If that alternative had been selected, sales would have been A, $54,000; B, $28,000; and C, $54,000.

The company expects to operate at the same level of production and sales in the forthcoming year.

Consider all the available information, and assume that all costs incurred after split off are variable.

1. Could the company increase operating income by altering its processing decisions? If so, what would be the expected overall operating income?
2. Which products should be processed further and which should be sold at split off?

6-A3 Role of Old Equipment Replacement

On January 2, 2004, the S. H. Park Company installed a brand-new $87,000 special molding machine for producing a new product. The product and the machine have an expected life of three years. The machine's expected disposal value at the end of three years is zero.

On January 3, 2004, Kimiyo Lee, a star salesperson for a machine tool manufacturer, tells Mr. Park, "I wish I had known earlier of your purchase plans. I can supply you with a technically superior machine for $99,000. The machine you just purchased can be sold for $16,000. I guarantee that our machine will save $35,000 per year in cash operating costs, although it too will have no disposal value at the end of three years."

Park examines some technical data. Although he has confidence in Lee's claims, Park contends, "I'm locked in now. My alternatives are clear: (a) Disposal will result in a loss, (b) keeping and using the 'old' equipment avoids such a loss. I have brains enough to avoid a loss when my other alternative is recognizing a loss. We've got to use that equipment until we get our money out of it."

The annual operating costs of the old machine are expected to be $60,000, exclusive of depreciation. Sales, all in cash, will be $910,000 per year. Other annual cash expenses will be $810,000 regardless of this decision. Assume that the equipment in question is the company's only fixed asset.

Ignore income taxes and the time value of money.

1. Prepare statements of cash receipts and disbursements as they would appear in each of the next three years under both alternatives. What is the total cumulative increase or decrease in cash for the three years?
2. Prepare income statements as they would appear in each of the next three years under both alternatives. Assume straight-line depreciation. What is the cumulative increase or decrease in net income for the three years?
3. Assume that the cost of the "old" equipment was $1 million rather than $87,000. Would the net difference computed in numbers 1 and 2 change? Explain.
4. As Kimiyo Lee, reply to Mr. Park's contentions.
5. What are the irrelevant items in each of your presentations for numbers 1 and 2? Why are they irrelevant?

6-A4 Straightforward Income Statements

The Columbia Company had the following manufacturing data for the year 2004 (in thousands of dollars).

Beginning and ending inventories	None
Direct material used	$400
Direct labor	330
Supplies	20
Utilities—variable portion	40
Utilities—fixed portion	12
Indirect labor—variable portion	90
Indirect labor—fixed portion	40
Depreciation	110
Property taxes	20
Supervisory salaries	50

Selling expenses were $300,000 (including $60,000 that were variable) and general administrative expenses were $144,000 (including $23,000 that were variable). Sales were $1.8 million.

Direct labor and supplies are regarded as variable costs.

1. Prepare two income statements, one using the contribution approach and one using the absorption approach.
2. Suppose that all variable costs fluctuate directly in proportion to sales and that fixed costs are unaffected over a very wide range of sales. What would operating income have been if sales had been $2.0 million instead of $1.8 million? Which income statement did you use to help obtain your answer? Why?

6-B1 Make or Buy

Suppose a **BMW** executive in Germany is trying to decide whether the company should continue to manufacture an engine component or purchase it from Frankfurt Corporation for 50 euros each. Demand for the coming year is expected to be the same as for the current year, 200,000 units. Data for the current year follow:

Direct material	€ 5,000,000
Direct labor	1,900,000
Factory overhead, variable	1,100,000
Factory overhead, fixed	2,500,000
Total costs	€10,500,000

If BMW makes the components, the unit costs of direct material will increase 10%.

If BMW buys the components, 40% of the fixed costs will be avoided. The other 60% will continue regardless of whether the components are manufactured or purchased. Assume that variable overhead varies with output volume.

1. Prepare a schedule that compares the make-or-buy alternatives. Show totals and amounts per unit. Compute the numerical difference between making and buying. Assume that the capacity now used to make the components will become idle if the components are purchased.
2. Assume also that the BMW capacity in question can be rented to a local electronics firm for €1,250,000 for the coming year. Prepare a schedule that compares the net relevant costs of the three alternatives: make, buy and leave capacity idle, buy and rent. Which is the most favorable alternative? By how much in total?

6-B2 Sell or Process Further

ConAgra, Inc., produces meat products with brand names such as Healthy Choice, Armour, and Butterball. Suppose one of the company's plants processes beef cattle into various products. For simplicity, assume that there are only three products: steak, hamburger, and hides, and that the average steer costs $700. The three products emerge from a process that costs $100 per steer to run, and output from one steer can be sold for the following net amounts.

Steak (100 pounds)	$ 400
Hamburger (500 pounds)	600
Hide (120 pounds)	100
Total	$1,100

Assume that each of these three products can be sold immediately or processed further in another ConAgra plant. The steak can be the main course in frozen dinners sold under the Healthy Choice label. The vegetables and desserts in the 400 dinners produced from the 100 pounds of steak would cost $120, and production, sales, and other costs for the 400 meals would total $350. Each meal would be sold wholesale for $2.15.

The hamburger could be made into frozen Salisbury steak patties sold under the Armour label. The only additional cost would be a $200 processing cost for the 500 pounds of hamburger. Frozen Salisbury steaks sell wholesale for $1.70 per pound.

The hide can be sold before or after tanning. The cost of tanning one hide is $80, and a tanned hide can be sold for $175.

1. Compute the total profit if all three products are sold at the split-off point.
2. Compute the total profit if all three products are processed further before being sold.
3. Which products should be sold at the split-off point? Which should be processed further?
4. Compute the total profit if your plan in number 3 is followed.

6-B3 Replacing Old Equipment

Consider these data regarding Douglas County's photocopying requirements:

	Old Equipment	Proposed Replacement Equipment
Useful life, in years	5	3
Current age, in years	2	0
Useful life remaining, in years	3	3
Original cost	$25,000	$15,000
Accumulated depreciation	10,000	0
Book value	15,000	Not acquired yet
Disposal value (in cash) now	3,000	Not acquired yet
Disposal value in 3 years	0	0
Annual cash operating costs for power, maintenance, toner, and supplies	14,000	7,500

The county administrator is trying to decide whether to replace the old equipment. Because of rapid changes in technology, she expects the replacement equipment to have only a three-year useful life. Ignore the effects of taxes.

1. Prepare a schedule that compares both relevant and irrelevant items for the next three years together. (*Hint:* See Exhibit 6-4, page 263.)
2. Prepare a schedule that compares all relevant items for the next three years together. Which tabulation is clearer, this one or the one in requirement 1? (*Hint:* See Exhibit 6-5, page 264.)
3. Prepare a simple "shortcut" or direct analysis to support your choice of alternatives.

6-B4 Decision and Performance Models

Refer to the preceding problem.

1. Suppose the "decision model" favored by top management consisted of a comparison of a three-year accumulation of cash under each alternative. As the manager of office operations, which alternative would you choose? Why?
2. Suppose the "performance evaluation model" emphasized the minimization of overall costs of photocopying operations for the first year. Which alternative would you choose?

6-B5 Contribution and Absorption Income Statements

The following information is taken from the records of the Kingland Manufacturing Company for the year ending December 31, 2004. There were no beginning or ending inventories.

Sales	$10,000,000	Long-term rent, factory	$ 100,000
Sales commissions	500,000	Factory superintendent's	
Advertising	200,000	salary	30,000
Shipping expenses	300,000	Supervisors' salaries	100,000
		Direct materials used	4,000,000
Administrative executive			
salaries	100,000	Direct labor	2,000,000
		Cutting bits used	60,000
Administrative clerical			
salaries (variable)	400,000	Factory methods research	40,000
		Abrasives for machining	100,000
Fire insurance on			
factory equipment	2,000	Indirect labor	800,000
Property taxes on			
factory equipment	10,000	Depreciation on	
		equipment	300,000

1. Prepare a contribution income statement and an absorption income statement. If you are in doubt about any cost behavior pattern, decide on the basis of whether the total cost in question will fluctuate substantially over a wide range of volume. Prepare a separate supporting schedule of indirect manufacturing costs subdivided between variable and fixed costs.
2. Suppose that all variable costs fluctuate directly in proportion to sales, and that fixed costs are unaffected over a wide range of sales. What would operating income have been if sales had been $10.5 million instead of $10 million? Which income statement did you use to help get your answer? Why?

Additional Assignment Material

Questions

6-1 Distinguish between an opportunity cost and an outlay cost.

6-2 "I had a chance to rent my summer home for two weeks for $800. But I chose to have it idle. I didn't want strangers living in my summer house." What term in this chapter describes the $800? Why?

6-3 "Accountants do not ordinarily record opportunity costs in the formal accounting records." Why?

6-4 Distinguish between an incremental cost and a differential cost.

6-5 "Incremental cost is the addition to costs from the manufacture of one unit." Do you agree? Explain.

6-6 "The differential costs or incremental costs of increasing production from 1,000 automobiles to 1,200 automobiles per week would be the additional costs of producing the additional 200 automobiles." If production were reduced from 1,200 to 1,000 automobiles per week, what would the decline in costs be called?

6-7 "Qualitative factors generally favor making over buying a component." Do you agree? Explain.

6-8 "Choices are often mislabeled as simply make or buy." Do you agree? Explain.

6-9 What are joint products? Name several examples of joint products.

6-10 What is the split-off point and why is it important in analyzing joint costs?

6-11 "No technique used to assign the joint cost to individual products should be used for management decisions regarding whether a product should be sold at the split-off point or processed further." Do you agree? Explain.

6-12 "Inventory that was purchased for $5,000 should not be sold for less than $5,000 because such a sale would result in a loss." Do you agree? Explain.

6-13 "Recovering sunk costs is a major objective when replacing equipment." Do you agree? Explain.

6-14 "Past costs are indeed relevant in most instances because they provide the point of departure for the entire decision process." Do you agree? Why?

6-15 Which of the following items are relevant to replacement decisions? Explain.
a. Book value of old equipment
b. Disposal value of old equipment
c. Cost of new equipment

6-16 "Some expected future costs may be irrelevant." Do you agree? Explain.

6-17 "Variable costs are irrelevant whenever they do not differ among the alternatives at hand." Do you agree? Explain.

6-18 There are two major reasons why unit costs should be analyzed with care in decision making. What are they?

6-19 "Machinery sales personnel sometimes erroneously brag about the low unit costs of using their machines." Identify one source of an error concerning the estimation of unit costs.

6-20 Give an example of a situation in which the performance evaluation model is not consistent with the decision model.

6-21 "Evaluating performance, decision by decision, is costly. Aggregate measures, such as the income statement, are frequently used." How might the wide use of income statements affect managers' decisions about buying equipment?

6-22 What is the advantage of the contribution approach as compared with the absorption approach?

6-23 "The primary classifications of costs are by variable- and fixed-cost behavior patterns, not by business functions." Name three commonly used terms that describe this type of income statement.

Critical Thinking Exercises

6-24 Measurement of Opportunity Cost
"Accountants cannot measure opportunity cost. Only managers have the knowledge to measure it." Do you agree with this statement? Why or why not?

6-25 Outsourcing Decisions
Decisions on whether to outsource services such a payroll accounting and systems development are much like make-or-buy decisions. What cost factors should influence the decision on whether to outsource payroll functions?

6-26 Unitized Costs
Suppose you are a manager in a manufacturing company. Your accountant has just presented you with a very detailed cost analysis for a decision whether to outsource or make a component of a product. You have to use this analysis in a meeting with other managers. Since the analysis is shown in totals and your colleagues prefer simple reports and unit costs, you divide the bottom-line amounts by the total units to be made or bought (outsourced) and present just these in a simple report. Your colleagues are pleased that your report is so easy to understand and simple to use. Then they begin to predict the total cost differences for several other possible number of units to be made or outsourced by simply multiplying the unit costs by the volume to be outsourced. Why should you feel uncomfortable?

6-27 Historical Costs and Inventory Decisions
Explain why it is sometimes best to sell inventory for less than the amount paid for it.

6-28 Income Statements and Sales Managers
Suppose Chee Wong is in charge of selling Nantucket Nectars Juice Cocktails. What type of income statement, absorption or contribution, would Wong find most useful for his decisions? Why?

Exercises

6-29 Opportunity Costs
Martina Bridgeman is an attorney employed by a large law firm at a salary of $90,000 per year. She is considering whether to become a sole practitioner, which would probably generate annually $320,000 in operating revenues and $220,000 in operating expenses.

1. Present two tabulations of the annual income effects of these alternatives. The second tabulation should include the opportunity cost of Bridgeman's compensation as an employee.
2. Suppose Bridgeman prefers less risk and chooses to stay an employee. Show a tabulation of the income effects of rejecting the opportunity of independent practice.

6-30 Opportunity Cost of Home Ownership
Oliver Kamp has just made the final payment on his mortgage. He could continue to live in the home; cash expenses for repairs and maintenance (after any tax effects) would be $500 monthly. Alternatively, he could sell the home for $200,000 (net of taxes), invest the proceeds in 6% municipal tax-free bonds, and rent an apartment for $10,000 annually. The landlord would then pay for repairs and maintenance.

Prepare two analyses of Kamps alternatives, one showing no explicit opportunity cost and the second showing the explicit opportunity cost of the decision to hold the present home.

6-31 Opportunity Cost at Nantucket Nectars

Suppose Nantucket Nectars has a machine for which it paid $160,000 several years ago and is currently not being used. It can use the machine to produce 12-oz. bottles of its Juice Cocktails or 12-oz. bottles of its 100% Juices. The contribution margin from the additional sales of 100% Juices would be $90,000. A third alternative is selling the machine for cash of $75,000. What is the opportunity cost of the machine when we analyze the alternative to produce 12-oz. bottles of Juice Cocktails?

6-32 Hospital Opportunity Cost

An administrator at Sacred Heart Hospital is considering how to use some space made available when the outpatient clinic moved to a new building. She has narrowed her choices, as follows:

a. Use the space to expand laboratory testing. Expected future annual revenue would be $320,000; future costs, $290,000.
b. Use the space to expand the eye clinic. Expected future annual revenue would be $500,000; future costs, $480,000.
c. The gift shop is rented by an independent retailer who wants to expand into the vacated space. The retailer has offered $11,000 for the yearly rental of the space. All operating expenses will be borne by the retailer.

The administrator's planning horizon is unsettled. However, she has decided that the yearly data given will suffice for guiding her decision.

Tabulate the total relevant data regarding the decision alternatives. Omit the concept of opportunity cost in one tabulation, but use the concept in a second tabulation. As the administrator, which tabulation would you prefer if you could receive only one?

6-33 Make or Buy

Assume that a division of **Bose** makes an electronic component for its speakers. Its manufacturing process for the component is a highly automated part of a just-in-time production system. All labor is considered to be an overhead cost, and all overhead is regarded as fixed with respect to output volume. Production costs for 100,000 units of the component are as follows:

Direct materials		$300,000
Factory overhead		
Indirect labor	$80,000	
Supplies	30,000	
Allocated occupancy cost	40,000	150,000
Total cost		$450,000

A small, local company has offered to supply the components at a price of $3.40 each. If the division discontinued its production of the component, it would save two-thirds of the supplies cost and $30,000 of indirect-labor cost. All other overhead costs would continue.

The division manager recently attended a seminar on cost behavior and learned about fixed and variable costs. He wants to continue to make the component because the variable cost of $3.00 is below the $3.40 bid.

1. Compute the relevant cost of (a) making and (b) purchasing the component. Which alternative is less costly and by how much?
2. What qualitative factors might influence the decision about whether to make or to buy the component?

6-34 Make or Buy at Nantucket Nectars

Assume that Nantucket Nectars reports the following costs to make 17.5 oz. bottles for its Juice Cocktails:

Nantucket Nectars Company
Cost of Making 17.5-Ounce Bottles

	Total Cost for 1,000,000 Bottles	Cost per Bottle
Direct materials	$ 85,000	$ .085
Direct labor	30,000	.030
Variable factory overhead	60,000	.060
Fixed factory overhead	85,000	.085
Total costs	$260,000	$ .260

Another manufacturer offers to sell Nantucket Nectars the bottles for $.25. The capacity now used to make bottles will become idle if the the company purchases the bottles. Further, one supervisor with a salary of $60,000, a fixed cost, would be eliminated if the bottles were purchased. Prepare a schedule that compares the costs to make and buy the 17.5 oz. bottles. Should Nantucket Nectars make or buy the bottles?

6-35 Make or Buy and the Use of Idle Facilities at Nantucket Nectars

Refer to the preceding exercise. Suppose Nantucket Nectars can use the released facilities in another manufacturing activity that makes a contribution to profits of $75,000 or can rent them out for $55,000. Prepare a schedule that compares the four alternative courses of action. Which alternative would yield the lowest net cost?

6-36 Sell or Process Further

An **Exxon** petrochemical factory produces two products, L and M, as a result of a particular joint process. Both products are sold to manufacturers as ingredients for assorted chemical products.

Product L sells at split off for $.25 per gallon; M, for $.30 per gallon. Data for April follow:

Joint processing cost	$1,600,000
Gallons produced and sold	
L	4,000,000
M	2,500,000

Suppose that in April the 2,500,000 gallons of M could have been processed further into Super M at an additional cost of $225,000. The Super M output would be sold for $.38 per gallon. Product L would be sold at split off in any event.

Should M have been processed further in April and sold as Super M? Show computations.

6-37 Joint Products, Multiple Choice

From a particular joint process, Edgerton company produces three products, A, B, and C. Each product may be sold at the point of split off or processed further. Additional processing requires no special facilities, and production costs of further processing are entirely variable and traceable to the products involved. In 2004, all three products were processed beyond split off. Joint production costs for the year were $72,000. Sales values and costs needed to evaluate Edgerton's 2004 production policy follow:

			Additional Costs and Sales Values if Processed Further	
Product	Units Produced	Net Realizable Values (Sales Values) at Split Off	Sales Values	Added Costs
A	6,000	$25,000	$42,000	$9,000
B	4,000	41,000	45,000	7,000
C	2,000	24,000	32,000	8,000

Answer the following multiple-choice questions:

1. For units of C, the unit production cost most relevant to a sell-or-process-further decision is (a) $5, (b) $12, (c) $4, (d) $9.
2. To maximize profits, Edgerton should subject the following products to additional processing (a) A only, (b) A, B, and C, (c) B and C only, (d) C only.

6-38 Obsolete Inventory

The Ohio State bookstore bought more "Buckeye Champs" calendars than it could sell. It was nearly June and 200 calendars remained in stock. The store paid $4.50 each for the calendars and normally sold them for $8.95. Since February, they had been on sale for $6.00, and two weeks ago the price was dropped to $5.00. Still, few calendars were being sold. The bookstore manager thought it was no longer worthwhile using shelf space for the calendars.

The proprietor of Hurricane Collectibles offered to buy all 200 calendars for $250. He intended to store them until the 2004 football season was over and then sell them as novelty items.

The bookstore manager was not sure she wanted to sell for $1.25 calendars that cost $4.50. The only alternative, however, was to scrap them because the publisher would not take them back.

1. Compute the difference in profit between accepting the $250 offer and scrapping the calendars.
2. Describe how the $4.50 × 200 = $900 paid for the calendars affects your decision.

6-39 Replacement of Old Equipment

Three years ago the Oak Street TCBY bought a frozen yogurt machine for $8,000. A salesman has just suggested to the TCBY manager that she replace the machine with a new, $12,500 machine. The manager has gathered the following data:

	Old Machine	New Machine
Original cost	$8,000	$12,500
Useful life in years	8	5
Current age in years	3	0
Useful life remaining in years	5	5
Accumulated depreciation	$3,000	Not acquired yet
Book value	$5,000	Not acquired yet
Disposal value (in cash) now	$2,000	Not acquired yet
Disposal value in 5 years	0	0
Annual cash operating cost	$4,500	$ 2,000

1. Compute the difference in total costs over the next five years under both alternatives, that is, keeping the original machine or replacing it with the new machine. Ignore taxes.
2. Suppose the Oak Street TCBY manager replaces the original machine. Compute the "loss on disposal" of the original machine. How does this amount affect your computation in number 1? Explain.

6-40 Unit Costs

Brandon Company produces and sells a product that has variable costs of $9 per unit and fixed costs of $110,000 per year.

1. Compute the unit cost at a production and sales level of 10,000 units per year.
2. Compute the unit cost at a production and sales level of 20,000 units per year.
3. Which of these unit costs is most accurate? Explain.

6-41 Relevant Investment

Roberta Thomas had obtained a new truck with a list price, including options, of $21,000. The dealer had given her a "generous trade-in allowance" of $4,500 on her old truck that had a wholesale price of $3,000. Sales tax was $1,260.

The annual cash operating costs of the old truck were $4,200. The new truck was expected to reduce these costs by one-third, to $2,800 per year.

Compute the amount of the original investment in the new truck. Explain your reasoning.

6-42 Weak Division

Lake Forest Electronics Company paid $7 million in cash four years ago to acquire a company that manufactures CD-ROM drives. This company has been operated as a division of Lake Forest and has lost $500,000 each year since its acquisition.

The minimum desired return for this division is that, when a new product is fully developed, it should return a net profit of $500,000 per year for the foreseeable future.

Recently, the IBM Corporation offered to purchase the division from Lake Forest for $5 million. The president of Lake Forest commented, "I've got an investment of $9 million to recoup ($7 million plus losses of $500,000 for each of four years). I have finally got this situation turned around, so I oppose selling the division now."

Prepare a response to the president's remarks. Indicate how to make this decision. Be as specific as possible.

6-43 Opportunity Cost

Renee Behr, M.D., is a psychiatrist who is in heavy demand. Even though she has raised her fees considerably during the past five years, Dr. Behr still cannot accommodate all the patients who wish to see her.

Behr has conducted six hours of appointments a day, six days a week, for 48 weeks a year. Her fee averages $140 per hour.

Her variable costs are negligible and may be ignored for decision purposes. Ignore income taxes.

1. Behr is weary of working a six-day week. She is considering taking every other Saturday off. What would be her annual income (a) if she worked every Saturday and (b) if she worked every other Saturday?
2. What would be her opportunity cost for the year of not working every other Saturday?
3. Assume that Dr. Behr has definitely decided to take every other Saturday off. She loves to repair her sports car by doing the work herself. If she works on her car during half a Saturday when she otherwise would not see patients, what is her opportunity cost?

6-44 Straightforward Absorption Statement

The Pierce Company had the following data (in thousands) for a given period:

Sales	$700
Direct materials	210
Direct labor	150
Indirect manufacturing costs	170
Selling and administrative expenses	150

There were no beginning or ending inventories. Compute the (1) manufacturing cost of goods sold, (2) gross profit, (3) operating income, and (4) conversion cost (total manufacturing cost less materials cost).

6-45 Straightforward Contribution Income Statement

Yoko Ltd. had the following data (in millions of yen) for a given period:

Sales	¥770
Direct materials	290
Direct labor	140
Variable factory overhead	60
Variable selling and administrative expenses	100
Fixed factory overhead	120
Fixed selling and administrative expenses	45

There were no beginning or ending inventories. Compute the (a) variable manufacturing cost of goods sold, (b) contribution margin, and (c) operating income.

6-46 Straightforward Absorption and Contribution Statement

Anzola Company had the following data (in millions) for a recent period. Fill in the blanks. There were no beginning or ending inventories.

a.	Sales	$920
b.	Direct materials used	350
c.	Direct labor	210
	Indirect manufacturing costs:	
d.	Variable	100
e.	Fixed	50
f.	Variable manufacturing cost of goods sold	—
g.	Manufacturing cost of goods sold	—
	Selling and administrative expenses:	
h.	Variable	90
i.	Fixed	80
j.	Gross profit	—
k.	Contribution margin	—

6-47 Absorption Statement

Raynard's Jewelry had the following data (in thousands of South African Rands, ZAR) for a given period. Assume there are no inventories. Fill in the blanks.

Sales	ZAR ___
Direct materials	370
Direct labor	___
Indirect manufacturing	___
Manufacturing cost of goods sold	780
Gross margin	120
Selling and administrative expenses	___
Operating income	20
Prime cost (direct materials + direct labor)	600

6-48 Contribution Income Statement

Marlinski Company had the following data (in thousands) for a given period. Assume there are no inventories.

Direct labor	$170
Direct materials	210
Variable indirect manufacturing	110
Contribution margin	200
Fixed selling and administrative expenses	100
Operating income	10
Sales	970

Compute the (a) variable manufacturing cost of goods sold, (b) variable selling and administrative expenses, and (c) fixed indirect manufacturing costs.

Problems

6-49 Hotel Rooms and Opportunity Costs

The **Marriott Corporation** operates many hotels throughout the world. Suppose one of its Chicago hotels is facing difficult times because of the opening of several new competing hotels.

To accommodate its flight personnel, **American Airlines** has offered Marriott a contract for the coming year that provides a rate of $50 per night per room for a minimum of 50 rooms for 365 nights. This contract would assure Marriott of selling 50 rooms of space nightly, even if some of the rooms are vacant on some nights.

The Marriott manager has mixed feelings about the contract. On several peak nights during the year, the hotel could sell the same space for $100 per room.

1. Suppose the Marriott manager signs the contract. What is the opportunity cost of the 50 rooms on October 20, the night of a big convention of retailers when every nearby hotel room is occupied? What is the opportunity cost on December 28, when only 10 of these rooms would be expected to be rented at an average rate of $80?
2. If the year-round rate per room averaged $90, what percentage of occupancy of the 50 rooms in question would have to be rented to make Marriott indifferent about accepting the offer?

6-50 Extension of Preceding Problem

Assume the same facts as in the preceding problem. However, also assume that the variable costs per room, per day are $10.

1. Suppose the best estimate is a 53% general occupancy rate for the 50 rooms at an average $90 room rate for the next year. Should Marriott accept the contract?
2. What percentage of occupancy of the 50 rooms in question would make Marriott indifferent about accepting the offer?

6-51 Make or Buy

Dana Corporation, based in Toledo, Ohio, is a global manufacturer of highly engineered products that serve industrial, vehicle, construction, commercial, aerospace, and semiconductor markets. Dana's 2002 sales were $10.3 billion. It frequently subcontracts work to other manufacturers, depending on whether Dana's facilities are fully occupied. Suppose Dana is about to make some final decisions regarding the use of its manufacturing facilities for the coming year.

The following are the costs of making part EC113, a key component of an emissions control system:

	Total Cost for 50,000 Units	Cost per Unit
Direct materials	$ 400,000	$8
Direct labor	300,000	6
Variable factory overhead	150,000	3
Fixed factory overhead	300,000	6
Total manufacturing costs	$1,150,000	$23

Another manufacturer has offered to sell the same part to Dana for $21 each. The fixed overhead consists of depreciation, property taxes, insurance, and supervisory salaries. All the fixed overhead would continue if Dana bought the component except that the cost of $100,000 pertaining to some supervisory and custodial personnel could be avoided.

1. Assume that the capacity now used to make parts will become idle if the parts are purchased. Should Dana buy or make the parts? Show computations.
2. Assume that the capacity now used to make parts will either (a) be rented to a nearby manufacturer for $65,000 for the year or (b) be used to make oil filters that will yield a profit contribution of $200,000. Should Dana buy or make part EC113? Show computations.

6-52 Relevant-Cost Analysis

Following are the unit costs of making and selling a single product at a normal level of 5,000 units per month and a current unit selling price of $90:

Manufacturing costs	
Direct materials	$35
Direct labor	12
Variable overhead	8
Fixed overhead (total for the year, $300,000)	5
Selling and administrative expenses	
Variable	15
Fixed (total for the year, $480,000)	8

Consider each requirement separately. Label all computations, and present your solutions in a form that will be comprehensible to the company president.

1. This product is usually sold at a rate of 60,000 units per year. It is predicted that a rise in price to $98 will decrease volume by 10%. How much may advertising be increased under this plan without having annual operating income fall below the current level?
2. The company has received a proposal from an outside supplier to make and ship this item directly to the company's customers as sales orders are forwarded. Variable selling and administrative costs would fall 40%. If the supplier's proposal is accepted, the company will use its own plant to produce a new product. The new product would be sold through manufacturer's agents at a 10% commission based on a selling price of $40 each. The cost characteristics of this product, based on predicted yearly normal volume, are as follows:

	Per Unit
Direct materials	$ 6
Direct labor	12
Variable overhead	8
Fixed overhead	6
Manufacturing costs	$32
Selling and administrative expenses	
Variable (commission)	10% of selling price
Fixed	$ 2

What is the maximum price per unit that the company can afford to pay to the supplier for subcontracting production of the entire old product? Assume the following:

- Total fixed factory overhead and total fixed selling expenses will not change if the new product line is added.
- The supplier's proposal will not be considered unless the present annual net income can be maintained.
- Selling price of the old product will remain unchanged.
- All $300,000 of fixed manufacturing overhead will be assigned to the new product.

6-53 Hotel Pricing and Use of Capacity

A growing corporation in a large city has offered a 200-room **Holiday Inn** a one-year contract to rent 40 rooms at reduced rates of $50 per room instead of the regular rate of $85 per room. The corporation will sign the contract for 365-day occupancy because its visiting manufacturing and marketing personnel are virtually certain to use all the space each night.

Each room occupied has a variable cost of $12 per night (for cleaning, laundry, lost linens, and extra electricity).

The hotel manager expects an 85% occupancy rate for the year, so she is reluctant to sign the contract. If the contract is signed, the occupancy rate on the remaining 160 rooms will be 95%.

1. Compute the total contribution margin for the year with and without the contract. Is the contract profitable to Holiday Inn?
2. Compute the lowest room rate that the hotel should accept on the contract so that the total contribution margin would be the same with or without the contract.

6-54 Special Air Fares

Denver-based **Frontier Airlines** provides service to 39 cities in the United States and Mexico. Frontier operates a fleet of 37 aircraft including 16 134-passenger Boeing 737-300 jets. The manager of operations of Frontier Airlines is trying to decide whether to adopt a new discount fare. Focus on one 134-seat 737 airplane now operating at a 56% load factor. That is, on average the airplane has $.56 \times 134 = 75$ passengers. The regular fares produce an average revenue of 12¢ per passenger mile.

Suppose an average 40% fare discount (which is subject to restrictions regarding time of departure and length of stay) will produce three new additional passengers. Also suppose that three of the previously committed passengers accept the restrictions and switch to the discount fare from the regular fare.

1. Compute the total revenue per airplane mile with and without the discount fares.
2. Suppose the maximum allowed allocation to new discount fares is 50 seats. These will be filled. As before, some previously committed passengers will accept the restrictions and switch to the discount fare from the regular fare. How many will have to switch so that the total revenue per mile will be the same either with or without the discount plan?

6-55 Joint Costs and Incremental Analysis

Jacque de Paris, a high-fashion women's dress manufacturer, is planning to market a new cocktail dress for the coming season. Jacque de Paris supplies retailers in Europe and the United States.

Four yards of material are required to lay out the dress pattern. Some material remains after cutting, which can be sold as remnants. The leftover material could also be used to manufacture a matching cape and handbag. However, if the leftover material is to be used for the cape and handbag, more care will be required in the cutting, which will increase the cutting costs.

The company expects to sell 1,250 dresses if no matching cape or handbag is available. Market research reveals that dress sales will be 20% higher if a matching cape and handbag are available. The market research indicates that the cape and handbag will not be sold individually, but only as accessories with the dress. The various combinations of dresses, capes, and handbags that are expected to be sold by retailers are as follows:

	Percent of Total
Complete sets of dress, cape, and handbag	70%
Dress and cape	6%
Dress and handbag	15%
Dress only	9%
Total	100%

The material used in the dress costs €80 a yard, or €320 for each dress. The cost of cutting the dress if the cape and handbag are not manufactured is estimated at €100 a dress, and the resulting remnants can be sold for €25 for each dress cut out. If the cape and handbag are to be manufactured, the cutting costs will be increased by €36 per dress. There will be no salable remnants if the capes and handbags are manufactured in the quantities estimated. The selling prices and the costs to complete the three items once they are cut are as follows:

	Selling Price per Unit	Unit Cost to Complete (Excludes Cost of Material and Cutting Operation)
Dress	€1,050	€400
Cape	140	100
Handbag	50	30

1. Calculate the incremental profit or loss to Jacque de Paris from manufacturing the capes and handbags in conjunction with the dresses.
2. Identify any nonquantitative factors that could influence the company's management in its decision to manufacture the capes and handbags that match the dress.

6-56 Relevant Cost

Debraceny Company's unit costs of manufacturing and selling a given item at the planned activity level of 10,000 units per month are

Manufacturing costs	
Direct materials	$4.20
Direct labor	.60
Variable overhead	.70
Fixed overhead	.80
Selling expenses	
Variable	3.00
Fixed	1.10

Ignore income taxes in all requirements. These four parts have no connection with each other.

1. Compute the planned annual operating income at a selling price of $12 per unit.
2. Compute the expected annual operating income if the volume can be increased by 20% when the selling price is reduced to $11. Assume the implied cost behavior patterns are correct.
3. The company desires to seek an order for 5,000 units from a foreign customer. The variable selling expenses for the order will be 40% less than usual, but the fixed costs for obtaining the order will be $6,000. Domestic sales will not be affected. Compute the minimum break-even price per unit to be considered.
4. The company has an inventory of 2,000 units of this item left over from last year's model. These must be sold through regular channels at reduced prices. The inventory will be valueless unless sold this way. What unit cost is relevant for establishing the minimum selling price of these 2,000 units?

6-57 New Machine

A new $300,000 machine is expected to have a five-year life and a terminal value of zero. It can produce 40,000 units a year at a variable cost of $4 per unit. The variable cost is $6 per unit with an old machine, which has a book value of $100,000. It is being depreciated on a straight-line basis at $20,000 per year. It too is expected to have a terminal value of zero. Its current disposal value is also zero because it is highly specialized equipment.

The salesperson of the new machine prepared the following comparison:

	New Machine	Old Machine
Units	40,000	40,000
Variable costs	$160,000	$240,000
Straight-line depreciation	60,000	20,000
Total cost	$220,000	$260,000
Unit cost	$ 5.50	$ 6.50

He said, "The new machine is obviously a worthwhile acquisition. You will save $1.00 for every unit you produce."

1. Do you agree with the salesperson's analysis? If not, how would you change it? Be specific. Ignore taxes.
2. Prepare an analysis of total and unit differential costs if the annual volume is 20,000 units.
3. At what annual volume would both the old and new machines have the same total relevant costs?

6-58 Conceptual Approach

A large automobile-parts plant was constructed four years ago in a Pennsylvania city served by two railroads. The PC Railroad purchased 40 specialized 60-foot freight cars as a direct result of the additional traffic generated by the new plant. The investment was based on an estimated useful life of 20 years.

Now the competing railroad has offered to service the plant with new 86-foot freight cars, which would enable more efficient shipping operations at the plant. The automobile-parts company has threatened to switch carriers unless PC Railroad buys ten new 86-foot freight cars.

The PC marketing management wants to buy the new cars, but PC operating management says, "The new investment is undesirable. It really consists of the new outlay plus the loss on the old freight cars. The old cars must be written down to a low salvage value if they cannot be used as originally intended."

Evaluate the comments. What is the correct conceptual approach to the quantitative analysis in this decision?

6-59 Book Value of Old Equipment

Consider the following data:

	Old Equipment	Proposed New Equipment
Original cost	$24,000	$12,000
Useful life in years	8	3
Current age in years	5	0
Useful life remaining in years	3	3
Accumulated depreciation	$15,000	0
Book value	9,000	*
Disposal value (in cash) now	3,000	*
Annual cash operating costs (maintenance, power, repairs, lubricants, etc.)	$10,000	$ 6,000

* Not acquired yet.

1. Prepare a cost comparison of all relevant items for the next three years together. Ignore taxes.
2. Prepare a cost comparison that includes both relevant and irrelevant items. (See Exhibit 6-4, p. 263.)
3. Prepare a comparative statement of the total charges against revenue for the first year. Would the manager be inclined to buy the new equipment? Explain.

6-60 Decision and Performance Models

Refer to problem 6-A3.

1. Suppose the "decision model" favored by top management consisted of a comparison of a three-year accumulation of wealth under each alternative. Which alternative would you choose? Why? (Accumulation of wealth means cumulative increase in cash.)
2. Suppose the "performance evaluation model" emphasized the net income of a subunit, such as a division, each year rather than considering each project, one by one. Which alternative would you expect a manager to choose? Why?
3. Suppose the same quantitative data existed, but the "enterprise" was a city and the "machine" was a computer in the treasurer's department. Would your answers to the first two parts change? Why?

6-61 Review of Relevant Costs

Since the early 1960s, Neil Simon has been one of Broadway's most successful playwrights. The *New York Times* reported that Neil Simon planned to open his play, *London Suite,* off-Broadway. Why? For financial reasons. Producer Emanuel Azenberg predicted the following costs before the play even opened:

	On Broadway	Off Broadway
Sets, costumes, lights	$ 357,000	$ 87,000
Loading in (building set, etc.)	175,000	8,000
Rehearsal salaries	102,000	63,000
Director and designer fees	126,000	61,000
Advertising	300,000	121,000
Administration	235,000	100,000
Total	$1,295,000	$440,000

Broadway ticket prices average $55, and theaters can seat about 1,000 persons per show. Off-Broadway prices average only $40, and the theaters seat only 500. Normally, plays run eight times a week, both on and off Broadway. Weekly operating expenses off Broadway average $82,000; they average an extra $124,000 on Broadway for a weekly total of $206,000.

1. Suppose 400 persons attended each show, whether on or off Broadway. Compare the weekly financial results from a Broadway production to one produced off Broadway.
2. Suppose attendance averaged 75% of capacity, whether on or off Broadway. Compare the weekly financial results from a Broadway production to one produced off Broadway.
3. Compute the attendance per show required just to cover weekly expenses (a) on Broadway and (b) off Broadway.
4. Suppose average attendance on Broadway was 600 per show and off Broadway was 400. Compute the total net profit for a 26-week run (a) on Broadway and (b) off Broadway. Be sure to include the pre-opening costs.
5. Repeat requirement 4 for a 100-week run.
6. Using attendance figures from numbers 4 and 5, compute (a) the number of weeks a Broadway production must run before it breaks even, and (b) the number of weeks an off-Broadway production must run before it breaks even.
7. Using attendance figures from numbers 4 and 5, determine how long a play must run before the profit from a Broadway production exceeds that from an off-Broadway production.
8. If you were Neil Simon, would you prefer *London Suite* to play on Broadway or off Broadway? Explain.

6-62 Make or Buy, Opportunity Costs, and Ethics

Agribiz Food Products, Inc., produces a wide variety of food and related products. The company's tomato canning operation relies partly on tomatoes grown on Agribiz's own farms and partly on tomatoes bought from other growers.

Agribiz's tomato farm is on the edge of Sharpestown, a fast-growing, medium-sized city. It produces 8 million pounds of tomatoes a year and employs 55 persons. The annual costs of tomatoes grown on this farm are

Variable production costs	$ 550,000
Fixed production costs	1,200,000
Shipping costs (all variable)	200,000
Total costs	$1,950,000

Fixed production costs include depreciation on machinery and equipment, but not on land because land should not be depreciated. Agribiz owns the land, which was purchased for $600,000 many years ago. A recent appraisal placed the value of the land at $15 million because it is a prime site for an industrial park and shopping center.

Agribiz could purchase all the tomatoes it needs on the market for $.25 per pound delivered to its factory. If it did this, it would sell the farmland and shut down the operations in Sharpestown. If the farm were sold, $300,000 of the annual fixed costs would be saved. Agribiz can invest excess cash and earn an annual rate of 10%.

1. How much does it cost Agribiz annually for the land used by the tomato farm?
2. How much would Agribiz save annually if it closed the tomato farm? Is this more or less than would be paid to purchase the tomatoes on the market?
3. What ethical issues are involved with the decision to shut down the tomato farm?

6-63 Irrelevance of Past Costs at Starbucks

Starbucks purchases and roasts high-quality, whole-bean coffees, its hallmark, and sells them, along with other coffee-related products, primarily through its company-operated retail stores.

Suppose that the quality-control manager at Starbucks discovered a 1,000-pound batch of roasted beans that did not meet the company's quality standards. Company policy would not allow such beans to be sold with the Starbucks name on it. However, it could be reprocessed, at which time it could be sold by Starbucks' retail stores, or it could be sold as is on the wholesale coffee-bean market.

Assume that the beans were initially purchased for $2,000, and the total cost of roasting the batch was $1,500, including $500 of variable cost and $1,000 of fixed costs (primarily depreciation on the equipment).

The wholesale price at which Starbucks could sell the beans was $2.65 per pound. Purchasers would pay the shipping costs from the Starbucks plant to their individual warehouses.

If the beans were reprocessed, the processing cost would be $600 because the beans would not require as much processing as new beans. All $600 would be additional costs, that is, costs that would not be incurred without the reprocessing. The beans would be sold to the retail stores for $3.70 per pound, and Starbucks would have to pay an average of $.20 per pound to ship the beans to the stores.

1. Should Starbucks sell the beans on the market as is for $2.65 per pound, or should the company reprocess the beans and sell them through its own retail stores? Why?
2. Compute the amount of extra profit Starbucks earns from the alternative you selected in number 1 compared to what it would earn from the other alternative.
3. What cost numbers in the problem were irrelevant to your analysis? Explain why they were irrelevant.

Cases

6-64 Make or Buy

The Minnetonka Corporation, which produces and sells to wholesalers a highly successful line of water skis, has decided to diversify to stabilize sales throughout the year. The company is considering the production of cross-country skis.

After considerable research, a cross-country ski line has been developed. Because of the conservative nature of the company management, however, Minnetonka's president has decided to introduce only one type of the new skis for this coming winter. If the product is a success, further expansion in future years will be initiated.

The ski selected is a mass-market ski with a special binding. It will be sold to wholesalers for $80 per pair. Because of available capacity, no additional fixed charges will be incurred to produce the skis. A $100,000 fixed charge will be absorbed by the skis, however, to allocate a fair share of the company's present fixed costs to the new product.

Using the estimated sales and production of 10,000 pair of skis as the expected volume, the accounting department has developed the following costs per pair of skis and bindings:

Direct labor	$35
Direct materials	30
Total overhead	15
Total	$80

Minnetonka has approached a subcontractor to discuss the possibility of purchasing the bindings. The purchase price of the bindings from the subcontractor would be $5.25 per binding, or $10.50 per pair. If the Minnetonka Corporation accepts the purchase proposal, it is predicted that direct-labor and variable-overhead costs would be reduced by 10% and direct-materials costs would be reduced by 20%.

1. Should the Minnetonka Corporation make or buy the bindings? Show calculations to support your answer.
2. What would be the maximum purchase price acceptable to the Minnetonka Corporation for the bindings? Support your answer with an appropriate explanation.
3. Instead of sales of 10,000 pairs of skis, revised estimates show sales volume at 12,500 pairs. At this new volume, additional equipment, at an annual rental of $10,000, must be acquired to manu-facture the bindings. This incremental cost would be the only additional fixed cost required, even if sales increased to 30,000 pairs. (The 30,000 level is the goal for the third year of production.) Under these circumstances, should the Minnetonka Corporation make or buy the bindings? Show calculations to support your answer.
4. The company has the option of making and buying at the same time. What would be your answer to number 3 if this alternative were considered? Show calculations to support your answer.
5. What nonquantifiable factors should the Minnetonka Corporation consider in determining whether they should make or buy the bindings?

6-65 Make or Buy

The Rohr Company's old equipment for making subassemblies is worn out. The company is considering two courses of action: (a) completely replacing the old equipment with new equipment or (b) buying subassemblies from a reliable outside supplier, who has quoted a unit price of $1 on a seven-year contract for a minimum of 50,000 units per year.

Production was 60,000 units in each of the past two years. Future needs for the next seven years are not expected to fluctuate beyond 50,000 to 70,000 units per year. Cost records for the past two years reveal the following unit costs of manufacturing the subassembly:

Direct materials	$ .30
Direct labor	.35
Variable overhead	.10
Fixed overhead (including $.10 depreciation and $.10 for direct departmental fixed overhead)	.25
	$1.00

The new equipment will cost $188,000 cash, will last seven years, and will have a disposal value of $20,000. The current disposal value of the old equipment is $10,000.

The sales representative for the new equipment has summarized her position as follows: The increase in machine speeds will reduce direct labor and variable overhead by 35¢ per unit. Consider last year's experience of one of your major competitors with identical equipment. They produced 100,000 units under operating conditions very comparable to yours and showed the following unit costs.

Direct materials	$.30
Direct labor	.05
Variable overhead	.05
Fixed overhead, including depreciation of $.24	.40
Total	$.80

For purposes of this case, assume that any idle facilities cannot be put to alternative use. Also assume that 5¢ of the old Rohr unit cost is allocated fixed overhead that will be unaffected by the decision.

1. The president asks you to compare the alternatives on a total-annual-cost basis and on a per-unit basis for annual needs of 60,000 units. Which alternative seems more attractive?

2. Would your answer to number 1 change if the needs were 50,000 units? 70,000 units? At what volume level would Rohr be indifferent between making and buying subassemblies? Show your computations.

3. What factors, other than the preceding ones, should the accountant bring to the attention of management to assist them in making their decision? Include the considerations that might be applied to the outside supplier.

6-66 Analysis with Contribution Income Statement

The following data have been condensed from LaGrande Corporation's report of 2004 operations (in millions of euros):

	Variable	Fixed	Total
Manufacturing cost of goods sold	€400	€180	€580
Selling and administrative expenses	140	60	200
Sales			900

1. Prepare the 2004 income statement in contribution form, ignoring income taxes.

2. LaGrande's operations have been fairly stable from year to year. In planning for the future, top management is considering several options for changing the annual pattern of operations. You are asked to perform an analysis of their estimated effects. Use your contribution income statement as a framework to compute the estimated operating income (in millions) under each of the following separate and unrelated assumptions:

   a. Assume that a 10% reduction in selling prices would cause a 30% increase in the physical volume of goods manufactured and sold.

   b. Assume that an annual expenditure of €30 million for a special sales promotion campaign would enable the company to increase its physical volume by 10% with no change in selling prices.

   c. Assume that a basic redesign of manufacturing operations would increase annual fixed manufacturing costs by €80 million and decrease variable manufacturing costs by 15% per product unit, but with no effect on physical volume or selling prices.

   d. Assume that a basic redesign of selling and administrative operations would double the annual fixed expenses for selling and administration and increase the variable expenses for selling and administration by 25% per product unit, but would also increase physical volume by 20%. Selling prices would be increased by 5%.

   e. Would you prefer to use the absorption form of income statement for the preceding analyses? Explain.

3. Discuss the desirability of alternatives a through d in number 2. If only one alternative could be selected, which would you choose? Explain.

EXCEL Application Exercise

6-67 Identifying Relevant Revenue, Costs, and Income Effects

Goal: Create an Excel spreadsheet to assist with sell-or-process-further decisions by identifying the relevant revenue, costs, and income effects. Use the results to answer questions about your findings.

Scenario: Mussina Chemical Company has asked you to prepare an analysis to help them make decisions about whether to sell joint products at the split-off point or process them further. The background data for the analysis appears in the Fundamental Assignment Material 6-A2. Prepare the analysis report using a format similar to Exhibit 6-2.

When you have completed your spreadsheet, answer the following questions:

1. How should the $117,000 be allocated to the three products?

2. Is the company currently making the right processing decisions? Explain.

3. If the company alters its processing decisions, what would be the expected combined operating income from the three products?

Step-by-Step:
1. Open a new Excel spreadsheet.
2. In column A, create a bold-faced heading that contains the following:
   Row 1: Chapter 6 Decision Guideline
   Row 2: Mussina Chemical Company
   Row 3: Sell-or-Process-Further Analysis
   Row 4: Today's Date
3. Merge and center the four heading rows across columns A through J.
4. In row 7, create the following bold-faced column headings:
   Column B: Chemical Product A
   Skip two columns
   Column E: Chemical Product B
   Skip two columns
   Column H: Chemical Product C
5. Merge and center the heading in row 7, column B across columns B through D.
   Merge and center the heading in row 7, column E across columns E through G.
   Merge and center the heading in row 7, column H across columns H through J.
6. In row 8, create the following center-justified column headings:
   Column B: Sell at Split-Off
   Column C: Process Further
   Column D: Difference
   Column E: Sell at Split-Off
   Column F: Process Further
   Column G: Difference
   Column H: Sell at Split-Off
   Column I : Process Further
   Column J : Difference
7. Change the format of the column headings in row 8 to permit the titles to be displayed on multiple lines within a single cell.

Alignment tab:	Wrap Text:	Checked

8. In column A, create the following bold-faced row headings:
   Row 9: Revenues
   Row 10: Costs beyond Split-Off
   Skip a row
   Row 11: Income Effects
   Note: Adjust width of column A to accommodate row headings.

9. Use the scenario data to fill in revenues and costs beyond split-off amounts for each of the products.
10. Use appropriate formulas to calculate the difference and income effects columns for each product as absolute values.
    =ABS(*formula*)
11. Format all amounts as

Number:	Category:	Accounting
	Decimal places:	0
	Symbol:	$

12. Change the format of the costs beyond split-off amounts to not display a dollar symbol.
13. Change the format of the income effects amounts to display as bold.
14. Change the format of the revenues amounts to display a top border, using the default line style.

Border tab:	Icon:	Top Border

15. Change the format of the costs beyond split-off amounts to display a bottom border, using the default line style.

Border tab: Icon: Bottom Border

16. Change the format of Row 7, Column B to display an outline border, using the default line style.

Border tab: Presets: Outline

Repeat this step for Column E.
Repeat this step for Column H.

17. Save your work to disk, and print a copy for your files.
Note: Print your spreadsheet using landscape in order to ensure that all columns appear on one page.

Collaborative Learning Exercise

6-68 Outsourcing

A popular term for make-or-buy decisions is *outsourcing decisions.* There are many examples of outsourcing, from **Nike**'s outsourcing of nearly all its production activities to small firms' outsourcing of their payroll activities. Especially popular outsourcing activities are warehousing and computer systems.

The purpose of this exercise is to share information on different types of outsourcing decisions. It can be done in small groups or as an entire class. Each student should pick an article from the literature that tells about a particular company's outsourcing decision. There are many such articles: a recent electronic search of the business literature turned up more than 4,000 articles. An easy way to find such an article is to search an electronic database of business literature. Magazines that have published outsourcing articles include *Fortune, Forbes, Business Week,* and *Strategic Finance.* Many business sections of newspapers also include such articles. The *Wall Street Journal* usually has a couple of articles on outsourcing each month.

1. List as many details about the outsourcing decision as you can. Include the type of activity that is being outsourced, the size of the outsourcing, and the type of company providing the outsourcing service.
2. Explain why the company decided to outsource the activity. If reasons are not given in the article, prepare a list of reasons that you think influenced the decision.
3. What disadvantages are there to outsourcing the activity?
4. Be prepared to make a 3- to 5-minute presentation to the rest of the group or to the class covering your answers to numbers 1, 2, and 3.

Internet Exercise   **www.prenhall.com/horngren**

6-68 Green Mountain Coffee Company

How do firms determine what type of information is useful for a given decision? Is it possible for firms to have too much information? While a look at a firm's Web site provides us with lots of information, not all of it is necessarily useful for a particular decision. Let's look at the **Green Mountain Coffee Company** and see what information on the site would be useful for some specific decisions.

1. Go to the home page of Green Mountain Coffee at http://www.greenmountaincoffee.com. What are the major topics on which a user can click and be taken to a page with more detailed information? Would you likely find the same type of information if you clicked on the links to any one of these? Why do you suppose Green Mountain Coffee chose those particular subtopics for its home page?
2. Where would you look on the site if you wanted to know more about Green Mountain Coffee's financial information? Did the company make a profit for the last year? What was the major expense that the firm encountered? Did the firm pay any dividends last year? If you were interested in an income-producing stock, would you want to invest in Green Mountain Coffee Roasters?

3. Which link would you want to use if you wanted to gain knowledge concerning differences in coffees? Click on this link now. This page has additional links about coffee. Which one(s) are likely to provide information to help you learn about differences in coffees? Click on one of the links you just identified. What type of information about coffee differences does it provide? Did your link provide any information concerning costs as being a difference? Do you think that this would be a difference between coffees?

4. The site provides extensive information about social and environmental initiatives. What areas in particular does the firm highlight? Is this information useful in helping determine if the company's coffee products taste good? What about the quality of the product? Would this information be useful to a potential investor in Green Mountain Coffee's common stock?

The Master Budget

CHAPTER

7

LEARNING OBJECTIVES
When you have finished studying this chapter, you should be able to:

1. Explain the major features and advantages of a master budget.
2. Follow the principal steps in preparing a master budget.
3. Prepare the operating budget and the supporting schedules.
4. Prepare the financial budget.
5. Explain the difficulties of sales forecasting.
6. Anticipate possible human relations problems caused by budgets.
7. Use a spreadsheet to develop a budget (Appendix 7).

If you have ever traveled, you will know that there is a

big difference between staying in a cheap motel and staying in a five-star, world-class hotel. You can think of the difference as that of riding in an old Ford Pinto versus riding in a Rolls-Royce. The first takes care of your basic needs, but the second surrounds you in comfort and luxury, catering to your every whim. The experience of staying in a luxurious hotel can simply take your breath away. No one knows that better than the managers of the **Ritz-Carlton** chain of hotels. After all, the word *ritzy,* which means glamorous and luxurious, is actually derived from the name of the Ritz Hotel. Thanks to fierce competition in the industry, though, Ritz-Carlton managers have their share of challenges in maintaining standards that keep their hotels successful.

What does it take to run a world-class hotel successfully? Good location, exquisite food, luxury, personalized service, and quality are all essential ingredients. But you might be surprised to learn that at the Ritz-Carlton hotels, the budgeting process is also a key to success. According to Ralph Vick, former general manager of the Phoenix Ritz-Carlton, "Budgets are crucial to the ultimate financial success of our hotels." Why are budgets so important? Mainly because they serve as a road map toward achieving goals. Budgets are a manager's tool to understand, plan, and control operations, and Ritz-Carlton wants to give its managers the best tools possible. As a result, the company takes the budgeting process very seriously.

At the Ritz-Carlton hotels, all employees, from the hotel manager, to the controller, to the newest housekeeper, are involved in the budgeting process. Working in teams, they set budget targets for the expenses they can control. These target figures help not only in planning, but also in controlling and evaluating employee performance. Managers compare actual results with previously budgeted target figures, and they

A Ritz-Carlton hotel projects an image of quality. High quality is expensive, so during the master budgeting process Ritz-Carlton managers must assess the planned expenditures for quality-enhancing features versus the added revenues these features will bring.

evaluate workers based on the differences. Even nonfinancial measures of performance are important. Ritz-Carlton managers use nonfinancial measures of quality and customer satisfaction in addition to financial reports to evaluate and reward employees.

Planning is the key to good management. This statement is certainly true for Ritz-Carlton, and it is also true for other types of business organizations—small, family-owned companies, large corporations, government agencies, and nonprofit organizations—as well as for individuals. For example, most successful students who earn good grades, finance their education, and finish their degrees on time do so because they plan their time, their work, and their recreation. These students are budgeting their scarce resources to make the best use of their time, money, and energy. Similarly, business owners and managers need to budget their resources—which include everything from raw materials to human resources to facilities—to make the best and most profitable use of what they have to work with. Budgeting can cover such diverse issues as how much time to spend sanding a piece of wood to how much money the company will allot to research and development in the coming year. Company budgets always aim to squeeze the most out of available resources.

In this chapter, we will look at the uses and benefits of budgets and consider the construction of the master budget. ■

Budgets and the Organization

Most people associate the word *budget* with limitations on spending. For example, governments often approve spending budgets for their various agencies. Then they expect the agencies to keep their expenditures within the limits prescribed by the budget. In contrast, most business organizations use budgets to focus attention on company operations and finances, not just to limit spending. Budgets highlight potential problems and advantages early, allowing managers to take steps to avoid these problems or use the advantages wisely.

A budget is a tool that aids managers in both their planning and control functions. Budgets help managers plan for the future. However, managers also use them to evaluate what happened in the past. They use budgets as a benchmark—a measure of estimated or desired performance—against which they compare actual performance. Keeping score is an American tradition, whether on the football field or in the boardroom, and budgets provide the standards for evaluating and "scoring" the company "players."

Recent surveys show just how valuable budgets can be. One study of over 150 organizations in North America listed budgeting as the most frequently used cost-management tool. It was also the tool with the highest value to the organization. Study after study has shown the budget to be one of the most widely used and highest rated cost-management tools for cost reduction and control. Advocates of budgeting go so far as to claim that the process of budgeting forces a manager to become a better administrator and puts planning in the forefront of the manager's mind. Actually, many seemingly healthy businesses have died because managers failed to draw up, monitor, and adjust budgets to changing conditions. While there has always been debate over the value of budgeting, as indicated in the Business First box that follows, the vast majority of managers continue to use budgeting as an effective cost-management tool.

Advantages of Budgets

In Chapter 1, we defined a budget as a quantitative expression of a plan of action. A budget is an example of a formal business plan. Sometimes plans are informal, perhaps even unwritten. Such plans might work in a small organization, but as an organization grows, seat-of-the-pants planning is not enough. A more formal plan—a budgetary system—becomes a necessity.

BUDGETING: VALUE DRIVER OR VALUE BUSTER?

Recently, some controversy has developed over the value of budgeting. Some critics claim that the budgeting process is not an effective cost-management tool. Critics focus on three problems with the budgeting process: (1) The process is too time-consuming and expensive; (2) the resulting annual budgets, operating and financial, are not accurate and hence not relevant—especially in industries where marketplace change is frequent and unpredictable; and (3) evaluating performance against a budget causes managers to bias their budgets, resulting in inaccurate planning.

Some studies suggest that the annual budgeting process can take up to 30% of management's time. Estimates place Ford Motor Company's cost of budgeting at $1.2 billion a year. Even after spending these resources, some companies react to changing economic conditions by ignoring the budget rather than changing it. In contrast, successful budget processes use the budget as the basis for making systematic adjustments to changing economic conditions.

Performance evaluation using budgets creates special problems if not done carefully. For a few companies, once they set the budget, managers attempt to manipulate performance measures to meet budget targets. This can lead to unethical behavior such as "cooking the books" (reporting false accounting numbers) or putting undue pressure on employees to meet budgeting numbers using whatever means possible. **WorldCom** and **Enron** used budgets inappropriately, motivating managers to do whatever was necessary to meet targeted goals. In other cases, managers anticipate the effect of performance evaluations when setting their budgets. Consequently, they present biased planning information to make sure that the budget targets are reachable.

Are companies that have experienced problems with their budgeting process abandoning traditional budgeting? No. Instead, they are modifying their approach to budgeting. Some companies are tying their budgets to benchmarks based on actual performance of peers and best-in-class operations. Some are separating planning budgets from control budgets. Most are tying their budgeting process more closely to their overall strategy. They then measure performance both in financial terms, such as cost to income, and in nonfinancial terms, such as time to market for new products or services, and compare actual performance to industry benchmarks in addition to budgeted performance.

Most managers still agree that budgeting, correctly used, has significant value to management. A recent survey of more than 150 North American organizations reported that budgeting was used by over 92% of the companies and was ranked among the top three cost-management tools.

Companies such as **Allstate**, **Owens Corning**, **Sprint**, **Battelle**, and **Texaco** are modifying their approach to budgeting by implementing new technologies. For example, at Battelle's Pacific Northwest National Laboratory, an intranet is used to reduce the time and expense of developing the annual budget. The new system enables support staff and managers to input their budget data and plans using this corporate intranet, eliminating the need for central business planning staff to upload data and the numerous changes made during the budgeting process. According to managers at Battelle, "This results in higher quality and more accurate budgeting, reporting, and analysis."

Sources: Adapted from R. Banham, "Better Budgets" *Journal of Accountancy,* February 2000, pp. 37–40, J. Hope and R. Fraser, "Who Needs Budgets?" *Harvard Business Review,* February 2003, pp. 108–115, P. Smith, C. Goranson, M. Astley, "Intranet Budgeting," *Strategic Finance,* May 2003, pp. 30–33, T. Hatch and W. Stratton, "Scorecarding in North America: Who is Doing What?" Paper presented at the CAM–I/CMS 3rd quarter meeting, Portland, Oregon, September 10, 2002, and M. Jensen, "Corporate Budgeting Is Broken, Let's Fix It," *Harvard Business Review,* (November 2001), pp. 94–101.

Skeptical managers have claimed, "I face too many uncertainties and complications to make budgeting worthwhile for me." Be wary of such claims. All managers do some kind of planning, and planning and budgeting are especially important in uncertain environments. A budget allows systematic rather than chaotic reaction to change. For example, the Natural Resources Group of **W. R. Grace & Co.** greatly reduced its planned expansion in reaction to a worldwide abundance of oil and gas. A top executive, quoted in the company's annual report, stated that "management used the business planning process to adjust to changes in operating conditions."

Three major benefits of budgeting are as follows:

1. Budgeting compels managers to think ahead by formalizing their responsibilities for planning.
2. Budgeting provides definite expectations that are the best framework for judging subsequent performance.
3. Budgeting aids managers in coordinating their efforts, so that the plans of an organization's subunits meet the objectives of the organization as a whole.

Let's look more closely at each of these benefits.

Formalization of Planning Budgeting forces managers to think ahead—to anticipate and prepare for changing conditions. The budgeting process makes planning an explicit management responsibility. Too often, managers operate on a day-to-day basis, extinguishing one business brush fire after another. They simply have "no time" for any tough-minded thinking beyond the next day's problems. Planning takes a back seat to or is actually obliterated by daily pressures.

The trouble with the day-to-day approach to managing an organization is that objectives are never crystallized. Managers react to current events rather than planning for the future. To prepare a budget, a manager should set goals and objectives and establish policies to aid their achievement. The objectives are the destination points, and budgets are the road maps guiding us to those destinations. Without goals and objectives, company operations lack direction, managers do not foresee problems, and results are difficult to interpret afterward.

Framework for Judging Performance Budgeted goals and performance are generally a better basis for judging actual results than is past performance. The news that a company had sales of $100 million this year, as compared with $80 million the previous year, may or may not indicate that the company has been effective and has met company objectives. Perhaps sales should have been $110 million this year. The major drawback of using historical results for judging current performance is that inefficiencies may be concealed in the past performance. Changes in economic conditions, technology, personnel, competition, and so forth also limit the usefulness of comparisons with the past.

MAKING MANAGERIAL DECISIONS

Level 3 Communications has focused its business strategy on providing "a broadband, continuously upgradeable, international IP infrastructure for leading Web-centric companies." Due to poor economic conditions and the impact from repositioning the company, the company had operating losses for several years. The loss from continuing operations decreased from $4,978 million in 2001 to $858 million in 2002. Suppose the company budgeted to breakeven for 2002. Evaluate performance for 2002.

Answer
Comparing Level 3's performance in 2002 to that in 2001 makes it appear that performance improved dra-matically because the loss was $4,120 million less in 2002 than it was in 2001. However, the loss was $858 million more than budgeted, showing that the company did worse than expected. During this period Level 3 was implementing a major shift in strategy to recognize the new Internet economy and a change in targeted market to major Web-centric companies such as America Online, AT&T Wireless, and Microsoft. The company stated that it is "well ahead of our original plans to position ourselves as the leading provider of broadband infrastructure services." Comparing actual results to plans gives a better picture of how well Level 3 is meeting its objectives than would a comparison to past results.

Communication and Coordination Budgets tell employees what is expected of them. Nobody likes to drift along, not knowing what the boss expects or hopes to achieve. A good budget process communicates both from the top down *and* from the bottom up. Top management makes clear the goals and objectives of the organization in its budgetary directives. Employees and lower-level managers then inform higher-level managers how they plan to achieve the goals and objectives.

Budgets also help managers coordinate objectives. For example, a budget forces purchasing personnel to integrate their plans with production requirements, while production managers use the sales budget and delivery schedule to help them anticipate and plan for the employees and physical facilities they will need. Similarly, financial officers use the sales budget, purchasing requirements, and so forth to anticipate the company's need for cash. Thus, the budgetary process forces managers to visualize the relationship of their department's activities to those of other departments and the company as a whole.

Types of Budgets

Businesses use several different types of budgets. The most forward-looking budget is the **strategic plan,** which sets the overall goals and objectives of the organization. Some business analysts won't classify the strategic plan as an actual budget, though, because it does not deal with a specific time frame and it does not produce forecasted financial statements. In any case, the strategic plan leads to **long-range planning,** which produces forecasted financial statements for five- to ten-year periods. The financial statements are estimates of what management would like to see in the company's future financial statements. Decisions made during long-range planning include addition or deletion of product lines, design and location of new plants, acquisitions of buildings and equipment, and other long-term commitments. Companies coordinate their long-range plans with **capital budgets,** which detail the planned expenditures for facilities, equipment, new products, and other long-term investments.

Long-range plans and budgets give the company direction and goals for the future, while short-term plans and budgets guide day-to-day operations. Managers who pay attention only to short-term budgets will quickly lose sight of long-term goals. Similarly, managers who pay attention only to the long-term budget could wind up mismanaging day-to-day operations. There has to be a happy medium that allows managers to pay attention to their short-term budgets while still keeping an eye on long-term plans. Enter the master budget.

The **master budget** is an extensive analysis of the first year of the long-range plan. It summarizes the planned activities of all subunits of an organization—sales, production, distribution, and finance. It also quantifies targets for sales, cost-driver activity, purchases, production, net income, cash position, and any other objective that management specifics. The master budget expresses these amounts in the form of forecasted financial statements and supporting operating schedules. These supporting schedules provide the information that is too highly detailed to appear in the actual financial statements.

Thus, the master budget is a periodic business plan that includes a coordinated set of detailed operating schedules and financial statements. It includes forecasts of sales, expenses, cash receipts and disbursements, and balance sheets. Master budgets (also called *pro forma statements*, another term for forecasted financial statements) might consist of 12 monthly budgets for the year or perhaps monthly budgets for only the first quarter and quarterly budgets for the three remaining quarters. In the process of preparing the master budget, managers make many important decisions about how to best deploy the organization's resources.

Continuous budgets or **rolling budgets** are a very common form of master budgets that simply add a month in the future as the month just ended is dropped. In this way, budgeting becomes an ongoing instead of periodic process. Continuous budgets force managers to always think about the next 12 months, not just the remaining months in a fixed budgeting cycle. As they add a new twelfth month to a continuous budget, managers may update the other 11 months as well. Then they can compare actual monthly results with both the original plan and the most recently revised plan.

strategic plan
A plan that sets the overall goals and objectives of the organization.

long-range planning
Producing forecasted financial statements for five- to ten-year periods.

capital budget
A budget that details the planned expenditures for facilities, equipment, new products, and other long-term investments.

O B J E C T I V E 1

Explain the major features and advantages of a master budget.

master budget
An extensive analysis of the first year of the long-range plan. It summarizes the planned activities of all subunits of an organization.

continuous budget (rolling budget)
A common form of master budget that adds a month in the future as the month just ended is dropped.

Components of Master Budget

The terms used to describe specific budget schedules vary from organization to organization. However, most master budgets have common elements. The usual master budget for a nonmanufacturing company has the following components:

A. Operating budget
   1. Sales budget (and other cost-driver budgets as necessary)
   2. Purchases budget
   3. Cost-of-goods-sold budget
   4. Operating expenses budget
   5. Budgeted statement of income
B. Financial budget
   1. Capital budget
   2. Cash budget
   3. Budgeted balance sheet

Exhibit 7-1 shows the relationships among the various parts of a master budget for a nonmanufacturing company. In addition to these categories, manufacturing companies that maintain inventories prepare ending inventory budgets and additional budgets for each type of resource activity such as labor, materials, and factory overhead.

operating budget (profit plan)
A major part of a master budget that focuses on the income statement and its supporting schedules.

The two major parts of a master budget are the operating budget and the financial budget. The **operating budget** focuses on the income statement and its supporting schedules. Although sometimes called the **profit plan**, an operating budget may show a budgeted

Exhibit 7-1
Preparation of Master Budget for Nonmanufacturing Company

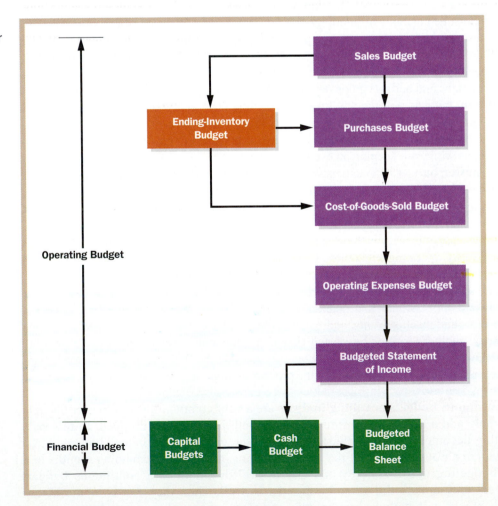

loss, or may even be used to budget expenses in an organization or agency with no sales revenues. In contrast, the **financial budget** focuses on the effects that the operating budget and other plans (such as capital budgets and repayments of debt) will have on cash.

In addition to the master budget, there are countless forms of special budgets and related reports. For example, a report might detail goals and objectives for improvements in quality or customer satisfaction during the budget period.

financial budget
The part of a master budget that focuses on the effects that the operating budget and other plans (such as capital budgets and repayments of debt) will have on cash.

Preparing the Master Budget

Let's return to Exhibit 7-1 and trace the preparation of the master budget components. Follow each step carefully and completely. Although the process may seem largely mechanical, remember that the master budgeting process generates key decisions regarding all aspects of the company's value chain. Therefore, the first draft of the budget leads to decisions that prompt subsequent drafts before top management accepts a final budget.

The Cooking Hut

We will illustrate the budgeting process using the Cooking Hut Company (CHC), a local retailer of a wide variety of kitchen and dining room items such as coffeemakers, silverware, and table linens. The company rents a retail store in a midsize community near Denver. CHC's management prepares a continuous budget to aid financial and operating decisions. For simplicity in this illustration, the planning horizon is only four months, April through July. In the past, sales have increased during this season. However, the company's collections have always lagged well behind its sales. As a result, CHC has often found itself pressed to come up with the cash for purchases, employee wages, and other operating outlays. To help meet this cash squeeze, CHC has used short-term loans from local banks, paying them back when cash comes in. The firm plans to keep on using this system.

Exhibit 7-2 is the closing balance sheet for the fiscal year ending March 31, 20X4. Sales in March were $40,000. Monthly sales are forecasted as follows:

April	$50,000
May	$80,000
June	$60,000
July	$50,000
August	$40,000

Management expects future sales collections to follow past experience: Customers pay 60% of the sales in cash and 40% on credit. CHC collects all credit accounts in the month following the sales. The $16,000 of accounts receivable on March 31 represents credit sales made in March (40% of $40,000). Uncollectible accounts are negligible and thus ignored. For simplicity's sake, we will ignore all local, state, and federal taxes for this illustration.

Because deliveries from suppliers and customer demands are uncertain, at the end of each month CHC wants to have on hand a basic inventory of items valued at $20,000 plus 80% of the expected cost of goods sold for the following month. The cost of merchandise sold averages 70% of sales. Therefore, the inventory on March 31 is $20,000 + .7(.8 × April sales of $50,000) = $20,000 + $28,000 = $48,000. The purchase terms available to CHC are net, 30 days. CHC pays for each month's purchases as follows: 50% during that month and 50% during the next month. Therefore, the accounts payable balance on March 31 is 50% of March's purchases, or $33,600 × .5 = $16,800.

CHC pays wages and commissions semimonthly, half a month after they are earned. They are divided into two portions: monthly fixed wages of $2,500 and commissions, equal to 15% of sales, which we will assume are uniform throughout each month. Therefore, the

Exhibit 7-2

The Cooking Hut
Company
Balance Sheet
March 31, 20X4

Assets		
Current assets		
Cash	$10,000	
Accounts receivable, net (.4 × March sales of $40,000)	16,000	
Merchandise inventory, $20,000 + .7 (.8 × April sales of $50,000)	48,000	
Unexpired insurance	1,800	$ 75,800
Plant assets		
Equipment, fixtures, and other	$37,000	
Accumulated depreciation	12,800	24,200
Total assets		$100,000

Liabilities and Owners' Equity		
Current liabilities		
Accounts payable (.5 × March purchases of $33,600)	$16,800	
Accrued wages and commissions payable ($1,250 + $3,000)	4,250	$ 21,050
Owners' equity		78,950
Total liabilities and owners' equity		$100,000

March 31 balance of accrued wages and commissions payable is (.5 × $2,500) + .5(.15 × $40,000) = $1,250 + $3,000 = $4,250. CHC will pay this $4,250 on April 15.

In addition to buying new fixtures for $3,000 cash in April, CHC has other monthly expenses as follows:

Miscellaneous expenses	5% of sales, paid as incurred
Rent	$2,000, paid as incurred
Insurance	$200 expiration per month
Depreciation, including new fixtures	$500 per month

The company wants to have a minimum of $10,000 as a cash balance at the end of each month. To keep this simple, we will assume that CHC can borrow or repay loans in multiples of $1,000. Management plans to borrow no more cash than necessary and to repay as promptly as possible. Assume that borrowing occurs at the beginning and repayment at the end of the months in question. CHC pays interest in cash when it repays the related loan. The interest rate is 12% per year.

Steps in Preparing the Master Budget

OBJECTIVE

Follow the principal steps
in preparing a master
budget.

The principal steps in preparing the master budget are:

Basic Data

1. Using the data given, prepare the following detailed schedules for each of the months of the planning horizon:
   a. Sales budget
   b. Cash collections from customers
   c. Purchases budget
   d. Disbursements for purchases
   e. Operating expense budget
   f. Disbursements for operating expenses

	Data	Source of Data
Sales	$240,000	Schedule a
Cost of goods sold	168,000	Schedule c
Gross margin	$ 72,000	
Operation expenses:		
Wages and commissions $46,000		Schedule e
Rent 8,000		Schedule e
Miscellaneous 12,000		Schedule e
Insurance 800		Schedule e
Depreciation 2,000	68,800	Schedule e
Income from operations	$ 3,200	
Interest expense	440	Exhibit 7-4
Net income	$ 2,760	

Exhibit 7-3
The Cooking Hut Company
Budgeted Income Statement for Four Months Ending July 31, 20X4

Operating Budget

2. Using these schedules, prepare a budgeted income statement for the four months ending July 31, 20X4 (Exhibit 7-3).

Financial Budget

3. Using the data given and the supporting schedules, prepare the following forecasted financial statements:
   a. Capital budget
   b. Cash budget, including details of borrowings, repayments, and interest for each month of the planning horizon (Exhibit 7-4)
   c. Budgeted balance sheet as of July 31, 20X4 (Exhibit 7-5)

	April	May	June	July
Beginning cash balance	$ 10,000	$ 10,550	$ 10,980	$ 10,080
Minimum cash balance desired	10,000	10,000	10,000	10,000
Available cash balance (x)	$ 0	$ 550	$ 980	$ 80
Cash receipts and disbursements:				
Collections from customers (Schedule b*)	$ 46,000	$ 68,000	$ 68,000	$ 54,000
Payments for merchandise (Schedule d)	(42,700)	(48,300)	(40,600)	(32,900)
Payments for operating expenses (Schedule f)	(13,750)	(18,250)	(18,000)	(15,250)
Purchase of new fixtures (given)	(3,000)			
Net cash receipts and disbursements (y)	$ (13,450)	$ 1,450	$ 9,400	$ 5,850
Excess (deficiency) of cash before financing (x + y)	$ (13,450)	$ 2,000	$ 10,380	$ 5,930
Financing:				
Borrowing (at beginning of month)	$ 14,000†			
Repayments (at end of month)	—	$ (1,000)	$(10,000)	$ (3,000)
Interest payments (at 12% per year‡)	—	(20)	(300)	(120)
Total cash increase (decrease) from financing (z)	$ 14,000	$ (1,020)	$(10,300)	$ (3,120)
Ending cash balance (beginning balance + y + z)	$ 10,550	$ 10,980	$ 10,080	$ 12,810

* Letters are keyed to the explanation in the text.
† Borrowing and repayment of principal are made in multiples of $1,000, at an interest rate of 12% per year.
‡ Interest computations: .12 × $1,000 × 2/12; .12 × $10,000 × 3/12; .12 × $3,000 × 4/12.

Exhibit 7-4
The Cooking Hut Company
Cash Budget for Four Months Ending July 31, 20X4

Exhibit 7-5
The Cooking Hut
Company
*Budgeted Balance
Sheet July 31, 20X4*

Assets		
Current assets		
Cash (Exhibit 7-4)	$ 12,810	
Accounts receivable, net (.4 × July sales of $50,000,		
Schedule a)	20,000	
Merchandise inventory (Schedule c)	42,400	
Unexpired insurance ($1,800 − $800)	1,000	$ 76,210
Plant assets		
Equipment, fixtures, and other ($37,000 + $3,000)	$ 40,000	
Accumulated depreciation ($12,800 + $2,000		
depreciation expense)	(14,800)	25,200
Total assets		$101,410

Liabilities and Owners' Equity		
Current liabilities		
Accounts payable (.5 × July purchases of		
$29,400, Schedule c)	$ 14,700	
Accrued wages and commissions payable		
(.5 × $10,000, Schedule e)	5,000	$ 19,700
Owners' equity ($78,950 + $2,760		
net income)		81,710
Total liabilities and owners' equity		$101,410

Note: Beginning balances are used as a start for the computations of unexpired insurance, plant, and owners' equity.

Organizations with effective budget systems have specific guidelines for the steps and timing of budget preparation. Although the details differ, the guidelines invariably include the preceding steps. As we follow these steps to prepare CHC's master budget, be sure that you understand the source of each figure in each schedule and budget.

Step 1: Preparing Basic Data

OBJECTIVE 3

Prepare the operating budget and the supporting schedules.

Step 1a: Sales Budget The sales budget (Schedule a in the following table) is the starting point for budgeting for CHC because inventory levels, purchases, and operating expenses are geared to the expected level of sales. Accurate sales forecasting is essential to effective budgeting. (We consider sales forecasting in a later section of this chapter.) Schedule a includes March sales because they affect cash collections in April. Trace the final column in Schedule a to the first row of Exhibit 7-3. In nonprofit organizations, forecasts of revenue or some level of services are also the focal points for budgeting. Examples are patient revenues and government reimbursement expected by hospitals and donations expected by churches. If an organization generates no revenues, as in the case of municipal fire protection, the "sales" budget simply specifies a desired level of service.

Step 1b: Cash Collections from Customers It is easiest to prepare Schedule b, cash collections, at the same time that we prepare the sales budget. Cash collections from customers include the current month's cash sales plus the previous month's credit sales. We will use total collections in preparing the cash budget—see Exhibit 7-4.

	March	April	May	June	July	April–July Total
Schedule a:						
Sales Budget						
Credit sales, 40%	$16,000	$20,000	$32,000	$24,000	$20,000	
Plus cash						
sales, 60%	24,000	30,000	48,000	36,000	30,000	
Total sales	$40,000	$50,000	$80,000	$60,000	$50,000	$240,000
Schedule b:						
Cash Collections						
Cash sales this month		$30,000	$48,000	$36,000	$30,000	
Plus 100% of last						
month's credit sales		16,000	20,000	32,000	24,000	
Total collections		$46,000	$68,000	$68,000	$54,000	

Step 1c: Purchases Budget After budgeting sales and cash collections, we prepare the purchases budget (Schedule c). The total merchandise needed will be the sum of the desired ending inventory plus the amount needed to fulfill budgeted sales demand. The total need will be partially met by the beginning inventory; the remainder must come from planned purchases. We can compute these purchases as follows:

$$\text{budgeted purchases} = \text{desired ending inventory} + \text{cost of goods sold} - \text{beginning inventory}$$

Trace the total purchases figure in the final column of Schedule c to the second row of Exhibit 7-3.

	March	April	May	June	July	April–July Total
Schedule c:						
Purchases Budget						
Desired ending						
inventory	$48,000*	$64,800	$ 53,600	$48,000	$42,400	
Plus cost of goods						
sold†	28,000	35,000	56,000	42,000	35,000	$168,000
Total needed	$76,000	$99,800	$109,600	$90,000	$77,400	
Less beginning						
inventory	42,400‡	48,000	64,800	53,600	48,000	
Purchases	$33,600	$51,800	$ 44,800	$36,400	$29,400	
Schedule d:						
Disbursements						
for Purchases						
50% of last month's						
purchases		$16,800	$ 25,900	$22,400	$18,200	
Plus 50% of this						
month's purchases		25,900	22,400	18,200	14,700	
Disbursements for						
purchases		$42,700	$ 48,300	$40,600	$32,900	

* $20,000 + (.8 × April cost of goods sold) = $20,000 + .8($35,000) = $48,000.
† .7 × March sales of $40,000 = $28,000; .7 × April sales of $50,000 = $35,000, and so on.
‡ $20,000 + (.8 × March cost of goods sold of $28,000) = $20,000 + $22,400 = $42,400.

Step 1d: Disbursements for Purchases We next use the purchases budget to develop Schedule d, disbursements for purchases. In our example, disbursements include 50% of the current month's purchases and 50% of the previous month's purchases. We will use total disbursements in preparing the cash budget, Exhibit 7-4.

Step 1e: Operating Expense Budget The budgeting of operating expenses depends on several factors. Month-to-month changes in sales volume and other cost-driver activities directly influence many operating expenses. Examples of expenses driven by sales volume include sales commissions and many delivery expenses. Other expenses, such as rent, insurance, depreciation, and salaries, are not influenced by sales within appropriate relevant ranges, and we regard them as fixed. Trace the total operating expenses in the final column of Schedule e, which summarizes these expenses, to the budgeted income statement, Exhibit 7-3.

	March	April	May	June	July	April–July Total
Schedule e: Operating Expense Budget						
Wages (fixed)	$2,500	$ 2,500	$ 2,500	$ 2,500	$ 2,500	
Commissions (15% of current month's sales)	6,000	7,500	12,000	9,000	7,500	
Total wages and commissions	$8,500	$10,000	$14,500	$11,500	$10,000	$46,000
Miscellaneous expenses (5% of current sales)		2,500	4,000	3,000	2,500	12,000
Rent (fixed)		2,000	2,000	2,000	2,000	8,000
Insurance (fixed)		200	200	200	200	800
Depreciation (fixed)		500	500	500	500	2,000
Total operating expenses		$15,200	$21,200	$17,200	$15,200	$68,800

Step 1f: Disbursements for Operating Expenses Disbursements for operating expenses are based on the operating expense budget. Disbursements include 50% of last month's and this month's wages and commissions, and miscellaneous and rent expenses. We will use the total of these disbursements in preparing the cash budget, Exhibit 7-4.

	March	April	May	June	July	April–July Total
Schedule f: Disbursements for Operating Expenses						
Wages and commissions:						
50% of last month's expenses		$ 4,250	$ 5,000	$ 7,250	$ 5,750	
50% of this month's expenses		5,000	7,250	5,750	5,000	
Total wages and commissions		$ 9,250	$12,250	$13,000	$10,750	
Miscellaneous expenses		2,500	4,000	3,000	2,500	
Rent		2,000	2,000	2,000	2,000	
Total disbursements		$13,750	$18,250	$18,000	$15,250	

Step 2: Preparing the Operating Budget

Steps 1a, 1c, and 1e provide enough information to construct a budgeted income statement from operations (Exhibit 7-3). The income statement will be complete after addition of the interest expense, which we can compute only after we prepare the cash budget. Budgeted income from operations is often a benchmark for judging management performance.

Step 3: Preparation of Financial Budget

O B J E C T I V E 4

Prepare the financial budget.

The second major part of the master budget is the financial budget, which consists of the capital budget, cash budget, and ending balance sheet. This chapter focuses on the cash budget and the ending balance sheet. Chapter 11 discusses the capital budget (Step 3a). In our illustration, the $3,000 purchase of new fixtures would be the only item included in the capital budget.

Step 3b: Cash Budget The **cash budget** is a statement of planned cash receipts and disbursements. The cash budget is heavily affected by the level of operations summarized in the budgeted income statement. The cash budget has the following major sections, where the letters *w, x, y,* and *z* refer to the lines in Exhibit 7-4 that summarize the effects of that section:

cash budget
A statement of planned cash receipts and disbursements.

- The available cash balance (x) equals the beginning cash balance less the minimum cash balance desired.
- Cash receipts and disbursements (y):
  1. Cash receipts depend on collections from customers' accounts receivable, cash sales, and on other operating cash income sources such as interest received on notes receivable. Trace total collections from Schedule b to Exhibit 7-4.
  2. Disbursements for purchases depend on the credit terms extended by suppliers and the bill-paying habits of the buyer. Trace payments for merchandise from Schedule d to Exhibit 7-4.
  3. Payroll depends on wage, salary, and commission terms and on payroll dates. Trace wages and commissions from Schedule f to Exhibit 7-4.
  4. Some costs and expenses depend on contractual terms for installment payments, mortgage payments, rents, leases, and miscellaneous items. Trace disbursements for operating expenses from Schedule f to Exhibit 7-4.
  5. Other disbursements include outlays for fixed assets, long-term investments, dividends, and the like. An example is the $3,000 expenditure for new fixtures.
- The cash needed from (or used for) financing (z) depends on the total available cash balance, x in Exhibit 7-4, and the net cash receipts and disbursements, y. If cash available plus net cash receipts less disbursements is negative, borrowing is necessary—Exhibit 7-4 shows that CHC will borrow $14,000 in April to cover the planned deficiency. If it is positive, CHC can repay loans—it repays $1,000, $10,000, and $3,000 in May, June, and July, respectively. This section of the cash budget also generally contains the outlays for interest expense. Trace the calculated interest expense, which in our example equals the total interest payments for the four months, to Exhibit 7-3, which then will be complete.
- The ending cash balance is the beginning cash balance + y + z. Financing, z, has either a positive (borrowing) or a negative (repayment) effect on the cash balance. The illustrative cash budget shows the pattern of short-term, "self-liquidating" financing. Seasonal peaks often result in heavy drains on cash—for merchandise purchases and operating expenses—before the company makes sales and collects cash from customers. The resulting loan is "self-liquidating"—that is, the company uses borrowed money to acquire merchandise for sale, and uses the proceeds from sales to repay the loan. This "working capital cycle" moves from cash to inventory to receivables and back to cash.

Cash budgets help management to avoid having unnecessary idle cash, on the one hand, and unnecessary cash deficiencies, on the other. A well-managed financing program keeps cash balances from becoming too large or too small.

Step 3c: Budgeted Balance Sheet The final step in preparing the master budget is to construct the budgeted balance sheet (Exhibit 7-5) that projects each balance sheet item in accordance with the business plan as expressed in the previous schedules. Specifically, the beginning balances at March 31 would be increased or decreased in light of the expected cash receipts and cash disbursements in Exhibit 7-4 and in light of the effects of noncash items appearing on the income statement in Exhibit 7-3. For example, unexpired insurance would decrease from its balance of $1,800 on March 31 to $1,000 on July 31, even though it is a noncash item.

When management has completed the master budget, it can consider all the major financial statements as a basis for changing the course of events. For example, the initial formulation of the financial statements may prompt management to try new sales strategies to generate more demand. Alternatively, management may explore the effects of various adjustments in the timing of receipts and disbursements. The large cash deficiency in April, for example, may lead to an emphasis on cash sales or an attempt to speed up collection of accounts receivable. In any event, the first draft of the master budget is rarely the final draft. As managers rework it, the budgeting process becomes an integral part of the management process itself—budgeting is planning and communicating. This is particularly true for a new company. Start-up companies require formal business plans but have no historical budgeting process in place. The Business First Box on page 309 describes how two start-up companies—**InfoSpace** and **EncrypTix**—used budgets.

MAKING MANAGERIAL DECISIONS

Some managers may focus on the operating budget, while others may be more concerned with the financial budget. How does the operating budget differ from the financial budget?

Answer

The operating budget focuses on the income statement, which is prepared using accrual accounting. It measures revenues and expenses. Line operating managers usually prepare and use the operating budget. In contrast, the financial budget focuses primarily on cash flow. It measures the receipts and disbursements of cash. Financial managers such as controllers and treasurers use the financial budget. The operating budget is a better measure of overall performance, but the financial budget is essential to plan for cash needs. A lack of cash rather than poor operating performance often gets companies into trouble. Thus, both operating and financial budgets are important to an organization.

Summary Problem For Your Review

You should be sure you understand every step in this chapter's CHC example before you tackle this problem.

PROBLEM

The Country Store is a retail outlet for a variety of hardware and housewares. The owner of The Country Store is eager to prepare a budget for the next quarter, which is typically quite busy. She is most concerned with her cash position because she expects that she will have to borrow to finance purchases in anticipation of sales. She has gathered all the data necessary to prepare the simplified budget shown in Exhibit 7-6. In addition, she will purchase equipment in April for $19,750 cash and pay dividends of $4,000 in June. Review the structure of the example in the chapter and then prepare The Country Store's

BUSINESS FIRST

ENTREPRENEURS, BUSINESS PLANS, AND BUDGETS

The decade of the 1990s saw a flurry of entrepreneurial activities. Start-up companies in a variety of high-tech industries mushroomed into multibillion dollar companies. Consider InfoSpace, Inc., as an example. Naveen Jain, former chairman and chief strategist, founded InfoSpace in April 1996 after leaving Microsoft. Jain took InfoSpace public in December 1998. By March 2000 the market value of InfoSpace stock was $30 billion. Jain's vision for InfoSpace was grand: "When the history of the impending [information] revolution is written, one name will be credited for helping map its route, and powering its progress. InfoSpace." InfoSpace's path to greatness has been somewhat bumpy, as with many dot-coms, but current CEO Jim Voelker has confidence in the company's future, stating "We are focused on our customers and improving product and service quality to maximize our long term growth and profitability."

How do start-up companies get started? An essential component in securing initial funding for a start-up is the development of a business plan. The federal government's Small Business Administration recommends a business plan with three sections:

1. The Business—includes a description of the business, a marketing plan, an assessment of the competition, a listing of operating procedures, and a roster of personnel.
2. Financial Data—includes the following items:
   Loan applications
   Capital equipment and supply list
   Balance sheet
   Break-even analysis
   Pro forma income projections (profit and loss statements):
       Three-year summary
       Detail by month, first year
       Detail by quarters, second and third years
       Assumptions upon which projections were based
   Pro forma cash flow

3. Supporting Documents—includes a variety of legal documents and information about the principals involved, suppliers, customers, etc.

Financial data are an important part of a business plan, the centerpiece of which is the budget. Without a well-developed budget, companies such as InfoSpace would not be able to raise the capital needed to start and expand their businesses. The budgeted income statement and budgeted cash flow statement are essential to predicting the future prospects of any business. They are especially critical to assessing the prospects of a new company that has little history to analyze.

The importance of a budget to a start-up company was emphasized by Jim Rowan, former senior vice president of Sun America, Inc., who left to form a new company, EncrypTix. He raised $36 million in investment funding to spin EncrypTix off from Stamps.com. The company focuses on Internet delivery and storage of tickets, coupons, and vouchers. Rowan stated, "The key thing for a start-up is to develop a budget and put it like a stake in the ground, so you can measure against it. It's not a ceiling, it's not carved in stone, but you have to have something that's a benchmark."

Budgeting is not often the most exciting task for entrepreneurs. However, lack of a credible budget is one of the main reasons venture capitalists will refuse funding for start-up companies. Further, it is one of the main causes of failure of the companies themselves. Anyone wanting to be an entrepreneur would be well advised to study budgeting and learn how it can be a powerful tool both for managing the company and for promoting the company to potential investors.

Sources: Adapted from Small Business Administration, *The Business Plan: Roadmap to Success* (http://www.sba.gov/starting/indexbusplans.html); InfoSpace 2000 Annual Report and 2003 First Quarter Report (http://www.infospace.com/about/annual_report/html/home.htm), and K. Klein, "Budgeting Helps Secure Longevity," *Los Angeles Times*, August 2, 2000, p. C6.

master budget for the months of April, May, and June. The solution follows after the budget data. Note that there are a few minor differences between this example and the one in the chapter. These are identified in Exhibit 7-6 and in the solution. The primary difference is in the payment of interest on borrowing. Borrowing occurs at the end of a month when the company needs cash. Repayments (if appropriate) occur at the end of a month when cash is available. The company also pays interest in cash at the end of the month at an annual rate of 12% on the amount of note payable outstanding during that month.

Balance Sheet as of March 31, 20X4

Assets

Cash	$ 9,000
Accounts receivable	48,000
Inventory	12,600
Plant and equipment (net)	200,000
Total assets	$269,600

Liabilities and equities

Interest payable	0
Note payable	0
Accounts payable	18,300
Capital stock	180,000
Retained earnings	71,300
Total liabilities and equities	$269,600

Budgeted expenses (per month):

Wages and salaries	$ 7,500
Freight out as a percent of sales	6%
Advertising	$ 6,000
Depreciation	$ 2,000
Other expense as a percent of sales	4%
Minimum inventory policy as a percent of next month's cost of goods sold	30%

Budgeted sales:

March (actual)	$60,000
April	70,000
May	85,000
June	90,000
July	50,000

Other data:

Required minimum cash balance	$ 8,000
Sales mix, cash/credit	
Cash sales	20%
Credit sales (collected the following month)	80%
Gross profit rate	40%
Loan interest rate (interest paid in cash monthly)	12%
Inventory paid for in	
Month purchased	50%
Month after purchase	50%

Exhibit 7-6
The Country Store
Budget Data

SOLUTION

Schedule a: Sales budget

	April	May	June	Total
Credit sales, 80%	$56,000	$68,000	$72,000	$196,000
Cash sales, 20%	14,000	17,000	18,000	49,000
Total sales	$70,000	$85,000	$90,000	$245,000

Schedule b: Cash collections

	April	May	June	Total
Cash sales	$14,000	$17,000	$18,000	$ 49,000
Collections from prior month	48,000	56,000	68,000	172,000
Total collections	$62,000	$73,000	$86,000	$221,000

Schedule c: Purchases budget

	April	May	June	Total
Desired ending inventory	$15,300	$16,200	$ 9,000	$ 40,500
Plus cost of goods sold	42,000	51,000	54,000	147,000
Total needed	$57,300	$67,200	$63,000	$187,500
Less beginning inventory	12,600	15,300	16,200	44,100
Total purchases	$44,700	$51,900	$46,800	$143,400

Schedule d: Cash disbursements for purchases

	April	May	June	Total
For March*	$18,300			$ 18,300
For April	22,350	$22,350		44,700
For May		25,950	$25,950	51,900
For June			23,400	23,400
Total disbursements	$40,650	$48,300	$49,350	$138,300

* The amount payable on the March 31, 20X4, balance sheet.

Schedules e and f: Operating expenses and disbursements for expenses (except interest)

	April	May	June	Total
Cash expenses:				
Salaries & wages	$ 7,500	$ 7,500	$ 7,500	$22,500
Freight-out	4,200	5,100	5,400	14,700
Advertising	6,000	6,000	6,000	18,000
Other expenses	2,800	3,400	3,600	9,800
Total disbursements for expenses	$20,500	$22,000	$22,500	$65,000
Noncash expenses:				
Depreciation	2,000	2,000	2,000	6,000
Total expenses	$22,500	$24,000	$24,500	$71,000

The Country Store
Cash Budget
April–June, 20X4

	April	May	June
Beginning cash balance	$ 9,000	$ 8,000	$ 8,000
Minimum cash balance desired	8,000	8,000	8,000
Available cash balance	1,000	0	0
Cash receipts and disbursements:			
Collections from customers	62,000	73,000	86,000
Inventory purchases	(40,650)	(48,300)	(49,350)
Operating expenses	(20,500)	(22,000)	(22,500)
Equipment purchases	(19,750)	0	0
Dividends	0	0	(4,000)
Interest*	0	(179)	(154)
Net cash receipts and disbursements	(18,900)	2,521	9,996
Excess (deficiency) of cash before financing	$(17,900)	$ 2,521	$ 9,996
Financing:			
Borrowing†	$ 17,900	$ 0	$ 0
Repayments	0	(2,521)	(9,996)
Total cash from financing	17,900	(2,521)	(9,996)
Ending cash balance	$ 8,000	$ 8,000	$ 8,000

* In this example, interest is paid on the loan amounts outstanding during the month. May: $(.12 \div 12) \times (\$17,900) = \$179$; June: $(.12 \div 12) \times (\$17,900 - \$2,521) = \$154$.

† In this example, borrowings are at the end of the month in the amounts needed. Repayments also are made at the end of the month as excess cash permits.

The Country Store
Budgeted Income Statement
April–June, 20X4

	April	May	June	April–June Total
Sales	$70,000	$85,000	$90,000	$245,000
Cost of goods sold	42,000	51,000	54,000	147,000
Gross margin	28,000	34,000	36,000	98,000
Operating expenses				
Salaries and wages	7,500	7,500	7,500	22,500
Freight-out	4,200	5,100	5,400	14,700
Advertising	6,000	6,000	6,000	18,000
Other	2,800	3,400	3,600	9,800
Interest*	—	179	154	333
Depreciation	2,000	2,000	2,000	6,000
Total operating expense	$22,500	$24,179	$24,654	$ 71,333
Net operating income	$ 5,500	$ 9,821	$11,346	$ 26,667

* Note that interest expense is the monthly interest rate times the borrowed amount held for the month.
May: (.12 ÷ 12) × $17,900 = $179; June: (.12 ÷ 12) × $15,379 = $154.

The Country Store
Budgeted Balance Sheets as of the Ends of April–June, 20X4

Assets	April	May	June*
Current assets			
Cash	$ 8,000	$ 8,000	$ 8,000
Accounts receivable	56,000	68,000	72,000
Inventory	15,300	16,200	9,000
Total current assets	79,300	92,200	89,000
Plant, less accumulated depreciation†	217,750	215,750	213,750
Total assets	$297,050	$307,950	$302,750
Liabilities and Equities			
Liabilities			
Accounts payable	$ 22,350	$ 25,950	$ 23,400
Notes payable	17,900	15,379	5,383
Total liabilities	40,250	41,329	28,783
Stockholders' equity			
Capital stock	180,000	180,000	180,000
Retained earnings	76,800	86,621	93,967
Total equities	256,800	266,621	273,967
Total liabilities and equities	$297,050	$307,950	$302,750

* The June 30, 20X4, balance sheet is the ending balance sheet for the quarter.
† $200,000 + $19,750 − $2,000 = $217,750.

Difficulties of Sales Forecasting

OBJECTIVE 5

Explain the difficulties of sales forecasting.

As you saw in the CHC example, the sales budget is the foundation of the entire master budget. The accuracy of estimated purchases budgets, production schedules, and costs depends on the detail and accuracy (in dollars, units, and mix) of the budgeted sales. At the Ritz-Carlton hotels, the process of developing the sales budget involves forecasting levels of room occupancy, group events, banquets, and other activities. Upper management initially sets the costs of these activities. Then, employee teams in each department provide ideas for improvements (cost reductions). Managers prepare monthly departmental budgets based on the annual master budget.

As we stated earlier, and as you might have noticed from Ritz-Carlton's budgeting practices, the sales budget depends entirely on sales forecasts. Although sales budget and sales forecast sound as if they might be the same thing, be aware that a forecast and a budget are not necessarily identical. A **sales forecast** is a prediction of sales under a given set of conditions. A **sales budget** is the result of decisions to create the conditions that will generate a desired level of sales. For example, you may have forecasts of sales at various levels of advertising. The forecast for the one level you decide to implement becomes the budget.

Sales forecasts are usually prepared under the direction of the top sales executive. Important factors considered by sales forecasters include the following:

sales forecast
A prediction of sales under a given set of conditions.

sales budget
The result of decisions to create conditions that will generate a desired level of sales.

1. Past patterns of sales: Past experience combined with detailed past sales by product line, geographical region, and type of customer can help predict future sales.
2. Estimates made by the sales force: A company's sales force is often the best source of information about the desires and plans of customers.
3. General economic conditions: The financial press regularly publish predictions for many economic indicators, such as gross domestic product and industrial production indexes (local and foreign). Knowledge of how sales relate to these indicators can aid sales forecasting.
4. Competitors' actions: Sales depend on the strength and actions of competitors. To forecast sales, a company should consider the likely strategies and reactions of competitors, such as changes in their prices, product quality, or services.
5. Changes in the firm's prices: Companies can usually increase sales by decreasing prices and vice versa. A company should consider the effects of price changes on customer demand (see Chapter 5).
6. Changes in product mix: Changing the mix of products often can affect not only sales levels but also overall contribution margin. Identifying the most profitable products and devising methods to increase their sales is a key part of successful management.
7. Market research studies: Some companies hire market experts to gather information about market conditions and customer preferences. Such information is useful to managers making sales forecasts and product mix decisions.
8. Advertising and sales promotion plans: Advertising and other promotional costs affect sales levels. A sales forecast should be based on anticipated effects of promotional activities.

Sales forecasting usually combines various techniques. In addition to the opinions of the sales staff, statistical analysis of correlations between sales and economic indicators (prepared by economists and members of the market research staff) provide valuable help. The opinions of line management also heavily influence the final sales forecasts. Ultimately, no matter how many technical experts a company uses in forecasting, the sales budget is the responsibility of line management.

Sales forecasting is still somewhat mystical, but companies are increasingly using more formalized procedures and reviewing their processes more seriously because of the intensity of global competitive pressures. Although this book does not include a detailed discussion of the preparation of the sales budget, we cannot overstress the importance of an accurate sales forecast.

Interestingly, governments and other nonprofit organizations also face a problem similar to sales forecasting. For example, the budget for city revenues may depend on a variety of factors, such as predicted property taxes, traffic fines, parking fees, license fees, and city income taxes. In turn, property taxes depend on the extent of new construction and, in most localities, general increases in real estate values. Thus, a municipal budget may require forecasting that is just as sophisticated as that required by a private firm.

Getting Employees to Accept the Budget

No matter how accurate sales forecasts are, if budgets are to benefit an organization, they need the support of all the firm's employees. The attitude of top management will heavily influence lower-level workers' and managers' attitudes toward budgets. Even with the support of top management, however, budgets—and the managers who implement them—can run into opposition.

Managers often compare actual results with budgets in evaluating subordinates. Few individuals are immediately ecstatic about techniques used to check their performance. Lower-level managers sometimes regard budgets as embodiments of restrictive, negative top-management attitudes. Accountants reinforce this view if they use a budget only to point out managers' failings. Such negative attitudes are even greater when the budget's primary purpose is to limit spending. For example, budgets are generally unpopular in government agencies where their only use is to request and authorize funding. To avoid negative attitudes toward budgets, accountants and top management must demonstrate how budgets can help each manager and employee achieve better results. Only then will the budgets become a positive aid in motivating employees at all levels to work toward goals, set objectives, measure results accurately, and direct attention to the areas that need investigation.

Another serious human relations problem that can negate the benefits of budgeting arises if budgets stress one set of performance goals but the company rewards employees and managers for different performance measures. For example, a budget may concentrate on current costs of production, but the company may reward managers and employees based on quality of production (defect rate) and on timely delivery of products to customers (percent on time). These measures of performance could be in direct conflict.

We can't overemphasize the overriding importance of the human aspects of budgeting. Too often, top management and accountants are overly concerned with the mechanics of budgets, ignoring the fact that the effectiveness of any budgeting system depends directly on whether the affected managers and employees understand and accept the budget. Budgets created with the active participation of all affected employees—called **participative budgeting**—are generally more effective than budgets imposed on subordinates.

For example, Ritz-Carlton's budgeting system involves all hotel employees and is thus a participative system. In fact, employee "buy-in" to the budget is so important at Ritz-Carlton that self-directed employee teams at all levels of the company have the authority to change operations based on budgets as they see fit.

participative budgeting
Budgets formulated with the active participation of all affected employees.

Activity-Based Master Budgets

functional budgeting
Budgeting process that focuses on preparing budgets for various functions such as production, selling, and administrative support.

activity-based budgets
Budgets that focus on the budgeted cost of activities required to produce and sell products and services.

The budget process we have described thus far in this chapter can be called **functional budgeting** because the focus is on preparing budgets for various functions such as production, selling, and administrative support. Organizations that have implemented activity-based cost accounting systems often use these systems as a vehicle to prepare **activity-based budgets**—budgets that focus on the budgeted cost of activities required to produce and sell products and services.

An activity-based budgetary system emphasizes the planning and control purpose of cost management. Our discussion of ABC in Chapter 4 focused on designing cost accounting and cost allocation systems that provided more accurate product and service costs. However, once a company has designed and implemented an ABC system, it can use the same framework for its budgetary system. Exhibit 7-7 highlights the main concepts and differences between ABC allocation of resource costs to activities and products, and activity-based budgeting (ABB).

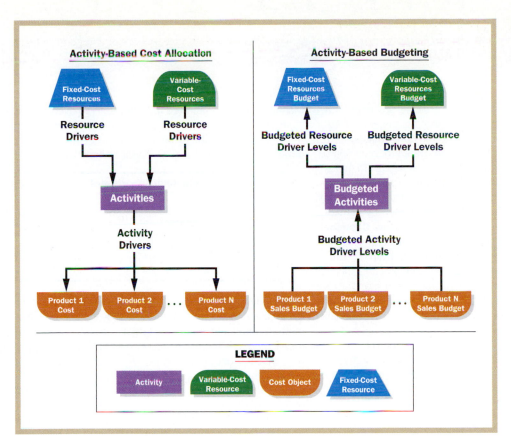

Exhibit 7-7
ABC and ABB
Compared

Just as in functional budgeting (see Exhibit 7-1), ABB begins with the forecasted demand for products or services—the sales budget. In functional budgeting, the next step is to determine the ending-inventory budget, then the material purchases, and the cost-of-goods-sold budget. In ABB, the focus is on estimating the demand for each activity's output as measured by its cost driver. Then, we use the rate at which activities consume resources to estimate or budget the resources needed. As we can see from comparing Exhibits 7-1 and Exhibit 7-7, functional budgeting determines the resources needed directly from the predicted sales of products or services, while ABB uses the sales predictions to estimate the required activities, which in turn determines the resources needed. Because of the emphasis on activities and their consumption of resources, some managers believe that ABB is more useful for controlling waste and improving efficiency—a primary objective of budgeting. The Business First box on p. 316 illustrates this point.

Financial Planning Models

Because a well-made budget considers all aspects of the company (the entire value chain), it serves as an effective model for decision making. For example, managers can use the master budget to predict how various decisions might affect the company in both the long run and the short run. Using the master budget in this way is a step-by-step process in which managers revise their tentative plans as they exchange views on various aspects of expected activities.

Today, most large companies have developed **financial planning models,** mathematical models of the master budget that can react to any set of assumptions about sales, costs, product mix, and so on. For instance, **Dow Chemical**'s model uses 140 separate, constantly revised cost inputs that are based on several different cost drivers.

financial planning models
Mathematical models of the master budget that can react to any set of assumptions about sales, costs, or product mix.

ACTIVITY BASED BUDGETING (ABB)

Activity-based costing (ABC) is growing in popularity. However, companies do not realize the real benefits of ABC until they totally integrate it into their budgeting system. Often accountants "own" the costing system of a company, but the budgeting system "belongs" to managers. To use an activity-based framework for budgeting means that all managers must focus on managing activities. They must prepare their budgets using the same framework used by the ABC system. For example, in 1997 and 1998, **Dow Chemical** integrated its new ABC system with its budgeting process. To be successful, this required a massive training effort attended by "controllers, accountants, work process subject matter experts, cost center owners, business manufacturing leaders, and site general managers." With budgets consistent with cost reports, Dow gained much greater benefit from its activity-based budgeting system.

To see how activity-based budgeting helps a company, let's compare methods using a company's purchasing department as an example. The purchasing department's previous-year results might appear as follows, based on a traditional view of costs:

Purchasing Department	
Salaries	$200,000
Benefits	75,000
Supplies	30,000
Travel	10,000
Total	$315,000

If management wants to reduce costs by 10% overall ($31,500) using the traditional view of costs, purchasing may simply reduce each cost category by 10%. Some critics refer to this method of cost reduction as "slash and burn." However, it is the managers who often wind up getting burned by this technique. For example, at **Borg-Warner Automotive**, virtually all managers expressed dissatisfaction with the budgeting process. Each year managers made cost estimates as part of the annual budgeting procedure. But, because the company used a slash-and-burn cost-cutting technique, top management almost always returned these budgets with a directive to cut costs across the board.

Managers got so frustrated that they started overestimating costs to compensate for the cuts they knew were coming.

Using activity-based cost information, the purchasing department's budget might appear as follows:

Purchasing Department	
Activity	
Certify 10 new vendors	$ 65,450
Issue 450 purchase orders	184,640
Issue 275 releases	64,910
Total	$315,000

ABB links financial data with the activity that consumes the related resource. Instead of using the slash-and-burn method, the department now targets specific activities that it can reduce without hurting its overall effectiveness. For example, the department may be able to reduce the number of vendor certifications to five. Assuming that vendor certification costs are variable with respect to the number of vendors, this would reduce certification costs by $5 \times (\$65,450 \div 10)$ or $32,725, enabling the department to meet or exceed its budget target.

Government organizations also are using ABB. In 2001, the U.S. Small Business Administration (SBA) began using ABB. The SBA is one of the five largest federal credit agencies with over $50 billion in loans. According to Thomas Dumaresq, the chief financial officer of the SBA, "Our goal is to clearly identify the activities that must be performed to produce critical outputs and then determine the level of resources that must be committed to successfully complete the activity. Once this is done, we can determine how various funding levels affect the outputs produced by the SBA. The ABB process provides SBA management the quality information necessary for sound decision making."

Sources: Adapted from G. Hanks, M. Fried, and J. Huber, "Shifting Gears at Borg-Warner Automotive," *Management Accounting*, February 1994, pp. 25–29; J. Damitio, G. Hayes, and P. Kintzele, "Integrating ANC and ABM at Dow Chemical," *Management Accounting Quarterly*, Winter 2000, pp. 22–26; and "Activity-based Budgeting," Office of the Chief Financial Officer, U.S. Small Business Administration, September 2002.

By mathematically describing the relationships among all the operating and financial activities covered in the master budget and among the other major internal and external factors that can affect the results of management decisions, financial planning models allow managers to assess the predicted impacts of various alternatives before they make final decisions. For example, a manager might want to predict the consequences of changing the mix of products offered for sale to emphasize several products with the highest prospects for growth. A financial planning model would provide operational and financial budgets well into the future under alternative assumptions about the product mix, sales levels, production constraints, quality levels, scheduling, and so on. Most importantly, managers can get answers to what-if questions, such as "What if sales are 10% below forecasts? What if material prices increase 8% instead of 4% as expected? What if the new union contract grants a 6% raise in consideration for productivity improvements?"

Financial planning models have shortened managers' reaction times dramatically. We can prepare in minutes (or even seconds) a revised plan for a large company that once took many accountants many days to prepare by hand. For example, **Public Service Electric & Gas**, a New Jersey utility company, can run its total master budget several times a day, if necessary.

The use of spreadsheet software on personal computers has put financial planning models within reach of even the smallest organizations. The ready access to powerful modeling, however, does not guarantee plausible or reliable results. Financial planning models are only as good as the assumptions and the inputs used to build and manipulate them—what computer specialists call GIGO (garbage in, garbage out). Nearly every chief financial officer has a horror story to tell about following the bad advice of a faulty financial planning model.

Highlights to Remember

1 **Explain the major features and advantages of a master budget.** A budget expresses, in quantitative terms, an organization's objectives and possible steps for achieving them. Thus, a budget is a tool that helps managers in both their planning and control functions. The two major parts of a master budget are the operating budget and the financial budget. Advantages of budgets include formalization of planning, providing a framework for judging performance, and aiding managers in coordinating their efforts.

2 **Follow the principal steps in preparing a master budget.** Master budgets typically cover relatively short periods—usually one month to one year. The steps involved in preparing the master budget vary across organizations but follow the general outline given on pages 302–303. Invariably, the first step is to forecast sales or service levels. The next step should be to forecast cost-driver activity levels, given expected sales and service. Using these forecasts and knowledge of cost behavior, collection patterns, and so on, managers can prepare the operating and financing budgets.

3 **Prepare the operating budget and the supporting schedules.** The operating budget is the income statement for the budget period. Managers prepare it using the following supporting schedules: sales budget, purchases budget, and operating expenses.

4 **Prepare the financial budget.** The second major part of the master budget is the financial budget. The financial budget consists of a cash budget, capital budget, and a budgeted balance sheet. Managers prepare the cash budget from the following supporting schedules: cash collections, disbursements for purchases, and disbursements for operating expenses.

5 **Explain the difficulties of sales forecasting.** Sales forecasting combines various techniques as well as opinions of sales staff and management. Sales forecasters must consider many factors such as past patterns of sales, economic conditions, and competitors' actions. Sales forecasting is difficult because of its complexity and the rapid changes in the business environment in which most companies operate.

6 **Anticipate possible human relations problems caused by budgets.** The success of a budget depends heavily on employee reaction to it. Negative attitudes toward budgets often prevent realization of many of the potential benefits. Such attitudes are usually caused by managers who use budgets to force behavior or to punish employees or who use budgets only to limit spending. Budgets generally are more useful when all affected parties participate in their preparation.

Appendix 7: Use of Spreadsheets for Budgeting

OBJECTIVE 7

Use a spreadsheet to develop a budget.

Spreadsheet software for personal computers is an extremely powerful and flexible tool for budgeting. An obvious advantage of the spreadsheet is that arithmetic errors are virtually nonexistent. The real value of spreadsheets, however, is that they can be used to make a mathematical model (a financial planning model) of the organization. This model can be used repeatedly at a very low cost and can be altered to reflect possible changes in expected sales, cost drivers, cost functions, and so on. The objective of this appendix is to illustrate sensitivity analysis, one aspect of the power and flexibility of spreadsheet software that has made this software an indispensable budgeting tool.

Recall the chapter's CHC example. Suppose CHC has prepared its master budget using spreadsheet software. To simplify making changes to the budget, we have placed the relevant forecasts and other budgeting details in Exhibit 7-8. Note that for simplification, we have included only the data necessary for the purchases budget. The full master budget would require a larger table with all the data given in the chapter.

A spreadsheet consists of a grid where every cell falls in one row and one column. We label each cell with its column (a letter) and its row (a number). For example, the beginning inventory for the budget period is in "D4," which is shown as $48,000.

By referencing the budget data's cell addresses, you can generate the purchases budget (Exhibit 7-9) within the same spreadsheet by entering formulas instead of numbers into the schedule. Consider Exhibit 7-9. Instead of typing $48,000 as April's beginning inventory in the purchases budget at cell D17, type a formula with the cell address for the beginning inventory from the preceding table, =D4 (the cell address preceded by an "=" sign—a spreadsheet rule to identify a formula; some spreadsheets use "+" to indicate a formula). Likewise, all the cells of the purchases budget will contain formulas that include cell addresses instead of numbers. The total inventory needed in April (D16) is =D13 + D14, and budgeted purchases in April (D19) are =D16 − D17. We can compute the figures for May, June, and July similarly within the respective columns. This approach gives the spreadsheet the most flexibility, because you could change any number in the budget data in Exhibit 7-8 (for example, a sales forecast), and the software automatically recalculates the numbers in the entire purchases budget. Exhibit 7-9 shows the formulas used for the purchases budget. Exhibit 7-10 is the purchases budget displaying the numbers generated by the formulas in Exhibit 7-9 using the input data in Exhibit 7-8.

Now, what if sales could be 10% higher than initially forecasted during April through August? What effect will this alternative forecast have on budgeted purchases? Even to revise this simple purchases budget would require a considerable number of manual recalculations. Merely changing the sales forecasts in spreadsheet Exhibit 7-8, however, results in a nearly instantaneous revision of the purchases budget. Exhibit 7-11 shows the alternative sales forecasts (in colored type) and other unchanged data along with the revised purchases budget. We could alter every piece of budget data in the table, and easily view or print out the effects on purchases. This sort of analysis, assessing the

	A	B	C	D	E	F	G
1	Budget data						
2	Sales forecasts		Other information				
3							
4	March (actual)	$40,000	Beginning inventory	$48,000			
5	April	50,000	Desired ending inventory:				
			Base amount	$20,000			
6	May	80,000	Plus percent of next month's cost of				
			goods sold				
7	June	60,000					
8	July	50,000		80%			
9	August	40,000	Cost of goods sold				
			as percent of sales	70%			
10							

Exhibit 7-8
The Cooking Hut Company
Budget Data (Column and row labels are given by the spreadsheet.)

	A	B	C	D	E	F	G
11	Schedule c						
12	Purchases budget			April	May	June	July
13	Desired ending inventory			=D5 + D8*(D10*B6)	=D5 + D8*(D10*B7)	=D5 + D8*(D10*B8)	=D5 + D8*(D10*B9)
14	Plus cost of goods sold			=D10*B5	=D10*B6	=D10*B7	=D10*B8
15							
16	Total needed			=D13 + D14	=E13 + E14	=F13 + F14	=G13 + G14
17	Less beginning inventory			=D4	=D13	=E13	=F13
18							
19	Purchases			=D16 − D17	=E16 − E17	=F16 − F17	=G16 − G17
20							

Exhibit 7-9
The Cooking Hut Company
Purchases Budget Formulas

effects of varying one of the budget inputs, up or down, is sensitivity analysis. **Sensitivity analysis** for budgeting is the systematic varying of budget data input to determine the effects of each change on the budget. This type of what-if analysis is one of the most powerful uses of spreadsheets for financial planning models. Note, though, that it is not generally a good idea to vary more than one of the types of budget inputs at a time, unless they are obviously related, because doing so makes it difficult to isolate the effects of each change.

We can prepare every schedule, operating budget, and financial budget of the master budget on the spreadsheet. We would link each schedule by the appropriate cell addresses just as we linked the budget input data (Exhibit 7-8) to the purchases budget (Exhibits 7-9 and 7-10). As in the purchases budget, ideally all cells in the master budget are formulas, not numbers. That way, every budget input can be the subject of sensitivity analysis, if desired, by simply changing the budget data in Exhibit 7-8.

Preparing the master budget on a spreadsheet is time-consuming—the first time. After that, the time savings and planning capabilities through sensitivity analysis are enormous compared with a manual approach. A problem can occur, however, if the master budget model is not well documented and a person other than the author attempts to modify the spreadsheet model. Any assumptions that are made should be described either within the spreadsheet or in a separate budget preparation document.

sensitivity analysis
In budgeting, the systematic varying of budget data input to determine the effects of each change on the budget.

	A	B	C	D	E	F	G
11	Schedule c						
12	Purchases budget			April	May	June	July
13	Desired ending inventory			$64,800	$ 53,600	$48,000	$42,400
14	Plus cost of goods sold			35,000	56,000	42,000	35,000
15							
16	Total needed			99,800	109,600	90,000	77,400
17	Less beginning inventory			48,000	64,800	53,600	48,000
18							
19	Purchases			$51,800	$ 44,800	$36,400	$29,400
20							

Exhibit 7-10
The Cooking Hut Company
Purchases Budget

	A	B	C	D	E	F	G
1	Budgeted data						
2	Sales forecasts		Other information				
3							
4	March (actual)	$40,000	Beginning inventory	$ 48,000			
5	April	55,000	Desired ending inventory:				
			Base amount	$ 20,000			
6	May	88,000	Plus percent of next				
7	June	66,000	month's cost of				
8	July	55,000	goods sold	80%			
9	August	44,000	Cost of goods sold				
10			as percent of sales	70%			
11	Schedule c						
12	Purchases budget			April	May	June	July
13	Desired ending inventory			$ 69,280	$ 56,960	$50,800	$44,640
14	Plus cost of goods sold			38,500	61,600	46,200	38,500
15							
16	Total needed			107,780	118,560	97,000	83,140
17	Beginning inventory			48,000	69,280	56,960	50,800
18							
19	Purchases			$ 59,780	$ 49,280	$40,040	$32,340
20							

Exhibit 7-11
The Cooking Hut Company
Purchases Budget

Accounting Vocabulary

activity-based budgets (ABB), p. 314
capital budget, p. 299
cash budget, p. 307
continuous budget, p. 299
financial budget, p. 301

financial planning model, p. 315
functional budgeting, p. 314
long-range planning, p. 299
master budget, p. 299
operating budget, p. 300
participative budgeting, p. 314

profit plan, p. 300
rolling budget, p. 299
sales budget, p. 313
sales forecast, p. 313
sensitivity analysis, p. 319
strategic plan, p. 299

Fundamental Assignment Material

Special note: Problems 7-A1 and 7-B1 provide single-problem reviews of most of the chapter topics. Those readers who prefer to concentrate on the fundamentals in smaller chunks should consider any of the other problems.

7-A1 Prepare Master Budget

Computer Superstores, Inc., has a strong belief in using highly decentralized management. You are the new manager of the company's store in the Mall of America. You know much about how to buy, how to display, how to sell, and how to reduce shoplifting. You know little about accounting and finance, however.

Top management is convinced that training for higher management should include the active participation of store managers in the budgeting process. You have been asked to prepare a complete master budget for your store for June, July, and August. You are responsible for its actual full preparation. All accounting is done centrally, so you have no expert help on the premises. In addition, tomorrow the branch manager and the assistant controller will be here to examine your work; at that time, they will assist you in formulating the final budget document. The idea is to have you prepare the budget a few times so that you gain more confidence about accounting matters. You want to make a favorable impression on your superiors, so you gather the following data as of May 31, 20X5:

		Recent and Projected Sales	
Cash	$ 29,000		
Inventory	420,000	April	$300,000
Accounts receivable	369,000	May	350,000
Net furniture and fixtures	168,000	June	700,000
Total assets	$986,000	July	400,000
Accounts payable	$475,000	August	400,000
Owners' equity	511,000	September	300,000
Total liabilities and owners' equities	$986,000		

Credit sales are 90% of total sales. Credit accounts are collected 80% in the month following the sale and 20% in the following month. Assume that bad debts are negligible and can be ignored. The accounts receivable on May 31 are the result of the credit sales for April and May:

$$(.20 \times .90 \times \$300,000) + (1.0 \times .90 \times \$350,000) = \$369,000.$$

The average gross profit on sales is 40%.

The policy is to acquire enough inventory each month to equal the following month's projected cost of goods sold. All purchases are paid for in the month following purchase.

Salaries, wages, and commissions average 20% of sales; all other variable expenses are 4% of sales. Fixed expenses for rent, property taxes, and miscellaneous payroll and other items are $55,000 monthly. Assume that these variable and fixed expenses require cash disbursements each month. Depreciation is $2,500 monthly.

In June, $55,000 is going to be disbursed for fixtures acquired in May. The May 31 balance of accounts payable includes this amount.

Assume that a minimum cash balance of $25,000 is to be maintained. Also assume that all borrowings are effective at the beginning of the month and all repayments are made at the end of the month of repayment. Interest is paid only at the time of repaying principal. The interest rate is 10% per annum; round interest computations to the nearest ten dollars. All loans and repayments of principal must be made in multiples of a thousand dollars.

1. Prepare a budgeted income statement for the coming quarter, a budgeted statement of monthly cash receipts and disbursements (for each of the next three months), and a budgeted balance sheet for August 31, 20X5. All operations are evaluated on a before-income-tax basis, so income taxes may be ignored here.
2. Explain why there is a need for a bank loan and what operating sources supply cash for repaying the bank loan.

7-B1 Prepare Master Budget

Victoria Kite Company, a small Melbourne firm that sells kites on the Web wants a master budget for the next three months, beginning January 1, 2005. It desires an ending minimum cash balance of $5,000 each month. Sales are forecasted at an average wholesale selling price of $8 per kite. In January, Victoria Kite is beginning just-in-time (JIT) deliveries from suppliers, which means that purchases equal expected sales.

On January 1, purchases will cease until inventory reaches $6,000, after which time purchases will equal sales. Merchandise costs average $4 per kite. Purchases during any given month are paid in full during the following month. All sales are on credit, payable within 30 days, but experience has shown that 60% of current sales are collected in the current month, 30% in the next month, and 10% in the month thereafter. Bad debts are negligible.

Monthly operating expenses are as follows:

Wages and salaries	$15,000
Insurance expired	125
Depreciation	250
Miscellaneous	2,500
Rent	$250/month + 10% of quarterly sales over $10,000

Cash dividends of $1,500 are to be paid quarterly, beginning January 15, and are declared on the fifteenth of the previous month. All operating expenses are paid as incurred, except insurance, depreciation, and rent. Rent of $250 is paid at the beginning of each month, and the additional 10% of sales is paid quarterly on the tenth of the month following the end of the quarter. The next settlement is due January 10.

The company plans to buy some new fixtures for $3,000 cash in March.

Money can be borrowed and repaid in multiples of $500 at an interest rate of 10% per annum. Management wants to minimize borrowing and repay rapidly. Interest is computed and paid when the principal is repaid. Assume that borrowing occurs at the beginning, and repayments at the end, of the months in question. Money is never borrowed at the beginning and repaid at the end of the *same* month. Compute interest to the nearest dollar.

Assets as of December 31, 2004		Liabilities as of December 31, 2004	
Cash	$ 5,000	Accounts payable	
Accounts receivable	12,500	(merchandise)	$35,550
Inventory*	39,050	Dividends payable	1,500
Unexpired insurance	1,500	Rent payable	7,800
Fixed assets, net	12,500		$44,850
	$70,550		

* November 30 inventory balance = $16,000.

Recent and forecasted sales:

October	$38,000	December	$25,000	February	$75,000	April	$45,000
November	25,000	January	62,000	March	38,000		

1. Prepare a master budget including a budgeted income statement, balance sheet, statement of cash receipts and disbursements, and supporting schedules for the months January through March 2005.
2. Explain why there is a need for a bank loan and what operating sources provide the cash for the repayment of the bank loan.

Additional Assignment Material

Questions

7-1 Is budgeting used primarily for scorekeeping, attention directing, or problem solving?

7-2 How do strategic planning, long-range planning, and budgeting differ?

7-3 "Capital budgets are plans for managing long-term debt and common stock." Do you agree? Explain.

7-4 "I oppose continuous budgets because they provide a moving target. Managers never know what to aim at." Discuss.

7-5 "Pro forma statements are those statements prepared in conjunction with continuous budgets." Do you agree? Explain.

7-6 Why is budgeted performance better than past performance as a basis for judging actual results?

7-7 "Budgets are okay in relatively certain environments. But everything changes so quickly in the electronics industry that budgeting is a waste of time." Comment on this statement.

7-8 What are the major benefits of budgeting?

7-9 "Budgeting is an unnecessary burden on many managers. It takes time away from important day-to-day problems." Do you agree? Explain.

7-10 Differentiate between an operating budget and a financial budget.

7-11 Why is the sales forecast the starting point for budgeting?

7-12 Distinguish between operating expenses and disbursements for operating expenses.

7-13 What is the principal objective of a cash budget?

7-14 Differentiate between a sales forecast and a sales budget.

7-15 What factors influence the sales forecast?

7-16 "Education and salesmanship are key features of budgeting." Explain.

7-17 What are the main differences between functional and activity-based budgets?

7-18 What are financial planning models?

7-19 "Financial planning models guide managers through the budget process so that managers do not really need to understand budgeting." Do you agree? Explain.

7-20 Study Appendix 7. "I cannot be bothered with setting up my monthly budget on a spread-sheet. It just takes too long to be worth the effort." Comment.

7-21 Study Appendix 7. How do spreadsheets aid the application of sensitivity analysis?

Critical Thinking Exercises

7-22 Budgets as Limitations on Spending

Many nonprofit organizations use budgets primarily to limit spending. Why does this limit the effectiveness of budgets?

7-23 Sales Personnel and Budgeting

The sales budget is the foundation of the entire master budget. How do sales personnel help formulate the budget? Compare the role of sales personnel to that of a central staff function such as market research.

7-24 Master Budgets for Research and Development

The text focuses on budgets for organizations that have revenues and expenses. Suppose you were the manager of a research and development division of a biotech company. How would budgets be helpful to you?

7-25 Production Budgets and Performance Evaluation

The Akron plant of American Tire Company prepares an annual master budget each November for the following year. At the end of each year it compares the actual costs incurred to the budgeted costs. How can American Tire get employees to accept the budget and strive to meet or beat the budgeted costs?

Exercises

7-26 Fill In the Blanks

Enter the word or phrase that best completes each sentence.

1. The financial budget process includes the following budgets:
   a. _____
   b. _____
   c. _____
   d. _____
2. The master budget process usually begins with the _____ budget.
3. The production budget process usually begins with the _____ budget.
4. A _____ budget is a plan that is revised monthly or quarterly, dropping one period and adding another.
5. Strategic planning sets the _____.

7-27 Cash Budgeting

Brenda Peterson and Molly Chan are preparing a plan to submit to venture capitalists to fund their business, Adventure.Com. The company plans to spend $300,000 on equipment in the first quarter of 2005. Salaries and other operating expenses (paid as incurred) will be $30,000 per month beginning in January 2005 and will continue at that level thereafter. The company will receive its first revenues in January 2006, with cash collections averaging $25,000 per month for all of 2006. In January 2007 cash collections are expected to increase to $100,000 per month and continue at that level thereafter.

How much venture capital funding should Adventure.Com seek? Assume that the company needs enough funding to cover all of its cash needs until cash receipts start exceeding cash disbursements.

7-28 Purchases and Cost of Goods Sold

The Bridgeford Co., a wholesaler of auto parts, budgeted the following sales for the indicated months:

	June 2005	July 2005	August 2005
Sales on account	$1,800,000	$1,920,000	$2,040,000
Cash sales	240,000	250,000	260,000
Total sales	$2,040,000	$2,170,000	$2,300,000

All merchandise is marked up to sell at its invoice cost plus 25%. Merchandise inventories at the beginning of each month are at 30% of that month's projected cost of goods sold.

1. Compute the budgeted cost of goods sold for the month of June 2005.
2. Compute the budgeted merchandise purchases for July 2005.

7-29 Purchases and Sales Budgets

All sales of Dunn's Building Supplies (DBS) are made on credit. Sales are billed twice monthly, on the tenth of the month for the last half of the prior month's sales and on the twentieth of the month for the first half of the current month's sales. The terms of all sales are 2/10, net 30. Based on past experience, the collection experience of accounts receivable is as follows:

Within the discount period	80%
On the 30th day	18%
Uncollectible	2%

The sales value of shipments for May 20X5 was $750,000. The forecast sales for the next four months are

June	$800,000
July	900,000
August	900,000
September	600,000

DBS's average markup on its products is 20% of the sales price.

DBS purchases merchandise for resale to meet the current month's sales demand and to maintain a desired monthly ending inventory of 25% of the next month's cost of goods sold. All purchases are on credit with terms of net 30. DBS pays for one-half of a month's purchases in the month of purchase and the other half in the month following the purchase.

All sales and purchases occur uniformly throughout the month.

1. How much cash can DBS plan to collect from accounts receivable collections during July 20X5?
2. How much can DBS plan to collect in September from sales made in August 20X5?
3. Compute the budgeted dollar value of DBS inventory on August 31, 20X5.
4. How much merchandise should DBS plan to purchase during June 20X5?
5. How much should DBS budget in August 20X5 for the payment for merchandise purchased?

7-30 Sales Budget

Suppose a **Gap** store has the following data:

- Accounts receivable, May 31: (.3 × May sales of $400,000) = $120,000
- Monthly forecasted sales: June, $400,000; July, $440,000; August, $500,000; September, $530,000

Sales consist of 70% cash and 30% credit. All credit accounts are collected in the month following the sales. Uncollectible accounts are negligible and may be ignored.

Prepare a sales budget schedule and a cash collections budget schedule for June, July, and August.

7-31 Sales Budget

A Tokyo clothing wholesaler was preparing its sales budget for the first quarter of 2005. Forecast sales are (in thousands of yen)

January	¥180,000
February	¥210,000
March	¥240,000

Sales are 20% cash and 80% on credit. Fifty percent of the credit accounts are collected in the month of sale, 40% in the month following the sale, and 10% in the following month. No uncollectible accounts are anticipated. Accounts receivable at the beginning of 2005 are ¥96 million (10% of November credit sales of ¥180 million and 50% of December credit sales of ¥156 million).

Prepare a schedule showing sales and cash collections for January, February, and March, 2005.

7-32 Cash Collection Budget

Pioneer Square Carpet Specialties has found that cash collections from customers tend to occur in the following pattern:

Collected within cash discount period in month of sale	50%
Collected within cash discount period in first month after month of sale	10
Collected after cash discount period in first month after month of sale	25
Collected after cash discount period in second month after month of sale	12
Never collected	3
Total sales in any month (before cash discounts)	100%
Cash discount allowable as a percentage of invoice price	1%

Compute the total cash budgeted to be collected in March if sales are predicted as $300,000 for January, $400,000 for February, and $450,000 for March.

7-33 Purchase Budget

Quantrill Furniture Mart plans inventory levels (at cost) at the end of each month as follows: May, $250,000; June, $220,000; July, $270,000; August, $240,000.

Sales are expected to be June, $440,000; July, $350,000; August, $400,000. Cost of goods sold is 60% of sales.

Purchases in April were $250,000; in May, $180,000. A given month's purchases are paid as follows: 10% during that month; 80% the next month; and the final 10% the next month.

Prepare budget schedules for June, July, and August for purchases and for disbursements for purchases.

7-34 Purchase Budget

The inventory of the Barcelona S.A. was €200,000 on May 31. The manager was upset because the inventory was too high. She has adopted the following policies regarding merchandise purchases and inventory. At the end of any month, the inventory should be €15,000 plus 90% of the cost of goods to be sold during the following month. The cost of merchandise sold averages 60% of sales. Purchase terms are generally net 30 days. A given month's purchases are paid as follows: 20% during that month and 80% during the following month.

Purchases in May had been €150,000. Sales are expected to be June, €300,000; July, €280,000; August, €340,000; and September, €400,000.

1. Compute the amount by which the inventory on May 31 exceeded the manager's policies.
2. Prepare budget schedules for June, July, and August for purchases and for disbursements for purchases.

7-35 Cash Budget

Consider the income statement in Exhibit 7-12.

The cash balance, May 31, 2004, is $15,000. Sales proceeds are collected as follows: 80% month of sale, 10% second month, 10% third month.

Accounts receivable are $40,000 on May 31, 2004, consisting of $16,000 from April sales and $24,000 from May sales.

Accounts payable on May 31, 2004, are $145,000. Raleigh Company pays 25% of purchases during the month of purchase and the remainder during the following month. All operating expenses requiring cash are paid during the month of recognition. Insurance and property taxes are paid annually in December, however.

Prepare a cash budget for June. Confine your analysis to the given data. Ignore income taxes and other possible items that might affect cash.

Problems

7-36 Cash Budget

Jean Kim is the manager of an airport gift shop, Kim News and Gifts. From the following data, Ms. Kim wants a cash budget showing expected cash receipts and disbursements for the month of April, and the cash balance expected as of April 30, 20X4.

- Bank note due April 10: $90,000 plus $4,500 interest
- Depreciation for April: $2,100

Exhibit 7-12

Raleigh Company
*Budgeted Income
Statement for the Month
Ended June 30, 2004
(in thousands)*

Sales		$290
Inventory, May 31	$ 50	
Purchases	192	
Available for sale	242	
Inventory, June 30	40	
Cost of goods sold		202
Gross margin		$ 88
Operating expenses		
Wages	$ 36	
Utilities	5	
Advertising	10	
Depreciation	1	
Office expenses	4	
Insurance and property taxes	3	59
Operating income		$ 29

- Two-year insurance policy due April 14 for renewal: $1,500, to be paid in cash
- Planned cash balance, March 31, 20X4: $80,000
- Merchandise purchases for April: $450,000, 40% paid in month of purchase, 60% paid in next month
- Customer receivables as of March 31: $60,000 from February sales, $450,000 from March sales
- Payrolls due in April: $90,000
- Other expenses for April, payable in April: $45,000
- Accrued taxes for April, payable in June: $7,500
- Sales for April: $1,000,000, half collected in month of sale, 40% in next month, 10% in third month
- Accounts payable, March 31, 20X4: $460,000

Prepare the cash budget.

7-37 Cash Budget

Prepare a statement of estimated cash receipts and disbursements for October 2004 for the Bouquet Company, which sells one product, herbal soap, by the case. On October 1, 2004, part of the trial balance showed

Cash	$ 4,800	
Accounts receivable	15,600	
Allowance for bad debts		$1,900
Merchandise inventory	9,000	
Accounts payable, merchandise		6,600

The company pays for its purchases within 10 days. Assume that one-third of the purchases of any month are due and paid for in the following month.

The cost of the merchandise purchased is $12 per case. At the end of each month it is desired to have an inventory equal in units to 50% of the following month's sales in units.

Sales terms include a 1% discount if payment is made by the end of the calendar month. Past experience indicates that 60% of the billings will be collected during the month of the sale, 30% in the following calendar month, 6% in the next following calendar month. Four percent will be uncollectible. The company's fiscal year begins August 1.

Unit selling price	$ 20
August actual sales	$ 12,000
September actual sales	36,000
October estimated sales	30,000
November estimated sales	22,000
Total sales expected in the fiscal year	360,000

Exclusive of bad debts, total budgeted selling and general administrative expenses for the fiscal year are estimated at $61,500, of which $24,000 is fixed expense (which includes a $13,200 annual depreciation charge). The Bouquet Company incurs these fixed expenses uniformly throughout the year. The balance of the selling and general administrative expenses varies with sales. Expenses are paid as incurred.

7-38 Budgeting at Ritz-Carlton

The Ritz-Carlton has four hotels and resorts in the Caribbean and Mexico. Suppose one of these hotels is a 300-room hotel. Management expects occupancy rates to be 95% in December, January, and February, 85% in November, March, and April, and 70% the rest of the year. The average room rental is $250 per night. Of this, on average 10% is received as a deposit the month before the stay, 60% is received in the month of the stay, and 28% is collected the month after. The remaining 2% is never collected.

Most of the costs of running the hotel are fixed. The variable costs are only $30 per occupied room per night. Fixed salaries (including benefits) run $400,000 per month, depreciation is $350,000 a month, other fixed operating costs are $120,000 per month, and interest expense is $500,000 per month. Variable costs and salaries are paid in the month they are incurred, depreciation is recorded at the end of each quarter, other fixed operating costs are paid as incurred, and interest is paid each June and December.

1. Prepare a monthly cash budget for this Ritz-Carlton hotel. For simplicity, assume that there are 30 days in each month.
2. How much would the hotel's annual profit increase if occupancy rates increased by five percentage points each month in the off-season (that is, from 70% to 75% in May through October)?

7-39 Activity-Based Budgeting

A recent directive from Helen Endicott, CEO of Warren Communications, had instructed each department to cut its costs by 10%. The traditional functional budget for the shipping and receiving department was as follows:

Salaries, 4 employees @ $42,000	$168,000
Benefits @ 20%	33,600
Depreciation, straight-line basis	76,000
Supplies	43,400
Overhead @ 35% of direct costs	112,350
Total	$433,350

Therefore, the shipping and receiving department needed to find $43,335 to cut.

Rick Tulchin, a recent MBA graduate, was asked to pare $43,335 from the shipping and receiving department's budget. As a first step, he recast the traditional budget into an activity-based budget.

Receiving, 620,000 pounds	$ 93,000
Shipping, 404,000 boxes	202,000
Handling, 11,200 moves	112,000
Record keeping, 65,000 transactions	26,350
Total	$433,350

1. What actions might Tulchin suggest to attain a $43,335 budget cut? Why would these be the best actions to pursue?
2. Which budget helped you most in answering number 1? Explain.

7-40 Budgeting, Behavior, and Ethics

Since Simon Dunlop had become president of Yukon Mining, Ltd., budgets had become a major focus for managers. In fact, making budget was such an important goal that the only two managers who had missed their budgets in 2004 (by 2% and 4%, respectively) had been summarily fired. This caused all managers to be wary when setting their 2005 budgets.

The YML Copper Division of Yukon Mining had the following results for 2004:

Sales, 1.6 million pounds @ $.95/pound	$1,520,000
Variable costs	880,000
Fixed costs, primarily depreciation	450,000
Pretax profit	$ 190,000

Sheila Kosta, general manager of YML Copper, received a memo from Dunlop that contained the following:

> We expect your profit for 2005 to be at least $209,000. Prepare a budget showing how you plan to accomplish this.

Kosta was concerned because the market for copper had recently softened. Her market research staff forecast that sales would be at or below the 2004 level and prices would likely be between $.92 and $.94 per pound. Her manufacturing manager reported that most of the fixed costs were committed and there were few efficiencies to be gained in the variable costs. He indicated that perhaps a 2% savings in variable costs might be achievable, but certainly no more.

1. Prepare a budget for Kosta to submit to headquarters. What dilemmas does Kosta face in preparing this budget?
2. What problems do you see in the budgeting process at Yukon Mining?
3. Suppose Kosta submitted a budget showing a $209,000 profit. It is now late in 2005, and she has had a good year. Despite an industry-wide decline in sales, YML Copper's sales matched last year's 1.6 million pounds, and the average price per pound was $.945, nearly at last year's level and well above that forecast. Variable costs were cut by 2% through extensive efforts. Still, profit projections were more than $9,000 below budget. Kosta was concerned for her job, so she approached the controller and requested that depreciation schedules be changed. By extending the lives of some equipment for two years, $15,000 of depreciation could be saved in 2005. Estimating the economic lives of equipment is difficult, and it would be hard to prove that the old lives were better than the new proposed lives. What should the controller do? What ethical issues does this raise?

7-41 Spreadsheets and Sensitivity Analysis of Income Statement

Study Appendix 7. A **Speedy-Mart Store** in Northcenter Mall has the following budgeted sales, which are uniform throughout the month:

May	$450,000
June	375,000
July	330,000
August	420,000

Cost of goods sold averages 70% of sales, and merchandise is purchased essentially as needed. Employees earn fixed salaries of $22,000 (total) monthly and commissions of 10% of the current month's sales, paid as earned. Other expenses are rent, $6,000, paid on the first of each month for that month's occupancy; miscellaneous expenses, 6% of sales, paid as incurred; insurance, $450 per month, from a one-year policy that was paid for on January 2; and depreciation, $2,850 per month.

1. Using spreadsheet software, prepare a table of budget data for the Speedy-Mart Store.
2. Continue the spreadsheet in number 1 to prepare budget schedules for (a) disbursements for operating expenses and (b) operating income for June, July, and August.
3. Adjust the budget data appropriately for each of the following scenarios independently and recompute operating income using the spreadsheet:
   a. A sales promotion that will cost $30,000 in May could increase sales in each of the following three months by 5%.
   b. Eliminating the sales commissions and increasing employees' salaries to $52,500 per month could decrease sales thereafter by a net of 2%.

7-42 Spreadsheets and Sensitivity Analysis of Operating Expenses

Study Appendix 7. The LCD Division (LCDD) of Micro Displays, Inc., produces highest quality displays for LCD TVs. The displays are assembled from purchased components. The costs (value) added by LCDD are indirect costs (which include assembly labor), packaging, and shipping. LCDD produces two sizes of displays: 15' and 17'. Cost behavior of LCDD is as follows:

	Fixed	Variable
Purchased components		
17' Displays		$100 per component
15' Displays		40 per component
Indirect costs	$40,000	16 per component
Packaging	8,000	4 per drive
Shipping	8,000	2 per drive

Both displays require five components. Therefore, the total cost of components for 17′ displays is $500 and for 15′ displays is $200. LCDD uses a six-month continuous budget that is revised monthly. Sales forecasts for the next eight months are as follows:

	17′ Displays	15′ Displays
October	3,200 units	4,000 units
November	2,400	3,000
December	5,600	7,000
January	3,200	4,000
February	3,200	4,000
March	2,400	3,000
April	2,400	3,000
May	2,800	3,500

Treat each event in succession.

1. Use spreadsheet software to prepare a table of budgeting information and an operating expense budget for the LCD Division for October through March. Incorporate the expectation that sales of 15′ displays will be 125% of 17′ displays. Prepare a spreadsheet that can be revised easily for succeeding months.
2. October's actual sales were 2,800 17′ displays and 3,600 15′ displays. This outcome has caused LCDD to revise its sales forecasts downward by 10%. Revise the operating expense budget for November through April.
3. At the end of November, LCDD decides that the proportion of 17′ to 15′ is changing. Sales of 15′ displays are expected to be 150% of 17′ displays sales. Expected sales of 17′ displays are unchanged from number 2. Revise the operating expense budget for December through May.

Cases

7-43 Comprehensive Cash Budgeting

Wilma Brown, treasurer of Columbia Civic Theater (CCT), was preparing a loan request to the Northeast National Bank in December 2004. The loan was necessary to meet the cash needs of the theater for year 2005. In a few short years, the CCT had established itself as a premier theater. In addition to its regular subscription series, it started a series for new playwrights and offered a very popular holiday production. In fact, the holiday production was the most financially successful of the theater's activities, providing a base to support innovative productions that were artistically important to the theater but did not usually succeed financially.

In total, the theater had done well financially, as shown in Exhibits 7-13 and 7-14. Its profitable operations had enabled it to build its own building and generally acquire a large number of assets. It had at least broken even every year since its incorporation, and management anticipates continued profitable operations. The Corporate Community for the Arts in Columbia and several private foundations had made many grants to the theater, and such grants are expected to continue. Most recently, the largest bank in town had agreed to sponsor the production of a new play by a local playwright. The theater's director of development, Richard Talman, expected such corporate sponsorships to increase in the future.

To provide facilities for the theater's anticipated growth, CCT began work on an addition to its building two years ago. The new facilities are intended primarily to support the experimental theater offerings that were becoming more numerous. The capital expansion was to be completed in 2005; all that remained was acquisition and installation of lighting, sound equipment, and other new equipment to be purchased in 2005.

Columbia Civic Theater had borrowed working capital from Northeast National Bank for the past several years. To qualify for the loans, the theater had to agree to

1. Completely pay off the loan for one month during the course of the year.
2. Maintain cash and accounts receivable balances equal to (or greater than) 120% of the loan.
3. Maintain a compensating cash balance of $200,000 at all times.

In the past, the theater has had no problem meeting these requirements. However, in 2004 the theater had been unable to reduce the loan to zero for an entire month. Although Northeast continued to extend the needed credit, the loan manager expressed concern over the situation. She asked for a quarterly cash budget to justify the financing needed for 2005. Ms. Brown began to assemble the data needed to prepare such a budget.

Exhibit 7-13
Columbia Civic
Theater
*Balance Sheets as
of December 31
(in thousands of dollars)*

	2002	2003	2004
Assets			
Cash	$2,688	$ 229	$ 208
Accounts receivable	2,942	3,372	4,440
Supplies inventory	700	700	500
Total current assets	$6,330	$4,301	$ 5,148
Plant and equipment	2,643	4,838	5,809
Total assets	$8,973	$9,139	$10,957
Liabilities and Equities			
Bank loan	$ 0	$ 0	$ 1,620*
Accounts payable	420	720	780
Accrued payroll expenses	472	583	646
Mortgage, current	250	250	250
Total current liabilities	$1,142	$1,553	$ 3,296
Other payables	270		
Mortgage payable, long-term	3,750	3,500	3,250
Net assets†	3,811	4,086	4,411
Total liabilities and equities	$8,973	$9,139	$10,957

* Includes $32 thousand of accrued interest.
† The "Net assets" account for a nonprofit organization is similar to "Stockholders' equity" for a corporation.

Exhibit 7-14
Columbia Civic
Theater
*Income Statements for
the Year Ended
December 31 (in
thousands of dollars)*

	2002	2003	2004
Ticket sales	$3,303	$4,060	$5,263
Contributions	1,041	1,412	1,702
Grants and other revenues	1,202	1,361	1,874
Total revenues	$5,546	$6,833	$8,839
Expenses*			
Production	$4,071	$4,805	$6,307
Operations	271	332	473
Public relations and community development	1,082	1,421	1,734
Total expenses	$5,424	$6,558	$8,514
Excess of revenues over expenses	$ 122	$ 275	$ 325

* Expenses include depreciation of $355, $370, and $470 and general and administrative expenses of $1,549, $1,688, and $2,142 in the years 2002, 2003, and 2004, respectively.

CCT received revenue from three main sources: ticket sales, contributions, and grants. Ms. Brown formed Exhibit 7-15 to calculate the accounts receivable balance for each of these sources for 2005. She assumed that CCT would continue its normal practices for collecting pledges and grant revenues.

Most expenses were constant from month to month. An exception was supplies, which were purchased twice a year in December and June. In 2005, CCT expects to purchase $200,000 of supplies in June and $700,000 in December on terms of net 30 days. The supplies inventory at the end of December was expected to be $600,000. Depreciation expense of $500,000 was planned for 2005, and other expenses were expected to run at a steady rate of $710,000 a month throughout the year, of which $700,000 was payroll costs. Salaries and wages were paid on the Monday of the first week following the end of the month. The other $10,000 of other expenses were paid as incurred.

The major portion of the new equipment to be installed in 2005 was to be delivered in September; payments totaling $400,000 would be made in four equal monthly installments beginning in September. In addition, small equipment purchases are expected to run $20,000 per month throughout the year. They will be paid for on delivery.

	Ticket Sales		Contributions		Grants	
	Revenues	End of Quarter Receivables	Revenues	End of Quarter Receivables	Revenues	End of Quarter Receivables
First Quarter	$ 852	$2,795	$ 75	$ 794	$ 132	$1,027
Second Quarter	1,584	3,100	363	888	448	1,130
Third Quarter	2,617	3,407	1,203	1,083	1,296	1,240
Fourth Quarter	1,519	3,683	442	1,170	528	1,342

Exhibit 7-15

Columbia Civic Theater

Estimated Quarterly Revenues and End of Quarter Receivables for the Year Ended December 31, 2005 (in thousands of dollars)

In late 2002 CCT had borrowed $4 million (classified as a mortgage payable) from Farmers' Life Insurance Company. The theater is repaying the loan over 16 years, in equal principal payments in June and December of each year. Interest at 5% annually is also paid on the unpaid balance on each of these dates. Total interest payments for 2005, according to Ms. Brown's calculations, would be $172,000.

Interest on the working capital loan from Northeast was at an annual rate of 8%; payment for 2004's interest would be made on January 10, 2005, and that for 2005's interest would be made on January 10, 2006. Working capital loans are taken out on the first day of the quarter that funds are needed and they are repaid on the last day of the quarter when extra funds are generated. CCT has tried to keep a minimum cash balance of $200,000 at all times, even if loan requirements do not require it.

1. Compute the cash inflows and outflows for each quarter of 2005. What are CCT's loan requirements each quarter?
2. Prepare a projected Income Statement and Balance Sheet for CCT for 2005.
3. Prepare the projected Statement of Cash Flows for 2005.
4. What financing strategy would you recommend for CCT?

7-44 Cash Budgeting for a Hospital

St. John Hospital provides a wide range of health services in its community. St. John's board of directors has authorized the following capital expenditures:

Intra-aortic balloon pump	$1,400,000
Computed tomographic scanner	850,000
X-ray equipment	550,000
Laboratory equipment	1,200,000
Total	$4,000,000

The expenditures are planned for October 1, 2004, and the board wishes to know the amount of borrowing, if any, necessary on that date. Jill Todd, hospital controller, has gathered the following information to be used in preparing an analysis of future cash flows.

Billings, made in the month of service, for the first six months of 2004 are

Month	Actual Amount
January	$5,300,000
February	5,300,000
March	5,400,000
April	5,400,000
May	6,000,000
June	6,000,000

Ninety percent of St. John's billings are made to third parties such as BlueCross, federal or state governments, and private insurance companies. The remaining 10% of the billings are made directly to patients. Historical patterns of billing collections are

	Third-Party Billings	Direct-Patient Billings
Month of service	20%	10%
Month following service	50	40
Second month following service	20	40
Uncollectible	10	10

Estimated billings for the last six months of 2004 are listed next. Todd expects the same billing and collection patterns that have been experienced during the first six months of 2004 to continue during the last six months of the year.

Month	Estimated Amount
July	$5,400,000
August	6,000,000
September	6,600,000
October	6,800,000
November	7,000,000
December	6,600,000

The following schedule presents the purchases that have been made during the past three months and the planned purchases for the last six months of 2004.

Month	Amount
April	$1,300,000
May	1,450,000
June	1,450,000
July	1,500,000
August	1,800,000
September	2,200,000
October	2,350,000
November	2,700,000
December	2,100,000

All purchases are made on account, and accounts payable are remitted in the month following the purchase.

- Salaries for each month during the remainder of 2004 are expected to be $1,800,000 per month plus 20% of that month's billings. Salaries are paid in the month of service.
- St. John's monthly depreciation charges are $150,000.
- St. John incurs interest expenses of $180,000 per month and makes interest payments of $540,000 on the last day of each calendar quarter.
- Endowment fund income is expected to continue to total $210,000 per month.
- St. John has a cash balance of $350,000 on July 1, 2004, and has a policy of maintaining a minimum end-of-month cash balance of 10% of the current month's purchases.
- St. John Hospital employs a calendar-year reporting period.

1. Prepare a schedule of budgeted cash receipts by month for the third quarter of 2004.
2. Prepare a schedule of budgeted cash disbursements by month for the third quarter of 2004.
3. Determine the amount of borrowing, if any, necessary on October 1, 2004, to acquire the capital items totaling $4,000,000.

7-45 Comprehensive Budgeting for a University

Suppose you are the controller of Western Idaho State University. The university president, Willa Redcloud, is preparing for her annual fund-raising campaign for 2004–2005. To set an appropriate target, she has asked you to prepare a budget for the academic year. You have collected the following data for the current year (2003–2004):

	Undergraduate Division	Graduate Division
Average salary of faculty member	$46,000	$46,000
Average faculty teaching load in semester credit-hours per year (eight undergraduate or six graduate courses)	24	18
Average number of students per class	30	20
Total enrollment (full-time and part-time students)	3,600	1,800
Average number of semester credit-hours carried each year per student	25	20
Full-time load, semester hours per year	30	24

For 2004–2005, all faculty and staff will receive a 6% salary increase. Undergraduate enrollment is expected to decline by 2%, but graduate enrollment is expected to increase by 5%.

- The 2003–2004 budget for operation and maintenance of facilities was $500,000, which includes $240,000 for salaries and wages. Experience so far this year indicates that the budget is accurate. Salaries and wages will increase by 6% and other operating costs will increase by $12,000 in 2004–2005.
- The 2003–2004 and 2004–2005 budgets for the remaining expenditures are

	2003–2004	2004–2005
General administrative	$500,000	$525,000
Library		
Acquisitions	150,000	155,000
Operations	190,000	200,000
Health services	48,000	50,000
Intramural athletics	56,000	60,000
Intercollegiate athletics	240,000	245,000
Insurance and retirement	520,000	560,000
Interest	75,000	75,000

- Tuition is $70 per credit hour. In addition, the state legislature provides $780 per full-time-equivalent student. (A full-time equivalent is 30 undergraduate hours or 24 graduate hours.) Tuition scholarships are given to 30 full-time undergraduates and 50 full-time graduate students.
- Revenues other than tuition and the legislative apportionment are

	2003–2004	2004–2005
Endowment income	$200,000	$210,000
Net income from auxiliary services	325,000	335,000
Intercollegiate athletic receipts	290,000	300,000

- The chemistry/physics classroom building needs remodeling during the 2004–2005 period. Projected cost is $575,000.

1. Prepare a schedule for 2004–2005 that shows, by division, (a) expected enrollment, (b) total credit hours, (c) full-time-equivalent enrollment, and (d) number of faculty members needed.
2. Calculate the budget for faculty salaries for 2004–2005 by division.
3. Calculate the budget for tuition revenue and legislative apportionment for 2004–2005 by division.
4. Prepare a schedule for President Redcloud showing the amount that must be raised by the annual fund-raising campaign.

7-46 Activity-Based Budgeting, Multi-Stage ABC, Process Map

(Review Appendix 4 on pages 162–169) **Gompf Brackets, Inc**. makes standard and custom brackets for such products as IBM PCs, **Apple Macintosh**, and **Sun Microsystems SPARC** Stations.

Gompf Brackets, Inc. utilizes sophisticated CAD technology to ensure absolute precision and quality. The company has developed more than 4,000 standard and custom brackets. In many cases Gompf offers customers the option of using a standard product, which provides a substantial cost savings. However, some customers fax in explicit engineering specifications and drawings. Others phone in to discuss a particular application and need direction. The answer may be a custom solution.

Suppose one of Gompf's operating units, the Spokane Bracket Division, has actual operating results for the year ending December 31, 2004 shown in Exhibits 7-16 and 7-17 on page 336. The amounts shown in Exhibit 7-16 can be derived using the 2004 data presented in Exhibit 7-17.

Spokane Bracket Division uses activity-based budgeting and a multi-stage activity-based costing system. Exhibit 7-18 on page 337 shows the process map for the division (unallocated resources are not shown in Exhibit 7-18) with the budgeted data from Exhibit 7-17 entered. Major activities included in the processing function include stamping, machining, fabrication, and tooling. The cost driver chosen for this function is machine hours. Activities included in the support function include engineering, inspection, printing, and shipping. The cost driver for this function is number of production runs. Fixed-cost resources consist mostly of expensive processing equipment such as die stamping, laser cutting, high-speed spindles, and deburring machines. Machine hours is the cost driver for these resources. Variable-cost resources are for the most part power and supplies. Management has found that a high correlation exists between the costs of these resources and the power consumed. So the cost driver chosen was megawatt hours.

a. Prepare a schedule that shows the 2005 budgeted gross margin for the Spokane Bracket Division and for each of the two product groups–standard brackets and custom solutions. Be sure to calculate the budgeted consumption of the three resources that have potential capacity constraints. Assume that if additional laborers or machines are required, the cost will behave as a step-fixed cost.

b. Prepare bar graphs giving the actual gross profit results for 2004 and the budgeted gross profit for 2005 in dollars by product group. Comment briefly about the budgeted changes in the components making up the gross profit.

EXCEL Application Exercise

7-47 Preparing a Cash Budget to Assist Long-Range Planning

Goal: Create an Excel spreadsheet to prepare a cash budget to assist with long-range planning. Use the results to answer questions about your findings.

Scenario: Adventure.com has asked you to prepare an analysis of their cash requirements until such time as their forecasted cash receipts begin to exceed their forecasted cash disbursements. The company will use your analysis to determine venture capital funding levels requests. Additional background information for your spreadsheet appears in assignment material 7-27.

When you have completed your spreadsheet, answer the following questions:

1. Based on their stated objective of stopping venture capital funding when cash receipts begin to exceed cash disbursements, in what month/year should Adventure.com no longer require venture capital funding? Why?
2. What is the total amount of expenditures Adventure.com will incur before their cash receipts begin to exceed their cash disbursements? What is the total amount of venture capital funding that Adventure.com should request?
3. Is the amount of venture capital funding that Adventure.com should request equal to their total expenditures? If not, why are the amounts different?

Step-by-Step:

1. Open a new Excel spreadsheet.
2. In column A, create a bold-faced heading that contains the following:
   Row 1: Chapter 7 Decision Guideline
   Row 2: Adventure.Com
   Row 3: Cash Budget for Venture Capital Requirements
   Row 4: Today's Date

3. Merge and center the four heading rows across columns A through F.
4. In row 7, create the following bold-faced, center-justified column headings with a column width of 10.57:
   Column B: 2003
   Column C: 2004
   Column D: 2005
   Column E: 2006
   Column F: Total
5. In column A, create the following row headings:
   Row 8:   Equipment Purchase
   Row 9:   Salaries and other Operating Expenses
   Row 10:   Revenues
   Row 11:   Net Cash Requirements
   Note: Adjust column width as necessary.

6. Use data from assignment 7-27 to enter the amounts for the yearly cash requirements for the three income/expense categories. Use formulas to calculate the appropriate yearly amounts within each category when necessary.
   Hint: Use different signs for the cash receipt (revenue) and cash disbursement (expense) amounts.

7. Use the SUM function to calculate totals for each column in row 11 and for each row in column F.
8. Format amounts in rows 8 and 11 as

Number tab:	Category:	Accounting
	Decimal:	0
	Symbol:	$

9. Format amounts in Rows 9 and 10 as

Number tab:	Category:	Accounting
	Decimal:	0
	Symbol:	None

10. Apply top and bottom borders to the amounts in row 11 by clicking the drop down indicator on the Borders icon from the toolbar. Select the "Top and Double Bottom Border."
11. Save your work to disk, and print a copy for your files.

Collaborative Learning Exercise

7-48 Personal Budgeting

Budgeting is useful to many different types of entities, including the individual. Consider the entity that you know best, the college or university student. Form a group of two to six students, and pool the information that you have about what it costs to spend a year as a full-time student.

Prepare a revenue and expense budget for an average prospective full-time student at your college or university. Identify possible sources of revenue and the amount to be received from each. Identify the costs a student is likely to incur during the year. You can assume that cash disbursements are made immediately for all expenses, so the budgeted income statement and cash budget are identical.

When all groups have completed their budgets, compare those budgets. What are the differences? What assumptions led to the differences?

Internet Exercises www.prenhall.com/horngren

7-49 Carnival Corporation

The budgeting process helps firms to identify sources of revenues and expenses as well as the timing of cash flows. While many parts of the budgeting process are confidential, there are some things that may be identifiable by someone outside the firm who would like to make some potential budget projections for the following year. Consider **Carnival Corporation**, the cruise ship firm. Go to the Carnival Web site at http://www.carnivalcorp.com.

1. Look at the list of Carnival Corporation's family of products. How many different brand lines operate under the corporation shell? What are they? Visit a couple of the links. Do the brands each

Exhibit 7-16

Spokane Bracket Division Operating Results For the Year Ending December 31, 2004

	Division Total	Standard Brackets	Custom Solutions
Revenue	$1,222,000	$952,000	$270,000
Expenses			
Direct material	280,200	224,400	55,800
Direct labor	84,000	56,000	28,000
Processing (allocated based on machine hours)	120,862	103,705	17,157
Production support (allocated based on number of production runs)	68,998	14,754	54,244
Total expenses	554,060	398,859	155,201
Contribution to unallocated overhead	$ 667,940	$553,141	$114,799
Unallocated division overhead	180,000		
Contribution to Corporate Income	$ 487,940		

Data Item	2004 Actual	2005 Budget
Standard bracket volume in packages	34,000	50,000
Standard bracket price per package	$28	$26
Custom solution volume in packages	750	1,000
Custom solution price per package	$360	$400
Standard direct labor consumption rate (hours per package)	0.1	0.1
Custom direct labor consumption rate (hours per package)	1.6	1.4
Direct labor wage per year	$28,000	$30,000
Number of standard direct laborers	2	?
Number of custom solution direct laborers	1	?
Standard direct material cost per package	$6.60	$6.00
Custom solution direct material cost per package	$77.4	$60
Standard bracket processing activity machine hours per package	0.08*	0.07
Custom solution processing activity machine hours per package	0.6	.5
Standard bracket production run per package**	.0006	.0005
Custom solution production run per package	0.1	0.1
Consumption rate of fixed-cost resources by processing activity (machine hours used for each processing machine hour)	1.05***	1.0
Consumption rate of variable-cost resources by processing activity (megawatt hours per machine hour)	0.11	0.1
Consumption rate of fixed-cost resources by production support activity	22	20
Consumption rate of variable-cost resources by production support activity (megawatt hours per machine hour)	1.7	1.5
Fixed operating cost per machine per year	$42,000	$40,625
Number of machines	3	?
Charge rate for variable-cost resources (per megawatt hour)	$125	$136
Utilization rates:		
• Standard direct labor	94.4%†	?
• Custom solutions direct labor	66.7%	?
• Fixed-cost resources	95.2%	?

* This consumption rate was computed by dividing the total of 2,720 machine hours required for processing standard brackets by 34,000 packages.

** The average number of packages produced during each production run is 1/.0006 = 1667.

*** In 2004, there was a 5% inefficiency rate, due to downtime for unscheduled repairs.

† In 2004, capacity was 1,800 hours. Utilization was (34,000 pkg. × 0.1 hours/pkg.) ÷ (2 × 1,800 hrs) = 94.4%. Capacity in 2005 will be lower due to training for process improvement programs.

Exhibit 7-17

Spokane Bracket Division Operating and Financial Data

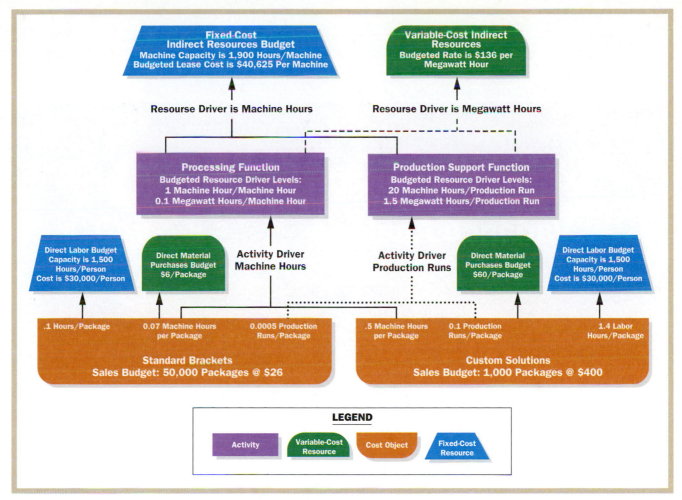

Exhibit 7-18
Process Map for Spokane Bracket Division—Budget for 2005

offer exactly the same services? Why might the firm have different names for the cruise lines serving different areas?

2. The sales figure is one of the most important pieces of information the firm uses in beginning the planning process. Carnival's sales figure is made up primarily of two parts—the number of passenger cruise days and the price charged for each passenger cruise day. Open Carnival's annual report for the most recent year. Notice the total revenues for the year and then turn to the section, Management's Discussion and Analysis of Financial Condition and Results of Operations, which follows the financial statements and footnotes. Notice the information about the number of cruise days and the occupancy percentage. When the firm does the budget for next year for passenger cruise days, if they add no new cruises or any new ships, and if they expect 100% occupancy, what number of days should they use? Read the information provided by management with respect to growth for the next year. Does the company expect any increase in passenger capacity during the next year?

3. Using the estimated increase in cruise capacity for the next year, what would be the expected cruise days available? Should the firm expect an increase in costs associated with the increase in capacity? When budgeting for these costs, would the costs be proportional to the increase in revenues? Why or why not?

4. The other component in revenue is how much the passenger pays for the cruise. Select one of the cruise line links from the main page. Find the subsequent link that takes you to information about cruise prices. Are all of the prices for the same length of cruise the same? Look at the fine print with respect to the cruise pricing. What does it tell about how the price is determined? Why might the capacity level of the cruise determine the price that is charged for the cruise?

Flexible Budgets and Variance Analysis

CHAPTER 8

LEARNING OBJECTIVES

When you have finished studying this chapter, you should be able to:

1. Distinguish between flexible budgets and master (static) budgets.

2. Use flexible-budget formulas to construct a flexible budget based on the volume of sales.

3. Prepare an activity-based flexible budget.

4. Explain the performance evaluation relationship between master (static) budgets and flexible budgets.

5. Compute flexible-budget variances and sales-activity variances.

6. Compute and interpret price and usage variances for inputs based on cost-driver activity.

7. Compute variable overhead spending and efficiency variances.

McDONALD'S

A recent survey ranked McDonald's as the world's

best-known brand. **McDonald's** opens about 1,000 new restaurants a year, most of them outside the United States. You can eat a Big Mac under the Golden Arches in nearly 120 countries. In addition, the company closes about 500 unprofitable restaurants each year.

With revenues exceeding $15 billion and more than 31,000 restaurants, the challenge is to ensure that the taste of each Big Mac is the same. How does McDonald's maintain cost and quality control? How does it ensure that each of the 46 million customers it serves daily receives the same value? It uses standards, budgets, and variance analysis. For example, the standards for material are the same for hamburgers wherever they are sold—1 bun, 1 hamburger patty, 1 pickle slice, 1/8 tablespoon of dehydrated onion, 1/4 tablespoon mustard, and 1/2 ounce of ketchup. Management determines material variances for each of these ingredients by computing the amount actually used compared to what should have been used, given the number and types of sandwiches sold.

McDonald's managers budget sales for each hour during the day. Based on the sales budgeted, they schedule labor. If sales are lower than budgeted, managers can control labor cost by sending some employees home early.

McDonald's also uses nonfinancial standards to help achieve its quality and service goals. For example, the standard time for a drive-through customer is 310 seconds, from pulling up to the menu board to driving away. Employees must destroy cooked meat that is not used in a sandwich within 30 minutes. Once employees make a sandwich and place it in the transfer bin, they must sell it within 10 minutes or throw it away.

Using flexible budgets to analyze performance is important to individual McDonald's restaurants, such as this one in Asia, as well as to the company as a whole.

As is the case at McDonald's, managers and employees of any organization want to know how they are doing in meeting their goals. Upper-level managers also want to know how the organization is meeting its financial objectives. Knowing what went wrong *and* what went right should help managers plan and manage more effectively in future periods.

This chapter introduces flexible budgets and budget variances. These tools direct management to areas of actual financial performance that deserve attention. Managers can apply this same basic process to the control of other important areas of performance such as quality and service. ■

Flexible Budgets: Bridge Between Static Budgets and Actual Results

Static Budgets

static budget
A budget that is based on only one level of activity.

A **static budget** is a budget that is based on only one level of activity. All the master budgets discussed in Chapter 7 are static budgets. Why? Because managers prepare a master budget for *only one level* of a given type of activity. When a company like McDonald's predicts its net income for the coming year or quarter, it uses a static budget—one that assumes one particular level of predicted sales.

Consider a company using a traditional costing system with only one cost driver. The Dominion Company is a one-department firm in Toronto that manufactures and sells a wheeled, collapsible suitcase carrier that is popular with airline flight crews. Manufacture of this suitcase carrier requires several manual and machine operations. The product has some variations, but we will assume for our purposes that it is a single product bearing one selling price. Assume that the cost driver is sales volume (that is, units sold), and the projected sales volume is 9,000 units. Thus, we base the master budget on projected sales of 9,000 units, as shown in column 2 of Exhibit 8-1.

Exhibit 8-1
Dominion Company
*Performance Report
Using a Master Budget
For the Month Ended
June 30, 20X1*

	Actual (1)	Master Budget (2)	Master Budget Variances (3)
Units	7,000	9,000	2,000 U
Sales	$217,000	$279,000	$62,000 U
Variable costs			
Variable manufacturing costs	$151,270	$189,000	$37,730 F
Shipping costs (selling)	5,000	5,400	400 F
Administrative costs	2,000	1,800	200 U
Total variable costs	$158,270	$196,200	$37,930 F
Contribution margin	$ 58,730	$ 82,800	$24,070 U
Fixed expenses			
Fixed manufacturing costs	$ 37,300	$ 37,000	$ 300 U
Fixed selling and administrative costs	33,000	33,000	—
Total fixed costs	$ 70,300	$ 70,000	$ 300 U
Operating income (loss)	$ (11,570)	$ 12,800	$24,370 U

U = Unfavorable cost variances occur when actual costs are more than budgeted costs.
F = Favorable cost variances occur when actual costs are less than budgeted costs.

We could compare the actual results with the original budgeted amounts, even though, for example, sales volume turned out to be only 7,000 units instead of the originally planned 9,000 units. The actual results for June 20X1 appear in column 1 of Exhibit 8-1. Differences or variances between actual results and the master budget are in column 3. The master budget called for production and sales of 9,000 units, but Dominion actually produced and sold only 7,000 units. There were no beginning or ending inventories, so the units made in June were sold in June.

The performance report in Exhibit 8-1 compares the actual results with the master budget. A helpful performance report will include variances that direct management's attention to significant deviations from expected results, allowing management by exception. (You might want to review pp. 12–13.) Recall that a variance is a deviation of an actual amount from the expected or budgeted amount. Exhibit 8-1 shows variances of actual results from the master budget. We call these **master-budget variances** or **static-budget variances.** Actual revenues that exceed expected revenues result in favorable revenue variances. When actual revenues are below expected revenues, variances are unfavorable. Similarly, actual costs that exceed budgeted costs result in **unfavorable cost variances.** Similarly, actual expenses that are less than budgeted expenses result in **favorable cost variances.** Each significant variance should cause a manager to ask, "Why?" By explaining why a variance occurs, managers are forced to recognize changes that have affected revenues or costs and that might affect future decisions.

Suppose the president of Dominion Company asks you to explain why there was an operating loss of $11,570 when you budgeted a profit of $12,800. First, the unfavorable sales variance means that sales were $62,000 below expectations. However, the favorable variances for the variable costs are misleading. Considering the lower-than-projected level of sales activity, was cost control really satisfactory? Would you really expect to pay $196,200 for variable costs when you produce only 7,000 units? Of course not! Therefore, the comparison of actual results with a master budget is not very useful for management by exception.

As another example, consider a particular McDonald's restaurant that expects to sell 10 million Big Macs in 2005 and budgets $1 million for the 10 million buns. Suppose the restaurant sells only 9 million Big Macs and pays $950,000 for buns. You would expect the buns to cost $900,000, not the $1 million originally budgeted. The $1,000,000 − $950,000 = $50,000 favorable variance is not meaningful; the restaurant really spent $950,000 − $900,000 = $50,000 more for buns than it should have for 9 million Big Macs.

Flexible Budgets

A more helpful benchmark for analysis is the flexible budget. A **flexible budget** (sometimes called **variable budget**) is a budget that adjusts for changes in sales volume and other cost-driver activities. The flexible budget is identical to the master budget in format, but managers may prepare it for any level of activity. So, when Dominion's sales turn out to be 7,000 units instead of 9,000, managers can use the flexible budget to prepare a new budget based on this new cost-driver level. We can then see what the total variable costs should be based on a sales level of 7,000 and compare this amount to the actual result. For performance evaluation, we would prepare the flexible budget at the actual level of activity achieved. In contrast, we keep the master budget fixed or static to serve as the original benchmark for evaluating performance. It shows revenues and costs at only the originally planned levels of activity.

The flexible-budget approach says, "Give me any activity level you choose, and I'll provide a budget tailored to that particular level." Many companies routinely "flex" their

OBJECTIVE 1
Distinguish between flexible budgets and master (static) budgets.

flexible budget (variable budget)
A budget that adjusts for changes in sales volume and other cost-driver activities.

budgets to help evaluate recent financial performance. For example, managers at **Ritz-Carlton** hotels evaluate monthly financial performance of all the company's hotels by comparing actual results to new, flexible budgets that they prepare for actual levels of activity.

Flexible-Budget Formulas

OBJECTIVE 2

Use flexible-budget formulas to construct a flexible budget based on the volume of sales.

To develop a flexible budget, managers determine revenue and cost behavior (within the relevant range) with respect to appropriate cost drivers. The cost functions that you used in Chapter 2 and estimated in Chapter 3 are essentially flexible-budget formulas. The flexible budget incorporates effects on each cost and revenue caused by changes in activity. Exhibits 8-2 and 8-3 show Dominion Company's simple flexible budget, which has a single cost driver, units of output. Managers believe that Dominion Company's cost functions or flexible-budget formulas are valid within the relevant range of 7,000 to

Exhibit 8-2

Dominion Company
Flexible Budgets

	Flexible-Budget Formula	Flexible Budgets for Various Levels of Sales/Production Activity		
Units		7,000	8,000	9,000
Sales	$ 31.00	$217,000	$248,000	$279,000
Variable costs				
Variable manufacturing costs	$ 21.00	$147,000	$168,000	$189,000
Shipping costs (selling)	.60	4,200	4,800	5,400
Administrative	.20	1,400	1,600	1,800
Total variable costs	$ 21.80	$152,600	$174,400	$196,200
Contribution margin	$ 9.20	$ 64,400	$ 73,600	$ 82,800
Fixed costs per month				
Fixed manufacturing costs	$37,000	$ 37,000	$ 37,000	$ 37,000
Fixed selling and administrative costs	33,000	33,000	33,000	33,000
Total fixed costs	$70,000	$ 70,000	$ 70,000	$ 70,000
Operating income (loss)		$ (5,600)	$ 3,600	$ 12,800

Exhibit 8-3

Dominion Company
Graph of Flexible Budget of Costs

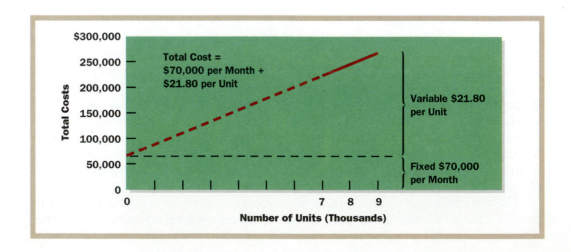

9,000 units. We prepare each column of Exhibit 8-2 (7,000, 8,000, and 9,000 units, respectively) using the same flexible-budget formula. We can use this formula to predict the cost of any activity level within this range, as shown in the graph in Exhibit 8-3. Of course, we expect fixed costs to be constant across this range of activity.

Activity-Based Flexible Budgets

Dominion Company's flexible budget in Exhibit 8-2 is based on a single cost driver—units of product. This is an appropriate approach to flexible budgeting when "units of product" is both a plausible and reliable cost driver for *all* of a company's costs. But what if some of a company's costs are caused by activities such as order processing and setting up for production? In this case, a more detailed budgeting system is needed.

Companies that have an activity-based costing system prepare an **activity-based flexible budget** by budgeting costs for each activity and related cost driver. Exhibit 8-4 shows an activity-based flexible budget for the Dominion Company. There are four

OBJECTIVE 3

Prepare an activity-based flexible budget.

activity-based flexible budget
A budget based on budgeted costs for each activity and related cost driver.

Exhibit 8-4
Dominion Company
Activity-Based Flexible Budget for the Month Ended June 30, 20X1

	BUDGET FORMULA	Units		
		7,000	8,000	9,000
Sales	$31.00	$217,000	$248,000	$279,000
ACTIVITY				
Processing		Cost Driver: Number of Machine Hours		
Cost-driver level		14,000	16,000	18,000
Variable costs	$10.50	$147,000	$168,000	$189,000
Fixed costs	$13,000	13,000	13,000	13,000
Total costs of processing activity		$160,000	$181,000	$202,000
Setup		Cost Driver: Number of Setups		
Cost-driver level		21	24	27
Variable costs	$500	$ 10,500	$ 12,000	$ 13,500
Fixed costs	$12,000	12,000	12,000	12,000
Total costs of setup activity		$ 22,500	$ 24,000	$ 25,500
Marketing		Cost Driver: Number of Orders		
Cost-driver level		350	400	450
Variable costs	$12.00	$ 4,200	$ 4,800	$ 5,400
Fixed costs	$15,000	15,000	15,000	15,000
Total costs of marketing activity		$ 19,200	$ 19,800	$ 20,400
Administration		Cost Driver: Number of Units		
Cost-driver level		7,000	8,000	9,000
Variable costs	$.20	$ 1,400	$ 1,600	$ 1,800
Fixed costs	$18,000	18,000	18,000	18,000
Total costs of administration activity		$ 19,400	$ 19,600	$ 19,800
Total costs		$221,100	$244,400	$267,700
Operating income (loss)		$ (4,100)	$ 3,600	$ 11,300

activities: processing, setup, marketing, and administration. Within each activity, costs depend on an appropriate cost driver. Compare the traditional flexible budget (Exhibit 8-2) and the activity-based flexible budget (Exhibit 8-4). Note that the 8,000-unit columns in Exhibits 8-4 and 8-2 are the same, but at other volumes the costs diverge. The key difference is that some manufacturing costs that are fixed with respect to units are variable with respect to the cost-driver "setups." That is, the fixed manufacturing costs ($37,000) in Exhibit 8-2 include setup costs that are largely fixed with respect to "units produced" but that vary with respect to the "number of setups." An example is the cost of supplies used to set up the production run. Each time employees perform a setup, they use supplies. Therefore, the cost of supplies varies directly with the number of setups. However, production itself uses no setup supplies, so there is little change in the cost of supplies over wide ranges of units produced. This basic difference is why the total budgeted costs differ using the two approaches—and why activity-based flexible budgets provide more accurate measures of cost behavior.

When should a company use activity-based flexible budgets? When a significant portion of its costs vary with cost drivers other than units of production. In our Dominion example, the $500 per setup is the only such cost. For the rest of this chapter, we will ignore the fact that this cost varies with number of setups, and go back to assuming that Dominion's operations are simple enough that a traditional flexible budget with a single cost driver is appropriate.

Evaluation of Financial Performance Using Flexible Budgets

OBJECTIVE 4

Explain the performance evaluation relationship between master (static) budgets and flexible budgets.

We saw earlier that comparing actual results to the master budget is not useful for management by exception. The problem stems from the comingling of two quite different causes for any differences. Actual results might differ from the master budget because (1) sales and other cost-driver activities were not the same as originally forecasted, or (2) revenues or variable costs per unit of activity and fixed costs per period were not as expected. Although these reasons may not be completely independent (for example, higher unit sales prices may have caused lower unit sales levels), it is useful to separate these effects because different people may be responsible for each and because it may take different management actions to correct deficiencies in each. The flexible budget allows us to separate these two effects.

Accountants use variances to isolate unexpected effects on actual results that managers can correct if adverse or enhance if beneficial. Because both the flexible budget and the actual results reflect the actual level of activity (in our example, sales volume), changes in the activity level cannot cause any variances between the flexible budget and actual results. Only departures of actual costs or revenues from flexible-budget formula amounts can cause such variances. We call these variances between the flexible budget and actual results **flexible-budget variances.**

flexible-budget variances
The variances between the flexible budget and the actual results.

In contrast, changes in activity levels, not cost control, cause any differences or variances between the master budget and the flexible budget. We call these differences between the master budget amounts and the amounts in the flexible budget **activity-level variances.** In other words, the original difference we saw between actual results and the original master budget, which we could not fully explain earlier, actually has two components: the sales-activity variance and the flexible-budget variance.

activity-level variances
The differences between the master budget amounts and the amounts in the flexible budget.

Consider Exhibit 8-5. The flexible budget (column 3) taken from Exhibit 8-2 (and simplified) provides an explanatory bridge between the master budget (column 5) and the actual results (column 1). The bottom of Exhibit 8-5 summarizes the variances for operating income. Note that the sum of the activity-level variances (here sales-activity variances, because sales is the only activity used as a cost driver) and the flexible-budget variances equals the total of the master-budget variances.

	Actual Results at Actual Activity Level* (1)	Flexible-Budget Variances† (2) = (1) − (3)	Flexible Budget for Actual Sales Activity‡ (3)	Sales-Activity Variances (4) = (3) − (5)	Master Budget (5)
Units	7,000	—	7,000	2,000 U	9,000
Sales	$217,000	—	$217,000	$62,000 U	$279,000
Variable costs	158,270	5,670 U	152,600	43,600 F	196,200
Contribution margin	$ 58,730	$5,670 U	$ 64,400	$18,400 U	$ 82,800
Fixed costs	70,300	300 U	70,000	—	70,000
Operating income	$(11,570)	$5,970 U	$ (5,600)	$18,400 U	$ 12,800

Total flexible-budget variances, $5,970 U   Total sales-activity variances, $18,400 U

Total master budget variances, $24,370 U

U = Unfavorable. F = Favorable.
* Figures are from Exhibit 8-1.
† Figures are shown in more detail in Exhibit 8-6.
‡ Figures are from the 7,000-unit column in Exhibit 8-2.

Exhibit 8-5
Dominion Company
Summary of Performance for the Month Ended June 30, 20X1

We next examine in more detail how managers can use variances to evaluate an operation's effectiveness and efficiency.

Isolating the Causes of Variances

Managers use comparisons between actual results, master budgets, and flexible budgets to evaluate organizational performance. When evaluating performance, they try to distinguish between **effectiveness**—the degree to which a goal, objective, or target is met—and **efficiency**—the degree to which an organization uses appropriate amounts of inputs to achieve a given level of outputs.

Performance may be effective, efficient, both, or neither. For example, Dominion Company set a master-budget objective of manufacturing and selling 9,000 units. It actually made and sold only 7,000 units. Performance, as measured by sales-activity variances, was ineffective because Dominion did not meet the sales objective.

Was Dominion's performance efficient? Managers judge the degree of efficiency by comparing actual outputs achieved (7,000 units) with actual inputs (such as the costs of direct materials and direct labor). The less input used to produce a given output, the more efficient the operation. As indicated by the flexible-budget variances, Dominion was inefficient because the actual cost of its inputs exceeded the cost expected for the actual level of output.

A McDonald's restaurant could use this same analysis. Its effectiveness—the difference between its master budget and flexible budget for the actual level of sales—depends on the degree to which it meets its sales objectives. Its efficiency—the difference between the actual results and the flexible budget—shows the difference between actual operating profit and the profit expected for the level of sales actually attained.

effectiveness
The degree to which a goal, objective, or target is met.

efficiency
The degree to which an organization uses appropriate amounts of inputs to achieve a given level of outputs.

MAKING MANAGERIAL DECISIONS

Consider a simple example of a company that plans to sell 1,000 units of a product for $2 per unit. Budgeted variable costs are $1 per unit, and the master-budget operating income is $400. Suppose the company actually sells 800 units and makes an operating income of $200. Compute and interpret the master-budget variance, the sales-activity variance, and the flexible-budget variance.

Answer

The master-budget variance is $400 − $200 = $200 U. The sales-activity variance is the lost contribution margin on the 200 units of lost sales: $1.00 × 200 = $200. Therefore, the flexible budget variance is $0. The entire shortfall in operating income was caused by failing to meet the unit sales target of 1,000 units. The operation was efficient but not effective.

Flexible-Budget Variances

OBJECTIVE 5

Compute flexible-budget variances and sales-activity variances.

Recall that flexible-budget variances measure the efficiency of operations at the actual level of activity. The first three columns of Exhibit 8-5 compare the actual results with the flexible-budget amounts. The flexible-budget variances are the differences between columns 1 and 3, which total $5,970 unfavorable:

$$\text{total flexible-budget variance} = \text{total actual results} - \text{total flexible budget,}$$
$$\text{planned results}$$
$$= (-\$11,570) - (-\$5,600)$$
$$= -\$5,970, \text{ or } \$5,970 \text{ unfavorable}$$

The total flexible-budget variance arises from sales prices received and the variable and fixed costs incurred. Dominion Company had no difference between actual sales price and the flexible-budgeted sales price, so we must focus on the differences between actual costs and flexible-budgeted costs at the actual 7,000-unit level of activity. Without the flexible budget in column 3, we cannot separate the effects of differences in cost behavior from the effects of changes in sales activity. The flexible-budget variances indicate whether operations were efficient or not and may form the basis for periodic performance evaluation. Operations managers are in the best position to explain flexible-budget variances.

Companies that use variances primarily to fix blame often find that managers resort to cheating and subversion to beat the system. Managers of operations usually have more information about those operations than higher-level managers. If supervisors use that information against them, lower-level managers might withhold or misstate valuable information for their own protection. For example, one manufacturing firm actually reduced the next period's departmental budget by the amount of the department's unfavorable variances in the current period. If a division had a $50,000 expense budget and experienced a $2,000 unfavorable variance, the following period's budget would be set at $48,000. This system led managers to cheat and to falsify reports to avoid unfavorable variances. We can criticize departmental managers' ethics, but the system was as much at fault as the managers.

Exhibit 8-6 gives an expanded, line-by-line computation of flexible-budget variances for all cost items at Dominion. Note how most of the costs that had seemingly favorable master-budget variances (see Exhibit 8-1) have unfavorable flexible-budget variances. Why is this so? Because sales fell short of the target, so costs in the flexible budget were much lower than costs in the master budget.

It is tempting to conclude that favorable flexible-budget variances are good and unfavorable flexible-budget variances are bad. Don't fall into that trap. Instead, interpret all

	Actual Costs Incurred	Flexible Budget*	Flexible-Budget Variances†	Explanation
Units	7,000	7,000	—	
Variable costs				
Direct materials	$ 69,920	$ 70,000	$ 80 F	Lower prices but higher usage
Direct labor	61,500	56,000	5,500 U	Higher wage rates and higher usage
Indirect labor	9,100	11,900	2,800 F	Decreased setup time
Idle time	3,550	2,800	750 U	Excessive machine breakdowns
Cleanup time	2,500	2,100	400 U	Cleanup of spilled solvent
Supplies	4,700	4,200	500 U	Higher prices and higher usage
Variable manufacturing costs	$151,270	$147,000	$4,270 U	
Shipping	5,000	4,200	800 U	Use of air freight to meet delivery
Administration	2,000	1,400	600 U	Excessive copying and long-distance calls
Total variable costs	$158,270	$152,600	$5,670 U	
Fixed costs				
Factory supervision	$ 14,700	$ 14,400	$ 300 U	Salary increase
Factory rent	5,000	5,000	—	
Equipment depreciation	15,000	15,000	—	
Other fixed factory costs	2,600	2,600	—	
Fixed manufacturing costs	$ 37,300	$ 37,000	$ 300 U	
Fixed selling and administrative costs	33,000	33,000	—	
Total fixed costs	$ 70,300	$ 70,000	$ 300 U	
Total variable and fixed costs	$228,570	$222,600	$5,970 U	

* From 7,000-unit column of Exhibit 8-2.

† This is a line-by-line breakout of the variances in column 2 of Exhibit 8-5.

Exhibit 8-6
Dominion Company
Cost-Control Performance Report for the Month Ended June 30, 20X1

variances as signals that actual operations have not occurred exactly as anticipated when managers set the flexible-budget formulas. Any cost that differs significantly from the flexible budget deserves an explanation. Sometimes managers can easily explain costs that exceed budget. For example, direct-labor costs may have increased because of an increase in pay rates. Costs that fall short of budget might mean that the company is spending too little. Maybe shipping costs are below budget because slow ground shipments replaced air shipments, and this might alienate customers. The last column of Exhibit 8-6 gives possible explanations for Dominion Company's variances.

Sales-Activity Variances

Sales-activity variances measure how effective managers have been in meeting the planned sales objective. Dominion Company's sales activity fell 2,000 units short of the planned level. The final three columns of Exhibit 8-5 show that changes in unit prices, unit variable costs, or fixed costs do not affect the sales-activity variances (totaling $18,400 U). Why? Because we use the same budgeted unit prices, unit variable costs, and total fixed costs in constructing both the flexible and master budgets. Notice that there can never be a sales-activity variance for fixed costs. Why? Because we include the same total budgeted fixed-cost amount in both the flexible budget and the master budget.

The total of the sales-activity variances informs the manager that falling short of the sales target by 2,000 units caused operating income to be $18,400 lower than initially

sales-activity variances
Variances that measure how effective managers have been in meeting the planned sales objective, calculated as actual unit sales less master budget unit sales times the budgeted unit contribution margin.

budgeted (a \$5,600 loss instead of a \$12,800 profit). In summary, the shortfall of sales by 2,000 units caused Dominion Company to incur a total sales activity variance of 2,000 units at a contribution margin of \$9.20 per unit (from the first column of Exhibit 8-2):

$$\text{total sales-activity variance} = (\text{actual sales units} - \text{master budgeted sales units})$$
$$\times \text{ budgeted contribution margin per unit}$$
$$= (9{,}000 - 7{,}000) \times \$9.20$$
$$= \$18{,}400 \text{ unfavorable}$$

Who has responsibility for the sales-activity variance? Marketing managers usually have the primary responsibility for reaching the sales level specified in the static budget. Of course many factors can cause variations in sales.[1] Nevertheless, marketing managers are typically in the best position to explain why actual sales levels differed from plans.

Think about the situation at **Dell**, **Compaq**, **Gateway**, **Intel**, **Cisco**, and other technology companies early this decade. An unforseen decline in computer sales caused actual sales to fall far short of predicted sales for these companies. Even if their operations were efficient (that is, no unfavorable flexible-budget variances), large unfavorable sales-activity variances caused operating income to fall short of predicted (master-budget) operating income levels.

Setting Standards

expected cost
The cost most likely to be attained.

standard cost
A carefully determined cost per unit that should be attained.

To establish flexible budgets, managers must determine expected costs or standard costs. An **expected cost** is the cost that is most likely to be attained. A **standard cost** is a carefully developed cost per unit that should be attained. It is often synonymous with the expected cost, but some companies intentionally set standards above or below expected costs to create desired incentives.

Standards are popular, used by more than 85% of U.S. companies. But standards mean different things to different companies. What standard of expected performance should a company use in its flexible budgets? Should a standard be so strict that the company rarely, if ever, meets it? Should the company attain it 50% of the time? 90%? 20%? Individuals who have worked a lifetime setting and evaluating standards for performance disagree, so there are no universal answers to this question. In fact, as described in the Business First box on page 349, more and more companies are adapting standards to fit their particular needs.

perfection standards (ideal standards)
Expressions of the most efficient performance possible under the best conceivable conditions, using existing specifications and equipment.

Perfection standards (also called **ideal standards**) are expressions of the most efficient performance possible under the best conceivable conditions, using existing specifications and equipment. They make no provision for waste, spoilage, machine breakdowns, and the like. Those who favor using perfection standards maintain that the resulting unfavorable variances will constantly remind personnel of the continuous need for improvement in all phases of operations. Though concern for continuous improvement is widespread, these standards are not widely used because they have an adverse effect on employee motivation. Employees tend to ignore unreasonable goals, especially if they would not share the gains from meeting imposed perfection standards. Many organizations attempt to achieve continuous improvement from "the bottom up," not by prescribing what should be achieved via perfection standards.

currently attainable standards
Levels of performance that managers can achieve by realistic levels of effort.

Currently attainable standards are levels of performance that managers can achieve by realistic levels of effort. They make allowances for normal defectives, spoilage, waste, and nonproductive time. There are at least two popular interpretations of the meaning of currently attainable standards. The first interpretation has standards set just tightly enough that employees regard their attainment as highly probable if normal effort and diligence are exercised.

---

[1]For example, managers can subdivide sales-activity variances into sales quantity, sales mix, market size, and market share variances. This more advanced treatment of sales-activity variances is covered in Charles T. Horngren, George Foster, and Srikant M. Datar, *Cost Accounting: A Managerial Emphasis*, 10th ed. (Upper Saddle River, NJ: Prentice Hall, 2000), pp. 573–580. These sales-activity variances might result from changes in the product, changes in customer demand, effective advertising, and so on.

THE NEED TO ADAPT STANDARD COST APPROACHES

The use of standard costs and variance analysis has come under attack during the last ten years. Critics maintained that comparing actual costs to predetermined standards is a static approach that does not work well in today's dynamic, fast-paced, just-in-time environment. However, companies continue to use standards and to measure performance against them. Surveys in five different countries have shown that between 65% and 86% of manufacturing companies use standard costs, with the high level of 86% being applied in the United States. Companies have apparently adapted the approach to fit their modern environments.

To apply standards in a dynamic environment, how should managers measure and report variances? First, they should continually evaluate their standards. If a company is in a state of continuous improvement, it must continually revise its standards. Second, standards and variances should measure key strategic variables. The concept of setting a benchmark, comparing actual results to the benchmark, and identifying causes for any differences is universal. We can apply it to many types of measures, such as production quantity or quality, as well as to costs. Finally, variances should not lead to affixing blame. Standards are plans, and things do not always go according to plan—often with no one being at fault.

One company that has adapted standard costs to meet its particular needs is the Brass Products Division (BPD) at **Parker Hannifin Corporation**, a $6 billion company that produces motion control products. The BPD uses standard costs and variances to pinpoint problem areas that need attention if the division is to meet its goal of continuous improvement. Among the changes that have increased the value of the standard cost information are more timely product cost information, variances computed at more detailed levels, and regular meetings held to help employees understand their impact on the variances.

The BPD also created three new variances: (1) the standard run quantity variance examines the effect of actual compared to optimal batch size for production runs; (2) the material substitution variance compares material costs to the costs of alternative materials; and (3) the method variance measures costs using actual machines compared to costs using alternative machines. All three variances use the concept of setting a standard and comparing actual results to the standard, but they do not apply the traditional standard cost variance formulas.

It was premature to declare standard costs dead. They are alive and well in many companies. However, there are fewer and fewer environments where traditional variance analysis is useful, and more and more environments where managers and accountants must adapt the standard cost concept to fit the particular needs of a company.

Sources: Adapted from D. Johnsen and P. Sopariwala, "Standard Costing Is Alive and Well at Parker Brass," *Management Accounting Quarterly*, Winter 2000, pp. 12–20; C. B. Cheatham and L. R. Cheatham, "Redesigning Cost Systems: Is Standard Costing Obsolete?" *Accounting Horizons*, December 1996, pp. 23–31; C. Horngren, G. Foster, and S. Datar, *Cost Accounting: A Managerial Emphasis* (Upper Saddle River, NJ: Prentice Hall, 2000), p. 226; and Parker Hannifin Corp., *Parker Hannifin 2002 Annual Report*.

That is, variances should be random and negligible. Hence, the standards are predictions of what will likely occur, anticipating some inefficiencies. Managers accept the standards as being reasonable goals. The major reasons for having "reasonable" standards, then, are

1. The resulting standards serve multiple purposes. For example, companies can use the same cost for financial budgeting, inventory valuation, and budgeting departmental performance. In contrast, they cannot use perfection standards for inventory valuation or financial budgeting, because they know that the costs are unrealistically low.
2. Reasonable standards have a desirable motivational impact on employees, especially when combined with incentives for continuous improvement. The standard represents reasonable future performance, not fanciful goals. Therefore, unfavorable variances direct attention to performance that is not meeting reasonable expectations.

A second interpretation of currently attainable standards is that standards are set tightly. That is, employees regard their fulfillment as possible, though unlikely. Managers can achieve such standards only by very efficient operations. Variances tend to be unfavorable; nevertheless, employees accept the standards as being tough but not unreasonable goals. Is it possible to achieve continuous improvement using currently attainable standards? Yes, but expectations must reflect improved productivity and management must also use incentive systems that reward continuous improvement.

Trade-Offs Among Variances

Because the operations of organizations are interrelated, the level of performance in one area will affect performance in other areas. Nearly any combination of effects is possible. Improvements in one area could lead to improvements in others and vice versa. Likewise, substandard performance in one area may be balanced by superior performance in others. For example, McDonald's may generate favorable labor variances by hiring less-skilled and thus lower-paid employees, but this favorable variance may lead to unfavorable customer satisfaction and future unfavorable sales-activity variances. In another situation, **General Motors** may experience unfavorable materials variances by purchasing higher-quality materials at a higher than planned price, but this variance may be more than offset by the favorable variances caused by less waste, fewer inspections, and higher-quality products.

Because of the many interdependencies among activities, an "unfavorable" or "favorable" label should not lead a manager to jump to conclusions. By themselves, such labels merely raise questions and provide clues to the causes of performance. They are attention directors, not problem solvers. Furthermore, the cause of unfavorable variances might be unrealistically high expectations rather than the substandard execution by managers. One of the first questions a manager should consider when explaining a large variance is whether expectations were valid.

When to Investigate Variances

When should management investigate a variance? Managers recognize that, even if everything operates as planned, variances are unlikely to be exactly zero. They predict a range of "normal" variances. This range is usually based on economic analysis of how big a variance must be before investigation could be worth the effort. For some critical items, any deviation may prompt a follow-up. For most items, a minimum dollar or percentage deviation from budget may be necessary before managers expect investigations to be worthwhile. For example, a 4% variance in a $1 million material cost may deserve more attention than a 20% variance in a $10,000 repair cost. Because knowing exactly when to investigate is difficult, many organizations have developed rules of thumb such as "Investigate all variances exceeding $5,000 or 25% of expected cost, whichever is lower."

Comparisons with Prior Period's Results

Some organizations compare the most recent budget period's actual results with last year's results for the same period rather than use flexible-budget benchmarks. For example, an organization might compare June 2004's actual results to June 2003's actual results. In general, these comparisons are not as useful for evaluating the performance of an organization as comparisons of actual outcomes with planned results for the same period. Why? Because many changes probably have occurred in the environment and in the organization. Such changes make a comparison across years invalid. Very few organizations and environments are so stable that the only difference between now and a year ago is merely the passage of time. For example, the turmoil in the stock market in 2001 and 2002 led **Merrill Lynch** to make some sweeping changes in operations to "enhance revenues in certain areas and reduce costs." Comparisons of operating results in 2003 to either 2002 or 2001 would not be appropriate because the company operated so differently in 2003. Even comparisons with last month's actual results may not be as useful as comparisons with flexible budgets. Comparisons over time may be useful for analyzing trends in such key variables as sales volume, market share, and product mix, but they do not help answer questions such as Dominion Company's "Why did we have a loss of $11,570 in June, when we expected a profit of $12,800?" or Merrill Lynch's "How could 2002 operating earnings increase by 7% when revenues fell by 15%?"

Summary Problem For Your Review

PROBLEM

Refer to the data in Exhibits 8-1 and 8-2. Suppose actual production and sales were 8,500 units instead of 7,000 units; actual variable costs were $188,800; and actual fixed costs were $71,200. The selling price remained at $31 per unit.

1. Compute the master-budget variance. What does this tell you about the efficiency of operations? The effectiveness of operations?
2. Compute the sales-activity variance. Is the performance of the marketing function the sole explanation for this variance? Why?
3. Using a flexible budget at the actual activity level, compute the budgeted contribution margin, budgeted operating income, and flexible-budget variance. What do you learn from this variance?

SOLUTION

1.
$$\text{actual operating income} = (8{,}500 \times \$31) - \$188{,}800 - \$71{,}200 = \$3{,}500$$

$$\text{master-budget operating income} = \$12{,}800 \text{ (from Exhibit 8-1)}$$

$$\text{master-budget variance} = \$12{,}800 - \$3{,}500 = \$9{,}300 \text{ U}$$

Three factors affect the master-budget variance: sales activity, efficiency, and price changes. There is no way to tell from the master-budget variance alone how much of the $9,300 U was caused by each of these factors.

2.
$$\text{sales-activity variance} = \text{budgeted unit contribution margin} \times \text{difference between the master-budget unit sales and the actual unit sales}$$

$$= \$9.20 \text{ per unit CM} \times (9{,}000 - 8{,}500)$$

$$= \$4{,}600 \text{ U}$$

This variance is the sales-activity variance because it quantifies the impact on operating income of the deviation from an original sales target while holding price and efficiency factors constant. This is a measure of the effectiveness of the operations. Dominion was ineffective in meeting its sales objective. Of course, management might attribute the failure to reach target sales to several causes beyond the control of marketing personnel, including material shortages, factory breakdowns, and so on.

3. The budget formulas in Exhibit 8-2 are the basis for the following answers.

$$\text{flexible-budget contribution margin} = \$9.20 \times 8{,}500 = \$78{,}200$$

$$\text{flexible-budget operating income} = \$78{,}200 - \$70{,}000 \text{ fixed costs} = \$8{,}200$$

$$\text{actual operating income} = \$3{,}500 \text{ (from number 1)}$$

$$\text{flexible-budget variance} = \$8{,}200 - \$3{,}500 = \$4{,}700 \text{ U}$$

The flexible-budget variance shows that the company spent $4,700 more to produce and sell the 8,500 units than it should have spent if operations had been efficient and unit sales prices had not changed. Note that this variance plus the $4,600 U sales-activity variance total to the $9,300 U master-budget variance.

Flexible-Budget Variances in Detail

The rest of this chapter probes the flexible-budget variance in detail, essentially subdividing labor-, materials-, and overhead-cost variances into their component parts. Note that in companies where direct-labor costs are small in relation to total costs (that is, in highly automated companies) direct-labor costs may be treated as an overhead-cost item. For example, the ABC system used by a wire-producing plant of **Insteel Industries** assigns both labor and overhead costs to a category called conversion costs. Such companies do not compute separate labor standards, budgets, or variances.

Variances from Material and Labor Standards

Consider Dominion Company's $10 standard cost of direct materials and $8 standard cost of direct labor. The company derived these standards per unit from two components: a standard quantity of an input and a standard price for the input.

| | Standards | | |
	Standard Inputs Expected per Unit of Output	Standard Price Expected per Unit of Input	Standard Cost Expected per Unit of Output
Direct materials	5 pounds	$ 2/pound	$10
Direct labor	1/2 hour	16/hour	8

Once we have set standards and observed actual results, we can measure variances from the flexible budget. To analyze the variances more fully, we will reconsider Dominion's direct-materials and direct-labor costs, as shown in Exhibit 8-6, and assume that the following actually occurred for the production of 7,000 units of output:

- Direct materials: Dominion purchased and used 36,800 pounds of material at an actual unit price of $1.90 for a total actual cost of $69,920.
- Direct labor: Dominion used 3,750 hours of labor at an actual hourly price (rate) of $16.40, for a total cost of $61,500.

Flexible budget variances for direct material and direct labor are $80 F and $5,500 U, respectively:

	(1) Actual Costs	(2) Flexible Budget	(3) Flexible- Budget Variance
Direct materials	$69,920	$70,000	$ 80 F
Direct labor	61,500	56,000	5,500 U

The flexible-budget totals [column (2)] for direct materials and direct labor are the amounts that Dominion would have spent with expected efficiency. We call this the total standard cost allowed, computed as follows:

$$\begin{array}{ccc} \text{flexible} \\ \text{budget or} \\ \text{total standard} \\ \text{cost allowed} \end{array} = \begin{array}{c} \text{units of good} \\ \text{output} \\ \text{achieved} \end{array} \times \begin{array}{c} \text{input allowed} \\ \text{per unit of} \\ \text{output} \end{array} \times \begin{array}{c} \text{standard unit} \\ \text{price of input} \end{array}$$

standard direct-materials cost allowed = 7,000 units $\times$ 5 pounds $\times$ \$2.00 per pound = \$70,000

standard direct-labor cost allowed = 7,000 units $\times$ 1/2 hour $\times$ \$16.00 per hour = \$56,000

Before reading on, note particularly that the flexible-budget amounts (that is, the standard costs allowed) depend on an initial question: What was the output achieved? Always ask yourself, What was the good output? Then proceed with your computations of the total standard cost allowed for the good output achieved.

Price and Usage Variances

Flexible-budget variances [column (3) in the table at the bottom of page 352] measure how efficiently Dominion produced its 7,000 units. Dominion's efficiency depends on whether it (1) used more or less of the resource than planned for the actual level of output achieved and (2) paid more or less than planned for each unit of the resources used. We measure these two components by computing price and usage variances, which subdivide each flexible-budget variance into the following two parts:

O B J E C T I V E 6

Compute and interpret price and usage variances for inputs based on cost-driver activity.

1. **Price variance**—difference between actual input prices and standard input prices multiplied by the actual quantity of inputs used.
2. **Usage variance**—difference between the quantity of inputs actually used and the quantity of inputs that the company should have used to achieve the actual quantity of output multiplied by the standard price of the input (also called a **quantity variance** or **efficiency variance**).

price variance
The difference between actual input prices and standard input prices multiplied by the actual quantity of inputs used.

usage variance (quantity variance, efficiency variance)
The difference between the quantity of inputs actually used and the quantity of inputs that the company should have used to achieve the actual quantity of output multiplied by the standard price of the input.

The objective of these variance calculations is to hold either price or usage constant so that we can isolate the effect of the other. When calculating the price variance, you hold use of inputs constant at the actual level of usage. When calculating the usage variance, you hold price constant at the standard price. For Dominion Company the price variances are

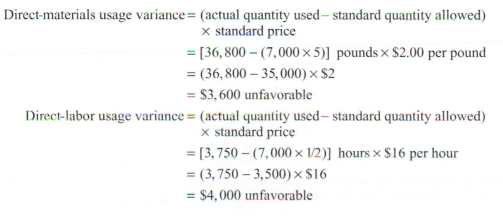

Direct-materials price variance = (actual price − standard price) × actual quantity

= (\$1.90 − \$2.00) per pound × 36,800 pounds

= \$3,680 favorable

Direct-labor price variance = (actual price − standard price) × actual quantity

= (\$16.40 − \$16.00) per hour × 3,750 hours

= \$1,500 unfavorable

The usage variances are

Direct-materials usage variance = (actual quantity used − standard quantity allowed) × standard price

= [36,800 − (7,000 × 5)] pounds × \$2.00 per pound

= (36,800 − 35,000) × \$2

= \$3,600 unfavorable

Direct-labor usage variance = (actual quantity used − standard quantity allowed) × standard price

= [3,750 − (7,000 × 1/2)] hours × \$16 per hour

= (3,750 − 3,500) × \$16

= \$4,000 unfavorable

To determine whether a variance is favorable or unfavorable, use logic rather than memorization of a formula. A price variance is favorable if the actual price is less than the standard. A usage variance is favorable if the actual quantity used is less than the standard quantity allowed. The opposite relationships imply unfavorable variances.

Note that the sum of the direct-labor price and usage variances equals the direct-labor flexible-budget variance. Furthermore, the sum of the direct-materials price and usage variances equals the total direct-materials flexible-budget variance.

$$\text{Direct-materials flexible-budget variance} = \$3,680 \text{ favorable} + \$3,600 \text{ unfavorable}$$
$$= \$80 \text{ favorable}$$
$$\text{Direct-labor flexible-budget variance} = \$1,500 \text{ unfavorable} + \$4,000 \text{ unfavorable}$$
$$= \$5,500 \text{ unfavorable}$$

Summary of Materials and Labor Variances

Exhibit 8-7 presents the analysis of direct materials and direct labor in a format that deserves close study. The general approach is at the top of the exhibit. The specific

Exhibit 8-7

General Approach to Analysis of Direct-Labor and Direct-Materials Variances

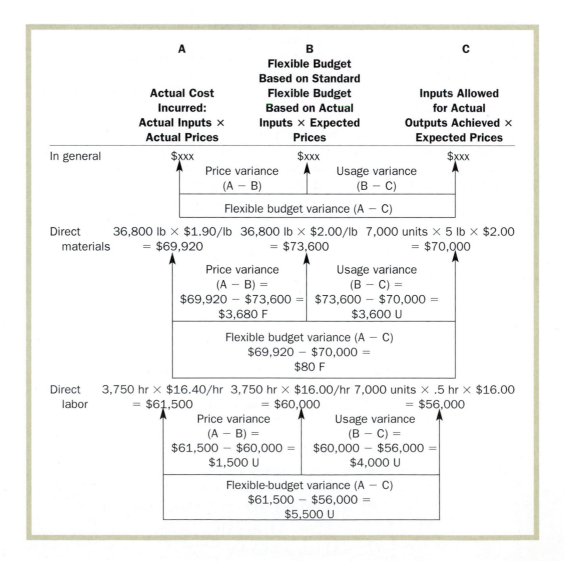

applications then follow. Even though the exhibit may seem complex at first, studying it will solidify your understanding of variance analysis.

Column A of Exhibit 8-7 contains the actual costs incurred for the inputs during the budget period. Column B is the expected costs for the actual inputs used, that is, the flexible budget with expected prices but actual usage. Column C is the flexible-budget amount using both expected prices and expected usage for the outputs actually achieved. (This is the flexible-budget amount from Exhibit 8-6 for 7,000 units.) We insert column B between A and C to separate price and usage effects. Managers can attribute the difference between columns A and B to changing prices because we hold usage at the same actual level in columns A and B. They can attribute the difference between columns B and C to changing usage because we hold price at the same expected level in columns B and C.

In column C, we measured output in units of product. However, most organizations manufacture a variety of products. To add disparate units together results in a nonsensical number (it is like adding apples and oranges). Therefore, we often express units of output in terms of the standard inputs allowed for their production. For example, labor hours may become the common denominator for measuring total output volume. Thus, a furniture manufacturer may express output as 20,000 standard hours allowed (or, more accurately, as standard hours of input allowed for outputs achieved) instead of 12,000 chairs and 3,000 sofas. Remember that standard hours allowed in this case is a measure of actual output achieved.

A key idea illustrated in Exhibit 8-7 is the versatility of the flexible budget. A flexible budget is geared to activity volume, and Exhibit 8-7 shows that activity volume can be measured in terms of either actual inputs used (columns A and B) or standard inputs allowed for actual outputs achieved (column C).

Interpretation of Price and Usage Variances

When feasible, managers try to separate the variances that they can directly influence from those that they cannot. The usual approach is to separate price factors from usage factors. Managers generally have less control over price factors than over usage factors. Why? Because external forces, such as general economic conditions, have more influence on prices. Even when managers do not control price factors, isolating them helps to focus on the efficient usage of inputs. For example, the commodity prices of wheat, oats, corn, and rice may be outside the control of **General Mills** managers. By separating price variances from usage variances, the breakfast-cereal maker can focus on whether managers used grain efficiently.

Price and usage variances are helpful because they provide feedback to those responsible for inputs. However, managers should not use these variances alone for decision making, control, or evaluation. Exclusive focus on material price variances by purchasing agents or buyers, for example, can work against an organization's JIT and total quality management goals. A buyer may earn favorable material price variances by buying in large quantities and buying low-quality material. The result could then be excessive inventory-handling and opportunity costs and increased manufacturing defects caused by faulty material. Similarly, exclusive focus on labor price and usage variances could motivate supervisors to use lower-skilled workers or to rush workers through critical tasks, both of which could impair quality of products and services.

Variances themselves do not show why the company achieved or failed to achieve the budgeted operating income. They simply raise questions, provide clues, and direct attention. For instance, one possible explanation for Dominion's set of variances is that a manager made a trade-off—the manager purchased substandard-quality materials at a favorable price, saving $3,680 (the materials price variance). Excessive waste of the materials nearly offset this savings, as indicated by the $3,600 unfavorable material usage variance and net flexible-budget variance of $80 favorable. The material waste also may have caused at least part of the excess use of direct labor. Why? Because Dominion used some labor on units that ended up being defective, thus wasting that labor. Suppose the labor wasted on the defective units was more than $80. Then the manager's trade-off was not successful. Why? Because the cost inefficiencies caused by using substandard materials exceeded the savings from the favorable price.

Exhibit 8-8 shows the price and usage variance computations for labor graphically. The standard cost (or flexible budget) is the standard quantity multiplied by the standard price—the rectangle shaded blue. The price variance is the difference between the actual and standard unit prices multiplied by actual quantity used—the rectangle shaded purple. The usage variance is the standard price multiplied by the difference between the actual quantity used and the standard quantity allowed for the good output achieved—the rectangle shaded green. (Note that for clarity the graph portrays only unfavorable variances.)

Exhibit 8-8
Graphical Representation of Price and Usage Variances for Labor

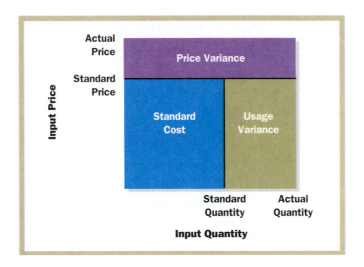

MAKING MANAGERIAL DECISIONS

The concept of variance analysis is not restricted to financial budgets. Consider a production plant that is supposed to produce 50 units per hour and work 8 hours each day. On March 23 the plant produced 325 units. Because of machine breakdowns, the plant operated for only 7.5 hours that day. Using the same conceptual framework as used for separating usage and price variances, determine how much of the 75 unit shortfall in production was caused by working only 7.5 hours and how much was caused by inefficiencies during the hours of actual operation.

Answer

Normal production would be 8 × 50 = 400 units per day. If the only difference from plan was the loss of 1/2 hour of productive time, production would have been 7.5 × 50 = 375 units. Therefore, 25 units of shortfall were caused by the machine breakdowns. The other 375 − 325 = 50 units were caused by producing fewer than 50 units per hour. The actual rate of production was 325 ÷ 7.5 = 43.3 units per hour, 6.7 units fewer than budgeted.

Overhead Variances

We have just seen that we can subdivide direct-materials and direct-labor variances into price and usage components. Some companies find it worthwhile to also subdivide the flexible-budget overhead variances, especially those for variable overhead. Part of the variable-overhead flexible-budget variance is related to control of the cost driver and part to the control of overhead spending itself. When actual cost-driver activity differs from the standard amount allowed for the actual output achieved, a **variable-overhead efficiency variance** will occur.

Consider Dominion Company's cost of supplies, a variable-overhead cost. The flexible-budget variance for supplies is $4,700 − $4,200 = $500 unfavorable, as shown in Exhibit 8-6. The variable-overhead cost rate of $.60 per unit is equivalent to $1.20 per direct-labor hour because each unit of output requires 1/2 hour of labor. Of the $500 unfavorable variance, $300 unfavorable is a variable-overhead efficiency variance caused by using 250 too many direct-labor hours (3,750 hours rather than the 3,500 allowed by the flexible budget):

$$\begin{array}{c}\text{variable-overhead}\\\text{efficiency variance}=\\\text{for supplies}\end{array}\left(\begin{array}{c}\text{actual direct-}\\\text{labor hours}\end{array}-\begin{array}{c}\text{standard direct-labor}\\\text{hours allowed}\end{array}\right)\times\begin{array}{c}\text{standard}\\\text{variable-overhead}\\\text{rate per hour}\end{array}$$

$$=\left(\begin{array}{c}3,750\ \text{actual}\\\text{hours}\end{array}-\begin{array}{c}3,500\ \text{standard}\\\text{hours allowed}\end{array}\right)\times\$1.20\ \text{per hour}$$

$$=\$300\ \text{unfavorable}$$

Whenever actual cost-driver activity exceeds that allowed for the actual output achieved, variable-overhead efficiency variances are unfavorable and vice versa. In essence, the variable-overhead efficiency variance tells management how much overhead cost it wastes (or saves, if the variance is favorable) by not controlling the use of cost-driver activity. The remainder of the flexible-budget variance measures control of overhead spending itself, given actual cost-driver activity.

That is, the **variable-overhead spending variance** is the difference between the actual variable overhead and the amount of variable overhead budgeted for the actual level of cost-driver activity.

$$\begin{array}{c}\text{variable-overhead spending}\\\text{variance for supplies}\end{array}=\begin{array}{c}\text{actual variable}\\\text{overhead}\end{array}-\left(\begin{array}{c}\text{standard variable-}\\\text{overhead rate}\end{array}\times\begin{array}{c}\text{actual direct-}\\\text{labor hours used}\end{array}\right)$$

$$=\$4,700-(\$1.20\times3,750\ \text{hours})$$

$$=\$4,700-\$4,500$$

$$=\$200\ \text{unfavorable}$$

Many organizations believe that it is not worthwhile to monitor individual overhead items to the same extent as labor and material variances. They do not subdivide overhead variances beyond the flexible-budget variances—they believe that the complexity of the analysis is not worth the effort. For example, Dominion Company's flexible-budget variance for supplies would be simply $4,700 − $4,200 = $500 unfavorable.

For analyzing performance, we seldom subdivide the fixed-overhead flexible-budget variance. For example, Dominion Company's factory supervision flexible-budget variance of $14,700 − $14,400 = $300 unfavorable is simply the difference between the original lump-sum budget and the actual cost of factory supervision.

Like other variances, the overhead variances by themselves cannot identify causes for results that differ from the static and flexible budgets. The only way for management to discover why overhead performance did not agree with the budget is to investigate possible

OBJECTIVE 7

Compute variable overhead spending and efficiency variables.

variable-overhead efficiency variance
An overhead variance caused by actual cost-driver activity differing from the standard amount allowed for the actual output achieved.

variable-overhead spending variance
The difference between the actual variable overhead and the amount of variable overhead budgeted for the actual level of cost-driver activity.

Exhibit 8-9
General Approach to
Analysis of Overhead
Variances

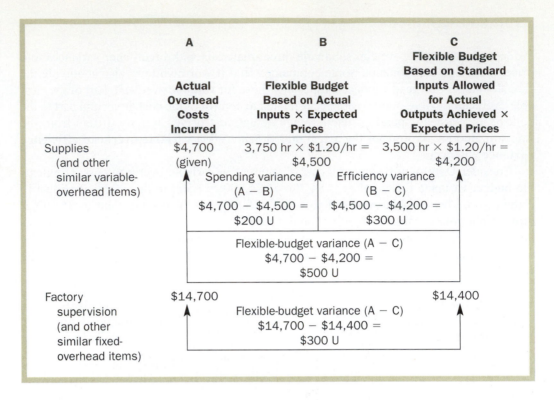

causes. The distinction between spending and usage variances for materials and labor and between efficiency and spending variances for variable overhead provides a springboard for more investigation, however.

Exhibit 8-9 summarizes a general approach to overhead variances. We do not subdivide the flexible-budget variances for fixed-overhead items here. We discuss fixed-overhead flexible-budget variances in more detail in Chapter 13.

Summary Problem For Your Review

PROBLEM

The following questions are based on the data contained in the Dominion Company illustration used in this chapter.

- Direct materials: standard, 5 pounds per unit @ $2 per pound
- Direct labor: standard, 1/2 hour @ $16 per hour

Suppose the following were the actual results for production of 8,500 units:

- Direct materials: Dominion purchased and used 46,000 pounds at an actual unit price of $1.85 per pound, for an actual total cost of $85,100
- Direct labor: Dominion used 4,125 hours of labor at an actual hourly rate of $16.80, for a total actual cost of $69,300
    1. Compute the flexible-budget variance and the price and usage variances for direct labor and direct material.
    2. In number 1 you should have computed a direct-materials price variance of $6,900 favorable. Is this a good outcome? Explain.

SOLUTION

1. The variances are

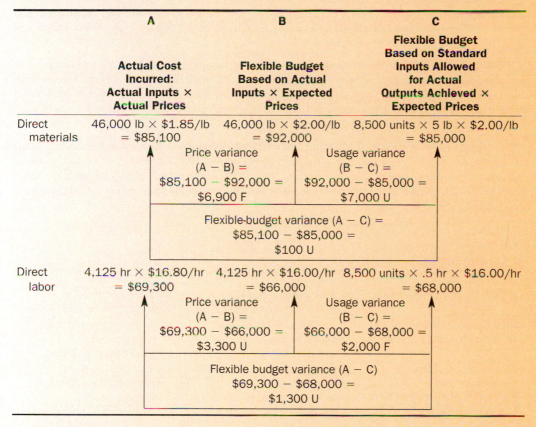

	A	B	C
	Actual Cost Incurred: Actual Inputs × Actual Prices	**Flexible Budget Based on Actual Inputs × Expected Prices**	**Flexible Budget Based on Standard Inputs Allowed for Actual Outputs Achieved × Expected Prices**
Direct materials	46,000 lb × $1.85/lb = $85,100	46,000 lb × $2.00/lb = $92,000	8,500 units × 5 lb × $2.00/lb = $85,000

Price variance
(A − B) =
$85,100 − $92,000 =
$6,900 F

Usage variance
(B − C) =
$92,000 − $85,000 =
$7,000 U

Flexible-budget variance (A − C) =
$85,100 − $85,000 =
$100 U

Direct labor	4,125 hr × $16.80/hr = $69,300	4,125 hr × $16.00/hr = $66,000	8,500 units × .5 hr × $16.00/hr = $68,000

Price variance
(A − B) =
$69,300 − $66,000 =
$3,300 U

Usage variance
(B − C) =
$66,000 − $68,000 =
$2,000 F

Flexible budget variance (A − C)
$69,300 − $68,000 =
$1,300 U

2. The favorable price variance may not be a good outcome. When prices are low, it may motivate Dominion Company managers to buy extra inventory in excess of its immediate needs, causing extra storage and handling costs. The favorable price variance may also mean that quality of the material is lower than planned. The favorable materials price variance is a good outcome only if it exceeds any unfavorable material, labor, or overhead variances caused by the volume and quality of materials purchased.

Highlights to Remember

1 **Distinguish between flexible budgets and master (static) budgets.** Flexible budgets are geared to changing levels of cost-driver activity rather than to the single static level of the master budget. Organizations may tailor flexible budgets to particular levels of sales or cost-driver activity—before or after the fact. They tell how much revenue and cost to expect for any level of activity.

2 **Use flexible-budget formulas to construct a flexible budget based on the volume of sales.** Cost functions, or flexible-budget formulas, reflect fixed- and variable-cost behavior and allow managers to compute budgets for any desired output or cost-driver activity level. We compute the flexible-budget amounts for variable costs by multiplying the variable cost per cost-driver unit times the level of activity, as measured in cost-driver units. The flexible-budgeted fixed cost is a lump sum, independent of the level of activity (within the relevant range).

3 **Prepare an activity-based flexible budget.** When a significant portion of operating costs varies with cost drivers other than units of production, a company benefits from using activity-based flexible budgets. These budgets are based on budgeted costs for each activity and related cost driver.

4 Explain the performance evaluation relationship between master (static) budgets and flexible budgets. The differences or variances between the master budget and the flexible budget are due to activity levels, not cost control. We call these variances activity-level variances.

5 Compute flexible-budget variances and sales-activity variances. The flexible-budget variance is the difference between the total actual results and the total flexible-budget amounts for the actual unit volume. We compute the sales-activity variances by multiplying actual unit sales less master-budget unit sales times the budgeted unit-contribution margin.

6 Compute and interpret price and usage variances for inputs based on cost-driver activity. Managers often want to subdivide flexible-budget variances for variable inputs into price (or spending) and usage (or efficiency) variances. Price variances reflect the effects of changing input prices, holding usage of inputs constant at actual input use. Usage variances reflect the effects of different levels of input usage, holding prices constant at expected prices.

7 Compute variable overhead spending and efficiency variances. The variable-overhead spending variance is the difference between the actual variable overhead and the amount of variable overhead budgeted for the actual level of cost-driver activity. The variable-overhead efficiency variance is the difference between the actual cost-driver activity and the amount allowed for the actual output achieved, costed at the standard variable-overhead rate.

Accounting Vocabulary

activity-based flexible budget, p. 343
activity-level variances, p. 344
currently attainable standards, p. 348
effectiveness, p. 345
efficiency, p. 345
efficiency variance, p. 353
expected cost, p. 348
favorable cost variance, p. 341

flexible budget, p. 341
flexible-budget variances, p. 344
ideal standards, p. 348
master-budget variances, p. 341
perfection standards, p. 348
price variance, p. 353
quantity variance, p. 353
sales-activity variances, p. 347
standard cost, p. 348

static budget, p. 340
static-budget variance, p. 341
unfavorable cost variance, p. 341
usage variance, p. 353
variable budget, p. 341
variable-overhead spending variance, p. 357
variable-overhead efficiency variance, p. 357

Fundamental Assignment Material

8-A1 Flexible and Static Budgets

Drake Shipping Company's general manager reports quarterly to the company president on the firm's operating performance. The company uses a budget based on detailed expectations for the forthcoming quarter. The general manager has just received the condensed quarterly performance report shown in Exhibit 8-10.

Although the general manager was upset about not obtaining enough revenue, she was happy that her cost performance was favorable; otherwise, her net operating income would be even worse.

The president was totally unhappy and remarked, "I can see some merit in comparing actual performance with budgeted performance because we can see whether actual revenue coincided with our best guess for budget purposes. But I can't see how this performance report helps me evaluate cost control performance."

1. Prepare a columnar flexible budget for Drake Shipping at revenue levels of $7,000,000, $8,000,000, and $9,000,000. Use the format of the last three columns of Exhibit 8-2, page 342. Assume that the prices and mix of products sold are equal to the budgeted prices and mix.
2. Express the flexible budget for costs in formula form.
3. Prepare a condensed table showing the master (static) budget variance, the sales activity variance, and the flexible-budget variance. Use the format of Exhibit 8-5, page 345.

8-A2 Activity Level Variances

The systems consulting department of Richland Textiles designs data collecting, encoding, and reporting systems to fit the needs of other departments within the company. An overall cost driver is the number of requests made to the systems consulting department. The expected variable cost of handling a request was $500, and the number of requests expected for June 20X1 was 75. Richland budgeted its monthly fixed costs for the department (salaries, equipment depreciation, space costs) at $65,000.

Exhibit 8-10
Drake Shipping
Operating
Performance Report
Second Quarter, 20X1

	Budget	Actual	Variance
Net revenue	$8,000,000	$7,600,000	$400,000 U
Fuel	$ 160,000	$ 157,000	$ 3,000 F
Repairs and maintenance	80,000	78,000	2,000 F
Supplies and miscellaneous	800,000	788,000	12,000 F
Variable payroll	5,360,000	5,200,000	160,000 F
Total variable costs*	$6,400,000	$6,223,000	$177,000 F
Supervision	$ 180,000	$ 183,000	$ 3,000 U
Rent	160,000	160,000	—
Depreciation	480,000	480,000	—
Other fixed costs	160,000	158,000	2,000 F
Total fixed costs	$ 980,000	$ 981,000	$ 1,000 U
Total costs charged against revenue	$7,380,000	$7,204,000	$176,000 F
Operating income	$ 620,000	$ 396,000	$224,000 U

U = Unfavorable. F = Favorable.

* For purposes of this analysis, assume that all these costs are totally variable with respect to sales revenue. In practice, many are mixed and have to be subdivided into variable and fixed components before a meaningful analysis can be made. Also assume that the prices and mix of services sold remain unchanged.

The actual number of requests serviced by systems consulting in June 20X1 was 90, and the total costs incurred by the department was $114,000. Of that amount, $77,000 was for fixed costs.

Compute the master (static) budget variances and the flexible-budget variances for variable and fixed costs for the systems consulting department for June 20X1.

8-A3 Direct-Material and Direct-Labor Variances

Los Angeles Lighting (LAL), Inc., manufactures sculpted metal railings, lamp posts, and other ornaments. The following standards were developed for a line of lampposts.

	Standard Inputs Expected for Each Unit of Output Achieved		Standard Price per Unit of Input
Direct materials	5 pounds	×	$10 per pound
Direct labor	5 hours		$25 per hour

During April, LAL scheduled 550 lampposts for production. However, the company produced only 525.

LAL purchased and used 2,700 pounds of direct materials at a unit price of $8.50 per pound. It used 2,850 hours of direct labor at an actual rate of $26.00 per hour.

1. Compute the standard cost per lamppost for direct materials and direct labor.
2. Compute the price variances and usage variances for direct materials and direct labor.
3. Based on these sketchy data, what clues for investigation are provided by the variances?

8-B1 Summary Performance Reports

Consider the following data for a tax preparation service such as **H&R Block**:

- Master budget data: sales, 2,500 clients at $350 each; variable costs, $250 per client; fixed costs, $150,000.
- Actual results at actual prices: sales, 3,000 clients at $360 per client; variable costs, $800,000; fixed costs, $159,500.
  1. Prepare a summary performance report similar to Exhibit 8-5, page 345.
  2. Fill in the blanks:

Master budget operating income		$ —
Variances		
Sales-activity variances	$ —	
Flexible-budget variances	—	—
Actual operating income		$

8-B2 Material and Labor Variances

Consider the following data for a manufacturing company:

	Direct Materials	Direct Labor
Actual price per unit of input (lb and hr)	$ 8	$12
Standard price per unit of input	$ 7	$13
Standard inputs allowed per unit of output	10	2
Actual units of input	115,000	30,000
Actual units of output (product)	14,400	14,400

1. Compute the price, usage, and flexible-budget variances for direct materials and direct labor. Use U or F to indicate whether the variances are unfavorable or favorable.
2. Prepare a plausible explanation for the performance.

8-B3 Variable-Overhead Variances

You have been asked to prepare an analysis of the overhead costs in the order processing department of a mail-order company like **Lillian Vernon Corporation.** As an initial step, you prepare a summary of some events that bear on overhead for the most recent period. The variable-overhead flexible-budget variance was $5,000 unfavorable. The standard variable-overhead price per order was $.06. The rate of ten orders per hour is regarded as standard productivity per clerk. The total overhead incurred was $203,200, of which $135,500 was fixed. There were no variances for fixed overhead. The variable-overhead spending variance was $2,500 favorable.

Find the following:

1. Variable-overhead efficiency variance
2. Actual hours of input
3. Standard hours allowed for output achieved

Additional Assignment Material

Questions

8-1 Distinguish between favorable and unfavorable variances.

8-2 "The flex in the flexible budget relates solely to variable costs." Do you agree? Explain.

8-3 "We want a flexible budget because costs are difficult to predict. We need the flexibility to change budgeted costs as input prices change." Does a flexible budget serve this purpose? Explain.

8-4 Explain the role of understanding cost behavior and cost-driver activities for flexible budgeting.

8-5 "An activity-based flexible budget has a 'flex' for every activity." Do you agree? Explain.

8-6 "Effectiveness and efficiency go hand in hand. You can't have one without the other." Do you agree? Explain.

8-7 Differentiate between a master-budget variance and a flexible-budget variance.

8-8 "Managers should be rewarded for favorable variances and punished for unfavorable variances." Do you agree? Explain.

8-9 "A good control system places the blame for every unfavorable variance on someone in the organization. Without affixing blame, no one will take responsibility for cost control." Do you agree? Explain.

8-10 Who is usually responsible for sales-activity variances? Why?

8-11 Differentiate between perfection standards and currently attainable standards.

8-12 What are two possible interpretations of "currently attainable standards"?

8-13 "A standard is one point in a band or range of acceptable outcomes." Evaluate this statement.

8-14 "Price variances should be computed even if prices are regarded as being outside of company control." Do you agree? Explain.

8-15 What are some common causes of usage variances?

8-16 "Failure to meet price standards is the responsibility of the purchasing officer." Do you agree? Explain.

8-17 "The variable overhead efficiency variance is not really an overhead variance." Evaluate this statement.

8-18 Why do the techniques for controlling overhead differ from those for controlling direct materials?

8-19 How does the variable-overhead spending variance differ from the direct-labor price variance?

Critical Thinking Exercises

8-20 Marketing Responsibility for Sales-Activity Variances

Suppose a company budgeted an operating profit of $100 on sales of $1,000. Actual sales were $900. The marketing department claimed that because sales were down 10%, it was responsible for a $10 drop in profit. Any further shortfall must be someone else's responsibility. Comment on this claim.

8-21 Production Responsibility for Flexible-Budget Variances

Suppose a plant manager planned to produce 100 units of product for $1,000. Instead, actual production was 110 units. When costs came in under $1,100, the plant manager claimed that she should get credit for a favorable variance equal to the amount by which the actual costs fell short of $1,100. Comment on this claim.

8-22 Responsibility of Purchasing Manager

A company's purchasing manager bought 5,000 pounds of material for $5.50 per pound instead of the budgeted $6.00 per pound, resulting in a favorable variance of $2,500. The company has a policy of rewarding employees with 20% of any cost savings they generate. Before awarding a $500 bonus to the purchasing manager, what other variances would you look at to determine the total effect of the purchasing decision? Explain.

8-23 Variable Overhead Efficiency Variance

Birmingham Company had a $1,000 U variable-overhead efficiency variance. Neither the plant manager, who was responsible primarily for labor scheduling, nor the administrative manager, who was responsible for most support services, felt responsible for the variance. Who should be held responsible? Why?

Exercises

8-24 Flexible Budget

Ralding Sports Equipment Company made 24,000 basketballs in a given year. Its manufacturing costs were $204,000 variable and $95,000 fixed. Assume that no price changes will occur in the following year and that no changes in production methods are applicable. Compute the budgeted cost for producing 30,000 basketballs in the following year.

8-25 Basic Flexible Budget

The superintendent of police of the city of Daytona is attempting to predict the costs of operating a fleet of police cars. Among the items of concern are fuel, $.15 per mile, and depreciation, $5,500 per car per year.

The manager is preparing a flexible budget for the coming year. Prepare the flexible-budget amounts for fuel and depreciation for each car at a level of 30,000, 40,000, and 50,000 miles.

8-26 Flexible Budget

Canadian Woolens has a department that makes wool scarves. Consider the following data for a recent month.

	Budget Formula per Unit	Various Levels of Output		
Units	—	6,000	7,000	8,000
Sales	$18	$?	$?	$?
Variable costs				
Direct materials	?	48,000	?	?
Hand labor	3	?	?	?
Fixed costs				
Depreciation		?	16,000	?
Salaries		?	?	42,000

Fill in the unknowns.

8-27 Basic Flexible Budget

The budgeted prices for materials and direct labor per unit of finished product are $13 and $5, respectively. The production manager is delighted about the following data.

	Master (Static) Budget	Actual Costs	Variance
Direct materials	$104,000	$99,000	$5,000 F
Direct labor	40,000	37,600	2,400 F

Is the manager's happiness justified? Prepare a report that might provide a more detailed explanation of why the static (master) budget was not achieved. Good output was 6,800 units.

8-28 Activity-Level Variances

Materials support costs for the Pittsburgh Steel Company (PSC) are variable costs that depend on the weight of material (plate steel, castings, etc.) moved. For the current budget period and based on scheduled production, PSC expected to move 750,000 pounds of material at a cost of $.25 per pound. Several orders were canceled by customers, and PSC moved only 650,000 pounds of material. Total materials support costs for the period were $170,000.

Compare actual support costs to the master-budget support costs by computing master budget, activity-level, and flexible-budget variances for materials support costs.

8-29 Direct-Material Variances

Bangkok Shirt Company uses a special fabric in the production of dress shirts. During August, Custom Shirt purchased and used 7,900 square yards in the production of 3,800 shirts. (B stands for the Thai baht. There are about 40 bahts to the U.S. dollar.) The standard allows two yards at B710 per yard for each shirt.

Calculate the material price variance and the material usage variance.

8-30 Labor Variances

The city of Sacramento has a sign shop where street signs of all kinds are manufactured and repaired. The manager of the shop uses standards to judge performance. Because a clerk mistakenly discarded some labor records, however, the manager has only partial data for April. She knows that the total direct-labor variance was $1,855 favorable, and that the standard labor price was $14 per hour. Moreover, a recent pay raise produced an unfavorable labor price variance for April of $1,015. The actual hours of input were 1,750.

1. Find the actual labor price per hour.
2. Determine the standard hours allowed for the output achieved.

8-31 Usage Variances

Singapore Toy Company produced 9,000 stuffed bears. The standard direct-material allowance is two pounds per bear, at a cost per pound of $3. Actually, 16,500 pounds of materials (input) were used to produce the 9,000 bears (output).

Similarly, it is supposed to take 5 direct-labor hours to produce one bear, and the standard hourly labor cost is $6. But 46,700 hours (input) were used to produce the 9,000 bears.

Compute the usage variances for direct materials and direct labor.

8-32 Labor and Material Variances

Standard direct-labor rate	$14.00
Actual direct-labor rate	$12.20
Standard direct-labor hours	12,000
Direct-labor usage variance—unfavorable	$14,140
Standard unit price of materials	$4.50
Actual quantity purchased and used	1,800
Standard quantity allowed for actual production	1,650
Materials purchase price variance—favorable	$288

1. Compute the actual hours worked, rounded to the nearest hour.
2. Compute the actual purchase price per unit of materials, rounded to the nearest penny.

8-33 Material and Labor Variances

Consider the following data:

	Direct Materials	Direct Labor
Costs incurred: actual inputs × actual prices incurred	$154,000	$79,200
Actual inputs × expected prices	165,000	74,000
Standard inputs allowed for actual outputs achieved × expected prices	172,500	71,300

Compute the price, usage, and flexible-budget variances for direct materials and direct labor. Use U or F to indicate whether the variances are unfavorable or favorable.

Problems

8-34 National Park Service

The National Park Service prepared the following budget for one of its national parks for 20X1:

Revenue from fees	$5,000,000
Variable costs (miscellaneous)	500,000
Contribution margin	$4,500,000
Fixed costs (miscellaneous)	4,500,000
Operating income	$ 0

The fees were based on an average of 25,000 vehicle-admission days (vehicles multiplied by number of days in parks) per week for the 20-week season, multiplied by average entry and other fees of $10 per vehicle-admission day.

The season was booming for the first four weeks. There were major forest fires during the fifth week, however. A large percentage of the park was scarred by the fires. As a result, the number of visitors to the park dropped sharply during the remainder of the season.

Total revenues fell $1 million short of the original budget. Variable costs fell as expected, and fixed costs were unaffected except for hiring extra firefighters at a cost of $410,000.

Prepare a columnar summary of performance, showing the original (static) budget, sales-activity variances, flexible budget, flexible-budget variances, and actual results.

8-35 Flexible and Static Budgets

Beta Gamma Sigma, the business honor society, recently held a dinner dance. The original (static) budget and actual results were as follows:

	Budget	Actual	Variance
Attendees	75	90	
Revenue	$2,625	$3,255	$630 F
Chicken dinners @ $17.60	1,320	1,670	350 U
Beverages, $6 per person	450	466	16 U
Club rental, $75 plus 8% tax	81	81	0
Music, 3 hours @ $250 per hour	750	875	125 U
Profit	$ 24	$ 163	$139 F

1. Subdivide each variance into a sales activity variance portion and a flexible-budget variance portion. Use the format of Exhibit 8-5, page 345.
2. Provide possible explanations for the variances.

8-36 Summary Explanation

Rameriz Company produced 80,000 units, 8,000 more than budgeted. Production data are as follows. Except for physical units, all quantities are in dollars.

	Actual Results at Actual Prices	Flexible-Budget Variances	Flexible Budget	Sales-Activity Variances	Static (Master) Budget
Physical units	80,000	—	?	?	72,000
Sales	?	6,400 F	?	?	720,000
Variable costs	492,000	?	480,000	?	?
Contribution margin	?	?	?	?	?
Fixed costs	?	10,000 U	?	?	200,000
Operating income	?	?	?	?	?

1. Fill in the unknowns.
2. Give a brief summary explanation of why the original target operating income was not attained.

8-37 Explanation of Variance in Income

Cortez Credit Services produces reports for consumers about their credit ratings. The company's standard contribution margins average 70% of dollar sales, and average selling prices are $50 per report. Average productivity is four reports per hour. Some employees work for sales commissions and others for an hourly rate. The master budget for 20X1 had predicted processing 800,000 reports, but Cortez processed only 700,000 reports.

Fixed costs of rent, supervision, advertising, and other items were budgeted at $21 million, but the budget was exceeded by $800,000 because of extra advertising in an attempt to boost revenue.

There were no variances from the average selling prices, but the actual commissions paid to preparers and the actual productivity per hour resulted in flexible-budget variances (i.e., total price and efficiency variances) for variable costs of $900,000 unfavorable.

The president of Cortez was unhappy because the budgeted operating income of $7 million was not achieved. He said, "Sure, we had unfavorable variable-cost variances, but our operating income was down far more than that. Please explain why."

Explain why the budgeted operating income was not attained. Use a presentation similar to Exhibit 8-5, page 345. Enough data have been given to permit you to construct the complete exhibit by filling in the known items and then computing the unknown. Complete your explanation by summarizing what happened, using no more than three sentences.

8-38 Activity and Flexible-Budget Variances at KFC

Suppose a chain of **KFC** franchises in Beijing had budgeted sales for 2005 of RMB 7.3 million (where RMB stands for the Chinese unit of currency, officially the Renminbi, also called the yuan). Cost of goods sold and other variable costs were expected to be 70% of sales. Budgeted annual fixed costs were RMB 1.8 million. A thriving Chinese economy caused actual 2005 sales to soar to RMB 9.2 million and actual profits to increase to RMB 570,000. Fixed costs in 2005 were as budgeted. The franchise was pleased with the increase in profit.

1. Compute the sales activity variance and the flexible budget variance for 2005. What can the franchisee learn from these variances?
2. Suppose that in 2006 the Chinese economy weakened, and the franchise's sales fell back to the RMB 7.3 million level. Given what happened in 2005, what do you expect to happen to profits in 2006?

8-39 Summary of Airline Performance

Consider the performance (in thousands of dollars) of San Juan Airlines for a given year in the following table.

	Actual Results at Actual Prices	Master Budget	Variance
Revenue	$?	$300,000	$?
Variable expenses	200,000	195,000*	5,000 U
Contribution margin	?	105,000	?
Fixed expenses	83,000	80,000	3,000 U
Operating income	$?	$ 25,000	$?

*Includes jet fuel of $90,000.

The master budget had been based on a budget of $.20 per revenue passenger mile. A revenue passenger mile is one paying passenger flown one mile. An average airfare decrease of 8% had helped generate an increase in passenger miles flown that was 10% in excess of the static budget for the year.

The price per gallon of jet fuel rose above the price used to formulate the static budget. The average jet fuel price increase for the year was 10%.

1. As an explanation for the president, prepare a summary performance report that is similar to Exhibit 8-5, page 345.
2. Assume that jet fuel costs are purely variable and the use of fuel was at the same level of efficiency as predicted in the static budget. What part of the flexible-budget variance for variable expenses is attributable to jet fuel expenses? Explain.

8-40 Hospital Costs and Explanation of Variances

The emergency room at Providence Hospital uses a flexible budget based on patients seen as a measure of activity. The hospital must maintain an adequate staff of attending and on-call physicians at all times, so patient activity does not affect physician scheduling. Nurse scheduling varies as volume changes, however. A standard of .5 nurse-hours per patient visit was set. Average hourly pay for nurses is $15, ranging from $9 to $18 per hour. The hospital considers all materials to be supplies, a part of overhead; there are no direct materials. A statistical study showed that the cost of supplies and other variable overhead is more closely associated with nurse-hours than with patient visits. The standard for supplies and other variable overhead is $10 per nurse-hour.

The head physician of the emergency room unit, Yolanda Mortensen, is responsible for control of costs. During October the emergency room unit treated 4,000 patients. The budget and actual costs were as follows:

	Budget	Actual	Variance
Patient visits	3,800	4,000	200
Nurse-hours	1,900	2,075	175
Nursing cost	$ 28,500	$ 33,150	$4,650
Supplies and other variable overhead	19,000	20,340	1,340
Fixed costs	92,600	92,600	0
Total cost	$140,100	$146,090	$5,990

1. Calculate price and usage variances for nursing costs.
2. Calculate spending and efficiency variances for supplies and other variable overhead.
3. The hospital's chief administrator has asked Dr. Mortensen to explain the variances. Provide possible explanations.

8-41 University Flexible Budgeting

The University of Scotland offers an extensive continuing education program in many cities throughout Scotland. For the convenience of its faculty and administrative staff and also to save costs, the university operates a motor pool. The motor pool operated with 25 vehicles until February of this year, when it acquired an additional automobile. The motor pool furnishes gasoline, oil, and other supplies for the cars and hires one mechanic who does routine maintenance and minor repairs. Major repairs are done at a nearby commercial garage. A supervisor manages the operations.

Each year the supervisor prepares an operating budget, informing university management of the funds needed to operate the pool. Depreciation on the automobiles is recorded in the budget in order to determine the cost per kilometer.

The schedule below presents the annual budget approved by the university. The actual costs for March are compared with one-twelfth of the annual budget.

University Motor Pool
Budget Report for March 20X1

	Annual Budget	One-Month Budget	March Actual	Over (Under)
Gasoline	£ 82,500	£ 6,875	£ 8,200	£1,325
Oil, minor repairs, parts, and supplies	15,000	1,250	1,290	40
Outside repairs	2,700	225	50	(175)
Insurance	4,800	400	416	16
Salaries and benefits	21,600	1,800	1,800	—
Depreciation	22,800	1,900	1,976	76
	£149,400	£12,450	£13,732	£1,282
Total kilometers	1,500,000	125,000	140,000	
Cost per kilometer	£ .0996	£ .0996	£ 0.981	
Number of automobiles	25	25	26	

The annual budget was constructed based on the following assumptions:

1. 25 automobiles in the pool
2. 60,000 kilometers per year per automobile
3. 8 kilometers per liter for each automobile
4. £0.44 per liter of gas
5. £.01 per kilometer for oil, minor repairs, parts, and supplies
6. £108 per automobile in outside repairs

The supervisor is unhappy with the monthly report comparing budget and actual costs for March; she claims it presents her performance unfairly. Her previous employer used flexible budgeting to compare actual costs with budgeted amounts.

1. Employing flexible-budgeting techniques, prepare a report that shows budgeted amounts, actual costs, and monthly variation for March.
2. Explain briefly the basis of your budget figure for outside repairs.

8-42 Activity-Based Flexible Budget

Cost behavior analysis for the four activity centers in the billing department of Oregon Power Company is given below.

Activity Center	Traceable Costs		Cost-Driver Activity
	Variable	Fixed	
Account inquiry	$ 79,910	$156,380	3,300 labor hours
Correspondence	9,800	25,584	2,800 letters
Account billing	154,377	81,400	2,440,000 lines
Bill verification	10,797	78,050	20,000 accounts

The billing department constructs a flexible budget for each activity center based on the following ranges of cost-driver activity.

Activity Center	Cost Driver	Relevant Range	
Account inquiry	Labor hours	3,000	5,000
Correspondence	Letters	2,500	3,500
Account billing	Lines	2,000,000	3,000,000
Bill verification	Accounts	15,000	25,000

1. Develop flexible-budget formulas for each of the four activity centers.
2. Compute the budgeted total cost in each activity center for each of these levels of cost driver activity: (a) the smallest activity in the relevant range, (b) the midpoint of the relevant range, and (c) the highest activity in the relevant range.
3. Determine the total cost function for the billing department.
4. The following table gives the actual results for the billing department. Prepare a cost-control performance report comparing the flexible budget to actual results for each activity center. Compute flexible budget variances.

Activity Center	Actual Cost-Driver Level	Actual Cost
Account inquiry	4,400 labor hours	$235,400
Correspondence	3,250 letters	38,020
Account billing	2,900,000 lines	285,000
Bill verification	22,500 accounts	105,320

8-43 Straightforward Variance Analysis

Duluth Metal Works, Inc., uses a standard cost system. The month's data regarding its iron castings follow:

- Materials purchased and used, 3,300 pounds
- Direct-labor costs incurred, 5,500 hours, 41,800
- Variable-overhead costs incurred, $4,730
- Finished units produced, 1,000
- Actual materials cost, $.96 per pound
- Variable-overhead rate, $.80 per hour
- Standard direct-labor cost, $8 per hour
- Standard materials cost, $1 per pound
- Standard pounds of material in a finished unit, 3
- Standard direct-labor hours per finished unit, 5

Prepare schedules of all variances, using the formats of Exhibits 8-7 and 8-9 on pages 354 and 358.

8-44 Variance Analysis

The Geneva Chocolate Company uses standard costs and a flexible budget to control its manufacture of fine chocolates. The purchasing agent is responsible for material price variances, and the production manager is responsible for all other variances. Operating data for the past week are summarized as follows:

1. Finished units produced: 4,000 boxes of chocolates.
2. Direct materials: Purchased and used, 4,300 pounds of chocolate @ 15.5 Swiss francs (SFR) per pound; standard price is 16 SFR per pound. Standard allowed per box produced, 1 pound.
3. Direct labor: Actual costs, 6,300 hours @ 30.5 SFR, or 192,150 SFR. Standard allowed per box produced, 1-1/2 hours. Standard price per direct-labor hour, 30 SFR.
4. Variable manufacturing overhead: Actual costs, 69,500 SFR. Budget formula is 10 SFR per standard direct-labor hour.

Compute the following:

1.
   a. Materials purchase-price variance
   b. Materials usage variance
   c. Direct-labor price variance
   d. Direct-labor usage variance
   e. Variable manufacturing-overhead spending variance
   f. Variable manufacturing-overhead efficiency variance
   (*Hint:* For format, see the solution to the Summary Problem for Your Review, pages 358–359.)
2.
   a. What is the budget allowance for direct labor?
   b. Would it be any different if production were 5,000 boxes?

8-45 Similarity of Direct-Labor and Variable-Overhead Variances

The T. K. Tan Company has had great difficulty controlling costs in Singapore during the past three years. Last month the company installed a standard cost and flexible-budget system. A condensation of results for a department follows.

	Expected Cost per Standard Direct-Labor Hour	Flexible-Budget Variance
Lubricants	$ .60	$330 F
Other supplies	.30	225 U
Rework	.60	450 U
Other indirect labor	1.50	450 U
Total variable overhead	$3.00	$795 U

F = Favorable. U = Unfavorable.

The department had initially planned to manufacture 9,000 audio speaker assemblies in 6,000 standard direct-labor hours allowed. Material shortages and a heat wave resulted in the production of 8,100 units in 5,700 actual direct-labor hours. The standard wage rate is $5.25 per hour, which was $.15 higher than the actual average hourly rate.

1. Prepare a detailed performance report with two major sections: direct labor and variable overhead.
2. Prepare a summary analysis of price and usage variances for direct labor and spending and efficiency variances for variable overhead.
3. Explain the similarities and differences between the direct-labor and variable-overhead variances. What are some of the likely causes of the overhead variances?

8-46 Material, Labor, and Overhead Variances

Poulsbo Kayak Company makes molded plastic kayaks. Standard costs for an entry-level whitewater kayak are

Direct materials, 60 lb @ $5.50/lb	$330
Direct labor, 1.5 hr @ $16/hr	24
Overhead, @ $12 per kayak	12
Total	$366

The overhead rate assumes production of 450 kayaks per month. The overhead cost function is $2,808 + $5.76 \times$ number of kayaks.

During March, Belfair produced 430 kayaks and had the following actual results.

Direct materials purchased and used	27,000 pounds @ $5.30/lb
Direct labor	660 hours @ $15.90/hr
Actual overhead	$5,335

1. Compute material, labor, and overhead variances.
2. Interpret the variances.
3. Suppose the cost function for variable overhead was $3.84 per labor hour instead of $5.76 per kayak. Compute the variable-overhead efficiency variance and the total overhead spending variance. Would these variances lead you to a different interpretation of the overhead variances from the interpretation in requirement 2? Explain.

8-47 Automation and Direct Labor as Overhead

Mississippi Precision Machining (MPM) has a highly automated manufacturing process for producing a variety of auto parts. Through the use of computer-aided manufacturing and robotics, the company has reduced its labor costs to only 5% of total manufacturing costs. Consequently, the company does not account for labor as a separate item but considers it part of overhead.

Consider a part used in antilock braking systems. The static budget for producing 750 units in March 20X1 is

Direct materials	$18,000*
Overhead	
Supplies	1,875
Power	1,310
Rent and other building services	2,815
Factory labor	1,500
Depreciation	4,500
Total manufacturing costs	$30,000

* 3 lb/unit × $8/lb × 750 units

Supplies and power are variable, and the other overhead items are fixed costs.

Actual costs in March 20X1 for producing 900 units of the brake part were

Direct materials	$21,645*
Overhead	
Supplies	2,132
Power	1,612
Rent and other building services	2,775
Factory labor	1,618
Depreciation	4,500
Total manufacturing costs	$34,282

*MPM purchased and used 2,775 pounds of materials @ $7.80 per pound

1. Compute (a) the direct-materials price and usage variances and (b) the flexible-budget variance for each overhead item.
2. Comment on the way MPM accounts for and controls factory labor.

8-48 Standard Material Allowances

Delaware Chemical Company supplies primarily industrial users. Your superior has asked you to develop a standard product cost for a new solution the company plans to introduce.

The new chemical solution is made by combining altium and bollium, boiling the mixture, adding credix, and bottling the resulting solution in 20-liter containers. The initial mix, which is 20 liters in volume, consists of 24 kilograms of altium and 19.2 liters of bollium. A 20% reduction in volume occurs during the boiling process. The solution is then cooled slightly before adding 10 kilograms of credix to each 20-liter container; the addition of credix does not affect the total liquid volume.

The purchase prices of the raw materials used in the manufacture of this new chemical solution are as follows:

Altium	$2.20 per kilogram
Bollium	1.95 per liter
Credix	2.80 per kilogram

Determine the standard quantity for each of the raw materials needed to produce 20 liters of Delaware Chemical Company's new chemical solution and the standard materials cost of 20 liters of the new product.

8-49 Role of Defective Units and Nonproductive Time in Setting Standards

Kee Kim owns and operates KimKee Machining, a subcontractor to several aerospace industry contractors. When Mr. Kim wins a bid to produce a piece of equipment, he sets standard costs for the production of the item. He then compares actual manufacturing costs with the standards to judge the efficiency of production.

In April 20X1, KimKee won a bid to produce 15,000 units of a shielded component used in a navigation device. Specifications for the components were very tight, and Mr. Kim expected that 20% of the components would fail his final inspection, even if employees exercise every care in production. There was no way to identify defective items before production was complete. Therefore, the company had to produce 18,750 units to get 15,000 good components. The company set standards to include an allowance for the expected number of defective items.

Each final component contained 3.2 pounds of direct materials, and the company expected normal scrap from production to average an additional .4 pounds per unit. It expected the direct material to cost $11.40 per pound plus $.80 per pound for shipping and handling.

Machining of the components required close attention by skilled machinists. Each component required four hours of machining time. KimKee paid the machinists $20 per hour, and they worked 40-hour weeks. Of the 40 hours, employees spent an average of 32 hours directly on production. The other eight hours consisted of time for breaks and waiting time when machines were broken down or there was no work to be done. Nevertheless, the company considered all payments to machinists to be direct labor, whether or not they represented time spent directly on production. In addition to the basic wage rate, KimKee paid fringe benefits averaging $6 per hour and payroll taxes of 10% of the basic wages.

Determine the standard cost of direct materials and direct labor for each good unit of output.

8-50 Review of Major Points in This Chapter

The following questions are based on the Dominion Company data contained in Exhibit 8-1 (p. 340) and in the table in the middle of p. 352.

1. Suppose actual production and sales were 8,000 units instead of 7,000 units. (a) Compute the sales-activity variance. Is the performance of the marketing function the sole explanation for this variance? Why? (b) Using a flexible budget, compute the budgeted contribution margin, the budgeted operating income, budgeted direct material, and budgeted direct labor.
2. Suppose the following were the actual results for the production of 8,000 units.

> Direct materials: 42,000 pounds were used at an actual unit price of $1.86, for a total actual cost of $78,120.
> Direct labor: 4,140 hours were used at an actual hourly rate of $16.40, for a total actual cost of $67,896.

Compute the flexible-budget variance and the price and usage variances for direct materials and direct labor. Present your answers in the form shown in Exhibit 8-7, p. 354.
3. Evaluate Dominion Company's performance based on the variances you calculated in numbers 1 and 2.

8-51 Review Problem on Standards and Flexible Budgets; Answers Are Provided

The Des Moines Leather Company makes a variety of leather goods. It uses standard costs and a flexible budget to aid planning and control. Budgeted variable overhead at a 45,000-direct-labor-hour level is $81,000.

During April the company had a favorable variable-overhead efficiency variance of $2,970. Material purchases were $241,900. Actual direct-labor costs incurred were $422,100. The direct-labor usage variance was $15,300 unfavorable. The actual average wage rate was $.60 lower than the standard average wage rate.

The company uses a variable-overhead rate of 20% of standard direct-labor cost for flexible-budgeting purposes. Actual variable overhead for the month was $92,250.

Compute the following amounts; use U or F to indicate whether variances are unfavorable or favorable.

1. Standard direct-labor cost per hour
2. Actual direct-labor hours worked
3. Total direct-labor price variance
4. Total flexible budget for direct-labor costs
5. Total direct-labor variance
6. Variable-overhead spending variance in total

Answers to Problem 8-51

1. $9. The variable-overhead rate is $1.80, obtained by dividing $81,000 by 45,000 hours. Therefore the direct-labor rate must be $1.80 ÷ .20 = $9.
2. 50,250 hours. Actual costs, $422,100 ÷ ($9 − $.60) = 50,250 hours.
3. $30,150 F. 50,250 actual hours × $.60 = $30,150.
4. $436,950. Usage variance was $15,300 U. Therefore, excess hours must have been $15,300 ÷ $9 = 1,700. Consequently, standard hours allowed must be 50,250 − 1,700 = 48,550. Flexible budget = 48,550 × $9 = $436,950.
5. $14,850 F. $436,950 − $422,100 = $14,850 F; or $30,150 F − $15,300 U = $14,850 F.
6. $7,830 U. Flexible budget = 48,550 × 1.80 = $87,390. Total variance = $92,250 − $87,390 = $4,860 U. Spending variance = Total variance − Efficiency variance = $4,860 + $2,970 = $7,830 U. Check: $92,250 − .20 × $422,100 = $7,830.

Cases

8-52 Activity and Flexible-Budget Variances

In 2000, County Hospital initiated its Substance Abuse Program, which focused on counseling current and potential substance abusers. The program was funded by a grant from the state department of health that paid $75 per visit for counseling. Reed Wylcinski, chief financial officer of County Hospital, was concerned about the Substance Abuse Program. It had never broken even, and thus was subsidized by the other patients in the hospital. In December 2003, Mr. Wylcinski was preparing the hospital's budget for 2004, and he did not like the Substance Abuse Program's financial situation. The results for 2003 (projected through the end of the year) are shown in Exhibit 8-11:

Revenues ($75 per visit; 17,000 visits)		$1,275,000
Cost of services:		
Supplies	$ 114,750	
Physician salaries	204,000	
Nurse salaries	153,000	
Overhead	676,200	
Total direct cost of services	1,147,950	
General and administrative expenses	194,250	
Total expenses	1,342,200	
Net loss	$ (67,200)	

Exhibit 8-11
Substance Abuse Program
2003 Results

A recent cost analysis had determined the following facts about the behavior of costs in the Substance Abuse Program:

a. Supplies and physician and nurse salaries were totally variable with respect to number of visits within the range of 15,000 to 30,000 visits.

b. Variable overhead was equal to 20% of labor costs in 2003; the remainder of the overhead was fixed.

c. $181,500 of the general and administrative cost was fixed; the remainder varied with number of visits.

d. Costs in 2004 are expected to behave the same as those in 2003, except that variable-overhead costs will be 21% of labor costs in 2004 compared to only 20% of labor costs in 2003. (Fixed overhead costs will remain the same in 2004 as in 2003.)

Wylcinski had been pressuring the director of the Substance Abuse Program, Rebecca Stein, for the last couple of years to try to get her costs under control. Ms. Stein responded that it was a very important program for the community. Besides, the program was so close to breaking even that all it needed was a little more time and the results would be better. In fact, she predicted 18,000 visits in 2004, an increase of nearly 6%, which would certainly make the financial picture brighter.

Wylcinski agreed on the importance of the program, but he also said that pressures were building from others in County Hospital to eliminate programs that were a drain on the hospital's resources. Thus, he believed that if the Substance Abuse Program were not at least at a break-even point in 2004, the program would be in jeopardy. He doesn't believe that even the increase of 1,000 visits would be enough to break even.

1. Compute the cost function for the Substance Abuse Program for use in budgeting for 2004. That is, compute the variable cost per visit and the total annual fixed cost based on the cost analysis that Wylcinski conducted.

2. Compute the budgeted profit (loss) for 2004, assuming that there will be 18,000 visits @ $75 each and the costs behave as expected.

3. Suppose that County Hospital accepted the budget for the Substance Abuse Program that you computed in number 2. At the end of 2004, the actual loss for the program was $15,500 and the actual number of visits was 18,400. Explain the difference between the amount of loss you budgeted in number 2 and the actual loss of $15,500 in as much detail as you can, given the information you have. Based on this, give a one-sentence answer to each of the following questions:

    a. What was the financial impact of the extra 400 visits?

    b. How well did the Substance Abuse Program control its costs in 2004?

8-53 Activity-Based Costing and Flexible Budgeting

The new printing department provides printing services to the other departments of Farmer & Teacher Life Insurance Company (FTLIC). Before the establishment of the in-house printing department, the departments contracted with external printers for their printing work. FTLIC's printing policy is to charge using departments for the variable printing costs on the basis of number of pages printed. The company recovers fixed costs in pricing of external jobs.

The first year's budget for the printing department was based on the department's expected total costs divided by the planned number of pages to be printed.

The projected annual number of pages to be printed was 420,000, and budgeted total variable costs were $420,000. Most government accounts and all internal jobs were expected to use only single-color printing. Commercial accounts use primarily four-color printing. FTLIC estimated its variable costs based on the average variable cost of printing a four-color page that is one-fourth graphics and three-fourths text. The expected annual costs for each division were as follows:

Department	Planned Pages Printed	Variable Cost per Page	Budgeted Charges
Government accounts	120,000	$1	$ 90,000
Commercial accounts	250,000	1	300,000
Central administration	50,000	1	30,000
Total	420,000		$420,000

After the first month of using the internal printing department, the printing department announced that its variable cost estimate of $1 per page was too low. The first month's actual costs were $50,000 to print 40,000 pages.

Government accounts	9,000 pages
Commercial accounts	27,500
Central administration	3,500

Three reasons were cited for higher-than-expected costs: All departments were using more printing services than planned, and government and internal jobs were using more four-color printing and more graphics than expected. The printing department also argued that it would have to purchase additional four-color printing equipment if demand for four-color printing continued to grow.

1. Compare the printing department actual results, static budget, and flexible budget for the month just completed.
2. Discuss possible reasons why the printing department static budget was inaccurate.
3. An activity-based costing (ABC) study completed by a consultant indicated that printing costs are driven by number of pages (@ $.35 per page), and use of colors (@ $1 extra per page for color).
   a. Discuss the likely effects of using the ABC results for budgeting and control of printing department use.
   b. Discuss the assumptions regarding cost behavior implied in the ABC study results.
   c. All commercial accounts during the first month (27,500 pages) used four colors per page. Compare the cost of commercial accounts under the old and the proposed ABC system.

8-54 Analyzing Performance

Bellevue Community Hospital operates an outpatient clinic in a town several miles from the main hospital. For several years the clinic has struggled just to break even. The clinic's financial budget for 2004 is in Exhibit 8-12.

On the average, billings for each patient-visit are expected to be $180. Costs in 2004 are expected to average $183 per patient-visit, as follows.

Physician time	$ 60
Nurse and technician time	45
Supplies	15
Overhead	63
Total	$183

Exhibit 8-12
Outpatient Clinic
2004 Budget

	Total	Per Patient
Revenues (4,000 patients @ $180 each)		$720,000	$180
Cost of services		
Physicians	$240,000	
Nurses and technicians	180,000	
Supplies	60,000	
Overhead	252,000	732,000	183
Net loss		$ (12,000)	$ (3)

The clinic is generally staffed by one physician, who must be present whether or not there is a patient to see. Currently about 10% of the physician's time is idle. The clinic employs nurses and technicians to meet the actual workload necessitated by patient appointments. Their cost averages $30 per hour, and usage varies proportionately with the number of patient-visits. Supplies cost is also variable with respect to patient-visits. Fixed overhead in 2004 was expected to be $180,000; the remaining $72,000 of overhead varies with respect to patient visits. Included in the fixed overhead was $30,000 of hospitalwide administrative costs that the hospital allocates to the clinic and $37,500 of depreciation on the clinic's property and equipment.

Renee Polanski, controller of Bellevue Community Hospital, has reported that the actual loss of $22,200 in 2004 represented the fifth straight year of losses. She explained that she did not feel it was right for patients in the main hospital to subsidize those using the clinic. Therefore, she suggested that unless the situation could be changed, the clinic should be closed. Emilio Martinez, Administrative Vice President of the hospital, who was charged with oversight of the clinic, disagreed. "We provide a valuable service to the community with the clinic. Even if we are losing money, it is worthwhile to keep it open."

At the end of 2004, the clinic's actual results for the year were

		Total
Revenues (3,800 patients @ $180)		$684,000
Cost of services		
Physicians	$233,000	
Nurses and technicians (5,800 hours)	182,700	
Supplies	58,500	
Overhead	232,000	706,200
Net loss		$ (22,200)

1. Would Bellevue Community Hospital have saved money in 2004 if the outpatient clinic was closed? Explain.
2. Explain the difference between the budgeted loss of $12,000 and the actual loss of $22,200 (that is, the master budget variance of $10,200) in as much detail as possible. From the analysis of the 2004 results, what actions would you suggest to avoid a loss in 2005?

8-55 Complete Variance Analysis

Balmer Video Games, Inc., manufactures video game machines. Market saturation and technological innovations have caused pricing pressures that have resulted in declining profits. To stem the slide in profits until the company can introduce new products, top management has turned its attention to both manufacturing economies and increased production. To realize these objectives, they developed an incentive program to reward production managers who contribute to an increase in the number of units produced and achieve cost reductions. In addition, the company instituted a just-in-time purchasing program so that it purchases raw materials on an as-needed basis.

The production managers have responded to the pressure to improve manufacturing performance in several ways that have resulted in an increase in the number of completed units over normal production levels. The video game machines put together by the assembly group require parts from both the printed circuit boards (PCB) and the reading heads (RH) departments. To attain increased production levels, the PCB and RH departments started rejecting parts from suppliers that previously would have been tested and modified to meet manufacturing standards. Preventive maintenance on machines used in the production of these parts has been postponed with only emergency repair work being performed to keep production lines moving. The maintenance staff is concerned that there will be serious breakdowns and unsafe operating conditions.

The more aggressive assembly group production supervisors have pressured maintenance personnel to attend to their machines at the expense of other groups. This has resulted in machine downtime in the PCB and RH departments which, when coupled with demands for accelerated parts delivery by the Assembly Department, has led to more frequent parts rejections and increased friction among departments. Balmer Video Games operates under a standard-costing system. The standard costs at a production level of 24,000 units per year are in part A of Exhibit 8-13.

Balmer Video Games prepares monthly income statements based on actual expenses. Part B of Exhibit 8-13 shows the statement for May, when production and sales both reached 2,200 units. The

Exhibit 8-13
Balmer Video
Games, Inc.

	Standard Cost per Unit		
	Quantity	Cost	Total
A. Standard Cost Report			
Direct materials:			
Housing unit	1 unit	$20	$ 20
Printed circuit boards	2 boards	15	30
Reading heads	4 heads	10	40
Direct labor:			
Assembly department	2.0 hours	$ 8	$ 16
PCB department	1.0 hour	9	9
RH department	1.5 hours	10	15
Overhead:			
Variable	4.5 hours	$ 2	$ 9
Fixed	4.5 hours	4	18
Total manufacturing cost per unit			$157
Selling & Administrative:			
Fixed		$10	$ 10
Total standard cost per unit			$167
B. Income Statement for May			
Revenues (2,200 units)		$440,000	
Variable costs:			
Direct materials	220,400		
Direct labor	93,460		
Variable overhead	18,800		
Fixed costs:			
Overhead	37,600		
Selling and administrative	22,000		
Total costs		392,260	
Income before taxes		$ 47,740	
C. Usage Report for May			
Cost Item	Actual Quantity	Actual Cost	
Direct materials:			
Housing units	2,200	$ 44,000	
Printed circuit boards	4,700 boards	75,200	
Reading heads	9,200 heads	101,200	
Direct labor:			
Assembly	3,900 hours	31,200	
Printed circuit boards	2,400 hours	23,760	
Reading heads	3,500 hours	38,500	
Overhead:			
Variable		18,800	
Fixed		37,600	
Total manufacturing costs		$370,260	

budgeted sales price was $200 per unit, and budgeted (normal) production and sales were 24,000 units per year. Top management was surprised by the low profit in spite of increased sales for May. The original budget had called for income before taxes of $66,000, and with the added sales, the president had expected at least $72,600 of income ($6,600 more income; 200 extra units × $33 per unit). The president called on Julie McGowan, Director of Cost Management, to report on the reasons for the shortfall in income. After a thorough review of the data, McGowan prepared the report in part C of Exhibit 8-13.

1. Prepare a budgeted income statement in contribution margin format for Balmer Video Games showing why the company expected income before taxes to be $66,000.
2. Assume that you have been given Julie McGowan's task. Prepare a complete analysis explaining the reason for the difference between the original projected income before taxes of $66,000 and the actual of $47,740. Compute all the variances that are helpful in explaining this difference, and explain what you learn from the variances.

EXCEL Application Exercise

8-56 Flexible-Budget and Sales-Activity Variances

Goal: Create an Excel spreadsheet to prepare a summary performance report that identifies flexible-budget and sales-activity variances. Use the results to answer questions about your findings.

Scenario: Tax Preparation Services, Inc., has asked you to prepare a summary performance report identifying their flexible-budget and sales-activity variances. The background data for the summary performance report appears in the Fundamental Assignment Material 8-B1. Prepare the summary performance report using a format similar to Exhibit 8-5. When you have completed your spreadsheet, answer the following questions:
1. What caused the flexible-budget variance for sales?
2. What was the change in actual operating income compared to the operating income calculated in the master budget?
3. Can the amount in question 2 be explained by the flexible-budget and sales-activity variances? Explain.

Step-by-Step:
1. Open a new Excel spreadsheet.
2. In column A, create a bold-faced heading that contains the following:
   Row 1: Chapter 8 Decision Guideline
   Row 2: Tax Preparation Services, Inc.
   Row 3: Summary Performance Report
   Row 4: Today's date
3. Merge and center the four heading rows across columns A through H.
4. In Column A, create the following row headings:
   Row 8: Clients
   Skip a row
   Row 10: Sales
   Row 11: Variable costs
   Row 12: Contribution margin
   Row 13: Fixed costs
   Skip a row
   Row 15: Operating income
5. Change the format of Contribution margin (Row 12) and Operating income (Row 15) to bold-faced headings.
   Note: Adjust width of Row A to accommodate row headings.

6. In Row 7, create the following bold-faced, center-justified column headings:
   Column B: Actual Results at Actual Activity
   Column C: Flexible-Budget Variances
   Skip a column
   Column E: Flexible Budget at Actual Activity

Column F: Sales-Activity Variances
Skip a column
Column H: Master Budget

7. Change the format of the column headings in Row 7 to permit the titles to be displayed on multiple lines within a single cell.

Alignment tab: Wrap Text: Checked

Note: Adjust column widths so that headings only use two lines.
  Adjust row height to insure that row is same height as adjusted headings.

8. Change format of the column width of columns D and G to a size of 2.
9. Use the scenario data to fill in client and fixed cost amounts for actual, flexible budget, and master budget columns as well as variable costs for the actual column.
10. Calculate variable costs for flexible-budget and master budget columns. Use appropriate formulas to calculate sales, contribution margin, and operating income amounts for actual, flexible budget, and master budget columns.
11. Use appropriate formulas to calculate flexible-budget and sales-activity variances and display as absolute values.
=ABS(*variance formula*)
12. Use one of the following formula templates to indicate whether variances are favorable (F) or unfavorable (U):

=IF(*variance formula*>0,"F",IF(*variance formula*<0,"U","–"))
For sales, margin and income variances only.
=IF(*variance formula*<0,"F",IF(*variance formula*>0,"U","–"))
For client, variable and fixed cost variances only.

Hint: Go to the "Help" text and type "copy formulas" in the search area to obtain instructions for copying formulas from one cell to another. If done correctly, you should have to type in each of the formula templates only once.

13. Format all amounts as:

Number: Category: Currency
            Decimal places: 0
            Symbol: None
            Negative numbers: Red with parenthesis

14. Change the format of the amounts for sales, contribution margin, and operating income to display a dollar symbol.
15. Change the format of the operating income amounts for actual, flexible budget, and master budget to display as bold.
16. Change the format of the row headings for contribution margin and operating income to display as indented.

Alignment tab: Horizontal: Left (Indent)
                              Indent: 1

Note: Adjust width of Row A to accommodate row headings.

17. Save your work to disk, and print a copy for your files.
Note: Print your spreadsheet using landscape format in order to ensure that all columns appear on one page.

Collaborative Learning Exercise

8-57 Setting Standards

Form groups of two to six persons each. The groups should each select a simple product or service. Be creative, but do not pick a product or service that is too complex. For those having difficulty choosing a product or service, some possibilities are

- One dozen chocolate-chip cookies
- A 10-mile taxi ride
- One copy of a 100-page course syllabus
- A machine-knit wool sweater
- A hand-knit wool sweater
- One hour of lawn mowing and fertilizing
- A hammer

1. Each student should individually estimate the direct materials and direct labor inputs needed to produce the product or service. For each type of direct material and direct labor, determine the standard quantity and standard price. Also, identify the overhead support needed, and determine the standard overhead cost of the product or service. The result should be a total standard cost for the product or service.

2. Each group should compare the estimates of its members. Where estimates differ, determine why there were differences. Did assumptions differ? Did some members have more knowledge about the product or service than others? Form a group estimate of the standard cost of the product or service.

3. After the group has agreed on a standard cost, discuss the process used to arrive at the cost. What assumptions did the group make? Is the standard cost an "ideal" standard or a "currently attainable" standard? Note how widely standard costs can vary depending on assumptions and knowledge of the production process.

Internet Exercise   www.prenhall.com/horngren

8-58 Flexible Budgets at Hershey Food Corporation

This chapter focused on flexible budgets and variance analysis. While the information used to determine both of these is generally for internal purposes only and not available to an outsider, it is possible to look at what information a firm reports and, based on that information, to make some judgments about what occurred.

1. Look at the **Hershey Food** home page at http://www.hersheys.com. Who is Hershey's home page directed to? Follow the link from "Our Products" to "New Products." What new products does Hershey list?

2. Click on "About Hershey Foods," and follow the link to a profile of the company. Hershey Foods has a variety of products. Is the company's product line limited only to the United States? In how many countries does Hershey sell its candy? With the large number of products offered, would a static or flexible budget be more useful for planning purposes? Why?

3. Examine Hershey's most recent income statement. Suppose that in the following year net sales were expected to increase by 5%, but there was no expected increase in selling prices. Also assume that cost of sales is the only variable cost. Prepare a master-budget income statement for the following year. Now suppose that selling prices were exactly as budgeted, but sales actually increased by 8% and net income increased by 10%. Determine the master-budget variance, the sales-activity variance, and the flexible-budget variance.

Management Control Systems and Responsibility Accounting

CHAPTER **9**

LEARNING OBJECTIVES

When you have finished studying this chapter, you should be able to:

1. Describe the relationship of management control systems to organizational goals.

2. Use responsibility accounting to define an organizational subunit as a cost center, a profit center, or an investment center.

3. Develop performance measures and use them to monitor the achievements of an organization.

4. Explain the importance of evaluating performance and how it impacts motivation, goal congruence, and employee effort.

5. Prepare segment income statements for evaluating profit and investment centers using the contribution margin and controllable-cost concepts.

6. Use a balanced scorecard to recognize both financial and nonfinancial measures of performance.

7. Measure performance against quality, cycle time, and productivity objectives.

8. Describe the difficulties of management control in service and nonprofit organizations.

It's 2:30 a.m. You don't feel well. Should you call your doctor? Go to the emergency room? Is what you're feeling really something to worry about? What you need is good quality health care and you need it now, not tomorrow morning, and you do not want to worry about its cost. Sound familiar? This is a dilemma that we have all faced at some time. One health care organization that has a solution is **Health Net, Inc.**

Health Net is one of the largest managed health care organizations in the United States. With more than 9,400 employees and 2002 revenues of more than $10 billion, it provides coverage to more than 5.3 million members.

Health care organizations must compete just as any other business, offering high quality health care at an affordable cost, and when it is needed. In order to maintain its competitive advantage, Health Net undertook a major information systems development program called "fourth generation medical management." According to Dr. Malik Hasan, former chairman and chief executive officer, this new management control system was created "because the greatest opportunity for increasing overall quality and decreasing the cost of health care lies in managing patient care by seamlessly linking the entire health care delivery system electronically." The system "gives physicians and health care providers instant, user-friendly electronic access to comprehensive information about a patient's medical history and the best clinical treatments recommended."

The result? A fast and pre-approved referral to the best clinical resource, whether it be a specialist, the emergency room or urgent care center, your regular physician, or safe self-care. In other words, a satisfied customer! And as a bonus, costs are reduced. As Medical Director John Danaher, M.D., explains, "Paper charting and duplicative lab and radiology tests are eliminated."

Doctors and managers at Health Net, Inc., use a state-of-the-art medical management system and management control system to offer the highest quality health care at an affordable price.

We presented many important cost-management tools used by management accountants in previous chapters. Tools such as activity-based costing, relevant costing, budgeting, and variance analysis are each useful by themselves. They are most useful, however, when they are parts of an integrated system—an orderly, logical plan to coordinate and evaluate all the activities of the organization's value chain. Just as in the case of Health Net, managers of most organizations today realize that long-run success depends on focusing on cost, quality, and service—the three components of the competitive edge. This chapter considers how the management control system helps managers focus organizational resources and employees' talents on such goals as cost, quality, and service. As you will see, no single management control system is inherently superior to another. The "best" system is the one that consistently leads to actions that meet the organization's goals and objectives.

This chapter builds on previous ones to present how managers blend the individual tools of management accounting to help achieve organizational goals. ■

Management Control Systems

management control system
A logical integration of techniques for gathering and using information to make planning and control decisions, for motivating employee behavior, and for evaluating performance.

A **management control system** is a logical integration of techniques for gathering and using information to make planning and control decisions, for motivating employee behavior, and for evaluating performance. The purposes of a management control system are

- to clearly communicate the organization's goals;
- to ensure that managers and employees understand the specific actions required of them to achieve organizational goals;
- to communicate results of actions across the organization; and
- to ensure that managers can adjust to changes in the environment.

Exhibit 9-1 shows the components of a management control system. We will refer to Exhibit 9-1 often as we consider the design and operation of management control systems.

Management Control Systems and Organizational Goals

OBJECTIVE 1

Describe the relationship of management control systems to organizational goals.

A well-designed management control system supports and coordinates the decision-making process and motivates individuals throughout the organization to act in concert. It also facilitates forecasting revenue- and cost-driver levels, budgeting, and measuring and evaluating performance.

The first and most basic component in a management control system is the organization's goals. Why? Because the focus of the management control system is on motivating decisions that help achieve the organization's goals. A basic adage of management control is that "you get what you measure." That is, measures of performance will influence managers' decisions, so those measures should be consistent with organizational goals. As shown in Exhibit 9-2, managers at all levels of the organization set goals and objectives and develop related performance measures for their section of the organization.

Exhibit 9-2 shows that top managers set organization-wide goals, performance measures, and targets and generally review them annually. These goals provide a long-term framework around which an organization will form its comprehensive plan for positioning itself in the market. As Exhibit 9-1 shows, goals answer the question, "What do we want to achieve?" However, goals without performance measures do not motivate managers.

Performance measures set direction and motivate managers. In their book, *Cracking the Value Code,* Boulton, Libert, and Samek state that we tend to "value what we measure but we do not always measure what we value." Measurements provide incentives, so it is important to tie performance measures to valuable goals. Otherwise, managers who

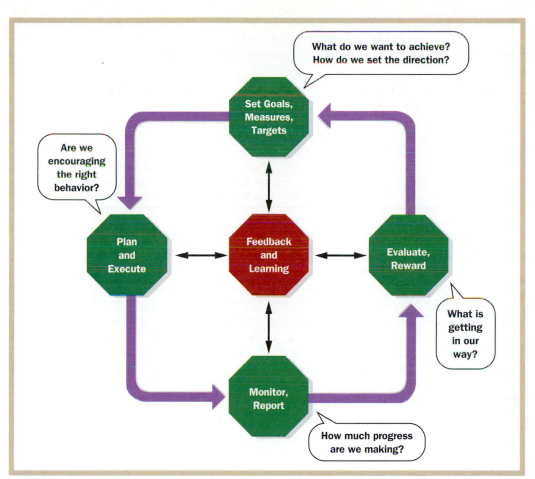

Exhibit 9-1
The Management Control System

Exhibit 9-2
Setting Goals, Objectives, and Performance Measures

achieve high performance measures may not create value for the company and its owners. For example, suppose a major Arizona-based luxury hotel chain, Scottdsale Luxury Suites, has the following goals and related performance measures:

Organizational Goals	Performance Measures
Exceed guest expectations	• Satisfaction index
	• Number of repeat stays
Maximize revenue yield	• Occupancy rate
	• Room rate
	• Income before fixed costs
Focus on innovation	• New products/services implemented per year
	• Number of employee suggestions

The company sets targets for goals at specific quantified levels of the measures. For example, a target for the performance measure occupancy rate might be "at least 70%."

As you can see, goals and their related performance measures are very broad. In fact, they are often too vague to guide managers and employees. As a result, top managers also identify key success factors. **Key success factors** are characteristics or attributes that managers must achieve in order to drive the organization toward its goals. Consider Scottsdale Luxury Suites. An example of a key success factor for the goal to exceed guest expectations is timeliness. That is, Scottsdale Luxury Suites must provide timely service to achieve its goal of exceeding guest expectations. Performance measures for timeliness would include time to check in, time to check out, and response time to guest requests (for example, number of rings before someone at the front desk answers the telephone).

Although key success factors and related performance measures give managers more focus than do overall, organization-wide goals, they still do not give lower-level managers and employees the direction they need to guide their daily actions. As shown in Exhibit 9-2, to set this direction, top managers work with lower-level managers within each business unit to select specific tangible short-term actions (or activities) that managers can carry out and their superiors can observe. Examples of specific actions related to timeliness are implementing an express check-in system and training staff to use it.

Balancing various goals is an important part of management control. Managers often face trade-off decisions. For example, a sales manager may increase employee satisfaction (measured by a survey of employees) by setting lower standards for responding to customer inquiries. However, this action may also decrease customer satisfaction measures.

key success factor
Characteristics or attributes that managers must achieve in order to drive the organization toward its goals.

Designing Management Control Systems

To design a management control system that meets the organization's needs, managers need to identify responsibility centers, develop performance measures, establish a monitoring and reporting structure, weigh costs and benefits, and provide motivation to achieve goal congruence and managerial effort. Let's look at each of these.

Identifying Responsibility Centers

responsibility center
A set of activities and resources assigned to a manager, a group of managers, or other employees.

Designers of management control systems must identify the responsibilities of each manager in an organization by establishing responsibility centers. A **responsibility center** is a set of activities and resources assigned to a manager, a group of managers, or other employees. A set of machines and machining activities, for example, may be a responsibility center for a production supervisor. The full production department may be a responsibility center for the department head. Finally, the entire organization may be a responsibility center for the president. In some organizations, groups of employees share management responsibility to create wide "ownership" of management decisions, to allow creative decision making, and to prevent one person's concern (or lack of concern) for risks of failure to dominate decisions.

An effective management control system gives each manager responsibility for a group of activities and actions and then, as Exhibit 9-1 shows, monitors and reports on (1) the results of the activities, and (2) the manager's influence on those results. Such a system has innate appeal for most top managers because it helps them delegate decision making and frees them to plan and control. Lower-level managers appreciate the autonomy of decision making they inherit. Thus, system designers apply **responsibility accounting** to identify what parts of the organization have primary responsibility for each action, develop performance measures and targets, and design reports of these measures by responsibility center. Responsibility centers usually have multiple goals and actions that the management control system monitors. We can classify responsibility centers as cost centers, profit centers, or investment centers based on their managers' primary financial responsibilities.

Cost, Profit, and Investment Centers In a **cost center** managers are responsible for costs only. A single cost center may encompass an entire department, or a department may contain several cost centers. For example, although one manager may supervise an assembly department, the department may contain several assembly lines and regard each assembly line as a separate cost center. Likewise, within each line, each separate machine may be its own cost center. The determination of the number of cost centers depends on cost-benefit considerations—do the benefits of smaller cost centers (for planning, control, and evaluation) exceed the higher costs of reporting?

Unlike cost center managers, **profit center** managers are responsible for controlling revenues as well as costs (or expenses)—that is, profitability. Despite the name, a profit center can exist in nonprofit organizations (though it might not be referred to as such) when a responsibility center receives revenues for its services. For example, the **Western Area Power Authority (WAPA)** is charged with recovering its costs of operations through sales of power to electric utilities in the western United States. WAPA essentially is a profit center with the objective of breaking even. All profit center managers are responsible for both revenues and costs, but they may not be expected to maximize profits.

An **investment center** adds responsibility for investment to profit center responsibilities. Investment-center success depends on both income and invested capital, perhaps measured by a ratio of income to the value of the capital employed. In practice, you will not often hear the term investment center. Instead, managers use the term profit center to describe centers that hold managers responsible for revenues and expenses, but may or may not hold them responsible for the capital investment.

Developing Performance Measures

Effective performance measures are essential for almost any organization. A typical attitude of managers is "You simply can't manage something you can't measure." Most responsibility centers have multiple goals and therefore multiple performance measures. Managers can express only some of these performance measures in financial terms, such as operating budgets, profit targets, or required return on investment. Other goals require nonfinancial measures. For example, many companies list environmental stewardship, social responsibility, and organizational learning as key goals. Therefore, well-designed management control systems develop and report both financial and nonfinancial measures of performance. Good performance measures will

1. Relate to the goals of the organization
2. Balance long-term and short-term concerns
3. Reflect the management of key actions and activities
4. Be affected by actions of managers and employees

OBJECTIVE 2

Use responsibility accounting to define an organizational subunit as a cost center, a profit center, or an investment center.

responsibility accounting
Identifying what parts of the organization have primary responsibility for each action, developing performance measures and targets, and designing reports of these measures by responsibility center.

cost center
A responsibility center in which managers are responsible for costs only.

profit center
A responsibility center in which managers are responsible for revenues as well as costs (or expenses)—that is, profitability.

investment center
A responsibility center whose success depends on both income and invested capital, perhaps measured by a ratio of income to the value of the capital employed.

OBJECTIVE 3

Develop performance measures and use them to monitor the achievements of an organization.

5. Be readily understood by employees
6. Be used in evaluating and rewarding managers and employees
7. Be reasonably objective and easily measured
8. Be used consistently and regularly

Sometimes accountants and managers focus too much on financial measures, such as profit or cost variances, because they are readily available from the accounting system. Managers, however, can improve operational control by also considering nonfinancial measures of performance. Such measures may be more timely and more closely affected by employees at lower levels of the organization, where the product is made or the service is rendered. Examples of this are in the Business First box on page 387.

Nonfinancial measures are often easier to quantify and understand. Hence, they can more easily motivate employees toward achieving performance goals. For example, **AT&T Universal Card Services**, which was awarded the prestigious Baldrige National Quality Award (presented by the U.S. Department of Commerce), uses 18 performance measures for its customer inquiries process. These measures include average speed of answer, abandon rate, and application processing time (three days compared to the industry average of 34 days).

Often the effects of poor nonfinancial performance (for example, lack of organizational learning and process improvement and low customer satisfaction) do not show up in the financial measures until the company has lost considerable ground. Financial measures often are lagging indicators that arrive too late to help prevent problems and ensure the organization's health. Rather, managers need leading indicators. As a result, many companies now stress management of the activities that drive revenues and costs rather than waiting to explain the revenues or costs themselves after the activities have occurred. Superior financial performance usually follows from superior nonfinancial performance.

Monitoring and Reporting Results

Notice that Exhibit 9-1 has feedback and learning at the center of the management control system. At all points in the planning and control process, it is vital to maintain effective communications among all levels of management and employees. In fact, organization-wide learning is a foundation for gaining and maintaining financial strength. Rich Teerlink, former CEO of **Harley-Davidson**, said, "If you empower dummies, they make dumb decisions faster." Harley-Davidson spends $1,000 per year per employee on training. Harley had 2002 sales of nearly $4.1 billion, one-year sales growth of 20%, and one-year earnings growth of 33%. Some management experts have said that the only sustainable competitive advantage is the rate at which a company's managers learn.

Once a company has superior intellectual capital, how can it best maintain its leadership? Exhibit 9-3 shows how organizational learning leads to financial strength. Measures such as training time, employee turnover, and staff satisfaction scores on employee surveys can monitor organizational learning. The result of learning is continuous process improvement. Measures such as cycle time, number of defects (quality), and activity cost can assess improvement. Customers will value improved response time (lower cycle time), higher quality, and lower prices, and thus increase their demand for products and services. Increased demand, combined with lower costs to make and deliver products and services, results in improved product profitability and earnings. It is important to note that the successful organization does not stop with one cycle of learning → process improvement → increased customer satisfaction → improved financial strength. It reinvests the excess financial resources that it gains to further support both continuous learning and continuous process improvement. The message from Exhibit 9-3 is that a key driver of enterprise performance is the culture within the company that fosters continual learning and growth at all levels of management. It is not adequate to use money to train managers if the resulting

PERFORMANCE MEASURES IN PRACTICE

An organization's performance measures depend on its goals and objectives. For example, a software company and an auto manufacturer will have vastly different performance measures. The measures also must span a variety of key success factors for the organization. Performance measures too focused on one aspect of performance may foster neglect of other important factors.

Let's look at a classic management control system, the one developed by General Electric in the 1950s. The system focused on eight "key result areas," as GE called them:

Financial Key Result Areas
- Profitability
- Productivity
- Market position

Nonfinancial Key Result Areas
- Product leadership
- Personnel development
- Employee attitudes
- Public responsibility
- Balance between short-run and long-range goals

Measures in each of these eight areas would be just as relevant today as in the 1950s. These are clearly long-run strategic goals. Measures might change as an organization adapts the means of achieving the goals, but the basic framework of a management control system need not change as management fads come and go.

A more recent example is Southwest Airlines. The mission of **Southwest Airlines** is "dedication to the highest quality of customer service delivered with a sense of warmth, friendliness, individual pride, and company spirit." Yet, until recently, the company focused mainly on financial measures in evaluating managers. Recently, Southwest introduced nonfinancial measures into the mix, including:

- Load factor (percentage of seats occupied)
- Utilization factors on aircraft and personnel
- On-time performance
- Available seat miles
- Denied boarding rate
- Lost bag reports per 10,000 passengers
- Flight cancellation rate
- Employee head count
- Cutomer complaints per 10,000 passengers

By including nonfinancial measures, Southwest could focus managers' attention on the key success factors that related most closely to Southwest's mission and goals.

Sources: David Solomons, *Divisional Performance: Measurement and Control* (Homewood, IL: Irwin, 1965); Southwest Airlines Web site (http://www.southwest.com).

---

learning does not translate into improved processes, products, and services. This requires a culture of learning that motivates managers to translate learning into growth.

There are no guarantees that each of the components "automatically" follows from success at the previous component. If no core business process improves, the cause-effect chain can be broken. For example, a lack of improvement in marketing and distribution techniques can lead to failure due to the inability to place the "new and improved" products or services at the location desired by the customer. For example, development of a great e-commerce Web site does no good if customers never visit the Web site. The point is that improvement in business processes must take place across all parts of the value chain.

General Electric Company (GE) provides a good example of the application of the enterprise learning culture. With sales of more than $130 billion, GE has demonstrated a remarkable ability to generate formidable profits in a wide range of industries, including broadcasting (**NBC**), transportation equipment, aircraft engines, appliances, lighting, electric distribution and control equipment, generators and turbines, nuclear reactors, medical imaging equipment, plastics, and financial services. In 1998 through 2002, GE was named Fortune magazine's "Most Admired Company in America," although it slipped to number five on the list in 2003.

Exhibit 9-3
The Components
of a Successful
Organization and
Measures of
Achievement

*Examples of performance measures used to monitor the achievement of the component.

In a GE annual report just before he retired, former CEO John Welch claimed GE's success is due to

> . . . *a General Electric culture that values the contributions of every*
> *individual, thrives on learning, thirsts for the better idea, and has the*
> *flexibility and speed to put the better idea into action every day. We are a*
> *learning company, a company that studies its own successes and failures and*
> *those of others—a company that has the self-confidence and the resources*
> *to take big swings and pursue numerous opportunities based on winning*
> *ideas and insights, regardless of their source. That appetite for learning, and*
> *the ability to act quickly on that learning, will provide GE with what we*
> *believe is an insurmountable and sustainable competitive advantage.*

Exactly what does John Welch mean by the "ability to act quickly on that learning"? He refers to a management leadership philosophy that ignores organizational boundaries when implementing learning. According to Welch, GE "opened [its] culture up to ideas from everyone, everywhere, killed NIH (Not Invented Here) thinking, decimated the bureaucracy, and made boundaryless behavior a reflexive and natural part of our culture, thereby creating the learning culture."

As shown in Exhibit 9-1, monitoring and reporting the results of business activities are key components of a management control system. Exhibit 9-2 indicates that managers identify actions and related performance measures that are linked to the achievement of goals and objectives. Once managers identify these performance measures and actions, they need periodic information on the achievement of desired outcomes. The performance-reporting system provides such information. Effective performance reports align results with managers' goals and objectives, provide guidance to managers, communicate goals and their level of attainment throughout the organization, and enable organizations to anticipate and respond to change in a timely manner.

Summary Problem For Your Review

PROBLEM

The Luxury Suites hotel chain is developing performance measures for each of its major goals. Top management established "exceed guest expectations" as one organization-wide goal. Among the key success factors are timeliness of customer service and quality of personalized service. Susan Pierce, vice president of sales, is the manager responsible for the actions required to meet the goal of exceeding guest expectations. She has already identified one action (objective) for the coming year—upgrade customer service department capabilities.

1. Identify several possible performance measures for the quality of personalized service key success factor.
2. Recommend several specific actions or activities associated with upgrading customer service department capabilities that would drive Luxury Suites to its goal of exceeding customer expectations.

SOLUTION

1. Performance measures for the quality of personalized service include number of changes to registration, rating on the "friendly, knowledgeable staff" question on the guest survey, number of complaints, percentage of return guests, and percentage of customers with completed customer profile (profiles special needs of customers).
2. Specific actions or activities include training employees, implementing a call checklist (list of services and options available to guest) and monitoring compliance with the list, developing a customer satisfaction survey, and reengineering the guest registration and reservation processes.

Goal Congruence, Managerial Effort, and Motivation

A first step in designing a management control system is to design performance measures that are consistent with the goals and objectives of the organization. An equally important second step is determining how employees will react to evaluations that use the performance measures. Designing performance measures is not a back-office accounting task. It requires the direct involvement of those affected. Stephen Kaufman, former chairman of the board of **Arrow Electronics** (quoted in *Harvard Business Review*), put it this way: "It's very difficult to define the right metric and anticipate exactly how your people will react to it. Your best chance of knowing whether it will have the intended effect is to talk to the people directly involved." This section discusses the motivation effects of management control systems.

Motivating Employees to Achieve Goal Congruence and Exert Managerial Effort Through Rewards

To achieve maximum benefits at minimum cost, a management control system must foster goal congruence and managerial effort. An organization achieves **goal congruence** when employees, working in their own perceived best interests, make decisions that help meet the overall goals of the organization. **Managerial effort**—exertion toward a goal or objective—must accompany goal congruence. Effort here means not merely working harder or faster but also working better. It includes all conscious actions (such as supervising, planning, and thinking) that result in more efficiency and effectiveness.

goal congruence
A condition where employees, working in their own personal interests, make decisions that help meet the overall goals of the organization.

managerial effort
Exertion toward a goal or objective including all conscious actions (such as supervising, planning, and thinking) that result in more efficiency and effectiveness.

OBJECTIVE 4

Explain the importance of evaluating performance and how it impacts motivation, goal congruence, and employee effort.

Goal congruence can exist with little accompanying effort, and vice versa, but good management control systems contain both. As we saw in Exhibit 9-1, the challenge of management control system design is to specify goals and actions and a performance evaluation and reward system that induce (or at least do not discourage) employee decisions that would achieve organizational goals. For example, an organization may specify one of its goals to be continuous improvement in employee efficiency and effectiveness. Employees, however, might perceive that continuous improvements will result in tighter standards, faster pace of work, and loss of jobs. Even though they may agree with management that continuous improvements are competitively necessary, management should not expect them to exert effort for continuous improvements unless rewards are in place to make this effort in their own best interests.

As another example, students may enroll in a college course because their goal is to learn about management accounting. The faculty and the students share the same goal, but goal congruence is not enough. Faculty also introduce rewards in the form of a grading system to spur student effort. Grading is a form of performance evaluation, as is use of management control reports for raises, promotions, and other forms of rewards in other settings. Performance evaluation is a widely used means of improving goal congruence and effort, because most individuals tend to perform better when performance reports lead directly to personal rewards. Thus, **Allen-Bradley Co.**, **Corning**, and other manufacturers that set quality improvements as critical goals put quality targets into the bonus plans of top managers. Corning has quality incentives for factory workers as well.

Motivation—the drive toward some selected goal that creates effort and action toward that goal—is key to management control. Yet employees differ widely in their motivations. This makes the system designer's task complex and ill structured. Each system must fit the specific organizational environment and behavioral characteristics of the employees. The system designer must align individuals' self-interest with the goals of the organization. Thus, the designer must predict the motivational impact of a particular system—how it will cause people to respond—and compare it to the motivational impact of other potential systems.

Responsibility accounting, budgets, variances, and the entire inventory of management control tools should constructively influence behavior. However, some managers misuse them as negative weapons to punish, place blame, or find fault. Viewed positively, they assist employees to improve decisions. Used negatively, they pose a threat to employees, who will resist and undermine the use of such techniques. Critics have pointed to **Enron's** management control system as a major cause of the company's problems. Employees were heavily rewarded for good performance. More important, the employees who were ranked lowest at each evaluation were fired. This created intense competition, which at first seemed to create exceptional performance levels for the company. Later, it became clear that some of this success came at the expense of undercutting other employees, and the pressure for good performance caused some employees to employ unethical methods to increase their performance measures.

motivation

The drive for some selected goal that creates effort and action toward that goal.

Weighing Costs and Benefits

The designer of a management control system must also weigh the costs and benefits of various alternatives, given the organization's needs. No system is perfect, but one system may be better than another if it can improve operating decisions at a reasonable cost.

Both benefits and costs of management control systems are often difficult to measure, and both may become apparent only after experimentation or use. For example, the director of accounting policy of **Citicorp** has stated that, after using a very detailed management control system for several years, the system has proved to be too costly to administer relative to the perceived benefits. Accordingly, Citicorp planned to return to a simpler, less costly—though less precise—management control system. In contrast, **Home Depot** added metrics to its management control system. When employees asked CEO Bob Nardelli why they should use the new metrics, he compared the metrics to gauges in a car: "Why do you need a gas gauge? Why do you need a speedometer?" He believed that the metrics were worth the cost because they helped headquarters know what is going on throughout the company.

Controllability and Measurement of Financial Performance

Management control systems often distinguish between controllable and uncontrollable events and between controllable and uncontrollable costs. Usually, responsibility center managers are in the best position to explain their center's results even if the managers had little influence over them. For example, an importer of grapes from Chile to the United States suffered a sudden loss of sales several years ago after a few of the grapes were found to contain poisonous cyanide. The tampering was beyond the import manager's control. The importer's management control system used a flexible budget (see Chapter 8) to separate the effects of activity volume—sales levels—from effects of efficiency. The company held the manager responsible for efficiency—the flexible-budget variance—but not for the sales volume effect. Nevertheless, the manager had to explain the reasons for and effects of the sales volume decline. Why? Because the manager had the best information about sales, even if he was not responsible for it.

An **uncontrollable cost** is any cost that the management of a responsibility center cannot affect within a given time span. For example, the manager of a **Dow Chemical** factory may not be able to control the market price of the crude oil used to make various chemicals. In contrast, **controllable costs** include all costs that a manager's decision and actions can influence. The chemical factory managers may be able to control the amount of crude oil used, the cost of labor, and most overhead costs in the factory.

In a sense, the term *controllable* is a misnomer because no cost is completely under the control of a manager. Nevertheless, we use the term to refer to any cost that a manager's decisions affect, even if not totally "controlled." Although the chemical factory manager may not totally control labor costs because union contracts place constraints on both hourly rates and labor usage, the company still considers the cost controllable.

The distinction between controllable and uncontrollable costs serves an information purpose. Costs that are completely uncontrollable tell nothing about a manager's decisions and actions because, by definition, nothing the manager does will affect the costs. Evaluations of the responsibility center manager's performance should ignore such costs. In contrast, measuring and reporting controllable costs provides evidence about a manager's performance.

Because responsibility for costs may be widespread, systems designers must depend on understanding operations and cost behavior to help identify controllable costs. By isolating activities and related cost drivers, activity-based costing (see Chapter 4) can help to point out controllable costs. For example, **Procter & Gamble** credited its activity-based management control system for identifying controllable costs in one of its detergent divisions, which led to major strategic changes.

uncontrollable cost
Any cost that the management of a responsibility center cannot affect within a given time span.

controllable cost
Any cost that a manager's decisions and actions can influence.

Contribution Margin

Many organizations combine the contribution approach to measuring income with responsibility accounting—that is, they report by cost behavior as well as by degrees of controllability.

	Company as a Whole	Company Breakdown into Two Divisions		Breakdown of West Division Only				Breakdown of West Division, Meats Only		
		East Division	West Division	Not Allocated†	Groceries	Produce	Meats	Not Allocated†	Store 1	Store 2
Net sales	$4,000	$1,500	$2,500	—	$1,300	$300	$900	—	$600	$300
Variable costs										
Cost of merchandise sold	$3,000	$1,100	$1,900	—	$1,000	$230	$670	—	$450	$220
Variable operating costs‡	260	100	160	—	100	10	50	—	35	15
Total variable costs	$3,260	$1,200	$2,060	—	$1,100	$240	$720	—	$485	$235
(a) Contribution margin	$ 740	$ 300	$ 440	—	$ 200	$ 60	$180	—	$115	$ 65
Less: fixed costs controllable by segment managers§	260	100	160	$ 20	40	10	90	$ 30	35	25
(b) Contribution controllable by segment managers	$ 480	$ 200	$ 280	$ (20)	$ 160	$ 50	$ 90	$ (30)	$ 80	$ 40
Less: fixed costs controllable by others¶	200	90	110	20	40	10	40	10	22	8
(c) Contribution by segments	$ 280	$ 110	$ 170	$ (40)	$ 120	$ 40	$ 50	$ (40)	$ 58	$ 32
Less: unallocated costs‖	100									
(d) Income before income taxes	$ 180									

* Three different types of segments are illustrated here: divisions, product lines, and stores. As you read across, note that the focus becomes narrower; from East and West divisions to West Division only, to meats in West Division only.

† Only those costs clearly identifiable to a product line should be allocated.

‡ Principally wages and payroll-related costs.

§ Examples are certain advertising, sales promotions, salespersons' salaries, management consulting, training and supervision costs.

¶ Examples are depreciation, property taxes, insurance, and perhaps the segment manager's salary.

‖ These costs are not clearly or practically allocable to any segment except by some highly questionable allocation base.

Exhibit 9-4
Retail Grocery Store
Contribution Approach: Model Income Statement, by Segments (thousands of dollars)

Exhibit 9-4 displays the contribution approach to measuring the financial performance of the various organizational units (or segments) of a retail grocery company like **Safeway.** You can see the relevant segments of the company's organization chart in Exhibit 9-5:

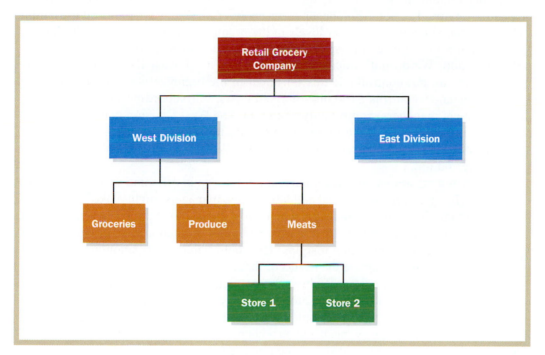

Segments are responsibility centers for which a company develops separate measures of revenues and costs. Study Exhibit 9-4 carefully. It provides perspective on how a management control system report can stress cost behavior, controllability, manager performance, and responsibility center performance simultaneously.

Line (a) in Exhibit 9-4 shows the contribution margin, sales revenues less all variable expenses. The contribution margin is especially helpful for predicting the impact on income of short-run changes in activity volume. Managers may quickly calculate any expected changes in income by multiplying increases in dollar sales by the contribution margin ratio. The contribution margin ratio for meats in the West Division is $180 \div $900 = .20. Thus, a $1,000 increase in sales of meats in the West Division should produce a $200 increase in income (.20 $\times$ $1,000 = $200) if there are no changes in selling prices, per unit operating expenses, or mix of sales between stores 1 and 2.

segments
Responsibility centers for which a company develops separate measures of revenues and costs.

OBJECTIVE 5

Prepare segment income statements for evaluating profit and investment centers using the contribution margin and controllable-cost concepts.

Contribution Controllable by Segment Managers

Lines (b) and (c) in Exhibit 9-4 separate the contribution that segment managers control (b) from the overall segment contribution (c). Designers of management control systems distinguish between the segment as an economic investment and the manager as a professional decision maker. For instance, an extended period of drought coupled with an aging population may adversely affect the desirability of continued economic investment in a ski resort, but the resort manager may be doing an excellent job under the circumstances.

The manager of store 1 may have influence over some local advertising but not other advertising, some fixed salaries but not other salaries, and so forth. Moreover, the meat manager at both the division and store levels may have zero influence over store depreciation or the president's salary. Therefore, Exhibit 9-4 separates costs by controllability.

Managers on all levels help explain the total segment contribution, but they are responsible only for the controllable contribution.

Note that we deduct the fixed costs controllable by the segment managers from the contribution margin to obtain the contribution controllable by segment managers. These controllable costs are usually discretionary fixed costs such as local advertising and some salaries, but not the manager's own salary. As we move to the right in Exhibit 9-4 we see the allocations to lower levels in the organization. Of the $160,000 that the West Division manager controls, groceries, produce, and meat departments control only $140,000. We do not allocate the other $20,000 of West Division fixed costs because they are not controllable this far down in the organization. That is, the West Division manager controls $160,000 of fixed costs, but subordinates (grocery, produce, and meat managers) control only $140,000. The West Division manager controls the remaining $20,000, but the lower managers do not. Similarly, the $30,000 in that same line are costs that the meat department of the West Division controls but the individual stores do not.

In many organizations, managers have latitude to trade off some variable costs for fixed costs. To save variable material and labor costs, managers might make heavier outlays for automation, quality management employee training programs, and so on. Moreover, decisions on advertising, research, and sales promotion have effects on sales activity and hence on contribution margins. The controllable contribution includes these expenses and attempts to capture the results of these trade-offs.

The classifications of costs in Exhibit 9-4 are generally not clear-cut. For example, determining controllability is always a problem when a company allocates service department costs to other departments. Should the store manager bear a part of the division headquarters' costs? If so, how much and on what basis? How much, if any, store depreciation or lease rentals should we deduct in computing the controllable contribution? There are no easy answers to these questions. Each organization picks ways that benefit it most with the lowest relative cost. (This differs from the situation in external financial accounting systems, which must follow strict regulations).

Contribution by Segments

The contribution by segments, line (c) in Exhibit 9-4, is an attempt to approximate the financial performance of the segment, as distinguished from the financial performance of its manager, which we measure in line (b). The "fixed costs controllable by others" typically include committed costs (such as depreciation and property taxes) and discretionary costs (such as the segment manager's salary). Although the segment manager does not control these costs, they are necessary for the operation of the segment.

Unallocated Costs

Exhibit 9-4 shows "unallocated costs" immediately before line (d). These costs might include central corporate costs such as the costs of top management and some corporate-level services (for example, legal and taxation). When an organization cannot find a persuasive cause-and-effect or activity-based justification for allocating such costs, they generally do not allocate them to segments.

The contribution approach highlights the relative objectivity of various means of measuring financial performance. The contribution margin itself tends to be the most objective. As you read downward in the report, the allocations become more subjective, and the resulting measures of contributions or income become more subject to dispute. Though such disputes may be unproductive uses of management time, the allocations do direct managers' attention to the costs of the entire organization and lead to organizational cost control.

MAKING MANAGERIAL DECISIONS

Managers should try to distinguish between controllable and uncontrollable events and costs when designing segment financial reports. For each of the following costs of a merchandising business (for example, a department store), indicate whether it is a variable cost, fixed cost controllable by segment managers, fixed cost controllable by someone other than the segment manager, or a cost that a company normally does not allocate.

> Property taxes
> Supervision of sales force
> Depreciation of store
> Cost of goods sold
> Local store advertising
> Corporate-level advertising
> Corporate-level public relations
> Temporary sales labor

Answers

Variable costs are generally controllable by the store manager. Cost of goods sold and temporary sales labor are examples.

Fixed costs controllable by the segment (store) manager include local store advertising and supervision of the local sales force. The store manager usually decides the appropriate level for these costs.

Fixed costs controllable by those other than the store manager include property taxes and depreciation of the store. These costs relate directly to the store, but the store manager cannot change them.

Unallocated costs include corporate-level advertising and public relations. These costs have a tenuous link to the store.

Nonfinancial Measures of Performance

For many years organizations have monitored their nonfinancial performance. For example, sales organizations have followed up on customers to ensure their satisfaction and manufacturers have tracked manufacturing defects and product performance. In recent years, most organizations have developed a new awareness of the importance of controlling nonfinancial performance areas. We will first discuss a popular, broad approach to performance reporting, the balanced scorecard, that explicitly balances financial and nonfinancial measures. Then we will examine specific nonfinancial performance measures such as quality, cycle time, and productivity.

OBJECTIVE 6

Use a balanced scorecard to recognize both financial and nonfinancial measures of performance.

The Balanced Scorecard

A **balanced scorecard** is a performance measurement and reporting system that strikes a balance between financial and operating measures, links performance to rewards, and gives explicit recognition to the diversity of organizational goals. It ties performance measurement directly to organizational goals and objectives. Companies such as **Microsoft, American Express, Exxon Mobile, Allstate,** and **Apple Computer** and government and nonprofit agencies such as the U.S. Department of Transportation and United Way of America have used the balanced scorecard to focus management's attention on key performance indicators—measures that drive an organization to achieve its goals. About 50% of the 1,000 largest U.S. firms use some version of the balanced scorecard. We describe some of the more successful in the Business First box on page 396.

One advantage of the balanced scorecard approach is that line managers can see the relationship between nonfinancial measures, which often more directly measure the results of their own actions, and the financial measures that relate to organizational goals. Another advantage of the balanced scorecard is its focus on performance

balanced scorecard
A performance measurement and reporting system that strikes a balance between financial and operating measures, links performance to rewards, and gives explicit recognition to the diversity of organizational goals.

Robert Kaplan and David Norton created the balanced scorecard (BSC) in 1992. In 2000, their company, **Balanced Scorecard Collaborative**, created a Balanced Scorecard Hall of Fame. In 2002, it inducted four organizations: St. Mary's/Duluth Clinic Health System, the U.K. Ministry of Defence, **Volvofinans**, and **Wendy's International**. (Already in the hall of fame were **Hilton Hotels Corporation**, **Verizon Communications**, Duke University Children's Hospital, **Siemens IC Mobile**, **Skandia**, **Borealis**, **DuPont**, Montifore Medical Center, National Reconnaissance Office, and **Saatchi & Saatchi**.) To be selected for the hall of fame, a company must apply one or more of the following five principles to create a strategy-focused organization: "mobilize change through executive leadership; translate the strategy into operational terms; align the organization around its strategy; make strategy everyone's job; and make strategy a continual process."

St. Mary's/Duluth Clinic Health System (SMDC) operates 20 clinics, four hospitals, and an array of specialty care services in northern Minnesota. It has gross revenue of nearly $1 billion. CEO Peter Person noted that "our monthly scorecard review sessions are incredibly valuable to me as CEO. The scorecard enables us to easily scan and digest overall organizational performance, and to identify any necessary course corrections." The strategic orientation of the BSC makes top management support and involvement essential to its success.

The mission of the U.K. Ministry of Defence is to defend the United Kingdom, its overseas territories, and its people and interests and to act as a force for good by strengthening international peace and security. Its budget for 2003–2004 is nearly £25 billion. It employs more than 300,000 military and civilian personnel, including 210,000 regular forces in the Royal Navy, Air Force, and Army. After implementing the BSC in 2000, Sir Kevin Tebbit, chairman of the Defence Management Board, stated that "the balanced scorecard is one of the most important management initiatives we have adopted. It ensures that we all share a common understanding—

from the top Board through major Commands to the Operational Units—of what we want to achieve and the individual contribution we all have to make." A key outcome of the BSC is tying strategy to operations.

Volvofinans is the leading vehicle-financing company in Sweden, with about 250,000 contracts in force and nearly 200 employees. According to its president, Bjorn Ingemanson, "most of our employees are involved in the BSC process and understand the strategic goals and targets of the company. Satisfied employees create satisfied customers, and satisfied customers become loyal customers both of the Volvo brand and to Volvofinans as a company." The BSC can help focus employees' attention on the key success factors such as customer satisfaction.

Wendy's International is one of the world's largest restaurant operating and franchising companies, with more than 8,800 restaurants and 2002 sales of $9.4 billion. The company implemented the BSC to get a better handle on intangible assets such as intellectual capital and customer focus. CEO Jack Schuessler lauded the BSC's success in "establishing targets and measuring our progress in key dimensions ranging from employee retention at the restaurant level, to restaurant evaluation scores, to business processes, to total revenue growth. They are all vitally important, not just the financial measures." The BSC provides a framework for balancing financial and nonfinancial measures.

The BSC has helped each of the four award-winning organizations in a slightly different way. It has gained wide acceptance and successful implementation in many companies since its introduction only a little more than a decade ago.

Sources: "Balanced Scorecard Collaborative Honors St. Mary's/Duluth Clinic Health System, the U.K. Ministry of Defence, Volvofinans, and Wendy's International with Prestigious Hall of Fame Award," *Financial Times Information,* October 16, 2002; Balanced Scorecard Collaborative Web site (http://www.bscol.com); St. Mary's/Duluth Clinic Health System Web site (http://www.smdc.org); U.K. Ministry of Defence Web site (http://www.mod.uk/index.shtml); Volvofinans, *Volvofinans 2002 Annual Report;* Wendy's Intl., Inc., *Wendy's International 2002 Annual Report.*

key performance indicators
Measures that drive the organization to achieve its goals.

measures from each of the four components of the successful organization shown in Exhibit 9-3 (p. 388). This enhances the learning process because managers learn the results of their actions and how these actions lead to attainment of the organization's goals.

What does a balanced scorecard look like? The classic balanced scorecard developed by Robert Kaplan and David Norton includes **key performance indicators**—measures

Financial	Processes
Economic profit realized	Percentage reduction in process cycle time
Income from operations	Number of engineering changes
Working capital	Capacity utilization
Operational cash flow	Order response time
Inventory turns	Process capability
Customers	**Competence**
Rank in customer survey	Leadership competence
Market share	Percentage of patent-protected turnover
Repeat order rate	Training days per employee
Complaints	Quality improvement team participation
Brand index	

Exhibit 9-6

Performance Indicators for Philips Electronics' Balanced Scorecard

that drive the organization to meet its goals—grouped into four categories: (1) financial, (2) customers, (3) internal processes, and (4) employee growth and learning. Some companies use other terminology or categories; the most common is to add a category for employees. However, all develop multiple performance measures for each category. For example, **Philips Electronics** uses the categories and performance indicators in Exhibit 9-6.

Most companies that use a balanced scorecard specify the categories that each business segment will use, but they allow the units to choose the key performance indicators. For example, every Microsoft division has measures for financial, customer, internal processes, and learning perspectives, but the Latin American division, for example, has different measures in each category than does the Seattle headquarters. The balanced scorecard should not be a straightjacket; rather it is a flexible framework for motivating and measuring performance.

MAKING MANAGERIAL DECISIONS

When top managers set organizational goals, they should attempt to provide a balance between financial and non-financial goals. Using the four components of a successful organization shown in Exhibit 9-3, indicate the component associated with the following goals of Whirlpool:

People commitment
Total quality
Customer satisfaction
Financial performance
Growth and innovation

Answer

The components listed in Exhibit 9-3 form a causal link from organizational learning to business process improvement, to customer satisfaction, and finally to financial strength. Using the five goals set by top managers at Whirlpool, we can make the following cause-effect statement:

If Whirlpool makes a solid commitment to its people, then growth and innovation will occur as part of the company's organizational learning. This will lead to business process improvements that increase the total quality of its products, which will then lead to increased customer satisfaction. The ultimate result of satisfied customers is improved financial performance. Sustainable financial strength should result in reinvestment in both Whirlpool's people and its internal processes.

Control of Quality

OBJECTIVE 7

Measure performance against quality, cycle time, and productivity objectives.

quality control
The effort to ensure that products and services perform to customer requirements.

Whether they use a balanced scorecard or not, most companies use performance metrics that measure the quality of their products or services. **Quality control** is the effort to ensure that products and services perform to customer requirements. In essence, customers or clients define quality by comparing their needs to the attributes of the product or service. For example, buyers judge the quality of an automobile based on reliability, performance, styling, safety, and image relative to their needs, budget, and the alternatives. Defining quality in terms of customer requirements is only half the battle. There remains the problem of reaching and maintaining the desired level of quality. There are many approaches to controlling quality. The traditional approach in the United States was to inspect products after completing them, and reject or rework those that failed the inspections. Because testing is expensive, companies often inspected only a sample of products. They judged the process to be in control as long as the number of defective products did not exceed an acceptable quality level. This meant that some defective products could still make their way to customers.

In recent years, however, many companies have learned that this is a costly way to control quality. All the resources consumed to make a defective product and to detect it are wasted, or considerable rework may be necessary to correct the defects. In addition, it is costly to repair products already in use by a customer or to win back a dissatisfied customer. IBM's[1] former chief executive officer John Akers was quoted in the *Wall Street Journal* as saying, "I am sick and tired of visiting plants to hear nothing but great things about quality and cycle time—and then to visit customers who tell me of problems." The high costs of achieving quality by "inspecting it in" are evident in a **cost of quality report,** which displays the financial impact of quality. The quality cost report shown in Exhibit 9-7 measures four categories of quality costs:

cost of quality report
A report that displays the financial impact of quality.

1. Prevention—costs incurred to prevent the production of defective products or delivery of substandard services including engineering analyses to improve product design for better manufacturing, improvements in production processes, increased quality of material inputs, and programs to train personnel
2. Appraisal—costs incurred to identify defective products or services including inspection and testing
3. Internal failure—costs of defective components and final products or services that are scrapped or reworked; also costs of delays caused by defective products or services
4. External failure—costs caused by delivery of defective products or services to customers, such as field repairs, returns, and warranty expenses

This report shows that internal or external failures caused most of the costs incurred by Eastside Manufacturing Company. These costs almost certainly are understated, however. Poor quality can result in large opportunity costs because of internal delays and lost sales. For example, quality problems in American-built automobiles in the 1980s probably caused forgone sales that were significantly more costly than the tangible costs measured in any quality cost report.

total quality management (TQM)
An approach to quality that focuses on prevention of defects and on customer satisfaction.

In recent years, more and more U.S. companies have been rethinking this approach to quality control. They have adopted an approach first espoused by an American, W. Edwards Deming, and embraced by Japanese companies decades ago: **total quality management (TQM).** Following the old adage "an ounce of prevention is worth a pound of cure," it focuses on prevention of defects and on achievement of customer satisfaction.

---

[1] Quoted in Graham Sharman, "When Quality Control Gets in the Way of Quality," *Wall Street Journal*, February 24, 1992, p. A14.

Month				Year to Date		
Actual	**Plan**	**Variance**	**Quality Cost Area**	**Actual**	**Plan**	**Variance**
			1. Prevention Cost			
3	2	1	A. Quality—administration	5	4	1
16	18	(2)	B. Quality—engineering	37	38	(1)
7	6	1	C. Quality—planning by others	14	12	2
5	7	(2)	D. Supplier assurance	13	14	(1)
31	33	(2)	Total prevention cost	69	68	1
5.5%	6.1%		% of Total quality cost	6.2%	6.3%	
			2. Appraisal cost			
31	26	5	A. Inspection	55	52	3
12	14	(2)	B. Test	24	28	(4)
7	6	1	C. Insp. & test of purchased mat.	15	12	3
11	11	0	D. Product quality audits	23	22	1
3	2	1	E. Maint. of insp. & test equip.	4	4	0
2	2	0	F. Mat. consumed in insp. & test	5	4	1
66	61	5	Total appraisal cost	126	122	4
11.8%	11.3%		% of Total quality cost	11.4%	11.3%	
			3. Internal failure cost			
144	140	4	A. Scrap & rework—manufacturing	295	280	15
55	53	2	B. Scrap & rework—engineering	103	106	(3)
28	30	(2)	C. Scrap & rework—supplier	55	60	(5)
21	22	(1)	D. Failure investigation	44	44	0
248	245	3	Total internal failure cost	497	490	7
44.3%	45.4%		% of Total quality cost	44.9%	45.3%	
345	339	6	Total internal quality cost (1 + 2 + 3)	692	680	12
61.6%	62.8%		% of Total quality cost	62.6%	62.8%	
			4. External failure quality cost			
75	66	9	A. Warranty exp.—manuf.	141	132	9
41	40	1	B. Warranty exp.—engineering	84	80	4
35	35	0	C. Warranty exp.—sales	69	70	(1)
46	40	6	D. Field warranty cost	83	80	3
18	20	(2)	E. Failure investigation	37	40	(3)
215	201	14	Total external failure cost	414	402	12
38.4%	37.2%		% of Total quality cost	37.4%	37.2%	
560	540	20	Total quality cost	1,106	1,082	24
9,872	9,800		Total product cost	20,170	19,600	
5.7%	5.5%		% Tot. qual. cost to tot. prod. cost	5.5%	5.5%	

* Adapted from Allen H. Seed III, *Adapting Management Accounting Practice to an Advanced Manufacturing Environment* (Montvale, NJ: National Association of Accountants, 1988), Table 5-2, p. 76.

Exhibit 9-7
Eastside Manufacturing Company
Quality Cost Report* (thousands of dollars)

The TQM approach builds on the assumption that an organization minimizes the cost of quality when it achieves high quality levels. Total quality management is the application of quality principles to all of the organization's endeavors to satisfy customers. The U.S. Department of Commerce presents the Baldrige Award to companies that excel in quality, based on their customer-oriented quality achievements. TQM has significant implications for organization goals, structure, and management control systems. For TQM to work, though, employees must be well trained in the process, the product or service, and the use of quality-control information.

To implement TQM, an organization trains employees to prepare, interpret, and act on quality-control charts, such as that shown in Exhibit 9-8. The **quality-control chart**

quality-control chart
The statistical plot of measures of various product dimensions or attributes.

Exhibit 9-8
Eastside
Manufacturing
Company
Quality-Control Chart

is a statistical plot of measures of various product dimensions or attributes. This plot helps detect process deviations before the process generates defects. These plots also identify excessive variation in product dimensions or attributes that process or design engineers should address. The chart in Exhibit 9-8 shows that the Eastside Manufacturing Company generally is not meeting its defects objective of .6% defects (which is a relatively high defect rate). Managers looking at this chart would know that they should take corrective action.

six sigma
An analytical method aimed at achieving near-perfect results on a production line.

The most recent trend in quality control is **six sigma,** an analytical method aimed at achieving near-perfect results on a production line. Literally, six sigma requires fewer than 3.4 defects per million. However, the six-sigma approach has broadened into a general process to define and measure a process, analyze the process, and improve the process to miminize errors. The focus is on measuring how many defects a company has in its process, because once it measures the defects it can take steps to eliminate them. Developed by **Motorola,** six sigma is making large impacts at companies such as **General Electric, Dow Chemical,** and **3M.** At Dow, each six sigma project has created an average of $500,000 in savings.

Control of Cycle Time

cycle time (throughput time)
The time taken to complete a product or service, or any of the components of a product or service.

Reducing cycle time is a key to improving quality. **Cycle time,** or **throughput time,** is the time taken to complete a product or service, or any of the components of a product or service. It is a summary measure of manufacturing or service efficiency and effectiveness and an important cost driver. The longer a product or service is in process, the more costs it consumes. Low cycle time means quick completion of a product or service (without defects). Lowering cycle time requires smooth-running processes and high quality. It also creates increased flexibility and quicker reactions to customer needs. As a company decreases cycle time, quality problems become apparent throughout the process. The company must solve the problems if it wants to improve quality. Decreasing cycle time also results in bringing products or services more quickly to customers, which makes for happy customers.

Firms measure cycle time for the important stages of a process and for the process as a whole. An effective means of measuring cycle time is to attach a bar code (similar to symbols on most grocery products) to each component or product and use a scanner to read the code at the end of each stage of completion. Cycle time for each stage is the time between readings of bar codes. Bar coding also permits effective tracking of materials and products for inventories, scheduling, and delivery.

Process Stage	Actual Cycle Time*	Standard Cycle Time	Variance	Explanation
Materials processing	2.1	2.5	0.4 F	
Circuit board assembly	44.7	28.8	15.9 U	Poor-quality materials caused rework
Power unit assembly	59.6	36.2	23.4 U	Engineering change required rebuilding all power units
Product assembly	14.6	14.7	0.1 F	
Functional and environmental test	53.3	32.0	21.3 U	Software failure in test procedures required retesting

F = Favorable. U = Unfavorable.
* Average time per stage over the week.

Exhibit 9-9
Eastside Manufacturing Company
Cycle Time Report for the Second Week of May

Exhibit 9-9 is a sample cycle-time report showing that Eastside Manufacturing Company is meeting its cycle-time objectives at two of its five production process stages. This report is similar to the flexible budget reports of Chapter 8. Explanations of the variances indicate that poor-quality materials and poor design led to extensive rework and retesting.

Control of Productivity

Another important performance measure for many companies is productivity. More than half the companies in the United States manage productivity as part of the effort to improve their competitiveness. **Productivity** is a measure of outputs divided by inputs. The fewer inputs needed to produce a given output, the more productive the organization. This simple definition, however, raises difficult measurement questions. How should the company measure outputs and inputs? Specific management control issues usually determine the most appropriate measures. Labor-intensive (especially service) organizations focus on increasing the productivity of labor, so labor-based measures are appropriate. Highly automated companies focus on machine use and productivity of capital investments, so capacity-based measures, such as the percentage of time machines are available, may be most important to them. Manufacturing companies in general monitor the efficient use of materials, and so for them measures of material yield (a ratio of material outputs over material inputs) may be useful indicators of productivity. In all cases of productivity ratios, a measure of the resource that management wishes to control is in the denominator (the input) and some measure of the objective of using the resource is in the numerator (the output).

Exhibit 9-10 shows 12 possible productivity measures. As you can see, they vary widely according to the type of resource that management wishes to use efficiently. The Business First box on page 403 shows how managers and analysts measure productivity in the auto industry.

productivity
A measure of outputs divided by inputs.

Choice of Productivity Measures

Which productivity measures should a company choose to manage? The choice depends on the behaviors desired. Managers generally concentrate on achieving the performance levels desired by their superiors. Thus, if top management evaluates subordinates' performance based on direct-labor productivity, lower-level managers will focus on

Exhibit 9-10
Measures of
Productivity

Resource	Possible Outputs (Numerator)		Possible Inputs (Denominator)
Labor	Standard direct-labor hours allowed for good output	÷	Actual direct-labor hours used
	Sales revenue	÷	Number of employees
	Sales revenue	÷	Direct-labor costs
	Bank deposit/loan activity (by a bank)	÷	Number of employees
	Service calls	÷	Number of employees
	Customer orders	÷	Number of employees
Materials	Weight of output	÷	Weight of input
	Number of good units	÷	Total number of units
Equipment, capital, physical capacity	Time (e.g., hours) used	÷	Time available for use
	Time available for use	÷	Time (e.g., 24 hours per day)
	Expected machine hours for good output	÷	Actual machine hours
	Sales revenue	÷	Direct-labor cost

improving that specific measure. "You get what you measure" is a favorite phrase to describe this.

The challenge in choosing productivity measures is that a manager may be able to improve a single measure but hurt performance elsewhere in the organization. For example, long production runs may improve machine productivity but result in excessive inventories. Alternatively, improved labor productivity in the short run may cause a high rate of product defects.

Use of a single measure of productivity is unlikely to result in overall improvements in performance. The choice of management controls requires anticipating the trade-offs that employees will make to improve their performance evaluations. Many organizations focus management control on the few most important activities, such as control of quality and service, and use productivity measures to monitor the actual benefits of improvements in these activities.

Productivity Measures Over Time

Be careful when comparing productivity measures over time. Changes in the process or in the rate of inflation can prove misleading. For example, consider labor productivity at **SBC Communications, Inc.** (the global U.S. telecommunications company). One measure of productivity tracked by SBC is sales revenue per employee.

	1999	2002	Percent Change
Total revenue (millions)	$49,489	$43,138	−12.8%
Employees	204,530	175,980	−14.0%
Revenue per employee (unadjusted for inflation)	$241,695	$245,130	+1.4%

By this measure, SBC appears to have achieved a 1.4% increase in the productivity of labor because the number of employees fell faster than the total revenue. However, total revenue has not been adjusted for the effects of inflation. Because of inflation, each 1999 dollar was equivalent to 1.08 2002 dollars. Therefore, SBC's 1999 sales revenue,

Productivity is an important component of profitability for auto manufacturers. In 2002, for the eighth year in a row, **Nissan** was rated by **Harbour and Associates** as the most productive auto assembly company in North America. The measure used was the number of hours per vehicle (HPV). Nissan averaged 17.92 hours to produce each vehicle. Two other foreign-owned manufacturers, **Honda** and **Toyota,** finished just behind Nissan. **General Motors**, **Ford,** and **Daimler-Chrysler** were far behind at 26, 27, and 31 HPV, respectively.

Although Nissan's plant in Smyrna, Tennessee, continued to have high productivity, its performance declined by 3.2% in 2002. For the first time ever, a General Motors plant (Oshawa #1) took the top place among individual plants with a 16.79 HPV. In addition, GM surpassed Ford in average HPV for the first time in history. Finally, **Mitsubishi's** plant in Normal, Illinois, showed exceptional improvement—8.6% in 2002 and 41% over the last four years, moving its HPV down to 21.82.

Other productivity measures indicate performance in specific parts of the manufacturing process. Harbor and Associates measures hours per engine (HPE) in the production of engines. For example, Toyota had the best productivity in 4-cylinder engines with an HPE of 2.71, Honda led in 6-cylinder productivity with an HPE of 3.47, and GM topped V8 productivity with an HPE of 4.55. Harbour also evaluates the stamping process, where it measures hits per hour (HPH) and pieces per hour (PPH), among other metrics.

Industry analysts look closely at these productivity numbers and their trends. They are a precursor of future profitability. Further, they want to find out how the various plants achieve their productivity levels so that other companies may copy successful methods and avoid others.

Nissan has more than 40% of its nearly $50 billion of sales in North America. Thus, productivity in its North American operations is important to the company. How has Nissan managed to achieve consistently high productivity? The key is a "highly motivated workforce," according to Barry Watson, Nissan's Smyrna plant department manager. A number of "simple but effective" efforts are at the heart of the plant's success. These efforts include

- Social events, such as family day and picnics
- Continuous training
- Manager and employee involvement through group meetings at the start of every shift—open, two-way discussions that focus on ideas for improving productivity and reducing costs
- Impact teams of managers and employees for evaluation and implementation of ideas

For example, an idea was submitted to build a special table that would significantly reduce the time it took to change equipment between production runs. The idea was implemented and resulted in a 15% increase in the number of units assembled on each production run.

Sources: Harbour and Associates, Inc., *Auto Manufacturing Productivity Report*, June, 2002 (http://www.harbourinc.com); Harbour and Associates, Inc., *Auto Manufacturing Productivity Report*, June, 1997; "Pick Me as Your Strike Target! No, Me!," *Business Week*, April 21, 2003; Nissan, *Nissan Motor Company Annual Report, Year Ended March 31, 2003*.

---

expressed in 2002 dollars (so we can compare it with 2002 sales revenue), is $49,489 × 1.08 = $53,448. The adjusted 1999 sales revenue per employee is as follows:

	1999 (adjusted)	2002	Percent Change
Total revenue (millions)	$53,448	$43,138	−19.3%
Employees	204,530	175,980	−14.0%
Revenue per employee (adjusted for inflation)	$261,321	$245,130	−6.2%

Adjusting for the effects of inflation reveals that SBC's labor productivity has actually decreased by 6.2% rather than increasing by 1.4%.

Management Control Systems in Service, Government, and Nonprofit Organizations

OBJECTIVE 8

Describe the difficulties of management control in service and nonprofit organizations.

Most service, government, and nonprofit organizations have more difficulty implementing management control systems than do manufacturing firms. Why? The main problem is that the outputs of service and nonprofit organizations are more difficult to measure than are the cars or computers that manufacturers produce. As a result, it may be more difficult to know quality or sometimes even the quantity of the service provided until long after the organization delivers the service. For example, what is a good measure of ouptut for a bank's call center (where service representatives answer customers' questions)? Number of calls or average minutes per call? Both of these might motivate many short calls that do not provide complete answers to customers. Total number of minutes on calls? This might motivate long, time-wasting calls. Because output is hard to measure, developing timely measures of input/output relationships is nearly impossible.

The key to successful management control in any organization is proper training and motivation of employees to achieve goal congruence and effort, followed by consistent monitoring of objectives set in accordance with critical processes and success factors. This is even more important in service-oriented organizations. It is just harder to achieve. **MBNA America,** a large issuer of bank credit cards, works hard to measure the amount and quality of its service. It identifies customer retention as its primary key success factor. MBNA trains its customer representatives carefully. Each day it measures and reports performance on 14 objectives consistent with customer retention, and it rewards every employee based on those 14 objectives. Measures include answering every call by the second ring, keeping the computer up 100% of the time, and processing credit-line requests within 1 hour. Employees have earned bonuses as high as 20% of their annual salaries by meeting those objectives.

Nonprofit and government organizations also have additional problems designing and implementing an objective that is similar to the financial "bottom line" that often serves as a powerful incentive in private industry. Furthermore, many people seek positions in nonprofit organizations primarily for nonmonetary rewards. For example, volunteers in the Peace Corps receive very little pay but derive much satisfaction from helping to improve conditions in underdeveloped countries. Thus, monetary incentives are generally less effective in nonprofit organizations. Control systems in nonprofit organizations probably will never be as highly developed as are those in profit-seeking firms because

1. Organizational goals and objectives are less clear. Moreover, they are often multiple, requiring difficult trade-offs.
2. Professionals (for example, teachers, attorneys, physicians, scientists, economists) tend to dominate nonprofit organizations. Because of their perceived professional status, they are often less receptive to the installation or improvement of formal control systems.
3. Measurements are more difficult because
   a. There is no profit measure.
   b. There are heavy amounts of discretionary fixed costs, which make the relationships of inputs to outputs difficult to specify and measure.
4. There is less competitive pressure from other organizations or "owners" to improve management control systems. As a result, for example, many cities in the United States are "privatizing" some essential services such as sanitation by contracting with private firms.
5. The role of budgeting, instead of being a rigorous planning process, is often more a matter of playing bargaining games with sources of funding to get the largest possible authorization.
6. Motivations and incentives of individuals may differ from those in for-profit organizations.

MAKING MANAGERIAL DECISIONS

Study Exhibit 9-3 again. Use the same four general components, but rearrange them a bit to reflect a framework that might help managers of a successful governmental or nonprofit organization.

Answer

For government and nonprofit organizations, the ultimate objective is not to focus on financial results but to deliver the maximum benefits to customers (or citizens) based on an available pool of financial resources. Thus the causal relationships might be

organizational learning → process improvements in delivering programs → fiscal or financial strength → greater program benefits for citizens or clients

Future of Management Control Systems

As organizations mature and as environments change, managers must expand and refine their management control tools. The management control techniques that were quite satisfactory 10 or 20 years ago may not be adequate for many organizations today.

A changing environment often means that organizations must set different goals or key success factors. Different goals create different actions and related targets as well as different benchmarks for evaluating performance. Obviously, the management control system must evolve, too, or the organization may not manage its resources effectively or efficiently. Certain management control principles that will always be important and that can guide the redesign of systems to meet new management needs follow.

1. Always expect that individuals will be pulled in the direction of their own self-interest. You may be pleasantly surprised that some individuals will act selflessly, but management control systems should be designed to take advantage of more typical human behavior. Be aware that managers in different cultures may perceive self-interest differently.

2. Design incentives so that individuals who pursue their own self-interest also achieve the organization's objectives. If there are multiple objectives (as is usually the case), then multiple incentives are appropriate. Do not underestimate the difficulty of balancing these incentives—some experimentation may be necessary to achieve multiple objectives.

3. Evaluate actual performance based on expected or planned performance, revised, if possible, for actual output achieved. You can apply the concept of flexible budgeting to most goals and actions, both financial and nonfinancial.

4. Consider nonfinancial performance to be just as important as financial performance. In the short run, a manager may be able to generate good financial performance while neglecting nonfinancial performance, but it is not likely over a longer haul.

5. Array performance measures across the entire value chain of the company. This ensures that the management control system incorporates all activities that are critical to the long-run success of the company.

6. Periodically review the success of the management control system. Is the organization achieving its overall goals? Do the actions motivated by the management control system lead to goal achievement? Do individuals have, understand, and use the management control information effectively?

7. Learn from the management control successes (and failures) of competitors around the world. Despite cultural differences, human behavior is remarkably similar. Managers can learn from successful applications of new technology and management controls by reading books or attending courses that describe management control systems at other companies.

Summary Problem For Your Review

PROBLEM

The Book & Game Company has two bookstores: Auntie's and Merlin's. Each store has managers who have a great deal of decision authority over their store. Advertising, market research, acquisition of books, legal services, and other staff functions, however, are handled by a central office. The Book & Game Company's current accounting system allocates all costs to the stores. Results for 20X1 were:

Item	Total Company	Auntie's	Merlin's
Sales revenue	$700,000	$350,000	$350,000
Cost of merchandise sold	450,000	225,000	225,000
Gross margin	250,000	125,000	125,000
Operating expenses			
Salaries and wages	63,000	30,000	33,000
Supplies	45,000	22,500	22,500
Rent and utilities	60,000	40,000	20,000
Depreciation	15,000	7,000	8,000
Allocated staff costs	60,000	30,000	30,000
Total operating expenses	243,000	129,500	113,500
Operating income (loss)	$ 7,000	$ (4,500)	$ 11,500

Each bookstore manager makes decisions that affect salaries and wages, supplies, and depreciation. In contrast, rent and utilities are beyond the managers' control because the managers did not choose the location or the size of the store.

Supplies are variable costs. Variable salaries and wages are equal to 8% of the cost of merchandise sold; the remainder of salaries and wages is a fixed cost. Rent, utilities, and depreciation also are fixed costs. Events at the individual bookstores do not affect staff costs; nevertheless, Book & Game Company allocates them as a proportion of sales revenue.

1. Using the contribution approach, prepare a performance report that distinguishes the performance of each bookstore from that of the bookstore manager.
2. Evaluate the financial performance of each bookstore.
3. Evaluate the financial performance of each manager.

SOLUTION

1. See Exhibit 9-11.
2. We can evaluate the financial performances of the bookstores (that is, segments of the company) using the line "contribution by bookstore." Merlin's has a substantially higher contribution, despite equal levels of sales revenues in the two stores. The major reason for this advantage is that Merlin's pays less for rent and utilities.
3. We can evaluate the financial performance of the managers using the line "contribution controllable by managers." By this measure, the performance of Auntie's manager is better than that of Merlin's. The contribution margin is the same for each store, but Merlin's manager paid $4,000 more in controllable fixed costs than did Auntie's manager. Of course, this decision could be beneficial in the long run. What is missing from each of these segment reports is the year's master budget and a flexible budget, which would be the best benchmark for evaluating both bookstore and bookstore manager.

Item	Total Company	Auntie's	Merlin's
Sales revenue	$700,000	$350,000	$350,000
Variable costs			
Cost of merchandise sold	450,000	225,000	225,000
Salaries and wages	36,000	18,000	18,000
Supplies	45,000	22,500	22,500
Total variable costs	531,000	265,500	265,500
Contribution margin by bookstore	169,000	84,500	84,500
Less: fixed costs controllable by			
bookstore managers			
Salaries and wages	27,000	12,000	15,000
Depreciation	15,000	7,000	8,000
Total controllable fixed costs	42,000	19,000	23,000
Contribution controllable by managers	127,000	65,500	61,500
Less: fixed costs controllable by others			
Rent and utilities	60,000	40,000	20,000
Contribution by bookstore	67,000	$ 25,500	$ 41,500
Unallocated costs	60,000		
Operating income	$ 7,000		

Exhibit 9-11
The Book & Game Company
Performance Report

Highlights to Remember

1 **Describe the relationship of management control systems to organizational goals.** The starting point for designing and evaluating a management control system is the identification of organizational goals as specified by top management.

2 **Use responsibility accounting to define an organizational subunit as a cost center, a profit center, or an investment center.** Responsibility accounting assigns particular revenue or cost objectives to the management of the subunit that has the greatest influence over them. Cost centers focus on costs only, profit centers on both revenues and costs, and investment centers on profits relative to the amount invested.

3 **Develop performance measures and use them to monitor the achievements of an organization.** A well-designed management control system measures both financial and nonfinancial performance. In fact, nonfinancial performance usually leads to financial performance in time. The performance measures should tell managers how well they are meeting the organizations goals.

4 **Explain the importance of evaluating performance and how it impacts motivation, goal congruence, and employee effort.** The way an organization measures and evaluates performance affects individuals' behavior. The more that it ties rewards to performance measures, the more incentive there is to improve the measures. Poorly designed measures may actually work against the organization's goals.

5 **Prepare segment income statements for evaluating profit and investment centers using the contribution margin and controllable-cost concepts.** The contribution approach to measuring a segment's income aids performance evaluation by separating a segment's costs into those controllable by the segment management and those beyond management's control. It allows separate evaluation of a segment as an economic investment and the performance of the segment's manager.

6 **Use a balanced scorecard to recognize both financial and nonfinancial measures of performance.** The balanced scorecard helps managers monitor actions that are designed to meet the various goals of the organization. It contains key performance indicators that measure how well the organization is meeting its goals.

7 **Measure performance against quality, cycle time, and productivity objectives.** Measuring performance in areas such as quality, cycle time, and productivity causes employees to direct attention to those areas. Achieving goals in these nonfinancial measures can help meet long-run financial objectives.

8 **Describe the difficulties of management control in service and nonprofit organizations.** Management control in service and nonprofit organizations is difficult because of a number of factors, chief of which is a relative lack of clearly observable outcomes.

Accounting Vocabulary

balanced scorecard, p. 395
controllable cost, p. 391
cost center, p. 385
cost of quality report, p. 398
cycle time, p. 400
goal congruence, p. 389
investment center, p. 385
key success factor, p. 384
key performance indicators,
    p. 396

management control system,
    p. 382
managerial effort, p. 389
motivation, p. 390
productivity, p. 401
profit center, p. 385
quality control, p. 398
quality-control chart, p. 399

responsibility accounting, p. 385
responsibility center, p. 384
segments, p. 393
six sigma, p. 400
throughput time, p. 400
total quality management
    (TQM), p. 398
uncontrollable cost, p. 391

Fundamental Assignment Material

9-A1 Responsibility of Purchasing Agent

Midwest Electronics Company, a privately held enterprise, has a subcontract from a large aerospace company in St. Louis. Although Midwest was a low bidder, the aerospace company was reluctant to award the business to the company because it was a newcomer to this kind of activity. Consequently, Midwest assured the aerospace company of its financial strength by submitting its audited financial statements. Moreover, Midwest agreed to a pay a penalty of $5,000 per day for each day of late delivery for whatever cause.

Jean Trudeau, the Midwest purchasing agent, is responsible for acquiring materials and parts in time to meet production schedules. She placed an order with a Midwest supplier for a critical manufactured component. The supplier, who had a reliable record for meeting schedules, gave Trudeau an acceptable delivery date. Trudeau checked up several times and was assured that the component would arrive at Midwest on schedule.

On the date specified by the supplier for shipment to Midwest, Trudeau was informed that the component had been damaged during final inspection. It was delivered ten days late. Trudeau had allowed four extra days for possible delays, but Midwest was six days late in delivering to the aerospace company and so had to pay a penalty of $30,000.

What department should bear the penalty? Why?

9-A2 Contribution Approach to Responsibility Accounting

Grant McGeorge owns and operates a small chain of convenience stores in Denver and Colorado Springs. The company's organization chart follows:

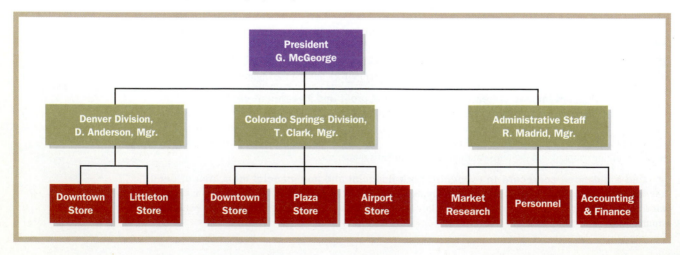

The company had the following financial results for 20X1 (in thousands):

Sales revenue	$8,000
Cost of merchandise sold	5,000
Gross margin	3,000
Operating expenses	2,200
Income before income taxes	$ 800

The following data about 20X1 operations were also available:

1. All five stores used the same pricing formula; therefore, all had the same gross margin percentage.
2. Sales were largest in the two Downtown stores, with 30% of the total sales volume in each. The Plaza and Airport stores each provided 15% of total sales volume, and the Littleton store provided 10%.
3. Variable operating costs at the stores were 10% of revenue for the Downtown stores. The other stores had lower variable and higher fixed costs. Their variable operating costs were only 5% of sales revenue.
4. The fixed costs over which the store managers had control were $125,000 in each of the Downtown stores, $160,000 at Plaza and Airport, and $80,000 at Littleton.
5. The remaining $910,000 of operating costs consisted of
   a. $180,000 controllable by the Colorado Springs division manager, but not by individual stores
   b. $130,000 controllable by the Denver division manager, but not by individual stores
   c. $600,000 controllable by the administrative staff
6. Of the $600,000 spent by the administrative staff, $350,000 directly supported the Colorado Springs division, with 20% for the Downtown store, 30% for each of the Plaza and Airport stores, and 20% for Colorado Springs operations in general. Another $140,000 supported the Denver division, 50% for the Downtown store, 25% for the Littleton store, and 25% supporting Denver operations in general. The other $110,000 was for general corporate expenses.

Prepare an income statement by segments using the contribution approach to responsibility accounting. Use the format of Exhibit 9-4, page 392. Column headings should be

			Breakdown of Denver Division			Breakdown of Colorado Springs Division			
Company as a whole	**Denver**	**Colorado Springs**	**Not allocated**	**Downtown**	**Littleton**	**Not allocated**	**Downtown**	**Plaza**	**Airport**

9-A3 Comparison of Productivity

Telemark and Intertel are communications companies. Comparative data for 1998 and 2004 are

		Telemark	Intertel
Sales revenue	1998	$5,831,000,000	$7,658,000,000
	2004	$6,764,000,000	$9,667,000,000
Number of employees	1998	56,600	75,900
	2004	54,800	76,200

Assume that each 1998 dollar is equivalent to 1.2 2004 dollars, due to inflation.

1. Compute 1998 and 2004 productivity measures in terms of revenue per employee for Telemark and Intertel.
2. Compare the change in productivity between 1998 and 2004 for Telemark with that for Intertel.

9-B1 Responsibility Accounting

The Hassan Company produces precision machine parts. Hassan uses a standard cost system, calculates standard cost variances for each department, and reports them to department managers. Managers use the information to improve their operations. Superiors use the same information to evaluate managers' performance.

Betty LaGrande was recently appointed manager of the assembly department of the company. She has complained that the system as designed is disadvantageous to her department. Included among the variances charged to the departments is one for rejected units. The inspection occurs at the end of the assembly department. The inspectors attempt to identify the cause of the rejection so that the department where the error occurred can be charged with it. Not all errors can be easily identified with a department, however. The nonidentified units are totaled and apportioned to the departments according to the number of identified errors. The variance for rejected units in each department is a combination of the errors caused by the department plus a portion of the unidentified causes of rejects.

1. Is LaGrande's complaint valid? Explain the reason(s) for your answer.
2. What would you recommend that the company do to solve its problem with LaGrande and her complaint?

9-B2 Divisional Contribution, Performance, and Segment Margins

The president of Golden Spike Railroad wants to obtain an overview of the company's operations, particularly with respect to comparing freight and passenger business. He has heard about "contribution" approaches to cost allocations that emphasize cost behavior patterns and contribution margins, contributions controllable by segment managers, and contributions by segments. The president has hired you as a consultant to help him. He has given you the following information.

Total revenue in 20X3 was $80 million, of which $72 million was freight traffic and $8 million was passenger traffic. Fifty percent of the latter was generated by Division 1; 40% by Division 2; and 10% by Division 3.

Total variable costs were $45 million, of which $36 million was caused by freight traffic. Of the $9 million allocable to passenger traffic, $3.3, $2.8, and $2.9 million could be allocated to Divisions 1, 2, and 3, respectively.

Total separable discretionary fixed costs were $8 million, of which $7.6 million applied to freight traffic. Of the remainder, $80,000 could not be allocated to specific divisions, although it was clearly traceable to passenger traffic in general. Divisions 1, 2, and 3 should be allocated $240,000, $60,000, and $20,000, respectively.

Total separable committed costs, which were not regarded as being controllable by segment managers, were $25 million, of which 80% was allocable to freight traffic. Of the 20% traceable to passenger traffic, Divisions 1, 2, and 3 should be allocated $3 million, $700,000, and $300,000, respectively; the balance was unallocable to a specific division.

The common fixed costs not clearly allocable to any part of the company amounted to $800,000.

1. The president asks you to prepare statements, dividing the data for the company as a whole between the freight and passenger traffic and then subdividing the passenger traffic into three divisions.
2. Some competing railroads actively promote a series of one-day sightseeing tours on summer weekends. Most often, these tours are timed so that the cars with the tourists are hitched on with regularly scheduled passenger trains. What costs are relevant for making decisions to run such tours? Other railroads, facing the same general cost picture, refuse to conduct such sightseeing tours. Why?
3. For purposes of this analysis, even though the numbers may be unrealistic, suppose that Division 2's figures represented a specific run for a train instead of a division. Suppose further that the railroad has petitioned government authorities for permission to drop Division 2. What would be the effect on overall company net income for 20X4, assuming that the figures are accurate and that 20X4 operations are in all other respects a duplication of 20X3 operations?

9-B3 Balanced Scorecard for a Law Firm

Young, Martinez, and Cheung (YMC) is a law firm in Chicago. The firm has had a very loose and relaxed management style that has served it well in the past. However, more aggressive law firms have been winning new clients faster than YMC has. Thus, the managing partner, Jerry Martinez, recently attended an ABA seminar on performance measurement in law firms, where he learned about the balanced scorecard. He thought it might be a good tool for YMC, one that would allow the firm to keep its culture yet still more aggressively seek new clients.

Martinez identified the following strategic objectives that fit with the firm's core values and provide a framework for assessing progress toward the firm's goals:

Financial
a. To steadily increase the firm's revenues and profits.

Customer
a. To understand the firm's customers and their needs.
b. To value customer service over self-interest.

Internal Business Process
a. Encourage knowledge sharing among the legal staff.
b. To communicate with each other openly, honestly, and often.
c. To empower staff to make decisions that benefit their clients.

Organizational Learning
a. To maintain an open and collaborative environment that attracts and retains the best legal staff.
b. To seek staff diversity.

Required
1. Develop at least one measure for each of the strategic objectives listed.
2. Explain how YMC can use this balanced scorecard to evaluate staff performance.
3. Should staff compensation be tied to the scorecard performance measures? Why or why not?

Additional Assignment Material

Questions

9-1 What is a management control system?

9-2 What are the purposes of a management control system?

9-3 What are the major components of a management control system?

9-4 What is a key success factor?

9-5 "Goals are useless without performance measures." Do you agree? Explain.

9-6 "There are corporate goals other than to improve profit." Name three.

9-7 How does management determine its key success factors?

9-8 Give three examples of how managers may improve short-run performance to the detriment of long-run results.

9-9 Name three kinds of responsibility centers.

9-10 How do profit centers and investment centers differ?

9-11 List five characteristics of a good performance measure.

9-12 What are four nonfinancial measures of performance that managers find useful?

9-13 "Performance evaluation seeks to achieve goal congruence and managerial effort." Describe what is meant by this statement.

9-14 "Managers of profit centers should be held responsible for the center's entire profit. They are responsible for profit even if they cannot control all factors affecting it." Discuss.

9-15 "Variable costs are controllable and fixed costs are uncontrollable." Do you agree? Explain.

9-16 "The contribution margin is the best measure of short-run performance." Do you agree? Explain.

9-17 Give four examples of segments.

9-18 "Always try to distinguish between the performance of a segment and its manager." Why?

9-19 "The contribution margin approach to performance evaluation is flawed because focusing on only the contribution margin ignores important aspects of performance." Do you agree? Explain.

9-20 What is a balanced scorecard and why are more and more companies using one?

9-21 What are key performance indicators?

9-22 There are four categories of cost in the quality cost report; explain them.

9-23 Why are companies increasing their quality control emphasis on the prevention of defects?

9-24 "Nonfinancial measures of performance can be controlled just like financial measures." Do you agree? Explain.

9-25 Identify three measures of labor productivity, one using all physical measures, one using all financial measures, and one that mixes physical and financial measures.

9-26 Discuss the difficulties of comparing productivity measures over time.

9-27 "Control systems in nonprofit organizations will never be as highly developed as in profit-seeking organizations." Do you agree? Explain.

Critical Thinking Exercises

9-28 Management Control Systems and Innovation
The president of a fast-growing, high-technology firm remarked, "Developing budgets and comparing performance with the budgets may be fine for some firms. But we want to encourage innovation and

entrepreneurship. Budgets go with bureaucracy, not innovation." Do you agree? How can a management control system encourage innovation and entrepreneurship?

9-29 Municipal Responsibility Accounting

After barely avoiding bankruptcy, New York City established one of the most sophisticated budgeting and reporting systems of any municipality. The Integrated Financial Management System (IFMS) "clearly identifies managers in line agencies and correlates allocations and expenditures with organizational structure. . . . In addition, managers have more time to take corrective measures when variances between budgeted and actual expenditures start to develop." (*FE—The Magazine for Financial Executives,* 1, no. 8, p. 26.)

Discuss how a responsibility accounting system such as IFMS can help manage a municipality such as New York City.

9-30 Control Systems and Customer Service Function of the Value Chain

Companies increasingly use nonfinancial measures to supplement financial measures of performance. One of the most important areas of nonfinancial performance is customer service. The last decade has brought a focus on the customer, and this focus is reflected in many companies' management control systems, where companies use "customer-value metrics." That is, they develop measures that monitor how well the company is meeting its customers' interests. What customer-value metrics might a company such as Volvo, the Swedish automobile company, use in its management control system?

9-31 Control Systems and the Production Function of the Value Chain

In recent years, many organizations have focused on the value of controlling nonfinancial performance as a key to improved productivity. In particular, to gain and maintain a competitive edge, companies focus on quality and cycle time. Discuss how quality, cycle time, and productivity are related.

Exercises

9-32 Key Performance Indicators

Research on performance management suggests that organizations can compete most effectively by identifying and monitoring those elements that are most closely linked to organizational success. A key performance indicator can be thought of as a measure that drives organizational success. For each of the following companies or organizations, identify two possible key performance indicators.

1. **Northwest Airlines**
2. **Wal-Mart**
3. **Hewlett Packard**
4. New York Department of Motor Vehicles

9-33 Responsibility for Stable Employment Policy

The Mid-Atlantic Metal Fabricating Company has been manufacturing machine tools for a number of years and has had an industrywide reputation for doing high-quality work. The company has been faced with irregularity of output over the years. It has been company policy to lay off welders as soon as there was insufficient work to keep them busy and to rehire them when demand warranted. The company, however, now has poor labor relations and finds it very difficult to hire good welders because of its lay-off policy. Consequently, the quality of the work has been declining steadily.

The plant manager has proposed that the welders, who earn $20 per hour, be retained during slow periods to do menial plant maintenance work that is normally performed by workers earning $14 per hour in the plant maintenance department.

You, as controller, must decide the most appropriate accounting procedure to handle the wages of the welders doing plant maintenance work. What department(s) should be charged with this work, and at what rate? Discuss the implications of your plan.

9-34 Salesclerk's Compensation Plan

You are manager of a department store in Tokyo. Sales are subject to month-to-month variations, depending on the individual salesclerk's efforts. A new salary-plus-bonus plan has been in effect for four months, and you are reviewing a sales performance report. The plan provides for a base salary of ¥50,000 per month, a ¥68,000 bonus each month if the salesclerk meets the monthly sales quota, and an additional commission of 5% of all sales over the monthly quota. The quota is set approximately 3% above the previous month's sales to motivate clerks toward increasing sales (in thousands).

		Salesclerk A	Salesclerk B	Salesclerk C
January	Quota	¥4,500	¥1,500	¥7,500
	Actual	1,500	1,500	9,000
February	Quota	¥1,545	¥1,545	¥9,270
	Actual	3,000	1,545	3,000
March	Quota	¥3,090	¥1,590	¥3,090
	Actual	5,250	750	9,000
April	Quota	¥5,400	¥ 775	¥9,270
	Actual	1,500	780	4,050

1. Compute the compensation for each salesclerk for each month.
2. Evaluate the compensation plan. Be specific. What changes would you recommend?

9-35 Common Measures on a Balanced Scorecard

Listed below are common performance measures appearing on balanced scorecards. Indicate whether the listed measure is primarily associated with the financial, customer, internal processes, or learning and growth perspective.

- Return on sales
- Retention of target customers
- Net cash flow
- Training hours
- Employee turnover rate
- Materials handling cost per unit
- Market share
- Product development cycle time
- Revenue growth in segments
- Occupational injuries and illness
- Days sales in inventory
- Average cost per invoice

9-36 Goals and Objectives at Health Net, Inc.

Health Net, Inc. provides health care to more than 5.3 million members. As a managed health care organization, the company strives to provide high-quality health care at a reasonable cost. Many stakeholders have an interest in Health Net's operations, including doctors and other medical personnel, patients, insurance companies, government regulators, and the general public.

Prepare a goal and one measure for assessing achievement of that goal for each of the following key areas:

Customer satisfaction
Efficient use of lab tests
Usage of physician time
Maintain state-of-the-art facilities
Overall financial performance

9-37 Performance Evaluation

Charles Merrill & Co. is a stock brokerage firm that evaluates its employees on sales activity generated. Recently, the firm also began evaluating its stockbrokers on the number of new accounts generated.

Discuss how these two performance measures are consistent and how they may conflict. Do you believe that these measures are appropriate for the long-term goal of profitability?

9-38 Simple Controllable Costs

Dan's BBQ is a restaurant in downtown Seattle. Dan expanded to a second location in suburban Jamesville three years ago. Recently, Dan decided to retire from active management of the individual restaurants but continued to oversee the entire company. He hired a manager for each restaurant. In 20X3 each restaurant had sales of $850,000. The Jamesville restaurant is still pricing lower than the downtown restaurant to establish a customer base. Variable expenses run 60% of sales for the downtown restaurant and 70% of sales for the Jamesville restaurant.

Each manager is responsible for the rent and some other fixed costs for his or her restaurant. These costs amounted to $125,000 for the downtown restaurant and $50,000 for the one in Jamesville. The difference is primarily due to the lower rent in Jamesville. In addition, several costs such as advertising, legal services, accounting, and personnel services were centralized. The managers had no control of these expenses, but some of them directly benefited the individual restaurants. Of the $360,000 cost in this category, $110,000 related to the downtown restaurant and $180,000 to the Jamesville restaurant. The Jamesville cost includes the cost of extra advertising to build up its customer base. The remaining $70,000 was general corporate overhead.

Required

1. Prepare income statements for each restaurant and for the company as a whole. Use a format that allows easy assessment of each manager's performance and each restaurant's economic performance.
2. Using only the information given in this exercise:
   a. Evaluate each restaurant as an economic investment.
   b. Evaluate each manager.

9-39 Quality Theories Compared

Examine the two graphs below. Compare the total quality management approach to the traditional theory of quality. Which theory do you believe represents the current realities of today's global competitive environment? Explain.

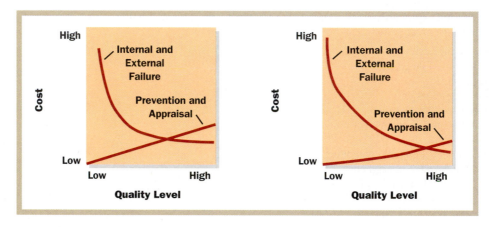

9-40 Quality Control Chart

San Angelo Manufacturing Company was concerned about a growing number of defective units being produced. At one time the company had the percentage of defective units down to less than 50 per thousand, but recently rates of defects have been near, or even above, 1%. The company decided to graph its defects for the last eight weeks (40 working days), beginning Monday, September 1 through Friday, October 24. The graph is shown in Exhibit 9-12.

1. Identify two important trends evident in the quality control chart.
2. What might management of San Angelo do to deal with each trend?

Exhibit 9-12
San Angelo Manufacturing Company
Quality Control Chart for September 1 through October 24

9-41 Cycle-Time Reporting

The Pierre plant of Global Electronics produces computers. The plant monitors its cycle time closely to prevent schedule delays and excessive costs. The standard cycle time for the manufacture of printed circuit boards for one of its computers is 26.0 hours. Consider the following cycle-time data from the past six weeks of circuit board production:

Week	Units Completed	Total Cycle Time
1	564	14,108 hours
2	544	14,592
3	553	15,152
4	571	16,598
5	547	17,104
6	552	16,673

Analyze circuit board cycle time performance in light of the 26.0-hour objective.

Problems

9-42 Multiple Goals and Profitability

The following multiple goals were identified by **General Electric**:

Profitability
Market position
Productivity
Product leadership
Personnel development
Employee attitudes
Public responsibility
Balance between short-range and long-range goals

General Electric is a huge, highly decentralized corporation. At the time it developed these goals, GE had approximately 170 responsibility centers called *departments,* but that is a deceptive term. In most other companies, these departments would be called divisions. For example, some GE departments had sales of more than $500 million.

Each department manager's performance was evaluated annually in relation to the specified multiple goals. A special measurements group was set up to devise ways of quantifying accomplishments in each of the areas. In this way, the evaluation of performance would become more objective as the various measures were developed and improved.

1. How would you measure performance in each of these areas? Be specific.
2. Can the other goals be encompassed as ingredients of a formal measure of profitability? In other words, can profitability per se be defined to include the other goals?

9-43 Responsibility Accounting, Profit Centers, and Contribution Approach

McBride Cadillac/Hummer had the following data for the year's operations:

Sales of vehicles	$2,400,000
Sales of parts and service	600,000
Cost of vehicle sales	1,920,000
Parts and service materials	180,000
Parts and service labor	240,000
Parts and service overhead	60,000
General dealership overhead	120,000
Advertising of vehicles	120,000
Sales commissions, vehicles	48,000
Sales salaries, vehicles	60,000

The president of the dealership has long regarded the markup on material and labor for the parts and service activity as the amount that is supposed to cover all parts and service overhead plus all general overhead of the dealership. In other words, the parts and service department is viewed as a cost-recovery operation, and the sales of vehicles as the income-producing activity.

1. Prepare a departmentalized operating statement that harmonizes with the views of the president.
2. Prepare an alternative operating statement that would reflect a different view of the dealership operations. Assume that $12,000 and $60,000 of the $120,000 general overhead can be allocated with confidence to the parts and service department and to sales of vehicles, respectively. The remaining $48,000 cannot be allocated except in some highly arbitrary manner.
3. Comment on the relative merits of numbers 1 and 2.

9-44 Incentives in Planned Economies

Often government-owned companies in planned economies reward managers based on nonfinancial measures. For example, the government might give managers a bonus for exceeding a five-year-plan target for production quantities. A problem with this method is that managers tend to predict low volumes so that officials will set the targets low. This hinders planning because managers do not provide accurate information about production possibilities.

The former Soviet Union developed an alternative performance measurement and reward system. Suppose F is the forecast of production, A is actual production, and X, Y, and Z are positive constants set by top officials, with $X, Y, Z > 0$. The following performance measure was designed to motivate both high production and accurate forecasts.

$$\text{performance} = (Y \times F) + [X \times (A - F)] \text{ if } F \leq A$$
$$(Y \times F) - [Z \times (F - A)] \text{ if } F > A$$

Assume that Cuba adopted this measure at a time when Soviet influence was great. Consider the Havana Television Manufacturing Company (HTMC). During 19X3 the factory manager, Che Chavez, had to predict the number of televisions that HTMC could produce during the next year. He was confident that at least 700,000 TVs could be produced in 19X4, and most likely they could produce 800,000 TVs. With good luck, they might even produce 900,000. Government officials told him that the new performance evaluation measure would be used, and that $X = .50$, $Y = .80$, and $Z = 1.00$ for 19X4 and 19X5.

1. Suppose Chavez predicted production of 800,000 TVs and HTMC actually produced 800,000. Calculate the performance measure.
2. Suppose again that HTMC produced 800,000 TVs. Calculate the performance measure if Chavez had been conservative and predicted only 700,000 TVs. Also calculate the performance measure if he had predicted 900,000 TVs.
3. Now suppose it is November 19X4 and it is clear that HTMC cannot achieve the 800,000 target. Does the performance measure motivate continued efforts to increase production? Suppose it is clear that the HTMC will easily meet the 800,000 target. Will the system motivate continued efforts to increase production?

9-45 Balanced Scorecard

Indianapolis Pharmaceuticals Company (IPC) recently revised its performance evaluation system. The company identified four major goals and several objectives required to meet each goal. Ruth Piniero, controller of IPC, suggested that a balanced scorecard be used to report on progress toward meeting the objectives. At a recent meeting, she told the managers of IPC that listing the objectives was only the first step in installing a new performance measurement system. Each objective has to be accompanied by one or more measures to monitor progress toward achieving the objectives. She asked the help of the managers in identifying appropriate measures.

The goals and objectives determined by the top management of IPC are

1. Maintain strong financial health.
   a. Keep sufficient cash balances to assure financial survival.
   b. Achieve consistent growth in sales and income.
   c. Provide excellent returns to shareholders.
2. Provide excellent service to customers.
   a. Provide products that meet the needs of customers.
   b. Meet customer needs on a timely basis.
   c. Meet customer quality requirements.
   d. Be the preferred supplier to customers.

3. Be among the industry leaders in product and process innovations.
    a. Bring new products to market before competition.
    b. Lead competition in production process innovation.
4. Develop and maintain efficient, state-of-the-art production processes.
    a. Excel in manufacturing efficiency.
    b. Meet or beat product introduction schedules.

Propose at least one measure of performance for each of the objectives of IPC.

9-46 Quality Cost Report

The manufacturing division of Red Lake Enterprises, Inc., makes a variety of home furnishings. The company prepares monthly reports on quality costs. In early 2004, Red Lake's president asked you, the controller, to compare quality costs in 2003 to those in 2001. He wanted to see only total annual numbers for 2003 compared with 2001. You have prepared the report shown in Exhibit 9-13.

1. For each of the four quality cost areas, explain what types of costs are included and how those costs have changed between 2001 and 2003.
2. Assess overall quality performance in 2003 compared with 2001. What do you suppose has caused the changes observed in quality costs?

9-47 Six Sigma, Mean, and Variance

A major objective of six sigma quality control programs is to better meet customers' needs. One place companies have applied six sigma is to order delivery times. They have directed efforts at reducing both the mean (average) time to delivery and the variance or standard deviation (dispersion) of the delivery times. Customers want to get their products sooner, as reflected in the mean. But they also want assurance that the product will arrive when promised. This requires delivery schedules to have little random variance.

Consider the following experience with the implementation of six sigma at a major manufacturing company:

Order Delivery Times (Days)	
Before Six Sigma	After Six Sigma
30	22
12	20
11	5
13	8
26	19
14	8
16	7
20	12
24	18
14	21

Exhibit 9-13

Red Lake Enterprises, Inc.

Quality Cost Report

(thousands of dollars)

Quality Cost Area	2001 Cost	2003 Cost
1. Prevention cost	45	107
% of Total quality cost	3.3%	12.4%
2. Appraisal cost	124	132
% of Total quality cost	9.1%	15.2%
3. Internal failure cost	503	368
% of Total quality cost	36.9%	42.5%
Total internal quality cost (1 + 2 + 3)	672	607
% of Total quality cost	49.3%	70.1%
4. External failure cost	691	259
% of Total quality cost	50.7%	29.9%
Total quality cost	1,363	866
Total product cost	22,168	23,462

Compute the mean and standard deviation of order delivery time before and after implementation of six sigma. From a customer's perspective, how would you view the results of this application of six sigma?

9-48 Productivity

In early 20X1, United Communications, a U.S.-based international telephone communications company, purchased the controlling interest in Bucharest Telecom, Ltd. (BTL) in Romania. A key productivity measure monitored by United is the number of customer telephone lines per employee. Consider the following data for United:

	20X1 without BTL	20X1 with BTL	20X0
Customer lines	15,054,000	19,994,000	14,615,000
Employees	74,520	114,590	72,350
Lines per employee	202	174	202

1. What are United's 20X0 productivity and 20X1 productivity without BTL?
2. What are BTL's 20X1 productivity and United's 20X1 productivity with BTL?
3. What difficulties do you foresee if United brings BTL's productivity in line?

9-49 Productivity Measurement

Cheng's Singapore Laundry had the following results in 20X1 and 20X3:

	20X1	20X3
Pounds of laundry processed	1,360,000 pounds	1,525,000 pounds
Sales revenue	$720,000	$1,394,000
Direct-labor hours worked	45,100 hours	46,650 hours
Direct-labor cost	$316,000	$498,000

The laundry used the same facilities in 20X3 as in 20X1. During the past three years, however, the company put more effort into training its employees. The manager of Cheng's was curious about whether the training had increased labor productivity.

1. Compute a measure of labor productivity for 20X3 based entirely on physical measures. Do the same for 20X1. That is, from the data given, choose measures of physical output and physical input, and use them to compare the physical productivity of labor in 20X3 with that in 20X1.
2. Compute a measure of labor productivity for 20X3 based entirely on financial measures. Do the same for 20X1. That is, from the data given, choose measures of financial output and financial input, and use them to compare the financial productivity of labor in 20X3 with that in 20X1.
3. Suppose the following productivity measure was used:

$$\text{productivity} = \frac{\text{sales revenue}}{\text{direct-labor hours worked}}$$

Because of inflation, each 20X1 dollar is equivalent to 1.4 20X3 dollars. Compute appropriate productivity numbers for comparing 20X3 productivity with 20X1 productivity.

Cases

9-50 Trade-Offs Among Objectives

Computer Data Services (CDS) performs routine and custom information systems services for many companies in a large midwestern metropolitan area. CDS has built a reputation for high-quality customer service and job security for its employees. Quality service and customer satisfaction have been CDS's primary subgoals—retaining a skilled and motivated workforce has been an important factor in achieving those goals. In the past, temporary downturns in business did not mean layoffs of employees, though some employees were required to perform other than their usual tasks. In anticipation of growth in business, CDS leased new equipment that, beginning in August, added $10,000 per month in operating costs. Three months ago, however, a new competitor began offering the same services to CDS customers at prices averaging 20% lower than those of CDS. Rico Estrada, the company founder and president, believes that a significant price reduction is necessary to maintain the company's market share and avoid financial ruin, but he is puzzled about how to achieve it without compromising quality, service, and the goodwill of his workforce.

CDS has a productivity objective of 20 accounts per employee. Estrada does not think that he can increase this productivity and still maintain both quality and flexibility to customer needs. CDS also monitors average cost per account and the number of customer satisfaction adjustments (resolutions of complaints). The average billing markup rate is 25% of cost. Consider the following data from the past six months:

	June	July	August	September	October	November
Number of accounts	797	803	869	784	723	680
Number of employees	40	41	44	43	43	41
Average cost per account	$ 153	$ 153	$ 158	$ 173	$ 187	$ 191
Average salary per employee	$3,000	$3,000	$3,000	$3,000	$3,000	$3,000

1. Discuss the trade-offs facing Rico Estrada.
2. Can you suggest solutions to his trade-off dilemma?

9-51 Six Sigma

The chapter mentions four companies that use six sigma for measuring and controlling quality: Motorola, General Electric, 3M, and Dow Chemical. Go to the Web site for each of these companies and find what each says about its six sigma efforts.

9-52 Review of Chapters 1–9

Joseph Whitebear, general manager of the Kamloops Division of Canada Enterprises, Inc., was preparing for a management meeting. His divisional controller gave him the following information:

1. The master budget for the fiscal year just ended on June 30, 20X4:

Sales (50,000 units of A and 70,000 units of B)	$920,000
Manufacturing cost of goods sold	740,000
Manufacturing margin	$180,000
Selling and administrative expenses	120,000
Operating income	$ 60,000

2. The standard variable manufacturing cost per unit:

	Product A		Product B	
Direct materials	10 pieces @ $.25	$2.50	5 pounds @ $.30	$1.50
Direct labor	1 hour @ $3.00	3.00	.3 hours @ $2.50	.75
Variable overhead	1 hour @ $2.00	2.00	.3 hours @ $2.50	.75
Total		$7.50		$3.00

3. All budgeted selling and administrative expenses are common, fixed expenses; 60% are discretionary expenses.
4. The actual income statement for the fiscal year ended June 30, 20X4:

Sales (53,000 units of A and 64,000 units of B)	$914,000
Manufacturing cost of goods sold	749,200
Manufacturing margin	$164,800
Selling and administrative expenses	116,000
Operating income	$ 48,800

5. The budgeted sales prices for products A and B were $10 and $6, respectively. Actual sales prices equaled budgeted sales prices.

6. The schedule of the actual variable manufacturing cost of goods sold by product (actual quantities in parentheses):

Product A:	Materials	$134,500	(538,000 pieces)
	Labor	156,350	(53,000 hours)
	Overhead	108,650	(53,000 hours)
Product B:	Materials	102,400	(320,000 pounds)
	Labor	50,000	(20,000 hours)
	Overhead	50,000	(20,000 hours)
Total		$601,900	

7. Products A and B are manufactured in separate facilities. Of the budgeted fixed manufacturing cost, $130,000 is separable as follows: $45,000 to product A and $85,000 to product B. Ten percent of these separate costs are discretionary. All other budgeted fixed manufacturing expenses, separable and common, are committed.
8. There are no beginning or ending inventories.

During the upcoming management meeting it is quite likely that some of the information from your controller will be discussed. In anticipation you set out to prepare answers to possible questions.

1. Determine the firm's budgeted break-even point in dollars, overall contribution-margin ratio, and contribution margins per unit by product.
2. Considering products A and B as segments of the firm, find the budgeted "contribution by segments" for each.
3. It is decided to allocate the budgeted selling and administrative expenses to the segments (in number 2) as follows: committed costs on the basis of budgeted unit sales mix and discretionary costs on the basis of actual unit sales mix. What are the final expense allocations? Briefly appraise the allocation method.
4. How would you respond to a proposal to base commissions to salespersons on the sales (revenue) value of orders received? Assume all salespersons have the opportunity to sell both products.
5. Determine the firm's actual "contribution margin" and "contribution controllable by segment managers" for the fiscal year ended June 30, 20X4. Assume no variances in committed fixed costs.
6. Determine the "sales-activity variance" for each product for the fiscal year ended June 30, 20X4.
7. Determine and identify all variances in variable manufacturing costs by product for the fiscal year ended June 30, 20X4.

EXCEL Application Exercise

9-53 Wages for new salary-plus-bonus plan

Goal: Create an Excel spreadsheet to calculate the impact on employee wages of a new salary-plus-bonus plan established to motivate salesclerks to increase sales. Use the results to answer questions about your findings.

Scenario: As the department store manager, you must determine if the new plan is the best way to motivate salesclerks and meet the objective of increasing sales. The background data for the compensation plan appear in exercise 9-34. Use only data for Salesclerk A and Salesclerk B to prepare your spreadsheet.

When you have completed your spreadsheet, answer the following questions:

1. Which salesclerk has the highest average total salary over the four-month period?
2. What part of the compensation plan had the most impact on the salesclerks' salaries? The least impact?
3. Do you see any problems with this compensation plan? Explain.

Step-by-Step:

1. Open a new Excel spreadsheet.
2. In column A, create a bold-faced heading that contains the following:
   Row 1: Chapter 9 Decision Guideline
   Row 2: Tokyo Department Store
   Row 3: Salary-Plus-Bonus Plan Analysis
   Row 4: Today's Date
3. Merge and center the four heading rows across columns A through H.
4. In column A, create the following row headings:
   Row 7: Salesclerk A
   Row 8: Month
   Row 9: January
   Row 10: February
   Row 11: March
   Row 12: April
   Skip 3 rows
   Row 16: Salesclerk B
   Row 17: Month
   Row 18: January
   Row 19: February
   Row 20: March
   Row 21: April
5. Change the format of salesclerk names (Rows 7, 16) to bold-faced, underlined headings.
6. Change the format of month (Rows 8, 17) to bold-faced headings.
7. In Rows 8 and 17, create the following bold-faced, right-justified column headings:
   Column B: Quota
   Column C: Sales
   Column D: Over Quota
   Column E: Base Salary
   Column F: Quota Bonus
   Column G: Commission
   Column H: Total Salary
   Note: Adjust column widths as necessary.

8. In column G, create the following right-justified cell headings:
   Row 14: Average:
   Row 23: Average:
9. Use the scenario data to fill in quota, sales, and base salary amounts from January–April for each salesclerk.
10. Use the appropriate IF statements to calculate over quota and quota bonus amounts when the clerks' sales met or exceeded their respective quotas (negative commissions should not be calculated).
    = IF(*formula*>0,*formula*,0)
         For Over Quota only.
    = IF(*formula*<0,0,68000)   OR   = IF(*formula*>=0,68000,0)
         For Quota Bonus only.
    Hint: Go to the "Help" text and type "copy formulas" in the search area to obtain instructions for copying formulas from one cell to another. If done correctly, you should have to type in each of the formulas only once.

11. Use appropriate formulas to calculate commission and total salary amounts for each month, as well as an average amount for the January–April period for each salesclerk.
12. Format all amounts as

Number tab:		
Category:	Currency	
Decimal places:	0	
Symbol:	None	
Negative numbers:	Black with parenthesis	

13. To format specific amounts to display with a yen symbol do the following:

    a. In an empty cell, hold down the Alt key and enter 0165 from the numeric keypad. When you stop holding the Alt key down, a yen sign will be displayed.
    Note: If your keyboard does not have a numeric keypad, use the shift and NumLk keys to activate the imbedded numeric keypad. Then follow the instructions in part a. Use the shift and NumLk keys to turn the feature off.

    b. Highlight the yen character you have just created, select Edit, Cut. This will paste the yen sign to the clipboard. To see the clipboard, select View, Toolbars, Clipboard.
    c. Select the average amount for salesclerk A and open the Format, Cells . . . dialog box.
    d. Select the custom category on the number tab. Scroll down toward the bottom of the type list and highlight the type shown below.

        Type: _($*#,##0_);_($*(#,##0);_($*"-"_);_(@_)

    Change the data between the quotation marks in the third grouping from "-" to "0". Paste the yen sign over EACH occurrence of the dollar sign.
    Hint: Highlight the $ sign; press "Ctrl" and "V". This will paste the yen sign from the clipboard over the $ sign that has been highlighted in the Type field.

    e. Click the OK button.
    f. Utilize the custom format, which should now be at the bottom of the type list, to print the yen sign for all January amounts for both clerks and the average amount for salesclerk B.

14. Save your work to disk, and print a copy for your files.
Note: Print your spreadsheet using landscape in order to ensure that all columns appear on one page.

Collaborative Learning Exercise

9-54 Goals, Objectives, and Performance Measures

There is increasing pressure on colleges and universities to develop measures of accountability. The objective is to specify goals and objectives and to develop measures to assess the achievement of those goals and objectives.

Form a group of four to six students to be a consulting team to the accounting department at your college or university. (If you are not using this book as part of a course in an accounting department, select any department at a local college or university.) Based on your collective knowledge of the department, its mission, and its activities, formulate a statement of goals for the department. From that statement, develop several specific objectives, each of which can be measured. Then develop one or more measures of performance for each objective.

An optional second step in this exercise is to meet with a faculty member from the department, and ask him or her to critique your objectives and measures. To the department member, do the objectives make sense? Are the proposed measures feasible, and will they correctly measure attainment of the objectives? Will they provide proper incentives to the faculty? If the department has created objectives and performance measures, compare them to those your group developed.

Internet Exercise   ● www.prenhall.com/horngren

9-55 Management Control System at Procter & Gamble

Setting up management control systems and determining measurement methods and who should be responsible for particular revenues, costs, and information can be a large task. The structure of the organization plays a part in how well a particular measure is likely to work. Ensuring that the goals of the organization are in concert with the management control system is also an important factor. It is not possible to evaluate a company's management control system from an Internet site. What we can do, however, is to use a site as an example and apply some of the concepts of the chapter to measures and tools that would be possibilities for a firm.

    1. A well-known and well-established company with worldwide acceptance is Procter & Gamble (P&G). Log on to the company's Web site at http://www.pg.com. Let's determine what P&G considers the most important factors in its success. P&G lists its "success drivers" in the "Letter

to Shareholders" section of the 2002 annual report. Locate the 2002 annual report. What are the success drivers of the firm? Give an example for each of the success drivers.

2. The company has numerous products and the Web site divides them into different categories and brands to help customers find relevant product information. What are the major categories the Web site uses? Visit the main page of the "household cleaners" category. What types of items are contained in this category? How could a system be set up to help measure the success of the firm's first goal to build established brands in the "household cleaners" category? What would be three possible financial measures? What about three nonfinancial measures?

3. To achieve maximum benefits at minimum cost, a management control system must foster goal congruence and managerial effort. Managerial effort is defined as exertion toward a goal or objective. Effort here means not merely working faster but also working better. As a result, effort includes all conscious actions (such as supervising, planning, and thinking) that result in more efficiency and effectiveness. Effort is a matter of degree—it is optimized when individuals and groups strive for their objectives. Return to the P&G home page and click on the "Corporate Information" tab of the "Jobs" section and then follow links to "Hiring Principles" and "Hiring Criteria" to find a section on "Succeeding at P&G." Which of the skill areas that they list as being necessary do you believe would be most important? Why?

Management Control in Decentralized Organizations

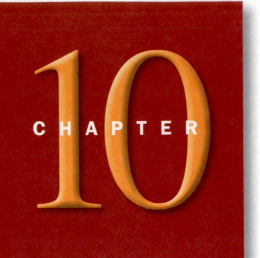

CHAPTER 10

LEARNING OBJECTIVES

When you have finished studying this chapter, you should be able to:

1. Define *decentralization* and identify its expected benefits and costs.

2. Distinguish between responsibility centers and decentralization.

3. Explain how the linking of rewards to responsibility center results affects incentives and risk.

4. Compute ROI, residual income, and economic value added (EVA) and contrast them as criteria for judging the performance of organization segments.

5. Compare the advantages and disadvantages of various bases for measuring the invested capital used by organization segments.

6. Define *transfer prices* and identify their purpose.

7. State the general rule for transfer pricing and use it to assess transfer prices based on total costs, variable costs, and market prices.

8. Identify the factors affecting multinational transfer prices.

9. Explain how controllability and management by objectives (MBO) aid the implementation of management control systems.

In thirty years, Nike has become the largest sports and

fitness company in the world. It has grown from a small Beaverton, Oregon, company into a global giant. Its world reach was apparent in 2003 when it announced a partnership with the Mexican National Soccer team to supply its new uniforms. Don Remlinger, global brand director of Nike Soccer, described **Nike**'s position: "As the exclusive product sponsor for the Mexico National Teams, we plan to provide the teams with our most innovative products to help them perform their best on the field." A major reason that Nike has been successful throughout the world is that it gives much authority to managers in each country or region. To manage effectively in this decentralized environment, Nike needs information to help coordinate and evaluate widely-dispersed operations. A well designed management control system is essential to global companies such as Nike.

From 1986 to 2003, Nike's revenues increased from $1 billion to more than $10 billion. During this same period, the percentage of revenues from outside the United States increased from 25% to 50%. While footwear still accounts for more than half of Nike's sales, apparel sales now account for nearly one-third. A sampling of endorsements (promotional contracts with famous sports teams, individuals, and organizations) gives another perspective of the company's global presence: Michael Jordan, the Italian National Soccer team, German tennis star Michael Stich, and golf star Tiger Woods. In fact, watch almost any sports event on television and you are likely to see the Nike "swoosh" logo.

Nike made a conscious decision to go global—a ten-year process that is now generating substantial financial rewards. What are some of the keys to success when a company such as Nike decides to significantly expand its operations abroad? One critical element is understanding the relevance of the brand to local markets. Nike has

Nike is a globally decentralized company. Customers throughout the world recognize its "swoosh" trademark, shown here on both the green jersey and blue shorts. Achieving the appropriate balance between autonomy at the local level and efficiencies at the corporate level is a challenge when designing Nike's management control system.

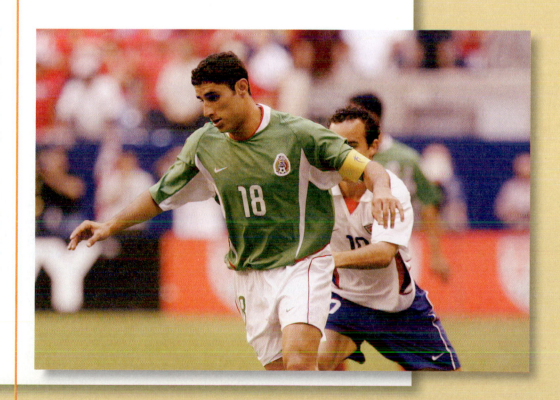

gained this understanding by delegating management decision making to the local market level. For example, local Nike managers in Germany made the decision to sign an endorsement contract with world champion racecar driver Michael Schumacher. According to CEO Philip Knight, "[Previously] it would have taken a move from within the company headquarters to strike such a deal. . . . But this time it was a decision made in country." The local German manager knew that Schumacher was extremely relevant to the German market and that this would be a "profit driven, culturally significant, and brand enhancing move." Knight credits this move toward decentralization for Nike's rapid increase in international sales. "It is a great example of what we are trying to do: Make decisions on the ground in faraway places."

decentralization
The delegation of freedom to make decisions. The lower in the organization that this freedom exists, the greater the decentralization.

As organizations like Nike grow and undertake more diverse and complex activities, many elect to delegate decision-making authority to managers throughout the organization. This delegation of the freedom to make decisions is called **decentralization.** The lower in the organization that this freedom exists, the greater the decentralization. Decentralization is a matter of degree along a continuum. Increasing sophistication of telecommunications—especially e-mail, fax machines, and worldwide cellular phone coverage—aids decentralization. Geographical separation no longer must mean lack of access to information. More and more companies are locating sales and production divisions far from headquarters without top management losing knowledge of what is happening in the units. While telecommunications can help Nike and others get information quickly, the management control system determines what information they receive.

This chapter focuses on the role of management control systems in decentralized organizations. After providing an overview of decentralization, the chapter discusses how companies can use performance measures to motivate managers of decentralized units, including various ways of measuring the profitability of these units to encourage goal-congruent actions by mangers. Finally, we address the special problems created when one segment of an organizaion charges another for providing goods or services.

Centralization Versus Decentralization

OBJECTIVE 1

Define decentralization and identify its expected benefits and costs.

Decentralization is not right for every firm. Both centralization and decentralization have their advantages. Sometimes it seems as if organizations and industries undergo cycles of decentralization, followed by centralization, and vice versa. For example, in the 1990s most airlines, such as **South China Airlines**, **Iberia Airlines**, and **Air France**, decentralized. In contrast, at the same time, **Sabena**, formerly Belgium's state-owned airline, undertook a centralization effort. In the insurance industry, **Aetna** decentralized at the same time **Equitable** was centralizing. Let's take a look at some of the reasons why companies choose to (or choose not to) decentralize.

Costs and Benefits

Some level of decentralization creates benefits for most organizations. For example, lower-level managers have the best information concerning local conditions and therefore may be able to make better decisions than their superiors. In addition, decentralization

BENEFITS AND COSTS OF DECENTRALIZATION

Many companies believe that decentralization is important to their success, including **PepsiCo**, **DuPont**, and **Procter & Gamble**. But one company stands out from the others in its efforts to decentralize—**Johnson & Johnson**. Johnson & Johnson (with 2002 sales of $36.3 billion, more than 108,000 employees, and operations in 54 countries) is the maker of products such as Tylenol, Band-Aids, Johnson's Baby Powder, and PEPCID AC. The company has a long history of decentralization, beginning in the 1930s. As stated in its *2002 Annual Report*, Johnson & Johnson considers it a primary competitive advantage that it empowers each of its 200 business units to act independently—"Our decentralized management system is also reflected in our strong performance, as it gives us focus and a sense of ownership in local markets through dedicated and empowered management groups. They can quickly pursue local avenues of opportunity."

Under the company's management structure, each of its operating companies is run autonomously. One benefit is that decisions are made by executives who are closer to the marketplace. One downfall is the expense, because many of the operating companies duplicate many overhead costs. Although ultimately accountable to executives at Johnson & Johnson headquarters in New Brunswick, New Jersey, some segment presidents see their bosses as few as four times a year. Bill Weldon, Johnson & Johnson CEO, extols the virtues of decentralization: "The magic around Johnson & Johnson is decentralization." He believes that the structure has been essential to its strategy of developing executives from within because young managers can be given responsibility for running whole companies. "This allows people to be entrepreneurial," he said, "and to grow."

Business Week summarized Weldon's approach as follows: "[Johnson & Johnson's] success has hinged on its unique culture and structure. . . . Each of its far-flung units operates pretty much as an independent enterprise. Businesses set their own strategies; they have their own finance and human resources departments, for example. While this degree of decentralization makes for relatively high overhead costs, no chief executive, Weldon included, has thought that too high a price to pay."

As you can see, decentralization has benefits and costs. Some companies have vacillated between decentralization and centralization, sometimes believing that the benefits of centralizing common activities dominates the benefits of decentralization, while at other times seeking the decision-making advantages of decentralization. In contrast, Johnson & Johnson has continued its policy of decentralization in good times and bad, through a long succession of top management leadership. The company has a long-term credo that mandates decentralization. It would take a brave (or foolhardy) leader to change Johnson & Johnson's philosophy of decentralization.

Sources: Adapted from Johnson & Johnson *2002 Annual Report*; M. Petersen, "From the Ranks, Unassumingly," *New York Times*, February 24, 2002; A. Barrett, "Staying on Top," *Business Week*, May 5, 2003.

---

gives managers decision-making ability and other management skills that help them move upward in the organization, ensuring continuity of leadership. Finally, managers enjoy higher status when they are independent and thus may be better motivated.

Of course, decentralization also has its costs. Managers may make decisions that are not in the organization's best interests. Why? Either because they act to improve their own segment's performance at the expense of the organization or because they are not aware of relevant facts from other segments. Managers in decentralized organizations also tend to duplicate services that might be less expensive if centralized (e.g., accounting, advertising, and personnel). Furthermore, costs of accumulating and processing information frequently rise under decentralization because top management needs additional accounting reports to learn about and evaluate decentralized units and their managers. Finally, managers in decentralized units may waste time negotiating with other units about goods or services one unit provides to the other. You can see some of the costs and benefits of decentralization in the Business First box above.

Decentralization is more popular in profit-seeking organizations—where accountants can measure outputs and inputs—than it is in nonprofit organizations. Top management can give managers more freedom when it can measure the results of their decisions and thereby hold the managers accountable for the results. Poor decisions in a profit-seeking firm become apparent from the inadequate profit generated. Most nonprofit organizations lack such a reliable performance measure, so granting their managers freedom is more risky.

Middle Ground

Philosophies of decentralization differ considerably. For every Nike that finds that the benefits of increased decentralization exceed the costs, another company finds that the benefits from increased centralization exceed the costs. Many companies find that decentralization works best in one part of the company, while centralization works better in other parts. To illustrate, many companies decentralize much of the controller's problem-solving and attention-directing functions and handle them at lower levels. In contrast, they generally centralize income tax planning and mass scorekeeping such as accounting for payroll.

Decentralization is most successful when an organization's segments are relatively independent of one another—that is, the decisions of a manager in one segment will not affect the fortunes of another segment. If segments do much internal buying or selling, much buying from the same outside suppliers, or much selling to the same outside markets, they are candidates for heavier centralization.

In Chapter 9, we stressed that managers should consider cost-benefit tests, goal congruence, and managerial effort when designing a management control system. If management has decided in favor of heavy decentralization, then **segment autonomy,** the delegation of decision-making power to managers of segments of an organization, is also crucial. For decentralization to work, however, this autonomy must be real, not just lip service. In most circumstances, top managers must be willing to abide by decisions made by segment managers.

segment autonomy
The delegation of decision-making power to managers of segments of an organization.

Responsibility Centers and Decentralization

OBJECTIVE 2

Distinguish between responsibility centers and decentralization.

Design of a management control system should consider two separate dimensions of control: (1) the responsibilities of managers and (2) the amount of autonomy they have. Some managers confuse these two dimensions by assuming that a profit center manager must have much decentralized decision-making authority and a cost center manager has less autonomy. This need not be the case. Although profit centers can aid decentralization, one can exist without the other. Some profit center managers possess vast freedom to make decisions concerning labor contracts, supplier choices, equipment purchases, personnel decisions, and so on. In contrast, other profit center managers may need top-management approval for almost all the decisions just mentioned. Indeed, cost centers may be more heavily decentralized than profit centers if cost center managers have more freedom to make decisions. The fundamental question in deciding between using a cost center or a profit center for a given segment is not whether heavy decentralization exists. Instead, the fundamental question is, for whatever level of decentralization that exists, "Will a profit center better solve the problems of goal congruence and management effort than a cost center?"

All control systems are imperfect. The choice among systems should be based on which one will bring more of the actions top management seeks. For example, a plant may seem to be a "natural" cost center because the plant manager has no influence over decisions concerning the marketing of its products. Nevertheless, some companies insist on evaluating a plant manager by the plant's profitability. Why? Because they believe this broader evaluation base will positively affect the plant manager's behavior. Instead of being concerned solely with running an efficient cost center, the system motivates the plant manager to consider quality control more carefully and react to customers' special requests more sympathetically. A profit center may thus obtain the desired plant-manager behavior better than a cost center does. In designing accounting control systems, top managers must consider the system's impact on behavior desired by the organization.

Performance Measures and Management Control

A major factor in designing decentralized management control systems is how the system's performance measures affect managers' incentives. When a company gives managers decision-making autonomy, it wants them to use this autonomy to meet the company's objectives, not to pursue other goals. For example, Nike executives wanted its manager of German operations to sign auto-racer Michael Schumacher to a contract only if it would create additional profits for Nike, not to provide an entree for the manager into the inner circles of auto racing.

Motivation, Performance, and Rewards

Exhibit 10-1 shows the criteria and choices that top management faces when designing a management control system. The motivational criteria established by the goal congruence and managerial efforts of the system affect managers' actions. The actions create outcomes that generate performance measures that then affect the managers' rewards. In turn, the measures and rewards provide feedback that influences the managers' goal congruence, effort, and actions. Essentially, the link between rewards and motivational criteria creates managerial **incentives**—informal and formal performance-based rewards that enhance managerial effort toward organizational goals. For example, how a company measures profit in a profit center affects the evaluation of a manager's performance, which, in turn, affects the manager's rewards.

We have described numerous performance measurement choices in this book, such as whether to use tight or loose standards, whether to measure divisional performance by contribution margins or operating incomes, and whether to use both financial and nonfinancial measures of performance. One rule for performance measurement is clear, simple, and important: You get what you measure! Managers tend to focus their efforts in areas where an organization measures their performance and where performance affects rewards. Further, the more objective the measures of performance, the more likely the manager will exert effort. Therefore, accounting measures, which provide relatively objective evaluations of performance, are important. Moreover, if individuals believe there is no connection between their behavior and their measure of performance, they will not know how to alter their performance to affect their rewards.

The choice of rewards is an important feature of management control systems. Rewards may be both monetary and nonmonetary. Examples include pay raises, bonuses, promotion, praise, self-satisfaction, elaborate offices, and private dining rooms. Accounting-based measures of performance often influence managers' rewards, but they are seldom the only basis for performance evaluation.

OBJECTIVE 3

Explain how the linking of rewards to responsibility center results affects incentives and risk.

incentives
Those informal and formal performance-based rewards that enhance managerial effort toward organizational goals.

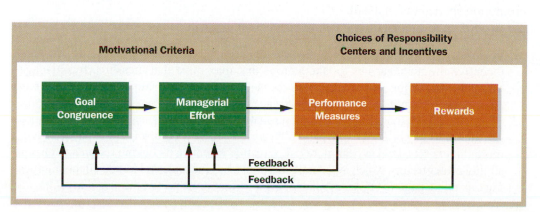

Exhibit 10-1
Criteria and Choices When Designing a Management Control System

Agency Theory, Performance, Rewards, and Risk

We just learned that linking rewards to performance is desirable. But often an organization cannot directly measure a manager's performance. For example, a company might easily measure responsibility center results, but it may not be able to isolate a manager's effect on those results. Ideally, companies should reward managers based on their individual performance, but in practice the rewards usually depend on the financial results in the manager's responsibility center. Managerial performance and responsibility center results are certainly related, but factors beyond a manager's control also affect results. The greater the influence of noncontrollable factors on responsibility center results, the more problems there are in using the results to represent a manager's performance.

Consider a particular Niketown store. Suppose its profits increased dramatically. The following factors all contributed to the increase in profit:

- A lengthy strike by employees of a competitor resulted in many customers switching to Nike.
- The store implemented a new cost management system resulting in a significant reduction in the costs of handling merchandise.
- Overall population growth in the store's region has been much higher than that in other Niketown locations.
- Labor costs in the region have not increased as much as in most Niketown locations.
- Employee turnover is lower than is the system average. Employees cite their excellent relationship with fellow employees and management as the reason for their high level of job satisfaction.

How should Nike evaluate the performance of the store manager? Should it measure the manager's performance by profit results compared to those of other Niketown stores? What other measures could Nike use? From the factors listed, it is likely that a significant portion of the store's profit increase was due to factors not controllable by the regional manager (the competitor's strike, population growth, and regional labor costs). In contrast, it is likely that the manager did a good job of refining the cost management system and creating a productive working environment for all employees. An ideal performance measure would measure and reward the manager for the controllable factors and neither reward nor punish the manager for uncontrollable factors.

Although this ideal is hard to achieve, understanding recent developments in agency theory can lead to insights that help to link performance measures and rewards. **Agency theory** deals with contracting between an organization and the managers that it hires to make decisions on its behalf. When top management hires a manager, both should agree to an employment contract that details performance measures and how they will affect rewards. For example, a manager might receive a bonus of 15% of her salary if her responsibility center achieves its budgeted profit. However, not all rewards are this explicit. A company can reward a manager with a promotion, but seldom are the requirements for promotion spelled out in detail.

According to agency theory, employment contracts will balance three factors:

1. Incentive: The more a manager's reward depends on a performance measure, the more incentive the manager has to take actions that maximize that measure. Top management should define the performance measure to promote goal congruence and base enough reward on it to achieve managerial effort.
2. Risk: The greater the influence of uncontrollable factors on a manager's reward, the more risk the manager bears. People generally avoid risk, so a company must pay managers more if it expects them to bear more risk. Creating incentive by linking rewards to responsibility center results, which is generally desirable, has the undesirable side effect of imposing risk on managers if noncontrollable factors affect some part of the center's results.
3. Cost of measuring performance: The incentive versus risk trade-off is not necessary if a manager's performance is perfectly measured. Why? Because then a manager could be

agency theory
A theory that deals with contracting between an organization and the managers that it hires to make decisions on its behalf.

paid a fixed amount if he or she performs as expected, and nothing if not. Because managers completely control their own performance, observation of the level of performance is all that is necessary to determine the compensation earned. But directly measuring a manager's performance is usually expensive and sometimes impossible. Responsibility center results are more readily available. The cost-benefit criterion usually indicates that perfect measurement of a manager's performance is not worth its cost.

Consider a concert promoter hired by a group of investors to promote and administer an outdoor rock performance. If the investors cannot directly measure the promoter's effort and judgment, they would probably pay a bonus based on the economic success of the concert. The bonus would motivate the promoter to put his effort toward generating a profit, but the promoter is taking a big risk. For example, what happens if it rains? Through no fault of the promoter, the weather might keep fans away and hurt the concert's economic success. The promoter might do an outstanding job and still not receive a bonus. Suppose the investors offer a contract with part guaranteed pay and part bonus. A larger bonus portion compared with the guaranteed portion creates more incentive, but it also means a larger expected total payment to compensate the promoter for the added risk. The investors must decide which is greater—the benefit from the added incentive created by a larger bonus or the extra total compensation to compensate for the added risk.

Regardless of how a company links rewards to performance measures, one pervasive performance measure is profitability. We next look at how various measures of profitability affect managers' incentives.

Measures of Profitability

A favorite objective of top management is to maximize profitability. Companies often evaluate segment managers in decentralized units based on their segment's profitability. The trouble is that profitability does not mean the same thing to all people. Is it income? If so, is it income before or after taxes? Is it an absolute amount? A percentage? If a percentage, is it a percentage of revenue or of investment? In this section we consider the strengths and weaknesses of several commonly used profitability measures.

OBJECTIVE 4

Compute ROI, residual income, and economic value added (EVA) and contrast them as criteria for judging the performance of organization segments.

Return on Investment

Too often, managers stress net operating income without tying the measure into the investment associated with generating the income. To say that division A has an operating income of $200,000 and division B has an operating income of $150,000 is an insufficient statement about profitability. A better test of profitability is the rate of **return on investment (ROI),** which is income (or profit) divided by the investment required to obtain that income or profit. Given the same risks, for any given amount of resources required, the investor wants the maximum income. If division A requires an investment of $500,000 and division B requires only $250,000, all other things being equal, where would you put your money?

return on investment (ROI)
A measure of income or profit divided by the investment required to obtain that income or profit.

$$ROI = \frac{income}{investment}$$

$$ROI \text{ division A} = \frac{\$200,000}{\$500,000} = 40\%$$

$$ROI \text{ division B} = \frac{\$150,000}{\$250,000} = 60\%$$

In all ROI calculations we should measure invested capital as an average for the period under review. Why? Because income is a flow of resources over a period of time, and we should measure the average investment that generates that flow over the same period. This average may be simply the average of the beginning and ending balances or it may be a more complicated average that weighs changes in investments through the months.

ROI is a useful basis of comparison. We can compare one unit's ROI with the ROI of other segments within the company or with similar units outside the company. ROI is the product to two items: **return on sales**—income divided by revenue—and **capital turnover**—revenue divided by invested capital.

return on sales
Income divided by revenue.

capital turnover
Revenue divided by invested capital.

$$\text{return on investment} = \frac{\text{income}}{\text{invested capital}}$$

$$= \frac{\text{income}}{\text{revenue}} \times \frac{\text{revenue}}{\text{invested capital}}$$

$$= \text{return on sales} \times \text{capital turnover}$$

An improvement in either of these rates without changing the other will improve the ROI. Consider an example of these relationships:

	Rate of Return on Invested Capital (%)		$\dfrac{\text{Income}}{\text{Revenue}}$	$\times$	$\dfrac{\text{Revenue}}{\text{Invested Capital}}$
Present outlook	20	=	$\dfrac{16}{100}$	$\times$	$\dfrac{100}{80}$
Alternatives:					
1. Increase return on sales by reducing expenses	25	=	$\dfrac{20}{100}$	$\times$	$\dfrac{100}{80}$
2. Increase capital turnover by decreasing investment	25	=	$\dfrac{16}{100}$	$\times$	$\dfrac{100}{64}$

Alternative 1 is a popular way to improve performance. Alert managers try to decrease expenses without reducing sales or increasing investment. Alternative 2 is less obvious, but it may be a quicker way to improve performance. Increasing the turnover of invested capital means using fewer assets such as cash, receivables, inventories, or equipment for each dollar of revenue generated.

There is an optimal level of investment in these assets. Having too much investment is wasteful, causing capital turnover to fall without an offsetting increase in return on sales. However, having too little investment may mean passing up revenues that would generate a return on sales that more than offsets the decrease in capital turnover. Increasing turnover is one of the advantages of implementing the just-in-time (JIT) philosophy (see Chapter 1). Many companies implementing JIT purchasing and production systems have realized dramatic improvements in their ROI because capital turnover increased and the return on sales stayed the same.

Residual Income (RI) and Economic Value Added (EVA)

Most managers agree that measuring return in relation to investment provides the ultimate test of profitability. ROI is only one such measure, focusing on income as a percentage of investment. However, some managers favor emphasizing an absolute amount of income rather than a percentage. They use **residual income (RI),** defined as after-tax operating income less a capital charge. The **capital charge** is the company's cost of capital multiplied by the amount of investment, where the **cost of capital** is what the firm must pay to acquire more capital—whether or not it actually has to immediately acquire more capital. In short, RI tells you how much a company's after-tax operating income exceeds what it is paying for capital. For example, suppose a division's after-tax operating income was $900,000, the average invested capital (total assets) in the division for the year was $10 million, and the company has a cost of capital of 8%:

Divisional after-tax operating income	$900,000
Minus capital charge on average invested capital (.08 × $10,000,000)	800,000
Equals residual income	$100,000

There are several different ways to calculate residual income, depending on how a company chooses to define the terms used. One popular variant coined and marketed by **Stern Stewart & Co.** is called **economic value added (EVA).** In formula form, Stern Stewart defines EVA as

$$\text{EVA} = \text{adjusted after-tax operating income} - \text{cost of invested capital (\%)} \times \text{adjusted average invested capital}$$

The cost of invested capital (%) is the cost of long-term liabilities and stockholders' equity weighted by their relative size for the company or division. Stern Stewart makes specific adjustments to financial-reporting measures of after-tax operating income and invested capital. These adjustments convert after-tax operating income into a closer approximation of cash income and invested capital into a closer approximation of the cash invested in the economic resources the company uses to create value. Examples of these adjustments include:

- Use taxes paid rather than tax expense,
- Capitalize research and development expenses,
- Use FIFO for inventory valuation (thus companies using LIFO must add back the LIFO reserve to invested capital and the change in the reserve to after-tax operating income),
- Add unrecorded goodwill and accumulated goodwill amortization to capital and add back goodwill amortization to after-tax operating income, and
- If a company deducts any interest expense in computing operating income, it must add this (after-tax) interest expense to its after-tax operating income.

To illustrate, suppose a division of Nike spends $4 million on January 2, 20X0, for research and development of a new shoe. The shoe proves to be a success with a product life cycle of four years (20X0 to 20X3). Before accounting for R&D, the division's operating income each year is $12 million and capital is $50 million. Assume that Nike's cost of capital is 10%. For simplicity, we will ignore income taxes, although EVA usually uses after-tax numbers.

Normally, financial reporting requires the company to expense the entire $4 million of R&D as incurred with no asset reported on the balance sheet. In short, generally accepted accounting principles assume that these expenditures reduce income immediately and create no future value. In contrast, EVA companies look upon R&D as a capital investment. For purposes of calculating EVA, Nike's division would capitalize these expenditures and expense them over the product's life cycle. In addition, the division would deduct from the operating income a capital charge of 10% of the average capital balance outstanding during the year, including the capitalized R&D. A comparison of

residual income (RI)
After-tax operating income less a capital charge.

capital charge
Company's cost of capital × amount of investment.

cost of capital
What a firm must pay to acquire more capital, whether or not it actually has to acquire more capital.

economic value added (EVA)
Equals adjusted after-tax operating income minus the cost of invested capital multiplied by the adjusted average invested capital.

the income and capital effects between traditional residual income and EVA follows (in millions):

Year	Accounting Operating Income	Adjusted Operating Income	Accounting Capital	Adjusted Average Capital†	Residual Income Capital Charge @ 10%‡	EVA Capital Charge @ 10%§	Residual Income	Economic Value Added
20X0	$ 8	8 + 4 − 1 = $11*	$50	$53.5	$ 5	$5.35	$ 3	$ 5.65
20X1	12	12 − 1 = 11	50	52.5	5	5.25	7	5.75
20X2	12	12 − 1 = 11	50	51.5	5	5.15	7	5.85
20X3	12	12 − 1 = 11	50	50.5	5	5.05	7	5.95
Total	$44	$44			$20	$20.8	$24	$23.20

* Accounting operating income + R&D expense − R&D amortization = $8 + $4 − $1 = $11.
† Adjusted average capital: 20X0, 1/2 × ($54 + $53); 20X1, 1/2 × ($53 + $52); etc.
‡ 10% × accounting capital.
§ 10% × adjusted average capital.

Total four-year operating income, the amount included on Nike's income statement, would be $44 million. Traditional residual income (without capitalizing R&D) would be $44 million less a capital charge of $20 million, or $24 million. EVA would also deduct a capital charge for the investment in R&D, making EVA = $44 million − $20.8 million = $23.2 million. That is, EVA deducts an additional $.8 million for the capital used for the R&D. Stern Stewart has identified more than 160 different adjustments such as the one for R&D. However, most often it recommends only a few for a specific client. Many companies make their own adjustments, as well. Nevertheless, all EVA companies use the basic concept of after-tax operating income less a capital charge.

RI and EVA have received much attention recently as scores of companies are adopting them as financial performance measures. **AT&T**, **Coca-Cola**, **CSX**, **FMC**, and **Quaker Oats** claim that using EVA motivated managers to make decisions that increased shareholder value. All these companies are successful. Why? Because they do a better job than their competitors at allocating, managing, and redeploying scarce capital resources (fixed assets such as heavy equipment, computers, real estate, and working capital). Because EVA explicitly recognizes the cost of the capital deployed, it may help managers in these companies make better capital allocation decisions.

MAKING MANAGERIAL DECISIONS

One company that improved its EVA performance dramatically during the 1990s is IBM. In 1993, its EVA was a negative $13 billion. By 2000, the company improved its EVA to $2.2 billion. Like most companies, the economic downturn in 2001 and 2002 hurt its EVA. Compute the EVA for IBM for 2002 using the following data (millions of dollars). As a manager, how would you explain this EVA to investors?

	2002
After-tax operating income	$5,706
Average stockholders' equity	23,115
Average long-term liabilities	35,444
Cost of capital (assumed)	10%

Answer

EVA = After-tax operating income − cost-of-capital percentage × capital invested

= $5,706 − .10 × ($23,115 + $35,444)

= $5,706 − .10 × $58,559

= $5,706 − $5,856

= $(150)

The improvement from 1993 to 2000 was dramatic. The decline in EVA in 2002 is not unexpected. A majority of companies lost value in 2002, and IBM's decline was smaller than most. (Note: We have used data reported in IBM's financial statements without adjustments that have been advocated by Stern Stewart or others.)

ROI or Residual Income?

Why do some companies prefer residual income (or EVA) to ROI? For a division with net operating income of $900,000 and average invested capital of $10,000,000, the ROI approach shows

Divisional net operating income after taxes	$ 900,000
Average invested capital	$10,000,000
Return on investment	9%

Under ROI, the basic message is: Go forth and maximize your rate of return, a percentage. Thus, if a company measures performance using ROI, managers of divisions currently earning 20% may be reluctant to invest in projects that earn only 15% because doing so would reduce their average ROI.

However, from the viewpoint of the company as a whole, top management may want this division manager to accept projects that earn 15%. Why? Suppose the company's cost of capital is 8%. Investing in projects earning 15% will increase the company's profitability. Why? For every $1.00 of investment, the company gets $.15 in operating income and pays $.08 for the capital, a net gain of $.15 − $.08 = $.07. When a company measures performance using residual income, managers tend to invest in any project earning more than the cost of capital and thus raise the firm's total profits. That is, the residual income approach fosters goal congruence and managerial effort. Its basic message is, Go forth and maximize residual income, an absolute dollar amount.

Suppose Nike has two divisions, Division A with net operating income of $200,000 and Division B with net operating income of $50,000. Both have average invested capital of $1 million. Suppose a project is proposed that can be undertaken by either A or B. The project will earn 15% annually on a $500,000 investment, or $75,000 a year. The cost of capital for the project is 8%. ROI and residual income with and without the project are as follows:

	Without Project		With Project	
	Division A	**Division B**	**Division A**	**Division B**
Net operating income	$ 200,000	$ 50,000	$ 275,000	$ 125,000
Invested capital	$1,000,000	$1,000,000	$1,500,000	$1,500,000
ROI (net operating income ÷ invested capital)	20%	5%	18.3%	8.3%
Capital charge (8% × invested capital)	$ 80,000	$ 80,000	$ 120,000	$ 120,000
Residual income (net operating income − capital charge)	$ 120,000	$ (30,000)	$ 155,000	$ 5,000

Suppose you are the manager of Division A. If top management at Nike bases your evaluation on ROI, would you invest in the project? No. It would decrease your ROI from 20 to 18.3%. But suppose you are in Division B. Would you invest? Yes, because ROI increases from 5% to 8.3%. In general, in companies using ROI, the least-profitable divisions have more incentive to invest in new projects than do the most profitable divisions.

Now suppose top management evaluates your performance using residual income. The project would be equally attractive to either division. Residual income increases by $35,000 for each division, $155,000 − $120,000 for A and $5,000 − (−$30,000) for B. Both divisions have the same incentive to invest in the project, and the incentive depends on the profitability of the project compared with the cost of the capital used by the project.

In general, use of residual income or EVA will promote goal congruence and lead to better decisions than using ROI. Many companies are convinced that EVA has played a large role in their success. James M. Cornelius, chairman of **Guidant Corporation**, a medical device company focused on cardiovascular disease, paid tribute to EVA on Stern Stewart's Web site:

> *From day one at Guidant, we linked management bonuses to EVA performance targets. . . . If a target acquisition isn't EVA positive here, we don't do it. We pay EVA performance bonuses to Guidant technologists who develop new products within specified time frames, and we are seeing product innovation here that we've never seen before. All of our employees. . . . are performing at levels we've never before experienced. I'm convinced these results are largely because of EVA. [Employees] keep looking for ways to improve our business because at the end of the day a significant share of their annual cash bonuses are tied to EVA improvement. . . . All that they have accomplished couldn't have been done without EVA.*

Siemens Corporation, Europe's largest electronics and electrical engineering firm and Stern Stewart's first EVA client in Europe reported in its annual report that "Siemens focuses on EVA as the yardstick by which we measure the success of our efforts. The EVA performance standard encourages our people to be efficient, productive and proactive in thinking about our customers and their customers. These attributes translate into profitable growth and higher returns." Examples of actions taken by Siemens to improve EVA include the sale of **Siecor**, the fiberoptic cable business, to **Corning**, and the sale of its retail and banking business. As stated by Siemens, "Divesting selected businesses has generated funds for more strategic investments."

Despite the success of residual income and EVA, most companies still use ROI. Why? Probably because it is easier for managers to understand, and it facilitates comparison across divisions. Furthermore, combining ROI with appropriate growth and profit targets can minimize ROI's dysfunctional motivations.

Summary Problem For Your Review

PROBLEM

A division has assets of $200,000, current liabilities of $20,000, and net operating income of $60,000.

1. What is the division's ROI?
2. If the weighted-average cost of capital is 14%, what is the EVA?
3. What effects on management behavior can be expected if ROI is used to gauge performance?
4. What effects on management behavior can be expected if EVA is used to gauge performance?

SOLUTION

1. ROI = $60,000 ÷ $200,000 = 30%. An alternative is $60,000 ÷ $180,000 = 33%.
2. EVA = $60,000 − .14 ($180,000) = $60,000 − $25,200 = $34,800.
3. If the company uses ROI to evaluate the manager, he is prone to reject projects that do not earn an ROI of at least 30%. From the viewpoint of the organization as a whole, this may be undesirable because its best investment opportunities may lie in that division and have a rate of, say, 22%. If a division is enjoying a high ROI, it is less likely to expand if top management judges it via ROI than if they judge it via EVA.

4. If the company uses EVA, the manager is inclined to accept all projects whose expected rate of return exceeds the weighted-average cost of capital. The manager's division is more likely to expand because his or her goal is to maximize a dollar amount rather than a rate.

A Closer Look at Invested Capital

To apply either ROI or residual income, we must measure both income and invested capital. However, there are many different interpretations of these concepts. To understand what ROI or residual income figures really mean for a particular company, you must first determine how the company defines and measures invested capital and income. We discussed various definitions of income in Chapter 9, pages 391–394, so we will not repeat them here. We will, however, explore various definitions of invested capital.

OBJECTIVE 5

Compare the advantages and disadvantages of various bases for measuring the invested capital used by organization segments.

Definitions of Invested Capital

Consider the following balance sheet classifications:

Current assets	$ 400,000	Current liabilities	$ 200,000
Property, plant, and		Long-term liabilities	400,000
equipment, net	800,000	Stockholders' equity	700,000
Construction in		Total liabilities and stockholders' equity	$1,300,000
progress	100,000		
Total assets	$1,300,000		

Possible definitions of invested capital and their values on the preceding balance sheet include

1. Total assets: All assets are included, $1,300,000.
2. Total assets employed: All assets except agreed-on exclusion of construction in progress, $1,300,000 − $100,000 = $1,200,000.
3. Total assets less current liabilities: All assets except that portion supplied by short-term creditors, $1,300,000 − $200,000 = $1,100,000. This is sometimes expressed as long-term invested capital; note that it can also be computed by adding the long-term liabilities and the stockholders' equity, $400,000 + $700,000 = $1,100,000, which is the definition used for EVA.
4. Stockholders' equity: Focuses on the investment of the owners of the business, $700,000.

For measuring the performance of division managers, we recommend any of the first three definitions rather than stockholders' equity. If the division manager's mission is to put all assets to their best use without regard to their financing, then total assets is best. If top management directs the manager to carry extra assets that are not currently productive, then total assets employed is best. If the manager has direct control over obtaining short-term credit and bank loans, then total assets less current liabilities is best. A key behavioral factor in choosing an investment definition is that managers will focus attention on reducing those assets and increasing those liabilities that a company includes in the definition. In practice, most companies using ROI or residual income include all assets in invested capital, and about half (primarily companies using EVA) deduct some portion of current liabilities.

Asset Allocation to Divisions

Just as cost allocations affect income, asset allocations affect the invested capital of particular divisions. Companies allocate capital when a particular asset serves two or more divisions. The aim is to allocate this capital in a manner that will be goal congruent, will spur managerial effort, and will recognize segment autonomy as much as possible. (As long as the managers feel that they are being treated uniformly, though, they tend to be more tolerant of the imperfections of the allocation.)

A frequent criterion for asset allocation is avoidability. That is, the amount a company allocates to any given segment for the purpose of evaluating the division's performance is the amount that the corporation as a whole could avoid by not having that segment. Commonly used bases for allocation, when assets are not directly identifiable with a specific division, include

Asset Class	Possible Allocation Base
Corporate cash	Budgeted cash needs
Receivables	Sales weighted by payment terms
Inventories	Budgeted sales or usage
Plant and equipment	Usage of services in terms of long-run forecasts of demand or area occupied

The allocation base should be the output measure or cost driver of the activity that caused the asset to be acquired. When the allocation of an asset would indeed be arbitrary (i.e., no causal activity can be identified), many managers think that it is better not to allocate.

There are two main reasons for allocating assets to divisions: (1) the division's managers influence the amount of the asset used to benefit their division's operations, or (2) the asset is an important part of the revenue-generating activities of the division. For example, consider a truck used to ship products for two Nike divisions. It is likely that the managers can influence how much of the truck's capacity is used to transport their division's products, and transportation of the products is essential to generating the revenues of each division. Nike should allocate the investment in the truck, possibly based on the cubic feet of product delivered for each division. In contrast, consider Nike's corporate public relations office. Divisional managers probably have little influence over the office, and it is not directly related to their revenue-generating activities. If this is the case, Nike should not allocate to divisions the investment in its public relations office.

Valuation of Assets

gross book value
The original cost of an asset before deducting accumulated depreciation.

net book value
The original cost of an asset less any accumulated depreciation.

Companies must measure whatever assets they include in a division's invested capital. Should they value the assets contained in the investment base at **gross book value**—the original cost of an asset—or **net book value**—the original cost of an asset less any accumulated depreciation? Should they base the values on historical cost or some version of current value? Practice is overwhelmingly in favor of using net book value based on historical cost. However, the alternatives are attractive in certain circumstances. We next examine the historical cost versus current cost issue and then discuss gross versus net asset values.

Most companies favor book value over any measure of current cost. Very few companies use replacement cost or any other type of current value. Yet, critics maintain that historical cost provides a faulty basis for decision making and performance evaluation. Recall that historical costs per se are irrelevant for making economic decisions. Despite these criticisms, managers have been slow to depart from historical cost.

Why is historical cost so widely used? Some critics would say that sheer ignorance is the explanation. But a more persuasive answer comes from cost-benefit analysis. Accounting systems are costly. Companies must keep historical records for many legal purposes, so historical records are already in place. A company spends no additional money to evaluate performance based on historical costs. Many top managers believe that a more sophisticated system would not improve collective operating decisions enough to warrant the added expense.

Historical costs may even improve some decisions because they are more objective than current costs. Because managers can better predict the historical-cost effects of their decisions, the control system may exert more influence on their decisions. Furthermore, the uncertainty involved with current-cost measures may impose undesirable risks on the managers. In short, the historical-cost system may be superior for the routine evaluation of performance. In nonroutine instances, such as replacing equipment or deleting a product line, managers should conduct special studies to gather any current valuations that seem relevant.

Finally, although historical-cost systems are common, most well-managed organizations do not use historical-cost systems alone. The alternatives available to managers are not

More accurately stated, the alternatives are

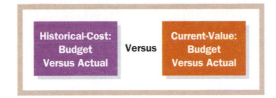

A budget system, whether based on historical cost or current value, causes managers to plan and control their operations. Most managers seem to prefer to concentrate on improving their existing historical-cost budget system.

Plant and Equipment: Gross or Net?

In valuing assets, we need to distinguish between net and gross book values. Most companies use net book value in calculating their investment base. However, a significant minority uses gross book value. The proponents of gross book value maintain that it facilitates comparisons between years and between plants or divisions.

Consider an example of a $600,000 piece of equipment with a three-year life and no residual value.

	Operating Income Before			Average Investment			
Year	Depreciation	Depreciation	Operating Income	Net Book Value*	Rate of Return	Gross Book Value	Rate of Return
1	$260,000	$200,000	$60,000	$500,000	12%	$600,000	10%
2	260,000	200,000	60,000	300,000	20	600,000	10
3	260,000	200,000	60,000	100,000	60	600,000	10

* ($600,000 + $400,000) ÷ 2; ($400,000 + $200,000) ÷ 2; and so on.

Notice that the rate of return on net book value increases as the equipment ages. In contrast, the rate of return on gross book value is unchanged if operating income does not change. Proponents of using gross book value for performance evaluation maintain that a performance measure should not improve simply because assets are getting older. In contrast, advocates of using net book value maintain that it is less confusing because it is consistent with the assets shown on the conventional balance sheet and with the net income computations.

Regardless of the theoretical arguments, companies should focus primarily on the effect on managers' motivation when choosing between net and gross book value. Managers evaluated using gross book value will tend to replace assets sooner than will those managers in firms using net book value. Consider a division of Nike that has a four-year-old machine with an original cost of $1,000 and net book value of $200. The division can replace the machine with a new one that also costs $1,000. The choice of net or gross book value does not affect net income. If Nike uses the net book value for measuring the investment base, replacement will increase the investment base from $200 to $1,000. However, the base remains at $1,000 if Nike uses gross book value. To maximize ROI or residual income, managers want a low investment base. Managers in firms using net book value will tend to keep old assets with their low book value. Those in firms using gross book value will have less incentive to keep old assets. Therefore, using gross book value will motivate managers to use more state-of-the-art production technology. Net asset value promotes a more conservative approach to asset replacement.

In sum, our cost-benefit approach provides no universal answers with respect to such controversial issues as historical values versus current values or gross versus net asset values. Instead, using a cost-benefit test and assessing the motivational effects of the alternatives, each organization must judge for itself whether a particular control system or accounting technique will improve collective decision making. The cost-benefit approach is not concerned with "truth" or "perfection" by itself. Instead it asks, Do you think your perceived "truer" or "more logical" system is worth its added cost? Will it achieve better goal congruence and managerial effort? Or will our existing imperfect system provide about the same set of decisions if it is skillfully administered?

Transfer Pricing

Now that you understand some of the issues in measuring profitability, we will look at something that can complicate the use of profitability as a performance measure. When all the segments of a decentralized organization are independent of one another, managers' motivations that result from using profitability measures for performance evaluations are generally consistent with overall organizational goals. Segment managers can then focus on only their own segments; what is best for their segment is generally best for the organization as a whole. In contrast, when segments interact greatly, there is an increased possibility that what is best for one segment hurts another segment badly enough to have a negative effect on the entire organization. For example, two Nike sales divisions may compete for the same customer by cutting prices and thereby reducing the company's overall margin on the business.

transfer price
The price that one segment of an organization charges another segment of the same organization for a product or service.

Conflicts between segment and organizational interests can easily occur when one segment sells products or services to another segment of the same company. The price that one segment charges another segment of the same organization for a product or service is a **transfer price.** Most items transferred are materials, parts, or finished goods, but they may also include services. The transfer price is revenue to the segment producing the product or service, and it is a cost to the acquiring segment.

Purposes of Transfer Pricing

Why do transfer-pricing systems exist? The principal reason is that management wants to create performance measurement systems that assure that managers who make decisions to improve their segment's performance also increase the performance of the organization as a whole. When a company evaluates a segment based on profitability, it wants to measure profitability in a way that rewards the segment manager for decisions that increase

OBJECTIVE 6

Define transfer prices and identify their purpose.

both a segment's profitability and the profitability of the entire company. For example, transfer prices should guide managers to make the best possible decisions regarding whether to buy or sell products and services inside or outside the total organization. Decisions made by the buying and selling segment managers, acting without top management intervention, should be the best decisions for their segment and for the entire organization. In other words, decisions that maximize a segment's profit should also maximize the profits of the entire company. In addition, multinational companies use transfer pricing to minimize their worldwide taxes, duties, and tariffs.

Another main goal of transfer-pricing systems is to preserve segment autonomy. Top management could always dictate how much of any product or service one segment transfers to another. However, if an organization has decided that decentralization, with its focus on autonomy of segment managers, is desirable, then segment managers must be free to make their own decisions. A transfer-pricing system essentially exerts top management's view through its performance measurement and evaluation system rather than through direct intervention in decisions.

Organizations use a variety of transfer prices, cost-based prices for some transfers, market-based prices for other transfers, and negotiated prices for others. Therefore, do not expect to obtain a single, universally applicable answer in the area of transfer pricing. It is a subject of continuous concern to top management. There is no perfect transfer-pricing system. Just ask any manager in a decentralized organization. Inevitably, such managers have had some experience with transfer-pricing systems that seems less than ideal. In fact, a manager in **Weyerhaeuser**, a large wood-products firm, called transfer pricing his firm's most troublesome management control issue.

A General Rule for Transfer Pricing

Although no single rule always meets the goals of transfer pricing, a general rule can provide guidance:

$$\text{transfer price} = \text{outlay cost} + \text{opportunity cost}$$

OBJECTIVE 7

State the general rule for transfer pricing and use it to assess transfer prices based on total costs, variable costs, and market prices.

Outlay cost is the additional amount the selling segment must pay to produce and transfer a product or service to another segment. It is often the variable cost for producing the item transferred. Opportunity cost is the maximum contribution to profit that the selling segment forgoes by transferring the item internally. For example, if capacity constraints force a segment to either transfer an item internally or sell it externally—that is, it cannot produce enough to do both—the opportunity cost for internal transfer is the contribution margin the segment could have gotten for the external sale.

Why does this rule generally work? Consider the following example, where the selling division is considering transferring a subcomponent to the buying division:

Suppose the selling division's opportunity cost arises because it can get $10 for the subcomponent on the market. Thus, the contribution from selling on the market is $10 − $6 = $4. At any transfer price less than $10, the division is better off selling the subcomponent on the market rather than transferring it. Thus, the minimum transfer price it would accept is $6 + ($10 − $6) = $6 + $4 = $10.

Now consider how much the item is worth to the buying division. For the subcomponent to be profitable to the buying division, it must be able to sell the final product for more than the transfer price plus the other costs it must incur to finish the product. Because it can sell the final product for $25 and its other costs are $12, it would be willing to pay up to $25 − $12 = $13 for it. But it will not pay more to the selling division than it would have to pay to an outside supplier. Thus, the largest transfer price acceptable to the buying division is the lesser of (1) $13 and (2) the cost charged by an outside supplier.

Now, from the company's point of view, transfer is desirable if (1) the total cost to the company for the subcomponent ($10 as determined by the selling division, including opportunity costs) is less than its value to the company ($13 as determined by the buying division), *and* (2) the selling division's costs (again including opportunity costs) are less than the price the buying division would have to pay to an outside supplier. The first criterion guarantees that the company does not pay more for the subcomponent than it is worth. The second guarantees that it does not pay more to produce the subcomponent internally than it would have to pay to buy it in the marketplace. The only transfer price that will always meet these criteria is $10, the outlay (variable) cost plus opportunity cost. Why? Any price between $10 and $13 meets the first criterion. However, only $10 meets the second if an outside supplier offers the subcomponent at a price between $10 and $13. At a $10 transfer price, we have the following result:

Outside Supplier Price	Decision by Division Managers	Decision Best for Company
<$10	Do not transfer—buying division rejects transfer because buying from outside supplier will maximize its profits	Buy from outside supplier because it is cheaper for the company as a whole
>$10	If value to buying division >$10: Transfer at $10—both divisions benefit	Transfer because internal price < external price
	If value to buying division <$10: Buying division rejects transfer	Do not transfer because the benefit of the subcomponent to the company is less than its cost

At a $10 transfer price, the division managers, acting independently, make the decision that is most profitable for the company as a whole. Any other transfer price creates a possibility of a manager making the decision that is best for his or her segment but not for the company as a whole. The selling division would reject the transfer at less than $10 regardless of how much profit it creates for the buying division. The buying division would reject the transfer whenever the transfer price is greater than the price from alternative sources. Any transfer price greater than $10 runs the risk of the buying division's purchasing outside the company even when the internal cost is lower. For example, with a transfer price of $12 and an outside bid of $11, the buying division would pay $11 to the outside supplier when the company could have spent only $10 (including opportunity cost) to produce the subcomponent in the selling division.

Because of the multiple goals of transfer pricing systems, this general rule doesn't always produce an ideal transfer price. But it is a good benchmark by which to judge transfer-pricing systems. We will analyze the following transfer-pricing systems, the most popular systems in practice, by examining how close the transfer price comes to the outlay cost plus opportunity cost:

1. Cost-based transfer prices
   a. Variable cost
   b. Full cost (possibly plus profit)

2. Market-based transfer prices
3. Negotiated transfer prices

In addressing these transfer-pricing systems, we will assume that a company has multiple divisions that transfer items to one another and that the company wants to preserve segment autonomy in a decentralized operation.

Transfers at Cost

About half the major companies in the world transfer items at cost. However, there are many possible definitions of cost. Some companies use only variable cost, others use full cost, and still others use full cost plus a profit markup. Some use standard costs, and some use actual costs. Let's examine these cost-based transfer-pricing systems.

Transfers at Variable Cost Companies that transfer items at variable cost implicitly assume that the selling division has no opportunity cost. Why? Because the outlay cost is generally about equal to variable cost: transfer price = outlay (variable) cost + $0. Therefore, a variable-cost transfer pricing system is most appropriate when the selling division forgoes no opportunities when it transfers the item internally. That generally implies that there is plenty of excess capacity.

Transfers at Full Cost or Full Cost Plus Profit Full-cost transfer pricing includes not only variable cost but also an allocation of fixed costs in the transfer price. In addition, some companies also add a markup for profit. This implicitly assumes that the allocation of fixed costs (and, if included, the profit markup) is a good approximation of the opportunity cost. In cases of constrained capacity, where the selling division cannot satisfy all internal and external demand for its products, the opportunity cost is positive. Thus, variable-cost transfer prices are problematic. A positive opportunity cost is surely warranted. However, there is no guarantee that the allocation of fixed costs, with or without a profit component added, is a good approximation of the opportunity cost. Yet, it may be a better approximation than assuming a zero opportunity cost. Some companies believe that using activity-based costing makes cost-based transfer prices appropriate, as described in the Business First box on page 444.

Cost-based transfer prices can also create problems if a company uses actual cost as a transfer price. Because the buying division will not know its actual cost in advance, it will not be able to accurately plan its costs. More important, a transfer price based on actual costs merely passes cost inefficiencies along to the buying division. Therefore, the supplying division lacks incentive to control its costs. Thus, we recommend using budgeted or standard costs instead of actual costs for cost-based transfer prices.

Finally, cost-based transfer prices can undercut segment autonomy and sometimes lead to conflicts between segment and organizational goals. Suppose managers believe that it's best for the company to transfer an item internally rather than purchasing it externally but also believe that the transfer price is unfair to their segment. They may either do what they think top management wants but resent its negative effect on their segment, or they may do what is best for their segment, ignoring its negative impact of the organization as a whole. Neither situation is desirable.

Market-Based Transfer Prices

If there is a competitive market for the product or service being transferred internally, using the market price as a transfer price will generally lead to the desired goal congruence and managerial effort. In such a case, the market price is equal to the variable cost

ACTIVITY-BASED COSTING AND TRANSFER PRICING

Teva Pharmaceutical Industries Ltd. is a global health care company specializing in pharmaceuticals. It is headquartered in Israel and had 2002 sales of $2.5 billion. Teva entered the lucrative generic drug market in the mid-1980s. As part of its strategy, the company decentralized its pharmaceutical business into cost and profit centers.

Each of the marketing divisions purchases generic drugs from the manufacturing division. Prior to decentralization, each marketing division was a revenue center. With the new organizational structure, management had to decide how to measure marketing division costs because profits were now the key financial performance measure.

A key cost to the marketing divisions is the transfer price paid for drugs purchased from the manufacturing division. Management considered several alternative bases for the company's transfer prices. They rejected market price because there was not a ready market. They rejected negotiated prices because they believed that the resulting debates over the proper price would be lengthy and disruptive. They adopted variable cost (raw material and packaging costs) for a short time. Eventually, however, they rejected it because it did not lead to congruent decisions—managers did not differentiate products using many scarce resources from those using few. Further, when a local source for the drug did exist, the market price was always above the variable-cost transfer price. Thus, managers in Teva's manufacturing division had little incentive to keep costs low.

Management also rejected full cost because the traditional costing system did not capture the actual cost structure of the manufacturing division. Specifically, the system undercosted the low volume products and overcosted the large volume products. The system traced only raw materials directly to products. It divided the remaining manufacturing costs into two cost pools and allocated them based on labor hours and machine hours. One problem with the traditional system was its inability to capture and correctly allocate the non-value-added cost of setup activity. Management did not know the size of the errors in product cost, but the lack of confidence in the traditional cost system led to rejection of full cost as the transfer-pricing base.

Then Teva's management adopted an activity-based-costing (ABC) system to improve the accuracy of its product costs. The ABC system has five activity centers and related cost pools: receiving, manufacturing, packaging, quality assurance, and shipping. Because of the dramatic increase in costing accuracy, management was able to adopt full activity-based cost as the transfer price.

Teva's managers are pleased with their transfer-pricing system. The benefits include increased confidence that the costs being transferred are closely aligned with the actual short- and long-run costs being incurred, increased communication between divisions, and an increased awareness of the costs of low-volume products and the costs of capacity required to support these products. They believe that their activity-based costs are the best approximation to outlay cost plus opportunity costs because the allocation of the fixed costs is a good measure of the value (opportunity cost) of the resources being consumed.

Sources: Adapted from Robert Kaplan, Dan Weiss, and Eyal Desheh, "Transfer Pricing with ABC," *Management Accounting,* May, 1997, pp. 20–28; Teva Pharmaceutical Industries, LTD, *2002 Annual Report.*

plus opportunity cost. Why? Because the opportunity cost equals the market price less the variable cost:

$$
\begin{aligned}
\text{transfer price} &= \text{variable cost} + \text{opportunity cost} \\
&= \text{variable cost} + (\text{market price} - \text{variable cost}) \\
&= \text{market price} + \text{variable cost} - \text{variable cost} \\
&= \text{market price}
\end{aligned}
$$

The market price may come from published price lists for similar products or services, or it may be the price the producing division charges its external customers. If the latter, the internal transfer price may be the external market price less the selling and delivery expenses that the company does not incur on internal business. The two major drawbacks to market-based prices are that (1) market prices are not always available for items transferred internally, and (2) in an imperfectly competitive market, the price one division has to pay to buy an item may be greater than the amount another division gets for selling the same item. The second of these drawbacks is not a major problem if the two prices are reasonably close. Many companies would simply use the lower of the two prices as a transfer price. But if no market exists or there are major differences in selling and buying prices for the item to be transferred, a company may need to use either cost-based or negotiated transfer prices.

To examine market-based transfer prices, consider two hypothetical divisions of Nike. One makes fabrics that it sells (transfers) to other divisions for use in many final products. It also sells the fabric directly to external customers. Another division buys the fabric from the first division and uses it to make jackets. A particular jacket requires two square yards of a special waterproof fabric. Should the Jacket Division obtain the fabric from the Fabric Division of Nike or purchase it from an external supplier?

Suppose the Fabric Division can sell the fabric externally for $25 per square yard and the Jacket Division can buy it from external suppliers for $25 per yard (or $2 \times \$25 = \$50$ per jacket). Assume for the moment that the Fabric Division can sell its entire production to external customers without incurring any marketing or shipping costs. The Jacket Division manager will refuse to pay a transfer price greater than $50 for the fabric for each jacket. Why? Because if the transfer price is greater than $50, she will purchase the fabric from the external supplier in order to maximize her division's profit.

Furthermore, the manager of the Fabric Division will not sell two square yards of fabric for less than $50. Why? Because he can sell it on the market for $50, so any lower price will reduce his division's profit. The only transfer price that allows both managers to maximize their division's profit is $50, the market price. If the managers had autonomy to make decisions, one of them would decline the internally produced fabric at any transfer price other than $50.

Now suppose the Fabric Division incurs a $2.50 per square yard marketing and shipping cost that it can avoid by transferring the fabric to the Jacket Division instead of marketing it to outside customers. Most companies would then use a transfer price of $22.50 per square yard, or $45 per jacket, often called a "market-price-minus" transfer price. The Fabric Division would get the same net amount from the transfer ($45 with no marketing or shipping costs) as from an external sale ($50 less $5 marketing and shipping costs), whereas the Jacket Division saves $5 per jacket. Thus, Nike overall benefits.

MAKING MANAGERIAL DECISIONS

Consider the following data concerning a subassembly that Wilamette Manufacturing Company produces in its Fabricating Division and uses in products assembled in its Assembly Division.

Fabricating Division
Variable cost of subassembly	$35
Excess capacity (in units)	1,000

Assembly Division
Market price for buying the subassembly from external sources	$50
Number of units needed	900

If you were manager of the Fabricating Division, what is the lowest transfer price you would accept for the subassembly? If you were the manager of the Assembly Division, what is the most you would be willing to pay for the subassembly? Is there a transfer price that would motivate production and transfer of the assembly? If so, what is the price?

Answer

The Fabricating Division has excess capacity, so its manager would be willing to accept any price above the variable cost of $35. The Assembly Division can buy the subassembly for $50 on the external market, so its manager would be willing to pay no more than $50 to buy it from the Fabricating Division. The transfer would take place at some price between $35 and $50.

Transfer Pricing when Market Prices Don't Exist

Now suppose that the Fabric Division cannot sell the fabric on the external market, either because there is no demand for the fabric or because Nike has a policy prohibiting such a sale. The prohibition may occur because Nike's strategy is to sell products only to final consumers, not to other manufacturers. Suppose the Fabric Division incurs variable production costs of $20 per square yard. On receiving two square yards of fabric, the Jacket Division spends an additional $56 to produce and sell each jacket, as shown in Exhibit 10-2. The Jacket Division manager predicts sales of 10,000 jackets, so its demand for fabric is 20,000 square yards. Whether it is best for Nike to have the Fabric Division manufacture and transfer the 20,000 square yards of fabric to the Jacket Division depends on whether the Fabric Division incurs any opportunity costs. Because there is no external market for the fabric, passing up external sales of the fabric cannot cause the opportunity cost. An opportunity cost will exist only if production of the fabric causes the Fabric Division to pass up using its production facilities for some other products that it can sell or transfer to another division.

First consider the case where there is no opportunity cost. That is, the Fabric Division passes up no opportunities because of its production of this fabric. Our rule gives a transfer price of $20 per square yard, the variable cost to the Fabric Division. This would provide a variable cost for the Jacket Division of $56 + (2 × $20) = $56 + $40 = $96 per jacket and a contribution margin of $100 − $96 = $4 per jacket. A full-cost or full-cost plus profit transfer price would potentially create **dysfunctional decisions**—decisions in conflict with the company's goals. Any transfer price above $44 would cause the Jacket Division manager to reject the transfer even though Nike is $4 better off with the transfer and production of the jacket—$100 of sales and a total additional cost of $40 + $56 = $96 for each jacket. In fact, any time the Jacket Division would find at least $40 of value in the transferred fabric, Nike would prefer the production and transfer of the fabric. The variable cost of $40 will motivate the two division managers to make this preferred decision. Any higher cost can cause the Jacket Division manager to buy too little fabric from the Fabric Division.

dysfunctional decision
Any decision that is in conflict with organizational goals.

With no opportunity cost, using the market price as a transfer price can create dysfunctional decisions. This could occur when there is an external market for the fabric, thus a market price, but Nike does not allow the Fabric Division to sell to that market. The market price in this case does not represent a real opportunity for the Fabric Division. Suppose the market price is $25 per square yard. A market-based transfer price would be $50 per jacket, making the total cost to the Jacket Division $106 and causing the rejection of the transfer. But it would still be best for Nike if the transfer took place because Nike still stands to gain $4 from the transfer and $0 with no transfer (and thus no jacket production).

Now suppose the Fabric Division has a $5-per-square-yard opportunity cost. This might arise because the division passes up $5 of contribution margin on other business when it uses its capacity to produce and transfer one square yard of this fabric. In this case, Nike would prefer production and transfer of the fabric only if it is worth at least $50

Exhibit 10-2
Contribution Margin on Jacket

Sales price of finished jacket			$100
Variable costs:			
Transfer price (T) for 2 square yards		$2 × T*	
Additional variable costs:			
Processing	$43		
Selling	13	56	
Total variable cost			56 + 2 × T
Contribution margin			$ 44 − 2 × T

* T = transfer price per yard.

to the Jacket Division. Why? Because the Fabric Division pays $40 of variable cost and passes up $10 of contribution to transfer the two square yards to the Jacket Division. At first it looks like a variable-cost transfer price might work. However, the Fabric Division manager would not produce and transfer the fabric at $20 per square yard because the division would be better off using its capacity for the other business. Nike would prefer not to transfer it because the $10 contribution to the Fabric Division from the other business is greater than the $4 contribution from production and sale of a jacket ($100 sales less $40 variable Fabric Division cost plus $56 variable Jacket Division cost). But what if the Jacket Division could sell the jacket for $110? The Fabric Division manager would still decline the business, even though Nike's contribution from the jacket would now be $110 − $96 = $14, which is greater than the $10 contribution the Fabric Division would receive. The variable-cost transfer price leads to a dysfunctional decision.

In summary, when the selling division cannot sell an item on the external market, using either a market-based or cost-based transfer for the item can lead to dysfunctional decisions. How do we resolve this dilemma? One possibility is for top management to impose a "fair" transfer price and insist that a transfer be made. But managers in a decentralized company often regard such orders as undermining their autonomy. Therefore, many companies turn to negotiated transfer prices.

Negotiated Transfer Prices

Companies heavily committed to segment autonomy often allow managers to negotiate transfer prices. The managers may consider both costs and market prices in their negotiations, but no policy requires them to do so. Supporters of negotiated transfer prices maintain that the managers involved have the best knowledge of what the company will gain or lose by producing and transferring the product or service, so open negotiation allows the managers to make optimal decisions. Critics of negotiated prices focus on the time and effort spent negotiating, an activity that adds nothing directly to the profits of the company.

Let's look at how our Fabric Division and Jacket Division managers might approach a negotiation of a transfer price. The Jacket Division manager might look at the selling price of the jacket, $100, less the additional cost the division incurs in making it, $56, and decide to purchase fabric at any transfer price less than $100 − $56 = $44. The Jacket Division will add to its profit by making the jacket if the transfer price is below $44.

Similarly, the Fabric Division manager will look at what it costs to produce and transfer the fabric. If there is no opportunity cost, any transfer price above $40 will increase the Fabric Division's profit. However, if there is a $5-per-square-yard opportunity cost, so that transferring two square yards of fabric causes the division to give up a contribution of $10 as well as paying variable costs of $40, the minimum transfer price acceptable to the Fabric Division is $50.

Negotiation will result in a transfer if the maximum transfer price the Jacket Division is willing to pay is greater than the minimum transfer price the Fabric Division is willing to accept. When the Fabric Division has no opportunity cost, a transfer will take place at a price between $40 and $44. The Fabric Division manager is willing to accept any price above $40 and the Jacket Division manager will pay up to $44. The exact transfer price may depend on the negotiating ability of the two division managers. The same result, agreeing to a transfer, will occur if the Fabric Division manager also has an opportunity cost if that cost is less than $2 per square yard. The transfer price will simply be at least equal to the $40 variable cost plus the opportunity cost for two square yards. However, if the Fabric Division has an opportunity cost of $2 or more per square yard, a transfer will not occur. This is exactly what Nike would prefer. When the Fabric Divison's opportuinty cost is less than $2, the jacket is more profitable than the Fabric Division's other business, and the transfer should occur. When the Fabric Division's opportunity cost is greater than $2, the additional contribution from the Fabric Division's other business will be greater than the Jacket Divison's contribution on a jacket, and the transfer should not occur. Therefore, the manager's decisions are congruent with the company's best interests.

What should top management of a decentralized organization do if it sees segment managers making dysfunctional decisions through their negotiations? As usual, the answer is, "It depends." Top management can step in and force the "correct" decision, but doing so undermines segment managers' autonomy and the overall notion of decentralization. It also assumes that top management has the information necessary to determine the correct decision. Most important, frequent intervention results in recentralization. Indeed, if more centralization is desired, the organization might want to reorganize by combining segments.

Top managers who wish to encourage decentralization will often make sure that both producing and purchasing division managers understand all the facts and then allow the managers to negotiate a transfer price. Even when top managers suspect that a dysfunctional decision might be made, they may swallow hard and accept the segment manager's judgment as a cost of decentralization. (Of course, repeated dysfunctional decision making may be a reason to change the organizational design or to change managers.)

Well-trained and informed segment managers who understand opportunity costs and fixed and variable costs will often make better decisions than will top managers. The producing division manager knows best the various uses of its capacity, and the purchasing division manager knows best what profit can be made on the items to be transferred. In addition, negotiation allows segments to respond flexibly to changing market conditions when setting transfer prices. One transfer price may be appropriate in a time of idle capacity, and another when demand increases and operations approach full capacity.

The Need for Many Transfer Prices

As you can see, there is seldom a single transfer price that will ensure the desired decisions. The "correct" transfer price depends on the economic and legal circumstances and the decision at hand. Organizations may have to make trade-offs between pricing for congruence and pricing to spur managerial effort. Furthermore, the optimal price for either may differ from that employed for tax reporting or for other external needs.

Income taxes, property taxes, and tariffs often influence the setting of transfer prices so that the firm as a whole will benefit, even though the performance of a segment may suffer. For example, to maximize tax deductions for percentage depletion allowances, which are based on revenue, a petroleum company may want to transfer crude oil to other segments at as high a price as is legally possible.

State fair-trade laws and national antitrust acts can also influence transfer pricing in some situations. Because of the differences in national tax structures around the world, or because of the differences in the incomes of various divisions and subsidiaries, the firm may wish to shift profits and "dump" goods, if legally possible. These considerations further illustrate the limits of decentralization where there are heavy interdependencies among segments and explain why the same companies may use different transfer prices for different purposes.

Multinational Transfer Pricing

OBJE8TIVE
Identify the factors affecting multinational transfer prices.

So far we have focused on how transfer pricing policies affect the motivation of managers. However, in multinational companies, other factors may dominate. For example, multinational companies use transfer prices to minimize worldwide income taxes, import duties, and tariffs. For example, Nike might prefer to make its profits in Canada, with its maximum corportate tax rate of 28%, rather than in the United States, where the rate is 35%.

Suppose a division in a high-income-tax-rate country produces a subcomponent for another division in a low-income-tax-rate country. By setting a low transfer price, the company can recognize most of the profit from the production in the low-income-tax-rate country, thereby minimizing taxes. Likewise, items produced by divisions in a low-income-tax-rate country and transferred to a division in a high-income-tax-rate country should have a high transfer price to minimize taxes.

Sometimes import duties offset income tax effects. Most countries base import duties on the price paid for an item, whether bought from an outside company or transferred from another division. Therefore, low transfer prices generally lead to low import duties.

Of course, tax authorities recognize the incentive to set transfer prices to minimize taxes and import duties. Therefore, most countries have restrictions on allowable transfer prices. United States multinationals must follow an Internal Revenue Code rule specifying that transfers be priced at "arm's-length" market values, or at the price one division would pay another if they were independent companies. Even with this rule, companies have some latitude in deciding an appropriate "arm's-length" price.

Consider a high-end running shoe produced by a Swiss Nike division with an 8% income tax rate and transferred to a division in Germany with a 40% income tax rate. In addition, suppose Germany imposes an import duty equal to 20% of the price of the item and that Nike cannot deduct this import duty for tax purposes. Suppose the full unit cost of a pair of the shoes is $100, and the variable cost is $60. If tax authorities allow either variable- or full-cost transfer prices, which should Nike choose? By transferring at $100 rather than at $60, the company gains $4.80 per unit:

Effect of Transferring at $100 Instead of at $60

Income of the Swiss division is $40 higher;	
therefore it pays 8% × $40 more income taxes	$(3.20)
Income of the German division is $40 lower;	
therefore it pays 40% × $40 less income taxes	16.00
Import duty is paid by the German division on an additional $100 − $60 = $40;	
therefore it pays 20% × $40 more duty	(8)
Net savings from transferring at $100 instead of $60	$ 4.80

Companies may also use transfer prices to avoid the financial restrictions imposed by some governments. For example, a country might restrict the amount of dividends paid to foreign owners. It may be easier for a company to get cash from a foreign division as payment for items transferred than as cash dividends.

In summary, transfer pricing is more complex in a multinational company than it is in a domestic company. Multinational companies try to achieve more objectives through transfer-pricing policies, and some of the objectives can conflict with one another.

Summary Problem For Your Review

PROBLEM

Reconsider Nike's Fabric Division and Jacket Division described on page 445. In addition to the data there, suppose the Fabric Division has annual fixed manufacturing costs of $800,000 and expected annual production of 200,000 square yards. The "fully allocated cost" per square yard was computed as follows:

Variable costs per square yard	$20.00
Fixed costs, $800,000 ÷ 200,000 square yards	4.00
Fully allocated cost per square yard	$24.00

Therefore, the "fully allocated cost" of the two square yards required for one jacket is 2 × $24 = $48.

Assume that the Fabric Division has idle capacity. The Jacket Division is considering whether to buy enough fabric for 10,000 jackets. It will sell each jacket for $100. The additional costs shown in Exhibit 10-2 for the Jacket Division would prevail. If Nike bases its transfer prices on fully allocated cost, would the Jacket Division manager buy? Explain. Would the company as a whole benefit if the Jacket Division manager decided to buy? Explain.

SOLUTION

The Jacket Division manager would not buy. The resulting transfer price of $48 would make the acquisition of the fabric unattractive to the Jacket Division:

Jacket Division			
Sales price of final product			$100
Deduct costs			
Transfer price paid to the Fabric Division			
(fully allocated cost)		$48	
Additional costs (from Exhibit 10-2)			
Processing	$43		
Selling	13	56	
Total costs to the Jacket Division			104
Contribution to profit of the Jacket Division			$ (4)
Contribution to company as a whole			
($100 − $40 − $56)			$ 4

The company as a whole would benefit by $40,000 (10,000 jackets × $4) if the Fabric Division produces and transfers the fabric.

The major lesson here is that, when there is idle capacity in the supplier division, transfer prices based on fully allocated costs may induce the wrong decisions. Working in her own best interests, the Jacket Division manager has no incentive to buy from the Fabric Division.

Keys To Successful Management Control Systems

Successful management control systems have several key factors in addition to appropriate measures of profitability and transfer-pricing policies. Like management in general, management control systems are more art than science. A company such as Nike will certainly include many subjective factors as well as more objective measures of profitability in its performance and evaluation system. Intelligent use of the available information is as important as generating the information itself. We next briefly explore three factors that help managers interpret and use management control information.

Focus on Controllability

OBJECTIVE 9

Explain how controllability and management by objectives (MBO) aid the implementation of management control systems.

As Chapter 9 explained (see Exhibit 9-4, page 392), top management should distinguish between the performance of the division manager and the performance of the division as an investment by the corporation. They should evaluate managers on the basis of their controllable performance (in many cases, some controllable contribution in relation to controllable investment). However, they should base decisions such as increasing or decreasing investment in a division on the economic viability of the division, not on the performance of its managers.

This distinction helps to clarify some vexing difficulties. For example, top management may want to use an investment base to gauge the economic performance of a retail store, but they might judge the store's manager by focusing on income and forgetting about any investment allocations. If top management assigns investment to the manager, the aim should be to assign only that investment that the manager can control. Controllability depends on what decisions managers can make regarding the size of the investment base. In a highly decentralized company, for instance, managers can influence the size of these assets and can exercise judgment regarding the appropriate amount of short-term credit and perhaps some long-term credit. Investment decisions that managers do not influence should not affect their performance evaluations.

Management by Objectives and Setting Expectations

Management by objectives (MBO) describes the joint formulation by a manager and his or her superior of a set of goals and plans for achieving the goals for a forthcoming period. For our purposes here, the terms *goals* and *objectives* are synonymous. The plans often take the form of a responsibility accounting budget (together with supplementary goals such as levels of management training and safety that managers may not incorporate into the accounting budget). The company then evaluates a manager's performance in relation to these agreed-on budgeted objectives. It is important that a manager's expectations be consistent with those of his or her superiors.

> **management by objectives (MBO)** *The joint formulation by a manager and his or her superior of a set of goals and plans for achieving the goals for a forthcoming period.*

An MBO approach tends to reduce complaints about lack of controllability because of its stress on budgeted results. That is, a particular manager and his or her superior negotiate a budget for a particular period and a particular set of expected outside and inside influences. By evaluating results compared to expectations, a manager may more readily accept an assignment to a less successful segment. Why? Because a manager of a segment that is economically struggling can still meet the agreed-upon goals. Thus, an MBO system is preferable to a system that emphasizes absolute profitability for its own sake. Unless evaluation focuses on meeting reasonable expectations, able managers will be reluctant to accept responsibility for segments that are in economic trouble. Whether using MBO or not, skillful budgeting and intelligent performance evaluation will go a long way toward overcoming the common lament: "I'm being held responsible for items beyond my control."

Budgets, Performance Targets, and Ethics

Organizations can minimize many of the troublesome motivational effects of performance evaluation systems by the astute use of budgets. We cannot overemphasize the desirability of tailoring budgets to a particular manager. For example, either an ROI or a residual income system can promote goal congruence and managerial effort if top management gets everybody to focus on what is currently attainable in the forthcoming budget period.

Using budgets as performance targets also has its dangers. Companies that make meeting a budget too important when evaluating managers can motivate unethical behavior. Top management at companies such as **WorldCom** made "making the numbers" such a high priority that, when it became clear that managers would not meet their goals, they fabricated the accounting reports. At **Enron**, the consequences of poor performance evaluations were so great that managers played bookkeeping games to make their performance look better. The lesson is that "astute" use of budgets is good, but using budgets to put unreasonable pressure on managers for performance rating can undermine the ethics of an organization.

As we said earlier in the chapter, "You get what you measure." It is important to use measures that are consistent with organizational goals. Yet, measurement is only part of the management control system. Accountants often focus too much on the measurements. Managers should also think hard about how they use the measures to achieve the organization's objectives. Even good measures can lead to dysfunctional decisions when managers misuse them. A management control system is only as good as the managers who use it.

Highlights to Remember

1 **Define decentralization and identify its expected benefits and costs.** As companies grow, the ability of managers to effectively plan and control becomes more and more difficult because top managers are further removed from day-to-day operations. One approach to effective planning and control in large companies is to decentralize decision making. This means that top management gives mid- and lower-level managers the freedom to make decisions that impact the subunit's performance. The more that decision making is delegated, the greater the decentralization. Often, the subunit manager is most knowledgeable of the factors that management should consider in the decision-making process.

2 **Distinguish between responsibility centers and decentralization.** Top management must design the management control system so that it motivates managers to act in the best interests of the company. This is done through the choice of responsibility centers and the appropriate performance measures and rewards. The degree of decentralization does not depend upon the type of responsibility center chosen. For example, a cost-center manager in one company may have more decision-making authority than does a profit-center manager in a highly centralized company.

3 **Explain how the linking of rewards to responsibility center results affects incentives and risk.** It is generally a good idea to link managers' rewards to responsibility center results. Top management should use performance measures for the responsibility center that promote goal congruence. However, linking rewards to results creates risk for the manager. The greater the influence of uncontrollable factors on a manager's reward, the more risk the manager bears.

4 **Compute ROI, residual income, and economic value added (EVA), and contrast them as criteria for judging the performance of organization segments.** It is typical to measure the results of investment centers using a set of performance measures that include financial measures such as return on investment (ROI), residual income (RI), or economic value added (EVA). ROI is any income measure divided by the dollar amount invested and is expressed as a percentage. Residual income, or economic value added, is after-tax operating income less a capital charge based on the capital invested (cost of capital). It is an absolute dollar amount.

5 **Compare the advantages and disadvantages of various bases for measuring the invested capital used by organization segments.** The way an organization measures invested capital determines the precise motivation provided by ROI, RI, or EVA. Managers will try to reduce assets or increase liabilities that a company includes in their division's investment base. They will adopt more conservative asset replacement policies if the company uses net book value rather than gross book value in measuring the assets.

6 **Define transfer prices and identify their purpose.** In large companies with many different segments, one segment often provides products or services to another segment. Deciding on the amount the selling division should charge the buying division for these transfers (transfer price) is difficult. Companies use various types of transfer pricing policies. The overall purpose of transfer prices is to motivate managers to act in the best interests of the company, not just the segment.

7 **State the general rule for transfer pricing and use it to assess transfer prices based on total costs, variable costs, and market prices.** As a general rule, transfer prices should approximate the outlay cost plus opportunity cost. Each type of transfer price has its own advantages and disadvantages. Each has a situation where it works best, and each can lead to dysfunctional decisions in some instances. Cost-based prices are readily available, but if a company uses actual costs, the receiving segment manager does not know the cost in advance, which makes cost planning difficult. When a competitive market exists for the product or service, using market-based transfer prices usually leads to goal congruence and optimal decisions. When idle capacity exists in the segment providing the product or service, the use of variable cost as the transfer price usually leads to goal congruence.

8 **Identify the factors affecting multinational transfer prices.** Multinational organizations often use transfer prices as a means of minimizing worldwide income taxes, import duties, and tariffs.

9 **Explain how controllability and management by objectives (MBO) aid the implementation of management control systems.** Regardless of what measures a management control system uses, when used to evaluate managers they should focus on only the controllable aspects of the measures. MBO can focus attention on performance compared to expectations, which is better than evaluations based on absolute profitability.

Accounting Vocabulary

agency theory, p. 430
capital charge, p. 433
capital turnover, p. 432
cost of capital, p. 433
decentralization, p. 426
dysfunctional decisions,
    p. 446

economic value added (EVA),
    p. 433
gross book value, p. 438
incentives, p. 429
management by objectives
    (MBO), p. 451
net book value, p. 438

residual income (RI), p. 433
return on investment (ROI),
    p. 431
return on sales, p. 432
segment autonomy, p. 428
transfer price, p. 440

Fundamental Assignment Material

10-A1 ROI and Residual Income Calculations

Consider the following data (in thousands):

	Division		
	A	B	C
Average invested capital	$1,000	$ 600	$ 900
Revenue	3,600	1,800	9,000
Income	180	126	90

1. For each division, compute the return on sales, the capital turnover, and the return on investment (ROI).
2. Which division is the best performer? Explain.
3. Suppose each division is assessed an imputed interest rate of 10% on invested capital. Compute the residual income for each division. Which division is the best performer based on residual income? Explain.

10-A2 Transfer-Pricing Dispute

Dixon Corporation, a transportation equipment manufacturer, is heavily decentralized. Each division head has full authority on all decisions regarding sales to internal or external customers. The Atlantic Division has always acquired a certain equipment component from the Southern Division. However, when informed that the Southern Division was increasing its unit price to $325, the Atlantic Division's management decided to purchase the component from outside suppliers at a price of $300.

The Southern Division had recently acquired some specialized equipment that was used primarily to make this component. The manager cited the resulting high depreciation charges as the justification for the price boost. He asked the president of the company to instruct the Atlantic Division to buy from Southern at the $325 price. He supplied the following data to back his request:

Atlantic's annual purchases of component	2,000 units
Southern's variable costs per unit	$ 285
Southern's fixed costs per unit	$ 30

1. Suppose there are no alternative uses of the Southern facilities. Will the company as a whole benefit if the Atlantic Division buys from the outside suppliers for $300 per unit? Show computations to support your answer.
2. Suppose internal facilities of Southern would not otherwise be idle. The equipment and other facilities would be assigned to other production operations that would otherwise require an additional annual outlay of $40,500. Should the Atlantic Division purchase from outsiders at $300 per unit?
3. Suppose that there are no alternative uses for Southern's internal facilities and that the outsiders' selling price drops by $30. Should the Atlantic Division purchase from outsiders?
4. As the president, how would you respond to the Southern Division manager's request? Would your response differ depending on the specific situations described in numbers 1 through 3 above? Why?

10-A3 Transfer Pricing

Refer to problem 10-A2, number 1 only. Suppose the Southern Division could modify the component at an additional variable cost of $12 per unit and sell the 2,000 units to other customers for $325. Then would the entire company benefit if the Atlantic Division purchased the 2,000 components from outsiders at $300 per unit?

10-A4 Rate of Return and Transfer Pricing

Consider the following data regarding budgeted operations of the Toronto Division of Machine Products, Inc.:

Average available assets	
Receivables	$ 160,000
Inventories	290,000
Plant and equipment, net	450,000
Total	$ 900,000
Fixed overhead	$ 300,000
Variable costs	$1 per unit
Desired rate of return on average	
available assets	25%
Expected volume	150,000 units

1. a. What average unit sales price does the Toronto Division need to obtain its desired rate of return on average available assets?
    b. What would be the expected asset turnover?
    c. What would be the return on sales?
2. a. If the selling price is as computed above, what rate of return will the division earn on available assets if sales volume is 180,000 units?
    b. If sales volume is 120,000 units?
3. Assume that the Toronto Division plans to sell 45,000 units to the Montreal Division of Machine Products, Inc., and that it can sell only 105,000 units to outside customers. The Montreal Division manager has balked at a tentative selling price of $4. She has offered $2.25, claiming that she can manufacture the units herself for that price. The Toronto Division manager has examined his own data. He had decided that he could eliminate $60,000 of inventories, $90,000 of plant and equipment, and $22,500 of fixed overhead if he did not sell to the Montreal Division and sold only 105,000 units to outside customers. Should he sell for $2.25? Show computations to support your answer.

10-B1 ROI or Residual Income

Brisbane Co. is a large integrated Australian conglomerate with shipping, metals, and mining operations throughout Asia. The general manager of the Heavy Metals Division plans to submit a proposed capital budget for 20X5 for inclusion in the companywide budget.

The division manager has for consideration the following projects, all of which require an outlay of capital. All projects have equal risk.

Project	Investment Required	Return
1	$4,800,000	$1,152,000
2	1,900,000	627,000
3	1,400,000	182,000
4	950,000	152,000
5	650,000	136,500
6	300,000	90,000

The division manager must decide which of the projects to take. The company has a cost of capital of 15%. An amount of $12 million is available to the division for investment purposes.

1. What will be the total investment, total return, return on capital invested, and residual income of the rational division manager if
    a. The company has a rule that managers should accept all projects promising a return on investment of at least 20%.

b. The company evaluates division managers on their ability to maximize the return on capital invested (assume that this is a new division with no invested capital).

c. The division manager is expected to maximize residual income as computed by using the 15% cost of capital.

2. Which of the three approaches will induce the most effective investment policy for the company as a whole? Explain.

10-B2 Computing EVA

Coca-Cola was one of the first companies to use EVA. The company's net income in 2002 was $3,976 million, up from $3,969 million in 2001 (before the effect of accounting changes). Coca-Cola reported the following results for 2001 and 2002 (in millions):

	2001	2002
Adjusted before-tax operating profit	$5,352	5,458
Cash taxes	1,496	1,508

Coca-Cola's average adjusted invested capital was $12,750 million in 2001 and $15,574 million in 2002, and its cost of capital decreased from 10% in 2001 to 9% in 2002.

Required

1. Compute Coca-Cola's EVA for 2001 and 2002.
2. Compare the company's performance in creating value for its shareholders in 2002 with that in 2001.

10-B3 Transfer Pricing

Arctic Enterprises runs a chain of drive-in ice cream stands in Anchorage during the ten-week summer season. Managers of all stands are told to act as if they owned the stand and are judged on their profit performance. Arctic Enterprises has rented an ice-cream machine for the summer to supply its stands with ice cream. Rent for the machine is $1,800. Arctic is not allowed to sell ice cream to other dealers because it cannot obtain a dairy license. The manager of the ice cream machine charges the stands $4 per gallon. Operating figures for the machine for the summer are as follows:

Sales to the stands (8,000 gallons at $4)		$32,000
Variable costs, @ $2.10 per gallon	$16,800	
Fixed costs		
Rental of machine	1,800	
Other fixed costs	5,000	23,600
Operating margin		$ 8,400

The manager of the Denali Drive-In, one of the Arctic drive-ins, is seeking permission to sign a contract to buy ice cream from an outside supplier at $3.35 a gallon. The Denali Drive-In uses 1,500 gallons of ice cream during the summer. Janet Gorton, controller of Arctic, refers this request to you. You determine that the other fixed costs of operating the machine will decrease by $480 if the Denali Drive-In purchases from an outside supplier. Gorton wants an analysis of the request in terms of overall company objectives and an explanation of your conclusion. What is the appropriate transfer price?

10-B4 Rate of Return and Transfer Pricing

The Kyoto division of B. Milton Toy Company manufactures units of the game Go and sells them in the Japanese market for ¥7,000 each. The following data are from the Kyoto Division's 20X2 budget:

Variable cost	¥ 4,800 per unit
Fixed overhead	¥ 6,080,000
Total assets	¥12,500,000

B. Milton has instructed the Kyoto Division to budget a rate of return on total assets (before taxes) of 20%.

1. Suppose the Kyoto Division expects to sell 3,400 games during 20X2.
   a. What rate of return will be earned on total assets?
   b. What would be the expected capital turnover?
   c. What would be the return on sales?
2. The Kyoto Division is considering adjustments in the budget to reach the desired 20% rate of return on total assets.
   a. How many units must be sold to obtain the desired return if no other part of the budget is changed?
   b. Suppose sales cannot be increased beyond 3,400 units. How much must total assets be reduced to obtain the desired return? Assume that for every ¥1,000 decrease in total assets, fixed costs decrease by ¥100.
3. Assume that only 2,400 units can be sold in the Japanese market. However, another 1,400 units can be sold to the European Marketing Division of B. Milton. The Kyoto manager has offered to sell the 1,400 units for ¥6,500 each. The European Marketing Division manager has countered with an offer to pay ¥6,000 per unit, claiming that she can subcontract production to a German producer at a cost equivalent to ¥6,000. The Kyoto manager knows that if his production falls to 2,400 units, he could eliminate some assets, reducing total assets to ¥10 million and annual fixed overhead to ¥4.9 million. Should the Kyoto manager sell for ¥6,000 per unit? Support your answer with the relevant computations. Ignore the effects of income taxes and import duties.

Additional Assignment Material

Questions

10-1 "Decentralization has benefits and costs." Name three of each.

10-2 Sophisticated accounting and communications systems aid decentralization. Explain how they accomplish this.

10-3 Why is decentralization more popular in profit-seeking organizations than in nonprofit organizations?

10-4 "The essence of decentralization is the use of profit centers." Do you agree? Explain.

10-5 What kinds of organizations find decentralization to be preferable to centralization?

10-6 What is the major benefit of the ROI technique for measuring performance?

10-7 What two major items affect ROI?

10-8 Define *economic value added (EVA)* and describe three ways a company can improve its EVA.

10-9 Division A's ROI is 20%, and B's is 10%. The company pays each division manager a bonus based on his or her division's ROI. Discuss whether each division manager would accept or reject a proposed project with a rate of return of 15%. Would either of them make a different decision if the company evaluated managers using residual income with a capital charge of 11%? Explain.

10-10 Give four possible definitions of invested capital that we can use in measuring ROI or residual income.

10-11 "Managers who use a historical-cost accounting system look backward at what something cost yesterday, instead of forward to what it will cost tomorrow." Do you agree? Why?

10-12 Ross Company uses net book value as a measure of invested capital when computing ROI. A division manager has suggested that the company change to using gross book value instead. What difference in motivation of division managers might result from such a change? Do you suppose most of the assets in the division of the manager proposing the change are relatively new or old? Why?

10-13 Why do companies need transfer-pricing systems?

10-14 Describe two problems that can arise when using actual full cost as a transfer price.

10-15 How does the presence or absence of idle capacity affect the optimal transfer-pricing policy?

10-16 "We use variable-cost transfer prices to ensure that we make no dysfunctional decisions." Discuss.

10-17 What is the major advantage of negotiated transfer prices? What is the major disadvantage?

10-18 Discuss two factors that affect multinational transfer prices but have little effect on purely domestic transfers.

10-19 Describe management by objectives (MBO).

Critical Thinking Exercises

10-20 Performance Measures and Economic Theory

Economists describe the formal choices of performance measures and rewards as agency theory. According to agency theory, employment contracts trade off three factors. Name and briefly describe the three.

10-21 Comparing Financial Measures of Performance

"Both ROI and residual income use profit and invested capital to measure performance. Therefore it really doesn't matter which we use." Do you agree? Explain.

10-22 Performance Measures and Ethics

"Financial performance measures cause managers to ignore ethics and focus just on meeting their profit targets. After all, look at what happened at **Enron**, **Global Crossing**, **WorldCom**, **Tyco**, **Health South**, and several other companies." Evaluate this quote. Can financial performance measures be compatible with ethical behavior?

10-23 Transfer Pricing and Organizational Behavior

The principle reason for transfer-pricing systems is to communicate data that will lead to goal-congruent decisions by managers of different business units. When managers take actions that conflict with organizational goals, dysfunctional behavior exists. Why does top management sometimes accept a division manager's judgments, even if the division manager appears to behave in a dysfunctional manner?

Exercises

10-24 Simple ROI Calculations

You are given the following data:

Sales	$130,000,000
Invested capital	$ 50,000,000
Net income	$ 6,000,000

Compute the following:
1. Turnover of capital
2. Return on sales
3. Return on investment (ROI)

10-25 Simple ROI Calculation

Fill in the blanks:

	Division		
	A	B	C
Return on sales	7%	3%	%
Capital turnover	3	___	4
Rate of return on invested capital	%	24%	20%

10-26 Simple ROI and Residual Income Calculations

Consider the following data:

	Division		
	X	Y	Z
Invested capital	$1,000,000	$	$1,250,000
Income	$	$ 182,000	$ 150,000
Revenue	$2,000,000	$3,640,000	$
Return on sales	5%	%	%
Capital turnover			3
Rate of return on invested capital	%	14%	%

1. Prepare a similar tabular presentation, filling in all blanks.
2. Which division is the best performer? Explain.
3. Suppose each division is assessed a capital charge based on a cost of capital of 12% of invested capital. Compute the residual income for each division.

10-27 EVA at Briggs & Stratton

Briggs & Stratton Corporation is the world's largest maker of air-cooled gasoline engines for outdoor power equipment. The company's engines are used by the lawn and garden equipment industry. According to the company's Annual Report, "management subscribes to the premise that the value of Briggs & Stratton is enhanced if the capital invested in its operations yields a cash return that is greater than that expected by the providers of capital."

The following data are from Briggs & Stratton's 2002 Annual Report (thousands of dollars):

	2002	2001
Adjusted before tax operating profit	$ 115,352	$107,593
Cash taxes	22,903	16,468
Adjusted average invested capital	1,154,653	942,811
Cost of capital	8.7%	9.6%

1. Compute the economic value added for Briggs & Stratton for 2001 and 2002.
2. Did Briggs & Stratton's overall performance improve from 2001 to 2002? Explain.

10-28 Comparison of Asset and Equity Bases

Fleet Footware has assets of $2 million and long-term, 10% debt of $800,000. Speedy Shoes has assets of $2 million and no long-term debt. The annual operating income (before interest) of both companies is $400,000. Ignore taxes.

1. Compute the rate of return on
   a. Assets available
   b. Stockholders' equity
2. Evaluate the relative merits of each base for appraising operating management.

10-29 Finding Unknowns

Consider the following data:

	Division		
	J	**K**	**L**
Income	$210,000	$	$
Revenue	$	$	$
Invested capital	$	$3,000,000	$16,000,000
Return on sales	7%	4%	%
Capital turnover	4		3
Rate of return on invested capital	%	20%	15%
Cost of capital	20%	12%	%
Residual income	$	$	$ 480,000

1. Prepare a similar tabular presentation, filling in all blanks.
2. Which division is the best performer? Explain.

10-30 Gross Versus Net Asset Value

The Ocala Division of Pinero Company just purchased an asset for $150,000. The asset has a three-year life. Pinero's top management evaluates Freida Carrasquel, manager of the Ocala Division, based on her division's ROI. She can choose to measure her assets using either gross asset value or net asset value. Her operating income before depreciation each year is $80,000.

Required

1. What is the Ocala Division's ROI for each of the three years using the gross asset value?
2. What is the Ocala Division's ROI for each of the three years using the net asset value?
3. If Carrasquel expects Pinero to transfer her to a different division in about a year, which asset valuation policy would she prefer?

10-31 Variable Cost as a Transfer Price

A desk calendar's variable cost is $5 and its market value is $6.30 at a transfer point from the Printing Division to the Binding Division. The Binding Division's variable cost of adding a simulated leather cover is $2.80, and the selling price of the final calendar is $8.50.

1. Prepare a tabulation of the contribution margin per unit for the Binding Division's performance and overall company performance under the two alternatives of (a) selling to outsiders at the transfer point and (b) adding the cover and then selling to outsiders.
2. As Binding Division manager, which alternative would you choose? Explain.

10-32 Maximum and Minimum Transfer Price

Biwheels Company makes bicycles. Various divisions make components and transfer them to the Omaha Division for assembly into final products. The Omaha Division can also buy components from external suppliers. The Lincoln Division makes the wheels, and it also sells wheels to external customers. All divisions are profit centers, and managers are free to negotiate transfer prices. Prices and costs for the Lincoln and Omaha divisions are

Lincoln Division	
Sales price to external customers	$13
Internal transfer price	?
Costs	
Variable costs per wheel	$9
Total fixed costs	$320,000
Budgeted production	64,000 wheels*

* Includes production for transfer to Omaha

Omaha Division	
Sales price to external customers	$160
Costs	
Wheels, per bicycle	?
Other components, per bicycle	$80
Other variable costs, per bicycle	$40
Total fixed costs	$640,000
Budgeted production	16,000 bicycles

Fixed costs in both divisions will be unaffected by the transfer of wheels from Lincoln to Omaha.

1. Compute the maximum transfer price per wheel the Omaha Division would be willing to pay to buy wheels from the Lincoln Division.
2. Compute the minimum transfer price per wheel at which the Lincoln Division would be willing to produce and sell wheels to the Omaha Division. Assume that Lincoln has excess capacity.

10-33 Multinational Transfer Prices

Glasgow Enterprises, Inc., has production and marketing divisions throughout the world. It produces one particular product in Japan, where the income tax rate is 30%, and transfers it to a marketing division in Sweden, where the income tax rate is 60%. Assume that Sweden places an import tax of 10% on the product and that import duties are not deductible for income tax purposes.

The variable cost of the product is £200 and the full cost is £400. Suppose the company can legally select a transfer price anywhere between the variable and full cost.

1. What transfer price should Glasgow Enterprises use to minimize taxes? Explain why this is the tax-minimizing transfer price.
2. Compute the amount of taxes saved by using the transfer price in number 1 instead of the transfer price that would result in the highest taxes.

Problems

10-34 Agency Theory

The U.K. International Trading Company plans to hire a manager for its division in Santiago, Chile. U.K. International's president and vice president of personnel are trying to decide on an appropriate incentive employment contract. The manager will operate far from the London corporate headquarters, so evaluation by personal observation will be limited. The president insists that a large incentive to produce profits is necessary; he favors a salary of £15,000 and a bonus of 10% of the profits above £120,000. If operations proceed as expected, profits will be £460,000, and the manager will receive £49,000. But both profits and compensation might be more or less than planned.

The vice president of personnel responds that £49,000 is more than most of U. K. International's division managers make. She is sure that the company can hire a competent manager for a guaranteed salary of £40,000. "Why pay £49,000 when we can probably hire the same person for £40,000?" she argued.

1. What factors would affect U.K. International's choice of employment contract? Include a discussion of the pros and cons of each proposed contract.
2. Why is the expected compensation more with the bonus plan than with the straight salary?

10-35 Margins and Turnover

Accountants often express return on investment as the product of two components—capital turnover and return on sales. You are considering investing in one of three companies, all in the same industry, and are given the following information:

	Company		
	Alpha	**Beta**	**Gamma**
Sales	$6,000,000	$ 2,500,000	$37,500,000
Income	$ 900,000	$ 375,000	$ 375,000
Capital	$3,000,000	$12,500,000	$12,500,000

1. Why would you desire the breakdown of return on investment into return on sales and turnover on capital?
2. Compute the return on sales, turnover on capital, and return on investment for the three companies, and comment on the relative performance of the companies as thoroughly as the data permit.
3. Notice that Beta and Gamma have the same income and capital but vastly different levels of sales. Discuss the types of industries that Beta and Gamma might be in.

10-36 ROI by Business Segment

Ruiz Media Inc. does business in three different business segments: (1) Entertainment, (2) Publishing/Information, and (3) Consumer/Commercial Finance. Results for a recent year were (in millions):

	Revenues	**Operating Income**	**Total Assets**
Entertainment	$1,272.2	$223.0	$1,120.1
Publishing/Information	$ 705.5	$122.4	$1,308.7
Consumer/Commercial Finance	$1,235.0	$244.6	$ 924.4

1. Compute the following for each business segment:
   a. Return on sales
   b. Capital turnover
   c. ROI
2. Comment on the differences in return on investment among the business segments. Include reasons for the differences.

10-37 EVA Versus Residual Income, Briggs & Stratton

This is an expansion of Exercise 10-27. The primary difference between the economic value added and residual income measures is the increased focus on cash flow by EVA. EVA companies make several adjustments to both operating income from the income statement and invested capital from the balance sheet. Common examples of these adjustments include capitalizing research and development costs and reporting warranty costs on a cash basis. Most EVA companies make only a few such adjustments (from 5 to 15).

The following data were taken from the 2002 Annual Report of **Briggs & Stratton** (thousands of dollars):

Income from operations	$ 118,358
Provision for income taxes	27,390
Net adjustments deducted from income from operations for EVA	3,006
Weighted average capital employed for EVA	1,154,653
Ending total shareholders' equity	449,646
Cash taxes	22,903
Ending total current liabilities	266,023
Ending total assets	1,349,033
Beginning total shareholders' equity	422,752
Beginning total current liabilities	242,182
Beginning total assets	1,296,195
Management's estimate of the cost-of-capital	8.7%

Prepare a schedule that calculates and compares economic value added to residual income for Briggs & Stratton.

10-38 Economic Value Added at Nike

Nike, Inc., is the largest seller of athletic footwear and athletic apparel in the world. Its financial results for the 2001 and 2002 fiscal years include (in millions):

	2002	2001
Revenues	$9,893	$9,489
Operating expenses	8,825	8,475
Interest expense	51	93
Income taxes	349	332
Average invested capital (total assets less current liabilities)	$4,320	$3,875

1. Suppose that Nike's cost of capital is 9.5%. Compute the company's economic value added (EVA) for 2001 and 2002. Assume definitions of after-tax operating income and invested capital as reported in Nike's annual reports without adjustments advocated by Stern Stewart or others.
2. Discuss the change in EVA between 2001 and 2002.

10-39 Economic Value Added

The **Coca-Cola Company** uses economic value added (EVA) to evaluate top management performance. In 2002, Coca-Cola had net operating income of $5,458 million, income taxes of $1,523 million, and average noncurrent liabilities plus stockholders' equity of $15,574 million. The company's capital is about 30% long-term debt and 70% equity. Assume that the after-tax cost of debt is 5% and the cost of equity is 11%.

1. Compute Coca-Cola's economic value added (EVA). Assume definitions of after-tax operating income and invested capital as reported in Coca-Cola's annual reports without adjustments advocated by Stern Stewart or others.
2. Explain what EVA tells you about the performance of the top management of Coca-Cola in 2002.

10-40 Evaluation of Divisional Performance

As the chief executive officer of Vernon Apparel Company, you examined the following measures of the performance of three divisions (in thousands of dollars):

	Net Assets Based On		Operating Income Based On*	
Division	Historical Cost	Replacement Cost	Historical Cost	Replacement Cost
Shoes	$15,000	$15,000	$2,700	$2,700
Clothing	44,000	55,000	6,750	6,150
Accessories	27,000	48,000	5,000	3,900

* The differences in operating income between historical and replacement cost are attributable to the differences in depreciation expenses.

1. Calculate for each division the rate of return on net assets and the residual income based on historical cost and on replacement cost. For purposes of calculating residual income, use 10% as the minimum desired rate of return.
2. Rank the performance of each division under each of the four different measures computed in number 1.
3. What do these measures indicate about the performance of the divisions? Of the division managers? Which measure do you prefer? Why?

10-41 Use of Gross or Net Book Value of Fixed Assets

Assume that an auto production plant acquires $400,000 of fixed assets with a useful life of four years and no residual value. The plant uses straight-line depreciation. The company judges the plant manager based on income in relation to these fixed assets. Annual net income, after deducting depreciation, is $40,000.

Assume that sales, and all expenses except depreciation, are on a cash basis. Dividends equal net income. Thus, cash in the amount of the depreciation charge will accumulate each year. The plant manager's performance is judged in relation to fixed assets because all current assets, including cash, are considered under central-company control. Assume (unrealistically) that any cash accumulated remains idle. Ignore taxes.

1. Prepare a comparative tabulation of the plant's rate of return and the company's overall rate of return based on
   a. Gross (i.e., original cost) assets.
   b. Net book value of assets.
2. Evaluate the relative merits of gross assets and net book value of assets as investment bases.

10-42 Role of Economic Value and Replacement Value

(This problem requires understanding of the concept of present values. See Appendix B.)

"To me, economic value is the only justifiable basis for measuring plant assets for purposes of evaluating performance. By economic value, I mean the present value of expected future services. Still, we do not even do this on acquisition of new assets—that is, we may compute a positive net present value, using discounted cash flow; but we record the asset at no more than its cost. In this way, the excess present value is not shown in the initial balance sheet. Moreover, the use of replacement costs in subsequent years is also unlikely to result in showing economic values. The replacement cost will probably be less than the economic value at any given instant of an asset's life.

"Market values are totally unappealing to me because they represent a second-best alternative value—that is, they ordinarily represent the maximum amount obtainable from an alternative that has been rejected. Obviously, if the market value exceeds the economic value of the assets in use, they should be sold. However, in most instances, the opposite is true; market values of individual assets are far below their economic value in use.

"The obtaining and recording of total present values of individual assets based on discounted-cash-flow techniques is an infeasible alternative. I, therefore, conclude that replacement cost (less accumulated depreciation) of similar assets producing similar services is the best practical approximation of the economic value of the assets in use. Of course, it is more appropriate for the evaluation of the division's performance than the division manager's performance."

Critically evaluate these comments. Please do not wander; concentrate on the issues described by the quotation.

10-43 Profit Centers and Transfer Pricing in an Automobile Dealership

A large automobile dealership in Houston is installing a responsibility accounting system and three profit centers: parts and service, new vehicles, and used vehicles. Top management has told the three department managers to run their shops as if they were in business for themselves. However, there are interdepartmental dealings. For example:

a. The parts and service department prepares new cars for final delivery and repairs used cars prior to resale.
b. The used-car department's major source of inventory has been cars traded in as partial payment for new cars.

The owner of the dealership has asked you to draft a company policy statement on transfer pricing, together with specific rules to be applied to the examples cited. He has told you that clarity is of paramount importance because he will rely on your statement for settling transfer pricing disputes.

10-44 Transfer Pricing

The Pump Division of Global Motors Company produces water pumps for automobiles. It has been the sole supplier of water pumps to the Automotive Division and charges $30 per unit, the current market price for very large wholesale lots. The Pump Division also sells to outside retail outlets, at $38 per unit. Normally, outside sales amount to 25% of a total sales volume of 1 million water pumps per year. Typical combined annual data for the division follow:

Sales	$32,000,000
Variable costs, @ $25 per water pump	$25,000,000
Fixed costs	$ 3,000,000
Total costs	$28,000,000
Gross margin	$ 4,000,000

Dearborn Pump Company, an entirely separate entity, has offered the Automotive Division comparable water pumps at a firm price of $28 per unit. The Pump Division of Global Motors claims that it cannot possibly match this price because it could not earn any margin at $28.

1. Assume that you are the manager of the Automotive Division of Global Motors. Comment on the Pump Division's claim. Assume that normal outside volume cannot be increased.
2. The Pump Division believes that it can increase outside sales by 750,000 water pumps per year by increasing fixed costs by $2 million and variable costs by $3 per unit while reducing the selling price to $36. Assume that maximum capacity is 1 million pumps per year. Should the division reject intracompany business and concentrate on outside sales?

10-45 Transfer Pricing Concession

You are the divisional controller of the U.S. Division of Japan Electronics, Inc. Your division is operating at capacity. The European Division has asked the U.S. Division to supply a sound system (chip and speaker), which it will use in a new model Game Box that it is introducing. The U.S. Division currently sells identical sound systems to outside customers at $11.00 each.

The European Division has offered to pay $6.90 for each sound system. The total cost of the Game Box is

Purchased parts from outside vendors	$28.10
Sound system from U.S. Division	6.90
Other variable costs	17.50
Fixed overhead	10.00
Total	$62.50

The European Division is operating at 50% of capacity, and this Game Box is an important new product introduction to increase its use of capacity. Based on a target-costing approach, the European Division management has decided that paying more than $6.90 for the sound system would make production of the Game Box infeasible because the predicted selling price for the boom box is only $62.50.

Japan Electronics evaluates divisional managers on the basis of pretax return on investment and dollar profits compared to the budget. Ignore taxes and tariffs.

1. As divisional controller of the U.S. Division, would you recommend supplying the sound system to the European Division for $6.90 each? Why or why not?
2. Would it be to the short-run economic advantage of Japan Electronics for the U.S. Division to supply the sound system to the European Division? Explain your answer.
3. Discuss the organizational and behavioral difficulties, if any, inherent in this situation. As the U.S. Division controller, what would you advise the Japan Electronics president to do in this situation?

10-46 Transfer Prices and Idle Capacity

The Ashville Division of National Woodcraft purchases lumber, which it uses to fabricate tables, chairs, and other wood furniture. It purchases most of the lumber from Georgolina Mill, also a division of National Woodcraft. Both the Ashville Division and Georgolina Mill are profit centers.

The Ashville Division proposes to produce a new Shaker-style chair that will sell for $94. The manager is exploring the possibility of purchasing the required lumber from Georgolina Mill. Production of 800 chairs is planned, using capacity in the Ashville Division that is currently idle.

The Ashville Division can purchase the lumber from an outside supplier for $72. National Woodcraft has a policy that internal transfers are priced at fully allocated cost.

Assume the following costs for the production of one chair and the lumber required for the chair:

Georgolina Mill		Ashville Division		
Variable cost	$48	Variable costs		
Allocated fixed cost	22	Lumber from Georgolina Mill		$70
Fully allocated cost	$70	Ashville Division variable costs		
		Manufacturing	$23	
		Selling	6	29
		Total variable cost		$99

1. Assume that the Georgolina Mill has idle capacity and therefore would incur no additional fixed costs to produce the required lumber. Would the Ashville division manager buy the lumber for the chair from the Georgolina Mill, given the existing transfer-pricing policy? Why or why not? Would the company as a whole benefit if the manager decides to buy from the Georgolina Mill? Explain.

2. Assume that there is no idle capacity at the Georgolina Mill and the lumber required for one chair can be sold to outside customers for $72. Would the company as a whole benefit if the Ashville manager buys from Georgolina? Explain.

10-47 Transfer-Pricing Principles

A consulting firm, Maxima, Inc., is decentralized with 25 offices around the country. The headquarters is based in San Francisco. Another operating division is located in San Jose, 50 miles away. A subsidiary printing operation, QualType, is located in the headquarters building. Top management has indicated the desirability of the San Jose office using QualType for printing reports. All charges are eventually billed to the client, but Maxima was concerned about keeping such charges competitive.

QualType charges San Jose the following:

Photographing page for offset printing (a setup cost)	$.25
Printing cost per page	.014

At this rate, QualType sales have a 60% contribution margin to fixed overhead.

Outside bids for 100 copies of a 120-page report needed immediately have been

Print 4U	$203.50
Jiffy Press	180.25
Kustom Print	184.00

These three printers are located within a five-mile radius of Maxima–San Jose and can have the reports ready in two days. A messenger would have to be sent to drop off the original and pick up the copies. The messenger usually goes to headquarters, but in the past, special trips have been required to deliver the original or pick up the copies. It takes three to four days to get the copies from QualType (because of the extra scheduling difficulties in delivery and pickup).

Quality control at QualType is poor. Reports received in the past have contained wrinkled pages, have occasionally been miscollated, or have had pages deleted altogether. (In one instance, an intracompany memorandum indicating Maxima's economic straits was inserted in a report prepared for an outside client. Fortunately, the San Jose office detected the error before the report was distributed to the client.) The degree of quality control in the three outside print shops is unknown.

(Although the differences in costs may seem immaterial in this case, regard the numbers as significant for purposes of focusing on the key issues.)

1. If you were the decision maker at Maxima–San Jose, to which print shop would you give the business? Is this an optimal economic decision from the entire corporation's viewpoint?
2. What would be the ideal transfer price in this case, if based only on economic considerations?
3. Time is an important factor in maintaining client goodwill. There is potential return business from this client. Given this perspective, what might be the optimal decision for the company?
4. Comment on the wisdom of top management in indicating that QualType should be used.

10-48 Negotiated Transfer Prices

The Assembly Division of Nathan Allen Office Furniture, Inc., needs 1,200 units of a subassembly from the Fabricating Division. The company has a policy of negotiated transfer prices. The Fabricating Division has enough excess capacity to produce 2,000 units of the subassembly. Its variable cost of production is $22. The market price of the subassembly is $38.

What is the natural bargaining range for a transfer price between the two divisions? Explain why no price below your range would be acceptable. Also explain why no price above your range would be acceptable.

10-49 Transfer Prices and Minority Interests

This chapter discussed transferring profits between divisions of a multinational company. Another situation where transfer prices have a similar effect is when a parent company transfers items to or from a subsidiary when there are minority shareholders in the subsidiary. Consider the **Michelin Group** and its Polish subsidiary, **Stomil Olsztyn**, of which Michelin owns 70%. Michelin buys tires from Stomil Olsztyn at a transfer price. Since Michelin owns a majority of Stomil Olsztyn, it controls the transfer-pricing policy. The holders of the other 30% of Stomil Olsztyn claim that Michelin sets the transfer prices too low, thereby reducing the profits of Stomil Olsztyn. They maintain that Stomil Olsztyn would be more profitable if it were allowed to sell its tires on the market rather than transfer them to Michelin. In reply, Michelin managers maintain that Stomil Olsztyn is more profitable than other members of the Michelin Group, and therefore the transfer prices must be fair.

Required

Discuss the incentives for Michelin to transfer tires at a low price from Stomil Olsztyn to its Michelin parent. What transfer price do the minority shareholders in Stomil Olsztyn favor? Use an example of a tire that Stomil Olsztyn produces at a variable cost of €20 that is transferred to Michelin for €25. How should Michelin and Stomil Olsztyn establish a fair transfer price?

10-50 Multinational Transfer Prices

Stockton's Medical Instruments, Inc., produces a variety of medical products at its plant in Ogden. The company has sales divisions worldwide. One of these sales divisions is located in Gothenberg, Sweden. Assume that the U.S. income tax rate is 34%, the Swedish rate is 60%, and a 15% import duty is imposed on medical supplies brought into Sweden.

One product produced in Ogden and shipped to Sweden is a heart monitor. The variable cost of production is $400 per unit, and the fully allocated cost is $650 per unit.

1. Suppose the Swedish and U.S. governments allow either the variable or fully allocated cost to be used as a transfer price. Which price should Stockton's Medical Instruments choose to minimize the total of income taxes and import duties? Compute the amount the company saves if it uses your suggested transfer price instead of the alternative. Assume import duties are not deductible for tax purposes.
2. Suppose the Swedish parliament passed a law decreasing the income tax rate to 50% and increasing the duty on heart monitors to 20%. Repeat number 1, using these new facts.

10-51 Review of Major Points in This Chapter

The Ohio Instruments Company uses the decentralized form of organizational structure and considers each of its divisions as an investment center. The Cleveland Division is currently selling 15,000 air filters annually, although it has sufficient productive capacity to produce 21,000 units per year. Variable manufacturing costs amount to $20 per unit, while the total fixed costs amount to $90,000. These 15,000 air filters are sold to outside customers at $40 per unit.

The Dayton Division, also a part of Ohio Instruments, has indicated that it would like to buy 1,500 air filters from the Cleveland Division, but at a price of $37 per unit. This is the price the Dayton Division is currently paying an outside supplier.

1. Compute the effect on the operating income of the company as a whole if the Dayton Division purchases the 1,500 air filters from the Cleveland Division.
2. What is the minimum price that the Cleveland Division should be willing to accept for these 1,500 air filters?

3. What is the maximum price that the Dayton Division should be willing to pay for these 1,500 air filters?

4. Suppose instead that the Cleveland Division is currently producing and selling 21,000 air filters annually to outside customers. What is the effect on the overall Ohio Instruments Company operating income if the Cleveland Division is required by top management to sell 1,500 air filters to the Dayton Division at (a) $20 per unit and (b) $37 per unit?

5. For this question only, assume that the Cleveland Division is currently earning an annual operating income of $36,000, and the division's average invested capital is $300,000. The division manager has an opportunity to invest in a proposal that will require an additional investment of $20,000 and will increase annual operating income by $2,200. (a) Should the division manager accept this proposal if the Ohio Instruments Company uses ROI in evaluating the performance of its divisional managers? (b) If the company uses economic value added? (Assume a cost of capital of 9%.)

Cases

10-52 Profit Centers and Central Services

Sun Manufacturing, Inc., manufacturer of Sunlite brand small appliances, has an Engineering Consulting Department (ECD). The department's major task has been to help the production departments improve their operating methods and processes.

For several years, Sun has charged the cost of consulting services to the production departments based on a signed agreement between the managers involved. The agreement specifies the scope of the project, the predicted savings, and the number of consulting hours required. The charge to the production departments is based on the costs to the Engineering Department of the services rendered. For example, senior engineer hours cost more per hour than junior engineer hours. An overhead cost is included. The agreement is really a "fixed-price" contract. That is, the production manager knows the total cost of the project in advance. A recent survey revealed that production managers have a high level of confidence in the engineers.

The ECD department manager oversees the work of about 40 engineers and 10 technicians. She reports to the engineering manager, who reports to the vice president of manufacturing. The ECD manager has the freedom to increase or decrease the number of engineers under her supervision. The ECD manager's performance evaluation is based on many factors including the annual incremental savings to the company in excess of the costs of operating the ECD department.

The production departments are profit centers. Their goods are transferred to subsequent departments, such as a sales department or sales division, at prices that approximate market prices for similar products.

Top management is seriously considering a "no-charge" plan. That is, production departments would receive engineering services at absolutely no cost. Proponents of the new plan maintain that it would motivate the production managers to take better advantage of engineering talent. In all other respects, the new system would be unchanged from the present system.

1. Compare the present and proposed plans. What are their strong and weak points? In particular, will the ECD manager tend to hire the "optimal" amount of engineering talent?

2. Which plan do you favor? Why?

10-53 Management by Objectives

Roger Chavez is the chief executive officer of Fresno Company. Chavez has a financial management background and is known throughout the organization as a "no-nonsense" executive. When Chavez became chief executive officer, he emphasized cost reduction and savings and introduced a comprehensive cost control and budget system. The company goals and budget plans were established by Chavez and given to his subordinates for implementation. Some of the company's key executives were dismissed or demoted for failing to meet projected budget plans. Under the leadership of Roger Chavez, Fresno has once again become financially stable and profitable after several years of poor performance.

Recently, Chavez has become concerned with the human side of the organization and has become interested in the management technique referred to as "management by objectives" (MBO). If there are enough positive benefits of MBO, he plans to implement the system throughout the company. However, he realizes that he does not fully understand MBO because he does not understand how it differs from the current system of establishing firm objectives and budget plans.

1. Briefly explain what MBO entails and identify its advantages and disadvantages.

2. Does Roger Chavez's management style incorporate the human value premises and goals of MBO? Explain your answer.

EXCEL Application Exercise

10-54 Return on investment and residual income

Goal: Create an Excel spreadsheet to calculate performance of divisional segments using the return on investment (ROI) and residual income (RI) methods. Use the results to answer questions about your findings.

Scenario: The company has asked you to calculate return on investment (ROI) and residual income (RI) for three divisions. The background data for your analysis appears in Fundamental Assignment Material 10-A1. Use an interest rate of 10% when calculating the capital charge.

When you have completed your spreadsheet, answer the following questions:
1. Which division has the best performance using the return on investment method? Using the residual income method?
2. Which division has the worst performance under both methods?
3. Based on your findings, what are your recommendations to management concerning which of these three divisions should receive an increase in invested capital?

Step-by-Step:
1. Open a new Excel spreadsheet.
2. In column A, create a bold-faced heading that contains the following:
   Row 1: Chapter 10 Decision Guideline
   Row 2: Divisions A, B and C
   Row 3: Measures of Profitability
   Row 4: Today's Date
3. Merge and center the four heading rows across columns A through I.
4. In row 7, create the following center-justified column headings:
   Column A: Division
   Column B: Invested Capital
   Column C: Revenue
   Column D: Income
   Column E: Capital Charge
   Column F: Residual Income
   Column G: Return on Investment
   Column H: Return on Sales
   Column I: Capital Turnover
5. Change the format of Residual Income and Return on Investment to bold-faced headings.
6. Change the format of the column headings in row 7 to permit the titles to be displayed on multiple lines within a single cell.

Alignment tab:	Wrap Text:	Checked

Note: Adjust column widths so the headings only use two lines.
Adjust row height to insure that row is same height as adjusted headings.

7. In column A, create the following center-justified row headings:
   Row 8: A
   Skip a row
   Row 10: B
   Skip a row
   Row 12: C
8. Use the scenario data to fill in invested capital, revenue, and income amounts for each division.
9. Use the scenario data and appropriate formulas to calculate capital charge amounts for each division.
10. Use the appropriate formulas from Chapter 10 to calculate residual income, return on investment, return on sales, and capital turnover amounts for each division.

11. Format amounts in columns B, C, D, E, and F for Division A as

Number tab:	Category:	Currency
	Decimal places:	0
	Symbol:	$
	Negative numbers:	Black with parenthesis

12. Format amounts in columns B, C, D, E, and F for Divisions B and C as

Number tab:	Category:	Currency
	Decimal places:	0
	Symbol:	None
	Negative numbers:	Black with parenthesis

13. Format amounts in columns G and H to display as percentages without decimal places.

Number tab:	Category:	Percentage
	Decimal places:	0

14. Format the capital turnover amounts to display two decimal places, followed by the word *times*.

Number tab:	Category:	Custom

From the Type list, highlight the type shown below:

	Type:	0.00

Change the data in the Type field from 0.00 to the following:

	Type:	0.00 "times"

Click the OK button.

15. Save your work to disk, and print a copy for your files.

Note: Print your spreadsheet using landscape in order to ensure that all columns appear on one page.

Collaborative Learning Exercise

10-55 Return on Investment

Form groups of three to six students. Each student should select a company. Coordinate the selection of companies so that each group has companies from a wide variety of industries. For example, a good mix of industries for a group of five students would be a retail company, a basic manufacturing company, a computer software company, a bank, and an electric utility.

1. Each student should find the latest annual report for his or her company. (The Internet is a good source. If you cannot find the company's home page, try http://www.sec.gov, and search the Security and Exchange Commission's Edgar files for the company's 10-K report, which will contain its financial statements.) Compute
   a. Return on sales.
   b. Capital turnover.
   c. Return on investment (ROI).

2. As a group, compare these performance measures for the chosen companies. Why do they differ across companies? What characteristic of the company and its industry might explain the differences in the measures?

Internet Exercise   www.prenhall.com/horngren

10-56 Decentralization at Marriott International

Decentralization of an organization can occur for many reasons. It may be that the organization is involved in multiple activities that are not closely related to each other, such as construction and auto sales. In other cases, the decision may be due to the structure of the firm's ownership and how it chooses to manage its image. Let's look at a firm that falls under this category—**Marriott International.**

1. Go to Marriott International's Web site at http://www.marriott.com. What does the home page emphasize about Marriott's operations? What promotional information does Marriott include on its home page?

2. How has Marriott decentralized its businesses? Do you suppose the divisions are cost centers, profit centers, or investment centers?

3. Go to the most recent annual report by clicking on "Corporate Information" on the home page and looking at SEC Filings. Locate the information on business segments in the footnotes. How many segments does Marriott identify? What are these segments? What information does the firm report with respect to each of the different segments?

4. Marriott provides both operating profit and assets for each of the segments. Calculate the operating return on average total assets for the past two years for each of the segments.

5. What was the operating return on average total assets for the corporation as a whole for each of the past two years? Given the different kinds of business segments the company has, do you think that operating return on average total assets would be a good measure for evaluating the individual segments? What factors might influence your answer?

6. Is Marriott likely to have any transfer prices? If Marriott has transfers, how do you suppose the company determines its transfer prices?

Capital Budgeting

CHAPTER 11

LEARNING OBJECTIVES

When you have finished studying this chapter, you should be able to:

1. Describe capital-budgeting decisions and use the net-present-value (NPV) method to make such decisions.

2. Evaluate projects using sensitivity analysis.

3. Calculate the NPV difference between two projects using both the total project and differential approaches.

4. Identify relevant cash flows for NPV analyses.

5. Compute the after-tax net present values of projects.

6. Explain the after-tax effect on cash of disposing of assets.

7. Use the payback model and the accounting rate-of-return model and compare them with the NPV model.

8. Reconcile the conflict between using an NPV model for making a decision and using accounting income for evaluating the related performance.

9. Appendix 11: Compute the impact of inflation on a capital-budgeting project.

Capital investment is probably the last thing you would

think of while schussing down the snow-covered slopes of the Rockies—unless you happen to be the manager of a ski resort. Where a resort guest sees slopes, chairlifts, and a nice warm lodge, a resort manager sees millions of dollars in investments.

Consider **Deer Valley Lodge**, a posh ski resort in the Wasatch Range in Utah. Deer Valley has a strong customer orientation—what Director of Finance Jim Madsen calls "the Deer Valley difference." From valets who help with skis to gourmet meals in the lodges, the offerings at Deer Valley make it a first-class resort. When facilities reach capacity, the resort limits sales of lift tickets to keep lift lines from getting too long. Each year Deer Valley officials invest in new, expanded, or remodeled facilities. For example, for the 2003–2004 season, they invested $6 million to expand their lodge, improve dining facilities, add glade skiing areas, and expand snowmaking into the Empire Canyon area.

Deer Valley keeps a ten-year plan for capital expansion. Recent investments included five new lifts that expanded operations into Empire Canyon, a day lodge, and a new parking facility. By continually measuring crowding, using measures such as waiting time for lifts and length of lines at restaurants and cafeterias, Deer Valley managers decide when the next capital expansion phase is needed.

Deer Valley completed a major capital expansion phase just before hosting part of the Olympic Winter Games in 2002. Deer Valley featured slalom and freestyle skiing, with slalom competition on a ski run called Know You Don't, moguls on Champion, and aerial events on White Owl. Now guests like you—if you are an excellent skier—can use these same runs yourself. Just as Olympic athletes hone their skills to compete in these events and weekend warriors test their ability and

Skiers do not often realize the planning and investment that go into preparing the slopes. However, managers at Deer Valley Lodge, a ski resort in Utah's Wasatch Range and one of the hosts of the 2002 Winter Olympics, understand this fully. Much effort goes into their capital-budgeting decisions—decisions that affect the enjoyment, comfort, and safety of their guests.

conditioning, Deer Valley managers must continually work to improve their facilities through additional capital investments. ■

Capital Budgeting for Programs or Projects

capital budgeting
The long-term planning for making and financing investments that affect financial results over a period longer than just the next year.

Ski resorts such as Deer Valley are not the only companies that face decisions about capital investment and expansion. At some time, every company needs to decide where and how to spend its money on major projects that will affect company financial results for years to come. This chapter concentrates on the planning and controlling decisions for programs or projects that affect financial results over a period longer than just the next year. Such decisions require investments of large amounts of resources—called capital outlays—in anticipation of future benefits. The term **capital budgeting** describes the long-term planning for making and financing such outlays.

Capital budgeting has three phases: (1) identifying potential investments, (2) choosing which investments to make (which includes gathering data to aid the decision), and (3) follow-up monitoring, or "postaudit," of the investments. Accountants usually are not involved in the first phase, but they play important roles in phases 2 and 3.

Why are accountants involved in capital-budgeting decisions? They function primarily as information specialists. One of the purposes of a cost management system is to provide cost measurements for strategic decisions such as major capital-budgeting decisions.

Accountants gather and interpret information to help managers make capital-budgeting decisions. To help organize what could be pages and pages worth of information, accountants rely on capital-budgeting models. Let's take a look at how some of these models work.

Discounted-Cash-Flow Models

discounted-cash-flow (DCF) models
A type of capital-budgeting model that focuses on cash inflows and outflows while taking into account the time value of money.

The most widely used capital-budgeting models are **discounted-cash-flow (DCF) models.** These models focus on a project's cash inflows and outflows while taking into account the time value of money. They are based on the old adage that a bird in the hand is worth two in the bush—that a dollar in the hand today is worth more than a dollar to be received (or spent) five years from today. This adage applies because the use of money has a cost (interest), just as the use of a building or an automobile may have a cost (rent). More than 85% of the large industrial firms in the United States use a DCF model. You can see how DCF applies to e-business companies in the Business First box on page 473.

Major Aspects of DCF

As the name suggests, DCF models focus on expected cash inflows and outflows rather than on net income. Companies invest cash today in order to receive cash in future periods. DCF models compare the value of today's cash outflows with the value of the future cash inflows.

DCF methods are based on the theory of compound interest, which you are probably familiar with from your course in financial accounting. If your knowledge of compound interest and time value of money is a little rusty, be sure to read Appendix B, pages 818–824. Do not try to learn about the DCF methods until you are able to use Tables 1 (p. 821) and 2 (p. 823) in Appendix B.

To illustrate how DCF models work, we will use the following example throughout the rest of this section: The ski-slope managers at Deer Valley Lodge are contemplating the purchase of new, more efficient snow-grooming equipment that they expect to

DOES DCF APPLY TO E-BUSINESS INVESTMENTS?

The e-business hype of the late 1990s seemed to crumble in the economic woes of 2001 and 2002. But by 2003, it became clear that e-business had not gone away. The economic shakeout identified the winners and losers—and there were plenty of both. The dot-com crash did not mark the end of e-business, but it more clearly defined what it took to be a winner in that venue. Companies who made wise investments in e-business prospered, while those who made unwise investments floundered or even disappeared.

One thing that differentiated winners from losers was how they evaluated capital investment decisions. In the e-business boom, many companies forgot the basic economics of investment analysis. Instead of focusing on cash flows and DCF analysis, companies touted their revenue per dollar of investment or, even worse, Web site hits per dollar of investment. They forgot that only net cash flows generate value. Increasing revenues are worthless if related expenses grow faster. And no one has gotten rich because of the number of visits to their Web site. There must be a way to turn these Web site visits into cash inflows.

Companies that focused on using the Internet and other e-business technologies to enhance profitability thrived. Those who used them simply to generate activity, with little attention to the profitability of that activity, struggled. *Business Week* identified some of the winners and losers:

Winners	Losers
Expedia	Hewlett-Packard
Amazon.com	Barnes & Noble
eBay	AOL Time Warner
Yahoo!	drkoop.com
Dell	many startups

How did the winners approach capital-budgeting decisions? First, they identified ways to generate cash—either new inflows or savings of outflows—that e-business solutions could produce. Their business plans showed at what point the company's e-business would become profitable and how profitable it would be. Second, they did not try to protect current business while simultaneously pursuing e-business. If customers were migrating to the Internet, brick-and-mortar companies would lose them anyway. And finally, they used DCF analysis. They realized that dollars in the future are worth less than those today so that they needed large future profits to justify investments that would not pay off in the short term.

Why did a company such as Amazon.com survive? Because the company met timelines for profitability of its individual product lines. Each new product line had a period of investment without profitability, but one by one its product lines met the cash flow predictions needed for ultimate profitablity. In fact, when Amazon announced a 28% sales increase in the first quarter of 2003, the press release first highlighted the positive cash flow that the company generated.

Also among the winners are many companies that the public does not see as e-business companies. The General Motors and Eli Lillys of the world have used e-business projects to great advantage. In fact, there was nearly $4 trillion worth of business-to-business e-business in 2003. Contrary to popular belief, investment in e-business projects continues to grow steadily, year after year, and predicted productivity growth was generally realized—much of that by mainstream companies that apply e-business principles to better achieve their objectives.

Investments in e-business ventures are still risky. However, companies that plan carefully for the cash flows using DCF analysis have a better chance of surviving and thriving than those who seek technology solutions for their own sake.

Sources: "The E-Business Surprise," *Business Week*, May 12, 2003, pp. 60–68; "Amazon.com Announces 28% Sales Growth Fueled by Lower Prices and Free Shipping," *Business Wire Press Release*, April 24, 2003.

increase efficiency and produce operating savings of $2,000 cash per year. The useful life of the equipment is four years, after which it will have a net disposal value of zero. The equipment will cost $6,075 now, and the minimum desired rate of return is 10% per year.

Net Present Value (NPV)

We will focus on the most popular version of DCF, the **net-present-value (NPV) method.** The NPV method computes the present value of all expected future cash flows using a minimum desired rate of return. The minimum desired rate of return depends on the risk

net-present-value (NPV) method
A discounted-cash-flow approach to capital budgeting that computes the present value of all expected future cash flows using a minimum desired rate of return.

Recent surveys have shown that nearly all large companies use discounted-cash-flow (DCF) methods for their capital-budgeting decisions. This is true in most of the developed countries in the world, not just the United States. But even as DCF is becoming dominant, it is being criticized by some for leading to overly cautious investment decisions in information technology (IT). The critics maintain that the benefits of IT investments are difficult to quantify and such investments lead to unforeseen opportunities. By ignoring some of the potential benefits and opportunities, companies pass up desirable IT investments.

Recently, experts have proposed two ways to rectify this situation. Both use the basic tenets of DCF analysis but add degrees of sophistication to help identify and value all the benefits of IT investments: (1) use of activity-based costing (ABC) to better define and quantify the benefits of IT investments, and (2) use of options pricing models to recognize the value of future options that result from IT investments.

Using ABC to better assess the benefits of an IT investment is simply a refinement in how to measure the cash flows for a DCF model. Scott Gamster of Grant Thornton's Performance Management Practice suggests that capital-budgeting analyses of IT investments often look primarily at the direct costs and benefits and ignore many of the savings in indirect costs. Because an ABC system focuses on indirect costs, it can help identify other cost impacts of new IT systems. The attention to activities lets managers better assess the various impacts on a new IT system. For example, an enterprise resource planning (ERP) system will transform much of the work in many of a company's activities. Examining each activity in light of the potential implementation of an ERP will help managers assess the full impact of the new system.

The other suggestion is to use options pricing theory for valuing IT investments. This is a refinement of DCF, not an alternative to it. The Yankee 24 shared electronic banking network in New England applied options pricing theory to the decision on timing of the deployment of point-of-sale debit services. The method explicitly recognizes the future opportunities created by a current investment decision, and it uses the complete range of possible outcomes to determine a potential investment's value. It is not our purpose to describe options pricing models; we leave that to the finance textbooks. However, the essence of the models is the impact of the possible future options on the value of a current investment decision. For example, investment today may eliminate the option of making a similar investment in six months when more information is available. Or investment today may create an infrastructure that will allow additional investments in the future that would not be otherwise possible. Limiting or expanding future options by today's investment decision can certainly affect the desirability of the investment.

Criticisms of DCF models for IT investments should lead to refinements of DCF, not rejection of it. Of course, if managers do not use refinements, they must use judgment regarding subjective impacts of the investment that are not measured in the DCF analysis.

Sources: Adapted from S. Gamster, "Using Activity Based Management to Justify ERP Implementations," *Journal of Cost Management*, September/October 1999, pp. 24–33; M. Benaroch and R. J. Kauffman, "A Case for Using Real Options Pricing Analysis to Evaluate Information Technology Project Investments," *Information Systems Research*, March 1999, pp. 70–76; G. C. Arnold and P. D. Aatzopoulos, "The Theory-Practice Gap in Capital Budgeting: Evidence from the United Kingdom," *Journal of Business Finance and Accounting*, June/July 2000, pp. 603–626; and M. Amram and K. M. Howe, "Real-Options Valuations: Taking Out the Rocket Science," *Strategic Management*, February 2003, pp. 10–13.

required rate of return (hurdle rate, discount rate)
The minimum desired rate of return, based on the firm's cost of capital.

of a proposed project—the higher the risk, the higher the rate. This minimum rate, called the **required rate of return, hurdle rate,** or **discount rate,** is based on the cost of capital—what the firm pays to acquire more capital. Using this required rate, managers determine the sum of the present values of all expected cash flows from the project. If this sum is positive, the project is desirable. If the sum is negative, the project is undesirable. Why? A positive NPV means that accepting the project will increase the value of the firm because the present value of the project's cash inflows exceeds the present value of its cash outflows. Similarly, a negative NPV means a decrease in the firm's value. (An NPV of zero means that the present value of the inflows equals the present value of the outflows, so the project will neither increase nor decrease the firm's value.) When choosing among several investments, managers should pick the one with the greatest net present value.

Applying the NPV Method

To apply the NPV method, you can use the following three steps, which we illustrate in Exhibit 11-1.

1. Prepare a diagram of relevant expected cash inflows and outflows: The right-hand side of Exhibit 11-1 shows how to sketch these cash flows. Outflows are in parentheses. Be sure to include the outflow at time zero, the date of acquisition. You do not have to use a sketch, but sketches do help you to see costs and cost relationships.
2. Find the present value of each expected cash inflow or outflow: Examine Table 1 in Appendix B on page 821. Find the present-value (PV) factor for each year's cash flow from the correct row and column of the table. Multiply each expected cash inflow or outflow by the appropriate present-value factor. For example, the $2,000 cash savings that will occur two years hence is worth $2,000 × .8264 = $1,653 today.
3. Sum the individual present values: The sum is the project's NPV. Accept a project whose NPV is positive, and reject a project whose NPV is negative.

The value today (at time zero) of the four $2,000 cash inflows is $6,340. The manager pays only $6,075 to obtain these cash inflows. Thus, the net present value is $6,340 − $6,075 = $265, so the investment is desirable.

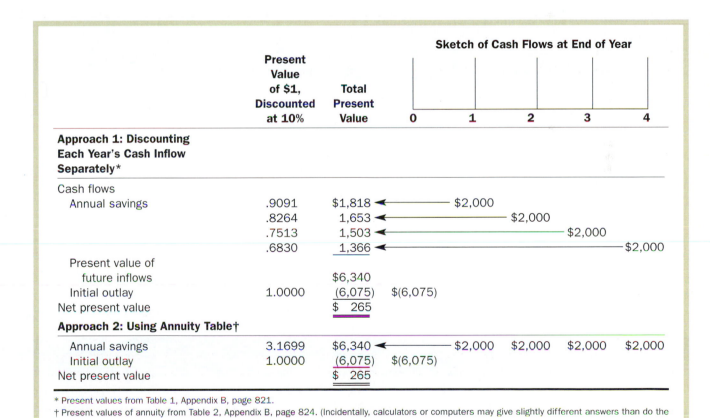

	Present Value of $1, Discounted at 10%	Total Present Value	Sketch of Cash Flows at End of Year				
			0	1	2	3	4
Approach 1: Discounting Each Year's Cash Inflow Separately*							
Cash flows							
Annual savings	.9091	$1,818 ◄———		$2,000			
	.8264	1,653 ◄———			$2,000		
	.7513	1,503 ◄———				$2,000	
	.6830	1,366 ◄———					$2,000
Present value of future inflows		$6,340					
Initial outlay	1.0000	(6,075)	$(6,075)				
Net present value		$ 265					
Approach 2: Using Annuity Table†							
Annual savings	3.1699	$6,340 ◄———		$2,000	$2,000	$2,000	$2,000
Initial outlay	1.0000	(6,075)	$(6,075)				
Net present value		$ 265					

* Present values from Table 1, Appendix B, page 821.
† Present values of annuity from Table 2, Appendix B, page 824. (Incidentally, calculators or computers may give slightly different answers than do the tables because of rounding differences.)

Exhibit 11-1
Net-Present-Value Method
Original investment, $6,075. Useful life, four years. Annual cash inflow from operations, $2,000. Minimum desired rate of return, 10%. Cash outflows are in parentheses; cash inflows are not. Total present values are rounded to the nearest dollar.

Choice of the Correct Table

Exhibit 11-1 also shows another way to calculate the NPV, shown as approach 2. The basic steps are the same as for approach 1. The only difference is that approach 2 uses Table 2 in Appendix B (see page 824) instead of Table 1. Table 2 is an annuity table that provides a shortcut to reduce hand calculations. It gives discount factors for computing the present value of a series of equal cash flows at equal intervals. Because the four cash flows in our example are all equal, you can use Table 2 to make one present-value computation instead of using Table 1 to make four individual computations. Table 2 merely sums up the pertinent present-value factors of Table 1. Therefore, the annuity factor for four years at 10% is[1]

$$.9091 + .8264 + .7513 + .6830 = 3.1698$$

Beware of using the wrong table. You should use Table 1 for discounting individual amounts, Table 2 for a series of equal amounts. Of course, Table 1 is the basis for Table 2, and you can use it for all present-value calculations if you wish.

You can avoid Tables 1 and 2 entirely by using the present-value function on a handheld calculator or the present-value function on a computer spreadsheet program. However, we encourage you to use the tables when learning the NPV method. Using the tables will let you better understand the process of present-value computation. Once you are comfortable with the method, you can take advantage of the speed and convenience of calculators and computers.

MAKING MANAGERIAL DECISIONS

Managers often find it useful to develop an intuitive feel for the effect of the time value of money. For each of the following three items, first estimate the amount and then compute the amount using a discount rate of 8%. Use Tables 1 and 2 from Appendix B.

1. Present value of $1,000 to be received in 5 years.
2. Present value of $1,000 to be received at the end of each year for 5 years.
3. Present value of $1,000 to be received at the end of years 3, 4, and 5.

Answers

Estimates will vary depending on your skill and experience with present value computations. The computed solutions follow.

The solution to number 1 requires the factor from row 5, 8% column of Table 1:

$$\$1,000 \times .6806 = \$680.60.$$

The solution to number 2 requires the factor from row 5, 8% column of Table 2:

$$\$1,000 \times 3.9927 = \$3,992.70.$$

The solution to number 3 can be done in several ways. Two of them are

Use only Table 2: $1,000 × (3.9927 − 1.7833) = $2,209.40
Use Tables 1 and 2: $1,000 × 2.5771 × .8573 = $2,209.35

These two solutions differ by a $.05 rounding error.

Effect of Minimum Rate

The minimum desired rate of return can have a large effect on NPVs. The higher the minimum desired rate of return, the lower the present value of each future cash inflow. Why? Because the higher the rate of return, the more it costs you to wait for the cash

---

[1]Rounding error causes a .0001 difference between the Table 2 factor and the summation of Table 1 factors.

rather than having it available to invest today. Thus, higher required rates lead to lower NPVs. For example, at a rate of 16%, the NPV of the project in Exhibit 11-1 would be −$479. That is, $2,000 × 2.7982 = $5,596, which is $479 less than the required investment of $6,075, instead of the +$265 computed with a 10% rate. (Present-value factor 2.7982 is taken from Table 2 in Appendix B on page 824.) When the desired rate of return is 16% rather than 10%, the project is undesirable at a cost of $6,075.

Assumptions of the NPV Model

We make two major assumptions when using the NPV model. First, we assume a world of certainty. That is, we act as if the predicted cash inflows and outflows are certain to occur at the times specified. Second, we assume perfect capital markets. That is, if we need to get extra cash or invest excess cash at any time, we can borrow or lend money at the same interest rate. This rate is our minimum desired rate of return. In a world that meets these assumptions, no model could possibly be better than the NPV model.

Unfortunately, the real world has neither certainty nor perfect capital markets. Nevertheless, the NPV model is usually preferred to other models because the assumptions of most other models are even less realistic. The NPV model is not perfect, but it generally meets our cost-benefit criterion. That is, the benefit of better decisions based on NPV is greater than the cost of applying it. More sophisticated models often do not improve decisions enough to be worth their cost.

Depreciation and NPV

NPV calculations do not include deductions for depreciation. Why not? Because NPV is based on inflows and outflows of cash and not on the accounting concepts of revenues and expenses.[2] Depreciation is not a cash flow. It is a way of allocating the cost of a long-lived asset (which a company usually pays for in cash upon purchase) to different periods. Because the company records and accounts for the cash outflow at the time of purchase, deducting depreciation from future cash flows would be like counting this cost twice—once at purchase and again over the asset's life.

Review of Decision Rules

Be sure that you understand why the NPV method works, not just how to apply it. The decision maker in our example cannot directly compare an immediate outflow of $6,075 with a series of future inflows of $2,000 each because of the time value of money. The NPV model aids comparison by expressing all amounts in today's monetary units (such as dollars, francs, marks, or yen) at time zero. The required rate of return measures the cost of using money. At a rate of 12%, the comparison is

Outflow in today's dollars	$(6,075)
Inflow equivalent in today's dollars @ 12%	6,075*
Net present value	$ 0

* $2,000 × 3.0373 from table 2 = $6,075.

Therefore, at a required rate of return of 12%, the decision maker is indifferent between having $6,075 now or having a stream of four annual inflows of $2,000 each. If

---

[2] Throughout this chapter, our examples often assume that cash inflows are equivalent to revenues and that cash outflows are equivalent to expenses (except for depreciation). Of course, if we account for the revenues and expenses on the accrual basis of accounting, there will be leads and lags of cash inflows and cash outflows that a precise DCF model must recognize. For example, we might record a $10,000 sale on credit as revenue in one period but not recognize the related cash inflow in a DCF model until collected, which may be in a second period. We do not make such refinements in this chapter.

the interest rate were 16%, the decision maker would find the project unattractive because the net present value would be a negative $479. The following graph shows the relationship between the required rate of return and the project's NPV.

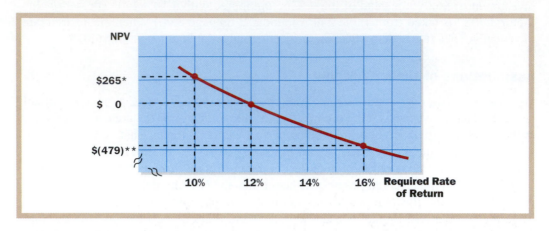

* ($2,000 × 3.1699) − $6,075 = $265
** ($2,000 × 2.7982) − $6,075 = $(479)

At 10%, the NPV is a positive $265, so the project is desirable. At all rates below 12%, the NPV is positive. At all rates above 12%, the NPV is negative.

Internal Rate of Return (IRR) Model

internal rate of return (IRR) model
A capital-budgeting model that determines the interest rate at which the NPV equals zero.

Another popular DCF model is the **internal rate of return (IRR) model.** This model determines the interest rate at which the NPV equals zero. If this rate, called the internal rate of return, is greater than the minimum desired rate of return, a project is desirable. If not, it is undesirable. Finance textbooks provide descriptions of the IRR method, and we will not go into details here. However, in most cases the IRR method gives equivalent decisions to the NPV method. In our example, the IRR is 12%; that is, the NPV of the equipment is zero using an interest rate of 12%. Thus, at our minimum desired rate of return of 10% (or any rate less than 12%) we accept the project. At any minimum desired rate above 12% we would reject it. In general, we find that:

> *If IRR > minimum desired rate of return, then NPV > 0 and we should accept the project*
> *If IRR < minimum desired rate of return, then NPV < 0 and we should reject the project*

Because of the equivalence of NPV and IRR models for most investment proposals, we will use the NPV model for all the illustrations in this chapter.

Real Options

real options model
A capital-budgeting model that recognizes the value of contingent investments— that is, investments that a company can adjust as it learns more about their potential for success.

Whereas the IRR model is generally equivalent to the NPV model, the use of real options is an improvement on NPV. It is more sophisticated, and only a few companies are using it for routine capital-budgeting decisions. But it is an important innovation that is sure to grow in popularity. Like the IRR model, we will leave the details to the finance textbooks. A **real options model** recognizes the value of contingent investments—that is, investments that a company can adjust as it learns more about their potential for success. For example, a project that a company can implement in stages, where investment in one stage occurs only if the previous stage was successful, has an advantage over an "all or nothing" project, one where the entire investment must take place up front. Even if the expected NPV of a staged investment is less (possibly because of the loss of efficiency when the entire investment process does not occur at the same time), it might be a preferred project if the company gains enough information in the early stages to make better decisions in the later stages.

Sensitivity Analysis and Risk Assessment in DCF Models

Because the future is uncertain, actual cash inflows may differ from what was expected or predicted. To quantify this uncertainty, managers often use sensitivity analysis, which shows the financial consequences that would occur if actual cash inflows and outflows differ from those expected. It can answer such what-if questions as: What will happen to my NPV if my predictions of useful life or cash flows change? The best way to understand sensitivity analysis is to see it in action, so let's take a look at an example.

Suppose the Deer Valley managers know that the actual cash inflows in Exhibit 11-1 could fall below the predicted level of $2,000. How far below $2,000 must the annual cash inflow drop before the NPV becomes negative? The cash inflow at the point where NPV = 0 is the "break-even" cash flow:

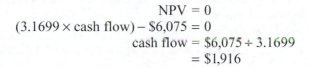

$$NPV = 0$$
$$(3.1699 \times \text{cash flow}) - \$6,075 = 0$$
$$\text{cash flow} = \$6,075 \div 3.1699$$
$$= \$1,916$$

If the annual cash inflow is less than $1,916, the NPV is negative, and the managers should reject the project. Therefore, annual cash inflows can drop only $2,000 − $1,916 = $84, or 4.2%, before the managers would change their decision.

Managers like sensitivity analysis because it can give them immediate answers about possible future events. It also shows managers how risky a given project might be by showing how sensitive the decision is to changes in predictions. If a project has a positive NPV that would become negative with only a small change in cash flows, it can be a risky project. Of course, sensitivity analysis can become complicated very quickly, and doing all of the calculations by hand can be tricky and tedious. Fortunately, there is a good deal of sensitivity analysis software available that lets managers and accountants sit back while computers do all the work.

The NPV Comparison of Two Projects

So far we have seen how to use the NPV method to evaluate a single given project. In practice, managers very rarely look at only one project or option at a time. Instead, managers need to compare several options to see which is the best or most profitable. We will now see how to use NPV to compare two or more alternatives.

Total Project Versus Differential Approach

Two common methods for comparing alternatives are (1) the total project approach and (2) the differential approach.

The **total project approach** computes the total impact on cash flows for each alternative and then converts these total cash flows to their present values. It is the most popular approach, and we can use it for any number of alternatives. The alternative with the largest NPV of total cash flows is best.

The **differential approach** computes the differences in cash flows between alternatives and then converts these differences to their present values. We cannot use this method to compare more than two alternatives. Often, the two alternatives being compared are (1) take on a project and (2) do nothing.

O B J E C T I V E **2**
Evaluate projects using sensitivity analysis.

O B J E C T I V E **3**
Calculate the NPV difference between two projects using both the total project and differential approaches.

total project approach
A method for comparing alternatives that computes the total impact on cash flows for each alternative and then converts these total cash flows to their present values.

differential approach
A method for comparing alternatives that computes the differences in cash flows between alternatives and then converts these differences in cash flows to their present values.

Let's compare the differential and total project approaches. Consider a motor that drives one of the ski lifts at Deer Valley Lodge. Assume that the lodge purchased the motor three years ago for $56,000. It has a remaining useful life of five years but will require a major overhaul at the end of two more years at a cost of $10,000. Its disposal value now is $20,000. Its predicted disposal value in five years is $8,000, assuming that the company does the $10,000 major overhaul on schedule. The predicted cash-operating costs of this motor are $40,000 annually. A sales representative has offered a substitute motor for $51,000. The new motor will reduce annual cash-operating costs by $10,000, will not require any overhauls, will have a useful life of five years, and will have a disposal value of $3,000. If the minimum desired rate of return is 14%, what should Deer Valley do to minimize long-run costs? (Try to solve this problem yourself before examining the solution that follows.)

Regardless of the approach used, perhaps the hardest part of making capital-budgeting decisions is predicting the relevant cash flows. Seeing which events will cause money to flow either in or out can be tricky, especially when there are many sources of cash flows. However, you cannot compare alternatives if you do not know their cash flows, so the first step for either the total project or differential approach is to arrange the relevant cash flows by project. Exhibit 11-2 sketches the cash flows for each alternative. The next step depends on the approach we choose.

Total Project Approach: Determine the net present value of the cash flows for each individual project. Choose the project with the largest positive net present value or smallest negative net present value. Exhibit 11-2 shows that the NPV of replacing the motor, −132,435, is better than the −$140,864 NPV of keeping the old motor. The advantage is $140,864 − $132,435 = $8,429. Most cash flows are negative because these are costs of operating the motor. The alternative with the lowest cost—the smallest negative NPV— is the most desirable.

Differential Approach: Compute the differential cash flows. In other words, subtract the cash flows for project B from the cash flows for project A for each year. Remember that cash inflows are positive numbers, while cash outflows are negative. Next, calculate the present value of the differential cash flows. If this present value is positive, choose project A; if it is negative, choose project B. Whereas the total project approach computed the difference in the NPVs of the two projects, the differential method computes the NPV of the difference in cash flows of the two projects. Both give the same total difference, a $8,429 advantage to replacement.

Exhibit 11-2 illustrates that both methods produce the same answer. As a result, you can use these methods interchangeably, as long as you are considering only two alternatives. If our example had more than two alternatives, our only choice would be to use the total project approach.

Relevant Cash Flows for NPV

OBJECTIVE 4

Identify relevant cash flows for NPV analyses.

As we said earlier, predicting cash flows is the hardest part of capital budgeting. When you array the relevant cash flows, be sure to consider four types of inflows and outflows: (1) initial cash inflows and outflows at time zero, (2) investments in receivables and inventories, (3) future disposal values, and (4) operating cash flows.

Initial Cash Inflows and Outflows at Time Zero These cash flows include both outflows for the purchases and installation of equipment and other items required by the new project and either inflows or outflows from disposal of any items that are replaced. In Exhibit 11-2, we subtracted the $20,000 received from selling the old machine from the $51,000 purchase price of the new machine, resulting in a net cash outflow of $31,000. If the company could not sell the old machine, we would have to add any cost incurred to dismantle and discard it to the purchase price of the new machine.

Sketch of After-Tax Cash Flows at End of Year

	Present Value Discount Factor, at 14%	Total Present Value	0	1	2	3	4	5
I. Total Project Approach								
A. Replace								
Recurring cash operating costs, using an annuity table*	3.4331	$ (102,993)		($30,000)	($30,000)	($30,000)	($30,000)	($30,000)
Disposal value, end of year 5	.5194	1,558						$3,000
Initial required investment	1.0000	(31,000)	($31,000)					
Present value of net cash outflows		$ (132,435)						
B. Keep								
Recurring cash operating costs, using an annuity table*	3.4331	$ (137,324)		($40,000)	($40,000)	($40,000)	($40,000)	($40,000)
Overhaul, end of year 2	.7695	(7,695)			$(10,000)			
Disposal value, end of year 5	.5194	4,155						$8,000
Present value of net cash outflows		$ (140,864)						
Difference in favor of replacement		$ 8,429						
II. Differential Approach								
A–B. Analysis confined to differences								
Recurring cash operating savings, using an annuity table*	3.4331	$ 34,331		$10,000	$10,000	$10,000	$10,000	$10,000
Overhaul avoided, end of year 2	.7695	7,695			$10,000			
Difference in disposal values, end of year 5	.5194	(2,597)						$(5,000)
Incremental initial investment	1.0000	(31,000)	($31,000)					
Net present value of replacement		$ 8,429						

* Table 2, Appendix B.

Exhibit 11-2

Total Project Versus Differential Approach to Net Present Value

Investments in Working Capital Companies that use predictions of *cash inflows* from sales (rather than revenues) and *cash outflows* for expenses (rather than accrual expenses such as cost of goods sold) in their capital-budgeting model need not be concerned with separately accounting for investments in working capital. However, companies that use accrual measures of revenue and expenses as approximations to cash flows must recognize their need for working capital, primarily receivables plus inventories less payables, as an additional investment. Investments in working capital are initial cash outflows just like investments in plant and equipment. In the NPV model, we enter the initial outlays in the sketch of cash flows at time zero. However, working capital often differs from plant and equipment at the end of the useful life of the project. We usually use up plant and equipment during the life of the project, leaving little, if any, salvage value. In contrast, the working capital is typically still available when the project ends. Therefore, we regard whatever working capital that remains as an inflow at the end of the project's useful life. The difference between the initial outlay for working capital (mostly receivables and inventory) and its present value when recovered at the end of the project's life is the cost of using working capital in the project.

MAKING MANAGERIAL DECISIONS

Consider the expansion of Deer Valley's gift shop. Suppose it entails an additional investment of $10,000 in a building and fixtures that have a 20-year life and a $1,000 salvage value at the end of 20 years. It also entails an initial investment of cash of $6,000 for inventories at time zero. Deer Valley will sell the initial inventory in year 1 and will replace it with a new inventory that it buys for $6,000 cash. It will do this each year through year 19. However, it will not replace the inventory that it sells in year 20 because no sales will occur beyond the end of the project's life. Assume that Deer Valley uses revenues and expenses as approximations to cash flows each year as shown in the table below. Complete the sketch of cash flows by adding the net cash flows for inventory (a, b, c, d, and e) in the table.

so on through year 19. Thus, years 1 through 19 have both an expense and a cash flow for inventory of $6,000. The expense is an acceptable measure of the cash flow each of those years. Thus, we record no additional investment in inventories, and $b = c = d = \$0$. However, in year 20 there is only an expense of $6,000 with no cash outflow. Since the expense overstates the cash outflow by $6,000, we must add a $6,000 cash inflow to the investment in working capital, making $e = \$6,000$. Essentially, this represents the recoupment of the $6,000 originally spent for inventory. The investment in working capital (in this case, only inventory) recognizes this difference between accrual measures of revenue and expense and the cash flow measure used for capital budgeting. As the table shows, the residual value of

Sketch of Cash Flows

End of year	0	1	2 ...	19	20
Investment in building and fixtures	$(10,000)				$1,000
Investment in working capital (inventories)	a	b	c	d	e
Revenue (an approximation for cash inflow)	$0	12,000	12,000 ...	12,000	12,000
Cost of goods sold (an approximation for cash outflow)	$0	(6,000)	(6,000) ...	(6,000)	(6,000)

Answer

We pay $6,000 at time zero for inventories, so $a = \$(6,000)$. This becomes a $6,000 expense (cost of goods sold) in year 1, when we spend another $6,000 to buy inventory, and

the building and fixtures might be small. However, the gift shop would ordinarily recover the entire investment in inventories when the company terminates the venture.

Future Disposal Values Assets may have relevant disposal values. The disposal value at the end of a project is an increase in the cash inflow in the year of disposal. Errors in forecasting terminal disposal values are usually not crucial because the present value is usually small.

Operating Cash Flows The major purpose of most investments is to affect operating cash inflows and outflows. Many of these effects are difficult to measure, and three points deserve special mention.

1. The only relevant cash flows are those that will differ among alternatives. Often fixed overhead will be the same under all the available alternatives. If so, you can safely ignore it. In practice, it is not easy to identify exactly which costs will differ among alternatives.
2. As mentioned earlier, ignore depreciation and book values. We recognize the cost of assets by the initial outlay, not by depreciation as computed under accrual accounting.
3. We treat a reduction in a cash outflow the same as a cash inflow. Both signify increases in value.

Cash Flows for Investments in Technology

Many capital-budgeting decisions compare undertaking a possible investment with doing nothing. One such decision is investment in a highly automated production system to replace a traditional system. Cash flows predicted for the automated system should be compared with those predicted for continuation of the present system into the future. The latter are not necessarily the cash flows currently being experienced. Why? Because the competitive environment is changing. If others invest in automated systems, failure to invest may cause a decline in sales and an uncompetitive cost structure. The future without an automated system might be a continual decline in cash flows.

Suppose a company has a $10,000 net cash inflow this year using a traditional system. Investing in an automated system will increase the net cash inflow to $12,000. Failure to invest will cause net cash inflows to fall to $8,000. The benefit from the investment is a cash inflow of $12,000 − $8,000 = $4,000, not $12,000 − $10,000 = $2,000.

Summary Problem For Your Review

PROBLEM

Review the problem and solution shown in Exhibit 11-2, page 481. Conduct a sensitivity analysis as indicated below. Consider each numbered item as independent of the others.

1. Compute the NPV if the minimum desired rate of return were 20%.
2. Compute the NPV if predicted cash operating costs were $35,000 instead of $30,000, using the 14% discount rate.
3. By how much may the cash operating savings fall short of the $30,000 predicted before the NPV of the project reaches zero, using the original discount rate of 14%?

SOLUTION

1. You can use either the total project approach or the differential approach. The differential approach shows

	Total Present Value
Recurring cash operating savings, using an annuity table (Table 2, p. 824): 2.9906 × $10,000 =	$29,906
Overhaul avoided: .6944 × $10,000 =	6,944
Difference in disposal values: .4019 × $5,000 =	(2,010)
Incremental initial investment	(31,000)
NPV of replacement	$ 3,840

2.

NPV value in Exhibit 11-2	$ 8,429
Present value of additional $5,000 annual operating costs 3.4331 × $5,000	(17,166)
New NPV	$ (8,737)

With $5,000 less in annual savings, the new machine has a negative NPV and therefore is not desirable.

3. Let X = annual cash operating savings and find the value of X so that NPV = 0. Then

$$0 = 3.4331(X) + \$7,695 - \$2,597 - \$31,000$$
$$3.4331X = \$25,902$$
$$X = \$7,545$$

(Note that the $7,695, $2,597, and $31,000 are at the bottom of Exhibit 11-2.)

If the annual savings fall from $10,000 to $7,545, a decrease of $2,455 or almost 25%, the NPV will hit zero.

An alternative way to obtain the same answer would be to divide the NPV of $8,429 (see bottom of Exhibit 11-2) by 3.4331, obtaining $2,455, the amount of the annual difference in savings that will eliminate the $8,429 of NPV.

Income Taxes and Capital Budgeting

We must consider another type of cash flow when making capital-budgeting decisions: income taxes. Income taxes paid by companies are cash outflows. Their basic role in capital budgeting does not differ from that of any other cash outflow. However, taxes tend to narrow the cash differences between projects. For example, if the cash savings from operations of one project over another were $1 million, a 40% tax rate would shrink the savings to $600,000. Why? Because the company would have to pay $400,000 (40% × $1 million) of the savings in taxes.

Corporations in the United States must pay both federal income taxes and state income taxes. Federal taxes are based on income, with tax rates rising as income rises. The current federal tax rate on ordinary corporate taxable income below $50,000 is 15%. Rates then increase until companies with taxable income over $335,000 pay between 34% and 38% on additional income. State tax rates vary widely from state to state. Therefore, the total tax rate a company has to pay, federal rates plus state rates, also varies widely.

In capital budgeting, the relevant tax rate is the **marginal income tax rate,** that is, the tax rate paid on additional amounts of pretax income. Suppose a corporation pays income taxes of 15% on the first $50,000 of pretax income and 30% on pretax income over $50,000. What is the company's marginal income tax rate when it has $75,000 of pretax

OBJECTIVE 5

Compute the after-tax net present values of projects.

marginal income tax rate

The tax rate paid on additional amounts of pretax income.

income? The marginal rate is 30%, because the company will pay 30% of any additional income in taxes. In contrast, the company's average income tax rate is only 20% (that is, 15% × $50,000 + 30% × $25,000 = $15,000 of taxes on $75,000 of pretax income). When we assess tax effects of capital-budgeting decisions, we will always use the marginal tax rate because that is the rate applied to the additional cash flows generated by a proposed project.

Effects of Depreciation Deductions

Organizations that pay income taxes generally keep two sets of books—one for reporting to the public and one for reporting to the tax authorities. In the United States, this practice is not illegal or immoral—in fact, it is necessary. Tax reporting must follow detailed rules designed to achieve certain social goals. These rules do not usually lead to financial statements that best measure an organization's financial results and position, so it is more informative to financial statement users if companies use a separate set of rules for financial reporting. In this chapter, we are concerned with measuring cash payments for taxes. Therefore, we focus on the tax reporting rules, not those for public financial reporting.

One item that often differs between tax reporting and public reporting is depreciation. Recall that depreciation spreads the cost of an asset over its useful life. Income tax laws and regulations generally permit companies to spread the cost over depreciable lives that are shorter than the assets' useful lives. In addition, U.S. tax authorities allow **accelerated depreciation,** which charges a larger proportion of an asset's cost to the earlier years and less to later years. In contrast, an asset's depreciation for public reporting purposes is usually the same each year, called straight-line depreciation. For example, a $10,000 asset depreciated over a five-year useful life results in straight-line depreciation of $10,000 ÷ 5 = $2,000 each year but accelerated depreciation of more than $2,000 per year in the early years and less than $2,000 in the later years.

Exhibit 11-3 shows the interrelationship of income before taxes, income taxes, and depreciation for a hypothetical asset owned by Deer Valley Lodge. Assume that Deer

accelerated depreciation
A pattern of depreciation that charges a larger proportion of an asset's cost to the earlier years and less to later years.

Exhibit 11-3
Deer Valley Lodge—
Snowmaking Machine
Basic Analysis of Income Statement, Income Taxes, and Cash Flows

	Traditional Annual Income Statement	
(S)	Sales	$130,000
(E)	Less: Expenses, excluding depreciation	$ 70,000
(D)	Depreciation (straight-line)	25,000
	Total expenses	$ 95,000
	Income before taxes	$ 35,000
(T)	Income taxes @ 40%	14,000
(I)	Net income	$ 21,000
	Total after-tax effect on cash is	
	either S − E − T = $130,000 − $70,000 − $14,000	
	= $46,000 or I + D = $21,000 + $25,000 = $46,000	

	Analysis of the Same Facts for Capital Budgeting	
	Cash effects of operations:	
(S − E)	Cash inflow from operations: $130,000 − $70,000	$ 60,000
	Income tax outflow @ 40%	24,000
	After-tax inflow from operations (excluding depreciation)	$ 36,000
	Cash effects of depreciation:	
(D)	Straight-line depreciation: $125,000 ÷ 5 = $25,000	
	Income tax savings @ 40%	10,000
	Total after-tax effect on cash	$ 46,000

recovery period
The number of years over which a company can depreciate an asset for tax purposes.

Valley has a snowmaking machine that it purchased for $125,000 cash. The machine has a five-year **recovery period,** which is the number of years over which a company can depreciate an asset for tax purposes. Using the machine produces annual sales revenue of $130,000 and expenses (excluding depreciation) of $70,000. The purchase cost of the machine is tax deductible in the form of yearly depreciation.

Depreciating a fixed asset such as the snowmaking machine creates future tax deductions. In this case, these deductions will total the full purchase price of $125,000. The present value of this deduction depends directly on its specific yearly effects on future income tax payments. Therefore, the recovery period, the depreciation method selected, the tax rates, and the discount rate all affect the present value.

Exhibit 11-4 analyzes Deer Valley's data for capital budgeting, assuming that the company uses straight-line depreciation for tax purposes. The net present value is $40,821 for the investment in this asset.

The $125,000 investment really buys two streams of cash: (1) net inflows from operations plus (2) savings of income tax outflows (which have the same effect in capital budgeting as do additions to cash inflows) because the company can deduct depreciation in computing taxable income. The choice of depreciation method will not affect the cash inflows from operations. But different depreciation methods will affect the cash outflows for income taxes. That is, a straight-line method will produce one present value of tax savings, and an accelerated method will produce a different present value.

Tax Deductions, Cash Effects, and Timing

Note that we computed the net cash effects of operations in Exhibit 11-4 by multiplying the pretax amounts by one minus the tax rate, or $1 - .40 = .60$. The total effect is the

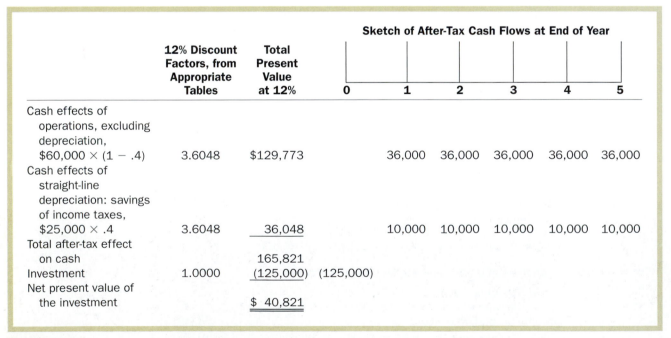

	12% Discount Factors, from Appropriate Tables	Total Present Value at 12%	Sketch of After-Tax Cash Flows at End of Year					
			0	1	2	3	4	5
Cash effects of operations, excluding depreciation, $60,000 × (1 − .4)	3.6048	$129,773		36,000	36,000	36,000	36,000	36,000
Cash effects of straight-line depreciation: savings of income taxes, $25,000 × .4	3.6048	36,048		10,000	10,000	10,000	10,000	10,000
Total after-tax effect on cash		165,821						
Investment	1.0000	(125,000)	(125,000)					
Net present value of the investment		$ 40,821						

Exhibit 11-4
Impact of Income Taxes on Capital-Budgeting Analysis
Assume: original cost of equipment, $125,000; 5-year life; zero terminal disposal value; pretax annual cash inflow from operations, $60,000; income tax rate, 40%; required after-tax rate of return, 12%. All items are in dollars except discount factors. The after-tax cash flows are from Exhibit 11-3.

cash flow itself less the tax effect. Each additional $1 of sales also adds $.40 of taxes, leaving a net cash inflow of $.60. Each additional $1 of cash expense reduces taxes by $.40, leaving a net cash outflow of $.60. Thus, the after-tax effect of the $130,000 − $70,000 = $60,000 net cash inflow from operations is an after-tax inflow of $130,000 × .6 − $70,000 × .6 = ($130,000 − $70,000) × .6 = $60,000 × .6 = $36,000.

In contrast, we compute the after-tax effects of the noncash expenses (depreciation) by multiplying the tax deduction of $25,000 by the tax rate itself, or $25,000 × .40 = $10,000. Note that this is a cash inflow because it is a decrease in the tax payment. The total cash effect of a noncash expense is only the tax-savings effect.

Throughout the illustrations in this chapter, we assume that all income tax flows occur at the same time as the related pretax cash flows. For example, we assume that both the net $60,000 pretax cash inflow and the related $24,000 tax payment occurred in year 1 and that the company could delay no part of the tax payment until year 2. We also assume that the companies in question are profitable. That is, the companies will have enough taxable income from all sources to use all income tax benefits in the situations described.

Accelerated Depreciation

Governments frequently allow accelerated depreciation to encourage investments in long-lived assets. To see why accelerated depreciation is attractive to investors, reconsider the facts in Exhibit 11-4. Suppose that, as is the case in some countries, companies can write off immediately the entire initial investment for income tax reporting. We see that net present value will rise from $40,821 to $54,773.

	Present Values	
	As in Exhibit 11-4	**Complete Write-Off Immediately**
Cash effects of operations	$129,773	$ 129,773
Cash effects of depreciation	36,048	50,000*
Total after-tax effect on cash	165,821	179,773
Investment	(125,000)	(125,000)
Net present value	$ 40,821	$ 54,773

* Assumes that the tax effect occurs simultaneously with the investment at time zero: $125,000 × .40 = $50,000.

In summary, the earlier you can take the depreciation, the greater the present value of the income tax savings. The total tax savings will be the same regardless of the depreciation method. In the example, the tax savings from the depreciation deduction is either .40 × $125,000 = $50,000 immediately or .40 × $25,000 = $10,000 per year for five years, a total of $50,000. However, the time value of money makes the immediate savings worth more than future savings. The mottoes in income tax planning are "When there is a legal choice, take the deduction sooner rather than later," and "Recognize taxable income later rather than sooner."

Managers have an obligation to stockholders to minimize and delay taxes to the extent permitted by law. For example, astute managers use accelerated depreciation instead of straight-line depreciation whenever the law permits its use. We call this tax avoidance. Careful tax planning can have large financial payoffs. In contrast, managers must not engage in tax evasion, which is illegally reducing taxes by recording fictitious deductions or failing to report income. Managers who avoid taxes get bonuses; those who evade taxes often land in jail.

Sometimes the line between tax avoidance and tax evasion is not clear. Pundits have called attempts to exploit this gray area "creative tax avoidance." Schemes that are not strictly illegal but are certainly at odds with the intent of the tax laws fall into this category. For example, authorities have accused executives at Tyco with minimizing taxes using methods that might be legal but are not ethical. While there is debate on whether everything that is legal is also ethical, there are certain tax minimizing schemes that are clearly illegal and unethical. If true, allegations that Tyco executives prepared false invoices and shipped empty boxes to the conglomerate's executive offices in New Hampshire to fool tax authorities represented behavior that is both illegal and unethical.

Modified Accelerated Cost Recovery System (MACRS)

modified accelerated cost recovery system (MACRS)
The method companies use to depreciate most assets under U.S. income tax laws.

Under U.S. income tax laws, companies depreciate most assets using the **modified accelerated cost recovery system (MACRS).** This system specifies a recovery period and an accelerated depreciation schedule for all types of assets. The MACRS system places each asset in one of the eight classes shown in Exhibit 11-5.

Exhibit 11-6 presents MACRS depreciation schedules for recovery periods of 3, 5, 7, and 10 years. Note that each schedule extends one year beyond the recovery period because MACRS assumes one half-year of depreciation in the first year and one half-year in the final year. Thus, a 3-year MACRS depreciation schedule has one half-year of depreciation in years 1 and 4 and a full year of depreciation in years 2 and 3. We can apply MACRS depreciation to the example in Exhibit 11-4 as follows, assuming that the snowmaking machine that Deer Valley purchased is a 5-year MACRS asset.

Exhibit 11-5
Examples of Assets in Modified Accelerated Cost Recovery System (MACRS) Classes

3-year	Special tools for several specific industries; tractor units for over-the-road.
5-year	Automobiles; trucks; research equipment; computers; machinery and equipment in selected industries.
7-year	Office furniture; railroad tracks; machinery and equipment in a majority of industries.
10-year	Water transportation equipment; machinery and equipment in selected industries.
15-year	Most land improvements; machinery and equipment in selected industries.
20-year	Farm buildings; electricity generation and distribution equipment.
27.5-year	Residential rental property.
31.5-year	Nonresidential real property.

Exhibit 11-6
Selected MACRS Depreciation Schedules

Tax Year	3-Year Property	5-Year Property	7-Year Property	10-Year Property
1	33.33%	20.00%	14.29%	10.00%
2	44.45	32.00	24.49	18.00
3	14.81	19.20	17.49	14.40
4	7.41	11.52	12.49	11.52
5		11.52	8.93	9.22
6		5.76	8.92	7.37
7			8.93	6.55
8			4.46	6.55
9				6.56
10				6.55
11				3.28

Year	Tax Rate (1)	PV Factor @ 12% (2)	Depreciation (3)	Present Value of Tax Savings (1) × (2) × (3)
1	.40	0.8929	$125,000 × .2000 = $25,000	$ 8,929
2	.40	0.7972	125,000 × .3200 = 40,000	12,755
3	.40	0.7118	125,000 × .1920 = 24,000	6,833
4	.40	0.6355	125,000 × .1152 = 14,400	3,660
5	.40	0.5674	125,000 × .1152 = 14,400	3,268
6	.40	0.5066	125,000 × .0576 = 7,200	1,459
				$36,904

How much did Deer Valley gain by using MACRS instead of straight-line depreciation? The $36,904 present value of tax savings is $856 higher with MACRS than the $36,048 achieved with straight-line depreciation (see Exhibit 11-4 on p. 486).

Present Value of MACRS Depreciation

In capital-budgeting decisions, managers often want to know the present value of the tax savings from depreciation. Exhibit 11-7 provides present values for $1 to be depreciated over MACRS schedules for 3-, 5-, 7-, and 10-year recovery periods for a variety of interest rates. For example, consider a company with a 3-year asset and 10% minimum desired rate of return. The present value of $1 of MACRS depreciation is

Year	Depreciation* (1)	PV Factor @ 10% (2)	PV of Depreciation (1) × (2)
1	$0.3333	0.9091	$0.3030
2	0.4445	0.8264	0.3673
3	0.1481	0.7513	0.1113
4	0.0741	0.6830	0.0506
Total Depreciation	$1.0000		
Present Value of $1 depreciation, shown in Exhibit 11-7			$0.8322

* From the 3-Year Property column of Exhibit 11-6.

Exhibit 11-7
Present Value of $1 of MACRS Depreciation

Discount Rate	3-year	5-year	7-year	10-year
3%	0.9439	0.9215	0.9002	0.8698
4%	0.9264	0.8975	0.8704	0.8324
5%	0.9095	0.8746	0.8422	0.7975
6%	0.8931	0.8526	0.8155	0.7649
7%	0.8772	0.8315	0.7902	0.7344
8%	0.8617	0.8113	0.7661	0.7059
9%	0.8468	0.7919	0.7432	0.6792
10%	0.8322	0.7733	0.7214	0.6541
12%	0.8044	0.7381	0.6810	0.6084
14%	0.7782	0.7055	0.6441	0.5678
15%	0.7657	0.6902	0.6270	0.5492
16%	0.7535	0.6753	0.6106	0.5317
18%	0.7300	0.6473	0.5798	0.4993
20%	0.7079	0.6211	0.5517	0.4702
22%	0.6868	0.5968	0.5257	0.4439
24%	0.6669	0.5740	0.5019	0.4201
25%	0.6573	0.5631	0.4906	0.4090
26%	0.6479	0.5526	0.4798	0.3985
28%	0.6299	0.5327	0.4594	0.3787
30%	0.6128	0.5139	0.4404	0.3606
40%	0.5381	0.4352	0.3632	0.2896

You can find the present value of tax savings in three steps:

1. Find the factor from Exhibit 11-7 for the appropriate recovery period and required rate of return.
2. Multiply the factor by the tax rate to find the tax savings per dollar of investment.
3. Multiply the result by the amount of the investment to find the total tax savings.

Consider our investment of $125,000 in a snowmaking machine with a 5-year MACRS recovery period. A 12% after-tax required rate of return and a 40% tax rate produce a tax savings with a present value of .7381 × .40 × $125,000 = $36,905. This differs from the $36,904 calculated earlier by a $1 rounding error.

MAKING MANAGERIAL DECISIONS

Why do managers like accelerated depreciation for tax purposes? Consider an investment of $100,000 in an asset with a ten-year economic life and a ten-year MACRS recovery period. The asset has no salvage value at the end of ten years. The tax rate is 40%, and the required rate of return is 10%. What is the present value of the depreciation tax savings using straight-line depreciation? What is the present value of the depreciation tax savings using MACRS depreciation? Which depreciation method is most beneficial to the company?

Answers

Straight-line depreciation = $10,000 per year, so tax savings is .40 × $10,000 = $4,000 per year. Thus, the present value of the tax savings is $4,000 × 6.1446 = $24,578.40.

The present value of MACRS depreciation is .6541 × .40 × $100,000 = $26,164.00. Although the total tax savings is $40,000 regardless of the depreciation method, the MACRS accelerated depreciation schedule creates a greater present value by $26,164.00 − $24,578.40 = $1,585.60.

Gains or Losses on Disposal

OBJECTIVE 6

Explain the after-tax effect on cash of disposing of assets.

The disposal of equipment for cash can also affect income taxes. Suppose Deer Valley sells its $125,000 snowmaking machine at the end of year 3 after taking three years of straight-line depreciation. If Deer Valley sells it for its book value, $125,000 − (3 × $25,000) = $50,000, there is no tax effect. If Deer Valley receives more than $50,000, there is a gain and an additional tax payment. If the company receives less than $50,000, there is a loss and a tax savings. The following table shows the effects on cash flow for sales prices of $70,000 and $20,000:

(a) Cash proceeds of sale	$70,000	$ 20,000
Book value: [$125,000 − 3 ($25,000)]	50,000	50,000
Gain (loss)	$20,000	$(30,000)
Effect on income taxes at 40%:		
(b) Tax savings, an inflow effect: .40 × loss		$ 12,000
(c) Tax paid, an outflow: .40 × gain	$ (8,000)	
Net cash inflow from sale:		
(a) plus (b)		$ 32,000
(a) minus (c)	$62,000	

Summary Problem For Your Review

PROBLEM

Consider the investment opportunity in Exhibit 11-4, page 486: original cost of machine, $125,000; 5-year economic life; zero terminal salvage value; pretax annual cash inflow from operations, $60,000; income tax rate, 40%; required after-tax rate of return, 12%. Assume the equipment is a 5-year MACRS asset for tax purposes. The net present value (NPV) is

	Present Values (PV)
Cash effects of operations,* $60,000 × (1 − .40) × 3.6048	$129,773
Cash effects of depreciation on income tax savings using MACRS,	
$125,000 × .40 × .7381†	36,905
Total after-tax effect on cash	$166,678
Investment	125,000
Net present value	$ 41,678

* See Exhibit 11-4, page 486, for details.
† Factor .7381 is from Exhibit 11-7, page 489.

Consider each requirement independently. Compute the NPV of the investment for each.

1. Suppose Deer Valley expects to sell the equipment for $20,000 cash immediately after the end of year 5.
2. Ignore the assumption in number 1. Return to the original data. Suppose the economic life of the machine was eight years, not five years. However, tax authorities still allow MACRS cost recovery over five years.

SOLUTION

1. Net present value as given		$41,678
Cash proceeds of sale	$ 20,000	
Book value	0	
Gain	$ 20,000	
Income taxes at 40%	8,000	
Total after-tax effect on cash	$ 12,000	
PV of $12,000 to be received in 5 years at 12%,		
$12,000 × .5674		6,809
NPV of investment		$48,487

2. Net present value as given		$41,678
Add the present value of $36,000 per year for 8 years		
Discount factor of 4.9676 × $36,000 =	$178,834	
Deduct the present value of $36,000 per year for 5 years	129,773	
Increase in present value		49,061
Net present value		$90,739

The investment would be very attractive. Note especially that the recovery period for tax purposes and the economic useful life of the asset need not be equal. The tax law specifies lives (or recovery periods) for various types of depreciable assets. The economic useful life of the asset does not affect the tax life. Thus, a longer useful life for an asset increases operating cash flows without decreasing the present value of the tax savings.

Confusion About Depreciation

The meanings of depreciation and book value are widely misunderstood. Let's review their role in decisions. Suppose Deer Valley Lodge is considering the replacement of some old copying equipment with a book value of $30,000, an expected terminal disposal value of zero, a current disposal value of $12,000, and a remaining useful life of three years. For simplicity, assume that Deer Valley will take straight-line depreciation of $10,000 yearly. The tax rate is 40%.

You should be careful to examine these data in perspective, as Exhibit 11-8 indicates. In particular, note that the inputs to the decision model are the predicted income tax effects on cash. Book values and depreciation may be necessary for making predictions. By themselves, however, they are not inputs to DCF decision model.

Other Models for Analyzing Long-Range Decisions

OBJECTIVE 7

Use the payback model and the accounting rate-of-return model and compare them with the NPV model.

Although more and more companies are using DCF models to make their capital-budgeting decisions, some companies still use simpler models, either in place of or in addition to the NPV model. We will examine two such models, the payback and accounting rate-of-return models.

Payback Model

Payback time or **payback period** is the time it will take to recoup, in the form of cash inflows from operations, the initial dollars invested in a project. Assume that Deer Valley Lodge spends $12,000 for a commercial stove in its restaurant. The stove has an estimated useful life of eight years. Deer Valley expects annual savings of $4,000 in cash outflows

payback time (payback period)

The time it will take to recoup, in the form of cash inflows from operations, the initial dollars invested in a project.

Exhibit 11-8
Perspective on Book Value and Depreciation

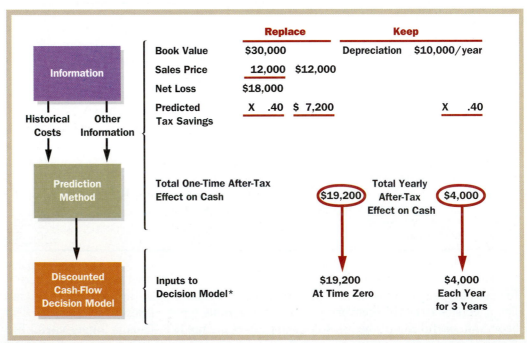

* There will, of course, be other related inputs to this decision model—for example, the cost of the new equipment and the differences in future annual cash flows from operations.

from operations. The payback method ignores depreciation. The payback period is three years, calculated as follows:

$$\text{payback time} = \frac{\text{initial incremental amount invested}}{\substack{\text{equal annual incremental cash} \\ \text{inflow from operations}}}$$

$$P = \frac{I}{O} = \frac{\$12,000}{\$4,000} = 3 \text{ years}$$

We can use this formula for payback time only when there are equal annual cash inflows from operations. When annual cash inflows are not equal, we must add up each year's net cash flows until they add up to the amount of the initial investment.

Assume the following cash flow pattern:

End of Year	0	1	2	3
Investment	($31,000)			
Cash inflows		$10,000	$20,000	$10,000

The calculation of the payback period is

	Initial	Net Cash Inflows	
Year	Investment	Each Year	Accumulated
0	$31,000	—	—
1	—	$10,000	$10,000
2	—	20,000	30,000
2.1	—	1,000	31,000

In this case, the payback time is slightly beyond the second year. Interpolation within the third year reveals that an additional .1 year is needed to recoup the final $1,000, making the payback period 2.1 years:

$$2 \text{ years} + \left(\frac{\$1,000}{\$10,000} \times 1 \text{ year} \right) = 2.1 \text{ years}$$

A major weakness of the payback model is that it does not measure profitability, which is a primary goal of businesses. The payback model merely measures how quickly a company will recoup its investment dollars. However, a project with a shorter payback time is not necessarily preferable to one with a longer payback time. After all, a company can recoup its entire investment immediately by not investing.

Sometimes managers use the payback period as a rough estimate of the riskiness of a project. Suppose a company faces rapid technological changes. Cash flows beyond the first few years may be extremely uncertain. In such a situation, projects that recoup their investment quickly may be less risky than those that require a longer wait until the cash starts flowing in.

Accounting Rate-of-Return Model

The **accounting rate-of-return (ARR) model** expresses a project's return as the increase in expected average annual operating income divided by the initial required investment.

accounting rate-of-return (ARR) model
A non-DCF capital-budgeting model expressed as the increase in expected average annual operating income divided by the initial required investment.

$$\text{accounting rate-of-return (ARR)} = \frac{\text{increase in expected average annual operating income}}{\text{initial required investment}}$$

$$= \frac{O - D}{I} = \frac{\text{average annual incremental cash inflow from operations} - \text{incremental average annual depreciation}}{\text{initial required investment}}$$

Its computations dovetail most closely with conventional accounting models of calculating income and required investment, and they show the effect of an investment on an organization's financial statements.

To see how ARR works, assume the same facts as in Exhibit 11-1: Investment is $6,075, useful life is four years, estimated disposal value is zero, and expected annual cash inflow from operations is $2,000. Annual depreciation is $6,075 ÷ 4 = $1,518.75, rounded to $1,519. Substitute these values in the accounting rate-of-return equation:

$$\text{ARR} = \frac{\$2,000 - \$1,519}{\$6,075} = 7.9\%$$

Some companies use the "average" investment (often assumed to be the average book value over the useful life) instead of original investment in the denominator. Therefore, the denominator[3] becomes $6,075 ÷ 2 = $3,037.50:

$$\text{ARR} = \frac{\$2,000 - \$1,519}{\$3,037.50} = 15.8\%$$

The accounting rate-of-return model is based on the familiar financial statements prepared under accrual accounting. Unlike the payback model, the accounting model at least has profitability as an objective. Nevertheless, it has a major drawback. The accounting model ignores the time value of money. Expected future dollars are erroneously regarded as equal to present dollars. DCF models explicitly allow for the force of interest and the timing of cash flows. In contrast, the accounting model uses annual averages. It uses concepts of investment and income that accountants originally designed for the quite different purpose of accounting for periodic income and financial position.

Performance Evaluation

Potential Conflict

OBJECTIVE 8

Reconcile the conflict between using an NPV model for making a decision and using accounting income for evaluating the related performance.

Many managers are reluctant to accept DCF models as the best way to make capital-budgeting decisions. Their reluctance stems from the wide usage of accounting income for evaluating performance. That is, managers become frustrated if their superiors instruct them to use a DCF model for making decisions but evaluate them later using a non-DCF model, such as the typical accounting rate-of-return model.

---

[3] The average investment committed to the project would decline at a rate of $1,519 per year from $6,075 to zero; hence, the average investment would be the beginning balance plus the ending balance ($6,075 + 0) divided by 2, or $3,037.50.

To illustrate, consider the potential conflict that might arise in the example of Exhibit 11-1. Recall that the NPV was $265 based on a 10% required rate of return, an investment of $6,075, cash savings of $2,000 for each of four years, and no terminal disposal value. Using accounting income computed with straight-line depreciation, the evaluation of performance for years 1 through 4 would be

	Year 1	Year 2	Year 3	Year 4
Cash-operating savings	$2,000	$2,000	$2,000	$2,000
Straight-line depreciation, $6,075 ÷ 4	1,519	1,519	1,519	1,519*
Effect on operating income	481	481	481	481
Book value at beginning of year	6,075	4,556	3,037	1,518
Accounting rate of return	7.9%	10.6%	15.8%	31.7%

* Total depreciation of 4 × $1,519 = $6,076 differs from $6,075 because of rounding error.

Many managers would be reluctant to replace equipment, despite the positive NPV, if superiors evaluated their performance by accounting income. They might be especially reluctant if they are likely to transfer to new positions every year or two. Why? This accrual accounting system understates the return in early years, especially in year 1 when the return is below the required rate, and a manager might not be around to reap the benefits of the later overstatement of returns.

As Chapter 6 indicated, managers are especially reluctant to replace assets if a heavy book loss on old equipment would appear in year 1's income statement—even though such a loss is irrelevant in a properly constructed decision model. Thus, performance evaluation based on typical accounting measures can cause the rejection of major, long-term projects such as investments in technologically advanced production systems. This pattern may help explain why many U.S. firms seem to be excessively short-term oriented.

Reconciliation of Conflict

The best way to reconcile any potential conflict between capital budgeting and performance evaluation is to use DCF for both capital-budgeting decisions and performance evaluation. Companies that use economic value added (EVA) for performance evaluation, as described in Chapter 10, p. 432, avoid some of the conflict. Although EVA has the weakness of using accrual accounting measures of profit and investment rather than cash flows, it has conceptual similarities to the NPV method of capital budgeting. Both EVA and NPV recognize that a firm creates value only after projects cover their cost of capital.

Another way to reconcile conflict is to conduct a follow-up evaluation of capital-budgeting decisions, often called a **postaudit.** Most large companies (76% in a recent survey) postaudit at least some capital-budgeting decisions. The purposes of a postaudit include

postaudit
A follow-up evaluation of capital-budgeting decisions.

1. Seeing that investment expenditures are proceeding on time and within budget.
2. Comparing actual cash flows with those originally predicted, in order to motivate careful and honest predictions.
3. Providing information for improving future predictions of cash flows.
4. Evaluating the continuation of the project.

By focusing the postaudit on actual versus predicted cash flows, we can make the evaluation consistent with the decision process.

However, postauditing of all capital-budgeting decisions is costly. Most accounting systems are best at evaluating operating performances of products, departments, divisions, territories, and so on, year by year. In contrast, capital-budgeting decisions frequently deal with individual projects, not the collection of projects that are usually being managed at the same time by division or department managers. Therefore, most companies audit only selected capital-budgeting decisions.

The conflicts between the longstanding, pervasive accrual accounting model and various formal decision models create some of the most serious unsolved problems in the design of management control systems. Top management cannot expect goal congruence if it favors the use of one type of model for decisions and the use of another type for performance evaluation.

Highlights to Remember

1 Describe capital-budgeting decisions and use the net-present-value (NPV) method to make such decisions. Capital budgeting is long-term planning for proposed capital outlays and their financing. The net-present-value (NPV) model aids this process by computing the present value of all expected future cash flows using a minimum desired rate of return. A company should accept projects with an NPV greater than zero.

2 Evaluate projects using sensitivity analysis. Managers use sensitivity analysis to aid risk assessment by examining the effects if actual cash flows differ from those expected.

3 Calculate the NPV difference between two projects using both the total project and differential approaches. The total project approach compares the NPVs of the cash flows from each project, while the differential approach computes the NPV of the difference in cash flows between two projects. Both produce the same results if there are two alternatives. You have to use the total project approach if you have more than two alternatives.

4 Identify relevant cash flows for NPV analyses. Predicting cash flows is the hardest part of capital budgeting. Managers should consider four categories of cash flows: initial cash inflows and outflows at time zero, investments in working capital, future disposal values, and operating cash flows.

5 Compute the after-tax net present values of projects. Income taxes can have a significant effect on the desirability of an investment. Additional taxes are cash outflows, and tax savings are cash inflows. Accelerated depreciation speeds up a company's tax savings. Generally, companies should take depreciation deductions as early as legally permitted.

6 Explain the after-tax effect on cash of disposing of assets. When companies sell assets for more than their book value, the gain generates additional taxes. When they sell assets for less than their book value, the loss generates tax savings.

7 Use the payback model and the accounting rate-of-return model and compare them with the NPV model. The payback model is simple to apply, but it does not measure profitability. The accounting rate-of-return model uses accounting measures of income and investment, but it ignores the time value of money. Both models are inferior to the NPV model.

8 Reconcile the conflict between using an NPV model for making a decision and using accounting income for evaluating the related performance. NPV is a summary measure of all the cash flows from a project. Accounting income is a one-period measure. A positive NPV project can have low (or even negative) accounting income in the first year. Managers may be reluctant to invest in such a project, despite its positive value to the company, especially if they expect to be transferred to a new position before they can benefit from the positive returns that come later.

9 Compute the impact of inflation on a capital-budgeting project (Appendix 11). Consistency is the key in adjusting capital-budgeting analyses for inflation. The required rate of return should include an element attributable to anticipated inflation, and cash-flow predictions should be adjusted for the effects of anticipated inflation.

OBJECTIVE 9

Compute the impact of inflation on a capital-budgeting project.

inflation
The decline in the general purchasing power of the monetary unit.

Appendix 11: Capital Budgeting and Inflation

Capital-budgeting decision makers should also consider the effects of inflation on their cash-flow predictions. **Inflation** is the decline in the general purchasing power of the monetary unit. For example, a dollar today will buy only half as much as it did in the mid-1980s. At a 5% annual inflation rate, average prices rise more than 60% over ten years. In countries such as Brazil and Argentina, triple-digit annual inflation rates (that is, average prices more than doubling each year) have been commonplace and have significantly affected business decisions. Recent inflation rates in the United States have been low—under 3%—but it is possible that rates in the future might increase. If a company expects significant inflation over the life of a project, it should specifically and consistently recognize inflation in its capital-budgeting decisions.

Watch for Consistency

The key to appropriate consideration of inflation in capital budgeting is consistent treatment of the minimum desired rate of return and the predicted cash inflows and outflows. We can achieve such consistency by including an element for inflation in both the minimum desired rate of return and in the cash-flow predictions.

Many firms base their minimum desired rate of return on market interest rates, also called **nominal rates,** that include an inflation element. For example, consider three possible components of a 12% nominal rate:

nominal rate
Quoted market interest rate that includes an inflation element.

(a)	Risk-free element—the "pure" rate of interest	3%
(b)	Business-risk element—the "risk" premium that is demanded for taking larger risks	5
(a) + (b)	Often called the "real rate"	8%
(c)	Inflation element—the premium demanded because of expected deterioration of the general purchasing power of the monetary unit	4
(a) + (b) + (c)	Often called the "nominal rate"	12%

Four percentage points out of the 12% return compensate an investor for receiving future payments in inflated dollars, that is, in dollars with less purchasing power than those invested. Therefore, basing the minimum desired rate of return on quoted market rates automatically includes an inflation element in the rate. Companies that base their minimum desired rate of return on market rates should also adjust their cash-flow predictions for anticipated inflation. For example, suppose a company expects to sell 1,000 units of a product in each of the next two years. Assume this year's price is $50, and inflation causes next year's price to be $52.50. This year's predicted cash inflow is $1,000 \times $50 = $50,000 and next year's inflation-adjusted cash inflow is $1,000 \times $52.50 = $52,500. Inflation-adjusted cash flows are the inflows and outflows expected after adjusting prices to reflect anticipated inflation.

Consider another illustration: purchase cost of equipment, $200,000; useful life, 5 years; zero terminal salvage value; pretax operating cash savings per year, $83,333 (in 20X0 dollars); income tax rate, 40%. For simplicity, we assume ordinary straight-line depreciation of $200,000 \div 5 = $40,000 per year. The after-tax minimum desired rate, based on quoted market rates, is 25%. It includes an inflation factor of 10%.

Exhibit 11-9 displays correct and incorrect ways to analyze the effects of inflation. The key words are *internal consistency.* The correct analysis (1) uses a minimum desired rate that includes an element attributable to inflation and (2) explicitly adjusts the predicted operating cash flows for the effects of inflation. Note that the correct analysis favors the purchase of the equipment, but the incorrect analysis does not.

The incorrect analysis in Exhibit 11-9 is inherently inconsistent. The predicted cash inflows exclude adjustments for inflation. Instead, they are stated in 20X0 dollars. However, the discount rate includes an element attributable to inflation. An analytical mistake like this might lead to an unwise refusal to purchase.

Role of Depreciation

The correct analysis in Exhibit 11-9 shows that we did not adjust the tax effects of depreciation for inflation. Why? Because U.S. income tax laws permit a depreciation deduction based on the original dollars invested, nothing more.

Critics of income tax laws emphasize that such laws discourage capital investment by not allowing companies to adjust depreciation deductions for inflationary effects. For instance, the net present value in Exhibit 11-9 would be larger if depreciation were not confined to the $40,000 amount per year. The latter generates a $16,000 savings in 20X1 dollars, then $16,000 in 20X2 dollars, and so forth. Defenders of existing U.S. tax laws assert that tax laws encourage capital investment in many other ways. The most prominent example is provision for accelerated depreciation over lives that are much shorter than the economic lives of the assets.

Sketch of Relevant Cash Flows (at End of Year)

Description	At 25% PV Factor	Present Value	0	1	2	3	4	5
Correct analysis (Be sure the discount rate includes an element attributable to inflation and adjust the predicted cash flows for inflationary effects.)								
Cash operating inflows:								
Pretax inflow in 20X0 dollars $83,333								
Income tax effect at 40% 33,333								
After-tax effect on cash $50,000	.8000	$ 44,000		$55,000*				
	.6400	38,720			$60,500			
	.5120	34,074				$66,550		
	.4096	29,985					$73,205	
	.3277	26,388						$80,526
Subtotal		$173,167						
Annual depreciation $200,000 ÷ 5 = $40,000								
Cash effect of depreciation								
Savings in income taxes @ 40% = $40,000 × .40 = $16,000	2.6893	43,029		$16,000†	$16,000	$16,000	$16,000	$16,000
Investment in equipment	1.0000	(200,000)	($200,000)					
Net present value		$ 16,196						
Incorrect analysis (A common error is to include an inflation element in the discount rate as above, but not adjust the predicted cash inflows.)								
Cash operating inflows after taxes	2.6893	$134,465		$50,000	$50,000	$50,000	$50,000	$50,000
Tax effect of depreciation	2.6893	43,029		16,000	16,000	16,000	16,000	16,000
Investment in equipment	1.0000	(200,000)	($200,000)					
Net present value		$ (22,506)						

* Each year is adjusted for anticipated inflation: $50,000 × 1.10, $50,000 × 1.10², $50,000 × 1.10³, and so on.
† Inflation will not affect the annual savings in income taxes from depreciation. Why? Because the income tax deduction must be based on original cost of the asset in 20X0 dollars.

Exhibit 11-9
Inflation and Capital Budgeting

Improvement of Predictions with Feedback

The ability to forecast and cope with changing prices is a valuable management skill, especially when inflation is significant. Auditing and feedback should help evaluate management's predictive skills.

The adjustment of the operating cash flows in Exhibit 11-9 uses a general-price-level rate of 10%. However, where feasible, managers should use specific rates or tailor-made predictions for price changes in materials, labor, and other items. These predictions may have different percentage changes from year to year.

Summary Problems For Your Review

PROBLEM

Examine the correct analysis in Exhibit 11-9, page 498. Suppose the cash-operating inflows persisted for an extra year. Compute the present value of the inflow for the sixth year. Ignore depreciation.

SOLUTION

The cash operating inflow would be $50,000 \times 1.10^6$, or $80,526 \times 1.10$, or $88,579. Its present value would be $88,579 \times .2621$, the factor from Table 1 of Appendix B (period 6 row, 25% column), or $23,217.

PROBLEM

Examine the MACRS depreciation schedule near the middle of page 489. Assume an anticipated inflation rate of 7%. How would you change the present values of depreciation to accommodate the inflation rate?

SOLUTION

The computations on page 489 would not change. Inflation does not affect the tax effects of depreciation. Income tax laws in the United States permit a deduction based on the original dollars invested, nothing more.

Accounting Vocabulary

accelerated depreciation, p. 485
accounting rate-of-return (ARR) model, p. 493
capital budgeting, p. 472
differential approach, p. 479
discount rate, p. 474
discounted-cash-flow (DCF) models, p. 472
hurdle rate, p. 474

inflation, p. 496
internal rate of return (IRR) model, p. 478
marginal income tax rate, p. 484
modified accelerated cost recovery system (MACRS), p. 488
net-present-value (NPV) method, p. 473

nominal rate, p. 497
payback period, p. 492
payback time, p. 492
postaudit, p. 495
real options model, p. 478
recovery period, p. 486
required rate of return, p. 474
total project approach, p. 479

Fundamental Assignment Material

Special note: In all assignment materials that include taxes, assume, unless directed otherwise, that (1) all income tax cash flows occur simultaneously with the pretax cash flows, and (2) the companies in question will have enough taxable income from other sources to use all income tax benefits from the situations described.

11-A1 Exercises in Compound Interest: Answers Supplied

Use the appropriate interest table from Appendix B (see pp. Bxx or Bxx) to complete the following exercises. The answers appear at the end of the assignment material for this chapter, page 518.

1. It is your 55th birthday. You plan to work five more years before retiring, at which point you and your spouse want to take $20,000 for a round-the-world tour. What lump sum do you have to invest now to accumulate the $20,000? Assume that your minimum desired rate of return is
   a. 5%, compounded annually
   b. 10%, compounded annually
   c. 20%, compounded annually
2. You want to spend $2,000 on a vacation at the end of each of the next five years. What lump sum do you have to invest now to take the five vacations? Assume that your minimum desired rate of return is
   a. 5%, compounded annually
   b. 10%, compounded annually
   c. 20%, compounded annually
3. At age 60, you find that your employer is moving to another location. You receive termination pay of $100,000. You have some savings and wonder whether to retire now.
   a. If you invest the $100,000 now at 5%, compounded annually, how much money can you withdraw from your account each year so that at the end of five years there will be a zero balance?
   b. Answer part a, assuming that you invest it at 10%.
4. Two NBA basketball players, Johnson and Jackson, signed five-year, $30-million contracts. At 16%, compounded annually, which of the following contracts is more desirable in terms of present values? Show computations to support your answer.

Annual Cash Inflows (000)		
Year	Johnson	Jackson
1	$10,000	$ 2,000
2	8,000	4,000
3	6,000	6,000
4	4,000	8,000
5	2,000	10,000
	$30,000	$30,000

11-A2 NPV for Investment Decisions

A manager of the Administrative Computer Center of Olympia State University is contemplating acquiring 120 computers. The computers will cost $325,000 cash, have zero terminal salvage value, and a useful life of three years. Annual cash savings from operations will be $150,000. The required rate of return is 14%. There are no taxes.

1. Compute the net present value.
2. Should the Computer Center acquire the computers? Explain.

11-A3 Taxes, Straight-Line Depreciation, and Present Values

A manager of eBooks.com is contemplating acquiring servers to operate its Web site. The servers will cost $660,000 cash and will have zero terminal salvage value. The recovery period and useful life are both three years. Annual pretax cash savings from operations will be $300,000. The income tax rate is 40%, and the required after-tax rate of return is 12%.

1. Compute the net present value, assuming straight-line depreciation of $220,000 yearly for tax purposes. Should eBooks.com acquire the computers? Explain.
2. Suppose the computers will be fully depreciated at the end of year 3 but can be sold for $90,000 cash. Compute the net present value. Should eBooks.com acquire the computers? Explain.
3. Ignore number 2. Suppose the required after-tax rate of return is 8% instead of 12%. Should eBooks.com acquire the computers? Show computations.

11-A4 MACRS and Present Values

The president of Interstate Manufacturing Company is considering whether to buy some equipment for its North Platte plant. The equipment will cost $1.5 million cash and will have a ten-year useful life and zero terminal salvage value. Annual pretax cash savings from operations will be $360,000. The income tax rate is 40%, and the required after-tax rate of return is 16%.

1. Compute the net present value, using a seven-year recovery period and MACRS depreciation for tax purposes. Should the company acquire the equipment?
2. Suppose the economic life of the equipment is 15 years, which means that there will be $360,000 additional annual cash savings from operations in each of years 11 to 15. Assume that a seven-year recovery period is used. Should the company acquire the equipment? Show computations.

11-A5 Gains or Losses on Disposal

On January 1, 20X1 Sydney Company sold an asset with a book value of $50,000 for cash.

Assume two selling prices: $65,000 and $30,000. For each selling price, prepare a tabulation of the gain or loss, the effect on income taxes, and the total after-tax effect on cash. The applicable income tax rate is 30%.

11-B1 Exercises in Compound Interest

Use the appropriate table to compute the following:

1. You have always dreamed of taking a trip to Machu Picchu. What lump sum do you have to invest today to have the $12,000 needed for the trip in three years? Assume that you can invest the money at
   a. 4%, compounded annually
   b. 10%, compounded annually
   c. 16%, compounded annually
2. You are considering partial retirement. To do so you need to use part of your savings to supplement your income for the next five years. Suppose you need an extra $15,000 per year. What lump sum do you have to invest now to supplement your income for five years? Assume that your minimum desired rate of return is
   a. 4%, compounded annually
   b. 10%, compounded annually
   c. 16%, compounded annually
3. You just won a lump sum of $400,000 in a local lottery. You have decided to invest the winnings and withdraw an equal amount each year for 10 years. How much can you withdraw each year and have a zero balance left at the end of 10 years if you invest at
   a. 5%, compounded annually
   b. 10%, compounded annually
4. A major league baseball player is offered the choice of two 4-year salary contracts, contract A for $1.4 million and contract B for $1.3 million:

	Contract A	Contract B
End of year 1	$ 200,000	$ 450,000
End of year 2	300,000	350,000
End of year 3	400,000	300,000
End of year 4	500,000	200,000
Total	$1,400,000	$1,300,000

Which contract has the higher present value at 14% compounded annually? Show computations to support your answer.

11-B2 NPV for Investment Decisions

The head of the radiology department of St. Vincent's Hospital is considering the purchase of some new x-ray equipment. The cost is $400,000, the economic life is five years, and there is no terminal disposal value. Annual cash inflows from operations would increase by $140,000 and the required rate of return is 14%. There are no taxes.

1. Compute the net present value.
2. Should the hospital acquire the equipment? Explain.

11-B3 Taxes, Straight-Line Depreciation, and NPV

The president of Genomics, Inc., a biotechnology company, is considering the purchase of some equipment used for research and development. The cost is $400,000, the economic life and the recovery period are both five years, and there is no terminal disposal value. Annual pretax cash inflows from operations would increase by $140,000, giving a total five-year pretax savings of $700,000. The income tax rate is 40%, and the required after-tax rate of return is 14%.

1. Compute the net present value, assuming straight-line depreciation of $80,000 yearly for tax purposes. Should Genomics acquire the equipment?

2. Suppose the asset will be fully depreciated at the end of year 5 but is sold for $25,000 cash. Should Genomics acquire the equipment? Show computations.
3. Ignore number 2. Suppose the required after-tax rate of return is 10% instead of 14%. Should Genomics acquire the equipment? Show computations.

11-B4 MACRS and Present Values

The general manager of a Wyoming mining company has a chance to purchase a new drill at a total cost of $250,000. The recovery period is five years. Additional annual pretax cash inflow from operations is $81,000, the economic life of the equipment is five years, there is no salvage value, the income tax rate is 35%, and the after-tax required rate of return is 16%.

1. Compute the net present value, assuming MACRS depreciation for tax purposes. Should the company acquire the equipment?
2. Suppose the economic life of the equipment is six years, which means that there will be an $81,000 cash inflow from operations in the sixth year. The recovery period is still five years. Should the company acquire the equipment? Show computations.

11-B5 Income Taxes and Disposal of Assets

Assume that the combined federal and state income tax rate for Garciaparra Company is 30%.

1. The book value of an old machine is $20,000. Garciaparra sold the machine for $10,000 cash. What is the effect of this decision on after-tax cash flows?
2. The book value of an old machine is $20,000. Garciaparra sold the machine for $35,000 cash. What is the effect of this decision on after-tax cash flows?

Additional Assignment Material

Questions

11-1 Capital budgeting has three phases: (a) identification of potential investments, (b) selection of investments, and (c) postaudit of investments. What is the accountant's role in each phase?

11-2 Why is discounted cash flow a superior method for capital budgeting?

11-3 "The higher the minimum desired rate of return, the higher the price that a company will be willing to pay for cost-saving equipment." Do you agree? Explain.

11-4 "The DCF model assumes certainty and perfect capital markets. Thus, it is impractical to use it in most real-world situations." Do you agree? Explain.

11-5 "Double-counting of costs occurs if depreciation is separately considered in DCF analysis." Do you agree? Explain.

11-6 Does the IRR model make significantly different decisions than does the NPV model? Why or why not?

11-7 What does the real options model recognize that the NPV and IRR models do not?

11-8 "We can't use sensitivity analysis because our cash-flow predictions are too inaccurate." Comment.

11-9 Why should the differential approach to alternatives always lead to the same decision as the total project approach?

11-10 "The NPV model should not be used for investment decisions about advanced technology such as computer-integrated manufacturing systems." Do you agree? Explain.

11-11 Distinguish between average and marginal tax rates.

11-12 "Congress should pass a law forbidding corporations to keep two sets of books." Do you agree? Explain.

11-13 Distinguish between tax avoidance and tax evasion.

11-14 "Companies that try to avoid taxes are unethical." Do you agree? Discuss.

11-15 Explain why accelerated depreciation methods are superior to straight-line methods for income tax purposes.

11-16 "An investment in equipment really buys two streams of cash." Do you agree? Explain.

11-17 Why should companies take tax deductions sooner rather than later?

11-18 "The MACRS half-year convention causes assets to be depreciated beyond the lives specified in the MACRS recovery schedules." Do you agree? Explain.

11-19 "When there are income taxes, depreciation is a cash outlay." Do you agree? Explain.

11-20 "If DCF approaches are superior to the payback and the accounting rate-of-return methods, why should we bother to learn the others? All it does is confuse things." Answer this contention.

11-21 What is the basic flaw in the payback model?

11-22 Explain how a conflict can arise between capital-budgeting decision models and performance evaluation methods.

11-23 Study Appendix 11. What are the three components of market (nominal) interest rates?

11-24 Study Appendix 11. Describe how internal consistency is achieved when considering inflation in a capital-budgeting model.

Critical Thinking Exercises

11-25 Investment in Research and Development

"It is impossible to use DCF methods for evaluating investments in research and development. There are no cost savings to measure, and we don't even know what products might come out of our R&D activities." This is a quote from an R&D manager who was asked to justify investment in a major research project based on its expected net present value. Do you agree with her statement? Explain.

11-26 Business Valuation and Net Present Value

When a company elects to invest in a project with a positive net present value, what will generally happen to the value of the company? What will happen to this value when the company invests in a negative net present value project?

11-27 Replacement of Production Facilities

A manufacturing company recently considered replacing one of its forming machines with a newer, faster, more accurate model. What cash flows would this decision be likely to affect? List both cash flows that would be easy to quantify and those for which measurement would be difficult.

11-28 Capital Budgeting, Taxes, and Ethics

The U.S. tax law is complex. Sometimes the line between tax avoidance and tax evasion is not clear. Discuss the legal and ethical implications of the following two capital investment decisions:

a. A company invested in an asset that it expects to grow rather than decline in value. Nevertheless, the tax law allows the company to deduct depreciation on the asset. Therefore, the company depreciated the asset for tax purposes using an accelerated MACRS schedule.

b. There are often tax advantages to investments "offshore." For example, in Bermuda there are no taxes on profits, dividends, or income, and there is no capital gains tax, no withholding tax, and no sales tax. A U.S. company decided to invest in a manufacturing plant in Bermuda and use transfer prices to move as much of the company's profits as possible to the Bermuda plant.

Exercises

11-29 Exercise in Compound Interest

Anita Chen wishes to purchase a $250,000 house. She has accumulated a $50,000 down payment, but she wishes to borrow $200,000 on a 30-year mortgage. For simplicity, assume annual mortgage payments at the end of each year and no loan fees.

1. What are Chen's annual payments if her interest rate is (a) 8%, (b) 10%, and (c) 12%, compounded annually?
2. Repeat number 1 for a 15-year mortgage.
3. Suppose Chen had to choose between a 30-year and a 15-year mortgage, either one at a 10% interest rate. Compute the total payments and total interest paid on (a) a 30-year mortgage and (b) a 15-year mortgage.

11-30 Exercise in Compound Interest

Suppose **Mitsubishi Motors North America** wishes to borrow money from **Citibank**. They agree on an annual rate of 12%.

1. Suppose Mitsubishi agrees to repay $600 million at the end of four years. How much will Citibank lend Mitsubishi?
2. Suppose Mitsubishi agrees to repay a total of $600 million at a rate of $150 million at the end of each of the next four years. How much will Citibank lend Mitsubishi?

11-31 Exercise in Compound Interest

Suppose you are a loan officer for a bank. A start-up company has qualified for a loan. You are pondering various proposals for repayment:

1. Lump sum of $800,000 four years hence. How much will you lend if your desired rate of return is (a) 12%, compounded annually, and (b) 16%, compounded annually?

2. Repeat number 1, but assume that the interest rates are compounded semiannually.
3. Suppose the loan is to be paid in full by equal payments of $200,000 at the end of each of the next four years. How much will you lend if your desired rate of return is (a) 12%, compounded annually, and (b) 16%, compounded annually?

11-32 Basic Relationships in Interest Tables

1. Suppose you borrow $150,000 now at 14% interest, compounded annually. You will repay the borrowed amount plus interest in a lump sum at the end of eight years. How much must you repay? Use Table 1 (p. 821) and the basic equation PV = future amount × conversion factor.
2. Assume the same facts as previously except that you will repay the loan in equal installments at the end of each of eight years. How much must you repay each year? Use Table 2 (p. 824) and the basic equation: PV = future annual amounts × conversion factor.

11-33 Present Value and Sports Salaries

Because of a salary cap, National Basketball Association teams are not allowed to exceed a certain annual limit in total player salaries. Suppose the San Antonio Spurs had scheduled salaries exactly equal to their cap of $60 million for 20X5. David Duncan, a star player, was scheduled to receive $12 million in 20X5. To free up money to pay a prize rookie, Duncan agreed to defer $4 million of his salary for two years, by which time the salary cap will have been increased. His contract called for salary payments of $12 million in 20X5, $14 million in 20X6, and $16 million in 20X7. Now he will receive $8 million in 20X5, still $14 million in 20X6, and $20 million in 20X7. For simplicity, assume that the team pays all salaries on July 1 of the year they are scheduled. Duncan's minimum desired rate of return is 12%.

Did the deferral of salary cost Duncan anything? If so, how much? Compute the present value of the sacrifice on July 1, 20X5. Explain.

11-34 Simple NPV

Fill in the blanks.

	Number of Years			
	8	**18**	**20**	**28**
Amount of annual cash inflow*	$10,000	$ _____	$ 9,000	$ 8,000
Required initial investment	$ _____	$ 80,000	$65,000	$30,000
Minimum desired rate of return	14%	20%	$ _____	25%
NPV	$ 5,613	($13,835)	$ 2,225	$ _____

* To be received at the end of each year.

11-35 New Equipment

The Livingston Office Equipment Company has offered to sell some new packaging equipment to the Chavez Company. The list price is $40,000, but Livingston has agreed to allow a trade-in allowance of $15,000 on some old equipment. The old equipment was carried at a book value of $8,700 and could be sold outright for $10,000 cash. Cash-operating savings are expected to be $5,000 annually for the next 12 years. The minimum desired rate of return is 12%. The old equipment has a remaining useful life of 12 years. Both the old and the new equipment will have zero disposal values 12 years from now.

Should Chavez buy the new equipment? Show your computations, using the NPV method. Ignore income taxes.

11-36 Present Values of Cash Inflows

Sea&ski.com, Inc., has just been established. Operating plans indicate the following expected cash flows:

	Outflows	Inflows
Initial investment now	$215,000	$ —
End of year: 1	150,000	200,000
2	200,000	250,000
3	250,000	300,000
4	300,000	400,000
5	350,000	450,000

1. Compute the NPV for all of these cash flows. This should be a single amount. Use a discount rate of 14%.
2. Suppose the minimum desired rate was 12%. Without further calculations, determine whether the NPV is positive or negative. Explain.

11-37 NPV and IRR

Albion Company is considering an investment in a machine that costs $36,048 and would result in cash savings per year of $10,000 per year for five years. The company's cost of capital is 10%.

1. Compute the project's NPV at 10%, 12%, and 14%.
2. Compute the project's IRR.
3. Suppose the company uses the NPV model. Would it accept the project? Why or why not?
4. Suppose the company uses the IRR model. Would it accept the project? Why or why not?

11-38 Sensitivity Analysis

Philadelphia Physicians is considering the replacement of an old billing system with new software that should save $5,000 per year in net cash operating costs. The old system has zero disposal value, but it could be used for the next 12 years. The estimated useful life of the new software is 12 years, and it will cost $25,000. The minimum desired rate of return is 10%.

1. What is the payback period?
2. Compute the net present value (NPV).
3. Management is unsure about the useful life. What would be the NPV if the useful life were (a) 5 years instead of 12 or (b) 20 years instead of 12?
4. Suppose the life will be 12 years, but the savings will be $3,500 per year instead of $5,000. What would be the NPV?
5. Suppose the annual savings will be $4,000 for eight years. What would be the NPV?

11-39 NPV and Sensitivity Analysis

Ojibwa County Jail currently has its laundry done by a local cleaners at an annual cost of $46,000. It is considering a purchase of washers, dryers, and presses at a total installed cost of $52,000 so that inmates can do the laundry. The county expects savings of $15,000 per year, and it expects the machines to last five years. The desired rate of return is 10%.

Answer each part separately.

1. Compute the NPV of the investment in laundry facilities.
2. a. Suppose the machines last only four years. Compute the NPV.
   b. Suppose the machines last seven years. Compute the NPV.
3. a. Suppose the annual savings are only $12,000. Compute the NPV.
   b. Suppose the annual savings are $18,000. Compute the NPV.
4. a. Compute the most optimistic estimate of NPV, combining the best outcomes in numbers 2 and 3.
   b. Compute the most pessimistic estimate of NPV, combining the worst outcomes in numbers 2 and 3.
5. Accept the expected life estimate of five years. What is the minimum annual savings that would justify the investment in the laundry facilities?

11-40 Depreciation, Income Taxes, Cash Flows

Fill in the unknowns (in thousands of dollars):

(S)	Sales	530
(E)	Expenses excluding depreciation	350
(D)	Depreciation	100
	Total expenses	450
	Income before income taxes	?
(T)	Income taxes at 40%	?
(I)	Net income	?
	Cash effects of operations	
	Cash inflow from operations	?
	Income tax outflow at 40%	?
	After-tax inflow from operations	?
	Effect of depreciation	
	Depreciation, ?	
	Income tax savings	?
	Total after-tax effect on cash	?

11-41 After-Tax Effect on Cash

The 20X0 income statement of CableNet Company included the following:

Sales	$1,200,000
Less: Expenses, excluding depreciation	$ 600,000
Depreciation	400,000
Total expenses	$1,000,000
Income before taxes	$ 200,000
Income taxes (35%)	70,000
Net income	$ 130,000

Compute the total after-tax effect on cash. Use the format of the second part of Exhibit 11-3, page 485, "Analysis of the Same Facts for Capital Budgeting."

11-42 MACRS Depreciation

In 2004, Electra Athletic Clothing Company acquired the following assets and immediately placed them into service.

1. Special tools (a three-year-MACRS asset) that cost $30,000 on February 1.
2. A desktop computer that cost $7,000 on December 15.
3. Special calibration equipment that was used in running-shoe research and cost $5,000 on July 7.
4. A set of file cabinets that cost $4,000, purchased on March 1.

Compute the depreciation for tax purposes, under the prescribed MACRS method, in 2004 and 2005.

11-43 Present Value of MACRS Depreciation

Compute the present value of the MACRS tax savings for each of the following five assets:

	Asset Cost	Recovery Period	Discount Rate	Tax Rate
(a)	$240,000	3-year	12%	35%
(b)	$560,000	5-year	10%	40%
(c)	$ 55,000	7-year	16%	50%
(d)	$910,000	10-year	8%	35%
(e)	$400,000	10-year	15%	25%

11-44 NPV, ARR, and Payback

Bob's Big Burgers is considering a proposal to invest in a speaker system that would allow its employees to service drive-through customers. The cost of the system (including installation of special windows and driveway modifications) is $30,000. Jenna Simon, manager of Bob's, expects the drive-through operations to increase annual sales by $25,000, with a 40% contribution margin ratio. Assume that the system has an economic life of six years, at which time it will have no disposal value. The required rate of return is 12%. Ignore taxes.

1. Compute the payback period. Is this a good measure of profitability?
2. Compute the NPV. Should Simon accept the proposal? Why or why not?
3. Using the accounting rate-of-return model, compute the rate of return on the initial investment.

11-45 Comparison of Capital-Budgeting Techniques

Rocky Mountain Swim Club is considering the purchase of a new pool heater at a cost of $12,000. It should save $3,000 in cash operating costs per year. Its estimated useful life is eight years, and it will have zero disposal value. Ignore taxes.

1. What is the payback time?
2. Compute the net present value if the minimum rate of return desired is 8%. Should the club buy? Why?
3. Using the accounting rate-of-return model, compute the rate of return on the initial investment.

11-46 Inflation and Capital Budgeting

Study Appendix 11. The head of the corporate tax division of a major law firm has proposed investing $300,000 in personal computers for the staff. The useful life and recovery period for the computers are both five years. The firm uses MACRS depreciation. There is no terminal salvage value. Labor savings of $125,000 per year (in year-zero dollars) are expected from the purchase. The income tax rate is 45%, the after-tax required rate of return is 20%, which includes a 4% element attributable to inflation.

1. Compute the net present value of the computers. Use the nominal required rate of return and adjust the cash flows for inflation. (For example, year 1 cash flow = 1.04 × year 0 cash flow.)
2. Compute the net present value of the computers using the nominal required rate of return without adjusting the cash flows for inflation.
3. Compare your answers in numbers 1 and 2. Which is correct? Would using the incorrect analysis generally lead to overinvestment or underinvestment? Explain.

11-47 Sensitivity of Capital Budgeting to Inflation

Study Appendix 11. Raef Moya, the president of a Mexican wholesale company, is considering whether to invest 420,000 pesos in new semiautomatic loading equipment that will last five years, have zero scrap value, and generate cash operating savings in labor usage of 160,000 pesos annually, using 20X0 prices and wage rates. It is December 31, 20X0.

The minimum desired rate of return is 18% per year after taxes.

1. Compute the net present value of the project. Use 160,000 pesos as the savings for each of the five years. Assume a 40% tax rate and, for simplicity, assume ordinary straight-line depreciation of 420,000 pesos ÷ 5 = 84,000 pesos annually for tax purposes.
2. Moya is wondering if the model in number 1 provides a correct analysis of the effects of inflation. He maintains that the 18% rate embodies an element attributable to anticipated inflation. For purposes of this analysis, he assumes that the existing rate of inflation, 10% annually, will persist over the next five years. Repeat number 1, adjusting the cash operating savings upward by using the 10% inflation rate.
3. Which analysis, the one in number 1 or 2, is correct? Why?

Problems

11-48 Replacement of Office Equipment

Western Kansas University is considering replacing some Ricoh copiers with faster copiers purchased from Kodak. The administration is very concerned about the rising costs of operations during the last decade.

To convert to Kodak, two operators would have to be retrained. Required training and remodeling would cost $4,000.

Western Kansas's three Ricoh machines were purchased for $10,000 each, five years ago. Their expected life was ten years. Their resale value now is $1,000 each and will be zero in five more years. The total cost of the new Kodak equipment will be $54,000; it will have zero disposal value in five years.

The three Ricoh operators are paid $8 an hour each. They usually work a 40-hour week. Machine breakdowns occur monthly on each machine, resulting in repair costs of $50 per month and overtime of four hours, at time-and-one-half, per machine per month, to complete the normal monthly workload. Toner, supplies, and so on, cost $100 a month for each Ricoh copier.

The Kodak system will require only two regular operators, on a regular work week of 40 hours each, to do the same work. Rates are $10 an hour, and no overtime is expected. Toner, supplies, and so on, will cost a total of $3,300 annually. Maintenance and repairs are fully serviced by Kodak for $1,050 annually. (Assume a 52-week year.)

1. Using DCF techniques, compute the present value of all relevant cash flows, under both alternatives, for the five-year period discounted at 12%. As a nonprofit university, Western Kansas does not pay income taxes.
2. Should Western Kansas keep the Ricoh copiers or replace them if the decision is based solely on the given data?
3. What other considerations might affect the decision?

11-49 Replacement Decision for Railway Equipment

Suppose the **Burlington Northern Sante Fe Railroad** is considering replacement of a power jack tamper, used for maintenance of track, with a new automatic raising device that can be attached to a production tamper.

The present power jack tamper cost $24,000 five years ago and had an estimated life of 12 years. A year from now, the machine will require a major overhaul estimated to cost $6,000. It can be disposed of now via an outright cash sale for $5,000. There will be no value at the end of another seven years.

The automatic raising attachment has a delivered selling price of $72,000 and an estimated life of 12 years. Because of anticipated future developments in combined maintenance machines, Burlington management believes that they would dispose of the machine at the end of the seventh year to take advantage of newly developed machines. Estimated sales value at the end of seven years is $5,000.

Tests have shown that the automatic raising machine will produce a more uniform surface on the track than does the power jack tamper now in use. The new equipment will eliminate one laborer whose annual compensation, including fringe benefits, is $30,000.

Track maintenance work is seasonal, and the equipment normally works from May 1 to October 31 each year. Machine operators and laborers are transferred to other work after October 31, at the same rate of pay.

The salesman claims that the annual normal maintenance of the new machine will run about $1,000 per year. Because the automatic raising machine is more complicated than the manually operated machine, it will probably require a thorough overhaul at the end of the fourth year, at an estimated cost of $7,000.

Records show the annual normal maintenance of the power jack tamper to be $1,200. Fuel consumption of the two machines is equal. Should Burlington keep or replace the power jack tamper? The company requires a 10% rate of return. Compute present values. Ignore income taxes.

11-50 Discounted Cash Flow, Uneven Revenue Stream, Relevant Costs

D. Bogey, the owner of a nine-hole golf course on the outskirts of a large city, is considering a proposal that the course be illuminated and operated at night. Ms. Bogey purchased the course early last year for $480,000. Her receipts from operations during the 28-week season were $135,000. Total disbursements for the year, for all purposes, were $84,000.

The required investment in lighting this course is estimated at $94,000. The system will require 300 lamps of 1,000 watts each. Electricity costs $.08 per kilowatt-hour. The expected average hours of operation per night is five. Because of occasional bad weather and the probable curtailment of night operation at the beginning and end of the season, it is estimated that there will be only 130 nights of operation per year. Labor for keeping the course open at night will cost $75 per night. Lightbulb cost is estimated at $1,500 per year; other maintenance and repairs, per year, will amount to 4% of the initial cost of the lighting system. Annual property taxes on this equipment will be about 1.7% of its initial cost. It is estimated that the average revenue, per night of operation, will be $450 for the first two years.

Considering the probability of competition from the illumination of other golf courses, Ms. Bogey decides that she will not make the investment unless she can make at least 10% per annum on her investment. Because of anticipated competition, revenue is expected to drop to $300 per night for years 3 through 5. It is estimated that the lighting equipment will have a salvage value of $35,000 at the end of the five-year period.

Using DCF techniques, determine whether Ms. Bogey should install the lighting system.

11-51 Investment in Machine and Working Capital

The Aberdeen Ale Company has an old brewing machine with a net disposal value of £15,000 now and £4,000 five years from now. A new brewing machine is offered for £62,000 cash or £47,000 with a trade-in. The new machine will result in an annual operating cash outflow of £40,000 as compared with the old machine's annual outflow of £52,000. The disposal value of the new machine five years hence will be £4,000.

The minimum desired rate of return is 20%. The company uses DCF techniques to guide these decisions.

Should Aberdeen Ale acquire the new brewing machine? Show your calculations. Company procedures require the computing of the present value of each alternative. The most desirable alternative is the one with the least cost. Assume that the PV of £1 at 20% for five years is £.40; the present value of an annuity of £1 at 20% for five years is £3.

11-52 Replacement Decision

Bay Area Commuter Rail (BACR), Inc., has included a cafeteria car on the passenger train it operates. Yearly operations of the cafeteria car have shown a consistent loss, which is expected to persist, as follows:

Revenue (in cash)		$200,000
Expenses for food, supplies, etc. (in cash)	$100,000	
Salaries	110,000	210,000
Net loss (ignore depreciation on the dining car itself)		$ (10,000)

The Auto-Vend Company has offered to sell automatic vending machines to BACR for $22,000, less a $3,000 trade-in allowance on old equipment (which is carried at $3,000 book value, and which can be sold outright for $3,000 cash) now used in the cafeteria car operation. The useful life of the vending equipment is estimated at ten years, with zero scrap value. Experience elsewhere has led executives to predict that the equipment will serve 50% more food than the dining car, but prices will be 50% less, so the new revenue will probably be $150,000. The variety and mix of food sold are expected to be the same as for the cafeteria car. A catering company will completely service and supply food and beverages for the machines, paying 10% of revenue to BACR and bearing all costs of food, repairs, and so on. All dining car employees will be discharged immediately. Their termination pay will total $32,000. However, an attendant who has some general knowledge of vending machines will be needed for one shift per day. The annual cost to BACR for the attendant will be $13,000.

For political and other reasons, the railroad will definitely not abandon its food service. The old equipment will have zero scrap value at the end of ten years.

Using the preceding data, compute the following. Label computations. Ignore income taxes.

1. Use the NPV method to analyze the incremental investment. Assume a minimum desired rate of return of 10%. For this problem, assume that the PV of $1 at 10% to be received at the end of ten years is $.400 and that the PV of an annuity of $1 at 10% for ten years is $6.000.
2. What would be the minimum amount of annual revenue that BACR would have to receive from the catering company to justify making the investment? Show computations.

11-53 Minimization of Transportation Costs without Income Taxes

The Luxor Company produces industrial and residential lighting fixtures at its manufacturing facility located in Phoenix. The company currently ships products to an eastern warehouse via common carriers at a rate of $.26 per pound of fixtures. The warehouse is located in Cleveland, 2,500 miles from Phoenix.

Marvella Harris, the treasurer of Luxor, is considering whether to purchase a truck for transporting products to the eastern warehouse. The following data on the truck are available:

Purchase price	$40,000
Useful life	5 years
Salvage value after 5 years	0
Capacity of truck	10,000 lb
Cash costs of operating truck	$.90 per mile

Harris feels that an investment in this truck is particularly attractive because of her successful negotiation with Retro, Inc., to back-haul Retro's products from Cleveland to Phoenix on every return trip from the warehouse. Retro has agreed to pay Luxor $2,400 per load of Retro's products hauled from Cleveland to Phoenix up to and including 100 loads per year.

Luxor's marketing manager has estimated that the company will ship 500,000 pounds of fixtures to the eastern warehouse each year for the next five years. The truck will be fully loaded on each round trip.

Ignore income taxes.

1. Assume that Luxor requires a minimum rate of return of 20%. Should it purchase the truck? Show computations to support your answer.
2. What is the minimum number of trips that Retro must guarantee to make the deal acceptable to Luxor, based on the preceding numbers alone?
3. What qualitative factors might influence your decision? Be specific.

11-54 Straight-Line Depreciation, MACRS Depreciation, and Immediate Write-Off

Mr. Tan bought a new $30,000 freezer for his grocery store on January 2, 2004. The freezer has a five-year economic life and recovery period, Mr. Tan's minimum desired rate of return is 12%, and his tax rate is 40%.

1. Suppose Mr. Tan uses straight-line depreciation for tax purposes. Compute the present value of the tax savings from depreciation. Assume that Mr. Tan takes a full year of depreciation at the end of 2004.
2. Suppose Mr. Tan uses MACRS depreciation for tax purposes. Compute the present value of the tax savings from depreciation.
3. Suppose Mr. Tan was allowed to immediately deduct the entire cost of the freezer for tax purposes. Compute the present value of the tax savings from depreciation.
4. Which of the three methods of deducting the cost of the freezer would Mr. Tan prefer if all three were allowable for tax purposes? Why?

11-55 MACRS, Residual Value

The Glavine Company estimates that it can save $10,000 per year in annual operating cash costs for the next five years if it buys a special-purpose machine at a cost of $33,000. Residual value is expected to be $5,000, although no residual value is being provided for in using MACRS depreciation (five-year recovery period) for tax purposes. The company will sell the equipment at the end of the fifth year. The minimum desired rate of return, after taxes, is 12%. Assume the income tax rate is 45%.

1. Using the net-present-value method, show whether the investment is desirable.
2. Suppose the equipment will produce savings for seven years instead of five. The company expects the residual value to be zero at the end of the seventh year. Using the net-present-value method, show whether the investment is desirable.

11-56 Purchase of Equipment

The Sacramento Clinic, a for-profit medical facility, is planning to spend $45,000 for modernized X-ray equipment. It will replace equipment that has zero book value and no salvage value, although the old equipment would have lasted another seven years.

The new equipment will save $14,000 in cash operating costs for each of the next seven years, at which time the clinic will sell it for $6,000. A major overhaul costing $5,000 will occur at the end of the fourth year; the old equipment would require no such overhaul. The entire cost of the overhaul is deductible for tax purposes in the fourth year. The equipment has a five-year recovery period. The clinic uses MACRS depreciation for tax purposes.

The minimum desired rate of return after taxes is 12%. The applicable income tax rate is 40%.

Compute the after-tax net present value. Is the new equipment a desirable investment?

11-57 MACRS and Low-Income Housing

Benjamin Rabinowitz is a real estate developer who specializes in residential apartments. A complex of 20 run-down apartments has recently come on the market for $310,000. Rabinowitz predicts that after remodeling, the 12 one-bedroom units will rent for $380 per month and the 8 two-bedroom apartments for $440. He budgets 15% of the rental fees for repairs and maintenance. It should be 30 years before the apartments need remodeling again, if the work is done well. Remodeling costs are $12,000 per apartment. Both purchase price and remodeling costs qualify as 27.5-year MACRS property.

Assume that the MACRS schedule assigns an equal amount of depreciation to each of the first 27 years and one-half year to the 28th year. The present value at 10% of $1 of cost recovery spread over the 28 years in this way is $.3372.

Rabinowitz does not believe he will keep the apartment complex for its entire 30-year life. Most likely he will sell it just after the end of the tenth year. His predicted sales price is $950,000.

Rabinowitz's after-tax required rate of return is 10%, and his tax rate is 38%.

Should Rabinowitz buy the apartment complex? What is the after-tax net present value? Ignore tax complications such as capital gains.

11-58 Present Value of After-Tax Cash Flows, Payback, and ARR

Osaka Company, a Japanese chemical company, is planning to buy new equipment to expand their production of a popular solvent. Estimated data are (monetary amounts are in thousands of Japanese yen):

Cash cost of new equipment now	¥380,000
Estimated life in years	10
Terminal salvage value	¥ 60,000
Incremental revenues per year	¥320,000
Incremental expenses per year other than depreciation	¥165,000

Assume a 60% flat rate for income taxes. The company receives all revenues and pays all expenses other than depreciation in cash. Use a 14% discount rate. Assume that the company uses ordinary straight-line depreciation based on a ten-year recovery period for tax purposes. Also assume that the company depreciates the original cost less the terminal salvage value.

Compute

1. Depreciation expense per year
2. Anticipated net income per year
3. Annual net cash flow
4. Payback period
5. Accounting rate of return on initial investment
6. Net present value

11-59 Investment Justification Analysis and Graphs

Consider a new integrated circuit (IC-968) developed by Analog Instruments Company (AIC). AIC's development team was formed at the end of 2000 and has been working on the development of IC-968 for several years. After spending $175,000 on the development of IC-968, the team has reached the point in 2004 where they must make a decision on whether to proceed with production of IC-968. Production of IC-968 will require an initial investment in facilities of $199,500 at the end of 2004.

The project has an expected life cycle of seven years (end of 2004 through 2011). Predicted cash flows for IC-968 are as follows (assuming that all cash flows occur at the end of the year):

End of Year	Cash Inflow	Cash Outflow
2004	$ 0	$199,500
2005	100,000	100,000
2006	220,000	180,000
2007	340,000	260,000
2008	460,000	320,000
2009	470,000	280,000
2010	410,000	200,000
2011	150,000	120,000

AIC's applicable tax rate is 40%, and Analog Instruments uses straight-line depreciation over the asset's expected life for tax purposes. The salvage value of the facilities will be zero in seven years. AIC uses two criteria to evaluate potential investments: payback time and NPV. It wants a payback period of three years or less and an NPV greater than zero. AIC has a cost of capital of 18%.

Required

1. Prepare a table that shows the after-tax annual net cash flows, cumulative net cash flow, and cumulative discounted net cash flow each year.
2. Would Analog Instruments invest in IC-968 production if it uses the payback period?
3. Would Analog Instruments invest in IC-968 production if it uses the NPV model?
4. Use graph paper to prepare a well-labeled line chart that shows the cumulative after-tax net cash flow and the cumulative after-tax discounted net cash flow of this investment over its life cycle. On your chart, clearly identify the payback time and the net present value for the project.
5. Would you recommend that AIC invest in this project? Explain.

11-60 Fixed and Current Assets; Evaluation of Performance

Bloomington Clinic has been under pressure to keep costs down. Indeed, the clinic administrator has been managing various revenue-producing centers to maximize contributions to the recovery of the operating costs of the clinic as a whole. The administrator has been considering whether to buy a special-purpose X-ray machine for $193,000. Its unique characteristics would generate additional cash operating income of $51,000 per year for the clinic as a whole.

The clinic expects the machine to have a useful life of six years and a terminal salvage value of $22,000. The machine is delicate. It requires a constant inventory of various supplies and spare parts. When the clinic uses some of these items, it instantly replaces them, so it maintains an investment of $16,000 at all times. However, the clinic fully recovers this investment at the end of the useful life of the machine.

1. Compute NPV if the required rate of return is 14%.
2. Compute the accounting rate of return on (a) the initial investment and (b) the "average" investment.
3. Why might the administrator be reluctant to base her decision on the DCF model?

11-61 Deer Valley Lodge

Deer Valley Lodge, a ski resort in the Wasatch Range of Utah, has plans to eventually add five new chairlifts. Suppose that one of the lifts costs $2 million, and preparing the slope and installing the lift costs another $1.3 million. The lift will allow 300 additional skiers on the slopes, but there are only 40 days a year when the lodge needs the extra capacity. (Assume that Deer Valley will sell all 300 lift tickets on those 40 days.) Running the new lift will cost $500 a day for the entire 200 days the lodge is open. Assume that lift tickets at Deer Valley cost $60 a day, and added cash expenses for each skier-day are $10. The new lift has an economic life of 20 years.

1. Assume that the before-tax required rate of return for Deer Valley is 14%. Compute the before-tax NPV of the new lift and advise the managers of Deer Valley about whether adding the lift will be a profitable investment.
2. Assume that the after-tax required rate of return for Deer Valley is 8%, the income tax rate is 40%, and the MACRS recovery period is ten years. Compute the after-tax NPV of the new lift and advise the managers of Deer Valley about whether adding the lift will be a profitable investment.
3. What subjective factors would affect the investment decision?

11-62 Minimization of Transportation Costs After Taxes, Inflation

Study Appendix 11. (This problem is a version of problem 11-53 that includes taxes and inflation elements.) The Luxor Company produces industrial and residential lighting fixtures at its manufacturing facility in Phoenix. The company currently ships products to an eastern warehouse via common carriers at a rate of 26¢ per pound of fixtures (expressed in year-zero dollars). The warehouse is located in Cleveland, 2,500 miles from Phoenix. The rate will increase with inflation.

Marvella Harris, the treasurer of Luxor, is currently considering whether to purchase a truck for transporting products to the eastern warehouse. The following data on the truck are available:

Purchase price	$40,000
Useful life	5 years
Terminal residual value	0
Capacity of truck	10,000 lb
Cash costs of operating truck	
(expressed in year-1 dollars)	$.90 per mile

Harris feels that an investment in this truck is particularly attractive because of her successful negotiation with Retro, Inc., to back-haul Retro's products from Cleveland to Phoenix on every return trip from the warehouse. Retro has agreed to pay Luxor $2,400 per load of Retro's products hauled from Cleveland to Phoenix for as many loads as Luxor can accommodate, up to and including 100 loads per year over the next five years.

Luxor's marketing manager has estimated that the company will ship 500,000 pounds of fixtures to the eastern warehouse each year for the next five years. The truck will be fully loaded on each round trip.

Make the following assumptions:

a. Luxor requires a minimum 20% after-tax rate of return, which includes a 10% element attributable to inflation.
b. A 40% tax rate.
c. MACRS depreciation based on five-year cost recovery period.
d. An inflation rate of 10%.

1. Should Luxor purchase the truck? Show computations to support your answer.
2. What qualitative factors might influence your decision? Be specific.

11-63 Inflation and Nonprofit Institution

Study Appendix 11. The city of Birmingham is considering the purchase of a photocopying machine for $7,300 on December 31, 20X0. The machine will have a useful life of five years and no residual value. The cash operating savings are expected to be $2,000 annually, measured in 20X0 dollars.

The minimum desired rate is 14%, which includes an element attributable to anticipated inflation of 6%. (Remember that the city pays no income taxes.)

Use the 14% minimum desired rate for numbers 1 and 2:

1. Compute the net present value of the project without adjusting the cash operating savings for inflation.
2. Repeat number 1, adjusting the cash operating savings upward in accordance with the 6% inflation rate.
3. Compare your results in numbers 1 and 2. What generalization seems applicable about the analysis of inflation in capital budgeting?

Cases

11-64 Investment in CAD/CAM

Gothenborg Fabrik, a Swedish manufacturing company, is considering the installation of a computer-aided design/computer-aided manufacturing (CAD/CAM) system. The current proposal calls for implementation of only the CAD portion of the system. Arvid Petterson, the manager in charge of production design and planning, has estimated that the CAD portion of CAD/CAM could do the work of five designers, who are each paid SKr 260,000 per year (52 weeks × 40 hours × SKr 125 per hour), where SKr is the symbol for Swedish krona.

Gothenborg Fabrik can purchase the CAD/CAM system for SKr 1.5 million. (It cannot purchase the CAD portion separately.) The annual out-of-pocket costs of running the CAD portion of the system are SKr 900,000. The company expects to use the system for eight years. The company's minimum desired rate of return is 12%.

1. Compute the NPV of the investment in the CAD/CAM system. Should Gothenborg Fabrik purchase the system? Explain.
2. Suppose Petterson was not certain about his predictions of savings and economic life. Possibly the company will replace only four designers, but if everything works out well, it may replace as many as six. If better systems become available, the company may use the CAD/CAM system for only five years, but it might last as long as ten years. Prepare pessimistic, most likely, and optimistic predictions of NPV. Would this analysis make you more confident or less confident in your decision in number 1? Explain.
3. What subjective factors might influence your decision?

11-65 Investment in Technology

Lexington Auto Parts Company is considering installation of a computer-integrated manufacturing (CIM) system as part of its implementation of a JIT philosophy. Carley Rupp, company president, is convinced that the new system is necessary, but she needs the numbers to convince the Board of Directors. This is a major move for the company, and approval at board level is required.

Leah Rupp, Carley's daughter, has been assigned the task of justifying the investment. She is a business school graduate and understands the use of NPV for capital-budgeting decisions. To identify relevant costs, she developed the following information.

Lexington Auto Parts Company produces a variety of small automobile components and sells them to auto manufacturers. It has a 40% market share, with the following condensed results expected for 2004:

Sales		$12,000,000
Cost of goods sold		
Variable	$4,000,000	
Fixed	4,300,000	8,300,000
Selling and administrative expenses		
Variable	$2,000,000	
Fixed	400,000	2,400,000
Operating income		$ 1,300,000

Installation of the CIM system will cost $5.5 million, and the company expects the system to have a useful life of six years with no salvage value. In 2005, the training costs for personnel will exceed any cost savings by $400,000. In years 2006 through 2010, variable cost of goods sold will decrease by 40%, an annual savings of $1.6 million. There will be no savings in fixed cost of goods sold—in fact, it will increase by the amount of the straight-line depreciation on the new system. Selling and administrative expenses will not be affected. The required rate of return is 12%. Assume that all cash flows occur at the end of the year, except the initial investment, which occurs at the beginning of 2005.

1. Suppose that Leah Rupp assumes that production and sales would continue for the next six years as they were in 2004 in the absence of investment in the CIM. Compute the NPV of investing in the CIM.
2. Now suppose Leah predicts that it will be difficult to compete without installing the CIM. In fact, she has undertaken market research that estimates a drop in market share of three percentage points a year starting in 2005 in the absence of investment in the CIM (i.e., market share will be 37% in 2005, 34% in 2006, 31% in 2007, etc.). Her study also showed that the total market sales level will stay the same, and she does not expect market prices to change. Compute the NPV of investing in the CIM.
3. Prepare a memo from Leah Rupp to the Board of Directors of Lexington Auto Parts Company. In the memo, explain why the analysis in number 2 is appropriate and why analyses such as that in number 1 cause companies to underinvest in high-technology projects. Include an explanation of qualitative factors that are not included in the NPV calculation.

11-66 Investment in Quality

The Perth Manufacturing Company produces a single model of a high-quality DVD player that it sells to Australian manufacturers of sound systems. It sells each DVD player for $210, resulting in a contribution margin of $70 before considering any costs of inspection, correction of product defects, or refunds to customers.

In 20X1, top management at Perth is contemplating a change in its quality control system. Currently, the company spends $40,000 annually on quality control inspections for the 50,000 DVD players it produces and ships each year. In producing those DVD players, the company produces an average of 2,000 defective units. The inspection process identifies 1,500 of these, and the company spends an average of $85 on each to correct the defects. The company ships the other 500 defective players to customers. When a customer discovers a defective DVD player, Perth Manufacturing refunds the $210 purchase price.

Many of Perth's customers build the DVDs into home-entertainment units. As more and more of these customers change to JIT inventory systems and automated production processes, the receipt of defective goods poses greater and greater problems for them. Sometimes a defective DVD player causes them to delay their whole production line while they replace the DVD player. Companies competing with Perth recognize this situation, and most have already begun extensive quality control programs. If Perth does not improve quality, sales volume is expected to fall by 5,000 DVD players a year, beginning after 20X2:

	Predicted Sales Volume in Units Without Quality Control Program	Predicted Sales Volume in Units with Quality Control Program
20X2	50,000	50,000
20X3	45,000	50,000
20X4	40,000	50,000
20X5	35,000	50,000

The proposed quality control program has two elements. First, Perth would spend $800,000 immediately to train workers to recognize and correct defects at the time they occur. This is expected to cut the number of defective DVD players produced from 2,000 to 500 without incurring additional manufacturing costs. Second, an earlier inspection point would replace the current inspection. This would require purchase of an X-ray machine at a cost of $250,000 plus additional annual operating costs of $50,000 more than the current inspection costs. Early detection of defects would reduce the average amount spent to correct defects from $85 to $50, and only 50 defective DVD players would be shipped to customers. To compete, Perth would refund one-and-one-half times the purchase price ($315) for defective DVD players delivered to customers.

Top management at Perth has decided that a four-year planning period is sufficient for analyzing this decision. The minimum required rate of return is 20%. For simplicity, assume that under the current quality control system, if the volume of production decreases, the number of defective DVD players produced remains at 2,000. Also assume that all annual cash flows occur at the end of the relevant year. Should Perth Manufacturing Company undertake the new quality control program? Explain, using the NPV model. Ignore income taxes.

11-67 Make or Buy and Replacement of Equipment

Nautical Creations is one of the largest producers of miniature ships in a bottle. An especially complex part of one of the ships needs special tools that are not useful for other products. The company purchased these tools on July 1, 2000, for $200,000.

It is now July 1, 2004. The manager of the Model Ships Division, Jeri Finley, is contemplating three alternatives. First, she could continue to produce the ship using the current tools; they will last another five years, at which time they would have zero terminal value. Second, she could sell the tools for $40,000 and purchase the parts from an outside supplier for $11 each. Third, she could replace the tools with new, more efficient tools costing $180,000.

Finley expects to produce 8,000 units of the ship each of the next five years. Manufacturing costs for the ship have been as follows, and no change in costs is expected:

Direct materials	$ 3.80
Direct labor	3.70
Variable overhead	1.70
Fixed overhead*	4.50
Total unit cost	$13.70

* Depreciation accounts for two-thirds of the fixed overhead. The balance is for other fixed overhead costs of the factory that require cash outlays, 60% of which would be saved if production of the parts were eliminated.

The outside supplier offered the $11 price as a once-only offer. It is unlikely they would make such a low price available later. Nautical Creations would also have to guarantee to purchase at least 7,000 parts for each of the next five years.

The new tools that are available would last for five years with a disposal value of $50,000 at the end of five years. The old tools are a five-year MACRS property, the new tools are a three-year MACRS property, and both use the current MACRS schedules. Nautical Creations uses straight-line depreciation for book purposes and MACRS for tax purposes. The sales representative selling the new tools stated, "The new tools will allow direct labor and variable overhead to be reduced by $2.10 per unit." Finley thinks this estimate is accurate. However, she also knows that a higher quality of materials would be necessary with the new tools. She predicts the following costs with the new tools:

Direct materials	$ 4.00
Direct labor	2.50
Variable overhead	.80
Fixed overhead	6.00*
Total unit cost	$13.30

* The increase in fixed overhead is caused by depreciation on the new tools.

The company has a 40% marginal tax rate and requires a 12% after-tax rate of return.

1. Calculate the net present value of each of the three alternatives. Recognize the tax implications. Which alternative should Finley select?
2. What are some factors besides the net present value that should influence Finley's selection?

EXCEL Application Exercise

11-68 Net present value and payback period for a purchase decision

Goal: Create a spreadsheet to compute the net present value and payback period to assist with a purchase decision. Use the results to answer questions about your findings.

Scenario: Amazon is planning to purchase a new bar-coding machine for one of its warehouses. You have been asked to prepare a simple analysis to determine whether the machine should be purchased. The bar-coding machine costs $60,000. It has a five-year economic life and an estimated residual value of $10,000. The estimated annual net cash flow from the machine is $16,000. Amazon's required rate of return is 16%. When you have completed your spreadsheet, answer the following questions:

1. What is the machine's net present value (NPV)?
2. What is the machine's payback period?
3. Should Amazon purchase the machine? Why or why not?

Step-by-Step:

1. Open a new Excel spreadsheet.
2. In column A, create a bold-faced heading that contains the following:
   Row 1: Chapter 11 Decision Guideline
   Row 2: Amazon
   Row 3: Analysis for Purchase of Bar-Coding Machine
   Row 4: Today's Date
3. Merge and center the four heading rows across columns A through H.
4. In row 7, create the following bold-faced headings:
   Column A: Cash Outflow
   Column B: Calculations
   Column D: Annualized Cash Flows
5. Center the heading in column A, row 7 and then shade the heading as follows:

Patterns tab:	Color:	Lightest grey (above white)

Note: Adjust column width as necessary.

6. Merge and center the heading in column B, row 7 across columns B through C.
7. Merge and center the heading in column D, row 7 across columns D through H and shade the heading as follows:

Patterns tab:	Color:	Lightest grey (above white)

8. In row 8, create the following bold-faced, center-justified column headings:
Column A: Investment
Column B: Net Present Value
Column C: Payback Period
Column D: Year 1
Column E: Year 2
Column F: Year 3
Column G: Year 4
Column H: Year 5
Note: Adjust the width of columns B and C as necessary.

9. Use the scenario data to fill in the investment and annualized cash flows for each of the five years.
Note: The amount in the Investment column should be entered as a negative amount because it represents cash outflow. Be sure to include the machine's residual value in the appropriate column when entering the Annualized Cash Flows data.

10. Use the NPV function to calculate the net present value of the machine in column B, row 9.
Click Insert on the tool bar and select Function. Then do the following:

Function category:	Financial
Function name:	NPV

Complete the fill-in form that appears with the appropriate data from the scenario.
Hint: Go to "Help" and search the topic "NPV." Review the help text that appears. Carefully read the examples given and their associated formulas. Use the formula that matches the Scenario data for the problem.

11. Enter a formula to calculate the payback period in column C, row 9. Ensure a positive result by using the absolute value function in your payback formula. (The formula can be found in the chapter.)
12. Modify the format of the payback period result by clicking in the cell containing the results. At the end of the formula that appears in the formula bar, type the following: & " years" Right justify the result.
13. Format row 9, columns A through B and columns D through H as

Number tab:	Category:	Currency
	Decimal places:	2
	Symbol:	$
	Negative numbers:	Red with parenthesis

14. Save your work to disk, and print a copy for your files.
Note: Print your spreadsheet using landscape to ensure that all columns appear on one page.

Collaborative Learning Exercise

11-69 Capital Budgeting, Sensitivity Analysis, and Ethics

Muriel Santelli had recently been appointed controller of the Breakfast Cereals Division of a major food company. The division manager, Ram Krishnamurthi, was known as a hard-driving, intelligent, uncompromising manager. He had been very successful and was rumored to be on the fast track to corporate top management, maybe even in line for the company presidency. One of Muriel's first assignments was to prepare the financial analysis for a new cold cereal, Krispie Krinkles. This product was especially important to Krishnamurthi because he was convinced that it would be a success and thereby a springboard for his ascent to top management.

Santelli discussed the product with the food lab that had designed it, with the market research department that had tested it, and with the finance people who would have to fund its introduction.

After putting together all the information, she developed the following optimistic and pessimistic sales projections:

	Optimistic	Pessimistic
Year 1	$ 1,600,000	$ 800,000
Year 2	3,600,000	1,200,000
Year 3	5,000,000	1,000,000
Year 4	8,000,000	800,000
Year 5	10,000,000	400,000

The optimistic predictions assume a successful introduction of a popular product. The pessimistic predictions assume that the product is introduced but does not gain wide acceptance and is terminated after five years. Santelli thinks the most likely results are halfway between the optimistic and pessimistic predictions.

Santelli learned from finance that this type of product introduction requires a predicted rate of return of 16% before top management will authorize funds for its introduction. She also determined that the contribution margin should be about 50% on the product, but could be as low as 42% or as high as 58%. Initial investment would include $3 million for production facilities, $2.5 million for advertising and other product introduction expenses, and $500,000 for working capital (inventory, etc.). The production facilities would have a value of $800,000 after five years.

Based on her preliminary analysis, Santelli recommended to Krishnamurthi that the product not be launched. Krishnamurthi was not pleased with the recommendation. He claimed that Santelli was much too pessimistic and asked her to redo her numbers so that he could justify the product to top management.

Santelli carried out further analysis, but her predictions came out no different. In fact, she became even more convinced that her projections were accurate. Yet, she was certain that if she returned to Krishnamurthi with numbers that did not support introduction of the product, she would incur his wrath. And, in fact, he could be right—that is, there is so much uncertainty in the forecasts that she could easily come up with believable numbers that would support going forward with the product. She would not believe them, but she believed she could convince top management that they were accurate.

The entire class could role-play this scenario, or it could be done in teams of three to six persons. Here, it is acted out by a team.

Choose one member of the team to be Muriel Santelli and one to be Ram Krishnamurthi.

1. With the help of the entire team except the person chosen to be Krishnamurthi, Santelli should prepare the capital-budgeting analysis used for her first meeting with Krishnamurthi.
2. Next, Santelli should meet again with Krishnamurthi. They should try to agree on the analysis to take forward to top management. As they discuss the issues and try to come to an agreement, the remaining team members should record all the ethical judgments each discussant makes.
3. After Santelli and Krishnamurthi have completed their role-playing assignment, the entire team should assess the ethical judgments made by each and recommend an appropriate position for Santelli to take in this situation.

Internet Exercise   www.prenhall.com/horngren

11-70 Capital Budgeting at Carnival Corporation

Many companies strive to continue to grow and develop. Some companies grow through the expansion of existing operations and increased utilization of existing assets. Others grow through the acquisition of firms within their industry or by purchasing a firm that opens up new direction for them. No matter which method a company selects, capital budgeting is an important part of a systematic expansion plan. Consider the expansion activities of **Carnival Corporation**, the cruise ship company.

1. Go to Carnival Corporation's home page at http://www.carnivalcorp.com. You should be on the page Investor Overview. What cruise lines does Carnival own or have an interest in? How many current ships does Carnival operate? What type of plans does the firm list for future expansion? What does this information indicate about the intent of the firm?
2. As we can see, the firm has looked ahead to buying new ships. To get additional information, click on the link to the annual reports, and then select the most recent annual report and open it. Go to the section on Management's Discussion and Analysis and find Selected Financial Data

near the end of the report. Looking at passengers carried and available lower berth days, examine how capacity available and capacity used have changed over the past five years.

3. Now, backtrack to the beginning of the annual report and read the CEO's letter. What does the letter tell the investor about new investment during the current year? What form did the investment/expansion take? What are the investment plans for the future?

4. While acquiring contracts for new ships and increasing ownership of other lines is noteworthy, the firm must in some manner plan to pay for this expansion. Let's look at the Statement of Cash Flows to see if we can determine where the firm got the cash to pay for the new ships. Based on your review of the cash flow statement, how much money did the firm invest in new assets? Where did Carnival generate these funds?

Solutions to Exercises in Compound Interest, Problem 11-A1

The general approach to these exercises centers on one fundamental question: Which of the two basic tables am I dealing with? No calculations should be made until after this question is answered with assurance. If you made any errors, it is possible that you used the wrong table.

1. From Table 1, Appendix B, page 821:
   a. $15,670
   b. $12,418
   c. $8,038

The $20,000 is an amount of future worth. You want the present value of that amount:

$$PV = \$20,000 \times \frac{1}{[(1+i)^n]}$$

The conversion factor, $1/(1+i)^n$, is on line 5 of Table 1. Substituting,

$$PV = \$20,000(.7835) = \$15,670$$
$$PV = \$20,000(.6209) = \$12,418$$
$$PV = \$20,000(.4019) = \$8,038$$

Note that the higher the interest rate, the lower the present value.

2. From Table 2, Appendix B, page 824:
   a. $8,659.00
   b. $7,581.60
   c. $5,981.20

The $2,000 withdrawal is a uniform annual amount, an annuity. You need to find the present value of an annuity for five years:

$$PV_A = \text{annual withdrawal} \times F, \text{ where F is the conversion factor.}$$

Substituting:
$$PV_A = \$2,000(4.3295) = \$8,659.00$$
$$PV_A = \$2,000(3.7908) = \$7,581.60$$
$$PV_A = \$2,000(2.9906) = \$5,981.20$$

3. From Table 2:
   a. $23,097.36
   b. $26,379.66

You have $100,000, the present value of your contemplated annuity. You must find the annuity that will just exhaust the invested principal in five years:

$$PV_A = \text{annual withdrawal} \times F$$
$$\$100,000 = \text{annual withdrawal} \times 4.3295$$
$$\text{annual withdrawal} = \$100,000 \div 4.3295$$
$$= \$23,097.36$$
$$\$100,000 = \text{annual withdrawal} \times 3.7908$$
$$\text{annual withdrawal} = \$100,000 \div 3.7908$$
$$= \$26,379.66$$

4. Amounts are in thousands. From Table 1: Johnson's contract is preferable; its present value exceeds that of Jackson's contract by $21,572 − $17,720 = $3,852. Note that the nearer dollars are more valuable than the distant dollars.

Year	Present Value @ 16% from Table 1	Present Value of Johnson's Contract	Present Value of Jackson's Contract
1	.8621	$ 8,621	$ 1,724
2	.7432	5,946	2,973
3	.6407	3,844	3,844
4	.5523	2,209	4,418
5	.4761	952	4,761
		$21,572	$17,720

Cost Allocation

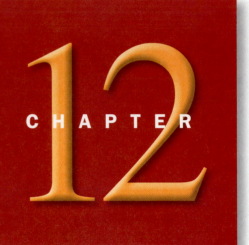

CHAPTER 12

Recall the last time you shopped in one of the following
stores—**Wal-Mart**, **Kmart**, **Dollar General**, **Best Buy**, **Walgreens**, or **Payless ShoeSource**. Do you remember anything about the store fixtures? Chances are, the answer is no. Store fixtures such as shelving, counters, garment racks, and displays are an important part of the merchandising programs of all leading discount, specialty, and department stores, but not many people are aware of them when shopping. One company that is an industry leader in store fixtures is **L. A. Darling Company**. L. A. Darling designs and manufactures metal, wood, and wire retail display systems for general merchandise, discount, department, drug, and specialty stores worldwide.

Recently, when a major retailer undertook an aggressive growth program, it selected Darling to meet its fixturing needs. According to Ray Watson, controller, "One of the advantages Darling offers companies is its large production capacity." But while this gives the company a competitive advantage, accounting for capacity costs, most of which are fixed manufacturing overhead, is a real challenge.

How should Darling allocate these fixed overhead costs to individual products, customers, or other cost objectives? Should Darling consider these costs when evaluating a manager's performance? Watson explains that the approach required for external reporting provides little value for measuring customer profitability. As a result, Darling uses the contribution approach (discussed in Chapter 6), combined with activity-based costing, for strategic decision making and operational control purposes.

Many companies base the evaluation of managers at least partly on the income of the organizational segment they manage. Therefore, managers strive to make their performance look good by making decisions that increase segment income. But how should we measure income? Accountants make many judgments when measuring income, and

L. A. Darling Company designs, makes, and installs displays, such as the ones shown here. The company uses many of the allocation concepts discussed in this chapter to ensure the cost information used for decision making and operational control is as accurate as possible.

one of the most important is choosing the appropriate method for calculating product costs. Some managers think product costing is a subject of interest only to accountants. However, when they realize that product costs affect their evaluations, they quickly begin to pay attention to the determination of product costs. Only by knowing what influences product costs will they be able to predict how their decisions will affect income and hence their evaluations.

Just as is the case for L. A. Darling, cost allocation is of strategic importance to most businesses. For example, faculty use a university's computer for teaching and for performing government-funded research. How much of its cost should we assign to the research projects? Or consider a special Los Angeles police unit set up to investigate a series of related assaults. What is the total cost of the effort? Finally, suppose a company uses a machine to make two different product lines. How much of the cost of the machine should we assign to each product line? These are all problems of cost allocation, the subject of this chapter. ■

Cost Allocation in General

In this section, we deal with two important questions: *Why* do companies allocate costs? *How* do companies allocate costs? As a manager, you make many important decisions that are based to a large degree on cost data. If the vast majority of costs were directly traceable—say, greater than 90%—cost allocation would be a minor issue. Unfortunately, for almost all companies, the proportion of all value-chain costs that can be directly traced to cost objectives is much less than 50%. So your choice is clear—base your decisions on a small fraction of total costs or attempt to find ways to allocate indirect costs that meets the cost/benefit criteria.

OBJECTIVE 1

Explain the major reasons for allocating costs.

As mentioned above, there are many reasons to allocate costs. So, before a manager can decide how to allocate costs, he or she needs to understand the reasons for allocation. We start with a discussion of why companies allocate costs.

Purposes of Cost Allocation

What logic should we use for allocating costs? The answer depends on the principal purpose(s) of the cost allocation for a specific organization. In short, there are no firm rules that we can rely on—there is no "best cost-allocation system." In fact, there are nearly as many schemes for allocation as there are companies. We focus on general concepts that provide guidance when managers are designing these systems.

Cost allocations support a company's cost management system (CMS) that provides cost measurements for strategic decision making, operational control, and external reporting. We list four puposes of cost allocation here; the first two support strategic decision making and operational control. The third supports external reporting. The last one has elements of both strategic decision making and external reporting.

1. *To predict the economic effects of strategic and operational control decisions:* Major strategic decisions include setting the optimal product and customer mix, establishing pricing policy, and setting policy about which value-chain functions to develop as core competencies. Managers also need to predict the economic effects—both benefits and costs—of process improvement efforts. Managers within an organizational unit should be aware of all the consequences of their decisions, even consequences outside of their unit. Examples are the addition of a new course in a university that causes additional work in the registrar's office, the addition of a new flight or an additional passenger on an airline that requires reservation and booking services, and the addition of a new specialty in a medical clinic that produces more work for the medical records department.

2. *To obtain desired motivation and to provide feedback for performance evaluation:* Cost allocations often influence management behavior and thus promote goal congruence and managerial effort. Consequently, some organizations do not allocate the costs of legal or internal auditing services or internal management consulting services because top

management wants to encourage their use. Other organizations allocate the costs of such items to spur managers to make sure the benefits of the specified services exceed the costs.

3. *To compute income and asset valuations:* Companies allocate costs to products and projects to measure inventory costs and cost of goods sold.

4. *To justify costs or obtain reimbursement:* Sometimes prices are based directly on costs. For example, government contracts often specify a price that includes reimbursement for costs plus some profit margin. In these instances, cost allocations become substitutes for the usual working of the marketplace in setting prices.

Ideally, a single cost allocation would serve all four purposes simultaneously. But thousands of managers and accountants will testify that most systems fail to achieve this ideal. Instead, cost allocations are often a major source of discontent and confusion to the affected parties. Allocating fixed costs usually causes the greatest problems. When a system cannot meet all purposes simultaneously, managers and accountants need to identify which of the purposes dominate the particular situation at hand.

Often inventory-costing rules for external reporting purposes dominate by default because they are externally imposed (GAAP). Thus, when managers need individual product or customer costs for decision making and performance evaluation, they often have to adjust the allocations used to satisfy inventory-costing purposes. Generally, the added benefit of using different allocations for planning and control than for inventory-costing purposes is much greater than the added cost. One company that learned this is Dow Chemical, as described in the Business First box on page 524.

Methods of Cost Allocation

Now let's turn to the question of *how* companies allocate costs. Cost-allocation methods comprise an important part of a company's **cost accounting system**—the techniques it uses to determine the cost of a product, service, customer, or other cost objective. Why? Because, for most companies, the percent of all resources whose costs can be directly traced to products and services is less than 50%. For the rest of a company's costs, the choice is either to apply cost-allocation methods or to leave costs unallocated. The latter choice is not perceived by managers as optimal.

> **cost accounting system**
> *The techniques used to determine the cost of a product, service, customer, or other cost objective.*

Because of the importance to all organizations of products or services as final cost objectives, we focus on how companies assign direct costs and allocated costs to these cost objectives. This generally includes all production-related costs, but it may omit other value-chain costs, such as R&D, marketing, or administrative expenses. Some companies assign nearly all value-chain costs to products or services, while others elect not to assign costs from parts of the value chain other than production. Companies must assign all production costs and only production costs for external financial reporting purposes. They can elect to assign or not assign all other costs for internal management purposes.

We will use the framework in Exhibit 12-1 to show how cost allocation fits into the overall cost accounting system. Each of the arrows in Exhibit 12-1 represents an assignment of some costs to a cost objective. We show three types of cost objectives—service departments, producing departments, and the final cost objective—products or services. The cost accounting system first accumulates costs and assigns them to organizational units which we will refer to as departments. We can physically trace the direct department costs to each department, shown by the arrows labeled "1". An example is the salaries of service department personnel in departments such as human resources or facilities maintenance. In contrast, we have to allocate the indirect costs such as rent for facilities used by more than one department. We label these allocations "2" in Exhibit 12-1.

Once a company has assigned resource costs 1 and 2 to service departments, it often chooses to move these costs into other service departments—allocation 3. **Service departments** exist only to support other departments, so the system totally reallocates their costs. Examples include personnel departments, laundry departments in hospitals,

> **service departments**
> *Units that exist only to support other departments.*

Dow Chemical believes that its ABC allocation system is the foundation of its cost management system. Dow, with annual revenues of more than $27 billion, is the largest chemical company in the United States. The company has three major business segments: plastics, chemicals, and agricultural products. Dow switched from a traditional allocation system to ABC in the mid-1990s as part of a major shift in its total strategy. It sold its pharmaceutical, energy, and consumer products businesses and set a goal to be the number one company in chemicals, plastics, and agroscience. Dow believed that to accomplish its goal, it needed to improve the quality and accuracy of its costing system, including the costs of internal services such as those provided by the human resources and maintenance departments.

Service providers such as human resources and maintenance identified the major activities performed, deter-mined the appropriate cost drivers for each activity, and computed costs for each activity and service provided to using departments. The focus on activities has led to a better understanding of costs by everyone and better cost control. One technique Dow's managers use to improve cost control is benchmarking. Service providers benchmark their costs against outside providers to ensure that the service or activity cost is competitive. Another advantage of the ABC system is improved resource planning and utilization. By focusing on activities and their related cost drivers, Dow's maintenance department managers can more effectively plan maintenance resource needs and availability. Overall, since the company integrated ABC into its cost management system it has realized significant benefits.

Sources: J. Damitio, G. Hayes, and P. Kintzele, "Integrating ABC and ABM at Dow Chemical," *Management Accounting Quarterly*, Winter 2000, pp. 22–26; Dow Chemical Company, *2002 Annual Report*.

and legal departments in industrial firms. After assignments 1, 2, and 3 have been made, managers can evaluate each service department as a cost objective.

In order to evaluate the costs of resources used in producing departments such as machine processing, installation, or assembly, many companies will develop allocation methods to move service department costs into the producing departments. Why? The reason is that managers want to know both producing-department costs and the costs of resources from other departments that are used. We show these assignments as 4 in Exhibit 12-1. Sometimes, producing departments transfer items to other producing departments as well as producing final products or services. For example, a producing department may process a chemical resulting in several final products and several products that need to be processed further. We transfer the costs of products that need further processing to other producing departments—labled "5" in Exhibit 12-1. It is important for you to recognize that any direct service department costs—labled "1"—become indirect costs when allocation 4 is performed. For example, the salaries of human resources personnel are a direct departmental cost for the human resources department. However, when these costs, along with all other human resource department costs, are allocated to producing departments, they become indirect to the producing department.

At this point, we have accumulated all service department and producing department costs into the producing departments. As you probably know, the most important cost objectives for a company as a whole are the products or services it sells. The final step in cost allocation is to assign costs to the final cost objectives, which are products or services. Again, we have changed the cost objectives and some costs that were directly traceable to the producing departments will be indirect when the cost objective is the various products or services. Examples include salaries of production supervisors, supplies, and most equipment costs. However, unlike service department cost allocations, there are significant producing department costs that are directly traceable to products and services. We indicate

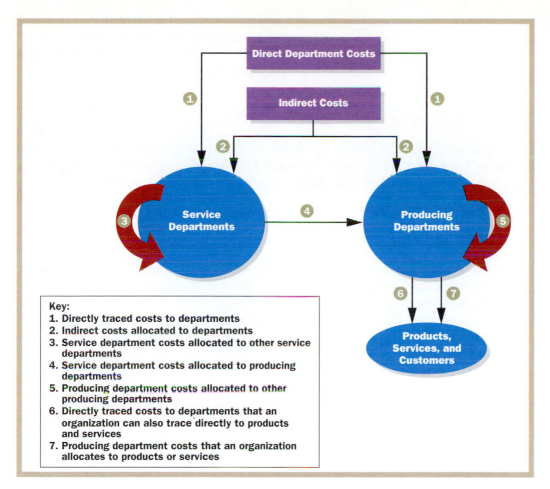

Exhibit 12-1
Framework for Cost
Accounting Systems

Key:
1. Directly traced costs to departments
2. Indirect costs allocated to departments
3. Service department costs allocated to other service departments
4. Service department costs allocated to producing departments
5. Producing department costs allocated to other producing departments
6. Directly traced costs to departments that an organization can also trace directly to products and services
7. Producing department costs that an organization allocates to products or services

these costs as "6". Examples are direct materials and direct labor. Last, all other producing department costs are allocated to products and services, labeled "7" in Exhibit 12-1.

The accounting system will assign to a department's output all of its direct costs plus all of the indirect costs allocated to it. This requires accountants to identify and measure a department's output (to which it will allocate costs) and determine the cost driver to use as a cost-allocation base for the indirect costs. The pediatrics department of a medical clinic might allocate its indirect costs to patients based on physician time per patient, the assembly activity of a manufacturing firm to units assembled based on machine hours used, and the tax department of a CPA firm to clients based on professional hours spent.

When we use a cost driver for allocating costs we call it a **cost-allocation base.** For example, a logical cost-allocation base for allocating rent costs to departments is the square feet that each department occupies. Other cost-allocation bases include cubic feet for allocating depreciation of heating and air conditioning equipment and total direct cost for allocating general administrative expense. Accountants use many different terms to describe cost allocation in practice. You may encounter terms such as *allocate, apply, absorb, attribute, reallocate, trace, assign, distribute, redistribute, load, burden, apportion,* and *reapportion* being used interchangeably to describe the allocation of costs to cost objectives.

Some individual indirect costs are important enough that we allocate them using obvious cost drivers. For example, we would allocate the cost of professional labor for a law firm to departments, jobs, and projects using labor hours used. We pool the other costs that are not important enough to justify being allocated individually and allocate them together. Recall that a cost pool is a group of individual costs that we allocate to cost objectives using a single cost driver. For example, building rent, utilities cost, and janitorial services may be in the same cost pool because a company allocates all of them on the basis of square footage of

cost-allocation base
A cost driver that is used for allocating costs.

space occupied. Or a university could pool all the operating costs of its registrar's office and allocate them to its colleges on the basis of the number of students in each college.

The next section looks in detail at allocation of service-department costs, and the following section focuses on allocation to the final cost objectives—products or services.

Allocation of Service Department Costs

In our general framework shown in Exhibit 12-1, service department allocations are labeled as 3 and 4. Before discussing methods of allocation, we give some general guidelines that managers should consider when designing allocation systems.

General Guidelines

The preferred guidelines for allocating service department costs are

1. Establish part or all of the details regarding cost allocation in advance of rendering the service rather than after the fact. This approach establishes the "rules of the game" so that all departments can plan appropriately.
2. Allocate variable- and fixed-cost pools separately. Note that one service department (such as a computer department) can contain multiple cost pools if more than one cost driver causes the department's costs. At a minimum, there should be a variable-cost pool and a fixed-cost pool.
3. Evaluate performance using budgets for each service (staff) department, just as for each production or operating (line) department. The performance of a service department is evaluated by comparing actual costs with a budget, regardless of how the costs are allocated. From the budget, variable-cost pools and fixed-cost pools can be identified for use in allocation.

Consider an example of a computer department of a university that serves two major users, the School of Business and the School of Engineering. Exhibit 12-2 shows the allocation system for this service department. Suppose there are two major reasons for the allocation: (1) predicting economic effects of the use of the computer, and (2) motivating the two schools and individuals to use its capabilities more fully. How should the university allocate the costs of the computer department (salaries, depreciation, energy, materials, and so on) to the two schools?

We begin by analyzing the costs of the computer department in detail. The primary activity performed is computer processing. The university acquired the computer mainframe on a five-year lease that is not cancelable unless it pays high cost penalties. Resources consumed include processing time, operator time, energy, materials, and building space. Suppose the university performed cost behavior analysis and the budget formula for the forthcoming year is $100,000 monthly fixed cost plus $200 variable cost per hour of computer time used. Refer to Exhibit 12-2 as we show how to apply guideline 2—the topic of the next two sections.

Variable-Cost Pool

Costs in the variable-cost pool include energy, operator labor costs, and materials. The cost driver for the variable-cost pool is actual hours of computer time used. Therefore, the university should allocate variable costs as follows:

$$\text{budgeted unit rate} \times \text{actual hours of computer time used}$$

The cause-and-effect relationship is clear: The heavier the usage, the higher the total costs. In this example, the budgeted cost-allocation rate is $200 per hour, determined by dividing the total budgeted costs of energy, operators, and materials by the total budgeted hours of computer time.

The use of budgeted cost rates rather than actual cost rates for allocating variable costs of service departments protects the user departments from intervening price fluctuations

Exhibit 12-2
Allocation of Variable-
and Fixed-Cost Pools

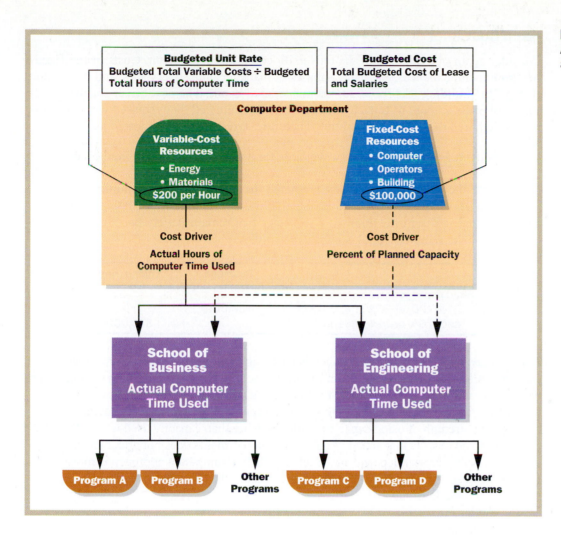

and also often protects them from inefficiencies in the service departments. When an organization allocates actual total service department cost, it holds user department managers responsible for costs beyond their control and provides less incentive for service departments to be efficient. Both effects are undesirable.

Consider the allocation of variable costs to a department that uses 600 hours of computer time. Suppose inefficiencies in the computer department caused the variable costs to be $140,000 instead of the 600 hours $\times$ $200 = $120,000 budgeted. A good cost-allocation scheme would allocate only the $120,000 to the consuming departments and would let the $20,000 remain as an unallocated unfavorable budget variance of the computer department. This scheme holds computer department managers responsible for the $20,000 variance and reduces the resentment of user managers. User department managers sometimes complain more vigorously about uncertainty over allocations and the poor management of a service department than about the choice of a cost driver (such as direct-labor dollars or number of employees). Such complaints are less likely if the service department managers have budget responsibility and the user departments are protected from short-run price fluctuations and inefficiencies.

Consider an automobile repair and maintenance department for a state government. Agencies that use the department's service should receive firm prices for various services. Imagine the feelings of an agency head who had an agency automobile repaired and was told, "Normally, your repair would have taken five hours. However, we had a new employee work on it, and the job took him ten hours. Therefore, we must charge you for ten hours of labor time."

Fixed-Cost Pool

Consider again our example of the university computer department. Costs in the fixed-cost pool include the lease payment, salaries of managers and supervisors, and occupancy costs of the building (depreciation, insurance, and so on). The cost driver for the fixed-cost pool is the amount of capacity the two schools estimated they required when the university acquired the computer facilities. Therefore, fixed costs are allocated as follows:

budgeted percent of capacity available for use × total budgeted fixed costs

Suppose the deans had originally predicted the long-run average monthly usage by Business at 210 hours, and by Engineering at 490 hours, a total of 700 hours. These estimates resulted in a set of committed fixed costs that remain largely uncontrollable over many years. The fixed-cost pool is allocated as follows:

	Business	Engineering
Fixed costs per month		
210/700, or 30% of $100,000	$30,000	
490/700, or 70% of $100,000		$70,000

This predetermined lump-sum approach is based on the long-run capacity available to the user, regardless of actual usage from month to month. The reasoning is that long-range planning regarding the overall level of service and the relative expected usage affect the level of fixed costs, not short-run fluctuations in service levels and relative actual usage.

A major strength of using capacity available rather than capacity used when allocating budgeted fixed costs is that actual usage by user departments does not affect the short-run allocations to other user departments. Such a budgeted lump-sum approach is more likely to have the desired motivational effects with respect to the ordering of services in both the short run and the long run.

In practice, companies often inappropriately allocate fixed-cost pools on the basis of capacity used, not capacity available. Suppose for two successive months the computer department's actual fixed costs were exactly the $100,000 budgeted. The university allocated these costs based on actual hours used by the consuming departments. Compare the costs borne by the two schools in the first month when Business uses 200 hours and Engineering 400 hours.

Total fixed costs incurred, $100,000	
Business: 200/600 × $100,000 =	$ 33,333
Engineering: 400/600 × $100,000 =	66,667
Total cost allocated	$100,000

What happens if Business uses only 100 hours during the following month, and Engineering still uses 400 hours?

Total fixed costs incurred, $100,000	
Business: 100/500 × $100,000 =	$ 20,000
Engineering: 400/500 × $100,000 =	80,000
Total cost allocated	$100,000

Engineering has done nothing differently, but it must bear an additional cost of $13,333, an increase of 20%. Its short-run costs depend on what other consumers have used, not solely on its own actions. This phenomenon is caused by a faulty allocation method for the fixed portion of total costs, a method whereby the allocations are highly sensitive to fluctuations in the actual volumes used by the various consuming departments. We can avoid this weakness by using a predetermined lump-sum allocation of fixed costs, based on budgeted usage.

Consider the preceding automobile repair shop example. You would not be happy if you came to get your car and were told, "Our daily fixed overhead is $1,000. Yours was the only car in our shop today, so we are charging you the full $1,000. If we had processed 100 cars today, your charge would have been only $10."

Trouble with Using Lump Sums

Using lump-sum allocations is not without problems, however. If a company allocates fixed costs on the basis of long-range plans, there is a natural tendency on the part of managers to underestimate their planned usage and thus obtain a smaller fraction of the cost allocation. Top management can counteract these tendencies by monitoring predictions and by following up and using feedback to keep future predictions more honest.

In some organizations, there are even definite rewards in the form of salary increases for managers who make accurate predictions. Moreover, some cost-allocation methods provide for penalties for underpredictions. For example, suppose a manager predicts usage of 210 hours and then demands 300 hours. The manager either doesn't get the hours or pays a dear price for every hour beyond 210 in such systems.

Reciprocal Services

In our computer department example, we assumed that computer services were provided only to two production units. Service departments often support other service departments in addition to producing departments. We call these services *reciprocal* or *interdepartmental services.*

Consider our chapter-opening vignette company L. A. Darling. Suppose one of L. A. Darling's display facilities assembles parts into custom and standard displays that Darling sells to WalMart, Kmart, and Walgreens. Exhibit 12-3 is a process map for the facility. There are two producing departments, processing and assembly, and two service departments, facilities management (rent, power, insurance, janitorial services, and some corporate resources such as administration and engineering) and human resources. In this section of the chapter, we focus on the processing and assembly departments as cost objectives. Let's assume that a single plausible and reliable cost driver exists for each service department and that all resource costs vary in proportion to this cost driver—these are variable-cost resources. Managers have decided that the best cost driver for facilities management costs is the square footage occupied and the best cost driver for human resources costs is the number of employees. Exhibit 12-3 shows the direct costs for a recent month when 200 custom and 1,200 standard displays were produced. Exhibit 12-3 shows the square footage occupied and number of employees for each department. Note that facilities management provides services for the human resources department in addition to providing services for the producing departments, and that human resources aids employees in facilities management as well as those in production departments.

There are two popular methods for allocating service department costs to producing departments in such cases: the direct method and the step-down method.

OBJECTIVE 3

Use the direct and step-down methods to allocate service department costs to user departments.

Direct Method As its name implies, the **direct method** ignores other service departments when allocating any given service department's costs to the operating departments. In other words, the direct method ignores the services that facilities management provides for human resources and the services that human resources provides to facilities management. The direct method allocates facilities management costs based on the relative square footage occupied by the processing and assembly departments only.

direct method
A method for allocating service department costs that ignores other service departments when any given service department's costs are allocated to the operating departments.

- Total square footage in production departments = 15,000 + 3,000 = 18,000
- Facilities management cost allocated to processing = (15,000 ÷ 18,000) × $1,260,000 = $1,050,000
- Facilities management cost allocated to assembly = (3,000 ÷ 18,000) × $1,260,000 = $210,000

Exhibit 12-3

L. A. Darling's
Processing Facility:
Service Department
Allocation

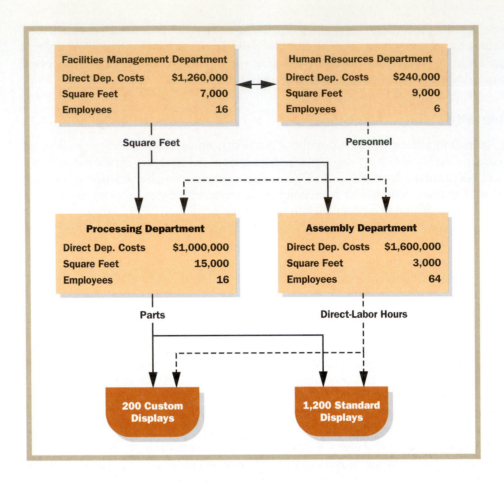

Likewise, human resources department costs are allocated only to the production departments on the basis of the relative number of employees in the production departments.

- Total employees in production departments = 16 + 64 = 80
- Human resources costs allocated to processing = (16 ÷ 80) × $240,000 = $48,000
- Human resources costs allocated to assembly = (64 ÷ 80) × $240,000 = $192,000

step-down method

*A method for allocating
service department costs
that recognizes that some
service departments
support the activities in
other service departments
as well as those in
operating departments.*

Step-Down Method The **step-down method** recognizes that some service departments support the activities in other service departments as well as those in operating departments. To apply the step-down method, we choose a sequence of service department allocations, starting with the service department that renders the greatest service (as measured by costs) to the greatest number of other service departments. The last service department in the sequence is the one that renders the least service to the least number of other service departments. We allocate the costs of one service department at a time, assigning the costs to the producing departments and to the remaining service departments. Once we allocate a department's costs to other departments, we never allocate other service department costs back to it.

In our example, we allocate facilities management department costs first. Why? Because facilities management renders more support to human resources than human resources provides for facilities management.[1] Examine Exhibit 12-4. After allocating facilities management costs, we do not allocate any costs back to facilities management,

---

[1]How should we determine which of the two service departments provides more service to the other? One way is to carry out step 1 of the step-down method with facilities management allocated first, and then repeat it assuming personnel is allocated first. With facilities management allocated first, $420,000 is allocated to human resources, as shown in Exhibit 12-4. If human resources had been allocated first, (16 ÷ 96) × $240,000 = $40,000 would have been allocated to facilities management. Because $40,000 is smaller than $420,000, facilities management is allocated first.

	Facilities Management	Human Resources	Processing	Assembly	Total
Direct department costs before allocation	$ 1,260,000	$ 240,000	$1,000,000	$1,600,000	$4,100,000
Step 1					
Facilities management	$(1,260,000)	(9 ÷ 27) × $1,260,000 = $ 420,000	(15 ÷ 27) × $1,260,000 = $ 700,000	(3 ÷ 27) × $1,260,000 = $ 140,000	
Step 2					
Human Resources		$(660,000)	(16 ÷ 80) × $660,000 = $ 132,000	(64 ÷ 80) × $660,000 = $ 528,000	
Total cost after allocation	$ 0	$ 0	$1,832,000	$2,268,000	$4,100,000

Exhibit 12-4
Step-Down Allocation

even though human resources does provide some services for facilities management. The human resources costs allocated to the production departments include the amount allocated to human resources from facilities management ($420,000) in addition to the direct human resources department costs of $240,000.

Examine the last column of Exhibit 12-4. Before allocation, the four departments incurred costs of $4,100,000. In step 1, we deducted $1,260,000 from facilities management and added it to the other three departments. There was no net effect on the total cost. In step 2, we deducted $660,000 from human resources and added it to the remaining two departments. Again, total cost was unaffected. After allocation, all $4,100,000 remains, but it is all in the processing and assembly departments. None was left in facilities management or human resources.

Comparison of the Methods Compare the costs of the production departments under direct and step-down methods, as shown in Exhibit 12-5. Note that the method of allocation can greatly affect the costs. Processing appears to be a more expensive operation to a manager using the direct method than it does to one using the step-down method. Conversely, assembly seems more expensive to a manager using the step-down method.

Which method is better? Generally, the step-down method.[2] Why? Because it recognizes the effects of the most significant support provided by service departments to other service departments. The greatest virtue of the direct method is its simplicity. If the two methods do not produce significantly different results, many companies elect to use the direct method because it is easier for managers to understand.

Costs Not Related to Cost Drivers Our example illustrating direct and step-down allocation methods assumed that we could use a single cost driver to allocate all costs in a given service department. For example, we assumed that we could use square footage occupied to allocate all facilities management costs. But what if some of the costs in facilities management do not vary proportionately to the cost driver square footage? For example, rent often is based on a single sum for the entire plant for a period of time. Another example occurs when the contract for an outside company to perform janitorial services specifies a fixed monthly charge plus an additional charge based on the square feet maintaned.

We suggest two guidelines that are helpful in situations where costs are not related to cost drivers:

1. Identify additional cost drivers. Divide facilities management costs into two or more different cost pools and use a different cost driver to allocate the costs in each pool. For example, rent and insurance costs often are fixed but we can allocate them using

Exhibit 12-5
Direct Versus
Step-Down Method

	Processing		Assembly	
	Direct	**Step-Down***	**Direct**	**Step-Down***
Direct department costs	$1,000,000	$1,000,000	$1,600,000	$1,600,000
Allocated from facilities management	1,050,000	700,000	210,000	140,000
Allocated from personnel	48,000	132,000	192,000	528,000
Total costs	$2,098,000	$1,832,000	$2,002,000	$2,268,000

* From Exhibit 12-4.

[2]The most defensible theoretical accuracy is generated by the reciprocal cost method, which is rarely used in practice because it is more difficult to understand. Simultaneous equations and linear algebra are used to solve for the impact of mutually interacting services.

square footage occupied by the various service departments. Power costs are mostly variable and we can allocate them using a driver such as megawatt hours. Janitorial services are either purely variable, purely fixed, or mixed costs. The allocation of the variable portion of janitorial services should be allocated based on the same measure used for billing—square feet maintained, for example. The fixed portion may not have a plausible or reliable cost driver and thus remains unallocated.

2. Allocate all costs by the direct or step-down method using square footage as the cost driver. In this alternative, we implicitly assume that, in the long run, square footage causes all facilities management costs—even if we cannot easily identify a short-term causal relationship. In other words, the need for more square footage may not cause an immediate increase in all facilities management costs, but eventually management will need to provide more space so the costs will increase.

MAKING MANAGERIAL DECISIONS

Suppose you are on a cross-functional team that is discussing how to allocate the costs of a purchasing department. One team member suggested that "number of purchase orders issued" is the best cost driver. However, a scatter graph of total costs versus number of purchase orders issued shows the following:

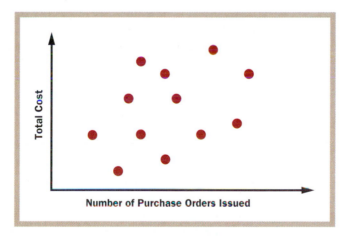

Because the data clearly indicate that the single cost driver "number of purchase orders issued" is not a reliable measure of the work done in the department (because there is too much scatter in the data), the team investigated. It discovered that a significant amount of work of the purchasing department was certifying new vendors in addition to issuing purchase orders. What alternative method of allocation would you recommend?

Answer

Because a large percentage of the work of the purchasing department is not related to the single cost driver "number of purchase orders," a second cost pool should be used with another cost driver, such as "number of new vendors."

Allocation of Costs to Final Cost Objects

After the allocation of service department costs, we have all costs residing in the producing departments. All that remains is to allocate those costs to the final cost objects. Examples of final cost objects are products, such as automobiles, furniture, and newspapers, services, such

OBJECTIVE 4

Integrate service-
department allocation
systems with traditional
and ABC systems to
allocate total systems
costs to final cost
objectives.

as banking, health care, and education, or customers. Some accountants call the allocation of total departmental costs to the revenue-producing products or services **cost application.**

A Traditional Approach

The traditional approach to cost application is as follows:

1. Divide the costs in each producing department, including both the direct department costs and all the costs allocated to it, into two categories: (1) the direct costs that you can physically trace to the final cost objectives and (2) the remainder, the indirect costs.
2. Assign the direct costs to the appropriate products, services, or customers. Note that some costs that are direct to the department will be indirect to the final cost objectives—for example, depreciation on the department's equipment.
3. Select one or more cost pools and related cost drivers in each production department, and assign all the indirect departmental costs to the appropriate cost pool. For example, you might assign a portion of the indirect departmental costs on the basis of direct-labor hours, another portion on the basis of machine hours, and the remainder on the basis of number of parts. Be sure to use separate cost pools for fixed and variable costs.
4. Allocate (apply) the costs in each cost pool to the products, services, or customers in proportion to their usage of the related cost driver. Apply variable costs on the basis of the actual cost-driver level achieved. Apply fixed costs on the basis of budgeted cost-driver levels.

Consider our example of the L. A. Darling display facility. Exhibit 12-6 shows the process map for the facility assuming that the facility uses the step-down method for allocating service department costs. We now shift our focus from the two operating departments as cost objectives to the two types of displays—the final cost objects for the L. A. Darling display facility.

The first step is to determine the operating department costs that can be directly traced to displays. There are a total of $1,832,000 costs in the processing department. Of this total, $800,000 are the variable costs of display parts. All of these costs can be directly traced to custom and standard displays, as shown in Exhibit 12-6. Similarly, of the $2,268,000 total costs in the assembly department, $200,000 can be directly traced to displays. These costs are the wages of workers who finish the displays and are variable costs at L. A. Darling. The remaining resources and allocated costs from service departments are indirect costs, and we will assume they are fixed-cost resources. Why is there no direct labor in the processing department? Because this is a machine intensive department with only indirect labor operating the machines.

In step 2, we trace the direct costs to the two display types as shown in Exhibit 12-6. Compare the processing department costs in Exhibits 12-3 and 12-6. How did $1,000,000 in direct processing department costs in Exhibit 12-3 decrease to only $800,000 direct costs in Exhibit 12-6? The answer lies in our change in cost objectives. When we were interested only in determining the cost of the processing department, $200,000 of costs such as depreciation on department equipment and supervision were wholly in support of the department—a single cost object—and did not need to be allocated. When we changed the cost objective to the two displays, these resources became shared. Since no economically feasible way could be found to trace their use directly, their costs needed to be allocated.

Next, in step 3, we select cost pools and related cost drivers for the indirect costs of each department. We assume that all the remaining $1,032,000 of indirect costs in the processing department can be assigned to one fixed-cost pool with budgeted number of parts as the cost driver. Similarly, all the remaining $2,068,000 indirect costs in the assembly department can be assigned to one fixed-cost pool with budgeted direct-labor hours as the cost driver.

Therefore, we allocate indirect departmental costs to the displays as follows:

Processing: $1,032,000 ÷ (10,400 + 24,000) parts = $30.00 per part
Assembly: $2,068,000 ÷ (1,600 + 4,800) direct-labor hours
= $323.125 per direct-labor hour

Exhibit 12-6
L. A. Darling's Display
Facility: Allocation to
Final Cost Objects
Using Traditional
Approach

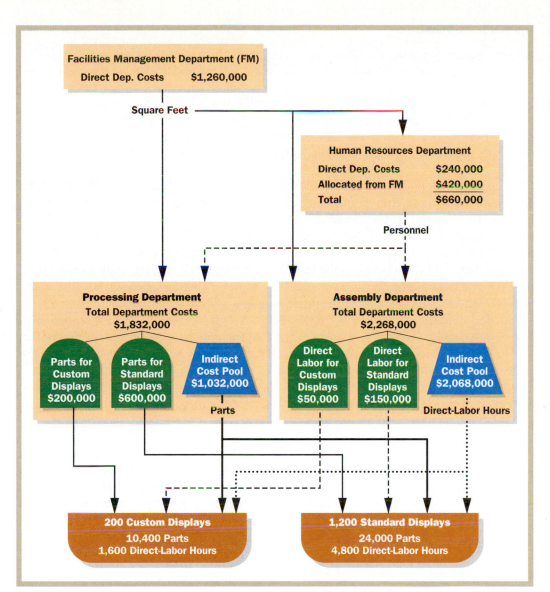

The total and unit costs of making 200 custom and 1,200 standard displays are

	200 Custom Displays		1,200 Standard Displays	
	Total	Unit	Total	Unit
Parts	$ 200,000	$1,000.00	$ 600,000	$ 500.00
Direct labor	50,000	250.00	150,000	125.00
Indirect costs— processing department	312,000*	1,560.00	720,000†	600.00
Indirect costs— assembly department	517,000‡	2,585.00	1,551,000§	1,292.50
	$1,079,000	$5,395.00	$3,021,000	$2,517.50

* $30.00 × 10,400 parts
† $30.00 × 24,000 parts
‡ $323.125 × 1,600 direct-labor hours
§ $323.125 × 4,800 direct-labor hours

The traditional approach to cost allocation focuses on accumulating and reporting costs by department. In the last couple decades an alternative approach, activity-based costing as described in Chapter 4, has become popular. Let's examine how the same facility of L. A. Darling Company might apply ABC to determine the costs of custom and standard displays.

An ABC Approach

Assume that management decides to apply ABC only to the operating departments, not to the service departments. We will still use the step-down method to allocate the costs of the facilities management department to the human resources department. Then the direct and allocated human resources department costs will be allocated to the specific activities identified in the operating department. Finally, the operating department activity cost pools will be allocated using the ABC system. Management implemented activity-based costing in this facility using the four-step procedure outlined in Chapter 4.

Step 1: Determine the Key Components of the System The costing objective is to determine the costs of custom and standard displays—the final cost objectives for L. A. Darling. The structure of the service department component of the cost allocation system is unchanged—we still use the step-down method. The major differences are in the operating departments. The ABC accounting system traces parts cost and direct labor to each product—this is the same as the traditional approach. During the implementation of the ABC, it is common to discover ways to improve costing accuracy. In this case, management decided to combine the processing and assembly departments into one new production department with three major activities—design, processing, and assembly. The design activity's resources, engineers and CAD equipment were previously part of the facilities management department. Managers believed that these costs are more accurately allocated if they are separately accumulated as part of a production department design activity and allocated using distinct parts as the cost driver. In summary, the cost drivers for design, processing, and assembly activities are distinct parts, machine hours, and direct-labor hours.

Step 2: Develop the Relationships Between Resources, Activities, and Cost Objectives Interviews with key personnel identified the interrelationships between the two service departments, three activities, resources, and final cost objects. Exhibit 12-7 is a process map that depicts these interrelationships. The newly formed production department is depicted by a dashed line in Exhibit 12-7. Why do we use a dashed line? The emphasis in the ABC approach is on allocations to activities without regard to departmental boundaries. Note that the exhibit also shows the cost behavior for each resource. Understanding the cost behavior of resources is vital during the planning process.

Step 3: Collect Relevant Data Concerning Costs and the Physical Flow of Cost-Driver Units Among Resources and Activities Using the process map as a guide, accountants collected the required cost and operational data by further interviews with relevant personnel. Data collected are given in Exhibit 12-7. Note that the total costs of the facilities management department is only $1,000,000 instead of $1,260,000 under the traditional approach. The difference is the cost of engineers and CAD equipment that is now treated as part of the production department. Each of the three activities shows the total cost pool. For example, the processing activity cost pool is $1,476,000. We calculate this as follows:

Resource Supporting the Processing Activity	Allocation Calculation	Allocated Cost
Facilities management department resources	$1,000,000 × [15,000/(9,000 + 3,000 + 15,000 + 3,000)]	$ 500,000
Human resources department resources	$540,000 × [16/(10 + 16 + 64)]	96,000
Machines, tools, mechanics, and supplies	$1,200,000 × 70%	840,000
Supervisors and equipment	$400,000 × 10%	40,000
Total		$1,476,000

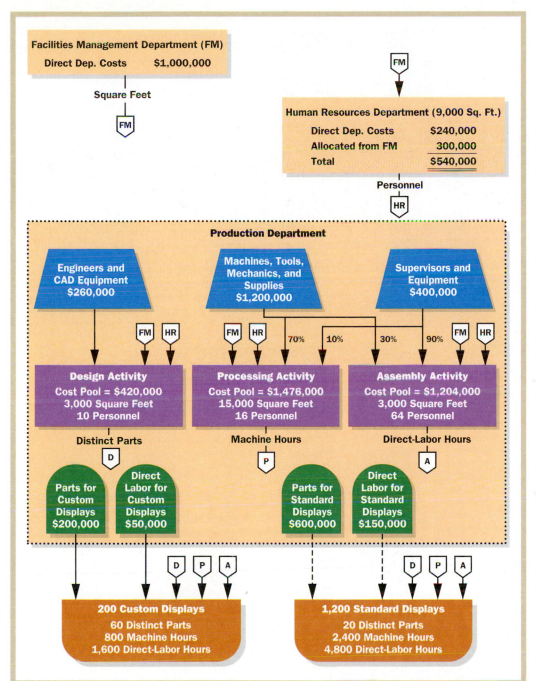

Exhibit 12-7

L. A. Darling's Display Facility: Allocation to Final Cost Objects Using the ABC Approach

Step 4: Calculate and Interpret the New Activity-Based Cost Information

Exhibit 12-8 includes the summary of the data collected for the two service departments and the activities identified in step 1. For each activity, the exhibit shows the indirect costs that result from allocations of service departments and the first stage of resource allocations.

Compare the cost per unit figures using the traditional and ABC approaches. There is a substantial difference in the reported cost as shown below:

	Allocated Cost	
	Custom Displays	Standard Displays
Traditional approach	$5,395.00	$2,517.50
ABC approach	$6,175.00	$2,387.50

Activity/Resource (Cost Driver)	Cost Pool	Physical Flow of Cost Driver	Cost per Driver Unit	Custom Displays		Standard Displays	
				Flow	Cost	Flow	Cost
Design (distinct parts)	$ 420,000	80	$5,250.000	60	$ 315,000	20	$ 105,000
Processing (machine hours)	1,476,000	3,200	461.250	800	369,000	2,400	1,107,000
Assembly (direct-labor hours)	1,204,000	6,400	188.125	1,600	301,000	4,800	903,000
Parts					200,000		600,000
Direct labor					50,000		150,000
Total direct and allocated cost					$1,235,000		$2,865,000
Units					÷ 200		÷ 1,200
Display cost per unit					$ 6,175.00		$ 2,387.50

Exhibit 12-8

L. A. Darling Display Facility: Allocation to Final Cost Objectives Using the ABC Appoach

How important are these differences? The $4,100,000 total facility cost includes all the research and development, design, production, and part of the corporate-level support functions of the value chain. However, we have not accounted for the costs to sell, distribute, provide cutomer support, and remaining general corporate-level support. Suppose the $4,100,000 is 40% of the total costs. If L. A. Darling desires an operating income of 20% of total costs, the required total revenue is [1.2 × ($4,100,000/0.4)] = 300% × $4,100,000 = $12,300,000 or three times the direct plus allocated costs. This is a pricing policy that requires a markup of 300% on reported cost. This means that the price for custom displays would be 3 × $5,395 = $16,185 under the traditional approach compared to 3 × $6,175 = $18,525 under the ABC approach. Assuming the ABC cost is the more accurate estimate of actual costs, using the traditional approach would underprice custom displays by $2,340 or 12.6%. The bottom-line question for L. A. Darling's decision makers—Is it worth the cost of maintaining the more expensive ABC system to be able to avoid strategic pricing errors of this magnitude?

This concludes our discussion of service department allocation. We will next consider two specific types of cost allocations—(1) allocation of central corporate costs such as public relations and legal costs and (2) allocation of joint and by-product costs.

MAKING MANAGERIAL DECISIONS

Confirm your understanding of traditional and ABC allocation by computing the allocation of overhead costs to the deluxe type speaker for the Louder Is Better Company. The company makes two types of speakers, a standard (S) and a deluxe (D) model. The diagrams below show how allocation would be done under ABC versus traditional allocation systems. The production department has overhead costs of $36,000. How would ABC versus traditional allocation differ?

Answer

In the traditional system, the deluxe product receives only 25% of the overhead costs because it uses only 25% of the machine hours. But in the ABC system, it receives 72% of the overhead because it uses 63% of the parts and 83% of the setups.

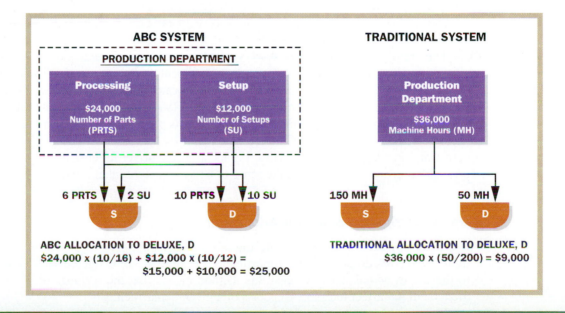

OBJECTIVE 5

Allocate the central
corporate costs of an
organization.

Allocation of Central Corporate Support Costs

Many managers believe it is desirable to fully allocate all costs to the revenue-producing (operating) parts of the organization. Such allocations are neither necessary from an accounting viewpoint nor useful as management information. For this reason, central costs are not considered part of the value chain in this text. However, most managers accept them as a fact of life — as long as all managers seem to be treated alike and thus "fairly."

Whenever possible, the preferred cost driver for central services is usage, either actual or estimated. But companies seldom allocate the costs of such services as public relations, top corporate management overhead, a real estate department, and a corporate-planning department on the basis of usage. They are more likely to choose usage as a cost driver for data processing, advertising, and operations research.

Companies that allocate central costs by usage tend to generate less resentment over allocations. Consider the experience of **J. C. Penney Co.** as reported in *Business Week*:

> *The controller's office wanted subsidiaries such as Thrift Drug Co. and the insurance operations to base their share of corporate personnel, legal, and auditing costs on their revenues. The subsidiaries contended that they maintained their own personnel and legal departments, and should be assessed far less. . . . The subcommittee addressed the issue by asking the corporate departments to approximate the time and costs involved in servicing the subsidiaries. The final allocation plan, based on these studies, cost the divisions less than they were initially assessed but more than they had wanted to pay. Nonetheless, the plan was implemented easily.*

Usage is not always an economically viable way to allocate central costs, however. Also, it is difficult to allocate many central costs, such as the president's salary and related expenses, public relations, legal services, income tax planning, company-wide advertising, and basic research, on the basis of cause and effect. As a result, some companies use cost drivers such as the revenue of each division, the cost of goods sold by each division, the total assets of each division, or the total costs of each division (before allocation of the central costs) to allocate central costs.

The use of the foregoing cost drivers might provide a rough indication of a cause-and-effect relationship. Basically, however, they represent an "ability to bear" philosophy of cost allocation. For example, a company might allocate the costs of company-wide advertising, such as the sponsorship of a program on a PBS station, to all products and divisions on the basis of the dollar sales in each. But such costs precede sales. They are discretionary costs as determined by management policies, not by sales results. Although 60% of the companies in a large survey use sales revenue as a cost driver for cost allocation purposes, it is seldom truly a cost driver in the sense of being an activity that causes the costs.

Use of Budgeted Sales for Allocation

If a company feels it must allocate the costs of central services based on sales, even though the costs do not vary in proportion to sales, the use of budgeted sales is preferable to the use of actual sales. At least this method means that the fortunes of other departments will not affect the short-run costs of a given department.

For example, suppose L. A. Darling Company budgets central advertising as 10% of forecasted sales in two countries — Mexico and Canada. The forecasted sales are

$500,000 in both Mexico and Canada so the total advertising budget, a fixed cost, is $100,000. Actual sales in Mexico and Canada are $300,000 and $600,000, respectively. How is the $100,000 advertising budget allocated if the company uses forecasted sales compared to actual sales?

Allocation of $100,000 Central Advertising Budget		
	Mexico	**Canada**
Forecast sales	$500,000	$500,000
Allocation based on forecast sales	50,000	50,000
Actual sales	300,000	600,000
Allocation based on actual sales	33,333	67,667

The preferred allocation is based on forecast sales. Why? Because it indicates a low ratio of sales to advertising in Mexico—it directs attention where it is deserved. In contrast, allocation based on actual sales soaks the Canadian operations with more advertising cost because of the achieved results and relieves Mexican operations despite its lower success. This is another example of the confusion that can arise when cost allocations to one consuming company unit depend on the activity of other consuming units.

Allocation of Joint Costs and By-Product Costs

Joint costs and by-product costs create especially difficult cost-allocation problems. By definition, such costs relate to more than one product and we cannot separately identify them with an individual product. Let's now examine these special cases, starting with joint costs.

OBJECTIVE 6

Allocate joint costs to products using the physical-units and relative-sales value methods.

Joint Costs

So far, we have assumed that we could identify cost drivers with an individual product. For example, if we are allocating activity costs to products or services on the basis of machine hours, we have assumed that we can measure the amount of machine time consumed in making each product. However, sometimes we add inputs to the production process before we can separately identify individual products (i.e., before the split-off point). Recall from Chapter 6 (page 260) that we call such costs joint costs. Joint costs include all inputs of material, labor, and overhead costs that are incurred before the split-off point.

Suppose a department has more than one product and some costs are joint costs. How should we allocate such joint costs to the products? Allocation of joint costs should not affect decisions about the individual products. Nevertheless, companies routinely allocate joint product costs to products for purposes of inventory valuation and income determination.

Consider the example of joint product costs that we used in Chapter 6. A department in Dow Chemical Company produces two chemicals, X and Y. The joint cost is $100,000, and production is 1,000,000 liters of X and 500,000 liters of Y. X sells for $.09 per liter and Y for $.06 per liter. We want to find a method to allocate some part of the $100,000 joint cost to the inventory of X and the rest to the inventory of Y. Such allocations are useful for inventory purposes only. You should ignore joint cost allocations for decisions such as selling a joint product or processing it further.

There are two conventional ways of allocating joint costs to products: physical units and relative sales values. If a company uses physical units, it would allocate the joint costs as follows:

	Liters	Weighting	Allocation of Joint Costs	Sales Value at Split-Off Point
X	1,000,000	10/15 × $100,000	$ 66,667	$ 90,000
Y	500,000	5/15 × $100,000	33,333	30,000
	1,500,000		$100,000	$120,000

This approach shows that the $33,333 joint cost of producing Y exceeds its $30,000 sales value at the split-off point seemingly indicating that the company should not produce Y. However, such an allocation is not helpful in making production decisions. We can produce neither of the two products separately.

A decision to produce Y must be a decision to produce X and Y. Because total revenue of $120,000 exceeds the total joint cost of $100,000, we should produce both. The allocation was not useful for this decision.

The physical-units method requires a common physical unit for measuring the output of each product. For example, board feet is a common unit for a variety of products in the lumber industry. However, sometimes such a common denominator is lacking. Consider the production of meat and hides from butchering a steer. You might use pounds as a common denominator, but pounds is not a good measure of the output of hides. As an alternative, many companies use the relative-sales-value method for allocating joint costs. The following allocation results from applying the relative-sales-value method to the Dow Chemical department:

	Relative Sales Value at Split-Off Point	Weighting	Allocation of Joint Costs
X	$ 90,000	90/120 × $100,000	$ 75,000
Y	30,000	30/120 × $100,000	25,000
	$120,000		$100,000

The weighting is based on the sales values of the individual products. Because the sales value of X at the split-off point is $90,000 and total sales value at the split-off point is $120,000, we allocate 90/120 of the joint cost to X.

This method might eliminate one problem, but it creates another. Note how the allocation of a cost to a particular product such as Y depends not only on the sales value of Y but also on the sales value of X. For example, suppose you were the product manager for Y. You planned to sell your 500,000 liters for $30,000, achieving a profit of $30,000 − $25,000 = $5,000. Everything went as expected except that the price of X fell to $.07 per liter for revenue of $70,000 rather than $90,000. Instead of 30/120 of the joint cost, Y received 30/100 × $100,000 = $30,000 and had a profit of $0. Despite the fact that Y operations were exactly as planned, the cost-allocation method caused the profit on Y to be $5,000 below plan.

We can also use the relative-sales-value method when we cannot sell one or more of the joint products at the split-off point. To apply the method, we approximate the sales value at split off as follows:

$$\text{sales value at split off} = \text{final sales value} - \text{separable costs}$$

For example, suppose the 500,000 liters of Y requires $20,000 of processing beyond the split-off point, after which we can sell it for $.10 per liter. The sales value at split off would be ($.10 × 500,000) − $20,000 = $50,000 − $20,000 = $30,000.

By-Product Costs

By-products are similar to joint products. A **by-product** is a product that, like a joint product, is not individually identifiable until manufacturing reaches a split-off point. By-products differ from joint products because they have relatively insignificant total sales values in comparison with the other products emerging at split off. In contrast, joint products have relatively significant total sales values at split off in comparison with the other jointly produced items. Examples of by-products are glycerine from soap making and mill ends of cloth and carpets.

If we account for an item as a by-product, we allocate only separable costs to it. We allocate all joint costs to the main products. We deduct any revenues from by-products, less their separable costs, from the cost of the main products.

Consider a lumber company that sells sawdust generated in the production of lumber to companies making particle board. Suppose the company regards the sawdust as a by-product. In 20X1, sales of sawdust totaled $30,000, and the cost of loading and shipping the sawdust (i.e., costs incurred beyond the split-off point) was $20,000. The inventory cost of the sawdust would consist of only the $20,000 separable cost. The company would allocate none of the joint cost of producing lumber and sawdust to the sawdust. It would deduct the difference between the revenue and separable cost, $30,000 − $20,000 = $10,000, from the cost of the lumber produced.

by-product
A product that, like a joint product, is not individually identifiable until manufacturing reaches a split-off point, but has relatively insignificant total sales value.

Summary Problem For Your Review

PROBLEM

Nonmanufacturing organizations often find it useful to allocate costs to final products or services. Consider a hospital. The output of a hospital is not as easy to define as the output of a factory. Assume the following measures of output in three revenue-producing departments:

Department	Measures of Output*
Radiology	X-ray films processed
Laboratory	Tests administered
Daily patient services†	Patient-days of care (i.e., the number of patients multiplied by the number of days of each patient's stay)

* These become the "product" cost objectives, the various revenue-producing activities of a hospital.
† There would be many of these departments, such as obstetrics, pediatrics, and orthopedics. Moreover, there may be both inpatient and outpatient care.

Budgeted output for 20X1 is 60,000 X-ray films processed in Radiology, 50,000 tests administered in the Laboratory, and 30,000 patient-days in Daily Patient Services.

In addition to the revenue-producing departments, the hospital has three service departments: Administrative and Fiscal Services, Plant Operations and Maintenance, and Laundry. (Of course, real hospitals have more than three revenue-producing departments and more than three service departments. This problem is simplified to keep the data manageable.)

The hospital has decided that the cost driver for Administrative and Fiscal Services costs is the direct department costs of the other departments. The cost driver for Plant

Operations and Maintenance is square feet occupied, and for Laundry is pounds of laundry. The pertinent budget data for 20X1 are

	Direct Department Costs	Square Feet Occupied	Pounds of Laundry
Administrative and fiscal services	$1,000,000	1,000	—
Plant operations and maintenance	800,000	2,000	—
Laundry	200,000	5,000	—
Radiology	1,000,000	12,000	80,000
Laboratory	400,000	3,000	20,000
Daily patient services	1,600,000	80,000	300,000
Total	$5,000,000	103,000	400,000

1. Allocate service department costs using the direct method.
2. Allocate service department costs using the step-down method. Allocate Administrative and Fiscal Services first, Plant Operations and Maintenance second, and Laundry third.
3. Compute the cost per unit of output in each of the revenue-producing departments using (a) the costs determined using the direct method for allocating service department costs (number 1) and (b) the costs determined using the step-down method for allocating service department costs (number 2).

SOLUTION

1. Exhibit 12-9 shows the solutions to all three problems. We present the direct method first. Note that we allocated no service department costs to another service department. Therefore, we base allocations on the relative amounts of the cost driver in the revenue-producing department only. For example, in allocating Plant Operations and Maintenance, we ignore square footage occupied by the service departments. The cost driver is the 95,000 square feet occupied by the revenue-producing departments.

   Note that the total cost of the revenue-producing departments after allocation, $1,474,386 + $568,596 + $2,957,018 = $5,000,000, is equal to the total of the direct department costs in all six departments before allocation.

2. The lower half of Exhibit 12-9 shows the step-down method. We allocate the costs of Administrative and Fiscal Services to all five other departments. Because we do not allocate a department's own costs to itself, the cost driver consists of the $4,000,000 direct department costs in the five departments excluding Administrative and Fiscal Services.

   We allocate Plant Operations and Maintenance second on the basis of square feet occupied. We allocate no cost to the department itself or back to Administrative and Fiscal Services. Therefore, the square footage used for allocation is the 100,000 square feet occupied by the other four departments.

   We allocate Laundry third. We allocate no cost back to the first two departments, even if they had used laundry services.

   As in the direct method, note that the total costs of the revenue-producing departments after allocation, $1,430,000 + $545,000 + $3,025,000 = $5,000,000, equals the total of the direct department costs before allocation.

3. We label the solutions 3a and 3b in Exhibit 12-9. Compare the unit costs derived from the direct method with those of the step-down method. In many instances, the final product costs may not differ enough to warrant investing in a cost-allocation method that is any fancier than the direct method. But sometimes even small differences may be significant to a government agency or anybody paying for a large volume of services based on costs. For example, in Exhibit 12-9 the "cost" of an "average" laboratory test is either $11.37 or $10.90. This may be significant for the fiscal committee of the hospital's board of trustees, who must decide on hospital prices. Thus, cost allocation often is a technique that helps answer the vital question, "Who should pay for what, and how much?"

Allocation Base	Administrative and Fiscal Services Accumulated Costs	Plant Operations and Maintenance Sq. Footage	Laundry Pounds	Radiology	Laboratory	Daily Patient Services
1. Direct method:						
Direct departmental costs before allocation	$1,000,000	$ 800,000	$200,000	$1,000,000	$400,000	$1,600,000
Administrative and Fiscal Services	(1,000,000)	—	—	333,333*	133,333	533,334
Plant Operations and Maintenance		(800,000)	—	101,053†	25,263	673,684
Laundry			(200,000)	40,000‡	10,000	150,000
Total costs after allocation				$1,474,386	$568,596	$2,957,018
Product output in films, tests, and patient-days, respectively				60,000	50,000	30,000
3a. Cost per unit of output				$24.573	$11.372	$98.567
2. Step-down method:						
Direct departmental costs before allocation	$1,000,000	$ 800,000	$200,000	$1,000,000	$400,000	$1,600,000
Administrative and Fiscal Services	(1,000,000)	200,000§	50,000	250,000	100,000	400,000
Plant Operations and Maintenance		(1,000,000)	50,000¶	120,000	30,000	800,000
Laundry			(300,000)	60,000#	15,000	225,000
Total costs after allocation				$1,430,000	$545,000	$3,025,000
Product output in films, tests, and patient-days, respectively				60,000	50,000	30,000
3b. Cost per unit of output				$23.833	$10.900	$100.833

* $1,000,000 ÷ (1,000,000 + 400,000 + 1,600,000) = $.33, 1/3 × 1,000,000 = $333,333; and so on.
† $800,000 ÷ (12,000 + 3,000 + 80,000) = $8.4210526; $8.4210526 × 12,000 sq. ft. = $101,053; and so on.
‡ $200,000 × (80,000 + 20,000 + 300,000) = $.50; $.50 × 80,000 = $40,000; and so on.
§ $1,000,000 ÷ (800,000 + 200,000 + 1,000,000 + 400,000 + 1,600,000) = $.25; .25 × 800,000 = $200,000; and so on.
¶ $1,000,000 × (5,000 + 12,000 + 3,000 + 80,000) = $10.00; $10.00 × 5,000 sq. ft. = $50,000; and so on.
# $300,000 ÷ (80,000 + 20,000 + 300,000) = $.75; $.75 × 80,000 = $60,000; and so on.

Exhibit 12-9
Allocation of Service Department Costs: Direct and Step-Down Methods

Highlights to Remember

1 **Explain the major reasons for allocating costs.** The four main purposes of cost allocation are to predict the economic effects of planning and control decisions, to motivate managers and employees, to measure the costs of inventory and cost of goods sold, and to justify costs for pricing or reimbursement.

2 **Allocate the variable and fixed costs of service departments to other organizational units.** The dual method of allocation is used for service department costs. Variable costs should be allocated using budgeted cost rates times the actual cost-driver level. Fixed costs should be allocated using budgeted percent of capacity available for use times the total budgeted fixed costs.

3 **Use the direct and step-down methods to allocate service department costs to user departments.** When service departments support other service departments in addition to producing departments, there are two methods for allocation. The direct method ignores other service departments when allocating costs. The step-down method recognizes other service departments' use of services.

4 **Integrate service department allocation systems with traditional and ABC systems to allocate total systems costs to final cost objectives.** When the cost objective is the products or services provided by a company, service department allocation must be integrated with the allocation system used to cost final cost objectives. Two approaches discussed that are frequently used are the traditional and ABC approaches. The ABC approach provides more accurate estimates of product or service costs than the traditional approach but is more costly to maintain.

5 **Allocate the central corporate costs of an organization.** Central costs include public relations, top corporate management overhead, legal, data processing, controller's department, and companywide planning. Often, it is best to allocate only those central costs of an organization for which measures of usage by departments are available.

6 **Allocate joint costs to products using the physical-units and relative-sales-value methods.** Joint costs are often allocated to products for inventory valuation and income determination using the physical-units or relative-sales-value method. However, such allocations should not affect decisions.

Accounting Vocabulary

by-product, p. 543
cost accounting system,
    p. 523

cost-allocation base, p. 525
cost application, p. 534
direct method, p. 529

service departments, p. 523
step-down method, p. 530

Fundamental Assignment Material

12-A1 Direct and Step-Down Methods of Allocation

Manriques Tool and Die has three service departments:

	Budgeted Department Costs
Cafeteria, revenue of $100,000	
less expenses of $250,000	$ 150,000
Engineering	2,500,000
General factory administration	950,000

Cost drivers are budgeted as follows:

Production Departments	Employees	Engineering Hours Worked for Production Departments	Total Labor Hours
Machining	120	50,000	300,000
Assembly	540	20,000	720,000
Finishing and painting	60	10,000	120,000

1. Manriques allocates all service department costs directly to the production departments without allocation to other service departments. Show how much of the budgeted costs of each service department are allocated to each production department. To plan your work, examine number 2 before undertaking this question.

2. The company has decided to use the step-down method of cost allocation. General factory administration would be allocated first, then cafeteria, then engineering. Cafeteria employees work 36,000 labor hours per year. There were 60 engineering employees with 120,000 total labor hours. Recompute the results in number 1, using the step-down method. Show your computations. Compare the results in numbers 1 and 2. Which method of allocation do you favor? Why?

12-A2 General Framework for Allocation, Service Departments, Activity-Based Costing, and Process Maps

Consider one of L. A. Darling's manufacturing facilities. Suppose this facility assembles parts for displays to be sold to **WalMart**, **Kmart**, and **Walgreens**. There are three departments—Assembly, Power, and Maintenance. The assembly department uses an ABC system. The general cost of occupancy is allocated to the maintenance department and the assembly department based on the space occupied. Power department costs are allocated based on megawatt hours used. The assembly process produces three different types of displays with diverse demands on various activities and resources. Display A consists of simple parts that are produced in high volume. Display type B has parts that are of medium volume and complexity. Display type C consists of complex parts that are produced in small lots.

Management implemented activity-based costing in this facility using the four-step procedure outlined in Chapter 4. The first steps have been completed and the results are depicted in the process map shown in Exhibit 12-10.

1. Refer to Exhibit 12-1 on page 525. For each type of cost assignment listed in Exhibit 12-1, give an example from L. A. Darling. If no example exists, so state.
2. What allocation method for service department costs does this facility use? Explain.
3. Calculate the allocations of service department and general costs to the assembly department activities.
4. Calculate the activity-based cost of each display type.

12-A3 Allocation of Central Costs

The Union Atlantic Railroad allocates all central corporate overhead costs to its divisions. Some costs, such as specified internal auditing and legal costs, are identified on the basis of time spent. However, other costs are harder to allocate, so the revenue achieved by each division is used as an allocation base. Examples of such costs are executive salaries, travel, secretarial, utilities, rent, depreciation, donations, corporate planning, and general marketing costs.

Allocations on the basis of revenue for 20X4 were (in millions):

Division	Revenue	Allocated Costs
Northeast	$120	$ 6
Mid-Atlantic	240	12
Southeast	240	12
Total	$600	$30

In 20X5, Northeast's revenue remained unchanged. However, Southeast's revenue soared to $280 million because of unusually large imports. The latter are troublesome to forecast because of variations in world markets. Mid-Atlantic had expected a sharp rise in revenue, but severe competitive conditions resulted in a decline to $200 million. The total cost allocated on the basis of revenue was again $30 million, despite rises in other costs. The president was pleased that central costs did not rise for the year.

1. Compute the allocations of costs to each division for 20X5.
2. How would each division manager probably feel about the cost allocation in 20X5 as compared with 20X4? What are the weaknesses of using revenue as a basis for cost allocation?
3. Suppose the budgeted revenues for 20X5 were $120, $240, and $280, respectively, and the budgeted revenues were used as a cost driver for allocation. Compute the allocations of costs to each division for 20X5. Do you prefer this method to the one used in number 1? Why?
4. Many accountants and managers oppose allocating any central costs. Why?

12-A4 Joint Products

Quebec Metals, Inc., buys raw ore on the open market and processes it into two final products, A and B. The ore costs $10 per pound, and the process separating it into A and B has a cost of $4 per pound. During 20X4, Benjamin plans to produce 200,000 pounds of A and 600,000 pounds of B from

Exhibit 12-10
L. A. Darling
Allocation of Service
Department Costs in
an ABC System

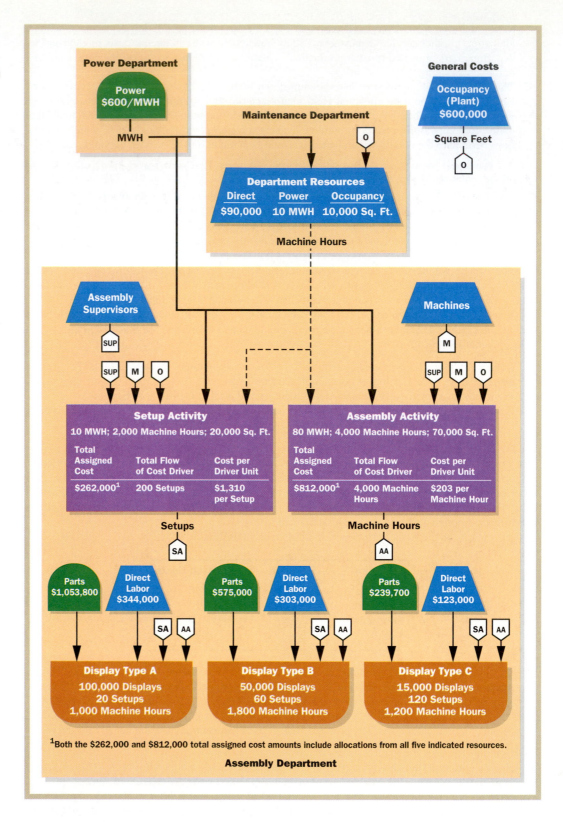

800,000 pounds of ore. A sells for $30 a pound and B for $15 a pound. The company allocated joint costs to the individual products for inventory valuation purposes.

1. Allocate all the joint costs to A and B using the physical-units method.
2. Allocate all the joint costs to A and B using the relative-sales-value method.

3. Suppose B cannot be sold in the form in which it emerges from the joint process. Instead, it must be processed further at a fixed cost of $300,000 plus a variable cost of $1 per pound. Then it can be sold for $21.50 a pound. Allocate all the joint costs to A and B using the relative-sales-value method.

12-B1 Allocation of Computer Costs

Review the section Allocation of Service Department Costs, pages 526–533, especially the example of the use of the computer by the university. Recall that the budget formula was $100,000 fixed cost monthly plus $200 per hour of computer time used. Based on long-run predicted usage, the fixed costs were allocated on a lump-sum basis, 30% to Business and 70% to Engineering.

1. Show the total allocation if Business used 210 hours and Engineering used 390 hours in a given month. Assume that the actual costs coincided exactly with the budgeted amount for total usage of 600 hours.
2. Assume the same facts as in number 1 except that the fixed costs were allocated on the basis of actual hours of usage. Show the total allocation of costs to each school. As the dean of Business, would you prefer this method or the method in number 1? Explain.

12-B2 Allocation of Service Department Costs

Dallas Cleaning, Inc., provides cleaning services for a variety of clients. The company has two producing departments, Residential and Commercial, and two service departments, Personnel and Administrative. The company has decided to allocate all service department costs to the producing departments—Personnel on the basis of number of employees and Administrative on the basis of direct department costs. The budget for 20X5 shows

	Personnel	Administrative	Residential	Commercial
Direct department costs	$70,000	$90,000	$240,000	$400,000
Number of employees	3	5	12	18
Direct-labor hours			24,000	36,000
Square feet cleaned			4,500,000	9,970,000

1. Allocate service department costs using the direct method.
2. Allocate service department costs using the step-down method. Personnel costs should be allocated first.
3. Suppose the company prices by the hour in the Residential Department and by the square foot cleaned in Commercial. Using the results of the step-down allocations in number 2,
   a. Compute the cost of providing one direct-labor hour of service in the Residential Department.
   b. Compute the cost of cleaning one square foot of space in the Commercial Department.

12-B3 Activity-Based Costing

The Maori Novelty Company makes a variety of souvenirs for visitors to New Zealand. The Otago Division manufactures stuffed kiwi birds using a highly automated operation. A recently installed activity-based-costing system has four activity centers:

Activity Center	Cost Driver	Cost per Driver Unit
Materials receiving and handling	Kilograms of materials	$1.20 per kg
Production setup	Number of setups	$60 per setup
Cutting, sewing, and assembly	Number of units	$.40 per unit
Packing and shipping	Number of orders	$10 per order

Two products are called "standard kiwi" and "giant kiwi." They require .20 and .40 kg of materials, respectively, at a materials cost of $1.30 for standard kiwis and $2.20 for giant kiwis. One computer-controlled assembly line makes all products. When a production run of a different product is started, a setup procedure is required to reprogram the computers and make other changes in the process. Normally, 600 standard kiwis are produced per setup, but only 240 giant kiwis. Products are packed and shipped separately, so a request from a customer for, say, three different products is considered three different orders.

The Auckland Zoo Gift Shop just placed an order for 100 standard kiwis and 50 giant kiwis.

1. Compute the cost of the products shipped to the Auckland Zoo Gift Shop.
2. Suppose the products made for the Auckland Zoo Gift Shop required "AZ" to be printed on each kiwi. Because of the automated process, printing the initials takes no extra time or materials, but

it requires a special production setup for each product. Compute the cost of the products shipped to the Auckland Zoo Gift Shop.

3. Explain how the activity-based-costing system helps Maori Novelty to measure costs of individual products or orders better than a traditional system that allocates all nonmaterials costs based on direct labor.

12-B4 Joint Products

Des Moines Milling buys oats at $.60 per pound and produces DMM Oat Flour, DMM Oat Flakes, and DMM Oat Bran. The process of separating the oats into oat flour and oat bran costs $.30 per pound. The oat flour can be sold for $1.50 per pound, the oat bran for $2.00 per pound. Each pound of oats has .2 pounds of oat bran and .8 pounds of oat flour. A pound of oat flour can be made into oat flakes for a fixed cost of $240,000 plus a variable cost of $.60 per pound. Des Moines Milling plans to process 1 million pounds of oats in 20X5, at a purchase price of $600,000.

1. Allocate all the joint costs to oat flour and oat bran using the physical-units method.
2. Allocate all the joint costs to oat flour and oat bran using the relative-sales-value method.
3. Suppose there were no market for oat flour. Instead, it must be made into oat flakes to be sold. Oat flakes sell for $2.90 per pound. Allocate the joint cost to oat bran and oat flakes using the relative-sales-value method.

Additional Assignment Material

Questions

12-1 Why do companies use a cost accounting system?

12-2 "A cost pool is a group of costs that is physically traced to the appropriate cost objective." Do you agree? Explain.

12-3 List five terms that are sometimes used as substitutes for the word *allocate*.

12-4 What are four purposes for cost allocation?

12-5 What are the seven types of cost assignments?

12-6 List three guidelines for the allocation of service department costs.

12-7 Explain how a direct department cost can become an indirect cost.

12-8 Why should budgeted cost rates, rather than actual cost rates, be used for allocating the variable costs of service departments?

12-9 "We used a lump-sum allocation method for fixed costs a few years ago, but we gave it up because managers always predicted usage below what they actually used." Is this a common problem? How might it be prevented?

12-10 Briefly describe the two popular methods for allocating service department costs.

12-11 "The step-down method allocates more costs to the producing departments than does the direct method." Do you agree? Explain.

12-12 What is a non-volume-related cost driver? Give two examples.

12-13 How are costs of various overhead resources allocated to products, services, or customers in an ABC system?

12-14 "A cost pool for a particular resource is either a variable cost pool or a fixed cost pool. There should be no mixed-cost pools." Do you agree? Explain.

12-15 Give four examples of activities and related cost drivers that can be used in an ABC system to allocate costs to products, services, or customers.

12-16 Chapter 6 explained that joint costs should not be allocated to individual products for decision purposes. For what purposes are such costs allocated to products?

12-17 Briefly explain each of the two conventional ways of allocating joint costs of products.

12-18 What are by-products and how do we account for them?

Critical Thinking Exercises

12-19 Allocation and Cost Behavior

There are three general guidelines to use when allocating service department (support) costs. One of these guidelines deals with the cost behavior of support costs. Why do many companies allocate fixed support costs separately from variable support costs?

12-20 Allocation and the Sales Function

Confusion can arise when cost allocations to one consuming department depend on the activity of another consuming department. "A commonly misused basis for allocation of central support costs is actual dollar sales." Explain.

12-21 Allocation and Marketing

Many companies are allocating more nonproduction costs because of the increasing magnitude of these value-chain costs. One value-chain function that is receiving more attention is marketing. How should national advertising costs be allocated to territories?

12-22 Cost Management Systems and Activity-Based Allocation

Many managers are confused regarding the value of activity-based allocation. A typical comment is, "Activity-based allocation is useful for product costing, but not for operational control." Do you agree? Explain.

Exercises

12-23 Fixed- and Variable-Cost Pools

The city of Castle Rock signed a lease for a photocopy machine at $2,500 per month and $.02 per copy. Operating costs for toner, paper, operator salary, and so on are all variable at $.03 per copy. Departments had projected a need for 100,000 copies a month. The City Planning Department predicted its usage at 36,000 copies a month. It made 42,000 copies in August.

1. Suppose one predetermined rate per copy was used to allocate all photocopy costs. What rate would be used and how much cost would be allocated to the City Planning Department in August?
2. Suppose fixed- and variable-cost pools were allocated separately. Specify how each pool should be allocated. Compute the cost allocated to the City Planning Department in August.
3. Which method, the one in number 1 or the one in number 2, do you prefer? Explain.

12-24 Sales-Based Allocations

Johnny's Markets has three grocery stores in the metropolitan Philadelphia area. Central costs are allocated using sales as the cost driver. Following are budgeted and actual sales during November:

	Sunnyville	Wedgewood	Independence
Budgeted sales	$600,000	$1,000,000	$400,000
Actual sales	600,000	700,000	500,000

Central costs of $200,000 are to be allocated in November.

1. Compute the central costs allocated to each store with budgeted sales as the cost driver.
2. Compute the central costs allocated to each store with actual sales as the cost driver.
3. What advantages are there to using budgeted rather than actual sales for allocating the central costs?

12-25 Direct and Step-Down Allocations, Activity-Based Allocation, and Process Map

Dallas Building Maintenance, Inc., provides cleaning services for a variety of clients. The company has two producing divisions, Residential and Commercial, and two service departments, Personnel and Administrative. The company uses an activity-based allocation system in each of its producing divisions. Previously, the costs of service support departments has been unallocated. However, the company has decided to allocate all service department costs to the producing departments — Personnel on the basis of number of employees and Administrative on the basis of the direct costs of the activities in each division. Dallas uses a process map as part of its activity-based allocation system. The map based on the budget for 20X5 is shown in Exhibit 12-11 on page 552.

1. Determine the costs allocated to the Residential and Commercial divisions using the direct method.
2. Determine the costs allocated to the Residential and Commercial divisions using the step-down method. The Personnel Department costs should be allocated first.
3. Explain how costs would be allocated to each customer in both the Residential and Commercial divisions.

12-26 Direct and Step-Down Allocations

Butler Home Products has two producing departments, Machining and Assembly, and two service departments, Personnel and Custodial. The company's budget for April 20X5 is

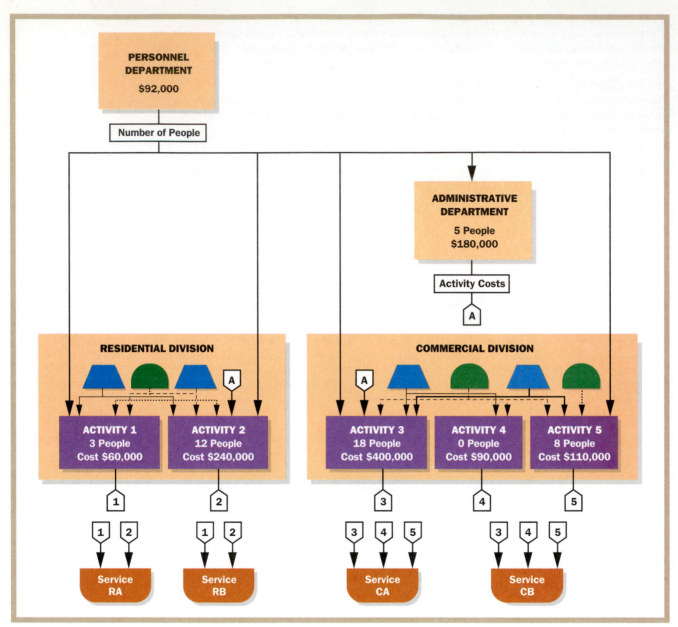

Exhibit 12-11
Dallas Building Maintenance, Inc., Allocation System

	Service Departments		Production Departments	
	Personnel	**Custodial**	**Machining**	**Assembly**
Direct department costs	$32,000	$70,000	$600,000	$800,000
Square feet	2,000	1,000	10,000	25,000
Number of employees	15	30	200	250

Butler allocates personnel costs on the basis of number of employees. Butler allocates custodial costs on the basis of square feet.

1. Allocate personnel and custodial costs to the producing departments using the direct method.
2. Allocate personnel and custodial costs to the producing departments using the step-down method. Allocate personnel costs first.

12-27 Joint Costs

Robinson Chemical Company's production process for two of its solvents can be diagrammed as follows:

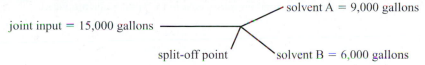

solvent A = 9,000 gallons

joint input = 15,000 gallons

split-off point solvent B = 6,000 gallons

The cost of the joint input, including processing costs before the split-off point, is $300,000. Solvent A can be sold at split off for $30 per gallon and solvent B for $45 per gallon.

1. Allocate the $300,000 joint cost to solvents A and B by the physical-units method.
2. Allocate the $300,000 joint cost to solvents A and B by the relative-sales-value method.

12-28 Joint Costs and Process Map

Hernandez Chemical Company's production process for two of its solvents can be diagrammed using a process map as shown in Exhibit 12-12.

The cost of the joint input, including processing costs before the split-off point, is $400,000. Solvent A can be sold at the split-off point for $20 per gallon and solvent B for $60 per gallon.

1. Allocate the $400,000 joint cost to solvents A and B by the physical-units method.
2. Allocate the $400,000 joint cost to solvents A and B by the relative-sales-value method.

12-29 By-Product Costing

The Wenatchee Apple Company buys apples from local orchards and presses them to produce apple juice. The pulp that remains after pressing is sold to farmers as livestock food. This livestock food is accounted for as a by-product.

During the 20X5 fiscal year, the company paid $1 million to purchase 8 million pounds of apples. After processing, 1 million pounds of pulp remained. Wenatchee spent $35,000 to package and ship the pulp, which was sold for $50,000.

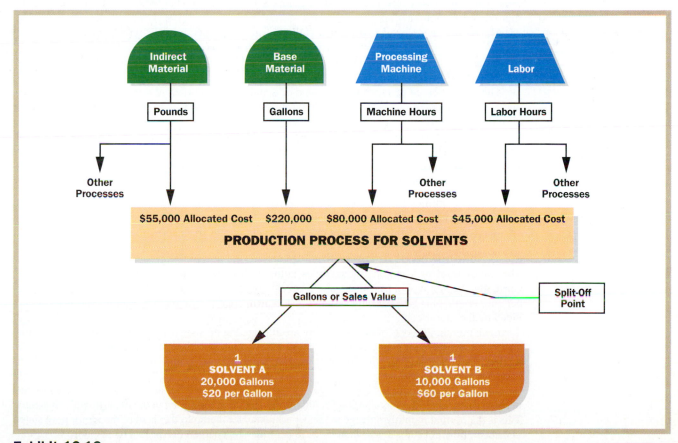

Exhibit 12-12
Hernandez Chemical Company's Joint Process

1. How much of the joint cost of the apples is allocated to the pulp?
2. Compute the total inventory cost (and therefore the cost of goods sold) for the pulp.
3. Assume that $130,000 was spent to press the apples and $150,000 was spent to filter, pasteurize, and pack the apple juice. Compute the total inventory cost of the apple juice produced.

Problems

12-30 Hospital Allocation Base

Jose Ortiz, the administrator of Brooklyn Community Hospital, has become interested in obtaining more accurate cost allocations on the basis of cause and effect. The $180,000 of laundry costs had been allocated on the basis of 600,000 pounds processed for all departments, or $.30 per pound.

Ortiz is concerned that government health care officials will require weighted statistics to be used for cost allocation. He asks you, "Please develop a revised base for allocating laundry costs. It should be better than our present base, but not be overly complex either."

You study the situation and find that the laundry processes a large volume of uniforms for student nurses and physicians and for dietary, housekeeping, and other personnel. In particular, the coats or jackets worn by personnel in the radiology department take an unusual amount of handwork.

A special study of laundry for radiology revealed that 7,500 of the 15,000 pounds were jackets and coats that were five times as expensive to process as regular laundry items. Several reasons explained the difference, but it was principally because of handwork involved.

Assume that no special requirements were needed in departments other than radiology. Revise the cost-allocation base and compute the new cost-allocation rate. Compute the total cost charged to radiology using pounds and using the new base.

12-31 Cost of Passenger Traffic

Southern Pacific Railroad (SP) has a commuter operation that services passengers along a route between San Jose and San Francisco. Problems of cost allocation were highlighted in a news story about SP's application to the Public Utilities Commission (PUC) for a rate increase. The PUC staff claimed that the "avoidable annual cost" of running the operation was $700,000, in contrast to SP officials' claim of a loss of $9 million. PUC's estimate was based on what SP would be able to save if it shut down the commuter operation.

The SP loss estimate was based on a "full-allocation-of-costs" method, which allocates a share of common maintenance and overhead costs to the passenger service.

If the PUC accepted its own estimate, a 25% fare increase would have been justified, whereas SP sought a 96% fare increase.

The PUC stressed that commuter costs represent less than 1% of the systemwide costs of SP and that 57% of the commuter costs are derived from some type of allocation method—sharing the costs of other operations.

SP's representative stated that "avoidable cost" is not an appropriate way to allocate costs for calculating rates. He said that "it is not fair to include just so-called above-the-rail costs" because there are other real costs associated with commuter service. Examples are maintaining smoother connections and making more frequent track inspections.

1. As public utilities commissioner, what approach toward cost allocation would you favor for making decisions regarding fares? Explain.
2. How would fluctuations in freight traffic affect commuter costs under the SP method?

12-32 Allocation of Automobile Costs

The motor pool of a major city provides automobiles for the use of various city departments. Currently, the motor pool has 50 autos. A recent study showed that it costs $2,400 of annual fixed cost per automobile plus $.10 per mile variable cost to own, operate, and maintain autos such as those provided by the motor pool.

Each month, the costs of the motor pool are allocated to the user departments on the basis of miles driven. On average, each auto is driven 24,000 miles annually, although wide month-to-month variations occur. In April 20X1, the 50 autos were driven a total of 50,000 miles. The motor pool's total costs for April were $19,000.

The chief planner for the city always seemed concerned about her auto costs. She was especially upset in April when she was charged $5,700 for the 15,000 miles driven in the department's five autos. This is the normal monthly mileage in the department. Her memo to the head of the motor pool stated, "I can certainly get autos at less than the $.38 per mile you charged in April." The response was, "I am under instructions to allocate the motor pool costs to the user departments. Your department was responsible for 30% of the April usage (15,000 miles ÷ 50,000 miles), so I allocated 30% of the motor pool's April costs to you (.30 × $19,000). That just seems fair."

1. Calculate the city's average annual cost per mile for owning, maintaining, and operating an auto.
2. Explain why the allocated cost in April ($.38 per mile) exceeds the average in number 1.
3. Describe any undesirable behavioral effects of the cost-allocation method used.
4. How would you improve the cost-allocation method?

12-33 Allocation of Costs

The Vigil Trucking Company has one service department and two regional operating departments. The budgeted cost behavior pattern of the service department is $750,000 monthly in fixed costs plus $.75 per 1,000 ton-miles operated in the North and South regions. (Ton-miles are the number of tons carried times the number of miles traveled.) The actual monthly costs of the service department are allocated using ton-miles operated as the cost driver.

1. Vigil processed 500 million ton-miles of traffic in April, half in each operating region. The actual costs of the service department were exactly equal to those predicted by the budget for 500 million ton-miles. Compute the costs that would be allocated to each operating region on an actual ton-miles basis.
2. Suppose the North region was plagued by strikes, so that the amount of freight handled was much lower than originally anticipated. North moved only 150 million ton-miles of traffic. The South region handled 250 million ton-miles. The actual costs were exactly as budgeted for this lower level of activity. Compute the costs that would be allocated to North and South on an actual ton-mile basis. Note that the total costs will be lower.
3. Refer to the facts in number 1. Various inefficiencies caused the service department to incur total costs of $1,250,000. Compute the costs to be allocated to North and South. Are the allocations justified? If not, what improvement do you suggest?
4. Refer to the facts in number 2. Assume that assorted investment outlays for equipment and space in the service department were made to provide a basic maximum capacity to serve the North region at a level of 360 million ton-miles and the South region at a level of 240 million ton-miles. Suppose fixed costs are allocated on the basis of this capacity to serve. Variable costs are allocated by using a predetermined standard rate per 1,000 ton-miles. Compute the costs to be allocated to each department. What are the advantages of this method over other methods?

12-34 Service Department Allocation and ABC, Product Costing

Fancy Fixtures makes displays for retail outlets. The company has three product lines—standard, deluxe, and custom. Fancy Fixtures integrates its service-department allocation system with its ABC system. There are two service departments—power and facilities management. Fancy allocates its two service department costs to the processing department using the direct method based on megawatt hours and machine hours consumed. There are two activity centers in the processing department—setup/maintenance and assembly. Parts and assembly labor are traced directly to each product. Setup/maintenance costs are allocated based on number of setups, and assembly costs are allocated based on machine hours.

Data for a recent reporting period follow:

	Product Line		
	Standard	Deluxe	Custom
Units produced and sold	100,000	10,000	1,000
Sales price per unit	$ 20	$ 50	$ 250
Total parts costs	$1,003,800	$115,080	$15,980
Total direct-labor costs	$ 298,000	$ 72,000	$68,000
Setups	20	12	8
Machine hours	1,000	400	100

			Activity Centers' Use of Driver Unit	
Resource/Department	Total Cost	Driver Unit	Setup/Maintenance	Assembly
Assembly supervisors	$ 92,400	%	2.6%	97.4%
Assembly machines	$247,000	Machine hours	400	1,500
Facilities management department	$ 95,000	Machine Hours	400	1,500
Power department	$ 54,000	Megawatt Hours	10	80

Prepare a schedule that calculates the contribution to cover other value-chain costs for each product and Fancy Fixtures as a whole company.

12-35 Service Department Allocation and ABC, Product Profitability, Process Map
(This problem is the same as problem 12-34, but uses a process map to provide data.) Fancy Fixtures makes displays for retail outlets. The company has three product lines—standard, deluxe, and custom. Fancy Fixtures integrates its service department allocation system with its ABC system. There are two service departments—power and facilities management. Fancy allocates its two service department costs to the processing department using the direct method based on megawatt hours and machine hours consumed. There are two activity centers in the processing department—setup/maintenance and assembly. Parts and assembly labor are traced directly to each product. Setup/maintenance costs are allocated based on number of setups and assembly costs are allocated based on machine hours.

Exhibit 12-13 is a process map for operations at Fancy Fixtures.

Prepare a schedule that calculates the contribution to cover other value-chain costs for each product and Fancy Fixtures as a whole company.

Exhibit 12-13
Allocation of Service Department Costs in Fancy Fixtures' ABC System

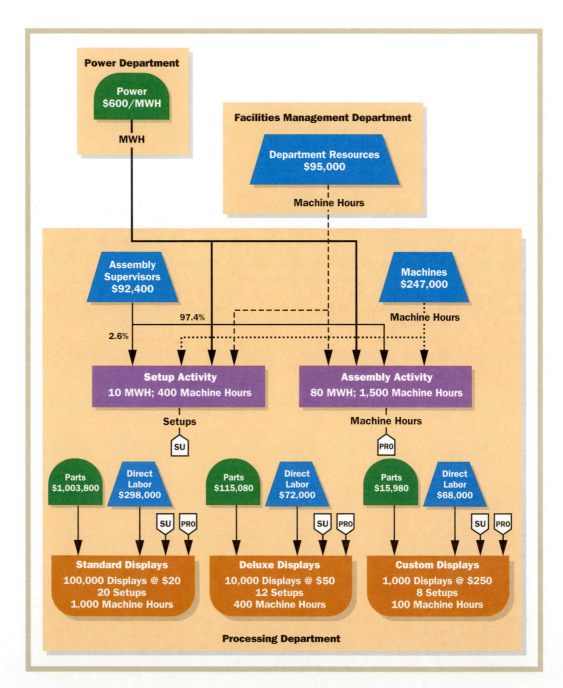

12-36 Service Department Allocation and ABC, Customer Profitability

(This problem should not be assigned unless problem 12-34 or problem 12-35 is also assigned.) Refer to problem 12-34 or problem 12-35. Fancy Fixtures has two types of customers. Customer type 1 purchases mostly standard displays. Customer type 2 purchases all three product lines but is the only customer type that purchases custom displays. Data regarding the product mix for each customer follows.

| | Units Sold by Product Line | | | |
	Standard	Deluxe	Custom	Total
Customer type 1	75,000	5,000	0	80,000
Customer type 2	25,000	5,000	1,000	31,000
Total	100,000	10,000	1,000	111,000

Prepare a schedule that calculates the contribution to cover other value-chain costs for each customer type.

12-37 Hospital Equipment

Many states have a hospital commission that must approve the acquisition of specified medical equipment before the hospitals in the state can qualify for cost-based reimbursement related to that equipment. That is, hospitals cannot bill government agencies for the use of the equipment unless the commission originally authorized the acquisition.

Two hospitals in one state proposed the acquisition and sharing of some expensive X-ray equipment to be used for unusual cases. The depreciation and related fixed costs of operating the equipment were predicted at $12,000 per month. The variable costs were predicted at $30 per patient procedure.

The commission asked each hospital to predict its usage of the equipment over its expected useful life of five years. University Hospital predicted an average usage of 75 X-rays per month; Children's Hospital of 50 X-rays. The commission regarded this information as critical to the size and degree of sophistication that would be justified. That is, if the number of X-rays exceeded a certain quantity per month, a different configuration of space, equipment, and personnel would be required that would mean higher fixed costs per month.

1. Suppose fixed costs are allocated on the basis of the hospitals' predicted average use per month. Variable costs are allocated on the basis of $30 per X-ray, the budgeted variable-cost rate for the current fiscal year. In October, University Hospital had 50 X-rays and Children's Hospital had 50 X-rays. Compute the total costs allocated to University Hospital and to Children's Hospital.
2. Suppose the manager of the equipment had various operating inefficiencies so that the total October costs were $16,500. Would you change your answers in number 1? Why?
3. A traditional method of cost allocation does not use the method in number 1. Instead, an allocation rate depends on the actual costs and actual volume encountered. The actual costs are totaled for the month and divided by the actual number of X-rays during the month. Suppose the actual costs agreed exactly with the budget for a total of 100 actual X-rays. Compute the total costs allocated to University Hospital and to Children's Hospital. Compare the results with those in number 1. What is the major weakness in this traditional method? What are some of its possible behavioral effects?
4. Describe any undesirable behavioral effects of the method described in number 1. How would you counteract any tendencies toward deliberate false predictions of long-run usage?

12-38 Direct Method for Service Department Allocation

Wheelick Controls Company has two producing departments, Mechanical Instruments and Electronic Instruments. In addition, there are two service departments, Building Services and Materials Receiving and Handling. The company purchases a variety of component parts from which the departments assemble instruments for sale in domestic and international markets.

The Electronic Instruments division is highly automated. The manufacturing costs depend primarily on the number of subcomponents in each instrument. In contrast, the Mechanical Instruments division relies primarily on a large labor force to hand-assemble instruments. Its costs depend on direct-labor hours.

The costs of Building Services depend primarily on the square footage occupied. The costs of Materials Receiving and Handling depend primarily on the total number of components handled.

Instruments M1 and M2 are produced in the Mechanical Instruments department, and E1 and E2 are produced in the Electronic Instruments department. Data about these products follow:

	Direct-Materials Cost	Number of Components	Direct-Labor Hours
M1	$74	25	4.0
M2	86	21	8.0
E1	63	10	1.5
E2	91	15	1.0

Budget figures for 20X5 include:

	Building Service	Materials Receiving and Handling	Mechanical Instruments	Electronic Instruments
Direct department costs (excluding direct materials cost)	$150,000	$120,000	$680,000	$548,000
Square footage occupied		5,000	50,000	25,000
Number of final instruments produced			8,000	10,000
Average number of components per instrument			10	16
Direct-labor hours			30,000	8,000

1. Allocate the costs of the service departments using the direct method.
2. Using the results of number 1, compute the cost per direct-labor hour in the Mechanical Instruments department and the cost per component in the Electronic Instruments department.
3. Using the results of number 2, compute the cost per unit of product for instruments M1, M2, E1, and E2.

12-39 Step-Down Method for Service Department Allocation

Refer to the data in problem 12-38.

1. Allocate the costs of the service departments using the step-down method.
2. Using the results of number 1, compute the cost per direct-labor hour in the Mechanical Instruments department and the cost per component in the Electronic Instruments department.
3. Using the results of number 2, compute the cost per unit of product for instruments M1, M2, E1, and E2.

12-40 Direct and Step-Down Methods of Allocation

General Textiles Company has prepared departmental overhead budgets for normal activity levels before allocations as follows:

Building and grounds	$ 20,000
Personnel	1,200
General factory administration*	28,020
Cafeteria operating loss	1,430
Storeroom	2,750
Machining	40,100
Assembly	71,500
Total	$165,000

* To be allocated before cafeteria.

Management has decided that the most sensible product costs are achieved by using departmental overhead rates. These rates are developed after allocating appropriate service department costs to production departments.

Cost drivers for allocation are to be selected from the following data:

Department	Direct-Labor Hours	Number of Employees	Square Feet of Floor Space Occupied	Total Labor Hours	Number of Requisitions
Building and grounds	—	—	—	—	—
Personnel*	—	—	2,000	—	—
General factory administration	—	35	7,000	—	—
Cafeteria operating loss	—	10	4,000	1,200	—
Storeroom	—	5	7,000	1,200	—
Machining	6,000	50	30,000	9,600	3,000
Assembly	18,000	100	50,000	20,400	1,500
	24,000	200	100,000	32,400	4,500

* Basis used is number of employees.

1. Allocate service department costs by the step-down method. Develop overhead rates per direct-labor hour for machining and assembly.
2. Same as in number 1, using the direct method.
3. What would be the plantwide factory-overhead application rate, assuming that direct-labor hours are used as a cost driver?
4. Using the following information about two jobs, prepare three different total overhead costs for each job, using rates developed in numbers 1, 2, and 3.

	Direct-Labor Hours	
	Machining	Assembly
Job K10	19	2
Job K12	3	18

12-41 ABC Allocations

Yamaguchi Company makes printed circuit boards in a suburb of Kyoto. The production process is automated with computer-controlled robotic machines assembling each circuit board from a supply of parts and then soldering the parts to the board. Materials-handling and quality-assurance activities use a combination of labor and equipment. Although a few resources that are used are variable with respect to changes in the demand of boards, these costs are not material compared to the fixed-cost resources that are used.

Yamaguchi makes three types of circuit boards, models 1, 2, and 3. Steps 1 to 3 of the design process for an ABC system have been completed. Exhibit 12-14 on page 560 shows the process-based map of Yamaguchi's operations.

1. Compute the cost of production for each of the three types of circuit boards and the cost per circuit board for each type.
2. Suppose the design of model 1 could be simplified so that it required only ten distinct parts (instead of 20) and took only three minutes of testing time (instead of five). Compute the cost of model 1 circuit boards and the cost per circuit board. Will the costs per circuit board for models 2 and 3 change? Explain.

12-42 Activity-Based Allocations

St. Louis Wholesale Distributors uses an activity-based-costing system to determine the cost of handling its products. One important activity is receiving shipments in the warehouse. Three resources support that activity: (1) recording and record keeping, (2) labor, and (3) inspection.

Recording and record keeping is a variable cost driven by number of shipments received. The cost per shipment is $16.50.

Labor is driven by pounds of merchandise received. Because labor is hired in shifts, it is fixed for large ranges of volume. Currently, labor costs are running $23,000 per month for handling 460,000 pounds. This same cost would apply to all volumes between 300,000 pounds and 550,000 pounds.

Finally, inspection is a variable cost driven by the number of boxes received. Inspection costs are $2.75 per box.

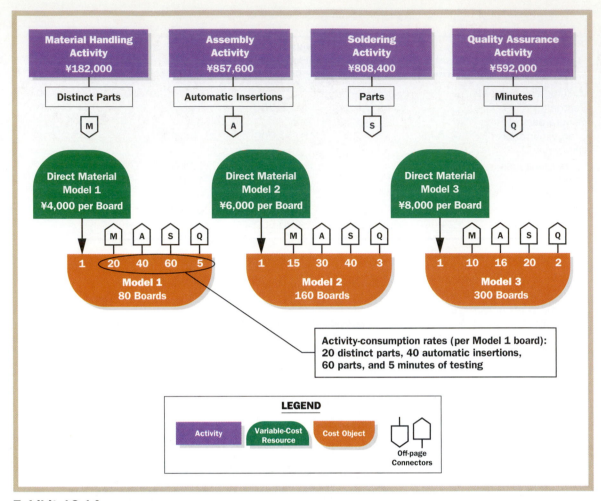

Exhibit 12-14
Yamaguchi Company's Two-Stage ABC System

One product distributed by St. Louis Wholesale Distributors is candy. There is a wide variety of candy, so many different shipments are handled in the warehouse. In July, the warehouse received 550 shipments, consisting of 4,000 boxes weighing a total of 80,000 pounds.

1. Compute the cost of receiving candy shipments during July.
2. Management is considering elimination of brands of candy that have small sales levels. This would reduce the warehouse volume to 220 shipments, consisting of 2,500 boxes weighing a total of 60,000 pounds. Compute the amount of savings from eliminating the small-sales-level brands.
3. Suppose receiving costs were estimated on a per-pound basis. What was the total receiving cost per pound of candy received in July? If management had used this cost to estimate the effect of eliminating the 20,000 pounds of candy, what mistake might be made?

12-43 Activity-Based Allocations at Dell Computer

Dell Computer Corporation installed an activity-based-costing system to help determine its product and customer profitability. The system is quite complex and took several years to fully implement. Consider a simplified hypothetical example of one component of such a system.

Dell offers two lines of notebook computers that use Pentium 4 processors and the 8600 which uses a Pentium M processor. Consider the 8600 line. Suppose that there are only three activities necessary to produce one of these computers: (1) receiving subcomponents, (2) assembling computers, and (3) inspecting computers. Computers are made to order, so each order potentially has a different cost. Therefore, to assess either product or customer profitability, it is important that Dell managers know how much each order costs. Assume that the cost of an order of computers is simply the cost of the subcomponents used plus the cost of the three activities needed to convert the subcomponents into final products.

Suppose that an activity analysis has revealed that the full cost of receiving subcomponents is 4% of the value of those subcomponents, the full cost of assembly is $24 per subcomponent, and the full cost of inspection is $56 per computer. The inspection cost is almost entirely variable, but only about one-half of the receiving and assembly costs is variable at current levels of operations.

Suppose Dell received an order from a CPA firm for 15 computers for its audit staff. The computers are identical, and each requires 12 subcomponents that cost Dell $1,100. The list price of the computers in the configuration required was $1,990.

1. Compute the cost per computer for the 15 computers ordered by the CPA firm.
2. Suppose the customer was negotiating for a 10% discount from list price. What would be Dell's profit on the order for 15 computers if it allows the discount?
3. What role should cost play in the pricing of Dell's computers?

12-44 Joint Costs and Decisions

A chemical company has a batch process that takes 1,000 gallons of a raw material and transforms it into 80 pounds of X1 and 400 pounds of X2. Although the joint costs of their production are $1,200, both products are worthless at their split-off point. Additional separable costs of $350 are necessary to give X1 a sales value of $1,000 as product A. Similarly, additional separable costs of $200 are necessary to give X2 a sales value of $1,000 as product B.

You are in charge of the batch process and the marketing of both products. (Show your computations for each answer.)

1. a. Assuming that you believe in assigning joint costs on a physical basis, allocate the total profit of $250 per batch to products A and B.
   b. Would you stop processing one of the products? Why?
2. a. Assuming that you believe in assigning joint costs on a net-realizable-value (relative-sales-value) basis, allocate the total operating profit of $250 per batch to products A and B. If there is no market for X1 and X2 at their split-off point, a net realizable value is usually imputed by taking the ultimate sales values at the point of sale and working backward to obtain approximated "synthetic" relative sales values at the split-off point. These synthetic values are then used as weights for allocating the joint costs to the products.
   b. You have internal product-profitability reports in which joint costs are assigned on a net-realizable-value basis. Your chief engineer says that, after seeing these reports, he has developed a method of obtaining more of product B and correspondingly less of product A from each batch, without changing the per-pound cost factors. Would you approve this new method? Why? What would the overall operating profit be if 40 pounds more of B were produced and 40 pounds less of A?

Cases

12-45 Allocation, Department Rates, and Direct-Labor Hours Versus Machine Hours

The Manning Manufacturing Company has two producing departments, Machining and Assembly. Mr. Manning recently automated the Machining department. The installation of a CAM system, together with robotic workstations, drastically reduced the amount of direct labor required. Meanwhile, the Assembly department remained labor intensive.

The company had always used one firmwide rate based on direct-labor hours as the cost driver for applying all costs (except direct materials) to the final products. Mr. Manning was considering two alternatives: (1) continue using direct-labor hours as the only cost driver, but use different rates in Machining and Assembly, and (2) using machine hours as the cost driver in the Machining department while continuing with direct-labor hours in Assembly.

Budgeted data for 20X5 are

	Machining	Assembly	Total
Total cost (except direct materials), after allocating service department costs	$630,000	$450,000	$1,080,000
Machine hours	105,000	*	105,000
Direct-labor hours	15,000	30,000	45,000

* Not applicable.

1. Suppose Manning continued to use one firmwide rate based on direct-labor hours to apply all manufacturing costs (except direct materials) to the final products. Compute the cost-application rate that would be used.
2. Suppose Manning continued to use direct-labor hours as the only cost driver but used different rates in Machining and Assembly.
   a. Compute the cost-application rate for Machining.
   b. Compute the cost-application rate for Assembly.
3. Suppose Manning changed the cost accounting system to use machine hours as the cost driver in Machining and direct-labor hours in Assembly.
   a. Compute the cost-application rate for Machining.
   b. Compute the cost-application rate for Assembly.
4. Three products use the following machine hours and direct-labor hours.

	Machine Hours in Machining	Direct-Labor Hours in Machining	Direct-Labor Hours in Assembly
Product A	10.0	1.0	14.0
Product B	17.0	1.5	3.0
Product C	14.0	1.3	8.0

   a. Compute the manufacturing cost of each product (excluding direct materials) using one firmwide rate based on direct-labor hours.
   b. Compute the manufacturing cost of each product (excluding direct materials) using direct-labor hours as the cost driver, but with different cost-application rates in Machining and Assembly.
   c. Compute the manufacturing cost of each product (excluding direct materials) using a cost-application rate based on direct-labor hours in Assembly and machine hours in Machining.
   d. Compare and explain the results in numbers 4a, 4b, and 4c.

12-46 Multiple Allocation Bases

The London Electronics Company produces three types of circuit boards; call them L, M, and N. The cost accounting system used by London until 2003 applied all costs except direct materials to the products using direct-labor hours as the only cost driver. In 2003, the company undertook a cost study. The study determined that there were six main factors that incurred costs. A new system was designed with a separate cost pool for each of the six factors. The factors and the costs associated with each are as follows:

1. Direct-labor hours—direct-labor cost and related fringe benefits and payroll taxes
2. Machine hours—depreciation and repairs and maintenance costs
3. Pounds of materials—materials receiving, handling, and storage costs
4. Number of production setups—labor used to change machinery and computer configurations for a new production batch
5. Number of production orders—costs of production scheduling and order processing
6. Number of orders shipped—all packaging and shipping expenses

The company is now preparing a budget for 2005. The budget includes the following predictions:

	Board L	Board M	Board N
Units to be produced	10,000	800	5,000
Direct-materials cost	£66/unit	£88/unit	£45/unit
Direct-labor hours	4/unit	18/unit	9/unit
Machine hours	7/unit	15/unit	7/unit
Pounds of materials	3/unit	4/unit	2/unit
Number of production setups	100	50	50
Number of production orders	300	200	70
Number of orders shipped	1,000	800	2,000

The total budgeted cost for 2005 is £3,712,250, of which £955,400 was direct-materials cost, and the amount in each of the six cost pools defined above is

Cost Pool*	Cost
1	£1,391,600
2	936,000
3	129,600
4	160,000
5	25,650
6	114,000
Total	£2,756,850

* Identified by the cost driver used.

1. Prepare a budget that shows the total budgeted cost and the unit cost for each circuit board. Use the new system with six cost pools (plus a separate direct application of direct-materials cost).
2. Compute the budgeted total and unit costs of each circuit board if the old direct-labor-hour system had been used.
3. How would you judge whether the new system is better than the old one?

12-47 Allocation of Data Processing Costs

The Gibraltar Insurance Co. (GIC) established a Systems department to implement and operate its own data processing systems. GIC believed that its own system would be more cost-effective than the service bureau it had been using.

GIC's three departments—Claims, Records, and Finance—have different requirements with respect to hardware and other capacity-related resources and operating resources. The system was designed to recognize these differing needs. In addition, the system was designed to meet GIC's long-term capacity needs. The excess capacity designed into the system would be sold to outside users until needed by GIC. The estimated resource requirements used to design and implement the system are shown in the following schedule:

	Hardware and Other Capacity-Related Resources	Operating Resources
Records	25%	60%
Claims	50	15
Finance	20	20
Expansion (outside use)	5	5
Total	100%	100%

GIC currently sells the equivalent of its expansion capacity to a few outside clients.

At the time the system became operational, management decided to redistribute total expenses of the Systems department to the user departments based on actual computer time used. The actual costs for the first quarter of the current fiscal year were distributed to the user departments as follows:

Department	Percentage Utilization	Amount
Records	60%	$330,000
Claims	15	82,500
Finance	20	110,000
Outside	5	27,500
Total	100%	$550,000

The three user departments have complained about the cost distribution method since the Systems department was established. The Records department's monthly costs have been as much as three times the costs experienced with the service bureau. The Finance department is concerned about the costs distributed to the outside user category because these allocated costs form the basis for the fees billed to the outside clients.

Mostafa al Rashed, GIC's controller, decided to review the cost-allocation method. The additional information he gathered for his review is reported in Tables 1, 2, and 3.

Table 1 Systems Department Costs and Activity Levels

| | Annual Budget | | First Quarter | | | |
| | | | Budget | | Actual | |
	Hours	Dollars	Hours	Dollars	Hours	Dollars
Hardware and other capacity-related costs	—	$ 600,000	—	$150,000	—	$155,000
Software development	18,750	562,500	4,725	141,750	4,250	130,000
Operations						
Computer related	3,750	750,000	945	189,000	920	187,000
Input/output related	30,000	300,000	7,560	75,600	7,900	78,000
Total		$2,212,500		$556,350		$550,000

Table 2 Historical Usage

| | Hardware and Other Capacity Needs | Software Development | | Operations | | | |
| | | | | Computer | | Input/Output | |
		Range	Average	Range	Average	Range	Average
Records	25%	0–30%	15%	55–65%	60%	10–30%	15%
Claims	50	15–60	40	10–25	15	60–80	75
Finance	20	25–75	40	10–25	20	3–10	5
Outside	5	0–25	5	3–8	5	3–10	5
	100%		100%		100%		100%

Table 3 Usage of Systems Department's Services
First Quarter (in hours)

| | Software Development | Operations | |
		Computer Related	Input/Output
Records	450	540	1,540
Claims	1,800	194	5,540
Finance	1,600	126	410
Outside	400	60	410
Total	4,250	920	7,900

Al Rashed has concluded that the method of cost allocation should be changed. He believes that the hardware and capacity-related costs should be allocated to the user departments in proportion to the planned long-term needs. Any difference between actual and budgeted hardware costs would not be allocated to the departments but remain with the Systems department.

The costs for software development and operations would be charged to the user departments based on actual hours used. A predetermined hourly rate based on the annual budget data would be used. The hourly rates that would be used for the current fiscal year are as follows:

Function	Hourly Rate
Software development	$ 30
Operations	
Computer related	200
Input/output related	10

Al Rashed plans to use first-quarter activity and cost data to illustrate his recommendations. The recommendations will be presented to the Systems department and the user departments for their comments and reactions. He then expects to present his recommendations to management for approval.

1. Calculate the amount of data-processing costs that would be included in the Claims department's first-quarter budget according to the method Mostafa Al Rashed has recommended.
2. Prepare a schedule to show how the actual first-quarter costs of the Systems department would be charged to the users if GIC adopts Al Rashed's recommended method.
3. Explain whether Al Rashed's recommended system for charging costs to the user departments will:
   a. Improve cost control in the Systems department
   b. Improve planning and cost control in the user departments

EXCEL Application Exercise

12-48 Allocating Costs Using Direct and Step-Down Methods

Goal: Create an Excel spreadsheet to allocate costs using the direct method and the step-down method. Use the results to answer questions about your findings.

Scenario: Dallas Cleaning, Inc., has asked you to help them determine the best method for allocating costs from their service departments to their producing departments. Additional background information for your spreadsheet appears in Fundamental Assignment Material 12-B2. Exhibit 12-4 illustrates the types of calculations that are used for allocating costs using the direct method and the step-down method.

When you have completed your spreadsheet, answer the following questions:
1. What are the total costs for the Residential department using the direct method? What are the total costs for the Commercial department using the direct method?
2. What are the total costs for the Residential department using the step-down method?
3. What are the total costs for the Commercial department using the step-down method?
4. Which method would you recommend that Dallas Cleaning, Inc., use to allocate their service departments' costs to their producing departments? Why?

Step-by-Step:
1. Open a new Excel spreadsheet.
2. In column A, create a bold-faced heading that contains the following:
   Row 1: Chapter 12 Decision Guideline
   Row 2: Dallas Cleaning, Inc.
   Row 3: Cost Allocations from Service Departments to Producing Departments
   Row 4: Today's Date
3. Merge and center the four heading rows across columns A through H.
4. In row 7, create the following bold-faced, center-justified column headings:
   Column B: Personnel
   Column C: Administrative
   Column D: Residential
   Column E: Commercial
   Column F: Total Res/Comm
   Column G: Total Admin/Res/Comm
   Column H: Grand Total
5. Change the format of the column headings in row 7 to permit the titles to be displayed on multiple lines within a single cell.

| Alignment tab: | Wrap Text: | Checked |

   Note: Adjust column widths so that headings use only two lines.
   Adjust row height to ensure that row is same height as adjusted headings.

6. In column A, create the following row headings:
   Row 8: Direct Department Costs
   Row 9: Number of Employees
   Skip 2 rows
   Note: Adjust the width of column A to 27.14.

7. In column A, create the following bold-faced, underlined row heading:
   Row 12: Direct Method:

8. In column A, create the following row headings:
   Row 13: Direct Department Costs
   Row 14: Personnel Allocation
   Row 15: Administrative Allocation
   Row 16: Total Costs
   Skip 2 rows
9. In column A, create the following bold-faced, underlined row heading:
   Row 19: Step-down Method:
10. In column A, create the following row headings:
    Row 20: Direct Department Costs
    Row 21: Step 1-Personnel Allocation
    Row 22: Step 2-Administrative Allocation
    Row 23: Total Costs
11. Use data from Fundamental Assignment 12-B2 to enter the amounts in columns B through E for rows 8, 9, 13 and 20.
12. Use the appropriate calculations to do the totals in row 8 for columns F and H.
    Use the appropriate calculations to do the totals in row 9 for columns F and G.
13. Use the appropriate formulas to allocate the costs from the service departments to the producing departments using each of the methods.
14. Use the appropriate calculations to do the totals in columns B through E and in column H, rows 16 and 23.
15. Format amounts in columns B through H, rows 8, 13, 16, 20 and 23 as

	Number tab:	Category:	Accounting
		Decimal:	0
		Symbol:	$

16. Format the amount in columns B through E, rows 14, 15, 21, and 22 as

	Number tab:	Category:	Accounting
		Decimal:	0
		Symbol:	None

17. Change the format of the total costs amounts in columns B through E, rows 16 and 23, to display a top border, using the default line style.

	Border tab:	Icon:	Top Border

18. Change the format of the amounts in row 9, columns B through G to center justified.
19. Save your work to disk, and print a copy for your files.
    Note: Print your spreadsheet using landscape in order to ensure that all columns appear on one page.

Collaborative Learning Exercise

12-49 Library Research on ABC

Form into groups of three to six students. Each student should choose a different article about activity-based costing (ABC) or activity-based management (ABM) from the current literature. The article should include information about at least one company's application of ABC. Such articles are available in a variety of sources. You might try bibliographic searches for "activity-based costing" or "activity-based management." Journals that will have articles on ABC and ABM include

Strategic Finance (USA)
Management Accounting (United Kingdom)
Journal of Cost Management
CMA Management (Canada)
Management Accounting Quarterly

1. After reading the article, note the following (if given in the article) for one company:
   a. The benefits of ABC or ABM
   b. The problems encountered in implementing ABC or ABM
   c. Suggestions by the author(s) about employing ABC or ABM
2. As a group, using the collective wisdom garnered from the articles, respond to the following:
   a. What kinds of companies can benefit from ABC or ABM?
   b. What kinds of companies have little to gain from ABC or ABM?
   c. What steps should be taken to ensure successful implementation of ABC or ABM?
   d. What potential pitfalls are there to avoid in implementing ABC or ABM?

Internet Exercise www.prenhall.com/horngren

12-50 Cost Allocation at Target Corporation

Allocating indirect costs can be a challenging task. Almost all firms have some type of cost centers (departments), whether it is the administration overseeing the corporation as a whole or the accounting department processing billing and invoicing customers. What to do with the costs generated by these cost centers can be a tricky task. Let's take a look at **Target Corporation**, a firm that has multiple divisions.

1. Go to the home page for Target, Inc., at http://www.target.com. How many companies are listed under the umbrella of "Target Corporation"? What are these companies? How many of them are located in the area where you are located? If one or more is not located in your area, have you heard of it before?

2. Go to the information on Marshall Field's. What type of a focus does this company have? Does the company have a separate Web site? Do you think that some of the cost of the Target Web site should be allocated to Marshall Field's? Why or why not? If the firm were to allocate costs, what measurement tool would you recommend that the firm consider?

3. Locate Target Corporation's most recent annual report by clicking on "Investor Information" at Target's home page. Click on "financial reports & filings" and then on the most recent annual report. Look at the financial review section. Did the firm provide any information on segment revenues? Sum the pretax segment profit of the segments for the current year. What is this figure? Now look at the income statement for the current year. What is the income before taxes and extraordinary items for the year? Why is it different from the sum of the segment pretax profit?

4. Assume that the difference in the pretax segment profit and the corporation's pretax profit is due to service department costs. If Target wants to allocate these costs to the major segments based on segment pretax income using the direct method, how much would be allocated to each segment? What would be the allocation if the corporation used the number of stores as the allocation basis?

Accounting for Overhead Costs

LEARNING OBJECTIVES

When you have finished studying this chapter, you should be able to:

1. Compute budgeted factory-overhead rates and apply factory overhead to production.

2. Determine and use appropriate cost drivers for overhead application.

3. Identify the meaning and purpose of normalized overhead rates.

4. Construct an income statement using the variable-costing approach.

5. Construct an income statement using the absorption-costing approach.

6. Compute the production-volume variance and show how it should appear in the income statement.

7. Explain why a company might prefer to use a variable-costing approach.

Dell Computer Corporation is the world's leading direct

marketer of made-to-order computer systems. Dell does not manufacture computer components (e.g., circuit boards, hard drives), but instead assembles them into computers on a made-to-order basis.

Dell pioneered the "direct business model"—selling directly to end users instead of using a network of dealers, which avoids the dealer markup and gives Dell a competitive price advantage. Customers can design their own computer systems to specifications they desire, choosing from among a full complement of options. Before ordering, customers can receive advice and price quotes for a wide variety of computer configurations.

Once an order is taken, Dell assembles it in a manufacturing work cell called a mod. There is a separate mod for each of Dell's "lines of business" (Dimension Desktop PCs, OptiPlex Desktops for networked environments, Latitude and Inspiron Notebooks, PowerEdge and PowerApp network servers, and Precision workstation products). Management considers rapid response to customer orders a key to gaining and maintaining a competitive edge.

Dell takes orders over the phone or over the Internet. In fact, Dell derives about 50% of its revenues from the company's Web site, http://www.dell.com, with daily revenues in excess of $40 million and weekly "hits" of over 3,000,000. Customers may review, configure, and price systems within Dell's entire product line. Web sites also offer personalized system-support pages and technical services. The Internet was tailor-made for Dell. Customers of all kinds prefer direct. They like the immediacy, convenience, savings, and personal touches the Internet-direct customer experience provides.

Dell Computer Corporation's workers assemble computers based on individual customer specifications. The assembly activity is a key part of the production process. Accounting for overhead costs is important at Dell, so much effort is given to ensure that appropriate costs are applied to its many computer products.

Why would managers at a highly profitable company like Dell be interested in knowing as much as possible about the cost of their individual product lines? With record profits being reported in their annual reports, is there a clear need for costs for other management purposes? The answer is yes—most of the reason why Dell's aggregate profitability measures are industry leading is the strategic and operational decisions its managers make. These decisions are based on detailed cost information. For example, Dell's cost accounting systems supply product costs to managers for evaluating pricing policy and product lines. Dell managers need to know the cost of each kind of computer being produced to set prices, to determine marketing and production strategies for various models, and to evaluate production operations. At the same time, product costs appear as cost of goods sold in income statements and as finished-goods inventory values in balance sheets. Although it would be possible to have two product-costing systems, one for management decision making and one for financial reporting, seldom do the benefits of using two completely separate systems exceed the costs. Therefore, both decision-making and financial-reporting needs influence the design of product-costing systems.

In Chapter 4, you learned about three types of costs in a manufacturing company, direct materials, direct labor, and factory overhead—that is, indirect manufacturing costs. In this chapter, we focus on overhead. ■

Accounting for Factory Overhead

OBJECTIVE 1

Compute budgeted factory-overhead rates and apply factory overhead to production.

Years ago, direct materials and direct labor were the largest costs for most companies. Today, automated companies such as Dell have less direct labor but much larger overhead costs. Thus, methods for assigning overhead costs to the products is an important part of accurately measuring product costs.

How to Apply Factory Overhead to Products

Managers need to know product costs in order to make ongoing decisions, such as which products to emphasize or deemphasize and how to price each product. Ideally, managers would know all costs precisely, including overhead, when they make these decisions. Because accountants directly trace direct materials and direct labor costs to products, these costs are available immediately on completion of production and they are known precisely. In contrast, because it is not economically feasible to know other indirect manufacturing costs immediately, accountants must estimate them. For this reason, accountants use budgeted (predetermined) overhead rates to apply overhead to jobs as they are completed, making an estimate of total product cost available for managerial decisions. When the relative size of the overhead costs is large, we can understand how important it is for companies to have an accurate system for factory overhead accounting.

The size of overhead costs in many manufacturing companies is large enough to motivate companies to search for ways to convert them into direct costs. Dell has increased the accuracy of its product cost information by converting some of its factory-overhead costs from indirect to direct costs. How did they do this? By dedicating assembly labor and factory equipment to specific product lines. Work cells (mods) do the assembly and software loading for specific product lines. This makes it easier to trace equipment costs to products. Nevertheless, significant overhead costs remain to be allocated. So let's look at how companies such as Dell allocate these overhead costs to products.

Budgeted Overhead Application Rates

The following steps summarize how to account for factory overhead:

1. Select one or more cost drivers to serve as a base for applying overhead costs. Examples include direct-labor hours, direct-labor costs, machine hours, and production setups. The cost driver should be an activity that is the common denominator for systematically relating a cost or a group of costs, such as machinery cost, set-up costs, or energy cost, with products. The cost driver(s) should be the most plausible and reliable measure available of the cause-and-effect relationships between overhead costs and production volume.
2. Prepare a factory-overhead budget for the planning period, ordinarily a year. The two key items are (a) budgeted overhead and (b) budgeted volume of the cost driver. There will be a set of budgeted overhead costs and an associated budgeted cost-driver level for each overhead cost pool.[1] In businesses with simple production systems, there may be just one set.
3. Compute the **budgeted factory-overhead rate**(s) by dividing the budgeted total overhead for each cost pool by the budgeted cost-driver level.
4. Obtain actual cost-driver data (such as machine hours) used for each product.
5. Apply the budgeted overhead to the products by multiplying the budgeted rate(s) in step 3 times the actual cost-driver data from step 4.
6. At the end of the year, account for any differences between the amount of overhead actually incurred and overhead applied to products.

> **budgeted factory-overhead rate**
> The budgeted total overhead for each cost pool divided by the budgeted cost-driver level.

Illustration of Overhead Application

Now that you know the steps in accounting for factory overhead, let's examine how they work in a realistic example. Consider the Enriquez Machine Parts Company.[2] Its manufacturing-overhead budget for 20X4 follows:

	Machining	Assembly
Indirect labor	$ 75,600	$ 36,800
Supplies	8,400	2,400
Utilities	20,000	7,000
Repairs	10,000	3,000
Factory rent	10,000	6,800
Supervision	42,600	35,400
Depreciation on equipment	104,000	9,400
Insurance, property taxes, etc.	7,200	2,400
Total	$277,800	$103,200

Enriquez selected a single cost driver in each department, machine hours in machining and direct-labor cost in assembly, for applying overhead. As Enriquez works on a product, it applies the factory overhead to the product using a budgeted overhead rate, computed as follows:

$$\text{budgeted overhead application rate} = \frac{\text{total budgeted factory overhead}}{\text{total budgeted amount of cost driver}}$$

---

[1] Cost pools were defined in Chapter 4, page 141, as a group of individual costs that a company allocates to activities or cost objectives using a single cost driver.

[2] If Chapter 14 and job-order costing have been assigned prior to this chapter, you will notice that the chapter illustration of Enriquez Machine Parts Company in both Chapters 13 and 14 are the same, with all data completely compatible.

The overhead rates for the two departments are as follows:

	Year 20X4	
	Machining	**Assembly**
Budgeted manufacturing overhead	$277,800	$103,200
Budgeted machine hours	69,450	
Budgeted direct-labor cost		$206,400
Budgeted overhead rate, per machine hour: $277,800 ÷ 69,450 =	$4	
Budgeted overhead rate, per direct-labor dollar: $103,200 ÷ $206,400 =		50%

Note that the overhead rates are budgeted; they are estimates. Accountants at Enriquez then use these budgeted rates to apply overhead based on actual events. That is, the total overhead applied to a particular product is the result of multiplying the budgeted overhead rates by the actual machine hours or labor cost used by that product. Thus, we would apply $44 of overhead to a product that uses six machine hours in machining and incurs direct-labor cost of $40 in assembly:

Machining: 6 actual machine hours × $4 per machine hour $24
Assembly: $40 of direct-labor cost × 50%   20
Total overhead $44

Suppose that at the end of the year Enriquez had used 70,000 machine hours in assembly and incurred $190,000 of direct-labor cost in assembly. It would have applied a total of $375,000 of overhead to the products produced:

Machining: 70,000 actual machine hours × $4 $280,000
Assembly: $190,000 actual direct-labor cost × .50   95,000
Total factory overhead applied $375,000

This $375,000 is an estimate of Enriquez's overhead for the year, and it will become part of the cost of goods sold expense on Enriquez's income statement either in the period of production or later. If the actual overhead costs differ from $375,000, the company will usually charge the difference to expense in the period of production. For example, if Enriquez's actual overhead in 20X4 were $392,000, it would add $392,000 − $375,000 = $17,000 additional expense in 2004.

This completes our six steps. Next let's go back to step one and explore how a company might choose appropriate cost drivers.

Choice of Cost Drivers

OBJECTIVE 2

Determine and use appropriate cost drivers for overhead application.

As you have seen several times in this text, no one cost driver is right for all situations. The accountant's goal is to find the driver that best links cause and effect. In the Enriquez machining department, use of machines causes most overhead cost, for example, depreciation and repairs. Therefore, machine hours is the cost driver and the appropriate base for applying overhead costs. Thus, Enriquez must keep track of the machine hours used for each job, creating an added data collection cost. That is, it must accumulate machine hours in addition to direct-materials costs and direct-labor costs for each job.

In contrast, direct labor is the principal cost driver in the Enriquez assembly department because employees assemble parts by hand. Suppose the company records the time each worker spends on each product (or batch of products). Then, all that is needed is to apply the 50% overhead rate to the cost of direct labor already recorded. No additional data are needed.

If the hourly labor rates for workers differ greatly for individuals performing identical tasks, Enriquez might use the hours of labor, rather than the dollars spent for labor, as a base. Otherwise, Enriquez would apply more overhead when a $10-per-hour worker works an hour than when an $8-per-hour worker works an hour, even though each employee uses the same facilities and generally receives the same overhead support. However, sometimes direct-labor cost is the best overhead cost driver even if wage rates vary within a department. For example, higher-skilled labor may use more costly equipment and have more indirect labor support. Moreover, many factory-overhead costs include costly labor fringe benefits such as pensions and payroll taxes. Direct-labor cost rather than direct-labor hours often drive such fringe-benefit costs.

If a department identifies more than one cost driver for overhead costs, it should accumulate a separate cost pool for each cost driver and put each overhead cost into the appropriate cost pool. In practice, such a system is too costly for many organizations. Instead, these organizations select a few cost drivers (often only one) to serve as a basis for allocating overhead costs. We often use the 80–20 rule in these situations–20% of the cost drivers drive 80% of the overhead costs. For example, suppose a company identifies ten separate overhead pools with ten different drivers. Often, it can accurately apply approximately 80% of the total overhead cost with only two drivers. It may be too costly to devise separate cost pools for the other 20%, so it arbitrarily assigns those costs to the two main cost pools.

The selected cost drivers should be the ones that cause most of the overhead costs. For example, suppose machine hours cause 70% of the overhead costs in a particular department, number of component parts causes 20%, and five assorted cost drivers cause the other 10%. Instead of using seven cost pools allocated on the basis of the seven cost drivers, most managers would use one cost driver—machine hours—to allocate all overhead costs. Others would assign all cost to two cost pools, one allocated on the basis of machine hours and one on the basis of number of component parts.

Consider Dell Computer Corporation. As we said earlier, Dell has converted many of its overhead costs into direct costs. However, two important costs that it cannot directly trace (that is, that remain indirect costs) are facilities and engineering. Facilities cost includes occupancy costs such as depreciation on the factory, insurance, and taxes. Dell allocates these costs using the cost driver "square footage used by each line of business (assembly line)." Dell incurs large product and process engineering costs as part of the design phase of the company's value chain. It allocates these costs to lines of business using a "complexity" cost driver such as number of distinct parts in the mother board. Server computer products, for example, require much more engineering time and effort due to the complexity of the product compared to laptops or PCs as measured by the number of distinct parts in the mother board. Thus, server products receive a much greater allocation of engineering costs than laptops or PCs.

Another example is Harley-Davidson, which changed from using direct labor as a cost allocation base to using process hours, as we describe in the Business First box on page 574.

Problems of Overhead Application

Normalized Overhead Rates

The Enriquez illustration demonstrated what we call the normal costing approach. Why the term *normal*? Because we use an annual average overhead rate consistently throughout the year for product costing, without altering it from day to day and from

OBJECTIVE 3

Identify the meaning and purpose of normalized overhead rates.

OVERHEAD ALLOCATION AT HARLEY-DAVIDSON

In August 2003, Milwaukee-based Harley-Davidson, the motorcycle manufacturer, celebrated its 100th birthday. As happy as everyone at Harley is today, it is a bit suprising to some how far the company has come over the past several decades. From near collapse, Harley turned its business around during the 1980s and 1990s, and in 1999 captured the number one market position from Honda for the first time in three decades. Harley-Davidson (2002 sales of $4.1 billion) is the only major U.S.-based motorcycle producer. One of the keys to the company's return to competitiveness was the adoption of a just-in-time (JIT) philosophy. It is not unusual for a company to discover that a change in an important component of operations requires a corresponding change in the company's accounting system. The main focus of the accounting system was direct labor, which not only made up a part of product cost itself, but also functioned as an all-purpose base for allocating overhead. However, direct labor was only 10% of total product cost. It certainly did not generate a majority of overhead costs. Although Harley-Davidson's production process had changed, the accounting system remained static.

The JIT system served to emphasize that detailed information on direct-labor costs was not useful to managers. It was costly to have each direct laborer record the time spent on each product or part and then enter the information from these time cards into the accounting system. For example, if each of 500 direct laborers works on 20 products per day, the system must record 10,000 entries per day, which is 200,000 entries per month. The time spent by direct laborers to record the time, by clerks to enter the data into the system, and by accountants to check the data's accuracy, is enormous—and all to produce product cost information that was used for financial reporting but was useless to managers.

The JIT system forced manufacturing managers to focus on satisfying customers and minimizing non-value-added activities. Gradually, accountants began to focus on the same objectives. Accounting's customers were the managers who used the accounting information, and effort put into activities that did not help managers was deemed counterproductive (non-value-added). Therefore, eliminating the costly, time-consuming recording of detailed labor costs became a priority. Direct labor was eliminated as a direct cost, and consequently it could not be used for overhead allocation. After considering process hours, flow-through time, materials value, and individual cost per unit as possible cost drivers for allocating overhead, the company selected process hours. Direct labor and overhead were combined to form conversion costs, which were applied to products on the basis of total process hours. This did not result in costs significantly different from the old system, but the new system was much simpler and less costly. Only direct material was traced directly to the product. Conversion costs were applied at completion of production based on a simple measure of process time.

Accounting systems should generate benefits greater than their costs. More sophisticated systems are not necessarily better systems. Harley-Davidson's main objective in changing its accounting system was simplification—elimination of unnecessary tasks and streamlining others. These changes resulted in a revitalized accounting system.

Sources: Adapted from W. T. Turk, "Management Accounting Revitalized: The Harley-Davidson Experience," in B. J. Brinker, ed., *Emerging Practices in Cost Management* (Boston: Warren, Gorham & Lamont, 1990), pp. 155–166; K. Barron, "Hog Wild," *Forbes*, May 15, 2000; Harley-Davidson *2002 Annual Report*.

normal costing system
The cost system in which the cost of the manufactured product is composed of actual direct material, actual direct labor, and normal applied overhead.

month to month. The resultant "normal" product costs include an average or normalized chunk of overhead. Hence, in a **normal costing system** the cost of the manufactured product is composed of actual direct material, actual direct labor, and normal applied overhead.

A department's actual overhead amount incurred will rarely equal the amount applied. Managers can analyze this variance between incurred and applied cost. The most common—and important—contributor to these variances is operating at a different level of volume than the level used as a denominator in calculating the budgeted overhead rate (for instance, using 100,000 budgeted direct-labor-hours as the denominator and then actually working only 80,000 hours). Other frequent contributory causes include poor forecasting, inefficient use of overhead items, price changes in individual overhead items, erratic behavior of individual overhead items (e.g., repairs made only during slack time), and calendar variations (e.g., 20 workdays in one month, 22 in the next).

Companies generally prefer to use an annual budgeted factory-overhead rate regardless of the month-to-month peculiarities of specific overhead costs. Such an approach is more defensible than, say, applying the actual overhead for each month. Why? Because a normal product cost is more useful for decisions, and more representative for inventory-costing purposes, than an "actual" product cost that is distorted by month-to-month fluctuations in production volume and by the erratic behavior of many overhead costs. For example, the employees of a gypsum plant using an "actual" product cost system had the privilege of buying company-made items "at cost." Employees joked about the benefits of buying "at cost" during high-volume months, when unit costs were lower because volume was higher, as the following table illustrates.

	Actual Overhead			Direct-Labor Hours	Actual Overhead Application Rate* per Direct-Labor Hour
	Variable	Fixed	Total		
Peak-volume month	$60,000	$40,000	$100,000	100,000	$1.00
Low-volume month	30,000	40,000	70,000	50,000	1.40

* Divide total overhead by direct-labor hours. Note that the presence of fixed overhead causes the fluctuation in unit overhead costs from $1.00 to $1.40. The variable component is $.60 an hour in both months, but the fixed component is $.40 in the peak-volume month ($40,000 ÷ 100,000) and $.80 in the low-volume month ($40,000 ÷ 50,000).

Disposition of Underapplied or Overapplied Overhead

The last step on page 571 dealt with differences between actual and applied overhead. Let's look in more detail at options for accounting for such differences. Recall that in 20X4 Enriquez applied $375,000 of overhead to its products but actually incurred $392,000 of overhead costs. Is the $17,000 difference an asset or an expense? Remember that the product has already been completed and most likely sold. Further, the sales price was probably set based on the applied overhead cost. So, because the extra $17,000 will not help the company generate any future revenue, it is normally treated as expense.

The $375,000 will become part of the Cost of Goods Sold expense when Enriquez sells the products produced in 20X4. The remaining $17,000 must also become expense by some method. We call it **underapplied overhead** because the amount applied is less than the amount incurred. The opposite, **overapplied overhead,** occurs when the amount applied exceeds the amount incurred. At year-end, the company disposes of under- or overapplied overhead through either an immediate write-off or through proration.

underapplied overhead
The excess of actual overhead over the overhead applied to products.

overapplied overhead
The excess of overhead applied to products over actual overhead incurred.

Immediate Write-Off The immediate write-off method regards the $17,000 underapplied overhead as a reduction in current income by *adding* it to the cost of goods sold. By the same logic we would *deduct* any overapplied overhead from the cost of goods sold.

One theory underlying the direct write-off is that the company has sold most of the goods worked on during the period, and a more elaborate method of disposition is not worth the extra trouble. Another justification is that the extra overhead costs represented by underapplied overhead do not qualify as part of ending inventory costs because they do not represent assets. They largely represent inefficiencies in the current period and thus are an expense of that period. Because of its simplicity, the immediate write-off method is most commonly used.

Proration Among Inventories Another method prorates over- or underapplied overhead among Work-In-Process (WIP), Finished Goods, and Cost of Goods Sold. To **prorate** underapplied overhead means to assign it in proportion to the sizes of the ending account balances. Theoretically, if the objective is to obtain as accurate an allocation of actual costs as possible, we should recompute all the overhead costs of the individual products, using the actual, rather than the budgeted, rates. This approach is rarely feasible, so a practical attack is to prorate on the basis of the ending balances in each of three accounts. Assume that the ending balances for Enriquez are WIP, $155,000; Finished Goods, $32,000; and Cost of Goods Sold, $2,480,000 (a total of $2,667,000). The results of proration follow:

	(1) Unadjusted Balance, End of 20X4	(2) Proration of Underapplied Overhead		(3) Adjusted Balance, End of 20X4
WIP	$ 155,000	155/2,667 × $17,000 = $	988	$ 155,988
Finished goods	32,000	32/2,667 × 17,000 =	204	32,204
Cost of goods sold	2,480,000	2,480/2,667 × 17,000 =	15,808	2,495,808
Total	$2,667,000		$17,000	$2,684,000

The amounts prorated to inventories here are not significant. In actual practice, prorating is done only when it would materially affect inventory valuations.

The Use of Variable and Fixed Application Rates

In general the cost of a product is the sum of direct costs and allocated costs. As we have seen, overhead application is the most troublesome aspect of product costing. The presence of fixed costs is a major reason for the costing difficulties. Many companies make no distinction between variable- and fixed-cost behavior in the design of their accounting systems. For instance, the machining department at Enriquez Machine Parts Company developed the following rate:

$$\text{budgeted overhead application rate} = \frac{\text{budgeted total overhead}}{\text{budgeted machine hours}}$$

$$= \frac{\$277,800}{69,450}$$

$$= \$4 \text{ per machine hour}$$

Some companies, though, do distinguish between variable overhead and fixed overhead for product costing as well as for control purposes. Suppose the machining department at Enriquez had made this distinction. Managers determined that rent, supervision, depreciation, and insurance were fixed costs and indirect labor, supplies, utilities, and repairs were variable costs. The department developed two rates:

$$\text{budgeted variable-overhead application rate} = \frac{\text{budgeted total variable overhead}}{\text{budgeted machine hours}}$$

$$= \frac{\$114,000}{69,450}$$

$$= \$1.64 \text{ per machine hour}$$

$$\text{budgeted fixed-overhead application rate} = \frac{\text{budgeted total fixed overhead}}{\text{budgeted machine hours}}$$

$$= \frac{\$163,800}{69,450}$$

$$= \$2.36 \text{ per machine hour}$$

Such rates can be used for product costing. However, it is more important to make distinctions between variable- and fixed-overhead rates for control purposes. Why? Because the explanations for over- or underapplied overhead are usually quite different for fixed and variable costs.

After the following summary problem, we will turn our attention to some other issues arising from differences between fixed and variable overhead.

Summary Problem For Your Review

PROBLEM

Review the Enriquez illustration. Suppose Enriquez had sales in 20X4 of $5,000,000. There were no beginning or ending inventories. That is, Enriquez sold everything it produced in 20X4. The company used the budgeted factory-overhead rates on page 572. Production in 20X4 required 85,000 machine hours in machining and $260,000 direct-labor cost in assembly. The materials used in 20X4 cost $2,400,000, and the total direct-labor cost was $490,000. Actual factory-overhead cost was $455,000. Prepare an income statement for 20X4 through the gross profit line. Include a separate line for the immediate write-off method for overapplied or underapplied overhead.

SOLUTION

See Exhibit 13-1. You can compute the overhead component of cost of goods sold as follows:

Machining: 85,000 machine hours × $4 per machine hour	$340,000
Assembly: $260,000 direct-labor cost × 50% of direct-labor dollars	$130,000
Total overhead	$470,000

Overapplied overhead is $470,000 − $455,000 = $15,000.

Sales		$ 5,000,000
Cost of goods sold:		
Direct materials	$2,400,000	
Direct labor	490,000	
Factory overhead	470,000	
Total		(3,360,000)
Overapplied overhead		15,000
Gross profit		$ 1,655,000

Exhibit 13-1
Enriquez Machine Parts Company
Incomes Statement, 20X4

VARIABLE COSTING AT NORTEL NETWORKS

Nortel Networks is a $11-billion Canada-based "global leader in telephone, data, wireless, and wireline solutions for the Internet." In the 1990s, while still known as Northern Telecom, Nortel gradually came to understand that its standard absorption costing income statement did not provide the information that managers needed. The company also realized that the problem was one of format more than it was of substance. The information needed for a more meaningful income statement was in the accounting system, but the traditional reported income statement did not present the information in the most useful way. Therefore, Nortel's accountants adopted a "variable costing" approach to the income statement.

Statutory and regulatory reporting requirements did not allow Northern Telecom to completely abandon absorption costing. The company's solution left the top line—revenue—and the bottom line—earnings before tax—unchanged. But everything in between was reported differently, in the following format:

Revenue
   Product cost
Product margin
   Manufacturing/operational costs
   Inventory provisions
   New product introduction
   Selling and marketing
Direct margin
   Administrative cost
   Other operating (income) expense
Operating profit
   Corporate assessments
   Other nonoperating (income) expense
Earnings before balance sheet adjustments
   Balance sheet adjustment
Earnings before tax

This format represents an extreme application of variable costing. Only direct-materials costs are considered product costs. All other costs, including direct labor and variable overhead, are period costs that are charged to expense when incurred, not added to inventory. For example, direct labor is part of manufacturing costs. The amount charged in any period is the amount actually incurred during that period, regardless of whether the labor is related to goods sold or those still in inventory. Four measures of "profit" are used by managers: product margin (to measure the value added), direct margin (to measure results of product production and sales), operating profit (to measure total results of operations), and earnings before balance sheet adjustments (to measure effect on company-wide profits).

The main difference between the old absorption-costing system and the new system is that the new system expenses all costs except materials costs, whereas the old system capitalized a portion of them. Reconciling the two systems was an accounting problem, unrelated to operating the business. Therefore, a final line was added to the income statement to provide a reconciliation—balance sheet adjustment. This represents the difference between the absorption and variable costing statements, as needed for statutory and regulatory reporting, but it can be ignored by managers.

Nortel's efforts illustrate two important points. First, it is possible to adapt accounting methods to meet the specific needs of managers. Second, companies often do not have to choose between absorption and variable costing—either format can be produced by the same basic accounting system.

Sources: From P. Sharman, "Time to Re-examine the P&L," *CMA Magazine*, September 1991, pp. 22–25, and Nortel Networks Corporation *2002 Annual Report* (http://www.nortelnetworks.com/corporate/investor/reports/index.html).

Variable Versus Absorption Costing

Accounting for Fixed Manufacturing Overhead

We compare two major methods of product costing in this section: variable costing (the contribution approach) and absorption costing (the functional, full-costing, or financial-reporting approach). You encountered these methods already in Chapter 6, but here we will provide more details. They differ in only one respect: Fixed manufacturing overhead is excluded from the cost of products under variable costing but is included in the cost of products under absorption costing.

Exhibit 13-2
Comparison of Flow
of Costs

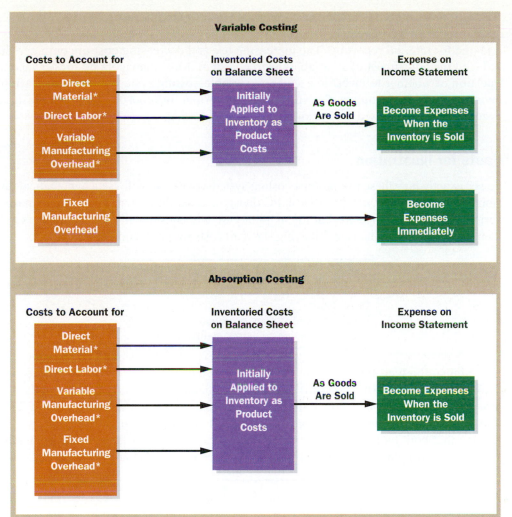

As goods are manufactured, the costs are "applied" to inventory, usually via the use of unit costs.

As Exhibit 13-2 shows, a variable-costing system treats fixed manufacturing overhead (fixed factory overhead) as a period cost that is immediately charged against sales—not as a product cost that is added to inventory and charged against sales as cost of goods sold when the company sells the inventory. Note that the only difference between variable and absorption costing is the accounting for fixed manufacturing overhead.[3]

Absorption costing is more widely used than variable costing. Why? Because neither the public accounting profession nor the U.S. IRS approves of variable costing for external-reporting or tax purposes. An example of how one company uses variable costing is shown in the Business First box on page 578.

However, the growing use of the contribution approach in performance measurement and cost analysis has led to increasing use of variable costing for internal-reporting purposes. Over half the major firms in the United States use variable costing for some internal reporting, and nearly a quarter use it as the primary internal format. For example, the Muncie, Indiana, plant of **BorgWarner Corporation** changed its product-line performance reporting from an absorption-costing approach to variable costing. Why? Because according to management, variable costing links manufacturing performance more closely with measures of that performance by removing the impact of changing inventory levels from financial results.

---

[3]Variable costing is sometimes called direct costing. However, variable costing is a more descriptive term, so we will use it exclusively in this text.

Until the last decade or two, use of variable costing for internal reporting was expensive. It requires a company to process information two ways, one for external reporting and one for internal reporting. The increasing use and decreasing cost of computers has reduced the added cost of a variable-costing system. Most managers no longer face the question of whether to invest in a separate variable-costing system. Rather, they simply choose a variable-costing or absorption-costing format for reports. Many well-designed accounting systems used today can produce either format.

Facts for Illustration

To see exactly how these two product costing systems work, we will use a hypothetical division of Dell Computer, call it the Desk PC division, as an illustration. The division makes a variety of desktop computers, but for simplicity we will consider all of the computers to be identical. The division had the following standard costs for production of computers:

Basic Production Data at Standard Cost	
Direct materials	$205
Direct labor	75
Variable manufacturing overhead	20
Standard variable costs per computer	$300

The annual budget for fixed manufacturing overhead (fixed factory overhead) is $1,500,000. Expected (or budgeted) production is 15,000 computers per year, and the sales price is $500 per computer. For simplicity, we will assume that the single cost driver for the $20 per-computer variable-manufacturing overhead is computers produced. Also, we will assume that both budgeted and actual selling and administrative expenses are $650,000 yearly fixed cost plus sales commissions at 5% of dollar sales. Actual product quantities are

	20X4	20X5
In units (computers)		
Opening inventory	—	3,000
Production	17,000	14,000
Sales	14,000	16,000
Ending inventory	3,000	1,000

There are no variances from the standard variable manufacturing costs, and the actual fixed manufacturing overhead incurred is exactly $1,500,000 each year.

Based on this information, we can

1. Prepare income statements for 20X4 and 20X5 under variable costing.
2. Prepare income statements for 20X4 and 20X5 under absorption costing.
3. Show a reconciliation of the difference in operating income for 20X4, 20X5, and the two years as a whole.

Variable-Costing Method

OBJECTIVE 4

Construct an income statement using the variable-costing approach.

We begin by preparing income statements under variable costing. The variable-costing statement shown in Exhibit 13-3 has a familiar contribution-approach format, the same format introduced in Chapter 6. The only new characteristic of Exhibit 13-3 is the presence of a detailed calculation of cost of goods sold, which is affected by changes in the beginning and ending inventories. In contrast, the income statements in earlier chapters assumed that there were no changes in the beginning and ending inventories.

We account for the costs of the product by applying all variable manufacturing costs to the goods produced, at a rate of $300 per computer; thus we value inventories at standard

			20X4	20X5
Sales, 14,000 and 16,000 computers, respectively	(1)		$7,000	$8,000
Variable expenses:				
Variable manufacturing cost of goods sold				
Opening inventory, at standard variable costs of $300			$ —	$ 900
Add: variable cost of goods manufactured at standard, 17,000 and 14,000 computers, respectively			5,100	4,200
Available for sale, 17,000 computers in each year			$5,100	$5,100
Deduct: ending inventory, at standard variable cost of $300			900*	300†
Variable manufacturing cost of goods sold			$4,200	$4,800
Variable selling expenses, at 5% of dollar sales			350	400
Total variable expenses	(2)		4,550	5,200
Contribution margin	(3) = (1) − (2)		$2,450	$2,800
Fixed expenses:				
Fixed factory overhead			$1,500	$1,500
Fixed selling and administrative expenses			650	650
Total fixed expenses	(4)		2,150	2,150
Operating income, variable costing	(3) − (4)		$ 300	$ 650

* 3,000 computers × $300 = $900,000.
† 1,000 computers × $300 = $300,000.

Exhibit 13-3
Desk PC Division: Comparative Income Statements Using Variable Costing
Years 20X4 and 20X5 (thousands of dollars)

variable costs. In contrast, we do not apply any fixed manufacturing costs to products but we regard them as expenses in the period they are incurred.

Before reading on, be sure to trace the facts from our Desktop PC division example to the presentation in Exhibit 13-3, step by step. Note that we deduct both variable cost of goods sold and variable selling and administrative expenses in computing the contribution margin. However, variable selling and administrative expenses are not inventoriable. Only the level of sales, not changes in inventory, affect them.

Absorption-Costing Method

Exhibit 13-4 shows the standard absorption-costing framework. As you can see, it differs from the variable-costing format in three ways.

First, the unit product cost used for computing cost of goods sold is $400, not $300. Why? Because we add fixed manufacturing overhead of $100 to the $300 variable manufacturing cost. The $100 of fixed manufacturing overhead applied to each unit is the **fixed-overhead rate.** We determine this rate by dividing the budgeted fixed overhead by the expected cost-driver activity, in this case expected volume of production, for the budget period:

$$\text{fixed - overhead rate} = \frac{\text{budgeted fixed manufacturing overhead}}{\text{expected volume of production}}$$

$$= \frac{\$1,500,000}{15,000 \text{ units}}$$

$$= \$100$$

Second, fixed factory overhead does not appear as a separate line in an absorption-costing income statement. Instead, the fixed factory overhead appears in two places: as

OBJECTIVE **5**

Construct an income statement using the absorption-costing approach.

fixed-overhead rate
The amount of fixed manufacturing overhead applied to each unit of production. It is determined by dividing the budgeting fixed overhead by the expected volume of production for the budget period.

Exhibit 13-4

Desk PC Division:
Comparative Income
Statements Using
Absorption Costing
*Years 20X4 and 20X5
(thousands of dollars)*

		20X4		20X5
Sales		$7,000		$8,000
Cost of goods sold:				
Opening inventory, at standard				
absorption cost of $400*	$ —		$1,200	
Cost of goods manufactured				
at standard of $400	6,800		5,600	
Available for sale	6,800		6,800	
Deduct: ending inventory at				
standard absorption cost of $400	1,200		400	
Cost of goods sold, at standard		5,600		6,400
Gross profit at standard		1,400		1,600
Production-volume variance†		200 F		100 U
Gross margin or gross profit,				
at "actual"		1,600		1,500
Selling and administrative expenses		1,000		1,050
Operating income		$ 600		$ 450

* Variable cost	$300	
Fixed cost ($1,500,000 ÷ 15,000)	100	
Standard absorption cost	$400	

† Computation of production-volume variance based on expected volume
of production of 15,000 computers:

	20X4	$200,000 F	(17,000 − 15,000) × $100
	20X5	100,000 U	(14,000 − 15,000) × $100
Two years together		$100,000 F	(31,000 − 30,000) × $100

U = Unfavorable, F = Favorable

production-volume variance

A variance that appears whenever actual production deviates from the expected volume of production used in computing the fixed overhead rate. It is calculated as (actual volume − expected volume) × fixed-overhead rate.

part of the cost of goods sold and as a production-volume variance.[4] A **production-volume variance** (which we explain further in the next section) appears whenever actual production deviates from the expected volume of production used in computing the fixed overhead rate:

$$\text{production-volume variance} = (\text{actual volume} - \text{expected volume}) \times \text{fixed-overhead rate}$$

Finally, the format for an absorption-costing income statement separates costs into the major categories of manufacturing and nonmanufacturing. In contrast, a variable-costing income statement separates costs into the major categories of fixed and variable. In an absorption-costing statement, revenue less manufacturing cost (both fixed and variable) is gross profit or gross margin. In a variable-costing statement, revenue less all variable costs (both manufacturing and nonmanufacturing) is the contribution margin. We illustrate this difference by a condensed comparison of 20X5 income statements (in thousands of dollars):

Variable Costing		**Absorption Costing**	
Revenue	$8,000	Revenue	$8,000
All variable costs	5,200	All manufacturing costs*	6,500
Contribution margin	2,800	Gross margin	1,500
All fixed costs	2,150	All nonmanufacturing costs	1,050
Operating income	$ 650	Operating income	$ 450

*Standard absorption cost of goods sold plus production-volume variance.

---

[4]In general, this will be a cost-driver activity variance. In our example, production volume is the only cost driver, so it can be called a production-volume variance.

MAKING MANAGERIAL DECISIONS

When making decisions, it is important for managers to distinguish between gross margin and contribution margin. List the ways in which these two margins differ.

Answer

Among the differences are the following:

- Gross margin appears in an absorption-costing income statement; contribution margin is in a variable-costing income statement.

- Gross margin is revenue less manufacturing cost; contribution margin is revenue less all variable costs.
- Gross margin is based on a categorization of costs by function; contribution margin divides costs by cost behavior.
- Gross margin is required for financial reporting; contribution margin is most useful for short-term management decisions.

Fixed Overhead and Absorption Costs of Product

All three differences between variable- and absorption-costing formats arise solely because the two formats treat fixed manufacturing overhead differently. In this and subsequent sections, we explore how to account for factory overhead in an absorption-costing system.

Variable and Fixed Unit Costs

Continuing our example of the Desktop PC division, we begin by comparing (1) the manufacturing overhead costs in the flexible budget used for departmental budgeting and control purposes with (2) the manufacturing overhead costs applied to products under an absorption-costing system. To stress the basic assumptions behind absorption costing, we will also split manufacturing overhead into variable and fixed components. (Most real absorption-costing systems do not make such a split.)

Consider the following graphs of variable-overhead costs:

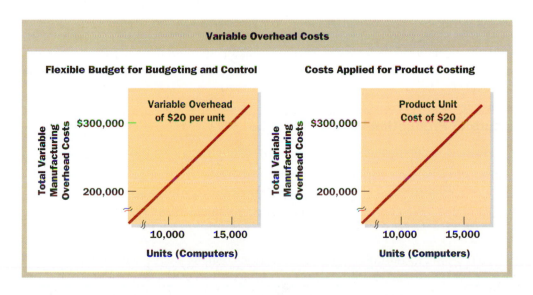

Note that the two graphs are identical. The expected variable-overhead costs from the flexible budget are the same as the variable-overhead costs applied to the products. Both budgeted and applied variable overhead are $20 per computer. Each time we produce 1,000 additional computers, we expect to incur an additional $20,000 of variable overhead, and we add $20,000 of variable-overhead cost to the inventory account for computers. The variable costs used for budgeting and control are the same as those used for product costing.

In contrast, the graph for applied fixed-overhead costs differs from that for the flexible budget:

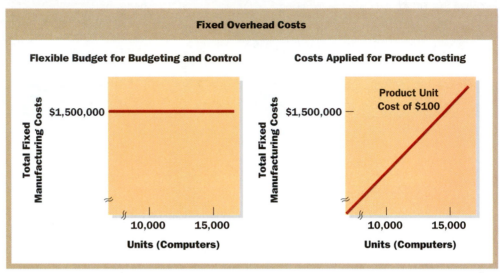

Note: These graphs are not to the same scale as the preceding graphs.

The flexible budget for fixed overhead is a lump-sum budgeted amount of $1,500,000. Volume does not affect it. In contrast, the applied fixed cost depends on actual volume.

$$\text{Fixed cost applied} = \text{actual volume} \times \text{fixed-overhead rate}$$

$$= \text{units produced} \times \$100$$

Suppose actual volume equals the expected volume of 15,000 computers. Applied fixed overhead would be 15,000 computers $\times$ $100 per computer = $1,500,000, the same as the flexible-budget amount. However, whenever actual volume differs from expected volume, the costs used for budgeting and control differ from those used for product costing. For budgeting and control purposes, managers use the actual cost behavior pattern for fixed costs. In contrast, as the graphs indicate, the absorption product-costing approach treats these fixed costs as though they had a variable-cost behavior pattern. The difference between applied and budgeted fixed overhead is the production-volume variance.

Nature of Production-Volume Variance

OBJECTIVE 6
Compute the production-volume variance and show how it should appear in the income statement.

We calculate the production-volume variance as follows:

$$\text{production-volume variance} = \text{applied fixed overhead} - \text{budgeted fixed overhead}$$

$$= (\text{actual volume} \times \text{fixed-overhead rate})$$
$$- (\text{expected volume} \times \text{fixed-overhead rate})$$

or

$$\text{production-volume variance} = (\text{actual volume} - \text{expected volume})$$
$$\times \text{fixed-overhead rate}$$

In practice, accountants often call the production-volume variance simply the **volume variance.** We use the term *production-volume variance* because it is a more precise description of the fundamental nature of the variance. Using production-volume variance also distinguishes it from the sales-volume variance described in Chapter 8. Despite similar nomenclature, they are completely different concepts.

A production-volume variance arises when the actual production volume achieved does not coincide with the expected volume of production used as a denominator for computing the fixed-overhead rate for product-costing purposes:

1. When expected production volume and actual production volume are identical, there is no production-volume variance.
2. When actual volume is less than expected volume, the production-volume variance is unfavorable because usage of facilities is less than expected and fixed overhead is underapplied. It is measured in Exhibit 13-4 for 20X5 as follows:

$$\text{production volume variance} = (\text{actual volume} - \text{expected volume})$$
$$\times \text{ budgeted fixed-overhead rate}$$
$$= (14,000 \text{ units} - 15,000 \text{ units}) \times \$100$$
$$= -\$100,000 \text{ or } \$100,000 \text{ U}$$

or

$$\text{production-volume variance} = \text{budget minus applied}$$
$$= \$1,500,000 - \$1,400,000 = \$100,000 \text{ U}$$

The $100,000 unfavorable production-volume variance increases the manufacturing costs shown on the income statement. Why? Recall that the department incurred $1,500,000 of fixed manufacturing cost, but applied only $1,400,000 to inventory. Therefore, the department will charge only $1,400,000 as expense when it sells the inventory. But it must charge the actual cost of $1,500,000 to expense sometime, so the extra $100,000 is an added expense in the current income statement.

3. When actual volume exceeds expected volume, as was the case in 20X4, the production-volume variance is favorable because use of facilities is better than expected, and fixed overhead is overapplied.

$$\text{production-volume variance} = (17,000 \text{ units} - 15,000 \text{ units}) \times \$100 = \$200,000 \text{ F}$$

In this case, the department will charge $1,700,000 through inventory. Because the department incurs actual costs of only $1,500,000, future expenses will be overstated by $200,000. Therefore, we reduce current period expenses by the $200,000 favorable variance.

The production-volume variance is the conventional measure of the cost of departing from the level of activity originally used to set the fixed-overhead rate. Most companies consider production-volume variances to be beyond immediate control, although sometimes a manager responsible for volume has to do some explaining or investigating. Sometimes, idle facilities caused by disappointing total sales, poor production scheduling, unusual machine breakdowns, shortages of skilled workers, strikes, storms, and the like are responsible for the failure to reach the expected volume.

There is no production-volume variance for variable overhead. The concept of production-volume variance arises for fixed overhead because of the conflict between accounting for control (by flexible budgets) and accounting for product costing (by application rates). Note again that the fixed-overhead budget serves the control purpose, whereas the development of a product-costing rate results in the treatment of fixed overhead as if it were a variable cost.

volume variance
A common name for production-volume variance.

Above all, remember that fixed costs are simply not divisible as variable costs are. Rather, they come in big chunks and are related to the provision of big chunks of production or sales capability, not to the production or sale of a single unit of product.

MAKING MANAGERIAL DECISIONS

Some accountants claim that the production-volume variance is a good measure of how well a company uses its capacity: Favorable (unfavorable) variances imply effective (ineffective) use of capacity. As a manager, be careful not to fall into that trap. Why?

Answer

The production volume variance tells you one thing and only one thing—whether actual production was above or below the predicted volume used in setting the fixed overhead rate. If a manager can avoid an unfavorable production-volume variance by lowering the price enough to use up the idle capacity but the result is a decline in contribution margin (i.e., the new price is less than the variable cost), this would not be an effective use of the capacity. If a favorable production-volume variance occurs because excess production is being forced through despite quality declines or other inefficiencies caused by overburdened production facilities, the "favorable" variance is certainly not desirable.

Reconciliation of Variable Costing and Absorption Costing

We can easily reconcile the operating incomes shown in Exhibits 13-3 and 13-4. The difference in income equals the difference in the total amount of fixed manufacturing overhead charged as an expense during a given year. Examine Exhibit 13-5. The $1,500,000 fixed manufacturing overhead incurred in 20X5 is automatically the amount recognized as an expense on a variable-costing income statement. Under absorption costing, fixed manufacturing overhead appears in two places: cost of goods sold and production-volume variance.

Under absorption costing, the department incurred $300,000 of the fixed costs before 20X5 and held it over in the beginning inventory. During 20X5, accountants added $1,400,000 of fixed manufacturing overhead to inventory, and $100,000 was still lodged in the ending inventory of 20X5. Thus, the fixed manufacturing overhead included in cost of goods sold for 20X5 was $300,000 + $1,400,000 − $100,000 = $1,600,000. In addition, the production-volume variance is $100,000, unfavorable. The total fixed manufacturing overhead charged as 20X5 expenses under absorption costing is $1,700,000, or $200,000 more than the $1,500,000 charged under variable costing. Therefore, 20X5 variable-costing income is higher by $200,000.

We can quickly explain the difference in variable-costing and absorption-costing operating income by multiplying the fixed-overhead product-costing rate by the change in the total units in the beginning and ending inventories. Consider 20X5: The change in inventory was 2,000 units, so the difference in net income would be 2,000 units $\times$ $100 = $200,000.

Remember that it is the relationship between sales and production that determines the difference between variable-costing and absorption-costing income. Whenever units sold exceed units produced, that is, when inventory decreases, variable-costing income is greater than absorption-costing income.

Why Use Variable Costing?

OBJECTIVE 7

Explain why a company might prefer to use a variable-costing approach.

Why do many companies use variable costing for internal statements? One reason is that production volume affects absorption-costing income but has no effect on variable-costing income. Consider the 20X5 absorption-costing statement in Exhibit 13-4, which

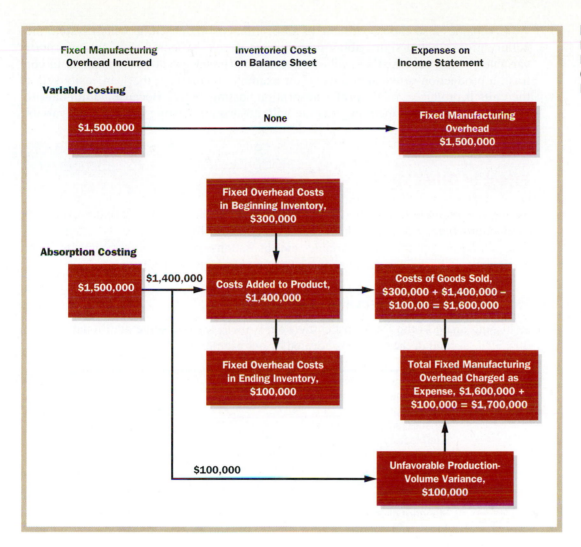

Exhibit 13-5
Flow of Fixed
Manufacturing
Overhead Costs
During 20X5

shows operating income of $450,000. Suppose a manager decides to produce 1,000 additional units in December 20X5 even though they will remain unsold. Will this affect operating income? First, note that the gross profit will not change. Why? Because it is based on sales, not production. However, the production-volume variance will change:

$$\text{If production} = 14,000 \text{ units}$$
$$\text{Production-volume variance} = (15,000 - 14,000) \times \$100 = \$100,000 \text{ U}$$
$$\text{If production} = 15,000 \text{ units}$$
$$\text{Production-volume variance} = (15,000 - 15,000) \times \$100 = 0$$

Because there is no production-volume variance when the department produces 15,000 units, the new operating income equals gross profit less selling and administrative expenses, $1,600,000 − $1,050,000 = $550,000. Therefore, increasing production by 1,000 units without any increase in sales increases absorption-costing operating income by $100,000, from $450,000 to $550,000.

How will such an increase in production affect the variable-costing statement in Exhibit 13-3? Nothing will change. Production does not affect operating income under variable costing.

Suppose the evaluation of a manager's performance is heavily based on operating income. If the company uses the absorption-costing approach, a manager might be tempted to produce unneeded units just to increase reported operating income. No such temptation exists with variable costing.

Companies also choose variable or absorption costing based on which system they believe gives a better signal about performance. A sales-oriented company may prefer variable costing because the level of sales is the primary effect on its income. In contrast, a production-oriented company, for example, a company that can easily sell all the units it produces, might prefer absorption costing. Why? Because additional production increases the operating income with absorption costing but not with variable costing.

Effect of Other Variances

So far, our example has deliberately ignored the possibility of any variance except the production-volume variance, which appears only on an absorption-costing statement. All other variances appear on both variable- and absorption-costing income statements. In this section, we will consider other variances that you encountered in Chapter 8.

Flexible-Budget Variances

Returning again to the Desktop PC division, we will assume some additional facts for 20X5 (the second of the two years covered by our example):

Flexible-budget variances	
Direct materials	None
Direct labor	$ 170,000 U
Variable factory overhead	$ 30,000 U
Fixed factory overhead	$ 70,000 U
Supporting data (used to compute the above variances as shown in Appendix 13):	
Standard direct-labor-hours allowed for 14,000 units of output produced	87,500
Standard direct-labor rate per hour	$12.00
Actual direct-labor-hours of inputs	100,000
Actual direct-labor rate per hour	$12.20
Variable manufacturing overhead actually incurred	$ 310,000
Fixed manufacturing overhead actually incurred	$1,570,000

As Chapter 8 explained, flexible-budget variances may arise for both variable overhead and fixed overhead. Consider the following:

	Actual Amounts	Flexible-Budget Amounts @14,000 Units	Flexible-Budget Variances
Variable factory overhead	$ 310,000	$ 280,000	$30,000 U
Fixed factory overhead	1,570,000	1,500,000	70,000 U

Exhibit 13-6 shows the relationship between the fixed-overhead flexible-budget variance and the production-volume variance. The difference between the actual fixed overhead and that applied to products is the underapplied (or overapplied) overhead. Because the actual fixed overhead of $1,570,000 exceeds the $1,400,000 applied, fixed overhead is underapplied by $170,000, which means that the variance is unfavorable. The $170,000 underapplied fixed overhead has two components: (1) a production-volume variance of $100,000 U and (2) a fixed-overhead flexible-budget variance (also called the fixed-overhead spending variance or simply the fixed-overhead budget variance) of $70,000 U.

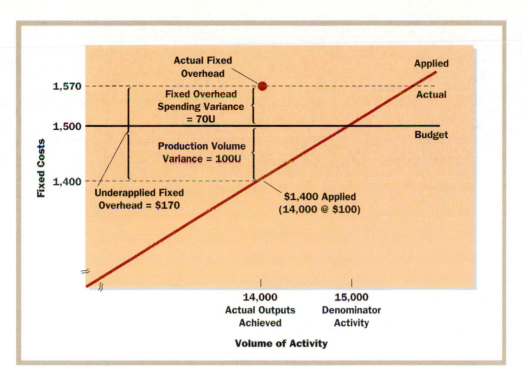

Exhibit 13-6
Fixed-Overhead
Variances for 20X5
(*dollar amounts
in thousands*)
*Data are from
Exhibit 13-4*

All variances other than the production-volume variance are essentially flexible-budget variances. They measure components of the differences between actual amounts and the flexible-budget amounts for the output achieved. Flexible budgets primarily assist planning and control rather than product costing. The production-volume variance is not a flexible-budget variance. It serves primarily a product costing purpose.

Exhibit 13-7 contains the income statement under absorption costing that incorporates these new facts. These new variances hurt income by $240,000 because, like the production-volume variance, they are all unfavorable variances that are charged against income in 20X5. When cost variances are favorable, they increase operating income.

	(in thousands)	
Sales, 16,000 at $500		$8,000
Opening inventory at standard, 3,000 at $400	$1,200	
Cost of goods manufactured at standard, 14,000 at $400	5,600	
Available for sale, 17,000 at $400	$6,800	
Deduct ending inventory at standard, 1,000 at $400	400	
Cost of goods sold at standard, 16,000 at $400		6,400
Gross profit at standard		$1,600
Flexible-budget variances, both unfavorable		
Variable manufacturing costs ($170,000 + $30,000)	$ 200	
Fixed factory overhead	70	
Production-volume variance (arises only because of		
fixed overhead), unfavorable	100	
Total variances		370
Gross profit at "actual"		$1,230
Selling and administrative expenses		1,050
Operating income		$ 180

Exhibit 13-7
Absorption Costing
Modification of
Exhibit 13-4 for 20X5
(*additional facts are
in text*)

Summary Problem For Your Review

PROBLEM

1. Reconsider Exhibits 13-3 and 13-4 on pages 581 and 582. Suppose production in 20X5 was 14,500 units instead of 14,000 units, but sales remained at 16,000 units. Assume that the net variances for all variable manufacturing costs were $200,000, unfavorable. Regard these variances as adjustments to the standard cost of goods sold. Also assume that actual fixed costs were $1,570,000. Prepare income statements for 20X5 under variable costing and under absorption costing.
2. Explain why operating income was different under variable costing from what it was under absorption costing. Show your calculations.
3. Without regard to number 1, would variable costing or absorption costing give a manager more leeway in influencing short-run operating income through production-scheduling decisions? Why?

SOLUTION

1. See Exhibit 13-8 and Exhibit 13-9. Note that the ending inventory will be 1,500 units instead of 1,000 units.
2. Decline in inventory levels is 3,000 − 1,500, or 1,500 units. The fixed-overhead rate per unit in absorption costing is $100. Therefore, $150,000 more fixed overhead was charged against operations under absorption costing than under variable costing. The variable-costing statement shows fixed factory overhead of $1,570,000, whereas the absorption-costing statement includes fixed factory overhead in three places: $1,600,000 in cost of goods sold, $70,000 U in fixed factory overhead flexible-budget variance, and $50,000 U as a production-volume variance, for a total of $1,720,000. Generally, when inventories

Sales		$8,000
Opening inventory, at variable		
standard cost of $300	$ 900	
Add: variable cost of goods manufactured	4,350	
Available for sale	$5,250	
Deduct: ending inventory, at variable		
standard cost of $300	450	
Variable cost of goods sold, at standard		$4,800
Net flexible-budget variances for		
all variable costs, unfavorable		200
Variable cost of goods sold, at actual		$5,000
Variable selling expenses, at 5% of dollar sales		400
Total variable costs charged against sales		5,400
Contribution margin		$2,600
Fixed factory overhead	$1,570*	
Fixed selling and administrative expenses	650	
Total fixed expenses		2,220
Operating income		$ 380†

* This could be shown in two lines, $1,500,000 budget plus $70,000 variance.

† The difference between this and the $650,000 operating income in Exhibit 13-3 occurs because of the $200,000 unfavorable variable-cost variances and the $70,000 unfavorable fixed-cost flexible-budget variance.

Exhibit 13-8
Desk PC Division
Income Statement (variable costing), Year 20X5 (thousands of dollars)

Sales		$8,000
Opening inventory, at standard cost of $4	$1,200	
Cost of goods manufactured, at standard	5,800	
Available for sale	$7,000	
Deduct: ending inventory, at standard	600	
Cost of goods sold, at standard	$6,400	
Net flexible-budget variances for all variable manufacturing costs, unfavorable	$200	
Fixed factory overhead flexible-budget variance, unfavorable	70	
Production-volume variance, unfavorable	50*	
Total variances	320	
Cost of goods sold, at actual		6,720†
Gross profit, at "actual"		$1,280
Selling and administrative expenses		
Variable	400	
Fixed	650	1,050
Operating income		$ 230‡

* Production-volume variance is $100 × (15,000 expected volume − 14,500 actual production).

† This format differs slightly from Exhibit 13-7. The difference is deliberate; it illustrates that the formats of income statements are not rigid.

‡ Compare this result with the $180,000 operating income in Exhibit 13-7. The only difference is traceable to the production of 14,500 units instead of 14,000 units, resulting in an unfavorable production-volume variance of $50,000 instead of $100,000.

Exhibit 13-9
Desk PC Division
Income Statement (absorption costing), Year 20X5 (thousands of dollars)

decline, absorption costing will show less income than will variable costing; when inventories rise, absorption costing will show more income than variable costing.

3. Absorption costing will give a manager more leeway in influencing operating income via production scheduling. Operating income will fluctuate in harmony with changes in net sales under variable costing, but both production and sales influence it under absorption costing. For example, compare the variable costing in Exhibits 13-3 and 13-8. As the second note to Exhibit 13-8 indicates, assorted variances (but not the production-volume variance) may affect operating income under variable costing, but production scheduling per se will have no effect on operating income.

On the other hand, compare the operating income of Exhibits 13-7 and 13-9. As the third note to Exhibit 13-9 explains, production scheduling as well as sales influence operating income. Production was 14,500 rather than 14,000 units. So $50,000 of fixed overhead became a part of ending inventory (an asset) instead of part of the production-volume variance (an expense)—that is, the production-volume variance is $50,000 lower and the ending inventory contains $50,000 more fixed overhead in Exhibit 13-9 than in Exhibit 13-7. The manager adds $100 to 20X5 operating income with each unit of production under absorption costing, even if the department does not sell the unit.

In summary, we note two important facts. First, each of the major topics covered in this chapter has an effect on income. Absorption- and variable-costing systems report different operating incomes because of their treatment of fixed factory overhead. Absorption-costing systems generate production-volume variances that also affect income. Exhibit 13-10 compares variable- and absorption-costing affects.

	Variable Costing	Absorption Costing	Comments
1. Fixed factory overhead inventoried?	No	Yes	Basic theoretical question of when a cost should become an expense.
2. Production-volume variance?	No	Yes	Choice of expected volume of production affects measurement of operating income under absorption costing.
3. Treatment of other variances?	Same	Same	Underscores the fact that the basic difference is the accounting for fixed factory overhead, not the accounting for variable factory overhead.
4. Classifications between variable and fixed costs are routinely made?	Yes	No	However, absorption cost can be modified to obtain subclassifications of variable and fixed costs, if desired.
5. Usual effects of changes in inventory levels on operating income			Differences are attributable to timing of the transformation of fixed factory overhead into expense.
Production = sales	Equal	Equal	
Production > sales	Lower*	Higher†	
Production < sales	Higher	Lower	
6. Cost-volume-profit relationships	Tied to sales	Tied to production and sales	Management control benefit: Effects of changes in volume on operating income are easier to understand under variable costing.

* That is, lower than absorption costing.
† That is, higher than variable costing.

Exhibit 13-10
Comparative Income Effects

Second, managers' performance measures and rewards are most often based on operating income. As a result of these two facts, managers are motivated to take action that improves current operating income.

Highlights to Remember

1 **Compute budgeted factory-overhead rates and apply factory overhead to production.** Accountants usually apply indirect manufacturing costs (factory overhead) to products using budgeted overhead rates. They compute the rates by dividing total budgeted overhead by a measure of cost-driver activity such as expected machine hours.

2 **Determine and use appropriate cost drivers for overhead application.** There should be a strong cause-and-effect relationship between cost drivers and the overhead costs that are allocated using these drivers.

3 **Identify the meaning and purpose of normalized overhead rates.** Budgeted overhead rates are usually annual averages. The resulting product costs are normal costs, consisting of actual direct materials plus actual direct labor plus applied overhead using the budgeted rates. Normal product costs are often more useful than true actual costs for decision-making and inventory-costing purposes.

4 **Construct an income statement using the variable-costing approach.** Two major methods of product costing are variable (contribution approach) and absorption costing. The variable-costing method emphasizes the effects of cost behavior on income. This method excludes fixed manufacturing overhead from the cost of products and expenses it immediately.

5 **Construct an income statement using the absorption-costing approach.** The absorption or traditional approach ignores cost behavior distinctions. As a result, all costs incurred in the production of goods become part of the inventory cost. Thus, we add fixed manufacturing overhead to inventory and it appears on the income statement only when the company sells the goods.

6 **Compute the production-volume variance and show how it should appear in the income statement.** Whenever a company employs the absorption method and the actual production volume does not equal the expected (budgeted) volume that it uses for computing the fixed-overhead rate, a production-volume variance arises. When the actual volume is less than budgeted, the variance is unfavorable and the amount is equal to the fixed-overhead rate times the difference between the budgeted and actual volume. The opposite is true when actual production volume exceeds budgeted production volume; that is, a favorable volume variance arises. Both types of variances are usually adjustments to the current period income. Favorable variances increase current-period income and unfavorable variances reduce current-period income.

7 **Explain why a company might prefer to use a variable-costing approach.** Companies that use operating income to measure results usually prefer variable costing. This is because changes in production volume affect absorption-costing income but not variable-costing income. A company that wants to focus managers' energies on sales would prefer to use variable costing, since the level of sales is the primary driver of variable-costing income.

Appendix 13: Comparisons of Production-Volume Variance with Other Variances

The only new variance introduced in this chapter is the production-volume variance, which arises because fixed-overhead accounting must serve two masters: the control-budget purpose and the product-costing purpose. Let's examine this variance in perspective by using the approach originally demonstrated in Exhibit 8-9. The results of the approach appear in Exhibit 13-11, which deserves your careful study, particularly the two footnotes. Please ponder the exhibit before reading on.

Exhibit 13-12 graphically compares the variable- and fixed-overhead costs analyzed in Exhibit 13-11. Note how the control-budget line and the product-costing line (the applied line) are superimposed in the graph for variable overhead but differ in the graph for fixed overhead.

Underapplied or overapplied overhead is always the difference between the actual overhead incurred and the overhead applied. An analysis may then be made:

$$\text{underapplied overhead} = \left(\begin{array}{c} \text{flexible-budget} \\ \text{variance} \end{array} \right) + \left(\begin{array}{c} \text{production-volume} \\ \text{variance} \end{array} \right)$$

$$\text{for variable overhead} = \$30,000 + 0 = \$30,000$$

$$\text{for fixed overhead} = \$70,000 + \$100,000 = \$170,000$$

Accounting Vocabulary

budgeted factory-overhead rate, p. 571	overapplied overhead, p. 576	underapplied overhead, p. 576
fixed-overhead rate, p. 581	production-volume variance, p. 582	volume variance, p. 585
normal costing system, p. 574	prorate, p. 576	

Fundamental Assignment Material

13-A1 Accounting for Overhead, Budgeted Rates

Donald Aeronautics Company uses a budgeted overhead rate in applying overhead to products on a machine-hour basis for Department A and on a direct-labor-hour basis for Department B. At the beginning of 20X4, the company's management made the following budget predictions:

	Department A	Department B
Direct-labor cost	$1,500,000	$1,200,000
Factory overhead	$2,170,000	$1,000,000
Direct-labor hours	90,000	125,000
Machine hours	350,000	20,000

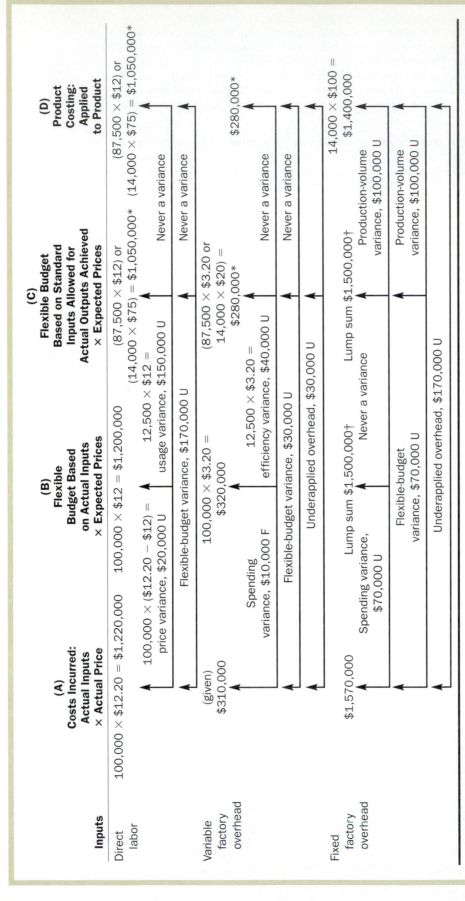

U = Unfavorable, F = Favorable.

* Note especially that the flexible budget for variable costs rises and falls in direct proportion to production. Note also that the control-budget purpose and the product-costing purpose harmonize completely. The total costs in the flexible budget will always agree with the standard variable costs applied to the product because they are based on standard costs per unit multiplied by units produced.

† In contrast with variable costs, the flexible-budget total for fixed costs will always agree with the standard variable costs applied to the product. However, the control-budget purpose and the product-costing purpose conflict; whenever actual production differs from expected production, the standard costs applied to the product will differ from the flexible budget. This difference is the production-volume variance. In this case, the production-volume variance may be computed by multiplying the $100 rate times the difference between the 15,000 expected volume and the 14,000 units of output achieved.

Exhibit 13-11
Analysis of Variances
(data are from text for 20X5)

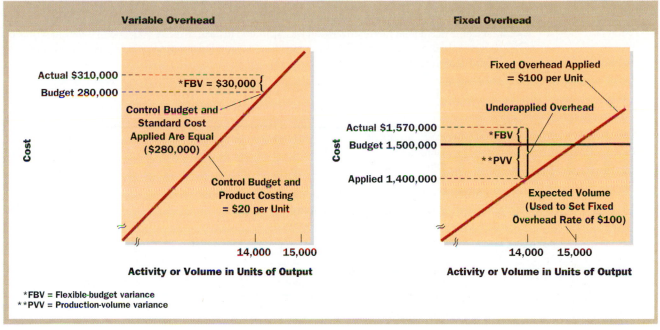

Exhibit 13-12

Comparison of Control and Product-Costing Purposes, Variable Overhead and Fixed Overhead (not to scale)

Cost records of recent months show the following accumulations for product M89:

	Department A	Department B
Material placed in production	$12,000	$32,000
Direct-labor cost	$10,800	$10,000
Direct-labor hours	900	1,250
Machine hours	3,500	150

1. What is the budgeted overhead rate that should be applied in Department A? In Department B?
2. What is the total overhead cost of product M89?
3. If 200 units of product M89 are produced, what is their unit cost?
4. At the end of 20X4, actual results for the year's operations were as follows:

	Department A	Department B
Actual overhead costs incurred	$1,600,000	$1,200,000
Actual direct-labor hours	80,000	120,000
Actual machine hours	300,000	25,000

Find the underapplied or overapplied overhead for each department and for the factory as a whole.

13-A2 Disposition of Overhead

Penski Precision Tooling applies factory overhead using machine hours and number of component parts as cost drivers. In 20X4, actual factory overhead incurred was $224,000 and applied factory overhead was $216,000. Before disposition of underapplied or overapplied factory overhead, the cost of goods sold was $525,000, gross profit was $70,000, and ending inventories were

Direct materials	$ 25,000
WIP	75,000
Finished goods	150,000
Total inventories	$250,000

1. Was factory overhead overapplied or underapplied? By how much?
2. Assume that Penski writes off overapplied or underapplied factory overhead as an adjustment to cost of goods sold. Compute adjusted gross profit.

3. Assume that Penski prorates overapplied or underapplied factory overhead based on end-of-the-year unadjusted balances. Compute adjusted gross profit.
4. Assume that actual factory overhead was $214,000 instead of $224,000, and that Penski writes off overapplied or underapplied factory overhead as an adjustment to cost of goods sold. Compute adjusted gross profit.

13-A3 Comparison of Variable Costing and Absorption Costing

Consider the following information pertaining to a year's operation of Blair Company:

Units produced	3,000
Units sold	2,400
Direct labor	$4,500
Direct materials used	$3,000
Selling and administrative expenses (all fixed)	$ 900
Fixed manufacturing overhead	$4,000
Variable manufacturing overhead	$2,500
All beginning inventories	$ 0
Gross margin (gross profit)	$2,400
Direct-materials inventory, end	$ 400
Work-in-process inventory, end	$ 0

1. What is the ending finished-goods inventory cost under variable costing?
2. What is the ending finished-goods inventory cost under absorption costing?
3. Would operating income be higher or lower under variable costing? By how much? Why? (Answer: $800 lower, but explain why.)

13-A4 Comparison of Absorption and Variable Costing

Examine the Trahn Company's simplified income statement based on variable costing. Assume that the budgeted volume for absorption costing in 20X4 and 20X5 was 1,400 units and that total fixed costs were identical in 20X4 and 20X5. There is no beginning or ending work in process.

Income Statement
Year Ended December 31, 20X5

Sales, 1,280 units @ $11		$14,080
Deduct variable costs		
Beginning inventory, 110 units @ $7	$ 770	
Variable manufacturing cost of goods manufactured, 1,200 units @ $7	8,400	
Variable manufacturing cost of goods available for sale	$9,170	
Ending inventory, 30 units @ $7	210	
Variable manufacturing cost of goods sold	$8,960	
Variable selling and administrative expenses	600	
Total variable costs		9,560
Contribution margin		$ 4,520
Deduct fixed costs		
Fixed factory overhead at budget	$2,800	
Fixed selling and administrative expenses	350	
Total fixed costs		3,150
Operating income		$ 1,370

1. Prepare an income statement based on absorption costing. Assume that actual fixed costs were equal to budgeted fixed costs.
2. Explain the difference in operating income between absorption costing and variable costing. Be specific.

13-B1 Disposition of Overhead

MacLachlan Mfg. Co. had overapplied overhead of $20,000 in 20X4. Before adjusting for overapplied or underapplied overhead, the ending inventories for direct materials, WIP, and finished goods were $75,000, $100,000, and $150,000, respectively. Unadjusted cost of goods sold was $250,000.

1. Assume that the $20,000 was written off solely as an adjustment to cost of goods sold. Compute the adjusted cost of goods sold.
2. Management has decided to prorate the $20,000 to the appropriate accounts (using the unadjusted ending balances) instead of writing it off solely as an adjustment of cost of goods sold. Would gross profit be higher or lower than in requirement 1? By how much?

13-B2 Application of Overhead Using Budgeted Rates

The Bellevue Clinic computes a cost of treating each patient. It allocates costs to departments and then applies departmental overhead costs to individual patients using a different budgeted overhead rate in each department. Consider the following predicted 20X4 data for two of Bellevue's departments:

	Pharmacy	Medical Records
Department overhead cost	$225,000	$300,000
Number of prescriptions filled	90,000	
Number of patient visits		60,000

The cost driver for overhead in Pharmacy is number of prescriptions filled; in Medical Records it is number of patient visits.

In June 20X4, David Li paid two visits to the clinic and had four prescriptions filled at the pharmacy.

1. Compute departmental overhead rates for the two departments.
2. Compute the overhead costs applied to the patient David Li in June 20X4.
3. At the end of 20X4, actual overhead costs were

Pharmacy	$217,000
Medical records	$325,000

The pharmacy filled 85,000 prescriptions, and the clinic had 63,000 patient visits during 20X4. Compute the overapplied or underapplied overhead in each department.

13-B3 Comparison of Variable Costing and Absorption Costing

Consider the following information pertaining to a year's operations of Cleveland Manufacturing, Inc.:

Units sold	1,200
Units produced	1,600
Direct labor	$4,200
Direct materials used	3,500
Fixed manufacturing overhead	2,200
Variable manufacturing overhead	300
Selling and administrative expenses (all fixed)	700
Beginning inventories	0
Contribution margin	5,600
Direct-material inventory, end	800

There are no work-in-process inventories.

1. What is the ending finished-goods inventory cost under absorption costing?
2. What is the ending finished-goods inventory cost under variable costing?

13-B4 Extension of Chapter Illustration

Reconsider Exhibits 13-3 and 13-4, pages 581 and 582. Suppose that in 20X5 production was 15,500 computers instead of 14,000 computers, and sales were 15,000 computers. Also assume that the net variances for all variable manufacturing costs were $18,000, unfavorable. Also assume that actual fixed manufacturing costs were $1,560,000.

1. Prepare income statements for 20X5 under variable costing and under absorption costing. Use a format similar to Exhibits 13-8 and 13-9, pages 590 and 591.
2. Explain why operating income was different under variable costing and absorption costing. Show your calculations.

Additional Assignment Material

Questions

13-1 Suppose a company uses machine hours as a cost driver for factory overhead. How does the company compute a budgeted overhead application rate? How does it compute the amounts of factory overhead applied to a particular job?

13-2 "Each department must choose one cost driver to be used for cost application." Do you agree? Explain.

13-3 "Sometimes direct-labor cost is the best cost driver for overhead allocation even if wage rates vary within a department." Do you agree? Explain.

13-4 Identify four cost drivers that a manufacturing company might use to apply factory overhead costs to jobs.

13-5 Is the comparison of actual overhead costs to budgeted overhead costs part of the product-costing process or part of the control process? Explain.

13-6 What are some reasons for differences between the amounts of incurred and applied overhead?

13-7 "Under actual overhead application, unit costs soar as volume increases, and vice versa." Do you agree? Explain.

13-8 Define normal costing.

13-9 What is the best theoretical method of allocating underapplied or overapplied overhead, assuming that the objective is to obtain as accurate a cost application as possible?

13-10 "As data processing becomes more economical, more costs than just direct materials and direct labor will be classified as direct costs wherever feasible." Give three examples of such costs.

13-11 "With variable costing, only direct materials and direct labor are inventoried." Do you agree? Why?

13-12 "Absorption costing regards more categories of costs as product costs." Explain. Be specific.

13-13 "An increasing number of companies are using variable costing in their corporate annual reports." Do you agree? Explain.

13-14 Why is variable costing used only for internal reporting and not for external financial reporting or tax purposes?

13-15 Compare the contribution margin with the gross margin.

13-16 How is fixed overhead applied to products?

13-17 Name the three ways that an absorption-costing format differs from a variable-costing format.

13-18 "The flexible budget for budgeting and control differs from the costs applied for product costing." What type of cost is being described? Explain.

13-19 "Variable costing is consistent with cost-volume-profit analysis." Explain.

13-20 "In a standard absorption-costing system, the amount of fixed manufacturing overhead applied to the products rarely equals the budgeted fixed manufacturing overhead." Do you agree? Explain.

13-21 "The dollar amount of the production-volume variance depends on what expected volume of production was chosen to determine the fixed-overhead rate." Explain.

13-22 Why is there no production-volume variance for direct labor?

13-23 "An unfavorable production-volume variance means that fixed manufacturing costs have not been well controlled." Do you agree? Explain.

13-24 "The fixed cost per unit is directly affected by the expected volume selected as the denominator." Do you agree? Explain.

13-25 "Absorption-costing income exceeds variable-costing income when the number of units sold exceeds the number of units produced." Do you agree? Explain.

13-26 Suppose a manager is paid a bonus only if standard absorption-costing operating income exceeds the budget. If operating income through November is slightly below budget, what might the manager do in December to increase his or her chance of getting the bonus?

13-27 Why are companies with small levels of inventory generally unconcerned with the choice of variable or absorption costing?

13-28 "Overhead variances arise only with absorption-costing systems." Do you agree? Explain.

Critical Thinking Exercises

13-29 Relationship Between Cost Drivers and Factory Overhead

"There should be a strong relationship between the factory overhead incurred and the cost driver chosen for its application." Why?

13-30 Cost Allocation in Service Firms

"Service firms trace only direct-labor costs to jobs. All other costs are applied as a percentage of direct-labor cost." Do you agree? Explain.

13-31 Accounting for Fixed Costs

Applying fixed costs to products seems to cause all kinds of problems. Why do companies continue to use accounting systems that assign fixed costs to products on a per unit basis?

13-32 Marketing Decisions and Absorption Costing

Product pricing and promotion decisions should usually be based on their effect on contribution margin, not on gross margin. Explain how using an absorption costing format for the income statement can provide misleading information on the effect of pricing and promotion decisions.

13-33 Evaluating Production Using the Production-Volume Variance

The sales-volume variance (see Chapter 8) highlights the effect on income of sales exceeding or falling short of sales targets. Does the production-volume variance provide parallel information for evaluating the effect of exceeding or falling short of production targets? Explain.

13-34 Absorption Costing and the Value Chain

Many costs on a product's value chain, such as research and development and product design costs, are considered period costs and are not assigned to units of product. An absorption-costing system could be expanded to apply such costs to the products. What would be the advantages and disadvantages of doing so? Would this help managers make better decisions?

Exercises

13-35 Discovery of Unknowns

The Hatch Manufacturing Company has the following budgeted overhead cost and other data for its machining department for the month of December.

Budgeted data:	
Indirect labor and supplies	$ 55,000
Factory rent	$ 12,000
Supervision	$ 64,000
Depreciation on equipment	$117,000
Cost driver for overhead application	Machine hours
Budgeted overhead application rate	$4 per machine hour
Other data:	
Actual machine hours during December	66,000
Actual overhead cost incurred during December	$256,000

Compute the total budgeted machine hours, total applied overhead cost, and indicate how any difference between the actual overhead cost incurred and applied overhead would be treated on Hatch's income statement for the month of December.

13-36 Discovery of Unknowns

The Lawson Manufacturing Company has the following budgeted overhead cost and other data for its assembly department for the month of April.

Budgeted data:	
Indirect labor and supplies	$110,000
Factory rent	$ 72,000
Supervision	$ 97,000
Depreciation on equipment	$246,000
Cost driver for overhead application	Direct labor hours
Total budgeted direct labor hours	75,000
Other data:	
Total applied overhead costs for April	$560,000
Actual overhead cost incurred during April	$567,000

Compute the budgeted factory overhead rate, actual direct labor hours, and indicate how the difference between the actual overhead cost incurred and applied overhead would be treated on Lawson's income statement for the month of April.

13-37 Relationship Among Overhead Items

Fill in the unknowns:

	Case 1	Case 2
a. Budgeted factory overhead	$750,000	$420,000
b. Cost driver, budgeted direct-labor cost	500,000	?
c. Budgeted factory-overhead rate	?	120%
d. Direct-labor cost incurred	570,000	?
e. Factory overhead incurred	825,000	415,000
f. Factory overhead applied	?	?
g. Underapplied (overapplied) factory overhead	?	25,000

13-38 Underapplied and Overapplied Overhead

Wosepka Welding Company applies factory overhead at a rate of $9.00 per direct-labor hour. Selected data for 20X4 operations are (in thousands):

	Case 1	Case 2
Direct-labor hours	30	36
Direct-labor cost	$220	$245
Indirect-labor cost	32	40
Sales commissions	20	15
Depreciation, manufacturing equipment	22	32
Direct-materials cost	230	250
Factory fuel costs	35	47
Depreciation, finished-goods warehouse	5	17
Cost of goods sold	420	510
All other factory costs	138	214

Compute for both cases

1. Factory overhead applied.
2. Total factory overhead incurred.
3. Amount of underapplied or overapplied factory overhead.

13-39 Disposition of Year-End Underapplied Overhead

Liz's Cosmetics uses a normal cost system and has the following balances at the end of its first year's operations.

WIP inventory	$200,000
Finished-goods inventory	200,000
Cost of goods sold	400,000
Actual factory overhead	409,000
Factory overhead applied	457,000

Compute gross profit for two different ways to dispose of the year-end overhead balances. By how much would gross profit differ?

13-40 Simple Comparison of Variable and Absorption Costing

Khalid Company began business on January 1, 20X4, with assets of $150,000 cash and equities of $150,000 capital stock. In 20X4, it manufactured some inventory at a cost of $60,000 cash, including $16,000 for factory rent and other fixed factory overhead. In 20X5, it manufactured nothing and sold half of its inventory for $42,000 cash. In 20X6, it manufactured nothing and sold the remaining half for another $42,000 cash. It had no fixed expenses in 20X5 or 20X6.

There are no other transactions of any kind. Ignore income taxes.

Prepare an ending balance sheet plus an income statement for 20X4, 20X5, and 20X6 under (1) absorption costing and (2) variable costing (direct costing). Explain the differences in net income between absorption and variable costing.

13-41 Comparisons Over Four Years

The Balakrishnan Corporation began business on January 1, 20X3, to produce and sell a single product. Reported operating income figures under both absorption and variable costing for the first four years of operation are

Year	Absorption Costing	Variable Costing
20X3	$70,000	$50,000
20X4	70,000	60,000
20X5	50,000	50,000
20X6	40,000	70,000

Standard production costs per unit, sales prices, application (absorption) rates, and expected volume levels were the same in each year. There were no flexible-budget variances for any type of cost. All nonmanufacturing expenses were fixed, and there were no nonmanufacturing cost variances in any year.

1. In what year(s) did "units produced" equal "units sold"?
2. In what year(s) did "units produced" exceed "units sold"?
3. What is the dollar amount of the December 31, 20X6 finished-goods inventory? (Give absorption-costing value.)
4. What is the difference between "units produced" and "units sold" in 20X6, if you know that the absorption-costing fixed-manufacturing-overhead application rate is $3 per unit? (Give answer in units.)

13-42 Variable and Absorption Costing

Chan Manufacturing Company data for 20X4 follow:

Sales: 12,000 units at $17 each	
Actual production	15,000 units
Expected volume of production	18,000 units
Manufacturing costs incurred	
Variable	$105,000
Fixed	63,000
Nonmanufacturing costs incurred	
Variable	$ 24,000
Fixed	18,000

1. Determine operating income for 20X4, assuming the firm uses the variable-costing approach to product costing. (Do not prepare a statement.)
2. Assume that there is no January 1, 20X4 inventory; no variances are allocated to inventory; and the firm uses a "full absorption" approach to product costing. Compute (a) the cost assigned to December 31, 20X4, inventory; and (b) operating income for the year ended December 31, 20X4. (Do not prepare a statement.)

13-43 Computation of Production-Volume Variance

Osaka Manufacturing Company budgeted its 20X4 variable overhead at ¥14,100,000 and its fixed overhead at ¥25,620,000. Expected 20X0 volume was 6,100 units. Actual costs for production of 5,800 units during 20X4 were

Variable overhead	¥14,160,000
Fixed overhead	25,620,000
Total overhead	¥39,780,000

Compute the production-volume variance. Be sure to label it favorable or unfavorable.

13-44 Reconciliation of Variable-Costing and Absorption-Costing Operating Income

Blackstone Tools, Inc., produced 12,000 electric drills during 20X4. Expected production was only 10,500 drills. The company's fixed-overhead rate is $7 per drill. Absorption-costing operating income for the year is $18,000, based on sales of 11,000 drills.

1. Compute
   a. Budgeted fixed overhead
   b. Production-volume variance
   c. Variable-costing operating income
2. Reconcile absorption-costing operating income and variable-costing operating income. Include the amount of the difference between the two and an explanation for the difference.

13-45 Overhead Variances

Study Appendix 13. Consider the following data for the Rivera Company:

	Factory Overhead	
	Fixed	**Variable**
Actual incurred	$14,200	$13,300
Budget for standard hours allowed for output achieved	12,500	11,000
Applied	11,600	11,000
Budget for actual hours of input	12,500	11,400

From the above information, fill in the blanks below. Be sure to mark your variances F for favorable and U for unfavorable.

a. Flexible-budget variance $———   Fixed $———
                                                    Variable $———

b. Production-volume variance $———   Fixed $———
                                                    Variable $———

c. Spending variance $———   Fixed $———
                                                    Variable $———

d. Efficiency variance $———   Fixed $———
                                                    Variable $———

13-46 Variances

Study Appendix 13. Consider the following data regarding factory overhead:

	Variable	**Fixed**
Budget for actual hours of input	$45,000	$70,000
Applied	41,000	64,800
Budget for standard hours allowed for actual output achieved	?	?
Actual incurred	48,500	68,500

Using the above data, fill in the following blanks with the variance amounts. Use F for favorable or U for unfavorable for each variance.

	Total Overhead	**Variable**	**Fixed**
1. Spending variance	———	———	———
2. Efficiency variance	———	———	———
3. Production-volume variance	———	———	———
4. Flexible-budget variance	———	———	———
5. Underapplied overhead	———	———	———

Problems

13-47 Choice of Cost Drivers in Accounting Firm

Brenda McCoy, the managing partner of McCoy, Brennan, and Cable, a public accounting firm, is considering the desirability of tracing more costs to jobs than just direct labor. In this way, the firm will be able to justify billings to clients.

Last year's costs were

Direct-professional labor	$ 5,000,000
Overhead	10,000,000
Total costs	$15,000,000

The following costs were included in overhead:

Computer time	$ 750,000
Secretarial cost	700,000
Photocopying	250,000
Fringe benefits to direct labor	800,000
Phone call time with clients	
(estimated but not tabulated)	500,000
Total	$3,000,000

The firm's data processing techniques now make it feasible to document and trace these costs to individual jobs.

As an experiment, in December Brenda McCoy arranged to trace these costs to six audit engagements. Two job records showed the following:

	Engagement	
	Eagledale Company	First Valley Bank
Direct-professional labor	$15,000	$15,000
Fringe benefits to direct labor	3,000	3,000
Phone call time with clients	1,500	500
Computer time	3,000	700
Secretarial costs	2,000	1,500
Photocopying	500	300
Total direct costs	$25,000	$21,000

1. Compute the overhead application rate based on last year's costs.
2. Suppose last year's costs were reclassified so that $3 million would be regarded as direct costs instead of overhead. Compute the overhead application rate as a percentage of direct labor and as a percentage of total direct costs.
3. Using the three rates computed in numbers 1 and 2, compute the total costs of engagements for Eagledale Company and First Valley Bank.
4. Suppose that client billing was based on a 30% markup of total job costs. Compute the billings that would be forthcoming in number 3.
5. Which method of costing and overhead application do you favor? Explain.

13-48 Allocated Costs and Public Services

The Napa County (California) Grand Jury charged the city of St. Helena with overbilling customers for water and sewer services. The city allocated "administrative overhead" to the water and sewer department's budget. These costs were then added to the "jobs," that is, to the accounts of the customers of the water and sewer department. The Grand Jury called the $76,581.20 allocated to the department in 1996–1997 "merely a ruse" to generate funds to cover city expenses that are unrelated to water and sewer services, resulting in "bloated water bills" for local customers.

The city finance director explained that the overhead allocation was the way in which the city bills the water and sewer department for time that other departments spend on water and sewer issues.

Mayor John Brown concluded that "it was very clear to me that they [the Grand Jury] didn't know what they were talking about."

1. Was the overhead charge to the water and sewer department a legitimate cost to be covered by water and sewer bills? Explain your reasoning to the citizens of St. Helena.
2. Assume that at least part of the overhead charge is a legitimate cost of the water and sewer department. Suggest possible changes in the accounting system that would provide a more accurate measure of the cost of services provided to the water and sewer department by other departments.

13-49 Overhead Accounting for Control and for Product Costing

The pickle department of a major food manufacturer has an overhead rate of $4.50 per direct-labor hour, based on expected variable overhead of $125,000 per year, expected fixed overhead of $325,000 per year, and expected direct-labor hours of 100,000 per year.

Data for the year's operations follow:

	Direct-Labor Hours Used	Overhead Costs Incurred*
First six months	55,000	$236,500
Last six months	41,000	206,500

* Fixed costs incurred were exactly equal to budgeted amounts throughout the year.

1. What is the underapplied or overapplied overhead for each six-month period? Label your answer as underapplied or overapplied.
2. Explain briefly (not more than 50 words for each part) the probable causes for the underapplied or overapplied overhead. Focus on variable and fixed costs separately. Give the exact figures attributable to the causes you cite.

13-50 Comparison of Variable Costing and Absorption Costing

Simple numbers are used in this problem to highlight the concepts covered in the chapter.

Assume that the Perth Woolen Company produces a rug that sells for $20. Perth uses a standard cost system. Total standard variable costs of production are $8 per rug, fixed manufacturing costs are $150,000 per year, and selling and administrative expenses are $30,000 per year, all fixed. Expected production volume is 25,000 rugs per year.

1. For each of the following nine combinations of actual sales and production (in thousands of units) for 20X4, prepare condensed income statements under variable costing and under absorption costing.

	(1)	(2)	(3)	(4)	(5)	(6)	(7)	(8)	(9)
Sales units	15	20	25	20	25	30	25	30	35
Production units	20	20	20	25	25	25	30	30	30

Use the following formats:

Variable Costing		Absorption Costing	
Revenue	$ aa	Revenue	$ aa
Cost of goods sold	(bb)	Cost of goods sold	(uu)
Contribution margin	$ cc	Gross profit at standard	$ vv
Fixed manufacturing costs	$(dd)	Favorable (unfavorable) production-volume	
Fixed selling and administrative expenses	(ee)	variance	ww
		Gross profit at "actual"	$ xx
		Selling and administrative expenses	(yy)
Operating income	$ ff	Operating income	$ zz

2. a. In which of the nine combinations is variable-costing income greater than absorption-costing income? In which is it lower? The same?
    b. In which of the nine combinations is the production-volume variance unfavorable? Favorable?
    c. How much profit is added by selling one more unit under variable costing? Under absorption costing?
    d. How much profit is added by producing one more unit under variable costing? Under absorption costing?
    e. Suppose sales, rather than production, is the critical factor in determining the success of Perth Woolen Company. Which format, variable costing or absorption costing, provides the better measure of performance?

13-51 All-Fixed Costs

The Gibraltar Company has built a massive water-desalting factory next to an ocean. The factory is completely automated. It has its own source of power, light, heat, and so on. The salt water costs nothing. All producing and other operating costs are fixed; they do not vary with output because the volume is governed by adjusting a few dials on a control panel. The employees have flat annual salaries.

The desalted water is not sold to household consumers. It has a special taste that appeals to local breweries, distilleries, and soft-drink manufacturers. The price, $.60 per gallon, is expected to remain unchanged for quite some time.

The following are data regarding the first two years of operations:

	In Gallons		Costs (All Fixed)	
	Sales	Production	Manufacturing	Other
20X4	1,500,000	3,000,000	$600,000	$200,000
20X5	1,500,000	0	600,000	200,000

Orders can be processed in four hours, so management decided, in early 20X5, to gear production strictly to sales.

1. Prepare three-column income statements for 20X4, for 20X5, and for the two years together using (a) variable costing and (b) absorption costing.
2. What is the break-even point under (a) variable costing and (b) absorption costing?
3. What inventory costs would be carried on the balance sheets on December 31, 20X0 and 20X1, under each method?
4. Comment on your answers in numbers 1 and 2. Which costing method appears more useful?

13-52 Semifixed Costs

The Plymouth Company differs from the Gibralter Company (described in problem 13-52) in only one respect: It has both variable and fixed manufacturing costs. Its variable costs are $.14 per gallon, and its fixed manufacturing costs are $390,000 per year.

1. Using the same data as in the preceding problem, except for the change in production-cost behavior, prepare three-column income statements for 20X4, for 20X5, and for the two years together using (a) variable costing and (b) absorption costing.
2. What inventory costs would be carried on the balance sheets on December 31, 20X4 and 20X5, under each method?

13-53 Absorption and Variable Costing

The Trapani Company had the following actual data for 20X4 and 20X5:

	20X4	20X5
Units of finished goods		
Opening inventory	—	2,000
Production	15,000	13,000
Sales	13,000	14,000
Ending inventory	2,000	1,000

The basic production data at standard unit costs for the two years were

Direct materials	$22
Direct labor	18
Variable factory overhead	4
Standard variable costs per unit	$44

Fixed factory overhead was budgeted at $98,000 per year. The expected volume of production was 14,000 units, so the fixed overhead rate was $98,000 ÷ 14,000 = $7 per unit.

Budgeted sales price was $75 per unit. Selling and administrative expenses were budgeted at variable, $9 per unit sold, and fixed, $80,000 per year.

Assume that there were absolutely no variances from any standard variable costs or budgeted selling prices or budgeted fixed costs in 20X4.

There were no beginning or ending inventories of work in process.

1. For 20X4, prepare income statements based on standard variable (direct) costing and standard absorption costing. (The next problem deals with 20X5.)
2. Explain why operating income differs between variable costing and absorption costing. Be specific.

13-54 Absorption and Variable Costing

Assume the same facts as in the preceding problem. In addition, consider the following actual data for 20X5:

Direct materials	$ 285,000
Direct labor	174,200
Variable factory overhead	36,000
Fixed factory overhead	95,000
Selling and administrative costs	
Variable	118,400
Fixed	80,000
Sales	1,068,000

1. For 20X5, prepare income statements based on standard variable (direct) costing and standard absorption costing.
2. Explain why operating income differs between variable costing and absorption costing. Be specific.

13-55 Fundamentals of Overhead Variances

The Durant Company is installing an absorption standard-cost system and a flexible-overhead budget. Standard costs have recently been developed for its only product and are as follows:

Direct materials, 3 pounds @ $20	$60
Direct labor, 2 hours @ $14	28
Variable overhead, 2 hours @ $5	10
Fixed overhead	?
Standard cost per unit of finished	
product	$?

Expected production activity is expressed as 7,500 standard direct-labor hours per month. Fixed overhead is expected to be $60,000 per month. The predetermined fixed-overhead rate for product costing is not changed from month to month.

1. Calculate the proper fixed-overhead rate per standard direct-labor hour and per unit.
2. Graph the following for activity from zero to 10,000 hours.
    a. Budgeted variable overhead
    b. Variable overhead applied to product
3. Graph the following for activity from zero to 10,000 hours.
    a. Budgeted fixed overhead
    b. Fixed overhead applied to product
4. Assume that 6,000 standard direct-labor hours are allowed for the output achieved during a given month. Actual variable overhead of $31,000 was incurred; actual fixed overhead amounted to $62,000. Calculate the
    a. Fixed-overhead flexible-budget variance
    b. Fixed-overhead production-volume variance
    c. Variable-overhead flexible-budget variance
5. Assume that 7,800 standard direct-labor hours are allowed for the output achieved during a given month. Actual overhead incurred amounted to $99,700, $62,000 of which was fixed. Calculate the
    a. Fixed-overhead flexible-budget variance
    b. Fixed-overhead production-volume variance
    c. Variable-overhead flexible-budget variance

13-56 Production-Volume Variance at L. A. Darling Company

Review the Chapter 12 opening vignette on **L. A. Darling Company** (pages 521–522). L. A. Darling receives about $6 billion of revenue each year from designing, manufacturing, and installing store fixtures in retail stores. Accounting for fixed manufacturing overhead is a challenge for the company. Suppose a manufacturing division of the company has the following budgeted costs for production of 700,000 shelving units in 2004:

Direct materials	$140,000,000
Direct labor	20,000,000
Other variable manufacturing costs	15,000,000
Fixed manufacturing costs	105,000,000
Total manufacturing cost	$280,000,000

During 2004, this division of L. A. Darling produced 750,000 of the shelving units and sold 720,000 of them for $360 million. Assume that L. A. Darling does not allocate selling or administrative costs to the individual products.

1. Compute the following budgeted unit costs for 2004:

Variable manufacturing costs per unit	?
Fixed manufacturing costs per unit	?
Total manufacturing costs per unit	?

2. Compute the production-volume variance for 2004. Be sure to label it favorable or unfavorable.
3. Compute the 2004 profit from the production and sales of the shelving using absorption costing. Ignore selling and administrative costs.
4. Compute the 2004 profit from the production and sales of the shelving using variable costing. Ignore selling and administrative costs.
5. Which measure of profit, absorption-costing profit or variable-costing profit, is a better measure of performance during 2004? Explain.

13-57 Fixed Overhead and Practical Capacity

The expected activity of the paper-making plant of Goldberg Paper Company was 45,000 machine hours per month. Practical capacity was 60,000 machine hours per month. The standard machine hours allowed for the actual output achieved in January were 54,000. The budgeted fixed-factory-overhead items were

Depreciation, equipment	$340,000
Depreciation, factory building	64,000
Supervision	47,000
Indirect labor	234,000
Insurance	18,000
Property taxes	17,000
Total	$720,000

Because of unanticipated scheduling difficulties and the need for more indirect labor, the actual fixed factory overhead was $747,000.

1. Using practical capacity as the base for applying fixed factory overhead, prepare a summary analysis of fixed-overhead variances for January.
2. Using expected activity as the base for applying fixed factory overhead, prepare a summary analysis of fixed-overhead variances for January.
3. Explain why some of your variances in numbers 1 and 2 are the same and why some differ.

13-58 Selection of Expected Volume

Rosanne McIntire is a consultant to Georgia Paper Products Company. She is helping one of the company's divisions to install a standard cost system for 20X2. For product-costing purposes, the system must apply fixed factory costs to products manufactured. She has decided that the fixed-overhead rate should be based on machine hours, but she is uncertain about the appropriate volume to use in the denominator. Georgia Paper has grown rapidly; the division has added production capacity approximately every four years. The last addition was completed in early 20X2, and the total capacity is now 2,800,000 machine hours per year. McIntire predicts the following operating levels (in machine hours) through 20X6:

Year	Capacity Used
20X2	2,250,000 hours
20X3	2,450,000 hours
20X4	2,700,000 hours
20X5	2,800,000 hours
20X6	2,900,000 hours

The current plan is to add another 500,000 machine hours of capacity in 20X6.

McIntire has identified three alternatives for the allocation base:

a. Predicted volume for the year in question
b. Average volume over the four years of the current production setup
c. Practical (or full) capacity

1. Suppose annual fixed factory overhead is expected to be $36,400,000 through 20X5. For simplicity, assume no inflation. Calculate the fixed-overhead rates (to the nearest cent) for 20X3, 20X4, and 20X5, using each of the three alternative allocation bases.
2. Provide a brief description of the effect of using each method of computing the allocation base.
3. Which method do you prefer? Why?

13-59 Analysis of Operating Results

Leeds Tool Company produces and sells a variety of machine-tooled products. The company employs a standard cost accounting system for record-keeping purposes.

At the beginning of 20X4, the president of Leeds Tool presented the budget to the company's board of directors. The board accepted a target 20X4 profit of £16,800 and agreed to pay the president a bonus if profits exceeded the target. The president has been confident that the year's profit would exceed the budget target, since the monthly sales reports that he has been receiving have shown that sales for the year will exceed budget by 10%. The president is both disturbed and confused when the controller presents an adjusted forecast as of November 30, 20X4, indicating that profit will be 14% under budget:

Leeds Tool Company
Forecasts of Operating Results

	Forecasts as of	
	1/1/X4	11/30/X4
Sales	£156,000	£171,600
Cost of sales at standard	108,000*	118,800
Gross margin at standard	£ 48,000	£ 52,800
Over- (under-) absorbed fixed		
manufacturing overhead	0	(6,000)
Actual gross margin	£ 48,000	£ 46,800
Selling expenses	£ 11,200	£ 12,320
Administrative expenses	20,000	20,000
Total operating expenses	£ 31,200	£ 32,320
Earnings before tax	£ 16,800	£ 14,480

* Includes fixed manufacturing overhead of £30,000.

There have been no sales price changes or product-mix shifts since the January 1, 20X4, forecast. The only cost variance on the income statement is the underapplied manufacturing overhead. This arose because the company produced only 16,000 standard machine hours (budgeted machine hours were 20,000) during 20X4, as a result of a shortage of raw materials while its principal supplier was closed by a strike. Fortunately, Leeds Tool's finished-goods inventory was large enough to fill all sales orders received.

1. Analyze and explain why the profit has declined despite increased sales and good control over costs. Show computations.
2. What plan, if any, could Leeds Tool Company adopt during December to improve its reported profit at year-end? Explain your answer.
3. Illustrate and explain how Leeds Tool Company could adopt an alternative internal cost-reporting procedure that would avoid the confusing effect of the present procedure. Show the revised forecasts under your alternative.
4. Would the alternative procedure described in number 3 be acceptable to the board of directors for financial-reporting purposes? Explain.

13-60 Standard Absorption and Standard Variable Costing

Schlosser Company has the following results for a certain year. All variances are written off as additions to (or deductions from) the standard cost of goods sold. Find the unknowns, designated by letters.

Sales: 150,000 units, @ $20	$3,000,000
Net variance for standard variable	
manufacturing costs	$33,000, unfavorable
Variable standard cost of goods manufactured	$11 per unit
Variable selling and administrative expenses	$3 per unit
Fixed selling and administrative expenses	$650,000
Fixed manufacturing overhead	$165,000
Maximum capacity per year	190,000 units
Expected production volume for year	150,000 units
Beginning inventory of finished goods	15,000 units
Ending inventory of finished goods	10,000 units
Beginning inventory: variable-costing basis	a
Contribution margin	b
Operating income: variable-costing basis	c
Beginning inventory: absorption-costing basis	d
Gross margin	e
Operating income: absorption-costing basis	f

13-61 Disposition of Variances

In January 20X4, Louisiana Garden Equipment Company started a division for making grass clippers. Management hoped that these grass clippers were significantly better than most competitors in the market. During 20X4, it produced 100,000 grass clippers. Financial results were as follows:

- Sales: 75,000 units @ $18
- Direct labor at standard: $100,000 \times \$8 = \$800,000$
- Direct-labor variances: $34,000 U
- Direct materials at standard: $100,000 \times \$5 = \$500,000$
- Direct-material variances: $9,500 U
- Overhead incurred at standard: $100,000 \times \$4 = \$400,000$
- Overhead variances: $3,500 F

Louisiana uses an absorption-costing system and allows divisions to choose one of two methods of accounting for variances:

a. Direct charge to income.
b. Proration to the production of the period. Method b requires variances to be spread equally over the units produced during the period.

1. Calculate the division's operating income (a) using method a and (b) using method b. Assume no selling and administrative expenses.
2. Calculate ending inventory value (a) using method a and (b) using method b. Note that there was no beginning inventory.
3. What is the major argument in support of each method?

13-62 Straightforward Problem on Standard Cost System

Study Appendix 13. The Winnipeg Chemical Company uses flexible budgets and a standard cost system.

- Direct-labor costs incurred, 12,000 hours, $150,000
- Variable-overhead costs incurred, $37,000
- Fixed-overhead flexible-budget variance, $1,600, favorable
- Finished units produced, 1,800
- Fixed-overhead costs incurred, $38,000
- Variable overhead applied at $3 per hour
- Standard direct-labor cost, $13 per hour
- Denominator production per month, 2,000 units
- Standard direct-labor hours per finished unit, 6

Prepare an analysis of all variances (similar to Exhibit 13-11, p. 594).

13-63 Straightforward Problem on Standard Cost System

Study Appendix 13. The München Company uses a standard cost system. The month's data regarding its single product follow (where € is the symbol for the euro, the currency of most countries of the European Union):

- Fixed-overhead costs incurred, €6,300
- Variable overhead applied at €11 per hour
- Standard direct-labor cost, €44 per hour
- Denominator production per month, 220 units
- Standard direct-labor hours per finished unit, 5
- Direct-labor costs incurred, 1,000 hours, €42,500
- Variable-overhead costs incurred, €10,400
- Fixed-overhead budget variance, €300, favorable
- Finished units produced, 180

Prepare an analysis of all variances (similar to Exhibit 13-11, p. 594).

Cases

13-64 Multiple Overhead Rates and Activity-Based Costing

A division of **Hewlett-Packard** assembles and tests printed circuit (PC) boards. The division has many different products. Some are high volume; others are low volume. For years, manufacturing overhead was applied to products using a single overhead rate based on direct-labor dollars. However, direct-labor has shrunk to 6% of total manufacturing costs.

Managers decided to refine the division's product-costing system. Abolishing the direct-labor category, they included all manufacturing labor as a part of factory overhead. They also identified several activities and the appropriate cost driver for each. The cost driver for the first activity, the start station, was the number of raw PC boards. The application rate was computed as follows:

$$\text{application rate for start station activity} = \frac{\text{budgeted total factory overhead at the activity}}{\text{budgeted raw PC boards for the year}}$$

$$= \frac{\$150,000}{125,000}$$

$$= \$1.20$$

Each time a raw PC board passes through the start station activity, $1.20 is added to the cost of the board. The product cost is the sum of costs directly traced to the board plus the indirect costs (factory overhead) accumulated at each of the manufacturing activities undergone.

Using assumed numbers, consider the following data regarding PC Board 37:

Direct materials	$55.00
Factory overhead applied	?
Total manufacturing product cost	?

The activities involved in the production of PC Board 37 and the related cost drivers were

Activity	Cost Driver	Factory-Overhead Costs Applied for Each Activity
1. Start station	No. of raw PC boards	1 × $1.20 = $1.20
2. Axial insertion	No. of axial insertions	39 × .07 = ?
3. Dip insertion	No. of dip insertions	? × .20 = 5.60
4. Manual insertion	No. of manual insertions	15 × ? = 6.00
5. Wave solder	No. of boards soldered	1 × 3.20 = 3.20
6. Backload	No. of backload insertions	8 × .60 = 4.80
7. Test	Standard time board is in test activity	.15 × 80.00 = ?
8. Defect analysis	Standard time for defect analysis and repair	.05 × ? = 4.50
Total		$?

1. Fill in the blanks.
2. How is direct labor identified with products under this product-costing system?
3. Why would managers favor this multiple-overhead rate, activity-based-costing system instead of the older system?

13-65 One or Two Cost Drivers

The Matterhorn Instruments Co. in Geneva, Switzerland, has the following 20X4 budget for its two departments in Swiss francs (SFr):

	Machining	Finishing	Total
Direct labor	SFr 300,000	SFr 800,000	SFr 1,100,000
Factory overhead	SFr 960,000	SFr 800,000	SFr 1,760,000
Machine hours	60,000	20,000	80,000

In the past, the company has used a single plantwide overhead application rate based on direct-labor cost. However, as the company's product line has expanded and as competition has intensified, Hans Volkert, the company president, has questioned the accuracy of the profits or losses shown on various products.

Matterhorn makes custom tools on special orders from customers. To be competitive and still make a reasonable profit, it is essential that the firm measure the cost of each customer order. Mr. Volkert has focused on overhead allocation as a potential problem. He knows that changes in costs are more heavily affected by machine hours in the machining department and by direct-labor costs in the finishing department. As company controller, you have gathered the following data regarding two typical customer orders:

	Order Number	
	K102	K156
Machining		
Direct materials	SFr 4,000	SFr 4,000
Direct labor	SFr 3,000	SFr 1,500
Machine hours	1,200	100
Finishing		
Direct labor	SFr 1,500	SFr 3,000
Machine hours	120	120

1. Compute six factory overhead application rates, three based on direct-labor cost and three based on machine hours for machining, finishing, and for the plant as a whole.
2. Use the application rates to compute the total costs of orders K102 and K156 as follows: (a) plantwide rate based on direct-labor cost and (b) machining based on machine hours and finishing based on direct-labor cost.
3. Evaluate your answers in number 2. Which set of job costs do you prefer? Why?

13-66 Absorption Costing and Incentive to Produce

Charlene Wolcott is manager of the Boulder division of Colorado Metals, Inc. Her division makes a single product that is sold to industrial customers. Demand is seasonal but is readily predictable. The division's budget for 20X4 called for production and sales of 120,000 units, with production of 10,000 units each month and sales varying between 8,000 and 13,000 units a month. The division's budget for 20X4 had operating income of $660,000:

Sales (120,000 × $55)	$6,600,000
Cost of goods sold (120,000 × $45)	5,400,000
Gross margin	$1,200,000
Selling and administrative expenses (all fixed)	540,000
Operating income	$ 660,000

By the end of November, sales had lagged projections, with only 105,000 units sold. Sales of 9,000 units were originally budgeted and are still expected in December. Production through November had remained stable at 10,000 units per month, and the cost of production had been exactly as budgeted:

Direct materials, 110,000 × $14	$1,540,000
Direct labor, 110,000 × $10	1,100,000
Variable overhead, 110,000 × $8	880,000
Fixed overhead	1,430,000
Total production cost	$4,950,000

The division's operating income for the first eleven months of 20X4 was

Sales (105,000 x $55)	$5,775,000
Cost of goods sold (105,000 x $45)	4,725,000
Gross margin	$1,050,000
Selling and administrative	
expenses (all fixed)	495,000
Operating income	$ 555,000

Wolcott receives an annual bonus only if her division's operating income exceeds the budget. She sees no way to increase sales beyond 9,000 units in December.

1. From the budgeted and actual income statements shown, determine whether Colorado Metals uses direct or absorption costing.
2. Suppose Colorado Metals uses a standard absorption-costing system. (a) Compute the 20X4 operating income if 10,000 units are produced and 9,000 units are sold in December. (b) How could Wolcott achieve her budgeted operating income for 20X4?
3. Suppose Colorado Metals uses a standard variable-costing system. (a) Compute the 20X4 operating income if 10,000 units are produced and 9,000 units are sold in December. (b) How could Wolcott achieve her budgeted operating income for 20X4?
4. Which system motivates Wolcott to make the decision that is in the best interests of Colorado Metals? Explain.

13-67 Inventory Measures, Production Scheduling, and Evaluating Divisional Performance

The Calais Company stresses competition between the heads of its various divisions, and it rewards stellar performance with year-end bonuses that vary between 5% and 10% of division net operating income (before considering the bonus or income taxes). The divisional managers have great discretion in setting production schedules.

The Brittany division produces and sells a product for which there is a long-standing demand but which can have marked seasonal and year-to-year fluctuations. On November 30, 20X4, Veronique Giraud, the Brittany division manager, is preparing a production schedule for December. The following data are available for January 1 through November 30 (€ is the symbol for euro, the currency for most countries of the European Union):

Beginning inventory, January 1, in units	10,000
Sales price, per unit	€ 400
Total fixed costs incurred for manufacturing	€ 9,350,000
Total fixed costs: other (not inventoriable)	€ 9,350,000
Total variable costs for manufacturing	€ 18,150,000
Total other variable costs (fluctuate with units sold)	€ 4,000,000
Units produced	110,000
Units sold	100,000
Variances	None

Production in October and November was 10,000 units each month. Practical capacity is 12,000 units per month. Maximum available storage space for inventory is 25,000 units. The sales outlook for December through February is 6,000 units monthly. To retain a core of key employees, monthly production cannot be scheduled at less than 4,000 units without special permission from the president. Inventory is never to be less than 10,000 units.

The denominator used for applying fixed factory overhead is regarded as 120,000 units annually. The company uses a standard absorption-costing system. All variances are disposed of at year-end as an adjustment to standard cost of goods sold.

1. Given the restrictions as stated, and assuming that Giraud wants to maximize the company's net income for 20X4,
   a. How many units should be scheduled for production in December?
   b. What net operating income will be reported in 20X4 as a whole, assuming that the implied cost behavior patterns will continue in December as they did throughout the year to date? Show your computations.
   c. If December production is scheduled at 4,000 units, what would reported net income be?
2. Assume that standard variable costing is used rather than standard absorption costing.
   a. What would net income for 20X4 be, assuming that the December production schedule is the one in part a of number 1?
   b. Assuming that December production was 4,000 units?
   c. Reconcile the net incomes in this requirement with those in number 1.
3. From the viewpoint of the long-run interests of the company as a whole, what production schedule should the division manager set? Explain fully. Include in your explanation a comparison of the motivating influence of absorption and variable costing in this situation.

4. Assume standard absorption costing. Giraud wants to maximize her after-income-tax performance over the long run. Given the data at the beginning of the problem, assume that income tax rates will be halved in 20X5. Assume also that year-end write-offs of variances are acceptable for income tax purposes. How many units should be scheduled for production in December? Why?

13-68 Performance Evaluation

A division of Iowa/Illinois Corn Company produces seed corn for farmers throughout the Midwest. Jens Jensen became president in 20X4. He is concerned with the ability of his division manager to control costs. To aid his evaluation, Jensen set up a standard cost system.

Standard costs were based on 20X4 costs in several categories. Each 20X4 cost was divided by 1,520,000 cwt, the volume of 20X4 production, to determine a standard for 20X5 (cwt means hundredweight, or 100 pounds):

	20X4 Cost (thousands)	20X5 Standard (per hundredweight)
Direct materials	$1,824	$1.20
Direct labor	836	.55
Variable overhead	1,596	1.05
Fixed overhead	2,432	1.60
Total	$6,688	$4.40

At the end of 20X5, Jensen compared actual results with the standards he established. Production was 1,360,000 cwt, and variances were as follows:

	Actual	Standard	Variance
Direct materials	$1,802	$1,632	$170 U
Direct labor	735	748	13 F
Variable overhead	1,422	1,428	6 F
Fixed overhead	2,412	2,176	236 U
Total	$6,371	$5,984	$387 U

Jensen was not surprised by the unfavorable variance in direct materials. After all, corn prices in 20X5 averaged 10% above those in 20X4. But he was disturbed by the lack of control of fixed overhead. He called in the production manager and demanded an explanation.

1. Prepare an explanation for the large unfavorable fixed-overhead variance.
2. Discuss the appropriateness of using one year's costs as the next year's standards.

EXCEL Application Exercise

13-69 Computing Budgeted Factory Overhead

Goal: Create an Excel spreadsheet to compute budgeted factory overhead rates and apply factory overhead to production. Use the results to answer questions about your findings.

Scenario: Donald Aeronautics Company has asked you to determine their budgeted factory overhead rates. They would also like you to apply the appropriate factory overhead amounts to actual production and determine any variances. Additional background information for your spreadsheet appears in Fundamental Assignment Material 13-A1. (Ignore data in the Fundamental Assignment Material for product M89.)

When you have completed your spreadsheet, answer the following questions:

1. What was the budgeted factory overhead rate for Department A? Department B?
2. What overhead amount was distributed to Department A? Was the overhead over- or underapplied? By what amount?
3. What overhead amount was distributed to Department B? Was the overhead over- or underapplied? By what amount?

Step-by-Step:

1. Open a new Excel spreadsheet.
2. In column A, create a bold-faced heading that contains the following:
   Row 1: Chapter 13 Decision Guideline
   Row 2: Donald Aeronautics Company
   Row 3: Overhead Allocations Using Budgeted Rates
   Row 4: Today's Date
3. Merge and center the four heading rows across columns A through G.
4. In row 7, create the following column headings:
   Column B: 20X1 Budget
   Column D: 20X1 Actual
   Column F: Variances
5. Merge and center the 20X1 Budget heading across columns B through C.
6. Merge and center the 20X1 Actual heading across columns D through E.
7. Merge and center the Variances heading across columns F through G.
8. In row 8, create the following center-justified column headings:
   Columns B, D, and F: Dept. A
   Columns C, E, and G: Dept. B
9. In column A, create the following row headings:
   Row 9: Factory overhead
   Row 10: Direct labor hours
   Row 11: Machine hours
   Skip a row
   Row 13: Overhead rate
   Row 14: Distributed overhead
   Row 15: Over/(under) applied
   Note: Recommended column widths: column A = 18, columns B through G = 12.

10. Use data from Fundamental Assignment Material 13-A1 to enter the amounts for the Department A and B 20X1 budget predictions and 20X1 actual results.
11. Use the appropriate formulas to calculate the following amounts:

20X1 budgeted overhead rates for depts. A and B	Row 13, columns B and C
20X1 distributed overhead for depts. A and B	Row 14, columns D and E
20X1 over/under applied overhead	Row 15, columns D and E
Flexible budget variances for depts. A and B	Row 9, columns F and G
Activity budget variance for dept. B	Row 10, column G
Activity budget variance for dept. A	Row 11, column F
Total variances for depts. A and B	Row 15, columns F and G

12. Format amounts in rows 10 and 11 as

Number tab:	Category:	Accounting
	Decimal:	0
	Symbol:	None

13. Format amounts in rows 9, 14 and 15 as

Number tab:	Category:	Accounting
	Decimal:	0
	Symbol:	$

14. Format amounts in row 13 as

Number tab:	Category:	Accounting
	Decimal:	2
	Symbol:	$

15. Modify the format of the total variances in row 15, columns F and G to display a top border using the default Line Style.

Border tab:	Icon:	Top Border

16. Save your work to disk, and print a copy for your files.
    Note: Print your spreadsheet using landscape in order to ensure that all columns appear on one page.

Collaborative Learning Exercise

13-70 Accounting for Overhead

Form into groups of four to six persons. Each group should identify a cost accountant at a local company to interview. The interviewee could be the top financial officer of a small company, but a division controller or cost analyst might be more appropriate for a large company. The essential factor is that the person chosen understands how overhead costs are allocated to products or services in the company.

Set up an interview with the cost accountant, and explore the following issues. Be prepared with follow-up questions if your question receives a superficial answer. Your goal should be to get as much operational detail as possible about the procedures used for allocating overhead costs at the company. If the company is large, you may want to focus on one department, one product line, or some other subdivision of the company.

The issues to explore are

1. What types of costs are included in overhead? How large is overhead compared with direct materials and labor costs?
2. What types of overhead cost pools exist? Are there different pools by department? By activity? By cost driver? By fixed or variable cost? Be prepared to explain what you mean by these terms, because terminology varies widely.
3. How is overhead applied to final products or services? What cost drivers are used?

After the interview, draw a diagram of the cost allocation system in as much detail as possible. Be prepared to share this with the entire class, using it to explain the overhead cost allocation system at the company your group studied.

Internet Exercise   www.prenhall.com/horngren

13-71 Dell Computers Company

Published income statements use the absorption-costing basis—after all, that is the method that is acceptable for use under the U.S. generally accepted accounting principles (GAAP). But the absorption-costing statement might not really provide the information that management needs to make future decisions because it does not separate fixed from variable costs. This exercise focuses on extracting contribution information from published absorption-costing financial statements of **Dell Computer Corporation**. As a manufacturer of computers, Dell has become a well-known, household name.

1. Go to the home page for Dell Computer Corporation at http://www.dell.com. Take a look at one of the new models being offered. Click on the "Products" drop-down menu and select the most recent model year. Once you've clicked in to that, choose a computer that you'd like to see. Once you've arrived at the product page, what type of information do you find about the computer? What information is available about prices? Is it possible that the model could have more than one price? Why or why not?
2. Now go to the Investor Relations section of the site by clicking on about Dell. Choose "Financial Information" from the pull-down menu. Click on the "Production and Marketing" information section of the report. Now look at the information for the most recent year with respect to shipments. What can you see in the shipping report? Did the number of units shipped increase or decrease over the prior year? Record the total number of computers shipped for the most recent full year of information.
3. Look at the most recent annual report for Dell. Go to the section, "Management's Discussion and Analysis of Financial Condition and Results of Operations." What was the total revenue for Latitude computers? What is the average selling price for a Latitude? How does this price compare to the suggested price for the Latitude computer? Why do you think that the prices differ?
4. Look at the most recent Consolidated Statement of Operations. What were the cost of goods sold and the selling, administrative, and engineering expenses for the current year? Refer to the cash

flow statement for the current year. How much was the depreciation and amortization for the current year? Assume that 80% of these expenses are related to PCs (since 80% of Dell's revenue comes from PC sales) and that depreciation and amortization is the only fixed expense that Dell had during the year. Compute the average variable cost of goods sold per unit for a PC. Compute the average contribution margin per PC. What would be the break-even number of PCs to produce and sell under this scenario? Does this seem reasonable, given the current income reported by the firm?

Job-Costing and Process-Costing Systems

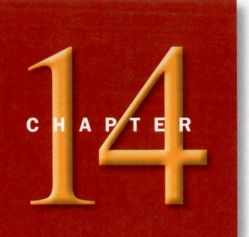

CHAPTER 14

LEARNING OBJECTIVES

When you have finished studying this chapter, you should be able to:

1. Distinguish between job-order costing and process costing.

2. Prepare summary journal entries for the typical transactions of a job-costing system.

3. Use an activity-based-costing system in a job-order environment.

4. Show how service organizations use job costing.

5. Explain the basic ideas underlying process costing and how they differ from job costing.

6. Compute output in terms of equivalent units.

7. Compute costs and prepare journal entries for the principal transactions in a process-costing system.

8. Demonstrate how the presence of beginning inventories affects the computation of unit costs under the weighted-average method.

9. Use backflush costing with a JIT production system.

Here is a trivia question.

Name the favorite candy of former President Ronald Reagan, the candy featured in the hit movie Harry Potter (with flavors like dirt, grass, and vomit), and the first candy to travel into outer space? Of course, the answer is jelly beans. And one of the most famous brands is Jelly Belly Candy. As noted by the authors of this text, this candy often shows up on the desks of students taking long, difficult management-accounting exams.

Jelly Belly is the world's #1 gourmet jelly bean. The **Jelly Belly Candy** company makes Candy Corn and more than 100 mouthwatering candies, including such delights as chocolates, gummies, sour candies, and confections for all the major seasons. To make a Jelly Belly jelly bean in either of its two factories, several processes are required. A hot kettle of gooey mix is flavored and colored with ingredients such as real peanut butter, peach puree, or milk chocolate. Then 1,260 tiny beans are placed in a tray, cooled, and coated with corn starch and sugar before a shell is added. The final processes include polishing, printing the Jelly Belly name on each piece, and packaging.

How do Jelly Belly's accountants, affectionately called bean counters, determine the cost of each of these processing steps? How is the cost of flavoring transferred to the sugar-coating process and then to the process that adds a shell? Finally, how are all these processing costs combined to determine the cost of the hundreds of products that are sold worldwide? The answers to these questions enable management to determine the profit of each of the products sold and to set prices. To answer such questions, the accountants at Jelly Belly have developed a process-costing system with capabilities that are carefully tailored to meet the decision-making needs of management. ■

---

[1]To take a tour of the Jelly Belly Candy factory, view the Prentice Hall video.

When a kid's eyes are larger and brighter than the yummiest jelly bean, you are not thinking about the methods used to determine the costs of the various processes used to make a handful of joy! But to the accountants at Jelly Belly Candy Company, process costing is a critical task. Managers use these costs to determine profitability and set price strategy.

Distinction Between Job Costing and Process Costing

The two most common systems of product costing are job-order costing and process costing. **Job-order costing** (or simply **job costing**) allocates costs to products that are readily identified by individual units or batches, each of which requires varying degrees of attention and skill. Industries that commonly use job-order methods include construction, printing, aircraft, furniture, special-purpose machinery, and any manufacturer of tailor-made or unique goods.

Process costing averages costs over large numbers of nearly identical products. It is most often found in such industries as chemicals, oil, plastics, rubber, lumber, food processing, glass, mining, cement, and meatpacking. These industries mass produce like units that usually pass in continuous fashion through a series of uniform production steps called operations or processes.

The distinction between the job-cost and the process-cost methods centers largely on how they measure product costs. Job costing applies costs to specific jobs, which may consist of either a single physical unit (such as a custom sofa) or a few like units (such as a dozen tables) in a distinct batch or job lot. In contrast, process costing deals with great masses of like units and broad averages of unit costs.

The most important point is that product costing is an averaging process. The unit cost used for inventory purposes is the result of taking some accumulated cost (e.g., the sum of production-related activity costs) of production and dividing it by some measure of production. The basic distinction between job-order costing and process costing is the breadth of the denominator: In job-order costing, the denominator is small (e.g., one painting, 100 advertising circulars, one special packaging machine, or one highway bridge); however, in process costing, the denominator is large (e.g., thousands of pounds, gallons, or board feet).

Job costing and process costing are extremes along a continuum of potential costing systems. Each company designs its own accounting system to fit its underlying production activities. Some companies use **hybrid costing systems,** which are blends of ideas from both job costing and process costing.

Illustration of Job Costing

Job costing is best learned by example. But first we examine the basic records used in a job-cost system. The centerpiece of a job-costing system is the **job-cost record** (also called a **job-cost sheet** or **job order**), shown in Exhibit 14-1. The job-cost record contains all costs for a particular product, service, or batch of products. A file of job-cost records for partially completed jobs provides supporting details for the Work-in-Process Inventory account, often simply called Work in Process (WIP). A file of completed job-cost records comprises the Finished-Goods Inventory account.

As Exhibit 14-1 shows, the job-cost record summarizes information contained on source documents such as materials requisitions and labor time tickets. **Materials requisitions** are records of materials used in particular jobs. **Labor time tickets** (or **time cards**) record the time a particular direct laborer spends on each job.

Today, job-cost records and source documents are likely to be computer files, not paper records. In fact, with online data entry, bar coding, and optical scanning, much of the information needed for such records enters the computer without ever being written on paper. Nevertheless, whether records are on paper or in computer files, the accounting system must collect and maintain the same basic information.

As each job begins, we create its own job-cost record. As units are worked on, we make entries on the job-cost record. We accumulate three classes of costs on the job-cost record as units pass through the departments: Materials requisitions are the source

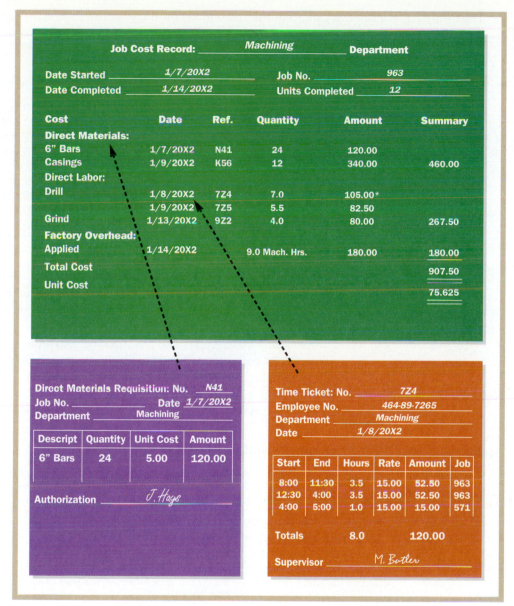

Exhibit 14-1
Completed Job-Cost
Record and Sample
Source Documents

* Note that 7 of the 8 hours and $105 of the $120 in time ticket 7Z4 belong to job no. 963.

of direct-materials costs, time tickets provide direct-labor costs, and budgeted overhead rates (a separate rate for each overhead cost pool) are used to apply factory overhead to products. (The computation of these budgeted rates will be described later in this chapter.)

Basic Records of Enriquez Machine Parts Company

To illustrate the functioning of a job-order-costing system, we will use the records and journal entries of the Enriquez Machine Parts Company. On December 31, 20X4, the firm had the following inventories:

Direct materials (12 types)	$110,000
Work in process	—
Finished goods (unsold units from two jobs)	12,000

The following is a summary of pertinent transactions for the year 20X5:

	Machining	Assembly	Total
1. Direct materials purchased on account	—	—	$1,900,000
2. Direct materials requisitioned for manufacturing	$1,000,000	$890,000	1,890,000
3. Direct-labor costs incurred	200,000	190,000	390,000
4a. Factory overhead incurred	290,000	102,000	392,000
4b. Factory overhead applied	280,000*	95,000	375,000
5. Cost of goods completed and transferred to finished-goods inventory	—	—	2,500,000
6a. Sales on account	—	—	4,000,000
6b. Cost of goods sold	—	—	2,480,000

* We explain the nature of factory overhead applied later in this chapter.

Exhibit 14-2 is an overview of the general flow of costs through the Enriquez Machine Parts Company's job-order-costing system.[1] The exhibit summarizes the effects of transactions on the key manufacturing accounts in the firm's books. As you proceed through the following transaction-by-transaction summary analysis, keep checking each explanation against the overview in Exhibit 4-2. (Companies usually make entries as transactions occur. However, to obtain a sweeping overview, our illustration uses summary entries for the entire year 20X5.) Essentially, we bring into WIP the costs of direct material used, direct labor, and factory overhead applied. In turn, we transfer the costs of completed goods from WIP to Finished Goods. As the company sells goods, their costs become expense in the form of Cost of Goods Sold.

Applying Direct Materials and Direct Labor Costs

OBJECTIVE 2

Prepare summary journal entries for the typical transactions of a job-costing system.

The first three transactions in Exhibit 14-2 trace direct materials and direct labor costs to WIP. The entries are straightforward.

1. Transaction: Direct materials purchased, $1,900,000.
   Analysis: The asset Direct-Materials Inventory is increased. The liability Accounts Payable is increased.
   Journal Entry: Direct-Materials Inventory 1,900,000
                       Accounts Payable 1,900,000
2. Transaction: Direct materials requisitioned, $1,890,000.
   Analysis: The asset Work in Process (WIP) Inventory is increased. The asset Direct-Materials Inventory is decreased.

---

[1] Exhibit 14-2 and the following explanation of transactions assume knowledge of basic accounting procedures. We will use the T-account format for a company's accounts. Entries on the left of the "T" are debits and those on the right are credits. Asset T-accounts, such as the inventory accounts, show increases on the left (debit) side and decreases on the right (credit) side of the "T":

Inventory	
Beginning Balance Increases	Decreases
Ending Balance	

We record transactions affecting the accounts as journal entries. We show debit (left-side) entries flush with the left margin, we indent credit (right-side) entries, and often we include an explanation. For example, we would show a $10,000 transfer from Direct Materials Inventory to WIP (Work in Process) Inventory as follows:

WIP Inventory   10,000
    Direct Materials Inventory 10,000
To increase WIP Inventory and decrease Direct
    Materials Inventory by $10,000.

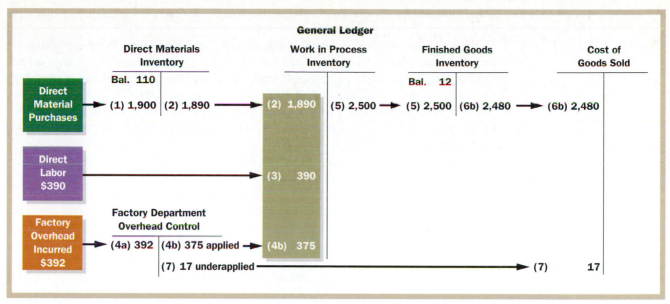

Exhibit 14-2
Job-Order Costing, General Flow of Costs (Thousands)

Journal Entry: WIP Inventory 1,890,000
               Direct-Materials Inventory 1,890,000
3. Transaction: Direct-labor cost incurred, $390,000.
      Analysis: The asset WIP Inventory is increased. The liability Accrued Payroll is increased.
Journal Entry: WIP Inventory 390,000
               Accrued Payroll 390,000

Applying Factory Overhead Costs

Transactions 4a and 4b deal with factory overhead costs. In transaction 4a we charge the actual factory overhead costs to a summary account called Factory Department Overhead Control, which we temporarily regard as an asset. Each department will have a variety of detailed overhead accounts to help control overhead, but for our purposes we summarize them all into the Factory Department Overhead Control account.

4a. Transaction: Factory overhead incurred, $392,000.
        Analysis: The temporary account Factory Department Overhead Control is increased.
                  Assorted asset accounts are decreased and/or liability accounts increased.
   Journal Entry: Factory Department Overhead Control 392,000
                  Cash, Accounts Payable, and various
                  other balance sheet accounts 392,000

In transaction 4b we apply factory overhead costs to WIP.[2] To make ongoing decisions such as which products to emphasize or deemphasize and how to price each product, managers would like to know all costs at the time production is completed. Because accountants directly trace direct materials and direct labor costs to products, these costs are available immediately on completion of production. In contrast, to apply factory overhead costs to products at the time of production, accountants must use budgeted (predetermined) overhead rates to apply overhead to jobs as they are completed, making an estimate of total product cost available for managerial decisions.

---

[2]This section on the application of overhead is a condensed version of the Chapter 13 section on pages 570–572. It is repeated here for courses that do not cover Chapter 13 prior to this discussion. You may wish to read the section in Chapter 13 for more detail.

The following steps summarize how to account for factory overhead in a job-cost system:

1. Determine the number of overhead cost pools to be used, and select a cost driver to serve as a base for applying overhead costs for each cost pool. Examples of cost drivers include direct-labor hours, direct-labor costs, machine hours, and production setups.
2. Prepare a factory-overhead budget for the planning period, ordinarily a year. The two key items are (a) budgeted overhead and (b) budgeted volume of the cost driver. There will be a set of budgeted overhead costs and an associated budgeted cost-driver level for each overhead cost pool.
3. Compute the budgeted factory-overhead rate(s) by dividing the budgeted total overhead for each cost pool by the budgeted cost-driver level.
4. Obtain actual cost-driver data (such as machine hours) used for each product.
5. Apply the budgeted overhead to the products by multiplying the budgeted rate(s) in step 3 times the actual cost-driver data from step 4.

Using these steps, let's account for factory overhead for the Enriquez Machine Parts Company. Its manufacturing-overhead budget for 20X5 follows:

	Machining	Assembly
Indirect labor	$ 75,600	$ 36,800
Supplies	8,400	2,400
Utilities	20,000	7,000
Repairs	10,000	3,000
Factory rent	10,000	6,800
Supervision	42,600	35,400
Depreciation on equipment	104,000	9,400
Insurance, property taxes, etc.	7,200	2,400
Total	$277,800	$103,200

Enriquez selected a single cost driver in each department, machine hours in machining and direct-labor cost in assembly, for applying overhead. As Enriquez works on a product, it applies the factory overhead to the product using a budgeted overhead rate, computed as follows:

$$\text{budgeted overhead application rate} = \frac{\text{total budgeted factory overhead}}{\text{total budgeted amount of cost driver}}$$

The overhead rates for the two departments are determined as follows:

	Year 20X5	
	Machining	Assembly
Budgeted manufacturing overhead	$277,800	$103,200
Budgeted machine hours	69,450	
Budgeted direct-labor cost		$206,400
Budgeted overhead rate, per machine hour: $277,800 ÷ 69,450 =	$ 4	
Budgeted overhead rate, per direct-labor dollar: $103,200 ÷ $206,400 =		50%

Note that the overhead rates are budgeted; they are estimates. Accountants at Enriquez then use these rates to apply overhead based on actual events. That is, the total overhead applied to a particular product is the result of multiplying the budgeted overhead rates by the actual machine hours or labor cost used by that product. Suppose that at the end of the year Enriquez had used 70,000 machine hours in Assembly and incurred $190,000 of direct-labor cost in Assembly. It would have applied a total of $375,000 of overhead to the products produced:

Machining: actual machine hours of 70,000 × $4   = $280,000
Assembly: actual direct-labor cost of $190,000 × .50 =   95,000
Total factory overhead applied $375,000

The summary journal entry for this application follows

4b. Transaction: Factory overhead applied, $95,000 + $280,000 = $375,000.
    Analysis: The asset WIP Inventory is increased. The asset Factory Department
                 Overhead Control is decreased.
    Journal Entry: WIP Inventory 375,000
                        Factory Department Overhead Control 375,000

Finished Goods, Sales, and Cost of Goods Sold

Transactions 5 and 6 recognize the completion of production and the eventual sale of the goods. When Enriquez completes a particular job, it transfers the costs assigned to that job to Finished Goods Inventory, and when it sells the job those same costs become Cost of Goods Sold.

5. Transaction: Cost of goods completed, $2,500,000.
   Analysis: The asset Finished Goods Inventory is increased. The asset WIP Inventory
                is decreased.
   Journal Entry: Finished Goods Inventory 2,500,000
                       WIP Inventory 2,500,000
6a. Transaction: Sales on account, $4,000,000.
    Analysis: The asset Accounts Receivable is increased. The revenue account Sales
                is increased.
    Journal Entry: Accounts Receivable 4,000,000
                        Sales 4,000,000
6b. Transaction: Cost of goods sold, $2,480,000.
    Analysis: The expense Cost of Goods Sold is increased. The asset Finished Goods
                Inventory is decreased.
    Journal Entry: Cost of Goods Sold 2,480,000
                        Finished Goods Inventory 2,480,000

Finally transaction 7 in Exhibit 14-2 deals with differences between actual and applied overhead. In 20X5, Enriquez applied $375,000 of overhead to its products but actually incurred $392,000 of overhead costs. Because the extra $17,000 will not help the company generate any future revenue, we normally treat it as an expense, not an asset. We call it under-applied overhead because the amount applied is less than the amount incurred. The opposite, over-applied overhead, occurs when the amount applied exceeds the amount incurred. At year-end, the Enriquez Company disposes of under- or over-applied overhead through an immediate write-off by charging the $17,000 of under-applied overhead to cost of goods sold:

7. Transaction: Under-applied overhead, $17,000.
   Analysis: Cost of Goods Sold in increased and Factory Department Overhead Control
                is decreased.
   Journal Entry: Cost of goods sold 17,000
                       Factory Department Overhead Control 17,000

These seven transactions have accounted for all direct materials, direct labor, and factory overhead costs incurred during 20X5. As shown in Exhibit 14-2, all of these costs ended up in either Direct Materials Inventory, Work in Process Inventory, Finished Goods Inventory, or Cost of Goods Sold.

MAKING MANAGERIAL DECISIONS

Suppose you are a manager of a manufacturing department. Confirm your understanding of product costing in a job-order environment by indicating the transactions that occurred for each of the following journal entries. Which of these transactions records actual costs versus cost estimates?

1. WIP Inventory XXX
       Accrued Payroll   XXX
2. WIP Inventory XXX
       Factory Department Overhead Control . . .   XXX
3. Cost of Goods Sold XXX
       Finished Goods   XXX

Answer

The first entry records the actual cost of direct labor that the accounting system traces to the specific order being costed. We make the second entry when the order is completed to record the application of factory overhead. This is an estimate of the costs of indirect resources used to complete the order. The last entry records the cost of goods sold when the company ships the order. This cost is a mix of actual costs (direct material and direct labor) and estimated costs (applied factory overhead).

Activity-Based Costing/Management in a Job-Costing Environment

Regardless of the nature of its production system, the firm will always find resources that it can share among different products. The costs of these resources are part of the overhead the company's cost accounting system must account for. In many cases, the magnitude of overhead is large enough to justify investing in a costing system that provides accurate cost information. Whether we use this cost information for inventory reporting, to cost jobs, or for cost planning and control, most often the benefits of more accurate costs exceed the costs of installing and maintaining the cost system. As we have seen, activity-based costing usually increases costing accuracy because it focuses on the cause-and-effect relationships between work performed (activities) and the consumption of resources (costs).

Illustration of Activity-Based Costing in a Job-Order Environment

OBJECTIVE 3

Use an activity-based-costing system in a job-order environment.

We illustrate an activity-based-costing (ABC) system in a job-order environment by considering Dell Computer Corporation. Recall that Dell was the subject of the introduction to Chapter 13, p. 569. A few years ago, Dell adopted an ABC job-order costing system. What motivated Dell to adopt activity-based costing? Company managers cite two reasons: (1) the aggressive cost reduction targets set by top management and (2) the need to understand product-line profitability. As is the case with any business, understanding profitability means understanding the cost structure of the entire business. One of the key advantages of an ABC system is its focus on understanding how work (activity) is related to the consumption of resources (costs). So, an ABC system was a logical choice for Dell. And, of course, once Dell's managers improved their understanding of the company's cost structure, cost reduction through activity-based management was much easier.

Like most companies that implement ABC, Dell began developing its ABC system by focusing on the most critical (core) processes across the value chain. These were the design and production processes. After it put the initial system in place, Dell added the remaining phases of the value chain. Exhibit 14-3 shows the functions (or core processes)

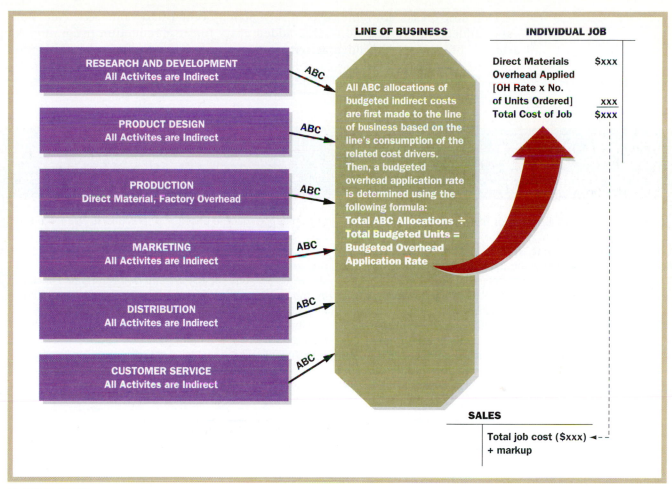

Exhibit 14-3
Dell Computer Corporation's Value Chain and ABC System

that add value to the company's products and how Dell assigns the costs of these functions to an individual job under the current ABC system.

To understand product-line profitability, Dell managers identified key activities for the research and development, product design, production, marketing, distribution, and customer service phases. Then, they used appropriate cost drivers to allocate activity costs to the produced product lines. While each of the phases shown in Exhibit 14-3 is important, we will focus on the product design and production phases. Product design is one of Dell's most important value-adding functions, providing a defect-free computer product that is easy to manufacture and reliable to use. Engineering costs (primarily salaries and CAD equipment depreciation) account for most of the design costs. These costs are indirect and thus Dell must allocate them to product lines using a cost driver.

The production costs include direct materials and factory overhead. Factory overhead consists of six activity centers and related cost pools: receiving, preparation, assembly, testing, packaging, and shipping. Facility costs (plant depreciation, insurance, taxes) are considered part of the production function and are allocated to each activity center based on the square feet occupied by the center.

Dell divided the total annual budgeted indirect cost allocated to a product line by the total budgeted units produced to find a budgeted overhead rate. It then used this rate, which is adjusted periodically to reflect changes in the budget, to cost individual jobs.

Dell now breaks down the costs in each activity center into value added and non-value added, and targets non-value-added costs for cost reduction programs. An example of a non-value-added activity is the preparation activity in the production function.

MAKING MANAGERIAL DECISIONS

Refer to Exhibit 14-3. One of the primary purposes of an ABC system is to increase the accuracy of product costs so that managers have a high level of confidence in cost-based decisions. Assume that you are a manager at Dell and that you have to determine prices for computers by adding a markup to the cost accumulated by the costing system. For example, if the accumulated total job cost is $1,200, a markup sufficient to "cover" all unallocated costs and provide a reasonable profit is added. Using the table below, determine whether the percentage markup under the ABC system is higher or lower than under the previous system. Which system gives you a higher degree of confidence that the price for a computer is adequate to cover all costs and provide a reasonable profit? Why?

Answer

Under the previous costing system, Dell determined prices by marking up only the cost of production. Thus, the markup was high so that the company would cover all the unallocated costs and also achieve a reasonable profit. Managers had a low level of confidence in this cost system. The ABC system provided estimates of all value-chain costs. The size of the markup was low, and the confidence level in the costs provided was high.

| | ABC or Unallocated | |
Value-Chain Function	Previous Costing System	ABC Costing System
Research and Development	Unallocated	ABC Allocations
Design	Unallocated	ABC Allocations
Production	Traditional Allocation	ABC Allocations
Marketing	Unallocated	ABC Allocations
Distribution	Unallocated	ABC Allocations
Customer Service	Unallocated	ABC Allocations

Summary Problem For Your Review

PROBLEM

Review the Enriquez illustration, especially Exhibit 14-2, page 623. Prepare an income statement for 20X5 through the gross profit line. Use the immediate write-off method for overapplied or underapplied overhead.

SOLUTION

Exhibit 14-4 recapitulates the final impact of the Enriquez illustration on the financial statements. Note how the immediate write-off means that we add the $17,000 to the cost of goods sold. As you study Exhibit 14-4, trace the three major elements of cost (direct materials, direct labor, and factory overhead) through the accounts.

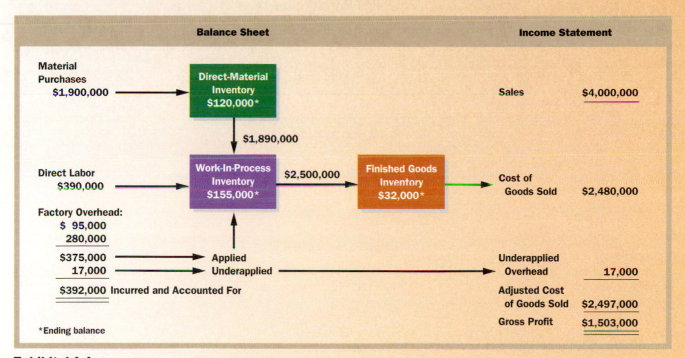

Exhibit 14-4
Relation of Costs to Financial Statements
* Ending balance.

Job Costing in Service and Nonprofit Organizations

So far, this chapter has concentrated on applying costs to manufactured products. However, the job-costing approach is used in nonmanufacturing situations, too. For example, universities have research "projects," airlines have repair and overhaul "jobs," and public accountants have audit "engagements." In such situations, the focus shifts from the costs of products to the costs of services, projects, or programs.

OBJECTIVE 4
Show how to use job costing in service organizations.

Service and nonprofit organizations do not usually call their "product" a "job order." Instead, they may call it a program or a class of service. A "program" is an identifiable group of activities that frequently produces outputs in the form of services rather than goods. Examples include a safety program, an education program, and a family counseling program. Accountants can trace costs or revenues to individual hospital patients, individual social welfare cases, and individual university research projects. However, departments often work simultaneously on many programs, so the "job-order" costing challenge is to "apply" the various department costs to the various programs. Only then can managers best allocate limited resources among competing programs.

In service industries—such as repairing, consulting, legal, and accounting services—each customer order is a different job with a special account or order number. Accountants can trace just costs, just revenues, or both to jobs. For example, automobile repair shops typically have a repair order for each car worked on, with space for allocating materials and labor costs. Customers see only a copy showing the retail prices of the materials, parts, and labor billed to their orders. Meanwhile, accountants trace the actual parts and labor costs of each order to a duplicate copy of the repair order, providing a measure of profit for each job. To get these actual costs, auto mechanics must enter their starting and stopping times on time tickets for each new order. This is why you might see them stamping a time card each time they start or end a job.

Budgets and Control of Engagements

In many service organizations and some manufacturing operations, job orders serve not only for product costing, but also for planning and control purposes. For example, a public accounting firm might have a condensed budget for 20X5 as follows:

Revenue	$10,000,000	100%
Direct labor (for professional hours charged to engagements)	2,500,000	25%
Contribution to overhead and operating income	$ 7,500,000	75%
Overhead (all other costs)	6,500,000	65%
Operating income	$ 1,000,000	10%

In this illustration,

$$\text{budgeted overhead rate} = \frac{\text{budgeted overhead}}{\text{budgeted direct labor}}$$
$$= \frac{\$6,500,000}{\$2,500,000}$$
$$= 260\%$$

To prepare a budget for each engagement, the partner in charge of the audit predicts the expected number of necessary direct-professional hours. Direct-professional hours are those that partners, managers, and subordinate auditors work to complete the engagement. The budgeted direct-labor cost is the pertinent hourly labor costs multiplied by the budgeted hours. Accounting firms charge partners' time to the engagement at much higher rates than subordinates' time.

How do such firms apply overhead? Accounting firms usually use either direct-labor cost or direct-labor hours as the cost driver for overhead application. In our example, the firm uses direct-labor cost. The budgeted total cost of an engagement is the direct-labor cost plus applied overhead, 260% of direct-labor cost in this illustration, plus any other direct costs.

This practice implies that partners require proportionately more overhead support for each of their hours charged. For example, one hour of partner work that has a direct-labor cost of $100 would result in a projected overhead support cost of $260. If this work can be done by a staff person whose charge rate is only $50, the projected overhead is only $130.

The engagement partner uses a budget for a specific audit that includes detailed scope and steps. For instance, the budget for auditing cash or receivables would specify the exact work to be done, the number of hours, and the necessary hours of partner time, manager time, and subordinate time. The partner monitors progress by comparing the hours logged to date with the original budget and with the estimated hours remaining on the engagement. Obviously, if the firm quoted a fixed audit fee, the profitability of an engagement depends on whether it can accomplish the audit within the budgeted time limits.

Accuracy of Costs of Engagements

Managers of service firms, such as auditing and consulting firms, frequently use either the budgeted or actual costs of engagements as guides to pricing and to allocating effort among particular services or customers. Hence, the accuracy of projected or actual costs of various engagements may affect pricing and operational decisions.

Suppose the accounting firm's policy for price quotes for engagements is 150% of total professional costs plus travel costs. The firm projects costs and sets the price on an auditing engagement as follows:

	Projected Cost	Price
Direct-professional labor	$ 50,000	$ 75,000
Applied overhead, 260% of direct-professional labor	130,000	195,000
Total costs excluding travel costs	$180,000	270,000
Travel costs	14,000	14,000
Total projected costs of engagement	$194,000	$284,000

Note that costs reimbursed by the client—such as travel costs—do not add to overhead costs and should not be subject to any markups in the setting of fees. Once the client accepts the offer, the firm needs to monitor the assignment of work as well as the overhead incurred to insure control of costs.

Process Costing Basics

Process Machinery, Inc., designs, builds, and installs conveyors that enable customers such as Nally & Gibson Georgetown, Inc., to access difficult quarry areas and lower operating costs. In this mine, owned and operated by Nally & Gibson Georgetown, Inc., limestone rock is mined from a quarry, and transported by a conveyor system built by Process Machinery to plant areas. Process Machinery uses a job-order costing system to determine the cost of building the conveyor for Nally & Gibson. Nally & Gibson uses a process-costing system to determine the costs of mining, crushing, transporting, processing, and storing limestone.

As indicated on page 620, an alternative to job costing is process costing. Before we examine the procedures of process costing, lets examine a real application. Don't look now, but you are most likely surrounded by the product produced by **Nally & Gibson Georgetown, Inc.** In fact, if you are in a typical residence or dormitory room, there are probably about 400 tons of this product close by—in the street and driveway, the sidewalk, the walls, and maybe even your toothpaste. What is it? Limestone. Nally & Gibson is a leading producer of limestone products used for industrial and commercial purposes. Limestone is used in highways, high school track beds, concrete sidewalks, buildings, soil enhancement products, residential homes, and about a million other places (yes, even in some toothpastes).

The making of limestone products is an excellent example of a process production system. A single output—limestone rock—is subjected to several processes that result in finished limestone products. The basic production processes that convert limestone rock into usable limestone are easy to understand and are reasonably simple. Basically, the limestone rock is mined from Nally & Gibson's quarry and mine in Georgetown, Kentucky, and transported to the processing facility. There it passes through several stages of crushing and grinding, depending on how fine the finished product needs to be. The ease and homogeneous nature of these processes might make you think that the cost accounting system used to track product costs should also be fairly simple and per-haps even unimportant to the success of the company. However, accurate and timely cost information is critical for both product costing and decision-making purposes at Nally & Gibson.

For example, the accurate allocation of the costs of mining and transporting limestone and then crushing the limestone to form the various products is essential to the success of the company. The company's cost accounting system accumulates the costs of these processes and then calculates an average cost per ton of product using a process-costing system. According to company president Frank Hamilton Jr., "If Nally & Gibson did not keep a handle on costs, we would not be here."

One of Nally Gibson's costs is transporting quarried rock from the mine to plants. Using trucks that have to travel up to a mile into the mine and then up a steep grade is expensive and hazardous. The solution was provided by **Process Machinery, Inc.**, who designed, constructed, and installed a 3,000-foot conveyor system used by Nally & Gibson. The accounting system used by Process Machinery for this job is an excellent example of a job-order system. There is a customer-specific product that requires a unique combination of resources.

The result—Nally & Gibson increased its production by up to 50% with increased safety and at a reduced cost. We can see from this example that the cost accounting sys-tem a company uses depends on the nature of its products and services. The cost infor-mation need by managers dictates the type of cost accounting system. Process Machinery's managers need costs for specific products that have unique features. Nally & Gibson's managers, whose product is crushed limestone, have much different cost-information needs.

Companies like Jelly Belly and Nally & Gibson that produce in a continuous process large quantities of a generic or homogeneous product, such as staples or sliced potato strips for french frying, do not use the job-costing techniques that you just learned. Why? Because a method called process costing is more efficient for such companies.

Why doesn't Nally & Gibson use a job-cost system to assign costs to its products? First, because there are no discrete jobs. The company does not wait for a specific cus-tomer order before producing the product. The company makes a forecast of the demand for the product and produces to meet this expected demand. Second, it is amazingly diffi-cult (and costly) to trace cost to a specific truckload of limestone. And there would be no benefit in doing so in terms of increased accuracy. So the cost-benefit criterion clearly dictates that the company determine unit costs using much larger quantities—say, a whole month's production.

As we noted early in this chapter, all product costing uses averaging to determine costs per unit of production. Sometimes those averages apply to a relatively small num-ber of units, such as a particular printing job produced in a job-order production sys-tem. Other times, the averages might have to be extremely broad, based on generic products from a continual-process production system, such as limestone road fill. Process-costing systems apply costs to like products that a company mass produces in continuous fashion through a series of production processes. These processes usually occur in separate departments, although a single department sometimes contains more than one process.

Process Costing Compared with Job Costing

It is easiest to understand process costing if you compare it with something you already know: job costing. Companies use job costing and process costing for different types of products. Firms in industries such as printing, construction, and furniture manufacturing, in which each unit or batch (job) of product is unique and easily identifiable, use job-order costing. When there is mass production through a sequence of several processes, such as mixing and cooking, we use process costing. Examples include chemicals, flour, glass, toothpaste, and limestone.

Exhibit 14-5 shows the major differences between job-order costing and process costing. Job order costing has one work-in-process for each job. In contrast, process costing requires one work-in-process account for each process. As goods move from process to process, accountants transfer their costs accordingly.

Consider Nally & Gibson's process-costing system. The company's production system has four core processes as shown in Exhibit 14-6. The company first obtains limestone rock from surface quarries or from mines. It then transports the rock to the plant by rail or truck. At the plant, the machines crush the rock and screen it to various sizes demanded by customers. The crushed limestone is then stocked in large piles of inventory for shipment. Each process requires resources. The direct-materials resource is the limestone rock itself. All four processes use direct-labor and overhead resources.

The process-costing approach does not distinguish among individual units of product. Instead, it accumulates costs for a period and divides them by quantities produced during that period to get broad, average unit costs. We can apply process costing to non-manufacturing activities as well as to manufacturing activities. For example, we can divide the costs of giving state automobile driver's license tests by the number of tests given, and we can divide the cost of a post office sorting department by the number of items sorted.

To get a rough feel for process costing, consider Magenta Midget Frozen Vegetables. This company quick-cooks tiny carrots, beans, and other vegetables before freezing them. It has only two processes, cooking and freezing. As the following T-accounts show, the costs of cooked vegetables (in millions of dollars) are transferred from the cooking department to the freezing department:

OBJECTIVE 5

Explain the basic ideas underlying process costing and how they differ from job costing.

Work in Process — Cooking			
Direct materials	14	Transfer cost of goods completed to next department	
Direct labor	4		
Factory overhead	8		
	26		24
Ending inventory	2		

Work in Process — Freezing			
Cost transferred in from cooking	24	Transfer cost of goods completed to finished goods	
Direct labor	1		
Factory overhead	2		
	27		25
Ending inventory	2		

We determine the amount of cost to be transferred by dividing the accumulated costs in the cooking department by the pounds of vegetables processed. We then multiply the resulting cost per pound by the pounds of vegetables physically transferred to the freezing department.

The journal entries for process-costing systems are similar to those for the job-order-costing system. That is, we account for direct materials, direct labor, and factory overhead as before. However, now there is more than a single work-in-process account for all units being manufactured. There is one work-in-process account for each processing department, Work in Process—Cooking and Work in Process—Freezing, in our example. The Magenta Midget data are recorded as follows:

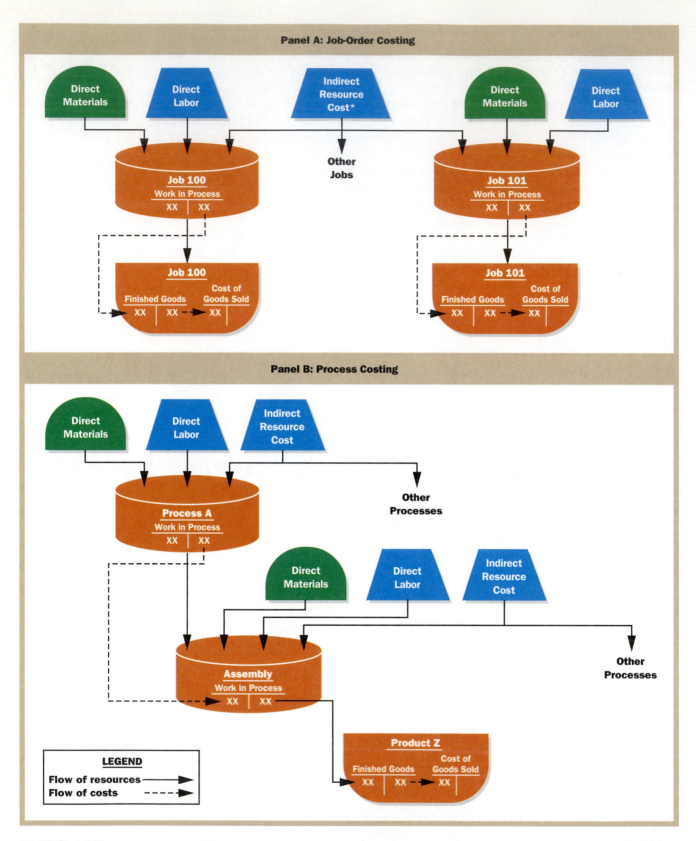

Exhibit 14-5
Comparison of Job-Order and Process Costing
* For simplicity, we show only one indirect-resource cost pool that has fixed-cost behavior. In reality, there would be several cost pools with fixed- and variable-cost behavior. Each of these indirect-resource-cost pools would be allocated using an appropriate cost driver.

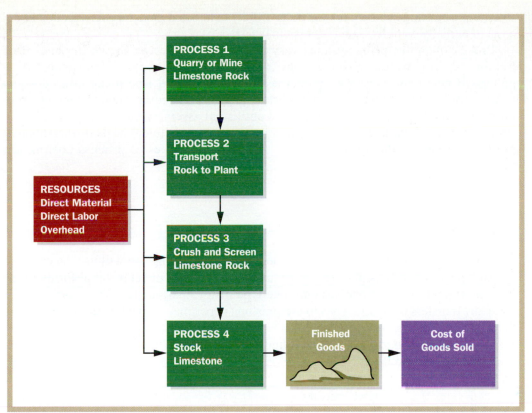

Exhibit 14-6
Process Costing at
Nally & Gibson

1. Work in Process—Cooking 14
   Direct-materials inventory 14
   To record direct materials used
2. Work in Process—Cooking 4
   Accrued payroll 4
   To record direct labor
3. Work in Process—Cooking 8
   Factory overhead 8
   To record factory overhead applied to product
4. Work in Process—Freezing 24
   Work in Process—Cooking 24
   To transfer goods from the cooking process
5. Work in Process—Freezing 1
   Accrued payroll 1
   To record direct labor
6. Work in Process—Freezing 2
   Factory overhead 2
   To record factory overhead applied to product
7. Finished goods 25
   Work in Process—Freezing 25
   To transfer goods from the freezing process

The central product-costing problem is how each department should compute the cost of goods transferred out and the cost of goods remaining in the department. If the same amount of work was done on each unit transferred and on each unit in ending inventory, the solution is easy. We simply divide total costs by total units. Then we use this unit cost to calculate the total cost of units transferred out and the remaining cost of unfinished units. However, if the units in the inventory are each partially completed, the product-costing system must distinguish between the costs of fully completed units transferred out and the costs of partially completed units not yet transferred.

Process manufacturing systems vary in design. The design shown in panel B of Exhibit 14-5 (as well as Exhibit 14-6) is sequential—units pass from process A to process B and so on until the product is finished. You will find many other designs in practice—each tailored to meet specific production requirements. For example, the firm can operate processes in parallel until final assembly. In this case, process A and process B might occur at the same time to produce different parts of the finished product. Whatever the specific layout, the basic principles of process costing are the same.

Application of Process Costing

To help you better understand our discussion of process costing, we will use the example of Oakville Wooden Toys, Inc. The company buys wood as a direct material for its forming department, which processes only one type of toy, marionettes. After forming, the company transfers the marionettes to the finishing department, where workers hand shape them and add strings, paint, and clothing.

The forming department manufactured 25,000 identical units during April, and its costs that month were

Direct materials		$ 70,000
Conversion costs		
Direct labor	$10,625	
Factory overhead	31,875	42,500
Costs to account for		$112,500

The unit cost of goods completed is simply $112,500 ÷ 25,000 = $4.50. An itemization would show

Direct materials, $70,000 ÷ 25,000	$2.80
Conversion costs, $42,500 ÷ 25,000	1.70
Unit cost of a whole completed marionette	$4.50

But what if not all 25,000 marionettes were completed during April? For example, assume that 5,000 were still in process at the end of April—only 20,000 were started and fully completed. All units—both those transferred out and those still in inventory—have received all the necessary direct materials. However, only the transferred units have received the full amount of conversion resources. The 5,000 marionettes that remain in process have received only 25% of conversion resources. How should the forming department calculate the cost of goods transferred and the cost of goods remaining in the ending work-in-process inventory? The answer lies in the following five key steps.

- Step 1: Summarize the flow of physical units.
- Step 2: Calculate output in terms of equivalent units.
- Step 3: Summarize the total costs to account for, which are the costs applied to work in process.
- Step 4: Calculate unit costs.
- Step 5: Apply costs to units completed and to units in the ending work in process.

We now work through each of these five steps. Keep in mind that each step provides managers with data that are useful for operational control purposes.

Physical Units and Equivalent Units (Steps 1 and 2)

Step 1, as the first column in Exhibit 14-7 shows, tracks the physical units of production. How should we measure the output—the results of the department's work? This tracking tells us we have a total of 25,000 physical units to account for, but not all these units count the same in the forming department's output. Why not? Because only 20,000 units were fully completed and transferred out. The remaining 5,000 units are only partially complete, and we cannot give partially completed units the same weight as the completed output. As a result, we have to state output not in terms of physical units but in terms of equivalent units.

Equivalent units are the number of completed units that the department could have produced from the inputs applied. For example, four units that are each one-half completed represent two equivalent units. If each unit had been one-fourth completed, the four together would have represented one equivalent unit. So, we determine equivalent units by multiplying physical units by the percent of completion.

In our example, as step 2 in Exhibit 14-7 shows, we measure the output as 25,000 equivalent units of direct-materials cost but only 21,250 equivalent units of conversion costs. Why do we have only 21,250 equivalent units of conversion costs but 25,000 of direct-materials cost? Because direct materials had been fully added to all 25,000 units. In contrast, only 25% of the conversion costs were applied to the 5,000 partially completed units, which would have been sufficient to complete only 1,250 units in addition to the 20,000 units that were actually completed.

Of course, to compute equivalent units, you need to estimate how much of a given resource was applied to units in process, which is not always an easy task. Some estimates are easier to make than others. For example, estimating the amount of direct materials used is fairly easy. However, how do you measure how much energy, maintenance labor, or supervision was used on a given unit? Conversion costs can involve a number of these hard-to-measure resources, which leaves you estimating both how much total effort it takes to complete a unit and how much of that effort has already been put into the units in process. Coming up with accurate estimates is further complicated in industries such as textiles, where there is a great deal of work in process at all times. To simplify estimation, some companies have decided that all work in process must be deemed either one-third, one-half, or two-thirds complete. In cases where continuous processing leaves roughly the same amount in process at the end of every month, accountants ignore work in process altogether and assign all monthly production costs to units completed and transferred out.

Measures in equivalent units are not confined to manufacturing situations. Such measures are a popular way of expressing workloads in terms of a common denominator. For example, radiology departments measure their output in terms of weighted units. Various X-ray procedures are ranked in terms of the time, supplies, and related costs devoted to each. A simple chest X-ray may receive a weight of one. But a skull X-ray may receive a

OBJECTIVE 6

Compute output in terms of equivalent units.

equivalent units
The number of completed units that could have been produced from the inputs applied.

Flow of Production	(Step 1) Physical Units	(Step 2) Equivalent Units	
		Direct Materials	Conversion
Started and completed	20,000	20,000	20,000
Work in process, ending inventory	5,000	5,000	1,250*
Units accounted for	25,000		
Work done to date		25,000	21,250*

* 5,000 physical units × .25 degree of completion of conversion costs.

Exhibit 14-7
Forming Department Output in Equivalent Units
Month Ended April 30, 20X4

weight of three because it uses three times the resources (for example, technicians' time) as does a procedure with a weight of one.

Calculation of Product Costs (Steps 3 to 5)

OBJECTIVE 7

Compute costs and prepare journal entries for the principal transactions in a process-costing system.

Exhibit 14-8 is a production-cost report. It shows steps 3 to 5 of process costing. Step 3 summarizes the total costs to account for (that is, the total costs in, or debits to, Work in Process — Forming). Step 4 obtains unit costs by dividing the two categories of total costs by the appropriate measures of equivalent units. The unit cost of a completed unit — materials cost plus conversion costs — is $2.80 + $2.00 = $4.80. Why is the unit cost $4.80 instead of the $4.50 calculated on page 636? Because the $42,500 conversion cost is spread over 21,250 units instead of 25,000 units. Step 5 then uses these unit costs to apply costs to products. The 20,000 finished units are complete in terms of both direct materials and conversion costs. Thus, we can multiply the full unit cost times the number of completed units to determine their costs. The 5,000 physical units in process are fully completed in terms of direct materials. Therefore, the direct materials applied to work in process are 5,000 equivalent units times $2.80, or $14,000. In contrast, the 5,000 physical units are 25% completed in terms of conversion costs. Therefore, the conversion costs applied to work in process are 1,250 equivalent units (25% of 5,000 physical units) times $2.00, or $2,500.

Journal entries for the data in our illustration would appear as

1. Work in Process — Forming 70,000
    Direct-materials inventory 70,000
   Materials added to production in April
2. Work in Process — Forming 10,625
    Accrued payroll 10,625
   Direct labor in April
3. Work in Process — Forming 31,875
    Factory overhead 31,875
   Factory overhead applied in April
4. Work in Process — Finishing 96,000
    Work in Process — Forming 96,000
   Cost of goods completed and transferred in April from Forming to Assembly

Exhibit 14-8
Forming Department Production Cost Report
Month Ended April 30, 20X4

		Total Costs	Details — Direct Materials	Details — Conversion Costs
(Step 3)	Costs to account for	$112,500	$70,000	$42,500
(Step 4)	Divide by equivalent units		÷25,000	÷21,250
	Unit costs	$ 4.80	$ 2.80	$ 2.00
(Step 5)	Application of costs			
	To units completed and transferred to the finishing department, 20,000 units @ $4.80	$ 96,000		
	To units not completed and still in process, April 30, 5,000 units			
	Direct materials	$ 14,000	5,000 ($2.80)	
	Conversion costs	2,500		1,250 ($2.00)
	Work in process, April 30	$ 16,500		
	Total costs accounted for	$112,500		

The $112,500 added to the Work in Process—Forming account less the $96,000 transferred out leaves an ending balance of $16,500:

Work in Process—Forming			
1. Direct materials	$ 70,000	4. Transferred out	
2. Direct labor	10,625	to finishing	$96,000
3. Factory overhead	31,875		
Costs to account for	112,500		
Bal. April 30	$ 16,500		

Summary Problem For Your Review

PROBLEM

Consider Nally & Gibson's plant operations in Georgetown. The plant processes limestone rock that is quarried in a nearby mine. Exhibit 14-6 (page 635) shows the various processing steps. Process 3 is crushing and screening the rock. To produce the crushed limestone, the company starts with limestone rocks from its quarry in Georgetown, Kentucky, and puts the rocks through a crushing process. Suppose that during May, the company quarried and shipped to its processing plant 288 tons of rock from its quarry, and at the end of the month 15 tons remained in process, on average 40% complete. The cost of rocks from the quarry for the last five months has been $120 per ton. Labor and overhead cost during May in the rock crushing process were $39,060. Assume there was no work-in-process at the beginning of May.

1. Compute the cost of crushed rock for production in May.
2. Compute the cost of the work in process inventory at the end of May.

SOLUTION

	(Step 1)	(Step 2) Equivalent Units in Tons	
Flow of Production	Physical Units (Tons)	Direct Materials	Conversion
Started and completed	273	273	273
Ending work in process	15	15*	6*
Units accounted for	288		
Work done to date		288	279

*15 × 100% = 15; 15 × 40% = 6.

		Details	
	Total Costs	Limestone Rock	Conversion Costs
(Step 3) Costs to account for	$73,620	$34,560	$39,060
(Step 4) Divide by equivalent units		÷ 288	÷ 279
Unit costs	$260.00*	$ 120.00	$ 140.00
(Step 5) Application of costs			
To units completed and			
transferred, 273 tons @ $260.00	$70,980		
To ending work in			
process, 15 tons			
Direct materials	$1,800	15 ($120.00)	
Conversion costs	840		6 ($140.00)
Work in process,			
ending inventory	$2,640		
Total costs accounted for	$73,620		

*Cost per ton ($260) = limestone rock costs ($120) + conversion costs ($140).

Effects of Beginning Inventories

OBJECTIVE 8

Demonstrate how the presence of beginning inventories affects the computation of unit costs under the weighted-average method.

So far, our example has been very straightforward because all units were started during the period. In other words, there were no units in beginning inventory. The presence of units in beginning inventory actually complicates matters a great deal.

So how do we account for product costs now that there are units in beginning inventory? We still use the same five steps as we did before, but now our results depend on which inventory system we use. The most popular inventory system is the weighted-average method. In the next two sections, we will explore this method using the following data from our Oakville example for the month of May. Recall that the ending work-in-process inventory for April in the forming department was 5,000 units. These units will be the beginning inventory for May.

Units
    Work in process, April 30: 5,000 units; 100% completed
       for materials, but only 25% completed for conversion costs
    Units started in May: 26,000
    Units completed in May: 24,000
    Work in process, May 31: 7,000 units; 100% completed
       for materials, but only 60% completed for conversion costs
Costs

Work in process, April 30		
Direct materials	$14,000	
Conversion costs	2,500	$ 16,500
Direct materials added during May		82,100
Conversion costs added during May ($14,560 + $42,160)		56,720
Total costs to account for		$155,320*

* Note that the $155,320 total costs to account for include the $16,500 of beginning inventory in addition to the $138,820 added during May.

Weighted-Average Method

weighted-average (WA) process-costing method

A process-costing method that adds the cost of (1) all work done in the current period to (2) the work done in the preceding period on the current period's beginning inventory of work in process, and divides the total by the equivalent units of work done to date.

The **weighted-average (WA) process-costing method** determines total costs by adding the cost of (1) all work done in the current period to (2) the work done in the preceding period on the current period's beginning inventory of work in process. Then you divide this total by the equivalent units of work done to date, whether that work was done in the current period or previously.

Why do we use the term *weighted-average* to describe this method? Primarily because the unit costs used for applying costs to products are based on the total cost incurred to date, regardless of whether those costs were incurred during or before the current period. If costs of materials, labor, or overhead changed from the last period, we use a weighted average to determine unit cost.

Exhibit 14-9 shows the first two steps in this method, computation of physical units and equivalent units. The computation of equivalent units ignores whether all 31,000 units to account for came from beginning work in process, or all were started in May, or some combination thereof. Exhibit 14-10 presents a production-cost report, summarizing steps 3 to 5 regarding computations of product costs.

Transferred-In Costs

transferred-in costs

In process costing, costs incurred in a previous department for items that have been received by a subsequent department.

Many companies that use process costing have sequential production processes. For example, Oakville Wooden Toys transfers the items completed in its forming department to the finishing department. The finishing department would call the costs of the items it receives **transferred-in costs**—costs incurred in a previous department for items that have been received by a subsequent department. They are similar to,

Flow of Production	(Step 1) Physical Units	(Step 2) Equivalent Units	
		Direct Materials	Conversion
Work in process, April 30	5,000 (25%)*		
Started in May	26,000		
To account for	31,000		
Completed and transferred out			
during current period	24,000	24,000	24,000
Work in process, May 31	7,000 (60%)*	7,000	4,200†
Units accounted for	31,000		
Work done to date		31,000	28,200

* Degrees of completion for conversion costs at the dates of inventories.
† .60 × 7,000 = 4,200.

Exhibit 14-9
Forming Department Output in Equivalent Units, Weighted-Average Method
Month Ended May 31, 20X4

but not identical to, additional direct-materials costs. Because transferred-in costs are a combination of all types of costs (direct-materials and conversion costs) incurred in previous departments, they should not be called a direct-materials cost in a subsequent department.

We account for transferred-in costs just as we account for direct materials, with one exception: We keep transferred-in costs separate from the direct materials added in the department. Therefore, reports such as Exhibits 14-10 will include three columns of costs instead of two: transferred-in costs, direct-materials costs, and conversion costs. The total unit cost will be the sum of all three types of unit costs. For an interesting look at how one major snack food company designed an ABC costing system with numerous transferred costs, see the Business First box on page 642–643.

		Totals	Details	
			Direct Materials	Conversion Costs
(Step 3)	Work in process, April 30	$ 16,500	$14,000	$ 2,500
	Costs added currently	138,820	82,100	56,720
	Total costs to account for	$155,320	$96,100	$59,220
(Step 4)	Divisor, equivalent units for work done to date*		31,000	28,200
	Unit costs (weighted averages)	$ 5.20	$ 3.10	$ 2.10
(Step 5)	Application of costs			
	Completed and transferred, 24,000 units ($5.20)	$124,800		
	Work in process, May 31, 7,000 units			
	Direct materials	$ 21,700	7,000 ($3.10)	
	Conversion costs	8,820		4,200* ($2.10)
	Total work in process	$ 30,520		
	Total costs accounted for	$155,320		

* Equivalent units of work done. For more details, see Exhibit 14-9.

Exhibit 14-10
Forming Department Production-Cost Report, Weighted-Average Method
Month Ended May 31, 20X4

Americans consume more than 300 million pounds of snack peanuts each year. The leading producer of snack peanuts is **Planters Specialty Products Company**, an operating unit of **Nabisco, Inc.** Planters markets regular-roast, dry-roast, salted, and unsalted peanuts in the United States. Processing a peanut snack food involves several activities. Most snack peanuts are blanched (removing the skins) before roasting. Peanuts can be oil-roasted or dry-roasted before being packaged and shipped.

What would an activity-based-costing system look like at a snack peanut company? First, let's look at the big picture. The major activities in the processing of peanuts are shown below. Note that in an ABC system, attention is focused on the operating relationships between major activities without regard to "departmental boundaries." In a traditional system, we typically would have a few operating departments such as the "blanching and frying department" and the "packing and shipping department." The receiving, moving, and storing activities would be part of the support (services) function or department in a

traditional system. While these departments still exist in a company using an ABC system, the focus is on understanding the interrelationships between activities without regard to departments. This focus translates into designing the cost accounting system to report costs by key activities.

Now, let's take a closer look at the blanching and frying activities and the related resources and the support activity, moving (see the top of page 643). To keep our presentation manageable, some resources, such as indirect materials and supervision, have been omitted. We describe the raw peanut blanching activity as follows, placing each resource consumed in italics. Blanching involves *operating labor* putting *raw peanuts* into a *blancher* machine. *Gas* is used to power the blanching activity and *maintenance labor* is also needed. The blanching machines occupy space, so a portion of *occupancy* costs are allocated to these machines. Note that cost behavior is depicted in this process map. For the blanching activity, raw peanuts and gas are variable-cost resources and the blancher, maintenance labor, operating labor, and occupancy are fixed-cost resources.

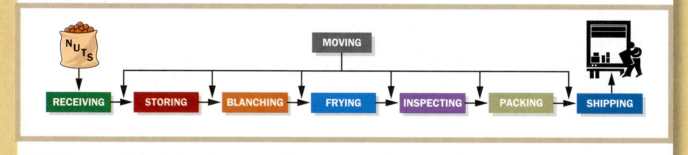

Summary Problem For Your Review

PROBLEM

Consider the cooking department of Middleton Foods, a British food-processing company. Compute the cost of work completed and the cost of the ending inventory of work in process using the weighted-average (WA) method.

Units
  Beginning work in process: 5,000 units; 100% completed for materials,
    40% completed for conversion costs
  Started during month: 28,000 units
  Completed during month: 31,000 units
  Ending work in process: 2,000 units; 100% completed
    for materials, 50% for conversion costs

BUSINESS FIRST

ACTIVITY-BASED COSTING AND PROCESS MAP AT A SNACK PEANUT COMPANY (Cont.)

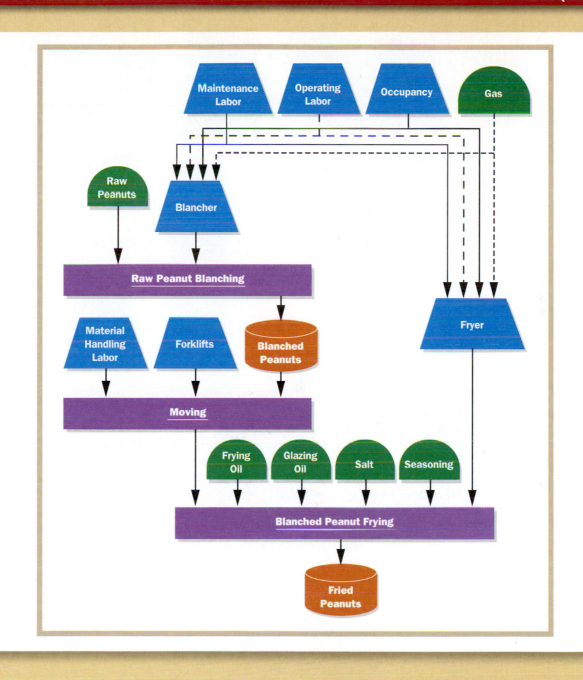

Costs

Beginning work in process		
Direct materials	£8,060	
Conversion costs	1,300	£ 9,360
Direct materials added in current month		41,440
Conversion costs added in current month		14,700
Total costs to account for		£65,500

SOLUTION

Flow of Production	(Step 1) Physical Units	(Step 2) Equivalent Units Material	(Step 2) Equivalent Units Conversion
Completed and transferred out	31,000	31,000	31,000
Ending work in process	2,000	2,000*	1,000*
Equivalent units	33,000	33,000	32,000

* 2,000 × 100% = 2,000; 2,000 × 50% = 1,000.

Weighted-Average Method	Total Cost	Direct Materials	Conversion Costs
Beginning work in process	£ 9,360	£ 8,060	£ 1,300
Costs added currently	56,140	41,440	14,700
Total costs to account for	£65,500	£49,500	£16,000
Equivalent units, weighted-average		÷33,000	÷32,000
Unit costs, weighted-average	£ 2.00	£ 1.50	£ 0.50
Transferred out, 31,000 × £2.00	£62,000		
Ending work in process			
Direct materials	£ 3,000	2,000 (£1.50)	
Conversion cost	500		1,000 (£.50)
Total work in process	£ 3,500		
Total costs accounted for	£65,500		

Process Costing in a JIT System: Backflush Costing

OBJECTIVE 9

Use backflush costing with a JIT production system.

Tracking costs through various stages of inventory—raw material, work-in-process, inventory for each process (or department), and finished goods inventory—makes accounting systems complex. If there were no inventories, we could charge all costs directly to cost of goods sold, and accounting systems would be much simpler. Organizations using just-in-time (JIT) production systems usually have very small inventories or no inventories at all. For them, a traditional accounting system that traces costs through several different types of inventories may be inappropriate or even useless. One such company is **Eagle-Gypsum Products Company.** The company operates in the Colorado Rockies and manufactures gypsum wallboard for commercial and residential use. Like many companies that use the JIT production system, Eagle-Gypsum has very low inventory levels and uses **backflush costing,** an accounting system that applies costs to products only when the production is complete. How does backflush costing work? As we shall see, it is a fairly simple costing system.

backflush costing

An accounting system that applies costs to products only when the production is complete.

Principles of Backflush Costing

Backflush costing has only two categories of costs: materials and conversion costs. Its unique feature is an absence of a work-in-process account. Accountants enter actual material costs into a materials inventory account, and they enter actual labor and overhead costs into a conversion costs account. They then transfer costs from these two temporary accounts directly into finished-goods inventories. Some backflush systems even eliminate the finished-goods inventory accounts and transfer costs directly to cost of goods sold, especially if the company does not keep finished goods in inventory but ships them immediately on completion. Backflush systems assume that production is completed so soon after the application of conversion activities that balances in the conversion costs accounts always should remain near zero. Costs are transferred out almost immediately after being initially recorded.

Example of Backflush Costing

Speaker Technology Inc. (STI) produces speakers for automobile stereo systems. STI recently introduced a JIT production system and backflush costing. Consider the July production for speaker model AX27. The standard material cost per unit of AX27 is $14, and the standard unit conversion cost is $21. During July, STI purchased materials for $5,600, incurred conversion costs of $8,400 (which included all labor costs and manufacturing overhead), and completed and sold 400 units of AX27.

Backflush costing is accomplished in three steps:

1. *Record actual materials and conversion costs.* For simplicity, we assume for now that actual materials and conversion costs were identical to the standard costs. As a company purchases materials, backflush systems add their cost to the materials inventory account:

```
Materials inventory ........................ 5,600
    Accounts payable (or cash) ........................ 5,600
To record material purchases
```

Similarly, we add direct labor and manufacturing overhead costs to the conversion-costs account when the company incurs them:

```
Conversion costs .......................... 8,400
    Accrued wages and other accounts ................... 8,400
To record conversion costs incurred
```

2. *Apply costs to completed units.* When production is complete, we transfer the costs from materials inventory and conversion-costs accounts to finished goods, based on the number of units completed and a standard cost of each unit:

```
Finished goods inventory (400 × $35) .......... 14,000
    Materials inventory ................................ 5,600
    Conversion costs .................................. 8,400
To record costs of completed production
```

Because of short production cycle times, there is little lag between additions to the conversion-costs account and transfers to finished goods. The conversion-costs account, therefore, remains near zero.

3. *Record cost of goods sold during the period.* We transfer the standard cost of the items sold from finished goods inventory to cost of goods sold:

```
Cost of goods sold ........................ 14,000
    Finished goods inventory ........................... 14,000
To record cost of 400 units sold @ $35 per unit
```

Suppose the company immediately delivers completed units to customers, so that finished goods inventories are negligible. We can combine steps 2 and 3 to eliminate the finished goods inventory account:

```
Cost of goods sold ........................ 14,000
    Material inventory ................................ 5,600
    Conversion costs .................................. 8,400
```

What if actual costs added to the conversion-costs account do not equal the standard amounts that are transferred to finished-goods inventory? We treat variances like overapplied or underapplied overhead. Backflush systems assume that account balances for conversion costs should be approximately zero at all times. We charge any remaining balance in the account at the end of an accounting period to cost of goods sold. Suppose actual conversion costs for July had been $8,600 and the amount transferred to finished goods (i.e., applied to the product) was $8,400. We would write off the $200 balance in the conversion-costs account to cost of goods sold at the end of the month:

```
Cost of goods sold . . . . . . . . . . . . . . . . . . . . . . . . 200
   Conversion costs  . . . . . . . . . . . . . . . . . . . . . . . . . . . . . . . 200
To recognize underapplied conversion costs
```

Summary Problem For Your Review

PROBLEM

The most extreme (and simplest) version of backflush costing makes product costing entries at only one point. Suppose Speaker Technology Inc. (STI) had no materials inventory account (in addition to no work-in-process inventory account). It purchases materials only when it needs them for production. Therefore, STI enters both materials and conversion costs directly into its finished goods inventory account.

Prepare journal entries (without explanations) and T-accounts for July's production of 400 units. As given earlier, materials purchases totaled $5,600, and conversion costs were $8,400. Why might a company use this extreme type of backflush costing?

SOLUTION

In one step, material and conversion costs are applied to finished goods inventories:

```
Finished goods inventories . . . . . . . . . . . . . . . . . . . 14,000
   Accounts payable  . . . . . . . . . . . . . . . . . . . . . . . . . . . . . . . . . 5,600
   Wages payable and other accounts  . . . . . . . . . . . . . . . . . . . 8,400
```

Finished Goods Inventories		Accounts Payable, Wages Payable, and Other Accounts	
Materials	5,600		5,600
Conversion costs	8,400		8,400

This example shows that backflush costing is simple and inexpensive. Backflush costing provides reasonably accurate product costs if (1) materials inventories are low (most likely because of JIT delivery schedules), and (2) production cycle times are short, so that at any time only inconsequential amounts of materials costs or conversion costs have been incurred for products that are not yet complete.

Highlights To Remember

1 **Distinguish between job-order costing and process costing.** Product costing is an averaging process. Process costing deals with broad averages and great masses of like units. Job-order costing deals with narrow averages and unique units or a small batch of like units.

2 **Prepare summary journal entries for the typical transactions of a job-costing system.** The focus of journal entries in a job-order-costing system is on inventory accounts. The WIP Inventory account receives central attention. Direct materials used, direct labor, and factory overhead applied are accumulated in WIP. In turn, the cost of completed goods is transferred from WIP to Finished Goods.

3 **Use an activity-based-costing system in a job-order environment.** Activity-based costing can be used for any type of business that has significant levels of shared resources. In a job-order system, ABC helps managers understand the cost structure of the business on a job-by-job basis. Overhead costs are assigned to activity centers and then to jobs based on appropriate cost drivers. Activity-based management uses ABC information and the increased understanding of the organization's cost structure to control and reduce overhead costs.

4 **Show how service organizations use job costing.** The job-costing approach is used in nonmanufacturing as well as in manufacturing. Examples include costs of services such as auto repair, consulting, and auditing. For example, the job order is a key device for planning and controlling an audit engagement by a public accounting firm.

5 **Explain the basic ideas underlying process costing and how they differ from job costing.** Process costing is used for inventory costing when there is continuous mass production of like units. Process-cost systems accumulate costs by department (or process); each department has its own work-in-process account. Job-order-cost systems differ because costs are accumulated and tracked by the individual job order.

6 **Compute output in terms of equivalent units.** The key concept in process costing is that of equivalent units, the number of fully completed units that could have been produced from the inputs applied.

7 **Compute costs and prepare journal entries for the principal transactions in a process-costing system.** There are five basic steps to process costing:

1. Summarize the flow of physical units.
2. Calculate output in terms of equivalent units.
3. Summarize the total costs to account for.
4. Calculate unit costs (step 3 ÷ step 2).
5. Apply costs to units completed and to units in the ending work in process.

Steps 3 and 5 provide the data for journal entries. These entries all involve the work-in-process accounts for the various departments (processes) producing products.

8 **Demonstrate how the presence of beginning inventories affects the computation of unit costs under the weighted-average method.** Process costing is complicated by the presence of beginning inventories. The weighted-average method includes the work done in previous periods on the current period's beginning inventory with work done in the current period to compute unit costs.

9 **Use backflush costing with a JIT production system.** Many companies with JIT production systems use backflush costing. Such systems have no work-in-process inventory account and apply costs to products only after the production process is complete.

Accounting Vocabulary

backflush costing, p. 644
equivalent units, p. 637
hybrid costing systems, p. 620
job costing, p. 620
job-cost record, p. 620

job-cost sheet, p. 620
job order, p. 620
job-order costing, p. 620
labor time tickets, p. 620
materials requisitions, p. 620

process costing, p. 620
time cards, p. 621
transferred-in costs, p. 640
weighted-average (WA) process-costing method, p. 640

Fundamental Assignment Material

14-A1 Job-Order Costing, Basic Journal Entries
The following data (in thousands) summarize the factory operations of the Hernandez Manufacturing Co. for the year 20X4, its first year in business:

a. Direct materials purchased for cash	$450
b. Direct materials issued and used	420
c. Labor used directly on production	125
d1. Indirect labor	80
d2. Depreciation of plant and equipment	55
d3. Miscellaneous factory overhead (ordinarily would be detailed)	40
e. Overhead applied: 180% of direct labor	?
f. Cost of production completed	705
g. Cost of goods sold	460

1. Prepare summary journal entries. Omit explanations. For purposes of this problem, combine the items in part d as "overhead incurred."
2. Show the T-accounts for all inventories, Cost of Goods Sold, and Factory Department Overhead Control. Compute the ending balances of the inventories. Do not adjust for underapplied or over-applied factory overhead.

14-A2 Basic Process Costing

CellTel, Inc., produces cellular phones in large quantities. For simplicity, assume that the company has two departments, assembly and testing. The manufacturing costs in the assembly department during February were

Direct materials added		$ 57,000
Conversion costs		
Direct labor	$50,000	
Factory overhead	40,000	90,000
Assembly costs to account for		$147,000

There was no beginning inventory of work in process. Suppose work on 19,000 phones was begun in the assembly department during February, but only 17,000 phones were fully completed. All the parts had been made or placed in process, but only half the labor had been completed for each of the phones still in process.

1. Compute the equivalent units and unit costs for February.
2. Compute the costs of units completed and transferred to the testing department. Also compute the cost of the ending work in process. (For journal entries, see problem 14-33.)

14-A3 Weighted-Average Process-Costing Method

The Magnatto Company manufactures electric drills. Material is introduced at the beginning of the process in the assembly department. Conversion costs are applied uniformly throughout the process. As the process is completed, goods are immediately transferred to the Finishing Department.

Data for the assembly department for the month of July 20X4 follow:

Work in process, June 30: $175,500 (consisting of $138,000 materials and $37,500 conversion costs); 100% completed for direct materials, but only 25% completed for conversion costs	10,000 units
Units started during July	80,000 units
Units completed during July	70,000 units
Work in process, July 31: 100% completed for direct materials, but only 50% completed for conversion costs	20,000 units
Direct materials added during July	$852,000
Conversion costs added during July	$642,500

1. Compute the total cost of goods transferred out of the assembly department during July.
2. Compute the total costs of the ending work in process. Prepare a production-cost report or a similar orderly tabulation of your work. Assume weighted-average product costing. (For journal entries, see problem 14-38.)

14-A4 Backflush Costing

Digital Controls, Inc., makes electronic thermostats for homes and offices. The Kansas City Division makes one product, Autotherm, which has a standard cost of $37, consisting of $22 of materials and $15 of conversion costs. In January, actual purchases of materials totaled $46,000, labor payroll costs were $11,000, and manufacturing overhead was $19,000. Completed output was 2,000 units.

The Kansas City Division uses a backflush-costing system that records costs in materials inventory and conversion costs accounts and applies costs to products at the time production is completed. There were no finished goods inventories on January 1 and 20 units on January 31.

1. Prepare journal entries (without explanations) to record January's costs for the Kansas City Division. Include the purchase of materials, incurrence of labor and manufacturing overhead costs, application of product costs, and recognition of cost of goods sold.
2. Suppose January's actual manufacturing overhead costs had been $21,000 instead of $19,000. Prepare the journal entry to recognize underapplied conversion costs at the end of January.

14-B1 Job-Order Costing, Basic Journal Entries

Consider the following data for Oxford Printing Company (in thousands):

Inventories, December 31, 20X4	
Direct materials	£ 18
Work in process	25
Finished goods	100

Summarized transactions for 20X5 are

a. Purchases of direct materials	£112
b. Direct materials used	98
c. Direct labor	105
d. Factory overhead incurred	90
e. Factory overhead applied, 80% of direct labor	?
f. Cost of goods completed and transferred to finished goods	280
g. Cost of goods sold	350
h. Sales on account	600

1. Prepare summary journal entries for 20X5 transactions. Omit explanations.
2. Show the T-accounts for all inventories, Cost of Goods Sold, and Factory Department Overhead Control. Compute the ending balances of the inventories. Do not adjust for underapplied or overapplied factory overhead.

14-B2 Basic Process Costing

Hassan Company produces digital watches in large quantities. The manufacturing costs of the Assembly Department were

Direct materials added		$1,620,000
Conversion costs		
Direct labor	$475,000	
Factory overhead	275,000	750,000
Assembly costs to account for		$2,370,000

For simplicity, assume that this is a two-department company, assembly and finishing. There was no beginning work in process.

Suppose 900,000 units were begun in the assembly department. There were 600,000 units completed and transferred to the Finishing Department. The 300,000 units in ending work in process were fully completed regarding direct materials but half-completed regarding conversion costs.

1. Compute the equivalent units and unit costs in the assembly department.
2. Compute the costs of units completed and transferred to the finishing department. Also compute the cost of the ending work in process in the assembly department. (For journal entries, see problem 14-34.)

14-B3 Weighted-Average Process-Costing Method

The Rainbow Paint Co. uses a process-costing system. Materials are added at the beginning of a particular process, and conversion costs are incurred uniformly. Work in process at the beginning of the month is 40% complete; at the end, 20%. One gallon of material makes one gallon of product. Data follow.

Beginning inventory	550 gal
Direct materials added	7,150 gal
Ending inventory	400 gal
Conversion costs incurred	$34,986
Cost of direct materials added	$65,340
Conversion costs, beginning inventory	$ 1,914
Cost of direct materials, beginning inventory	$ 3,190

Use the weighted-average method. Prepare a schedule of output in equivalent units and a schedule of application of costs to products. Show the cost of goods completed and cost of ending work in process. (For journal entries, see problem 14-37.)

14-B4 Backflush Costing

Audio Components, Inc., recently installed a backflush-costing system. One department makes four-inch speakers with a standard cost as follows:

Materials	$10.00
Conversion costs	4.20
Total	$14.20

Speakers are scheduled for production only after orders are received, and products are shipped to customers immediately on completion. Therefore, no finished goods inventories are kept, and product costs are applied directly to cost of goods sold.

In October, 1,500 speakers were produced and shipped to customers. Materials were purchased at a cost of $16,000, and actual conversion costs (labor plus manufacturing overhead) of $6,300 were recorded.

1. Prepare journal entries to record October's costs for the production of four-inch speakers.
2. Suppose October's actual conversion costs had been $5,900 instead of $6,300. Prepare a journal entry to recognize overapplied conversion costs.

Additional Assignment Material

Questions

14-1 "There are different product costs for different purposes." Name at least two purposes.

14-2 Distinguish between job costing and process costing.

14-3 Describe the supporting details for work in process in a job-cost system.

14-4 What types of source documents provide information for job-cost records?

14-5 State three examples of service industries that use the job-costing approach.

14-6 "Law firms use job-costing to cost engagements. Thus, the markup required to cover overhead costs is not as great as in companies that use a process costing system." Do you agree? Explain.

14-7 Give three examples of industries where process-costing systems are probably used.

14-8 Give three examples of nonprofit organizations where process-costing systems are probably used.

14-9 "There are five key steps in process-cost accounting." What are they?

14-10 Identify the major distinction between the first two and the final three steps of the five major steps in accounting for process costs.

14-11 Suppose a university has 10,000 full-time students and 5,000 half-time students. Using the concept of equivalent units, compute the number of "full-time equivalent" students.

14-12 Present an equation that describes the physical flow in process costing when there are beginning inventories in work in process.

14-13 How are transferred-in costs similar to direct materials costs? How are they different?

14-14 Explain what happens in a backflush-costing system when the amount of actual conversion cost in a period exceeds the amount applied to the products completed during that period.

Critical Thinking Exercises

14-15 Purposes of Accumulating Job Costs
"Job costs are accumulated for purposes of inventory valuation and income determination." State two other purposes.

14-16 Job-Order Compared to Process Costing
"The basic distinction between job-order costing and process costing is the breadth of the denominator." Explain.

14-17 Cost Allocation in Service Firms
"Service firms trace only direct-labor costs to jobs. All other costs are applied as a percentage of direct-labor cost." Do you agree? Explain.

14-18 Purpose of Product Costing in a Process Production Environment
All product costing uses averages to determine costs per unit of product produced. In job-order production systems, the averages are based on a relatively small number of units. In a process production environment, the number of units is much larger. Once the average unit cost is determined, what is the central product-costing problem in process costing?

14-19 Process Costing in a JIT Environment
Companies using JIT production systems usually have very small inventories or no inventories at all. As a result, a traditional accounting system may be inappropriate. Many of these companies have adopted backflush-costing systems. Do backflush-costing systems work only for companies using a JIT production system? Explain.

Exercises

14-20 Direct Materials
For each of the following independent cases, fill in the blanks (in millions of dollars):

	1	2	3	4
Direct-materials inventory, Dec. 31, 20X4	8	8	5	—
Purchased	5	9	—	8
Used	7	—	7	3
Direct-materials inventory, Dec. 31, 20X5	—	6	8	7

14-21 Direct Materials
Vermont Textile Company had an ending inventory of direct materials of $9 million. During the year, the company had acquired $15 million worth of additional direct materials and had used $12 million. Compute the beginning inventory.

14-22 Use of WIP Inventory Account
April production resulted in the following activity in a key account of Cheung Casting Company (in thousands):

WIP Inventory

April 1 balance	12
Direct materials used	50
Direct labor charged to jobs	25
Factory overhead applied to jobs	55

Job Orders A13 and A37, with total costs of $72,000 and $56,000, respectively, were completed in April.

1. Journalize the completed production for April.
2. Compute the balance in WIP Inventory, April 30, after recording the completed production.
3. Journalize the credit sale of Job A13 for $101,000.

14-23 Job-Cost Record

Western State University uses job-cost records for various research projects. A major reason for such records is to justify requests for reimbursement of costs on projects sponsored by the federal government.

Consider the following summarized data regarding a cancer research project in the Medical School:

- Jan. 5   Direct materials, various medical supplies, $925
- Jan. 7   Direct materials, various chemicals, $780
- Jan. 5–12 Direct labor, research associates, 120 hours
- Jan. 7–12 Direct labor, research assistants, 180 hours

Research associates receive $32 per hour; assistants, $19. The overhead rate is 70% of direct-labor cost.

Sketch a job-cost record. Post all the data to the project-cost record. Compute the total cost of the project through January 12.

14-24 Analysis of Job-Cost Data

Job-cost records for Ganz Construciton, Inc., contained the following data:

Job No.	Dates			Total Cost of Job at May 31
	Started	Finished	Sold	
1	April 19	May 14	May 15	$3,200
2	April 26	May 22	May 25	8,800
3	May 2	June 6	June 8	6,500
4	May 9	May 29	June 5	8,100
5	May 14	June 14	June 16	3,900

Compute Ganz's (1) WIP Inventory at May 31, (2) Finished-Goods Inventory at May 31, and (3) Cost of Goods Sold for May.

14-25 Analysis of Job-Cost Data

The Cabrillo Construction Company constructs houses on speculation. That is, the houses are begun before any buyer is known. Even if the buyer agrees to purchase a house under construction, no sales are recorded until the house is completed and accepted for delivery. The job-cost records contained the following (in thousands):

Job No.	Dates			Total Cost of Job at Sept. 30	Total Construction Cost Added in Oct.
	Started	Finished	Sold		
43	4/26	9/7	9/8	$180	
51	5/17	9/14	9/17	170	
52	5/20	9/30	10/4	150	
53	5/28	10/14	10/18	200	$50
61	6/3	10/20	11/24	115	20
62	6/9	10/21	10/27	180	25
71	7/7	11/6	11/22	118	36
81	8/7	11/24	12/24	106	48

1. Compute Cabrillo's cost of (a) construction-in-process inventory at September 30 and October 31, (b) finished-houses inventory at September 30 and October 31, and (c) cost of houses sold for September and October.
2. Prepare summary journal entries for the transfer of completed houses from construction in process to finished houses for September and October.
3. Record the cash sale (price = $345,000) and cost of house sold for Job 53.

14-26 Discovery of Unknowns

DeMond Chemicals has the following balances (in millions) on December 31, 20X4:

Factory overhead applied	$200
Cost of goods sold	500
Factory overhead incurred	215
Direct-materials inventory	30
Finished-goods inventory	160
WIP inventory	120

The cost of goods completed was $420. The cost of direct materials requisitioned for production during 20X4 was $210. The cost of direct materials purchased was $225. Factory overhead was applied to production at a rate of 160% of direct-labor cost.

Compute the beginning inventory balances of direct materials, WIP, and finished goods. Make these computations before considering any possible adjustments for overapplied or underapplied overhead.

14-27 Discovery of Unknowns

The Ramakrishnan Manufacturing Company has the following balances (in millions) as of December 31, 20X4:

WIP inventory	$ 14
Finished-goods inventory	205
Direct-materials inventory	65
Factory overhead incurred	180
Factory overhead applied	
at 150% of direct-labor cost	150
Cost of goods sold	350

The cost of direct materials purchased during 20X4 was $305. The cost of direct materials requisitioned for production during 20X4 was $265. The cost of goods completed was $523, all in millions.

Before considering any year-end adjustments for overapplied or underapplied overhead, compute the beginning inventory balances of direct materials, WIP, and finished goods.

14-28 Relationships Among Overhead Items

Fill in the unknowns:

	Case A	Case B	Case C
Budgeted factory overhead	$3,400,000	$?	$1,750,000
Budgeted cost drivers			
Direct-labor cost	$2,000,000		
Direct-labor hours		450,000	
Machine hours			250,000
Overhead application rate	?	$5	?

14-29 Process Map and Process Costing

Refer to Exhibit 14-5, panel B, on page 634. Identify an example of (1) a transferred-in cost, (2) a variable-cost resource, (3) a direct fixed-cost resource, and (4) an indirect resource cost for the process-costing system.

14-30 Equivalent Units

Confirm your understanding of the equivalent units concept by computing the equivalent units for material, direct labor, and overhead for the following hypothetical case at Nally & Gibson (refer to Exhibit 14-6, page 635).

In process 3—crush and screen limestone rock—400 tons of limestone rock were transported to the plant during March. There was no beginning inventory of rock. During March, 320 tons were crushed, screened, and stocked. At the end of March, 80 tons of rock were 40% crushed and screened. Direct labor and overhead are incurred evenly during the crushing and screening process.

14-31 Basic Process Costing

A department of Jamestown Textiles produces cotton fabric. All direct materials are introduced at the start of the process. Conversion costs are incurred uniformly throughout the process.

In April, there was no beginning inventory. Units started, completed, and transferred: 650,000. Units in process, April 30: 220,000. Each unit in ending work in process was 60% converted. Costs incurred during April: direct materials, $3,741,000; conversion costs, $860,200.

1. Compute the total work done in equivalent units and the unit cost for April.
2. Compute the cost of units completed and transferred. Also compute the cost of units in ending work in process.

14-32 Uneven Flow

One department of Dallas Instruments Company manufactures basic handheld calculators. Several materials are added at various stages of the process. The outer front shell and the carrying case, which represent 10% of the total materials cost, are added at the final step of the assembly process. All other materials are considered to be "in process" by the time the calculator reaches a 50% stage of completion.

Seventy-four thousand calculators were started in production during 20X4. At year-end, 6,000 calculators were in various stages of completion, but all of them were beyond the 50% stage and, on the average, they were regarded as being 70% completed.

The following costs were incurred during the year: direct materials, $205,520; conversion costs, $397,100. There were no work-in-process inventories.

1. Prepare a schedule of physical units and equivalent units.
2. Tabulate the unit costs, cost of goods completed, and cost of ending work in process.

14-33 Journal Entries

Refer to the data in problem 14-A2. Prepare summary journal entries for the use of direct materials, direct labor, and factory overhead applied. Also prepare a journal entry for the transfer of goods completed and transferred. Show the postings to the Work-in-Process account.

14-34 Journal Entries

Refer to the data in problem 14-B2. Prepare summary journal entries for the use of direct materials, direct labor, and factory overhead applied. Also prepare a journal entry for the transfer of goods completed and transferred. Show the posting to the Work-in-Process—Assembly Department account.

14-35 Physical Units

Fill in the unknowns in physical units:

| | Case | |
Flow of Production	A	B
Work in process, beginning inventory	1,500	4,000
Started	6,500	?
Completed and transferred	?	8,000
Work in process, ending inventory	2,000	3,300

14-36 Compute Equivalent Units

Consider the following data for 20X4:

	Physical Units
Started in 20X4	80,000
Completed in 20X4	90,000
Ending inventory, work in process	10,000
Beginning inventory, work in process	20,000

The beginning inventory was 80% complete regarding direct materials and 40% complete regarding conversion costs. The ending inventory was 20% complete regarding direct materials and 30% complete regarding conversion costs.

Prepare a schedule of equivalent units for the work done to date.

14-37 Journal Entries

Refer to the data in problem 14-B3. Prepare summary journal entries for the use of direct materials and conversion costs. Also prepare a journal entry for the transfer of goods completed, assuming that the goods are transferred to another department.

14-38 Journal Entries

Refer to the data in problem 14-A3. Prepare summary journal entries for the use of direct materials and conversion costs. Also prepare a journal entry for the transfer of the goods completed and transferred from the assembly department to the finishing department.

Problems

14-39 Job Costing at Dell Computer

Dell Computer Corporation's manufacturing process at its Austin, Texas, facility consists of assembly, functional testing, and quality control of the company's computer systems. The company's build-to-order manufacturing process is designed to allow the company to quickly produce customized computer systems. For example, the company contracts with various suppliers to manufacture unconfigured base Latitude notebook computers and then Dell customizes these systems for shipment to customers. Quality control is maintained through the testing of components, parts, and subassemblies at various stages in the manufacturing process.

Describe how Dell might set up a job-costing system to determine the costs of its computers. What is a "job" to Dell? How might the costs of components, assembly, testing, and quality control be allocated to each "job"?

14-40 Relationships of Manufacturing Costs

Selected data concerning the past fiscal year's operations of the Woodson Manufacturing Company are (in thousands)

	Inventories		
	Beginning	**Ending**	
Raw materials	$ 55	$ 75	
WIP	75	35	
Finished goods	90	110	
Other data:			
Raw materials used			$ 455
Total manufacturing costs charged to production during the year (includes raw materials, direct labor, and factory overhead applied at a rate of 80% of direct-labor cost)			851
Cost of goods available for sale			981
Selling and general expenses			50

Answer for each of the following items:

1. Compute the cost of raw materials purchased during the year.
2. Compute the direct-labor costs charged to production during the year.
3. Compute the cost of goods manufactured during the year.
4. Compute the cost of goods sold during the year.

14-41 Relationship of Subsidiary and General Ledgers, Journal Entries

The following summarized data are available on three job-cost records of Red Lake Manufacturing Company, a producer of packaging equipment.

| | Job 412 | | Job 413 | | Job 414 |
	April	May	April	May	May
Direct materials	$9,000	$2,500	$12,000	—	$13,000
Direct labor	4,000	1,500	5,000	2,500	2,000
Factory overhead applied	8,000	?	10,000	?	?

The company's fiscal year ends on May 31. Factory overhead is applied as a percentage of direct-labor costs. The balances in selected accounts on April 30 were direct-materials inventory, $19,000; finished-goods inventory, $18,000.

Job 412 was completed during May and transferred to finished goods. Job 413 was still in process at the end of May, as was Job 414, which had begun on May 24. These were the only jobs worked on during April and May.

Job 412 was sold, along with other finished goods, by May 30. The total cost of goods sold during May was $33,000. The balance in Cost of Goods Sold for sales through April 30 was $450,000.

1. Prepare a schedule showing the balance of the WIP Inventory, April 30. This schedule should show the total costs of each job record. Taken together, the job-cost records are the subsidiary ledger supporting the general ledger balance of work in process.
2. What is the overhead application rate?
3. Prepare summary general journal entries for all costs added to WIP during May. Also prepare entries for all costs transferred from WIP to Finished Goods and from Finished Goods to Cost of Goods Sold. Post to the appropriate T-accounts.
4. Prepare a schedule showing the balance of the WIP Inventory, May 31.

14-42 Job Costing in a Consulting Firm

Lubbock Engineering Consultants is a firm of professional civil engineers. It mostly does surveying jobs for the heavy construction industry throughout Texas. The firm obtains its jobs by giving fixed-price quotations, so profitability depends on the ability to predict the time required for the various subtasks on the job. (This situation is similar to that in the auditing profession, where times are budgeted for such audit steps as reconciling cash and confirming accounts receivable.)

A client may be served by various professional staff, who hold positions in the hierarchy from partners to managers to senior engineers to assistants. In addition, there are secretaries and other employees.

Lubbock Engineering has the following budget for 20X5:

Compensation of professional staff	$3,600,000
Other costs	1,449,000
Total budgeted costs	$5,049,000

Each professional staff member must submit a weekly time report, which is used for charging hours to a client job-order record. The time report has seven columns, one for each day of the week. Its rows are as follows:

- Chargeable hours
    Client 156
    Client 183
    Etc.
- Nonchargeable hours
    Attending seminar on new equipment
    Unassigned time
    Etc.

In turn, these time reports are used for charging hours and costs to the client job-order records. The managing partner regards these job records as absolutely essential for measuring the profitability of various jobs and for providing an "experience base for improving predictions on future jobs."

1. This firm applies overhead to jobs at a budgeted percentage of the professional compensation charged directly to the job ("direct labor"). For all categories of professional personnel,

chargeable hours average 85% of available hours. Nonchargeable hours are regarded as additional overhead. What is the overhead rate as a percentage of "direct labor," the chargeable professional compensation cost?

2. A senior engineer works 48 weeks per year, 40 hours per week. His compensation is $60,000. He has worked on two jobs during the past week, devoting 10 hours to Job 156 and 30 hours to Job 183. How much cost should be charged to Job 156 because of his work there?

14-43 Weighted Average Process Costing at Nally & Gibson

Nally & Gibson produces crushed limestone, among other products, used in highway construction. To produce the crushed limestone, the company starts with limestone rocks from its quarry in Georgetown, Kentucky, and puts the rocks through a crushing process. Suppose that on May 1, Nally & Gibson has 24 tons of rock (75% complete) in the crushing process. The cost of that beginning work-in-process inventory was $6,000. During May, the company added 288 tons of rock from its quarry, and at the end of the month 15 tons remained in process, on average one-third complete. The cost of rocks from the quarry for the last five months has been $120 per ton. Labor and overhead cost during May in the rock crushing process were $40,670. Nally & Gibson uses weighted-average process costing.

1. Compute the cost per ton of crushed rock for production in May.
2. Compute the cost of the work in process inventory at the end of May.
3. Suppose the flexible budget for labor and overhead was $16,000 plus $80 per ton. Evaluate the control of overhead and labor costs during May.

14-44 Process and Activity-Based Costing

Consider the potato chip production process at a company such as **Frito-Lay**. Frito-Lay uses a continuous flow technology that is suited for high volumes of product. At the Plano, Texas, facility, between 6,000 and 7,000 pounds of potato chips are produced each hour. The plant operates 24 hours a day. It takes 30 minutes to completely produce a bag of potato chips from the raw potato to the packed end product.

1. What product and process characteristics of potato chips dictate the cost accounting system used? Describe the costing system best suited to Frito-Lay.
2. What product and process characteristics dictate the use of an activity-based-costing system? What implications does this have for Frito-Lay?
3. When beginning inventories are present, product costing becomes more complicated. Estimate the relative magnitude of beginning inventories at Frito-Lay compared to total production. What implication does this have for the costing system?

14-45 Nonprofit Basic Process Costing

The IRS must process millions of income tax returns yearly. When the taxpayer sends in a return, documents such as withholding statements and checks are matched against the data submitted. Then various other inspections of the data are conducted. Of course, some returns are more complicated than others, so the expected time allowed to process a return is geared to an "average" return.

Some work-measurement experts have been closely monitoring the processing at a particular branch. They are seeking ways to improve productivity.

Suppose 3 million returns were received on April 15. On April 22, the work-measurement teams discovered that all supplies (punched cards, inspection check-sheets, and so on) had been affixed to the returns, but 40% of the returns still had to undergo a final inspection. The other returns were fully completed.

1. Suppose the final inspection represents 25% of the overall processing time in this process. Compute the total work done in terms of equivalent units.
2. The materials and supplies consumed were $600,000. For these calculations, materials and supplies are regarded just like direct materials. The conversion costs were $4,725,000. Compute the unit costs of materials and supplies and of conversion.
3. Compute the cost of the tax returns not yet completely processed.

14-46 Two Materials, Basic Process Costing

The following data pertain to the blending department at Pennsylvania Chemicals for April:

Units	
Work in process, March 31	0
Units started	60,000
Completed and transferred	
to finishing department	40,000
Costs	
Materials	
Plastic compound	$300,000
Softening compound	$ 80,000
Conversion costs	$240,000

The plastic compound is introduced at the start of the process, while the softening compound is added when the product reaches an 80% stage of completion. Conversion costs are incurred uniformly throughout the process.

The ending work in process is 40% completed for conversion costs. None of the units in process reached the 80% stage of completion.

1. Compute the equivalent units and unit costs for April.
2. Compute the total cost of units completed and transferred to finished goods. Also compute the cost of the ending work in process.

14-47 Materials and Cartons in Basic Process Costing

A Manchester, England, company manufactures and sells small portable tape recorders. Business is booming. Several materials are added at various stages in the assembly department. Costs are accounted for on a process-cost basis. The end of the process involves conducting a final inspection and adding a cardboard carton.

The final inspection requires 5% of the total processing time. All materials, besides the carton, are added by the time the recorders reach an 80% stage of completion of conversion.

There were no beginning inventories. One hundred fifty thousand recorders were started in production during 20X4. At the end of the year, which was not a busy time, 5,000 recorders were in various stages of completion. All the ending units in work in process were at the 95% stage. They awaited final inspection before being placed in cartons.

Total direct materials consumed in production, except for cartons, cost £2,250,000. Cartons used cost £290,000. Total conversion costs were £1,198,000.

1. Present a schedule of physical units, equivalent units, and unit costs of direct materials, cartons, and conversion costs.
2. Present a summary of the cost of goods completed and the cost of ending work in process.

14-48 Backflush Costing

Adirondak Meter manufactures a variety of measuring instruments. One product is an altimeter used by hikers and mountain climbers. Adirondak adopted a JIT philosophy with an automated, computer-controlled, robotic production system. The company schedules production only after an order is received, materials and parts arrive just as they are needed, the production cycle time for altimeters is less than one day, and completed units are packaged and shipped as part of the production cycle.

Adirondak's backflush-costing system has only three accounts related to production of altimeters: materials and parts inventory, conversion costs, and finished goods inventory. At the beginning of April (as at the beginning of every month), each of the three accounts had a balance of zero. Following are the April transactions related to the production of altimeters:

Materials and parts purchased	$287,000
Conversion costs incurred	$ 92,000
Altimeters produced	11,500 units

The budgeted (or standard) cost for one altimeter is $24 for materials and parts and $8 for conversion costs.

1. Prepare summary journal entries for the production of altimeters in April.
2. Compute the cost of goods sold for April. Explain any assumptions you make.

3. Suppose the actual conversion costs incurred during April were $94,600 instead of $92,000, and all other facts were as given. Prepare the additional journal entry that would be required at the end of April. Explain why the entry was necessary.

EXCEL Application Exercise

14-49 Value of Units Produced

Goal: Create an Excel spreadsheet to compute the value of units produced utilizing the weighted-average process costing method. Use the results to answer questions about your findings.

Scenario: The Magnatto Company has asked you to compute costs for the electric drills produced in their assembly department during the month of July. You will need to use the weighted-average process costing method to determine costs for beginning WIP, completed units and ending WIP. Additional background information for your spreadsheet appears in Fundamental Assignment Material 14-A3.

When you have completed your spreadsheet, answer the following questions:
1. At the end of July, what is the value of the 20,000 units remaining in the WIP ending inventory?
2. What were the materials, conversion, and total cost of goods amounts for the units transferred to the finishing department during the month of July?
3. What are the materials and conversion cost per unit amounts for the accumulated units and costs in July?

Step-by-Step:
1. Open a new Excel spreadsheet.
2. In column A, create a bold-faced heading that contains the following:
   Row 1: Chapter 14 Decision Guideline
   Row 2: Magnatto Company
   Row 3: Weighted-Average Process Costing for July, 20X4
   Row 4: Today's Date
3. Merge and center the four heading rows across columns A through K.
4. In row 7, create the following column headings justified as indicated:
   Column B: Number   Center-justify
   Column C: Percent Complete Merge and center across columns C and D
   Column E: Equivalent Units Merge and center across columns E and F
   Column G: Cost of Goods   Merge and center across columns G through I
   Column J: Cost per Unit   Merge and center across columns J and K
5. In row 8, create the following center-justified column headings:
   Column B: of Units
   Columns C, E, G, and J: Materials
   Columns D, F, H, and K: Conversion
   Column I: Total
6. In column A, create the following row headings:
   Row 9: Beginning WIP
   Skip a row
   Row 11: Units started
   Row 12: Less: Ending units
   Row 13: Units started & completed in July
   Row 14: Beginning units completed
   Skip a row
   Row 16: Accumulated units & costs in July
   Skip a row
   Row 18: Value of transferred units
   Note: Recommended column widths:
   Column A = 28
   Column B = 7
   Columns C, E, and J = 8
   Columns D, F, G, H, and K = 9
   Column I = 11

7. Format columns C and D as

| | **Number tab:** | Category: | Percentage |
| | | Decimal places: | 0 |

8. Use data from Fundamental Assignment Material 14-A3 to enter the following amounts:

Beginning WIP:	units, percent complete, cost of goods
Units started:	units
Less: Ending units:	units, percent complete
Accumulated units & costs in July:	cost of goods for materials and conversion
Value of transferred units:	units

9. Calculate the following amounts:

Units started & completed in July:	units, percent complete
Beginning units completed:	units, percent complete

10. In the sequence listed, use formulas to calculate the following amounts:

Equivalent units for:	Beginning WIP
	Less: Ending units
	Units started & completed in July
	Beginning units completed
	Accumulated units & costs in July
Cost per unit for:	Beginning WIP
	Accumulated units & costs in July
Materials cost of goods for:	Less: Ending units
	Units started & completed in July
	Beginning units completed
	Value of transferred units
Conversion cost of goods for:	Less: Ending units
	Units started & completed in July
	Beginning units completed
	Value of transferred units
Total cost of goods for:	Less: Ending units
	Units started & completed in July
	Beginning units completed
	Accumulated units & costs in July
	Value of transferred units
Cost per unit for:	Value of transferred units

11. Format columns B, E, F, G, H, and I as

	Number tab:	Category:	Number
		Decimal places:	0
		Use 1000 Separator (,):	Checked
		Negative numbers:	Red with parenthesis

12. Format columns J and K as

	Number tab:	Category:	Currency
		Decimal places:	2
		Symbol:	$
		Negative numbers:	Red with parenthesis

13. Format the cost of goods rows 9, 12, 16, and 18 as

	Number tab:	Category:	Accounting
		Decimal places:	0
		Symbol:	$

14. Modify the format of column B, rows 13 and 18, and row 16, columns E through I to display a top border using the default Line Style.

Border tab:	Icon:	Top Border

15. Modify the format of row 7, columns C, D, G, H, and I, and row 8, columns E, F, J, and K to display with a light gray fill.

Patterns tab:	Color:	Lightest Grey (above white)

16. Save your work to disk, and print a copy for your files.
Note: Print your spreadsheet using landscape in order to ensure that all columns appear on one page.

Collaborative Learning Exercise

14-50 Job and Process Costing

Form into groups of three to six students. For each of the following production processes, assess whether a job-cost or process-cost system is most likely to be used to determine the cost of the product or service. Also, explain why you think that system is most logical. (This can be done by individuals, but it is a much richer experience when done as a group, because the knowledge and judgment of several students interact to produce a much better analysis than a single student can produce.)

a. Producing Cheerios by **General Mills**.
b. Processing an application for life insurance by **Prudential**.
c. Producing a couch by **Ethan Allen**.
d. Building a bridge by **Kiewit Construction Co**.
e. Producing gasoline by **Chevron**.
f. Producing 200 copies of a 140-page course packet by **Kinkos**.
g. Producing a superferry by **Todd Shipyards**.

Internet Exercise ● www.prenhall.com/horngren

14-51 Process Costing at a Variety of Companies

Process costing assigns costs by measuring overall production costs and averaging them based on total production in units over a period of time, usually a month. The resulting average unit costs are then used to determine inventory cost and the cost of goods sold. Let's look at some companies and see if any of them might be candidates for using a process-costing system.

1. Log on to **Lands' End**'s Web site at http://www.landsend.com. Click on "General Information" on the left panel. What type of firm is Lands' End? What is its main activity? Do you think that the firm would be a good candidate for using a process-costing system? Why or why not?

2. Log on to **La-Z-Boy**'s Web site at http://www.lazboy.com. Click on "about LA-Z-BOY." What type of firm is La-Z-Boy? What is its main activity? Do you think that the firm would be a good candidate for using a process-costing system? Why or why not?

3. Log on to **Tasty Baking Company**'s Web site at http://www.tastykake.com. What type of firm is Tasty Baking Company? What is its main activity? Do you think that the firm would be a good candidate for using a process-costing system? Why or why not?

4. Refer to Tasty Baking Company's most recent annual report. What type of inventory accounts do you find? Where did you locate the information on inventory? Can you tell from the information provided what type of costing system that Tasty Baking Company uses?

Recommended Readings

APPENDIX

The following readings will aid readers who want to pursue some topics in more depth than is possible in this book. There is a hazard in compiling a group of recommended readings. Inevitably, some worthwhile books or periodicals are omitted. Moreover, such a list cannot include books published subsequent to the compilation date. The list is not comprehensive, but it suggests many excellent readings.

Periodicals

Professional Journals

The following professional journals are typically available in university libraries and include articles on the application of management accounting:

- **Accounting Horizons.** Published by the American Accounting Association; stresses current practice-oriented articles in all areas of accounting.
- **CMA Management.** Published by CMA Canada; includes much practice-oriented research in management accounting.
- **Cost Management.** Published by Thompson/RIA; stresses cost management tools.
- **Financial Executive.** Published by the Financial Executives International; emphasizes general policy issues for accounting and finance executives.
- **GAO Journal.** Covers managerial accounting issues of interest to the General Accounting Office of the U.S. government.
- **Harvard Business Review.** Published by Harvard Business School; directed to general managers, but contains excellent articles on applications of management accounting.
- **Journal of Accountancy.** Published by the American Institute of CPAs; emphasizes financial accounting and is directed at the practicing CPA.
- **Journal of Strategic Performance Measurement.** Covers issues related to performance measurement.
- **Management Accounting Quarterly.** Published by the Institute of Management Accountants; practical articles with an academic bent.
- **Strategic Finance.** Published by the Institute of Management Accountants; many articles on actual applications by individual organizations.
- **Business Week, Forbes, Fortune, The Economist, The Wall Street Journal.** Popular publications that cover a variety of business and economics topics; often their articles relate to management accounting.

Academic Journals

The academic journal that focuses most directly on current management and cost accounting research is the *Journal of Management Accounting Research*, published by the Management Accounting section of the American Accounting Association. *Accounting Horizons* is an American Accounting publication that bridges the gap between accounting research and practice. *The Accounting Review*, the general research publication of the American Accounting Association, and *Journal of Accounting Research*, published at the University of Chicago, and *Contemporary Accounting Research*, published by the Canadian Academic Association, cover all accounting topics at a more theoretical level. *Accounting, Organizations and Society*, a British journal, publishes much research on behavioral aspects of management accounting. *The Journal of Accounting and Economics* covers economics-based accounting research.

Books In Management Accounting

Most of the topics in this text are covered in more detail in the many books entitled *Cost Accounting* including *Cost Accounting: A Managerial Emphasis* by C. T. Horngren, G. Foster, and Srikant Datar (Prentice Hall, 2002). You can find more advanced coverage in *Advanced Management Accounting*, 3rd ed., by R. S. Kaplan and Anthony A. Atkinson (Prentice Hall, 1998).

The Financial Executives Institute, 200 Campus Drive, P.O. Box 674, Florham Park NJ 07960, and the Institute of Management Accounting, 10 Paragon Drive, P.O. Box 433, Montvale, NJ 07932–0674, have long lists of accounting research publications.

Handbooks, General Texts, and Case Books

The books in this list have wide application to management accounting issues. The handbooks are basic references. The textbooks are designed for classroom use but may be useful for self-study. The case books present applications from real companies.

- Bierman, H., Jr., C. Bonini, and W. Hausman, *Quantitative Analysis for Management*, 9th ed. Homewood, IL: Richard D. Irwin, 1997.
- Bierman, H., Jr., and S. Smidt, *The Capital Budgeting Decision*, 8th ed. New York: Macmillan, 1992. Expands the capital budgeting discussion in Chapter 11.
- Brinker, B. (ed.), *Guide to Cost Management*. New York: John Wiley & Sons, 2000.
- Davidson, S., and R. Weil, *Handbook of Cost Accounting*. Aspen Publishers, 1989.
- Lukka, K., and T. Groot (eds.), *Cases in Management Accounting: Practices in European Companies*. London: Financial Times Management, 2000.
- Manning, G., *Financial Investigation and Forensic Accounting*. Boca Raton, FL: CRC Press, 1999.
- Pryor, T., et al., *Activity Dictionary: A Comprehensive Reference Tool for ABM and ABC*: 2000 Edition. Arlington, TX: ICMS, Inc., 2000.
- Rotch, W., B. Allen, and R. Brownlee, *Cases in Management Accounting and Control Systems*, 3rd ed. Upper Saddle River, NJ: Prentice Hall, 1995.
- Shank, J., *Cases in Cost Management: A Strategic Emphasis*, 2nd ed. Cincinnati, OH: South-Western, 2000.

Strategic Nature of Management Accounting

Management accountants realize that cost and performance information is most useful to organizations when it helps define strategic alternatives and helps in the management of resources to achieve strategic objectives. The books in this list, though not necessarily accounting books, provide valuable foundation to the interaction of strategy and accounting information.

- Ansari, S., and J. Bell, *Target Costing: The Next Frontier in Strategic Cost Management*. Chicago: Irwin, 1997.
- Grant, J. L., Foundations of Economic Valued Added, 2nd ed. New York: Wiley, 2002.
- Hronec, S., *Vital Signs*. New York: Amacom, 1993.
- Porter, M., *The Michael Porter Trilogy*. New York: Free Press, 1998.
- Rappaport, A., *Creating Shareholder Value: A Guide for Manager's and Investors*. New York: Free Press, 1997.
- Small, P., *The Ultimate Game of Strategy: Establishing a Personal Niche in the World of e-Business*. Upper Saddle River, NJ: Prentice Hall, 2001.
- Stern, J., J. Shiely, and I. Ross, *The EVA Challenge: Implementing Value Added Change in an Organization*. New York: Wiley, 2001.
- Stewart, G., *The Quest for Value*. New York: Harper Business, 1999.

owns and expects to provide future benefits. **Liabilities** are the entity's economic obliga-tions to nonowners. **Owners' equity** is the excess of the assets over the liabilities. You can think of the balance sheet as an equation:

$$\text{assets} = \text{liabilities} + \text{owners' equity}$$

Because the owners of a corporation are its stockholders, we call the owners' equity of a corporation **stockholders' equity.** In turn, the stockholders' equity is composed of (1) **paid-in capital,** the ownership claim arising from funds paid in by the owners, plus (2) **retained earn-ings** (or **retained income**) the ownership claim arising from reinvestment of previous profits:

$$\begin{aligned}\text{assets} &= \text{liabilities} + \text{stockholders' equity}\\ &= \text{liabilities} + (\text{paid-in capital} + \text{retained earnings})\end{aligned}$$

Consider a summary of King Hardware's transactions in March (including the initial investment on February 28):

1. Initial investment by owners, $100,000 cash.
2. Acquisition of inventory for $75,000 cash.
3. Acquisition of inventory for $35,000 on open account. A purchase on open account allows the buyer to pay cash some time after the date of sale, often in 30 days. Amounts owed to vendors for purchases on open accounts are **accounts payable,** liabilities of the purchasing entity.
4. Merchandise carried in inventory at a cost of $100,000 was sold on open account for $120,000. The amounts due from customers for sales on open accounts are **accounts receivable,** assets of the selling entity.
5. Cash collections of accounts receivable, $15,000.
6. Cash payments of accounts payable, $20,000.
7. On March 1, King Hardware paid $3,000 cash for store rent for March, April, and May. Rent is $1,000 per month, payable quarterly in advance, beginning March 1.

We can analyze the preceding transactions using the balance sheet equation, as shown in Exhibit 15-1. Note that most of these are summarized transactions. For example, all the sales did not occur at once, nor did all purchases of inventory, collections from customers, or dis-bursements to suppliers. Many repetitive transactions occur in practice, and accountants use specialized data collection techniques to measure and aggregate the effects of the transactions on the organization. Consider Microsoft's sales of Xboxes. It sells thousands of Xboxes during a year, but accountants add together all the sales amounts as a single number for sales.

King Hardware's transaction 1, the initial investment by owners, increases assets and increases stockholders' equitiy. That is, cash increases and so does paid-in capital—the claim arising from the owners' total initial investment in the corporation.

Transaction 2, the purchase of inventory for cash, is an exchange of one asset for another. Neither total assets nor claims on those assets changes. Transaction 3 adds both an asset and a liability.

Transaction 4 is the sale of $100,000 of inventory for $120,000. Two things happened simultaneously: The company acquires a new asset, Accounts Receivable (4a), in exchange for the giving up of Inventory (4b), and the retained earnings portion of Stockholders' Equity increases by the amount of the asset received ($120,000) and decreases by the amount of the asset given up ($100,000). The $20,000 net increase in retained earnings represents stockholders' claims arising from the profitable sale.

Transaction 5, cash collection of accounts receivable, is another example of an event that has no impact on stockholders' equity. Collections are merely the transformation of one asset (Accounts Receivable) into another (Cash).

Transaction 6, cash payment of accounts payable, also does not affect stockholders' equity—it affects assets and liabilities only. In general, collections from customers and payments to suppliers have no direct impact on stockholders' equity.

OBJECTIVE 2

Analyze typical business transactions using the balance sheet equation.

Management Accounting in Nonprofit Organizations

Many books discuss management accounting in nonprofit organizations, especially in health care. Four examples are

- Anthony, R.N., and D.W. Young, *Management Control in Nonprofit Organizations*, 7th ed. Homewood, IL: Irwin, 2003.
- Brimson, J., and J. Antos, *Activity Based Management for Service Industries, Government Entities, and Non-Profit Organizations*. New York: Wiley, 1998.
- Herzlinger, R., and D. Nitterhouse, *Financial Accounting and Managerial Control for Nonprofit Organizations*. Cincinnati, OH: South-Western Publishing Co., 1994.
- Neumann, B., and K. Boles, *Management Accounting for Healthcare Organizations*, 5th ed. Precept Press, 1998.

Books in Financial Accounting

This book's companion volume, *Introduction to Financial Accounting*, provides an expansion of the financial accounting material (Chapters 15–17). A more detailed coverage of the topics can be found in books entitled *Intermediate Accounting* including that by D. Kieso, J. Weygandt, and T. Warfield (John Wiley, 2003).

Opinions of the Accounting Principles Board are available from the American Institute of CPAs, 1211 Avenue of the Americas, New York, NY 10036–8775. The institute also has a series of research studies on a variety of topics. The pronouncements of the Financial Accounting Standards Board are available from the board's offices, 401 Merritt 7, P.O. Box 5116, Norwalk, CT 06856–5116.

Financial accounting has such an extensive body of literature that it is impossible to provide a short list of books that adequately covers the field. However, we will mention a few books that cover a wide range of issues. For a historical perspective on the large firms practicing accounting, see two books by M. Stevens, *The Accounting Wars* (Macmillan, 1985) and *The Big Six* (Touchstone Books, 1992). The interaction of financial reporting and management's economic incentives is covered in text and readings in R. Ball and C. Smith, *The Economics of Accounting Policy Choice* (McGraw-Hill, 1992). Application of this research to financial statement analysis is provided in C. Stickney, J. Wahlen, and P. Brown *Financial Reporting and Statement Analysis*, 4th ed. (South-Western, 2003) or G. White, A. Sondi and D. Fried, The *Analysis and Use of Financial Statements*, 3rd ed. (New York: Wiley, 2003).

Online Resources

The online resources are too extensive for a comprehensive list. The best way to access them may be to use a good search routine. However, we will list a few URLs that can help you get started:

- AICPA's Center for Excellence in Financial Management: Information for CPAs in business and industry at http://www.aicpa.org/cefm/index.htm.
- Better Management.com: Includes materials on both activity-based management and balanced scorecard at http://www.bettermanagement.com.
- CMA Canada: Many services including Strategic Management Accounting Practices and Management Accounting Standards at http://www.cma-canada.org/cmacan.
- Consortium for Advanced Manufacturing International (CAM-I): Online library at http://www.cam-i.org/Web_store/web_store.cgi?page=management.html.

- Economic Profit Frontiers: Additional information about economic value added at http://www.epfrontiers.com.
- Financial Executives International: Information for corporate financial officers at http://www.fei.org.
- Hyperion Solutions: Software for both activity-based management and the balanced scorecard at http://www.hyperion.com/.
- Institute of Management Accountants: A variety of services including index of research publications at http://www.imanet.org/.
- Metrus Group: A variation of the balance scorecard at http://www.metrus.com/spg.shtml.
- Stern Stewart: Information about economic value added by the firm that developed the technique at http://www.eva.com/.

The following King Hardware income statement summarizes the company's revenues and expenses for the month of March:

King Hardware Co.
Income Statement for the Month Ended March 31, 20X1

Revenues (sales)		$120,000
Expenses		
Cost of goods sold	$100,000	
Rent	1,000	
Total expenses		101,000
Net income		$ 19,000

The income statement is the major link between balance sheets:

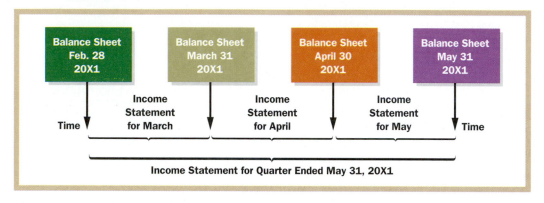

Income Statement for Quarter Ended May 31, 20X1

Notice that each balance sheet is a snapshot at the end of a month. In contrast, each income statement summarizes events during the month that caused changes in the balance sheet. Examine the changes in retained earnings in Exhibit 15-1. The revenues and expenses during March explain why retained earnings changed from $0 at the beginning of the month to $19,000 at the end of the month. The income statement measures financial performance during the month, while the balance sheet measures financial position at the end of the month.

account
Each item in a financial statement.

Each item in a financial statement is an **account**. Expense accounts are basically negative elements of the stockholders' equity account. Similarly, the sales (revenue) account is a positive element of stockholders' equity.

Real income statements and balance sheets use the same formats as those for King Hardware, though they usually contain more details. Consider Microsoft, the world's largest software company. A simplified version of its balance sheet follows (in millions):

Microsoft Corporation
Balance Sheet June 30, 2003

Assets		Liabilities and Stockholders' Equity	
Cash and short-term investments	$49,048	Liabilities	$18,551
Accounts receivable	5,196	Stockholders' equity:	
Other assets	25,327	Paid-in capital	35,344
		Retained earnings	25,676
Total assets	$79,571	Total liabilities & stockholders' equity	$79,571

Microsoft's condensed income statement shows that retained earnings increased by $9,993 million because of profitable operations in 2003 (in millions):

Microsoft Corporation
Income Statement for the Year Ended June 30, 2003

Sales	$32,187
Expenses	22,194
Net income	$ 9,993

Nature of Interest

Interest is the cost of using money. It is the rental charge for cash, just as rental charges are often made for the use of automobiles or boats.

Interest does not always entail an outlay of cash. The concept of interest applies to ownership funds as well as to borrowed funds. The reason why interest must be considered on *all* funds in use, regardless of their source, is that the selection of one alternative necessarily commits funds that could otherwise be invested in some other opportunity. The measure of the interest in such cases is the return foregone by rejecting the alternative use. For instance, a wholly owned home or business asset is not cost free. The funds so invested could alternatively be invested in government bonds or in some other venture. The measure of this opportunity cost depends on what alternative incomes are available.

Newspapers often contain advertisements of financial institutions citing interest rates that are "compounded." This appendix explains compound interest, including the use of present-value tables.

Simple interest is calculated by multiplying an interest rate by an unchanging principal amount. In contrast, *compound interest* is calculated by multiplying an interest rate by a principal amount that is increased each interest period by the previously accumulated (unpaid) interest. The accumulated interest is added to the principal to become the principal for the new period. For example, suppose you deposited $10,000 in a financial institution that promised to pay 10% interest per annum. You then let the amount accumulate for three years before withdrawing the full balance of the deposit. The *simple-interest* deposit would accumulate to $13,000 at the end of three years:

	Principal	Simple Interest	Balance, End of Year
Year 1	$10,000	$10,000 × 0.10 = $1,000	$11,000
Year 2	10,000	10,000 × 0.10 = 1,000	12,000
Year 3	10,000	10,000 × 0.10 = 1,000	13,000

Compound interest provides interest on interest. That is, the principal changes from period to period. The deposit would accumulate to $10,000 \times (1.10)^3 = \$10,000 \times 1.331 = \$13,310$:

	Principal	Compound Interest	Balance, End of Year
Year 1	$10,000	$10,000 × 0.10 = $1,000	$11,000
Year 2	11,000	11,000 × 0.10 = 1,100	12,100
Year 3	12,100	12,100 × 0.10 = 1,210	13,310

The "force" of compound interest can be staggering. For example, the same deposit would accumulate as follows:

	At End of		
	10 Years	*20 Years*	*40 Years*
Simple interest			
$10,000 + 10 ($1,000) =	$20,000		
$10,000 + 20 ($1,000) =		$30,000	
$10,000 + 40 ($1,000) =			$50,000
Compound interest			
$10,000 \times (1.10)^{10} = \$10,000 \times 2.5937 =$	$25,937		
$10,000 \times (1.10)^{20} = \$10,000 \times 6.7275 =$		$67,275	
$10,000 \times (1.10)^{40} = \$10,000 \times 45.2593 =$			$452,593

Hand calculations of compound interest quickly become burdensome. Therefore compound interest tables have been constructed to ease computations. (Indeed, many hand-held calculators contain programs that provide speedy answers.) Hundreds of tables are available, but we will use only the two most useful for capital budgeting.[1]

Table 1: Present Value of $1

How shall we express a future cash inflow or outflow in terms of its equivalent today (at time zero)? Table 1 provides factors that give the present value of a single, lump-sum cash flow to be received or paid at the end of a future period.[2]

Suppose you invest $1.00 today. It will grow to $1.06 in one year at six percent interest; that is, $1 \times 1.06 = $1.06. At the end of the second year its value is ($1 \times 1.06) \times 1.06 = $1 \times (1.06)^2 = $1.124, and at the end of the third year it is $1 \times (1.06)^3 = 1.191. In general, $1.00 grows to $(1 + i)^n$ in n years at i percent interest.

To determine *the present value*, you reverse this accumulation process. If $1.00 is to be received in one year, it is worth $1 \div 1.06 = $0.9434 today at an interest rate of 6%. Suppose you invest $0.9434 today. In one year you will have $0.9434 \times 1.06 = $1.00. Thus $0.9434 is the *present value* of $1.00 a year hence at 6%. If the dollar will be received in two years, its present value is $1.00 \div (1.06)^2 = $0.8900. The general formula for the present value (*PV*) of an amount S to be received or paid in n periods at an interest rate of $i\%$ per period is

$$PV = \frac{S}{(1+i)^n}$$

Table 1 on page 821 gives factors for the present value of $1.00 at various interest rates over several different periods. Present values are also called *discounted* values, and the process of finding the present value is *discounting.* You can think of this as discounting (decreasing) the value of a future cash inflow or outflow. Why is the value discounted? Because the cash is to be received or paid in the future, not today.

Assume that a prominent city is issuing a 3-year non-interest-bearing note payable that promises to pay a lump sum of $1,000 exactly three years from now. You desire a rate of return of exactly 6%, compounded annually. How much would you be willing to pay now for the 3-year note? The situation is sketched as follows:

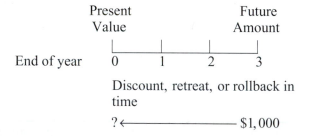

The factor in the period 3 row and 6% column of Table 1 is 0.8396. The present value of the $1,000 payment is $1,000 \times 0.8396 = $839.60. You would be willing to pay $839.60 for the $1,000 to be received in three years.

---

[1]*For additional tables, see R. Vichas,* Handbook of Financial Mathematics, Formulas and Tables *(Upper Saddle River, NJ: Prentice Hall, 1979).*

[2]*The factors are rounded to four decimal places. The examples in this text use these rounded factors. If you use tables with different rounding, or if you use a calculator or personal computer, your answers may differ from those given because of a small rounding error.*

Table 1

Present Value of $1

$$PV = \frac{1}{(1+i)^n}$$

Periods	3%	4%	5%	6%	7%	8%	10%	12%	14%	16%	18%	20%	22%	24%	25%	26%	28%	30%	40%
1	.9709	.9615	.9524	.9434	.9346	.9259	.9091	.8929	.8772	.8621	.8475	.8333	.8197	.8065	.8000	.7937	.7813	.7692	.7143
2	.9426	.9246	.9070	.8900	.8734	.8573	.8264	.7972	.7695	.7432	.7182	.6944	.6719	.6504	.6400	.6299	.6104	.5917	.5102
3	.9151	.8890	.8638	.8396	.8163	.7938	.7513	.7118	.6750	.6407	.6086	.5787	.5507	.5245	.5120	.4999	.4768	.4552	.3644
4	.8885	.8548	.8227	.7921	.7629	.7350	.6830	.6355	.5921	.5523	.5158	.4823	.4514	.4230	.4096	.3968	.3725	.3501	.2603
5	.8626	.8219	.7835	.7473	.7130	.6806	.6209	.5674	.5194	.4761	.4371	.4019	.3700	.3411	.3277	.3149	.2910	.2693	.1859
6	.8375	.7903	.7462	.7050	.6663	.6302	.5645	.5066	.4556	.4104	.3704	.3349	.3033	.2751	.2621	.2499	.2274	.2072	.1328
7	.8131	.7599	.7107	.6651	.6227	.5835	.5132	.4523	.3996	.3538	.3139	.2791	.2486	.2218	.2097	.1983	.1776	.1594	.0949
8	.7894	.7307	.6768	.6274	.5820	.5403	.4665	.4039	.3506	.3050	.2660	.2326	.2038	.1789	.1678	.1574	.1388	.1226	.0678
9	.7664	.7026	.6446	.5919	.5439	.5002	.4241	.3606	.3075	.2630	.2255	.1938	.1670	.1443	.1342	.1249	.1084	.0943	.0484
10	.7441	.6756	.6139	.5584	.5083	.4632	.3855	.3220	.2697	.2267	.1911	.1615	.1369	.1164	.1074	.0992	.0847	.0725	.0346
11	.7224	.6496	.5847	.5268	.4751	.4289	.3505	.2875	.2366	.1954	.1619	.1346	.1122	.0938	.0859	.0787	.0662	.0558	.0247
12	.7014	.6246	.5568	.4970	.4440	.3971	.3186	.2567	.2076	.1685	.1372	.1122	.0920	.0757	.0687	.0625	.0517	.0429	.0176
13	.6810	.6006	.5303	.4688	.4150	.3677	.2897	.2292	.1821	.1452	.1163	.0935	.0754	.0610	.0550	.0496	.0404	.0330	.0126
14	.6611	.5775	.5051	.4423	.3878	.3405	.2633	.2046	.1597	.1252	.0985	.0779	.0618	.0492	.0440	.0393	.0316	.0254	.0090
15	.6419	.5553	.4810	.4173	.3624	.3152	.2394	.1827	.1401	.1079	.0835	.0649	.0507	.0397	.0352	.0312	.0247	.0195	.0064
16	.6232	.5339	.4581	.3936	.3387	.2919	.2176	.1631	.1229	.0930	.0708	.0541	.0415	.0320	.0281	.0248	.0193	.0150	.0046
17	.6050	.5134	.4363	.3714	.3166	.2703	.1978	.1456	.1078	.0802	.0600	.0451	.0340	.0258	.0225	.0197	.0150	.0116	.0033
18	.5874	.4936	.4155	.3503	.2959	.2502	.1799	.1300	.0946	.0691	.0508	.0376	.0279	.0208	.0180	.0156	.0118	.0089	.0023
19	.5703	.4746	.3957	.3305	.2765	.2317	.1635	.1161	.0829	.0596	.0431	.0313	.0229	.0168	.0144	.0124	.0092	.0068	.0017
20	.5537	.4564	.3769	.3118	.2584	.2145	.1486	.1037	.0728	.0514	.0365	.0261	.0187	.0135	.0115	.0098	.0072	.0053	.0012
21	.5375	.4388	.3589	.2942	.2415	.1987	.1351	.0926	.0638	.0443	.0309	.0217	.0154	.0109	.0092	.0078	.0056	.0040	.0009
22	.5219	.4220	.3418	.2775	.2257	.1839	.1228	.0826	.0560	.0382	.0262	.0181	.0126	.0088	.0074	.0062	.0044	.0031	.0006
23	.5067	.4057	.3256	.2618	.2109	.1703	.1117	.0738	.0491	.0329	.0222	.0151	.0103	.0071	.0059	.0049	.0034	.0024	.0004
24	.4919	.3901	.3101	.2470	.1971	.1577	.1015	.0659	.0431	.0284	.0188	.0126	.0085	.0057	.0047	.0039	.0027	.0018	.0003
25	.4776	.3751	.2953	.2330	.1842	.1460	.0923	.0588	.0378	.0245	.0160	.0105	.0069	.0046	.0038	.0031	.0021	.0014	.0002
26	.4637	.3607	.2812	.2198	.1722	.1352	.0839	.0525	.0331	.0211	.0135	.0087	.0057	.0037	.0030	.0025	.0016	.0011	.0002
27	.4502	.3468	.2678	.2074	.1609	.1252	.0763	.0469	.0291	.0182	.0115	.0073	.0047	.0030	.0024	.0019	.0013	.0008	.0001
28	.4371	.3335	.2551	.1956	.1504	.1159	.0693	.0419	.0255	.0157	.0097	.0061	.0038	.0024	.0019	.0015	.0010	.0006	.0001
29	.4243	.3207	.2429	.1846	.1406	.1073	.0630	.0374	.0224	.0135	.0082	.0051	.0031	.0020	.0015	.0012	.0008	.0005	.0001
30	.4120	.3083	.2314	.1741	.1314	.0994	.0573	.0334	.0196	.0116	.0070	.0042	.0026	.0016	.0012	.0010	.0006	.0004	.0000
40	.3066	.2083	.1420	.0972	.0668	.0460	.0221	.0107	.0053	.0026	.0013	.0007	.0004	.0002	.0001	.0001	.0001	.0000	.0000

Suppose interest is compounded semiannually rather than annually. How much would you be willing to pay? The three years become six interest payment periods. The rate per period is half the annual rate, or 6% ÷ 2 = 3%. The factor in the period 6 row and 3% column of Table 1 is 0.8375. You would be willing to pay $1,000 × 0.8375 or only $837.50 rather than $839.60.

As a further check on your understanding, review the earlier example of compound interest. Suppose the financial institution promised to pay $13,310 at the end of three years. How much would you be willing to deposit at time zero if you desired a 10% rate of return compounded annually? Using Table 1, the period 3 row and the 10% column show a factor of 0.7513. Multiply this factor by the future amount:

$$PV = 0.7513 \times \$13,310 = \$10,000$$

A diagram of this computation follows:

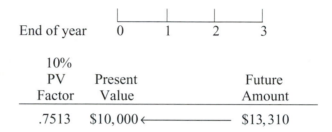

| End of year | 0 | 1 | 2 | 3 |

| 10% PV Factor | Present Value | | | Future Amount |
| .7513 | $10,000 ⟵ | | | $13,310 |

Pause for a moment. Use Table 1 to obtain the present values of

1. $1,700, at 20%, at the end of 20 years
2. $8,300, at 10%, at the end of 12 years
3. $8,000, at 4%, at the end of 4 years

Answers:

1. $1,700 (0.0261) = $44.37
2. $8,300 (0.3186) = $2,644.38
3. $8,000 (0.8548) = $6,838.40

Table 2: Present Value of an Ordinary Annuity of $1

An ordinary annuity is a series of equal cash flows to take place at the end of successive periods of equal length. Its present value is denoted PV_A. Assume that you buy a note from a municipality that promises to pay $1,000 at the end of *each* of three years. How much should you be willing to pay if you desire a rate of return of 6%, compounded annually?

You could solve this problem using Table 1. First, find the present value of each payment, and then add the present values as in Exhibit B-1. You would be willing to pay $943.40 for the first payment, $890.00 for the second, and $839.60 for the third, a total of $2,673.00.

Since each cash payment is $1,000 with equal one-year periods between them, the note is an ordinary annuity. Table 2 provides a shortcut method. The present value in Exhibit B-1 can be expressed as

$$PV_A = \$1,000 \times \frac{1}{1.06} + \$1,000 \times \frac{1}{(1.06)^2} + \$1,000 \times \frac{1}{(1.06)^3}$$

$$= \$1,000 \left[\frac{1}{1.06} + \frac{1}{(1.06)^2} + \frac{1}{(1.06)^3} \right]$$

Hardware Co. had acquired some store equipment for $14,000 on March 1. The predicted life of the equipment is ten years, and the estimated residual value is $2,000:

$$\text{straight-line depreciation per year} = \frac{\text{original cost} - \text{estimated residual value}}{\text{years of useful life}}$$

$$= \frac{\$14,000 - \$2,000}{10}$$

$$= \$1,200 \text{ per year, or } \$100 \text{ per month}$$

We discuss depreciation in more detail in subsequent chapters. But you should recognize the essence of the general concept of expense by now. The purchase and use of a resource (that is, a good or service such as inventories, rent, or equipment) ordinarily consists of two basic steps: (1) the acquisition of the asset (transactions 2, 3, and 7a) and (2) the expiration of the asset as an expense (transactions 4b and 7b). When an asset expires, we decrease both the value of the asset and owners' equity.

Summary Problem For Your Review

PROBLEM

We analyzed the King Hardware Co. transactions for March in Exhibit 15-1, page 666. The balance sheet showed the following balances as of March 31, 20X1:

Assets		Liabilities and Stockholders' Equity
Cash	$ 17,000	
Accounts receivable	105,000	
Inventory	10,000	
Prepaid rent	2,000	
Accounts payable		$ 15,000
Paid-in capital		100,000
Retained earnings		19,000
	$134,000	$134,000

Here is a summary of the transactions that occurred during the next month, April:

1. Cash collections of accounts receivable, $88,000.
2. Cash payments of accounts payable, $24,000.
3. Acquisitions of inventory on open account, $80,000.
4. Merchandise carried in inventory at a cost of $70,000 was sold on open account for $85,000.
5. Adjustment for recognition of rent expense for April.

Using the accrual basis of accounting, prepare an analysis of transactions, employing the equation approach demonstrated in Exhibit 15-1.

SOLUTION

1. The answer is in the top half of Exhibit 15-2. We will explain the bottom half of the exhibit in the following sections.

Table 2
Present Value of Ordinary Annuity of $1

$$PV_A = \frac{1}{i}\left[1 - \frac{1}{(1+i)^n}\right]$$

Periods	3%	4%	5%	6%	7%	8%	10%	12%	14%	16%	18%	20%	22%	24%	25%	26%	28%	30%	40%
1	.9709	.9615	.9524	.9434	.9346	.9259	.9091	.8929	.8772	.8621	.8475	.8333	.8197	.8065	.8000	.7937	.7813	.7692	.7143
2	1.9135	1.8861	1.8594	1.8334	1.8080	1.7833	1.7355	1.6901	1.6467	1.6052	1.5656	1.5278	1.4915	1.4568	1.4400	1.4235	1.3916	1.3609	1.2245
3	2.8286	2.7751	2.7232	2.6730	2.6243	2.5771	2.4869	2.4018	2.3216	2.2459	2.1743	2.1065	2.0422	1.9813	1.9520	1.9234	1.8684	1.8161	1.5889
4	3.7171	3.6299	3.5460	3.4651	3.3872	3.3121	3.1699	3.0373	2.9137	2.7982	2.6901	2.5887	2.4936	2.4043	2.3616	2.3202	2.2410	2.1662	1.8492
5	4.5797	4.4518	4.3295	4.2124	4.1002	3.9927	3.7908	3.6048	3.4331	3.2743	3.1272	2.9906	2.8636	2.7454	2.6893	2.6351	2.5320	2.4356	2.0352
6	5.4172	5.2421	5.0757	4.9173	4.7665	4.6229	4.3553	4.1114	3.8887	3.6847	3.4976	3.3255	3.1669	3.0205	2.9514	2.8850	2.7594	2.6427	2.1680
7	6.2303	6.0021	5.7864	5.5824	5.3893	5.2064	4.8684	4.5638	4.2883	4.0386	3.8115	3.6046	3.4155	3.2423	3.1611	3.0833	2.9370	2.8021	2.2628
8	7.0197	6.7327	6.4632	6.2098	5.9713	5.7466	5.3349	4.9676	4.6389	4.3436	4.0776	3.8372	3.6193	3.4212	3.3289	3.2407	3.0758	2.9247	2.3306
9	7.7861	7.4353	7.1078	6.8017	6.5152	6.2469	5.7590	5.3282	4.9464	4.6065	4.3030	4.0310	3.7863	3.5655	3.4631	3.3657	3.1842	3.0190	2.3790
10	8.5302	8.1109	7.7217	7.3601	7.0236	6.7101	6.1446	5.6502	5.2161	4.8332	4.4941	4.1925	3.9232	3.6819	3.5705	3.4648	3.2689	3.0915	2.4136
11	9.2526	8.7605	8.3064	7.8869	7.4987	7.1390	6.4951	5.9377	5.4527	5.0286	4.6560	4.3271	4.0354	3.7757	3.6564	3.5435	3.3351	3.1473	2.4383
12	9.9540	9.3851	8.8633	8.3838	7.9427	7.5361	6.8137	6.1944	5.6603	5.1971	4.7932	4.4392	4.1274	3.8514	3.7251	3.6059	3.3868	3.1903	2.4559
13	10.6350	9.9856	9.3936	8.8527	8.3577	7.9038	7.1034	6.4235	5.8424	5.3423	4.9095	4.5327	4.2028	3.9124	3.7801	3.6555	3.4272	3.2233	2.4685
14	11.2961	10.5631	9.8986	9.2950	8.7455	8.2442	7.3667	6.6282	6.0021	5.4675	5.0081	4.6106	4.2646	3.9616	3.8241	3.6949	3.4587	3.2487	2.4775
15	11.9379	11.1184	10.3797	9.7122	9.1079	8.5595	7.6061	6.8109	6.1422	5.5755	5.0916	4.6755	4.3152	4.0013	3.8593	3.7261	3.4834	3.2682	2.4839
16	12.5611	11.6523	10.8378	10.1059	9.4466	8.8514	7.8237	6.9740	6.2651	5.6685	5.1624	4.7296	4.3567	4.0333	3.8874	3.7509	3.5026	3.2832	2.4885
17	13.1661	12.1657	11.2741	10.4773	9.7632	9.1216	8.0216	7.1196	6.3729	5.7487	5.2223	4.7746	4.3908	4.0591	3.9099	3.7705	3.5177	3.2948	2.4918
18	13.7535	12.6593	11.6896	10.8276	10.0591	9.3719	8.2014	7.2497	6.4674	5.8178	5.2732	4.8122	4.4187	4.0799	3.9279	3.7861	3.5294	3.3037	2.4941
19	14.3238	13.1339	12.0853	11.1581	10.3356	9.6036	8.3649	7.3658	6.5504	5.8775	5.3162	4.8435	4.4415	4.0967	3.9424	3.7985	3.5386	3.3105	2.4958
20	14.8775	13.5903	12.4622	11.4699	10.5940	9.8181	8.5136	7.4694	6.6231	5.9288	5.3527	4.8696	4.4603	4.1103	3.9539	3.8083	3.5458	3.3158	2.4970
21	15.4150	14.0292	12.8212	11.7641	10.8355	10.0168	8.6487	7.5620	6.6870	5.9731	5.3837	4.8913	4.4756	4.1212	3.9631	3.8161	3.5514	3.3198	2.4979
22	15.9369	14.4511	13.1630	12.0416	11.0612	10.2007	8.7715	7.6446	6.7429	6.0113	5.4099	4.9094	4.4882	4.1300	3.9705	3.8223	3.5558	3.3230	2.4985
23	16.4436	14.8568	13.4886	12.3034	11.2722	10.3711	8.8832	7.7184	6.7921	6.0442	5.4321	4.9245	4.4985	4.1371	3.9764	3.8273	3.5592	3.3254	2.4989
24	16.9355	15.2470	13.7986	12.5504	11.4693	10.5288	8.9847	7.7843	6.8351	6.0726	5.4509	4.9371	4.5070	4.1428	3.9811	3.8312	3.5619	3.3272	2.4992
25	17.4131	15.6221	14.0939	12.7834	11.6536	10.6748	9.0770	7.8431	6.8729	6.0971	5.4669	4.9476	4.5139	4.1474	3.9849	3.8342	3.5640	3.3286	2.4994
26	17.8768	15.9828	14.3752	13.0032	11.8258	10.8100	9.1609	7.8957	6.9061	6.1182	5.4804	4.9563	4.5196	4.1511	3.9879	3.8367	3.5656	3.3297	2.4996
27	18.3270	16.3296	14.6430	13.2105	11.9867	10.9352	9.2372	7.9426	6.9352	6.1364	5.4919	4.9636	4.5243	4.1542	3.9903	3.8387	3.5669	3.3305	2.4997
28	18.7641	16.6631	14.8981	13.4062	12.1371	11.0511	9.3066	7.9844	6.9607	6.1520	5.5016	4.9697	4.5281	4.1566	3.9923	3.8402	3.5679	3.3312	2.4998
29	19.1885	16.9837	15.1411	13.5907	12.2777	11.1584	9.3696	8.0218	6.9830	6.1656	5.5098	4.9747	4.5312	4.1585	3.9938	3.8414	3.5687	3.3317	2.4999
30	19.6004	17.2920	15.3725	13.7648	12.4090	11.2578	9.4269	8.0552	7.0027	6.1772	5.5168	4.9789	4.5338	4.1601	3.9950	3.8424	3.5693	3.3321	2.4999
40	23.1148	19.7928	17.1591	15.0463	13.3317	11.9246	9.7791	8.2438	7.1050	6.2335	5.5482	4.9966	4.5439	4.1659	3.9995	3.8458	3.5712	3.3332	2.5000

Adjustment Type II: Recognition (Earning) of Unearned Revenues

Consider the following transaction for King Hardware:

6. Some customers paid $3,000 in advance for merchandise that they ordered but that King did not expect to deliver until mid-May.

See transaction 6 in Exhibit 15-2. We call this $3,000 **unearned revenue** or **deferred revenue.** Why? Because King Hardware collected it from customers and recorded it before the company earned it. It is a liability because King Hardware is obligated to deliver the goods ordered or to refund the money if it does not deliver the goods. Some companies call this account *advances from customers* or *customer deposits,* but it is an unearned revenue account no matter what its label. Advance collections of rent and magazine subscriptions are other examples.

unearned revenue (deferred revenue) Collections from customers that companies receive and record before they earn the revenue.

Sometimes it is easier to see how accountants analyze transactions by visualizing the financial positions of both parties to a contract. For instance, consider the rent transaction of March 1. Compare the financial impact on King Hardware with the impact on the landlord who received the rental payment:

	Owner of Property (Landlord, Lessor)				King Hardware Co. (Tenant, Lessee)		
	A	=	L	+	SE	A	=	L + SE
			Unearned				Prepaid		Rent
			Rent		Rent				
	Cash		Revenue		Revenue	Cash	Rent		Expense
(a) Explicit transaction (advance payment of three months' rent)	+3,000	=	+3,000			−3,000	+3,000	=	
(b) March adjustment (for one month's rent)		=	−1,000		+1,000		−1,000	=	−1,000
(c) April adjustment (for one month's rent)		=	−1,000		+1,000		−1,000	=	−1,000
(d) May adjustment (for one month's rent)		=	−1,000		+1,000		−1,000	=	−1,000

You are already familiar with the King Hardware analysis. The $1,000 monthly entries for King Hardware are examples of the first type of adjustments, the expiration of unexpired costs.

Now study the transactions from the viewpoint of the owner of the rental property. The first transaction recognizes unearned revenue, which is a liability because the lessor is obligated to deliver the rental services (or to refund the money if it does not deliver the services).

As you can see from the table above, adjustments for the expiration of unexpired costs (Type I) and adjustments for the realization of unearned revenues (Type II) are really mirror images of each other. If one party to a contract has a prepaid expense, the other has unearned revenue. We can make a similar analysis for, say, a three-year fire insurance policy or a three-year magazine subscription. The buyer recognizes a prepaid expense (asset) and uses adjustments to spread the initial cost to expense over the life of the services. In turn, the seller, such as a magazine publisher, must initially recognize its liability, unearned subscription revenue. It then recognizes the unearned revenue as earned revenue when the company delivers magazines throughout the life of the subscription.

You have now seen how two types of adjustments might occur: (1) expiration of unexpired costs and (2) recognition (earning) of unearned revenues. Next we consider the third type of adjustment: accrual of unrecorded expenses.

Adjustment Type III: Accrual of Unrecorded Expenses

accrue
To accumulate a receivable or payable during a given period, even though no explicit transaction occurs.

Accrue means to accumulate a receivable or payable during a given period, even though no explicit transaction occurs. Examples of accruals are the wages of employees for partial payroll periods and the interest that accumulates on borrowed money before the interest payment date. The receivables or payables grow as the clock ticks or as a company continuously acquires and uses some services. We say that such amounts are accruing (or accumulating).

Computerized accounting systems can make weekly, daily, or even "real-time" recordings in the accounts for many accruals. However, such frequent entries are often costly and unnecessary. Usually, accountants make adjustments to bring each expense (and corresponding liability) account up to date just before they prepare the formal financial statements.

Accounting for Payment of Wages

Consider the following two transactions relating to wages paid by King Hardware to its employees:

7. King Hardware paid employees $1,500 each Friday in April, for total wages of $6,000 (which we ignored for simplicity in March). King Hardware recognizes these payments for employee services by increasing Wages Expense and decreasing Cash.
8. King Hardware incurred wages of $600 near the end of April, but it did not pay the employees until after April 30. Accordingly, the accountant increased Wages Expense and increased a liability, Accrued Wages Payable.

Most companies pay their employees at predetermined times. For example, the University of Washington pays employees the 10th and 25th of each month. King Hardware pays its employees each Friday for services rendered during that week. Here is a sample calendar for April:

King Hardware's wages paid on April 26 are compensation for the week ended April 26. The cumulative total wages paid on the Fridays during April were $6,000. King Hardware accounts for wages expense using the shortcut procedure described earlier for goods and services that a company routinely consumes in the period of their purchase. Transaction 7 in Exhibit 15-2 (and summarized below) shows King Hardware's entry for April's wages through April 26:

	Assets (A)	=	Liabilities (L)	+	Stockholders' Equity (SE)
	Cash	=			Wages Expense
7. Routine entry for explicit transactions	−6,000	=			−6,000

Accounting for Accrual of Wages

King Hardware's wages are $300 per day. At the end of April, in addition to the $6,000 already paid, King Hardware owes $600 for employee services rendered during the last two days of April. King Hardware will not pay the employees for these services until the next regular weekly payday, May 3, so an accrual is necessary. Periodic adjustments ensure that the financial statements adhere to accrual accounting. King Hardware accomplishes this with entry 8:

	A	=	L	+	SE
			Accrued Wages Payable		**Wages Expense**
8. Adjustment for implicit transaction, the accrual of unrecorded wages		=	+600		−600

Conceptually, we could divide entries 7 and 8 into the asset acquisition and asset expiration sequence, but companies seldom use this two-step sequence in practice for expenses that represent services that they purchase and use in the same accounting period.

Accrued expenses arise when payment follows the rendering of services; prepaid expenses arise when payment precedes the services. Other examples of accrued expenses include sales commissions, property taxes, income taxes, and interest on borrowed money. Consider interest, which is rent paid for the use of money, just as you pay rent for the use of buildings or automobiles. The interest accumulates (accrues) as time unfolds, regardless of when the company actually pays the interest in cash. So when **McDonald's** showed interest expense of $374 million on its 2002 income statement, it means that it accrued $374 million on interest that year, not necessarily that it paid $374 million in cash.

Adjustment Type IV: Accrual of Unrecorded Revenues

The final type of adjustment, the realization of revenues that a company has earned but has not yet recorded in its accounts, does not appear in Exhibit 15-2. It is the mirror image of the accrual of unrecorded expenses. Suppose Security State Bank lends cash to King Hardware Co. on a three-month promissory note for $50,000 with interest at 1% per month payable at maturity. The following tabulation shows the mirror-image effect of the adjustment for interest at the end of the first month (.01 × $50,000 = $500):

Security State Bank (Lender)					King Hardware Co. (Borrower)				
A	=	L	+	SE	A	=	L	+	SE
Accrued Interest Receivable				**Interest Revenue**			**Accrued Interest Payable**		**Interest Expense**
+500	=			+500		=	+500		−500

This completes our discussion of the four types of accruals. We summarize these in Exhibit 15-3—a 2 × 2 matrix showing accruals of expenses or revenues in the columns and the timing of the accrual compared to the cash flows in the rows.

	Expense	Revenue
Payment precedes recognition of expense or revenue	I Expiration of unexpired costs. Illustration: The write-off of prepaid rent as rent expense (Exhibit 15-2, entry 5)	II Recognition (earning) of unearned revenues. Illustration: The mirror image of Type I, whereby the landlord recognizes rent revenue and decreases unearned rent revenue (rent collected in advance)
Recognition of expense or revenue precedes payments	III Accrual of unrecorded expenses. Illustration: Wage expense for wages earned by employees but not yet paid (Exhibit 15-2, entry 8)	IV Accrual of unrecorded revenues. Illustration: Interest revenue earned but not yet collected by a financial institution

Exhibit 15-3
Four Major Types of Accounting Adjustments Before Preparation of Financial Statements

MAKING MANAGERIAL DECISIONS

The manager of the DVD division of a large electronics firm complained: "I don't understand all this accrual stuff. Why can't you just measure my performance based on cash in and cash out?" Provide a brief answer to this complaint.

Answer

Accural accounting more accurately matches accomplishment with effort. When you buy a machine that will last five years, do you think the entire cost of the machine should be charged against your performance at the time of purchase? Or when you sell a carton of DVD players on credit, should your credit for the sale await eventual payment? Accrual accounting gives you credit for accomplishments when you achieve them and charges for the expenses associated with those accomplishments. Thus, it provides a much better measure of performance than does "cash in and cash out."

Dividends and Retained Earnings

OBJECTIVE 5

Explain the nature of dividends and retained earnings.

We have now covered all the entries in Exhibit 15-2 that show how revenues increase and expenses decrease the retained earnings portion of stockholders' equity. Now let's turn our attention to transaction 9, which shows another type of transaction that affects retained earnings—payment of dividends:

9. Cash dividends declared by the board of directors and disbursed to stockholders on April 29 equaled $18,000.

Dividends Are Not Expenses

dividends

Distributions of assets to stockholders that reduce retained earnings.

Dividends are distributions of assets to stockholders that reduce retained earnings. (Cash dividends are distributions of cash rather than some other asset.) Dividends are not expenses like rent and wages. Companies do not deduct them from revenues when measuring income because dividends do not relate directly to the generation of sales or the conduct of operations.

Profitable operations create the ability to pay dividends. Retained earnings increases as a company accumulates profits and decreases as it pays dividends. A company's board of directors decides when to pay dividends and how much to pay.

You can think of the entire right-hand side of the balance sheet equation as claims against the total assets. The liabilities are the claims of creditors. The stockholders' equity represents the claims of owners arising out of their initial investment (paid-in capital) and subsequent profitable operations (retained earnings). As a company grows, the retained earnings account can soar enormously if the company does not pay large dividends. Retained earnings is frequently the largest stockholders' equity account, especially for older companies. For example, **General Electric** had retained earnings of $79 billion in 2003 compared to paid-in capital of only $18 billion. In contrast, Microsoft is a younger company that has not had as much time to accumulate retained earnings. Despite paying no dividends, Microsoft's retained earnings on June 30, 2003, was $26 billion, compared with paid-in-capital of $35 billion.

Retained Earnings Is Not Cash

Although retained earnings is a result of profitable operations, it is not a pot of cash awaiting distribution to stockholders. We can illustrate this for Dollar & Cent Stores, a start-up retail operation (in thousands):

Step 1. Shareholders invested $100,000, giving an opening balance sheet of

Cash	$100	Paid-in capital	$100

Step 2. The company purchases inventory for $50,000 cash. The balance sheet now reads

Cash	$ 50	Paid-in capital	$100
Inventory	50		
	$100		

Steps 1 and 2 demonstrate a fundamental point. Ownership equity (paid-in capital, here) is an undivided claim against the total assets. For example, half the shareholders do not have a specific claim on cash, and the other half do not have a specific claim on inventory. Instead, all the shareholders have an undivided claim against (or, if you prefer, an undivided interest in) all the assets.

Step 3. Now the company sells the inventory for cash of $80,000, which produces a retained earnings of $80,000 − $50,000 = $30,000:

Cash	$130	Paid-in capital	$100
		Retained earnings	30
		Total liabilities and stockholders' equity	$130

At this stage, steps 2 and 3 may imply that the retained earnings is related to the $30,000 increase in cash, from $100,000 initially to $130,000 now. But that inference would be incorrect. The $30,000 in retained earnings connotes only a general claim against total assets. It appears to be a claim against cash because, at this time, cash is the only asset. Let's take our example one step further.

Step 4. The company purchases equipment and inventory, in the amounts of $70,000 and $50,000, respectively. Now cash is $130,000 − $70,000 − $50,000 = $10,000:

Cash	$ 10	Paid-in capital	$100
Inventory	50	Retained earnings	30
Equipment	70		
Total assets	$130	Total liabilities and stockholders' equity	$130

To what assets is the $30,000 in retained earnings related? Is it linked to Cash, to Inventory, or to Equipment? The answer is, to all three. This example helps to explain the nature of the Retained Earnings account. It is a claim, not a pot of gold. You cannot buy a loaf of bread with retained earnings. Retained earnings (and also paid-in capital) is a general claim against, or undivided interest in, total assets, not a specific claim against cash or against any other particular asset. Do not confuse the assets themselves with the claims against the assets.

Nature of Dividends

We've seen that dividends are distributions of assets that reduce ownership claims. The cash assets that companies disburse typically arise from profitable operations. Thus, journalists often write about dividends or withdrawals as "distributions of profits" or "distributions of retained earnings." Sometimes they erroneously describe dividends as being "paid out of retained earnings." In reality, cash dividends are distributions of assets, usually cash, that liquidate a portion of the ownership claim. The distribution is made possible by profitable operations.

The amount of cash dividends declared by the board of directors of a company depends on many factors, the least important of which is usually the balance in retained earnings. Although profitable operations are generally essential, the company's cash position and future needs for cash to pay debts or to purchase additional assets also influences its dividend policy. In addition, many companies maintain a stable dividend policy. Under a stable policy, a company may pay dividends consistently even if it encounters a few years of little or no net income. For years, the classic example of stable dividends was the utility industry. Many retired investors counted on utility dividends for their living expenses. Regulations kept their cash flows reasonably steady, so the companies could easily maintain a stable dividend. With deregulation of utilities, the stable cash flows often disappeared, as did their stable dividend policies.

OBJECTIVE 6

Select relevant items from a set of data and assemble them into a balance sheet, an income statement, and a statement of retained earnings.

Preparing Financial Statements

You can use the balance sheet equation to prepare a company's financial statement. We can use the data in Exhibit 15-2 to prepare King Hardware's April financial statements. The income statement and balance sheet, shown in Exhibits 15-4 and 15-5, are similar to those illustrated earlier. The balance sheet uses the totals at the bottom of Exhibit 15-2,

Assets		Liabilities and Stockholders' Equity		
Cash	$ 60,000	Liabilities		
Accounts receivable	102,000	Accounts payable	$ 71,000	
Inventory	20,000	Accrued wages payable	600	
Prepaid rent	1,000	Unearned sales revenue	3,000	$ 74,600
		Stockholders' equity		
		Paid-in capital	$100,000	
		Retained earnings	8,400	108,400
Total assets	$183,000	Total liabilities and stockholders' equity		$183,000

Exhibit 15-4
King Hardware Company
Balance Sheet as of April 30, 20X1

Sales		$85,000
Cost of goods sold		70,000
Gross profit		$15,000
Operating expenses		
Rent	$1,000	
Wages	6,600	7,600
Net income		$ 7,400

Exhibit 15-5
King Hardware
Company
Income Statement for the Month Ended April 30, 20X1

Retained earnings, March 31, 20X1	$19,000
Net Income for April	7,400
Total	$26,400
Dividends	18,000
Retained earnings, April 30, 20X1	$ 8,400

Exhibit 15-6
King Hardware
Company
Statement of Retained Earnings for the Month Ended April 30, 20X1

and the income statement uses the revenue and expense entries in the retained earnings column. Exhibit 15-6 presents the third financial statement, the Statement of Retained Earnings. This is a formal presentation of the items affecting retained earnings during April. It starts with the beginning balance, adds net income for the period, and deducts cash dividends, to arrive at the ending balance. Frequently, companies tack this statement on to the bottom of an income statement. If so, the result is a combined statement of income and retained earnings.

Accountants call the income statement in Exhibit 15-5 a "multiple-step" statement because it includes a subtotal for gross profit. **Gross profit** (sometimes called **gross margin**) is the excess of sales over the cost of the inventory that was sold. A "single step" statement would merely list all the expenses, including cost of goods sold, and deduct the total from sales.

gross profit (gross margin)
The excess of sales over the cost of the inventory that was sold.

Sole Proprietorships and Partnerships

This chapter has focused on the accounting for a corporation. However, the basic accounting concepts that underlie the owners' equity in a corporation also apply to a **sole proprietorship**—a business entity with a single owner, or a **partnership**—an organization that joins two or more individuals together as co-owners. However, financial statements for proprietorships and partnerships rarely make distinctions between paid-in capital (i.e., the investments by owners) and retained earnings. Let's compare the owners' equity section of King Hardware Co. as of April 30 to similar presentations for a sole prietorship and a partnership:

OBJECTIVE 7

Distinguish between the reporting of corporate owners' equity and the reporting of owners' equity for partnerships and sole proprietorships.

sole proprietorship
A business entity with a single owner.

partnership
An organization that joins two or more individuals together as co-owners.

Owners' Equity for a Corporation		
Stockholders' equity		
Capital stock (paid-in capital)	$100,000	
Retained earnings	8,400	
Total stockholders' equity		$108,400

Owner's Equity for a Sole Proprietorship	
Alice Walsh, capital	$108,400

Owners' Equity for a Partnership	
Susan Zingler, capital	$ 54,200
John Martin, capital	54,200
Total partners' equity	$108,400

Notice that, unlike corporations, sole proprietorships and partnerships do not account separately for paid-in capital (i.e., proceeds from issuances of capital stock) and retained earnings. Instead, they typically accumulate a single amount for each owner's original investment, subsequent investments, share of net income, and withdrawals. In the case of a sole proprietorship, then, the owner's equity will consist of a lone capital account.

net worth
A synonym for owner's equity.

Some accountants call owners' equity **net worth.** This is unfortunate because naïve users of financial statements might interpret this as meaning that owners' equity is a measure of the "current value" of the business to an outside buyer. It is not. The selling price of a business depends on future profit projections that may have little relationship to the existing assets, liabilities, or stockholders' equity of the entity as measured by its accounting records. For example, Microsoft's shareholders' equity (or net worth) in 2003 was about $61 billion, while its market value was approximately $600 billion. Even more extreme was **Amazon.com**, with a negative net worth of about $1.3 billion and a market value of $14 billion.

MAKING MANAGERIAL DECISIONS

When entrepreneurs start a company, they must decide whether the company will be a sole proprietorship, a partnership, or a corporation. As the accountant for such a start-up company, explain how the accounting system would differ for each of the three types of organization structures.

Answer

Most important aspects of the accounting system are the same for all three types of organizational structures. The only difference will be in the owners' equity section.

For a sole proprietorship, there is only one owner's equity account. A partnership has one owner's equity account for each partner. This requires the accountant to assign all increases or decreases in owners' equity to a particular partner. For example, income will be split among the partners according to a predetermined formula. Finally, a corporation divides owners' equity into paid-in capital and retained earnings to distinguished resources contributed by the owners from those generated by profitable operations.

generally accepted accounting principles (GAAP)
The conventions, rules, and procedures that together make up accepted accounting practice at any given time.

Generally Accepted Accounting Principles

Accounting is more an art than a science. It is based on a set of principles on which there is general agreement, not on rules that can be "proved." We call the conventions, rules, and procedures that together make up accepted accounting practice at any given time **generally accepted accounting principles (GAAP).**

Auditor's Independent Opinion

To ensure that companies abide by GAAP, the financial statements of publicly held corporations are subject to an independent audit that forms the basis for a professional accounting firm's opinion, typically including the following key phrasing found in Microsoft's 2003 annual report:

> *In our opinion, such consolidated financial statements present fairly, in all material respects, the financial position of Microsoft Corporation and subsidiaries as of June 30, 2002 and 2003, and the results of their operations and their cash flows for each of the three years in the period ended June 30, 2003, in conformity with accounting principles generally accepted in the United States of America.*

An accounting firm must conduct an audit before it can render an opinion. An **audit** is an "examination" or in-depth inspection of financial statements and companies' records made in accordance with auditing standards that have been developed primarily by the American Institute of Certified Public Accountants (AICPA), the leading organization of auditors. Starting in 2003, the Public Company Accounting Oversight Board must also approve auditing standards. After auditing a company, an accountant issues an independent opinion—the accountant's assurance that management's financial statements are in conformity with generally accepted accounting principles.

audit
An "examination" or in-depth inspection of financial statements and companies' records made in accordance with auditing standards

The auditor's opinion usually appears at the end of annual reports prepared for the stockholders and other external users. Investors often mistakenly rely on the opinion as an infallible guarantee of financial truth. Somehow, accounting is thought to be an exact science, perhaps because of the aura of precision that financial statements possess. But, as noted earlier, accounting is more art than science. The financial reports may appear accurate because of their neatly integrated numbers, but they are the result of a complex measurement process that rests on a huge bundle of assumptions and conventions.

Although audits are not perfect, financial statement users rely on them being honest assessments of the quality of the financial statements. In several cases recently, including **Enron**, **WorldCom**, **Global Crossing**, and **Tyco**, shareholders have accused auditors of being either negligent or deceitful (and sometimes both). These companies experienced financial troubles after receiving a "clean bill of health" from their auditors. It is essential that auditors have the expertise to determine if financial statements are inaccurate and the integrity to disclose problems when they find them. The accounting profession and government regulators are trying hard to restore the image of accountants and auditors so that once again investors can rely on their opinions.

Financial Accounting Standards Board (FASB)
The body that sets generally accepted accounting principles in the United States.

Accounting Standard Setters

Auditors and the investing public rely on generally accepted accounting principles that are largely the work of the **Financial Accounting Standards Board (FASB)** in the United States and the **International Accounting Standards Board (IASB)** in much of the rest of the world. The FASB, consisting of seven full-time members, is an independent creation of the private sector. It is financially supported by various companies and professional accounting associations. The IASB is a similar independent organization whose pronouncements become GAAP in the European Union and many other countries.

International Accounting Standards Board (IASB)
The group that establishes international GAAP.

By federal law, the **Securities and Exchange Commission (SEC),** a government agency, has the ultimate responsibility for specifying GAAP for U.S. companies with publically traded stock. However, the SEC has informally delegated much rule-making

Securities and Exchange Commission (SEC)
By federal law, the agency with the ultimate responsibility for specifying the generally accepted accounting principles for U.S. companies whose stock is publically traded.

power to the FASB. This public-sector–private-sector relationship may be sketched as follows:

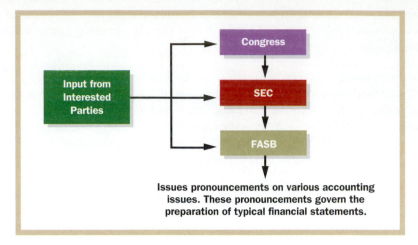

The FASB issues pronouncements on various accounting issues. These pronouncements govern the preparation of typical financial statements.

Consider this three-tiered structure. Note that Congress can overrule both the SEC and FASB, and the SEC can overrule the FASB. The SEC and FASB work closely together in developing standards, so there is seldom disagreement once the FASB has issued a standard. Until recently, Congress rarely intervened in accounting matters. However, the financial reporting problems in 2001 and 2002 brought more congressional oversight. The Sarbanes-Oxley Act of 2002 dictates more regulatory contol of both accounting and auditing standards. Corporations and other interested parties exert pressure on all three tiers—Congress, SEC, and FASB—if they think an impending pronouncement is "wrong." Hence, the setting of accounting principles is a complex process involving heavy interactions among the affected parties: public regulators (Congress and SEC), private regulators (FASB), companies, the public accounting profession, representatives of investors, and other interested groups.

Ethics

Regardless of what the accounting standards say, they do no good if accountants disobey them. A hallmark of the accounting profession has been its ethics and integrity. Despite some recent evidence to the contrary, most accountants and auditors are highly ethical and truthfully report their financial results in accordance with GAAP. The media have feasted on a few allegations of untruthful reporting in companies such as **HealthSouth** and **Freddie Mac**, but these are the exceptions. The Business First box on p. 685 highlights some of the companies that won 2003 good citizenship awards from *Business Ethics* magazine. Confidence in financial information is important to the smooth functioning of the world's capital markets, and confidence in financial statements depends on the competence and integrity of accountants and auditors. The leading professional organization of accountants in the United States, the AICPA, has a code of professional conduct that specifies the ethical obligations of accountants. The accounting problems in recent years have just highlighted the importance of accurate financial information and, therefore, the importance of recognizing and adhering to these standards.

Identify how the measurement conventions of recognition, matching and cost recovery, and stable monetary unit affect financial reporting.

Three Measurement Conventions

Generally accepted accounting principles in the United States are based on a conceptual framework that the FASB established in the 1970s. Among the most important concepts are three broad measurement or valuation conventions (principles) that underlie accrual accounting: recognition (when to record revenue), matching and cost recovery (when to record expense), and the stable monetary unit (what unit of measure to use).

Recognition

We discussed the first convention, **recognition,** earlier in this chapter in the section "Revenues and Expenses." In general, companies recognize revenue when it has earned and realized the revenue. Consequently, most companies recognize revenue when they deliver the goods or services to customers. However, in some industries revenue recognition can be problematic. Suppose **Oracle** sells some enterprise resource planning (ERP) software to a client and promises to help until the installation is complete. When has Oracle earned the revenue? At the point of sale? At the time the installation is complete? Or some time in between? This might be further complicated if the customer is a small start-up company that may run out of cash before it is able to pay for the software. How certain must Oracle be that it will receive payment before it can recognize the revenue? These are judgment issues, and Oracle's accountants together with its auditor will decide when earning and realization are sufficiently complete to recognize the revenue.

recognition
The principle that states that a company records revenue in its accounts only when it has earned and realized the revenue.

Matching and Cost Recovery

The timing of revenue recognition is important because it leads to the recording of expenses through the concept of matching. **Matching** is the linking of revenues (as measured by the selling prices of goods and services delivered) with the expenses (as measured by the cost of goods and services used) incurred to generate them.

Accountants apply matching as follows:

1. Identify the revenue recognized during the period.
2. Link the expenses to the recognized revenue directly (e.g., sales commissions or costs of inventories sold to customers) or indirectly (e.g., wages of janitors and supplies

matching
The linking of revenues (as measured by the selling prices of goods and services delivered) with the expenses (as measured by the cost of goods and services used) incurred to generate them.

used). The latter expenses are costs of operations during a specific time period that have no measurable benefit for a future period and thus must be linked to the current period's revenues.

cost recovery
A concept in which companies carry forward as assets such items as inventories, prepayments, and equipment because they expect to recover the costs of these assets in the form of cash inflows (or reduced cash outflows) in future periods.

The heart of recognizing expense is the **cost recovery** concept. That is, companies carry forward as assets such items as inventories, prepayments, and equipment. Why? Because companies expect to recover the costs of these assets in the form of cash inflows (or reduced cash outflows) in future periods. At the end of each period, accountants will examine evidence to assure themselves that they should not write off these assets—these unexpired costs—as an expense of the current period. For instance, in our chapter example, King Hardware carried forward the asset Prepaid Rent of $2,000 on March 31 because the accountant is virtually certain that it represents a future benefit. Why? Because without the prepayment, King Hardware would have to pay $2,000 in April and May. So the presence of the prepayment is a benefit in the sense that it reduces future cash outflows by $2,000. Furthermore, future revenue (sales) will be high enough to ensure the recovery of the $2,000.

Stable Monetary Unit

The monetary unit (for example, the dollar in the United States, the yen in Japan, or the euro in the European Union) is the principal means for measuring assets, liabilities, and stockholders' equity. It is the common denominator for quantifying the effects of a wide variety of transactions.

Such measurement assumes that the monetary unit—the dollar, for example—is an unchanging yardstick. Yet, we all know that a 2005 dollar does not have the same purchasing power as a 1995 or 1985 dollar. Therefore, users of accounting statements that include dollars from different years must recognize the limitations of the basic measurement unit.

Some accountants have criticized the FASB and IASB for not making explicit and formal adjustments to remedy the defects of the measuring unit. Supporters of the status quo maintain that price-level adjustments would lessen objectivity and would add to the general confusion. They claim that critics have exaggerated the price-level problem and that the adjustments would not significantly affect the vast bulk of corporate statements. Why? Because many accounts, such as cash, receivables, and payables, are already in current or nearly current dollars, and inflation rates have been low in recent years.

On the other hand, inflation has been steady and its effects are sometimes surprisingly pervasive. Companies in several countries that have experienced high inflation rates, including Brazil and Argentina, have had to adjust their accounting numbers for the effects of inflation for them to make sense. In addition, even low inflation rates can create large changes in value across a long enough time period. The most troublesome aspect of adjusting accounting numbers for inflation, however, is how to interpret the results after we measure them. Investors and managers in the United States are accustomed to the conventional statements. The intelligent interpretation of statements adjusted for changes in the price level would require extensive changes in the habits of users, and therefore faces widespread opposition. Rather than explicitly adjusting values for inflation, most users prefer to live with an "elastic" measuring stick.

The body of generally accepted accounting principles contains more than the measurement conventions just discussed. We discuss some other major concepts, including going concern, objectivity, materiality, and cost benefit, in Appendix 15A. In Chapter 16 we will look in more detail at the income statement and balance sheet and introduce the third major financial statement, the statement of cash flows.

Summary Problem For Your Review

PROBLEM

Suppose a friend approaches you after learning that you have taken an accounting course. He makes the following interpretations and remarks regarding financial statements. Do you agree or disagree? Explain fully.

1. "If I purchase 100 shares of the outstanding common stock of Microsoft, I invest my money directly in that corporation. Microsoft must record that transaction."
2. "Sales show the cash coming in from customers and the various expenses show the cash going out for goods and services. The difference is net income."
3. Consider the following recent accounts of Microsoft (in millions):

Paid-in capital	$35,344
Retained earnings	25,676
Total stockholders' equity	$61,020

A shareholder commented, "Why can't that big software company pay higher wages and dividends? It can use its billions of dollars of retained earnings to do so."
4. "The total Microsoft stockholders' equity measures the amount that the shareholders would get today if the corporation were liquidated."

SOLUTION

1. Money is invested directly in a corporation only upon original issuance of the stock by the corporation. For example, a corporation might issue 100,000 shares of stock at $80 per share, bringing in $8 million to the corporation. This is a transaction between the corporation and the stockholders. It affects the corporate financial position:

Cash	$8,000,000	Stockholders' equity	$8,000,000

In turn, an original stockholder (A) may sell 100 shares of that stock to another individual (B) for $92 per share. This is a private transaction; no cash comes to the corporation. Of course, the corporation records the fact that 100 shares originally owned by A are now owned by B, but the corporate financial position is unchanged. Accounting focuses on the business entity; the private dealings of the owners have no direct effect on the financial position of the entity and hence are unrecorded except for detailed records of the owners' identities.

2. Cash receipts and disbursements are not the fundamental basis for the accounting recognition of revenues and expenses. Credit, not cash, lubricates the economy. Therefore, if a company delivers goods or renders services to a customer, a collectible claim to cash in the form of a receivable is sufficient justification for recognizing revenue; similarly, if a company uses up goods or services, an obligation in the form of a payable is justification for recognizing expense.

This approach to the measurement of net income is the accrual basis. Companies recognize revenue as they earn and realize it. They recognize expenses or losses when they use goods or services in obtaining revenue (or when they can no longer justify carrying forward such goods or services as an asset because they have no potential future benefit). Companies deduct the expenses and losses from the revenue, and the result of this matching process is net income, the net increase in stockholders' equity from the conduct of operations.

3. Remember, retained earnings is not cash. It is a stockholders' equity account that represents the accumulated increase in ownership claims because of profitable operations. A company may partially liquidate this claim or interest by the payment of cash dividends, but a growing company will reinvest cash to increase the investments in receivables, inventories, plant, equipment, and other assets so necessary for expansion. As a result, the ownership claims reflected by retained earnings may become "permanent" in the sense that, as a practical matter, the company will never liquidate them as long as the company remains in business.

This linking of retained earnings and cash is only one example of erroneous interpretation. As a general rule, there is no direct relationship between the individual items on the two sides of the balance sheet. For example, Microsoft had cash of only $6 billion when its retained earnings were nearly $26 billion. General Electric has an even larger difference between cash and retained earnings, with a recent cash balance of less than $7 million when its retained earnings were nearly $79 billion.

4. Stockholders' equity is a difference, the excess of assets over liabilities. If companies carried their assets at their liquidating value today and their liabilities at the exact amounts needed for their extinguishment, the remark would be true. However, companies customarily carry assets at historical cost expressed in an unchanging monetary unit. Intervening changes in markets and general price levels in inflationary times may mean that the assets are woefully understated. Investors may make a critical error if they think that balance sheets indicate current values.

Furthermore, daily trading conducted in the financial marketplaces such as the New York Stock Exchange generally determines the "market values" for publicly owned shares. Numerous factors affect these values, including the expectations of (a) price appreciation and (b) cash flows in the form of dividends. The focus is on the future; investors examine the present and the past only as clues to what may be forthcoming. Therefore, the present stockholders' equity is usually of only incidental concern. For example, stockholders' equity for Microsoft was $61,020,000,000 ÷ 10,771,000,000 shares, or $5.67 per share, while the company's market price per common share fluctuated between about $25 and $30.

Highlights to Remember

1 **Read and interpret basic financial statements.** An underlying structure of concepts, techniques, and conventions provides a basis for accounting practice. We present two basic financial statements, the balance sheet (or statement of financial position) and income statement, in this chapter. Their main elements are assets, liabilities, owners' equity, revenues, and expenses. Income statements and balance sheets are linked because the revenues and expenses appearing on income statements are components of stockholders' equity. Revenues increase stockholders' equity; expenses decrease stockholders' equity.

2 **Analyze typical business transactions using the balance sheet equation.** The balance sheet equation provides a framework for recording accounting transactions: assets = liabilities + owners' equity.

3 **Distinguish between the accrual basis of accounting and the cash basis of accounting.** The accrual basis is the heart of accounting. Under accrual accounting, companies recognize revenues as they earn and realize them, and they record expenses as they use resources, not necessarily when they receive or disburse cash. Do not confuse expense with the term *cash disbursement,* or revenue with the term *cash receipt.*

4 **Relate the measurement of expenses to the expiration of assets.** At the end of each accounting period, companies must make adjustments so that they can present financial statements on a full-fledged accrual basis. The major adjustments are for (a) expiration of unexpired costs, (b) recognition (earning) of unearned revenues, (c) accrual of unrecorded expenses, and (d) accrual of unrecorded revenues.

5 **Explain the nature of dividends and retained earnings.** Dividends are not expenses; they are distributions of assets that reduce ownership claims. Similarly, retained earnings is not cash; it is a claim against total assets.

6 **Select relevant items from a set of data and assemble them into a balance sheet, an income statement, and a statement of retained earnings.** After a company records transactions and makes adjustments, it can compile the data into financial statements. The remaining balances in the accounts comprise the balance sheet. The changes in the retained earnings account form the basis for the income statement and the statement of retained earnings.

7 **Distinguish between the reporting of corporate owners' equity and the reporting of owners' equity for partnerships and sole proprietorships.** Entities can be organized as corporations, partnerships, or sole proprietorships. The type of organization does not affect most accounting entries. Only the owners' equity section will differ among organizational types.

8 **Identify how the measurement conventions of recognition, matching and cost recovery, and stable monetary unit affect financial reporting.** Three major conventions that affect accounting are recognition, matching and cost recovery, and stable monetary unit. Recognition determines when companies record revenues in the income statement, matching and cost recovery specify when to record expenses, and stable monetary units justify use of a unit of currency (the dollar in the United States) to measure accounting transactions.

Appendix 15A: Additional Accounting Concepts

This appendix describes several concepts that are prominent parts of the body of generally accepted accounting principles: continuity or going concern, objectivity or verifiability, materiality, conservatism, and cost-benefit.

The Continuity or Going Concern Convention

The **continuity** or **going concern convention** is the assumption that an organization will continue to exist and operate. This notion implies that a company will use existing resources, such as plant assets, to fulfill the general purposes of a continuing entity rather than sell them in tomorrow's real estate or equipment markets. It also implies that the company will pay existing liabilities at maturity in an orderly manner.

Suppose some old specialized equipment has a depreciated cost (i.e., original cost less accumulated depreciation) of $10,000, a replacement cost of $12,000, and a realizable value of $7,000 on the used-equipment market. Accountants often cite the continuity convention as the justification for adhering to acquisition cost less depreciation, $10,000 in this example, as the primary basis for valuing assets such as inventories, land, buildings, and equipment. Some critics of these accounting practices believe that such valuations are not as informative as their replacement cost ($12,000) or their realizable values on sale ($7,000). Defenders of using $10,000 as an appropriate asset valuation argue that a going concern will generally use the asset as originally intended. Therefore, the recorded cost (the acquisition cost less depreciation) is the preferable basis for accountability and evaluation of performance. Hence, other values are not germane because replacement or disposal will not occur en masse as of the balance sheet date.

The opposite view to this going concern or continuity convention is an immediate-liquidation assumption, whereby a company values all items on a balance sheet at the amounts appropriate if it were to sell its assets and pay off its liabilities in piecemeal fashion within a few days or months. A company would use this liquidation approach to valuation only when it is in severe, near-bankrupt straits.

continuity convention (going concern convention) *The assumption that an organization will continue to exist and operate.*

Objectivity or Verifiability

Users want assurance that management or accountants have not fabricated the numbers in the financial statements to mislead or falsify the firm's financial position and performance. Consequently,

objectivity (verifiability)
Accuracy supported by a high extent of consensus among independent measures of an item.

accountants seek and prize **objectivity** (or **verifiability**) as an essential characteristic of measurement. A financial statement item is objective or verifiable if there would be a high extent of consensus among independent measures of the item. For example, the amount paid for assets is usually highly verifiable, but the predicted cost to replace assets often is not.

Many critics of existing accounting practices want to trade objectivity for what they conceive as more relevant or valid information. For example, the accounting literature is peppered with suggestions that accounting should attempt to measure "economic income," even though it may reduce objectivity. This particular suggestion often involves introducing asset valuations at replacement costs when these are higher than historical costs. The accounting profession has generally rejected these suggestions, even when reliable replacement price quotations are available, because many accountants believe that only a bona fide sale is sufficient to justify income recognition.

Materiality

materiality
The accounting convention that justifies the omission of insignificant information when its omission or misstatement would not mislead a user of the financial statements.

Because accounting is a practical art, accountants often temper their reports by applying judgments about **materiality.** A financial statement item is material if its omission or misstatement would be likely to mislead a user of the financial statements. Items with a sufficiently small value are immaterial. For example, accountants write off as expenses many small outlays that they should theoretically record as assets. Why? Because they are small enough to be immaterial. For example, many corporations have a rule that requires the immediate write-off to expense of all outlays under a specified minimum of, say, $100, regardless of the useful life of the asset acquired. In such a case, a company might acquire coat hangers that will last many years but never add them to its balance sheet as assets. Why? The resulting $100 understatement of assets and stockholders' equity would be too trivial to worry about. The cost of recording and carrying forward an asset is greater than the benefit of more accurate financial statements.

When is an item material? There will probably never be a definitive answer. What is trivial to **IBM** may be material to a two-person e-commerce start-up. A working rule is that an item is material if its proper accounting would probably affect the decision of a knowledgeable user. In sum, although materiality is an important convention, it is difficult to use anything other than prudent judgment to tell whether an item is material.

The Conservatism Convention

conservatism convention
Selecting the method of measurement that yields the gloomiest immediate results.

Conservatism has been a hallmark of accounting. In a technical sense, the **conservatism convention** means selecting the method of measurement that yields the gloomiest immediate results. This attitude affects such working rules as "Anticipate no gains, but provide for all possible losses," and "If in doubt, write it off."

Accountants have traditionally regarded the historical costs of acquiring an asset as the ceiling for its valuation. Asset values may be increased (written up) only upon an exchange, but they may be reduced (written down) without an exchange. For example, companies write down inventories (and recognize a loss) when replacement costs decline, but they never write them up when replacement costs increase.

Critics maintain that conservatism is inherently inconsistent. If replacement market prices are sufficiently objective and verifiable to justify write-downs, why aren't they just as valid for write-ups? Furthermore, the critics maintain, conservatism is not a fundamental concept. Accounting reports should try to present the most accurate picture feasible—neither too high nor too low. Accountants defend their attitude by saying that erring in the direction of conservatism would usually have less severe economic consequences than erring in the direction of overstating assets and net income.

In a way, conservatism is a double-edged sword. Conservatism that leads to understating net income in one period also creates an overstatement of net income in a future period. For example, suppose a company writes down inventory from $100 to $80. The company's operating income falls by $20 in the period of the write-down, but it increases by $20 in the period it sells the inventory.

Cost-Benefit

cost-benefit criterion
An approach that implicitly underlies the decisions about the design of accounting systems. As companies change their accounting systems, the potential benefits should exceed the additional costs.

Accounting systems vary in complexity from the minimum crude records kept to satisfy government authorities to the sophisticated budgeting and feedback schemes that are at the heart of management planning and controlling. Recent innovations include huge, multimillion dollar enterprise resource planning (ERP) systems. As companies change their accounting systems, the potential benefits should exceed the additional costs. Often, the benefits are difficult to measure but this **cost-benefit criterion** at least implicitly underlies the decisions about the design of accounting systems. Sometimes, the reluctance to adopt suggestions for new ways of measuring financial position and performance is because of inertia. More often, it is because the apparent benefits do not exceed the obvious costs of gathering and interpreting the information. Some companies, such as **Hershey Foods**, have found out too late that huge investments in accounting systems sometimes do not deliver the benefits promised.

Room for Judgment

Accounting is commonly misunderstood as being a precise discipline that produces exact measurements of a company's financial position and performance. As a result, many individuals regard accountants as little more than mechanical tabulators who grind out financial reports after processing an imposing amount of detail in accordance with stringent predetermined rules. Although accountants take methodical steps with masses of data, their rules of measurement allow much room for judgment. Managers and accountants who exercise this judgment have more influence on financial reporting than is commonly believed. These judgments are guided by the basic concepts, techniques, and conventions included in GAAP. Examples of the latter include the basic concepts just discussed. Their meaning will become clearer as we apply these concepts in future chapters.

Appendix 15B: Using Ledger Accounts

Chapter 15 focused on the balance sheet equation, the general framework used by accountants to record economic transactions. This appendix focuses on some of the main techniques that accountants use to record the transactions illustrated in the chapter.

The Account

To begin, consider how the accountant would record the King Hardware Co. transactions that you encountered in the chapter. Exhibit 15-1 (p. 666) showed their effects on the elements of the balance sheet equation:

	A		=	L	+	SE
	Cash	Inventory		Accounts Payable		Paid-In Capital
1. Initial investment by owners	+100,000		=			+100,000
2. Acquire inventory for cash	−75,000	+75,000	=			
3. Acquire inventory on credit		+35,000	=	+35,000		

This balance-sheet-equation approach emphasizes the concepts, but it can become unwieldy if many transactions occur. Changes in the balance sheet equation can occur many times daily. In large businesses, such as in a discount department store like **Target**, hundreds or thousands of repetitive transactions occur hourly. In practice, accountants use **ledger accounts** to keep track of how these multitudes of transactions affect each particular asset, liability, revenue, expense, and so forth. We use simplified versions of ledger accounts called T-accounts. We call them T-accounts because they take the form of the capital letter T. The following T-accounts illustrate the preceding transactions:

ledger accounts
A method of keeping track of how multitudes of transactions affect each particular asset, liability, revenue, and expense.

Assets		=	**Liabilities + Stockholders' Equity**	
Cash			**Accounts Payable**	
Increases	Decreases		Decreases	Increases
(1) 100,000	(2) 75,000			(3) 35,000
Bal. 25,000				

Inventory			**Paid-in Capital**	
Increases	Decreases		Decreases	Increases
(2) 75,000				(1) 100,000
(3) 35,000				
Bal. 110,000				

double-entry system
A method of record keeping in which each transaction affects at least two accounts.

We made the T-account entries using a **double-entry system,** whereby each transaction affects at least two accounts. Asset accounts have balances on the left side of the T-account. Entries on the left side increase the accounts and entries on the right side decrease them.

Liabilities and stockholders' equity accounts have right-side balances. We increase them by entries on the right side and decrease them by entries on the left side.

Each T-account is similar to a column in the balance sheet equation. However, the format of the T-account eliminates the use of negative numbers. We add any entry that reduces an account balance to the side of the account that decreases the account balance.

Each T-account summarizes the changes in a particular asset, liability, or stockholders' equity. We key each transaction in some way, such as by the numbering used in this illustration or by date or both. This keying facilitates the rechecking (auditing) process by helping accountants trace transactions to their original sources. You can compute the balance of any account by totaling each side of the account and deducting the smaller total amount from the larger. Accounts exist to keep an up-to-date summary of the changes in specific assets, liabilities, and stockholders' equity.

Accountants can prepare a balance sheet at any time if the accounts are up to date. The accounts contain all the necessary information. For example, the balance sheet for King Hardware after the first three transactions is

	Assets		Liabilities and Stockholders' Equity	
Cash	$ 25,000		Liabilities	
Inventory	110,000		Accounts payable	$ 35,000
			Stockholders' equity	
			Paid-in capital	100,000
Total assets	$135,000		Total liabilities and stockholders' equity	$135,000

General Ledger

general ledger
A collection of the group of accounts that supports the items shown in the major financial statements.

We show King Hardware's general ledger in Exhibit 15-7. A **general ledger** is a collection of the group of accounts that supports the items shown in the major financial statements.[3] Exhibit 15-7 is merely a recasting of the facts that we analyzed in Exhibit 15-1. Study Exhibit 15-7 by comparing its analysis of each transaction against its corresponding analysis in Exhibit 15-1, page 666.

Debits and Credits

debit
An entry on the left side of an account.

credit
An entry on the right side of an account.

When placing transaction amounts in the appropriate accounts, accountants often use the technical terms *debit* and *credit*. **Debit** means one thing and one thing only—"left side of an account." **Credit** means one thing and one thing only—"right side of an account." Neither debit or credit has a connotation of "good" or "bad." In our everyday conversation, we sometimes use the words *debit* and *credit* in a general sense that may completely diverge from their technical accounting uses. For instance, we may give praise by saying, "She deserves plenty of credit for her good deed" or critizize someone by saying "That misplay is a debit on his ledger." When you study accounting, forget these general uses and misuses of the words. Merely think right-side or left-side entries to T-accounts.

For example, if you asked an accountant what entry to make for transaction 4b, the answer would be "I would debit (or charge) Cost of Goods Sold for $100,000; and I would credit Inventory for $100,000." This is an abbreviated way of saying, "Place $100,000 on the left (debit) side of the Cost of Goods Sold T-account and place $100,000 on the right (credit) side of the Inventory T-account." Note that the total dollar amounts of the debits (entries on the left side of the account[s] affected) will always equal the total dollar amount of credits (entries on the right side of the account[s] affected) because the whole accounting system is based on an equation.

---

[3]The general ledger is usually supported by various subsidiary ledgers that provide details for accounts in the general ledger. For instance, an accounts receivable subsidiary ledger would contain a separate account for each credit customer. For example, the accounts receivable balance that appears in the Target balance sheet is in a single account in the Target general ledger. However, that single balance is the sum of the detailed individual accounts receivable balances of millions of credit customers.

Assets
(increases on left, decreases on right)

Liabilities and Stockholders' Equity
(decreases on left, increases on right)

Cash

(1)	100,000	(2)	75,000
(5)	15,000	(6)	20,000
		(7a)	3,000
3/31 Bal.	17,000		

Accounts Payable

(6)	20,000	(3)	35,000
		3/31 Bal.	15,000

Accounts Receivable

(4a)	120,000	(5)	15,000
3/31 Bal.	105,000		

Paid-In Capital

		(1)	100,000
		3/31 Bal.	100,000

Inventory

(2)	75,000	(4b)	100,000
(3)	35,000		
3/31 Bal.	10,000		

Retained Earnings

		3/31 Bal.	19,000*

Prepaid Rent

(7a)	3,000	(7b)	1,000
3/31 Bal.	2,000		

*Expense and Revenue Accounts

Sales

		(4a)	120,000

Cost of Goods Sold

(4b)	100,000

Rent Expense

(7b)	1,000

Exhibit 15-7
General Ledger of King Hardware Co.

You can use debit and credit as verbs, adjectives, or nouns. The instruction "debit $1,000 to cash" uses debit as a verb, meaning that you should place $1,000 on the left side of the cash account. When you say "make a debit to cash," debit is a noun. In the statement "cash has a debit balance of $12,000," debit is an adjective that describes the status of a particular account.

Assets generally have left-side (debit) balances. Why do expenses also carry debit balances? Expense accounts are places to temporarily record reductions in stockholders' equity. To reduce stockholders' equity, we place entries on the left side of the accounts. Why? Because they offset the normal (i.e., right-side) stockholders' equity balances. Because expenses decrease stockholders' equity, we carry them as left-side (debit) balances.

To recapitulate:

Because revenues increase stockholders' equity, we record them as credits. Because expenses decrease stockholders' equity, we record them as debits.

Accounting Vocabulary

More new terms were introduced in this chapter (and its appendices) than in any other, so be sure that you understand them thoroughly.

account, p. 668
accounts payable, p. 665
accounts receivable, p. 665
accrual basis, p. 669
accrue, p. 676
adjustments, p. 671
assets, p. 665
audit, p. 683
balance sheet, p. 664
cash basis, p. 670
conservatism convention, p. 690
continuity convention, p. 689
corporation, p. 664
cost-benefit criterion, p. 690
cost recovery, p. 686
credit, p. 692
debit, p. 692
deferred revenue, p. 675
dividends, p. 678
double-entry system, p. 692
earnings, p. 667

expenses, p. 667
explicit transactions, p. 671
Financial Accounting Standards
    Board (FASB), p. 683
general ledger, p. 692
generally accepted accounting
    principles (GAAP), p. 682
going concern convention, p. 689
gross margin, p. 681
gross profit, p. 681
implicit transactions, p. 671
income, p. 667
income statement, p. 667
International Accounting
    Standards Board (IASB),
    p. 683
ledger accounts, p. 691
liabilities, p. 665
matching, p. 685
materiality, p. 690
net worth, p. 682

objectivity, p. 690
owners' equity, p. 665
paid-in capital, p. 665
partnership, p. 681
profits, p. 667
recognition, p. 685
residual value, p. 672
retained earnings, p. 665
retained income, p. 665
revenue, p. 667
Securities and Exchange
    Commission (SEC), p. 683
sole proprietorship, p. 681
source documents, p. 671
statement of financial position,
    p. 664
stockholders' equity, p. 665
transaction, p. 664
unearned revenue, p. 675
unexpired cost, p. 671
verifiability, p. 690

Assignment Material

The assignment material for each remaining chapter is divided as follows:
- Fundamental Assignment Material
    General Exercises and Problems
    Understanding Published Financial Reports
- Additional Assignment Material
    Questions

General Exercises and Problems
Understanding Published Financial Reports
- Excel Application Exercise
- Collaborative Learning Exercise
- Internet Exercise

The General Exercises and Problems subgroups focus on concepts and procedures that are applicable to a wide variety of specific settings. Many instructors believe that these "traditional" types of exercises and problems have proved their educational value over many years of use in introductory textbooks.

The Understanding Published Financial Reports subgroups focus on real-life situations. They have the same basic aims as the General Exercises and Problems subgroups. Indeed, some instructors may confine their assignments to the Understanding Published Financial Reports subgroups. The distinctive characteristic of the latter subgroups is the use of actual companies and news events to enhance the student's interest in accounting. Many students and instructors get more satisfaction out of a course that frequently uses actual situations as a means of learning accounting methods and concepts.

Fundamental Assignment Material

General Exercises and Problems

15-A1 Balance Sheet Equation

For each of the following independent cases, compute the amounts (in thousands) for the items indicated by letters, and show your supporting computations:

	Case		
	1	**2**	**3**
Revenues	$150	$ K	$300
Expenses	120	170	270
Dividends declared	–0–	5	Q
Additional investment by stockholders	–0–	30	35
Net income	E	20	P
Retained earnings			
Beginning of year	40	50	100
End of year	D	J	110
Paid-in capital			
Beginning of year	15	10	N
End of year	C	H	85
Total assets			
Beginning of year	85	F	L
End of year	95	275	M
Total liabilities			
Beginning of year	A	100	105
End of year	B	G	95

15-A2 Analysis of Transactions, Preparation of Statements

The Srinivas Company was incorporated on April 1, 20X1. Srinivas had ten holders of common stock. Diveesh Srinivas, who was the president and chief executive officer, held 51% of the shares. The company rented space in chain discount stores and specialized in selling ladies' shoes. Srinivas's first location was a store in Import Market Centers, Inc.

The following events occurred during April:

a. The company was incorporated. Common stockholders invested $120,000 cash.
b. Purchased merchandise inventory for cash, $35,000.
c. Purchased merchandise inventory on open account, $25,000.
d. Merchandise carried in inventory at a cost of $40,000 was sold for cash for $30,000 and on open account for $70,000, a grand total of $100,000. Srinivas carries and will collect these accounts receivable.
e. Collection of the above accounts receivable, $15,000.

f. Payments of accounts payable, $18,000. See transaction c.
g. Special display equipment and fixtures were acquired on April 1 for $36,000. Their expected useful life was 36 months with no terminal scrap value. Straight-line depreciation was adopted. This equipment was removable. Srinivas paid $12,000 as a down payment and signed a promissory note for $24,000.
h. On April 1, Srinivas signed a rental agreement with Import Market Centers. The agreement called for a flat $2,000 per month, payable quarterly in advance. Therefore, Srinivas paid $6,000 cash on April 1.
i. The rental agreement also called for a payment of 10% of all sales. This payment was in addition to the flat $2,000 per month. In this way, Import Market Centers would share in any success of the venture and be compensated for general services such as cleaning and utilities. This payment was to be made in cash on the last day of each month as soon as the sales for the month were tabulated. Therefore, Srinivas made the payment on April 30.
j. Wages, salaries, and sales commissions were all paid in cash for all earnings by employees. The amount was $43,000.
k. Depreciation expense was recognized. See transaction g.
l. The expiration of an appropriate amount of prepaid rental services was recognized. See transaction h.

1. Prepare an analysis of Srinivas Company's transactions, employing the equation approach demonstrated in Exhibit 15-1. Two additional columns will be needed: Equipment and Fixtures, and Note Payable. Show all amounts in thousands.
2. Prepare a balance sheet as of April 30, 20X1, and an income statement for the month of April. Ignore income taxes.
3. Given these sparse facts, analyze Srinivas's performance for April and its financial position as of April 30, 20X1.

15-A3 Cash Basis Versus Accrual Basis

Refer to the preceding problem. If Srinivas Company measured income on the cash basis, what revenue would be reported for April? Which basis (accrual or cash) provides a better measure of revenue? Why?

Understanding Published Financial Reports

15-B1 Balance Sheet Equation

Micron Technology is one of the leading producers of semiconductor components. The company's actual data (in millions of dollars) follow for its fiscal year ended August 29, 2002:

Assets, beginning of period	$8,363.2
Assets, end of period	E
Liabilities, beginning of period	A
Liabilities, end of period	1,888.8
Paid-in capital, beginning of period	4,213.5
Paid-in capital, end of period	D
Retained earnings, beginning of period	2,921.3
Retained earnings, end of period	C
Revenues	2,589.0
Costs and expenses	B
Net income (loss)	(907.0)
Dividends	0.0
Other increase in retained earnings	2.2
Additional investments by stockholders	136.6

Find the unknowns (in millions), showing computations to support your answers.

15-B2 Analysis of Transactions, Preparation of Statements

PACCAR produces Kenworth and Peterbilt trucks. The company's actual condensed balance sheet data for January 1, 2003 follows (in millions):

Assets		Liabilities and Stockholders' Equity	
Cash and cash equivalents	$ 773	Accounts payable	$1,275
Receivables	5,064	Other liabilities	4,827
Inventories	311		
Prepaid expenses and other assets	978	Stockholders' equity	2,601
Property, plant, and equipment	1,577		
Total	$8,703	Total	$8,703

Suppose the following summarizes some major transactions during January, 2003 (in millions):

a. Sold trucks for cash of $155 and on open account of $500, a grand total of $655. PACCAR carried the trucks in inventory for $390.
b. Acquired inventory on account, $500.
c. Collected receivables, $300.
d. On January 2, used $250 cash to prepay some rent and insurance for 2003.
e. Payments on accounts payable (for inventories), $450.
f. Paid selling and administrative expenses in cash, $100.
g. A total of $90 of prepaid expenses for rent and insurance expired in January 2003.
h. Recognized depreciation expense of $20 for January.

1. Prepare an analysis of the PACCAR transactions, employing the equation approach demonstrated in Exhibit 15-1, p. 666. Show all amounts in millions of dollars. (For simplicity, only a few major transactions are illustrated here.)
2. Prepare an income statement for the month ended January 31, 2003, and a balance sheet as of January 31, 2003. Ignore income taxes.

15-B3 Cash Basis Versus Accrual Basis

Refer to the preceding problem. If PACCAR measured income on the cash basis, what revenue would the company report for January? Which basis (accrual or cash) provides a better measure of revenue? Why?

Additional Assignment Material

Questions

15-1 What types of questions are answered by the income statement and balance sheet?

15-2 Define *assets* and *liabilities*.

15-3 How are the income statement and balance sheet related?

15-4 Criticize: "Net income is the difference in the ownership capital account balances at two points in time."

15-5 Distinguish between the accrual basis and the cash basis of accounting.

15-6 How do adjusting entries differ from routine entries?

15-7 Explain why some accountants want to record advertising as an asset on acquisition.

15-8 Why is it better to refer to the costs, rather than values, of assets such as plant or inventories?

15-9 "Depreciation is cost allocation, not valuation." Do you agree? Explain.

15-10 Criticize: "As a stockholder, I have a right to more dividends. You have millions stashed away in retained earnings. It's about time that you let the true owners get their hands on that pot of gold."

15-11 Criticize: "Dividends are distributions of profits."

15-12 Explain the relationship between the FASB and the SEC.

15-13 Why are ethics and integrity important to accountants?

15-14 When do accountants recognize revenue? Why is this so important in an accrual accounting system?

15-15 What is the major criticism of the dollar as the principal accounting measure?

15-16 What does the accountant mean by *going concern*?

15-17 What does the accountant mean by *objectivity*?

15-18 What is the role of cost-benefit (economic feasibility) in the development of accounting principles?

Critical Thinking Exercises

15-19 Accounting Valuation of Fixed Assets

Consider two types of assets held by **Weyerhaeuser Company**: timber-growing land purchased in 1910 when the company was known as Weyerhaeuser Timber Company and machinery purchased and installed at its paper processing plant in Saskatchewan, Canada, in 1998. How close do you suppose the December 31, 2004, balance sheet value of each asset is to the market value of the asset at that date?

15-20 Marketing, the Income Statement, and the Balance Sheet

The marketing manager of a major consumer products company said, "The balance sheet isn't of much use to me. It is so static. But the income statement is a primary tool for managing my dynamic business." Why would a marketing manager find the income statement more useful than the balance sheet?

15-21 Revenue Recognition and Evaluation of Sales Staff

Revenue on an accrual-accounting basis must be both earned and realized before it is recognized in the income statement. Revenue in cash-basis accounting must be received in cash. Is an accrual-basis or cash-basis recognition of revenue more relevant for evaluating the performance of a sales staff? Why?

15-22 Relationship Between the Balance Sheet and the Income Statement

Suppose a company has no transactions with its owners during 20X1. That is, paid-in capital remains unchanged and retained earnings increases by the entire amount of the net income. During 20X1 the company's net income is $100,000. At the beginning of the year, the company's balance sheet equation was:

$$\text{assets} = \text{liabilities} + \text{stockholders' equity}$$
$$\$500,000 = \$200,000 + \$300,000$$

What do you know about the balance sheet equation at the end of 20X1?

General Exercises and Problems

15-23 True or False

Use T or F to indicate whether each of the following statements is true or false. Change each false statement into one that is true.

1. Accounts receivable should be classified as a stockholders' equity item.
2. Retained earnings should be accounted for as an asset item.
3. Machinery used in the business should be recorded at replacement cost.
4. The large cash balance is the best evidence of previous profitable operations.
5. It is not possible to determine changes in the condition of a business from a single balance sheet.
6. From a single balance sheet, you can find stockholders' equity for a period but not for a specific day.

15-24 Nature of Retained Earnings

This is an exercise on the relationships among assets, liabilities, and ownership equities. The numbers are small, but the underlying concepts are large.

1. Prepare an opening balance sheet of

Cash	$1,500	Paid-in capital	$1,500

2. Purchase inventory for $600 cash. Prepare a balance sheet. A heading is unnecessary in this and subsequent requirements.

3. Sell the entire inventory for $850 cash. Prepare a balance sheet. Where is the retained earnings in terms of relationships within the balance sheet? That is, what is the meaning of the retained earnings? Explain in your own words.
4. Buy inventory for $400 cash and equipment for $750 cash. Prepare a balance sheet. Where is the retained earnings in terms of relationships within the balance sheet? That is, what is the meaning of the retained earnings? Explain in your own words.
5. Buy inventory for $350 on open account. Prepare a balance sheet. Where is the retained earnings and account payable in terms of the relationships within the balance sheet? That is, what is the meaning of the account payable and the retained earnings? Explain in your own words.

15-25 Income Statement

Here is a proposed income statement of an antiques dealer:

Basin Street Antiques
Statement of Profit and Loss, December 31, 20X1

Revenues		
Sales	$1,400,000	
Increase in market value of land and		
building	100,000	
Cash received from loan	200,000	$1,700,000
Deduct expenses		
Advertising	$ 100,000	
Sales commissions	60,000	
Utilities	20,000	
Wages	150,000	
Dividends	200,000	
Cost of antiques purchased	800,000	1,330,000
Net profit		$ 370,000

List and describe any shortcomings of this statement.

15-26 Customer and Airline

Suppose **Sony** decided to hold a managers' meeting in Cancun in February. To take advantage of special fares, Sony purchased airline tickets in advance from **United Airlines** at a total cost of $70,000. Sony acquired the tickets on December 1 for cash.

Using the balance sheet equation format, analyze the impact of the December payment and the February travel on the financial position of both Sony and United.

15-27 Tenant and Landlord

Winsted Hardware, a franchise of **Ace Hardware Corporation**, pays quarterly rent on its store at the beginning of each quarter. The rent per quarter is $6,000. The owner of the building in which the store is located is the Hutchinson Corporation.

Using the balance sheet equation format, analyze the effects of the following on the tenant's and the landlord's financial position:

1. Winsted Hardware pays $6,000 rent on July 1.
2. Adjustment for July.
3. Adjustment for August.
4. Adjustment for September.

15-28 Find Unknowns

The following data pertain to Similan Cruises, a company in Thailand where the currency is the baht (B). Total assets at January 1, 20X1, were B100,000; at December 31, 20X1, B125,000. During 20X1, sales were B265,000, cash dividends were B16,000, and operating expenses (exclusive of costs of goods sold) were B50,000. Total liabilities at December 31, 20X1, were B55,000; at January 1, 20X1, B40,000. There was no additional capital paid in during 20X1.

Calculate the following items. (These need not be computed in any particular order.)

1. Stockholders' equity, for January 1, 20X1
2. Net income for 20X1
3. Cost of goods sold for 20X1

15-29 Balance Sheet Equation; Solving for Unknowns
Compute the unknowns (X, Y, Z, A, and B) in each of the individual cases, columns 1 through 7, in Exhibit 15-8.

15-30 Fundamental Transaction Analysis and Preparation of Statements
Three former dot-com workers have decided to pool a variety of work experiences by opening a store near a college campus to sell wireless equipment to students. The first products were Palm Pilots and **Nokia** cell phones. The business has been incorporated as University Wireless. The following transactions occurred during October:

Given	1	2	3	4	5	6	7
Assets at beginning of period		$ 9,000				B	$ 8,200
Assets at end of period		11,000					9,600
Liabilities at beginning of period		6,000				$12,000	4,000
Liabilities at end of period		Y					6,000
Stockholders' equity at beginning of period	$9,000	X				A	X
Stockholders' equity at end of period	X	5,000				10,000	Y
Sales			$15,000		X	14,000	20,000
Inventory at beginning of period			6,000	$ 8,000		Z	
Inventory at end of period			7,000	6,000		7,000	
Purchase of inventory			10,000	12,000		6,000	
Gross profit			Y		$3,000	6,000	A
Cost of goods sold*			X	X	4,500	X	B
Other expenses			4,000			4,000	5,000
Net profit	3,000	Z	Z			Y	Z
Dividends	2,000	–0–				1,500	400
Additional investments by stockholders						5,000	–0–

*Note that cost of goods sold = beginning inventory + purchases − ending inventory.

Exhibit 15-8
Data for Exercise 15-29

a. On October 1, 20X1, each of the three invested $12,000 in cash in exchange for 1,000 shares of stock each.
b. The corporation quickly acquired $40,000 in inventory, half of which had to be paid for in cash. The other half was acquired on open accounts that were payable after 30 days.
c. A store was rented for $500 monthly. A lease was signed for one year on October 1. The first two months' rent were paid in advance. Monthly payments were to be made on the second of each month.
d. Advertising during October was purchased on open account for $3,000 from a newspaper owned by one of the stockholders. Additional advertising services of $6,000 were acquired for cash.
e. Sales were $60,000. Merchandise was sold for twice its purchase cost. Sales of $50,000 were on open account, and the remaining $10,000 were for cash.
f. Wages and salaries incurred in October amounted to $11,000, of which $5,000 was paid in cash.
g. Miscellaneous services paid for in cash were $1,510.
h. On October 1, fixtures and equipment were purchased for $6,000 with a downpayment of $1,000 plus a $5,000 note payable in one year.
i. See transaction h and make the October 31 adjustment for interest expense accrued at 9.6%. (The interest is not due until the note matures.)
j. See transaction h and make the October 31 adjustment for depreciation expense on a straight-line basis. The estimated life of the fixtures and equipment is 10 years with no expected terminal scrap value. Straight-line depreciation here would be $6,000 ÷ 10 years = $600 per year, or $50 per month.
k. Cash dividends of $6,000 were declared and disbursed to stockholders on October 30.

1. Using the accrual basis of accounting, prepare an analysis of transactions, employing the equation approach demonstrated in Exhibit 15-1, page 666. Use the following headings: Cash, Accounts Receivable, Inventory, Prepaid Rent, Fixtures and Equipment, Accounts Payable, Notes Payable, Accrued Wages Payable, Accrued Interest Payable, Paid-in Capital, and Retained Earnings.
2. Prepare a balance sheet and a multiple-step income statement. Also prepare a statement of retained earnings.
3. What advice would you give the owners based on the information compiled in the financial statements?

15-31 Debits and Credits

Study Appendix 15B. Determine for the following transactions whether the account named in parentheses is to be debited or credited.

1. Bought merchandise on open account (Accounts Payable), $5,000.
2. Sold merchandise (Merchandise Inventory), $1,000.
3. Borrowed money from a bank (Notes Payable), $12,000.
4. Paid Johnson Associates $3,000 owed them (Accounts Payable).
5. Paid dividends (Cash), $500.
6. Delivered merchandise to customers (Merchandise Inventory), $3,000.
7. Received cash from customers on accounts due (Accounts Receivable), $2,000.

15-32 True or False

Study Appendix 15B. Use T or F to indicate whether each of the following statements is true or false. For each false statement, explain why it is false.

1. Debit entries must always be recorded on the left. Credit entries can be recorded either on the right or on the left.
2. Money borrowed from the bank should be credited to Cash and debited to Notes Payable.
3. Decreases in accounts must be shown on the credit side.
4. Both increases in liabilities and decreases in assets should be entered on the right.
5. Equipment purchases for cash should be debited to Equipment and credited to Cash.
6. Asset credits should be entered on the right and liability credits on the left.
7. Payments on mortgages should be debited to Cash and credited to Mortgages Payable. Mortgages are long-term debts.
8. Increases in asset accounts must always be entered on the left.

9. Increases in stockholders' equity always should be entered as credits.
10. Purchase of inventory on account should be credited to Inventory and debited to Accounts Payable.
11. Decreases in liability accounts should be recorded on the right.

15-33 Use of T-Accounts

Study Appendix 15B. The YMCA of Adams County had the following transactions during June:

a. Collected $300 of dues that had been billed in May.
b. Sold an old computer for $150 cash and a promise to pay $200 in one month. The book value of the computer was $350.
c. Bought a postage meter on credit for $120.
d. Received the $200 promised in transaction b.

1. Set up T-accounts for the following accounts:
   Cash
   Dues receivable
   Accounts receivable
   Equipment
   Accounts payable
2. Make entries for each of the four transactions into the T-accounts. Label each entry a, b, c, or d.

15-34 Use of T-Accounts

Study Appendix 15B. Refer to problem 15-A2. Make entries for April in T-accounts. Key your entries and check to see that the ending balances agree with the financial statements.

15-35 Use of T-Accounts

Study Appendix 15B. Refer to problem 15-30. Use T-accounts to present an analysis of October transactions. Key your entries and check to see that the ending balances agree with the financial statements.

15-36 Measurement of Income for Tax and Other Purposes

The following are the summarized transactions of Dr. Veronica Bridge, a dentist, for 20X1, her first year in practice.

a. Acquired equipment and furniture for $72,000. Its expected useful life is six years. Dr. Bridge will use straight-line depreciation, assuming zero terminal disposal value.
b. Fees collected, $81,000. These fees included $2,000 paid in advance by some patients on December 31, 20X1.
c. Rent is paid at the rate of $500 monthly, payable quarterly on the 25th of March, June, September, and December for the following quarter. Total disbursements during 20X1 for rent were $7,500 including an initial payment on January 1.
d. Fees billed but uncollected, December 31, 20X1, $20,000.
e. Utilities expense paid in cash, $600. Additional utility bills unpaid at December 31, 20X1, $100.
f. Salary expense for dental assistant and secretary, $16,000 paid in cash. In addition, $1,000 was earned but unpaid on December 31, 20X1.

Dr. Bridge may elect either the cash basis or the accrual basis of measuring income for income tax purposes, provided that she uses it consistently in subsequent years. Under either alternative, the original cost of the equipment and furniture must be written off over its six-year useful life rather than being regarded as a lump-sum expense in the first year.

1. Prepare income statements on both the cash and accrual bases, using one column for each basis.
2. Which basis do you prefer as a measure of Dr. Bridge's performance? Why? What do you think is the justification for the government's allowing the use of the cash basis for income tax purposes?

Understanding Published Financial Reports

15-37 Balance Sheet Effects

Seattle-based **Washington Mutual, Inc.,** one of the largest financial institutions in the United States with total assets of nearly $300 billion, showed the following items (among others) on its balance sheet at January 1, 2003 (in millions):

Cash (an asset)	$ 7,208
Total deposits (a liability)	$155,516

1. Suppose you deposited $1,000 in the bank. How would each of the bank's assets, liabilities, and stockholders' equities be affected? How much would each of your personal assets, liabilities, and owner's equities be affected? Be specific.
2. Suppose Washington Mutual makes an $800,000 loan to a local hospital for remodeling purposes. What would be the effect on each of the bank's assets, liabilities, and stockholders' equities immediately after it makes the loan? Be specific.
3. Suppose you borrowed $10,000 from Washington Mutual on a personal loan. How would such a transaction affect each of your personal assets, liabilities, and owner's equities?

15-38 Preparation of Balance Sheet for Kellogg Company

Kellogg Company produces breakfast cereals and other food products. Its annual report included the following items at March 29, 2003 (in millions of dollars):

Accrued liabilities	$ 1,227.9
Cash and cash equivalents	138.8
Total stockholders' equity	b
Total liabilities	c
Long-term liabilities	5,830.5
Net sales	2,147.5
Accounts receivable	811.1
Common stock	148.4
Inventories	a
Accounts payable	583.3
Property, net of accumulated depreciation	2,776.2
Retained earnings	760.6
Other assets	5,937.7
Other liabilities	1,707.3
Total assets	10,258.0

Prepare a condensed balance sheet including amounts for

a. Inventory
b. Total stockholders' equity
c. Total liabilities

15-39 Net Income and Retained Earnings

Walt Disney Company is a well-known entertainment company. The following data are from its 2002 annual report (in millions):

Walt Disney Company			
Retained earnings, end of year	$12,979	Dividends paid	$?
Revenues	25,329	Retained earnings, beginning of year	12,171
Net interest expense	453	Operating costs and expenses	22,924
Income taxes	853	Cash and cash equivalents	1,239
Other income, net	137		

1. Prepare the following for the year:
    a. Income statement. The final three lines of the income statement were labeled as income before taxes, income taxes, and net income.
    b. Statement of retained earnings. Compute the amount of dividends paid.
2. Comment briefly on the relative size of the cash dividend.

15-40 Earnings Statement, Retained Earnings

The **Procter & Gamble Company** has many well-known, diverse products, including Tide detergent, Crest toothpaste, Jif peanut butter, and Prell shampoo. The following is a reproduction of the terms and amounts in the financial statements contained in a recent annual report regarding the fiscal year ended June 30, 2002 (in millions):

Net sales	$40,238	Retained earnings at	
Cash	3,421	beginning of year	$10,451
Interest and other expense	295	Cost of products sold	20,989
Income taxes	2,031	Dividends to shareholders	1,971
Accounts payable	2,209	Marketing, research, and	
Other decreases in		administrative expenses	12,571
retained earnings	852		

Choose the relevant data and prepare (1) the income statement for the fiscal year and (2) the statement of retained earnings for the fiscal year. The final three lines of the income statement were labeled as earnings before income taxes, income taxes, and net earnings.

EXCEL Application Exercise

15-41 Monthly Transactions Using Balance Sheet Equation

Goal: Create an Excel spreadsheet to analyze the monthly transactions of a company using the balance sheet equation. Use the results to answer questions about your findings.

Scenario: Srinivas Company has asked you to prepare a transaction analysis report to help them analyze what transpired during their first month of operation. They would like you to record the transactions and calculate the appropriate totals using the balance sheet equation. The background data for your analysis appears in Fundamental Assignment Material 15-A2. Prepare the transaction analysis using a format similar to Exhibit 15-1.

When you have completed your spreadsheet, answer the following questions:
1. What are the total Assets of the firm at the end of April, 20X1?
2. Did the Stockholders' Equity increase or decrease as of the end of April, 20X1? What caused the change?
3. Discuss what occurred in the Cash account and its implications.

Step-by-Step:
1. Open a new Excel spreadsheet.
2. In column A, create a bold-faced heading that contains the following:
    Row 1: Chapter 15 Decision Guideline
    Row 2: Srinivas Company
    Row 3: Transaction Analysis (in Dollars) for April 20X1
    Row 4: Today's Date
3. Merge and center the four heading rows across columns A through L.
4. In row 7, create the following bold-faced column headings:
    Column B: Assets
    Column H: Liabilities
    Column J: Stockholders' Equity
5. Merge and center the Assets heading across columns B through G.
6. Merge and center the Liabilities heading across columns H through I.
7. Merge and center the Stockholders' Equity heading across columns J through L.

8. Create a border around each of the headings created in row 7.

        Border tab: Presets: Outline

9. In row 8, create the following center-justified column headings:
Column B: Cash
Column C: A/R
Column D: Inven.
Column E: Ppd. Rent
Column F: Equip.
Column G: Acc. Dep.
Column H: A/P
Column I: N/P
Column J: PIC
Column K: Revenue
Column L: Expense

10. Create a border around each of the column headings created in row 8.

        Border tab: Presets: Outline

11. In column A, create the following row headings:
Row 9: Transactions:
Row 10:   a. Incorporation
Row 11:   b. Inven. for cash
Row 12:   c. Inven. for credit
Row 13: d1. Merch. sold
Row 14: d2. COGS
Row 15:   e. Collect A/R
Row 16:   f. Payment of A/P
Row 17:   g. Equip. purchased
Row 18:   h. Prepaid rent
Row 19:   i. Add'l. rental fees
Row 20:   j. Wage expense
Row 21:   k. Depreciation exp.
Row 22:   l. Rent expense
Skip a row
Row 24: Balance, 4/30/X1
Skip 2 rows
Row 27: Totals
Note: Adjust width of row A to accommodate row headings.

12. Use the data from Fundamental Assignment Material 15-A2 and enter the amounts for transactions 1 through 8 and 10 in the appropriate columns.
13. Use formulas to compute the adjusting entries needed for transactions 9, 11, and 12.
14. Use formulas to calculate the totals in each of the columns for row 24, Balance, 4/30/X1.
15. Use formulas to generate totals for Assets, Liabilities, and Stockholders' Equity in row 27.

Print the total for Assets in column B.
Merge and center the total across columns B through G.

Print the total for Liabilities in column H.
Merge and center the total across columns H through I.

Print the total for Stockholders' Equity in column J.
Merge and center the total across columns J through L.

Change the format of the three totals amounts to display as bold-faced.
16. Format all amounts in rows 10 through 22 as:

        Number tab: Category: Currency
                              Decimal places: 0
                              Symbol: None
                            Negative numbers: Black with parenthesis

17. Format amounts on row 24 as:

Number tab:	Category:	Accounting
	Decimal places:	0
	Symbol:	$

18. Format amounts on row 27 as:

Number tab:	Category:	Currency
	Decimal places:	0
	Symbol:	$
	Negative numbers:	Black with parenthesis

19. Modify the Page Setup by selecting File, Page Setup.

Page tab:	Orientation:	Landscape
Sheet tab:	Gridlines:	Checked

20. Save your work to disk, and print a copy for your files.

Collaborative Learning Exercise

15-42 Implicit Transactions

Form groups of from three to six "players." Each group should have a die and paper (or board) with four columns labeled

1. Expiration of unexpired costs
2. Realization of unearned revenues
3. Accrual of unrecorded expenses
4. Accrual of unrecorded revenues

The players should select an order in which they wish to play. Then, the first player rolls the die. If he or she rolls a 5 or 6, the die passes to the next player. If he or she rolls a 1, 2, 3, or 4, he or she must, within 20 seconds, name an example of a transaction that fits in the corresponding category; for example, if a 2 is rolled, the player must give an example of realization of unearned revenues.

Each time a correct example is given, the player receives one point. If someone doubts the correctness of a given example, he or she can challenge it. If the remaining players unanimously agree that the example is incorrect, the challenger gets a point and the player giving the example does not get a point for the example and is out of the game. If the remaining players do not unanimously agree that the answer is incorrect, the challenger loses a point and the player giving the example gets a point for a correct example.

If a player fails to give an example within the time limit or gives an incorrect example, he or she is out of the game (except for voting when an example is challenged), and the remaining players continue until everyone has failed to give a correct example within the time limit. Each correct answer should be listed under the appropriate column. The player with the most points is the group winner.

When all groups have finished a round of play, a second level of play can begin. All the groups should get together and list all the examples for each of the four categories by group. Discussion can establish the correctness of each entry; the faculty member or an appointed discussion leader will be the final arbitrator of the correctness of each entry. Each group gets one point for each correct example and loses one point for each incorrect entry. The group with the most points is the overall winner.

Internet Exercise   **www.prenhall.com/horngren**

15-43 McDonalds' Financial Statements

Go to http://www.mcdonalds.com to find **McDonalds'** home page. Under the "Corporate" heading, select "Investors," and click on the most recent annual report (McDonalds may call it the "financial report").

Answer the following questions:

1. First open the balance sheet. Name two items on McDonalds' balance sheet that most likely represent unexpired (prepaid) costs. Name two items that most likely represent accruals of unrecorded expenses.
2. Has McDonalds grown in the past year? What did you look at to determine this?
3. Now look at McDonalds' income statement. Did the company's sales (revenues) grow during the past year? By how much? Did its income increase or decrease? By how much? Do the sales and income changes bode well or poorly for McDonalds' future?
4. Which financial statements provide evidence that McDonalds is a corporation, not a sole proprietorship or partnership?
5. Where can you find evidence in McDonalds' annual report that the financial statements were prepared using GAAP?
6. Explain how McDonalds' financial statements illustrate one of the basic concepts or principles found in this chapter of the text.

Understanding Corporate Annual Reports: Basic Financial Statements

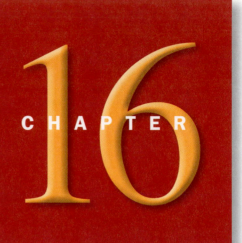

CHAPTER 16

LEARNING OBJECTIVES

When you have finished studying this chapter, you should be able to:

1. Recognize and define the main types of assets in the balance sheet of a corporation.

2. Recognize and define the main types of liabilities in the balance sheet of a corporation.

3. Recognize and define the main elements of the stockholders' equity section of the balance sheet of a corporation.

4. Recognize and define the principal elements in the income statement of a corporation.

5. Recognize and define the elements in the statement of retained earnings.

6. Identify activities that affect cash, and classify them as operating, investing, or financing activities.

7. Assess financing and investing activities using the statement of cash flows.

8. Use both the direct method and the indirect method to explain cash flows from operating activities.

9. Explain the role of depreciation in the statement of cash flows.

10. Describe and assess the effects of the four major methods of accounting for inventories (Appendix 16A).

"Just do it!" Competitive athletes, armchair athletes, and nonathletes around the world recognize **Nike**'s slogan and its "swoosh" logo. In just two decades, the company grew from a small shoe company to a major producer of athletic footwear and other leisure wear, with annual sales of more than $10 billion. The "Just do it!" slogan would also have been apt for early investors in Nike. A dollar invested in Nike stock in the mid-1980s would be worth more than $50 today. But is Nike stock a good investment today? Prospective investors look to the company's financial statements to help answer that question. Let's look at the kind of information that Nike includes in its financial statements.

Each year, Nike issues an annual report summarizing the 12 months ended on May 31. This is Nike's *fiscal year*. All companies issue such annual reports, but others choose different fiscal years. A majority of firms use the calendar year, January 1 through December 31.

Like most companies, Nike uses its annual report partly as a promotion piece. For example, the 2003 annual report contained information about its successful products. But, for investors, the most important part of Nike's annual report is the financial section, which contains four financial statements, footnotes to those statements, and reports by management and auditors. You can examine the financial statements to learn about Nike's financial position at the beginning and end of the year. You can also glean information about its performance during the year. Of course, investors want to know about the future, not just about the past. Accountants do not predict the future. However, the history recorded in the financial statements gives a baseline for investors like you to evaluate past performance and position and make judgments about how likely it is that future performance will be similar to that in the past. This chapter

Nearly everyone, athlete or not, recognizes the Nike "swoosh," shown here on both the jersey and the finish-line tape. But how many of them know about Nike's financial performance and status? To learn this, you can look at the details in Nike's financial statements, which form the basis for the discussion in this chapter.

focuses on what you can learn from financial statements such as those of Nike. It extends our discussion of balance sheets and income statements from the preceding chapter and introduces another major financial statement, the statement of cash flows.

A common misunderstanding is that accounting is a precise discipline that produces exact measurements of a company's financial position and performance. Although accountants do take methodical steps with masses of data, their rules of measurement allow room for judgment. Managers and accountants who exercise this judgment have a major effect on a company's financial statements. To understand financial statements fully, you must recognize the judgmental decisions that go into their construction. Controversial accounting judgments by **Enron**, **WorldCom**, **Tyco**, **HealthSouth**, **Global Crossing**, **Freddie Mac**, and many others in the last few years have illustrated just how important accountants' decisions are to users of financial statements. ■

Classified Balance Sheet

OBJECTIVE 1

Recognize and define the main types of assets in the balance sheet of a corporation.

Exhibit 16-1 shows the 2002 and 2003 classified balance sheets for Nike, Inc. We will examine the five main sections of Nike's balance sheet: current assets, noncurrent assets, current liabilities, noncurrent liabilities, and shareholders' equity. By understanding what items Nike and other companies include in each of these categories you will be able to better interpret their financial position and performance. Be sure to locate each of these items in the exhibit as you read the description of the item in the following pages.

Current Assets

current assets
Cash and all other assets that a company reasonably expects to convert to cash or sell or consume within one year or during the normal operating cycle, if longer than a year.

operating cycle
The time span during which a company spends cash to acquire goods and services that it uses to produce the organization's output, which it in turn sells to customers, who in turn pay for their purchases with cash.

Current assets include cash and all other assets that a company reasonably expects to convert to cash or sell or consume within one year or during the normal operating cycle, if longer than a year. An **operating cycle** is the time span during which a company spends cash to acquire goods and services that it uses to produce the organization's output, which in turn it sells to customers, who in turn pay for their purchases with cash. The following diagram illustrates what Nike's operating cycle might look like (figures are hypothetical):

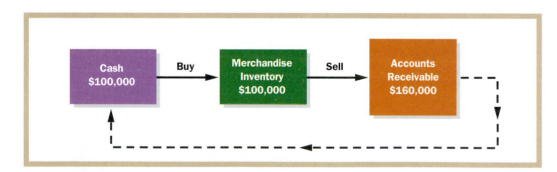

The box for Accounts Receivable (amounts owed to the business by customers) is larger than the other two boxes because the objective of a business is to sell goods at a price higher than their acquisition cost. The total amount of profit a firm earns during a particular period depends on how much its selling prices exceed its costs of producing or purchasing the products and additional expenses incurred during the period. The time span represented by the cycle might be as short as a few days — for a grocery store chain such as **Albertsons** — or many years — for a timber company such as **Georgia Pacific**.

As Exhibit 16-1 shows, Nike's current assets include cash and cash equivalents, accounts receivable, inventories, prepaid expenses, and other current assets. *Cash*

Exhibit 16-1

Nike, Inc.

Balance Sheet
(in millions)

	May 31	
	2003	**2002**
ASSETS		
Current assets		
Cash and equivalents	$ 634.0	$ 575.5
Accounts receivable, less allowance for		
doubtful accounts of $87.9 and $80.4	2,101.1	1,804.1
Inventories	1,514.9	1,373.8
Prepaid expenses	266.2	260.5
Other current assets	163.7	140.8
Total current assets	4,679.9	4,154.7
Noncurrent assets		
Property, plant, and equipment		
At cost	2,988.8	2,741.7
Less: accumulated depreciation	1,368.0	1,127.2
Net property, plant, and equipment	1,620.8	1,614.5
Identifiable intangible assets	118.2	206.0
Goodwill	65.6	232.7
Other assets	229.4	232.1
Total noncurrent assets	2,034.0	2,285.3
Total assets	$6,713.9	$6,440.0
LIABILITIES AND SHAREHOLDERS' EQUITY		
Current liabilities		
Notes payable	$ 75.4	$ 425.2
Accounts payable	572.7	504.4
Accrued liabilities	1,054.2	765.3
Income taxes payable	107.2	83.0
Current portion of long-term debt	205.7	55.3
Total current liabilities	2,015.2	1,833.2
Noncurrent liabilities		
Long-term debt	551.6	625.9
Deferred income taxes and		
other liabilities	156.1	141.6
Total noncurrent liabilities	707.7	767.5
Total liabilities	2,722.9	2,600.7
Shareholders' equity		
Redeemable preferred stock	0.3	0.3
Common stock at stated value	2.8	2.8
Capital in excess of stated value	589.0	538.7
Retained earnings	3,639.2	3,495.0
Other	(240.3)	(197.5)
Total shareholders' equity	3,991.0	3,839.3
Total liabilities and shareholders' equity	$6,713.9	$6,440.0

consists of bank deposits in checking accounts plus money on hand. **Cash equivalents** are short-term investments that a company can easily convert into cash with little delay, such as money market funds and Treasury bills. They represent an investment of excess cash that a company does not immediately need. The balance sheet usually shows these securities at their market price. In 2003, Nike had $634.0 million in cash and cash equivalents.

Accounts receivable is the total amount owed to the company by its customers. Accountants classify all accounts receivable as current assets, even though they may not fully collect them within one year. Because some customers ultimately will not pay their

cash equivalents
Short-term investments that a company can easily convert into cash with little delay.

bill, we reduce the total by an allowance or provision for "doubtful accounts" or "bad debts." The result represents the net amount the company will probably collect. At the end of the 2003 fiscal year,[1] Nike had gross accounts receivable of $2,189.0 million, but after deducting $87.9 million for doubtful accounts, the company expects to collect $2,101.1 million from its accounts receivable.

Inventories consist of merchandise, finished products of manufacturers, goods in the process of being manufactured, and raw materials. Accountants assume that companies do not hold inventories longer than one operating cycle. Thus, they regard all inventories as current assets. Companies state inventories at their cost or market price (defined as replacement cost), whichever is lower. Cost of manufactured products normally includes raw material cost plus the costs of converting it into a finished product (direct labor and manufacturing overhead). Companies in the United States can choose among four alternative methods to account for inventories: FIFO (first-in, first-out), LIFO (last-in, last-out), weighted-average cost, or specific identification. Appendix 16A describes these four methods. Nike uses FIFO for some of its inventories and weighted-average cost for others. Its 2003 inventories stood at $1,514.9 million.

Prepaid expenses are advance payments to suppliers. They are usually unimportant in relation to other assets. Examples are prepayment of rent and insurance premiums for coverage over the coming operating cycle. They belong in current assets because, if they were not present, the company would need more cash to conduct current operations. In 2003, Nike shows $266.2 million of prepaid expenses, which is less than 6% of total current assets.

Other current assets are miscellaneous current assets that do not fit into the listed categories. They might include notes receivable and short-term investments that are not cash equivalents. For Nike, such assets amounted to $163.7 million in 2003.

Noncurrent Assets: Property, Plant, and Equipment

**fixed assets
(tangible assets)**
Physical items that a person can see and touch, such as property, plant, and equipment.

Property, plant, and equipment are examples of **fixed assets** or **tangible assets**—physical items that a person can see and touch. Companies usually provide details about property, plant, and equipment in a footnote to the financial statements, such as the one for Nike shown in Exhibit 16-2. Footnotes are an integral part of financial statements. They contain explanations for the summary figures that appear in the statements.

Companies typically show *land* as a separate asset and carry it indefinitely at its original cost. They also initially record *buildings* and *machinery and equipment* at cost: the invoice amount, plus freight and installation, less cash discounts. However, unlike land, buildings, machinery, and equipment gradually decline in value through depreciation (see Chapter 15, page 662). The major challenge to firms is choosing a depreciation method—that is, deciding how to allocate the original cost to the particular periods or products that benefit from the use of the assets. Remember that depreciation only means allocating the original cost of plant and equipment, not valuing them in the ordinary sense of the term. Balance sheets typically do not show replacement cost, resale value, or the price changes since acquisition. The balance sheet amount is simply the original cost less the accumulated depreciation, which is the sum of all depreciation taken to date on the asset.

The amount of depreciation charged as expense each year depends on three factors:

1. The depreciable amount, which is the difference between the total acquisition cost and the estimated residual value. The residual value is the amount a company expects to receive when selling the asset at the end of its economic life.
2. The estimate of the asset's useful life or economic life. This estimate often depends more on technological changes and economic obsolescence than on physical wear and tear. Thus, the useful life is usually less than the physical life.

---

[1]A fiscal year is defined as the year established for accounting purposes for the preparation of annual reports. Nike's fiscal year is June 1 through May 31.

Note 3. Property, Plant, and Equipment (millions)		
	2003	**2002**
Land	$ 191.1	$ 178.3
Buildings	785.0	739.9
Machinery and equipment	1,538.7	1,356.9
Leasehold improvements	433.4	394.2
Construction-in-progress	40.6	72.4
	2,988.8	2,741.7
Less: accumulated depreciation	1,368.0	1,127.2
Net property, plant, and equipment	$1,620.8	$1,614.5

Exhibit 16-2

Nike, Inc.
Footnote 3 to the 2003 Financial Statements

3. The depreciation method. There are three general methods of depreciation: straight line, accelerated, and units of production. The straight-line method allocates the same cost to each year of an asset's useful life. Accelerated methods allocate more of the cost to the early years and less to the later years.[2] The units-of-production method allocates cost based on the amount of production rather than the passage of time.

Which method is best? It depends on the firm's goals, the asset involved, and the type of financial statement being prepared. The straight-line method is most popular. More than 90% of all firms use it for at least some assets when preparing financial statements for reporting to the public. They believe that it best matches the cost of an asset with the benefits from its use. In contrast, most U.S. firms use accelerated depreciation when preparing financial statements for tax reporting to the IRS. Why? Because it is the most beneficial method allowed under U.S. tax laws.

Suppose a business spends $42,000 to buy equipment with an estimated useful life of four years and an estimated residual value of $2,000. If we use the straight-line method of depreciation, the annual depreciation expense in each of the four years would be as follows:

$$= \frac{\text{original cost} - \text{estimated residual value}}{\text{years of useful life}}$$

$$= \frac{(\$42,000 - \$2,000)}{4}$$

$$= \$10,000 \text{ per year}$$

Exhibit 16-3 shows how we would display the asset in the balance sheet. In Exhibits 16-1 and 16-2, the original cost of fixed assets on Nike's 2003 balance sheet is $2,988.8 million. There is accumulated depreciation of $1,368.0 million, the portion of the original cost of the asset that Nike previously charged as depreciation expense, so the net property, plant, and equipment at May 31, 2003 is $2,988.8 million − $1,368.0 million = $1,620.8 million.

Depreciation represents the part of an asset that a company has already used. It is gone. It is not a pool of cash set aside to replace the asset. If a company decides to accumulate specific cash to replace assets, we would label such cash a "fund," such as a "cash fund for replacement and expansion." **Overseas Shipholding Group**, one of the world's largest bulk-shipping companies and owner of 52 vessels, has such a fund for new ships, calling it a capital construction fund. Its balance in 2003 was $232 million. Such funds are quite rare because most companies can earn better returns by investing any available cash

[2]Accelerated depreciation is described in Chapter 11. However, knowledge of accelerated depreciation methods is not necessary for understanding this chapter.

Exhibit 16-3
Straight-Line
Depreciation
(figures assumed)

	Balances at End of Year			
	1	2	3	4
Plant and equipment (at original acquisition cost)	$42,000	$42,000	$42,000	$42,000
Less: accumulated depreciation (the portion of original cost that has already been charged to operations as depreciation expense)	10,000	20,000	30,000	40,000
Net book value (the portion of original cost not yet charged as expense)	$32,000	$22,000	$12,000	$ 2,000

in ordinary operations rather than in special funds. Typically, companies use or acquire cash for the replacement and expansion of plant assets only as specific needs arise.

Leasehold improvements are investments made by a lessee (tenant) in items such as painting, decorating, fixtures, and airconditioning equipment that it cannot remove from the premises when a lease expires. Companies write off the costs of leasehold improvements in the same manner as depreciation, but we call their periodic write-off amortization rather than depreciation. Nike's leasehold improvements of $433.4 million are 15% of its property, plant, and equipment.

Nike shows *construction in progress* separately from other assets because the assets are not yet ready for use. It represents assets that will be part of buildings or machinery and equipment when completed.

Nike does not have natural resource assets, such as mineral deposits, but if it did it would group them with plant assets. Companies write off the original cost of natural resources in the form of depletion as they use the resources. For example, if a coal mine originally cost $10 million and contained an estimated 5 million tons, the depletion rate would be $10,000,000 ÷ 5,000,000 tons = $2 per ton. If the company mined 500,000 tons during the first year, depletion would be $2 × 500,000 = $1,000,000 for that year. If it mined 300,000 tons the second year, depletion would be $2 × 300,000 = $600,000. Such depletion charges would continue until the company had charged the entire $10 million as depletion expense.

Long-term investments are also noncurrent assets. They include long-term holdings of securities of other firms. We discuss the accounting for such investments in Chapter 17. Nike does not have any long-term investments, unless they are combined with other small, miscellaneous noncurrent assets in the $229.4 million of other assets shown in Exhibit 16-1.

Intangible Assets

intangible assets
Long-lived assets that are not physical in nature. Examples are goodwill, franchises, patents, trademarks, and copyrights.

goodwill
The excess of the cost of an acquired company over the sum of the fair market values of its identifiable individual assets less its liabilities.

We can physically observe tangible assets such as cash or equipment. In contrast, **intangible assets** are a class of long-lived assets that are not physical in nature. They are rights to expected future benefits deriving from their acquisition and continued possession. Examples are goodwill, franchises, patents, trademarks, and copyrights. In Exhibit 16-1, Nike shows intangible assets and goodwill of $118.2 million + $65.6 million = $183.8 million at May 31, 2003.

Goodwill, which we will discuss in more detail in the next chapter, is the excess of the cost of an acquired company over the sum of the fair market values of its identifiable individual assets less its liabilities. For example, Nike acquired Cole Haan for $95 million. It could assign only $13 million to various identifiable assets such as receivables, plant, and patents less liabilities assumed by Nike. It recorded the remainder, $82 million, as goodwill. This $82 million represents a value that Nike saw in Cole Haan beyond its recorded assets less liabilities. Accountants record it as an asset only because Nike was willing to pay $82 million more than the identifiable value of the assets less liabilities it acquired. The same value may have existed when Cole Haan was an independent company, but it would not appear on its balance sheet. This illustrates how an exchange transaction is a basic concept of accounting. After all, many owners, like those of Cole Haan, could obtain a premium price if they sold their companies. But we never record such goodwill. The only goodwill you will find on a balance sheet arises from an actual acquisition when a purchaser pays more than the amount assigned to individual assets.

Goodwill remains on a company's books until management determines that its value is impaired. Companies do not depreciate or amortize goodwill. However, they must annually apply an impairment test to assure that the goodwill has kept its value. If the goodwill has lost value, a company must reduce goodwill by the amount of the value decrease and charge that same amount as an impairment expense on the income statement. The accounting rule requiring an impairment test for goodwill is new, and Nike applied it for the first time in 2003. It found that goodwill from its Cole Haan acquisition as well as that from other acquisitions was impaired, and Nike reduced its goodwill by $266.1 million and charged an expense of the same amount on its 2003 income statement. (Note that Nike also added $99 million of goodwill in 2003.) An even larger impact of the impairment test occured in the fourth quarter of 2002 when **AOL-Time Warner** determined that its goodwill, which was listed on its books at $81.671 billion, was worth only $36.986 billion. Thus, the company reduced goodwill by $81.671 billion − $36.986 billion = $44.685 billion and recognized an expense of the same amount, contributing greatly to the company's nearly $100 billion net loss.

Companies in many countries also regard research and development costs as assets. For example, many Australian companies, such as **SSH Medical** (a medical devices company near Sydney) and **Advanced Energy Systems** (a renewable energy company in Perth), list "capitalized research and development costs" on their balance sheets. Accounting authorities in those countries assume that companies incur research costs to benefit future operations and thus record the costs the same way they would the purchase of equipment. They then amortize the costs over the years, usually three to six, of expected benefit. In the United States, however, the FASB requires companies to write off these costs to expense as incurred. The FASB admits that research and development costs may generate many long-term benefits, but the general high degree of uncertainty about the extent and measurement of future benefits has led to conservative accounting in the form of immediate write-off.

Liabilities

Assets are, of course, only part of the picture of any organization's financial health. Its liabilities, both current and noncurrent, are equally important.

Current liabilities are an organization's debts that fall due within the coming year or within the normal operating cycle if longer than a year. Turn again to Exhibit 16-1 on page 711. *Notes payable* are short-term debts backed by formal promissory notes held by a bank or business creditors. *Accounts payable* are amounts owed to suppliers who extended credit for purchases on open account. *Accrued liabilities* (also called accrued expenses payable) are amounts owed for wages, salaries, interest, and similar items. The accountant recognizes expenses as they occur—regardless of when a company pays for them in cash. *Income taxes payable* is a special accrued expense of enough magnitude to warrant a separate classification. The *current portion of long-term debt* shows the payments due within the next year on bonds and other long-term debt. This concludes Nike's current liabilities, which total $2,015.2 million.

In addition to the current liabilities that Nike lists, some companies also list unearned revenue, also called deferred revenue. Such revenue occurs when a company receives cash before delivering the related goods or services. For example,

OBJECTIVE 2

Recognize and define the main types of liabilities in the balance sheet of a corporation.

current liabilities
An organization's debts that fall due within the coming year or within the normal operating cycle if longer than a year.

The Washington Post Company has about $135 million in such an account because it agrees to send newspapers and magazines (including *Newsweek*) to subscribers with prepaid subscriptions. Nike had no unearned revenue in 2003. Now that you understand both current assets and current liabilities, we can introduce a commonly used term, **working capital,** which is current assets less current liabilities. Investors watch working capital carefully to assess whether a company has enough current assets to pay current liabilities as they come due.

Noncurrent liabilities, also called **long-term liabilities,** are an organization's debts that fall due beyond one year. Exhibit 16-1 shows Nike's noncurrent liabilities for 2003 as $707.7 million, making its total liabilities $2,722.9 million. Nike has two noncurrent liabilities, long-term debt (which we will discuss in more depth in a moment) and deferred income taxes. The latter rather technical and controversial item arises because the financial statements used for reporting to shareholders differ legitimately from those used for reporting to the income tax authorities. Appendix 16B provides more details about deferred taxes.

Exhibit 16-4 is a footnote from Nike's financial statements that provides details about its long-term debts. Note especially the next-to-last line in this exhibit, "Less: current maturities." This item refers to payments due in the next year. Nike subtracts the $205.7 million noted on this line from long-term debt because the company has already included it in current liabilities. Nike shows the remaining $551.6 million as "Long-term debt" in Exhibit 16-1.

Long-term debt may be secured or unsecured. Secured debt provides debt holders with first claim on specified assets. Mortgage bonds are an example of secured debt. If the company is unable to meet its regular obligations on the bonds, it may sell the specified assets and use the proceeds to pay off the firm's obligations to its bondholders, in which case secured debt holders have first claim.

Unsecured debt consists of **debentures** (bonds, notes, or loans), which are formal certificates of indebtedness accompanied by a promise to pay interest at a specified annual rate. Unsecured debt holders are general creditors who have a general claim against total assets rather than a specific claim against particular assets. Most of Nike's long-term debt is unsecured. Holders of **subordinated** bonds or debentures are junior to the other creditors in exercising claims against assets.

---

working capital
Current assets less current liabilities.

noncurrent liabilities (long-term liabilities)
An organization's debts that fall due beyond one year.

debentures
Formal certificates of indebtedness that are accompanied by a promise to pay interest at a specified annual rate.

subordinated
A creditor claim that is junior to the other creditors in exercising claims against assets.

Exhibit 16-4
Nike, Inc
Footnote 7 to the 2003 Financial Statements

	May 31	
Note 7. Long-Term Debt (millions)	**2003**	**2002**
6.69% Corporate bond, payable June 17, 2002	$ —	$ 50.0
6.375% Corporate bond, payable December 1, 2003	200.0	199.8
5.5% Corporate bond, payable August 15, 2006	266.3	248.2
4.8% Corporate bond, payable July 9, 2007	27.1	—
5.375% Corporate bond, payable July 8, 2009	27.6	—
5.66% Corporate bond, payable July 23, 2012	28.1	—
5.4% Corporate bond, payable August 7, 2012	16.4	—
4.3% Japanese yen note, payable June 26, 2011	90.1	83.4
2.6% Japanese yen note, maturing August 20, 2001 through November 20, 2020	69.2	67.8
2.0% Japanese yen note, maturing August 20, 2001 through November 20, 2020	30.8	30.2
Other	1.7	1.8
Subtotal	757.3	681.2
Less: current maturities	205.7	55.3
Total	$551.6	$625.9

Consider the following simplified example. Suppose a corporation is liquidated. **Liquidation** means converting assets to cash and using the cash to pay off outside claims. The company had a single asset, a building, that it sold for $120,000 cash:

Assets		Liabilities and Stockholders' Equity	
Cash	$120,000	Accounts payable	$ 60,000
		First-mortgage bonds payable	80,000
		Subordinated debentures payable	40,000
		Total liabilities	$180,000
		Stockholders' equity (negative)	(60,000)
Total assets	$120,000	Total liabilities and stockholders' equity	$120,000

The company would pay the mortgage (secured) bondholders in full ($80,000). It would pay trade creditors, such as suppliers, the remaining $40,000 for their $60,000 claim ($.67 on the dollar). Other claimants would get nothing. If the debentures were unsubordinated, the company would use the $40,000 of cash remaining after paying $80,000 to the mortgage holders to settle the $100,000 claims of the unsecured creditors proportionately as follows:

To trade creditors	6/10 × $40,000 = $24,000
To debenture holders	4/10 × $40,000 = 16,000
Total cash distributed	$40,000

To increase the appeal of their bonds, many companies issue debt that is convertible into common stock. Convertibility allows bondholders to participate in a company's success without the risk of holding common stock. Suppose Nike issued convertible bonds for $1,000 when its stock price was $22, with a provision that investors can convert each bond into 40 common shares. If the stock price increases by 50% to $33 a share, the bondholder could exchange the $1,000 bond for 40 shares worth 40 × $33 = $1,320. If the stock price falls (or does not increase beyond $25 a share), the bondholder can keep the bond and receive $1,000 at maturity.

Stockholders' Equity

The final element of a balance sheet is stockholders' equity (also called shareholders' equity or owners' equity or net worth), the total residual interest in the business. As we saw in Chapter 15, it is the excess of total assets over total liabilities. The main elements of stockholders' equity arise from two sources: (1) contributed or paid-in capital, and (2) retained income.

Paid-in capital typically comes from owners who invest in the business in exchange for stock certificates that specify their ownership interest. Holders of stock certificates are stockholders or shareholders. There are two major classes of capital stock: common stock and preferred stock. Some companies have several categories of each, all with a variety of different attributes.

All corporations have **common stock.** Such stock has no predetermined rate of dividends and is the last to obtain a share in the assets when the corporation liquidates. It usually confers voting power to elect the board of directors of the corporation. Common stock is generally the riskiest investment in a corporation, being unattractive in dire times but attractive in prosperous times because, unlike other stocks, there is no limit to the stockholder's potential participation in earnings. The corporate form of ownership provides one additional benefit to shareholders—**limited liability.** This means that a company's creditors cannot seek payment from stockholders as individuals if the corporation itself cannot pay its debts.

preferred stock
*Stock that typically has
some priority over other
shares in the payment
of dividends or the
distribution of assets
upon liquidation.*

**par value (legal value,
stated value)**
*The value often printed
on the face of stock
certificates.*

Exhibit 16-1 shows that Nike has a small amount of preferred stock, in addition to common stock. About 40% of the major companies in the United States issue **preferred stock.** It typically has some priority over other shares in the payment of dividends or the distribution of assets on liquidation. For example, Nike pays an annual preferred stock dividend of $.10 per share, or $30,000 in total. Nike must pay these dividends in full before it pays dividends to any other classes of stock. Preferred shareholders in Nike, like preferred shareholders in other corporations, have no voting privileges.

A **par** or **legal** or **stated value** is often printed on the face of stock certificates. For preferred stock, par is a basis for designating the amount of dividends or interest. Many preferred stocks have $100 par values. That is, a 9%, $100-par preferred stock would carry a $9 annual dividend. In contrast, par value has no practical importance for common stock. Historically, the par amount of common stock specified the maximum legal liability of the stockholder in case the corporation could not pay its debts. Currently, companies set par at a nominal amount (for example, $1) in relation to the market value of the stock on issuance (say, $70). It is generally illegal for a corporation to sell an original issue of its common stock below par.

Capital in excess of stated value is the difference between the amount a company receives when issuing new shares and the stated, par, or legal value of the shares issued. Suppose Nike had issued all its outstanding common shares for cash. The cumulative balance sheet effect at May 31, 2003, would be

Cash	$591,800,000	Common stock, at stated value	$ 2,800,000
		Capital in excess of stated value	589,000,000
		Total paid-in capital	$591,800,000

Retained earnings, also called retained income, is the increase in stockholders' equity caused by profitable operations (see Chapter 15). Retained earnings is the dominant item of stockholders' equity for most companies. For instance, as of May 31, 2003, Nike had common stockholders' equity of $3,990.7 million of which $3,639.2 million or 91% was retained earnings.

treasury stock
*A corporation's own
stock that it has issued
and subsequently
repurchased to hold for
a specific purpose.*

Many companies have **treasury stock,** which is a corporation's own stock that the company issued and subsequently repurchased to hold for a specific purpose. Such a repurchase is a decrease in ownership claims. Therefore, it should appear on a balance sheet as a deduction from total stockholders' equity. The stock is not retired; it is only held temporarily "in the treasury" to be distributed later, possibly as a part of an employee stock purchase plan or as an executive bonus or for use in acquiring another company. A company does not pay cash dividends on shares held in the treasury. Companies distribute dividends only to the outstanding shares (those in the hands of stockholders). Nike had no treasury stock in 2003. In contrast, **McDonald's Corporation** had nearly $9 billion of treasury stock on January 1, 2003:

Shareholders' equity before deducting treasury stock	$ 19,268,600,000
Treasury stock	(8,987,700,000)
Total shareholders' equity	$ 10,280,900,000

Summary Problems For Your Review

PROBLEM

"The book value of plant assets is the amount that a company would have to spend today for their replacement." Do you agree? Explain.

SOLUTION

Net book value of the plant assets is the result of deducting accumulated depreciation from original cost. This process does not attempt to capture all the technological and economic events that may affect replacement value. Consequently, there is little likelihood that net book value will approximate replacement cost.

PROBLEM

On December 31, 20X1, a magazine publishing company receives $150,000 in cash for three-year subscriptions. It regards this sum as unearned revenue. Show the balances in that account at December 31, 20X2, 20X3, and 20X4. How much revenue would the company earn in each of those three years?

SOLUTION

The balance in unearned revenue would decline at the rate of $50,000 yearly. The company would recognize $50,000 as earned revenue in each of the three years.

	December 31			
	20X1	**20X2**	**20X3**	**20X4**
Unearned revenue	$150,000	$100,000	$50,000	$0

Income Statement

Most investors are vitally concerned about a company's ability to produce long-run earnings and dividends. In this regard, income statements are more important than balance sheets. Income statements show revenue first; this represents the total sales value of products delivered and services rendered to customers. Then they list expenses, which we deduct to get net income. We next examine how the format of the income statement can help users judge a company's performance.

OBJECTIVE 4

Recognize and define the principal elements in the income statement of a corporation.

Operating Performance

An income statement can take one of two major forms: single step or multiple step. A single-step statement merely lists all expenses without drawing subtotals. It provides an overall measure of performance, but it does not allow direct assessment of performance in specific areas. In contrast, a multiple-step statement contains one or more subtotals. By dividing expenses into categories, we can monitor a company's performance in different dimensions—primarily assessing operating management separately from financial management.

Exhibit 16-5 illustrates the two most common subtotals used to assess operating performance: *gross profit* and *income from operations* (also called operating income or operating profit). Gross profit or gross margin is sales less cost of goods sold. It measures the size of the margin above merchandise costs and is an important statistic for many managers and analysts. A shrinking gross profit can indicate increasing competition in the market for the company's goods or services. If you try to compare gross margins for two companies, you should be aware that a company's inventory method affects its gross profit. Why? Because the cost of goods sold is the inventory value for the items sold. Thus, understanding the inventory methods described in Appendix 16A is important to interpreting differences in gross margin.

Exhibit 16-5
Nike, Inc.
*Statement of Income
(millions except per
share data)*

	Year Ended May 31	
	2003	**2002**
Revenues	$10,697.0	$ 9,893.0
Cost of sales	6,313.6	6,004.7
Gross profit	$ 4,383.4	$ 3,888.3
Selling and administrative expenses	3,137.6	2,820.4
Income from operations	$ 1,245.8	$ 1,067.9
Other expense (income)		
Interest expense	$ 42.9	$ 47.6
Other income/expense, net	79.9	3.0
Total other expense	$ 122.8	$ 50.6
Income before income taxes	$ 1,123.0	$ 1,017.3
Income taxes	382.9	349.0
Income before cumulative effect of		
accounting change	740.1	668.3
Cumulative effect of accounting change	266.1	5.0
Net income	$ 474.0	$ 663.3
Earnings per share*	$ 1.79	$ 2.48

* Computation of earnings per share:

	2003	**2002**
Net income	$474,000,000	$663,300,000
Divided by average common shares		
outstanding	264,500,000	267,700,000
Earnings per share	$1.79	$2.48

Operating income (or loss) summarizes the results of the basic operating activities of the company—the day-to-day activities that generate sales revenue. Income statements often group depreciation expense, selling expenses, and administrative expenses as "operating expenses" and deduct them from the gross profit to obtain operating income. (Of course, cost of goods sold is also an operating expense. Why? Because we also deduct it from sales revenue to obtain "operating income.") In 2003, Nike had a gross profit of $4,383.4 million and operating income of $1,245.8 million. This summarizes Nike's success in producing and selling its products.

MAKING MANAGERIAL DECISIONS

To intelligently interpret a company's financial statements, it is important to identify whether a particular account is an asset, liability, stockholders' equity, revenue, or expense account. Identify the type of account for each of the following: accounts receivable, accounts payable, investments in marketable securities, depreciation, paid-in capital, cost of goods sold, income taxes, income taxes payable, bank loans, common stock, and inventories.

Answer
Asset accounts are accounts receivable, investments in marketable securities, and inventories. Liability accounts are accounts payable and bank loans. Stockholders' equity accounts are paid-in capital and common stock. No revenue accounts are listed. Expense accounts are depreciation, cost of goods sold, and income taxes.

Financial Management

Management of a company is responsible for financial management as well as operating management. Financial management focuses on where to get cash and how to use cash for the benefit of the organization. That is, financial management attempts to answer such questions as: How much cash should we hold in our checking accounts? Should we pay a dividend? Should we borrow money or issue common stock? The best managers are superb at both operating management and financial management. However, many managers are better operating managers than financial managers, or vice versa.

Because financial decisions and operating decisions each have their own effect on income, it is useful to separate the two effects in the income statement. Financing decisions affect primarily interest income and expense, so we present them as separate items after operating income. This approach facilitates comparisons of operating income between years and between companies. Some companies make heavy use of debt, which causes high interest expense, whereas other companies incur little debt and interest expense. Other nonoperating items might also include income or loss on investments and gains or losses from foreign exchange transactions or from disposals of fixed assets.

Income, Earnings, and Profits

Although this book tends to use the term *income* most often, you will also see the terms *earnings* and *profits* used as synonyms. Other names for the income statement include statement of earnings, statement of profit and loss, and P&L statement. Most companies still use *net income* on their income statements, but the term *earnings* is becoming increasingly popular. Nike's 2003 net income was $474.0 million.

The term **net income** is the popular "bottom line"—the residual amount after we deduct all expenses including income taxes. Income taxes are often a prominent expense that companies do not merely list with operating expenses. Instead, income statements usually deduct income taxes as a separate item placed immediately before net income. Nike's 2003 income statement in Exhibit 16-5 shows income taxes followed by a subtotal labeled "income before effect of accounting change." If Nike had no changes in accounting method, which is usually the case, the line after income taxes would have been net income.

> **net income**
> The "bottom line"—the residual amount after we deduct from revenues all expenses, including income taxes.

Why does Nike deduct the effect of a change in accounting methods on a separate line? In 2003, the company implemented the impairment test for goodwill for the first time, and as a result it charged $266.1 million to income for reductions in goodwill. Because this represents a cumulative effect of impairments over several years, Nike elected to show it separately so that investors did not think that the entire charge was a result of 2003's activities. The line "income before effect of accounting change" is a better summary of 2003's performance than is net income.

Income statements conclude with the disclosure of **earnings per share.** Exhibit 16-5 illustrates this as the net income divided by the average number of common shares outstanding during the year. Nike earned $1.79 per share in 2003.

> **earnings per share**
> Net income divided by the average number of common shares outstanding during the year.

OBJECTIVE 5

Recognize and define the elements in the statement of retained earnings.

Statement of Retained Earnings

To explain the changes in retained earnings, companies frequently include a separate financial statement, the **statement of retained earnings** (also called **statement of retained income**). This may also be one part of a larger statement, the statement of changes in stockholders' equity. As Exhibit 16-6 demonstrates, the major reasons for changes in retained earnings are dividends and net income. Net income increases retained earnings, and losses and dividends reduce retained earnings. Note especially that dividends are not expenses; companies do not deduct them in computing net income, as explained in Chapter 15 on page 678. Nike also reduced retained earnings by buying back some of its common shares, essentially giving some shareholders cash in exchange for their equity claims.

> **statement of retained earnings (statement of retained income)**
> A financial statement that explains changes in the retained earnings or retained income account for a given period.

Exhibit 16-6
Nike, Inc.
Statement of Retained Earnings for the Year Ended May 31, 2003 (millions of dollars)

Retained earnings, May 31, 2002	$3,495.0
Net income (Exhibit 16-5)	474.0
Total	3,969.0
Deduct: Dividends on common stock	142.7
Repurchase of common stock	186.2
Other	0.9
Retained earnings, May 31, 2003	$3,639.2

Summary Problem For Your Review

PROBLEM

Companies sometimes combine the income statement and statement of retained earnings into a single statement. Prepare a combined income statement and statement of retained earnings from the following data. Use a multiple-step format for the income statement.

Cost of goods sold	$420,000
Net sales	750,000
Income taxes	80,000
Beginning retained earnings	440,000
Dividends	30,000
Interest expense	20,000
Selling and administrative expenses	110,000

SOLUTION

Statement of Income and Retained Earnings	
Net sales	$750,000
Cost of goods sold	420,000
Gross margin	330,000
Selling and administrative expenses	110,000
Operating income	220,000
Interest expense	20,000
Income before income taxes	200,000
Income taxes	80,000
Net income	120,000
Beginning retained earnings	440,000
Dividends	(30,000)
Ending retained earnings	$530,000

Statement of Cash Flows

Until recently, many decision makers focused primarily on the income statement and the balance sheet. However, an increasing number of decision makers are now carefully examining another required statement, the statement of cash flows. A **statement of cash flows** reports the cash receipts and cash payments of an organization during a particular period. The statement has the following purposes:

statement of cash flows
A statement that reports the cash receipts and cash payments of an organization during a particular period.

1. It shows the relationship of net income to changes in cash balances. Cash balances can decline despite positive net income and vice versa.

2. It reports past cash flows as an aid to
   a. Predicting future cash flows
   b. Evaluating management's generation and use of cash
   c. Determining a company's ability to pay interest and dividends, and to pay debts when they are due
3. It reveals commitments to assets that may restrict or expand future courses of action.

Basic Concepts

Recall that balance sheets show the status of an entity at a point in time. In contrast, statements of cash flows, income statements, and statements of retained income cover periods of time. They explain why the balance sheet items have changed. The accompanying diagram depicts this linkage, where the arrows represent the flow of events that affect a company's balance sheet during the year:

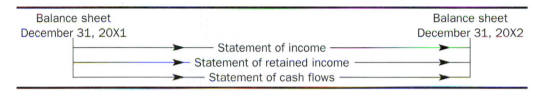

The income and retained income statements summarize events that explain the change in retained earnings. The statement of cash flows summarizes events that explain the change in cash—where cash came from during a period and where it was spent.

The statement of cash flows explains changes in cash and cash equivalents, both of which a company can use almost immediately to meet obligations. Recall from p. 711 that cash equivalents are highly liquid short-term investments that a company can easily convert into cash with little delay. Hereafter, when we refer to cash, we mean both cash and cash equivalents.

Typical Activities Affecting Cash

The fundamental approach to the statement of cash flows is simple: (1) List the activities that increased cash (cash inflows) and those that decreased cash (cash outflows), and (2) place each cash inflow and outflow into one of three categories according to the type of activity that caused it: operating activities, investing activities, and financing activities.

The following activities are those found most often in statements of cash flows:

OBJECTIVE 6

Identify activities that affect cash, and classify them as operating, investing, or financing activities.

Operating Activities

Cash Inflows:	*Cash Outflows:*
Collections from customers	Cash payments to suppliers
Interest and dividends collected	Cash payments to employees
Other operating receipts	Interest paid
	Taxes paid
	Other operating cash payments

Investing Activities

Cash Inflows:	*Cash Outflows:*
Sale of property, plant, and equipment	Purchase of property, plant, and equipment
Sale of securities that are not cash equivalents	Purchase of securities that are not cash equivalents
Receipt of loan repayments	Making loans

Financing Activities

Cash Inflows:	*Cash Outflows:*
Borrowing cash from creditors	Repayment of amounts borrowed
Issuing equity securities	Repurchase of equity shares (including the purchase of treasury stock)
	Payment of dividends

Liabilities and Stockholders' Equity

Transaction	Assets					=	Liabilities			Stockholders' Equity	
	Cash	Accounts Receivable	Inventories	Fixed Assets, Gross	Accumulated Depreciation	=	Accounts Payable	Wages & Salaries Payable	Long-Term Debt	Paid-In Capital	Retained Earnings
Balance, 12/31/X1	+25	+25	+60	+330	−110	=	+6	+4	+5	+210	+105
1a. Purchase inventory on account			+140			=	+140				
1b. Payments to suppliers	−72					=	−72				
2a. Sales on credit		+200				=					+200
2b. Cash collections from customers	+180	−180				=					
2c. Cost of goods sold			−100			=					−100
3a. Wages & salaries expense						=		+36			−36
3b. Payments to employees	−15					=		−15			
4. Depreciation expense					−17	=					−17
5. Interest expense—paid in cash	−4					=					−4
6. Income tax expense—paid in cash	−20					=					−20
7. Purchase of fixed assets for cash	−287			+287		=					
8. Sales of fixed assets*	+10			−36	+26	=					
9. Issue long-term debt for cash	+120					=			+120		
10. Issue common stock for cash	+98					=				+98	
11. Pay cash dividends	−19					=					−19
Balance, 12/31/X2	+16	+45	+100	+581	−101	=	+74	+25	+125	+308	+109

* Balmer Company sold assets with a gross book value of $36,000 and accumulated depreciation of $26,000, receiving cash of $10,000.

Exhibit 16-7
Balmer Company Summarized Transactions, 20X2 (in thousands of dollars)

Let's look briefly at each of the three categories. As the lists of activities indicate, **cash flows from operating activities** are generally the effects of transactions that affect the income statement. **Cash flows from investing activities** include (1) lending and collecting on loans and (2) acquiring and selling long-term assets. **Cash flows from financing** activities include obtaining cash from creditors and owners, repaying creditors or buying back stock from owners, and paying cash dividends.

Perhaps the most troublesome classifications are the receipts and payments of interest and the receipts of dividends. After all, these items are a result of investment and financing activities. After much debate, the FASB decided to include these items with cash flows from operating activities. Why? Mainly because they affect the computation of income. In contrast, payments of cash dividends are financing activities because they do not affect income.

Focus of a Statement of Cash Flows

To see the basic ideas underlying the statement of cash flows, we will first consider a simple hypothetical company, the Balmer Company, and later we will look at the real statement of cash flows for Nike. Exhibit 16-7 shows Balmer Company's summary transactions for 20X2, Exhibit 16-8 shows its 20X2 income statement, and Exhibit 16-9 shows condensed balance sheets for 20X1 and 20X2.

Because the statement of cash flows explains the causes for the change in cash, our first step is to compute the amount of the change (which represents the net effect we need to explain):

Cash, December 31, 20X1	$25,000
Cash, December 31, 20X2	16,000
Net decrease in cash	$ 9,000

Exhibit 16-10 illustrates a statement of cash flows that explains this $9,000 decrease in cash. Let's look at each of the three sections of this cash flow statement.

Cash Flows from Financing Activities

Although most companies list operating activities as the first section of the cash flow statement, it is better to begin our discussion with the more easily described and understood section of the cash flow statement, cash flows from financing activities. This section shows cash flows to and from providers of capital. The easiest way to determine cash flows from financing activities is to examine changes in the cash account in the balance sheet equation and identify those associated with financing activities. Balmer Company had three such transactions in 20X2, as shown in Exhibit 16-7:

transaction 9, Issue long-term debt, $120,000
transaction 10, Issue common stock, $98,000
transaction 11, Pay dividends, $19,000

Sidebar definitions

cash flows from operating activities
The section in the statement of cash flows that lists the cash-flow effects of transactions that affect the income statement.

cash flows from investing activities
The section in the statement of cash flows that lists the cash-flow effects of (1) lending and collecting on loans and (2) acquiring and selling long-term assets.

cash flows from financing activities
The section in the statement of cash flows that lists the cash-flow effects of obtaining cash from creditors and owners, repaying creditors or buying back stock from owners, and paying cash dividends.

OBJECTIVE 7

Assess financing and investing activities using the statement of cash flows.

Sales		$200
Costs and expenses		
Cost of goods sold	$100	
Wages and salaries	36	
Depreciation	17	
Interest	4	
Total costs and expenses		157
Income before income taxes		43
Income taxes		20
Net income		$ 23

Exhibit 16-8
Balmer Company
Statement of Income for the Year Ended December 31, 20X2 (in thousands)

	Assets				Liabilities and Stockholders' Equity		
	20X2	**20X1**	**Increase (Decrease)**		**20X2**	**20X1**	**Increase (Decrease)**
Current assets				Current liabilities			
Cash	$ 16	$ 25	$ (9)	Accounts payable	$ 74	$ 6	$ 68
Accounts receivable	45	25	20	Wages and salaries			
Inventory	100	60	40	payable	25	4	21
Total current assets	161	110	51	Total current liabilities	99	10	89
Fixed assets, gross	581	330	251	Long-term debt	125	5	120
Less accum. depreciation	(101)	(110)	9	Stockholders' equity	417	315	102
Net fixed assets	480	220	260	Total liabilities and			
Total assets	$641	$330	$311	stockholders' equity	$641	$330	$311

Exhibit 16-9
Balmer Company
Balance Sheet as of December 31 (in thousands)

The first two of these transactions are cash inflows, and the last is a cash outflow. Therefore, Balmer's net cash inflow from financing activities totals $199,000:

Balmer Company
Cash Flows from Financing Activities, 20X2

Proceeds from issuance of long-term debt	$120,000
Proceeds from issuance of common stock	98,000
Payment of dividends	(19,000)
Net cash provided by financing activities	$199,000

Exhibit 16-10
Balmer Company
Statement of Cash Flows for the Year Ended December 31, 20X2 (in thousands)

Cash Flows from Operating Activities		
Cash collections from customers		$180
Cash payments		
To suppliers	$72	
To employees	15	
For interest	4	
For taxes	20	
Total cash payments		(111)
Net cash provided by operating activities		$ 69

Cash Flows from Investing Activities		
Purchases of fixed assets	$(287)	
Proceeds from sale of fixed assets	10	
Net cash used in investing activities		(277)

Cash Flows from Financing Activities		
Proceeds from issue of long-term debt	$120	
Proceeds from issue of common stock	98	
Dividends paid	(19)	
Net cash provided by financing activities		199
Net decrease in cash		$ (9)
Cash, December 31, 20X1		25
Cash, December 31, 20X2		$ 16

If you did not have access to the balance sheet equation entries, you could also look at the changes in Balmer's balance sheet during 20X2. As a general rule for financing activities,

- Increases in cash (cash inflows) stem from increases in liabilities or paid-in-capital
- Decreases in cash (cash outflows) stem from decreases in liabilities or paid-in-capital or payment of dividends

Following is a list of some financing activities and their effect on cash:

Type of Transaction	Increase (+) or Decrease (−) in Cash
Increase long-term or short-term debt	+
Reduce long-term or short-term debt	−
Sell common or preferred shares	+
Repurchase common shares	−
Pay dividends	−
Convert debt to common stock	No effect

Cash Flows from Investing Activities

The section of the cash flow statement called cash flows from investing activities lists cash flows from the purchase or sale of plant, property, equipment, and other long-lived assets. It is usually the second section in the statement. To determine the cash flows from investing activities, you need to look at transactions that increase or decrease long-lived assets, loans made by the company, or securities it owns that are not cash equivalents. Balmer Company has only one such asset, fixed assets, and its related accumulated depreciation account. There were two cash transactions relating to fixed assets during 20X2:

transaction 7, Purchase fixed assets for cash, $287,000
transaction 8, Sale of fixed assets for cash, $10,000

The first of these transactions is a cash outflow, and the second is a cash inflow. The investing activities section of Balmer's cash flow statement is

Balmer Company
Cash Flows from Investing Activities, 20X2

Purchase of fixed assets	$(287,000)
Proceeds from sale of fixed assets	10,000
Net cash used by investing activities	$(277,000)

Notice that we place cash outflows in parentheses. Because there is a net cash outflow, investing activities used cash during January. This contrasts with financing activities, which provided cash.

The general rule for investing activities is that

- Increases in cash (cash inflows) stem from decreases in long-lived assets, loans, and investments
- Decreases in cash (cash outflows) stem from increases in long-lived assets, loans, and investments

Following is a list of investing activities and their effects on cash:

Type of Transaction	Increase (+) or Decrease (−) in Cash
Purchase fixed assets for cash	−
Purchase fixed assets by issuing debt	No effect
Sell fixed assets for cash	+
Purchase securities that are not cash equivalents	−
Sell securities that are not cash equivalents	+
Make a loan	−
Collect a loan	+

Noncash Investing and Financing Activities

Sometimes financing or investing activities do not affect cash but are very similar to transactions that have a cash flow effect. Companies must list such activities in a separate schedule accompanying the statement of cash flows. In our example, Balmer Company did not have any noncash investing or financing activities. However, suppose Balmer's purchase of fixed assets was not for cash but was financed as follows:

A. Balmer acquired $150,000 of the fixed assets by issuing common stock, and
B. Balmer acquired the other $137,000 of fixed assets by signing a note payable for $137,000.

Balmer could have taken the $150,000 and $137,000 in cash and then used that cash to buy fixed assets, but it never actually received the cash. Thus, there is no entry to the statement of cash flows. However, because of the similarities between this noncash transaction and the purchase for cash, readers of statements of cash flows want to be informed of such noncash activities. We must report such items in a schedule of noncash investing and financing activities. Balmer Company's schedule for these hypothetical transactions would be

Balmer Company
Schedule of noncash investing and financing activities, 20X2

Common stock issued to acquire store equipment	$150,000
Mortgage payable for acquisition of store equipment	$137,000

OBJECTIVE 8

Use both the direct method and the indirect method to explain cash flows from operating activities.

direct method
A method for computing cash flows from operating activities that subtracts operating cash disbursements from cash collections to arrive at cash flows from operations.

indirect method
A method for computing cash flows from operating activities that adjusts the previously calculated accrual net income from the income statement to reflect only cash receipts and cash disbursements.

Cash Flow from Operating Activities

Analyzing the results of financing and investing activities informs investors about management's ability to make financial and investment decisions. However, users of financial statements are even more concerned with assessing management's operating decisions. They focus on the first major section of cash flow statements, cash flows from operating activities (or cash flows from operations). This section shows the cash effects of transactions that affect the income statement.

Approaches to Calculating the Cash Flow from Operating Activities

We can use either of two approaches to compute cash flows from operating activities (or cash flow from operations). The **direct method** subtracts operating cash disbursements from cash collections to arrive at cash flows from operations. The **indirect method** adjusts the previously calculated accrual net income from the income statement to reflect only cash receipts and cash disbursements. Both methods show the same amount of cash provided by (or used for) operating activities. The only difference is the format of the statement.

The FASB prefers the direct method because it is a straightforward listing of cash inflows and cash outflows and is easier for investors to understand. However, 99% of all companies use the indirect method. Why? Because it links cash flows directly with net income, emphasizing how income and cash flows differ. We will discuss the direct method first because, as a newcomer to accounting, you will probably find it easier to understand. However, to understand cash flow statements for real companies, it is essential to also understand the indirect method that most companies use.

Consider first the types of cash flows that accountants classify as operating activities. Exhibit 16-11 lists many such activities. These cash flows are associated with revenues and expenses on the income statement. Notice that recording revenues from the sales of goods or services does not necessarily increase cash immediately. Only sales for cash immediately increase cash. There is no cash effect of credit sales until the customer actually pays. Balmer Company must collect its accounts receivable to generate any cash.

The cash effects of expenses are similar. Sometimes—depreciation is an example—the cash outflow precedes the recording of the expense on the income statement. For example, Balmer Company paid $287,000 in cash for its fixed assets and recorded the purchase as an investing cash outflow. The company then records depreciation expenses as it uses the equipment, long after the cash payment. Thus, depreciation is not a cash flow.

In contrast, sometimes the cash outflow follows the recording of the expense. For example, most companies pay salaries and wages after employees have earned them. Suppose that Balmer Company pays salaries and wages on the 10th of each month for the amount earned the previous month. Then the accrual of the expense would occur one month and the related cash outflow would come the following month. The expense appears in the first month's income statement, but the cash outflow appears in the second month's statement of cash flows.

Now that you know some of the operating transactions that affect cash and how the cash inflow or outflow can occur at a different time than the recording of the related revenue or expense, let's examine the two formats used for showing the cash flow effects of operations.

Type of Transaction	Increase (+) or Decrease (−) in Cash
Operating activities	
Sales of goods and services for cash	+
Sales of goods and services on credit	No effect
Collection of accounts receivable	+
Receive dividends or interest	+
Recognize cost of goods sold	No effect
Purchase inventory for cash	−
Purchase inventory on credit	No effect
Pay accounts payable	−
Accrue operating expenses	No effect
Pay operating expenses	−
Accrue taxes	No effect
Pay taxes	−
Accrue interest	No effect
Pay interest	−
Prepay expenses for cash	−
Record the using up of prepaid expenses	No effect
Charge depreciation	No effect

Exhibit 16-11
Analysis of Effects of Transactions on Cash Flows from Operating Activities

Cash Flow from Operations—The Direct Method

The direct method consists of a listing of cash receipts (inflows) and cash disbursements (outflows). The easiest way to construct the statement of cash flows from operations using the direct method is to examine the Cash column of the balance sheet equation. The following entries from Exhibit 16-7 affect cash and were not financing and investing activities:

Transaction	Cash Effect
(1b) Payments to suppliers	−72,000
(2c) Collections from customers	+180,000
(3b) Payments to employees	−15,000
(5) Interest expense and payment	−4,000
(6) Income tax expense and payment	−20,000

From these transactions we can construct the cash flows from operating activities section of the cash flow statement:

Balmer Company
Cash Flows from Operating Activities, 20X2

Cash collections from customers	$180,000
Cash payments:	
To suppliers	(72,000)
To employees	(15,000)
For interest	(4,000)
For taxes	(20,000)
Net cash provided by operating activities	$ 69,000

This completes the statement of cash flows in Exhibit 16-10. We can see that operations generated $69,000 of cash, but Balmer Company needed an additional $199,000 from financing activities to cover the $277,000 needed for investing. Even after raising those funds, cash still declined $9,000 over the year.

Cash Flow from Operations—The Indirect Method

The direct method gives a straightforward picture of where cash came from and how it was spent. However, it does not address the issue of how the cash flows from operating activities differ from net income. To do this, we use the indirect method. We can construct the indirect method cash flow statement for Balmer Company from 20X2's income statement and the beginning and ending balance sheets in Exhibits 16-8 and 16-9. Each income statement item has a parallel item or items in the statement of cash flows. Each sale eventually results in cash inflows; each expense entails cash outflows at some time. When the cash inflow from a sale or the cash outflow for an expense occurs in one accounting period and we record the sales revenue or expense in another, net income can differ from the cash flows from operations. The indirect method highlights such differences by beginning with net income and then listing all the adjustments necessary to compute cash flows from operating activities. Exhibit 16-12 illustrates the indirect method, and we will next explain the entries in this exhibit.

If Balmer's sales were all for cash and it paid all expenses in cash as incurred, the cash flows from operating activities would be identical to the net income. Thus, you can think of the first line of the Exhibit 16-12, net income, as the cash flow from operating activities when revenues equal cash inflows and expenses equal cash outflows. The subsequent adjustments recognize the differences between revenues and cash inflows and between expenses and cash outflows.

Net income	$23,000
Adjustments to reconcile net income to net	
cash provided (used) by operating activities:	
Depreciation	17,000
Net increase in accounts receivable	(20,000)
Net increase in inventories	(40,000)
Net increase in accounts payable	68,000
Net increase in wages and salaries payable	21,000
Net cash provided by operating activities	$69,000

Exhibit 16-12
Balmer Company
*Cash Flows from
Operating Activities—
Indirect Method*

The first adjustment is to add the depreciation expense to net income. We do this because we deducted depreciation of $17,000 when computing the net income of $23,000, but it does not cause an operating cash outflow in 20X2. Depreciation is an expense, but the related cash flow occured as an investing activity when Balmer purchased the equipment. Because we deducted $17,000 of depreciation in computing 20X2's net income, adding it back simply cancels the deduction. There is no cash flow effect of depreciation.

Depreciation represents an expense for which there is never an operating cash flow. The related cash flow was an investing outflow. The remaining adjustments represent situations where only timing creates differences between net income and cash flows from operations. That is, the timing of revenues or expenses differs from that of the related operting cash inflow or outflow.

The sales revenues of $200,000 shown on the income statement immediately affects the accounts receivable account on the balance sheet and eventually will affect cash. If all sales were for cash, sales would not affect accounts receivable, the associated cash flows would occur at the time of sale, and the cash inflow would equal the sales. However, Balmer's sales are all on open account. Thus, the sale initially increases accounts receivable, and the cash inflow occurs when Balmer collects the receivables. You can compute the amount of cash collections from income statement and balance sheet data in one of two ways. First, you can compute the total collections Balmer could possibly collect during the year, which is the accounts receivable balance at the beginning of the year plus the sales during the year. From this, you subtract the amount that Balmer has not yet collected, the accounts receivable at the end of the year. This gives collections in 20X2 of $180,000:

Beginning accounts receivable	$ 25,000
+ Sales	200,000
Potential collections	$225,000
− Ending accounts receivable	(45,000)
Cash collections from customers	$180,000

Alternatively, you can start with the sales for the year. If accounts receivable had remained unchanged, cash collections would equal sales. If accounts receivable increased, collections fell short of the sales, causing net income to be higher than cash flows from operations. If accounts receivable decreased, collections exceeded sales, causing net income to be lower than cash flows from operations. In 20X2, Balmer's accounts receivables increased from $25,000 to $45,000, so cash collections were only $180,000:

Sales	$200,000
Decrease (increase) in accounts receivable*	(20,000)
Cash collections from customers	$180,000

* The format "decrease (increase)" means that decreases are positive amounts and increases are negative amounts.

Because Balmer's accounts receivable increased in 20X2, we need to deduct the $20,000 from net income to get cash provided by operating activities. Entry 1 in Exhibit 16-13 shows this adjustment.

Just as we adjusted sales to compute cash collections from customers, we can adjust the cost of goods sold from the income statement to compute cash outflow for payments to suppliers. To do this, we look at one income statement account, cost of goods sold, and two balance sheet accounts, inventory and accounts payable. We adjust cost of goods sold to get cash payments to suppliers in two steps:

$$\text{Cost of Goods Sold} \rightarrow \text{Purchases} \rightarrow \text{Payments to Suppliers}$$

These two steps yield the following:

Step 1:	
Ending inventory, December 31, 20X2	$100,000
+ Cost of goods sold in 20X2	100,000
Inventory to account for	$200,000
− Beginning inventory, December, 31, 20X1	(60,000)
Inventory purchased in 20X2	$140,000
Step 2:	
Inventory purchased in 20X2	$140,000
+ Beginning accounts payable, December 31, 20X1	6,000
Total amount to be paid	$146,000
− Ending accounts payable, December 31, 20X2	(74,000)
Amount paid in cash during 20X2	$ 72,000

In step 1, we compute the amount of inventory purchased in 20X2, independent of whether we purchase the inventory for cash or credit. The calculation requires taking the amount of inventory used in 20X2 (that is, the cost of goods sold), plus the amount of inventory left at the end of the year, less the amount that was already in inventory at the beginning of the year. If Balmer had bought all its inventory for cash, we could stop at this point. Its cash outflow to suppliers would be equal to the amount purchased, $140,000. However, because Balmer purchased some inventory on credit, we must take step 2.

Net Income		Adjustments		Cash Provided by Operating Activities	
1) Sales revenues	$200,000	Increase in accounts receivable	$(20,000)	Cash collections from customers	$180,000
		Increase in inventories	(40,000)		
2) Cost of goods sold	(100,000)	Increase in accounts payable	68,000	Cash payments to suppliers	(72,000)
3) Wages and salaries expense	(36,000)	Increase in wages and salaries payable	21,000	Cash payments to employees	(15,000)
4) Interest	(4,000)	None		Cash payments for interest	(4,000)
5) Income taxes	(20,000)	None		Cash payments for income taxes	(20,000)
6) Depreciation	(17,000)	Depreciation	17,000		0
Net income	$ 23,000	Total adjustments	$ 46,000	Net cash provided by (used for) operating activities	$ 69,000

Exhibit 16-13
Balmer Company
Comparison of Net Income and Cash Provided by Operating Activities

If Balmer had paid off all its accounts payable by the end of the year, it would have paid an amount equal to the beginning accounts payable plus the purchases in 20X2, a total of $146,000. But $74,000 remained payable at the end of 20X2, meaning that of the $146,000 of potential payments, Balmer paid only $146,000 − $74,000 = $72,000 in 20X2.

From these two steps we can determine the two adjustments to net income needed to adjust it to a cash outflow number:

Cost of goods sold in 20X2	$100,000
Increase (decrease) in inventory during 20X2	40,000
Decrease (increase) in trade accounts payable during 20X2	(68,000)
Payments to suppliers during 20X2	$ 72,000

Now consider the adjustment to net income required to compute cash provided by operating activities. Exhibit 16-13 shows this in entry 2. First, remember that we subtract cost of goods sold in computing net income just as we subtract the cash payments to suppliers in determining cash provided by operating activities. Any adjustment showing a cash outflow greater than the cost of goods sold will lead to cash provided by operations that is less than net income. Because the increase in inventory caused the cash outflow to exceed the cost of goods sold by $40,000, net income will be $40,000 more than cash provided by operations. In contrast, the increase in accounts payable caused the cash outflow to fall short of cost of goods sold by $68,000, which results in net income that is $68,000 less than cash provided by operations.

Before considering the other adjustments in Exhibit 16-13, let's create a general approach to adjustments. Then we can apply the approach to wages and salaries.

- Adjust for revenues and expenses not requiring cash
    Add back depreciation
    Other adjustments are beyond the scope of this chapter
- Adjust for changes in noncash assets and liabilities relating to operating activities
    Add decreases in assets
    Deduct increases in assets
    Add increases in liabilities
    Deduct decreases in liabilities

Adjustments discussed so far have included adding back the $17,000 of depreciation (entry 6 in Exhibit 16-13), deducting the $20,000 increase in accounts receivable (an asset), deducting the $40,000 increase in inventory (an asset), and adding the $68,000 increase in accounts payable (a liability). Take time now to verify that each of these adjustments is consistent with the rules in the general approach.

Now let's consider the wages and salaries expense. Notice that wages and salaries payable, a liability account, increased from $4,000 at the beginning of the year to $25,000 at the end of the year. Thus, we need to add a $21,000 adjustment for wages and salaries, as shown in entry 3 of Exhibit 16-13. This $21,000 balance is the result of charging $36,000 for wages and salaries in the income statement but paying only $15,000 in cash. This means that Balmer's expense exceeded the cash outflow by $21,000, as shown in the adjustment we made.

Finally, Balmer pays both interest expense and taxes in cash when incurred. Thus, they require no adjustment—the cash flow equals the expense, as shown in entries 4 and 5.

To summarize, look again at Exhibit 16-13. The comparison of net income to cash flows from operating activities in Exhibit 16-13 begins with the net income of $23,000 from the first column of Exhibit 16-13, adds the adjustments of $46,000 in the middle column, and ends with the $69,000 net cash provided by operating activities in the right-hand column. Exhibit 16-12 shows this same information in the proper indirect-method format.

MAKING MANAGERIAL DECISIONS

Managers often want quick approximations of financial statement effects of their decisions. Suppose we have a simple company that sells only on a cash basis and pays all expenses except depreciation in cash. In a recent month, the company had sales of $100,000 and expenses of $85,000, of which $20,000 was depreciation. Therefore, it had net income of $15,000. Prepare two statements of cash flows from operating activities,

one using the direct method and one using the indirect method. Which is easier to prepare?

Answer

Both statements are easy to prepare if one has all the underlying information. For someone without access to the company's detailed records, the indirect method may be easier.

Direct Method		Indirect Method	
Cash collections from customers	$100,000	Net income	$15,000
Cash expenses	65,000	Add: Depreciation	20,000
Cash provided by operating activities	$35,000	Cash provided by operating activities	$35,000

Reconciliation Statement

When a company uses the direct method for reporting cash flows from operating activities, users of the financial statements would miss information that relates net income to operating cash flows. Thus, the FASB requires direct-method statements to include a supplementary schedule reconciling net income to net cash provided by operations. Such a supplementary statement is essentially an indirect-method cash flow statement. In essence, companies that choose to use the direct method must also report using the indirect method. In contrast, those using the indirect method never explicitly report the information on a direct-method statement. The supplementary statement included with direct-method cash flow statements would be identical to the body of Exhibit 16-12, but we would label it "Reconciliation of Net Income to Net Cash Provided by Operating Activities." No wonder 99% of firms use the indirect method!

Interpreting the Cash Flow Statement

Let's look back on what we learned from Balmer Company's cash flow statement. For growing companies that have a strong cash position at the outset, cash often declines. Why? Because growing companies usually need cash for investment in various business assets required for expansion, including investment in accounts receivable and inventories. Notice that Balmer Company's total assets nearly doubled between 20X1 and 20X2, so we should not be surprised at the decrease in cash.

The statement in Exhibit 16-10 on page 226 gives a direct picture of where Balmer's cash came from and where it went. Operations generated $69,000 of cash, investing activities used $277,000, and the company raised a net of $199,000 from financing activities. The excess of cash outflows over cash inflows reduced cash in total by $9,000. Without the statement of cash flows, the readers of the annual report would have to conduct their own analyses of the beginning and ending balance sheets, the income statement, and the statement of retained income to get a grasp of the impact of financial management decisions. The Business First box on p. 735 provides more information about what one can learn from a company's cash flow statement.

BUSINESS FIRST

HOW MUCH CASH IS ENOUGH?

On July 27, 2002, **Cisco** had $12.5 billion in cash and short-term investments, about 25% of its total assets. On December 31, 2002, **Ford Motor Company** had about $30 billion in cash and marketable securities, more than 10% of total assets. In managing our personal lives, we need to do cash planning so that we will have the money we need when we need it, and the corporate world is no different. However, these amounts seem to exceed normal needs for liquidity. Investors might reasonably ask why such significant asset levels are committed to such low return investments as cash and U.S. Treasury notes and bonds.

There are conventional answers. Cash and cash equivalents provide flexibility. It is often the currency used in merger transactions, something both Cisco and Ford do regularly. In cyclical industries, such as autos, cash helps you through the money-losing years when car and truck sales drop sharply. In unstable industries, such as hardware for computer networks, cash can prevent financial insolvency when sales drop. You might describe the cash levels as precautions against bad economic times, as the minimum level to cover ongoing transactions, or as the speculative amounts needed to fund major unspecified investments.

Even in the lean times of 2000 through 2002, Cisco generated cash from operations of more than $6 billion each year. Because of slow demand for its products, Cisco did not have investment uses for all the cash being generated. Cisco does not pay dividends, so it had a choice of accumulating cash, starting to pay dividends, or buying back stock. It chose the first and last of the options.

Ford's cash and marketable securities grew by about $12 billion in 2002, mainly because it generated $15 billion more cash from operations than it used in investing activities. Ford management faces the question of whether this is too much cash or whether it provides an appropriate safety net.

Although Cisco and Ford have lived with high cash levels, other companies are devoted to operating with as little cash as possible. A chief financial officer of **Verizon** has said, "I hate cash on hand. It is anathema to me." He kept only about ten days' cash on hand. Firms that take such strategies typically use short-term debt to manage through ups and downs in the cash-flow cycle. They set up collection and cash management processes so that whenever balances are above the minimum, they pay down any existing debt.

Sources: Cisco Systems, *2002 Annual Report;* Ford Motor Company, *2002 Annual Report.*

A concept that has received notice recently is **free cash flow**—cash flows from operations less capital expenditures. This is the cash flow left over after undertaking the firm's operations and making the investments necessary to ensure its continued operation. Some also subtract dividends, assuming that they are necessary to keep the shareholders happy. Companies that cannot generate enough cash from opertions to cover their investments need to raise more capital, either by selling assets or by issuing debt or equity. If investment is for growth, this situation may be acceptable. If the investment is merely to maintain the status quo, the company is probably in trouble. In recent years, many utilities, such as **Aquila Corporation,** have resorted to selling off assets because they could not generate enough free cash flow to meet their needs. Balmer Company has a large negative free cash flow, $69,000 − $287,000 = −$218,000, meaning that it cannot maintain its current plans without raising substantial capital, which it did during 20X2.

The Balmer Company illustration demonstrates how a firm may simultaneously (1) have a significant amount of net income, as computed by accountants on the accrual basis, and yet (2) have a decline in cash that could become severe. Indeed, many growing businesses are desperate for cash even though reported net income zooms upward. For example, in the years leading up to **Enron**'s bankruptcy, it had annual net income between $500,000 million and $1 billion, but it used much more cash for investment

free cash flow
Cash flows from operations less capital expenditures.

activities than it generated from operations—an average of about $2 billion a year more. Examining its free cash flow might have provided a warning to investors of bad things to come.

Role of Depreciation

OBJECTIVE 9

Explain the role of depreciation in the statement of cash flows.

Readers of statements of cash flows sometimes misunderstand the reason for adding depreciation to net income when computing cash flows from operating activities. Depreciation is an allocation of historical cost to expense. Therefore, depreciation expense does not entail a current outflow of cash. Consider again the comparison of Balmer Company's net income and cash flows in Exhibit 16-13 on page 732. Why do we add the $17,000 of depreciation to net income to compute cash flow? We do so simply to cancel its deduction in calculating net income. Unfortunately, use of the indirect method may at first glance create an erroneous impression that we add depreciation because it, by itself, is a source of cash. If that were really true, a corporation could merely double or triple its bookkeeping entry for depreciation expense when it needs cash! What would happen? Income would decline, but cash provided by operations would not change. Suppose we doubled Balmer Company's depreciation:

	With Depreciation of $17,000	With Depreciation of $34,000
Sales	$200,000	$200,000
All expenses except depreciation (including income taxes)*	(160,000)	(160,000)
Depreciation	(17,000)	(34,000)
Net income	$ 23,000	$ 6,000
Nondepreciation adjustments†	29,000	29,000
Add depreciation	17,000	34,000
Net cash provided by operating activities	$ 69,000	$ 69,000

* $100,000 + $36,000 + $4,000 + $20,000 = $160,000
† $(20,000) + $(40,000) + $68,000 + $21,000 = $29,000

The doubling would affect depreciation and net income, but it would have no direct influence on cash provided by operations, which would still amount to $69,000.

Statement of Cash Flows for Nike, Inc.

Exhibit 16-14 contains the 2003 statement of cash flows for Nike, Inc. Most publicly held corporations use this general format for their statement of cash flows. Like Nike, they use the indirect method in the body of the statement of cash flows to report the cash flows from operating activities.

We have discussed most of the items in Exhibit 16-14 earlier in the chapter, but three deserve mention here. First, Nike adds deferred income taxes back to net income. These taxes are charged as expense but are not currently payable. Therefore, they are a noncash expense, similar to depreciation. Second, the cumulative effect of the accounting change is essentially a noncash charge. It reduces goodwill by a charge to income, but it entails no cash effect. Third, proceeds from the exercise of options are cash received from issuance of shares to executives as part of a stock option compensation plan. You might also notice that we cannot compute changes in account balances directly from the balance sheets in Exhibit 16-1. This is a result of factors beyond the scope of this text, primarily the incorporation of the accounts of companies that Nike acquired during fiscal 2003.

Exhibit 16-14
Nike, Inc.
*Statement of Cash
Flows for the Year
Ended May 31, 2003
(millions)*

Cash provided (used) by operations:

Net income	$474.0
Income charges (credits) not affecting cash	
Depreciation	239.3
Deferred income taxes	50.4
Amortization and other	23.2
Cumulative effect of accounting change	266.1
Changes in certain working capital components:	
Increase in inventories	(102.8)
Increase in accounts receivable	(136.3)
Decrease in other current assets	60.9
Increase in accounts payable, accrued	
liabilities, and income taxes payable	30.1
Other	12.5
Cash provided by operations	917.4

Cash provided (used) by investing activities:

Additions to property, plant, and equipment	(185.9)
Disposals of property, plant, and equipment	14.8
Increase in other assets	(46.3)
Increase in other liabilities	1.8
Cash used by investing activities	(215.6)

Cash provided (used) by financing activities:

Proceeds from long-term debt issuance	90.4
Reductions in long-term debt including current portion	(55.9)
Decrease in notes payable	(349.8)
Proceeds from exercise of stock options and other stock issuances	44.2
Repurchase of stock	(196.3)
Dividends—common and preferred	(137.8)
Cash used by financing activities	(605.2)
Other	(38.1)
Net increase in cash and equivalents	58.5
Cash and equivalents, beginning of year	575.5
Cash and equivalents, end of year	$634.0

Summary Problem For Your Review

PROBLEM

The Buretta Company has prepared the data in Exhibit 16-15. In December 20X1, Buretta paid $54 million cash for a new building acquired to accommodate an expansion of operations. This was financed partly by a new issue of long-term debt for $40 million cash. During 20X1, the company also sold fixed assets for $5 million cash, which was equal to their book value. All sales and purchases of merchandise were on credit.

Because the net income of $4 million was the highest in the company's history, Mr. Buretta, the chairman of the board, was perplexed by the company's extremely low cash balance.

1. Prepare a statement of cash flows. Ignore income taxes. You may wish to use Exhibit 16-10, page 726, as a guide. Use the direct method for reporting cash flows from operating activities.
2. Prepare a supporting schedule that reconciles net income to net cash provided by operating activities.
3. What is revealed by the statement of cash flows? Does it help you reduce Mr. Buretta's puzzlement? Why?

Income Statement and Statement of Retained Earnings for the Year Ended December 31, 20X1 (millions)

Sales		$100
Less cost of goods sold		
Inventory, December 31, 20X0	$ 15	
Purchases	104	
Cost of goods available for sale	$119	
Inventory, December 31, 20X1	46	73
Gross profit		$ 27
Less other expenses		
General expenses	$ 8	
Depreciation	8	
Property taxes	4	
Interest expense	3	23
Net income		$ 4
Retained earnings, December 31, 20X0		7
Total		$ 11
Dividends		1
Retained earnings, December 31, 20X1		$ 10

Balance Sheets as of December 31 (millions)

Assets	20X1	20X0	Increase (Decrease)
Cash	$ 1	$20	$(19)
Accounts receivable	20	5	15
Inventory	46	15	31
Prepaid general expenses	4	2	2
Fixed assets, net	91	50	41
	$162	$92	$70

Equities	20X1	20X0	Increase (Decrease)
Accounts payable for merchandise	$ 39	$14	$25
Accrued property tax payable	3	1	2
Long-term debt	40	—	40
Capital stock	70	70	—
Retained earnings	10	7	3
	$162	$92	$70

Exhibit 16-15
Buretta Co. Financial Statements

SOLUTION

1. See Exhibit 16-16 We can explain cash flows from operating activities as follows (in millions):

Sales	$100
Less increase in accounts receivable	(15)
Cash collections from customers	$ 85
Cost of goods sold	$ 73
Plus increase in inventory	31
Purchases	$104
Less increase in accounts payable	(25)
Cash paid to suppliers	$ 79

Cash Flows from Operating Activities		
Cash collections from customers		$85
Cash payments		
Cash paid to suppliers	$(79)	
General expenses	(10)	
Interest paid	(3)	
Property taxes	(2)	(94)
Net cash used by operating activities		$ (9)
Cash Flows from Investing Activities		
Purchase of fixed assets (building)	$(54)	
Proceeds from sale of fixed assets	5	
Net cash used by investing activities		(49)
Cash Flows from Financing Activities		
Long-term debt issued	$ 40	
Dividends paid	(1)	
Net cash provided by financing activities		39
Net decrease in cash		$(19)
Cash balance, December 31, 20X1		20
Cash balance, December 31, 20X2		$ 1

Exhibit 16-16
Buretta Company
Statement of Cash Flows for the Year Ended December 31, 20X1 (in millions)

General expenses	$ 8
Plus increase in prepaid general expenses	2
Cash payment for general expenses	$10
Property taxes	$ 4
Less increase in accrued property tax payable	(2)
Cash paid for property taxes	$ 2
Cash paid for interest	$ 3

2. Exhibit 16-17 reconciles net income to net cash provided by operating activities.

3. The statement of cash flows shows where cash has come from and where it has gone. Operations used $9 million of cash. Why? Exhibit 16-17 shows that large increases in accounts receivable ($15 million) and inventory ($31 million), plus a $2 million increase in prepaid expenses, used $48 million of cash. In contrast, Buretta generated only $39 million (i.e., $4 + $8 + $25 + $2 million). Exhibit 16-16 explains the $9 million use of cash slightly differently. It shows directly the $85 million of cash receipts and $94 million in disbursements. Investing activities also consumed cash because Buretta invested $54 million in a building, and it received only $5 million from sales of fixed assets. Financing activities generated $39 million cash, which was $19 million less than the $58 million used by operating and investing activities.

Mr. Buretta should no longer be puzzled. The statement of cash flows shows clearly that cash payments exceeded receipts by $19 million. However, he may still be concerned about the depletion of cash. Either Buretta must change operations so that they do not require so much cash, or it must curtail investment, or it must raise more long-term debt or ownership equity. Otherwise, Buretta Company will soon run out of cash.

Supporting Schedule to Statement of Cash Flows	
Net income (from income statement)	$ 4
Adjustments to reconcile net income to net	
cash provided by operating activities	
Add: depreciation, which was deducted in the computation	
of net income but does not decrease cash	8
Deduct: increase in accounts receivable	(15)
Deduct: increase in inventory	(31)
Deduct: increase in prepaid general expenses	(2)
Add: increase in accounts payable	25
Add: increase in accrued property tax payable	2
Net cash provided by operating activities	$ (9)

Exhibit 16-17
Buretta Company
Reconciliation of Net Income to Net Cash Provided by Operating Activities for the Year Ended December 31, 20X1 (millions)

Highlights to Remember

1 **Recognize and define the main types of assets in the balance sheet of a corporation.** Assets are divided into current and noncurrent categories. Common current assets are cash, accounts receivable, inventories, and prepaid expenses. The largest noncurrent (or fixed) asset is generally property, plant, and equipment, which accountants list at acquisition cost less accumulated depreciation.

2 **Recognize and define the main types of liabilities in the balance sheet of a corporation.** Liabilities are divided into current liabilities and long-term liabilities. Current liabilities include notes payable and accounts payable. Long-term debt in the form of debentures or mortgages is the most common noncurrent liability.

3 **Recognize and define the main elements of the stockholders' equity section of the balance sheet of a corporation.** Stockholders' equity contains paid-in capital and retained earnings. Paid-in capital is often divided into a par value amount and an amount in excess of par value.

4 **Recognize and define the principal elements in the income statement of a corporation.** Income statements contain revenues and expenses. Multistep income statements have some of the following subtotals: gross profit (gross margin), operating income, and income before income taxes.

5 **Recognize and define the elements in the statement of retained earnings.** Net income increases retained earnings and losses and dividends decrease them. For large profitable companies, retained earnings may be by far the largest component of stockholders' equity.

6 **Identify activities that affect cash, and classify them as operating, investing, or financing activities.** The statement of cash flows lists cash inflows and cash outflows in one of three categories. Operating cash flows include collections from customers and payments to suppliers. Investing cash flows include purchases and sales of fixed assets. Financing cash flows include borrowings and repayment of borrowings, sales of shares of stock, and payment of dividends.

7 **Assess financing and investing activities using the statement of cash flows.** Financing activities include cash flows to and from providers of capital. Investing activities include cash flows from the purchase or sale of plant, property, equipment, and other long-lived assets.

8 **Use both the direct method and the indirect method to explain cash flows from operating activities.** In the direct method, cash flows from operating activities include all cash receipts from customers and all cash payments to suppliers, employees, the government, and others for activities supporting basic operations. The indirect method reconciles net income and cash flow from operations.

It begins with net income, adds depreciation and other noncash expenses, adds (subtracts) decreases (increases) in operating current assets, and adds (subtracts) increases (decreases) in operating current liabilities.

9 **Explain the role of depreciation in the statement of cash flows.** Depreciation is not a cash inflow. When using an indirect method cash flow statement, we add it to net income to get cash flow from operating activities only to offset the fact that we deducted it in computing net income.

Appendix 16A: Accounting for Inventory

A company's inventory method affects its income statement as well as its balance sheet. This appendix focuses on how choices in accounting for inventory can significantly affect a company's reported net income.

Each period, accountants must divide the costs of merchandise acquired between cost of goods sold and cost of items remaining in ending inventory. Various inventory methods accomplish this division. If unit prices and costs did not fluctuate, all inventory methods would show identical results. But prices change, and these changes raise central issues regarding cost of goods sold (income measurement) and inventories (asset measurement).

Let's explore inventory accounting using a simple example. Consider a new vendor of a cola drink at the fairgrounds. He began the week with no inventory. He bought one can of cola on Monday for 30 cents; a second can on Tuesday for 40 cents; and a third can on Wednesday for 56 cents. He then sold one can on Thursday for 90 cents. What is his gross profit? What is his ending inventory?

Four Major Inventory Methods

U.S. GAAP accepts four principal inventory methods: specific identification, weighted average, FIFO, and LIFO. Exhibit 16-18 provides a quick glimpse into the nature of these four methods and applies them to our example of the cola vendor. As you can see, the choice of an inventory method often can

OBJECTIVE 10

Describe and assess the effects of the four major methods of accounting for inventories.

| | (1) Specific Identification | | | (2) | (3) | (4) |
	(1A)	(1B)	(1C)	FIFO	LIFO	Weighted Average
Income statement for the period Monday through Thursday						
Sales (1 unit @ 90)	90	90	90	90	90	90
Deduct cost of goods sold*						
1 30-cent (Monday) unit	30			30		
1 40-cent (Tuesday) unit		40				
1 56-cent (Wednesday) unit			56		56	
1 weighted-average unit						
[(30 + 40 + 56) ÷ 3 = 42]						42
Gross profit for Monday through Thursday	60	50	34	60	34	48
Ending inventory, Thursday, 2 units:						
[(30 + 40 + 56) − cost of goods sold]	96	86	70	96	70	84

* The cost of goods sold can also be computed as follows, using FIFO cost of goods sold as an example:

Beginning inventory	0
+ Purchases	126
= Cost of goods available for sale	126
− Ending inventory	96
= Cost of goods sold	30

Exhibit 16-18
Comparison of Inventory Methods for Cola Vendor (all monetary amounts are in cents)

significantly affect gross profit and hence net income (and also ending inventory valuation for balance sheet purposes).

Specific Identification

specific identification
An inventory method that recognizes the actual cost paid for the specific physical item sold.

The **specific identification** method (column 1) recognizes the actual cost paid for the specific physical item sold. Gross profit depends on which can the vendor sells. As Exhibit 16-18 shows, gross profit for operations of Monday through Thursday could be 60 cents, 50 cents, or 34 cents, depending on the particular can handed to the customer. By reaching for the "Monday" can instead of the "Wednesday" can, the vendor makes a gross profit of 60 cents instead of 34 cents.

Specific identification, which uses physical observation or the labeling of items in stock with individual numbers or codes, is easy and economically justifiable for relatively expensive merchandise such as custom artwork, diamond jewelry, and automobiles. However, many organizations have vast segments of inventories that are too numerous and insufficiently valuable per unit to warrant such individualized attention. In addition, because the specific item handed to the customer affects the cost of goods sold, the specific identification method permits managers to manipulate income and inventory values when filling a sales order by selecting a particular item from several physically equivalent items with different historical costs.

First-In, First-Out (FIFO) Method

first-in, first-out (FIFO)
An inventory method that assumes that a company sells or uses up first the stock acquired earliest.

The **first-in, first-out (FIFO)** method (column 2) assumes that a company sells or uses up first the stock acquired earliest. Thus, FIFO assumes that the vendor sells the "Monday" can before the "Tuesday" can regardless of the actual can he delivers to the customer.

By using the latest costs to measure the ending inventory, FIFO tends to provide inventory valuations that closely approximate the actual market value of the inventory at the balance sheet date. In addition, in periods of rising prices, FIFO leads to higher gross profit (60 cents in Exhibit 16-18). Why? Because older, lower costs become the cost of goods sold expense.

Higher reported incomes may favorably affect investor attitudes toward the company. Similarly, higher reported incomes may lead to higher salaries, higher bonuses, or higher status for the management of the company. Unlike specific identification, FIFO dictates the order in which acquisition costs will become cost of goods sold. Therefore, managers cannot affect income by choosing to sell one item rather than another, identical one.

Last-In, First-Out (LIFO) Method

last-in, first-out (LIFO)
An inventory method that assumes that a company sells or uses up first the stock acquired most recently.

The **last-in, first-out (LIFO)** method (column 3) assumes that a company sells or uses up first the stock acquired most recently. That is, FIFO associates the most recent costs with inventories, whereas LIFO treats the most recent costs as cost of goods sold. Thus, LIFO assumes that the vendor sells the "Wednesday" can first, regardless of the actual can delivered. Many accountants believe that LIFO provides a more realistic income number because net income measured using LIFO combines current sales prices and current acquisition costs.

In contrast, LIFO inventory values on the balance sheet are less realistic because they are older costs. In a period of rising prices and constant or growing inventories, LIFO yields lower net income than the other inventory methods (34 cents in Exhibit 16-18) because it charges recent higher costs as cost of goods sold. Why is lower net income such an important feature of LIFO? Because the IRS accepts LIFO for U.S. income tax purposes. When a company reports lower income to the tax authorities, it pays lower taxes. Because the Internal Revenue Code requires companies to use LIFO for financial reporting purposes if they use it for tax purposes, it is not surprising that almost two-thirds of U.S. corporations use LIFO for at least some of their inventories.

A disadvantage of LIFO is that it permits management to influence income by the timing of purchases of inventory items. Consider our cola vendor. Suppose acquisition prices increase from 56 cents on Wednesday to 68 cents on Thursday, the day of the sale of the one unit. How does the acquisition of one more unit on Thursday affect net income? Under LIFO, cost of goods sold would change from 56 cents to 68 cents (the cost of the last unit purchased, the one bought on Thursday), and profit would fall by 12 cents. In contrast, a FIFO valuation of the cost of goods sold and gross profit would be unchanged:

	LIFO		FIFO	
	Without Thursday Purchase (cents)	**With Thursday Purchase (cents)**	**Without Thursday Purchase (cents)**	**With Thursday Purchase (cents)**
Sales	90	90	90	90
Cost of goods sold	56	68	30	30
Gross profit	34	22	60	60
Ending inventory (cents)				
(30 + 40)	70			
(30 + 40 + 56)		126		
(40 + 56)			96	
(40 + 56 + 68)				164

Another disadvantage of LIFO is that income can soar when a company reduces its inventories. Under LIFO, inventory consists of **LIFO layers** (or **LIFO increments**), which are separately identifiable additions to inventory. All units in a particular LIFO layer have the same cost. For example, on Wednesday our cola vendor had three LIFO layers:

LIFO layers (LIFO increments) Separately identifiable additions to a LIFO inventory.

- Layer 1: 30-cent unit purchased on Monday
- Layer 2: 40-cent unit purchased on Tuesday
- Layer 3: 56-cent unit purchased on Wednesday

As a company grows, the LIFO layers tend to pile on one another as the years go by. Thus, many LIFO companies show inventories that have ancient layers (going back to 1940, in some instances). The reported LIFO value may therefore be far below what FIFO values might otherwise show.

When a company reduces its inventory, old LIFO layers become the cost of goods sold. These old values may be much below current replacement values, leading to overstatement of income. In other words, the LIFO method usually gives lower net income because it uses the most recent values for the cost of goods sold. But when a company reduces its inventories, LIFO can lead to just the opposite effect. Cost of goods sold includes old values, and net income is higher under LIFO than under other methods.

Suppose our cola vendor worked the fair for 20 years and never had less than one can of cola in inventory. By the end of the 20 years, he could buy a can of cola for $3 and sell it for $4. Now he decides to get out of the cola business and sells his last can for $4. What would be his profit on that last can under LIFO? It would be $4 − $.30 = $3.70. Why? Because the original cost of the Monday can would finally become the cost of goods sold. Under FIFO, it would be only $4 − $3 − $1 because the cost of goods sold would be the cost of a recently purchased can of cola.

Weighted-Average Cost

The **weighted-average cost** method assigns the same unit cost to each unit available for sale. The unit cost is the cost of all units available for sale divided by the number of units available, as shown in Exhibit 16-18. The weighted-average method usually produces a gross profit somewhere between that obtained under FIFO and that under LIFO (48 cents as compared with 60 cents and 34 cents in Exhibit 16-18).

weighted-average cost An inventory method that assigns the same unit cost to each unit available for sale.

To better understand the term *weighted average,* assume that our cola vendor bought two cans rather than one on Monday at 30 cents each. To get the weighted average, we must consider not only the price paid, but also the number of units purchased:

weighted average = cost of goods available for sale ÷ units available for sale

weighted average = $[(2 \times 30 \text{ cents}) + (1 \times 40 \text{ cents}) + (1 \times 56 \text{ cents})] \div 4$

= 156 cents ÷ 4 = 39 cents

Choice and Use of Inventory Methods

Each of the four inventory methods has different strengths and weaknesses. Among the issues facing management when choosing a method are the following: Which method provides the highest reported net income? Which method provides management the most flexibility to affect reported earnings? How do the methods affect income tax obligations? Which method produces an inventory valuation that approximates the actual value of the inventory?

In choosing an inventory method, it is important to recognize the link between the cost of goods sold and the valuation of ending inventory. The cola vendor began his business, acquired three cans of cola during the week, and had a total cost of goods available for sale of $1.26. At the end of the period, he must allocate this $1.26 either to cans sold or to cans in ending inventory. The higher the cost of goods sold, the lower the ending inventory. Exhibit 16-19 illustrates this interdependence. At one extreme, FIFO treats the 30-cent cost of the first can acquired as the cost of goods sold and 96 cents as ending inventory. At the other extreme, LIFO treats the 56-cent cost of the last can acquired as the cost of goods sold and the 70 cents as ending inventory.

One thing to consider in choosing among inventory methods is how physical units flow. Consider four different ways that our cola vendor might physically store and sell his cola. One way—specific identification—is to mark each can with its cost, and record that cost as a cost of goods sold when he hands the can to a customer. Companies can use this method only when the physical procedure allows the seller to track each item of inventory. Another way—LIFO—is to put each new can acquired into the top of a cooler. As each customer arrives, the vendor sells the top can. In contrast, if he places each new can at the back of the cooler to chill and sells the oldest, coldest can first, FIFO captures the physical flow. Finally, if the cans are just mixed together, the weighted-average method is a rough approximation of what we know about the cost of the can sold.

Although we can relate the four methods to the physical flow of the cola cans, the accounting profession has concluded that this is not important to the choice of the inventory accounting method. Why? Many vendors have substantial choice over the physical flow of their products, but that choice often has little importance to the financial success of the business. Therefore, companies may choose any of the four methods to record the cost of goods sold, but they must apply the method consistently. That is, they cannot change the choice of method from period to period.

Exhibit 16-20 shows the results of selling the remaining two cans of inventory on Friday. Note that cumulative gross profit over the life of the vendor's business would be the same $1.44 under any of the inventory methods. These methods are important only because we must match particular costs to particular periods during the life of the business to prepare financial statements and evaluate performance. We must understand how the inventory method affects a company's financial statements for a particular period before we can use the statements to evaluate performance over that period.

lower-of-cost-or-market (LCM)

An inventory method in which accountants compare the current market price of inventory with its cost (derived by specific identification, FIFO, LIFO, or weighted average) and select the lower of the two as the inventory value.

Lower-of-Cost-or-Market (LCM) Method

Regardless of the inventory method used, accountants must decrease the inventory value if the inventory's market price drops below its acquisition cost. As a general rule, the acquisition cost provides a ceiling for the valuation of all assets; companies can decrease inventory values when prices fall, but they cannot increase values when prices rise.

Inventory accounting uses the **lower-of-cost-or-market (LCM)** method, whereby accountants compare the current market price of inventory with its cost (derived by specific identification, FIFO, LIFO, or weighted average) and select the lower of the two as the inventory value.

Exhibit 16-19
Diagram of Inventory Methods (data are from Exhibit 16-18; monetary amounts are in cents)

Beginning inventory	+	Merchandise purchases	=	Cost of goods available for sale
0	+	126	=	126
Cost of goods available for sale	−	Cost of goods sold	=	Ending inventory
1 @ 30		30		96	
		or		or	
1 @ 40	−	40	=	86	Specific identification
		or		or	
1 @ 50		56		70	
126	−	30	=	96	FIFO
	−	56	=	70	LIFO
	−	42	=	84	Weighted average

	(1) Specific Identification			(2)	(3)	(4) Weighted
	(1A)	(1B)	(1C)	FIFO	LIFO	Average
Sales, 2 units @ 90 on Friday	180	180	180	180	180	180
Cost of goods sold (Thursday ending inventory from Exhibit 16-18)	96	86	70	96	70	84
Gross profit, Friday only	84	94	110	84	110	96
Gross profit, Monday through Thursday (from Exhibit 16-18)	60	50	34	60	34	48
Gross profit, Monday through Friday (3 cans sold)	144	144	144	144	144	144

Exhibit 16-20
Income Statements for Friday Only and for Monday Through Friday for Cola Vendor (all monetary amounts are in cents)

Market generally means the current replacement cost or its equivalent. It ordinarily does not mean the ultimate selling price to customers. Consider the following facts. A company has 100 units in its ending FIFO inventory on December 31, 20X0. Its tentative gross profit for 20X0 is $990:

Sales		$2,180
Cost of goods available for sale	$1,980	
Ending inventory, at cost of 100 units	790	
Cost of goods sold		$1,190
Gross profit		$ 990

However, market prices during the final week of December suddenly declined to $4 per unit. If the lower market price is indicative of lower ultimate sales prices, an inventory write-down of $790 − (100 × $4), or $390, is in order. Therefore reported income for 20X0 would be $990 − $390 = $600. The theory states that of the $790 cost, $390 expired during 20X0 because we cannot justify carrying the cost forward to the future as an asset.

Now suppose the replacement prices rise to $8 per unit in January 20X1. Authorities do not permit restoration of the December write-down. In short, the lower-of-cost-or-market method would regard the $4 cost as of December 31 as the "new cost" of the inventory.

Summary Problem For Your Review

PROBLEM

Refer to Exhibit 16-18, page 741. Suppose the vendor sold two cans on Thursday for 90 cents each. All other data are unchanged.

1. Compute (a) the gross profit for Monday through Wednesday, (b) the gross profit for Thursday, and (c) the ending inventory on Thursday, under FIFO and under LIFO.
2. Assume the same facts as in number 1, except that the vendor purchased one additional can of cola on Thursday for 65 cents. Compute Thursday's gross profit under FIFO and under LIFO.

SOLUTION

All amounts are in cents.
1. a. The vendor would recognize no gross profit on Monday through Wednesday because he had no sales.

b.

	FIFO		LIFO	
Sales	180		180	
Cost of goods sold				
Beginning inventory (from Exhibit 16-18)	126		126	
Purchases	0		0	
Cost of goods available for sale	126		126	
Ending inventory	56		30	
Cost of goods sold		70		96
Gross profit, Thursday		110		84

c. The ending inventory on Thursday was one Wednesday unit @ 56 cents under FIFO and one Monday unit @ 30 cents under LIFO.

2. Note how the late purchase affects LIFO gross profit but not FIFO gross profit:

	FIFO		LIFO	
Sales	180		180	
Cost of goods sold				
Beginning inventory (from Exhibit 16-18)	126		126	
Purchases	65		65	
Cost of goods available for sale	191		191	
Ending inventory*	121		70	
Cost of goods sold		70		121
Gross profit, Thursday		110		59

* Wednesday and Thursday units for FIFO (56 cents + 65 cents) and Monday and Tuesday units for LIFO (30 cents + 40 cents).

Appendix 16B: Shareholder Reporting, Income Tax Reporting, and Deferred Taxes

In the United States, reports to stockholders must abide by "generally accepted accounting principles (GAAP)." In contrast, reports to income tax authorities must abide by the income tax rules and regulations. Tax regulations comply with GAAP in many respects, but in others they diverge. Therefore, there is nothing immoral or unethical about "keeping two sets of books." In fact, it is necessary.

Keep in mind that the income tax laws are patchworks that legislators often design to give taxpayers special incentives for making investments. For example, tax authorities in some countries have permitted taxpayers to write off the full cost of new equipment as expense in the year acquired. Although tax authorities may permit (or even require) such a total write-off, GAAP does not permit it for shareholder reporting purposes.

Depreciation causes the largest differences between tax and shareholder reporting in the United States. Most companies use straight-line depreciation for reporting to shareholders. Why? Managers believe that it best matches expenses with revenues. But companies use accelerated depreciation for tax reporting because it postpones (or defers) tax payments. Congress provided this deferral opportunity to motivate companies to increase their investment.

For reporting to shareholders, accountants must match income tax expense with the revenues and expenses that cause the taxes. When revenues and expenses on the statement to tax authorities differ from the revenues and expenses on the shareholders' report, deferred taxes can arise. Most often, deferred taxes arise when tax expenses exceed book expenses. The result is a deferred tax liability.

Exhibit 16-21
Illustration of
Deferred Taxes

	20X0	20X1	Total
Income statement for tax purposes			
Revenue	$100,000	$100,000	$200,000
Expenses, except depreciation	80,000	80,000	160,000
Depreciation	20,000	0	20,000
Operating income			
(or taxable income)	$ 0	$ 20,000	$ 20,000
Taxes payable @ 40%	0	8,000	8,000
Net income	$ 0	$ 12,000	$ 12,000
Income statement for			
shareholder reporting			
Revenue	$100,000	$100,000	$200,000
Expenses, except depreciation	80,000	80,000	160,000
Depreciation	10,000	10,000	20,000
Operating income	$ 10,000	$ 10,000	$ 20,000
Less income taxes			
Paid or payable almost			
immediately	0	8,000	8,000
Deferred	4,000	(4,000)	0
Net income	$ 6,000	$ 6,000	$ 12,000

	December 31	
	20X0	20X1
Balance sheet effect		
Liability: Deferred income taxes	$4,000	$0

Consider a simple example. The total depreciation on a company's only asset over a two-year period, 20X0–20X1, was $20,000. Revenue was $100,000 each year, expenses (other than depreciation) were $80,000, and the combined federal and state income tax rate was 40%. For tax purposes, the company charged the entire $20,000 of depreciation as an expense in 20X0; for shareholder reporting, it charged $10,000 each year. Such differences in timing of expenses are completely legitimate.

Exhibit 16-21 illustrates tax deferral. Total operating income over the two years was $20,000, and total taxes were $8,000. According to U.S. tax law, all $20,000 of operating income and $8,000 of taxes applied to 20X1. In contrast, for financial reporting, the company recognized half of the operating income each year, so it should recognize half of the taxes each year. Although $4,000 of taxes was related to 20X0 revenues and expenses, the payment was postponed (deferred) to 20X1. The 20X0 financial reporting income statement included a $4,000 expense for deferred taxes, and the obligation for future payment of the tax is a liability on the 20X0 balance sheet. In 20X1, $4,000 of tax expense was again related to the revenues and expenses of the period. However, the tax payment was $8,000. The payment covers the $4,000 expense for 20X1 and pays off the $4,000 of taxes deferred from 20X0.

Accounting Vocabulary

accumulated depreciation, p. 712
cash equivalents, p. 711
cash flows from financing
    activities, p. 725
cash flows from investing
    activities, p. 725
cash flows from operating
    activities, p. 725
common stock, p. 717
current assets, p. 710
current liabilities, p. 715

debentures, p. 716
direct method, p. 728
earnings per share, p. 721
first-in, first-out (FIFO), p. 742
fixed assets, p. 712
free cash flow, p. 735
goodwill, p. 714
indirect method, p. 728
intangible assets, p. 714
last-in, first-out (LIFO),
    p. 742

legal value, p. 718
LIFO increments, p. 743
LIFO layers, p. 743
limited liability, p. 717
liquidation, p. 717
long-term liabilities, p. 716
lower-of-cost-or-market (LCM),
    p. 744
net income, p. 721
noncurrent liabilities, p. 716
operating cycle, p. 710

Fundamental Assignment Material

16-A1 Balance Sheet and Income Statement

The Weikart Company had the following items on its December 31, 20X0, balance sheet and 20X0 income statement (in dollars except for number of shares outstanding):

Cash and equivalents	$ 49,000
Revenues	800,000
Notes payable	40,000
Long-term debt, excluding current portion	210,000
Accounts receivable, net	48,000
Provision for income taxes	60,000
Other long-term assets	110,000
Interest expense	55,000
Deferred income tax liability	44,000
Retained earnings	202,000
Income taxes payable	37,000
Cost of sales	460,000
Inventories	36,000
Prepaid expenses	15,000
Common stock (50,000 shares outstanding)	25,000
Property, plant, and equipment, at cost	580,000
Accounts payable	48,000
Interest income	20,000
Goodwill, patents, and trademarks	75,000
Current portion of long-term debt	16,000
Less: accumulated depreciation	170,000
Selling and administrative expenses	150,000
Additional paid-in capital	?

Prepare in proper form the December 31, 20X0, balance sheet and the 20X0 income statement for Weikart Company. Include the proper amount for additional paid-in capital.

16-A2 Statement of Cash Flows, Direct Method

Altobelli Auto Parts had a cash balance on December 31, 20X0, of $50,000. Its net income for 20X1 was $364,000. Its 20X1 transactions affecting income or cash were (in thousands):

1. Sales of $1,600, all on credit. Cash collections from customers, $1,450.
2. The cost of items sold, $850. Purchases of inventory totaled $900; inventory and accounts payable were affected accordingly.
3. Cash payments on trade accounts payable, $775.
4. Salaries and wages: accrued, $190; paid in cash, $180.
5. Depreciation, $45.
6. Interest expense, all paid in cash, $11.
7. Other expenses, all paid in cash, $100.
8. Income taxes accrued, $40; income taxes paid in cash, $30.
9. Bought plant and facilities for $335 cash.
10. Issued debt for $110 cash.
11. Paid cash dividends of $39.

Prepare a statement of cash flows using the direct method for reporting cash flows from operating activities. Omit supporting schedules.

16-A3 Reconciliation of Net Income and Net Cash Provided by Operating Activities

Refer to Problem 16-A2. Prepare a supporting schedule that reconciles net income to net cash provided by operating activities.

16-A4 Depreciation and Cash Flows

O'Malley Company had sales of $720,000, all received in cash. Total operating expenses were $600,000. All except depreciation were paid in cash. Depreciation of $90,000 was included in the $600,000 of operating expenses. Ignore income taxes.

1. Compute net income and net cash provided by operating activities.
2. Assume that depreciation is tripled. Compute net income and net cash provided by operating activities.

Understanding Published Financial Reports

16-B1 Classified Balance Sheet

Intel, the world's largest microprocessor chip company, lists the following balance sheet items for December 28, 2002 (in millions):

Property, plant, and equipment, at cost	$36,912
Short-term investments	5,183
Common stock and capital in excess of par value	7,641
Cash and cash equivalents	7,404
Other accrued liabilities	1,697
Accounts receivable	2,574
Other current assets	1,488
Accumulated depreciation	(19,065)
Accounts payable	?
Inventories	2,276
Deferred income on shipments to distributors	475
Income taxes payable	1,157
Other assets	1,888
Goodwill	4,330
Accrued compensation and benefits	1,287
Long-term investments	1,234
Deferred tax liabilities	1,232
Short-term debt	436
Long-term debt	929
Retained earnings	27,827

Prepare a balance sheet in proper form for Intel. Include the proper amount for accounts payable.

16-B2 Preparation of Statement of Cash Flows

Walgreens Co., the largest drugstore chain in the United States, had the following items in its financial statements for the fiscal year ended August 31, 2002 (in millions):

Net sales	$28,681.1
Net earnings	1,019.2
Additions to property and equipment	(934.4)
Depreciation and amortization	307.3
Cash dividends paid	(147.0)
Other non-cash expenses	48.2
Proceeds from the surrender of corporate-owned life insurance	14.4
Increases in inventories	(162.8)
Repayments of short-term borrowings	(440.7)
Increases in trade accounts payable	289.6

Decreases in other current assets	30.7
Other cash used for financing activities	(12.3)
Net proceeds from employee stock plans	111.1
Increases in accrued expenses and other liabilities	75.0
Increases in accounts receivable	(170.6)
Retained earnings	5,401.7
Deferred income taxes	22.9
Increases in income taxes payable	14.3
Disposition of property and equipment	368.1
Total assets	9,878.8
Cash and cash equivalents at beginning of year	?
Cash and cash equivalents at end of year	449.9
Net increase in cash and cash equivalents	433.0

Select the items from this list that would appear in Walgreens' statement of cash flows and prepare the statement in proper form. Fill in the appropriate amount for cash and cash equivalents at beginning of year. Use the indirect method for reporting cash flows from operating activities. (*Note:* Deferred income taxes is a noncash expense, proceeds from the surrender of corporate-owned life insurance is an investing activity, and net proceeds from employee stock plans is a financing activity.)

16-B3 Cash Provided by Operations

Target Corporation, operator of retail stores such as Target, Mervyn's, and Marshall Field's, had net earnings of $1,654 million in the fiscal year ending February 1, 2003. Additional information follows (in millions):

	Year Ended February 1, 2003	
Depreciation and amortization	$1,212	
Other noncash charges affecting earnings	$ 934	
Interest expense	$ 588	
Provision for income taxes	$1,022	
Other operating cash inflows	$ 30	
Changes in noncash working capital accounts		
Accounts receivable	$2,194	Increase
Inventories	$ 311	Increase
Other assets	$ 159	Increase
Accrued liabilities	$ 21	Decrease
Accounts payable	$ 524	Increase
Income taxes payable	$ ·79	Decrease

Compute the net cash provided by operating activities. Explain why the net cash provided by operating activities is less than the net income.

Additional Assignment Material

Questions

16-1 "The operating cycle for a company is one year." Do you agree? Why?

16-2 Why should short-term prepaid expenses be classified as current assets?

16-3 Enumerate the items most commonly classified as current assets.

16-4 "Accumulated depreciation is the cumulative amount charged as expense." Explain.

16-5 "Accumulated depreciation is a sum of cash being accumulated for the replacement of fixed assets." Do you agree? Explain.

16-6 Criticize: "Depreciation is the loss in value of a fixed asset over a given span of time."

16-7 What factors influence the estimate of useful life in depreciation accounting?

16-8 "Goodwill may have nothing to do with the personality of the manager or employees." Do you agree? Explain.

16-9 What is a subordinated debenture?

16-10 "Common shareholders have limited liability." Explain.

16-11 What is the role of the par value of stocks or bonds?

16-12 "Treasury stock is negative stockholders' equity." Do you agree? Explain.

16-13 What advantages does a multiple-step income statement have over a single-step statement?

16-14 "The statement of cash flows is an optional statement included by most companies in their annual reports." Do you agree? Explain.

16-15 What are the purposes of a statement of cash flows?

16-16 What three types of activities are summarized in the statement of cash flows?

16-17 Name four major operating activities included in a statement of cash flows.

16-18 Name three major investing activities included in a statement of cash flows.

16-19 Name three major financing activities included in a statement of cash flows.

16-20 Where does interest received or paid appear on the statement of cash flows? Explain.

16-21 "Borrowing cash or repayment of borrowings are investing activities because companies borrow when they need cash for investments." Comment on this quote.

16-22 The Lawrence Company sold fixed assets for cash of $8,000. The assets had a book value of $5,000. How should this be reported in the investing activities section of a statement of cash flows?

16-23 Why are noncash investing and financing activities listed on a separate schedule accompanying the statement of cash flows?

16-24 What are the two major ways of computing net cash provided by operating activities? How do they differ?

16-25 The indirect method for reporting cash flows from operating activities can create an erroneous impression about noncash expenses (such as depreciation). What is the impression and why is it erroneous?

16-26 Why is there usually a difference between the cash collections from customers and sales revenue in a period's financial statements?

16-27 "Net losses mean drains on cash." Do you agree? Explain.

16-28 Why do analysts focus on free cash flow rather than just on cash flow from operating activities?

16-29 "Depreciation is an integral part of a statement of cash flows." Do you agree? Explain.

16-30 An investor's newsletter had the following item: "The company expects increased cash flow in 2002 because depreciation charges will be substantially greater than they were in 2001." Comment.

16-31 Study Appendix 16A. Name and briefly describe each of the four inventory methods that are generally accepted in the United States.

16-32 Study Appendix 16A. Suppose prices are rising and inventories are increasing. Which of the four generally accepted inventory methods will usually result in the highest net income? Explain.

16-33 Study Appendix 16A. "Purchases of inventory at the end of a fiscal period can have a direct effect on income under LIFO." Do you agree? Explain.

16-34 Study Appendix 16A. "In applying the lower-of-cost-or-market method to inventories, inventory values are written down when replacement cost falls. If the replacement cost then increases, inventory values are written up, but not to an amount greater than the original cost." Do you agree? Explain.

16-35 Study Appendix 16B. "The presence of a deferred tax liability on the balance sheet means that cumulative tax payments have exceeded the cumulative tax expense charged on financial reports to shareholders." Do you agree? Explain.

Critical Thinking Exercises

16-36 Production Facilities and Depreciation

A manager complained about the amount of depreciation charged on the plant for which she was responsible: "The market value of my plant just continues to increase, yet I am hit with large depreciation charges on my income statement and the value of my plant and equipment on the balance sheet goes down each year. This doesn't seem fair." Comment on this statement, focusing on the relation of asset values on the balance sheet to market values of the assets.

16-37 Research and Development and the Recognition of Intangible Assets

In the United States, companies must charge expenditures for research and development directly to expense. In some other countries companies can recognize such costs as assets. Suppose you were a manager of a research and development department. Which method of accounting for research and development would be most consistent with the information you use for decision making? Explain.

16-38 Using the Income Statement to Evaluate Sales Success

The net income of a company is the result of many factors. Sometimes managers want to measure the performance of one part of the organization separate from the effects of other parts. How might a company evaluate the success of its sales efforts using a classified income statement? Assume that the sales department is responsible for pricing and thus influences both the total amount sold and the margin on the items sold.

16-39 Capital Investment and the Statement of Cash Flows

Growing companies often need capital to purchase or build additional facilities. There are many potential sources of such capital. Describe how an investor might use the statement of cash flows to learn how a company financed its capital expansion.

16-40 Purchasing Operations and LIFO Versus FIFO

Study Appendix 16A. Suppose that the evaluation of the purchasing officer for a refinery is based on the gross margin on the oil products produced and sold during the year. During the year, the price of a barrel of oil has increased from $20 to $30. All the inventory of oil at the beginning of the year is valued at $20 or less. On the last day of the year, the purchasing agent is contemplating the purchase of additional oil at $30 per barrel. Is she more likely to purchase additional oil if the company uses the FIFO or the LIFO method for its inventories? Explain.

General Exercises and Problems

16-41 Meaning of Book Value

Schindler Properties purchased an office building near Munich, 25 years ago, for the equivalent of 1.1 million euros (€), 300,000 of which was attributable to land. The mortgage has been fully paid. The current balance sheet follows:

Cash		€ 400,000	Stockholders'	
Land		300,000	equity	€ 860,000
Building at cost	€ 800,000			
Accumulated				
depreciation	640,000			
Book value		160,000		
Total assets		€ 860,000		

The company is about to borrow € 1.8 million on a first mortgage to modernize and expand the building. This amounts to 60% of the combined appraised value of the land and building before the modernization and expansion.

Prepare a balance sheet after the loan is made and the building is expanded and modernized, but before any further depreciation is charged. Comment on its significance.

16-42 Balance Sheet and Income Statement

The fiscal year for Hokkaido Company ends on May 31. Results for the year ended May 31, 20X1, included (in millions of Japanese yen except for number of shares outstanding):

Cash and cash equivalents	¥ 31,000
Cost of goods sold	190,000
Inventories	29,000
Other current assets	6,000
Fixed assets, net	217,000

Net sales	410,000
Receivables	22,000
Debentures	77,000
Research and development expenses	42,000
Administrative and general expenses	65,000
Other income (expenses), net	(12,000)
Capital construction fund	28,000
Selling and distribution expenses	41,000
Other current liabilities	9,000
Less: treasury stock	(13,000)
Long-term investments	?
Retained income, appropriated for self-insurance	16,000
Accounts payable	19,000
Mortgage bonds	84,000
Deferred income tax liability	12,000
Redeemable preferred stock	15,000
Common stock, at par (50,000 shares outstanding)	5,000
Paid-in capital in excess of par	102,000
Income tax expense	51,000
Accrued expenses payable	16,000
Retained income, unrestricted	27,000
Intangible assets	21,000

Prepare in proper form the balance sheet as of May 31, 20X1, and the income statement for the year ended May 31, 20X1. Include the proper amount for long-term investments.

16-43 Cash Received from Customers

Sales for Tahoe Construction Company during 20X1 were $650,000, 80% of them on credit and 20% for cash. During the year, accounts receivable increased from $66,000 to $74,000, an increase of $8,000. What amount of cash did Tahoe receive from customers during 20X1?

16-44 Cash Paid to Suppliers

Cost of goods sold for Tahoe Construction Company during 20X1 was $360,000. Beginning inventory was $95,000 and ending inventory was $120,000. Beginning trade accounts payable were $24,000, and ending trade accounts payable were $51,000. What amount of cash did Tahoe pay to suppliers?

16-45 Cash Paid to Employees

Tahoe Construction Company reported wage and salary expenses of $195,000 on its 20X1 income statement. It reported cash paid to employees of $165,000 on its statement of cash flows. The beginning balance of accrued wages and salaries payable was $15,000. What was the ending balance in accrued wages and salaries payable? Ignore payroll taxes.

16-46 Simple Cash Flows from Operating Activities

Ekern and Associates provides consulting services in Oslo. In 20X0, net income was NOK 200,000 on revenues of NOK 480,000 and expenses of NOK 280,000 (NOK stands for Norwegian kroner). The only noncash expense was depreciation of NOK 50,000. The company has no inventory. Accounts receivable increased by NOK 9,000 during 20X0, and accounts payable and salaries payable were unchanged.

Prepare a statement of cash flows from operating activities. Use the direct method. Omit supporting schedules.

16-47 Net Income and Cash Flow

Refer to Problem 16-46. Prepare a schedule that reconciles net income to net cash provided by operating activities.

16-48 Net Loss and Cash Flows from Operating Activities

The Hernandez Company had a net loss of $39,000 in 20X2. The following information is available:

Depreciation	$22,000
Decrease in accounts receivable	4,000
Increase in inventory	2,000
Increase in accounts payable	17,000
Increase in salaries and wages payable	5,000

Present a schedule that reconciles net income (loss) to net cash provided by operating activities.

16-49 Preparation of a Statement of Cash Flows

New Ulm Bottlers is a microbrewery in Milwaukee. By the end of 20X1, the company's cash balance had dropped to $8,000, despite net income of $239,000 in 20X1. Its transactions affecting income or cash in 20X1 were (in thousands):

1. Sales were $3,003, all on credit. Cash collections from customers were $2,901.
2. The cost of items sold was $2,096.
3. Inventory increased by $56.
4. Cash payments on trade accounts payable were $2,140.
5. Payments to employees were $305; accrued wages payable decreased by $24.
6. Other operating expenses, all paid in cash, were $105.
7. Interest expense, all paid in cash, was $26.
8. Income tax expense was $105; cash payments for income taxes were $108.
9. Depreciation was $151.
10. A warehouse was acquired for $540 cash.
11. Equipment was sold for $37 cash; original cost was $196, accumulated depreciation was $159.
12. Received $28 for issue of common stock.
13. Retired long-term debt for $25 cash.
14. Paid cash dividends of $89.

Prepare a statement of cash flows using the direct method for reporting cash flows from operating activities. Omit supporting schedules.

16-50 Reconciliation of Net Income and Net Cash Provided by Operating Activities

Refer to Problem 16-49. Prepare a supporting schedule to the statement of cash flows that reconciles net income to net cash provided by operating activities.

16-51 Depreciation and Cash Flows

The following condensed income statement and reconciliation schedule are from the annual report of Okanogan Company (in millions):

Sales	$215
Expenses	188
Net income	$ 27

Reconciliation Schedule of Net Income to Net Cash Provided by Operating Activities	
Net income	$27
Add noncash expenses	
Depreciation	17
Deduct net increase in noncash	
operating working capital	(15)
Net cash provided by operating activities	$29

A shareholder has suggested that the company switch from straight-line to accelerated depreciation on its annual report to shareholders. He maintains that this will increase the cash flow provided by operating activities. According to his calculations, using accelerated methods would increase depreciation to $29 million, an increase of $12 million; net cash flow from operating activities would then be $41 million.

1. Suppose Okanogan Company adopts the accelerated depreciation method proposed. Compute net income and net cash flow from operating activities. Ignore income taxes.
2. Use your answer to number 1 to prepare a response to the shareholder.

16-52 Cash Flows, Indirect Method

The Juneau Company has the following balance sheet data (in millions):

| | December 31 | | | | December 31 | | |
	20X2	20X1	Change		20X2	20X1	Change
Current assets				Current liabilities			
Cash	$ 25	$ 31	$ (6)	(detailed)	$105	$ 30	$ 75
Receivables, net	65	30	35	Long-term debt	120	—	120
				Stockholders'			
Inventories	100	50	50	equity	235	181	54
Total current assets	$190	$111	$ 79				
Plant assets (net of accumulated depreciation)	270	100	170				
				Total liabilities and stockholders'			
Total assets	$460	$211	$249	equity	$460	$211	$249

Net income for 20X2 was $60 million. Net cash inflow from operating activities was $70 million. Cash dividends paid were $6 million. Depreciation was $20 million. Fixed assets were purchased for $190 million, $120 million of which was financed via the issuance of long-term debt, the balance outright for cash.

Jennifer Tallman, the president and majority stockholder of Juneau, was a superb operating executive. She was imaginative and aggressive in marketing and ingenious and creative in production. But she had little patience with financial matters. After examining the most recent balance sheet and income statement, she muttered, "We've enjoyed ten years of steady growth; 20X2 was our most profitable ever. Despite such profitability, we're in the worst cash position in our history. Just look at those current liabilities in relation to our available cash! This whole picture of the more you make, the poorer you get, just does not make sense. These statements must be cockeyed."

1. Prepare a statement of cash flows using the indirect method, which includes a schedule reconciling net income to net cash provided by operating activities in the body of the statement.
2. Using the statement of cash flows and other information, write a short memorandum to Tallman, explaining why there is such a squeeze on cash.

16-53 Preparation of Statement of Cash Flows

The Shanghai Imports Company has assembled the (a) balance sheet and (b) income statement and statement of retained earnings for 20X1 shown in Exhibit 16-22. On December 30, 20X1, Shanghai Imports paid $102 million in cash to acquire a new plant to expand operations. This was partly financed by an issue of long-term debt for $50 million cash. Plant assets were sold for their book value of $6 million during 20X1. Because net income was $24 million, the highest in the company's history, James Chen, the chief executive officer, was distressed by the company's extremely low cash balance.

Exhibit 16-22
Shanghai Imports Co.
Financial Statements

Balance Sheet December 31, 20X1 (in millions)

	20X1	20X0	Change
Assets			
Cash	$ 6	$ 25	$(19)
Accounts receivable	55	28	27
Inventory	70	50	20
Prepaid general expenses	4	3	1
Plant assets, net	206	150	56
	$341	$256	$ 85
Liabilities and shareholders' equity			
Accounts payable for merchandise	$ 74	$ 60	$ 14
Accrued tax payable	3	2	1
Long-term debt	50	—	50
Capital stock	100	100	—
Retained earnings	114	94	20
	$341	$256	$ 85

Income Statement and Statement of Retained Earnings for the Year Ended December 31, 20X1 (in millions)

Sales		$265
Less cost of goods sold		
Inventory, December 31, 20X0	$ 50	
Purchases	160	
Cost of goods available for sale	$210	
Inventory, December 31, 20X1	70	140
Gross profit		$125
Less other expenses		
General expense	$ 51	
Depreciation	40	
Taxes	10	101
Net income		$ 24
Dividends		4
Net income of the period retained		$ 20
Retained earnings, December 31, 20X0		94
Retained earnings, December 31, 20X1		$114

1. Prepare a statement of cash flows using the direct method for reporting cash flows from operating activities. You may wish to use Exhibit 16-10, page 726, as a guide.
2. Prepare a schedule that reconciles net income to net cash provided by operating activities.
3. What is revealed by the statement of cash flows? Does it help you reduce Mr. Chen's distress? Why? Briefly explain to Mr. Chen why cash has decreased even though net income was $24 million.

16-54 LIFO and FIFO

Study Appendix 16A. The inventory of the Pinero Gravel Company on June 30 shows 500 tons at $7 per ton. A physical inventory on July 31 shows a total of 600 tons on hand. Revenue from sales of gravel for May totals $16,000. The following purchases were made during May:

July 5	1,000 tons @ $ 8 per ton
July 15	250 tons @ $ 9 per ton
July 25	300 tons @ $10 per ton

1. Compute the inventory value as of July 31, using (a) FIFO and (b) LIFO.
2. Compute the gross profit using each method.

16-55 Lower of Cost or Market

Study Appendix 16A. Potter Toy Company uses cost or market, whichever is lower, for its inventories. There were no sales or purchases during the periods indicated, although selling prices generally fluctuated in the same directions as replacement costs. What amount for merchandise inventories would you show on the balance sheet on the dates listed below?

	Invoice Cost	Replacement Cost
December 31, 20X0	$100,000	$ 75,000
April 30, 20X1	100,000	90,000
August 31, 20X1	100,000	110,000
December 31, 20X1	100,000	70,000

16-56 LIFO, FIFO, Cash Effects

Study Appendix 16A. Skykomish Machine Company had sales revenue of $360,000 in 20X1. Pertinent data for its only product in 20X1 included:

Inventory, December 31, 20X0	15,000 units @ $6	$ 90,000
February purchases	20,000 units @ $7	140,000
August purchases	32,000 units @ $8	256,000
Sales for the year	30,000 units	

1. Prepare a statement of gross margin for 20X1. Use two columns, one assuming LIFO and one assuming FIFO.
2. Assume a 40% income tax rate. Suppose all transactions are for cash. Which inventory method results in more cash for Skykomish? By how much?

16-57 LIFO, FIFO, Purchase Decisions, and Earnings per Share

Study Appendix 16A. Suppose the LeBron Company has 1 million shares of common stock outstanding and has had the following transactions during 20X1, its first year in business:

Sales	1,000,000 units @ $7
Purchases	800,000 units @ $3
	300,000 units @ $4

The current income tax rate is a flat 50%; the rate next year is expected to be 40%. Prices on inventory increased from $3 to $4 during the year.

It is December 20, and, as the president, you are trying to decide whether you should buy the 600,000 units you need for inventory now or early next year. The current price is $5 per unit. Prices on inventory are expected to remain stable; in any event, no decline in prices is anticipated.

You have not chosen an inventory method as yet, but you will pick either LIFO or FIFO. Other expenses for the year will be $2.4 million.

1. Using LIFO, prepare a comparative income statement assuming the 600,000 units (a) are not purchased, (b) are purchased. The statement should end with reported earnings per share.
2. Repeat number 1, using FIFO.
3. Comment on the results obtained. What method would you choose? Why? Be specific.
4. Suppose that in year 2 the tax rate drops to 40%, prices remain stable, 1 million units are sold at $7, enough units are purchased at $5 so that the ending inventory will be 700,000 units, and other expenses are reduced to $1,800,000.
   a. Prepare a comparative income statement for the second year showing the impact of each of the four alternatives in numbers 1 and 2 on net income and earnings per share.
   b. Explain any difference in net income that you encounter among the four alternatives.
   c. Why is there a difference in ending inventory values under LIFO, even though the same amount of physical inventory is in stock?
   d. What is the total cash outflow for income taxes for the two years together, under the four alternatives?
   e. Would you change your answer in number 3 now that you have completed number 4? Why?

16-58 LIFO, FIFO, Prices Rising and Falling

Study Appendix 16A. The Chavez Fertilizer Company had inventory on December 31, 20X0, of 20,000 bags at $10 = $200,000. Purchases during 20X1 were 30,000 bags. Sales were 28,000 bags for sales revenue of $22 per bag.

Prepare a four-column comparative statement of gross margin for 20X1:

1. Assume that purchases were at $12 per unit. Assume FIFO and then LIFO (columns 1 and 2).
2. Assume that purchases were at $8 per unit. Assume FIFO and LIFO (columns 3 and 4).
3. Assume an income tax rate of 40%. Suppose all transactions are for cash.
   a. Which inventory method in number 1 results in more cash for Chavez Company? By how much?
   b. Which inventory method in number 2 results in more cash for Chavez Company? By how much?

Understanding Published Financial Reports

16-59 Various Intangible Assets

Consider the following:

1. a. **Dow Chemical Company's** annual report indicated that research and development (R&D) expenditures were $1,066 million during 2002. How did this amount affect operating income, which was $1,100 million?
   b. Suppose the entire $1,066 million arose from outlays for patents acquired from various outside parties on December 30, 2002. What would be the operating income for 2002?
   c. How would the Dow balance sheet, December 31, 2002, be affected by your treatment of R&D in a?
2. Suppose that on December 30, 2004, **Verizon Wireless** acquired new patents on some communications equipment for $40 million. Technology changes quickly. The equipment's useful life is expected to be four years rather than the 17-year life of the patent. What will be the amortization for 2005?
3. **Hilton Hotels** had an account classified under assets in its balance sheet called pre-opening costs. A footnote said that these costs "are deferred and charged to income over a three-year period after the opening date." Suppose expenditures for pre-opening costs in 2003 were $2,100,000 and the pre-opening costs account balance on December 31, 2003, was $1,840,000 and on December 31, 2002, it was $2,390,000. What amount was amortized for 2003?
4. **Philip Morris** purchased **Kraft** for approximately $13 billion. Of the $13 billion purchase price, only about $2 billion could be assigned to identifiable individual assets. What was the total amount of goodwill from the purchase recorded on the Philip Morris balance sheet? How will Philip Morris account for the goodwill in the years after the acquisition?

16-60 Various Liabilities

For each of the following items, indicate how the financial statements will be affected. Identify the affected accounts specifically.

1. **Maytag Corporation** sells electric appliances, including washing machines. Suppose that experience in recent years has indicated that warranty costs average 3.2% of sales. Sales of washing machines for October were $4 million. Cash disbursements and obligations for warranty service on washing machines during October totaled $114,000.
2. **Pepsi-Cola Company** of New York gets cash deposits for its returnable bottles. In August, it received $99,000 cash and disbursed $93,000 for bottles returned.
3. **Washington Mutual** received a $2,000 savings deposit on April 1. On June 30, it recognized interest thereon at an annual rate of 5%. On July 1, the depositor closed her account with the bank.
4. The Intiman Theater sold for $160,000 cash a "season's series" of tickets in advance of December 31 for four plays, each to be held in successive months beginning in January. (a) What is the effect on the balance sheet, December 31? (b) What is the effect on the balance sheet, January 31?

16-61 Exercises in Assets, Liabilities, and Stockholders' Equity

Gateway Inc., is a leading direct marketer of computers. In 2002, the company lost almost $300 million on sales of slightly more than $4 billion.

1. On December 31, 2001, Gateway had accounts receivable totaling $224,443,000 on its books and, after subtracting estimated uncollectible accounts of $4,469,000, the company reported net accounts receivable of $219,974,000 on its balance sheet. In 2002, accounts receivable before subtracting estimated uncollectibles decreased by $21,506,000 and estimated uncollectible accounts increased by $651,000. What amount was reported for net accounts receivable on Gateway's December 31, 2002, balance sheet?

2. Gateway began the 2002 fiscal year with approximately $102,706,000 in its liabilities for warranties account. The company repaid $167,252,000 during the year to settle warranty claims, and it accrued warranty expenses of $131,687,000. What was the liability for warranties shown on Gateway's December 31, 2002, balance sheet?

3. Retained earnings at the end of 2001 were shown at $616,420,000 on Gateway's balance sheet. During 2002, Gateway's net loss was $297,718,000 and the company paid $11,323,000 in dividends. What was the balance in retained earnings in Gateway's December 31, 2002, balance sheet?

16-62 Classified Balance Sheet — Britain

Johnson Matthey, the large British specialty chemical company, had annual net income of more than £135 million on sales of more than £4 billion for fiscal 2003. The company presented its classified balance sheet for March 31, 2003, as follows:

Johnson Matthey
March 31, 2003 (in millions of pounds)

Fixed assets	
Goodwill	£369.1
Tangible fixed assets	601.1
Investments	6.4
	976.6
Current assets	
Stocks	438.4
Debtors: due within one year	369.3
Debtors: due after more than one year	124.3
Short-term investments	15.3
Cash at bank and in hand	100.4
	1,047.7
Creditors: Amounts falling due within one year	
Borrowings and finance leases	(46.5)
Precious metal leases	(128.0)
Other creditors	(386.0)
Net current assets less current liabilities	487.2
Total assets	1,463.8
Creditors: Amounts falling due after more than one year	
Borrowings and finance leases	(456.4)
Other creditors	(0.6)
Provisions for liabilities and charges	(100.4)
Net assets	**906.4**
Capital and reserves	
Called up share capital	219.5
Share premium account	131.8
Reserves	5.0
Profit and loss account	539.3
Shareholders' funds	895.6
Minority interests	10.8
	£906.4

Suppose Johnson Matthey used the format adopted by most U.S. companies for its balance sheet. How would the format of its balance sheet differ from that shown?

16-63 Gain on Airplane Crash

Several years ago, a Delta Airlines 727 crashed in Dallas. The crash resulted in a gain of $.11 per share of Delta. How could this happen? Consider the accounting for airplanes. Airlines insure their craft at market value, $6.5 million for Delta's 727. However, the planes' book values are often much less because of large accumulated depreciation amounts. The book value of Delta's 727 was only $962,000.

1. Suppose Delta received the insurance payment and immediately purchased another 727 for $6.5 million. Compute the effect of the crash on pretax income. Also compute the effect on Delta's total assets.
2. Do you think a casualty loss should generate a reported gain? Why?

16-64 Identification of Operating, Investing, and Financing Activities

The items listed below were found on the statement of cash flows of **Level 3 Communications, Inc.,** a broadband infrastructure provider to Internet service providers, applications service providers, Web-hosting companies, streaming media companies, and many other Web-centric companies. For each item, indicate which section of the statement should contain the item—the operating, investing, or financing section.

a. Net earnings (loss)
b. Proceeds from sale of property, plant, and equipment
c. Change in working capital items
d. Repurchases of common stock
e. Long-term debt borrowings
f. Capital expenditures
g. Dividends paid
h. Issuances of common shares
i. Depreciation and amortization

16-65 Interest Expense

J. M. Smucker Company has three main brands, Smucker's, Jif, and Crisco. In 2003, the company reported interest expense of $8,752,000 on its income statement. Its supplemental cash flow information showed a cash payment for interest of $10,613,000. Suppose that accrued interest, a current liability on the balance sheet, was $3,105,000 at the beginning of 2003.

1. Describe how the transactions relating to interest would be shown in the body of the statement of cash flows. Assume that J. M. Smucker Company uses the direct method for reporting cash flows from operating activities. Be specific, including amounts shown.
2. Describe how the transactions relating to interest would be shown on a supplementary schedule that reconciles net income and net cash provided by operating activities.

16-66 Indirect and Direct Cash Flows from Operations

ConAgra Foods is the third-largest food company in the world, with brands such as Healthy Choice, Armour, and Swiss Miss and sales of nearly $30 billion. The following items were in the company's statement of cash flows for the fiscal year ending May 26, 2002 (in millions):

Decrease in inventories	$ 658.4
Net income	783.0
Depreciation and amortization	623.2
Other noncash expenses	133.2
Decrease in accounts payable and accrued liabilities	(17.8)
Decrease in receivables	$169.5

The company's income statement showed (in millions):

Net sales	$ 27,629.6
Cost of goods sold	(23,536.5)
Selling, general, and administrative expenses	(2,423.4)
Operating income	1,669.7
Interest and other expense	403.5
Income before income taxes	1,266.2
Income tax	(483.2)
Net income	$ 783.0

1. Prepare a statement of cash flows from operating activities using the indirect method.
2. Prepare a statement of cash flows from operating activities using the direct method. Assume that all other interest, other expenses, and income taxes were paid in cash, and that all depreciation and other noncash expenses are included in selling, general, and administrative expenses.

16-67 Statement of Cash Flows, Direct and Indirect Methods

Nordstrom, Inc., the Seattle-based department store, had the following income statement for the year ended January 31, 2003 (in millions):

Net sales		$5,975
Costs and expenses		
Cost of sales	$3,971	
Selling, general, and administrative	1,814	
Interest	82	
Less: Other income, net	(74)	
Total costs and expenses		5,793
Earnings before income taxes		$ 182
Income taxes		92
Net earnings		$ 90

The company's net cash provided by operating activities, prepared using the indirect method, was

Net earnings	$ 90
Adjustments to reconcile net earnings to net cash	
provided by operating activities	
Depreciation and amortization	234
Other noncash expenses	54
Changes in	
Accounts receivable	(58)
Merchandise inventories	(117)
Prepaid expenses	1
Accounts payable	(10)
Accrued salaries and wages	24
Other liabilities	17
Income taxes payable	44
Net cash provided by operating activities	$279

Prepare a statement showing the net cash provided by operating activities using the direct method. Assume that all "other income" was received in cash and that prepaid expenses, accrued salaries and wages, and other liabilities relate to selling, general, and administrative expenses.

16-68 Comparison of Inventory Methods

Study Appendix 16A. **Unisys Corporation** is a producer of computer-based information systems. The following actual data and descriptions are from the company's 2002 annual report as of December 31 (in millions):

	2001	2002
Inventories	$399.4	$345.8

A footnote states that "Inventories are valued at the lower of cost or market. Cost is determined principally on the first-in, first-out method."

The income statement for 2002 included (in millions):

Total revenues	$6,607.4
Cost of revenue	3,918.9

Suppose a division of Unisys had the accompanying data regarding computer parts that it acquires and resells to customers for maintaining equipment (dollars are not in millions):

	Units	Total
Inventory (December 31, 2002)	100	$ 400
Purchase (February 20, 2003)	200	1,000
Sales (March 17, 2003)	150	1,200
Purchase (April 25, 2003)	140	840
Sales (June 27, 2003)	160	1,280

1. For these computer parts only, prepare a tabulation of the cost-of-goods-sold section of the income statement for the six months ended June 30, 2003. Support your computations. Round totals to the nearest dollar. Show your tabulation for four different inventory methods: (a) FIFO, (b) LIFO, (c) weighted-average, and (d) specific identification.

   For part d, assume that the purchase of February 20 was identified with the sale of March 17. Also assume that the purchase of April 25 was identified with the sale of June 27; the additional units sold were identified with the beginning inventory.
2. By how much would income taxes differ if Unisys used (a) LIFO instead of FIFO for this inventory item? (b) LIFO instead of weighted average? Assume a 40% tax rate.

16-69 Effects of Late Purchases

Study Appendix 16A. Refer to the preceding problem. Suppose Unisys acquired 60 extra units at $7 each on June 29, 2003, a total of $420. How would gross margin and income taxes be affected under FIFO? That is, compare FIFO results before and after the purchase of 60 extra units. Under LIFO? That is, compare LIFO results before and after the purchase of 60 extra units. Show computations and explain.

16-70 LIFO and FIFO at Home Depot

Study Appendix 16A. **Home Depot**, the eighth-largest retailer in the United States, uses the FIFO inventory method. On February 2, 2002, the company reported merchandise inventory of $8.3 billion; at the beginning of the year the inventory amount was only $6.7 billion. Cost of merchandise sold for the year ended February 2, 2003 (fiscal 2003), was $40.1 billion, and operating income was $5.8 billion. During the year, Home Depot purchased merchandise for $41.7 billion.

Suppose Home Depot had changed to LIFO on the first day of fiscal 2003, using the current inventory amount ($6.7 billion) as the first LIFO layer. Assume that its LIFO inventory on February 2, 2003, was $8.0 billion instead of the FIFO value of $8.3 billion.

1. Compute Home Depot's cost of merchandise sold and operating income for the year ended February 2, 2003, assuming that the switch to LIFO had been made at the beginning of fiscal 2003.
2. How would the switch to LIFO have affected Home Depot's fiscal 2003 income taxes, assuming a 40% tax rate?
3. Were the prices Home Depot paid for merchandise inventory rising or falling during fiscal 2003? How do you know?

16-71 Effect of LIFO

Study Appendix 16A. **General Mills**, producer of Wheaties, Cheerios, Gold Medal Flour, and many other food products, reported fiscal 2003 income before taxes of $1,925 million. Part of footnote 1 to the financial statements stated

> *Inventories are valued at the lower of cost or market. We generally use the LIFO method of valuing inventory because we believe that it is a better match with current revenues. However, FIFO is used for most foreign operations.*

Inventories are valued at the lower of LIFO cost or market as follows (in millions):

	May 26, 2002	**May 25, 2003**
Inventories	$1,055	$1,082

If LIFO inventories were valued at the lower of FIFO cost or market, the inventories would have been $31 million and $27 million higher than those reported for fiscal 2002 and 2003, respectively.

Suppose the FIFO method had always been used for all inventories. Calculate General Mills's operating income for fiscal 2003. By how much would the cumulative operating income for all years through 2003 differ from that reported? Would it be more or less than that reported?

EXCEL Application Exercise

16-72 Analyzing Differences Between Inventory Valuation Methods

Goal: Create an Excel spreadsheet to analyze differences between inventory valuation methods during inflationary and deflationary economies. Use the results to answer questions about your findings.

Scenario: The Chavez Fertilizer Company has asked you to compute their cost of goods sold and ending inventories for 20X1 using both FIFO and LIFO inventory valuation methods. Your computations will include scenarios for both rising and declining purchase prices. The company has a beginning inventory balance on January 1, 20X1, of 20,000 bags purchased at $10 per bag. For Scenario 1, assume that the company purchased 30,000 bags of fertilizer at $12 per bag in 20X1. For Scenario 2, assume that the company purchased 30,000 bags of fertilizer at $8 per bag in 20X1. The company sold 28,000 bags of fertilizer at $22 per bag during 20X1.

Note: This scenario is based on data in General Exercises and Problems 16-58. It requires study of Appendix 16A.

When you have completed your spreadsheet, answer the following questions:
1. In Scenario 1, which assumes rising prices, which method's ending inventory most accurately reflects current replacement cost? Why?
2. In Scenario 2, which assumes declining prices, which method's ending inventory most accurately reflects current replacement cost? Why?
3. Does LIFO always show the highest cost of goods sold (COGS)? Explain.

Step-by-Step:
1. Open a new Excel spreadsheet.
2. In column A, create a bold-faced heading that contains the following:
   Row 1: Chapter 16 Decision Guideline
   Row 2: Chavez Fertilizer Company
   Row 3: Inventory Valuation Analysis
   Row 4: Today's Date
3. Merge and center the four heading rows across columns A through F.
4. In row 7, create the following column headings:
   Column B: Beginning Inventory
   Column C: Inventory Purchases
   Column D: Available Inventory
   Column E: COGS
   Column F: Ending Inventory
5. Change the format of the column headings in row 7 to permit the titles to be displayed on multiple lines within a single cell.

Alignment tab:	Wrap text:	Checked

6. Change the format of the column headings in row 7 to display as bold-faced.
   Note: Adjust column widths so that headings only use two lines.
   Adjust row height to ensure that row is same height as adjusted headings.

7. Change the format of each column heading in row 7 to be center justified.
8. In row 8, create the following bold-faced row heading:

Column A:	Scenario #1 ($12 per bag):

Note: Adjust the column width as necessary.

9. In row 9, create the following right-justified row heading:

Column A:	FIFO

10. Use formulas to calculate the amounts for columns B through F in row 9.
   Note: Formulas for COGS and Ending Inventory (columns E and F, respectively) will need a multistep formula if they are composed of items that do not all have the same inventory/purchase price. An example of the multistep formula needed in this situation would be $=(a*b) + (c*d)$
   See Exhibit 16–18 for examples on how to calculate COGS and Ending Inventory.

11. Skip a row.
12. In row 11, create the following right-justified row heading:

Column A:	LIFO

13. Use formulas to calculate the amounts for columns B through F in row 11.
14. Skip two rows.
15. In row 14, create the following bold-faced row heading:

Column A:	Scenario #2 ($8 per bag):

16. In row 15, create the following right-justified row heading:

Column A:	FIFO

17. Use formulas to calculate the amounts for columns B through F in row 15.
18. Skip a row.
19. In row 17, create the following right-justified row heading:

Column A:	LIFO

20. Use formulas to calculate the amounts for columns B through F in row 17.
21. Format all amounts in rows 9, 11, 15 and 17 as:

Number tab:	Category:	Currency
	Decimal places:	0
	Symbol:	$
	Negative numbers:	Black with parenthesis

22. Accentuate the COGS and Ending Inventory columns by applying cell-shading to columns E and F for rows 7 through 17.

Patterns tab:	Color:	Lightest grey

23. Save your work to disk, and print a copy for your files.

Collaborative Learning Exercise

16-73 Income Statement and Balance Sheet Accounts

Form teams of two persons each. Each person should make a list of ten account names, with approximately half being income statement accounts and half being balance sheet accounts. Give the list to the other member of the team, who is to write beside each account name the financial statement (I for income statement or B for balance sheet) on which it belongs. If there are errors or disagreements in classification, discuss the account and come to an agreement about which financial statement it belongs to.

Internet Exercise   www.prenhall.com/horngren

16-74 Safeway's Financial Statements

Go to www.safeway.com to locate **Safeway**'s home page and financial information. You can follow the links to Our Company, then Investor Relations, and then Annual Reports.

Answer the following questions about the company:

1. What is Safeway's main business? How many stores does it operate?
2. Examine Safeway's income statement. What does the company call this statement? Does it use the single-step or multiple-step format? What subtitles does Safeway use in its income statement? What was Safeway's net income in the most recent year? Was this more or less income than the company had in the preceding year?
3. Now look at Safeway's balance sheet. What is the company's largest current asset? Its largest current liability? How much goodwill does the company show? How was this goodwill created?
4. In its stockholders' equity section, Safeway lists treasury stock. What does this represent?
5. Examine Safeway's statement of cash flows. Is the company's cash flow from operating activities more or less than its net income? Why? Did cash increase or decrease during the year? By how much?
6. Compare Safeway's depreciation and amortization to its cash used for additions to its property. Which is larger? What does this tell you?

Understanding and Analyzing Consolidated Financial Statements

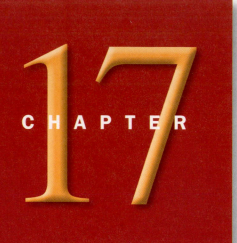

CHAPTER 17

LEARNING OBJECTIVES

When you have finished studying this chapter, you should be able to:

1. Contrast accounting for investments using the equity method and the market method.

2. Explain the basic ideas and methods used to prepare consolidated financial statements.

3. Describe how goodwill arises and how to account for it.

4. Explain and use a variety of popular financial ratios.

5. Identify the major implications that efficient stock markets have for accounting.

6. Explain and illustrate four methods of measuring income.

Deciding how to buy and finance a new car is one of

life's more important decisions. If you have gone through this process, you know that auto dealers sell financing (auto loans) as well as automobiles. If you buy a General Motors car, you can finance it on the spot at the dealership, through a fully owned subsidiary of GM, General Motors Acceptance Corporation (GMAC). Just what is the relationship between General Motors and GMAC? They are separate entities, each with its own financial records. However, they are so closely related that authorities require them to combine their financial records when preparing financial statements for the public.

GM is not the only company that has to combine the financial records of its subsidiaries. Pick up the annual report of almost any major company and you will find *consolidated financial statements*. This term means that the company has combined the books of two or more separate legal entities into one set of financial statements. General Motors describes its statements as follows: "The consolidated financial statements include the accounts of General Motors Corporation and domestic and foreign subsidiaries that are more than 50% owned, principally General Motors Acceptance Corporation (GMAC) and Hughes Electronics Corporation."

The consolidated General Motors statements you see in the company's annual report combine the financial results of companies making millions of transactions in many different currencies throughout the world. And if you buy a GM car or finance one through GMAC, GM will consolidate your transaction into the overall GM financial statements as well.

If General Motors (GM) had to rely on customers to pay cash for an auto like this one, it would not sell many cars. So GM created a subsidiary company, General Motors Acceptance Corporation (GMAC), to help customers finance the purchase of GM cars. Because of GMAC, General Motors sells more automobiles and earns profits from the interest paid by borrowers. The financial results of GM and GMAC are consolidated into one set of financial statements. In this chapter, we learn how to read and analyze such consolidated statements.

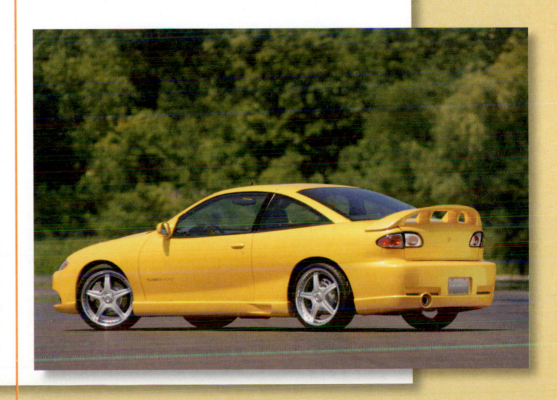

This chapter contains two parts. You can study either part or both, depending on your specific interest. Part One shows how to account for the investments one company makes in another, such as General Motors's investment in GMAC, with a focus on consolidated financial statements. Part Two covers the analysis of consolidated financial statements. ■

Part One: Intercorporate Investments Including Consolidations

Firms often invest in the equity securities of another company. The investing company may be simply investing excess cash, or it may be seeking some degree of control over the investee. The way we account for these investments depends on management's reasons for making the investment.

Accountants assume an investor that holds less than 20% of another company is a passive investor—it cannot significantly influence the decisions of the investee—and account for such an investment using the *market method*. Investors with between 20% and 50% have the ability to exert significant influence on the investee. They use the equity method. For example, **Ford** uses the *equity method* to account for its 33% interest in **Mazda Motor Corporation** of Japan. Companies with an interest in excess of 50% must use the *consolidation approach*. We will next discuss each of these three methods.

Market and Equity Methods

OBJECTIVE 1

Contrast accounting for investments using the equity method and the market method.

market method
The method of accounting for investments in equity securities that shows the investment on the balance sheet at market value.

trading securities
Investments that the investor company intends to sell in the near future.

available-for-sale securities
Investments that the investor company has no intention of selling in the near future.

Companies that hold less than 50% of the common stock of another company must use either the market method or the equity method. Let's look at each method.

Market Method

An investment in less than 20% of the common stock of another company requires use of the market method. An investor using the **market method** shows the investment on its balance sheet at market value (also called fair value). Companies often call such investments "marketable securities" in the financial statements.

The effect of such securities on the income statement depends on whether management classifies them as trading securities or available-for-sale securities. **Trading securities** are investments that the investor company intends to sell in the near future. **Available-for-sale securities** are investments that the investor company has no intention of selling in the near future. This title may be counterintuitive, but it simply means that the company can sell such securities at any time but it does not plan to sell them. Trading securities and available-for-sale securities provide returns to the investor in two ways: (1) dividend revenue, and (2) changes in market value. The investor company records dividend revenue on its income statement when received for both types of investments. However, we account for changes in market value differently for trading securities than for available-for-sale securities.

As the market value of trading securities changes, companies report the gains from increases in price and losses from decreases in price in the income statement. In contrast, as market values of available-for-sale securities rise and fall, there is no income statement effect. Instead, we add such unrealized gains and losses to a separate valuation allowance account in the stockholders' equity section of the balance sheet. This account increases stockholders' equity for securities whose price has increased since purchase. It decreases stockholders' equity for securities that have experienced a drop in prices.

Equity Method

Now consider investing companies that hold 20% to 50% of the common shares of another company and thus must use the equity method. The **equity method** accounts for the investment at the acquisition cost adjusted for dividends received and the investor's share of earnings or losses of the investee after the date of investment. Investors increase both income and the carrying amount of the investment by their share of the investee's earnings and reduce both income and the carrying amount by dividends received from the investee and by their share in the investee's losses.

equity method
Accounts for the investment at the acquisition cost adjusted for dividends received and the investor's share of earnings or losses of the investee after the date of investment.

Let's compare the market and equity methods. Suppose **IBM** acquires 40% of the voting stock of Start-Up Computer Corporation (SCC) for $80 million. In year 1, SCC has a net income of $30 million and pays cash dividends of $10 million. IBM's 40% shares of income and dividends would be $12 million and $4 million, respectively. At the end of the year, the market value of IBM's investment is $90 million. For illustrative purposes, suppose that IBM could use either the market or equity method. (In reality, IBM must use the equity method.) The following balance sheet equation shows how to record the transactions under each of the methods (in millions):

	Equity Method					Market Method				
	Assets		=	Liab. & Stk. Eq.		Assets		=	Liab. & Stk. Eq.	
	Cash	Investments		Liab.	Stk. Eq.	Cash	Investments		Liab.	Stk. Eq.
1. Acquisition	−80	+80	=			−80	+80	=		
2. Net income of SCC		+12	=		+12		No entry and no effect			
3. Dividends from SCC	+4	−4	=			+4		=		+4
4. Increase in SCC market value		No entry and no effect					+10			+10
Effects for year	−76	+88	=		+12	−76	+90	=		+14

The investment account will have a net increase of $8 million for the year. The dividend will increase the cash account by $4 million.

The investment account will increase by the $10 million increase in market value. The dividend will increase the cash account by $4 million.

Under the market method, the $10 million increase in stockholders' equity would be part of retained earnings if IBM classified the investment as a trading security. It would be in a separate stockholders' equity valuation allowance account if IBM classified the investment as an available-for-sale security.

Under the equity method, IBM would recognize income as SCC earns it rather than when SCC pays dividends or when market values change. Cash dividends do not affect net income; they increase cash and decrease the investment balance. In a sense, IBM's "claim" on SCC grows by its share of SCC's net income. The dividend is a partial liquidation of IBM's claim. The receipt of a dividend is similar to the collection of an account receivable, from an accounting standpoint. A company recognizes the revenue from a sale of merchandise on account when it creates the receivable, so to include the collection also as revenue would be double-counting. Similarly, it would be double-counting to include the $4 million of dividends as income because IBM already recognizes the $12 million of income as SCC earns it.

Suppose accounting rules allowed IBM to account for this investment using the market method. IBM would receive cash and recognize income each time SCC pays a dividend. In addition, at the end of each accounting period, IBM would find the market price of the shares and increase income (if it is a trading security) or the valuation allowance (if it is an available-for-sale security) for increases in price and decrease the same accounts for decreases in price.

General Motors recently reduced its share of ownership of **Isuzu** from 49% to 12%. As part of this decision, GM managers probably considered the effect of droppping below 20% ownership. Suppose GM was considering whether to retain either 20.5% or 19.5% of Isuzu. This is a strategic decision and GM plans to hold the stock indefinitely. What difference would it make if GM retains 19.5% of the stock rather than 20.5%?

Answer

The accounting for the investment would be different under these two options. If GM retains only 19.5% (or any percentage less than this), it must treat this as an available-for-sale investment and use the market method. This means that GM's balance sheet will include the market value of the investment, and its income statement will include only the dividends received from Isuzu. In contrast, if GM retains 20.5% (or more) of the stock, it will use the equity method. The investment account on the balance sheet will grow with the net income of Isuzu less dividends received. The balance sheet amount will not fluctuate with market values. In addition, GM's income statement will include its share of Isuzu's net income, regardless of dividend payments or changes in market prices.

If GM expects Isuzu to have increasing earnings but to pay few dividends, GM would recognize more income from the investment under the equity method. Further, wide swings in the market value of Isuzu will not affect GM's books under the equity method. However, because of this, GM's books would get no immediate benefit from large increases in Isuzu's market value. The choice of the amount of investment can have a major impact on GM's future financial statements. Depending on what GM wants to accomplish, it might prefer either the market or the equity method. The only way to select one or the other is to retain the right investment in Isuzu.

Consolidated Financial Statements

Now let's consider a firm that owns more than 50% of the stock in another business. The stockholding firm obviously has a great deal of influence over the other business, so we call it the **parent company.** We call the other business the **subsidiary.** Although parent and subsidiary companies typically are separate legal entities, in many regards they function as one unit.

Why have subsidiaries? Why not have the corporation take the form of a single legal entity? Subsidiaries often limit the liabilities in a risky venture, save income taxes, help conform to government regulations, and allow the parent to do business in a foreign country and expand in an orderly way. For example, there are often tax advantages in acquiring the capital stock of a going concern rather than buying its individual assets.

The parent-subsidiary relationship requires special accounting treatment. Parent companies must issue **consolidated financial statements** that combine the financial statements of the parent company with those of its subsidiaries. That is, we account for the parent and subsidiary companies as if they were a single entity. Why? Because consolidated statements give investors a more accurate picture of the whole organization's health. Let's look at the issues that arise when consolidating financial statements.

The Acquisition

When consolidating parent and subsidiary financial statements, accountants must avoid double-counting of assets, liabilities, and stockholders' equities. Accomplishing this is a complex process in real companies, but we can see the basic principles in a simple example. Suppose company P (parent) acquired 100% of the common stock of S (subsidiary)

---

parent company
A company owning more than 50% of another business's stock.

subsidiary
A company owned by a parent company that owns more than 50% of its stock.

O B J E C T I V E 2

Explain the basic ideas and methods used to prepare consolidated financial statements.

consolidated financial statements
Financial statements that combine the financial statements of the parent company with those of various subsidiaries, as if they were a single entity.

for $210 million cash at the beginning of the year.[1] The following table analyzes the balance sheet accounts of both companies. (Investment in S appears in the first column because it is a focal point in this chapter, not because it comes first in actual balance sheets.) Figures in this and subsequent tables are in millions of dollars:

	Assets			=	Liabilities	+	Stockholders' Equity
	Investment in S	+	Cash and Other Assets	=	Accounts Payable, Etc.	+	Stockholders' Equity
P's accounts, January 1							
Before acquisition			650	=	200	+	450
Acquisition of S	+210		−210	=			
S's accounts, January 1			400	=	190	+	210
Intercompany eliminations for a consolidated							
balance sheet	−210			=			−210
Consolidated, January 1	0	+	840	=	390	+	450

Note that P pays the $210 million to the former owners of S as private investors. The $210 million is not an addition to the existing assets and stockholders' equity of S. That is, P's purchase of stock in S does not affect S's books. S does not disappear, but it lives on as a separate legal entity. Each legal entity has its individual set of books. The consolidated entity does not keep a separate set of books.

Let's prepare a consolidated balance sheet immediately after the acquisition. The consolidated statement shows the details of all assets and liabilities of both the parent and the subsidiary. The Investment in S account on P's books is the evidence of P's ownership interest in all the assets and liabilities of S. The consolidated statements cannot show both the evidence of interest plus the detailed underlying assets and liabilities. To avoid such double-counting, we eliminate the evidence of ownership present in two places: (1) the Investment in S on P's books and (2) the Stockholders' Equity on S's books.

In summary, if the $210 million elimination of the reciprocal accounts did not occur, there would be a double-counting in the consolidated statement:

Entity	Types of Records
P	Parent books
+ S	Subsidiary books
= Preliminary consolidated report	No separate books for the consolidated entity, but periodically P and S assets and liabilities are added together via work sheets
− E	"Eliminating entries" to remove double-counting
= Consolidated report to investors	

After Acquisition

Now let's look at how we combine a parent's and subsidiary's income. A parent company carries its investment in subsidiaries, such as this investment in S, on its balance sheet by the equity method, described earlier in this chapter. Suppose S has a net income of $50 million for the year. If P were reporting alone, it would account for the net income of its subsidiary by increasing its Investment in S account and its Stockholders' Equity account (in the form of Retained Earnings) by 100% of $50 million.

---

[1] In this example, the purchase price equals the stockholders' equity of the acquired company. On pages 776–777, we discuss the preparation of consolidated statements in situations in which these two amounts differ.

The income statements for the year would be (numbers in millions):

	P	S	Consolidated
Sales	$900	$300	$1,200
Expenses	800	250	1,050
Operating income	$100	$ 50	$ 150
Pro-rata share (100%) of subsidiary net income	50	—	
Net income	$150	$ 50	

P's parent-company–only income statement (the first column) shows its own sales and expenses plus its pro rata share of S's net income (as the equity method requires). The consolidated statement (the last column) adds together all the revenues and expenses of the parent and the subsidiary.

Reflect on the changes in P's accounts, S's accounts, and the consolidated accounts in the following table (in millions of dollars):

	Assets			=	Liabilities	+	Stockholders' Equity
	Investment in S	+	Cash and Other Assets	=	Accounts Payable, Etc.	+	Stockholders' Equity
P's accounts							
Beginning of year	210	+	440	=	200	+	450
Operating income			+100	=			+100*
Share of S income	+ 50			=			+ 50*
End of year	260	+	540	=	200	+	600
S's accounts							
Beginning of year			400	=	190	+	210
Net income			+ 50	=			+ 50*
End of year			450	=	190	+	260
Intercompany eliminations	−260			=			−260
Consolidated, end of year	0	+	990	=	390	+	600

* Changes in the retained earnings portion of stockholders' equity.

Note that consolidated statements summarize the individual accounts of two or more separate legal entities, eliminating double-counting.[2] The income statement for P shows a $150 million net income; for S, a $50 million net income; for P and S consolidated, a $150 million net income.

Minority Interests

minority interests
An account that shows the outside stockholders' interest, as opposed to the parent's interest, in a subsidiary corporation.

In the preceding example, P owned 100% of S. What happens when a parent holds less than 100% of the stock of a subsidiary? In such a case, a consolidated balance sheet includes an account on the equities side called minority interests in subsidiaries, or simply **minority interests.** The account shows the outside stockholders' interest, as opposed to the parent's interest, in a subsidiary corporation. It arises because the consolidated balance sheet includes all the assets and liabilities of a subsidiary. Suppose

---

[2]Another example of double-counting is sales by P to S (or by S to P), which do not exist in this example. A consolidated income statement should not include the sale when P sells the item to S and again when S sells it to an outsider. Suppose P bought an item for $1,000 and sold it to S for $1,200. P recognized revenue of $1,200, cost of goods sold of $1,000, and income of $200. S recorded an inventory item of $1,200. In consolidation, this transaction must be eliminated. After adding together the individual accounts of P and S, you must deduct $1,200 from revenue, $1,000 from cost of goods sold, and $200 from inventory. This eliminates the $200 of income that P recognized and reduces inventory to the original $1,000 that P paid for the item.

the parent owns 90% of the subsidiary stock, and outsiders to the consolidated group own the other 10%. The Minority Interests account is a measure of the outside stockholders' interest. The diagram that follows shows the area encompassed by the consolidated statements; it includes all the subsidiary's assets and liabilities, item by item. However, because of the outsiders' ownership interests, P does not have a claim on all the assets and liabilities listed. The creation of an account for minority interests, in effect, corrects this overstatement. The remainder after deducting minority interests is P's total ownership interest:

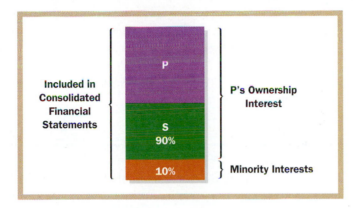

The next table, using the basic figures of the previous example, shows the overall approach to a consolidated balance sheet immediately after the acquisition. Suppose P bought 90% of the stock of S for a cost of 0.90 × $210, or $189 million. The minority interest is 10%, or $21 million.

	Assets		=	Liabilities	+		+	Stockholders' Equity
	Investment in S	+ Cash and Other Assets	=	Accounts Payable, Etc.	+	Minority Interest	+	Stockholders' Equity
P's accounts, January 1								
Before acquisition		650	=	200			+	450
Acquisition of 90% of S	+189	−189	=					
S's accounts, January 1		400	=	190			+	210
Intercompany eliminations	−189		=			+21		−210
Consolidated, January 1	0	+ 861	=	390	+	21	+	450

Again, suppose S has a net income of $50 million for the year. P and S follow the same basic procedures, regardless of whether P owns 100% or 90% of S. However, the presence of a minority interest changes the consolidated income statement slightly, as follows:

	P	S	Consolidated
Sales	$900	$300	$1,200
Expenses	800	250	1,050
Operating income	$100	$ 50	$ 150
Pro rata share (90%) of subsidiary net income	45	—	
Net income	$145	$ 50	
Minority interest (10%) in subsidiaries' net income			5
Net income to consolidated entity			$ 145

The minority interest also changes the consolidated balance sheets at the end of the year, as follows:

	Assets		=	Liabilities	+	Stockholders' Equity		
	Investment in S	+	Cash and Other Assets	=	Accounts Payable, Etc.	+	Minority Interest	+	Stockholders' Equity
P's accounts								
Beginning of year, before acquisition		650	=	200		+		450
Acquisition	189	−189	=					
Operating income		+100	=					+100
Share of S income	+ 45		=					+ 45
End of year	234	+	561	=	200		+		595
S's accounts								
Beginning of year		400	=	190		+		210
Net income		+ 50	=					+ 50
End of year		+	450	=	190		+		260
Intercompany eliminations	−234		=			+26*		−260
Consolidated, end of year	0	+	1,011	=	390	+	26	+	595

* Beginning minority interest plus minority interest in net income: $21 + (0.10 \times 50) = 21 + 5 = 26$.

Notice that the entry to consolidate the statements eliminates $260 million of stockholders' equity (on S's books) and $234 million of investment in S (on P's books). The $26 million difference is the minority interest (on consolidated statements). It identifies the interest of those shareholders who own the 10% of the subsidiary stockholders' equity that we do not eliminate by consolidation.

Perspective on Consolidated Statements

To get a clear idea of how investments in other companies affect income statements and balance sheets, consider Exhibits 17-1 and 17-2, the 2002 income statement and balance sheet of General Motors. We have simplified the statements and highlighted the items of

Exhibit 17-1
General Motors Corporation
Consolidated Balance Sheet
December 31, 2002
(in millions)

Assets	
Cash and cash equivalents	$21,449
Other marketable securities	*16,825*
Receivables	150,362
Inventories	9,967
Deferred income taxes	41,649
Property and equipment—net	72,784
Equity in net assets of unconsolidated associates	*5,044*
Intangible assets	17,954
Other assets	34,748
Total assets	$370,782
Liabilities and Stockholders' Equity	
Total liabilities	$363,134
Minority interests	*834*
Stockholders' equity:	
Paid-in capital	$22,615
Retained earnings	10,031
Net unrealized gains on securities	*372*
Other adjustments	(26,204)
Total stockholders' equity	6,814
Total liabilities and stockholders' equity	$370,782

Total net sales and revenues	$186,763
Cost of sales and other expenses	184,683
Income before income taxes and minority interests	2,080
Income tax expense	533
Equity income (loss) and minority interests	*189*
Net income	$ 1,736

Exhibit 17-2

General Motors Corporation
*Consolidated Statement of Income
Year Ended
December 31, 2002
(in millions)*

interest by showing them in italics. However, we have used GM's terminology for all the items we will discuss in this section.

First look at the headings of both exhibits. GM highlights the fact that the statements are consolidated. This means that the accounts listed include both GM's parent company amounts and those of its subsidiaries. Consolidated subsidiaries include General Motors Acceptance Corporation, Hughes Electronics, **Saturn Corporation, Saab Automobile AB** (Sweden), and **Vauxhall Motors Ltd.** (U.K.). GM has added the assets, liabilities, revenues, and expenses of these subsidiaries to their own and eliminated double counting to produce the consolidated statements.

Now look at the balance sheet (Exhibit 17-1). In addition to consolidated assets and liabilities, GM shows two assets related to investments in other companies: "Other marketable securities" and "Equity in net asets of unconsolidated associates." A footnote to GM's financial statements explains that other marketable securities consists mainly of available-for-sale securities—securities in which GM owns less than 20% of the company. These include a 10% interest in **Adam Opel AG** and a 12% interest in **Isuzu Motors Limited.** The $16,825 million is the current market value of these securities because GM accounts for them using the market method. The "equity in net assets of unconsolidated associates" account means that GM owns between 20% and 50% of some companies. These companies include **Fiat S.p.A., Suzuki Motor Corporation**, and **Fuji Heavy Industries** (maker of Subaru). The $5,044 million shown is the original price GM paid for these associates plus GM's proportional interest in their net income since acquisition less dividends paid to GM.

GM's liabilities and stockholders' equity includes two items we will discuss: "Minority interests" and "Net unrealized gains on securities." Minority interest is the part of the equity in consolidated subsidiaries that GM doesn't own. Minority shareholders own it. All the subsidiaries' assets and liabilities are consolidated, but only part belong to the owners of GM. The total stockholders' equity is the equity of the GM stockholders and the minority interest is the equity of the minority shareholders. Finally, the net unrealized gains on securities arises because of the available-for-sale securities. GM's available-for-sale securities have increased in market value by $372 million since GM purchased them. This amount appears as a separate line in stockholders' equity.

Next we will examine the income statement (Exhibit 17-2). In addition to consolidated revenues and expenses, GM has a line for "Equity income (loss) and minority interests." This combines the effects of two items. First is the equity in the income or loss of unconsolidated affiliates. When an unconsolidated affiliate company earns income, GM recognizes its share of this income on its income statement. The second item is minority interest—the proportion of GM's total income that belongs to minority shareholders. This is a proportion of the income of any subsidiary that GM does not completely own.

Exhibit 17-3 summarizes all the relationships depicted in Exhibits 17-1 and 17-2. Take a few moments to review all three exhibits. In particular, note that minority interests arise only in conjunction with consolidated subsidiaries. Why? Because consolidated balance sheets and income statements aggregate 100% of the detailed assets, liabilities, sales, and expenses of the subsidiary companies. Thus, if we do not recognize a minority interest, the financial statements would overstate the stockholders' equity and net income of the consolidated enterprise.

Percentage of Ownership	Type of Accounting	Balance Sheet Effects	Income Statement Effects
100%	Consolidation	Individual assets, individual liabilities added together	Individual revenues, individual expenses added together
Greater than 50% and less than 100%	Consolidation	Same as 100% ownership, but recognition given to minority interest in liability section	Same as 100% ownership, but recognition given to minority interest near bottom of statement when consolidated income is computed
20% to and including 50%	Equity method	Investment carried at cost plus pro rata share of subsidiary earnings less dividends received	Equity in earnings of affiliated or associated companies shown on one line as addition to income

Exhibit 17-3
Summary of Equity Method and Consolidations

In contrast, minority interests do not arise in connection with the accounting for investments in affiliated companies. Why? Because consolidated statements do not contain detailed assets, liabilities, revenues, and expenses of the affiliated companies. Investors record their interests in these companies on a pro rata basis only.

Accounting for Goodwill

OBJECTIVE 3

Describe how goodwill arises and how to account for it.

Now we will consider one more complication that arises when a company purchases more than 50% of another company. Our previous example of companies P and S assumed that the acquisition cost of S by P was equal to the amount of the stockholders' equity, or the book value, of S. However, the total purchase price paid by P often exceeds the book values of the assets acquired. In fact, the purchase price also often exceeds the sum of the fair market values (current values) of the identifiable individual assets less the liabilities. For example, when **Philip Morris** paid $13 billion for **Kraft**, it assigned only $2 billion to identifiable individual assets. It assigned the remainder to goodwill. Recall from Chapter 16 that goodwill is the excess of the purchase price over the fair (market) value of net identifiable assets of businesses acquired.

Goodwill is frequently misunderstood. The layperson often thinks of goodwill as the friendly attitude of the neighborhood store manager. But companies cannot record that type of goodwill. We record goodwill as an asset only when one company purchases another. A purchaser may be willing to pay more than the current values of the individual assets received because the acquired company is able to generate abnormally high earnings. We might trace this excess earning to personalities, skills, locations, operating methods, and so forth. For example, a purchaser may be willing to pay extra because excess earnings can be forthcoming from

1. Saving in time and costs by purchasing a corporation having a share of the market in a type of business or in a geographical area where the acquiring corporation planned expansion
2. Excellent general management skills or a unique product line
3. Potential efficiency by combination, rearrangement, or elimination of duplicate facilities and administration

To see the impact of goodwill on the consolidated statements, refer to our initial example on consolidations, where P acquired a 100% interest in S for $210 million. Suppose the price were $40 million higher, or a total of $250 million cash. For simplicity, assume that the fair values of the individual assets of S are equal to their book values. The balance sheets immediately after the acquisition are

	Assets				=	Liabilities	+	Stockholders' Equity
	Cash and Investment + in S		Goodwill	+	Other = Assets		Accounts Payable, + Etc.	Stockholders' Equity
P's accounts								
Before acquisition					650 =	200 +		450
Acquisition	+250				−250 =			
S's accounts					400 =	190 +		210
Intercompany								
eliminations	−250	+	40		=			−210
Consolidated	0	+	40*	+	800 =	390 +		450

* The $40 million "goodwill" would appear in the consolidated balance sheet as a separate intangible asset account. It often is the final item in a listing of assets.

What if the book values of the individual assets of S are not equal to their fair values? The usual procedures are

1. S continues as a going concern and keeps its accounts on the same basis as before.
2. P records its investment at its acquisition cost (the agreed purchase price).
3. For consolidated reporting purposes, we first assign part of the excess of the acquisition cost over the book value of S to the individual assets, item by item, to increase each to its fair market value at the time of the acquisition. We label any remaining excess as purchased goodwill.

Suppose the fair value of the assets of S exceeded their book value by $30 million in our example. The balance sheets immediately after acquisition would be the same as previously, with a single exception. The $40 million goodwill would now be only $10 million. The remaining $30 million would appear in the consolidated balance sheet as an integral part of the individual assets. That is, S's equipment would be shown at $30 million higher in the consolidated balance sheet than the carrying amount on S's books. Similarly, the depreciation expense on the consolidated income statement would be higher. For instance, if the equipment had five years of useful life remaining, the straight-line depreciation would be $30 million ÷ 5 = $6 million higher per year.

As in the preceding tabulation, the $10 million "goodwill" would appear in the consolidated balance sheet as a separate intangible asset account. Like any goodwill account, it will remain on the balance sheet until management judges that its value is impaired—that is, until it is evident that whatever advantages created the goodwill are no longer present.

Summary Problem For Your Review

PROBLEM

1. Review the section on minority interests, pages 772–774. Suppose P purchases 60% of the stock of S for a cost of .60 × $210, or $126 million cash. The total assets of P consist of this $126 million plus $524 million of other assets, a total of $650 million. The assets, liabilities, and shareholders' equity of S are unchanged from the amounts given in the example on minority interests. Prepare an analysis showing what amounts would appear in a consolidated balance sheet immediately after the acquisition.
2. Suppose S has a net income of $50 million for the year, and P has an operating income of $100 million. Other details are described in the example on page 773. Prepare an analysis showing what amounts would appear in a consolidated income statement and year-end balance sheet.

SOLUTION

1.

	Assets		= Liabilities +		Stockholders' Equity	
	Investment + in S	Cash Other Assets	= Accounts Payable, Etc.	+ Minority Interest	+ Stockholders' Equity
P's accounts, January 1:						
Before acquisition		650	=	200	+	450
Acquisition of 60% of S	+126	−126	=			
S's accounts, January 1		400	=	190	+	210
Intercompany eliminations	−126		=		+84	−210
Consolidated, January 1	0	+ 924	=	390	+ 84	+ 450

2.

	P	S	Consolidated
Sales	$900	$300	$1,200
Expenses	800	250	1,050
Operating income	$100	$ 50	$ 150
Pro rata share (60%) of unconsolidated subsidiary net income	30	—	
Net income	$130	$ 50	
Minority interest (40%) in consolidated subsidiary net income			20
Net income to consolidated entity			$ 130

	Assets		= Liabilities +		Stockholders' Equity	
	Investment + in S	Cash and Other Assets	= Accounts Payable, Etc.	+ Minority Interest	+ Stockholders' Equity
P's accounts						
Beginning of year, before acquisition		650	=	200	+	450
Acquisition	126	−126	=			
Operating income		+100	=			+100
Share of S income	+30		=			+ 30
End of year	156	+ 624	=	200	+	580
S's accounts						
Beginning of year		400	=	190	+	210
Net income		+ 50	=			+ 50
End of year		450	=	190	+	260
Intercompany eliminations	−156		=		+104*	−260
Consolidated, end of year	0	+ 1,074	=	390	+ 104	+ 580

* 84 beginning of year + (0.40 × 50) = 84 + 20 = 104.

Part Two: Analysis of Financial Statements

For financial statements to be useful, managers and investors need to be able to analyze and interpret the statements. Careful analysis of financial statements can help decision makers evaluate an organization's past performance and predict its future performance. Such evaluations help managers, investors, and others make intelligent, informed financial decisions. We use the 2001 and 2002 financial statements of **Microsoft Corporation** in Exhibits 17-4 and 17-5 to focus on financial statement analysis.

Exhibit 17-4
Microsoft Corporation
Balance Sheet (millions)

	June 30	
	2001	**2002**
Assets		
Current assets		
Cash and short-term investments	$31,600	$38,652
Accounts receivable	3,671	5,129
Other	3,939	4,795
Total current assets	$39,210	$48,576
Long-term assets*		
Property, plant and equipment, net	2,309	2,268
Equity and other investments	14,361	14,191
Other assets	2,950	2,611
Total assets	$58,830	$67,646
Liabilities and stockholders' equity		
Current liabilities		
Accounts payable	$ 1,188	$ 1,208
Income taxes payable	1,468	2,022
Accrued compensation	742	1,145
Unearned revenue	4,395	5,920
Other	1,461	2,449
Total current liabilities	$ 9,254	$12,744
Long-term liabilities	$ 2,287	$ 2,722
Stockholders' equity		
Paid-in capital	$28,390	$31,647
Retained earnings	18,899	20,533
Total shareholders' equity	$47,289	$52,180
Total liabilities and shareholders' equity	$58,830	$67,646

* Companies frequently omit this caption. Instead, they merely list the long-term assets as separate items following the current assets.

Exhibit 17-5
Microsoft Corporation
Statement of Income (millions, except earnings per share)

	For the Year Ended June 30			
	2001		**2002**	
Net revenues		$25,296		$28,365
Cost of revenues*		3,455		5,191
Gross profit		21,841		23,174
Operating expenses:				
General and administrative	$ 857		$1,550	
Research and development	4,379		4,307	
Sales and marketing	4,885	10,121	5,407	11,264
Operating income		11,720		11,910
Other income (expense)†		(570)		(397)
Income before income taxes		11,150		11,513
Provision for income taxes		3,804		3,684
Net income		$ 7,346		$ 7,829
Earnings per share‡		$ 1.38		$ 1.45

* Also called cost of goods sold.
† Primarily investment revenue.
‡ Microsoft paid no dividends in 2001 or 2002. Publicly held companies must show earnings per share on the face of the income statement, but it is not necessary to show dividends per share. Average shares outstanding for computation of EPS are approximately 5,341 million in 2001 and 5,406 million in 2002.

What sort of decisions are based on comparisons of financial statements? They span a wide range. For example, investors use them to decide whether to buy, sell, or hold common stock. Managers and the financial community (such as bank officers and stockholders) use them as clues to help evaluate the operating and financial outlook for an organization. Budgets or pro forma statements—carefully formulated expressions of predicted results, including a schedule of the amounts and timing of cash repayments—are helpful to extenders of credit, who want assurance of being paid in full and on time. For example, a set of budgeted financial statements is one of the first things a banker will request from an entrepreneur proposing a new business. Even well-established companies usually need to provide pro forma statements to assure creditors that the company will pay back the amounts borrowed. Let's look at some ways that users analyze financial statements.

Component Percentages

component percentages
Analysis and presentation of financial statements in percentage form to aid comparability, frequently used when companies differ in size.

When comparing companies that differ in size, analysts often apply percentage relationships, called **component percentages,** to income statements and balance sheets (see Exhibit 17-6). We call the resulting statements **common-size statements.** For example, it is difficult to compare Microsoft's $48,576 million of current assets with the $1,995 million of **Intuit**, maker of Quicken and QuickBooks software. It's much easier to compare Microsoft's 72% current asset percentage (shown in Exhibit 17-6) with Intuit's $1,195 million ÷ $2,963 million = 40%.

common-size statements
Financial statements expressed in component percentages.

Income statement percentages are usually based on sales = 100%. Microsoft seems reasonably profitable, but such percentages can tell us more when we compare them with

| | For the Year Ended June 30 | | | |
Statement of Income	2001		2002	
Net revenues	$ 25,296*	100%	$ 28,365	100%
Cost of revenues	3,455	14	5,191	18
Gross profit (or gross margin)	$ 21,841	86%	$ 23,174	82%
General and administrative	$ 857	4%	$ 1,550	6%
Research and development	4,379	17	4,307	15
Sales and marketing	4,885	19	5,407	19
Operating expenses	$ 10,121	40%	$ 11,264	40%
Operating income	$ 11,720	46%	$ 11,910	42%
Other income (expense)	(570)	−2	(397)	−1
Income before income taxes	$ 11,150	44%	$ 11,513	41%
Provision for income taxes	3,804	15	3,684	13
Net income	$ 7,346	29%	$ 7,829	28%
Balance sheet				
Current assets	$ 39,210	67%	$ 48,576	72%
Plant, property, and equipment, net	2,309	4	2,268	3
Other assets	17,311	29	16,802	25
Total assets	$ 58,830	100%	$ 67,646	100%
Current liabilities	$ 9,254	16%	$ 12,744	19%
Long-term liabilities	2,287	4	2,722	4
Stockholders' equity	47,289	80	52,180	77
Total liabilities and stockholders' equity	$ 58,830	100%	$ 67,646	100

* Note the use of dollar signs in columns of numbers. Frequently, companies use them at the top and bottom only and not for every subtotal. Their use by companies depends on the preference of management.

Exhibit 17-6
Microsoft Corporation
Common-Size Statements (millions, except percentages)

the budgeted performance for the current year (not shown here). Both the gross margin rate and net income percentage seem outstanding. However, averages for these items vary greatly by industry. Comparison with other similar firms or industry averages is necessary to interpret the rates fully. Changes between one year and the next can also reveal important information. Microsoft's net income fzell from 29% to 28% of sales, primarily because of an increase in cost of revenues.

Balance sheet percentages are usually based on total assets = 100%. Note in Exhibit 17-6 that Microsoft's current assets and current liabilities percentages increased, while other assets and stockholders' equity percentages decreased.

Corporate annual reports to the public must contain a section called management's discussion and analysis (or MD&A). This section concentrates on explaining the major changes in the income statement, changes in liquidity and capital resources, and the impact of inflation. The focus is on a comparison of one year with the next. For example, Microsoft's annual report had several pages of detailed discussions, including the following:

> The Company's revenue growth rate was 16% in fiscal 2000, 10% in fiscal 2001, and 12% in fiscal 2002. Revenue growth in fiscal 2002 was led by the addition of Xbox video game system revenue and the strong penetration of Microsoft Windows XP Professional and Home operating stystems. . . . Cost of revenue as a percent of revenue was 13.1% in 2000, 13.7% in 2001, and 18.3% in 2002. Cost of revenue in fiscal 2002 increased primarily due to costs related to Xbox. . . . The Company's cash and short-term investment portfolio totaled $38.65 billion at June 30, 2002. The portfolio consists primarily of fixed-income securities, diversified among industries and individual issuers. . . . Management believes existing cash and short-term investments together with funds generated from operations will be sufficient to meet operating requirements. . . . Microsoft has not paid cash dividends on its common stock.

Comparing component percentages across time or to those of other companies is only one way of analyzing financial statements. Next we will see what we can learn from several financial ratios.

Uses of Ratios

A favorite way for investors and creditors to analyze financial statements is to use ratios. In Exhibit 17-7 we calculate some typical ratios for Microsoft. We could compute many more ratios, but these few popular ratios included in Exhibit 17-7 will illustrate how useful ratios can be.

Data for computing ratios are available from many sources. Each company files its annual financial statements with the Securities and Exchange Commission as part of its form 10K. The SEC makes these available online in its Edgar database (http://www.sec.gov/edgar.shtml). In addition, **Standard & Poor's Corporation** sells a COMPUSTAT service that provides more than 20 years of computer-readable data on companies. The information includes more than 300 financial statement items on an annual basis and more than 100 items on a quarterly basis, plus limited footnote information. By using technology, analysts are able to use a much more extensive set of information about companies, as indicated in the Business First box on page 783.

Comparisons

Evaluation of a financial ratio requires a comparison. There are three main types of comparisons: (1) **time-series comparisons** with a company's own historical ratios, (2) **benchmark comparisons** with general rules of thumb or "best-practices" ratios,

OBJECTIVE 4
Explain and use a variety of popular financial ratios.

time-series comparisons
Comparison of a company's financial ratios with its own historical ratios.

benchmark comparisons
Comparison of a company's financial ratios with general rules of thumb or best-practices ratios.

Typical Name of Ratio	Numerator	Denominator	Appropriate Microsoft Numbers Applied to June 30 of Year	
			2001	2002
Short-term ratios				
Current ratio	Current assets	Current liabilities	39,210 ÷ 9,254 = 4.2	48,576 ÷ 12,744 = 3.8
Average collection period in days	Average accounts receivable† × 365	Sales on account	[1/2(3,671 + 3,250) × 365] ÷ 25,296 = 50 days*	[1/2(5,129 + 3,671) × 365] ÷ 28,365 = 57 days
Debt-to-equity ratio				
Total debt to equity	Total liabilities	Stockholders' equity	11,541 ÷ 47,289 = 24.4%	15,466 ÷ 52,180 = 29.6%
Profitability ratios				
Gross profit rate or percentage	Gross profit or gross margin	Sales	21,841 ÷ 25,296 = 86.3%	23,174 ÷ 28,365 = 81.7%
Return on sales	Net income	Sales	7,346 ÷ 25,296 = 29.0%	7,829 ÷ 28,365 = 27.6%
Return on stockholders' equity	Net income	Average stockholders' equity†	7,346 ÷ 1/2(47,289 + 41,368) = 16.6%	7,829 ÷ 1/2(52,180 + 47,289) = 15.7%
Earnings per share	Net income less dividends on preferred stock, if any	Average common shares outstanding	7,346 ÷ 5,341 = $1.38	7,829 ÷ 5,406 = $1.45
Price earnings	Market price per share of common stock‡	Earnings per share	73 ÷ 1.38 = 52.9	55 ÷ 1.45 = 37.9
Dividend ratios				
Dividend yield	Dividends per common share	Market price per common share‡	0 ÷ 73 = 0.0%	0 ÷ 55 = 0.0%
Dividend payout	Dividends per common share	Earnings per share	0 ÷ 1.38 = 0.0%	0 ÷ 1.45 = 0.0%

* This may be easier to see as follows:

Average receivables = 1/2 (3,671 + 3,250) = 3,460.5

Average receivables as a percentage of annual sales 3,460.5 ÷ 25,296 = 13.68%

Average collection period = 13.68% × 365 days = 50 days

† Relevant 2000 amounts: accounts receivable, $3,250 million; stockholders' equity, $41,368 million.

‡ Market price: June 30, 2001, $73; June 30, 2002, $55.

Exhibit 17-7
Some Typical Financial Ratios

BUSINESS FIRST

TECHNOLOGY CHANGES FINANCIAL STATEMENT ANALYSIS

The key to financial analysis is the availability of data. Companies can accumulate, categorize, and summarize basic financial data in many ways. In the past, investors and analysts had access only to the published summary data in quarterly and annual financial statements. Analysts then used the methods discussed in this chapter, along with many others, to try to predict the future financial performance of a company. Enter technology. By making more data available on a more timely basis and making mathematical analysis easier and faster, technology is enabling investors and analysts to obtain and analyze more information about a company than ever before.

Some companies are providing tools to help investors and analysts. For example, Microsoft includes items on its Web site called "Financial History Pivot Table" and "FY 2003 Microsoft What If?" The former provides line-item financial information as far back as 1985 and sophisticated analytical tools to help examine historical trends in many categories. The latter uses Microsoft historical data together with assumptions entered by the investor to project future net income. Tools such as these allow individual investors easy access to some of the analysis tools that have been primarily the domain of analysts in the past.

Another innovation that is sure to make a big impact is XBRL (eXtensible Business Reporting Language). A group of technology firms and consultants formed XBRL International to create a common XML-based computer language for the reporting of business information. Today, a consortium of over 170 companies and agencies supports the efforts. XBRL provides "an XML-based framework that the global business information supply chain will use to create, exchange, and analyze financial reporting information including, but not limited to, regulatory filings such as annual and quarterly financial statements, general ledger information, and audit schedules." XBRL will make it easier to share information. As Robert Elliott, former chair of the AICPA and a partner at the accounting firm **KPMG** said, "While sharing business information has always been necessary, it has been a significant challenge. [XBRL] will revolutionize the way financial information is communicated, accessed and used." XBRL is the language of the future for exchanging financial information. It has the potential to make vast sums of data available in an easily accessible format.

With improved communication of detailed financial information and enhanced modeling and analysis tools, the future for financial analysis looks good.

Sources: Microsoft Web site (www.microsoft.com); XBRL International Web site (www.xbrl.org); L. Watson, B. McGuire, and E. Cohen, "Looking at Business Reports Through XBRL-Tinted Glasses," *Strategic Finance*, September 2000, pp. 40–45; "Pilot Program Uses XBRL for Reports," *Financial Executive*, October 2002, p. 8.

---

and (3) **cross-sectional comparisons** with ratios of similar companies or with industry averages for the same period.

Consider first time-series comparisons. Because analysts rely heavily on the trend of a company's ratios, annual reports typically contain a table of comparative statistics for five or ten years. For example, consider the trends in three of Microsoft's profitability ratios.

cross-sectional comparisons

Comparisons of a company's financial ratios with ratios of similar companies or with industry averages for the same period.

	1998	1999	2000	2001	2002
Return on sales	29.4%	39.4%	41.0%	29.0%	27.6%
Return on stockholders'equity	32.8%	34.6%	27.0%	16.6%	15.7%
Earnings per share	$.92	$1.54	$1.81	$1.38	$1.45

Note that return on sales increased significantly in 1999 and 2000 but decreased in 2001 and 2002. Return on stockholders' equity peaked in 1999 and fell in 2000, 2001, and 2002. Earnings per share had a large fall in 2001 but resumed its upward climb in 2002. One danger in comparing earnings numbers across time is that earnings are measured in dollars of different purchasing power. If inflation is significant, this can create inappropriate comparisons—like comparing apples and oranges. Appendix 17 shows methods of adjusting for changes in the purchasing power of the dollar.

At first glance, you might think that 2001 and 2002 were bad years for Microsoft. In many ways they were. It was a bad time for all technology stocks. However, compared with other software and hardware companies, Microsoft endured the technology crash well. Nevertheless, you can see the negative effect on its profitability in 2001 and 2002.

The second type of comparison uses benchmarks. One type of benchmark is a general consensus on appropriate levels for ratios, or rules of thumb. For instance, the most quoted benchmark is a current ratio of 2 to 1. Others are described in *Key Business Ratios* by **Dun & Bradstreet**, a financial services firm. For example,

> Total debt to equity. *In general, total liabilities shouldn't exceed net worth [equity] (100%) since in such cases creditors have more at stake than owners.* Return on equity. *Generally, a relationship of at least 10% is regarded as a desirable objective.*

Recently, more studies have developed "best-practices" benchmarks, that is, ratios of companies that experts acknowledge as best in their field. Each analyst can pick a relevant best-practices benchmark for each ratio analyzed.

Obviously, rule-of-thumb benchmarks are only general guides. When best-practices benchmarks are not available or are not relevant, many analysts use the third type of comparison, examining ratios of similar companies or industry averages. Consider Dun & Bradstreet, a company that informs its subscribers of the creditworthiness of thousands of individual companies. D&B regularly compiles and published statistics on many ratios of the companies it monitors. Using these data, we can compare each ratio in Exhibit 17-7 with industry statistics. For example, some of the D&B ratios for 140 prepackaged software companies showed:

	Current Ratio (times)	Collection Period (days)	Total Debt to Equity (percent)	Return on Sales (percent)	Return on Stockholders' Equity (percent)
140 companies					
Upper quartile*	2.2	35	26.6	5.6	20.5
Median	1.2	61	64.0	(4.2)	(2.7)
Lower quartile	0.7	89	138.7	(42.6)	(60.1)
Microsoft†	3.8	57	29.6	27.6	15.7

* The individual ratios are ranked from best to worst. The middle figure is the median. The figure ranked halfway between the median and the best is the upper quartile. Similarly, the figure ranked halfway between the median and the worst is the lower quartile.

† Ratios are from Exhibit 17-7. Please consult that exhibit for an explanation of the components of each ratio.

Our illustration focuses on one company and one or two years. This is sufficient as a start, but analysts also examine other firms in the industry, industry averages, and a series of years to get a better perspective. Above all, recognize that a ratio by itself is of limited use. There must be a standard for comparison—a history, a similar entity, an industry average, a benchmark, or a budget.

Discussion of Specific Ratios

Consider again the ratios in Exhibit 17-7. First is the current ratio, a widely used statistic. Other things being equal, the higher the current ratio, the more assurance the creditor has about being paid in full and on time. Microsoft's current ratio of 3.8 is down slightly from 4.2, but it is still well into the top quartile in the industry.

Microsoft's average collection period of 57 days places it slightly better than the median of prepackaged software firms, according to Dun & Bradstreet industry data. A lengthening collection period might indicate increasing acceptance of poor credit risks or less energetic collection efforts.

The third column of the Dun & Bradstreet tabulation shows the total debt-to-equity ratio. Both creditors and shareholders watch this ratio to judge the risk of insolvency and stability of profits. Typically, companies with heavy debt in relationship to ownership capital are in greater danger of suffering net losses or even bankruptcy when business conditions sour. Why? Because revenues and many expenses decline, but interest expenses and maturity dates do not change. Microsoft's ratio of 29.6% is well below the median for the industry; it reflects low levels of risk or uncertainty concerning the company's ability to pay its debts on time.

Investors find profitability ratios especially helpful. Examine the gross profit rate and the return on sales. Microsoft's gross profit rate decreased from 86.3% in 2001 to 81.7% in 2002, and its return on sales decreased from 29.0% to 27.6%. These are both measures of operating success. Dun & Bradstreet does not report gross profit rates, but Microsoft's return on sales is high enough to put the firm high in the top quartile of prepackaged software companies.

More important to shareholders is the rate of return on their invested capital, a measure of overall accomplishment. Microsoft's 2002 rate of 15.7% is down from the 16.6% of 2001, but it is well above the industry median and almost in the top quartile.

The final four ratios in Exhibit 17-7 are based on earnings and dividends. The first, earnings per share of common stock (EPS), is the most popular of all ratios. Companies must present the EPS on the face of the income statement. Most companies calculate it as in Exhibit 17-7: net income less dividends on preferred stock divided by average common shares outstanding. For companies holding securities that can be exchanged for or converted to common shares, EPS calculations are more complex. Such computations are beyond the scope of this discussion.

The computation of three other ratios is shown in Exhibit 17-7: price earnings, dividend yield, and dividend payout. These ratios are especially useful to investors in the common stock of the company. Because Microsoft paid no dividends, the last two ratios are both zero. Investors use the price-earnings ratio to help determine if the market price of a share of stock is reasonable based on the company's earnings. Microsoft's price-earnings ratio of 37.9 is lower than Microsoft's historical average, but it is still quite high compared to the ratios of other companies.

Operating Performance Ratios

In addition to the more focused ratios just cited, businesspeople often look at the rate of return on invested capital as an important measure of overall accomplishment:

$$\text{rate of return on investment} = \frac{\text{income}}{\text{invested capital}} \quad (1)$$

On the surface, this measure is straightforward, but its ingredients may differ according to the purpose it is to serve. What is invested capital, the denominator of the ratio? What income figure is appropriate?

The measurement of operating performance (how profitably managers employ assets) should not be influenced by the management's financial decisions (i.e., how they obtain and finance assets). The best measure of operating performance is pretax operating rate of return on average total assets:

$$\text{pretax operating rate of return on average total assets} = \frac{\text{operating income}}{\text{average total assets}} \quad (2)$$

For Microsoft, this ratio is $11,910 \div \frac{1}{2} \times (\$58,830 + \$67,646) = 18.8\%$

The right-hand side of equation (2) consists, in turn, of two important ratios:

$$\frac{\text{operating income}}{\text{average total assets}} = \frac{\text{operating income}}{\text{sales}} \times \frac{\text{sales}}{\text{average total assets}} \quad (3)$$

The right-hand terms in equation (3) are the operating return on sales and total asset turnover, respectively. Therefore, Microsoft's operating performance can be expressed as

$$\begin{array}{ll}\text{pretax operating rate}\\ \text{of return on average total assets}\end{array} = \begin{array}{c}\text{operating return}\\ \text{on sales}\end{array} \times \begin{array}{c}\text{total asset}\\ \text{turnover}\end{array} \qquad (4)$$

$$= 42.0\% \times .448 = 18.8\%$$

When analysts use ratios to evaluate operating performance, they usually exclude extraordinary items. They do not expect such items to recur, and therefore we do not include them in measures of normal performance.

By studying equation (4), you will see that there are two basic factors in profit making: operating margin percentages and turnover. An improvement in either will, by itself, increase the rate of return on total assets.

MAKING MANAGERIAL DECISIONS

Which is better, an investment in **Wal-Mart** or one in **Saks, Inc.**, operators of Saks Fifth Avenue? How might one use financial ratios to better understand the different ways that Wal-Mart and Saks create value for investors? Would you expect Wal-Mart and Saks to have different pretax operating rate of return on average total assets? Would you expect them to have different operating return on sales and total asset turnover?

Answers

Investors have many different alternative investments. If either Wal-Mart or Saks offered lower returns to investors, they would not find many people willing to invest. (This assumes that the riskiness of investing in the two companies is about the same.) However, even if the two companies seek the same total return on assets, they pursue this return quite differently. Wal-Mart has a high total asset turnover and a low operating return on sales, while Saks has the opposite (dollar amounts are in millions):

Wal-Mart: Operating return on sales = $13,644 ÷ $244,524 = 5.6%

Total asset turnover = $244,524 ÷ ½ ($94,685 + $83,527) = 2.74

Return on assets = 5.6% × 2.74 = 15.3 %

Saks : Operating return on sales = $233.1 ÷ $5,911.1 = 3.94%

Total asset turnover = $5,911.1 ÷ ½ ($4,595.5 + $4,579.4) = 1.29

Return on assets = 3.94% × 1.29 = 5.1%

The fiscal year 2003 was better for Wal-Mart than for Saks as judged by their return on assets. Wal-Mart had a slightly higher operating return on sales, but it had a significantly higher total asset turnover.

Efficient Markets and Investor Decisions

OBJECTIVE 5

Identify the major implications that efficient stock markets have for accounting.

efficient capital market
A market in which market prices fully reflect all information available to the public.

How investors use accounting information such as ratios depends on whether they believe stock markets are efficient. An **efficient capital market** is one in which market prices fully reflect all information available to the public. Therefore, searching for underpriced securities in such a market would be fruitless unless an investor has information that is not generally available. If the real-world markets are indeed efficient, a relatively inactive portfolio approach would be an appropriate investment strategy for most investors. The hallmarks of the approach are risk control, high diversification, and low turnover of securities. The role of accounting information would mainly be to help investors identify the different degrees of risk among various stocks so that they can maintain desired levels of risk and diversification.

Research has shown that financial ratios and other data such as reported earnings help predict such economic phenomena as financial failure or earnings growth. Furthermore, analysts use many ratios simultaneously rather than one at a time for such predictions. Above all, the research shows that accounting reports are only one source of information and that in the aggregate the market is not fooled by companies that choose the least-conservative accounting policies. In sum, the market as a whole generally sees through any attempts by companies to gain favor through the choice of accounting policies that tend to boost immediate income. Thus, there is evidence that the stock markets may indeed be "efficient," at least in their reflection of most accounting data.[3]

Suppose you are the chief executive officer of a company with reported earnings of $4 per share and a stock price of $40. You are contemplating changing your method of depreciation for investor-reporting purposes from accelerated to straight line. Your competitors use straight line. You think your company's stock price unjustifiably suffers in comparison with other companies in the same industry.

If you adopt straight-line depreciation, your company's reported earnings will be $5 instead of $4 per share. Would the stock price rise accordingly, from $40 to $50? No, the research on these issues indicates that the stock price would remain at $40 (all other things equal).

Many managers share the chief executive's beliefs illustrated in the preceding example. They essentially adhere to an extremely narrow view of the role of an income statement. Such a "bottom-line" mentality is slowly, surely, and sensibly falling into disrepute. At the risk of unfair exaggeration, the view is summarized as

1. The income statement is the sole (or at least the primary) source of information about a company.
2. Lenders and shareholders invest in a company because of its reported earnings. For instance, the higher the reported earnings per share, the higher the stock price, and the easier it is to raise capital.

These arguments assume that companies can mislead investors by the way they measure reported earnings. But there is considerable evidence that accounting changes that have no effect on cash flows do not fool the securities markets. Why? Because the change generally reveals no new information, so no significant change in stock price is likely.

Remember that the market is efficient only with respect to publicly available information. Therefore, accounting issues that deal with the disclosure of new information are more important than those that simply change the format for reporting already available data.

Be aware also that accounting statements are not the only source of financial information about companies. Some alternative sources are the following: company press releases (e.g., capital expenditure announcements); trade association publications (e.g., reports with industry statistics); brokerage house analyses (e.g., company or industry studies); and government economic reports (e.g., gross national product and unemployment figures). For accounting reports to be useful, they must have some advantage over alternative sources in disclosing new information. Financial statement information may be more directly related to the item of interest, and it may be more reliable, less costly, or more timely than information from alternative sources.

In the end, investors have two basic choices: (1) trust their investment decisions to experts such as investment advisers or mutual fund portfolio managers, or (2) carefully

---

[3]Several "anomalies" prevent unqualified endorsement of stock market efficiency. Recent research shows that accounting data may be combined to yield information that is not reflected in stock prices. Nevertheless, the evidence that stock prices efficiently reflect basic accounting data is quite strong.

analyze information from a variety of sources, including companies' financial statements, and make their own investment decisions. Those who try the latter will soon learn that they cannot undertake intelligent analysis without understanding how to analyze financial statements, including appreciation of the assumptions and limitations of the financial statements.

Summary Problem For Your Review

PROBLEM

Examine Exhibits 17-4 and 17-5, page 779. Assume some new data in place of certain old data for the June 30, 2002, balance sheet (in millions):

	Old Data	New Data
Accounts receivable	$ 5,129	$ 5,629
Total current assets	48,576	51,276
Paid-in capital	31,647	35,467
Total stockholders' equity	52,180	56,000

Compute the following ratios applicable to June 30, 2002, or to the fiscal year 2002, as appropriate: current ratio, average collection period, and return on stockholders' equity. Compare this new set of ratios with the old set of ratios. Are the new ratios more desirable? Explain.

SOLUTION

All the ratios would be affected.

$$\text{current ratio} = \frac{\text{current assets}}{\text{current liabilities}}$$

$$= \frac{\$51,276}{\$12,744} = 4.0 \text{ instead of } 3.8$$

$$\text{average collection period} = \frac{\text{average accounts receivable} \times 365}{\text{sales on account}}$$

$$= \frac{\frac{1}{2}(\$5,629 + \$3,671) \times 365}{\$28,365}$$

$$= \frac{\$4,650 \times 365}{\$28,365} = 60 \text{ days instead of } 57 \text{ days}$$

$$\text{return on stockholders' equity} = \frac{\text{net income}}{\text{average stockholders' equity}}$$

$$= \frac{\$7,829}{\frac{1}{2}(\$56,000 + \$47,289)}$$

$$= 15.2\% \text{ instead of } 15.7\%$$

The new set of ratios has good news and bad news. The good news is that the company would appear to be slightly more liquid (a current ratio of 4.0 instead of 3.8). The bad news is that the average collection period and the rate of return on stockholders' equity are less attractive.

Highlights to Remember

1 **Contrast accounting for investments using the equity method and the market method.** Companies often invest in the equity securities of another company. If they own less than 20% of a company, they use the market method to account for the investment. Under the market method, the balance sheet shows the market value of the securities. If a company expects to sell the securities shortly, it calls them trading securities, and changes in market value are part of income. If there is no intention to sell the securities in the near future, they are available-for-sale securities, and the company places changes in market value in a separate valuation allowance account in stockholders' equity.

2 **Explain the basic ideas and methods used to prepare consolidated financial statements.** When a parent company owns more than 50% of another company, the owned company is a subsidiary and the companies must prepare consolidated financial statements. Each company continues to keep its own books, but for reporting to the public they combine their assets and liabilities, eliminating double-counting. If the parent owns less than 100% of a subsidiary, the statements will show a minority interest.

3 **Describe how goodwill arises and how to account for it.** If a parent pays more than the fair market value of the net assets when acquiring a subsidiary, it must record the difference as goodwill. Goodwill is an intangible asset that remains on the company's books until its value is impaired.

4 **Explain and use a variety of popular financial ratios.** Financial ratios aid the intelligent analysis of financial statements. To compare companies that differ in size, analysts use component percentages. They also prepare a variety of ratios and compare them with the company's own historical ratios, with general benchmarks, and with ratios of other companies or industry averages. They use short-term ratios, debt-to-equity ratios, profitability ratios, and dividend ratios. An especially important ratio for assessing operating performance is the rate of return on invested capital.

5 **Identify the major implications that efficient stock markets have for accounting.** Financial statements are only one source of information used by investors. Evidence indicates that stock prices fully reflect most publicly available information, including accounting numbers. The format of the information apparently does not fool investors. Therefore, accounting regulators should focus on disclosure issues, not format.

Appendix 17: Changing Prices and Income Measurement

The use of historical cost in measuring income is one of the most controversial subjects in accounting. This appendix focuses on how inflation affects the income statement. Recall that inflation is the decline in the general purchasing power of the monetary unit (the dollar in the United States).

Complaints About Historical Cost

Accountants have traditionally maintained that net income is a return on the capital invested by shareholders. Suppose shareholders receive cash dividends equal to the amount of net income of a period. In the absence of inflation, such a payment leaves the shareholders' invested capital at the end of the period equal to the beginning capital. However, price changes alter this relationship between income and capital. In times of generally rising prices, paying dividends equal to net income, as conventionally measured, usually amounts to paying out some capital itself, as well as the return on capital.

In particular, industries with huge investments in plant and equipment claim that accrual accounting based on historical costs badly misstate their profits in times of inflation. For example, consider NYNEX a company that emerged from the breakup of the Bell System and has since merged into Verizon. During a year of high inflation in the 1980s, NYNEX reported net income of $1,095 million. However, if the company had adjusted its depreciation for inflation, it would have reported a net loss of $82 million. Because inflation rates have been small in the last decade, such dramatic differences are rare. However, even an inflation rate of 4% results in a doubling of prices every 18 years, which is less than the economic life of many assets.

U.S. Companies have never had to adjust their financial statements for inflation. However, several South American countries have experienced high enough inflation rates that companies in those countries had to adjust statements for inflation for them to make any sense at all. Even though you will not see inflation-adjusted financial statements in today's annual reports, a basic knowledge about reporting the effects of changing prices is useful for at least three reasons: (1) High inflation is still present in many countries, and accounting reports in those countries must cope with the effects of inflation; (2) if history is any indication, higher inflation rates will return to the United States sooner or later, and when they do, users of financial statements will again become concerned with inflation-adjusted statements; and (3) understanding the limitations of traditional financial statements is enhanced by knowing how inflation affects (or does not affect) such financial statements.

Income or Capital

To understand inflation's effects on financial statements, you must understand the concepts of income and capital. Stockholders invest financial resources (capital) and expect an eventual return *of* that capital, together with additional amounts representing the return *on* that capital (income). Separating returns *of* capital from returns *on* capital is difficult in inflationary times.

Consider an example. Owners invest $1,000 in a new company. The company immediately buys $1,000 worth of inventory. It then sells the inventory a year later for $1,500. Meanwhile, the cost of replacing the inventory has risen to $1,200.

Most accountants and managers believe that income emerges after investors recover their financial resources, a concept called **financial capital maintenance.** After the company sets aside $1,000 for the return *of* capital to investors, the remaining $500 is a return *on* capital, or income. This is the concept underlying traditional historical-cost accounting.

On the other hand, some accountants believe that income emerges only after setting aside an amount that allows a company to maintain physical operating capability, called **physical capital maintenance.** Because $1,200 is the current cost of inventory (cost of maintaining physical capability) at the date of sale, the company must set aside $1,200 to maintain the same level of invested (physical) capital, leaving only $300 of income.

financial capital maintenance

The concept that income emerges after investors recover their financial resources.

physical capital maintenance

The concept that income emerges only after setting aside an amount that allows physical operating capability to be maintained.

	Financial Capital Maintenance	Physical Capital Maintenance
Sales	$1,500	$1,500
Cost of goods sold	1,000	1,200
Income	$ 500	$ 300

We will now explore methods of measuring income based on both financial and physical capital maintenance.

Measurement Alternatives Under Inflation

Inflation has caused accountants to consider two types of changes in financial reporting:

nominal dollars

Dollar measurements that are not restated for inflation.

1. Switch from measuring transactions in **nominal dollars**—dollar measurements that are not restated for inflation—to **constant dollars**—dollars that are restated in terms of current purchasing power.

constant dollars

Nominal dollars that are restated in terms of current purchasing power.

2. Instead of reporting the **historical cost** of an asset—the amount originally paid to acquire it—use the **current cost**—generally, the cost to replace it. Using historical costs implies maintenance of financial capital; current costs imply physical capital maintenance.

historical cost

The amount originally paid to acquire an asset.

Traditional accounting uses nominal (rather than constant) dollars and historical (rather than current) costs. Historical cost/nominal dollar accounting has almost exclusively dominated financial reporting throughout the past century. Yet, as noted earlier, criticism of this type of accounting abounds when inflation is present.

current cost

The cost to replace an asset, as opposed to its historical cost.

The two nontraditional alternatives, which we can apply separately or in combination, address separate but related problems caused by inflation: (1) Constant-dollar disclosures account for general changes in the purchasing power of the dollar, and (2) current-cost disclosures account for changes in prices of specific assets. The two approaches create the following four alternatives for measuring income:

OBJECTIVE 6

Explain and illustrate four methods of measuring income.

	Historical Cost	Current Cost
Nominal Dollars	1 Historical Cost/ Nominal Dollars	2 Current Cost/ Nominal Dollars
Constant Dollars	3 Historical Cost/ Constant Dollars	4 Current Cost/ Constant Dollars

In the following discussion of these alternatives, we will consider the situation of the Marsalis Company. Marsalis has the following traditional balance sheets at December 31 (based on historical costs in nominal dollars):

	20X0	20X1
Cash	$ 0	$10,500
Inventory, 400 and 100 units, respectively	8,000	2,000
Total assets	$8,000	$12,500
Original paid-in capital	$8,000	$ 8,000
Retained income	—	4,500
Stockholders' equity	$8,000	$12,500

The company acquired all 400 units of inventory at $20 per unit (total of $8,000) on December 31, 20X0, and held the units until December 31, 20X1, when it sold 300 units for $35 per unit (total of $10,500 cash). The replacement cost of the inventory at that date was $30 per unit. The general price level index was 100 on December 31, 20X0, and 110 on December 31, 20X1. We will assume that these are the only transactions, and we will focus on operating income before taxes.

Historical Cost/Nominal Dollars

Exhibit 17-8 is the basis for the explanations that follow. The first two columns of Exhibit 17-8 show financial statements prepared using the time-honored historical cost/nominal dollars approach (HC/ND). This method measures invested capital in nominal dollars. It is the most popular approach to income measurement, and most people simply call it the historical-cost method. Operating income is the excess of revenue ($10,500 in 20X1) over the original acquisition costs of assets used in obtaining that revenue. As we have already seen, when using the conventional accrual basis of accounting, we need an exchange transaction before recording revenues (and resulting incomes). Thus, no income generally appears until the company sells the asset. We ignore the intervening price fluctuations.

Current Cost/Nominal Dollars

The second set of financial statements in Exhibit 17-8 illustrates the current cost/nominal dollar approach (CC/ND), sometimes called simply the **current-cost method,** that has especially strong advocates in the United Kingdom and Australia. This model emphasizes that operating income should be "distributable" income. That is, Marsalis Company could pay dividends of only $1,500 and still leave enough assets to allow for replacement of the inventory that it has just sold.

Critics of traditional accounting claim that the $4,500 historical-cost measure of operating income is misleading because it overstates the real income. If Marsalis were to pay a $4,500

current-cost method
The measurement method that uses current costs and nominal dollars.

| | Nominal Dollars* | | | | Constant Dollars* | | | |
	Historical Cost HC/ND		Current Cost CC/ND		Historical Cost HC/CD		Current Cost CC/CD	
Balance Sheets as of December 31	20X0	20X1	20X0	20X1	20X0	20X1	20X0	20X1
Cash	—	10,500	—	10,500	—	10,500	—	10,500
Inventory, 400 and 100 units, respectively	8,000	2,000^b	8,000	3,000^c	8,800^e	2,200^e	8,800^e	3,000^c
Total assets	8,000	12,500	8,000	13,500	8,800	12,700	8,800	13,500
Original paid-in capital	8,000	8,000	8,000	8,000	8,800^f	8,800^f	8,800^f	8,800^f
Retained income (confined to operating income)		4,500		1,500		3,900		1,500
Revaluation equity (accumulated holding gains)			—	4,000				3,200
Total liabilities and shareholders' equity	8,000	12,500	8,000	13,500	8,800	12,700	8,800	13,500
Income statements for 20X1								
Sales, 300 units @ $35		10,500		10,500		10,500		10,500
Cost of goods sold, 300 units		6,000^b		9,000^c		6,600^e		9,000^c
Operating income (to retained income)		4,500		1,500		3,900		1,500
Holding gains^a								
On 300 units sold				3,000^d				2,400^g
On 100 units unsold				1,000^d				800^g
Total holding gains^a (to revaluation equity)				4,000				3,200

* Nominal dollars are not restated for a general price index, whereas constant dollars are restated.

a Many advocates of this current-cost method favor showing these gains in a completely separate statement of holding gains rather than as a part of the income statement. Others favor including some or all of these gains as a part of income for the year.

b 100 × $20,   c 100 × $30,   d 300 × ($30 – $20),   e 110/100 × $8,000,   f 110/100 × $8,000.
300 × $20,   300 × $30,   100 × ($30 – $20).   110/100 × $2,000,
   110/100 × $6,000.

g $9,000 – [(110/100) × $6,000] = $2,400. $3,000 – [(110/100) × $2,000] = $800
or   or
300 × [$30 – (110/100) × $20] = $2,400.   100 × [$30 – (110/100) × $20] = $800.

Exhibit 17-8
Four Major Methods to Measure Income and Capital (dollars)

dividend, the company would not be able to continue operations at the same level as before. Accountants frequently call the $3,000 difference between the two operating incomes ($4,500 − $1,500 = $3,000) an "inventory profit." Why? Because Marsalis now needs $9,000 instead of $6,000 to replace the 300 units sold (300 × the increase in price from $20 to $30 equals the $3,000 difference). It is not really profit or income because the company needs it to maintain its inventory at the original level.

The CC/ND approach stresses a separation between operating income—the excess of revenue over the current costs of the assets consumed in obtaining that revenue—and **holding gains (or losses)**—increases (or decreases) in the replacement costs of the assets held during the current period. Accountants differ sharply on how to account for holding gains or losses. If income cannot occur until invested capital is "recovered" or "maintained," we have to agree on how to measure capital maintenance. Exhibit 17-8 illustrates this issue. Advocates of a physical concept of capital maintenance claim that companies should exclude from income all holding gains (both those gains related to the units sold and the gains related to the units unsold). Instead, they should become a part of stockholders' equity called **revaluation equity.** Why? Because holding gains represent the amount that a company must reinvest to maintain physical capital at its beginning-of-the-year level. Holding gains become part *of* capital, not a return *on* capital.

holding gains (or losses)
Increases (or decreases) in the replacement costs of the assets held during the current period.

revaluation equity
A portion of stockholders' equity that shows all accumulated holding gains.

Historical Cost/Constant Dollars

The third column of Exhibit 17-8, historical cost/constant dollars (HC/CD), shows the results of applying a general price index adjustment to historical costs. For our purpose, a **general price index** compares the average price of a group of goods and services at one date with the average price of a similar group at another date. To apply the HC/CD method, we restate the income measurements in each year from nominal dollars (possessing different general purchasing powers of various years) to constant dollars (possessing the same general purchasing power of the current year). Because of inflation, dollars spent or received in 20X1 have a different value than dollars spent or received in 20X0. Comparing 20X0 dollars to 20X1 dollars is like comparing apples and oranges. Constant-dollar accounting measures all items on the 20X1 financial statements in 20X1 dollars.

general price index
A comparison of the average price of a group of goods and services at one date with the average price of a similar group at another date.

Consider the objections to the HC/ND method. Deducting 6,000 20X0 dollars from 10,500 20X1 dollars to obtain $4,500 is akin to deducting 60 centimeters from 105 inches and calling the result 45. In either case, the result is nonsense.

The HC/CD method attempts to remedy the objections. It uses general price indexes to restate the amounts of the HC/ND method. Examples of such indexes are the gross national product implicit price deflator and the consumer price index for all urban consumers (CPI). Index numbers gauge the relationship between current conditions and some norm or baseline condition (to which we assign the index number of 100).

A price index is an average. It does not measure the behavior of the individual component prices. Some individual prices may rise and others may fall. The general consumer price level may soar while the prices of eggs and chickens decline.

Do not confuse general indexes, which are used in constant-dollar accounting, with specific indexes. The two have entirely different purposes. Some companies use **specific price indexes** to approximate the current costs of particular assets or types of assets. That is, companies use specialized indexes to get approximations of current costs without having to pay professional appraisers. For example, **Inland Steel** used the *Engineering News Record* construction cost index to value most of its property, plant, and equipment for purposes of using the current-cost method.

specific price index
An index used to approximate the current costs of particular assets or types of assets.

Note that the HC/CD approach is not a fundamental departure from historical costs. Instead, it restates all historical costs in order to express all revenues and expenses in dollars of the same purchasing power. The restated figures are historical costs expressed in constant dollars via the use of a general price index. They are not current costs.

Constant-dollar financial statements generally measure all amounts using the most recent dollar. Why? Because users tend to think in terms of current purchasing power. The company would update the cost of the units in beginning inventory on each year's balance sheet along with the effect on stockholders' equity. For example, Marsalis Company would restate the December 31, 20X0, balance sheet for comparative purposes on December 31, 20X1:

	Original Cost	Multiplier	Restated Cost
Inventory	$8,000	110/100	$8,800
Original paid-in capital	8,000	110/100	8,800

To extend the illustration, suppose Marsalis held all the inventory for two full years and that the general price index rose from 110 to 132 during 20X2. Marsalis would restate the December 31, 20X1, balance sheet items for comparative purposes on December 31, 20X2, using 20X2 dollars:

	Restated Cost, 12/31/X2	Multiplier	Restated Cost, 12/31/X3
Inventory	$8,800	132/110	$10,560*
Original paid-in capital	8,800	132/110	10,560*

* We could compute the same result using the original acquisition cost
  of the inventory:
  Inventory $8,000 × 132/100 = $10,560
  Original paid-in capital $8,000 × 132/100 = $10,560

The restated amount is just that—a restatement of original cost in terms of current (20X2) dollars. It is not a gain in any sense. Therefore, this approach differs from an application of "current-cost" accounting. Using this approach, fluctuations in the specific current cost of the inventory do not affect the amount of inventory shown on the balance sheet.

The HC/CD approach maintains the general purchasing power of the total invested capital, a financial concept of capital maintenance, rather than maintaining the physical level of the inventory.

Current Cost/Constant Dollars

The last column of Exhibit 17-8 shows the results of applying general index numbers to current costs, the current cost/constant dollar method (CC/CD). As the footnotes of the exhibit explain in more detail, Marsalis adjusts the nominal gains reported under the CC/ND method so that it reports only gains in constant dollars. For example, suppose you buy 100 units on December 31, 20X0, for $2,000 cash and hold it until December 31, 20X1, when its replacement cost is $3,000. Suppose also that the general price index has risen from 100 to 110. Your nominal gain is $1,000, but your "real" gain in constant dollars in 20X1 is only $800: the $3,000 current cost minus the restated historical cost of $2,000 × 1.10 = $2,200.

Suppose Marsalis holds the 100 units throughout 20X2. The general price index rises from 110 to 132. The replacement cost rises from $30 to $34, a nominal holding gain for 20X2 of $4 × 100 = $400. However, because the original cost adjusted for price increases is $2,000 × (132 ÷ 100) = $2,200 × (132 ÷ 110) = $2,640 at the end of 20X1, an increase of $440 over the beginning-of-the-year amount, the CC/CD approach would report a real holding loss:

	12/31/X0	12/31/X1	12/31/X2
Original cost restated for changes in the price level	$2,000	$2,200	$2,640
Current cost	2,000	3,000	3,400
Increase in current cost		1,000*	400*
Increase due to price level		200†	440†
Holding gain (loss)		$ 800	$ (40)

* 3,000 − 2,000 = 1,000, and 3,400 − 3,000 = 400
† 2,200 − 2,000 = 200, and 2,640 − 2,200 = 440

Many accountants disagree on the relative merits of historical-cost versus current-cost approaches to income measurement. But there is general agreement among most accountants that restatements in constant dollars would be an improvement regardless of whether a company uses historical or current costs (ignoring practical barriers). Without price-level adjustments, income includes illusory gains caused by using an unstable measuring unit, not by the company's performance.

MAKING MANAGERIAL DECISIONS

Consider the concept of a holding gain on inventory. Holding gains arise only when using current rather than historical costs. They measure the specific price increases of inventory held by a company compared to some benchmark. Under the current-cost/nominal-dollars method, the benchmark is the original cost of the inventory. Under the current-cost/constant-dollars method, the benchmark is the price-level adjusted historical cost of the inventory. Suppose a company purchased $5,000 of inventory at the beginning of the year and held it until the end of the year, when its replacement cost was $6,000. The price-level index was 100 at the beginning of the year and 112 at the end of the year. Compute the holding gain under (1) the current-cost/nominal-dollars method and (2) the current-cost/constant-dollars method. How would a manager explain each holding gain?

Answer

Under the current-cost/nominal-dollars method, the entire $1,000 price increase is a holding gain. It reflects the fact that inventory purchased for $5,000 is now worth $6,000. Under the current-cost/constant-dollar method, only $400 of the price increase is a holding gain. The original $5,000 of inventory is worth $5,000 × (112 ÷ 100) = $5,600 in end-of-year dollars. The only real gain is $6,000 − $5,600 = $400; the other $600 increase in value merely offsets the decline in the value of the dollar.

Summary Problem For Your Review

PROBLEM

In 1985, a company purchased a parcel of land, call it parcel 1, for $1,200. The company purchased an identical parcel, 2, today for $3,000. The general price level index has risen from 100 in 1985 to 250 now. Fill in the blanks in the following table:

Parcel	(1) Historical Cost Measured in 1985 Purchasing Power	(2) Historical Cost Measured in Current Purchasing Power	(3) Historical Cost as Originally Measured
1	___	___	___
2	___	___	___
Total	___	___	___

1. Compare the figures in the three columns. Which total presents a nonsense result? Why?
2. Does the write-up of parcel 1 in column 2 result in a gain? Why?
3. Assume that these parcels are the only assets of the business. There are no liabilities. Prepare a balance sheet for each of the three columns.

SOLUTION

Parcel	(1) Historical Cost Measured in 1985 Purchasing Power	(2) Historical Cost Measured in Current Purchasing Power	(3) Historical Cost as Originally Measured
1	$1,200	$3,000	$1,200
2	1,200	3,000	3,000
Total	$2,400	$6,000	$4,200

1. The addition in column 3 produces a nonsense result. In contrast, the other two sums are the results of applying a standard unit of measure. The computations in columns 1 and 2 are illustrations of a restatement of historical cost in terms of a common dollar, a standard unit of measure. Whether the company makes the restatement using the 1985 dollar or the current dollar is a matter of personal preference; columns 1 and 2 yield equivalent results. Restatement in terms of the current dollar (column 2) is most popular because the current dollar has more meaning than the old dollar to readers of the financial statements.

2. The mere restatement of identical assets in terms of different but equivalent measuring units does not create a gain. Expressing parcel 1 as $1,200 in column 1 and $3,000 in column 2 is like expressing parcel 1 in terms of, say, either 1,200 square yards or $9 \times 1,200 = 10,800$ square feet. Surely the "write-up" from 1,200 square yards to 10,800 square feet is not a gain; it is merely another way of measuring the same asset. That is basically what general price level accounting is all about. It says you cannot measure one plot of land in square yards and another in square feet and add them together. You must first convert them to some common measure. Unfortunately, column 3 fails to perform such a conversion before adding the two parcels together; hence the total is internally inconsistent.

3. The balance sheets would be

	(1)	(2)	(3)
Land	$2,400	$6,000	$4,200
Paid-in capital	$2,400	$6,000	$4,200

Note that we expressed (1) in 1985 dollars, (2) in current dollars, and (3) in a mixture of 1985 and current dollars.

Accounting Vocabulary

For various financial ratios, see Exhibit 17-7, page 782. Also become familiar with the following terms.

available-for-sale securities, p. 768
benchmark comparisons, p. 781
common-size statements, p. 780
component percentages, p. 780
consolidated financial statements, p. 770
constant dollars, p. 790
cross-sectional comparisons, p. 783

current cost, p. 790
current-cost method, p. 791
efficient capital market, p. 786
equity method, p. 769
financial capital maintenance, p. 790
general price index, p. 793
historical cost, p. 790
holding gains (or losses), p. 793
market method, p. 768

minority interests, p. 772
nominal dollars, p. 790
parent company, p. 770
physical capital maintenance, p. 790
revaluation equity, p. 793
specific price index, p. 793
subsidiary, p. 770
time-series comparisons, p. 781
trading securities, p. 768

Fundamental Assignment Material

Special Note: Problems relating to Part One of the chapter are presented first in each subgrouping of the assignment material.

General Exercises and Problems

17-A1 Market or Equity Method

Suppose General Motors acquired 25% of the voting stock of Akron Tire Co. for $72 million cash. In year 1, Akron Tire had a net income of $48 million and paid a cash dividend of $32 million. The investment had a market value of $76 million at the end of the year.

1. Using the equity method, show the effects of the three transactions on the accounts of General Motors. Use the balance sheet equation format.
2. Assume that General Motors could use the market method for this investment and that General Motors classified the investment as an available-for-sale security. Show the effects of the three transactions on the accounts of General Motors. Use the balance sheet equation format.

17-A2 Consolidated Financial Statements

Suppose Vancouver Publishing Company acquired all the common shares of Trudeau Book Company for $50 million cash at the start of the year. Immediately before the business combination, each company had the following condensed balance sheet accounts (in millions):

	Vancouver	Trudeau
Cash and other assets	$330	$70
Accounts payable, etc.	$110	$20
Stockholders' equity	220	50
Total equities	$330	$70

1. Prepare a tabulation of the consolidated balance sheet accounts immediately after the acquisition. Use the balance sheet equation format.
2. Suppose Vancouver and Trudeau have the following results for the year:

	Vancouver	Trudeau
Sales	$330	$100
Expenses	245	90

Prepare income statements for the year for Vancouver, Trudeau, and the consolidated entity. Assume that neither Vancouver nor Trudeau sells items to the other.

3. Present the effects of the operations for the year on Vancouver's accounts and on Trudeau's accounts, using the balance sheet equation. Also tabulate the consolidated balance sheet accounts at the end of the year. Assume that liabilities are unchanged.
4. Suppose Trudeau paid a cash dividend of $7 million. What accounts in requirement 3 would be affected and by how much?

17-A3 Minority Interests

This modifies and extends the preceding problem. However, this problem is self-contained because all the facts are reproduced below. Vancouver Publishing Company acquired 80% of the common shares of Trudeau Book Company for $40 million cash at the start of the year. Immediately before the business combination, each company had the following condensed balance sheet accounts (in millions):

	Vancouver	Trudeau
Cash and other assets	$330	$70
Accounts payable, etc.	$110	$20
Stockholders' equity	220	50
Total equities	$330	$70

1. Prepare a tabulation of the consolidated balance sheet accounts immediately after the acquisition. Use the balance sheet equation format.
2. Suppose Vancouver and Trudeau have the following results for the year:

	Vancouver	Trudeau
Sales	$330	$100
Expenses	245	90

Prepare income statements for the year for Vancouver, Trudeau, and the consolidated entity.

3. Using the balance sheet equation format, present the effects of the operations for the year on Vancouver's accounts and Trudeau's accounts. Also tabulate consolidated balance sheet accounts at the end of the year. Assume that liabilities are unchanged.

4. Suppose Trudeau paid a cash dividend of $7 million. What accounts in number 3 would be affected and by how much?

17-A4 Goodwill and Consolidation

This modifies and extends Problem 17-A2. However, this problem is self-contained because all the facts are reproduced below. Vancouver Publishing Company acquired all the common shares of Trudeau Book Company for $80 million cash at the start of the year. Immediately before the business combination, each company had the following condensed balance sheet accounts (in millions):

	Vancouver	Trudeau
Cash and other assets	$330	$70
Accounts payable, etc.	$110	$20
Stockholders' equity	220	50
Total equities	$330	$70

Assume that the fair values of Trudeau's individual assets were equal to their book values.

1. Prepare a tabulation of the consolidated balance sheet accounts immediately after the acquisition. Use the balance sheet equation format.

2. Suppose the book values of Trudeau's individual assets are equal to their fair market values except for equipment. The net book value of equipment is $15 million and its fair market value is $27 million. The equipment has a remaining useful life of four years. Straight-line depreciation is used.
   a. Describe how the consolidated balance sheet accounts immediately after the acquisition would differ from those in number 1. Be specific as to accounts and amounts.
   b. By how much will consolidated income differ in comparison with the consolidated income that would be reported when the entire excess of purchase cost over book value of assets was assigned to goodwill? Assume no amortization of goodwill.

17-A5 Rate-of-Return Computations

1. Harkins Chemical Company reported a 6% operating margin on sales, a 12% pretax operating return on total assets, and $400 million of average total assets. Compute the (a) operating income, (b) total sales, and (c) total asset turnover.

2. Osaka Electronics Corporation reported ¥300 million of sales, ¥15 million of operating income, and a total asset turnover of 5 times. (¥ is Japanese yen.) Compute the (a) total assets, (b) operating return on sales, and (c) pretax operating return on total assets.

Understanding Published Financial Reports

17-B1 Equity and Market Methods

Suppose **Microsoft** acquired one-third of the common shares of Jain Software Corporation for $55 million cash. In year 1, Jain had a net income of $60 million and paid cash dividends of $24 million. At the end of the year, the market value of the investment had fallen to $43 million.

Prepare a tabulation that compares the equity method and the market method of accounting for Microsoft's investment in Jain. Show the effects on the balance sheet equation under each method. (Assume that under the market method this investment is a trading security.) What is the year-end balance in the Investment in Jain account under the equity method? Under the market method? Which method should Microsoft use for reporting its investment in Jain?

17-B2 Consolidated Financial Statements

Consider the actual purchase of boat maker **Bayliner, Inc.**, by **Brunswick Corporation**. The purchase price was $400 million for a 100% interest.

Assume that the book value and the fair market value of Bayliner's net assets was $400 million. The balance sheet accounts immediately after the transaction were approximately (in millions):

	Brunswick	Bayliner
Investment in Bayliner	$ 400	—
Cash and other assets	1,000	$600
Total assets	$1,400	$600
Liabilities	$ 800	$200
Stockholders' equity	600	400
Total equities	$1,400	$600

1. Using the balance sheet equation format, prepare a tabulation of the consolidated balance sheet accounts immediately after the acquisition.
2. Suppose Bayliner had sales of $600 million and expenses of $500 million for the year, and Brunswick had sales of $1,800 million and expenses of $1,300 million. Prepare income statements for Brunswick, for Bayliner, and for the consolidated company. Assume that neither Brunswick nor Bayliner sold items to the other.
3. Using the balance sheet equation, present the effects of the operations for the year on the accounts of Bayliner and Brunswick. Also tabulate the consolidated balance sheet accounts at the end of the year. Assume that liabilities are unchanged.
4. Suppose Bayliner paid a cash dividend of $15 million. What accounts in number 3 would be affected and by how much?

17-B3 Investment in Equity Securities

Ford owns 33% of the stock of Mazda Corporation. In 2002, Mazda reported a net income of approximately $67 million and declared cash dividends of $20 million. Ford accounted for its investment in Mazda by the equity method.

1. Compute the amount of income recognized by Ford in 2002 from its investment in Mazda.
2. Suppose Ford had a balance of $2.1 billion in its "Investment in Mazda" account at the beginning of 2002. Compute the balance in the account at the end of 2002.
3. Suppose Ford had used the market method to account for its investment in Mazda and had classified this investment as an available-for-sale security. Assume that the market value of Ford's Mazda securities was $2.1 billion at the end of 2001 and $2.5 billion at the end of 2002.
   a. Compute the amount of income recognized by Ford in 2002 from its investment in Mazda.
   b. Assume that Ford had a balance of $2.1 billion in its "Investment in Mazda" account at the beginning of 2002. Compute the balance in the account at the end of 2002.
   c. Explain how Ford would account for the $400 million increase in market value.
4. Indicate briefly how the following three classes of investments should be accounted for: (a) greater than 50% interest, (b) 20% through 50% interest, and (c) less than 20% interest.

17-B4 Income Ratios and Asset Turnover

A semiannual report to the stockholders of Texaco included the following comments on earnings:

> On an annualized basis, net income represented an 8.9% return on average total assets of approximately $27.3 billion and an 18.9% return on average stockholders' equity. . . . Net income per gallon on all petroleum products sold worldwide averaged 3.6 cents. Net income was 4 cents on each dollar of revenue.

Using only this information, compute the (1) total asset turnover, (2) net income, (3) total revenues, (4) average stockholders' equity, and (5) gallons of petroleum products sold.

17-B5 Financial Ratios

Albertson's has more than 2,300 stores in 31 states and is one of the largest retail food and drug chains in the United States. Excerpts from the company's 2003 annual report are in Exhibit 17-9. Albertson's paid cash dividends of $.76 per common share in fiscal 2003, and an average of 397 million shares were outstanding during the year. Assume that Albertson's has no stock options or convertible securities. The company's market price on January 30, 2003, was $21 per share. Compute the following financial ratios for fiscal 2003:

1. Current ratio
2. Total debt to equity
3. Gross profit rate
4. Return on sales
5. Return on stockholders' equity

Income statement for the year ended January 30, 2003

Sales	$35,626
Cost of sales	25,242
Gross profit	$10,384
Other expenses (summarized)	9,359
Earnings before income taxes	$ 1,025
Income taxes	540
Net earnings	$ 485

Balance sheet	January 30, 2003	January 31, 2002
Assets		
Inventories	$ 2,973	$ 3,196
Other current assets (summarized)	1,295	1,427
Total current assets	$ 4,268	$ 4,623
Land, buildings, and equipment (net)	9,029	9,282
Other assets	1,914	2,076
Total assets	$ 15,211	$15,981
Liabilities and stockholders' equity		
Current liabilities (summarized)	$ 3,448	$ 3,596
Long-term liabilities (summarized)	6,566	6,470
Total liabilities	$ 10,014	$10,066
Stockholders' equity (summarized)	5,197	5,915
Total liabilities and stockholders' equity	$ 15,211	$15,981

Exhibit 17-9
Albertson's, Inc.
Income Statement and Balance Sheet (in millions)

6. Earnings per share
7. Price earnings
8. Dividend yield
9. Dividend payout

Additional Assignment Material

Questions

17-1 Distinguish between trading securities and available-for-sale securities.

17-2 What is the equity method?

17-3 Contrast the market method and the equity method.

17-4 "The equity method is usually used for long-term investments." Do you think this is appropriate? Explain.

17-5 Distinguish between control of a company and a significant influence over a company.

17-6 What criterion is used to determine whether a parent-subsidiary relationship exists?

17-7 Why have subsidiaries? Why not have the corporation take the form of a single legal entity?

17-8 "A consolidated financial statement simply adds together the separate accounts of a parent company and its subsidiaries." Do you agree? Explain.

17-9 What is a minority interest?

17-10 "Goodwill is the excess of purchase price over the book values of the individual assets acquired." Do you agree? Explain.

17-11 "It is better to recognize goodwill than to write up assets to their fair market values." Do you agree? Why?

17-12 "Pro forma statements are the formal financial statements that companies file with the Securities and Exchange Commission." Do you agree? Explain.

17-13 Name the three types of comparisons made with ratios.

17-14 Why is it useful to analyze income statements and balance sheets by component percentages?

17-15 What two ratios are multiplied together to give the pretax operating rate of return on average total assets?

17-16 "Ratios are mechanical and incomplete." Explain.

17-17 "An efficient capital market is one where securities are traded through stockbrokers." Do you agree? Explain.

17-18 Give three sources of information for investors besides accounting information.

17-19 Evaluate the following quotation from Forbes: "If IBM had been forced to expense [the software development cost of] $785 million, its earnings would have been cut by 72 cents a share. With IBM selling at 14 times earnings, expensing the costs might have knocked over $10 off IBM's share price."

17-20 Suppose the president of your company wanted to switch depreciation methods to increase reported net income: "Our stock price is 10% below what I think it should be; changing depreciation method will increase income by 10%, thus getting our share price up to its proper level." How would you respond?

17-21 Study Appendix 17. Explain the difference between return *on* capital and return *of* capital.

17-22 Study Appendix 17. Distinguish between the physical and the financial concepts of maintenance of invested capital.

17-23 Study Appendix 17. "The choice among accounting measures of income is often expressed as either historical-cost accounting or general price level accounting or current-cost accounting." Do you agree? Explain.

17-24 Study Appendix 17. "All holding gains should be excluded from income." What is the major logic behind this statement?

Cognitive Exercises

17-25 Depreciation in Consolidated Financial Statements

Suppose Company P buys 100% of the common stock of Company S for more than the book value of S. After one year, the consolidated entity prepares financial statements. Two expense items appear on the consolidated income statement that are not on the individual statements of P and S:

1. Depreciation on equipment in excess of that in the individual statements
2. Write-off of goodwill

Explain why these two accounts exist. That is, what was there about the acquisition that generated the need for these two accounts?

17-26 Market Method, Equity Method, and Total Assets

Suppose **Disney** bought 20% of the common shares of a small software company that recently went public. The management of Disney believed that patents developed by the software company would make the company very valuable in a year or two. Near-term profits may not be high, but large increases in the share price are likely. No dividends are expected. How would the choice of accounting method, the market method or the equity method, affect Disney's total assets reported on its balance sheet in the next couple years if its expectations about the software firm come true? Explain.

17-27 Just-in-Time (JIT) Inventory and Current Ratio

Many companies have adopted JIT inventory methods to reduce the size of their inventories. What would you expect to happen to the current ratios of such companies? Would you interpret the current ratio differently for JIT companies compared to other companies? Explain.

17-28 Inflation and Financing Decisions

Study Appendix 17. Investors expect a return on their investments and an eventual return of their investments. Suppose that the treasurer of a company decides to pay dividends that will be a reasonable return on investment but not return any of the original investment. Since the original investment, there has been substantial inflation. How should the treasurer decide the amount of dividends to pay if he uses the concept of financial capital maintenance? How should he decide if he uses the concept of physical capital maintenance? If you were an investor in this company, which concept of capital maintenance would you prefer the treasurer to use?

General Exercises and Problems

17-29 Equity Method

Company X acquired 25% of the voting stock of Company Y for $45 million cash. In year 1, Y had a net income of $20 million and paid cash dividends of $12 million. At the end of the year, the total market value of Company Y was $200 million.

Prepare a tabulation that compares the equity method and the market method of accounting for X's investment in Y. Show the effects on the balance sheet equation under each method. What is the year-end balance in the Investment in Y account under the equity method? Under the market method? What difference in accounting would there be if the investment were a trading security instead of an available-for-sale security?

17-30 Consolidated Financial Statements

Salt Lake Development Company (the parent) acquired 100% of the common stock of Provo Company (the subsidiary) at the start of 20X1. Their financial statements follow:

	Salt Lake Development (Parent)	Provo (Subsidiary)
Income statement for 20X1		
Revenue and "other income"	$5,400,000	$1,100,000
Expenses	5,100,000	1,000,000
Net income	$ 300,000	$ 100,000
Balance sheets, December 31, 20X1		
Assets	$1,000,000	$ 400,000
Liabilities to creditors	$ 450,000	$ 100,000
Stockholders' equity	550,000	300,000
Total liabilities and stockholders' equity	$1,000,000	$ 400,000

1. Provo had enjoyed a fantastically profitable year in 20X1. Salt Lake Development prepared its income statement by showing its claim to Provo's income as part of "other income." On the other hand, Salt Lake Development's balance sheet is really not completed. The $1 million of assets of Salt Lake Development includes a $200,000 investment in Provo and does not include Salt Lake Development's claim to Provo's 20X1 net income.

   Prepare a consolidated income statement and a consolidated balance sheet. Use the balance sheet equation format for the latter.

2. Suppose Salt Lake Development Company owned 60% of Provo Company. Liabilities to creditors are unchanged. The assets of Salt Lake Development include a $120,000 investment in Provo instead of $200,000. However, assume the total assets are $1 million. The balance sheet is really not completed because the investment account does not reflect the claim to Provo's 20X1 net income. Similarly, Salt Lake Development's revenue and other income is $5.36 million, not $5.4 million, but expenses remain at $5.1 million as in number 1.

   Prepare a consolidated income statement and a consolidated balance sheet. Use the balance sheet equation format for the latter.

17-31 Determination of Goodwill

Refer to the preceding problem, number 1. Suppose the investment in Provo 1 was $300,000 instead of the $200,000 as stated. This would mean that the "other assets" at the end of 20X1 would be $700,000 instead of $800,000. Would the consolidated income differ? How? Be as specific as possible. Would the consolidated balance sheet differ? How? Be as specific as possible.

17-32 Purchased Goodwill

Consider the following balance sheets (in millions):

	El Paso Minerals Company	Tulsa Oil Company
Cash	$ 700	$ 80
Inventories	350	70
Plant assets, net	390	60
Total assets	$1,440	$210
Common stock and paid-in capital	$ 470	$120
Retained income	970	90
Total liabilities and stockholders' equity	$1,440	$210

El Paso paid $290 million to Tulsa stockholders for all their stock. The "fair value" of the plant assets of Tulsa is $140 million. The fair value of cash and inventories is equal to their carrying amounts. El Paso and Tulsa still keep separate books.

1. Prepare a tabulation showing the balance sheets of El Paso, of Tulsa, Intercompany Eliminations, and Consolidated immediately after the acquisition.

2. Suppose only $100 million rather than $140 million of the total purchase price of $290 million could be logically assigned to the plant assets. How would the consolidated accounts be affected?

3. Refer to the facts in number 1. Suppose El Paso had paid $340 million rather than $290 million. State how your tabulation in number 1 would change.

17-33 Amortization and Depreciation

Refer to the preceding problem, number 3. Suppose a year passes, and El Paso and Tulsa generate individual net incomes of $105 million and $35 million, respectively. The latter is after a deduction by Tulsa of $12 million of straight-line depreciation. Compute the consolidated net income if (1) goodwill is not impaired and (2) half of the goodwill is written off at the end of the year. Ignore income taxes.

17-34 Allocating Total Purchase Price to Assets

Two Hollywood companies had the following balance sheet accounts as of December 31, 20X0 and net income for 20X0 (in millions):

	MCM Films	TeeWarn Productions		MCM Films	TeeWarn Productions
Cash and receivables	$ 30	$ 22	Current liabilities	$ 50	$ 20
Inventories	120	3	Common stock	100	10
Plant assets, net	150	95	Retained income	150	90
Total assets	$300	$120	Total liab. and stk. eq.	$300	$120
Net income for 20X0	$ 19	$ 4			

On January 4, 20X1, these firms merged. MCM issued $170 million of its shares (at market value) in exchange for all the shares of TeeWarn, a motion picture division of a large company. The inventory of films acquired through the combination had been fully amortized on TeeWarn's books.

During 20X1, TeeWarn received revenue of $21 million from the rental of films from its inventory. MCM earned $20 million on its other operations (i.e., excluding TeeWarn) during 20X1. TeeWarn broke even on its other operations (i.e., excluding the film rental contracts) during 20X1.

1. Prepare a consolidated balance sheet for the combined company immediately after the combination. Assume that $70 million of the purchase price was assigned to the inventory of films.

2. Prepare a comparison of MCM's net income between 20X0 and 20X1 where the cost of the film inventories would be amortized on a straight-line basis over four years. What would be the net income for 20X1 if the $70 million were assigned to goodwill rather than to the inventory of films and the value of goodwill was maintained?

17-35 Preparation of Consolidated Financial Statements

The Ramnath Medical Instruments Company's fiscal year ends on December 31. The company had the following items on its 20X1 income statement and balance sheet (in millions):

Net sales and other operating revenue	$900
Investments in affiliated companies	100
Common stock, 9,000,000, $1 par	9
Depreciation and amortization	20
Accounts payable	210
Cash	30
Paid-in capital in excess of par	103
Interest expense	25
Retained income	198
Accrued income taxes payable	20
Cost of goods sold and operating expenses, exclusive of depreciation and amortization	650
Subordinated debentures, 11% interest, due December 31, 20X7	100
Minority interest in consolidated subsidiaries' net income	20
Goodwill	95
First-mortgage bonds, 10% interest, due December 31, 20X9	80
Property, plant, and equipment, net	125
Preferred stock, 2,000,000 shares, $50 par, dividend rate is $3.5 per share, each share is convertible into one share of common stock	100

Short-term investments at market value	45
Income tax expense	90
Accounts receivable, net	175
Minority interest in subsidiaries	90
Inventories at average cost	340
Dividends declared and paid on preferred stock	10
Equity in earnings of affiliated companies	20

Prepare Ramnath's consolidated 20X1 income statement and its consolidated balance sheet for December 31, 20X1.

17-36 Financial Ratios

The annual reports of Svalbard Fiske, a Norwegian fishing supply company, included the following selected data (in millions):

	20X2	20X1	20X0
Annual amounts:			
Net income	NOK 95*	NOK 60	NOK 25
Gross margin on sales	520	380	200
Cost of goods sold	980	620	300
Operating expenses	380	295	165
Income tax expense	45	25	10
Dividends declared	30	15	5
End-of-year amounts:			
Long-term assets	NOK 240	NOK 220	NOK 180
Long-term debt	80	65	40
Current liabilities	70	55	35
Cash	30	5	10
Accounts receivable	85	70	40
Merchandise inventory	120	85	60
Paid-in capital	205	205	205
Retained income	120	55	10

* NOK is Norwegian kroner. In recent years, the exchange rate has varied between seven and ten NOK per dollar.

During each of the three years, there were outstanding 10 million shares of capital stock, all common. Assume that all sales were on account and that the applicable market prices per share of stock were NOK 30 for 20X1 and NOK 40 for 20X2.

1. Compute each of the following for each of the last two years, 20X1 and 20X2:
   a. Current ratio
   b. Rate of return on sales
   c. Rate of return on stockholders' equity
   d. Ratio of total debt to stockholders' equity
   e. Ratio of current debt to stockholders' equity
   f. Gross profit rate
   g. Average collection period for accounts receivable
   h. Price-earnings ratio
   i. Dividend-payout percentage
   j. Dividend yield
2. Answer yes or no to each of these questions and indicate which of the computations in number 1 support your answer:
   a. Has gross profit rate improved?
   b. Has the rate of return on sales deteriorated?
   c. Has the rate of return on owners' investment increased?
   d. Is there a decrease in the effectiveness of collection efforts?
   e. Are dividends relatively more generous?
   f. Have the risks of insolvency changed significantly?
   g. Has the market price of the stock become cheaper relative to earnings?
   h. Have business operations improved?

   i. Has there been a worsening of the company's ability to pay current debts on time?

   j. Has there been a decline in the cash return on the market value of the capital stock?

   k. Did the collectibility of the receivables improve?

3. Basing your observations on only the available data and the ratios you computed, prepare some brief comments on the company's operations and financial changes during the three years.

17-37 Concepts of Income

Study Appendix 17. Suppose you are in the business of investing in land and holding it for resale. On December 31, 20X0, a parcel of land has a historical cost of $100,000 and a current value of $400,000; the general price index had tripled since the land was acquired. Suppose that the land is sold on December 31, 20X1, for $460,000. The general price level rose by 5% during 20X1.

1. Prepare a tabulation of income from continuing operations and holding gains for 20X1, using the four methods illustrated in Exhibit 17-8, page 792.
2. In your own words, explain the meaning of the results, giving special attention to what income represents.

17-38 Four Versions of Income and Capital

Study Appendix 17. Zamora Company has the following comparative balance sheets as of December 31 (based on historical costs in nominal dollars):

	20X0	20X1
Cash	$ —	$3,900
Inventory, 100 and 40 units, respectively	5,000	2,000
Total assets	$5,000	$5,900
Paid-in capital	$5,000	$5,000
Retained income	—	900
Stockholders' equity	$5,000	$5,900

The general price level index was 100 on December 31, 20X0, and 115 on December 31, 20X1. The company had acquired 100 units of inventory on December 31, 20X0, for $50 each and had held them throughout 20X1. The company sold 60 units on December 31, 20X1, for $70 cash each. The replacement cost of the inventory at that date was $60 per unit. Assume that these are the only transactions. Ignore income taxes.

    Use four columns to prepare comparative balance sheets as of December 31, 20X0, and December 31, 20X1, and income statements for 20X1 under (1) historical cost/nominal dollars, (2) current cost/nominal dollars, (3) historical cost/constant dollars, and (4) current cost/constant dollars.

Understanding Published Financial Reports

17-39 Classification on Balance Sheet

The following accounts appeared in the annual report of the **Mitsubishi Kasei Corporation**, Japan's premier integrated chemical company:

1. Minority interests in consolidated subsidiaries
2. Current maturities of long-term debt
3. Investments in and advances to nonconsolidated subsidiaries and affiliates
4. Prepaid expenses
5. Accrued income taxes
6. Treasury stock at cost

Indicate in detail in which section of the balance sheet each account should appear.

17-40 Meaning of Account Descriptions

The following account descriptions were found in an annual report of **E. I. du Pont de Nemours & Company**:

- Minority interests in earnings of consolidated subsidiaries
- Minority interest in consolidated subsidiaries
- Investments in affiliates
- Equity in earnings of affiliates

In your own words, explain what each type of account represents. Indicate whether the item appears on the balance sheet or the income statement.

17-41 Effect of Transactions Under the Equity Method

ConocoPhillips is the third-largest integrated energy company in the United States and the largest refiner. It holds between 30% and 50% ownership in six companies. The company uses the equity method to account for these companies and calls them affiliated companies on its balance sheet (in millions):

	December 31	
	2002	**2001**
Investments in affiliated companies	$5,900	$2,788

ConocoPhillips's equity in the earnings of affiliated companies in 2002 was approximately $337 million, and it received dividends of $313 from these affiliates. ConocoPhillips had pretax income of $2,164 million.

1. How much did ConocoPhillips's investments in affiliated companies add to its pretax income in 2002? What percentage of this income came from these investments?
2. Compute the additional investment that ConocoPhillips made in its affiliated companies in 2002. (*Hint:* Use a T-account to aid your analysis.)
3. Suppose ConocoPhillips received only $113 million rather than $313 million in dividends from its affiliated companies in 2002. What income would ConocoPhillips recognize from its affiliated companies in 2002?

17-42 Consolidations in Japan

A few years ago, Japan's finance ministry issued a directive requiring the 600 largest Japanese companies to produce consolidated financial statements. The previous practice had been to use parent-company-only statements. A story in *Business Week* said, "Financial observers hope that the move will help end the tradition-honored Japanese practice of 'window dressing' the parent company financial results by shoving losses onto hapless subsidiaries, whose red ink was seldom revealed. . . . When companies needed to show a bigger profit, they would sell their product to subsidiaries at an inflated price. . . . Or the parent company charged a higher rent to a subsidiary company using its building."

Could a parent company follow the quoted practices and achieve window dressing in its parent-only financial statements if it used the equity method of accounting for its intercorporate investments? Explain.

17-43 Minority Interests

Toyota Motor Company has 49 consolidated subsidiaries, 26 in Japan and 23 outside of Japan. It owns 100% of 25 of these companies and percentages ranging from 50% to 94% in the others. Toyota's 2002 income statement showed (in millions of yen):

Income before taxes and minority interests	¥47,866
Income taxes	19,707
Minority interests	848
Net income	¥27,311

Toyota's balance sheet included an amount of ¥18,856 million for "Minority interest in consolidated subsidiaries."

1. What would Toyota's net income have been if it owned 100% of all 49 subsidiaries?
2. Suppose Toyota's average ownership percentage of these consolidated subsidiaries is 90%. What was the total 2002 net income of the subsidiaries?
3. Suppose that none of the subsidiaries paid any dividends and Toyota neither bought nor sold any interest in its subsidiaries during 2002. What was Toyota's balance in "Minority interest in consolidated subsidiaries" at the end of 2001?

17-44 General Motors and GMAC

The consolidated financial statements of **General Motors** include the results of **GMAC**, its financing subsidiary. Some investors think the business of a financing subsidiary is so different from that of its parent that the two should not be consolidated. In 2002, General Motors reported consolidated net income of $1,736, and GMAC reported net income of $1,870 million.

1. What would be the 2002 net income of General Motors if it did not consolidate GMAC but accounted for it on an equity basis?

2. What would General Motors' net income be if it did not own GMAC but all other results were as reported?

3. What advantages does the consolidated statement have? What advantages does the unconsolidated statement that accounts for GMAC on an equity basis have?

17-45 Goodwill

In 2002 **Procter & Gamble** (P&G) bought the Clairol business from **Bristol-Myers Squibb** for $5.0 billion in cash. The purchase added $700,000 tangible assets and $500,000 liabilities to P&G's balance sheet. In addition, P&G identified $1.5 billion of specific intangible assets acquired, and these assets had an average life of nine years.

1. How much goodwill did P&G record as a result of the acquisition of Clairol? How much of this goodwill will still be on P&G's balance sheet in 2005?

2. Suppose P&G had not identified the $1.5 billion of specific intangible assets but instead had recorded an extra $1.5 billion worth of goodwill. How would this affect P&G's income in 2003?

3. Why might a manager want this $1.5 billion to be recorded as goodwill rather than as part of the value of identifiable intangible assets?

17-46 Accounting for Goodwill

On April 12, 2002, **Medtronic, Inc.**, the Minneapolis-based medical technology company, bought 100% of **VidaMed**, a company that designs, develops, and markets technologically and clinically advanced systems for urological conditions. The purchase price was $328.6 million. At the time of acquisition, VidaMed's liabilities exceeded the fair value of its tangible assets by $38.4 million. However, included in the acquisition were technology-based intangible assets with a useful life of 15 years that were valued at $165.8 million.

1. Compute the amount of goodwill recognized at the time of purchase.

2. Medtronic had net earnings of $984.0 million in 2002. (Assume that these are without any earnings or losses from VidaMed.) VidaMed had a net loss of $9.4 million in 2001. Assume that these same VidaMed results occurred in 2002, when the results of the two companies would be consolidated. What would be the consolidated net income?

3. How would the consolidated net income computed in number 2 change if the entire excess of the purchase price over the value of assets less liabilites had been assigned to goodwill?

17-47 Income Ratios and Asset Turnover

Briggs & Stratton is the world's largest producer of air-cooled gasoline engines for outdoor power equipment. Its 2000 annual report to stockholders included the following data (in millions):

Net income	$80,638
Total assets	
Beginning of year	1,356,601
End of year	1,475,193
Net income as a percent of	
Total revenue	4.865%
Average stockholders' equity	16.719%

Using only the data given, compute the (1) net income percent of average assets, (2) total revenues, (3) average stockholders' equity, and (4) asset turnover (using two different approaches).

17-48 Financial Ratios

Honda Motor Company is a Japanese company with sales equivalent to nearly $70 billion. The company's income statement and balance sheet for the year ended March 31, 2003, are shown in Exhibits 17-10 and 17-11. Monetary amounts are in Japanese yen (¥).

1. Prepare a common-size income statement, that is, one showing component percentages.
2. Compute the following ratios:
   a. Current ratio
   b. Total debt to equity
   c. Gross profit rate
   d. Return on stockholders' equity (2002 stockholders' equity was ¥2,574 billion)
   e. Price-earnings ratio (the market price on March 31, 2002 was approximately ¥4,000 per share)
   f. Dividend-payout ratio
3. What additional information would help you interpret the percentages and ratios you calculated?

Exhibit 17-10

Honda Motor
Company, Ltd.

*Income Statement for
the Year Ended March
31, 2003 (in billions,
except per-share
amounts)*

Net sales	¥7,971
Cost of sales	5,410
Gross profit	¥2,561
Selling and administrative	1,435
Research and development	437
Operating income	¥ 689
Other income (expenses)	
Interest income	¥ 7
Interest expense	(11)
Other	(13)
Total	(17)
Income before income taxes	¥ 672
Income taxes	245
Net income	¥ 427
Amounts per share	
Net income	¥ 439
Cash dividends	¥ 31

17-49 Intercorporate Investments and Ethics

Hans Rasmussen and Alex Renalda were best friends at a small college, and they fought side-by-side in the jungles of Vietnam. After their military service, they went their separate ways to pursue MBA degrees, Hans to a prestigious East Coast business school and Alex to an equally prestigious West Coast school. But 30 years later, their paths crossed again.

By 2001, Alex had become president and CEO of Medusa Electronics, after 21 years with the firm. Hans had started out working for **American Airlines**, but left after nine years to start his own firm, Rasmussen Transport. In April 2001, Rasmussen Transport was near bankruptcy when Hans approached his old friend for help. Alex Renalda answered his friend's call, and Medusa Electronic bought 19% of Rasmussen Transport.

In 2004, Rasmussen was financially stable and Medusa was struggling. In fact, Alex Renalda thought his job as CEO might be in jeopardy if Medusa did not report income up to expectations. Late in 2004, Alex approached Hans with a request—quadruple Rasmussen's dividends so that Medusa could recognize $760,000 of investment income. Medusa had listed its investment in Rasmussen as an available-for-sale security, so changes in the market value of Rasmussen were recorded directly in stockholders' equity. However, dividends paid were recognized in Medusa's income statement.

Although Rasmussen had never paid dividends of more than 25% of net income, and it had plenty of uses for excess cash, Hans felt a deep obligation to Alex. Thus, he agreed to a $4 million dividend on net income of $4.17 million.

1. Why does the dividend policy of Rasmussen Transport affect the income of Medusa Electronics? Is this consistent with the intent of the accounting principles relating to the market and equity methods for intercorporate investments? Explain.
2. Comment on the ethical issues in the arrangements between Hans Rasmussen and Alex Renalda.

17-50 Accounting for Changing Prices

Study Appendix 17. **ConAgra**, the food products company with brands such as Healthy Choice, Wesson, Hunt's, Armour, and Swiss Miss, had historical-cost inventory of $3,275 million at the end of fiscal year 2003. Suppose ConAgra purchased the entire 2003 inventory on the last day of the year when the price index was 100. Half the inventory was sold for $2,000 million one year later, when the price index was 110; the other half remained in inventory. An amount of inventory identical to the amount sold was immediately purchased for $1,900 million.

1. Compute the amount ConAgra would show in its annual report for fiscal year 2004 for (a) beginning inventory; (b) ending inventory; (c) cost of goods sold; and (d) holding gains (losses), under each of the following four measurement methods: historical cost/nominal dollars, current cost/nominal dollars, historical cost/constant dollars, and current cost/constant dollars.
2. Suppose the sale of this inventory was ConAgra's only revenue in fiscal year 2004. Compute ConAgra's gross margin under historical cost/nominal dollars, current cost/nominal dollars, historical cost/constant dollars, and current cost/constant dollars.

Exhibit 17-11
Honda Motor
Company, Ltd.
*Balance Sheet March
31, 2003 (in billions)*

Assets	
Current assets	
Cash and cash equivalents	¥ 547
Receivables	1,542
Inventories	752
Other	451
Total current assets	¥3,292
Property, plant, and equipment, net	1,394
Investments	413
Other assets	2,582
Total assets	¥7,681
Liabilities and Stockholders' Equity	
Current liabilities	
Short-term debt	¥ 878
Payables	831
Accrued expenses	777
Current portion of long-term debt	304
Other	332
Total current liabilities	¥3,122
Long-term liabilities	
Long-term debt	¥1,140
Other	789
Total long-term liabilities	¥1,929
Stockholders' equity	
Common stock	¥ 86
Additional paid-in capital	202
Retained earnings	3,162
Other	(820)
Total stockholders' equity	¥2,630
Total liabilities and stockholders' equity	¥7,681

17-51 Effects of General Versus Specific Price Changes

Study Appendix 17. The following data are from the annual reports of **Gannett Co.** (owner of 125 newspapers), **Zayre Corp.** (operator of over 360 discount stores and over 700 specialty stores), and **Goodyear Tire and Rubber Company**, respectively (in millions):

	Gannett	Zayre	Goodyear
Increase in specific prices of assets held during the year	$45.8	$ 24.9	$ (4.7)
Less: effect of increase in general price level	37.5	55.5	252.0
Excess of increase in specific prices over increase in the general price level	$ 8.3	$(30.6)	$(256.7)

Compare and contrast the relationship between changes in the general price level and changes in the price of specific assets of each of the three companies.

EXCEL Application Exercise

17-52 Calculating Financial Ratios

Goal: Create an Excel spreadsheet to calculate financial ratios. Use the results to answer questions about your findings.

Scenario: Albertson's, Inc., has asked you to calculate financial ratios for their company based on Income Statement and Balance Sheet data presented in Exhibit 17-9.

Additional background information for your calculations appears in problem 17-B5. The formulas for the financial ratios can be found in Exhibit 17-7.

When you have completed your spreadsheet, answer the following questions:

1. Discuss Albertson's current ratio calculations and their meaning. Compare the results to the benchmark data presented in the chapter for this calculation.
2. Discuss Albertson's total debt to equity calculations and their meaning. Compare the results to the benchmark data presented in the chapter for this calculation.
3. Discuss the results of the dividend payout calculation and your opinion regarding its percentage.

Step-by-Step:

1. Open a new Excel spreadsheet.
2. In column A, create a bold-faced heading that contains the following:
   Row 1: Chapter 17 Decision Guideline
   Row 2: Albertson's, Inc.
   Row 3: Financial Ratio Analysis
   Row 4: Today's Date
3. Merge and center the four heading rows across columns A through C.
4. In row 7, create the following bold-faced column headings:
   Column A: Financial Data (in millions):
   Column B: January 30, 2003
   Column C: January 31, 2002
   Note: Adjust column widths as necessary.
5. Modify the format of the date headings in columns B and C as follows:

Number tab:	Category:	Date
	Type:	March 14, 1998

6. In column A, create the following row headings:
   Row 8: Current Assets
   Row 9: Current Liabilities
   Row 10: Total Liabilities
   Row 11: Stockholders' Equity
   Row 12: Sales
   Row 13: Gross Profit
   Row 14: Net Income
   Row 15: Market Price of Stock
   Row 16: Dividends Paid
   Row 17: Avg. Common Shares Outstanding
   Note: Adjust the column width as necessary.

7. Use data from Exhibit 17-9 and problem 17-B5 to enter the amounts for rows 8 through 17 in columns B and C.
8. Skip a row.
9. In row 19, create the following bold-faced column heading:
   Column A: Financial Ratios:
10. In column A, create the following row headings:
    Row 20: Current ratio
    Row 21: Total debt to equity
    Row 22: Gross profit percentage
    Row 23: Return on sales
    Row 24: Return on stockholders' equity
    Row 25: Earnings per share
    Row 26: Price earnings
    Row 27: Dividend yield
    Row 28: Dividend payout
11. Use cell-referenced formulas to calculate the amounts in columns B and C for rows 20 through 28.
    Hint: By using cell-referenced formulas, the data in rows 8 through 17 can be changed without invalidating the Excel formulas coded in rows 20 through 28.
    Example: The Excel formula for the Current Ratio in cell B20 would be =B8/B9
    Note: The ratio formulas can be found in Exhibit 17-7.

12. Format amounts in column B, rows 8 through 15 and column C, rows 8 through 11 as

Number tab:	Category:	Accounting
	Decimal:	0
	Symbol:	$

13. Format the amount in column B, row 16 as

Number tab:	Category:	Accounting
	Decimal:	2
	Symbol:	$

14. Format the amount in column B, row 25 as

Number tab:	Category:	Currency
	Decimal:	2
	Symbol:	$
	Negative numbers:	Black with parenthesis

15. Format amounts in columns B and C, row 20 and column B, row 26 as

Number tab:	Category:	Number
	Decimal:	2
	Negative numbers:	Black with parenthesis

16. Format amounts in column B, rows 21 through 24 and 27 through 28, and column C, row 21 as

Number tab:	Category:	Percentage
	Decimal:	2

17. Save your work to disk, and print a copy for your files.

Collaborative Learning Exercise

17-53 Financial Ratios

Form groups of four to six persons each. Each member of the group should pick a different company and find the most recent annual report for that company. (If you do not have printed annual reports, try searching the Internet for one.)

1. Each member should compute the following ratios for his or her company:
   a. Earnings per share
   b. Price-earnings ratio
   c. Dividend-yield ratio
   d. Dividend-payout ratio
2. As a group, list two possible reasons that each ratio differs across the selected companies. Focus on comparing the companies with the highest and lowest values for each ratio, and explain how the nature of the company might be the reason for the differences in ratios.

Internet Exercise www.prenhall.com/horngren

17-54 General Electric's Annual Report

Go to http://www.ge.com and follow the links to Investors and then to **General Electric's (GE)** most recent annual report.

Answer the following questions about GE:

1. Look at GE's income statement. Does GE consolidate parent and subsidiary accounts in the statement? Does GE hold less than 100% interest in any of its subsidiaries? How do you know?
2. Turn to GE's balance sheet. What does GE call this statement? GE omits some subtotals that most companies include on their balance sheets. What are these subtotals? How much "Minority interest in equity of consolidated affiliates" does GE show? What does this mean?
3. Does GE pay cash dividends? If so, what was the payout ratio in the most recent year?
4. Compute GE's return on stockholders' equity for the last two years. Is the change in a positive or negative direction?
5. What kinds of contributions to the community does GE emphasize in its annual report?

Recommended Readings

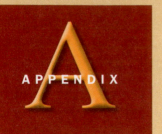

APPENDIX A

The following readings will aid readers who want to pursue some topics in more depth than is possible in this book. There is a hazard in compiling a group of recommended readings. Inevitably, some worthwhile books or periodicals are omitted. Moreover, such a list cannot include books published subsequent to the compilation date. The list is not comprehensive, but it suggests many excellent readings.

Periodicals

Professional Journals

The following professional journals are typically available in university libraries and include articles on the application of management accounting:

- **Accounting Horizons.** Published by the American Accounting Association; stresses current practice-oriented articles in all areas of accounting.
- **CMA Management.** Published by CMA Canada; includes much practice-oriented research in management accounting.
- **Cost Management.** Published by Thompson/RIA; stresses cost management tools.
- **Financial Executive.** Published by the Financial Executives International; emphasizes general policy issues for accounting and finance executives.
- **GAO Journal.** Covers managerial accounting issues of interest to the General Accounting Office of the U.S. government.
- **Harvard Business Review.** Published by Harvard Business School; directed to general managers, but contains excellent articles on applications of management accounting.
- **Journal of Accountancy.** Published by the American Institute of CPAs; emphasizes financial accounting and is directed at the practicing CPA.
- **Journal of Strategic Performance Measurement.** Covers issues related to performance measurement.
- **Management Accounting Quarterly.** Published by the Institute of Management Accountants; practical articles with an academic bent.
- **Strategic Finance.** Published by the Institute of Management Accountants; many articles on actual applications by individual organizations.
- **Business Week, Forbes, Fortune, The Economist, The Wall Street Journal.** Popular publications that cover a variety of business and economics topics; often their articles relate to management accounting.

Academic Journals

The academic journal that focuses most directly on current management and cost accounting research is the *Journal of Management Accounting Research*, published by the Management Accounting section of the American Accounting Association. *Accounting Horizons* is an American Accounting publication that bridges the gap between accounting research and practice. *The Accounting Review*, the general research publication of the American Accounting Association, and *Journal of Accounting Research*, published at the University of Chicago, and *Contemporary Accounting Research*, published by the Canadian Academic Association, cover all accounting topics at a more theoretical level. *Accounting, Organizations and Society*, a British journal, publishes much research on behavioral aspects of management accounting. *The Journal of Accounting and Economics* covers economics-based accounting research.

Books In Management Accounting

Most of the topics in this text are covered in more detail in the many books entitled *Cost Accounting* including *Cost Accounting: A Managerial Emphasis* by C. T. Horngren, G. Foster, and Srikant Datar (Prentice Hall, 2002). You can find more advanced coverage in *Advanced Management Accounting*, 3rd ed., by R. S. Kaplan and Anthony A. Atkinson (Prentice Hall, 1998).

The Financial Executives Institute, 200 Campus Drive, P.O. Box 674, Florham Park NJ 07960, and the Institute of Management Accounting, 10 Paragon Drive, P.O. Box 433, Montvale, NJ 07932–0674, have long lists of accounting research publications.

Handbooks, General Texts, and Case Books

The books in this list have wide application to management accounting issues. The handbooks are basic references. The textbooks are designed for classroom use but may be useful for self-study. The case books present applications from real companies.

- Bierman, H., Jr., C. Bonini, and W. Hausman, *Quantitative Analysis for Management*, 9th ed. Homewood, IL: Richard D. Irwin, 1997.
- Bierman, H., Jr., and S. Smidt, *The Capital Budgeting Decision*, 8th ed. New York: Macmillan, 1992. Expands the capital budgeting discussion in Chapter 11.
- Brinker, B. (ed.), *Guide to Cost Management*. New York: John Wiley & Sons, 2000.
- Davidson, S., and R. Weil, *Handbook of Cost Accounting*. Aspen Publishers, 1989.
- Lukka, K., and T. Groot (eds.), *Cases in Management Accounting: Practices in European Companies*. London: Financial Times Management, 2000.
- Manning, G., *Financial Investigation and Forensic Accounting*. Boca Raton, FL: CRC Press, 1999.
- Pryor, T., et al., *Activity Dictionary: A Comprehensive Reference Tool for ABM and ABC*: 2000 Edition. Arlington, TX: ICMS, Inc., 2000.
- Rotch, W., B. Allen, and R. Brownlee, *Cases in Management Accounting and Control Systems*, 3rd ed. Upper Saddle River, NJ: Prentice Hall, 1995.
- Shank, J., *Cases in Cost Management: A Strategic Emphasis*, 2nd ed. Cincinnati, OH: South-Western, 2000.

Strategic Nature of Management Accounting

Management accountants realize that cost and performance information is most useful to organizations when it helps define strategic alternatives and helps in the management of resources to achieve strategic objectives. The books in this list, though not necessarily accounting books, provide valuable foundation to the interaction of strategy and accounting information.

- Ansari, S., and J. Bell, *Target Costing: The Next Frontier in Strategic Cost Management*. Chicago: Irwin, 1997.
- Grant, J. L., Foundations of Economic Valued Added, 2nd ed. New York: Wiley, 2002.
- Hronec, S., *Vital Signs*. New York: Amacom, 1993.
- Porter, M., *The Michael Porter Trilogy*. New York: Free Press, 1998.
- Rappaport, A., *Creating Shareholder Value: A Guide for Manager's and Investors*. New York: Free Press, 1997.
- Small, P., *The Ultimate Game of Strategy: Establishing a Personal Niche in the World of e-Business*. Upper Saddle River, NJ: Prentice Hall, 2001.
- Stern, J., J. Shiely, and I. Ross, *The EVA Challenge: Implementing Value Added Change in an Organization*. New York: Wiley, 2001.
- Stewart, G., *The Quest for Value*. New York: Harper Business, 1999.

Modern Manufacturing

The following books provide background on the nature of modern manufacturing.

- Chase, R., N. Aquilano, and F. R. Jacobs, *Production and Operation Management: Manufacturing and Services*. Homewood, IL: Irwin, 1999.
- *Heizer, J. and B. Render, Principles of Operations Management and Student CD-ROM*. 5th ed. Upper Saddle River, NJ: Prentice Hall, 2003.
- Schonberger, R., *World Class Manufacturing: The Next Decade*. New York, Free Press, 1996.

Management Accounting in Modern Manufacturing Settings

These books present responses of management accountants and others to changes in manufacturing methods and practices.

- Atkinson, A., R. Banker, R. Kaplan, and S. Young, *Management Accounting*, 3rd ed. Upper Saddle River, NJ: Prentice Hall, 2000.
- Bennett, R., J. Hendricks, D. Keys, and E. Rudnicki, *Cost Accounting for Factory Automation*. Montvale, NJ: National Association of Accountants, 1987.
- Cooper, R. and R. Kaplan, *Design of Cost Management Systems*, 2nd ed. Upper Saddle River, NJ: Prentice Hall, 1999.
- Goldratt, E., and J. Cox, *The Goal*. Croton-On-Hudson, NY: North River Press, Inc., 1992. A novel illustrating the new manufacturing environment.
- Goldratt, E., *Theory of Constraints*. Croton-On-Hudson, NY: North River Press, Inc., 2000.
- Kaplan R. and R. Cooper, *Cost & Effect*. Boston: Harvard Business School Press, 1998.
- Kaplan, R. (ed.), *Measures for Manufacturing Excellence*. Boston, MA: Harvard Business School Press, 1990.

Management Control Systems

The topics of Chapters 7 to 10 can be explored further in several books, including:

- Anthony, R. N., and V. Govindarajan, *Management Control Systems*, 11th ed. Irwin/McGraw-Hill, 2003.
- Arrow, K.J., *The Limits of Organization*. New York: Norton, 1974. A readable classic by the Nobel laureate.
- Brimson, J. and J. Antos, *Driving Value Using Activity-Based Budgeting*. New York: Wiley, 1999.
- Emmanuel, C., K. Merchant, and D. Otley, *Accounting for Management Control*. Chapman & Hall, 1990.
- Gupta, P., *Six Sigma Business Scorecard: Creating a Comprehensive Corporate Performance Measurement System*. New York: McGraw-Hill, 2003.
- Kaplan, R., and D. Norton, *The Balanced Scorecard: Translating Strategy into Action*. Boston: Harvard Business School Press, 1996.
- Maciariello, J. A. and C. Kirby, *Management Control Systems: Using Adaptive Systems to Attain Control*. Upper Saddle River, NJ: Prentice Hall, 1994.
- Merchant, K., *Modern Management Control Systems: Text and Cases*. Upper Saddle River, NJ: Prentice Hall, 1998.
- Merchant K., and W. Van der Stede, *Management Control Systems*. Upper Saddle River, NJ: Prentice Hall, 2003.
- Simons, R., *Performance Measurement and Control Systems for Implementing Strategy*. Upper Saddle River, NJ: Prentice Hall, 2000.
- Solomons, D., *Divisional Performance: Measurement and Control*. New York: Markus Wiener, 1983. A reprint of a 1965 classic that is still relevant.

Management Accounting in Nonprofit Organizations

Many books discuss management accounting in nonprofit organizations, especially in health care. Four examples are

- Anthony, R.N., and D.W. Young, *Management Control in Nonprofit Organizations*, 7th ed. Homewood, IL: Irwin, 2003.
- Brimson, J., and J. Antos, *Activity Based Management for Service Industries, Government Entities, and Non-Profit Organizations*. New York: Wiley, 1998.
- Herzlinger, R., and D. Nitterhouse, *Financial Accounting and Managerial Control for Nonprofit Organizations*. Cincinnati, OH: South-Western Publishing Co., 1994.
- Neumann, B., and K. Boles, *Management Accounting for Healthcare Organizations*, 5th ed. Precept Press, 1998.

Books in Financial Accounting

This book's companion volume, *Introduction to Financial Accounting*, provides an expansion of the financial accounting material (Chapters 15–17). A more detailed coverage of the topics can be found in books entitled *Intermediate Accounting* including that by D. Kieso, J. Weygandt, and T. Warfield (John Wiley, 2003).

Opinions of the Accounting Principles Board are available from the American Institute of CPAs, 1211 Avenue of the Americas, New York, NY 10036–8775. The institute also has a series of research studies on a variety of topics. The pronouncements of the Financial Accounting Standards Board are available from the board's offices, 401 Merritt 7, P.O. Box 5116, Norwalk, CT 06856–5116.

Financial accounting has such an extensive body of literature that it is impossible to provide a short list of books that adequately covers the field. However, we will mention a few books that cover a wide range of issues. For a historical perspective on the large firms practicing accounting, see two books by M. Stevens, *The Accounting Wars* (Macmillan, 1985) and *The Big Six* (Touchstone Books, 1992). The interaction of financial reporting and management's economic incentives is covered in text and readings in R. Ball and C. Smith, *The Economics of Accounting Policy Choice* (McGraw-Hill, 1992). Application of this research to financial statement analysis is provided in C. Stickney, J. Wahlen, and P. Brown *Financial Reporting and Statement Analysis*, 4th ed. (South-Western, 2003) or G. White, A. Sondi and D. Fried, The *Analysis and Use of Financial Statements*, 3rd ed. (New York: Wiley, 2003).

Online Resources

The online resources are too extensive for a comprehensive list. The best way to access them may be to use a good search routine. However, we will list a few URLs that can help you get started:

- AICPA's Center for Excellence in Financial Management: Information for CPAs in business and industry at http://www.aicpa.org/cefm/index.htm.
- Better Management.com: Includes materials on both activity-based management and balanced scorecard at http://www.bettermanagement.com.
- CMA Canada: Many services including Strategic Management Accounting Practices and Management Accounting Standards at http://www.cma-canada.org/cmacan.
- Consortium for Advanced Manufacturing International (CAM-I): Online library at http://www.cam-i.org/Web_store/web_store.cgi?page=management.html.

- Economic Profit Frontiers: Additional information about economic value added at http://www.epfrontiers.com.
- Financial Executives International: Information for corporate financial officers at http://www.fei.org.
- Hyperion Solutions: Software for both activity-based management and the balanced scorecard at http://www.hyperion.com/.
- Institute of Management Accountants: A variety of services including index of research publications at http://www.imanet.org/.
- Metrus Group: A variation of the balance scorecard at http://www.metrus.com/spg.shtml.
- Stern Stewart: Information about economic value added by the firm that developed the technique at http://www.eva.com/.

Fundamentals of Compound Interest and the Use of Present-Value Tables

APPENDIX

B

Nature of Interest

Interest is the cost of using money. It is the rental charge for cash, just as rental charges are often made for the use of automobiles or boats.

Interest does not always entail an outlay of cash. The concept of interest applies to ownership funds as well as to borrowed funds. The reason why interest must be considered on *all* funds in use, regardless of their source, is that the selection of one alternative necessarily commits funds that could otherwise be invested in some other opportunity. The measure of the interest in such cases is the return foregone by rejecting the alternative use. For instance, a wholly owned home or business asset is not cost free. The funds so invested could alternatively be invested in government bonds or in some other venture. The measure of this opportunity cost depends on what alternative incomes are available.

Newspapers often contain advertisements of financial institutions citing interest rates that are "compounded." This appendix explains compound interest, including the use of present-value tables.

Simple interest is calculated by multiplying an interest rate by an unchanging principal amount. In contrast, *compound interest* is calculated by multiplying an interest rate by a principal amount that is increased each interest period by the previously accumulated (unpaid) interest. The accumulated interest is added to the principal to become the principal for the new period. For example, suppose you deposited $10,000 in a financial institution that promised to pay 10% interest per annum. You then let the amount accumulate for three years before withdrawing the full balance of the deposit. The *simple-interest* deposit would accumulate to $13,000 at the end of three years:

	Principal	Simple Interest	Balance, End of Year
Year 1	$10,000	$10,000 × 0.10 = $1,000	$11,000
Year 2	10,000	10,000 × 0.10 = 1,000	12,000
Year 3	10,000	10,000 × 0.10 = 1,000	13,000

Compound interest provides interest on interest. That is, the principal changes from period to period. The deposit would accumulate to $10,000 \times (1.10)^3 = \$10,000 \times 1.331 = \$13,310$:

	Principal	Compound Interest	Balance, End of Year
Year 1	$10,000	$10,000 × 0.10 = $1,000	$11,000
Year 2	11,000	11,000 × 0.10 = 1,100	12,100
Year 3	12,100	12,100 × 0.10 = 1,210	13,310

The "force" of compound interest can be staggering. For example, the same deposit would accumulate as follows:

	At End of		
	10 Years	20 Years	40 Years
Simple interest			
$10,000 + 10 ($1,000) =	$20,000		
$10,000 + 20 ($1,000) =		$30,000	
$10,000 + 40 ($1,000) =			$50,000
Compound interest			
$10,000 × (1.10)^{10} = $10,000 × 2.5937 =	$25,937		
$10,000 × (1.10)^{20} = $10,000 × 6.7275 =		$67,275	
$10,000 × (1.10)^{40} = $10,000 × 45.2593 =			$452,593

Hand calculations of compound interest quickly become burdensome. Therefore compound interest tables have been constructed to ease computations. (Indeed, many hand-held calculators contain programs that provide speedy answers.) Hundreds of tables are available, but we will use only the two most useful for capital budgeting.[1]

Table 1: Present Value of $1

How shall we express a future cash inflow or outflow in terms of its equivalent today (at time zero)? Table 1 provides factors that give the present value of a single, lump-sum cash flow to be received or paid at the end of a future period.[2]

Suppose you invest $1.00 today. It will grow to $1.06 in one year at six percent interest; that is, $1 \times 1.06 = $1.06. At the end of the second year its value is ($1 \times 1.06) \times 1.06 = $1 \times (1.06)^2 = 1.124, and at the end of the third year it is $1 \times (1.06)^3 = 1.191$. In general, $1.00 grows to $(1 + i)^n$ in n years at i percent interest.

To determine *the present value*, you reverse this accumulation process. If $1.00 is to be received in one year, it is worth $1 \div 1.06 = $0.9434 today at an interest rate of 6%. Suppose you invest $0.9434 today. In one year you will have $0.9434 \times 1.06 = $1.00. Thus $0.9434 is the *present value* of $1.00 a year hence at 6%. If the dollar will be received in two years, its present value is $1.00 \div (1.06)^2 = $0.8900. The general formula for the present value (*PV*) of an amount S to be received or paid in n periods at an interest rate of i% per period is

$$PV = \frac{S}{(1 + i)^n}$$

Table 1 on page 821 gives factors for the present value of $1.00 at various interest rates over several different periods. Present values are also called *discounted* values, and the process of finding the present value is *discounting*. You can think of this as discounting (decreasing) the value of a future cash inflow or outflow. Why is the value discounted? Because the cash is to be received or paid in the future, not today.

Assume that a prominent city is issuing a 3-year non-interest-bearing note payable that promises to pay a lump sum of $1,000 exactly three years from now. You desire a rate of return of exactly 6%, compounded annually. How much would you be willing to pay now for the 3-year note? The situation is sketched as follows:

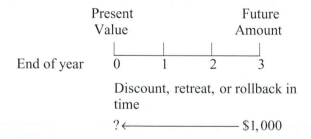

The factor in the period 3 row and 6% column of Table 1 is 0.8396. The present value of the $1,000 payment is $1,000 \times 0.8396 = $839.60. You would be willing to pay $839.60 for the $1,000 to be received in three years.

---

[1]*For additional tables, see R. Vichas,* Handbook of Financial Mathematics, Formulas and Tables *(Upper Saddle River, NJ: Prentice Hall, 1979).*

[2]*The factors are rounded to four decimal places. The examples in this text use these rounded factors. If you use tables with different rounding, or if you use a calculator or personal computer, your answers may differ from those given because of a small rounding error.*

Table 1
Present Value of $1

$$PV = \frac{1}{(1+i)^n}$$

Periods	3%	4%	5%	6%	7%	8%	10%	12%	14%	16%	18%	20%	22%	24%	25%	26%	28%	30%	40%
1	.9709	.9615	.9524	.9434	.9346	.9259	.9091	.8929	.8772	.8621	.8475	.8333	.8197	.8065	.8000	.7937	.7813	.7692	.7143
2	.9426	.9246	.9070	.8900	.8734	.8573	.8264	.7972	.7695	.7432	.7182	.6944	.6719	.6504	.6400	.6299	.6104	.5917	.5102
3	.9151	.8890	.8638	.8396	.8163	.7938	.7513	.7118	.6750	.6407	.6086	.5787	.5507	.5245	.5120	.4999	.4768	.4552	.3644
4	.8885	.8548	.8227	.7921	.7629	.7350	.6830	.6355	.5921	.5523	.5158	.4823	.4514	.4230	.4096	.3968	.3725	.3501	.2603
5	.8626	.8219	.7835	.7473	.7130	.6806	.6209	.5674	.5194	.4761	.4371	.4019	.3700	.3411	.3277	.3149	.2910	.2693	.1859
6	.8375	.7903	.7462	.7050	.6663	.6302	.5645	.5066	.4556	.4104	.3704	.3349	.3033	.2751	.2621	.2499	.2274	.2072	.1328
7	.8131	.7599	.7107	.6651	.6227	.5835	.5132	.4523	.3996	.3538	.3139	.2791	.2486	.2218	.2097	.1983	.1776	.1594	.0949
8	.7894	.7307	.6768	.6274	.5820	.5403	.4665	.4039	.3506	.3050	.2660	.2326	.2038	.1789	.1678	.1574	.1388	.1226	.0678
9	.7664	.7026	.6446	.5919	.5439	.5002	.4241	.3606	.3075	.2630	.2255	.1938	.1670	.1443	.1342	.1249	.1084	.0943	.0484
10	.7441	.6756	.6139	.5584	.5083	.4632	.3855	.3220	.2697	.2267	.1911	.1615	.1369	.1164	.1074	.0992	.0847	.0725	.0346
11	.7224	.6496	.5847	.5268	.4751	.4289	.3505	.2875	.2366	.1954	.1619	.1346	.1122	.0938	.0859	.0787	.0662	.0558	.0247
12	.7014	.6246	.5568	.4970	.4440	.3971	.3186	.2567	.2076	.1685	.1372	.1122	.0920	.0757	.0687	.0625	.0517	.0429	.0176
13	.6810	.6006	.5303	.4688	.4150	.3677	.2897	.2292	.1821	.1452	.1163	.0935	.0754	.0610	.0550	.0496	.0404	.0330	.0126
14	.6611	.5775	.5051	.4423	.3878	.3405	.2633	.2046	.1597	.1252	.0985	.0779	.0618	.0492	.0440	.0393	.0316	.0254	.0090
15	.6419	.5553	.4810	.4173	.3624	.3152	.2394	.1827	.1401	.1079	.0835	.0649	.0507	.0397	.0352	.0312	.0247	.0195	.0064
16	.6232	.5339	.4581	.3936	.3387	.2919	.2176	.1631	.1229	.0930	.0708	.0541	.0415	.0320	.0281	.0248	.0193	.0150	.0046
17	.6050	.5134	.4363	.3714	.3166	.2703	.1978	.1456	.1078	.0802	.0600	.0451	.0340	.0258	.0225	.0197	.0150	.0116	.0033
18	.5874	.4936	.4155	.3503	.2959	.2502	.1799	.1300	.0946	.0691	.0508	.0376	.0279	.0208	.0180	.0156	.0118	.0089	.0023
19	.5703	.4746	.3957	.3305	.2765	.2317	.1635	.1161	.0829	.0596	.0431	.0313	.0229	.0168	.0144	.0124	.0092	.0068	.0017
20	.5537	.4564	.3769	.3118	.2584	.2145	.1486	.1037	.0728	.0514	.0365	.0261	.0187	.0135	.0115	.0098	.0072	.0053	.0012
21	.5375	.4388	.3589	.2942	.2415	.1987	.1351	.0926	.0638	.0443	.0309	.0217	.0154	.0109	.0092	.0078	.0056	.0040	.0009
22	.5219	.4220	.3418	.2775	.2257	.1839	.1228	.0826	.0560	.0382	.0262	.0181	.0126	.0088	.0074	.0062	.0044	.0031	.0006
23	.5067	.4057	.3256	.2618	.2109	.1703	.1117	.0738	.0491	.0329	.0222	.0151	.0103	.0071	.0059	.0049	.0034	.0024	.0004
24	.4919	.3901	.3101	.2470	.1971	.1577	.1015	.0659	.0431	.0284	.0188	.0126	.0085	.0057	.0047	.0039	.0027	.0018	.0003
25	.4776	.3751	.2953	.2330	.1842	.1460	.0923	.0588	.0378	.0245	.0160	.0105	.0069	.0046	.0038	.0031	.0021	.0014	.0002
26	.4637	.3607	.2812	.2198	.1722	.1352	.0839	.0525	.0331	.0211	.0135	.0087	.0057	.0037	.0030	.0025	.0016	.0011	.0002
27	.4502	.3468	.2678	.2074	.1609	.1252	.0763	.0469	.0291	.0182	.0115	.0073	.0047	.0030	.0024	.0019	.0013	.0008	.0001
28	.4371	.3335	.2551	.1956	.1504	.1159	.0693	.0419	.0255	.0157	.0097	.0061	.0038	.0024	.0019	.0015	.0010	.0006	.0001
29	.4243	.3207	.2429	.1846	.1406	.1073	.0630	.0374	.0224	.0135	.0082	.0051	.0031	.0020	.0015	.0012	.0008	.0005	.0001
30	.4120	.3083	.2314	.1741	.1314	.0994	.0573	.0334	.0196	.0116	.0070	.0042	.0026	.0016	.0012	.0010	.0006	.0004	.0000
40	.3066	.2083	.1420	.0972	.0668	.0460	.0221	.0107	.0053	.0026	.0013	.0007	.0004	.0002	.0001	.0001	.0001	.0000	.0000

Suppose interest is compounded semiannually rather than annually. How much would you be willing to pay? The three years become six interest payment periods. The rate per period is half the annual rate, or 6% ÷ 2 = 3%. The factor in the period 6 row and 3% column of Table 1 is 0.8375. You would be willing to pay $1,000 × 0.8375 or only $837.50 rather than $839.60.

As a further check on your understanding, review the earlier example of compound interest. Suppose the financial institution promised to pay $13,310 at the end of three years. How much would you be willing to deposit at time zero if you desired a 10% rate of return compounded annually? Using Table 1, the period 3 row and the 10% column show a factor of 0.7513. Multiply this factor by the future amount:

$$PV = 0.7513 \times \$13,310 = \$10,000$$

A diagram of this computation follows:

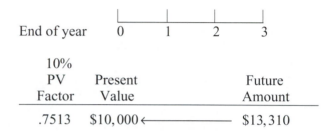

Pause for a moment. Use Table 1 to obtain the present values of

1. $1,700, at 20%, at the end of 20 years
2. $8,300, at 10%, at the end of 12 years
3. $8,000, at 4%, at the end of 4 years

Answers:

1. $1,700 (0.0261) = $44.37
2. $8,300 (0.3186) = $2,644.38
3. $8,000 (0.8548) = $6,838.40

Table 2: Present Value of an Ordinary Annuity of $1

An ordinary annuity is a series of equal cash flows to take place at the end of successive periods of equal length. Its present value is denoted PV_A. Assume that you buy a note from a municipality that promises to pay $1,000 at the end of *each* of three years. How much should you be willing to pay if you desire a rate of return of 6%, compounded annually?

You could solve this problem using Table 1. First, find the present value of each payment, and then add the present values as in Exhibit B-1. You would be willing to pay $943.40 for the first payment, $890.00 for the second, and $839.60 for the third, a total of $2,673.00.

Since each cash payment is $1,000 with equal one-year periods between them, the note is an ordinary annuity. Table 2 provides a shortcut method. The present value in Exhibit B-1 can be expressed as

$$PV_A = \$1,000 \times \frac{1}{1.06} + \$1,000 \times \frac{1}{(1.06)^2} + \$1,000 \times \frac{1}{(1.06)^3}$$

$$= \$1,000 \left[\frac{1}{1.06} + \frac{1}{(1.06)^2} + \frac{1}{(1.06)^3} \right]$$

Exhibit B-1

Payment	End of Year Table 1 Factor	0 Present Value	1	2	3
1	$\dfrac{1}{1.06} = .9434$	$ 943.40	$1,000		
2	$\dfrac{1}{(1.06)^2} = .8900$	890.00		1,000	
3	$\dfrac{1}{(1.06)^3} = .8396$	839.60			$1,000
Total		$2,673.00			

The three terms in brackets are the first three numbers from the 6% column of Table 1, and their sum is in the third row of the 6% column of Table 2: .9434 + .8900 + .8396 = 2.6730. Instead of calculating three present values and adding them, you can simply multiply the PV factor from Table 2 by the cash payment: 2.6730 × $1,000 = $2,673.

This shortcut is especially valuable if the cash payments or receipts extend over many periods. Consider an annual cash payment of $1,000 for 20 years at 6%. The present value, calculated from Table 2, is $1,000 × 11.4699 = $11,469.90. To use Table 1 for this calculation, you would perform 20 multiplications and then add the 20 products.

The factors in Table 2 can be calculated using the following general formula:

$$PV_A = \frac{1}{i}\left[1 - \frac{1}{(1+i)^n}\right]$$

Applied to our illustration:

$$PV_A = \frac{1}{.06}\left[1 - \frac{1}{(1.06)^3}\right] = \frac{1}{.06}(1 - .8396) = \frac{.1604}{.06} = 2.6730$$

Use Table 2 to obtain the present values of the following ordinary annuities:

1. $1,600 at 20% for 20 years
2. $8,300 at 10% for 12 years
3. $8,000 at 4% for 4 years

Answers:

1. $1,600 (4.8696) = $7,791.36
2. $8,300 (6.8137) = $56,553.71
3. $8,000 (3.6299) = $29,039.20

In particular, note that the higher the interest rate, the lower the present value.

Table 2
Present Value of Ordinary Annuity of $1

$$PV_A = \frac{1}{i}\left[1 - \frac{1}{(1+i)^n}\right]$$

Periods	3%	4%	5%	6%	7%	8%	10%	12%	14%	16%	18%	20%	22%	24%	25%	26%	28%	30%	40%
1	.9709	.9615	.9524	.9434	.9346	.9259	.9091	.8929	.8772	.8621	.8475	.8333	.8197	.8065	.8000	.7937	.7813	.7692	.7143
2	1.9135	1.8861	1.8594	1.8334	1.8080	1.7833	1.7355	1.6901	1.6467	1.6052	1.5656	1.5278	1.4915	1.4568	1.4400	1.4235	1.3916	1.3609	1.2245
3	2.8286	2.7751	2.7232	2.6730	2.6243	2.5771	2.4869	2.4018	2.3216	2.2459	2.1743	2.1065	2.0422	1.9813	1.9520	1.9234	1.8684	1.8161	1.5889
4	3.7171	3.6299	3.5460	3.4651	3.3872	3.3121	3.1699	3.0373	2.9137	2.7982	2.6901	2.5887	2.4936	2.4043	2.3616	2.3202	2.2410	2.1662	1.8492
5	4.5797	4.4518	4.3295	4.2124	4.1002	3.9927	3.7908	3.6048	3.4331	3.2743	3.1272	2.9906	2.8636	2.7454	2.6893	2.6351	2.5320	2.4356	2.0352
6	5.4172	5.2421	5.0757	4.9173	4.7665	4.6229	4.3553	4.1114	3.8887	3.6847	3.4976	3.3255	3.1669	3.0205	2.9514	2.8850	2.7594	2.6427	2.1680
7	6.2303	6.0021	5.7864	5.5824	5.3893	5.2064	4.8684	4.5638	4.2883	4.0386	3.8115	3.6046	3.4155	3.2423	3.1611	3.0833	2.9370	2.8021	2.2628
8	7.0197	6.7327	6.4632	6.2098	5.9713	5.7466	5.3349	4.9676	4.6389	4.3436	4.0776	3.8372	3.6193	3.4212	3.3289	3.2407	3.0758	2.9247	2.3306
9	7.7861	7.4353	7.1078	6.8017	6.5152	6.2469	5.7590	5.3282	4.9464	4.6065	4.3030	4.0310	3.7863	3.5655	3.4631	3.3657	3.1842	3.0190	2.3790
10	8.5302	8.1109	7.7217	7.3601	7.0236	6.7101	6.1446	5.6502	5.2161	4.8332	4.4941	4.1925	3.9232	3.6819	3.5705	3.4648	3.2689	3.0915	2.4136
11	9.2526	8.7605	8.3064	7.8869	7.4987	7.1390	6.4951	5.9377	5.4527	5.0286	4.6560	4.3271	4.0354	3.7757	3.6564	3.5435	3.3351	3.1473	2.4383
12	9.9540	9.3851	8.8633	8.3838	7.9427	7.5361	6.8137	6.1944	5.6603	5.1971	4.7932	4.4392	4.1274	3.8514	3.7251	3.6059	3.3868	3.1903	2.4559
13	10.6350	9.9856	9.3936	8.8527	8.3577	7.9038	7.1034	6.4235	5.8424	5.3423	4.9095	4.5327	4.2028	3.9124	3.7801	3.6555	3.4272	3.2233	2.4685
14	11.2961	10.5631	9.8986	9.2950	8.7455	8.2442	7.3667	6.6282	6.0021	5.4675	5.0081	4.6106	4.2646	3.9616	3.8241	3.6949	3.4587	3.2487	2.4775
15	11.9379	11.1184	10.3797	9.7122	9.1079	8.5595	7.6061	6.8109	6.1422	5.5755	5.0916	4.6755	4.3152	4.0013	3.8593	3.7261	3.4834	3.2682	2.4839
16	12.5611	11.6523	10.8378	10.1059	9.4466	8.8514	7.8237	6.9740	6.2651	5.6685	5.1624	4.7296	4.3567	4.0333	3.8874	3.7509	3.5026	3.2832	2.4885
17	13.1661	12.1657	11.2741	10.4773	9.7632	9.1216	8.0216	7.1196	6.3729	5.7487	5.2223	4.7746	4.3908	4.0591	3.9099	3.7705	3.5177	3.2948	2.4918
18	13.7535	12.6593	11.6896	10.8276	10.0591	9.3719	8.2014	7.2497	6.4674	5.8178	5.2732	4.8122	4.4187	4.0799	3.9279	3.7861	3.5294	3.3037	2.4941
19	14.3238	13.1339	12.0853	11.1581	10.3356	9.6036	8.3649	7.3658	6.5504	5.8775	5.3162	4.8435	4.4415	4.0967	3.9424	3.7985	3.5386	3.3105	2.4958
20	14.8775	13.5903	12.4622	11.4699	10.5940	9.8181	8.5136	7.4694	6.6231	5.9288	5.3527	4.8696	4.4603	4.1103	3.9539	3.8083	3.5458	3.3158	2.4970
21	15.4150	14.0292	12.8212	11.7641	10.8355	10.0168	8.6487	7.5620	6.6870	5.9731	5.3837	4.8913	4.4756	4.1212	3.9631	3.8161	3.5514	3.3198	2.4979
22	15.9369	14.4511	13.1630	12.0416	11.0612	10.2007	8.7715	7.6446	6.7429	6.0113	5.4099	4.9094	4.4882	4.1300	3.9705	3.8223	3.5558	3.3230	2.4985
23	16.4436	14.8568	13.4886	12.3034	11.2722	10.3711	8.8832	7.7184	6.7921	6.0442	5.4321	4.9245	4.4985	4.1371	3.9764	3.8273	3.5592	3.3254	2.4989
24	16.9355	15.2470	13.7986	12.5504	11.4693	10.5288	8.9847	7.7843	6.8351	6.0726	5.4509	4.9371	4.5070	4.1428	3.9811	3.8312	3.5619	3.3272	2.4992
25	17.4131	15.6221	14.0939	12.7834	11.6536	10.6748	9.0770	7.8431	6.8729	6.0971	5.4669	4.9476	4.5139	4.1474	3.9849	3.8342	3.5640	3.3286	2.4994
26	17.8768	15.9828	14.3752	13.0032	11.8258	10.8100	9.1609	7.8957	6.9061	6.1182	5.4804	4.9563	4.5196	4.1511	3.9879	3.8367	3.5656	3.3297	2.4996
27	18.3270	16.3296	14.6430	13.2105	11.9867	10.9352	9.2372	7.9426	6.9352	6.1364	5.4919	4.9636	4.5243	4.1542	3.9903	3.8387	3.5669	3.3305	2.4997
28	18.7641	16.6631	14.8981	13.4062	12.1371	11.0511	9.3066	7.9844	6.9607	6.1520	5.5016	4.9697	4.5281	4.1566	3.9923	3.8402	3.5679	3.3312	2.4998
29	19.1885	16.9837	15.1411	13.5907	12.2777	11.1584	9.3696	8.0218	6.9830	6.1656	5.5098	4.9747	4.5312	4.1585	3.9938	3.8414	3.5687	3.3317	2.4999
30	19.6004	17.2920	15.3725	13.7648	12.4090	11.2578	9.4269	8.0552	7.0027	6.1772	5.5168	4.9789	4.5338	4.1601	3.9950	3.8424	3.5693	3.3321	2.4999
40	23.1148	19.7928	17.1591	15.0463	13.3317	11.9246	9.7791	8.2438	7.1050	6.2335	5.5482	4.9966	4.5439	4.1659	3.9995	3.8458	3.5712	3.3332	2.5000

GLOSSARY

absorption approach   A costing approach that considers all indirect manufacturing costs (both variable and fixed) to be product (inventoriable) costs that become an expense in the form of manufacturing cost of goods sold only as sales occur.

accelerated depreciation   A pattern of depreciation that charges a larger proportion of an asset's cost to the earlier years and less to later years.

account   Each item in a financial statement.

account analysis   Selecting a plausible cost driver and classifying each account as a variable cost or as a fixed cost.

accounting rate-of-return (ARR) model   A non-DCF capital-budgeting model expressed as the increase in expected average annual operating income divided by the initial required investment.

accounting system   A formal mechanism for gathering, organizing, and communicating information about an organization's activities.

accounts payable   Amounts owed to vendors for purchases on open accounts.

accounts receivable   Amounts due from customers for sales on open account.

accrual basis   A process of accounting that recognizes the impact of transactions on the financial statements in the time periods when revenues and expenses occur instead of when the company pays or receives cash.

accrue   To accumulate a receivable or payable during a given period, even though no explicit transaction occurs.

accumulated depreciation   The sum of all depreciation charged to past periods.

activity analysis   The process of identifying appropriate cost drivers and their effects on the costs of making a product or providing a service.

activity-based budgets   Budgets that focus on the budgeted cost of activities required to produce and sell products and services.

activity-based costing (ABC) systems   A system that first accumulates overhead costs for each of the activities of the area being costed, and then assigns the costs of activities to the products, services, or other cost objects that require that activity.

activity-based flexible budget   A budget based on budgeted costs for each activity and related cost driver.

activity-based management (ABM)   Using an activity-based costing system to improve the operations of an organization.

activity-level variances   The differences between the master budget amounts and the amounts in the flexible budget.

adjustments   Entries that record implicit transactions, in contrast to the explicit transactions that trigger nearly all day-to-day routine entries.

agency theory   A theory that deals with contracting between an organization and the managers that it hires to make decisions on its behalf.

assets   Economic resources that a company owns and expects to benefit future activities.

attention directing   Reporting and interpreting information that helps managers to focus on operating problems, imperfections, inefficiencies, and opportunities.

audit   An "examination" or in-depth inspection of financial statements and companies' records made in accordance with auditing standards.

available-for-sale securities   Investments that the investor company has no intention of selling in the near future.

avoidable costs   Costs that will not continue if an ongoing operation is changed or deleted.

B2B   Electronic commerce from one business to another business.

B2C   Electronic commerce from business to consumer.

backflush costing   An accounting system that applies costs to products only when the production is complete.

balance sheet (statement of financial position)   A snapshot of the financial status of an organization at an instant of time.

balanced scorecard   A performance measurement and reporting system that strikes a balance between financial and operating measures, links performance to rewards, and gives explicit recognition to the diversity of organizational goals.

behavioral implications   The accounting system's effect on the behavior, specifically the decisions, of managers.

benchmark comparisons   Comparison of a company's financial ratios with general rules of thumb or best-practices ratios.

benchmarking   The continuous process of comparing products, services, and activities against the best industry standards.

book value (net book value)   The original cost of equipment less accumulated depreciation.

break-even point   The level of sales at which revenue equals expenses and net income is zero.

budget   A quantitative expression of a plan of action and an aid to coordinating and implementing the plan.

budgeted factory-overhead rate   The budgeted total overhead for each cost pool divided by the budgeted cost-driver level.

business process reengineering   The fundamental rethinking and radical redesign of business processes to improve performance in areas such as cost, quality, service, and speed.

by-product   A product that, like a joint product, is not individually identifiable until manufacturing reaches a split-off point, but has relatively insignificant total sales value.

capacity costs   The fixed costs of being able to achieve a desired level of production or to provide a desired level of service while maintaining product or service attributes, such as quality.

capital budget   A budget that details the planned expenditures for facilities, equipment, new products, and other long-term investments.

capital budgeting The long-term planning for making and financing investments that affect financial results over a period longer than just the next year.

capital charge Company's cost of capital × amount of investment.

capital turnover Revenue divided by invested capital.

cash basis A process of accounting where revenue and expense recognition would occur when the company receives and disburses cash.

cash budget A statement of planned cash receipts and disbursements.

cash equivalents Short-term investments that a company can easily convert into cash with little delay.

cash flows from financing activities The section in the statement of cash flows that lists the cash-flow effects of obtaining cash from creditors and owners, repaying creditors or buying back stock from owners, and paying cash dividends.

cash flows from investing activities The section in the statement of cash flows that lists the cash-flow effects of (1) lending and collecting on loans and (2) acquiring and selling long-term assets.

cash flows from operating activities The section in the statement of cash flows that lists the cash-flow effects of transactions that affect the income statement.

certified management accountant (CMA) The management accountant's counterpart to the CPA.

certified public accountant (CPA) In the United States, independent accountants who reassure the public about the reliability of companies' published financial statements.

chartered accountant (CA) The equivalent to the CPA in many countries.

chief financial officer (CFO) The top executive who deals with all finance and accounting issues in an organization. The CFO generally oversees the accounting function.

code of conduct A document specifying the ethical standards of an organization.

coefficient of determination (R2) A measurement of how much of the fluctuation of a cost is explained by changes in the cost driver.

committed fixed costs Costs arising from the possession of facilities, equipment, and a basic organization.

common costs Those costs of facilities and services that are shared by users.

common stock Stock that has no predetermined rate of dividends and is the last to obtain a share in the assets when the corporation liquidates. It usually confers voting power to elect the board of directors of the corporation.

common-size statements Financial statements expressed in component percentages.

component percentages Analysis and presentation of financial statements in percentage form to aid comparability, frequently used when companies differ in size.

computer-integrated manufacturing (CIM) systems Systems that use computer-aided design, computer-aided manufacturing, robots, and computer-controlled machines.

conservatism convention Selecting the method of measurement that yields the gloomiest immediate results.

consolidated financial statements Financial statements that combine the financial statements of the parent company with those of various subsidiaries, as if they were a single entity.

constant dollars Nominal dollars that are restated in terms of current purchasing power.

continuity convention (going concern convention) The assumption that an organization will continue to exist and operate.

continuous budget (rolling budget) A common form of master budget that adds a month in the future as the month just ended is dropped.

contribution approach A method of internal (management accounting) reporting that emphasizes the distinction between variable and fixed costs for the purpose of better decision making.

contribution margin A term used for either unit contribution margin or total contribution margin.

contribution-margin percentage Total contribution margin divided by sales or 100% minus the variable cost percentage.

contribution-margin ratio Contribution margin percentage expressed as a ratio.

controllable cost Any cost that a manager's decisions and actions can influence.

controller (comptroller) The top accounting officer of an organization who deals mainly with operating matters such as aiding management decision making.

controlling Implementing plans and using feedback to attain objectives.

corporation A business organized as a separate legal entity and owned by its stockholders.

cost A sacrifice or giving up of resources for a particular purpose, frequently measured by the monetary units that an organization must pay for goods and services.

cost accounting That part of the cost management system that measures costs for the purposes of management decision making and financial reporting.

cost accounting system The techniques used to determine the cost of a product, service, customer, or other cost objective.

cost accumulation Collecting costs by some natural classification such as activities performed, labor, or materials.

cost allocation Assigning indirect costs to cost objects using plausible and reliable cost drivers.

cost application The allocation of total departmental costs to the revenue-producing products or services.

cost assignment Tracing or allocating costs to one or more cost objectives such as activities, departments, customers, or products.

cost behavior How the activities of an organization affect its costs.

cost center A responsibility center in which managers are responsible for costs only.

cost driver Any output measure that causes costs (that is, causes the use of costly resources).

cost function An algebraic equation used by managers to describe the relationship between a cost and its cost driver(s).

cost management system (CMS) A collection of tools and techniques that identify how management's decisions affect costs, by first measuring the resources used in performing the organization's activities and then assessing the effects on costs of changes in those activities.

cost measurement   Estimating or predicting costs as a function of appropriate cost drivers.

cost objective (cost object)   Anything for which decision makers desire a separate measurement of costs. Examples include departments, products, activities, and territories.

cost of capital   What a firm must pay to acquire more capital, whether or not it actually has to acquire more capital.

cost of goods sold   The cost of the merchandise that a company acquires or produces and then sells.

cost of quality report   A report that displays the financial impact of quality.

cost pool   A group of individual costs that a company allocates to cost objectives using a single cost driver.

cost recovery   A concept in which companies carry forward as assets such items as inventories, prepayments, and equipment because they expect to recover the costs of these assets in the form of cash inflows (or reduced cash outflows) in future periods.

cost-allocation base   A cost driver that is used for allocating costs.

cost-benefit balance   Weighing estimated costs against probable benefits, the primary consideration in choosing among accounting systems and methods.

cost-benefit criterion   An approach that implicitly underlies the decisions about the design of accounting systems. As companies change their accounting systems, the potential benefits should exceed the additional costs.

cost-volume-profit (CVP) analysis   The study of the effects of output volume on revenue (sales), expenses (costs), and net income (net profit).

credit   An entry on the right side of an account.

cross-sectional comparisons   Comparisons of a company's financial ratios with ratios of similar companies or with industry averages for the same period.

current assets   Cash and all other assets that a company reasonably expects to convert to cash or sell or consume within one year or during the normal operating cycle, if longer than a year.

current cost   The cost to replace an asset, as opposed to its historical cost.

current liabilities   An organization's debts that fall due within the coming year or within the normal operating cycle if longer than a year.

current-cost method   The measurement method that uses current costs and nominal dollars.

currently attainable standards   Levels of performance that managers can achieve by realistic levels of effort.

cycle time (throughput time)   The time taken to complete a product or service, or any of the components of a product or service.

debentures   Formal certificates of indebtedness that are accompanied by a promise to pay interest at a specified annual rate.

debit   An entry on the left side of an account.

decentralization   The delegation of freedom to make decisions. The lower in the organization that this freedom exists, the greater the decentralization.

decision making   The purposeful choice from among a set of alternative courses of action designed to achieve some objective.

decision model   Any method for making a choice, sometimes requiring elaborate quantitative procedures.

depreciation   The periodic cost of equipment that a company spread over the future periods in which the company will use the equipment.

differential approach   A method for comparing alternatives that computes the differences in cash flows between alternatives and then converts these differences in cash flows to their present values.

differential cost (revenue)   The difference in total cost or revenue between two alternatives.

direct costs   Costs that can be identified specifically and exclusively with a given cost objective in an economically feasible way.

direct method   1. A method for allocating service department costs that ignores other service departments when any given service department's costs are allocated to the operating departments. 2. A method for computing cash flows from operating activities that subtracts operating cash disbursements from cash collections to arrive at cash flows from operations.

direct-labor costs   The wages of all labor that a company can trace specifically and exclusively to the manufactured goods in an economically feasible way.

direct-material costs   The acquisition costs of all materials that a company identifies as a part of the manufactured goods and traces to the manufactured goods in an economically feasible way.

discounted-cash-flow (DCF) models   A type of capital-budgeting model that focuses on cash inflows and outflows while taking into account the time value of money.

discretionary fixed costs   Costs determined by management as part of the periodic planning process in order to meet the organization's goals. They have no obvious relationship with levels of capacity or output activity.

discriminatory pricing   Charging different prices to different customers for the same product or service.

dividends   Distributions of assets to stockholders that reduce retained earnings.

double-entry system   A method of record keeping in which each transaction affects at least two accounts.

dysfunctional decision   Any decision that is in conflict with organizational goals.

earnings per share   Net income divided by the average number of common shares outstanding during the year.

economic value added (EVA)   Equals adjusted after-tax operating income minus the cost of invested capital multiplied by the adjusted average invested capital.

effectiveness   The degree to which a goal, objective, or target is met.

efficiency   The degree to which an organization uses appropriate amounts of inputs to achieve a given level of outputs.

efficient capital market   A market in which market prices fully reflect all information available to the public.

electronic commerce (e-commerce)   Conducting business online.

engineering analysis   The systematic review of materials, supplies, labor, support services, and facilities needed for products and services; measuring cost behavior according to what costs should be, not by what costs have been.

enterprise resource planning (ERP) systems   Integrated information systems that support all functional areas of a company.

equity method   Accounts for the investment at the acquisition cost adjusted for dividends received and the investor's share of earnings or losses of the investee after the date of investment.

equivalent units   The number of completed units that could have been produced from the inputs applied.

ethics   Doing what is right.

expected cost   The cost most likely to be attained.

expenses   Decreases in ownership claims arising from delivering goods or services or using up assets.

explicit transactions   Transactions such as credit sales, credit purchases, cash received on account, and cash disbursed on account, that are supported by source documents.

favorable cost variance   A variance that occurs when actual costs are less than budgeted costs.

financial accounting   The branch of accounting that develops information for external decision makers such as stockholders, suppliers, banks, and government regulatory agencies.

Financial Accounting Standards Board (FASB)   The body that sets generally accepted accounting principles in the United States.

financial budget   The part of a master budget that focuses on the effects that the operating budget and other plans (such as capital budgets and repayments of debt) will have on cash.

financial capital maintenance   The concept that income emerges after investors recover their financial resources.

financial planning models   Mathematical models of the master budget that can react to any set of assumptions about sales, costs, or product mix.

first-in, first-out (FIFO)   An inventory method that assumes that a company sells or uses up first the stock acquired earliest.

fixed assets (tangible assets)   Physical items that a person can see and touch, such as property, plant, and equipment.

fixed cost   A cost that is not immediately affected by changes in the cost-driver level.

fixed-overhead rate   The amount of fixed manufacturing overhead applied to each unit of production. It is determined by dividing the budgeting fixed overhead by the expected volume of production for the budget period.

flexible budget (variable budget)   A budget that adjusts for changes in sales volume and other cost-driver activities.

flexible-budget variances   The variances between the flexible budget and the actual results.

foreign Corrupt Practices Act   A U.S. law forbidding bribery and other corrupt practices. The law also requires all public companies to maintain their accounting records in reasonable detail and accuracy and have an appropriate system of internal controls.

free cash flow   Cash flows from operations less capital expenditures.

full cost (fully allocated cost)   The total of all manufacturing costs plus the total of all selling and administrative costs.

functional budgeting   Budgeting process that focuses on preparing budgets for various functions such as production, selling, and administrative support.

general ledger   A collection of the group of accounts that supports the items shown in the major financial statements.

general price index   A comparison of the average price of a group of goods and services at one date with the average price of a similar group at another date.

generally accepted accounting principles (GAAP)   1. A set of standards to which public companies' published financial statements must adhere. 2. The conventions, rules, and procedures that together make up accepted accounting practice at any given time.

goal congruence   A condition where employees, working in their own personal interests, make decisions that help meet the overall goals of the organization.

goodwill   The excess of the cost of an acquired company over the sum of the fair market values of its identifiable individual assets less its liabilities.

gross book value   The original cost of an asset before deducting accumulated depreciation.

gross margin   The excess of sales over the total cost of goods sold.

gross profit   The excess of sales over the total cost of goods sold.

high-low method   A simple method for measuring a linear-cost function from past cost data, focusing on the highest-activity and lowest-activity points and fitting a line through these two points.

historical cost   The amount originally paid to acquire an asset.

holding gains (or losses)   Increases (or decreases) in the replacement costs of the assets held during the current period.

hybrid costing systems   An accounting system that is a blend of ideas from both job costing and process costing.

imperfect competition   A market in which the price a firm charges for a unit will influence the quantity of units it sells.

implicit transactions   Events (such as the passage of time) that day-to-day recording procedures temporarily ignore. Examples of implicit transactions are unpaid wages, prepaid rent, interest owed, and the like.

incentives   Those informal and formal performance-based rewards that enhance managerial effort toward organizational goals.

income statement   A statement that summarizes a company's revenues and expenses. It measures the performance of an organization by matching its accomplishments (revenue from customers, which is usually called sales) and its efforts (cost of goods sold and other expenses).

income (profits, earnings)   The excess of revenues over expenses.

incremental cost   Another term for differential cost when one alternative includes all the costs of the other plus some additional costs.

incremental effect   The change in total results (such as revenue, expenses, or income) under a new condition in comparison with some given or known condition.

indirect costs   Costs that cannot be identified specifically and exclusively with a given cost objective in an economically feasible way.

indirect method   A method for computing cash flows from operating activities that adjusts the previously calculated accrual net income from the income statement to reflect only cash receipts and cash disbursements.

indirect production costs (indirect manufacturing costs, factory burden, factory overhead, manufacturing overhead) All costs other than direct material or direct labor that are associated with the manufacturing process.

inflation The decline in the general purchasing power of the monetary unit.

Institute of Management Accountants (IMA) The largest U.S. professional organization of accountants focused on internal accounting. It oversees the CMA program.

intangible assets Long-lived assets that are not physical in nature. Examples are goodwill, franchises, patents, trademarks, and copyrights.

internal controls Policies to protect and make the most efficient use of an organization's assets.

internal rate of return (IRR) model A capital-budgeting model that determines the interest rate at which the NPV equals zero.

International Accounting Standards Board (IASB) The group that establishes international GAAP.

inventory turnover The number of times the average inventory is sold per year.

investment center A responsibility center whose success depends on both income and invested capital, perhaps measured by a ratio of income to the value of the capital employed.

job-cost record (job-cost sheet, job order) A document that shows all costs for a particular product, service, or batch of products.

job-order costing (job costing) The method of allocating costs to products that are readily identified by individual units or batches, each of which requires varying degrees of attention and skill.

joint costs The costs of manufacturing joint products prior to the split-off point.

joint products Two or more manufactured products that (1) have relatively significant sales values and (2) are not separately identifiable as individual products until their split-off point.

just-in-time (JIT) philosophy A philosophy to eliminate waste by reducing the time products spend in the production process and eliminating the time products spend on activities that do not add value.

kaizen costing The Japanese term for continuous improvement during manufacturing.

key performance indicators Measures that drive the organization to achieve its goals.

key success factor Characteristics or attributes that managers must achieve in order to drive the organization toward its goals.

labor time tickets (time cards) The record of the time a particular direct laborer spends on each job.

last-in, first-out (LIFO) An inventory method that assumes that a company sells or uses up first the stock acquired most recently.

least-squares regression (regression analysis) Measuring a cost function objectively by using statistics to fit a cost function to all the data.

ledger accounts A method of keeping track of how multitudes of transactions affect each particular asset, liability, revenue, and expense.

liabilities The entity's economic obligations to nonowners.

LIFO layers (LIFO increments) Separately identifiable additions to a LIFO inventory.

limited liability A provision that a company's creditors cannot seek payment from stockholders as individuals if the corporation itself cannot pay its debts.

limiting factor (scarce resource) The item that restricts or constrains the production or sale of a product or service.

line managers Managers who are directly involved with making and selling the organization's products or services.

linear-cost behavior Activity that can be graphed with a straight line because costs are assumed to be either fixed or variable.

liquidation Converting assets to cash and using the cash to pay off outside claims.

long-range planning Producing forecasted financial statements for five- to ten-year periods.

lower-of-cost-or-market (LCM) An inventory method in which accountants compare the current market price of inventory with its cost (derived by specific identification, FIFO, LIFO, or weighted average) and select the lower of the two as the inventory value.

management accounting The branch of accounting that produces information for managers within an organization. It is the process of identifying, measuring, accumulating, analyzing, preparing, interpreting, and communicating information that helps managers fulfill organizational objectives.

management audit A review to determine whether managers are implementing the policies and procedures specified by top management.

management by exception Concentrating on areas that deviate from the plan and ignoring areas that are presumed to be running smoothly.

management by objectives (MBO) The joint formulation by a manager and his or her superior of a set of goals and plans for achieving the goals for a forthcoming period.

management control system A logical integration of techniques for gathering and using information to make planning and control decisions, for motivating employee behavior, and for evaluating performance.

managerial effort Exertion toward a goal or objective including all conscious actions (such as supervising, planning, and thinking) that result in more efficiency and effectiveness.

margin of safety The planned unit sales less the break-even unit sales; it shows how far sales can fall below the planned level before losses occur.

marginal cost The additional cost resulting from producing and selling one additional unit.

marginal income tax rate The tax rate paid on additional amounts of pretax income.

marginal revenue The additional revenue resulting from the sale of an additional unit.

market method The method of accounting for investments in equity securities that shows the investment on the balance sheet at market value.

markup The amount by which price exceeds cost.

master budget An extensive analysis of the first year of the long-range plan. It summarizes the planned activities of all sub-units of an organization.

master budget variance (static budget variance) The variance of actual results from the master (static) budget.

matching The linking of revenues (as measured by the selling prices of goods and services delivered) with the expenses (as measured by the cost of goods and services used) incurred to generate them.

materiality The accounting convention that justifies the omission of insignificant information when its omission or misstatement would not mislead a user of the financial statements.

materials requisitions Records of materials used in particular jobs.

measurement of cost behavior Understanding and quantifying how activities of an organization affect its levels of costs.

minority interests An account that shows the outside stockholders' interest, as opposed to the parent's interest, in a subsidiary corporation.

mixed costs Costs that contain elements of both fixed- and variable-cost behavior.

modified accelerated cost recovery system (MACRS) The method companies use to depreciate most assets under U.S. income tax laws.

motivation The drive for some selected goal that creates effort and action toward that goal.

multistage ABC (MSABC) systems Costing systems with more than two stages of allocations and cost drivers other than percentages.

net book value The original cost of an asset less any accumulated depreciation.

net income The "bottom line"—the residual amount after we deduct from revenues all expenses, including income taxes.

net worth A synonym for owner's equity.

net-present-value (NPV) method A discounted-cash-flow approach to capital budgeting that computes the present value of all expected future cash flows using a minimum desired rate of return.

nominal dollars Dollar measurements that are not restated for inflation.

nominal rate Quoted market interest rate that includes an inflation element.

noncurrent liabilities (long-term liabilities) An organization's debts that fall due beyond one year.

non-value-added costs Costs that a company can eliminate without affecting a product's value to the customer.

normal costing system The cost system in which the cost of the manufactured product is composed of actual direct material, actual direct labor, and normal applied overhead.

objectivity (verifiability) Accuracy supported by a high extent of consensus among independent measures of an item.

operating budget (profit plan) A major part of a master budget that focuses on the income statement and its supporting schedules.

operating cycle The time span during which a company spends cash to acquire goods and services that it uses to produce the organization's output, which it in turn sells to customers, who in turn pay for their purchases with cash.

operating leverage A firm's ratio of fixed to variable costs.

opportunity cost The maximum available contribution to profit forgone (or passed up) by using limited resources for a particular purpose.

outlay cost A cost that requires a future cash disbursement.

overapplied overhead The excess of overhead applied to products over actual overhead incurred.

owners' equity The excess of the assets over the liabilities.

paid-in capital The ownership claim arising from funds paid in by the owners.

par value (legal value, stated value) The value often printed on the face of stock certificates.

parent company A company owning more than 50% of another business's stock.

participative budgeting Budgets formulated with the active participation of all affected employees.

partnership An organization that joins two or more individuals together as co-owners.

payback time (payback period) The time it will take to recoup, in the form of cash inflows from operations, the initial dollars invested in a project.

perfect competition A market in which a firm can sell as much of a product as it can produce, all at a single market price.

perfection standards (ideal standards) Expressions of the most efficient performance possible under the best conceivable conditions, using existing specifications and equipment.

performance reports Feedback provided by comparing results with plans and by highlighting variances.

period costs Costs that are deducted as expenses during the current period without going through an inventory stage.

physical capital maintenance The concept that income emerges only after setting aside an amount that allows physical operating capability to be maintained.

planning Setting objectives for an organization and outlining how it will attain them.

postaudit A follow-up evaluation of capital-budgeting decisions.

predatory pricing Establishing prices so low that they drive competitors out of the market. The predatory pricer then has no significant competition and can raise prices dramatically.

preferred stock Stock that typically has some priority over other shares in the payment of dividends or the distribution of assets upon liquidation.

price elasticity The effect of price changes on sales volume.

price variance The difference between actual input prices and standard input prices multiplied by the actual quantity of inputs used.

problem-solving The aspect of accounting that often involves a special study to assess possible courses of action and recommends the best course to follow.

process costing The method of allocating costs to products by averaging costs over large numbers of nearly identical products.

process map A schematic diagram capturing interrelationships between cost objects, activities, and resources.

product costs   Costs identified with goods produced or purchased for resale.

product life cycle   The various stages through which a product passes, from conception and development to introduction into the market to maturation and, finally, withdrawal from the market.

production-volume variance   A variance that appears whenever actual production deviates from the expected volume of production used in computing the fixed overhead rate. It is calculated as (actual volume − expected volume) × fixed-overhead rate.

productivity   A measure of outputs divided by inputs.

profit center   A responsibility center in which managers are responsible for revenues as well as costs (or expenses)-that is, profitability.

prorate   To assign underapplied overhead or overapplied overhead in proportion to the sizes of the ending account balances.

quality control   The effort to ensure that products and services perform to customer requirements.

quality-control chart   The statistical plot of measures of various product dimensions or attributes.

real options model   A capital-budgeting model that recognizes the value of contingent investments-that is, investments that a company can adjust as it learns more about their potential for success.

recognition   The principle that states that a company records revenue in its accounts only when it has earned and realized the revenue.

recovery period   The number of years over which a company can depreciate an asset for tax purposes.

relevant information   The predicted future costs and revenues that will differ among alternative courses of action.

relevant range   The limit of cost-driver activity level within which a specific relationship between costs and the cost driver is valid.

required rate of return (hurdle rate, discount rate)   The minimum desired rate of return, based on the firm's cost of capital.

residual income (RI)   After-tax operating income less a capital charge.

residual value   The predicted sales value of a long-lived asset at the end of its useful life.

responsibility accounting   Identifying what parts of the organization have primary responsibility for each action, developing performance measures and targets, and designing reports of these measures by responsibility center.

responsibility center   A set of activities and resources assigned to a manager, a group of managers, or other employees.

retained earnings (retained income)   The ownership claim arising from the reinvestment of previous profits.

return on investment (ROI)   A measure of income or profit divided by the investment required to obtain that income or profit.

return on sales   Income divided by revenue.

revaluation equity   A portion of stockholders' equity that shows all accumulated holding gains.

revenue   Increases in ownership claims arising from the delivery of goods or services.

sales budget   The result of decisions to create conditions that will generate a desired level of sales.

sales forecast   A prediction of sales under a given set of conditions.

sales mix   The relative proportions or combinations of quantities of products that constitute total sales.

sales-activity variances   Variances that measure how effective managers have been in meeting the planned sales objective, calculated as actual unit sales less master budget unit sales times the budgeted unit contribution margin.

Sarbanes-Oxley Act   A 2002 law that requires more top-management oversight of a company's accounting policies and procedures.

scorekeeping   The accumulation and classification of data.

Securities and Exchange Commission (SEC)   By federal law, the agency with the ultimate responsibility for specifying the generally accepted accounting principles for U.S. companies whose stock is publicly traded.

segment autonomy   The delegation of decision-making power to managers of segments of an organization.

segments   Responsibility centers for which a company develops separate measures of revenues and costs.

sensitivity analysis   In budgeting, the systematic varying of budget data input to determine the effects of each change on the budget.

separable costs   Any cost beyond the split-off point.

service departments   Units that exist only to support other departments.

Six Sigma   1. A continuous process improvement effort designed to reduce costs by improving quality. 2. An analytical method aimed at achieving near-perfect results on a production line.

sole proprietorship   A business entity with a single owner.

source documents   Explicit evidence of transactions, such as sales slips, purchase invoices, and employee time records.

specific identification   An inventory method that recognizes the actual cost paid for the specific physical item sold.

specific price index   An index used to approximate the current costs of particular assets or types of assets.

split-off point   The juncture of manufacturing where the joint products become individually identifiable.

staff managers   Managers who are advisory to the line managers. They have no authority over line managers, but they help the line managers by providing information and advice.

standard cost   A carefully determined cost per unit that should be attained.

Standards of Ethical Conduct for Practitioners of Management Accounting and Financial Management   Codes of conduct developed by the Institute of Management Accountants; these codes include competence, confidentiality, integrity, and objectivity.

statement of cash flows   A statement that reports the cash receipts and cash payments of an organization during a particular period.

statement of retained earnings (statement of retained income)   A financial statement that explains changes in the retained earnings or retained income account for a given period.

static budget   A budget that is based on only one level of activity.

step costs   Costs that change abruptly at intervals of activity because the resources and their costs come in indivisible chunks.

step-down method   A method for allocating service department costs that recognizes that some service departments support the activities in other service departments as well as those in operating departments.

stockholders' equity   The owners' equity of a corporation.

strategic plan   A plan that sets the overall goals and objectives of the organization.

subordinated   A creditor claim that is junior to the other creditors in exercising claims against assets.

subsidiary   A company owned by a parent company that owns more than 50% of its stock.

sunk cost   A historical or past cost, that is, a cost that the company has already incurred and, therefore, is irrelevant to the decision-making process.

target costing   A cost management tool for making cost reduction a key focus throughout the life of a product.

time-series comparisons   Comparison of a company's financial ratios with its own historical ratios.

total contribution margin   Total number of units sold times the unit contribution margin.

total project approach   A method for comparing alternatives that computes the total impact on cash flows for each alternative and then converts these total cash flows to their present values.

total quality management (TQM)   1. An approach to quality that focuses on prevention of defects and on customer satisfaction. 2. Initiatives that minimize costs by maximizing quality.

trading securities   Investments that the investor company intends to sell in the near future.

traditional costing systems   One that does not accumulate or report costs of activities or processes.

transaction   Any event that affects the financial position of an organization and requires recording.

transfer price   The price that one segment of an organization charges another segment of the same organization for a product or service.

transferred-in costs   In process costing, costs incurred in a previous department for items that have been received by a subsequent department.

treasurer   A manager who is concerned mainly with the company's financial matters such as raising and managing cash.

treasury stock   A corporation's own stock that it has issued and subsequently repurchased to hold for a specific purpose.

two-stage ABC system   A costing system with two stages of allocation to get from the original cost to the final product or service cost. The first stage allocates resource costs to activity-cost pools. The second stage allocates activity costs to products or services.

unallocated costs   Costs for which we can identify no relationship to a cost objective.

unavoidable costs   Costs that continue even if a company discontinues an operation.

uncontrollable cost   Any cost that the management of a responsibility center cannot affect within a given time span.

underapplied overhead   The excess of actual overhead over the overhead applied to products.

unearned revenue (deferred revenue)   Collections from customers that companies receive and record before they earn the revenue.

unexpired cost   Any asset that ordinarily becomes an expense in future periods, for example, inventory and prepaid rent.

unfavorable cost variance   A variance that occurs when actual costs are more than budgeted costs.

unit contribution margin (marginal income)   The sales price minus the variable cost per unit.

usage variance (quantity variance, efficiency variance)   The difference between the quantity of inputs actually used and the quantity of inputs that the company should have used to achieve the actual quantity of output multiplied by the standard price of the input.

value chain   The set of business functions or activities that add value to the products or services of an organization.

value engineering   A cost-reduction technique, used primarily during design, that uses information about all value chain functions to satisfy customer needs while reducing costs.

value-added cost   The necessary cost of an activity that cannot be eliminated without affecting a product's value to the customer.

variable cost   A cost that changes in direct proportion to changes in the cost-driver level.

variable-cost percentage   Total variable costs divided by total sales.

variable-cost ratio   Variable cost percentage expressed as a ratio.

variable-overhead efficiency variance   An overhead variance caused by actual cost-driver activity differing from the standard amount allowed for the actual output achieved.

variable-overhead spending variance   The difference between the actual variable overhead and the amount of variable overhead budgeted for the actual level of cost-driver activity.

variances   Deviations from plans.

visual-fit method   A method in which the cost analyst visually fits a straight line through a plot of all the available data.

volume variance   A common name for production-volume variance.

weighted-average (WA) process-costing method   A process-costing method that adds the cost of (1) all work done in the current period to (2) the work done in the preceding period on the current period's beginning inventory of work in process, and divides the total by the equivalent units of work done to date.

weighted-average cost   An inventory method that assigns the same unit cost to each unit available for sale.

working capital   Current assets less current liabilities.

XBRL   An XML-based accounting language that helps communicate financial information electronically.

INDEX

PHOTO CREDITS

PHOTO CREDITS